Business Organizations

ASPEN CASEBOOK SERIES

BUSINESS ORGANIZATIONS
Cases, Problems, and Case Studies

Third Edition

D. GORDON SMITH
Glen L. Farr Professor of Law
J. Reuben Clark School of Law
Brigham Young University

CYNTHIA A. WILLIAMS
Professor of Law
University of Illinois College of Law

Wolters Kluwer
Law & Business

Published by Wolters Kluwer Law & Business in New York.

Wolters Kluwer Law & Business serves customers worldwide with CCH, Aspen Publishers, and Kluwer Law International products. (www.wolterskluwerlb.com)

To contact Customer Service, e-mail customer.service@wolterskluwer.com, call 1-800-234-1660, fax 1-800-901-9075, or mail correspondence to:

Wolters Kluwer Law & Business
Attn: Order Department
PO Box 990
Frederick, MD 21705

Printed in the United States of America.

1 2 3 4 5 6 7 8 9 0

ISBN 978-1-4548-0268-6

Library of Congress Cataloging-in-Publication Data

Smith, D. Gordon, 1962-
   Business organizations : cases, problems, and case studies / D. Gordon Smith, Cynthia A. Williams. — 3nd ed.
     p. cm. — (Aspen casebook series)
   Includes index.
   ISBN 978-1-4548-0268-6
   1. Business enterprises — Law and legislation — United States — Cases. 2. Corporation law — United States — Cases. I. Williams, Cynthia A., 1955- II. Title.

   KF1355.S63 2012
   346.73'065 — dc23

                                      2012021491

About Wolters Kluwer Law & Business

Wolters Kluwer Law & Business is a leading global provider of intelligent information and digital solutions for legal and business professionals in key specialty areas, and respected educational resources for professors and law students. Wolters Kluwer Law & Business connects legal and business professionals as well as those in the education market with timely, specialized authoritative content and information-enabled solutions to support success through productivity, accuracy and mobility.

Serving customers worldwide, Wolters Kluwer Law & Business products include those under the Aspen Publishers, CCH, Kluwer Law International, Loislaw, Best Case, ftwilliam.com and MediRegs family of products.

CCH products have been a trusted resource since 1913, and are highly regarded resources for legal, securities, antitrust and trade regulation, government contracting, banking, pension, payroll, employment and labor, and healthcare reimbursement and compliance professionals.

Aspen Publishers products provide essential information to attorneys, business professionals and law students. Written by preeminent authorities, the product line offers analytical and practical information in a range of specialty practice areas from securities law and intellectual property to mergers and acquisitions and pension/benefits. Aspen's trusted legal education resources provide professors and students with high-quality, up-to-date and effective resources for successful instruction and study in all areas of the law.

Kluwer Law International products provide the global business community with reliable international legal information in English. Legal practitioners, corporate counsel and business executives around the world rely on Kluwer Law journals, looseleafs, books, and electronic products for comprehensive information in many areas of international legal practice.

Loislaw is a comprehensive online legal research product providing legal content to law firm practitioners of various specializations. Loislaw provides attorneys with the ability to quickly and efficiently find the necessary legal information they need, when and where they need it, by facilitating access to primary law as well as state-specific law, records, forms and treatises.

Best Case Solutions is the leading bankruptcy software product to the bankruptcy industry. It provides software and workflow tools to flawlessly streamline petition preparation and the electronic filing process, while timely incorporating ever-changing court requirements.

ftwilliam.com offers employee benefits professionals the highest quality plan documents (retirement, welfare and non-qualified) and government forms (5500/PBGC, 1099 and IRS) software at highly competitive prices.

MediRegs products provide integrated health care compliance content and software solutions for professionals in healthcare, higher education and life sciences, including professionals in accounting, law and consulting.

Wolters Kluwer Law & Business, a division of Wolters Kluwer, is headquartered in New York. Wolters Kluwer is a market-leading global information services company focused on professionals.

To my wife, Sue, and our children.
For constant support and understanding.
D. Gordon Smith

To my family — Franz, Simone, Emily and Caroline.
Thank you for everything.
Cynthia A. Williams

Summary of Contents

Contents

CHAPTER 3

Limited Liability Companies

CHAPTER 4

Organization and Structure of a Corporation

CHAPTER 5

Control of the Closely Held Firm

CHAPTER 6

Shareholder Voting in the Publicly Held Firm

CHAPTER 7

Duty of Care

CHAPTER 8

Duty of Loyalty

CHAPTER 9

Litigation to Enforce Fiduciary Duties

CHAPTER 10

Friendly Mergers and Acquisitions

CHAPTER 11

Defending Against Hostile Takeovers

CHAPTER 12

Regulation of Disclosure, Fraud, and Insider Trading

Preface

The law governing business associations is voluminous and expanding. Over the past several decades, new business associations (limited liability companies and limited liability partnerships) have been developed and have gained widespread acceptance in the business world. The law relating to corporations underwent a dramatic reconsideration during the hostile takeover era of the 1980s, and the repercussions of those changes continue to be worked out by courts, legislatures, and regulators. Modern business developments — particularly, the globalization of the economy and the increasing importance of joint ventures, venture capital, franchising, and cross-border governance structures — inevitably impose stress on legal rules designed to address the problems of a different time. Finally, there has been an explosion in agency law, as fundamental principles of the common law are adapted to the modern regulatory state.

Despite the complexity surrounding business associations, we believe that (with limited exceptions) the legal principles central to the law of business associations are actually quite straightforward. Most issues in this course arise simply because one person has acted on behalf of another person. Whenever this occurs, there is a risk that the actor will not behave in accordance with the other person's wishes. Hence the adage, "If you want something done right you have to do it yourself." But doing everything by oneself is an onerous burden on all but the smallest of small business operators. In the business world, therefore, people attempt to structure their relationships in way that minimizes the risk of having others deviate from their wishes. The law relating to business associations may be viewed as providing legal rules to accomplish this goal.

Much of the difficulty (and fascination) for students, practicing attorneys, and scholars lies in applying the fundamental principles to complex factual situations, and in understanding the business contexts in which those legal principles operate. Because many students come into the basic course with little knowledge of business and finance, one of the major goals of this casebook, in addition to exploring the applicable legal principles, is to increase the business sophistication of the students. That goal significantly informs our pedagogical approach, which may be summarized in the following three principles:

First, we share a conviction that students learn this subject best by wrestling with real-world situations and materials. As a result, we have included discussion problems based on actual problems faced by identified companies, as reported in decided cases or in the business press, although we may mask their identities. Moreover, we include at various points excerpts from transactional and litigation documents. The premise underlying this approach is that "the law of business associations" is more than the words of the statutes or the holdings of the cases, but includes the practices of those who work in the field. One side benefit to this approach is that such materials provide an excellent opportunity to explore ethical issues faced by practicing attorneys.

Second, we have found that most students in the basic Business Associations course are uninterested in reading law review articles exploring the nuances of legal theory, but that they are nevertheless interested in constructing a theoretical framework to assist in understanding the law. As a result, we emphasize fundamental concepts in the textual materials that introduce the cases. We hope most students will find it unnecessary to use outside materials to understand the issues presented here, although we do encourage reading a good business newspaper daily to supplement your learning. In addition, we have structured the materials in a manner that is designed to evoke comparisons between the various sections on a conceptual level. More specifically, the materials relating to each major section explore formation, management, financial attributes, fiduciary duties, and termination/dissolution. Also, we have edited the materials in a manner that evokes discussion of legal theory in the context of problem solving.

Third, we find that the law governing business associations is most fascinating when viewed from many perspectives. In writing text and selecting cases and materials, therefore, we have consciously included historical, economic, progressive, comparative/international, sociological, and psychological perspectives.

This book begins with a section on the law of agency, which at one time was considered a fundamental common law topic (of nearly equal magnitude with contract law, property law, and tort law) and remains an area of heavy traffic among modern courts. Mysteriously, the law of agency is largely neglected at most modern law schools. The remainder of the casebook covers partnerships (including limited liability partnerships), limited liability companies, and corporations.

The laws governing business associations come from courts, legislatures, regulatory agencies, and business practice. While some of the cases in the book are "classics," many are recent cases that apply the legal principles being studied to modern business structures or "hot" industries to engage the students and increase their business sophistication. Although this book is full of cases, it needs to be supplemented by a book of statutes and regulations. In most cases, judges endeavor to interpret the statutes and regulations. This book, therefore, may not be used effectively without delving into the statutes.

We believe that the law of business associations is one of the most important subjects taught in law schools. We hope that you will find these materials engaging, informative, and, at times, provocative.

Gordon Smith and
Cynthia Williams
June 2012

Acknowledgments

At the risk of being redundant, we remain grateful for the folks at Wolters Kluwer, nee Aspen, for their consistent good humor and professionalism. We feel very fortunate to have our book with such a high-quality publisher.

We are also indebted to several professors who taught from the prior editions and offered useful suggestions for improvement. In particular, Rachel Anderson, Barbara Bucholtz, Christine Hurt, Brett McDonnell, John Ohnesorge, Karl Okamoto, Danny Sokol, David Walker, and Kaimi Wenger all made helpful suggestions for this new edition. David Armond of BYU has been invaluable in developing the casebook and teaching resources.

The new edition of this book has also benefitted greatly from several years of Business Associations students at the BYU Law School and the University of Illinois College of Law. And many research assistants have made valuable contributions to this volume. We express particular thanks to Eden Burkett, James Dunkelberger, Tyler Hawkes, Alyssa Munguia, Brett Nichols, Sara Elizabeth Payne, Nathan Prete, Heath Waddingham, and Ryan Wallace of BYU Law School for their assistance. At Illinois, Emily Heller deserves special recognition, as does Justin Lang from Osgoode Hall Law School, Toronto.

Business Organizations

CHAPTER
1

The Law of Agency

MOTIVATING HYPOTHETICAL

When the first Cloudberry Frozen Yogurt store opened in 2005, the venture seemed destined to fail. In fact, so few people came to the tiny frozen yogurt shop in New York City, that sales totaled only $70 after the first month. Word spread quickly, however, and soon people from miles around were lining up to sample Cloudberry's unique blend of tangy frozen yogurt and fresh fruit toppings. Within a year, Cloudberry became a local phenomenon. So many people came that New York City forced the shop to post guards at the door to control the massive crowds. Parking problems created by the yogurt-hungry masses prompted the New York Times to dub Cloudberry's product "the taste that launched 1,000 parking tickets." Hordes of Cloudberry fans gave their new-found addiction a different unofficial nickname: Crackberry.

Cloudberry fever soon spread beyond New York to Los Angeles and other major U.S. markets. By early 2011, Cloudberry had locations nationwide. Cloudberry also plans to continue expanding globally, partnering with selected "area developers" to open frozen-yogurt shops in Mexico and the Middle East. Area developers license territories, usually defined by metropolitan statistical areas, and agree to build numerous stores within that area. Area developers must enter into an area development agreement with Cloudberry (which establishes the number of stores to be developed in an area) and a franchise agreement for each store opened.

Generally speaking, an agent is any person who is authorized to act on behalf of another (known as the principal). The law of agency governs the interactions among principals, agents, and the third parties with whom agents deal on behalf of principals. In the preface to one of the first treatises on the law of agency, William Paley wrote: "The law of Principal and Agent appears at first view to be founded upon principles so few and simple, and in general so easy of application, that a treatise upon such a subject may seem altogether superfluous." William Paley, *A Treatise on the Law of Principal and Agent* at iii. Paley found sufficient justification for his treatise, however, in the "vast extension of modern commerce, [and] the novelty and variety of the channels through which it is carried on."

Today agency issues are, if anything, more pervasive than in Paley's day, and they are certainly more complicated than Paley's skeptics would have been willing to concede. Personal injury law, commercial law, and employment law — not to mention partnership law and corporate law — all involve issues of agency law. The following materials do not attempt to cover the entire breadth of agency law, but instead strive to explore the fundamental principles relating to creation of an agency relationship and the potential liabilities flowing from that relationship. These principles are essential to the transaction of business generally and to the understanding of the law of business associations covered in subsequent chapters.

The law of agency developed as part of the common law. In 1812 Paley wrote that "the decisions upon this branch of the law which are to be met with in the older reports are neither numerous nor important." In the 19th century, however, the law of agency came into full flower. As business transactions became increasingly complicated, the law of agency became concomitantly necessary to bring order and equity. Justice Joseph Story published his magnificent *Commentaries on the Law of Agency* in 1839, and it quickly became the leading authority on agency law cited by American courts. Although the last edition of Story's treatise (the 9th edition, published in 1882, as revised by Charles P. Greenough) was cited well into the 20th century, it was largely displaced by Floyd R. Mechem's *A Treatise on the Law of Agency* in 1888. The second edition of Mechem's treatise, which appeared in 1914, was widely cited by American courts, especially before the publication of the first edition of the Restatement of the Law of Agency by the American Law Institute in 1933, but Mechem is still cited by modern courts.

The 900-pound gorilla in this field, however, is the Restatement. Originally published in 1933, the Restatement was again published in 1958 in the Restatement (Second) of the Law of Agency, and the American Law Institute published Restatement (Third) of the Law of Agency in 2006. Although several of the cases in this chapter cite the Restatement (Second), the text of this chapter will highlight the relevant provisions of the Restatement (Third). The Restatement is not binding on courts, but it is cited in many modern decisions invoking agency law. The Restatement has helped to unify the law of agency among different states. Despite the apparent certainty that the Restatement conveys, however, underlying the principles are many challenging legal issues with which business lawyers and courts often struggle.

A. CREATION OF THE AGENCY RELATIONSHIP

Paley's treatise on agency law devoted only a single sentence to the creation of the agency relationship: "The authority of an agent is created either by deed, by simple writing, by parol, or by mere employment, according to the capacity of the parties, or the nature of the act to be done." Paley, *A Treatise on the Law of Principal and Agent* at 2. The common law cases offered a more detailed exploration of agency formation, starting from the proposition that an agency relationship is a consensual relationship between a principal and an agent. According to Restatement (Third), an agency relationship is created when (1) the principal "manifests assent" to have the agent act on the principal's behalf and under the principal's control, and (2) the agent "manifests assent or otherwise consents" so to act. Restatement (Third) of Agency § 1.01. In Restatement (Third), use of the word "assent" is "intended to emphasize that unexpressed reservations or limitations . . . do not restrict the [party's] expression of consent." Restatement (Third) of Agency § 1.01, note d.

Although the parties must agree to enter into the type of relationship described, no contract is required to form an agency relationship. Restatement (Third) of Agency § 1.01, note d (observing, "Many agents act or promise to act gratuitously"). Indeed, the parties need not have an intent to enter into something called an agency relationship. As stated in Restatement (Third) of Agency § 1.02, "Whether a relationship is characterized as agency in an agreement between parties or in the context of industry or popular usage is not controlling."

The "legal consequences of agency" will be explored more fully in subsequent sections. For present purposes, suffice it say that the creation of an agency relationship has — in the words of Restatement (Third) — both "inward-looking" and "outward-looking" consequences. Restatement (Third) of Agency § 1.01, note c. Inward-looking consequences relate to the relationship between the principal and the agent and are largely governed by the contracts between the parties and by the law of fiduciary duties. Outward-looking consequences relate to the relationship among the principal, the agent, and a third party and are governed by the various "principles of attribution" examined in Section C later in this chapter.

Outward-looking consequences tend to be the primary focus in cases where the central issue is agency formation. The following case, Nears v. Holiday Hospitality Franchising, Inc., involves a very common form of outward-looking consequence — a claim by a third party that a principal is liable for the tortious conduct of an agent.

NEARS v. HOLIDAY HOSPITALITY FRANCHISING, INC.

Court of Appeals of Texas, Texarkana
295 S.W.3d 787 (2010)

Opinion by Justice MOSELEY.

Sharon Nears appeals the entry of orders granting summary judgments which disposed of her claims against Holiday Hospitality Franchising, Inc. . . . We affirm.

I. FACTUAL AND PROCEDURAL HISTORY

. . . The circumstances giving rise to Nears's complaints against Holiday Hospitality Franchising, Inc. ("HHFI") began when she was working for VI-MTLS, Ltd. ("Holiday Inn") as the guest services manager at its Mount Pleasant, Texas, Holiday Inn hotel. During Nears's employment, Jack Marshall was made the interim general manager of the hotel July 26, 1999. Nears alleged that Marshall routinely engaged in violent outbursts, attacking the honesty, character, and competency of all of the employees of the hotel. Nears alleged that Marshall drank excessively, a practice which exacerbated the general environment of fear and hostility among the hotel employees, and that Marshall directed the worst of his vitriol toward her. Nears contends that Marshall curtailed her work duties, ransacked her office, and threw away her files and possessions. Marshall's conduct, according to Nears, was outrageous and unpredictable, causing Nears to feel threatened and fearful that Marshall would physically harm her. Nears claims to have experienced a number of stress-related health problems as a result of Marshall's conduct toward her.

Nears was fired November 5, 1999, and was given no reason for her termination. Nears claims she was wrongfully terminated as a result of her filing of a worker's compensation claim (stemming from an on-the-job May 24, 1999, injury).

In Nears's third amended petition . . . , she had asserted claims against a number of defendants, including the following: (a) Marshall, her supervisor, (b) Holiday Inn, (c) ETEX Hotel Management Co., Inc. (which was hired by Holiday Inn to manage the Mount Pleasant hotel), (d) Dewey Neely and Robert Brewer (respectively, ETEX's director of operations and president), and (e) HHFI. Nears alleged intentional infliction of emotional distress by Marshall and claimed that Marshall acted as HHFI's agent and that HHFI was vicariously liable for Marshall's actions. . . .

Nears alleges that she advised Brewer of Marshall's conduct and asked for his assistance in dealing with this matter, but her pleas fell on deaf ears because Brewer did nothing to ameliorate the situation. Nears also contends that she wrote Neely a detailed letter outlining Marshall's conduct; Neely made no response. . . .

IV. ANALYSIS

. . . Nears argues that HHFI exercised sufficient specific control over conduct of ETEX and/or Marshall concerning employees of the hotel to establish an agency relationship. . . . In support of this contention, Nears relies on the standards manual promulgated by Holiday Inn Worldwide for all Holiday Inn owners, licensees, and general managers to follow. The manual required all general managers (the position held by Marshall at the Mount Pleasant Holiday Inn hotel), to be certified through the Holiday Inn Worldwide Property Executive Training Program. The general manager was supposed to be required to attend the annual Holiday Inn Worldwide Conference for management training, and the evidence shows that the management training is supposed to be completed by the general manager within 180 days of assuming the position. However, although Nears has shown that Marshall was supposedly required to attend this particular program, there is no evidence as to what this specific training was intended to entail. The evidence further shows that Marshall never attended this program. Likewise, the Holiday Inn Worldwide standards manual is shown to contain minimum training requirements for the guest services manager, but there is no evidence regarding what this specific training was intended to entail.

Nears contends that HHFI's control of the Mount Pleasant hotel is further evidenced by quarterly unannounced property inspections. These inspections related to housekeeping, front office procedures, guest comments, food and beverage, cleanliness, maintenance issues, life safety factors, and the condition of the exterior of the property. Based upon these inspections, the hotel was given an overall score. The evidence shows that the general manager prior to Marshall was dismissed by ETEX after receiving low scores on the quarterly inspections conducted by HHFI. Nears argues that the activity of conducting quarterly inspections, the fact that guests' comment cards were sent directly to HHFI, and the dismissal of Marshall's predecessor as general manager due to low inspection scores create more than a scintilla of evidence that ETEX was HHFI's agent.

The basis of Nears's claims is the manner in which Marshall and ETEX conducted themselves as her employment superiors, including the competence of their management skills. Nears argues that because Marshall and ETEX received training from HHFI regarding the management of the hotel, together with the other factors listed above, there exists a genuine issue of material fact as to whether HHFI should be liable for the actions of ETEX and Marshall.

The inspections, guest comment cards, and training requirements are geared toward ensuring guest satisfaction, not toward the treatment of hotel employees. Standards are established by HHFI and presumably enforced for the purpose of enhancing customer satisfaction. Quality control standards for operating a franchise should not be construed to create an agency relationship. The implementation of standards to ensure guest satisfaction in this case does not evidence express or implied actual authority flowing from HHFI to ETEX or Marshall pertaining to the treatment of hotel employees. As stated in the commentary from the Restatement of Agency: "[S]etting standards in an agreement for acceptable service quality does not of itself create a right of control." Restatement (Third) of Agency § 1.01 cmt. f (2006).

The evidence here simply does not reveal a genuine issue of material fact on the issue of whether HHFI had the right to control the acts giving rise to the lawsuit, i.e., Marshall's supervisory interactions with Nears. There is no evidence that HHFI had the right to control or, in fact, did control Marshall's day-to-day supervisory interactions with Nears. To impose vicarious liability, there must be evidence that such control was exercised.

In this case, HHFI introduced evidence that:

- HHFI had no ownership interest in or financial control over the hotel and provided no funds for operating expenses, managers' salaries, or for any other purpose;
- There is no comingling of funds or sharing in profits or losses between HHFI and the Mount Pleasant hotel;
- HHFI was not involved in any decision with respect to the terms and conditions of employment for workers at the hotel;
- HHFI did not have authority to hire or fire workers at the hotel;
- HHFI did not pay any compensation to workers at the hotel, and paid no employment taxes on its behalf;
- While she worked at the Mount Pleasant hotel, Nears did not report to anybody at HHFI; and

- Nears received her paycheck from ETEX while employed as guest services manager at the hotel. (Nears was previously directly employed by Holiday Inn, the limited partnership that owns the hotel, when she worked at the front desk.)

Taking this evidence into account and given that Nears failed to produce any evidence that HHFI either did control or had the right to control Marshall's supervisory interactions with Nears, there is no genuine issue of material fact on the issue of whether HHFI expressly or impliedly delegated authority to ETEX and/or Marshall to manage the hotel in such a manner as to control the supervisory interactions with Nears in this case.

Because the evidence of the allegations does not rise to a level that would "enable reasonable and fair-minded people to differ in their conclusions," we find there to be no genuine issue of material fact regarding the question of whether ETEX and Marshall has . . . authority to act as agents of HHFI, we affirm the judgment of the trial court.

PROBLEM 1-1

The franchise relationship is a contractual relationship and both franchisors and franchisees contribute significantly to its success. The Franchise Agreement is the basic governance document for the franchising relationship. Both parties value uniformity within the system and strive to maintain the competitiveness of the system. The terms of a franchising agreement require a balance between predictability (to avoid opportunism) and flexibility (to respond to a changing business environment).

As with most franchises, Cloudberry contributes three things to the franchising relationship: (1) trademarks and trade dress; (2) trade secrets, which are part of what is often referred to as the "System"; and (3) services, often including site selection, training, promotion, bookkeeping, compliance with laws and system standards, and insurance. In exchange for these things, the franchisees pay a one-time franchise fee ($45,000 in the case of Cloudberry) and ongoing royalties (6% of gross sales). Also, the franchisees are required to pay for the development of the franchise store according to the franchisor's specifications, which may cost anywhere from $400,000 to $1,500,000, depending on size and location.

To ensure uniformity within the system, franchisors like Cloudberry impose systemwide standards, usually contained in an operations manual. These requirements are notoriously detailed and wide ranging. For instance, the Cloudberry License Agreement regulates everything from ingredients and menu items to display signs to advertising formats to hours of operation. Failure to comply with these standards could result in termination of the franchise.

Cloudberry also requires the managers and assistant managers of its outlets to complete a training program prior to opening an outlet. Once the outlet is open, Cloudberry has the right to inspect the outlet, which includes the right to speak to employees of the franchisee. Cloudberry requires franchisees to submit weekly, monthly, quarterly, and annual reports. Often, these reports contain routine financial information regarding Gross Sales. However, Cloudberry may also require franchisees to submit additional operational and statistical information to assist in product purchasing, product development, or System refinements. Finally, Cloudberry explicitly provides for a right to audit each franchisee's books.

Denise Hernandez stopped at a Cloudberry store in Long Beach, California. When Hernandez approached the counter, the store cashier, Rachel Jones, began to insult Hernandez, using profanity and racial epithets, including "go back to where you came from you poor, f***ing Mexicans." Hernandez, a PhD candidate in biophysics at UCLA, was born and raised in Los Angeles. Before Hernandez had a chance to recover from the shock of being so insulted, Jones also threw a counter display in her direction. After Hernandez retreated from the inside of the store, Jones continued to yell racial epithets and made obscene gestures through the window.

Jones is employed by the Long Beach franchisee for Cloudberry, and the law is clear that Jones is the franchisee's agent. Moreover, the franchisee, as the principal in an agency relationship, would almost certainly be liable to Hernandez for the agent's actions. ***Could the franchisor, Cloudberry, also be liable to Hernandez for Jones's actions?***

In answering this question, please consider the following provision from Cloudberry's License Agreement:

> <u>Relationship of Licensee to Company</u>. It is expressly agreed that the parties intend by this Agreement to establish between Company and Licensee the relationship of franchisor and franchisee. It is further agreed that Licensee has no authority to create or assume in Company's name or on behalf of Company, any obligation, express or implied, or to act or purport to act as agent or representative on behalf of Company for any purpose whatsoever. Neither Company nor Licensee is the employer, employee, agent, partner or co-venturer of or with the other, each being independent.
>
> . . .
>
> Company and Licensee agree that the relationship created by this Agreement is one of independent contractor and is not a fiduciary relationship.

B. AGENT'S FIDUCIARY DUTIES TO PRINCIPAL

Principals and agents owe duties to each other within an agency relationship. *See* Restatement (Third) of Agency, Ch. 8. The principal's duties include performance of contract obligations, good faith and fair dealing, and indemnification under certain circumstances. Restatement (Third) of Agency §§ 8.13-8.15. The agent's duties include performance of contract obligations, care, competence, diligence, obedience, and disclosure. Restatement (Third) of Agency §§ 8.07-8.12. But the most important duty in the law of agency — and the focus of attention here — is the agent's duty of loyalty to the principal. The essence of this duty is that the agent must act "loyally for the principal's benefit in all matters connected with the agency relationship." Restatement (Third) of Agency § 8.01. The agent's duty of loyalty is multifaceted and includes, among other obligations, a duty "not to use or communicate confidential information of the principal for the agent's own purposes or those of a third party" (§ 8.05), a duty not to compete with the principal in any matter within the scope of the agency relationship (§ 8.04), and a duty not to act as an adverse party to the principal in a transaction connected with the agency relationship (§ 8.03). If the agent breaches the duty of loyalty, the principal's primary remedies are damages and disgorgement of profits, if any.

The following case introduces the duty of loyalty, which is a fundamental element of entity law, and as such will reappear in numerous permutations throughout this book.

FOOD LION, INC. v. CAPITAL CITIES/ABC, INC.

194 F.3d 505
United States Court of Appeals, Fourth Circuit
October 20, 1999

MICHAEL, Circuit Judge.

Two ABC television reporters, after using false resumes to get jobs at Food Lion, Inc. supermarkets, secretly videotaped what appeared to be unwholesome food handling practices. Some of the video footage was used by ABC in a Prime-Time Live broadcast that was sharply critical of Food Lion. The grocery chain sued Capital Cities/ABC, Inc., American Broadcasting Companies, Inc., Richard Kaplan and Ira Rosen, producers of PrimeTime Live, and Lynne Dale and Susan Barnett, two reporters for the program (collectively, "ABC" or the "ABC defendants"). Food Lion did not sue for defamation, but focused on how ABC gathered its information through claims for fraud, breach of duty of loyalty, trespass, and unfair trade practices. Food Lion won at trial, and judgment for compensatory damages of $1,402 was entered on the various claims. Following a substantial (over $5 million) remittitur, the judgment provided for $315,000 in punitive damages. The ABC defendants appeal the district court's denial of their motion for judgment as a matter of law, and Food Lion appeals the court's ruling that prevented it from proving publication damages. Having considered the case, we (1) reverse the judgment that the ABC defendants committed fraud and unfair trade practices, (2) affirm the judgment that Dale and Barnett breached their duty of loyalty and committed a trespass, and (3) affirm, on First Amendment grounds, the district court's refusal to allow Food Lion to prove publication damages.

I

In early 1992 producers of ABC's PrimeTime Live program received a report alleging that Food Lion stores were engaging in unsanitary meat-handling practices. The allegations were that Food Lion employees ground out-of-date beef together with new beef, bleached rank meat to remove its odor, and re-dated (and offered for sale) products not sold before their printed expiration date. The producers recognized that these allegations presented the potential for a powerful news story, and they decided to conduct an undercover investigation of Food Lion. ABC reporters Lynne Dale (Lynne Litt at the time) and Susan Barnett concluded that they would have a better chance of investigating the allegations if they could become Food Lion employees. With the approval of their superiors, they proceeded to apply for jobs with the grocery chain, submitting applications with false identities and references and fictitious local addresses. Notably, the applications failed to mention the reporters' concurrent employment with ABC and otherwise misrepresented their educational and employment experiences. Based on these applications, a South Carolina Food Lion store hired Barnett as a deli clerk in April 1992, and a North Carolina Food Lion store hired Dale as a meat wrapper trainee in May 1992.

Barnett worked for Food Lion for two weeks, and Dale for only one week. As they went about their assigned tasks for Food Lion, Dale and Barnett used tiny cameras ("lipstick" cameras, for example) and microphones concealed on their bodies to secretly record Food Lion employees treating, wrapping and labeling meat, cleaning machinery, and discussing the practices of the meat department. They gathered footage from the meat cutting room, the deli counter, the employee break room, and a manager's office. All told, in their three collective weeks as Food Lion employees, Dale and Barnett recorded approximately 45 hours of concealed camera footage.

Some of the videotape was eventually used in a November 5, 1992, broadcast of PrimeTime Live. ABC contends the footage confirmed many of the allegations initially leveled against Food Lion. The broadcast included, for example, videotape that appeared to show Food Lion employees repackaging and redating fish that had passed the expiration date, grinding expired beef with fresh beef, and applying barbeque sauce to chicken past its expiration date in order to mask the smell and sell it as fresh in the gourmet food section. The program included statements by former Food Lion employees alleging even more serious mishandling of meat at Food Lion stores across several states. The truth of the PrimeTime Live broadcast was not an issue in the litigation we now describe.

Food Lion sued ABC and the PrimeTime Live producers and reporters. Food Lion's suit focused not on the broadcast, as a defamation suit would, but on the methods ABC used to obtain the video footage. The grocery chain asserted claims of fraud, breach of the duty of loyalty, trespass, and unfair trade practices, seeking millions in compensatory damages. Specifically, Food Lion sought to recover (1) administrative costs and wages paid in connection with the employment of Dale and Barnett and (2) broadcast (publication) damages for matters such as loss of good will, lost sales and profits, and diminished stock value. Punitive damages were also requested by Food Lion.

The district court, in a remarkably efficient effort, tried the case with a jury in three phases. At the liability phase, the jury found all of the ABC defendants liable to Food Lion for fraud and two of them, Dale and Barnett, additionally liable for breach of the duty of loyalty and trespass. Based on the jury's fraud verdict and its special interrogatory findings that the ABC defendants had engaged in deceptive acts, the district court determined that the ABC defendants had violated the North Carolina Unfair and Deceptive Trade Practices Act (UTPA). Prior to the compensatory damages phase, the district court ruled that damages allegedly incurred by Food Lion as a result of ABC's broadcast of PrimeTime Live — "lost profits, lost sales, diminished stock value or anything of that nature" — could not be recovered because these damages were not proximately caused by the acts (fraud, trespass, etc.) attributed to the ABC defendants in this case. Operating within this constraint, the jury in the second phase awarded Food Lion $1,400 in compensatory damages on its fraud claim, $1.00

each on its duty of loyalty and trespass claims, and $1,500 on its UTPA claim. (The court required Food Lion to make an election between the fraud and UTPA damages, and the grocery chain elected to take the $1,400 in fraud damages.) At the final stage the jury lowered the boom and awarded $5,545,750 in punitive damages on the fraud claim against ABC and its two producers, Kaplan and Rosen. The jury refused to award punitive damages against the reporters, Dale and Barnett. In post-trial proceedings the district court ruled that the punitive damages award was excessive, and Food Lion accepted a remittitur to a total of $315,000.

After trial the ABC defendants moved for judgment as a matter of law on all claims, the motion was denied, and the defendants now appeal. Food Lion cross-appeals, contesting the district court's ruling that the damages the grocery chain sought as a result of the PrimeTime Live broadcast were not recoverable in this action. We now turn to the legal issues.

II

A.

. . .

ABC argues that Dale and Barnett cannot be held liable for a breach of duty of loyalty to Food Lion under existing tort law in North and South Carolina. It is undisputed that both reporters, on behalf of ABC, wore hidden cameras to make a video and audio record of what they saw and heard while they were employed by Food Lion. Specifically, they sought to document, for ABC's PrimeTime Live program, Food Lion employees engaging in unsanitary practices, treating products to hide spoilage, and repackaging and redating out-of-date products. The jury found that Dale and Barnett breached their duty of loyalty to Food Lion, and nominal damages of $1.00 were awarded.

As a matter of agency law, an employee owes a duty of loyalty to her employer. . . . The courts of North and South Carolina have not set out a specific test for determining when the duty of loyalty is breached. Disloyalty has been described in fairly broad terms, however. Employees are disloyal when their acts are "inconsistent with promoting the best interest of their employer at a time when they were on its payroll," Lowndes Prods., Inc. v. Brower, 259 S.C. 322, 191 S.E.2d 761, 767 (S.C. 1972), and an employee who "deliberately acquires an interest adverse to his employer . . . is disloyal," Long v. Vertical Techs., Inc., 113 N.C. App. 598, 439 S.E.2d 797, 802 (N.C. Ct. App. 1994).

ABC is correct to remind us that employee disloyalty issues are usually dealt with in the context of the employment contract: unfaithful employees are simply discharged, disciplined, or reprimanded. Up to now, disloyal conduct by an employee has been considered tortious in North and South Carolina in three circumstances. First, the tort of breach of duty of loyalty applies when an employee competes directly with her employer, either on her own or as an agent of a rival company. Second, the tort applies when the employee misappropriates her employer's profits, property, or business opportunities. Third, the tort applies when the employee breaches her employer's confidences.

Because Dale and Barnett did not compete with Food Lion, misappropriate any of its profits or opportunities, or breach its confidences, ABC argues that the reporters did not engage in any disloyal conduct that is tortious under existing law. Indeed, the district court acknowledged that it was the first court to hold that the conduct in question "would be recognized by the Supreme Courts of North Carolina and South Carolina" as tortiously violating the duty of loyalty. Food Lion, Inc. v. Capital Cities/ABC, Inc., 964 F. Supp. 956, 959 n.2 (M.D.N.C. 1997). We believe the district court was correct to conclude that those courts would decide today that the reporters' conduct was sufficient to breach the duty of loyalty and trigger tort liability.

What Dale and Barnett did verges on the kind of employee activity that has already been determined to be tortious. The interests of the employer (ABC) to whom Dale and Barnett gave complete loyalty were adverse to the interests of Food Lion, the employer to whom they were unfaithful. ABC and Food Lion were not business competitors but they were adverse in a fundamental way. ABC's interest was to expose Food Lion to the public as a food chain that engaged in unsanitary and deceptive practices. Dale and Barnett served ABC's interest, at the expense of Food Lion, by engaging in the taping for ABC while they were on Food Lion's payroll. In doing this, Dale and Barnett did not serve Food Lion faithfully, and their interest (which was the same as ABC's) was diametrically opposed to Food Lion's. In these circumstances, we believe that the highest courts of North and South Carolina would hold that the reporters—in promoting the interests of one master, ABC, to the detriment of a second, Food Lion—committed the tort of disloyalty against Food Lion.

Our holding on this point is not a sweeping one. An employee does not commit a tort simply by holding two jobs or by performing a second job inadequately. For example, a second employer has no tort action for breach of the duty of loyalty when its employee fails to devote adequate attention or effort to her second (night shift) job because she is tired. That is because the inadequate performance is simply an incident of trying to work two jobs. There is no intent to act adversely to the second employer for the benefit of the first. Because Dale and Barnett had the requisite intent to act against the interests of their second employer, Food Lion, for the benefit of their main employer, ABC, they were liable in tort for their disloyalty.

We hold that, insofar as North and South Carolina law is concerned, the district court did not err in refusing to set aside the jury's verdict that Dale and Barnett breached their duty of loyalty to Food Lion.

PROBLEM 1-2

An agent's fiduciary duty of loyalty to her principal ends the day the agency relationship ends, and thus the former agent may begin to compete with the former principal. Employers will often protect themselves from competition with their former employees by requiring their employees to sign agreements not to compete with the company after the employment relationship ends. Such agreements will be enforced in most states so long as they are "reasonable," which means so long as they are limited in time (three years or less, typically), and so long as there are sensible geographic boundaries to the noncompetition agreement.

Paul Rockham worked in marketing for Cloudberry for five years and ultimately became responsible for marketing of Cloudberry's franchises. As part of marketing, Cloudberry obtained raw market research data and used it to develop models of consumers' preferences to determine the product areas that were most successful in different geographic areas. Rockham's particular expertise was international marketing — that is, determining which products to sell in which foreign countries, based upon marketing strategies and advertising claims. As a member of worldwide, multifunctional teams at Cloudberry, just prior to leaving the company Rockham developed a confidential ten-year global marketing plan for Cloudberry's franchises.

When Rockham was hired by Cloudberry, he was offered stock options, as were all of the company's top management employees. As a condition for getting the options, Rockham was required to sign an agreement not to compete with Cloudberry for three years after leaving the company.

In 2011, Rockham was offered the job of president of Red Mango, Inc., another frozen yogurt franchisor that competed directly with Cloudberry. Soon after Rockham joined Red Mango, Cloudberry brought an injunctive action against Rockham to enforce the covenant not to compete, claiming that Rockham's knowledge of how Cloudberry cross-indexed its market research (in order to be able to determine which products were most successful among which consumers in which countries) and how Cloudberry organized its area developers was confidential information and constituted a trade secret.

While the court hearing Cloudberry's case found that Rockham's agreement to the covenant not to compete was "entirely voluntary," the court also found that failing to agree would have required Rockham to give up the stock options. Rockham was also required to sign a confidentiality agreement when he was hired, as were all other Cloudberry employees, in which he agreed not to disclose any of Cloudberry's trade secrets or confidential information, particularly how it cross-indexed its market research. The trial court ruled in Rockham's favor, finding this was not confidential information and refusing to enforce the covenant not to compete.

How should the court of appeals rule on Cloudberry's appeal? How would you advise someone like Rockham (in advance), who is being asked to sign a broad confidentiality agreement and covenant not to compete?

C. PRINCIPLES OF ATTRIBUTION

As stated above, the existence of an agency relationship has both inward-looking consequences, through, among other things, the imposition of fiduciary duties, and outward-looking consequences. The outward-looking consequences come about because principals can be held liable for the tortious actions of their agents, and can be required to fulfill contracts into which their agents have entered. In this section, we will explore the factors used by courts to justify holding principals responsible for the consequences of their agents' actions.

The official comment to Restatement (Third) of Agency § 1.01 states:

> The chief justifications for the principal's accountability for the agent's acts are the principal's ability to select and control the agent and to terminate the agency relationship, together with the fact that the agent has agreed expressly or implicitly to act on the principal's behalf.

Reduced to its simplest terms, this passage invokes the concepts of *control*, *benefit*, and *consent*, all of which are commonly found in the cases. The primary rationale for imposing liability based on the existence of control is neatly summarized by the ancient maxim, *"Qui facit per alium facit per se"* ("he who acts through another, acts himself"). The rationale for imposing liability based on the existence of benefits to the principal is simply that those who gain from the actions of another should sometimes be held to answer for costs inflicted by those actions. In addition to control and benefit, courts also seem to rely at times on the notion of *consent* to justify liability. As noted above, consent is central to the determination of when an agency relationship exists, and thus when it is fair to impose liability on the principal for actions of the agent.

As you work through the materials in this section, consider what level of control is necessary to prompt a finding of liability, and think about why control, standing alone, is (usually) insufficient for such a finding. Similarly, the existence of benefits to the principal does not necessarily lead to liability for the agent's actions. It is useful, therefore, to identify the circumstances in which benefit seems to play an important role in a court's decision, and to try to determine whether benefit, standing alone, may be sufficient to justify the imposition of liability. In thinking about each of these issues, it is also useful to separate the rationales for imposing liability in the tort context from the rationales for holding principals responsible for fulfilling contracts into which their agents have entered.

The following sections examine several bases for holding one person or entity — the principal — responsible for the actions of another person — the agent. The doctrines of authority, both actual authority and apparent authority, are distinctive to agency law. In addition to these doctrines of attribution based on principles of authority, principals may incur liability for the actions of their agents based on the general doctrine of vicarious liability — *respondeat superior* — which we do not cover here on the assumption that most students will have encountered this doctrine in Torts.

1. *Actual Authority*

When an agent acts with authority, her action has legal consequences for the principal. Such action, when taken "in accordance with the principal's manifestations to the agent that the principal wishes the agent so to act" is known as "actual authority." The Restatement (Third) of Agency § 2.01.

Actual authority is created by a manifestation from the principal to the agent that the principal consents to the agent taking actions on the principal's behalf. Restatement (Third) of Agency § 3.01. Thus, in evaluating the actual authority of an agent, one would evaluate the communications from the principal to the agent. Actual authority may exist even though there is no written contract between a principal and an agent, although certain kinds of authority (such as the authority to sell real estate for another) must be in writing based on individual state law requirements.

An agent's actual authority typically includes both express and implied aspects. The "express actual authority" of an agent to act on a principal's behalf may be conveyed orally or in writing; the "implied actual authority" is the power to do those things necessary to fulfill the agency. Thus, the express actual authority to "run my used car business" would imply actual authority to buy used cars, presumably on credit; advertise the cars; hire additional employees as necessary; and enter binding contracts with customers. When potential liability arises from the actions of an agent, principals may seek to narrowly construe their agent's actual authority, both express and implied, as in the following case.

CASTILLO v. CASE FARMS OF OHIO, INC.

United States District Court, Western District of Texas
96 F. Supp. 2d 578
December 1, 1999

JUSTICE, Senior District Judge.

Th[is] civil action was filed on December 19, 1997, by a group of migrant farm workers, claiming violations of the Migrant and Seasonal Agricultural Worker Protection Act ("AWPA"), the Fair Labor Standards Act ("FLSA"), and various state laws. The primary defendant is Case Farms of Ohio, a chicken processing plant located in Winesburg, Ohio.

A bench trial in this civil action commenced on March 29, 1999, and was completed on April 1, 1999. In accordance with Federal Rule of Civil Procedure 52(a), the following memorandum opinion constitutes the court's findings of fact and conclusions of law in this civil action. . . .

INTRODUCTION

I. BACKGROUND

Defendant Case Farms of Ohio, Inc. ("Case Farms"), is a chicken processing plant in Winesburg, Ohio. At this facility, approximately 400,000 live chickens per week, year-round, are live-hung, slaughtered, eviscerated, cleaned, cut and deboned, and ultimately packaged for market. Case Farms employees perform a range of jobs, which include eviscerating, deboning, receiving, grading, wrapping, weighing, and washing chickens.

In consideration of its historically high turnover rate, Case Farms actively recruited workers for its processing plant during 1996 and 1997. Andy Cilona, primarily responsible for recruiting workers for Case Farms, served as Case Farms' Human Resources Director from his date of hire until February 1996, and as Case Farms' Director of Corporate Development, from February 1996 until mid-1997. During one of his recruiting trips in Florida, Cilona initiated contact with a labor agency for temporary employees, America's Tempcorps ("ATC"). In conformity with an unwritten agreement with Case Farms, ATC worked in Texas, recruiting and hiring a number of people to work at Case

Farms' chicken processing plant in Ohio. During this recruitment process, ATC gave some of its recruits the telephone number of Alvaro Hernandez, a Case Farms employee, and instructed them to call Hernandez upon their arrival in Ohio. ATC also usually gave its recruits a free bus ticket or other free transportation to Ohio, as well as $20.00 each in traveling expenses. Case Farms ceased doing business with ATC in February 1996. . . .

[The] plaintiffs generally claim that they were recruited in Texas to work at Case Farms' Winesburg facility, and that, upon arriving at Case Farms, they discovered that the actual terms and conditions of their employment, transportation, and housing in Ohio did not coincide with the promises made to them in Texas. At the trial of this case, plaintiffs testified to the inadequate housing conditions and transportation provisions they encountered upon arrival in Ohio.

Thus, the bases for this civil action are the defendants' alleged misrepresentations and mistreatment of the plaintiffs in the recruitment process in Texas, and, as well, the working and living conditions afforded them in Ohio. Plaintiffs contend that defendants violated a number of the statutory rights of employees created by the Migrant and Seasonal Agricultural Worker Protection Act ("AWPA"), 29 U.S.C. §1801 et seq., and the Fair Labor Standards Act ("FLSA"), 29 U.S.C. §216(b). Plaintiffs further allege that defendants were guilty of breach of contract, fraud, and negligent misrepresentation with regard to the bases of plaintiffs' claims.

Defendant Case Farms responded to these allegations with primarily legal defenses. Generally speaking, rather than refute the veracity of most of the plaintiffs' factual claims, Case Farms' primary defense at trial was that it cannot be held legally responsible for the plaintiffs' alleged mistreatment. . . .

PART I

AN OVERVIEW OF THE LAW

The Migrant and Seasonal Agricultural Worker Protection Act ("AWPA") is a broad-ranging network of migrant and seasonal worker protections that requires, in part, written and forthright disclosures, in the workers' language, of working conditions at the time of recruitment. It prohibits false and misleading representations concerning employment policies and practices, housing conditions, and transportation arrangements for workers. It also regulates housing and transportation standards for covered workers. . . .

The bulk of the plaintiffs' claims arise out of the AWPA's statutory protections. The specific statutory provisions of the AWPA that are at issue in this civil action are as follows:

(1) utilization of an unregistered farm labor contractor,
(2) failure to provide written disclosures,
(3) the use of false and misleading information,
(4) violations of the terms of the working agreement,
(5) failure to ensure that the housing met applicable health and safety codes,
(6) failure to secure certification that the housing met the applicable health and safety codes,
(7) failure to post or to provide a statement of the terms and conditions of housing,

(8) failure to properly insure and inspect transportation vehicles,
(9) failure to ensure that each plaintiff received a proper pay statement, and
(10) "wages owed when due" violations.

In the event of violation of these provisions, the AWPA provides for statutory or actual damages, or equitable relief, at the discretion of the court.

Plaintiffs also allege violations of the minimum wage, and overtime wage, provisions of the Fair Labor Standards Act. The FLSA establishes a minimum wage, maximum working hours, record keeping and reporting requirements, and child labor prohibitions, as well as a system of civil and criminal penalties for its violation.

The remainder of the plaintiffs' claims, for breach of contract, fraud, and negligent misrepresentation, are based on state law.

PART II

GENERAL APPLICABLE LIABILITY PRINCIPLES

The distressing and deplorable conditions allegedly encountered and endured by [the] plaintiffs upon arriving in Ohio stand largely unrefuted. Often with little more than the $20.00 they were given for food during the three day bus ride from the Rio Grande Valley, the majority of the plaintiffs left behind their homes and families in Texas for the promise of suitable work in Ohio. Once there, many of the plaintiffs found themselves sleeping on floors in bare houses or apartments, often with a dozen or more other workers. One young woman described the frightening experience of sleeping in [an] unfurnished, one-bathroom house with approximately seventeen other people, mostly men. From the stand, she expressed her gratitude to several other male recruits, whom she had met just days before living with them in Ohio, for their willingness to allow her to sleep between them and the wall for protection. Another plaintiff testified that he and his sister were forced to sleep outside their apartment on concrete steps to escape the stench of the raw sewage that was seeping into their apartment. Other plaintiffs described their unremitting encounters with cockroaches and rats. With harrowing detail, plaintiffs related the discomfort and dangerousness of traveling to work in an overcrowded van that not only had only boards laid on cement blocks in lieu of seats, but which also was filled with exhaust fumes. For the most part, these disturbing and unsettling accounts were uncontested by Case Farms.

There can be no doubt that such living and transportation conditions were appalling, and would be, in many contexts, illegal. The plaintiffs' express challenge in this civil action, however, was to establish Case Farms' liability for such conditions. That is, before considering each of the many statutory violations alleged by the plaintiffs, an important threshold issue must be resolved. Does the law allow the plaintiffs to recover for their maltreatment from Case Farms? Can the plaintiffs, recruited and purportedly "employed" by ATC, recover from Case Farms? . . .

B. An Agricultural Employer's Liability Under Common Law Agency Principles

The fact that Congress has created a statutory framework of protections for migrant workers in no way exempts agricultural employers, recruiters, and over-seers from common law agency principles. Rather, the protections afforded by the AWPA are designed to supplement traditional common law principles. Thus, one theory under which the plaintiffs could prove that Case Farms itself committed the alleged violations would be to demonstrate that the ATC defendants' misdeeds were committed by ATC within the scope of its role as an agent of Case Farms.

ATC's Agency

Plaintiffs' supplementary theory of Case Farms liability is, therefore, based on traditional, pre-AWPA common law tenets of agency. Plaintiffs argue that an agency relationship existed between ATC and Case Farms, and that the scope of that relationship included both the express authority to recruit and hire people to work at Case Farms' plant, and the implied authority to do all things proper, usual, and necessary to exercise that authority. Case Farms responds that to the extent any agency relationship existed between ATC and Case Farms, the scope of that agency was limited solely to informing recruits about the availability of work in Ohio at Case Farms' processing plant.

The fundamental precepts of the law of agency are well settled. At common law, a principal may be held liable for the acts of its purported agent based on an actual agency relationship created by the principal's express or implied delegation of authority to the agent. Both forms of agency are at issue here. Express actual authority exists "where the principal has made it clear to the agent that he [or she] wants the act under scrutiny to be done." Pasant v. Jackson Nat'l Life Ins. Co., 52 F.3d 94, 97 (5th Cir. 1995). Further, giving an agent express authority to undertake a certain act also includes the implied authority to do all things proper, usual, and necessary to exercise that express authority.

Applying these principles, the plaintiffs assert that the scope of the agency relationship between Case Farms and ATC expressly authorized ATC to recruit and hire people to work at Case Farms' Ohio plant. Such a contention is certainly well-supported by the evidence. Former Case Farms' Director of Corporate Development, Andy Cilona, among others, testified that "the arrangement with ATC was for it to hire workers for Case Farms' production." Based on Case Farms' explicit agreement with ATC, it is found, by a preponderance of the evidence, that such an express agency relationship, the scope of which included recruiting and hiring migrant workers to perform jobs at Case Farms' plant, did exist between Case Farms and ATC.

A principal is liable for the actions of an agent only if those actions are taken in the scope of the agent's employment. While Case Farms acknowledges that ATC was expressly authorized to recruit and hire workers for its plant, the chicken processing company maintains that the scope of that relationship was extremely narrow, and that the vagueness of the plaintiffs' claim that ATC was Case Farms' agent glosses over the exact nature of the relationship between ATC and Case Farms.[16] The plaintiffs, on the other hand, argue that the scope of ATC's express authority to recruit and hire people to work at Case Farms' plant included the implied authority to do all things proper, usual, and necessary to exercise that authority.

---

16. This court again notes with some astonishment that the entire relationship between Case Farms and ATC was oral. No written contract or record of this agreement exists. Such an agreement, of course, would have been invaluable in the resolution of these issues.

A preponderance of the evidence supports the plaintiffs' contention. Credible evidence, adduced at trial, reveals that housing and transportation issues were well within the class of activities proper, usual, and necessary to recruit and hire workers for Case Farms' Ohio processing plant. It is uncontested that the combination of its high turnover rate, and relative isolation from metropolitan areas, complicates Case Farms' recruitment process. For Case Farms, recruitment was, at all relevant times, an on-going, virtually nation-wide undertaking. The very fact that this Ohio chicken processing plant was recruiting workers in Florida and Texas attests to the difficulties it faces finding workers. Furthermore, once the workers arrived in Ohio, it was difficult for workers to find housing on their own because of language barriers, lack of personal transportation, and their unfamiliarity with the area. So, it was essential to the success of Case Farms' hiring practices to assist out-of-state workers with housing. Case Farms, before any relationship with ATC, actually did assist incoming workers with housing and transportation in Ohio. Furthermore, it was clear from the evidence adduced at trial that Case Farms meant for ATC to perform these duties. Thus, it is found that Case Farms knew that these duties were proper, usual, and necessary in order to recruit and retain a workforce primarily migrating from out-of-state.

Case Farms points out, and places much weight on the fact, that its representatives Cilona and Kohli both testified that ATC was not authorized to hire workers and make them full fledged "Case Farms" employees. Rather, under the arrangement with ATC, the workers would supposedly remain "ATC employees," despite the fact that they worked in the Case Farms plant, doing the same work, at the same rate of pay, under the supervision of the same supervisors, as Case Farms workers.

Whether or not a plaintiff would become a "full-fledged" Case Farms employee, however, cannot be dispositive of the agency issue at hand. At issue in this civil action is precisely the question of whether superficial differences (such as which company's name appeared on a plaintiff's pay stub) somehow immunize the company that owns and operates the plant from liability. Given the fact that housing and transportation were necessary components of Case Farms' recruitment process, ATC's actions in those arenas were within the scope of its relationship as an agent of Case Farms.

For the foregoing reasons, it is found that the ATC defendants were clearly acting as Case Farms' agent in all of their actions relating to the recruitment and hiring of workers for Case Farms' chicken processing plant in Winesburg, Ohio. And, under the AWPA, recruitment by an agricultural employer includes recruitment through an agent. Hence, ATC's interactions with the plaintiffs may be attributed to Case Farms for the purpose of assessing compliance with AWPA. . . .

C. Case Farms' Liability for the Actions of ATC . . .

It is against the background of these general principles of liability that the many claims brought by the plaintiffs in this civil action will be considered. . . . ATC's actions, under common law precepts of agency, can be attributed directly to Case Farms for the purpose of assessing compliance with the AWPA. . . .

[After a lengthy review of the law, the court concluded that "Case Farms violated the law in its treatment of the plaintiffs, in the manners and ways set forth herein, and that plaintiffs should be awarded judgment therefor."]

Problem 1-3

Utah Cloudberry, Inc. (UCI) is an area developer of Cloudberry franchises in the state of Utah. UCI has opened several Cloudberry outlets, including one in Salt Lake City near the University of Utah. Kevin Macaulay is the general manager of this outlet.

According to his employment contract, Macaulay is responsible for running a "clean, orderly, lawful and respectable place of business in accordance with the standards established in the Franchise Agreement and Operations Manual." In furtherance of his responsibilities as general manager, Macaulay took the following actions:

- Purchased various cleaning supplies, including an automatic toilet bowl cleaner. The Franchise Agreement and Operations Manual did not specify the supplies to be used in cleaning.
- Purchased the point of sale system (a.k.a., a "cash register") specified by the Franchisor in the Operations Manual.
- Hired an interior decorator to redesign the store. The Franchise Agreement provides, "No furnishings, interior and exterior decor items, fixtures, or equipment shall be used in or upon any Shop unless expressly approved by Franchisor."
- Closed the shop on Sundays to conform to local business norms, even though the Franchise Agreement provides that the shop "shall be open and operational a minimum of 7 days per week, 12 hours per day, every day of the year."
- Terminated a male employee who showed up at work unshaven, even though being clean shaven was not an employment requirement imposed by the Franchise Agreement or Operations Manual.

How would you analyze whether Macaulay had actual authority to take each of the foregoing actions?

2.   Apparent Authority

One person may bind another in a transaction with a third person, even in the absence of actual authority, when the third person reasonably believes — based on "manifestations" by the purported principal — that the actor is authorized to act on behalf of the purported principal. We say "purported principal" because this "apparent authority" does not require the prior existence of an agency relationship. In other words, apparent authority may be the basis for liability in two situations: (1) where persons appear to be agents, even though they do not qualify under the definition discussed above (often referred to as "apparent agency"), and (2) where agents act beyond the scope of their actual authority.

The primary difficulties with the doctrine of apparent authority revolve around the notion of "manifestation." "Manifestation" was not defined in Restatement (Second), though the term appeared in many sections. The commentary on Restatement (Second) of Agency § 27 provides the following examples:

> [Manifestations from the principal to a] third person may come directly from the principal by letter or by word of mouth, from authorized statements of the agent, from documents or other indicia of authority given by the principal to the agent, or from third persons who have heard of the agent's authority from authorized or permitted channels of communication. Likewise, as in the case of authority, apparent authority can be created by appointing a person to a position, such as that of manager or treasurer, which carries with it generally recognized duties; to those who know of the appointment there is apparent authority to do the things ordinarily entrusted to one occupying such a position, regardless of unknown limitations which are imposed on a particular agent.

One of the most important innovations in Restatement (Third) of Agency is the inclusion of a new section defining "manifestation":

> A person manifests consent or intention through written or spoken words or other conduct.

Restatement (Third) of Agency § 1.03.

This definition was intended to broaden the concept of manifestation. As noted in the commentary to § 1.03, "conduct may constitute a manifestation sufficient to create apparent authority even though it does not use the word 'authority' and even though it does not consist of words targeted specifically to a third party." The primary purpose behind broadening the scope of this concept was to eliminate the separate doctrine of inherent agency power, which is discussed later in this section.

Given the commentary on Restatement (Second) of Agency § 27 quoted above — notably that manifestations may come "from third persons who have heard of the agent's authority" or merely from appointing a person to a position — one might be excused for wondering whether the concept of manifestation needed to be expanded. According to the drafters of the Restatement (Third) of Agency, the most important implication of the new definition of "manifestation" is that communications from the principal need not be directed to third persons before apparent authority is created. The necessity of finding a direct link between the principal and third persons could reasonably be drawn from the Restatement (Second) of Agency's definition of "apparent authority," which required "manifestations to such third persons," yet courts have traditionally not been so restrictive in requiring such manifestations prior to finding apparent authority. Consistent with what the courts have done, the Restatement (Third) of Agency now clearly permits the creation of apparent authority when manifestations reach the third party through an intermediary (as long as the manifestations are traceable to the principal), or simply by placing a person in a certain position. The importance of the new definition of "manifestation," therefore, probably lies in the fact that it has now made explicit in the primary sections of the Restatement what previously appeared only in the commentary, and that it endorses what courts were already doing.

In any event, there are two key points to finding apparent authority: (1) the manifestation (however defined) must emanate from the principal (or purported principal) and must be received (either directly or indirectly) by the third person; and (2) the scope of the agent's apparent authority depends on the third person's reasonable interpretation of that manifestation. Whether it was reasonable for a third person to believe that the agent with whom she transacted business had the authority to enter into a particular transaction has subjective and objective components. Courts consider prior dealings between the parties, customs that apply in the particular setting, and the nature of the proposed transaction (for example, whether the agent proposes a transaction that would benefit the purported principal). Reliance is not technically required to establish apparent authority—rather, it is an element of estoppel, which is discussed briefly below—though some courts inquire about reliance in some circumstances when evaluating apparent authority.

Estoppel is a non-agency doctrine that is similar to apparent authority in that both are created when the principal leads a third party to believe that an agent is authorized to act on the principal's behalf, even though no such actual authority has been granted. Two things distinguish estoppel from apparent authority: (1) estoppel requires the third party to change position in reliance on the principal, whereas a principal may be bound under apparent authority even in the absence of such detrimental reliance; and (2) estoppel allows the third party to hold the principal liable but does not give the principal any rights against the third party (although the principal can often cure that deficiency by ratifying the transaction).

Because estoppel and apparent authority are so similar, many courts treat them as synonymous and often use the terms interchangeably or impose a detrimental reliance requirement in cases decided on the basis of "apparent authority." Nevertheless, the Restatement (Third) of Agency retains the distinction between apparent authority and estoppel "to clarify the law and to make clear when and why it is necessary for a plaintiff to show detrimental reliance." Restatement (Third) of Agency, Introductory Note. The following case examines the doctrine of apparent authority and reminds us that apparent authority depends on a manifestation from the principal.

BETHANY PHARMACAL CO. v. QVC, INC.

241 F.3d 854
United States Court of Appeals, Seventh Circuit
February 23, 2001

RIPPLE, Circuit Judge.

Bethany Pharmacal Company, Inc. ("Bethany") brought this action against QVC, Inc. ("QVC"). It claimed that QVC had agreed to allow Bethany to appear on QVC's televised shopping program in order to sell its skin moisturizer. QVC moved for summary judgment. Bethany responded to QVC's motion and also sought leave to amend its complaint to add a promissory estoppel claim against QVC. The district court denied Bethany's request for leave to amend and granted QVC's motion for summary judgment. Bethany now seeks review of both rulings. For the reasons set forth in the following opinion, we affirm the judgment of the district court.

I

BACKGROUND

A. Facts

QVC operates a televised home shopping network. In 1997, QVC conducted a tour that it titled "The Quest for America's Best — QVC's 50 in 50 Tour" ("the Tour"). The purpose of the Tour was to find local vendors in each of the fifty states to appear on QVC's televised broadcast in order to sell their products. QVC hired Network Trade Associates, Inc. ("NTA") to serve as its contact with economic development offices or agencies in each of the fifty states. NTA, in turn, contacted the Illinois Department of Commerce and Community Affairs ("DCCA") for assistance in conducting the Illinois leg of the Tour. Roberta Janis was the DCCA employee responsible for the QVC/NTA project. Although Janis' responsibilities dealt primarily with the logistical aspects of the Tour, she self-titled herself the "QVC Project Manager" in her correspondence concerning this project. At no time, however, did QVC enter into a contract with either DCCA or Janis.

QVC held two trade shows in Illinois in April 1997. The purpose of the trade shows was to choose twenty Illinois vendors who would sell their products on QVC's broadcast. QVC also intended to choose five additional vendors as alternates. Prior to the trade shows, NTA gave Janis the names and addresses of several Illinois vendors. Janis sent those vendors a QVC solicitation packet; the information in this packet listed her as a contact person. In order to participate in the trade shows, vendors had to complete a product information sheet included in the solicitation packet. On that sheet, the vendor described the product that the vendor proposed to sell on QVC's program. The information sheet also included the following written disclaimer:

> The data provided on this sheet is for information purposes only. QVC's acceptance of your completed form does not constitute acceptance or agreement that the information you have provided is correct or complete. It is also not a waiver of any of QVC's rights, remedies or defenses with respect to you or your product. Any sales of the product to QVC shall be governed by a purchase order issued by QVC. An authorized QVC Purchase Order is the only valid contract. Verbal statements or discussions do not constitute a commitment to do business and should not be considered as such.

Bethany was one of the Illinois businesses that received a QVC solicitation packet. Bethany is a pharmaceutical company that manufactures a moisturizing skin lotion called Ti-Creme. Bethany's chairman, Jack J. Scott, Sr., completed a product information sheet describing Ti-Creme on behalf of Bethany, in which he indicated that Bethany had 15,000 to 50,000 jars of Ti-Creme available on hand. The product information sheet also asked Scott to indicate the "[m]anufacturer lead time required for $10,000 wholesale order"; Scott responded, "On Hand."

Scott represented Bethany at QVC's Springfield, Illinois, trade show in April 1997. Janis also attended the trade show and her DCCA business cards were on display at the registration desk. James Plutte and Julie Campbell, both buyers for

QVC, were also at the trade show. Plutte and Campbell explained to the vendors that, if their products were selected, they would receive a purchase order from QVC and that the vendors should not do anything until they heard directly from QVC.

Following the trade show, NTA notified Janis that it would send her a list of the twenty vendors and five alternates from Illinois that QVC had selected to appear on its broadcast, but it told Janis not to contact any of the listed vendors until QVC had notified the vendors of their selection itself. Apparently, Janis did not receive this list right away. Janis may not have received the list until after QVC had contacted the selected vendors, although the record is not clear on this point. What is clear is that Janis thought QVC had already contacted the vendors by the time she received the list. She therefore prepared a letter that she sent to the twenty participants and the five alternates in which she gave them logistical information about the broadcast and alerted them to a potential shortage in hotel accommodations during the time of the broadcast ("the Janis letter").[2] The Janis letter was printed on DCCA stationery, was addressed to "QVC Participants," congratulated them on being selected to participate in QVC's broadcast, and concluded by stating, "See you at the Fair." Although the same letter was sent to both participants and alternates, Janis directed her subordinates to attach a "post-it note" to the letters sent to the alternates with the word "Alternate."

In selecting the program participants, QVC chose Bethany as an alternate vendor. However, although Bethany received the Janis letter, it did not receive the post-it note informing it that it was only an alternate rather than a confirmed participant. After receiving the Janis letter, Scott telephoned Janis to thank her for notifying him that QVC had selected Bethany as a participant. The parties disagree as to the content of the conversation that followed. Scott claims that, in response to his call, Janis said, "We'll be seeing you at the show." Janis, however, claims that she told Scott that her records indicated that he was only an alternate and that she asked him whether he had received information from QVC indicating that he was a participant. The parties agree, however, that, in the course of the conversation, Janis did not say anything definitive that clearly would have dispelled Scott's misperception.

---

2. Given the importance of the Janis letter to this litigation, we set forth its text in full:

Dear QVC Participants:

Congratulations! We just received the news from QVC identifying the twenty companies who will be participating in the QVC broadcast in Springfield at the Illinois State Fair on August 9th.

The Department of Commerce and Community Affairs Small Business Division will be preparing a press release and distributing it statewide. When it is ready, we will provide a copy to you for your use.

The broadcast will be held on the first Saturday of the State Fair, which usually draws close to 150,000 attendees that day. The broadcast itself will be three (3) hours in length. The actual time for the broadcast is yet to be determined. The site selected for the broadcast is a 40,000 square foot area within the Farm Expo area. The site is in direct proximity to the Fair's main entrance.

Hotel rooms will be filling up fast. A listing of some Springfield hotels is provided to assist you in locating accommodations. A map of the State Fairgrounds is also provided.

Look forward to assisting you during the broadcast. See you at the Fair!

Sincerely,

Roberta Janis, QVC Project Manager

Scott claims that, in reliance on the Janis letter, he spent $100,000 to buy 60,000 units of Ti-Creme. This amount was what he predicted he would need on hand to meet the demand for Ti-Creme when QVC's broadcast aired. His calculation was based on a QVC press release describing the financial success of the vendors who had participated in the broadcasts. No one at QVC suggested to Scott that he should purchase additional product or that he would need more than the $10,000 worth of product that he already claimed to have on hand.

B. Earlier Proceedings

QVC eventually learned that Scott's receipt of the Janis letter had led him to believe that Bethany had been selected to participate in the broadcast, but it did not change Bethany's status from an alternate to a participant. Consequently, Bethany filed this breach of contract action against QVC. In Bethany's view, the Janis letter constituted a binding contract between Bethany and QVC; the letter constituted a promise that Bethany would be allowed to sell Ti-Creme on QVC's broadcast. Bethany sought to recover the $100,000 it spent to purchase additional product in reliance on QVC's alleged promise. QVC filed a motion for summary judgment. When Bethany replied to QVC's motion, it also filed a motion seeking leave to amend its complaint to add a promissory estoppel claim.

The district court granted QVC's motion for summary judgment. The court first considered whether Janis was QVC's apparent agent, which would allow her to bind QVC to a contract. The court held that Janis was not QVC's apparent agent because QVC had done nothing to indicate to Scott that Janis had any authority to act on QVC's behalf. The court determined that, because Janis had initiated her contact with the vendors, her conduct did not constitute a manifestation by QVC to third parties that Janis had the authority to transact business on QVC's behalf.

The district court further held that, even if Janis was QVC's apparent agent, there still was no valid contract between Bethany and QVC. It concluded that Scott's belief that the Janis letter was an offer to enter into a contract was not reasonable because the Janis letter did not specify the terms of the purported offer or the identities of the offeror and offeree. The court also concluded that, even if there was a valid contract, Bethany could not establish that the contract had been breached because it could not show that it suffered damages or had a reasonable basis for computing the damages it claimed to have suffered.

Finally, the court refused to allow Bethany to amend its complaint to include a promissory estoppel claim against QVC. The court determined that Bethany would be unable to succeed on such a claim because the Janis letter did not clearly promise that QVC would allow Bethany to appear on its broadcast to promote Ti-Creme. Additionally, the court believed that Bethany's promissory estoppel claim would fail because Bethany's reliance on the Janis letter in purchasing additional product was unreasonable, given that QVC never had indicated that this purchase would be necessary.

II

DISCUSSION

In appealing the district court's judgment, Bethany submits that the district court erred in concluding that Janis was not QVC's apparent agent and that the Janis letter could not form the basis of a binding contract. Bethany also argues that the district court abused its discretion in refusing to allow it to amend its complaint in order to add a promissory estoppel claim. We shall examine each of these contentions.

A. Breach of Contract . . .

Under Illinois' law of agency, an apparent agency exists if (1) the principal consents to or knowingly acquiesces in the agent's conduct, (2) the third party has a reasonable belief that the agent possesses authority to act on the principal's behalf, and (3) the third party relied to his detriment on the agent's apparent authority. An agent's apparent authority can only be determined by evaluating the principal's conduct toward the third party. Specifically, the principal must do something to lead the third party to believe that the agent is authorized to act on its behalf. The agent cannot unilaterally create an apparent agency through her own words or conduct. An apparent agency may arise, however, "from silence of the alleged principals when they knowingly allow another to act for them as their agent." Mateyka v. Schroeder, 504 N.E.2d 1289, 1295 (1987). In such a situation, the scope of the apparent agent's authority is determined by the authority that a reasonably prudent person might believe the agent to possess based on the actions of the principal.

Bethany maintains that QVC created the appearance that Janis was its agent by allowing her to correspond with vendors and to act as an intermediary between QVC and the vendors. Bethany further maintains that QVC should be responsible for the consequences of the Janis letter because it knew about the letter but never told Janis not to send it. QVC responds that Janis herself initiated the conduct to which Bethany points, and, therefore, the conduct cannot be attributed to any manifestation or authorization on QVC's part. Additionally, QVC maintains that Bethany's perception of Janis as a QVC agent with the authority to bind QVC to a contract was unreasonable, given QVC's statement on the product information sheet that the only valid contract with QVC was a purchase order.

We cannot accept Bethany's argument. Bethany has not established that QVC took any steps that would make a reasonable person believe that Janis had the authority to contract on its behalf. QVC consistently maintained that the only way in which it would enter a binding contract was through a purchase order issued by QVC. QVC clearly stated this principle in the product information sheet that it distributed to all interested vendors, including Bethany. QVC representatives again stated this principle to the vendors attending the trade show when they verbally reminded the vendors of the importance of a purchase order. Bethany has produced no evidence to demonstrate that QVC ever indicated that Janis or DCCA could contract on its behalf through some means other than a purchase order. Indeed, we can find no evidence in the appellate record that QVC ever indicated to any vendor that someone other than a QVC buyer had the authority to contract on QVC's behalf.

Bethany's argument that QVC created an apparent agency in Janis by allowing her to interact with the vendors on its behalf misses the mark. QVC did allow Janis to work with the vendors by providing logistical information about the trade shows and the broadcast; however, given QVC's repeated disclaimers regarding the need for a purchase order, that relationship cannot reasonably be interpreted as including the authority to contract on QVC's behalf. Moreover, QVC did not stand idly by and accept the benefits of contracts Janis allegedly had procured on its behalf. Instead, upon realizing that Bethany had misinterpreted the Janis letter, QVC notified Bethany of Janis' error and made clear that Bethany would not be allowed to appear on its broadcast. In short, QVC consistently stated to Bethany that a valid contract could be created only by a purchase order. Furthermore, after learning of Bethany's misperception because of Janis' mistake, QVC consistently maintained that Bethany was only an alternate. Under these circumstances, it was unreasonable for Bethany to believe that Janis had any authority to bind QVC to a contract with a vendor.

B. Bethany's Motion to Amend Its Complaint . . .

The district court determined that allowing Bethany to amend its complaint to add a promissory estoppel claim would be futile because Bethany would be unable to succeed on that claim. Bethany takes issue with this conclusion. It argues that the Janis letter constitutes an unambiguous promise by QVC to allow Bethany to appear on its broadcast and that Scott relied on this promise to Bethany's detriment by purchasing $100,000 worth of product in order to meet the anticipated demand for Ti-Creme following the broadcast. QVC responds that the Janis letter was not an unambiguous promise, that Bethany's reliance on the Janis letter was unreasonable, that Bethany delayed unduly in seeking the amendment, and that allowing the amendment in the face of Bethany's undue delay would prejudice QVC.

In order to succeed on its promissory estoppel claim, Bethany would have to prove that QVC made an unambiguous promise, that Bethany relied on that promise to its detriment, and that its reliance was reasonable and foreseeable by QVC. Bethany has failed to establish that the Janis letter was an unambiguous promise or that its reliance on that letter was reasonable. The Janis letter contains no words of promise or obligation; instead, it merely states that QVC notified DCCA of the vendors it had chosen to participate in the broadcast. Such a statement does not amount to an unambiguous promise on QVC's part to have Bethany promote Ti-Creme on its broadcast. More fundamentally, as we have discussed in the previous section, it was unreasonable for Scott to rely on the Janis letter in purchasing $100,000 worth of Ti-Creme after QVC had stated expressly to Scott and the other vendors that the sale of any product to QVC would be governed by a purchase order. The district court did not abuse its discretion in refusing to allow the amendment on the grounds that it would be futile . . . .

CONCLUSION

The district court properly granted summary judgment. It also acted well within its discretion in denying Bethany leave to amend its complaint to add a promissory estoppel claim. Accordingly, the judgment of the district court is affirmed.

PROBLEM 1-4

Under the terms of the Cloudberry Franchise Agreement, a franchisee may sell only Authorized Cloudberry Products, a term that is defined as follows:

"Authorized Cloudberry Products" means the foods, yogurts, frozen yogurts, yogurt drinks, frozen desserts, smoothies and beverages, and other food items and other products, which may include specialty foods, packaged foods, books, hats, CDs, DVDs and other media, apparel, retail items, and gift or loyalty cards, as specified by Cloudberry Ventures, Inc. (the "Company") from time to time in the operations manual, or as otherwise directed by Company in writing, for sale at a Shop (or the Licensed Shop), prepared, sold, and/or manufactured in strict accordance with Company's recipes, and Standards, including specifications as to ingredients, brand names, preparation, and presentation.

As noted above, Utah Cloudberry, Inc. (UCI) is the area developer of Cloudberry franchises in the state of Utah. Kevin Macaulay, the general manager of an outlet in Salt Lake City, is an employee of UCI and is responsible for overseeing the operation of the Salt Lake City store.

Macaulay entered into a long-term contract, purportedly on behalf of UCI, with a supplier of organically grown fruits in Park City, Utah. Macaulay believes that the store's clientele would be interested in locally grown, organic produce, but this produce is not specified in the Cloudberry operations manual or otherwise directed by the Company in writing. Because organic produce is more expensive than produce grown using pesticides and chemical fertilizers, UCI's profits have declined. Recent rumblings from Cloudberry's attorneys about this state of affairs, using terms like "default on UCI's obligations under the License Agreement," have caused UCI to want to disavow the supply agreement.

What facts would be most important in determining whether UCI would be bound by Macaulay's contract with the produce supplier?

CHAPTER
2

Partnerships

MOTIVATING HYPOTHETICAL

Lloyd Park was admitted to the California Bar in 1992, and opened his own law office in Newport Beach. He built a successful practice, focusing on family law and estate planning. John Blaylock was admitted to the California Bar in 2001, the year he graduated from law school, and he immediately began working in Lloyd Park's law office.

General partnerships are plentiful in the United States. Despite the widespread availability of limited liability entities—including corporations, limited liability companies, and limited partnerships—general partnerships are a popular business entity. The primary virtues of general partnerships are simplicity and favorable tax treatment. As will be discussed in more detail below, general partnerships are simple to form and flexible in their organization. In addition, general partnerships are not taxed as separate business entities, unlike corporations.

Like the law of agency, partnership law first developed through common law. Several states codified partnership law in the second half of the 19th century, but the primary vehicle of standardization of partnership law in the United States was the Uniform Partnership Act (UPA), which was proposed by the National Conference of Commissioners on Uniform State Laws (NCCUSL) in 1914 and subsequently adopted, with minor amendments, by 49 states (Louisiana excepted).

At the time of the drafting of the UPA, there was much debate about the value of codification. After all, the United States was built on the tradition of the common law of England rather than the civil law tradition of the European continent. Nevertheless, the desire for uniformity was strong. Uniformity was not sought for its own sake but for the sake of business efficiency. As noted by William Draper Lewis, one of the principal draftsmen of the UPA, uniformity in partnership law was desirable because "a considerable proportion of existing partnerships do business in more than one state." William Draper Lewis, *The Desirability of Expressing the Law of Partnership in Statutory Form*, 60 U. Pa. L. Rev. 93,

95 (1911). Lewis contended that conflicts among state partnership laws induced confusion among partners and third parties.

Even more important to Lewis than uniformity, however, was the clarifying effect of a uniform partnership statute. He attributed the existing conflicts among states to "a confusion, and to what we may call a haziness, in respect to fundamental legal conceptions." *Id.* at 96. Lewis hoped the UPA would shed light on those fundamental concepts, thus revealing his view of the value of codification.

The most fundamental concept is the nature of the partnership: Are partnerships treated as entities separate from the individual partners or merely as aggregations of individuals, with the partnership having no separate legal status? The answer to this question has profound implications for almost all legal rules that govern partnerships. Under the common law, partnerships usually were treated as aggregates. Nevertheless, courts often employed the entity theory. This equivocation caused Professor Scott Rowley, in his treatise on partnerships, to remark, "There is no other relation known to law which, in its nature, is so complicated as is partnership." Scott Rowley, *Rowley on Partnership* 15 (2d ed. 1960). Frustration over the crazy quilt of rules produced by the common law moved Judge Learned Hand to write in support of universal recognition of the entity theory:

> The whole subject of partnership has undoubtedly always been exceedingly confused, simply because our law has failed to recognize that partners are not merely joint debtors. It could be straightened out into great simplicity, and in accordance with business usages and business understanding, if the entity of the firm, through a fiction, were consistently recognized and enforced. Like the concept of a corporation, it is for many purposes a device of the utmost value in clarifying ideas and in making easy the solution of legal relations.

In re Samuels & Lesser, 207 Fed. 195, 198 (S.D.N.Y. 1913).

Although the drafters of the UPA claimed to embrace the aggregate theory of partnership, the UPA is schizophrenic on the issue of partnership personality. Some provisions suggest that partnerships have a separate legal existence (for example, UPA § 9 provides that each partner is considered an agent of the partnership, not of the other partners) while other sections suggest that a partnership is merely an aggregation of partners (for example, UPA § 15 imposes liability on partners individually for obligations of the partnership). This confusion within the UPA is partially explained by its drafting history. The initial drafting committee was charged with drafting a statute following the entity approach, and the first drafts of the UPA were prepared by Dean James Barr Ames of Harvard Law School, an enthusiastic advocate of the entity approach. When Ames died in 1910, he was replaced by Dean William Draper Lewis of the University of Pennsylvania Law School, who believed in an aggregate approach to partnership. Under Lewis's guidance, the drafting committee changed some provisions in the early drafts to reflect an aggregate approach, thus creating the mix of entity and aggregate provisions.

The utility of the entity theory, so obvious today, was not so obvious to the drafters of the UPA, and vigorous debates surrounded the issue. Recounting a meeting of the UPA drafting committee and commentators, Lewis explained that three reasons persuaded the group to unanimously recommend a statute based on the aggregate theory: (1) existing common law was based on the aggregate theory; (2) the aggregate theory better reflected the expectations of third persons dealing with the partnership (creditors expected to hold partners directly liable for partnership obligations); and (3) the draft before the committee had overcome the most serious objections to the aggregate theory (primarily those relating to ownership of partnership property). William Draper Lewis, *The Uniform Partnership Act—A Reply to Mr. Crane's Criticism*, 29 Harv. L. Rev. 158, 172-173 (1915). Interestingly, Lewis also noted: "[T]hose with the largest practical experience present were opposed to regarding the partnership as a 'legal person' because of the effect of the theory in lessening the partner's sense of moral responsibility for partnership acts." *Id.* at 173.

Although the UPA is still immensely important to partnership law in the United States, discontent with its provisions—largely the result of the incoherence of the aggregate view of the partnership—prompted Georgia and California to adopt substantial amendments to their versions of the UPA in the 1980s. In 1986 the American Bar Association (ABA) recommended changes to the UPA. Finally, in 1987 the NCCUSL created a drafting committee to draft a revision of the UPA. After years of work, the committee produced a "final" version of the new act in 1991. Following ABA objections, the committee produced several subsequent revisions to the act. The latest version of the Revised Uniform Partnership Act (RUPA) is dated 1994, but it contains amendments adopted in 1996 and 1997. As of 2011, 35 states and the District of Columbia have adopted RUPA.

The committee that drafted RUPA did not begin with a mandate to treat the partnership as an entity or an aggregate. Over the course of drafting, however, the committee settled on the entity theory of partnership because it "provides simpler rules and is consistent with RUPA's attempt to give partnerships greater stability." As a result of this recognition, the committee added RUPA § 201 to clarify that a "partnership is an entity distinct from its partners." Donald J. Weidner & John W. Larson, *The Revised Uniform Partnership Act: The Reporters' Overview*, 49 Bus. Law. 1, 3 (1993).

RUPA makes many important changes to the UPA, most of which can be traced to RUPA's commitment to the entity theory throughout. Some of the more important changes RUPA makes, a number of which will be explored in more detail in later sections of the book, include the following: (1) RUPA § 203 makes partnership property the property of the entity, not of the individual partners. (2) RUPA does away with the UPA rule that the departure of a partner causes a dissolution of the partnership. This rule reflected the concept that every aggregation of partners is unique and any change causes a new partnership to be formed. The UPA did not account for the fact that some departures trigger the winding up of the partnership business and some simply trigger a buyout of the departing partner. RUPA has different rules for each of these situations, thus tracking business practice more closely. (3) RUPA provides for the merger or conversion of partnerships into limited partnerships. Mergers or conversions of partnership would be unthinkable under UPA because partnerships were not an entity.

A.   FORMATION

The rules contained in the uniform partnership acts apply only to relationships that meet the definition of a "partnership." UPA § 6(1) and RUPA § 202(a) both define "partnership" as an "association of two or more persons to carry on as co-owners a business for profit." Despite several centuries of judicial consideration—including 90 years of experience with the foregoing statutory definition—partnership formation still poses some of the most challenging issues in partnership law. This is largely attributable to the fact that no formalities are required to form a partnership. Although people may create a partnership through formal agreement, the most difficult formation questions arise in the context of inadvertent partnerships. Courts often find that a partnership has been created in the absence of a written agreement, conscious intent to form a partnership, or knowledge that a partnership has been formed.

The UPA definition of "partnership" comports with prior common law definitions in all essential respects. Nevertheless, no general definition of "partnership" can adequately explain all of the cases. This difficulty is best understood by reflecting on the fact that partnership formation issues are raised almost exclusively in cases where one person is attempting to avoid liability to another—either to a purported partner or to a third party—where such liability is founded on the existence of a partnership. Partnership liability rules will be examined in more detail in Section D. For the present, it is sufficient to understand two general principles: (1) one partner may be bound to third parties by the act of another partner; and (2) partners are personally liable for obligations of the partnership. As a result of these principles, partnership formation issues take on great importance. The finding of a partnership can impose personal liability on an individual who did not act or even know of the action of another partner. Against this backdrop, courts tend to strive for fairness rather than doctrinal purity. The definition of "partnership," therefore, is necessarily flexible.

Courts often state that the existence of a partnership depends on whether the partners had the requisite intent. But what must the parties have intended? Consider Bass v. Bass, 814 S.W.2d 38, 41 (Tenn. 1991):

> [T]he existence of a partnership depends upon the intention of the parties, and the controlling intention in this regard is that ascertainable from the acts of the parties. Although a contract of partnership, either express or implied, is essential to the creation of partnership status, it is not essential that the parties actually intend to become partners. The existence of a partnership is not a question of the parties' undisclosed intention or even the terminology they use to describe their relationship, nor is it necessary that the parties have an understanding of the legal effect of their acts. It is the intent to do the things which constitute a partnership that determines whether individuals are partners, regardless if it is their purpose to create or avoid the relationship. Stated another way, the existence of a partnership may be implied from the circumstances where it appears that the individuals involved have entered into a business relationship for profit, combining their property, labor, skill, experience, or money.

Courts are not bound by statements of parties disavowing an intention to enter into a partnership. Nevertheless, expressions of intent by the parties are probably highly persuasive. Courts are most likely to override the expressed intentions of the parties where the rights of third parties are involved.

As in other areas of the law, intent is difficult to discern from a distance. The informality of most partnerships ensures that intent is rarely expressed in written form. As a result, most courts focus on a few indicia of partnership in an attempt to ascertain whether the parties intended to enter into a partnership. The most important of these indicia of partnership is whether a purported partner receives a share of the profits of the business. UPA § 7(4) states that "receipt by a person of a share of profits of a business is prima facie evidence that he is a partner in the business." *Cf.* RUPA § 202(c)(3) (receipt of profits raises a presumption of partnership).

This test originated in the well-known English case, Waugh v. Carver, 2 H. Bl. 235, 126 Eng. Rep. 525 (C.P.D., Nov. 23, 1793), in which Erasmus Carver and William Carver agreed with Archibald Giesler to cooperate in generating business. Under the agreement, each side would "take a moiety" — that is, one half — of the proceeds, but each side would bear its own losses. As to liability, the agreement explicitly stated that neither side would be liable for the acts of the other. The court characterized the moiety as "profit" and held that the parties had formed a partnership because they agreed to share profits. The rationale for this holding was "the principle that by taking a part of the profits, he takes from the creditors a part of that fund which is the proper security to them for the payment of their debts."

Waugh does not admit any possible exceptions to the general rule that sharing of profits results in the formation of a partnership vis-à-vis third parties. Nevertheless, courts readily recognized an exception for employees who are paid for their services out of the profits of the firm. Often, distinguishing between employees and partners is easier said than done. Similarly, if creditors receive payments from the profits of the firm, courts will refrain from finding that a partnership has been formed. The analysis in these cases is highly textured. Given that the sharing of profits is present, courts examine other aspects of the relationship closely.

The following case explores some of the difficult questions that surround partnership formation. As you consider the claim in *Holmes*, contemplate the difference (if any) between forming a partnership and preparing to incorporate a business. Moreover, try to identify why it matters whether a partnership has been formed.

HOLMES v. LERNER

Court of Appeal, First District, Division 1, California
74 Cal. App. 4th 442
August 20, 1999 (as modified Sept. 7, 1999)

MARCHIANO, Judge.

This case involves an oral partnership agreement to start a cosmetics company known as "Urban Decay." Patricia Holmes prevailed on her claim that Sandra Kruger Lerner breached her partnership agreement and that David Soward interfered with the Holmes-Lerner contract, resulting in Holmes's ouster from the business. Lerner and Soward appeal from the judgment finding them liable to Holmes for compensatory and punitive damages of over $1 million. . . .

We affirm the judgment against Lerner, primarily because we determine that an express agreement to divide profits is not a prerequisite to prove the existence of a partnership. We also determine that the oral partnership agreement between Lerner and Holmes was sufficiently definite to allow enforcement. . . .

BACKGROUND . . .

Sandra Lerner is a successful entrepreneur and an experienced business person. She and her husband were the original founders of Cisco Systems. When she sold her interest in that company, she received a substantial amount of money, which she invested, in part, in a venture capital limited partnership called "& Capital Partners." By the time of trial in this matter, Lerner was extremely wealthy. Patricia Holmes met Lerner in late 1993, when Lerner visited Holmes's horse training facility to arrange for training and boarding of two horses that Lerner was importing from England. Holmes and Lerner became friends, and after an initial six-month training contract expired, Holmes continued to train Lerner's horses without a contract and without cost.

In 1995, Lerner and Holmes traveled to England to a horse show and to make arrangements to ship the horses that Lerner had purchased. On this trip, Lerner decided that she wanted to celebrate her 40th birthday by going pub crawling in Dublin. Lerner was wearing what Holmes termed "alternative clothes" and black nail polish, and encouraged Holmes to do the same.[1] Holmes, however, did not like black nail polish, and was unable to find a suitable color in the English stores. At Lerner's mansion outside of London, Lerner gave Holmes a manicuring kit, telling her to see if she could find a color she would wear. Holmes looked through the kit, tried different colors, and eventually developed her own color by layering a raspberry color over black nail polish. This produced a purple color that Holmes liked. Holmes showed the new color to Lerner, who also liked it.

On July 31, 1995, the two women returned from England and stayed at Lerner's West Hollywood condominium while they waited for the horses to clear quarantine. While sitting at the kitchen table, they discussed nail polish, and colors. Len Bosack, Lerner's husband, was in and out of the room during the conversations. For approximately an hour and a half, Lerner and Holmes worked with the colors in a nail kit to try to recreate the purple color Holmes had made in England so they could have the color in a liquid form, rather than layering two colors. Lerner made a different shade of purple, and Holmes commented that it looked just like a bruise. Holmes then said that she wanted to call the purple color she had made "Plague." Holmes had been reading about 16th-century England, and how people with the plague developed purple sores, and thought the color looked like the plague sores.[2] Lerner and Holmes discussed the fact that the names they were creating had an urban theme, and tried to think of other names to fit the theme. Starting with "Bruise" and "Plague," they also discussed the names "Mildew," "Smog," "Uzi," and "Oil Slick." Len Bosack

1. There were references throughout the trial to Lerner's "alternative" look and to "alternative" culture. Lerner, who referred to herself as an "edgy cosmetics queen," described "alternative culture" as "not really mainstream," "edgy," and "fashion forward." As an example, she noted her own purple hair. She defined "edgy" as not trying to be cute, and being unconventional.
2. Plague is described as "rich violet with a blue sheen."

walked into the kitchen at that point, heard the conversation about the urban theme, and said "What about decay?" The two women liked the idea, and decided that "Urban Decay" was a good name for their concept.[3]

Lerner said to Holmes: "This seems like a good [thing], it's something that we both like, and isn't out there. Do you think we should start a company?" Holmes responded: "Yes, I think it's a great idea." Lerner told Holmes that they would have to do market research, determine how to have the polishes produced, and that there were many things they would have to do. Lerner said: "We will hire people to work for us. We will do everything we can to get the company going, and then we'll be creative, and other people will do the work, so we'll have time to continue riding the horses." Holmes agreed that they would do those things. They did not separate out which tasks each of them would do, but planned to do it all together.

Lerner went to the telephone and called David Soward, the general partner of & Capital, and her business consultant. Holmes heard her say "Please check Urban, for the name, Urban Decay, to see if it's available and if it is, get it for us." Holmes knew that Lerner did not joke about business, and was certain, from the tone of her voice, that Lerner was serious about the new business. The telephone call to secure the trademark for Urban Decay confirmed in Holmes's mind that they were forming a business based on the concepts they had originated in England and at the kitchen table that day. Holmes knew that she would be taking the risk of sharing in losses as well as potential success, but the two friends did not discuss the details at that time. Lerner's housekeeper heard Lerner tell Holmes: "It's going to be our baby, and we're going to work on it together." After Holmes left, the housekeeper asked what gave Lerner the idea to go into the cosmetics business, since her background was computers. Lerner replied: "It was all Pat's idea over in England, but I've got the money to make it work." Lerner told her housekeeper that she hoped to sell Urban Decay to Estee Lauder for $50 million.

Although neither of the two women had any experience in the cosmetics business, they began work on their idea immediately. Holmes and Lerner did market research by going to stores, talking with people about nail polish, seeing what nail polishes were available, and buying samples to bring back to discuss with each other. They met frequently in August and September at Lerner's home, and experimented with nail colors. They took pictures of various color mixing sessions. In early August, they met with a graphic artist, Andrea Kelly, and discussed putting together a logo and future advertising work for Urban Decay.

Prior to the first scheduled August meeting, Holmes told Lerner she was concerned about financing the venture. Lerner told her not to worry about it because Lerner thought they could convince Soward that the nail polish business would be a good investment. She told Holmes that Soward took care of Lerner's investment money. Holmes and Lerner discussed their plans for the company, and agreed that they would attempt to build it up and then sell it. Lerner and Holmes discussed the need to visit chemical companies and hire people to handle the daily operations of the company. However, the creative aspect, ideas, inspiration, and impetus for the company came from Holmes and Lerner.

___

3. At the trial, Lerner testified that she had an idea prior to July of 1995 that there might be a market for unusual nail colors, but was missing a "unifying theme" to identify the concept.

Lerner, Holmes, Soward, and Kelly attended the first scheduled meeting. The participants in these meetings referred to them as "board meetings," even though there was no formal organizational structure, and technically, no board. They discussed financing, and Soward reluctantly agreed to commit $500,000 towards the project. Urban Decay was financed entirely by & Capital, the venture capital partnership composed of Soward as general partner, and Lerner and her husband as the only limited partners. Neither Lerner nor Holmes invested any of their individual funds.

Lerner and Soward went to Kirker Chemical Company later in August of 1995 and learned about mixing and manufacturing nail polish colors. Lerner discouraged Holmes from accompanying them. Although Lerner returned to Kirker, she never took Holmes with her. At the second board meeting, in late August, Soward introduced Wendy Zomnir, a friend of Soward's former fiancé, as an advertising and marketing specialist. After Zomnir and Kelly left the meeting, Holmes, Lerner and Soward discussed her presentation. Holmes was enthusiastic about Zomnir and they decided to hire her. At the conclusion of the September board meeting, after Holmes had left, Lerner and Soward secretly made Zomnir an offer of employment, which included a percentage ownership interest in Urban Decay. It wasn't until a couple of meetings later, when Lerner or Soward referred to Zomnir as the "Chief Operating Officer" of Urban Decay, that Holmes learned of the terms of the offer.

In early October, after Holmes learned of the secret offer to Zomnir, she asked Lerner to define her role at Urban Decay. Lerner responded: "Your role is anything you want it to be." When Holmes asked to discuss the issue in more detail, Lerner turned and walked away. Holmes believed that Lerner was nervous about an upcoming photo session, and decided to discuss it with Lerner at a later date. At their regular board meetings, Holmes participated with Soward, Lerner, Zomnir, Kelly, and another person in discussing new colors, and deciding which ones they wanted to sell, and which names would be used.

In September of 1995, Soward signed an application for trademark registration as president of Urban Decay. In December of 1995, Urban Decay was incorporated. Holmes asked for a copy of the articles of incorporation, but was given only two pages showing the name and address of the company. On December 31, Holmes sent a fax to Lerner stating that it had been difficult to discuss her position in Urban Decay with Lerner. Holmes asked Lerner: "What are my responsibilities and obligations, and what are my rights or entitlements?" Holmes also asked: "What are my current and potential liabilities and assets?" She requested that Lerner provide the information in writing. At this point, Holmes wanted to memorialize the agreement she and Lerner had made on July 31.

Soward intercepted the fax and called Holmes, asking: "What's going on?" Holmes explained that she wanted a written agreement, and Soward apologized, telling her that Lerner had asked him to get "something . . . in writing" to Holmes. Soward told Holmes that no one in the company had a written statement of their percentage interest in the company yet. Soward asked: "What do you want, one percent, two percent?" When Holmes did not respond, he told her that 5 percent was high for an idea. Holmes told him: "I'm not selling an idea. I'm a founder of this company." Soward exclaimed: "Surely you don't think you have fifty percent of this company?" Holmes told him that it was a matter between herself and Lerner, and that Soward should speak to Lerner. Soward agreed to talk to Lerner.

On January 11, 1996, Lerner and Holmes met at a coffee shop to discuss the fax. Holmes explained that she wanted "something in writing" and an explanation of her interest and position in the company. Lerner responded that a start up business is "like a freight train . . . you can either run and catch up, and get on, and take a piece of this company and make it your own, or get out of the way." As a result of this conversation, Holmes decided to double her efforts on behalf of Urban Decay. Because she was most comfortable working at the warehouse, she focused on that aspect of the business.[4] Holmes was reimbursed for mileage, but received no pay for her work.

During January and February, Urban Decay was launching its new nail polish product. Publicity included press releases, brochures, and newspaper interviews with Lerner. An early press release stated: "The idea for Urban Decay was born after Lerner and her horse trainer, Pat Holmes, were sitting around in the English countryside." Lerner approved the press release. In February of 1996, an article was printed in the San Francisco Examiner containing the following quotes from Lerner. "Since we couldn't find good nail polish, in cool colors there must be a business opportunity here. Pat had the original idea. Urban Decay was my spin." The Examiner reporter testified at trial that the quote attributed to Lerner was accurate. Lerner was also interviewed in April by CNN. In that interview she told the story of herself and Holmes looking for unusual colors, mixing their own colors at the kitchen table, and that "we came up with the colors, and it just sort of suggested the urban thing."[5]

Lerner had always notified Holmes whenever there was a board meeting, and she sent Holmes an agenda for the February 20, 1996, meeting. Lerner also sent a memo stating that she thought they should have an "operations meeting" with the warehouse supervisor first. Lerner's memo continued: "and then have a regular board meeting, including [Zomnir], me, David, and Pat, and no one else." Holmes understood that the regular board meeting would be for the purpose of discussing general Urban Decay business. At the operations meeting, Holmes made a presentation regarding the warehouse operations. The financial report showed $205,000 in revenues and $431,000 in expenses. The "directors" thought this early sales figure was "terrific." Soward handed out an organizational chart, which showed Lerner, with the title "CEO" at the top; Soward, as "President" beneath her; and Zomnir, as "COO" beneath Soward. Holmes asked "Where am I?" Lerner responded by pointing to the top of the chart and telling Holmes that she was a director, and was at the top of the chart, above all the other names.

In March of 1996, Holmes received a document from Soward offering her a one percent ownership interest in Urban Decay. Soward explained that Urban

---

4. Holmes testified that her work at the warehouse included responding to requests for brochures, developing a system for handling increased telephone inquiries, and negotiating a contract with a skills center to assist with the mail-order business. She had authority to hire and fire employees and to sign checks on the Urban Decay account. Only Holmes, Soward, Lerner, Zomnir, and the warehouse manager were authorized to sign on the account. Only the manager's authority was limited to $1,500. Holmes was spending four to five days a week at the warehouse. Urban Decay accountant Sharon Land testified that Holmes "contributed a great deal" to Urban Decay, and directed the retail business. Soward, Lerner, and Zomnir seldom came to the office. Soward told Land that Holmes was on the board of directors.

5. When asked at trial why she used the word "we," Lerner responded that she was stressed. Lerner testified that almost every statement she made in the CNN interview was false, and a result of stress.

Decay had been formed as a limited liability company, which was owned by its members. For the first time, Holmes realized that Lerner and Soward had produced an organizational document that did not include her, and she was now being asked to become a minor partner. When she studied the document, she discovered that it referred to an exhibit A, which was purported to show the distribution of ownership interests in Urban Decay. Soward had given Zomnir a copy of exhibit A when he offered her an ownership interest in Urban Decay. However, when Holmes asked Soward for a copy of exhibit A, he told her it did not exist.[10] By this time, Holmes was planning to consult an attorney about the document.

Despite the deterioration of her friendship with Lerner, and her strained relationship with Soward, Holmes continued to attend the scheduled board meetings, hoping that her differences with Lerner could be resolved. She also continued to work at the warehouse on various administrative projects and on direct mail order sales. As late as the April board meeting, Holmes was still actively engaged in Urban Decay business. She made a presentation on a direct mail project she had been asked to undertake. As a result of Holmes's attendance at a sales presentation when she referred to herself as a cofounder of Urban Decay, Lerner instructed Zomnir to draft a dress code and an official history of Urban Decay. Lerner told Zomnir that it was a "real error in judgment" to allow Holmes to attend the sales presentation because she did not project the appropriate image. The official history, proposed in the memo, omitted any reference to Holmes. Finally, matters deteriorated to the point that Soward told Holmes not to attend the July board meeting because she was no longer welcome at Urban Decay.

On August 27, 1996, Holmes filed a complaint against Lerner and Soward, alleging 10 causes of action, including breach of an oral contract, intentional interference with contractual relations, fraud, breach of fiduciary duty, and constructive fraud. Holmes eventually dismissed some of her claims and the court dismissed others, sending the case to the jury on the causes of action noted above. At the trial, cosmetic industry expert Gabriella Zuckerman testified that Urban Decay was not just a fad. In her opinion, Urban Decay had discovered and capitalized on a trend that was just beginning. She reviewed projected sales figures of $19.9 million in 1997, going up to $52 million in 2003, and found them definitely obtainable. Arthur Clark, Holmes's expert at valuing startup businesses, valued Urban Decay under different risk scenarios. In Clark's opinion, the value of Urban Decay to a potential buyer was between $4,672,000 and $6,270,000. Lerner's expert, who had never valued a cosmetics company, testified that Urban Decay had $2.7 million in sales in 1996. He estimated the value of Urban Decay as approximately $2 million, but concluded that it was not marketable.

Lerner and Soward claimed that Holmes was never a director, officer, or even an employee of Urban Decay. According to Lerner, she was just being nice to Holmes by letting her be present during Urban Decay business. Lerner denied

---

10. Holmes was never given exhibit A, and did not see it until trial. It showed & Capital Partners, L.P. with a 92 percent interest, having contributed $489,900. It also showed Lerner and her husband with contributions of $5,050 each, and 1 percent apiece. Zomnir's contribution was listed as $5,050, but she had a 5 percent interest. None of the individuals actually paid in the listed contributions.

Holmes had any role in creating the colors, names, or concepts for Urban Decay. When Holmes asked Lerner about her assets and liabilities in Urban Decay, Lerner thought she was asking for a job. She explained her statements to the press regarding Urban Decay being Holmes's idea as misquotes or the product of her stress.

The jury found in favor of Holmes on every cause of action. The jury assessed $480,000 in damages against Lerner, and $320,000 against Soward. Following presentation of evidence as to net worth, the jury awarded punitive damages of $500,000 against Lerner and $130,000 against Soward. In the judgment, the court declined to add the two amounts together, but stated that the verdict of $320,000 was against Lerner and Soward, jointly and severally, and that the additional $160,000 verdict was against Lerner individually. Lerner and Soward moved for a judgment notwithstanding the verdict, which was denied on December 16, 1997. They appealed from the judgment and the order denying their postverdict motion. . . .

DISCUSSION

Lerner and Soward argue that there was no partnership agreement as a matter of law. . . .

I. THERE WAS NO ERROR IN THE DETERMINATION THAT A PARTNERSHIP WAS FORMED

Holmes testified that she and Lerner did not discuss sharing profits of the business during the July 31, "kitchen table" conversation. Throughout the case, Lerner and Soward have contended that without an agreement to share profits, there can be no partnership. Lerner and Soward begin their argument on appeal by quoting a statement from Westcott v. Gilman (1915) [150 P. 777], that profit sharing is "an essential element of every partnership. . . ." They argue that nothing has changed since the "ancient truth" regarding profit sharing was expressed in *Westcott*. However, an important element supporting the *Westcott* decision has changed, because *Westcott* relied on the language of former section 2395 of the Civil Code. That statutory predecessor of the Uniform Partnership Act defined a partnership as: ". . . the association of two or more persons, for the purpose of carrying on business together, and dividing its profits between them." Civil Code former section 2395 was repealed and replaced with the UPA in 1949.

The applicable version of the UPA omitted the language regarding division of profits and defined a partnership as: "an association of two or more persons to carry on as co-owners a business for profit." When the Legislature enacts a new statute, replacing an existing one, and omits express language, it indicates an intent to change the original act. We can only conclude that the omission of the language regarding dividing profits from the definition of a partnership was an intentional change in the law.[13] The UPA relocated the provision regarding

---

13. The significance of the change in the definition of a partnership is noted in the article by Professor Wright, California Partnership Law and the Uniform Partnership Act (1921) 9 Cal. L. Rev. 117, 127-128, criticizing the Civil Code provision because it "emphasizes the division of profits unduly," and noting that deletion of the "'dividing the profit between them'" language of the Civil Code would theoretically allow a partnership to be formed in which all profits went to one partner, or all profits were reinvested.

profits to former section 15007, subdivision (4), which provided that in deter-mining whether a partnership exists, "[t]he receipt by a person of a share of the profits of a business is prima facie evidence that he is a partner. . . ." This relocation of the element of sharing the profits indicates that the Legislature intends profit sharing to be evidence of a partnership, rather than a required element of the definition of a partnership. The presence or absence of any of the various elements set forth in former section 15007, including sharing of profits and losses, is not necessarily dispositive. As explained in Cochran v. Board of Supervisors (1978) [149 Cal. Rptr. 304], the rules to establish the existence of a partnership in [former section] 15007 should be viewed in the light of the crucial factor of the intent of the parties revealed in the terms of their agree-ment, conduct, and the surrounding circumstances when determining whether a partnership exists.

The UPA provides for the situation in which the partners have not expressly stated an agreement regarding sharing of profits. Former section 15018 provided in relevant part: "The rights and duties of the partners in relation to the partnership shall be determined, subject to any agreement between them, by the following rules: (a) Each partner shall . . . share equally in the profits and surplus remaining after all liabilities, including those to partners, are satisfied." This provision states, subject to an agreement between the parties, partners "shall" share equally in the profits. Lerner and Soward argue that using former section 15018 to supply a missing term regarding profit sharing ignores the provision of former section 15007, subdivision (2). That section, headed "rules for determining existence of partnership," provided that mere joint ownership of common property "does not of itself establish a partnership, whether such co-owners do or do not share any profits made by the use of the property." Lerner and Soward are mistaken. The def-inition in former section 15006 provides that the association with the intent to carry on a business for profit is the essential requirement for a partnership. Following that definition does not transform mere joint ownership into the essence of a partnership. . . .

The trial court in this case refused to add additional elements to the statu-tory definition and properly instructed the jury in the language of former section 15006. We agree with the trial court's interpretation of the law. The actual sharing of profits (with exceptions which do not apply here) is prima facie evidence, which is to be considered, in light of any other evidence, when determining if a partnership exists. In this case, there were no profits to share at the time Holmes was expelled from the business, so the evidentiary provi-sion . . . is not applicable. According to former section 15006, parties who expressly agree to associate as co-owners with the intent to carry on a business for profit, have established a partnership. Once the elements of that definition are established, other provisions of the UPA and the conduct of the parties supply the details of the agreement. Certainly implicit in the Holmes-Lerner agreement to operate Urban Decay together was an understanding to share in profits and losses as any business owners would. The evidence supported the jury's implicit finding that Holmes birthed an idea which was incubated jointly by Lerner and Holmes, from which they intended to profit once it was fully matured in their company.

II. THE AGREEMENT WAS SUFFICIENTLY DEFINITE

Lerner and Soward argue that the agreement between Lerner and Holmes was too indefinite to be enforced. . . .

The agreement between Holmes and Lerner was to take Holmes's idea and reduce it to concrete form. They decided to do it together, to form a company, to hire employees, and to engage in the entire process together. The agreement here, as presented to the jury, was that Holmes and Lerner would start a cosmetics company based on the unusual colors developed by Holmes, identified by the Urban theme and the exotic names. The agreement is evidenced by Lerner's statements: "We will do . . . everything," "[i]t's going to be our baby, and we're going to work on it together." Their agreement is reflected in Lerner's words: "We will hire people to work for us." "We will do everything we can to get the company going, and then we'll be creative, and other people will do the work, so we'll have time to continue riding the horses." The additional terms were filled in as the two women immediately began work on the multitude of details necessary to bring their idea to fruition. The fact that Holmes worked for almost a year, without expectation of pay, is further confirmation of the agreement. Lerner and Soward never objected to her work, her participation in board meetings and decisionmaking, or her exercise of authority over the retail warehouse operation. Even as late as the trial in this matter, when Lerner was claiming that everything Holmes said was a lie, Lerner admitted: "It was not only my intention to give Pat every opportunity to be a part of this, but I had hoped that she would." . . . Holmes was not seeking specific enforcement of a single vague term of the agreement. She was frozen out of the business altogether, and her agreement with Lerner was completely renounced. The agreement that was made and the subsequent acts of the parties supply sufficient certainty to determine the existence of a breach and a remedy. . . .

[T]he judgment and postjudgment order are affirmed. . . .

PROBLEM 2-1

For the first four years of their association, Lloyd Park paid John Blaylock a salary from which income taxes were withheld. Park also paid Blaylock one-third of all fees collected in relation to any matters that Blaylock brought into the office.

In 2005 Park and Blaylock entered into an agreement (Agreement) redefining their relationship. The Agreement provided that the name of the firm would be changed to "Park & Blaylock," but the Agreement specified that the name change did "not represent a partnership but was only a change in firm name." Beyond this provision, the Agreement did not characterize the relationship as employer-employee or as a partnership. Instead, the Agreement referred to an "arrangement" based on Park and Blaylock's prior "excellent relationship in the law practice heretofore owned solely by Park."

The preamble to the Agreement stated that Blaylock did not "wish to invest any capital to purchase a share of said practice for cash," but it also provided that Blaylock would "share in the net income of the practice" at a rate of 20 percent. The Agreement discontinued the salary and fee-sharing provisions in their prior agreement but provided for a specified minimum annual payment "regardless of the amount of net practice income." That minimum amount started at $52,000 in 2005 and increased annually to $60,000 in 2010. From 2011 forward, Blaylock's annual share of the net income was fixed at 25 percent with no guaranteed minimum payment.

Although the preamble to the Agreement characterized the practice as having been "heretofore" owned solely by Park, Paragraph 8 specifically provided that the practice would "continue to be owned solely by Park, who alone shall make all decisions with respect to management of the practice." It also characterized Blaylock as "an independent contractor" who would be "solely responsible for all taxes payable upon his remuneration."

After the Agreement was signed, no taxes were withheld from Blaylock's checks and, in contrast to prior years, his income was reported to the taxing authorities on a Form 1099 rather than a W-2. The firm never filed a partnership tax return.

Which of the foregoing facts would be most important in determining whether Park and Blaylock formed a general partnership? Are there other facts that you would investigate to shed light on the formation issue?

B. MANAGEMENT

Management issues concern decision making in the ongoing operations of the partnership. In the absence of an agreement to the contrary, all partners have equal rights in the management and conduct of the partnership business. UPA § 18(e); RUPA § 401(f). If partners disagree about ordinary matters within the scope of the partnership business, the vote of a majority of partners controls. UPA § 18(h); RUPA § 401(j).

The UPA requires the unanimous consent of partners to authorize amendments to the partnership agreement (UPA § 18(h)) and to add new partners (UPA § 18(g)) and lists certain extraordinary transactions in UPA § 9(3) that require the unanimous consent of partners. But the UPA does not have a general provision covering authorization of extraordinary transactions. As a result, most courts have reasoned from the existing provisions that any extraordinary transaction requires the unanimous consent of partners. This unanimity requirement was codified by RUPA § 401(j), which addresses "act[s] outside the ordinary course of business of a partnership."

The *Vecchitto* case involves a simple disagreement among multiple partners. While the narrow doctrinal lesson of the case is straightforward—all of the partners must consent to acts outside the partnership's ordinary course of business—the value of the case lies in its discussion of control over the partnership entity. This is the first case in the book examining the manner in which a business organization (as opposed to an individual agent) is controlled. Is the court right to conclude that if the filing of the lawsuit were within the partnership's ordinary course of business, no approval of the partners would be required? Is the court correct that the filing of the lawsuit is outside the ordinary course of business of the partnership? How should a court decide what is the ordinary course of business of a partnership?

VECCHITTO v. VECCHITTO

2008 WL 4210784
Superior Court of Connecticut
Aug. 26, 2008

CLARANCE J. JONES, Judge.

The plaintiffs, Christopher Vecchitto and Vecchitto Lemon Ice,[1] filed an eighteen-count complaint against the defendants, alleging various claims on March 17, 2008. This action arises out of the alleged breach of a partnership agreement that Christopher Vecchitto and his brothers, named defendants in this matter, entered into on January 23, 1957. All of the odd counts are brought on behalf of the individual partner, Christopher Vecchitto, and all of the even counts are brought on behalf of Vecchitto Lemon Ice, the partnership.

Two of the partners are named as defendants in this action. The fourth has allegedly been disassociated with the partnership for some time. The complaint alleges that the defendant partners have breached the provisions of the partnership agreement by either transferring his interests in the partnership and/or introducing other persons into the business of the partnership without the consent required in the partnership agreement. The plaintiff partnership essentially argues that it would be futile to try to come to an agreement to file suit on behalf of the partnership because the remaining two partners would not have agreed to file suit because they are also defendants in this action. The plaintiff partnership has cited no case law to support this argument.

The plaintiff partnership argues that in this circumstance, it would set bad precedent to not allow the individual partner, without the consent of the other partners, to file a lawsuit on behalf of the partnership.

The defendants have filed a motion to dismiss all counts brought on behalf of the partnership arguing that the partnership lacks standing to bring suit because it never authorized such action. . . .

The defendants argue that the counts brought on behalf of the partnership should be dismissed because the partnership did not authorize such action, but rather, an individual partner, Christopher Vecchitto, brought the action on behalf of the partnership without the partnership's approval. Furthermore, the defendants argue that General Statutes § 34-335(j) supports their argument because it states that "[a] difference arising as to a matter in the ordinary course of business of a partnership may be decided by a majority of the partners. An act outside the ordinary course of business of a partnership and an amendment to the partnership agreement may be undertaken only with the consent of all of the partners." The partnership, on the other hand, argues that it has standing to "commence this action to preserve, protect, reacquire and prevent the further loss of property, profits and other associated economic damage to partnership interests." Further, the partnership argues that it is authorized to commence the suit pursuant to General Statutes § 34-328[2] and § 34-339.[3] Lastly, the partnership

---

1. Vecchitto Lemon Ice is a Connecticut Partnership, formerly known as Vecchitto Brothers Froze Rite Ice Cream.

2. General Statutes § 34-328 provides in relevant part that "(a) A partnership may sue and be sued in the name of the partnership. (b) An action may be brought against the partnership and any or all of the partners in the same action or in separate actions."

3. General Statutes § 34-339 provides in relevant part that "(a) A partnership may maintain an action against a partner for a breach of the partnership agreement, or for the violation of a duty to the partnership, causing harm to the partnership."

argues that Connecticut law does not require a single partner, or the partnership itself, to seek authorization to sue.

General Statutes § 34-339(a) provides in relevant part that "[a] partnership may maintain an action against a partner for a breach of the partnership agreement." Furthermore, General Statutes § 34-303(a) states that "relations among the partners and between the partners and the partnership are governed by the partnership agreement. To the extent the partnership agreement does not otherwise provide, sections 34-300 to 34-399, inclusive, govern relations among the partners and between the partners and the partnership." The partnership argues that it has a statutory right to file an action based on the language of these statutes. In this case, the partnership agreement is silent as to the filing of a lawsuit or what must be done given the circumstances of this case. The plaintiff argues that this silence means that the partnership agreement does not require the majority consent of the partners prior to the commencement of a lawsuit on behalf of the partnership, as argued by the defendants. Further, it is argued that to require the consent of the other partners prior to the commencement of the lawsuit "would render meaningless those provisions of the act authorizing the partnership to commence suit against a partner for violation of the partnership agreement of violation of a duty owed to it." The partnership argues that based on § 34-339(a) and § 34-328(a), the partnership can bring an action against a partner for breach of the partnership agreement, just as is alleged in the complaint. This, however, does not take into account the language of § 34-335(j). [As is stated in 34-303(a), if the partnership agreement is silent, which it is in this matter, then the court must look at sections § 34-300 to § 34-399 to determine the relationship among the partners and partnership. That includes the sections cited by the plaintiff which state that a partnership may file suit, as well as § 34-335(j) cited by the defendants.]

General Statutes § 34-335(j) indicates that matters that are within the ordinary course of business *may* be decided by a majority of the partners, however, acts outside of the ordinary course of business may be undertaken *only with the consent of all of the partners*. The issue then becomes whether the filing of this lawsuit is within the partnership's ordinary course of business. If it is, then the defendants' argument fails, however, if it is not, then the opposite is true.

It is alleged in the complaint that the partnership's primary purpose is to engage in the sale of ice cream and frozen ice. The partnership agreement . . . also states that the purpose of the partnership is to carry on an ice cream and frozen ice business, and any other business the partners shall agree upon. Based on the allegations of the complaint and the partnership agreement itself, it is clear that filing a lawsuit is not within the ordinary course of the partnership's business, which is to sell "frozen treats." Furthermore, the partnership agreement states that the partners shall agree upon any other business. Also, based on the affidavits submitted by the parties, the partners never agreed to file this lawsuit on behalf of the partnership. The filing of this lawsuit is not within the ordinary course of the partnership's business. In accordance with § 34-335(j) acts outside of the ordinary course of business must be consented to by all of the partners and in this case, the partners never consented to the filing of this lawsuit.

. . . There are four equal partners in this partnership and the partnership agreement does not authorize or give one partner the power to bring litigation on behalf of the partnership. The partners never consented to the filing of this lawsuit, and, therefore, the partnership cannot request that the issues complained of be adjudicated. Simply stated, the partnership lacks standing. Since the partnership does not have standing to file this lawsuit, this court lacks subject matter jurisdiction, and therefore, the defendants' motion to dismiss should be granted.

Despite the failure of the partners to consent to the filing of this lawsuit on behalf of the partnership, the partnership argues that it would have been futile to try to come to an agreement to file suit, and therefore, the motion to dismiss should be denied. In support of its futility argument, the partnership cites to *Santana v. Hartford,* 94 Conn.App. 445, 462, 894 A.2d 307 (2006). The court in *Santana* held that the "Supreme Court has grudgingly carved several exceptions from the exhaustion doctrine . . . although only infrequently and only for narrowly defined purposes. . . . One of the limited exceptions to the exhaustion rule arises when recourse to the administrative remedy would be demonstrably futile. . . . An action is futile when such action could not result in a favorable decision and invariably would result in further judicial proceedings. . . . The guiding principle in determining futility is that the law does not require the doing of a useless thing." *Id.,* at 462, 894 A.2d 307.

General Statutes § 34-335(j) provided that there must be consent of all of the partners regarding acts outside of the partnership's ordinary course of business. There is no statutory authority that states that when an individual partner feels that the partnership is going in a direction other than what is described in the partnership agreement, despite objections from the other partners, that individual partner can file a lawsuit on behalf of the partnership against the other partners. . . .

For the foregoing reasons, the Court finds that since the partnership does not have standing in this case, the defendants' motion to dismiss should be and hereby is granted as to counts two, four, six, eight, ten, twelve, fourteen, sixteen and eighteen.

PROBLEM 2-2

One of the vexing problems in partnership law involves management rights in partnerships with only two partners. In the event of an internal dispute about a matter of partnership business, William Draper Lewis suggested that the UPA as written made the result clear: "A contract made by one of two partners against the protest of the other is not made by a majority. The implication from the section as worded, therefore, is that such a contract, the third person knowing of the protest, would not be a partnership contract." William Draper Lewis, *The Uniform Partnership Act — A Reply to Mr. Crane's Criticism,* 29 Harv. L. Rev. 291, 302 (1911). This view has not always prevailed in the courts. In the well-known case of National Biscuit Company, Inc. v. Stroud, 106 S.E.2d 692 (N.C. 1959), the Supreme Court of North Carolina faced this issue in the context of a partnership that operated a grocery store. One of the two partners (Stroud) decided that he no longer wanted to purchase bread from Nabisco, and he told Nabisco that he would not be personally liable for any future orders. When the other partner (Freeman) subsequently ordered bread, Nabisco delivered. Upon the failure of the partnership to pay for the bread, Nabisco sued Stroud for payment. The court held Stroud personally liable, reasoning:

Freeman as a general partner with Stroud, with no restrictions on his authority to act within the scope of the partnership business so far as the agreed statement of facts shows, had under the Uniform Partnership Act "equal rights in the management and conduct of the partnership business." Under [UPA § 18(h)], Stroud, his co-partner, could not restrict the power and authority of Freeman to buy bread for the partnership as a going concern, for such a purchase was an "ordinary matter connected with the partnership business," for the purpose of its business and within its scope, because in the very nature of things Stroud was not, and could not be, a majority of the partners. Therefore, Freeman's purchases of bread from plaintiff for Stroud's Food Center as a going concern bound the partnership and his co-partner Stroud. . . .

While this case neatly displays the tension between the rules governing management rights and the rules governing authority, cases involving third-party claims against divided two-person partnerships are fairly rare.[1] A more common problem arises when a rogue partner acts in a manner that exposes other partners to liability. As you evaluate that problem, consider the possible justifications for holding partners responsible for fraudulent behavior that they did not condone.

For the sake of discussing the remaining problems in this chapter, assume that Lloyd Park and John Blaylock formed a general partnership, later adding a third partner named Kenneth Wheeler, who had expertise in real estate development. Wheeler was not licensed to practice in California, but he was licensed to practice in Arizona. In December 2010, Wheeler engaged in the unauthorized practice of law in several real estate transactions and began misappropriating client funds in connection with those transactions. *If parties to the foregoing real estate transactions sued the law firm partnership because of Wheeler's actions, under what circumstances would the law firm or its partners incur liability for Wheeler's actions? If the law firm instructed Wheeler not to practice law until he obtained his license, would that influence your answer? Would it matter to your answer that the misappropriations would have been difficult for the other partners to detect?*

---

1. The *Nabisco* case is often contrasted with Summers v. Dooley, 481 P.2d 318 (Idaho 1971), in which one partner hired an employee over the objection of another. When the employee attempted to recover wages from the dissenting partner, the court refused to uphold the claim, reasoning as follows:

> A careful reading of the statutory provision indicates that [UPA § 18] bestows equal rights in the management and conduct of the partnership business upon all of the partners. The concept of equality between partners with respect to management of business affairs is a central theme and recurs throughout the Uniform Partnership law, which has been enacted in this jurisdiction. Thus the only reasonable interpretation of [UPA § 18(h)] is that business differences must be decided by a majority of the partners provided no other agreement between the partners speaks to the issues.

This case is usually rationalized with *Nabisco* with the notion that partners cannot change the status quo (their existing ordinary business practices), except by majority vote. In *Nabisco*, the dissenting partner wanted to change; in *Summers*, the initiating partner wanted to change. In both instances, the court refused to honor the change.

C. FIDUCIARY DUTIES

Fiduciary duties traditionally have developed through common law. Although UPA § 21 purports to contain a description of the fiduciary duties of partners, it is very narrow in its literal terms, providing only that partners must not steal from the partnership. Other sections of the UPA often are said to supplement this duty of loyalty. For example, UPA § 19 provides for access to partnership records, UPA § 20 requires partners to render "true and full information" about the partnership to the other partners, and UPA § 22 gives partners the right to an accounting under certain specified circumstances as well as when "other circumstances render it just and reasonable." In addition to the weak duty of loyalty provisions, the UPA contains no provision for the duty of care, although some courts have implied a duty of care. The explicit duties in the UPA are flimsy indeed, compared with the expansive duties of an agent to a principal. Perhaps because UPA § 4(3) explicitly incorporates the law of agency, courts have been very generous about imposing fiduciary duties on partners under the UPA.

RUPA goes far to change the statutory structure of fiduciary duties under partnership law. Under RUPA § 404, partners owe duties of loyalty and care. RUPA attempts to narrow the broad duties imposed by courts under UPA, providing that the duty of loyalty "is limited to the following," and specifying three discrete duties: (1) an anti-theft duty that corresponds to the anti-theft duty in UPA § 21, except that the word "formation" has been dropped to indicate that fiduciary duties arise only after the partnership is created; (2) a prohibition against self-dealing; and (3) a prohibition against competing against the partnership. RUPA § 404(b). If these provisions were interpreted literally by courts, they would narrow the scope of a partner's duty of loyalty from most common law standards. Partners are allowed to narrow the duty of loyalty still further by contract, but they are not allowed to eliminate the duty of loyalty completely. RUPA § 103(b)(3).

The duty of care in RUPA § 404(c) establishes that conduct showing gross negligence, recklessness, intentional misconduct, or knowing violation of the law would violate the requisite standard of care. This default standard forces partners to share any losses resulting from the negligence of one of the partners. The RUPA Reporters believed that losses from negligence are perceived as an inevitable series of costs that over time will be imposed randomly and equally on all partners. This is because partners are open to unlimited liability and therefore have an incentive to exercise due care and to monitor the behavior of other partners. In addition, if the partners know of disparities in ability or attitude toward care, they are likely to contract to alter the default loss-sharing rule. Therefore, the Reporters argue, there is no need to allocate risk of loss from negligence among the partners. Gross negligence was the standard applied by courts that have implied a duty of care. Donald J. Weidner & John W. Larson, *The Revised Uniform Partnership Act: The Reporters' Overview*, 49 Bus. Law. 1, 22 (1993). While the partners may modify the duty of care by contract, they are not allowed to "unreasonably reduce the duty of care." RUPA § 103(b)(4).

In addition to the duties of loyalty and care, RUPA adds an obligation of good faith and fair dealing. RUPA § 404(d). This obligation was not expressly required in the UPA except in a single, narrowly defined clause dealing with expulsions, but courts often implied a duty of good faith and fair dealing.

The RUPA obligation is expressly made nonwaivable (mandatory), except that the parties may "determine the standards by which performance is to be measured, if the standards are not manifestly unreasonable." RUPA § 103(b)(5). By failing to define the meaning of good faith and fair dealing in the partnership context, it is uncertain how this broad obligation will be interpreted and applied. The drafting committee has made it clear that the omission of any definition of good faith and fair dealing in RUPA is not an oversight: "The meaning of 'good faith' is not defined nor is it firmly fixed under present law. . . . [The Drafting Committee] concluded that it would be preferable to leave the term undefined. . . ."

The following is perhaps the most-cited partnership case ever, although, as you will see, it is not actually a partnership case. Judge Cardozo's vaulting rhetoric has ensured Meinhard v. Salmon a prominent place among the great articulations of fiduciary duty. It is followed by a problem exploring the tension between management rights and fiduciary obligation and a more recent case that illustrates a modern approach to fiduciary duties in the context of a large law firm partnership.

MEINHARD v. SALMON
249 N.Y. 458, 164 N.E. 545
Court of Appeals of New York
December 31, 1928

CARDOZO, Chief Justice.

On April 10, 1902, Louisa M. Gerry leased to the defendant Walter J. Salmon the premises known as the Hotel Bristol at the northwest corner of Forty-Second street and Fifth avenue in the city of New York. The lease was for a term of 20 years, commencing May 1, 1902, and ending April 30, 1922. The lessee undertook to change the hotel building for use as shops and offices at a cost of $200,000. Alterations and additions were to be accretions to the land.

Salmon, while in course of treaty with the lessor as to the execution of the lease, was in course of treaty with Meinhard, the plaintiff, for the necessary funds. The result was a joint venture with terms embodied in a writing. Meinhard was to pay to Salmon half of the moneys requisite to reconstruct, alter, manage, and operate the property. Salmon was to pay to Meinhard 40 per cent of the net profits for the first five years of the lease and 50 per cent for the years thereafter. If there were losses, each party was to bear them equally. Salmon, however, was to have sole power to "manage, lease, underlet and operate" the building. There were to be certain pre-emptive rights for each in the contingency of death.

The two were coadventurers, subject to fiduciary duties akin to those of partners. As to this we are all agreed. The heavier weight of duty rested, however, upon Salmon. He was a coadventurer with Meinhard, but he was manager as well. During the early years of the enterprise, the building, reconstructed, was operated at a loss. If the relation had then ended, Meinhard as well as Salmon would have carried a heavy burden. Later the profits became large with the result that for each of the investors there came a rich return. For each the venture had its phases of fair weather and of foul. The two were in it jointly, for better or for worse.

When the lease was near its end, Elbridge T. Gerry had become the owner of the reversion. He owned much other property in the neighborhood, one lot adjoining the Bristol building on Fifth avenue and four lots on Forty-Second street. He had a plan to lease the entire tract for a long term to someone who would destroy the buildings then existing and put up another in their place. In the latter part of 1921, he submitted such a project to several capitalists and dealers. He was unable to carry it through with any of them. Then, in January, 1922, with less than four months of the lease to run, he approached the defendant Salmon. The result was a new lease to the Midpoint Realty Company, which is owned and controlled by Salmon, a lease covering the whole tract, and involving a huge outlay. The term is to be 20 years, but successive covenants for renewal will extend it to a maximum of 80 years at the will of either party. The existing buildings may remain unchanged for seven years. They are then to be torn down, and a new building to cost $3,000,000 is to be placed upon the site. The rental, which under the Bristol lease was only $55,000, is to be from $350,000 to $475,000 for the properties so combined. Salmon personally guaranteed the performance by the lessee of the covenants of the new lease until such time as the new building had been completed and fully paid for.

The lease between Gerry and the Midpoint Realty Company was signed and delivered on January 25, 1922. Salmon had not told Meinhard anything about it. Whatever his motive may have been, he had kept the negotiations to himself. Meinhard was not informed even of the bare existence of a project. The first that he knew of it was in February, when the lease was an accomplished fact. He then made demand on the defendants that the lease be held in trust as an asset of the venture, making offer upon the trial to share the personal obligations incidental to the guaranty. The demand was followed by refusal, and later by this suit. A referee gave judgment for the plaintiff, limiting the plaintiff's interest in the lease, however, to 25 per cent. The limitation was on the theory that the plaintiff's equity was to be restricted to one-half of so much of the value of the lease as was contributed or represented by the occupation of the Bristol site. Upon cross-appeals to the Appellate Division, the judgment was modified so as to enlarge the equitable interest to one-half of the whole lease. With this enlargement of plaintiff's interest, there went, of course, a corresponding enlargement of his attendant obligations. The case is now here on an appeal by the defendants.

Joint adventurers, like copartners, owe to one another, while the enterprise continues, the duty of the finest loyalty. Many forms of conduct permissible in a workaday world for those acting at arm's length, are forbidden to those bound by fiduciary ties. A trustee is held to something stricter than the morals of the market place. Not honesty alone, but the punctilio of an honor the most sensitive, is then the standard of behavior. As to this there has developed a tradition that is unbending and inveterate. Uncompromising rigidity has been the attitude of courts of equity when petitioned to undermine the rule of undivided loyalty by the "disintegrating erosion" of particular exceptions. Wendt v. Fischer, 243 N.Y. 439, 444, 154 N.E. 303. Only thus has the level of conduct for fiduciaries been kept at a level higher than that trodden by the crowd. It will not consciously be lowered by any judgment of this court.

The owner of the reversion, Mr. Gerry, had vainly striven to find a tenant who would favor his ambitious scheme of demolition and construction. Baffled in the search, he turned to the defendant Salmon in possession of the Bristol, the keystone of the project. He figured to himself beyond a doubt that the man in possession would prove a likely customer. To the eye of an observer, Salmon held the lease as owner in his own right, for himself and no one else. In fact he held it as a fiduciary, for himself and another, sharers in a common venture. If this fact had been proclaimed, if the lease by its terms had run in favor of a partnership, Mr. Gerry, we may fairly assume, would have laid before the partners, and not merely before one of them, his plan of reconstruction. The pre-emptive privilege, or, better, the pre-emptive opportunity, that was thus an incident of the enterprise, Salmon appropriated to himself in secrecy and silence. He might have warned Meinhard that the plan had been submitted, and that either would be free to compete for the award. If he had done this, we do not need to say whether he would have been under a duty, if successful in the competition, to hold the lease so acquired for the benefit of a venture then about to end, and thus prolong by indirection its responsibilities and duties. The trouble about his conduct is that he excluded his coadventurer from any chance to compete, from any chance to enjoy the opportunity for benefit that had come to him alone by virtue of his agency. This chance, if nothing more, he was under a duty to concede. The price of its denial is an extension of the trust at the option and for the benefit of the one whom he excluded.

No answer is it to say that the chance would have been of little value even if seasonably offered. Such a calculus of probabilities is beyond the science of the chancery. Salmon, the real estate operator, might have been preferred to Meinhard, the woolen merchant. On the other hand, Meinhard might have offered better terms, or reinforced his offer by alliance with the wealth of others. Perhaps he might even have persuaded the lessor to renew the Bristol lease alone, postponing for a time, in return for higher rentals, the improvement of adjoining lots. We know that even under the lease as made the time for the enlargement of the building was delayed for seven years. All these opportunities were cut away from him through another's intervention. He knew that Salmon was the manager. As the time drew near for the expiration of the lease, he would naturally assume from silence, if from nothing else, that the lessor was willing to extend it for a term of years, or at least to let it stand as a lease from year to year. Not impossibly the lessor would have done so, whatever his protestations of unwillingness, if Salmon had not given assent to a project more attractive. At all events, notice of termination, even if not necessary, might seem, not unreasonably, to be something to be looked for, if the business was over and another tenant was to enter. In the absence of such notice, the matter of an extension was one that would naturally be attended to by the manager of the enterprise, and not neglected altogether. At least, there was nothing in the situation to give warning to any one that while the lease was still in being, there had come to the manager an offer of extension which he had locked within his breast to be utilized by himself alone. The very fact that Salmon was in control with exclusive powers of direction charged him the more obviously with the duty of disclosure, since only through disclosure could opportunity be equalized. If he might cut off renewal by a purchase for his own benefit when four months were to pass before the lease would have an end, he might do so with equal right while there remained as many years. He might steal a march on his comrade under cover of the darkness, and then hold the captured ground. Loyalty and comradeship are not so easily abjured. . . .

We have no thought to hold that Salmon was guilty of a conscious purpose to defraud. Very likely he assumed in all good faith that with the approaching end of the venture he might ignore his coadventurer and take the extension for himself. He had given to the enterprise time and labor as well as money. He had made it a success. Meinhard, who had given money, but neither time nor labor, had already been richly paid. There might seem to be something grasping in his insistence upon more. Such recriminations are not unusual when coadventurers fall out. They are not without their force if conduct is to be judged by the common standards of competitors. That is not to say that they have pertinency here. Salmon had put himself in a position in which thought of self was to be renounced, however hard the abnegation. He was much more than a coadventurer. He was a managing coadventurer. For him and for those like him the rule of undivided loyalty is relentless and supreme. A different question would be here if there were lacking any nexus of relation between the business conducted by the manager and the opportunity brought to him as an incident of management. For this problem, as for most, there are distinctions of degree. If Salmon had received from Gerry a proposition to lease a building at a location far removed, he might have held for himself the privilege thus acquired, or so we shall assume. Here the subject-matter of the new lease was an extension and enlargement of the subject-matter of the old one. A managing coadventurer appropriating the benefit of such a lease without warning to his partner might fairly expect to be reproached with conduct that was underhand, or lacking, to say the least, in reasonable candor, if the partner were to surprise him in the act of signing the new instrument. Conduct subject to that reproach does not receive from equity a healing benediction.

A question remains as to the form and extent of the equitable interest to be allotted to the plaintiff. The trust as declared has been held to attach to the lease which was in the name of the defendant corporation. We think it ought to attach at the option of the defendant Salmon to the shares of stock which were owned by him or were under his control. The difference may be important if the lessee shall wish to execute an assignment of the lease, as it ought to be free to do with the consent of the lessor. On the other hand, an equal division of the shares might lead to other hardships. It might take away from Salmon the power of control and management which under the plan of the joint venture he was to have from first to last. The number of shares to be allotted to the plaintiff should, therefore, be reduced to such an extent as may be necessary to preserve to the defendant Salmon the expected measure of dominion. To that end an extra share should be added to his half. . . .

The judgment should be modified by providing that at the option of the defendant Salmon there may be substituted for a trust attaching to the lease a trust attaching to the shares of stock, with the result that one-half of such shares together with one additional share will in that event be allotted to the defendant Salmon and the other shares to the plaintiff, and as so modified the judgment should be affirmed with costs.

ANDREWS, J. (dissenting).

. . . Morton H. Meinhard was a woolen merchant. At some period during the negotiations between Mr. Salmon and Mrs. Gerry, so far as the findings show without the latter's knowledge, he became interested in the transaction. Before the lease was executed he advanced $5,000 toward the cost of the proposed alterations. Finally, on May 19th he and Salmon entered into a written agreement. "During the period of twenty years from the 1st day of May, 1902," the parties agree to share equally in the expense needed "to reconstruct, alter, manage and operate the Bristol Hotel property"; and in all payments required by the lease, and in all losses incurred "during the full term of the lease, *i.e.*, from the first day of May, 1902, to the 1st day of May, 1922." During the same term net profits are to be divided. Mr. Salmon has sole power to "manage, lease, underlet and operate" the premises. If he dies, Mr. Meinhard shall be consulted before any disposition is made of the lease, and if Mr. Salmon's representatives decide to dispose of it, and the decision is theirs, Mr. Meinhard is to be given the first chance to take the unexpired term upon the same conditions they could obtain from others.

The referee finds that this arrangement did not create a partnership between Mr. Salmon and Mr. Meinhard. In this he is clearly right. He is equally right in holding that while no general partnership existed the two men had entered into a joint adventure and that while the legal title to the lease was in Mr. Salmon, Mr. Meinhard had some sort of an equitable interest therein. Mr. Salmon was to manage the property for their joint benefit. He was bound to use good faith. He could not willfully destroy the lease, the object of the adventure, to the detriment of Mr. Meinhard. . . .

Were this a general partnership between Mr. Salmon and Mr. Meinhard, I should have little doubt as to the correctness of this result, assuming the new lease to be an offshoot of the old. Such a situation involves questions of trust and confidence to a high degree; it involves questions of good will; many other considerations. As has been said, rarely if ever may one partner without the knowledge of the other acquire for himself the renewal of a lease held by the firm, even if the new lease is to begin after the firm is dissolved. Warning of such an intent, if he is managing partner, may not be sufficient to prevent the application of this rule.

We have here a different situation governed by less drastic principles. I assume that where parties engage in a joint enterprise each owes to the other the duty of the utmost good faith in all that relates to their common venture. Within its scope they stand in a fiduciary relationship. I assume prima facie that even as between joint adventurers one may not secretly obtain a renewal of the lease of property actually used in the joint adventure where the possibility of renewal is expressly or impliedly involved in the enterprise. I assume also that Mr. Meinhard had an equitable interest in the Bristol Hotel lease. Further, that an expectancy of renewal inhered in that lease. Two questions then arise. Under his contract did he share in that expectancy? And if so, did that expectancy mature into a graft of the original lease? To both questions my answer is "No." . . .

What then was the scope of the adventure into which the two men entered? It is to be remembered that before their contract was signed Mr. Salmon had obtained the lease of the Bristol property. Very likely the matter had been earlier discussed between them. The $5,000 advance by Mr. Meinhard indicates that fact. But it has been held that the written contract defines their rights and duties. Having the lease, Mr. Salmon assigns no interest in it to Mr. Meinhard. He is to manage the property. It is for him to decide what alterations shall be made and to fix the rents. But for 20 years from May 1, 1902, Salmon is to make all advances from his own funds and Meinhard is to pay him personally on demand one-half of all expenses incurred and all losses sustained "during the full term of said lease," and during the same period Salmon is to pay him a part of the net profits. There was no joint capital provided.

It seems to me that the venture so inaugurated had in view a limited object and was to end at a limited time. There was no intent to expand it into a far greater undertaking lasting for many years. The design was to exploit a particular lease. Doubtless in it Mr. Meinhard had an equitable interest, but in it alone. This interest terminated when the joint adventure terminated. There was no intent that for the benefit of both any advantage should be taken of the chance of renewal — that the adventure should be continued beyond that date. Mr. Salmon has done all he promised to do in return for Mr. Meinhard's undertaking when he distributed profits up to May 1, 1922. . . .

The judgment of the courts below should be reversed and a new trial ordered, with costs in all courts to abide the event.

PROBLEM 2-3

Assume for the sake of evaluating this problem that Park and Blaylock continue to work in their law firm partnership, and that Wheeler (see Problem 2-2) has been expelled for his unauthorized practice of law. In the course of their work on estate planning, both Park and Blaylock routinely interacted with wealthy and accomplished individuals. While preparing a trust for Thomas Hunter, a serial entrepreneur and founder of several successful software companies, Blaylock complained about the lack of a cost-effective electronic document management system for small law firms. Over the course of several meetings, Hunter and Blaylock refined an idea for a new software program that they called eKabinett.

Hunter and Blaylock decided to develop and commercialize the software. They formed a company, and they each invested $10,000 of personal funds as seed financing. Employees of the company visited the offices of Park & Blaylock and several other small law firms to observe the flow of documents and to interview attorneys and staff. Blaylock spent many hours with the software engineers, describing features and testing the product. As a result of his work on eKabinett, his billable hours for Park & Blaylock over a three-month period declined by approximately 15% from the same months in the prior year.

After the software was sufficiently developed, Blaylock started using it in connection with his work at Park & Blaylock. Pricing for eKabinett started at approximately $1,000, but Park & Blaylock paid only $250 — just enough to cover materials and training costs.

The product struck a chord with small law firms, and after a positive review in the *ABA Journal*, sales increased at a rapid pace. The company founded by Hunter and Blaylock became very profitable, but neither Park individually nor the Park & Blaylock partnership received any revenue from the venture.

California has adopted the Revised Uniform Partnership Act (RUPA). Did Blaylock breach his duty of loyalty as specified by RUPA to the partnership or to Park?

GIBBS v. BREED, ABBOTT & MORGAN

710 N.Y.S.2d 578
New York Supreme Court, Appellate Division
July 13, 2000

MAZZARELLI, J.

Plaintiffs Charles Gibbs and Robert Sheehan are former partners of Breed Abbott & Morgan ("BAM") who specialize in trust and estate law. They withdrew from BAM in July 1991 to join Chadbourne & Parke ("Chadbourne"), and brought this action for monies due to them under their BAM partnership agreement. Defendants asserted various counterclaims alleging that plaintiffs breached their fiduciary duty to BAM. The counterclaims were severed and tried without a jury. Plaintiffs appeal from the trial court's determination that, in the course of both partners' planning and eventually implementing their withdrawal from BAM, they breached their fiduciary duty to the partnership. Plaintiffs also appeal from the trial court's determination that $1,861,045 in damages resulted from these transgressions.

From January 1991 until July 1991, plaintiffs were the only partners in the Trusts and Estates department ("T/E") at BAM; plaintiff Gibbs was the head of the department. A third partner, Paul Lambert, had been the former head of the department, and he had obtained many, if not most of the department's clients. In 1989 he had left the firm to become the United States Ambassador to Ecuador and was still on leave in 1991. Lambert intended to return to the firm upon completion of his term as ambassador. The BAM trusts and estates department also employed three associate attorneys, Warren Whitaker (fifteenth year), Austin Wilkie (fourth year), and Joseph Scorese (first year); two accountants, Lois Wetzel and Ellen Furst; and two paralegals, Lee Ann Riley and Ruth Kramer.

Gibbs had become dissatisfied with BAM, and in January 1991 he began interviews to locate a new affiliation. He also approached Sheehan to persuade him to move with him. Sheehan and Gibbs subsequently conducted a number of joint interviews with prospective employers. In May 1991, Ambassador Lambert visited BAM, and Gibbs told him that he had been interviewing. Lambert relayed this information to the other partners. In early June, plaintiffs informed the executive committee that they had received an offer from two firms: McDermott, Will & Emory and Bryan Cave.

On June 19, 1991, both plaintiffs informed Stephen Lang, BAM's presiding partner, that they had accepted offers to join Chadbourne. Lang asked Gibbs not to discuss his departure with any of the T/E associates, and Gibbs agreed not to do so. On June 20, 1991, Lawrence Warble, a BAM partner who was named temporary head of the T/E department, met with its associates and non-legal personnel to inform them that plaintiffs were leaving the firm.

On June 24, 1991, Gibbs and Sheehan sent Chadbourne a memo listing the names of the personnel in the T/E department at BAM, their respective salaries, their annual billable hours, and the rate at which BAM billed out these employees to clients. The memo included other information about the attorneys, including the colleges and law schools they attended, and their bar admissions. This list had been prepared by Sheehan on April 26, 1991, months before the partners announced they were leaving. Sheehan specifically testified that the memo was prepared in anticipation of discussions with prospective firms, and both Gibbs and Sheehan testified at trial that the recruitment of certain associates and support personnel was discussed with different firms between March and May, as the partners were considering various affiliations. While Gibbs and Sheehan were still partners at BAM, Chadbourne interviewed four BAM employees that Gibbs had indicated he was interested in bringing to Chadbourne with him. On June 27, 1991, plaintiffs submitted their written resignations. Before Gibbs and Sheehan left BAM, they wrote letters to clients served by them, advising that they were leaving BAM and that other attorneys at BAM could serve them. These letters did not mention the fact that the two partners were moving to Chadbourne. Although the partnership agreement required 45 days notice of an intention to withdraw, BAM waived this provision upon plaintiffs' production of their final billings for work previously performed. Gibbs left BAM on July 9, 1991, and Sheehan left on July 11, 1991, both taking various documents, including their respective "chronology" or desk files. With the assistance of his chronology file, Gibbs began to contact his former clients on July 11, 1991. On July 11th, Chadbourne made employment offers to Whitaker, Wilkie, Wetzel, and Riley. Wilkie, Wetzel, and Riley accepted that same day; Whitaker accepted on July 15, 1991. In the following weeks, 92 of the 201 BAM T/E clients moved their business to Chadbourne.

After hearing all the testimony and the parties' arguments, the trial court determined that Gibbs' actions in persuading his partner Sheehan to leave BAM, "and the way in which the leave was orchestrated, were done, at least partially, with the intention of crippling BAM's Trusts and Estates ("T/E") department," and constituted a breach of loyalty to BAM. The court also found that Gibbs and Sheehan had breached their fiduciary duties to BAM by sending Chadbourne the April 26, 1991 memo detailing personal information about the individuals in the T/E Department at BAM, because this gave Chadbourne a competitive advantage in offering employment to other members of the department. Finally, the court found that Gibbs and Sheehan breached their fiduciary duties to BAM by taking their chronology files with them to Chadbourne. Specifically, the court concluded that by taking their respective chronology files, the partners "to a large degree hobbled their former partners in their effort to rebuild the Trusts and Estates department, in order to maintain a viable department, and in their ability to serve clients without undue disruption."

With respect to damages, the court concluded that both Gibbs and Sheehan were entitled to recover their share of BAM profits accruing until the end of July 1991, and that Sheehan was entitled to the remainder of his capital account with the firm. Although there was no evidence that the partners had improperly solicited former BAM clients, the court found that despite BAM's efforts to mitigate damages by hiring a new partner and two associates into the T/E Department, that department suffered financial losses as a result of plaintiffs' conduct, and concluded that it was entitled to recover lost profits for a reasonable period following plaintiffs' departure. The court directed that lost profits be calculated from July 1991, when the partners left the firm, to November 1993, when BAM dissolved. Gibbs and Sheehan were held jointly and severally liable for $1,861,045. The court also awarded defendants prejudgment interest and attorneys' fees. The court's liability finding should be modified, the damage award vacated, and the matter remanded for a determination of the financial loss, if any, occasioned by plaintiffs' disloyal act of supplying competitors with BAM's confidential employee data.

The members of a partnership owe each other a duty of loyalty and good faith. . . . According the trial court's findings on issues of fact and credibility appropriate deference, we uphold that portion of the court's liability determination which found that plaintiffs breached their fiduciary duty as partners of the firm they were about to leave by supplying confidential employee information to Chadbourne while still partners at BAM. However, we find no breach with respect to Gibbs' interactions with Sheehan, or with respect to either partner's removal of his desk files from BAM.

Defendants did not establish that Gibbs breached any duty to BAM by discussing with Sheehan a joint move to another firm, or that Sheehan's decision was based upon anything other than his own personal interests. In addition, while in certain situations "[A] lawyer's removal or copying, without the firm's consent, of materials from a law firm that do not belong to the lawyer, that are the property of the law firm, and that are intended by the lawyer to be used in his new affiliation, could constitute dishonesty, which is professional misconduct under [Model] Rule 8.4(c)" (D.C. Bar Legal Ethics Comm. Op. 273 at 192), here, the partners took their desk copies of recent correspondence with the good faith belief that they were entitled to do so.

Contrary to the finding of the trial court, and applying the principle that "[t]he distinction between motive and process is critical to a realistic application of fiduciary duties" [Robert Hillman, *Loyalty in the Firm: A Statement of General Principles on the Duties of Partners Withdrawing from Law Firms*, 55 Wash & Lee L. Rev. 997, 999 (1998)], we find no breach of duty in plaintiffs' taking their desk files. These were comprised of duplicates of material maintained in individual client files, the partnership agreement was silent as to these documents, and removal was apparently common practice for departing attorneys.

However, the record supports the court's finding that both partners committed a breach of their fiduciary duty to the BAM partners by supplying Chadbourne, and presumably the other partnerships they considered joining, with the April 26, 1991 memorandum describing the members of BAM's T/E department, their salaries, and other confidential information such as billing rates and average billable hours, taken from personnel files. Moreover, a closer examination of the record does not support the dissent's conclusion that these partners did not engage in surreptitious recruiting. The partners may not have discussed with firm employees the possibility of moving with them prior to June 20, 1991, but they indicated to Chadbourne the employees they were interested in prior to this date, and Gibbs specifically testified that he refrained from telling one of his partners, to whom he had a duty of loyalty, about his future plans to recruit specific associates and support staff from the partnership.

There is no evidence of improper client solicitation in this case, nor is it an issue on this appeal. Although the analogy could be useful in concluding that Gibbs did not breach his fiduciary duty to the partnership by working with Sheehan to find a new affiliation, the fiduciary restraints upon a partner with respect to client solicitation are not analogous to those applicable to employee recruitment. By contrast to the lawyer-client relationship, a partner does not have a fiduciary duty to the employees of a firm which would limit its duty of loyalty to the partnership. Thus, recruitment of firm employees has been viewed as distinct and "permissible on a more limited basis than . . . solicitation of clients" (Hillman, *supra* at 1031). Pre-withdrawal recruitment is generally allowed "only after the firm has been given notice of the lawyer's intention to withdraw" (*id.*).

However, here, Sheehan prepared a memo in April of 1991, well in advance of even deciding, much less informing his partners, of his intention to withdraw. There is ample support in the record for the trial court's finding that the preparation and sending of the April 26, 1991 memo, combined with the subsequent hiring of certain trusts and estates personnel, constituted an egregious breach of plaintiff's fiduciary duty to BAM. Moreover, it is not speculative to infer more widespread dissemination given Sheehan's trial testimony that the memo "was prepared in connection with talking to other firms," and that "he was sure the subject of staffing was discussed at firms other than Chadbourne." Sheehan's disclosure of confidential BAM data to even one firm was a direct breach of his duty of loyalty to his partners. Because the memo gave Chadbourne confidential BAM employment data as well as other information reflecting BAM's valuation of each employee, Chadbourne was made privy to information calculated to give it an unfair advantage in recruiting certain employees.

While partners may not be restrained from inviting qualified personnel to change firms with them, here Gibbs and Sheehan began their recruiting while still members of the firm and prior to serving notice of their intent to withdraw. They did so without informing their partners that they were disseminating confidential firm data to competitors. Their actions, while still members of the firm, were intended to and did place BAM in the position of not knowing which of their employees were targets and what steps would be appropriate for them to take in order to retain these critical employees. The dissent's analysis, that once the firm was notified of the partners' departure, there was no breach of fiduciary duty, is flawed. The breach occurred in April of 1991 and could not be cured by any after-the-fact notification by the fiduciary who committed the breach that he was withdrawing from the firm. Chadbourne still had the unfair advantage of the confidential information from the April 1991 memo, and still had the upper hand, which was manifested by its ability to tailor its offers and incentives to the BAM recruits.

Contrary to the dissent, I would characterize the memo distributed to prospective competitors as confidential. The data was obtained from BAM personnel files which Sheehan had unique access to as a BAM partner. The dissent's statement that such financial information is generally known to "head-hunters" is without foundation. While the broad outlines of the partners' profits at a select number of large New York firms and the incremental increases in the base compensation of young associates at some firms are published in professional publications such as the New York Law Journal, or known to some recruitment firms, the available figures often vary substantially from the actual compensation received by specific individuals.

For example, the BAM partnership agreement, which is included in the record, reveals that the approximately 40 partners in the firm earn substantially different percentages of the firm's earnings. No professional publication would be privy to these financials. With respect to the specific associates and support staff whose compensation was disseminated in the April 1991 memo, the information disclosed to Chadbourne incorporated these individuals' bonuses. Bonus payments are confidential, often voted by the partnership, based upon the unique quality of an individual's work, the number of hours billed, and many other intangible factors. These lump sum payments often constitute a substantial portion of an associate's salary, and the payments are certainly not available to the public. Finally, support staff also receive bonuses paid to them at the discretion of the individual partners, from their personal accounts. This information is highly individualized and also privileged. Sheehan abused his fiduciary duty to the partnership by accessing personnel files to obtain the actual gross compensation of the associates and support staff he and Gibbs wished to bring with them, including bonuses, and disclosing this information to Chadbourne.

Moreover, the memo contained more than a list of salaries. It itemized each of the employees' annual billable hours, and the rates at which BAM billed these employees out to their clients, information which was not otherwise publically available. These facts go directly to a potential employee's value and were accessible only to members of the BAM partnership. Selected partners providing BAM's confidential information, which they were able to obtain by virtue of their position as fiduciaries, to Chadbourne was an act of disloyalty to their partnership. The confidential information placed Chadbourne, as a competing prospective employer, in the advantageous position of conducting interviews of the associates and support staff with more knowledge than any firm could obtain through independent research, as well as providing it with information BAM partners did not know it had, thereby prejudicing their own efforts to retain their associates and support staff.

The calculation of damages in cases such as this is difficult. "[B]reaches of a fiduciary relationship in any context comprise a special breed of cases that often loosen normally stringent requirements of causation and damages" (Milbank, Tweed, Hadley & McCloy v. Boon, 13 F.3d 537, 543 [2d Cir. 1994]). This is because the purpose of this type of action "'is not merely to *compensate* the plaintiff for wrongs committed . . . [but also] to *prevent* them, by removing from agents and trustees all inducement to attempt dealing for their own benefit in matters which they have undertaken for others, or to which their agency or trust relates'" (Diamond v. Oreamuno, 24 N.Y.2d 494, 498 [emphasis in original]). However, the proponent of a claim for a breach of fiduciary duty must, at a minimum, establish that the offending parties' actions were "a substantial factor" in causing an identifiable loss.

A reasonable assessment of lost profits has been deemed an appropriate measure of damages in cases where there was evidence that the fiduciary improperly solicited clients to move with him or her, or where the fiduciary's acts could otherwise be connected to a subsequent loss of business. Here, the court based its damage award on what it believed to be a series of disloyal acts. Defendants did not establish how the only act of plaintiffs which this Court finds to be disloyal, that of supplying employee information to Chadbourne, in and of itself, was a substantial cause of BAM's lost profits. We therefore vacate the court's award to defendants of the total profits lost by BAM between the time of plaintiffs departure in July 1991 and BAM's dissolution in November 1993, and remand for consideration of the issue of whether plaintiff's disloyal act of sending Chadbourne the April 26, 1991 memorandum was a significant cause of any identifiable loss, and, if so, the amount of such loss.

Accordingly, the order, Supreme Court, New York County (Herman Cahn, J.), entered October 1, 1998, which, after a nonjury trial on defendants' counterclaims, determined that plaintiffs had breached their fiduciary duty to defendants, should be modified, on the law, to limit such conclusion to the act of disseminating confidential employee information, and otherwise affirmed, without costs.

SAXE, J. (concurring in part and dissenting in part).

Much has been written about the ethical and fiduciary obligations of attorneys upon withdrawal from their law firms, particularly with regard to their solicitation of firm clients. However, rather than involving the improper solicitation of former clients, this case concerns claims of wrongful "solicitation" or "taking" of a withdrawing attorney's own partners, associates, and support staff. We are also required to address the propriety of departing attorneys removing the duplicate copies of letters and memos in their possession that they personally prepared and issued over the preceding years, which plaintiffs term "desk chronology files" or "correspondence chronology files."

In view of the limited case authorities directly on point, resolution of this appeal requires a review of the general principles concerning client solicitation and attorneys' covenants not to compete, as well as the general policy considerations discussed in numerous scholarly articles concerning the competing interests in law firm breakups. The trial court's liability determination runs counter to these principles and policies and it is not supported by the evidence. Therefore, I would reverse the judgment in its entirety. To the extent the majority affirms one aspect of the liability determination, I dissent. As to the remainder of the majority opinion, I concur in the result, based upon the following discussion. . . .

The evidence before the trial court fails to support its findings that plaintiffs violated their fiduciary duty to their partners at Breed, Abbott. I agree with the majority's holding that Gibbs's pre-departure discussions with Sheehan cannot constitute a breach of Gibbs's fiduciary duty to Breed, Abbott, and that plaintiffs' removal of their desk chronology files breached no obligation to their former partners. However, I disagree with the conclusion that defendants are entitled to damages based upon plaintiffs having provided Chadbourne with information about other employees of the firm's trusts & estates department, which information was provided in the interests of bringing these employees along with them in their move to Chadbourne.

PERSUADING A PARTNER TO LEAVE THE FIRM AS A TEAM

Turning first to the trial court's finding that Gibbs "actively encouraged" or "persuaded" Sheehan to leave the firm with him, and "orchestrated" their move to cripple Breed, Abbott's trusts and estates department, there is no established fiduciary duty that can be stretched to cover Gibbs's conduct. The standard employed by the trial court, if applied generally, would too severely restrict attorneys' rights to change affiliations, compete with former partners, and offer clients full freedom of choice with respect to retaining counsel.

Initially, the "solicitation" of one's own partners to make a joint move simply does not qualify as a breach of fiduciary duty. . . . The "solicitation" of one's own partners to make a joint move is fundamentally different than the solicitation of firm clients; the analysis which concludes that surreptitious solicitation of clients or secreting client files is improper is irrelevant to partners' conduct toward one another. "Soliciting" another member of one's firm does not involve the same concerns.

Although clients are not, technically, an "asset" or "property" of the firm, subject to possession, the rules regarding their solicitation treat them as something of an equivalent. The wrongfulness in preresignation solicitation of clients lies in directly and unfairly competing with the firm for business, while still a partner of it, taking unfair advantage of knowledge the firm lacks.

While it is arguable whether clients should be treated, for purposes of this analysis, as assets of the firm, it is clear that partners in a law firm cannot be treated as such.

Law partners "are bound by a fiduciary duty requiring 'the punctilio of an honor the most sensitive'" (see, Graubard Mollen Dannett & Horowitz v. Moskovitz, 86 N.Y.2d 112, 118, 629 N.Y.S.2d 1009, 653 N.E.2d 1179, *supra*, quoting Meinhard v. Salmon, 249 N.Y. 458, 464, 164 N.E. 545). Yet, neither this duty nor any rules of ethics prohibit partners in a law firm from leaving the firm, or from competing with their former firm immediately upon their departure, or even from making plans while still a member of the firm to compete with it following their departure. What is prohibited is actual competition with the firm while still a member of it.

An overall guiding principle limiting the conduct of departing partners is that the process must be handled properly and fairly, so that the withdrawing partner, while in possession of information that the firm lacks (namely, his impending departure), may not take unfair advantage of that information. Thus, where a partner surreptitiously approaches firm clients to obtain assurances that the clients will remain with him if he forms a new law firm, the partner has breached his duty to his partners and his firm. The prohibition against secretly soliciting clients, or removing client files, prior to one's resignation, is founded upon the prohibition against taking unfair advantage of the knowledge of his impending departure, while his partners are still unaware of it. It constitutes not a mere plan to compete in the future with his former law partners, but a present act of direct competition with those to whom he still owes a duty of loyalty. . . .

A partner planning a move necessarily makes numerous arrangements in anticipation of withdrawal, to ensure a smooth transition, including ensuring the capability of continuing to serve those former clients who choose to retain the departing partner. The same considerations apply equally when two partners plan a joint move. The fact that one partner conceived of the move first and approached the other with the idea, or even convinced an initially content colleague to embark upon a joint departure, cannot change the attorneys' right to leave their firm.

The observation of the trial court that plaintiffs' joint departure "denuded" Breed, Abbott's trusts and estates department is irrelevant to the issue of breach of fiduciary duty. Where a department of a law firm contains two active partners, a few associates and support staff, a decision by the two partners to withdraw from the firm will of necessity "denude" the department, and may indeed even "cripple" it, at least temporarily. However, it does not follow that the departure violates the duty owed by the departing partners to the firm. Partners' freedom to withdraw from a firm simply cannot be reconciled with a requirement that their departure be arranged in such a way as to protect the integrity of the department, and ensure its continued profit levels.

Partners who choose to leave a firm and join another presumably believe they will do better at their new affiliation. We can thus assume that as a result of the withdrawal, the old firm may well be economically damaged. Yet, the mere fact of such damage does not make it compensable.

Associates and Other Staff

Once it is recognized that partners in law firms do not breach their duty to the other members of their firm by speaking to colleagues about leaving the firm, there is no logic to prohibiting partners from inviting selected employees to apply for a position at the new firm as well, absent contractual obligations not at issue here. Support staff, like clients, are not the exclusive property of a firm with which they are affiliated. . . .

Even assuming that a partner's duty of loyalty to the other members of his firm prohibits any recruitment of department support staff before the firm is notified of the partner's intended departure, here, there is no showing that members of the staff were contacted prior to the firm being notified. Once the firm is notified of the partners' planned withdrawal, both the firm and the departing partners are on equal footing in competing for these employees; the departing partners no longer have any unfair advantage.

Since plaintiffs were entitled to inform the department staff at issue of their move, and to invite these individuals to submit applications to Chadbourne themselves, there was no impropriety in the manner in which Chadbourne extended offers to members of plaintiffs' staff. The real damage to the firm, namely, the loss of the knowledgeable and experienced attorneys and support staff, was caused not by a breach of fiduciary duty, but simply by the departure of these people — an act that each one of them had an absolute right to do, despite the damage their joint departure would cause the firm.

THE APRIL 26, 1991 MEMO

Under the circumstances, plaintiffs' preliminary compilation of information regarding the salaries, billable hours and standard billing rates of the employees they sought to bring with them, and their providing it to Chadbourne after giving notice to Breed, Abbott, provides no support for a liability determination against them.

First of all, there is no showing, nor did the trial court find, that the purportedly confidential information was provided to Chadbourne — or any other firm — during the period that plaintiffs were interviewing, or at any time before they gave notice to Breed, Abbott. The April 26, 1991 memo was simply a compilation of information of which a lead partner of a practice group is normally aware as a matter of course. Testimony that "the subject of staffing was discussed" during plaintiffs' interviews with firms — a discussion which we must presume will occur any time partners inquire into the possibility of changing firm affiliations — in no way establishes that the April 26, 1991 memo was turned over at that time. The suggestion of the majority that plaintiffs disseminated this information prior to giving notice to Breed, Abbott is speculation.

Furthermore, although the salaries and bonuses paid to associates may be termed "confidential," in fact this information is often the greatest unkept secret in the legal profession. Unlike the earnings of law firm partners, which vary widely even within most firms, depending upon such factors as billable hours and "rainmaking" ability, the earnings of associates and support staff at large firms are relatively circumscribed, with each firm setting standard rates for both salaries and bonuses. Such information is widely known outside the firms themselves: the salary levels and bonuses paid to associates at large New York firms are regularly published in professional publications such as the New York Law Journal. Salary levels, bonuses and other financial information regarding employees' billing rates are well known to professional "headhunters," the agencies that specialize in recruiting and placing lawyers and law firm support staff, and associates' background information is available from sources such as the Martindale-Hubbell directory. . . .

I conclude that the information plaintiffs disclosed to Chadbourne should not be treated as a "trade secret" or "confidential matter" since if it were, a departing attorney might have a continuing obligation not to disclose it, even after leaving the firm.

It is only the partners' fiduciary duty, rather than the label "confidential information," that limits their right to disclose information about their present firm to members of a contemplated new affiliation, and this limitation applies only where disclosure of the information would constitute an act of direct competition with their present firm.

Finally, assuming that plaintiffs had a duty not to disclose financial information known to them concerning the department staff prior to June 19, 1991, I fail to see how Chadbourne obtained any unfair advantage in recruitment. Since no actual recruitment took place until Breed Abbott knew of plaintiffs' intentions, Breed Abbott's ability to take appropriate steps to attempt to retain the employees was in no way diminished. Consequently, no actionable damage can have been suffered by the disclosure of the information.

DESK CHRONOLOGY FILES

[The dissent agreed with the majority that there was no breach of fiduciary duty in the partners taking copies of their own chronology files, since these were duplicates of documents and letters the firm had in its central filing system.]

D. FINANCIAL ATTRIBUTES

Perhaps the most important consequence of the partnership formation determination discussed above is that partners are personally liable for all debts and obligations of the partnership. Of course, partners also are entitled to share in the profits of a partnership, but inadvertent sharing of profits is a rare and happy event. Inadvertent — or even anticipated — sharing of losses is a different matter. Issues relating to the financial attributes of the partnership can be broken down into two major parts: (1) How are profits and losses ultimately allocated among the partners? (2) Who is responsible to pay third parties for partnership liabilities? The following sections begin with a brief introduction to partnership accounting, and then take up these two major issues.

1. *Partnership Accounting*

A brief introduction to partnership accounting is useful in understanding the legal rules governing partnerships. The fundamental concept of partnership accounting is the *capital account*. Roughly speaking, a capital account tracks each partner's ownership claim against the partnership. That ownership claim is determined by the following: (1) *contributions* made by each partner to the partnership; (2) each partner's share of *profits or losses* from partnership operations; (3) any *withdrawals* of funds from the partnership; and (4) each partner's *gains or losses* upon sale of the partnership or its assets. The capital account does not reflect loans made by partners to the partnership.

Contributions. Consider a restaurant with three partners: Andy, Beth, and Conrad. Upon formation of the partnership, each partner contributed $20,000 in cash. In addition, Andy loaned the partnership $50,000 for the purchase of kitchen equipment and restaurant furniture. Moreover, Conrad agreed to assume the additional responsibilities of managing the business affairs of the partnership.

These contributions would result in a *credit* to each partner's capital account in the amount of $20,000. Andy's loan to the partnership would not be reflected in his capital account — that is, the loan would not be considered an ownership interest in the partnership — but it remains a separate obligation of the partnership. Even if Conrad's services required him to work more hours than his partners, he would not receive any increase in his capital account (though the partnership agreement may stipulate additional compensation for Conrad) because labor is not considered to be a capital contribution.

Sharing of Profits and Losses. The relative amount of capital contributions does not necessarily determine each partner's share of profits and losses from the ongoing business of the partnership. Equal sharing of profits and losses is the default rule under both the UPA (§ 18(a)) and RUPA (§ 401(b)), but partners often change that allocation by contract. In this restaurant business, the partners each contributed one-third of the capital of the partnership, but the partners may have agreed to allocate profits and losses as follows: Andy = 50%, Beth = 20%, and Conrad = 30%. Using this allocation and assuming that the business earned a profit of $300,000 in the first year of operation, the capital accounts of the partners would be credited with the following amounts:

Andy	$150,000
Beth	60,000
Conrad	90,000

Assuming that the partners had made no other contributions or withdrawals from the partnership, their capital accounts after one year would appear as follows:

Andy	$20,000 + $150,000 = $170,000
Beth	20,000 + 60,000 = 80,000
Conrad	20,000 + 90,000 = 110,000[1]

To appreciate the importance of these numbers, assume that the partners sell their business at this point. According to both the UPA and RUPA, they must use the proceeds of that sale to pay any debts of the partnership (including Andy's $50,000 loan). Once the partnership's debts have been paid, any remaining amount — called the "surplus" — belongs to the partners. But how should the surplus be allocated? The capital accounts provide useful information to resolve this issue.

Assume for the sake of simplicity that the surplus exactly equals the amount of the total capital accounts. We will relax this assumption below when discussing gains and losses, but for the moment we will assume a surplus equal to $360,000. This money would be distributed to the partners according to the amounts in their capital accounts.

But what if the partners have a negative amount in their capital account? In our hypothetical partnership, this would require a loss following the initial capital contributions. Partners usually allocate losses in the same proportion as profits, following the default rule under both the UPA and RUPA. If we assume that, instead of a handsome profit, the partnership had incurred a $50,000 loss in its first year of operation, the capital accounts of the partners would be *charged* with the following amounts:

Andy	$25,000
Beth	10,000
Conrad	15,000

---

1. Notice that none of the partners received interest on the amount of the initial capital contribution. While the partners can agree to pay interest, the default rules under the UPA and RUPA do not provide for interest payments.

Assuming that the partners had made no other contributions or withdrawals from the partnership during the first year, their capital accounts after one year would appear as follows:

Andy	$20,000 − $25,000	= $(5,000)
Beth	20,000 − 10,000	= 10,000
Conrad	20,000 − 15,000	= 5,000

If the partnership is sold at this point and the surplus exactly equals the amount of the total capital accounts — that is, $10,000 — Beth and Conrad will receive payments of $10,000 and $5,000, respectively, but Andy will owe the partnership $5,000. Andy's obligation to the partnership arises from the fact that partners are personally liable for all obligations of the partnership (unlike shareholders, who have limited liability for the obligations of their corporation).

Withdrawals. As illustrated by the foregoing examples, the sharing of profits and losses is a bookkeeping transaction. The partners in our business did not receive any actual distributions of money until the business was sold. In most partnerships, of course, the partners do not wait until a sale of the partnership before withdrawing funds. Instead, they take periodic distributions from the partnership in the form of *draws*. When made in regular installments (say, monthly), a draw is akin to a salary or wages. Although the amount of a partner's draw is determined by agreement among the partners — and can be more or less than the partner's share of partnership profits — most partnerships attempt to calibrate the amount of a partner's draw to the partner's share of partnership profits. As an actual outflow of cash, draws are *charged* to the capital account.

In the case of our business, assume that each of the partners withdraws $50,000 during a profitable first year of operation. The capital accounts of the partnership would reflect these withdrawals as follows:

Andy	$170,000 − $50,000 =	$120,000
Beth	80,000 − 50,000 =	30,000
Conrad	110,000 − 50,000 =	60,000

The partners probably established the amount of the draws at the beginning of the year, and it is clear that the partnership earned more profits than the partners withdrew. The profits, therefore, might be viewed as earnings that are reinvested in the partnership. By contrast, the draws are earnings that are removed from the partnership. In many partnerships, the partners take a regular draw determined at the beginning of the year, then take an additional draw at year's end, the size of which depends on the profitability of the partnership. For example, following the highly successful first year, Andy may take an additional draw of $100,000, assuming the other partners or the partnership agreement permit him to make such a withdrawal. In that event, his capital account — that is, his claim against the partnership's assets — would be reduced to $20,000.

Gains and Losses Upon Sale or Liquidation. The amounts shown in the capital accounts do not necessarily correspond to the value of the partnership. For example, assume that the capital accounts of the partners in our hypothetical partnership show the following amounts:

Andy	$25,000
Beth	10,000
Conrad	15,000

In addition, assume that Andy's $50,000 loan is the only outstanding debt. If the partners sell their business for $130,000, they will have a surplus that exceeds the total capital accounts:

$130,000 (proceeds from sale) − $50,000 (Andy's loan) = $80,000 (surplus)

In this event, the sale of the partnership generated a "gain" (sometimes called a "profit") of $30,000:

$80,000 (surplus) − $50,000 (total of capital accounts) = $30,000 (gain)

Each partner would receive the amount in his or her capital account prior to the sale of the partnership *plus* an additional amount equal to his or her share of the gain. In this instance, the partners would receive the following amounts:

Andy	$25,000	+ $15,000 =	$40,000
Beth	10,000	+ 6,000 =	16,000
Conrad	15,000	+ 9,000 =	24,000

Notice that the total amount distributed to the partners is $80,000 — the exact amount of the surplus.

If the surplus is less than the total capital accounts, the partnership is said to have a *loss* on the sale. That loss is allocated in that same way as operating losses. For example, in our hypothetical partnership, we will assume that the business is sold for $70,000, resulting in a surplus of only $20,000:

$70,000 (proceeds from sale) − $50,000 (Andy's loan) = $20,000 (surplus)

This, in turn, would result in a loss on the sale of $30,000:

$20,000 (surplus) − $50,000 (total of capital accounts) = $(30,000) (loss)

Each partner would receive the amount in his or her capital account prior to the sale of the partnership *minus* an amount equal to his or her share of the loss. In this instance, the partners would receive the following amounts:

Andy	$25,000	− $15,000 =	$10,000
Beth	10,000	− 6,000 =	4,000
Conrad	15,000	− 9,000 =	6,000

Notice that the total amount distributed to the partners is $20,000 — again, the exact amount of the surplus.

2.   Sharing Profits and Losses Among Partners

The allocation of profits and losses is determined by each partner's interest in the partnership. In the absence of a contrary agreement, partners share in profits equally, even if unequal amounts of capital have been contributed, and losses are shared in the same proportion as profits. UPA § 18(a); RUPA

§ 401(b). Partnerships often change the default rule of equal sharing, however, and provide for different sharing arrangements depending on each partner's partnership interest.

Partners are entitled to a repayment of any capital contributions or advances made to the partnership, UPA § 18(a); RUPA § 401(a) and (d), and the partnership must reimburse a partner for payments made and indemnify a partner for liabilities incurred in the ordinary course of partnership business or for preservation of the partnership's business or property. UPA § 18(b); RUPA § 401(c). Any partner who makes a payment or advance beyond the amount agreed to be contributed as capital is entitled to interest on the amount of the payment or advance. UPA § 18(c); RUPA § 401(e).

Profits from the partnership normally are paid out on a periodic basis, usually annually, during the life of the partnership. Capital contributions normally are repaid when a partner withdraws from the partnership or when the partnership terminates. Advances and indemnification for liabilities incurred often are paid during the course of the partnership, but if not, partners have a right to such amounts when the partnership terminates and the accounts of the partners are settled. The UPA does not expressly provide for partnership accounts, but RUPA § 401(a) provides that each partner is deemed to have a capital account that is credited with contributions made and profits allocated and charged for any distributions from the partnership and losses allocated.

Assets of the partnership are used to pay liabilities of the partnership in the following order: (1) amounts owed to creditors of the partnership who are not partners; (2) amounts owed to partners other than for capital and profits; (3) amounts owing to partners for repayment of capital; and (4) amounts owing to partners for any remaining profits. If partnership assets are insufficient to cover any partnership liabilities, partners must contribute to the payment of those liabilities. UPA § 40; RUPA § 807.

The following case considers the sharing of profits and losses among partners in a so-called "service partnership" (*i.e.,* a partnership in which one of the partners provides only service — or human capital — not financial capital). Notice that *Kovacik* is at odds with the language of the partnership statutes.

KOVACIK v. REED

49 Cal.2d 166, 315 P.2d 314
Supreme Court of California
September 20, 1957

SCHAUER, Justice.

In this suit for dissolution of a joint venture and for an accounting, defendant appeals from a judgment that plaintiff recover from defendant one half the losses of the venture. We have concluded that inasmuch as the parties agreed the plaintiff was to supply the money and defendant the labor to carry on the venture, defendant is correct in his contention that the trial court erred in holding him liable for one half the monetary losses, and that the judgment should therefore be reversed.

. . . From the "condensed statement of the oral proceedings" included in the settled statement, it appears that plaintiff, a licensed building contractor in San Francisco, operated his contracting business as a sole proprietorship under the fictitious name of "Asbestos Siding Company." Defendant had for a number of years worked for various building contractors in that city as a job superintendent and estimator.

Early in November, 1952, "Kovacik (plaintiff) told Reed (defendant) that Kovacik had an opportunity to do kitchen remodeling work for Sears Roebuck Company in San Francisco and asked Reed to become his job superintendent and estimator in this venture. Kovacik said that he had about $10,000.00 to invest in the venture and that, if Reed would superintend and estimate the jobs, Kovacik would share the profits with Reed on a 50-50 basis. Kovacik did not ask Reed to agree to share any loss that might result and Reed did not offer to share any such loss. The subject of a possible loss was not discussed in the inception of this venture. Reed accepted Kovacik's proposal and commenced work for the venture shortly after November 1, 1952. . . . Reed's only contribution was his own labor. Kovacik provided all of the venture's financing through the credit of Asbestos Siding Company, although at times Reed purchased materials for the jobs in his own name or on his account for which he was reimbursed. . . ."

"The venture bid on and was awarded a number of . . . remodeling jobs . . . in San Francisco. Reed worked on all of the jobs as job superintendent. . . . During . . . August, 1953, Kovacik, who at that time had had all of the financial records of the venture in his possession, . . . informed Reed that the venture had been unprofitable and demanded contribution from Reed as to amounts which Kovacik claimed to have advanced in excess of the income received from the venture. Reed at no time promised, represented or agreed that he was liable for any of the venture's losses and he consistently and without exception refused to contribute to or pay any of the loss resulting from the venture. . . . The venture was terminated on August 31, 1953."

Kovacik thereafter instituted this proceeding, seeking an accounting of the affairs of the venture and to recover from Reed one half of the losses. Despite the evidence above set forth from the statement of the oral proceedings, showing that at no time had defendant agreed to be liable for any of the losses, the trial court "found" — more accurately, we think, concluded as a matter of law — that "plaintiff and defendant were to share equally all their joint venture profits and losses between them," and that defendant "agreed to share equally in the profits and losses of said joint venture." Following an accounting taken by a referee appointed by the court, judgment was rendered awarding plaintiff recovery against defendant of some $4,340, as one half the monetary losses[6] found by the referee to have been sustained by the joint venture.

---

6. The record is silent as to the factors taken into account by the referee in determining the "loss" suffered by the venture. However, there is no contention that defendant's services were ascribed any value whatsoever. It may also be noted that the trial court "found" that "neither plaintiff nor defendant was to receive compensation for their services rendered to said joint venture, but plaintiff and defendant were to share equally all their joint venture profits and losses between them." Neither party suggests that plaintiff actually rendered services to the venture in the same sense that defendant did. And, as is clear from the settled statement, plaintiff's proposition to defendant was that plaintiff would provide the money as against defendant's contribution of services as estimator and superintendent.

(1) It is the general rule that in the absence of an agreement to the contrary the law presumes that partners and joint adventurers intended to participate equally in the profits and losses of the common enterprise, irrespective of any inequality in the amounts each contributed to the capital employed in the venture, with the losses being shared by them in the same proportions as they share the profits.

(2) However, it appears that in the cases in which the above stated general rule has been applied, each of the parties had contributed capital consisting of either money or land or other tangible property, or else was to receive compensation for services rendered to the common undertaking which was to be paid before computation of the profits or losses. Where, however, as in the present case, one partner or joint adventurer contributes the money capital as against the other's skill and labor, all the cases cited, and which our research has discovered, hold that neither party is liable to the other for contribution for any loss sustained. Thus, upon loss of the money the party who contributed it is not entitled to recover any part of it from the party who contributed only services. The rationale of this rule, as expressed in Heran v. Hall[, 40 Ky. 159, 35 Am. Dec. 178 (1840),] and Meadows v. Mocquot, [110 Ky. 220, 61 S.W. 28, 22 Ky. Law. Rep. 1646 (1901)], is that where one party contributes money and the other contributes services, then in the event of a loss each would lose his own capital the one his money and the other his labor. Another view would be that in such a situation the parties have, by their agreement to share equally in profits, agreed that the value of their contributions the money on the one hand and the labor on the other were likewise equal; it would follow that upon the loss, as here, of both money and labor, the parties have shared equally in the losses. Actually, of course, plaintiff here lost only some $8,680 or somewhat less than the $10,000 which he originally proposed and agreed to invest.

* * *

It follows that the conclusion of law upon which the judgment in favor of plaintiff for recovery from defendant of one half the monetary losses depends is untenable, and that the judgment should be reversed. . . .

The judgment is reversed.

3. Liability of Partners to Third Parties

With respect to the responsibility of partners to third parties, it has always been the case that partners may be forced to fulfill the obligations of the partnership to third parties out of their personal funds. Although this aspect of the issue is beyond question, the details implementing that policy have engendered much debate. William Draper Lewis recalled that upon being appointed as the primary draftsman of the UPA, "[h]e found that his first problem was to determine the relation of the partners and the persons having claims on the partnership." William Draper Lewis, *The Uniform Partnership Act — A Reply to Mr. Crane's Criticism*, 29 Harv. L. Rev. 158, 165 (1915). Lewis was then operating under instructions from NCCUSL to adopt the entity theory of partnership. He concluded that under this theory, partners should be viewed as "contributors" to the partnership, "having an obligation to the partnership to furnish it with the necessary funds to meet its obligations to third persons, but that those having claims against the partnership have, as such claimants, no claims against the partners." *Id.* at 166. This view of partnership had, in Lewis's opinion, severe drawbacks because partnership creditors would be forced to first exhaust the assets of the partnership and then institute new proceedings to attach the claims of the partnership against the partners as contributors. In addition to being complicated, argued Lewis, this procedure would change existing partnership law rather dramatically, and would be based on a false assumption "that third persons dealing with a partnership do not deal directly with the partners as principals." *Id.* at 166.

Having rejected the entity approach to partner liability, Lewis drafted UPA § 15, under which partners are jointly liable for all debts and other obligations of the partnership except wrongful acts (UPA § 13) or breaches of trust (UPA § 14) of one of the partners, for which the other partners are jointly and severally liable. ("Joint and several liability," you may recall from your torts class, means that each partner could be responsible for paying an entire judgment against the partnership.) The liability of individual partners for obligations of the partnership may not be altered by agreement among the partners because it affects the rights of third parties. UPA § 15 reveals its roots in the aggregate theory of partnership by making partners directly liable for partnership obligations. In addition, the provision does not require exhaustion of the partnership's assets prior to collection from individual partners.

Despite Lewis's efforts to avoid the exhaustion requirement by providing for direct liability of partners, many courts interpreting the UPA have required plaintiffs to exhaust partnership assets prior to seeking the personal assets of the partners. Traditionally, courts have imposed this exhaustion requirement only when the underlying claims create joint liability, allowing immediate suit against partners when the underlying claims create joint and several liability.

The drafters of RUPA perceived two main problems with the UPA's liability provisions. First, by providing for joint liability in some circumstances, UPA § 15 creates practical problems for plaintiffs, who are required to join all partners as defendants in such litigation. Recognizing this problem, several states amended their version of the UPA to provide for joint and several liability of partners in all matters. Likewise, RUPA § 306(a) makes all partnership liability joint and several. Note that, although this RUPA provision solves the practical problems engendered by joint liability, it retains direct personal liability of partners for obligations of the partnership and thus compromises the entity approach that RUPA elsewhere has explicitly embraced.

Second, omission of an exhaustion requirement was beneficial to creditors but inconvenient for the partners, who were required to pay an obligation out of their personal assets and then seek indemnification from the partnership. In the end, whether the exhaustion requirement is good policy probably depends on whether it accurately reflects the expectations of the parties. After all, both the UPA (implicitly) and RUPA (explicitly in § 307(d)(3)) permit the parties to contract for whatever arrangement they desire.

The following case illustrates the effect of the partnership liability rules. As you read this case, consider the effect of rules holding Billauer and Ho'okano liable for actions of their partners. Is the result fair? What incentives do these rules produce?

IN RE KECK, MAHIN & CATE

274 B.R. 740
United States Bankruptcy Court, N.D. Illinois
March 6, 2002

CAROL A. DOYLE, Bankruptcy Judge.

This matter is before the court on plaintiff Jacob Brandzel's ("plaintiff") adversary complaint seeking a determination of defendants' liability under the Illinois Uniform Partnership Act ("IUPA"). The plaintiff is the plan administrator for the debtor Keck, Mahin & Cate ("Keck") pursuant to the chapter 11 plan ("Plan") confirmed by the bankruptcy court on December 16, 1999. The plaintiff seeks recovery for malpractice claims filed by Bank of Orange County and Pacific Inland Bancorp (collectively, "Pacific Inland") and Wozniak Industries, Inc. ("Wozniak"), a claim filed by Citizens Commercial Leasing Corporation ("Citizens") and administrative claims allowed in the bankruptcy case as of December 16, 1999. Defendants Barbara P. Billauer and Thomas E. Ho'okano (collectively, "defendants") are former capital partners of Keck. Pursuant to the Plan, the plaintiff is the assignee of all allowed claims, and has the right to seek recovery from partners who did not participate in a settlement of partners' outstanding liabilities. Ms. Billauer and Mr. Ho'okano dispute any liability for allowed claims against Keck. For the reasons stated below, the court finds for the plaintiff regarding the Pacific Inland, Wozniak and administrative claims. The court finds for the defendants regarding the Citizens claim.

After holding a trial on the merits, the court makes the following findings of fact and conclusions of law:

A. BACKGROUND

Keck was an Illinois partnership whose partners engaged in the practice of law. On December 16, 1997, some of Keck's creditors filed an involuntary chapter 7 bankruptcy petition against the partnership. On December 31, 1997, the bankruptcy court granted Keck's motion to convert the case to chapter 11 of the Bankruptcy Code. The Plan was confirmed on December 16, 1999. Under the confirmation order ("Order"), Jacob Brandzel was appointed plan administrator.

Ms. Billauer and Mr. Ho'okano are former capital partners of Keck. Ms. Billauer was a partner from July 2, 1990 until August 31, 1993. Mr. Ho'okano was a partner from June 24, 1991 until March 26, 1993. Pursuant to the Plan, all Keck partners had the option to pay a specified settlement amount for partnership liabilities and become "participating partners," or to decline to pay the settlement amount and become "non-participating partners." Non-participating partners potentially faced maximum liability for Keck's obligations. Ms. Billauer and Mr. Ho'okano chose not to participate in the settlement and are being sued for their liability with regard to the Pacific Inland, Wozniak, Citizens and administrative claims, totaling $5,483,189.96.

B. ADMINISTRATIVE CLAIMS

The plaintiff seeks to hold the defendants liable for administrative claims allowed in the bankruptcy case as of December 16, 1999, in the amount of approximately $2.1 million. Under section 9.8 of the Plan and paragraph F of the Order, the plaintiff is entitled to recover allowed administrative claims as of December 16, 1999 from all non-participating partners. Neither Mr. Ho'okano nor Ms. Billauer dispute the validity of the Plan or Order granting the plaintiff the authority to recover administrative claims allowed as of December 16, 1999. They also have not contested the amount of administrative claims as of December 16, 1999. Therefore, the court finds for the plaintiff against both defendants with respect to the $2,177,787.73 in administrative claims allowed as of December 16, 1999.

C. PACIFIC INLAND, WOZNIAK AND CITIZENS CLAIMS

The plaintiff contends that the defendants are jointly and severally liable under section 13 of the IUPA, and the partnership agreement ("Agreement") for the Pacific Inland, Wozniak and Citizens claims. He asserts that each of these claims arose before or during the time the defendants were partners. Ms. Billauer and Mr. Ho'okano dispute any liability for the Pacific Inland, Wozniak and Citizens claims. Both Ms. Billauer and Mr. Ho'okano argue that: (1) the allowed claims were not in existence when they withdrew from the partnership; (2) Keck paid Citizens the full amount incurred while the defendants were partners; (3) the partnership dissolved upon their withdrawal and the new partnership assumed all prior debts, thereby terminating their liabilities; (4) liability is barred under the terms of the Agreement; . . . and (6) they are not liable because Keck was solvent when they left the partnership. Ms. Billauer also argues that (7) the Agreement is void as against public policy and (8) the doctrine of laches bars suit against her. Each of these defenses is discussed below.

1. EXISTENCE OF WOZNIAK AND PACIFIC INLAND CLAIMS

Ms. Billauer and Mr. Ho'okano first argue that no obligations to Wozniak or Pacific Inland existed at the time they left Keck. They assert that they are liable under paragraph 8(a) of the Agreement only for "Firm Obligations" that arose before they left the partnership.[4] They further contend that the Wozniak and Pacific Inland malpractice claims did not become Firm Obligations until those claimants had a judgment entered against them or the malpractice claims were settled, which the defendants assert occurred after they left the partnership.

This argument is not persuasive. Sections 13 and 15 of the Illinois Uniform Partnership Act determine the scope of Ms. Billauer's and Mr. Ho'okano's liability to third parties (which includes the plaintiff in this case). That liability is not limited to "Firm Obligations" as that phrase is used in paragraph 8(a) of the

---

4. Neither Ms. Billauer nor Mr. Ho'okano contest that they are liable under the Agreement for partnership debts that arose before they joined the firm. Under the IUPA, partner liability for preexisting partnership debts is generally limited to partnership assets. However, an incoming partner can be held personally liable where there is an express assumption of liability. Magrini v. Jackson, 150 N.E.2d 387, 392 (1958). In this case, the partnership agreement expressly provides for the assumption of preexisting Firm Obligations by incoming partners.

Agreement. Section 13 of the Act provides that "[w]here, by any wrongful act or omission of any partner acting in the ordinary course of the business of the partnership, . . . loss or injury is caused to any person, . . . the partnership is liable therefor to the same extent as the partners so acting or omitting to act." Under the language of section 13, it is the "wrongful act or omission" of a partner that gives rise to the liability of all other partners. The only reasonable interpretation of this provision is that the liability of all partners arises at the time of "any wrongful act or omission" by any partner.

A partner cannot escape liability simply by leaving the partnership after the malpractice is committed but before the client wins or settles a malpractice claim. Courts have consistently held that, within the context of partnership dissolution, withdrawing partners remain liable for matters pending at the time of dissolution. These cases support the conclusion that liability under section 13 of the IUPA arises at the time of the offending conduct. . . .

[Applying that standard, the court found that the malpractice alleged in the Wozniack and Pacific Island claims was committed while Mr. Ho'okano and Ms. Billauer were still partners, but that the debt to Citizens on a line of credit was incurred after they withdrew from the partnership.]

3. DISSOLUTION OF PARTNERSHIP

Ms. Billauer and Mr. Ho'okano argue that they are not liable for the Pacific Inland and Wozniak claims because the partnership dissolved when they withdrew from the firm and a new partnership was formed. They contend that the new partnership assumed any debts from the old partnership, and that therefore no liabilities against them now exist. However, whether the partnership dissolved and a new partnership was formed, or the old partnership continued by virtue of paragraph 15(b) of the Agreement without the defendants, the result is the same. The general rule under Illinois law is that "dissolution of the partnership does not of itself discharge the existing liability of any partners." As noted earlier, that liability can stem from prior contractual obligations, including those that give rise to malpractice claims.

In addition, partners cannot release one another from liability to third parties. Illinois law requires consent by the third party itself to release the liability of any partner. This consent may be express or inferred based on the third party's course of conduct after it learned of the dissolution. Without this consent, partners cannot shield themselves from the rights of creditors. There is no evidence that either Wozniak or Pacific Inland consented to releasing Ms. Billauer and Mr. Ho'okano of their liability. Therefore, whether the partnership dissolved or the old partnership continued without the defendants, they are liable for debts incurred to the third-party claimants before their departure dates.

4. FIVE YEAR LIMITATION ON LIABILITY IN PARTNERSHIP AGREEMENT

Ms. Billauer and Mr. Ho'okano also argue that they can be pursued for partnership liabilities only during the first five years after they withdrew from the partnership. The defendants rely on paragraph 8(b)(2) of the Agreement, which attempts to reduce a partner's liability by twenty percent per year following a partner's departure from the firm. However, this provision does not absolve the defendants of liability under the Plan and Illinois law.

The Plan grants the plaintiff the authority to pursue the defendants for the full amount of the allowed claims at issue in this case. Section 9.8 of the Plan specifically states that "[i]n any legal action or proceeding of any kind against a Non-Participating Partner, the Plan Administrator shall have any and all rights available under applicable law to assert, and seek recovery for, . . . any amount up to the full amount of the Allowed Claims." Section 16.8 states that "[e]xcept as otherwise expressly provided [in the Plan], to the extent the Plan is inconsistent with any other documents, the provisions of the Plan shall be controlling." Therefore, the Plan grants the plaintiff the right to seek recovery for the full amount allowable under Illinois law, and the Plan controls over the terms of the partnership agreement to the extent there are any inconsistencies.

Under Illinois law and the Agreement, Ms. Billauer and Mr. Ho'okano are liable for claims arising before or during the time they were partners. Keck is a general partnership subject to Illinois law. Under Illinois law, partners are jointly and severally liable to creditors of the partnership. Illinois law does not limit this liability with respect to innocent co-partners. As noted above, partners cannot release their liability to third parties without their consent. There is no evidence of any such consent, so paragraph 8(b)(2) of the Agreement is not binding on claimants like Wozniak and Pacific Inland. Because the plaintiff stands in the shoes of these two creditors, the defendants cannot escape liability based on paragraph 8(b)(2) of the Agreement. . . .

D. Conclusion

For the foregoing reasons, the court finds that Mr. Ho'okano and Ms. Billauer are jointly and severally liable to the plaintiff in the amount of $775,000.00 for the Wozniak claim, $825,000.00 for the Pacific Inland claim and $2,177,787.73 for the administrative claims. The court finds for the defendants regarding the Citizens claim.

PROBLEM 2-4

Somehow the partnership between Lloyd Park and John Blaylock survived the formation of eKabinett (see Problem 2-3), but it would not survive Blaylock's next entrepreneurial venture. The partners had a bank account in the name of the partnership at Longview National Bank (Longview), and Blaylock developed a habit of writing checks for amounts exceeding the funds in the partnership's account and later covering the overdrafts with deposits. At some point, this relatively common and innocuous practice took a nefarious turn, as Blaylock embarked on a full-blown check-kiting scheme.

Check kiting is fraud, plain and simple. Here's how it worked: Park & Blaylock had $500 in its account with Longview, but Blaylock wrote a check from that account for $1,000 and deposited the check in another bank. Blaylock knew that checks take some time to work their way through the banking system, and he attempted to take advantage of this lag. Before the check had circled back to Longview, Blaylock withdrew money from the second bank and deposited it in the Longview account. Then he started the whole process over again. Ultimately, the goal of a person engaged in a check-kiting scheme is to withdraw a substantial amount of money and abscond with it.

Blaylock never got that far. He was caught, prosecuted, and sent to jail, leaving Longview with over $380,000 in losses. Unable to recover from Blaylock or the partnership, Longview turned to Park, who was completely unaware of the check-kiting scheme.

Assuming all of the assets of the partnership have been exhausted, should Park be responsible to Longview for Blaylock's criminal activity? Is it relevant that Blaylock's activities were contrary to the company's express written financial policies?

4.   Limited Liability Partnerships

Limited liability partnerships (LLPs) are general partnerships that have registered with the state and as a result of such registration obtain a certain level of limited liability protection for the partners. That is, the partners' responsibilities for partnership obligations are limited to the amount of their investment. The first LLPs were authorized under a Texas statute passed in 1991 at the behest of accountants and lawyers, all of whom traditionally practiced in general partnerships. The LLP form is now authorized in all 50 states in the United States.

The primary purpose of the early LLP statutes was to protect the personal assets of partners from the risk of negligence or malpractice by another partner. Under more recent statutes, partners in an LLP are not personally liable for any of the obligations of the partnership unless the partners become personally liable as a result of their own conduct or have participated in or supervised the wrongful conduct of another partner. (Supervisory liability is required by professional ethics rules.)

Like a general partnership, a limited liability partnership requires that two or more persons join to conduct a business activity for profit. To become an LLP, the partnership must file an application with the secretary of state and include information such as the name and address of the partnership, the number of partners, and a brief description of the nature of the partnership's business.

Though LLPs have many of the advantages of limited liability companies (LLCs), which are the focus of Chapter 3, many more LLCs are created than LLPs. Though one might posit several reasons for this — for example, the fact that one person can create an LLC in most states or the fact that some states limit LLPs to professional firms — the available evidence suggests no clear answers to why this pattern occurs. Larry E. Ribstein & Bruce H. Kobayashi, *Choice of Form and Network Externalities*, 43 William & Mary L. Rev. 79 (2001).

One thing is clear: LLPs are most popular among professional firms, where access to non-partnership entities often is limited by professional ethics rules. Even in this arena, however, patterns of LLP adoption are puzzling. Scott Baker and Kimberly Krawiec studied New York law firms and found that movement into the LLP form was slower than they expected. Their hypothesis was based on interviews: "Law firms will go to great lengths (in this case, risking full personal liability) in order to avoid being perceived in a negative light relative to firms that they consider competitors for prestige and clients." Scott Baker & Kimberly D. Krawiec, *The Economics of Limited Liability: An Empirical Study of New York Law Firms*, 2005 U. Ill. L. Rev. 107, 154. In another article, however, Professor Krawiec subjected this hypothesis to quantitative examination and found only limited support. Kimberly D. Krawiec, *Organizational Form as Status and Signal*, 40 Wake Forest L. Rev. 977 (2005).

FRODE JENSEN & PILLSBURY WINTHROP, LLP: A CASE STUDY

When Frode Jensen announced his intention to leave Pillsbury Winthrop LLP (Pillsbury) for Latham & Watkins LLP (Latham) in August 2002, hardly anyone outside the two firms took notice. But when Pillsbury issued a press release downplaying Jensen's productivity and stating that he had been the subject of a complaint alleging sexual harassment, suddenly everyone seemed interested.[1]

Frode Jensen was, by virtually all accounts, a solid if unspectacular corporate lawyer. He had begun his legal career as an associate with Davis Polk & Wardwell, a top New York law firm. After five years, he left Davis Polk for a smaller firm in Stamford, Connecticut, where he was elevated to partner within a year. A few years later, he moved again, this time to the Stamford office of Winthrop Stimson Putnam & Roberts.

Shortly after his arrival, Winthrop's biggest client in Stamford — the Singer Corporation — was acquired in a hostile takeover and moved its legal work to another firm. Jensen proceeded to build his stable of clients afresh, and ultimately came to represent Merck, Smith-Corona, and many less recognizable but substantial companies.[2] According to Jensen's complaint, filed in response to a Pillsbury press release, "During the period 1988 through 2001 his annual billings for the firm grew from approximately $1 million to a peak of approximately $10 million, and have averaged in excess of $5 million for the past six years. During several of those years his billings were the highest of any Winthrop partner in the firm."[3]

Jensen had enhanced his stature at Winthrop and, according to his complaint, he "took a central role" in merger talks with Pillsbury Madison & Sutro. The two firms merged in the fall of 2001. As of early 2003, the combined firm had approximately 800 attorneys in 17 offices, mostly in the United States, but also in London, Singapore, Sydney, and Tokyo. After the merger, Jensen sat on Pillsbury's managing board and was co-head of the international mergers and acquisitions practice.

Despite this apparent success, Jensen claims that he became dissatisfied with the firm after the merger. According to the complaint,

> . . . he had serious concerns about the relentless, and, in his view, unrealistic focus of senior management at Pillsbury on achieving American Lawyer 100 "first quartile profitability," and the elevation within the firm of that goal over the goals of professional excellence and successfully serving the firm's clients. Moreover, the firm faced serious financial challenges, and upheaval in personnel. . . . In addition, Jensen also became disappointed by Pillsbury's failure to appreciate the contributions of Pillsbury's Stamford office, where Jensen worked. . . . Jensen also was disappointed by the firm's widespread morale problems, particularly amongst the firm's associates, due to decisions to lay off associates, due to incomplete or misleading statements made by Pillsbury's senior management to the firm's lawyers, as well as due to the firm's management style.

1. Reports on the ensuing events appeared in the Wall Street Journal, the New York Times, and many periodicals that cover the legal industry. For the most detailed account of Jensen's side of the story, see Carlyn Kolkere, *Take Down*, Am. Law. 68 (Feb. 2003).

2. For a discussion of Jensen's clients, see Thomas Scheffey, *Assessing Jensen's Book of Business*, Leg. Times 14 (Nov. 11, 2002).

3. Jensen's most successful year was 1999, when he billed $10 million, mostly as a result of his work in the Astra-Zeneca merger.

In August 2002, Jensen was offered a position with Latham, which would appear to most outsiders as a step up in the hierarchy of firms.[4] Jensen accepted the position after notifying Pillsbury. Prior to announcing his departure publicly, Jensen negotiated the terms of his departure with John F. Pritchard, Pillsbury's vice chairperson. According to the complaint, "Pritchard specifically promised Jensen that his withdrawal would not be the subject of a negative or 'defensive' press statement by Pillsbury, and it was agreed and understood that there would be mutual non-disparagement."

On September 3, Latham issued a press release touting Jensen's hiring, calling him "a very capable lawyer [with] extensive contacts and experience in several industries, including the biotechnology sector." The next day, Pillsbury responded with a release of its own:

> Pillsbury Winthrop, in response to a press release issued by Latham & Watkins on September 3, 2002 announcing that Frode Jensen, a corporate securities partner in Pillsbury Winthrop's Stamford, Connecticut, office is joining the New York Office of Latham & Watkins, would like to correct some possible misconceptions caused by the Latham release. Pillsbury Winthrop previously had intended not to comment on Mr. Jensen's departure in order to downplay the event. However, as a result of Latham's press release Pillsbury Winthrop Chair, Mary Cranston, explained that Mr. Jensen's departure comes on the heels of sexual harassment allegations involving Mr. Jensen and a significant decline in his productivity. According to Ms. Cranston, Mr. Jensen has been largely absent from the Stamford office since the start of this year. "Our firm values respect and integrity above all else. We investigated the harassment claims, concluded that there was a reasonable likelihood that harassment had occurred and responded with a variety of measures. It is always sad to lose a friend and colleague to another firm, however, under the circumstances of the past year, Mr. Jensen's move is probably in the best interest of all concerned, and we wish him well with his new firm." Ms. Cranston further stated that to her knowledge, Latham & Watkins did not contact anyone in Pillsbury Winthrop's management in connection with a reference check for Mr. Jensen.

While the charges of sexual harassment and productivity decline may have had some basis,[5] the press release was still shocking to most lawyers. Why would

---

4. In the 2002 ranking of law firms by the American Lawyer, Latham ranks fourth in total revenues, while Pillsbury ranks 26th. Latham had 1,165 lawyers; Pillsbury had 733.

5. Jensen denies being unproductive, and as to the sexual harassment claims, the complaint asserts: "These allegations are untrue in their entirety." Despite Jensen's protestations, it appears that his billings had declined from 1999, when he billed an extraordinary sum of $10 million. *See* Carlyn Kolkere, *Take Down*, Am. Law. 72-74 (Feb. 2003). In addition, Jensen admits in the complaint that he, Pillsbury, and "a third-party" had entered into a "Separation Agreement, General Release of Claims and Covenant Not to Sue" on December 10, 2001. In addition, the American Lawyer reported that a female partner who was leaving the firm in December 2001 had complained about Jensen, alleging that Jensen had twice asked to kiss her, and that the firm paid the departing partner to release the firm and Jensen from liability and to keep the incidents confidential.

Jensen included a potentially explosive claim regarding sexual harassment in the complaint:

> There are presently partners of Pillsbury who, in the recent past, have been charged with sexual harassment, which charges — unlike the false charges against Jensen — were founded, and which were settled by agreements that included confidentiality provisions that have been honored by Pillsbury. It is thus apparent that the only purpose of the public disclosure by Pillsbury regarding the unfounded allegations against Jensen was to destroy his relationship with Latham.

Pillsbury issue this press release? What did it have to gain? Surely, it was more than spite. According to Jensen's complaint, his former firm was motivated by competition:

> 24. Particularly revealing, however, is that Pillsbury's conduct appears to have been motivated in part by the advice of a legal headhunter consulted by Pillsbury. On information and belief, on or about September 3, 2002, certain of the defendants consulted with a legal headhunter regarding Jensen's withdrawal and Latham's September 3 press release.
>
> 25. On information and belief, the headhunter advised defendants that Jensen's departure to Latham would be viewed in the legal community as a serious blow to Pillsbury, and that it would make it difficult for Pillsbury to recruit lateral partners from other law firms in the future, and that Pillsbury had to take some action to counter the consequences to Pillsbury of Jensen's departure. Defendant Park partially confirmed this set of events in an interview reported in "law.com Connecticut" on September 19, 2002 during which Park acknowledged that "Pillsbury also had received third-party feedback that perception of Jensen's departure could hurt the firm's ability to attract lateral partners."
>
> 26. It is plain that defendants feared that Jensen's move to Latham would impair Pillsbury's ability to attract lateral partners. Although Pillsbury throughout 2001 and 2002 identified the hiring of lateral partners as a key initiative for improving the firm's profitability, including in a study of the firm conducted by McKinsey & Co., Inc., it has experienced little, if any, success in this regard. When Jensen's departure was publicly received as a "coup" for Latham, Pillsbury lashed out in an unlawful and desperate manner because its senior management feared that Jensen's departure would make it even more difficult to attract lateral partners to the firm and, perhaps, serve to encourage other partners to leave.

Initially, Jensen assumed that he would maintain his partnership with Latham, but Latham was troubled that Jensen had not disclosed the sexual harassment charge during the interview process—a lapse that Jensen attributes to the confidentiality agreement signed in settlement of the claim. Moreover, Latham was concerned about the distractions Jensen was causing and the negative media attention the firm might receive if they decided to bring Jensen on board. On September 15, Jensen was forced to withdraw from Latham, leaving behind over $1 million in annual draw.[6] Considering his options, Jensen decided to sue Pillsbury, along with Mary Cranston, John Pritchard, Marina Park, and five "John or Jane Does," who are "outside advisors of defendants, including a headhunting firm and its principal, who conspired with defendants to cause injury to Jensen." The following are representative paragraphs from Jensen's complaint:

COUNT ONE

(Conspiracy—against all defendants) . . .

> 33. On or about September 4, 2002, defendants, together with John or Jane Does 1 through 5, including on information and belief a headhunting firm that encouraged and advised defendants, conspired together in person, by telephone and, on

---

6. According to Jensen's court filings, he was making an annual income of approximately $700,000 at Pillsbury.

information and belief, by e-mail and other writings for the purpose of unlawfully defaming Jensen and interfering with his partnership contract at Latham.

34. In furtherance of that conspiracy, (i) Defendant Cranston issued the false and defamatory September 4 Release and caused it to be broadly disseminated amongst the legal and business community, and to the public generally, (ii) Defendant Park placed an unsolicited telephone call to Gordon and Davenport at Latham and read them the substance of the September 4 Release for the sole purpose of undermining Jensen's partnership at Latham, (iii) Defendant Cranston stated publicly that Pillsbury "dragged [Jensen] through the mud," and (iv) on information and belief, Defendants John or Jane Does 1-5 encouraged Pillsbury's misconduct by advising Pillsbury that a failure to disparage Jensen would make Pillsbury's lateral partner acquisitions even more difficult. Defendant Park acknowledged and admitted the defendants' conspiracy by stating publicly that the September 4 Release "is out there and makes the point we [defendants] wanted to make."

35. By reason of the foregoing, the defendants are jointly and severally liable for conspiring to defame Jensen and to interfere with and destroy his partnership at Latham, in an amount not less than $15 million, the exact amount to be proven at trial.

36. Because of the willful, wanton and intentional nature of defendants' conduct, they also are liable for punitive damages in an amount to be determined at trial.

COUNT THREE

(Interference with Business Relations — against all defendants) . . .

45. On or about August 2002 Jensen was offered and accepted a partnership with Latham to commence October 1, 2002, and agreed to compensation of a minimum of $1,050,000 per year.

46. Each of the defendants was given notice of Jensen's acceptance of the Latham partnership.

47. On or about September 4, 2002, defendants sought to interfere with and destroy Jensen's business relations with Latham by (i) Cranston's issuing the defamatory September 4 Release and defendants causing it to be broadly disseminated to the public, (ii) Park's placing an unsolicited telephone call to Gordon and Davenport at Latham to read them the substance of the September 4 Release for the purpose of undermining Jensen's partnership at Latham, (iii) Cranston's and Park's continuing efforts to attack and defame Jensen in the media after the issuance of the September 4 Release and Park's telephone call to Latham, and (iv) on information and belief, Defendants John or Jane Does 1-5 encouraging Pillsbury's misconduct by advising Pillsbury that a failure to disparage Jensen would make Pillsbury's lateral partner acquisitions even more difficult.

48. By reason of the foregoing, defendants are jointly and severally liable for interfering with Jensen's business relations in an amount not less than $15 million, the exact amount to be determined at trial.

49. Because of the willful, wanton and intentional nature of defendants' conduct, they also are liable for punitive damages in an amount to be determined at trial.

COUNT FIVE

(Defamation per se, Defamation — against all defendants) . . .

56. On or about September 3, 2002, defendants together with John or Jane Does 1 through 5 acted to defame Jensen by, among other things, disparaging his skill and integrity as an attorney.

57. As part of their effort to defame Jensen, defendants made the following writings and statements: (i) Cranston issued the September 4 Release . . . which falsely disparages Jensen's integrity and his skills as an attorney, and falsely accuses Jensen of engaging in sexual harassment, and caused that Release to be broadly disseminated to the public through numerous media that Jensen presently is identifying, in addition to those set forth herein, (ii) Defendant Park telephoned Gordon and Davenport at Latham and read them the substance of the September 4 Release, (iii) Defendant Cranston publicly stated that Pillsbury "dragged [Jensen] through the mud", and (iv) on information and belief, Defendants John or Jane Does 1-5 encouraged Pillsbury's misconduct by advising Pillsbury that a failure to disparage Jensen would make Pillsbury's lateral partner acquisitions even more difficult. Defendant Park acknowledged and admitted that defendants intended to defame Jensen by stating publicly that the September 4 Release "is out there and makes the point we wanted to make."

58. The September 4 Release, and the other statements listed above and described throughout this pleading are false and were known, or should have been known, by defendants to be false. Defendants were not privileged to publish those statements, and the statements unlawfully disparage Jensen's skill and integrity as a lawyer, and his ability to function productively as a lawyer, and are calculated to cause injury to Jensen in his profession.

59. As a result of defendants' defamatory statements, Jensen was obliged to withdraw from his partnership at Latham.

60. By reason of the foregoing, the defendants are jointly and severally liable for defamation per se and defamation, in an amount not less than $15 million, the exact amount to be proven at trial.

61. Because of the willful, wanton and intentional nature of defendants' conduct, they also are liable for punitive damages in an amount to be determined at trial.

COUNT SEVEN

(Breach of Contract — against defendant Pillsbury) . . .

70. On or about December 10, 2001, Jensen, Pillsbury and a third-party entered into the Separation Agreement. The Separation Agreement includes a broad confidentiality clause, which provides in part as follows:

> The Firm, including, without limitation, Jensen, agrees to keep all information which it has concerning the Potential Claims and the terms of this Separation Agreement, as well as the terms of and the reason for your departure, confidential, except as is necessary to administer this Separation Agreement and as required by law.

71. Pillsbury breached the Separation Agreement by issuing the September 4 Release.

72. As a result of Pillsbury's breach of contract, Jensen has suffered substantial direct and consequential damage, including, but not limited to, the loss of his partnership at Latham, the disparagement of his personal and professional reputation, and the severe impairment of his prospects for future employment.

73. By reason of the foregoing, Pillsbury is liable to Jensen for breach of contract in an amount of at least $15 million, the exact amount to be proven at trial.

COUNT EIGHT

(Breach of Contract — against defendants Pillsbury and Pritchard) . . .

75. On or about August 30, 2002, Pritchard, on behalf of Pillsbury, entered into a contract with Jensen concerning the terms and conditions of his departure.

Among other things, Pritchard specifically approved the terms of the Latham press release announcing Jensen's partnership, and committed to Jensen that Pillsbury would not make any negative or "defensive" public statements regarding Jensen's departure and agreed to the terms of a draft press release to be released by Latham.

76. On or about August 30, 2002, Pritchard, on behalf of Pillsbury, sent an e-mail to Jensen stating "we're done": that the terms of his withdrawal were agreed.

77. Consistent with his agreement with Pritchard, Jensen formally withdrew from Pillsbury on August 31, 2002, and on or about September 3, 2002, Latham issued its press release, as approved by Pritchard, announcing Jensen's joining Latham.

78. By issuing the September 4 Release, by calling Gordon and Davenport and reading them the substance of the September 4 Release, and by the other defamatory public statements made by defendants, Pillsbury and Pritchard breached the terms of their agreement with Jensen.

79. As a result of the breach of contract by Pillsbury and Pritchard, Jensen has suffered substantial direct and consequential damages, including, but not limited to, the loss of his partnership at Latham, the disparagement of his personal and professional reputation, and the severe impairment of his prospects for future employment.

80. By reason of the foregoing, Pillsbury and Pritchard are liable to Jensen in an amount of at least $15 million, the exact amount to be proven at trial.

In addition to the $15 million in compensatory damages, Jensen asked the court for "punitive damages in an amount of at least $30 million, and such other and further relief as to the Court may be just and proper."

Pillsbury's initial reaction to the lawsuit was defiance. Pillsbury's general counsel, Ronald E. Van Buskirk, was quoted as saying, "Mr. Jensen is a disgruntled ex-partner making unjustified allegations. While we regret the filing of the lawsuit, we've thoroughly reviewed all the facts and absolutely stand by those individuals named in the case." *Law Firm Sued by Ex-Partner Over Statements*, N.Y. Times C8 (Oct. 9, 2002). Pillsbury's managing partner, Marina Park, stated flatly, "The press release is out there and makes the point we wanted to make."[7]

The case took another turn in January 2003, when Jensen requested a $19 million prejudgment remedy lien.[8] According to this filing, Pillsbury was in "poor financial condition," evidenced by reduced revenues in 2002, coupled

---

7. Jonathan D. Glater & Andrew Ross Sorkin, *Bitter Exchange by Law Firms Over the Hiring of a Lawyer*, N.Y. Times C2 (Sept. 9, 2002). Not long before the Jensen story broke, Ms. Park published a short advice column for lawyers on teamwork called "Hair of the Dog" in California Law Business (July 1, 2002). In that column, she wrote: "My colleague, Mary Cranston, likes to say that an important part of achieving one's vision is to learn to pat the obstacles on the head and move on."

8. The amount was calculated as follows:

Loss of 3 months of compensation from Latham	$262,500
Loss of 14 years of future compensation from Latham	$22,400,000
Loss of 14 years of future bonuses and benefits from Latham	$5,665,625
Loss of unfunded retirement benefits at Latham	$2,500,000
Subtotal	$30,828,125
Present value (reduce total by multiplying by .7)	$21,579,687
Mitigation of damages (assuming Jensen has 50 percent chance of finding job equivalent to Pillsbury partnership)	.65
New subtotal	$14,026,796
Plus general damages for per se defamation	$5,000,000
TOTAL	$19,026,796

with attorney and staff layoffs, salary freezes, and buyouts.[9] Moreover, Jensen alleged that the firm did not have sufficient insurance to cover the damages that would result from his lawsuit. The parties settled the dispute on April 2, 2003. Pillsbury issued a statement recanting its previous statements about Jensen and calling him "a valued and respected member of the firm and . . . one of the firm's most productive corporate partners."

Pillsbury is a limited liability partnership registered in Delaware, despite the fact that it has no offices there. Mary Cranston works out of the San Francisco office; John Pritchard works out of the New York office; and Marina Park works out of the Silicon Valley office. Of course, Frode Jensen was based in Connecticut and brought his lawsuit there.

State limited liability partnership statutes determine which state's laws apply. Many LLP statutes include an "internal affairs" rule to resolve difficult choice-of-law issues involving so-called "foreign" LLPs (that is, LLPs registered outside the state in which the relevant partners are located). Named after a comparable rule in state corporation law, the internal affairs rule would allow an LLP to be governed by the liability provisions of the jurisdiction in which it is registered. Regardless of the rule embedded in the particular statute, choice-of-law provisions are mandatory and cannot be changed by the LLP's operating agreement. Connecticut's choice-of-law provision for foreign LLPs is a typical internal affairs provision:

> The internal affairs of a foreign registered limited liability partnership, including the liability of partners for debts, obligations and liabilities of or chargeable to the partnership, shall be subject to and governed by the laws of the state in which it is registered as a registered limited liability partnership.

Conn. Stat. § 34-400.

So, too, with California: "The laws of the jurisdiction under which a foreign limited liability partnership is organized shall govern its organization and internal affairs and the liability and authority of its partners."

The Delaware statute according to which Pillsbury was organized provides the following liability shield:

> (c) An obligation of a partnership incurred while the partnership is a limited liability partnership, whether arising in contract, tort or otherwise, is solely the obligation of the partnership. A partner is not personally liable, directly or indirectly, by way of indemnification, contribution, assessment or otherwise, for such an obligation solely by reason of being or so acting as a partner.

6 Del. C. 15-306(c).

As with all limited liability entities, the owners of a Delaware LLP may become personally liable for their own actions:

> (e) Notwithstanding the provisions of subsection (c) of this section, under a partnership agreement or under another agreement, a partner may agree to be personally liable, directly or indirectly, by way of indemnification, contribution,

---

9. Despite lower revenues, the firm increased profits per partner because it had ten fewer equity partners at the end of the year than at the beginning. *Red Scare: After Years in the Black, Bay Area Firms Saw Their Revenues Plummet in 2002*, the Recorder 1 (Jan. 6, 2003).

assessment or otherwise, for any or all of the obligations of the partnership incurred while the partnership is a limited liability partnership.

Id., 15-306(e).

For matters that are not "internal affairs," states follow various choice-of-law rules. In this case, the choice-of-law rules of Connecticut would determine which state's laws on the merits would apply to the trial if it were to proceed since the case was brought there. Connecticut follows the "significant relationship" test advanced in the Restatement (Second) Conflicts of Law to determine choice-of-law issues in tort cases. *See* O'Connor v. O'Connor, 201 Conn. 632, 650, 519 A.2d 13, 16-23 (1986).

Under the significant relationship test, the applicable law is that of the state with the "most significant relationship to the occurrence and the parties." Restatement (Second) Conflicts of Law § 145 (2002). The relevant contacts are (1) the place where the injury occurred; (2) the place where the conduct causing the injury occurred; (3) the domicile, residence, nationality, place of incorporation, and place of business of the parties; and (4) the place where the relationship, if any, between the parties is centered. *Id.* "[I]t is the significance, and not the number, of § 145(2) contacts that determines the outcome of the choice of law inquiry under the Restatement approach." O'Connor, 201 Conn. 652-653.

QUESTIONS

1. Would the actions of Mary Cranston, John Pritchard, and Marina Park bind the LLP? Would it matter if Cranston, Pritchard, and Park had not been in management positions? What if they were associates rather than partners?

2. If the actions of Cranston, Pritchard, or Park result in liability to the firm, would the other partners be entitled to bring claims for breach of fiduciary duty against the perpetrator?

E. DISSOLUTION

Dissolution has long been one of the most complex aspects of partnership law. William Draper Lewis attributed the complexity to a lack of precision in common law decisions: "The subject of dissolution and winding up of a partnership is involved in considerable confusion principally because of the various ways in which the word 'dissolution' is employed." William Draper Lewis, *The Uniform Partnership Act*, 24 Yale L.J. 617, 626-627 (1915). Courts used the term "dissolution" to refer variously to the departure of a partner from the partnership, the process of liquidating and winding up a partnership, or the completion of that process. Lewis's straightforward solution to this confusion was to codify the definitions of each stage of the process of ending a partnership.

"Dissolution" under the UPA means simply any "change in the relation of the partners caused by any partner ceasing to be associated in the carrying on as distinguished from the winding up of the business." UPA § 29. The dissolution of a partnership is an event that triggers the process of winding up. As explained by the official comments, "[D]issolution designates the point in time when the partners cease to carry on the business together; termination is the point in time when all the partnership affairs are wound up; winding up, the process of settling partnership affairs after dissolution." Official Comment, UPA § 29. The dissolution of a partnership, therefore, does not result in its immediate termination. UPA § 30. It is important to note that termination of a partnership as a legal entity is not the same as termination of the partnership business. Partners often elect to continue a partnership business by forming a new partnership or some other business entity.

The technical definition of "dissolution" emanates from the aggregate theory of partnership. If any partner departs from an existing partnership, the aggregation is altered and thus the partnership is dissolved. Note that dissolution occurs only when a partner ceases to be associated with the partnership, not when a partner is added. Although some courts have treated admission of a new partner as a dissolution, this view of dissolution isn't very useful, since the consequences of dissolution contemplate some breakup of the partnership.

Despite Lewis's confidence in the superiority of the UPA's approach to dissolution, subsequent cases have revealed that courts are often confused by the concept. In addition, strict adherence to the statutory definition of "dissolution" can lead to seemingly unjust results. The RUPA Reporters criticized the UPA definition as follows:

> The problem with the UPA's use of the term *dissolution* is ... much more fundamental than the absence of a clear definition of the concept. The UPA's definition and use of the concept of dissolution is a bad idea because it reflects an aggregate concept of partnerships that fails to recognize the stability of many partnerships. The UPA unnecessarily destabilizes many partnerships, particularly those that have continuation agreements, and actually undercuts the attempts of partners to contract for stability. The UPA suggests that the partnership business is coming to a close when all that may be coming to a close is one partner's participation. In short, the UPA does not distinguish adequately a departure that triggers a winding up of the business from a departure that is governed by a buyout or continuation agreement.

Donald J. Weidner & John W. Larson, *The Revised Uniform Partnership Act: The Reporters' Overview*, 49 Bus. Law. 1, 5 (1993).

RUPA does away with the UPA rule that the departure of a partner causes a dissolution of the partnership and has different rules for continuation and winding up of the partnership business. Under RUPA the departure of a partner is called a "dissociation" in recognition of the fact that under RUPA the departure may or may not result in the winding up and termination of the partnership. RUPA Article 6 defines all "dissociations." Whether a dissociation results in a buyout of the dissociated partner and continuation of the partnership business or a winding up and termination of the partnership business depends on Article 8.

Within that Article, RUPA § 801 lists all of the events that trigger a winding up, or liquidation, of the partnership business. The most common dissolution events are dissociations, but it is not necessary to have a dissociation to cause a dissolution and winding up. For example, a partnership may be dissolved by the express will of all of the partners (RUPA § 801(2)(ii)) or by an event agreed to in the partnership agreement (RUPA § 801(3)).

If a dissociation does not cause the dissolution and winding up of the partnership business, the dissociating partner must be bought out pursuant to Article 7. The main consequences of Article 7 are (1) the dissociated partner's interest must be purchased for "the greater of the liquidation value or the value based on a sale of the entire business as a going concern without the dissociated partner" (§ 701(c)); and (2) the dissociated partner's liability and ability to bind the partnership are terminated (§ 702).

In analyzing the effect of dissociation on the rights of the partners, a key issue is whether the dissociation was "rightful" or "wrongful," and resolution of that issue often depends on the nature of the partnership. A partnership can be a partnership for a specified term, a partnership for a particular undertaking, or a partnership at will. Generally speaking, dissociation is "rightful" when it is accomplished without violating the agreement between the partners.

A partner may dissociate at any time. RUPA § 602(a). But if a partner dissociates in breach of the partnership agreement or, in a partnership for a definite term or for a particular undertaking, before the expiration of the term or completion of the undertaking (under specified circumstances), the dissociation has been wrongful, RUPA § 602(b), and the dissociating partner is liable to the partnership and the other partners for damages. RUPA § 602(c).

Below is a recent "dissolution" case decided under the UPA. Do you agree with the majority or with the concurrence on whether the partnership is for a particular undertaking? Is the concurring opinion correct in asserting that the consequences are the same, regardless how that issue is resolved? Would this case be decided in the same way under RUPA? Following the case is a problem raising the issue of expulsion.

FISCHER v. FISCHER

197 S.W.3d 98
Supreme Court of Kentucky
June 15, 2006

LAMBERT, Chief Justice.

Appellant, Todd A. Fischer, seeks reversal of the Court of Appeals' opinion, wherein it reversed a Boone Circuit Court summary judgment in favor of Appellant, that enforced a buy-sell provision in a partnership agreement. Appellee, Jacquelyn Fischer, argues that we should affirm the opinion of the Court of Appeals overturning the trial court. For the reasons herein stated, we now reverse the decision of the Court of Appeals and reinstate the judgment of the Boone Circuit Court.

Appellant is the son of Richard Fischer, now deceased, and the stepson of Appellee. On November 1, 1994, Richard and Appellant formed the partnership D & T Enterprises, executing a written agreement to govern the partnership. The partnership agreement stated that its purpose was "the purchasing, leasing, and selling of real estate at 8415 U.S. 42, Florence, Kentucky." One of the partnership lessees was DAL,[1] a closely held corporation owned wholly by

---

1. DAL stands for Dental Arts Laboratory which was a tenant at the location in question, and was jointly operated by Appellant and Richard Fischer.

Richard. Although Appellant had no ownership interest in DAL, he was involved in its management and operation as a corporate officer.

Article XI of the 1994 agreement included a provision whereby, at the end of each year, a partner could retire from the partnership, giving the other partner an option to purchase the retiring partner's interest or terminate and liquidate the partnership business. Article XII of the 1994 agreement also included a buy-sell clause stating that:

> Upon the death of any Partner, the surviving Partners may either purchase the decedent's interest in the Partnership or may terminate and liquidate the Partnership business. If the election is to purchase the decedent's interest, the surviving Partners shall serve notice in writing of the election, within three months after the death of the decedent. The notice [is] to be served upon the executor or administrator of the decedent, or upon the known legal heirs of the decedent if no legal representative has been appointed at that time.
>
> If the surviving Partners do not elect to purchase the interest of the decedent in the Partnership, they shall proceed with reasonable promptness to liquidate the business of the partnership. The decedent's estate shall not be liable for losses in excess of the decedent's interest in the Partnership at the time of his death. No compensation shall be paid to the surviving partners for their services and liquidation. The proceeds of the liquidation shall be distributed as realized, 50 percent to Richard Fischer and 50 percent to Todd A. Fischer.

On April 18, 1995, the property at 8415 U.S. 42, Florence, Kentucky, was conveyed to the partnership D & T Enterprises. On June 19, 1995, Appellant and Richard entered into an amended partnership agreement, modifying the previous buy-sell provision. In the amended agreement, the buy-sell provision stated that:

> Upon the death of any Partner, the surviving Partners shall purchase the decedent's interest in the Partnership. The notice [is] to be served upon the executor or administrator of the decedent, or upon the known legal heirs of the decedent if no legal representative has been appointed at that time. Said purchase price shall be $50,000.00 payable over five years with interest at the prime rate to a cap of 10 percent.

Both the original agreement and the amended agreement required changes of any of the terms or provisions of the agreement to be in writing and signed by each of the parties.

Several years after the partnership was formed, Richard learned that he was terminally ill. Thereafter, he communicated with Appellant, by counsel, on July 27, 2000, stating in relevant part as follows:

> As Mr. Richard Fischer's attorney, I am putting you on notice that effective immediately Mr. Fischer is exercising his right pursuant to K.R.S. 362.300(1)(b) to dissolve the partnership since no definite term or particular undertaking has been specified.
>
> The reason for this dissolution is that the buy-sell provision is grossly unfair to Mr. Richard Fischer. Article IX provides for a buy-out in the event of the death of Mr. Richard Fischer of his interest in the partnership property for $50,000.00. The current mortgage on the property is approximately $200,000.00 and the property

is valued in excess of $600,000.00. The result of such a buy-out would be a loss to Mr. Richard Fischer's estate of approximately $150,000.00

Mr. Richard Fisher will certainly consider reforming a new partnership with his son upon more equitable terms.

For the time being, the parties will own the property as joint tenants and should continue filing tax returns as though a partnership exist [*sic*]. From this point, no formal partnership agreement exists due to the dissolution. Please let me know how your client wishes to proceed.

Thereafter, Richard executed a new will on March 13, 2001, leaving his entire estate to his second wife, Appellee, Jacquelyn Fischer. Appellee was also named as executrix. Richard named Chad Fischer, his minor son with Appellee, as the first contingent beneficiary. But in the event that both Appellee and Chad predeceased Richard, four of five of Richard's children from his first marriage were named secondary contingent beneficiaries. Appellant was left out.

Richard died on June 28, 2001. The property which D & T Enterprises purchased was titled in the name of D & T Enterprises and it so remains. Tax returns were filed for D & T Enterprises in 2000 and 2001 as a partnership, per Richard's request. Appellant contends that Richard did not wind up the partnership, but that both parties merely entered into negotiations to reach an agreement to work out their differences. Appellee contends that the wind up was initiated by the letter of dissolution from Richard's attorney to Appellant, and the winding up of the partnership's business was ongoing but not completed before Richard's death.

Appellee, individually and as executrix of Richard's estate, filed suit in the Boone Circuit Court. After a period of discovery, Appellant, the defendant at trial, moved for partial summary judgment seeking enforcement of the buy-sell provision of the partnership agreement. Appellant argued that despite Richard's letter, "no affirmative act was carried out by the Partners to wind up the affairs of the Partnership." There being no wind up, Appellant argues that the partnership continued in fact, and accordingly, the partnership agreement remained in effect governing the partnership. The trial court granted partial summary judgment, holding that the buy-sell agreement was enforceable. Appellant was ordered to pay to Richard's estate the sum of $50,000.00 for Richard's interest in the partnership, and to dissolve, wind-up, and terminate D & T Enterprises. Appellee was ordered to convey to Appellant, by general warranty deed, title to the property at 8415 U.S. 42, Florence, Kentucky.

The Court of Appeals reversed, holding that the letter of July 27, 2000, from Richard's attorney to Appellant's attorney dissolved the partnership; that the buy-sell provision was extinguished and became unenforceable on that date; and that nothing in the Kentucky Uniform Partnership Act required Richard and Appellant to complete the winding up of partnership affairs before Richard's death. We granted review, and oral argument was heard.

. . .

Appellant first argues that the Court of Appeals erred by failing to determine whether D & T Enterprises was a partnership for a particular undertaking pursuant to KRS 362.300. He contends that if the partnership was for a particular undertaking, then Richard would have been in contravention of the partnership agreement by attempting to dissolve the partnership, and subject to contractual liability. "[I]n the absence of some contrary showing a partnership is deemed to be at will and any partner may withdraw at any time without incurring liability, such a withdrawal is wrongful if it is in violation of an express or implied agreement that the relationship would continue for a definite term or until a particular undertaking is completed." [68th Street Apts., Inc. v. Lauricella, 362 A.2d 78, 86-87 (1976).]

Adopted verbatim from § 31 of the Uniform Partnership Act (UPA) of 1914, KRS 362.300 deals with causes of dissolution, and the relevant portions of the statute for this case are reprinted below:

> Dissolution is caused:
> (1) Without violation of the agreement between the partners:
> . . .
> (b) By the express will of any partner when no definite term or particular undertaking is specified,
> . . .
> (4) By the death of any partner[.]

It is undisputed that the partnership was not for a definite term, as no time length was included in the amended partnership agreement. However, whether the partnership was for a particular undertaking has been in much dispute. If the partnership was for a particular undertaking, one capable of accomplishment at some time, then Richard would have been unable to rightly dissolve the partnership via the letter from his counsel under the authority of KRS 362.300(1)(b). If, however, the partnership was not for a particular undertaking, then the letter would have been effective to dissolve the partnership without violating the agreement, and this Court would have to decide whether the dissolution eliminated the partnership agreement.

. . .

Appellee asserts that the partnership agreement was not for a definite term or for a particular undertaking, and the partnership could be properly dissolved at the express will of either Richard or Appellant. However, the language suggests otherwise. The amended partnership agreement's stated purpose was for the "purchasing, leasing, and selling of real estate at 8415 U.S. 42, Florence, KY." Both sides have cited the case of Girard Bank v. Haley [332 A.2d 443 (Pa. 1975)] favorably, and both contend that the case buttresses their argument. *Girard Bank* is not a Kentucky case, but it has been relied on in many other states, and its holding is instructive to the case at bar.

In *Girard Bank*, Mrs. Reid and three other partners entered into a written partnership agreement for the purpose of leasing real property in Pennsylvania. Mrs. Reid was designated as the manager of the property, and the three other parties were to perform manual labor on the parcel. In a letter addressed to the other partners, Mrs. Reid advised them that she was dissolving the partnership and requested that the partnership assets be liquidated. Meetings between all the partners failed to develop a plan of liquidation, and suit was initiated by Mrs. Reid, naming the other partners as defendants. Mrs. Reid died before finality of the controversy, and the question became whether her letter, or her death, dissolved the partnership.

As Pennsylvania had enacted the Uniform Partnership Act, the Supreme Court of Pennsylvania decided that the case turned on the applicability of § 31 of the UPA. The partnership agreement in *Girard Bank* is very similar to the case at bar, in that both partnerships existed for the buying and leasing of property, with the Fischer partnership adding the word "selling" to its partnership purpose. The Pennsylvania court concluded pursuant to § 31, that dissolution of the partnership is caused "by the express will of any partner," and "the expression of that will need not be supported by any justification." Furthermore, that court went on to explain:

> If no "definite term or particular undertaking [is] specified in the partnership agreement," such an at-will dissolution does not violate the agreement between the partners; indeed, an expression of a will to dissolve is effective as a dissolution even if in contravention of the agreement. . . . If dissolution results in a breach of contract, the aggrieved partners may recover damages for the breach and, if they meet certain conditions, may continue the firm business for the duration of the agreed term or until the particular undertaking is completed. [Girard Bank, 332 A.2d at 446-47.]

The Pennsylvania Court went on to hold that the letter by Mrs. Reid was an unequivocal dissolution of the partnership, and was not in contravention of the partnership agreement. In doing so, the court noted that there was no provision fixing a definite term, and the undertaking to which the agreement referred was for the maintaining and leasing of real property. The court stated its rationale regarding the particular undertaking as follows: "Leasing property, like many other trades or businesses, involves entering into a business relationship which may continue indefinitely; there is nothing 'particular' about it." We accept the view of the Pennsylvania Court that the undertaking in *Girard Bank* was one of a general purpose, and could not be considered a "particular undertaking" under the UPA. "A 'particular undertaking' under the statute must be capable of accomplishment at some time, although the exact time may be unknown and unascertainable at the date of the agreement."

Appellee cites the case of Chandler Med. Bldg. Partners v. Chandler Dental Group [855 P.2d 787 (1993)] for the proposition that a partnership agreement that includes among its purposes the selling of particular real estate is not a partnership for a particular undertaking. However, the partnership agreement at issue in *Chandler* stated that its purpose was developing, constructing, operating, leasing, *or* selling a two-story medical office building in Chandler, Arizona. The conjunction "or," as it is used in *Chandler*, operates very differently than the conjunction "and," as it is used in the case at bar. The usage of "or" allows the partnership flexibility to pick and choose which purpose it operates under, and thereby removes any particularity it might otherwise have. In contrast, the use of "and" does not allow the partnership the flexibility to choose which purpose it wishes to pursue, rather, the partnership must pursue all of the purposes listed in the partnership agreement. Simply stated, "or" is flexible, while "and" is rigid.

Perhaps even more instructive, the Arizona Court of Appeals stated as follows [in *Chandler*]:

> In contrast, a partnership formed for the purpose of developing and selling real property is one for a particular undertaking and is not terminable at will. As stated in *Lauricella*: It is true that where a partnership is not limited as to time, and there is nothing to show the intention of the parties as to its duration, it will be held to be a

partnership at will. But where a partnership has for its object the completion of a specified piece of work, or the effecting of a specified result, it will be presumed that the parties intended the relation to continue until the object has been accomplished. There is, then, a term fixed by the copartnership agreement, and until that time arrives one partner cannot terminate the partnership and continue the enterprise for his own benefit. In keeping with this analysis, a number of cases have found agreements to develop real estate to be partnership or joint venture obligations which are to continue until the undertaking is accomplished.

Here, section 3 of the partnership agreement provides that the purpose and business of this partnership shall be to "sponsor, for a profit, the promotion, development, and construction of a two-story medical office building . . . to own, hold for investment, improve, *lease, manage, operate or sell* such building." According to the record, at the time the complaint was filed, the building had been constructed and was being leased, managed, or operated, but had not been sold. CMBP claims that the particular undertaking was the sale of the building, which had not been accomplished. We reject the argument because the agreement does not require that the building ever be sold; conceivably, it can be leased for an indefinite period of time. Under these circumstances, and given the fact that section 20 provides for voluntary dissolution at any time upon agreement of 60 percent in interest of the partners, we believe that CMBP has not established this was a partnership for a particular undertaking. [*Id.* at 793-94.]

If the partnership agreement between Appellant and Richard was for the sole purpose of "buying and leasing property," our conclusion would follow *Girard Bank,* and we would conclude that the letter from counsel giving notice of dissolution was not in contravention of the partnership agreement. However for our purposes, the most instructive language in *Girard Bank* is not contained in the main body of the decision, but is in footnote 9. Referring to the buying and leasing provision of the partnership agreement, the Pennsylvania Court stated in the footnote that "[i]n contrast, a partnership formed for the purpose of developing and selling a particular tract of land would be one for a particular undertaking, and hence not rightfully terminable at will until the purpose was accomplished."

At first glance, the language of the partnership agreement in the case at bar appears to designate the lot located at 8415 U.S. 42, Florence, KY, as one used for a real estate business office. This is because of the use of the word "at" in the phrase "purchasing, leasing, and selling of real estate at 8415 U.S. 42, Florence, KY." However, neither side has contended that this was the intended use of the parcel; rather, both sides have conceded that the land was to be bought, leased variously, and eventually sold. This supports the view that the partnership was for a particular undertaking, because it could be accomplished at some point in the future. The absence of an exact date for accomplishment of the ultimate undertaking does not change this feature of the agreement. Additionally, the inclusion of a specific address in the partnership agreement, as opposed to just a general statement of the partnership's purpose, adds to the weight of finding that this partnership was for a particular undertaking. Because the partnership agreement itself uses specificity to designate one unique parcel of land that will be bought, leased, and sold, there is no question as to when the partnership will terminate; *i.e.,* when the land at 8415 U.S. 42, in Florence, Kentucky, is sold.

Whether a partnership is for a particular undertaking has generally been regarded as a question of fact. However, as the facts regarding the purpose of the partnership appear in this agreement, there is no dispute as to the facts. . . . This case turns on the legal effect of the facts regarding the purpose of the partnership. We hold that in this case, no trier of fact need address whether the partnership was for a particular undertaking, and that the question was properly decided by the trial court as a matter of law.

Richard's attempted dissolution prejudiced valuable contract rights belonging to Appellant. Whether dissolution was conditional or unconditional defined Appellant's rights and remedies. The letter from Richard's counsel relied on incorrect statutory authority, and in the context of our analysis, was no more than an attempt to circumvent what the partnership agreement expressly provided. Effective dissolution was conditional on KRS 362.300(1)(b) being applicable, but since that section is not a proper basis of dissolution under the facts of this case, the dissolution was ineffective. A dissolution must be unequivocal, and this one was not. The partnership agreement was in operation, and Richard could not rightly dissolve it under KRS 362.300(1)(b). If the letter had been an unequivocal dissolution, Appellant could have sued under a breach of contract theory for Richard's wrongful dissolution. But as Richard tried to have it both ways and did not manifest an unequivocal intent to dissolve, there was no dissolution, and the agreement must be enforced. Dissolution occurred only upon Richard's death and those provisions of the agreement are controlling.

For the foregoing reasons we reverse the Court of Appeals, and reinstate the judgment of the trial court.

GRAVES, JOHNSTONE, SCOTT, and WINTERSHEIMER, J. J., concur.

COOPER, J., files a separate concurring opinion.

ROACH, J., concurs in the majority opinion and in Justice Cooper's concurring opinion as an alternative ground for resolving the matter.

COOPER, Concurring Justice.

I concur in the result reached in this case because the winding up of the partnership affairs was not completed prior to Richard Fischer's death. KRS 362.295. However, I do not regard the "purpose" statement in Article II of the amended partnership agreement, *i.e.*, "the purchasing, leasing and selling of real estate at 8415 U.S. 42, Florence, Kentucky," to be dispositive of whether the partnership was one of definite term or particular undertaking. KRS 362.300(1)(b).

. . .

One can assume that a partnership would retain the right to sell, as well as purchase and lease, its real estate. While the majority opinion finds footnote 9 in Girard Bank v. Haley, 460 Pa. 237, 332 A.2d 443, 447 n. 9 (1975), to be dispositive, that footnote describes a hypothetical partnership "formed for the purpose of developing and selling a particular tract of land" as being one for a particular undertaking. *Girard Bank* obviously was referring to the type of real estate development enterprise in which the primary purpose is to subdivide a tract of land into and sell, *e.g.*, residential lots, so that when the last lot is sold, the particular undertaking for which the partnership was formed is concluded.

Here, the primary purpose of the enterprise was to generate income by purchasing and leasing the partnership property. "Leasing property, like many other trades or businesses, involves entering into a business relationship which may continue indefinitely; there is nothing 'particular' about it." *Id.* at

447. Thus, KRS 362.300(1)(b) applied, and Richard Fischer had the power to unilaterally dissolve the partnership. However, the only immediate effect of a dissolution is that the partner ceases to be associated in the carrying on of as distinguished from the winding up of the business. KRS 362.290. Dissolution does not terminate the partnership; rather, the partnership continues until the winding up of the partnership affairs is completed. KRS 362.295. . . .

Here, the parties never even ceased carrying on the partnership business.

Since the winding up of D & T Enterprises was never completed, the partnership agreement and its buy-sell provision were still in effect at the time of Richard Fischer's death.

Accordingly, I concur in the result reached by the majority opinion, though not in its reasoning.

PROBLEM 2-5

Despite various conflicts between Lloyd Park and John Blaylock, the law firm has expanded under Park's skillful management. Although Blaylock is no longer a member of the bar after his conviction for check kiting, Park has a dozen new partners, and the firm is servicing clients in a wide range of legal matters.

Before joining Park's firm as an associate in 2008, Coleen Bradley had obtained valuable experience as a lawyer for the California Public Utilities Commission (CPUC). This experience seemed particularly well tailored for her new practice: representing several southern California companies before CPUC. After laboring as an associate for three years, Bradley achieved partner status.

Shortly after obtaining her new status, Bradley began to have concerns about another partner, Bill Hopkins. Once she began receiving internal billing reports, Bradley became concerned that Hopkins was overbilling some of their utility clients. Her concern was based completely on her personal observations of Hopkins's work habits.

Although Bradley never saw the actual bills, she became convinced that Hopkins was reporting too many hours. Moreover, she felt that she had an obligation under the California Rules of Professional Conduct to report her concerns to Lloyd Park. After she did so, Park promised to investigate.

The next day, Hopkins met with Bradley and told her that the utility clients were dissatisfied with her work. He said that the clients had asked that her work be supervised. Bradley later testified that she had never before heard criticism of her work for the utility clients. From that day forward, Bradley never again received an assignment to work for those clients.

Over the next month, Park investigated Bradley's charges, reviewing the bills and finding that in all but one instance fewer hours were billed than were shown on internal computer printouts as having been worked. Park also discussed the bills with corporate counsel for all of the utility clients. These counsel—all of whom had longstanding relationships with Hopkins—concluded that the firm's bills were reasonable. One of the corporate counsel also confirmed that he had complained to Hopkins several months earlier about the quality of Bradley's work.

During the investigation, Bradley wrote to Park that she believed Hopkins had overcharged clients $20,000 to $25,000 per month for his work. In fact, in the preceding six months Hopkins had billed on average less than $24,000 per month for his work. In August, Park told Bradley that the firm's investigation revealed no basis for her contentions, and he advised her to seek new employment.

The firm continued to pay Bradley a monthly draw of $7,500 and provided her with an office and a secretary while she looked for a new position until halfway through the following year. Although the firm did not immediately expel her as a partner, it did not pay her any partnership distribution other than her draw. She finally found a new position in September of the following year, over a year after she was advised to seek new employment. The firm voted formally to expel her from the partnership in October of the following year.

Assuming that the firm complied with the expulsion provision of the firm's partnership agreement (which provides for expulsion of any partner upon the vote of a majority of the partners), can Bradley nevertheless prevail in a claim that the partners breached their fiduciary duties by expelling her?

CHAPTER
3

Limited Liability Companies

MOTIVATING HYPOTHETICAL

Eve Drew is a young, energetic turophile, that is, she loves cheese. Drew spent her formative years in Wisconsin, where she discovered a taste for fresh cheese curds as a young girl. As she matured, she developed a taste for specialty cheeses, including Hook's 10-year-old cheddar and Pleasant Ridge Reserve, a *Comté*-style cheese manufactured in southern Wisconsin.

Drew decided to attend college in Arizona, which is, comparatively, a cheese desert. During her freshman year, she introduced her roommate, Amanda Carder, to specialty cheeses, most of which she acquired through online distributors. Carder was hooked immediately, and the two began discussing the possibility of opening a cheese shop near the university.

General partnerships have many appealing attributes. They are easy to form and the default rules provided by the uniform partnership statutes—equal sharing of profits, direct participation in management, restrictions on the transfer of management rights, and easy dissolution—are attractive to many small businesses. Moreover, the default rules are easily adapted to each partnership's special needs simply by changing the terms of the partnership agreement. Indeed, the only major drawback of general partnerships is that the partners are personally liable for partnership obligations.

In this regard, corporations would seem to be more advantageous. Investors in a corporation have limited liability—that is, their responsibility for corporate obligations is limited to the amount of their investment. But this limited liability benefit comes at the cost of increased formality, and there is sometimes an awkward fit between corporate default rules and the needs of small businesses. In particular, the corporate norms of centralized management (through a board of directors), free transferability of voting rights, and difficulty of dissolution are anathema to many small businesses. And unlike general partnerships, corporations are difficult to tailor to the particular needs of the owners because many changes to the default rules must be embodied in the corporation's charter, which may be amended only by board recommendation followed by shareholder approval and a public filing.

Corporations also suffer from the dreaded problem of "double" taxation — the notion that corporate profits are taxed once at the corporate level and then again at the level of the individual shareholder after payment of dividends. General partnerships avoid this negative tax treatment because the Internal Revenue Service (IRS) does not treat general partnerships as separate entities for tax purposes. When a general partnership earns profits, therefore, those profits are allocated to the individual partners in the year that they are earned, even if the money is not actually distributed until a later time. Similarly, any losses incurred by the partnership will be available as tax deductions to the individual partners. Because of this tax treatment, general partnerships are said to be "pass-through" tax entities.

While some investors might prefer corporate tax treatment as a means of delaying the consequences of any taxable events until the time when the investment is sold, investors in businesses that distribute earnings on a regular basis usually prefer pass-through tax treatment. Subchapter S of the Internal Revenue Code offers relief from double taxation to corporations that meet its eligibility requirements. Among other things, such corporations (1) cannot have more than 100 shareholders; (2) must have only one class of stock (meaning that the corporation cannot have both common and preferred shares); and (3) may have as individual shareholders only U.S. citizens or resident aliens. Many corporations understandably find these restrictions unpalatable.

Hybrid entities are the result of a search for a business entity that combines the best feature of general partnerships, pass-through taxation, and the best feature of corporations, limited liability. In Chapter 2, we introduced the limited liability partnership (LLP), a hybrid entity that is popular with professional firms. In this chapter, we examine the limited liability company (LLC), which has quickly become the entity of choice for most small businesses. A recent study shows that "the number of new LLCs formed in America in 2007 now outpaces the number of new corporations formed by a margin of nearly two to one." Rodney D. Chrisman, *LLCs Are the New King of the Hill: An Empirical Study of the Number of New LLCs, Corporations, or LLPs Formed in the United States Between 2004-2007 and How LLCs Were Taxed for Tax Years 2002-2006*, 15 Fordham J. Corp. & Fin. L. 459, 460 (2010).

Another hybrid entity that you may have encountered is the limited partnership (LP). The first LP statutes in the United States were adopted in the early 1800s, providing an alternative investment vehicle to corporations, which at the time required special legislative action before they could be formed. As corporations became more accessible through the adoption of general incorporation statutes, the popularity of LPs faded. LPs waged a comeback in the 1970s, however, when they were employed as tax shelters — investors used losses generated by the LPs to "shelter" other income from federal taxation — but changes in federal income tax law have dramatically reduced this use of LPs.

Most states have adopted a form of the Revised Uniform Limited Partnership Act (RULPA), which provides the default rules for LPs. The first Uniform Limited Partnership Act was promulgated in 1916, but its effectiveness was constrained by the fact that it viewed limited partnerships as small, local entities. As limited partnerships became popular vehicles for tax shelters, shortcomings in the 1916 act became apparent. This led to a major rewriting of that statute in 1976 and the creation of RULPA. RULPA was further revised in 1985 and remains the most popular limited partnership statute today. A new Uniform

Limited Partnership Act was promulgated in 2001 (ULPA), and as of early 2012, 18 states and the District of Columbia had adopted the new statute.

LPs must have at least one general partner, who exercises management responsibilities (GP), and at least one limited partner, who traditionally has been a passive investor. ULPA § 102(11). The traditional advantage of a limited partnership over a general partnership is simply that a general partnership subjects *all* partners to unlimited personal liability, while a limited partnership requires only one partner to be subject to unlimited personal liability. By creating a corporation to act as the general partner, business planners can effectively obtain limited liability for all participants in the LP. Following the lead of many states, the drafters of the new ULPA have opened another avenue for universal limited liability: the limited liability limited partnership (LLLP). Under this version of the LP, even general partners obtain limited liability to the same extent as general partners in an LLP. Under the new statute, LPs can register as LLLPs by simply including a statement to that effect in the certificate of limited partnership. Under ULPA § 404(c), the effect of such a statement on the general partner's liability is as follows:

> An obligation of a limited partnership incurred while the limited partnership is a limited liability limited partnership, whether arising in contract, tort, or otherwise, is solely the obligation of the limited partnership. A general partner is not personally liable, directly or indirectly, by way of contribution or otherwise, for such an obligation solely by reason of being or acting as a general partner.

While limited partners typically have limited personal liability, traditional LP law includes several exceptions to this rule, the most important of which holds that a limited partner who "participates in the control of the business" is liable to persons who transact business with the LP reasonably believing, based on the limited partner's conduct, that the limited partner is a general partner. This so-called "control rule" has been removed from the new ULPA. Referring to the rule as an "anachronism" in the age of LLCs, LLPs, and LLLPs, the drafting committee included the following provision as ULPA § 303:

> A limited partner is not personally liable, directly or indirectly, by way of contribution or otherwise, for an obligation of the limited partnership solely by reason of being a limited partner, even if the limited partner participates in the management and control of the limited partnership.

As a result of their long history, LPs have developed a rich and textured law separate from — but related to — the law governing general partnerships and the law governing corporations. As noted by the drafters of ULPA, however, the importance of LPs as a business entity is fading quickly:

> The new Act has been drafted for a world in which limited liability partnerships and limited liability companies can meet many of the needs formerly met by limited partnerships. This Act therefore targets two types of enterprises that seem largely beyond the scope of LLPs and LLCs: (i) sophisticated, manager-entrenched commercial deals whose participants commit for the long term, and (ii) estate planning arrangements (family limited partnerships).

In light of the waning relevance of LP law to modern business practice, we have elected to omit materials on LPs from this casebook.

A. BIRTH AND DEVELOPMENT OF LLCs

The most important development in recent years in the area of business associations is the widespread acceptance of limited liability companies (LLCs) as an alternative entity for small businesses. The impetus for this rapid development was a 1988 revenue ruling providing that Wyoming LLCs would be treated as partnerships for tax purposes. That ruling sanctioned the use of an entity that combined limited liability and pass-through tax treatment for businesses that found LPs cumbersome or could not qualify for Subchapter S status (perhaps because they had more than the requisite number of investors or a financial structure more complicated than that permitted by the one class of stock requirement of Subchapter S).

The first LLC statute in the United States was adopted by Wyoming in 1977, but LLCs did not become widely popular until the passage of the Tax Reform Act of 1986, which increased the federal income tax rate on corporations and eliminated the so-called *General Utilities* doctrine (*see* General Utilities & Operating Co. v. Helvering, 296 U.S. 200 (1935)), which permitted a corporation to distribute appreciated property to its shareholders without realizing taxable gain, thus avoiding double taxation. Shortly thereafter, the IRS issued the revenue ruling discussed above, and the rush was on. States quickly adopted LLC statutes, and the popularity of LLCs has been increasing ever since.

Until the mid-1990s, the IRS evaluated each LLC separately in an attempt to discern whether the entity was more like a corporation or a partnership. If the entity was more like a corporation, then it would be taxed as such. This evaluation began with four of the so-called *Kintner* factors — centralized management, continuity of life, free transferability of ownership interests, and limited liability. These factors were named after United States v. Kintner, 216 F.2d 418 (9th Cir. 1954), and later embodied in an IRS regulation. According to the IRS, an entity could have any two of these characteristics and still be treated as a partnership for tax purposes. Of course, every LLC entity wanted limited liability, and this left little room for flexibility in the remaining governance decisions.

Early LLC statutes were cut-and-paste productions, using provisions from state partnership, corporation, and limited partnership statutes to create a new entity whose primary goal was to allow for the combination of limited liability and partnership tax treatment. To ensure that all entities formed under the statute would obtain partnership tax treatment under the *Kintner* factors, many early statutes included numerous mandatory provisions. Before long, it became apparent that the *Kintner* factors were inhibiting the development of business forms, and the IRS decided to abandon individualized evaluation in favor of a system of election. Under the "check-the-box" regulation, which became effective in 1997, all unincorporated firms were allowed to select their tax classification. In other words, every LLC that wanted partnership tax treatment would obtain partnership tax treatment, even if the governance structure was effectively indistinguishable from a corporation.

LLC statutes have now been adopted in all 50 states and in the District of Columbia. The variety among LLC statutes is great. The National Conference of Commissioners on Uniform Laws proposed the Uniform Limited Liability Company Act (ULLCA) in 1996 in an attempt to unify the laws governing LLCs, but that effort was unsuccessful, as only five states adopted ULLCA. As of early 2012, the Revised Uniform Limited Liability Company Act (RULLCA), promulgated in 2006, has also been adopted in five states, plus the District of Columbia, and four other states are scheduled to introduce the statute in 2012. According to a recent study, "Delaware seems to have emerged as the national leader in the competition to attract LLC charters." Mohsen Manesh, *Delaware and the Market for LLC Law: A Theory of Contractability and Legal Indeterminacy*, 52 B.C. L. Rev. 189, 201 (2011). We use RULLCA, the Delaware LLC Act (DLLCA), and several other state statutes as reference points in this chapter.

B. FORMATION

Like other limited liability associations, LLCs are formed through a formal filing of a certification of organization or certificate of formation with the state, RULLCA § 201(a); DLLCA § 18-201(a). Most certificates of organization contain only minimal information about the company, including the name and mailing address of the company and a statement as to whether the company has members at the time of filing, RULLCA § 201(b); DLLCA § 18-201(a). Agreements among the members of an LLC are typically contained in an operating agreement, which is analogous to a partnership agreement. If the certificate of organization and the operating agreement conflict, under RULLCA § 112(d) the operating agreement controls with respect to members, dissociated members, transferees, and managers, while the certificate of organization controls with respect to third parties who reasonably rely on it. If the articles of organization or the operating agreement conflict with the statute, the statute prevails with respect to mandatory provisions, and an agreement between the parties prevails with respect to nonmandatory provisions. RULLCA § 110. The Delaware policy is "to give the maximum effect to the principle of freedom of contract and to the enforceability of limited liability company agreements," DLLCA § 18-1101(b), and the Delaware Supreme Court has held that a limited liability company agreement will be invalidated only when "the agreement is inconsistent with mandatory statutory provisions." Elf Atochem North America, Inc. v. Jaffari, 727 A.2d 286, 292 (Del. 1999).

The formation process is simple, but it is an important formality. Unlike agency relationships and general partnerships, LLCs cannot be created informally, and if the filing of the certificate of organization is never made, the default rules of the underlying LLC statute generally do not adhere. The short case below illustrates the importance of the filing to the formation of an LLC. It also illustrates how courts appeal to corporate law to guide their decisions regarding LLCs and their interpretations of LLC statutes. The appellant in the case below unsuccessfully invokes two old corporate law doctrines — "de facto corporation" and "corporation by estoppel" — in an attempt to argue that an LLC existed, even though the organizers of the LLC did not complete the formal filing in a timely manner.

By way of background, the concepts "de facto corporation" and "corporation by estoppel" were created by courts to deal with potential inequities that sometimes result from a failure to incorporate. If a person (usually called a "promoter") commences business without attempting to incorporate, the promoter generally will be personally liable for any obligations incurred. On the other hand, if the promoter attempted to incorporate but failed to follow the proper formalities, courts might conclude that the corporation existed "in fact" (*de facto*), even if not "in law" (*de jure*). The implication of this conclusion would be the recognition of limited liability to protect the promoter from personal liability. Similarly, a "corporation by estoppel" allows for the recognition of limited liability vis-à-vis third parties who deal with a promoter on the assumption that the promoter represents an existing corporation, even if the corporation has not been formed.

As you might imagine, these doctrines have resulted in no end of complications for courts. The drafters of the Model Business Corporation Act, which is the corporation statute referenced in the case below, attempted to resolve questions surrounding pre-incorporation contracts with the following deceptively simple rule: "All persons purporting to act as or on behalf of a corporation, knowing there was no incorporation under this Act, are jointly and severally liable for all liabilities created while so acting," MBCA § 2.04. In the comments to that section, the drafters observed:

> Incorporation under modern statutes is so simple and inexpensive that a strong argument may be made that nothing short of filing the articles of incorporation should create the privilege of limited liability. A number of situations have arisen, however, in which the protection of limited liability arguably should be recognized even though the simple incorporation process established by modern statutes has not been completed: (1) where a corporate organizer reasonably and honestly believes that the articles have been filed, but in fact they have not been due, for example, to attorney neglect; (2) where the articles have been mailed or delivered for filing, but not received by the secretary of state through no fault of the corporate organizer; (3) where the third party knows the articles have not been filed and looks only to the corporation in formation; (4) where the third party relies on the corporation's credit even though no corporation exists, and the corporate organizer knows that; and (5) where inactive investors have not authorized the commencement of business without the protection of the corporate shield and business is commenced without their knowledge.

Official Comment, MBCA § 2.04.

Despite this comment, some courts, such as the Minnesota court below, have held that the doctrine of de facto corporation has been abolished, and the application of the doctrine of corporation by estoppel is often accompanied by uncertainty regarding its proper scope. We do not need to resolve these quandaries, but you should consider how all of this reflects on the question: Why might courts be willing to recognize informal agency relationships and partnerships, but not informal LLCs?

STONE v. JETMAR PROPERTIES, LLC

733 N.W.2d 480
Court of Appeals of Minnesota
June 12, 2007

LANSING, Judge.

This appeal arises out of a series of real-estate transactions that resulted in the foreclosure sale of property that respondent Dale Stone had quitclaimed to a limited-liability company that was not yet organized when he attempted delivery. The foreclosure sale was initiated by Selwin Ortega, to whom the property had been mortgaged. Ortega appeals from an order establishing Stone's title to the property and providing damages. Ortega argues that the district court erred by concluding that the quitclaim deed was void. . . . Because we conclude that the quitclaim deed was void and that Stone is not legally or equitably precluded from asserting his interest in the property, we affirm.

FACTS

Keith Hammond drafted and signed articles of organization for Jetmar Properties, LLC, in November 2002, but he did not file the articles with the secretary of state. Later that same year, Hammond, acting as president of Jetmar, offered to buy commercial property from Selwin Ortega. Hammond and Ortega signed a purchase agreement, but the sale did not close because Hammond did not have the money. Nonetheless, based on Hammond's representation that he needed cash to develop the property into condominiums, Ortega gave Hammond a three-day, unsecured $200,000 loan, which Hammond failed to repay.

In April 2003 Hammond met Dale Stone, a retiree, and convinced him to invest in several of Jetmar's "real estate ventures." During the course of their relationship, Stone gave Hammond more than $50,000 in cashiers' checks for Jetmar's various projects. Sometime in May 2003, Hammond asked Stone to quitclaim a duplex to Jetmar to improve Jetmar's balance sheet, which would allow it to secure financing for a large condominium development. Stone was renting out the property to supplement his social-security income. In exchange for the deed, Hammond promised Stone an interest in the development. Hammond also told Stone that he would deed the property back to Stone "free and clear" in sixty days and that Stone could continue to collect rent. On May 14, 2003, Stone quitclaimed the property to Jetmar. Hammond purported to accept the deed as Jetmar's president and recorded it the same day.

On May 15, 2003, Hammond mortgaged the duplex to Ortega in exchange for an extension on the $200,000 loan. Ortega recorded the mortgage on May 20, 2003, after checking the title and determining that Jetmar had title to the property by virtue of a quitclaim deed from Stone.

Hammond did not repay the loan or deed the property back to Stone. Sometime around December 2003, Ortega began foreclosure proceedings. Ortega sent the duplex tenants a notice of foreclosure, which they passed along to Stone. Stone confronted Hammond about the mortgage, but he was told that there would be time to redeem and regain title to the property. Based on Hammond's assurances, Stone did not alert Ortega of his claimed interest. On March 2, 2004, Ortega conducted a sale under the foreclosure-by-advertisement procedures. Because there were no higher bidders, Ortega purchased the property in exchange for the surrender of his $200,000 claim against Jetmar. Hammond filed Jetmar's articles of organization on March 11, 2004, and received a certificate of organization.

Stone brought this action in October 2004, alleging that Hammond and Jetmar had defrauded him. . . . Stone sought damages and a declaratory judgment that he was the owner of the duplex. Ortega filed an answer, but Hammond and

Jetmar failed to respond. The district court concluded that, because Jetmar did not exist at the time of delivery, it was therefore incapable of taking title to land, and the quitclaim deed was void. Because the quitclaim deed was void, both the mortgage and the foreclosure were also void. . . . Based on these conclusions, the court awarded Stone damages and title to the duplex. This appeal followed.

ISSUES

I. Did the district court correctly conclude that Dale Stone's quitclaim deed to Jetmar Properties, LLC, was void?
II. Is Stone barred by the corporation-by-estoppel doctrine from challenging Selwin Ortega's title to the property?
. . .

ANALYSIS

I

Selwin Ortega argues that the district court erred by concluding that Dale Stone's quitclaim deed to Jetmar Properties, LLC, was void. Ortega claims that Jetmar was a de facto corporation when the deed was delivered, and, alternatively, that Jetmar was not per se barred from accepting delivery of the deed despite its nonexistence at the time of transfer. Because Ortega's de facto-corporation claim raises an issue of statutory construction, it is subject to de novo review. Ortega's claim that a deed can be delivered to an entity that did not exist at the time of transfer is also subject to de novo review.

Ortega first argues that, although Jetmar had not filed its articles of organization when Stone delivered the quitclaim deed, Jetmar could accept the deed under the de facto-corporation doctrine. Ortega claims that any suggestion that the de facto-corporation doctrine has been abolished in Minnesota is unfounded because it appeared only in the Reporter's Notes to Chapter 302A of the Minnesota Statutes. Minnesota cases continue to refer to the doctrine even after the enactment of chapter 302A, and it is unclear whether any prohibition against de facto corporations found in chapter 302A necessarily extends to limited-liability companies (LLC), which are governed by chapter 322B. The law and the facts do not support these arguments.

Historically, a de facto corporation could exist in Minnesota when there was "(1) some law under which a corporation with powers assumed might lawfully have been created; (2) a colorable and *bona fide* attempt to perfect an organization under such a law; and (3) user of the rights claimed to have been conferred by the law." Evens v. Anderson, 155 N.W. 1040, 1041 (1916). Ortega's claim that the de facto-corporation doctrine applies in this case fails as a matter of fact because, as he acknowledges, there had been *no* colorable attempt to organize Jetmar under the LLC statute when Stone signed the deed. The LLC statute provides that an LLC is organized by filing articles of organization with the secretary of state. Hammond made no attempt to file Jetmar's articles of organization with the secretary of state. As a result, even if the de facto-corporation doctrine had not been abolished, it would not apply.

We conclude, however, that the doctrine has been abolished in the context of business-corporation law and, by extension, in the context of LLC law.

The 1981 notes accompanying the business-corporations statute that sets the effective date of a corporation's articles of incorporation specifically provide that "the doctrine of de facto corporations is inapplicable in this state after the enactment of this act." Minn. Stat. Ann. § 302A.153, reporter's notes (West 2006). The rationale for the abolition of de facto corporations is that the process for incorporating is so simple that no one could ever make a "colorable attempt" to incorporate and fail. This court recognized the abolition of de facto corporations in *Warthan v. Midwest Consol. Ins. Agencies, Inc.*, 450 N.W.2d 145, 147-48 (Minn.App.1990), when, after quoting the reporter's notes, we observed that the "use of advisory committee reports is recognized in this state as a tool for ascertaining legislative intent." *Id.* at 148 n. 2.

Minnesota cases that continue to refer to the availability of the de facto-corporation doctrine after the enactment of the business-corporation statute are distinguishable. . . .

We also reject Ortega's claim that even if the de facto-corporation doctrine was abolished for purposes of business corporations it has not been abolished for LLC purposes. The 1992 notes to the LLC statute explain that "[t]o the extent a chapter 322B provision resembles a chapter 302A provision in substance, the case law and Reporter's Notes of chapter 302A should be used to interpret and apply the chapter 322B provision." Minn. Stat. Ann. § 322B.01, reporter's notes (West 2006). The LLC statute setting the effective date of articles of organization lists section 302A.153 as its source. Because section 302A.153 serves as the basis for section 322B.175, and the law relevant to corporations guides our interpretation and application of the law relevant to LLCs, the prohibition against de facto corporations must extend to LLCs.

Like the business-corporations statute, the LLC statute provides organizers with an indisputably simple route to formal organization. Thus it is doubtful that one could actually make an unsuccessful "colorable attempt" to organize a de jure LLC. Accordingly, the district court did not err by concluding that Jetmar was not a de facto corporation when Stone executed the deed.

Ortega next argues that Jetmar's nonexistence at the time Stone executed the deed is not determinative of whether Jetmar could take title to the property. To transfer title, a deed must be delivered. Ortega argues that when a deed is delivered to an "incipient" LLC, the transfer of title may take effect upon the LLC's formal organization. We disagree.

Under Minnesota law deeds cannot be delivered to nonexistent entities, whether the entities are natural or legal. A deed cannot be delivered to a deceased grantee, for example. Similarly, the supreme court has held that because an organization was not a corporation de jure or de facto, it could not take title to real estate. We can find no basis in Minnesota law for delaying transfer of title to some indeterminate future date when the grantee might come into existence. In fact, "many, but not all, courts have denied validity to deeds conveying property to corporations which are not incorporated at the time of conveyance." 14 Richard R. Powell, *Powell on Real Property* § 81A.04[1][a][iii] (Michael Allan Wolf ed., 2006). . . . According to these courts, "[t]he effective date of a deed is usually stated to be the date of delivery, and if at that date the corporation is 'non-existent,' the ordinary rule governs and the deed is treated as a nullity." 9 *Thompson on Real Property* § 82.08(a)(2) (David A. Thomas ed., 1994) (footnote omitted).

. . .

II

Ortega next argues that the doctrine of corporation-by-estoppel prevents Stone from taking title to the property. The district court did not expressly address Ortega's equitable claims, but it implicitly denied them by granting Stone's request for a declaratory judgment establishing title in him. The issue of estoppel is generally a question of fact. We review fact questions for clear error.

Ortega argues that under the corporation-by-estoppel doctrine Stone cannot take title to the property because Stone obtained an advantage by entering into a contract with Jetmar acting as an LLC, and Stone cannot now question the organization of the LLC. Although section 302A.153 abolished the de facto-corporation doctrine, the reporter's notes to the same statute indicate that the corporation-by-estoppel doctrine "has nothing to do with the efficacy of an attempted incorporation, and may apply even where no documents have been filed with the secretary of state." Minn. Stat. Ann. § 302A.153, reporter's notes. Thus, the corporation-by-estoppel doctrine survives in Minnesota despite the inapplicability of the de facto-corporation doctrine.

Even if we assume, without deciding, that the corporation-by-estoppel doctrine applies to LLCs, Ortega's claim fails. Stone treated Jetmar as a "corporation" when he executed the deed. But the estoppel doctrine does not apply when the acts forming the basis for an estoppel claim are induced by fraud. [A] court may refuse to apply the doctrine of corporation-by-estoppel when the corporation is used to accomplish fraud. The district court found that Stone executed the quitclaim deed while "relying on the false representations, promises, and assurances of Hammond." Because Stone was fraudulently induced to sign the deed and treat Jetmar as a "corporation," the district court could reject Ortega's corporation-by-estoppel argument.

. . .

The district court did not err by concluding that the quitclaim deed was void and that neither law nor equity prevented Stone from asserting his interest in the property.

Affirmed.

PROBLEM 3-1

Eve Drew and Amanda Carder seek out Drew's father, who is a corporate lawyer, for advice on forming a business. In the course of the discussion, they touch on many issues, including the leasing of space for their cheese shop, the acquiring of state licenses to distribute food, and the raising of capital to purchase equipment and build an inventory. The conversation also turns to their personal relationship. They call each other "partners," but they do not use the term in a technical, legal sense. They want advice on structuring their relationship. What business entity should they form? A general partnership? An LLP? An LLC? *What factors should drive this analysis?*

C. MANAGEMENT

The first and most important management issue regarding LLCs is whether they are to have centralized management (like a corporation) or decentralized management (like a partnership). LLC statutes provide for both types, with member management as the default rule. Both RULLCA and DLLCA require a statement in the operating agreement if the LLC is to be manager managed. RULLCA § 407(a); DLLCA § 18-402. Under RULLCA, members in a member-managed LLC have equal management rights and decide all ordinary business matters by a majority of the members. RULLCA § 407(b). Extraordinary matters and amendments to the operating agreement require the consent of all of the members. *Id.* DLLCA allocates management rights in a member-managed LLC "in proportion to the then current percentage or other interest of members in the profits of the limited liability company owned by all of the members." DLLCA § 18-402. The decisions of members are made by majority vote. *Id.*

Members in manager-managed LLCs have limited powers. In RULLCA managers have exclusive management rights and decide all ordinary business matters by a majority of the managers. RULLCA § 407(c). All members must consent to (1) sell, lease, exchange, or otherwise dispose of all, or substantially all, of the company's property, with or without the goodwill, outside the ordinary course of the company's activities; (2) approve a merger, conversion, or domestication under Article 10; (3) undertake any other act outside the ordinary course of the company's activities; and (4) amend the operating agreement. RULLCA § 407(c)(4). In DLLCA managers have whatever rights are provided in the limited liability company agreement. DLLCA § 18-402. Some other LLC statutes allow for extraordinary transactions upon the consent of a majority of the members. The argument for unanimity is that LLCs are likely to be closely held; therefore, members are likely to want a veto power over extraordinary transactions, and the unanimity requirement is the easiest method of providing that. The arguments against are numerous: (1) obtaining consent may be costly because it may require individual negotiations; (2) the veto power may not be as justified in an LLC as it is in a general partnership because members cannot impose unlimited liability for their actions on each other; and (3) a disgruntled member has the right to withdraw and be paid for his or her interest in the LLC.

Another management issue concerns the authority of members or managers to bind the LLC. In RULLCA members who are not managers, like shareholders in a corporation, have no inherent right to bind the LLC. RULLCA § 301(a). Managers, on the other hand, hold the exclusive power to make decisions with regard to the activities of the LLC, and each manager has equal management rights, with differences as to a matter in the ordinary course of the activities of the company being resolved by a majority of the managers. RULLCA § 407(c)(4). DLLCA relies on the limited liability company agreement to define authority: "Unless otherwise provided in a limited liability company agreement, each member and manager has the authority to bind the limited liability company." DLLCA § 18-402.

The following cases illustrate the management rules in action. The first case involves an extraordinary transaction that requires the Supreme Court of Wisconsin to examine both the LLC statute and the operating agreement. Generally speaking, the management provisions of an LLC statute are default rules, meaning that they can by changed by the operating agreement. RULLCA § 110; DLLCA § 18-1101(b). In the second case, however, the court interprets the Utah LLC statute in a manner that places the innocent LLC members in a very vulnerable position. The case raises issues relating to the power of an LLC operating agreement to limit the authority of a manager to act on behalf of the LLC. As you read this case, consider ways in which the innocent members might have avoided exposing themselves to this sort of liability.

GOTTSACKER v. MONNIER

697 N.W.2d 436
Supreme Court of Wisconsin
June 8, 2005

BRADLEY, Justice.

. . .

I

On September 4, 1998, Julie Monnier (hereinafter Monnier) formed New Jersey LLC as a vehicle to own investment real estate. Ten days later, the company acquired a 40,000-square-foot warehouse located at 2005 New Jersey Avenue in Sheboygan, Wisconsin. The warehouse had a single tenant on a year-to-year lease. New Jersey LLC purchased the property for $510,000, with the financing arranged for and guaranteed by Monnier.

Brothers Paul Gottsacker (hereinafter Paul) and Gregory Gottsacker (hereinafter Gregory) became members of New Jersey LLC in January 1999. They entered into a Member's Agreement, which expressed their intent to operate under Wisconsin's limited liability company laws. That document stated in relevant part:

(4) Julie A. Monnier shall own a 50% interest in the capital, profits and losses of Company and shall have 50% of the voting rights of Company.

(5) Paul Gottsacker and Gregory Gottsacker, collectively, shall own a 50% interest in the capital, profits and losses of Company and shall have 50% of the voting rights of Company.

New Jersey LLC later purchased additional property in Sheboygan on Wilson Avenue. When it was sold, the proceeds were distributed to the members as follows: 50% to Julie, 25% to Paul, and 25% to Gregory. After the sale of the Wilson Avenue property, the only remaining asset of New Jersey LLC was the warehouse on New Jersey Avenue.

Relationships among the members of New Jersey LLC subsequently became strained. In May 2000, Paul and Gregory had a falling-out, allegedly due to Gregory's lack of contribution to the enterprise. Thereafter, communication between the brothers was virtually nonexistent. Monnier also testified that she had not spoken with Gregory since 1998.

On June 7, 2001, Monnier executed a warranty deed transferring the warehouse property owned by New Jersey LLC to a new limited liability company called 2005 New Jersey LLC for $510,000, the same amount as the original purchase price. The new limited liability company consisted of two members: Monnier with a 60% ownership interest and Paul with a 40% ownership interest. Neither one had discussed the transfer with Gregory before it occurred.

Following the transfer, Monnier sent a check to Gregory for $22,000, which purportedly represented his 25% interest in the warehouse property previously owned by New Jersey LLC. Gregory did not cash the check. Monnier and Paul, meanwhile, did not receive any cash payment but instead left their equity in the recently created 2005 New Jersey LLC.

Gregory commenced suit against Monnier, Paul, and 2005 New Jersey LLC, alleging that they had engaged in an illegal transaction under Wis. Stat. Ch. 183. After a bench trial, the circuit court agreed, noting that the sole purpose of the transfer of the warehouse property was to eliminate Gregory's ownership interest in the asset.

Because the transfer served no legitimate business purpose, and because Monnier and Paul both profited from it, the circuit court determined that Monnier and Paul were precluded by the conflict of interest rules under Wis. Stat. Ch. 183 from voting to authorize the transfer. In the alternative, it concluded that Paul did not have authority to act without the assent of Gregory because the two brothers held a "collective" interest in the ownership. Ultimately, the circuit court ordered that 2005 New Jersey LLC return the warehouse property to New Jersey LLC. Monnier, Paul, and 2005 New Jersey LLC appealed.

The court of appeals affirmed the decision of the circuit court on different grounds. Contrary to the circuit court, the court of appeals reasoned that the provisions of Wis. Stat. Ch. 183, specifically Wis. Stat. §§ 183.0402 and 183.0404, do not prevent a member who has a material conflict of interest from dealing with matters of the LLC. Rather, those statutes prohibit a member who has a material conflict of interest from dealing unfairly with the LLC or its members. Thus, a member with a material conflict of interest can vote to transfer property but is required to do so fairly.

Applying this standard to the present case, the court of appeals held that the transfer of property was unfair in two respects. First, the conveyance was not an "arm's length transaction" because it did not occur on the open market. Second, the sale made it impracticable for New Jersey LLC to carry on with its intended business (i.e., to hold the commercial property as a long-term investment). Accordingly, the court of appeals did not reach the issue of whether Paul and Gregory each held a 25% ownership interest or whether the term "collectively" in the Member's Agreement required both brothers to jointly vote the entire 50%.

. . .

IV

The first issue we address is whether the petitioners possessed the majority necessary to authorize the transfer in question. Gregory submits that they did not. He notes that under the Member's Agreement for New Jersey LLC, Monnier had 50% of the voting rights, while he and his brother "collectively" had the other 50%. Thus, Gregory asserts, Monnier needed the approval of both brothers in order to transfer the commercial real estate.[7]

The petitioners, meanwhile, maintain that Paul and Gregory each possessed 25% of the voting rights. They argue that there is nothing in the Member's Agreement to indicate that the brothers could not vote independently. Furthermore, they contend that the term "collectively" simply refers to the sum of the brothers' individual interests, which are 25% each. According to the petitioners, such an understanding is consistent with the practice and past experience of the company.

Resolution of this dispute involves interpretation of a contract. When the terms of a contract are plain and unambiguous, we will construe it as it stands. However, a contract is ambiguous when its terms are reasonably susceptible to more than one construction.

We conclude that the Member's Agreement here is ambiguous as to the voting rights of Paul and Gregory. To begin, the term "collectively" is not defined in the document. Moreover, the dictionary definition relied upon by the circuit court in its decision is reasonably susceptible of more than one construction. That definition provided: "formed by collecting; gathered into a whole . . . designating or any enterprise in which people work together as a group, especially under a system of collectivism. . . ." Although the definition supports an interpretation that the brothers, together, have a 50% voting interest, it fails to conclusively answer whether they have to act in concert.

When interpreting an ambiguous contract provision, we must reject a construction that renders an unfair or unreasonable result. Likewise, we should adopt a construction that will render the contract a rational business instrument so far as reasonably practicable.

Applying these principles to the case at hand, we are satisfied that the term "collectively" refers to the sum of the brothers' individual 25% interests. To conclude otherwise would require unanimous approval by the members in order to perform any act that concerns the business of the company. Here, there is no express language indicating that the parties intended such a result. Construing the Member's Agreement to allow one minority member to effectively deadlock the LLC is unreasonable absent express language.

V

Having determined that the petitioners possessed the majority necessary to authorize the transaction, we consider next whether they were nonetheless prohibited from voting to transfer the property because of a material conflict of interest. Here, the circuit court found that "[t]he conveyance of the property by Julie Monnier and Paul Gottsacker to themselves in the guise of a newly created LLC, unquestionably, represents a material conflict of interest." This finding is supported by the facts of the case. Not only did Monnier and Paul engage in self-dealing, but in doing so they also increased their individual interests in the new LLC which received the property. Monnier's ownership improved from 50% to 60%, while Paul's interest improved from 25% to 40%.

---

7. Both parties agree that an affirmative vote of more than 50% was required to decide any matter connected with the business of New Jersey LLC.

The question therefore becomes what, if any, impact did this conflict of interest have on Monnier and Paul's ability to vote to transfer the property. Wisconsin Stat. § 183.0404 governs voting in LLCs and contemplates situations that would prevent a member from exercising that voting power. Subsection (3) of the statute explicitly states that members can be "precluded from voting." However, that subsection does not address how or when that preclusion would occur. Wisconsin Stat. § 183.0404 provides in relevant part:

> (1) Unless otherwise provided in an operating agreement or this chapter . . . an affirmative vote, approval or consent as follows shall be required to decide any matter connected with the business of a limited liability company:
>> (a) If management of a limited liability company is reserved to the members, an affirmative vote, approval or consent by members whose interests in the limited liability company represent contributions to the limited liability company of more than 50% of the value. . . .
>
> . . .
>
> (3) Unless otherwise provided in an operating agreement, *if any member is precluded from voting with respect to a given matter,* then the value of the contribution represented by the interest in the limited liability company with respect to which the member would otherwise have been entitled to vote shall be excluded from the total contributions made to the limited liability company for purposes of determining the 50% threshold under sub. (1)(a) for that matter.

(Emphasis added.)

Because Wis. Stat. § 183.0404 does not address how or when a member is precluded from voting, Gregory asks that we look to Wis. Stat. § 183.1101 for guidance. Wisconsin Stat. § 183.1101 pertains to the authority to sue on behalf of an LLC. It states that, "the vote of any member who has an interest in the outcome of the action that is adverse to the interest of the limited liability company shall be excluded." Wis. Stat. § 183.1101(1). According to Gregory, if one wishes to harmonize this section with Wis. Stat. § 183.0404, then it must follow that a member who has an interest adverse to the interest of the LLC is precluded from voting.

The petitioners, however, contend that members are not precluded from voting on a matter affecting the LLC, even if they have a material conflict of interest. For support, the petitioners rely upon Wis. Stat. § 183.0402, the statute defining duties of managers and members. That statute anticipates members having a material conflict of interest and requires them to "deal fairly" with the LLC and its other members. . . .

We have previously recognized that statutes relating to the same subject matter should be read together and harmonized when possible. Like the court of appeals, we discern a stronger relationship between Wis. Stat. §§ 183.0404 and 183.0402 than §§ 183.0404 and 183.1101. Here, Wis. Stat. §§ 183.0404 and 183.0402 appear in the same subchapter entitled "Rights and Duties of Members and Managers." The position of a statutory subsection is significant when construing the statute.

Reading Wis. Stat. §§ 183.0404 and 183.0402 together in harmony, we determine that the WLLCL does not preclude members with a material conflict of interest from voting their ownership interest with respect to a given matter. Rather, it prohibits members with a material conflict of interest from acting in a manner that constitutes a willful failure to deal fairly with the LLC or its other members. We interpret this requirement to mean that members with a material conflict of interest may not willfully act or fail to act in a manner that will have the effect of injuring the LLC or its other members. This inquiry contemplates both the conduct along with the end result, which we view as intertwined. The inquiry also contemplates a determination of the purpose of the LLC and the justified expectations of the parties.

Here, the circuit court made no express determination as to whether the petitioners willfully failed to deal fairly in spite of the conflict of interest. Under the circuit court's analysis, there was no need to reach this issue because the court reasoned that a material conflict of interest precluded any vote to transfer the property. . . .

Accordingly, we remand the cause to the circuit court for further findings and application of the foregoing standard. Consistent with Wis. Stat. § 183.0402(2), Monnier and Paul on remand shall also "account to the limited liability company and hold as trustee . . . any improper personal profit derived by that member . . . without the consent of a majority of the disinterested members" for the transfer in question. If it is determined by the court that this statute was violated, then the court will determine the appropriate remedy under the circumstances. . . .

The decision of the court of appeals is reversed and the cause is remanded to the circuit court.

ROGGENSACK, Justice (concurring).

I write in concurrence to further explain the foundation for decisions under the provisions of Wis. Stat. ch. 183 (2001-02), Wisconsin's limited liability company statute. In so doing, I focus on the nature of a member's interest in a limited liability company and on the specifics of New Jersey LLC, which drive the remedy available to Gregory Gottsacker on remand. . . .

I begin by noting that the nature of a member's interest in a limited liability company is personal property. As a member, Gregory has a right to receive a share of the profits and losses of New Jersey LLC and the right to "vote or participate" in the management of New Jersey LLC. However, Gregory never had an interest in real property in regard to the Sheboygan warehouse.

I agree with the majority opinion that Gregory had the right to be dealt with fairly by members of New Jersey LLC who had a "material conflict of interest" in regard to the sale of the Sheboygan warehouse. I also agree that if Julie and Paul acquired any "improper personal profit" in connection with the sale of the Sheboygan warehouse, they hold such improper personal profit in trust for Gregory.

Gregory contends that Julie and Paul could not vote to sell the warehouse because they had a conflict of interest in the matter. Again, I agree with the majority opinion's conclusion that ch. 183 does not preclude a member who has a material conflict of interest in a transaction from casting a valid vote on it. Accordingly, the sale is valid, but what remains on remand is to assess whether Gregory is due a payment different from that which he has received.

The majority has concluded that Gregory held a 25% interest in profits, losses and votes in New Jersey LLC. I concur in the majority opinion's interpretation of the Member's Agreement. In addition, the majority opinion's interpretation is consistent with the K-1 form Gregory filed with his federal taxes. On his K-1, Gregory declared that he had a 25% interest in the "profit sharing," "loss sharing" and "ownership of capital" for New Jersey LLC.

Gregory further claims that his right to vote on the proposed sale of the Sheboygan warehouse was violated because Julie and Paul did not give him notice of the potential sale and ask for his consent to the transaction. The majority opinion does not address this contention. Both Wis. Stat. § 183.0102(11) and Wis. Stat. § 183.0404(1) address a member's vote on matters connected with the business of a limited liability company.[7] Julie and Paul do not contend that Gregory had no right to vote, and I found nothing to support such a position. Accordingly, I conclude that Gregory did have a right to vote, give approval or consent on the sale of the Sheboygan warehouse, according to these provisions. Therefore, I compare Gregory's 25% member interest with the requirements of § 183.0404(1)(a) to determine if he had sufficient member interest to preclude the sale.

Wisconsin Stat. § 183.0404(1)(a) establishes that the member vote, approval or consent necessary must be "*more than 50%* of the value . . . of the total contributions made to the limited liability company." (Emphasis added.) It is uncontested that Julie contributed 50% of the value of the contributions made to New Jersey LLC. The majority opinion concludes that Paul contributed 25% of the contributions to New Jersey LLC and that Gregory contributed 25% of the contributions. Accordingly, Gregory's interest is insufficient to satisfy the statutory criteria for member participation that will determine whether a transaction occurs. Therefore, the fact that Gregory was not given the opportunity to vote against the sale of the Sheboygan warehouse had no effect on whether a valid sale occurred. . . .

I am authorized to state that Justice Jon P. Wilcox joins in this concurrence.

BUTLER, JR., Justice. (dissenting).

At times, issues are complex and therefore are in need of complex resolutions. At times, we tend to see complexity where none exists. This, I conclude, is one of those occasions where the issue and its resolution are simple. Because there was no affirmative vote, approval, or consent to transfer the warehouse property owned by New Jersey LLC to a new limited liability company called 2005 New Jersey LLC, as required by the Member's Agreement and Wis. Stat. § 183.0404(1), no legal transfer of the property took place. As such, I would affirm the court of appeals, albeit on different grounds. I therefore respectfully dissent.

I agree with the majority's overall analysis of the overview and history of limited liability companies. The majority correctly notes that the overriding goal of the Wisconsin Limited Liability Company Law (WLLCL) was to create a business entity providing, among other things, simplicity. The drafters of Wis. Stat. ch. 183 emphasized the importance of flexibility and freedom of contract and hoped that the LLC would provide an inexpensive vehicle that did not require legal counsel at every step.

---

7. Wisconsin Stat. § 183.0102(11) provides that a member's interest "means a member's rights in the limited liability company, including the member's . . . right . . . to vote or participate in management of the limited liability company."

The meaning of the Member's Agreement signed on January 13, 1999, by Julie Monnier, Paul Gottsacker, and Gregory Gottsacker is at issue here. . . . Because I see no ambiguity, I would use the terms of the agreement to ascertain its meaning.

Part (4) of the agreement clearly states that Julie Monnier owns a 50 percent interest in the Company, and *shall* have 50 percent of the voting rights of Company. Part (5) clearly provides that the Gottsacker brothers collectively own a 50 percent interest in the Company and "*shall* have 50% of the voting rights of Company." (emphasis added). There is no ambiguity in the construction of this agreement. Part (4) defines a separate 50 percent interest and voting right, and part (5) defines a separate 50 percent interest and voting right. Part (5) could have been written to provide each brother with a 25 percent share of the collective interest and voting right, but it was not drafted in that manner. Instead, the interest *and* the voting right were created as a collective.

The term "collectively" is not defined in the document. Accepting the definition for collectively that the majority adopts which was relied upon by the trial court creates no ambiguity. That definition provided: "formed by collecting; gathered into a whole . . . designating or any enterprise in which people work together as a group, especially under a system of collectivism. . . ." I disagree with the conclusion that the definition relied upon, or any definition for that matter, supports Monnier and Paul's position that Paul and Gregory each had an individual 25 percent voting right in the LLC.

If a "collective" is formed by collecting, it is the collective that remains, not the individual collected items. If it is gathered into a whole, it is the whole that remains. If it is an enterprise in which people work together as a group, it is the group that remains. I concur with the majority's conclusion that the term "collectively" refers to the sum of the brothers' interests, but that does not alter the fact that it is the sum that remains, and not the individual interests. Any other construction effectively rewrites the agreement entered into by these individuals.

Of course we must reject a construction resulting in unfair or unreasonable results, and give a construction that will render the contract a rational business instrument. There is nothing unfair nor unreasonable about construing this agreement as the parties wrote it. Nor is the agreement an irrational business instrument. It was the parties that specified the two separate 50 percent interests in New Jersey LLC. It was the parties that specified the two separate voting blocks. They could have chosen to draft the agreement to take into account each person's individual interest and voting rights, but the parties chose not to do so. If the parties choose to set forth an agreement that requires the brothers to vote together as one interest, this court should not stand in their way. If the drafters of Wis. Stat. ch. 183 emphasized the importance of flexibility and freedom of contract, then we ought to respect the flexibility and freedom of this agreement. In short, the trial court got it right when it concluded that Paul Gottsacker lacked the authority to act without the assent of his brother.

Gregory Gottsacker did not agree to or even know about the transfer of the warehouse engineered by petitioners in this matter. Thus, the collective provided in part (5) of the agreement never voted, approved, or consented to that transfer, as is required by Wis. Stat. § 183.0404(1). I therefore agree with the trial court that the warehouse should be returned from 2005 New Jersey LLC to New Jersey LLC. Accordingly, I respectfully dissent.

PROBLEM 3-2

Drew and Carder decided to form a company called Turophile LLC. They chose to form the company under the DLLCA. Although Drew and Carder each took 50% ownership shares in the company, the limited liability company agreement (LLC Agreement) drafted by Drew's father designates Drew as the Manager of Turophile LLC. The LLC Agreement does not provide a term limit or any method of removal of the Manager.

DLLCA § 18-402 provides in relevant part:

> [I]f a limited liability company agreement provides for the management, in whole or in part, of a limited liability company by a manager, the management of the limited liability company, to the extent so provided, shall be vested in the manager who shall be chosen in the manner provided in the limited liability company agreement. The manager shall also hold the offices and have the responsibilities accorded to the manager by or in the manner provided in a limited liability company agreement. Subject to § 18-602 of this title [providing for "Resignation of manager"], a manager shall cease to be a manager as provided in a limited liability company agreement.

In the early stages of their business relationship, Drew and Carder work well together, but if the day ever came when Carder wanted to remove Drew as manager of Turophile LLC, what would be her options?

TAGHIPOUR v. JEREZ

52 P.3d 1252
Supreme Court of Utah
July 30, 2002

RUSSON, Justice.

On a writ of certiorari, Namvar Taghipour, Danesh Rahemi, and Jerez, Taghipour and Associates, LLC, seek review of the decision of the court of appeals affirming the trial court's dismissal of their causes of action against Mount Olympus Financial, L.C. ("Mt. Olympus"). We affirm.

BACKGROUND

Namvar Taghipour, Danesh Rahemi, and Edgar Jerez ("Jerez") formed a limited liability company known as Jerez, Taghipour and Associates, LLC (the "LLC"), on August 30, 1994, to purchase and develop a particular parcel of real estate pursuant to a joint venture agreement. The LLC's articles of organization designated Jerez as the LLC's manager. In addition, the operating agreement between the members of the LLC provided: "No loans may be contracted on behalf of the [LLC] . . . unless authorized by a resolution of the [m]embers."

On August 31, 1994, the LLC acquired the intended real estate. Then, on January 10, 1997, Jerez, unbeknownst to the LLC's other members or managers, entered into a loan agreement on behalf of the LLC with Mt. Olympus.

According to the agreement, Mt. Olympus lent the LLC $25,000 and, as security for the loan, Jerez executed and delivered a trust deed that conveyed the LLC's real estate property to a trustee with the power to sell the property in the event of default. Mt. Olympus then dispensed $20,000 to Jerez and retained the $5,000 balance to cover various fees. In making the loan, Mt. Olympus did not investigate Jerez's authority to effectuate the loan agreement beyond determining that Jerez was the manager of the LLC.

After Mt. Olympus dispersed the funds pursuant to the agreement, Jerez apparently misappropriated and absconded with the $20,000. Jerez never remitted a payment on the loan, and because the other members of the LLC were unaware of the loan, no loan payments were ever made by anyone, and consequently, the LLC defaulted. Therefore, Mt. Olympus foreclosed on the LLC's property. The members of the LLC, other than Jerez, were never notified of the default or pending foreclosure sale.

On June 18, 1999, Namvar Taghipour, Danesh Rahemi, and the LLC (collectively, "Taghipour") filed suit against Mt. Olympus and Jerez. Taghipour asserted three claims against Mt. Olympus: (1) declaratory judgment that the loan agreement and subsequent foreclosure on the LLC's property were invalid because Jerez lacked the authority to bind the LLC under the operating agreement, (2) negligence in failing to conduct proper due diligence in determining whether Jerez had the authority to enter into the loan agreement, and (3) partition of the various interests in the property at issue. In response, Mt. Olympus moved to dismiss all three claims, asserting that pursuant to Utah Code section 48-2b-127(2), the loan agreement documents are valid and binding on the LLC since they were signed by the LLC's manager. This section provides:

> Instruments and documents providing for the acquisition, mortgage, or disposition of property of the limited liability company shall be valid and binding upon the limited liability company if they are executed by one or more managers of a limited liability company having a manager or managers or if they are executed by one or more members of a limited liability company in which management has been retained by the members.

The trial court granted Mt. Olympus' motion and dismissed Taghipour's claims against Mt. Olympus, ruling that under the above section, "instruments and documents providing for the mortgage of property of a limited liability company are valid and binding on the limited liability company if they are executed by the manager," that the complaint alleges that Jerez is the manager of the LLC, and that therefore the loan documents Jerez executed are valid and binding on the LLC.

Taghipour appealed to the Utah Court of Appeals. Taghipour argued that the trial court's interpretation of section 48-2b-127(2) was in error, inasmuch as it failed to read it in conjunction with Utah Code section 48-2b-125(2)(b), which provides that a manager's authority to bind a limited liability company can be limited by the operating agreement. That section provides in relevant part:

> If the management of the limited liability company is vested in a manager or managers, any manager has authority to bind the limited liability company, unless otherwise provided in the articles of organization or operating agreement.

The Utah Court of Appeals affirmed the trial court, concluding that the plain language of section 48-2b-127(2) provided no limitation on a manager's authority to execute certain documents and bind a limited liability company, and specifically stated such documents shall be valid and binding upon the limited liability company if executed by one or more managers. Further, the court of appeals concluded that this specific statute prevailed over the general statute, section 48-2b-125(2)(b), and that the loan documents executed by Jerez were therefore binding upon the LLC in this case. It also held that Mt. Olympus did all that it was required to do under section 48-2b-127(2) and that Taghipour waived the right to appeal the dismissal of the partition claim by failing to object to the dismissal of that claim. Taghipour petitioned this court for certiorari, which we granted.

Taghipour asks this court to reverse the court of appeals, arguing that (1) sections 48-2b-125(2)(b) and 48-2b-127(2) should be read in harmony to require that managers "be properly authorized to bind the limited liability company in all situations," and therefore Jerez lacked authority to bind the LLC under the operating agreement, and (2) a commercial lender has a due diligence obligation to determine the authority of a manager of a limited liability company before that manager can encumber the assets of the company, which Mt. Olympus failed to do by neglecting to determine whether Jerez had the authority to bind the LLC. In reply, Mt. Olympus contends that under Utah Code section 48-2b-127(2), Mt. Olympus could properly rely on Jerez's execution of the loan agreement as the manager of the LLC without further inquiry. . . .

ANALYSIS . . .

I. COMPETING STATUTORY PROVISIONS

To determine whether the loan agreement in this case is valid and binding on the LLC, it must first be determined whether this case is governed by section 48-2b-127(2), which makes certain kinds of documents binding on a limited liability company when executed by a manager, or section 48-2b-125(2)(b), which provides that a manager's authority to bind a limited liability company can be limited or eliminated by an operating agreement.

When two statutory provisions purport to cover the same subject, the legislature's intent must be considered in determining which provision applies. To determine that intent, our rules of statutory construction provide that "when two statutory provisions conflict in their operation, the provision more specific in application governs over the more general provision." Hall v. State Dep't of Corr., 2001 UT 34, ¶ 15, 24 P.3d 958.

In this case, the Utah Court of Appeals, affirming the trial court, concluded that section 48-2b-127(2) was more specific than section 48-2b-125(2)(b), and therefore took precedence over it. However, Taghipour contends that in determining which of the two provisions is more specific, the more restrictive clause is more specific because it is more limiting and "would require authority in all situations." Accordingly, Taghipour contends that section 48-2b-125(2)(b) is the more restrictive, and consequently, the more specific, provision.

The question of which statute the legislature intended to apply in this case is determined by looking to the plain language of the statutes that purport to cover the same subject. Section 48-2b-125(2)(b) provides in relevant part:

> If the management of the limited liability company is vested in a manager or managers, any manager has authority to bind the limited liability company, unless otherwise provided in the articles of organization or operating agreement.

Utah Code Ann. § 48-2b-125(2)(b) (1998). In contrast, section 48-2b-127(2) provides:

> Instruments and documents providing for the acquisition, mortgage, or disposition of property of the limited liability company shall be valid and binding upon the limited liability company if they are executed by one or more managers of a limited liability company having a manager or managers or if they are executed by one or more members of a limited liability company in which management has been retained by the members.

Section 48-2b-127(2) is the more specific statute because it applies only to documents explicitly enumerated in the statute, *i.e.*, the section expressly addresses "[i]nstruments and documents" that provide "for the acquisition, mortgage, or disposition of property of the limited liability company." Thus, this section is tailored precisely to address the documents and instruments Jerez executed, *e.g.*, the trust deed and trust deed note. For example, a trust deed is similar to a mortgage in that it secures an obligation relating to real property, and a trust deed "is a conveyance" of title to real property, which is a disposition of property as contemplated by the statutory provision. Conversely, section 48-2b-125(2)(b) is more general because it addresses *every* situation in which a manager can bind a limited liability company.

Further, a statute is more specific according to the content of the statute, not according to how restrictive the statute is in application. Indeed, a specific statute may be either more or less restrictive than the statute more general in application, depending upon the intent of the legislature in enacting a more specific statute.

Moreover, if we were to hold that section 48-2b-125(2)(b) is the more specific provision, we would essentially render section 48-2b-127(2) "superfluous and inoperative," because section 48-2b-127(2) would simply restate section 48-2b-125(2)(b) and would therefore be subsumed by section 48-2b-125(2)(b). Accordingly, the court of appeals correctly concluded that section 48-2b-127(2) is more specific, and therefore, the applicable statute in this case.

II. VALID AND BINDING LOAN AGREEMENT DOCUMENTS

Section 48-2b-127(2) must be applied to the facts of this case to determine whether the documents are valid and bind the LLC. At the time relevant to this case, section 48-2b-127(2), the statute applicable to the issue in this case, provided:

> *Instruments and documents providing for the* acquisition, *mortgage,* or disposition *of property of the limited liability company shall be valid and binding upon the limited liability company if they are executed by one or more managers* of a limited liability company

having a manager or managers or if they are executed by one or more members of a limited liability company in which management has been retained by the members.

Utah Code Ann. § 48-26-127(2) (1998) (emphasis added). According to this section, the documents are binding if they are covered by the statute and if executed by a manager. There are no other requirements for such documents to be binding on a limited liability company.

In this case, as Taghipour acknowledges in the complaint and Taghipour's brief on appeal, Jerez was designated as the LLC's manager in the articles of organization. Jerez, acting in his capacity as manager, executed loan agreement documents, *e.g.*, the trust deed and trust deed note, on behalf of the LLC that are specifically covered by the above statute. As such, these documents are valid and binding on the LLC under section 48-2b-127(2). Therefore, the court of appeals correctly concluded that the LLC was bound by the loan agreement and, consequently, that Mt. Olympus was not liable to Taghipour for Jerez's actions. . . .

PROBLEM 3-3

Drew and Carder's cheese shop is so successful that they have been able to hire employees to take care of the day-to-day operations. While Drew continues to oversee the purchasing of cheese, Carder has become a passive owner, turning her attention to a new online business that promotes specialty food sales over the internet. Described in informal discussions as "Groupon for Foodies," the business has started to get traction in San Francisco, where Carder's family maintains a residence.

Carder decided to further her online business by using email addresses collected from customers of the cheese shop. Using these addresses in this way violated Turophile's written privacy policy, which was sent to each customer who provided an email address. *If some of Turophile's customers sued Turophile for breach of contract, would Turophile be liable for Carder's actions?* DLLCA § 18-402 provides in relevant part: "Unless otherwise provided in a limited liability company agreement, each member and manager has the authority to bind the limited liability company."

D. LIMITED LIABILITY

Whether an LLC is member managed or manager managed, the members of an LLC are not personally liable for any obligation of the LLC simply because they are members or managers. RULLCA § 304(a); DLLCA § 303(a). Of course, members and managers of an LLC are responsible for their own acts or omissions and for obligations undertaken by agreement, but they are not personally responsible for the acts, omissions, or obligations of other members. This is the essence of "limited liability."

In the corporate context, courts have developed a doctrine called "piercing the corporate veil" as a means of circumventing limited liability and holding shareholders personally liable for the obligations of the corporation. This doctrine is employed only in exceptional circumstances. Generally speaking, it is designed to impose personal liability on shareholders when they have failed to treat the corporation as a separate legal entity. While the justification for the doctrine remains elusive, many courts seem to be reasoning along the following lines: If a shareholder treats the corporation's funds as interchangeable with the shareholder's personal funds, courts will do the same. In these circumstances, courts often refer to the corporation as an "alter ego" of the shareholder. We will examine this doctrine more closely in Chapter 4, but we pause here to consider its application in the LLC context.

When LLCs first started to grow in popularity in the mid-1990s, many commentators wondered whether courts would apply the doctrine of "piercing the corporate veil" in the LLC context. While many courts have not hesitated to transfer the doctrine to this new setting, some courts have suggested that "piercing the LLC veil" is a slightly different concept than "piercing the corporate veil." In the corporate context, courts confronted with a piercing claim place great weight on the maintenance of "corporate formalities," such as having a separate bank account or holding regular meetings of the board of directors. But LLCs may well lack such formalities by design. For example, in Kaycee Land and Livestock v. Flahive, 46 P.3d 323, 328 (Wyo. 2002), the Wyoming Supreme Court explained why the piercing doctrine might be an awkward fit:

> Certainly, the various factors which would justify piercing an LLC veil would not be identical to the corporate situation for the obvious reason that many of the organizational formalities applicable to corporations do not apply to LLCs. The LLC's operation is intended to be much more flexible than a corporation's.

Because of the inherent informality of LLCs, many statutes expressly provide that piercing shall not be based on the failure to maintain formalities. For example, RULLCA § 304(b) provides:

> The failure of a limited liability company to observe any particular formalities relating to the exercise of its powers or management of its activities is not a ground for imposing liability on the members or managers for the debts, obligations, or other liabilities of the company.

The DLLCA does not mention piercing, but in the following case, the United States Court of Appeals for the Second Circuit offers a careful analysis of piercing in the LLC context, using Delaware common law to motivate the analysis.

NETJETS AVIATION, INC. v. LHC COMMUNICATIONS, LLC

537 F.3d 168
United States Court of Appeals, Second Circuit
August 8, 2008

KEARSE, Circuit Judge:

. . .

I. Background

[Plaintiffs NetJets Aviation, Inc., and NetJets Sales, Inc. (collectively "NetJets") are] engaged in the business of leasing fractional interests in airplanes and providing related air-travel services. [Defendant LHC Communications, LLC ("LHC")] is a Delaware limited liability company whose sole member-owner is [Laurence S. Zimmerman]. Most of the facts with respect to the relationship between NetJets and LHC are not in dispute.

A. THE CONTRACTS BETWEEN NETJETS AND LHC

On August 1, 1999, LHC entered into two contracts with NetJets. In the first (the "Lease Agreement"), NetJets leased to LHC a 12.5 percent interest in an airplane, for which LHC was to pay NetJets a fixed monthly rental fee. The lease term was five years, with LHC having a qualified right of early termination. The second contract (the "Management Agreement") required NetJets to manage LHC's interest in the leased airplane and to provide services such as maintenance and piloting with respect to that airplane, or substitute aircraft, at specified hourly rates. It required LHC to pay a monthly management fee, as well as fuel charges, taxes, and other fees associated with LHC's air travel. The Management Agreement allotted to LHC use of the airplane for an average of 100 hours per year for the five-year term of the lease ("LHC air hours"), and it provided that if the leased airplane were unavailable at a time when LHC wished to use it, NetJets would provide substitute aircraft. NetJets regularly sent LHC invoices for the services provided under the Lease and Management Agreements. . . .

In July 2000, LHC terminated its agreements with NetJets. LHC's chief financial officer ("CFO") James P. Whittier sent a letter, addressed to a NetJets vice president, stating, in pertinent part, that "[t]he present outstanding is $440,840.39 and we are requesting that you apply the deposit of $100,000 against the outstanding and contact this office to resolve the balance." (Letter from James P. Whittier to Ron Miller dated July 24, 2000 ("LHC Termination Letter").)

As requested, NetJets contacted LHC and applied the $100,000 deposit against LHC's debt; however, it did not receive payment of the remaining balance of $340,840.39. In 2001, LHC ceased operations.

B. THE PRESENT ACTION AND THE DECISION OF THE DISTRICT COURT

. . . In a Memorandum and Order dated June 12, 2006, the district court granted NetJets's summary judgment motion in part, awarding it $340,840.39 against LHC. . . . The court concluded that, in light of the LHC Termination Letter, whose authenticity was unchallenged, there was no genuine issue to be tried with respect to LHC's liability to NetJets in the amount of $340,840.39. . . .

The district court . . . denied NetJets's motion for summary judgment on its . . . claims against Zimmerman. It stated that under Delaware law, in order to recover against Zimmerman for the debts of LHC, NetJets would be required to meet a two-pronged test showing "(1) that the business entity and its owner 'operated as a single economic entity' and (2) that [there was] an 'overall element of injustice or unfairness.'" *NetJets Aviation, Inc. v. LHC Communications LLC*, No. 02 Civ. 7441, 2006 WL 1627899 at *4 (S.D.N.Y. June 12, 2006) (quoting *Fletcher v. Atex, Inc.*, 68 F.3d 1451, 1458 (2d Cir.1995), which applied Delaware law). The court concluded that although NetJets had "shown that Zimmerman and LHC functioned as a single economic unit," NetJets had not "set forth any facts from which a jury could reasonably conclude that Zimmerman formed LHC with the specific fraudulent intent of evading liability to Plaintiffs." The court noted that while "something other than specific fraudulent intent could satisfy the second prong, wherever courts have given shape to the second prong, they primarily have focused on the need to show fraud or bad faith"; it stated that NetJets had "not proven as a matter of law that Zimmerman conducted a sophisticated shell game to the purposeful detriment of creditors, namely Net-Jets." The district court rejected the proposition that the requisite unfairness was shown by the evidence that "Zimmerman allowed LHC to default on its payments to NetJets even as he was siphoning money from the company coffers, transferring funds to other companies he controlled, and making payments through LHC on a mortgage and luxury cars that were in his own name." The court stated that "each of these actions are factors in considering the first prong of the alter ego analysis and cannot simultaneously be used by Plaintiffs to satisfy the second prong. 'To hold otherwise would render the fraud or injustice element meaningless. . . .'" *Id.* (quoting *Mobil Oil Corp. v. Linear Films, Inc.*, 718 F.Supp. 260, 268 (D.Del.1989)).

Although Zimmerman had not moved for summary judgment in his favor, the court *sua sponte* granted summary judgment dismissing all of NetJets's claims against him.

II. Discussion

. . . For the reasons that follow, we conclude that NetJets is entitled to trial on its . . . claims against Zimmerman as LHC's alter ego.

. . .

B. NETJETS'S CLAIMS AGAINST ZIMMERMAN

1. Limitations on Limited Liability

A limited liability company (or "LLC"), formed by one or more entities and/or individuals as its "members," is an entity that, as a general matter, provides "tax benefits akin to a partnership and limited liability akin to the corporate form." *Elf Atochem North America, Inc. v. Jaffari*, 727 A.2d 286, 287 (Del.1999). . . . The shareholders of a corporation and the members of an LLC generally are not liable for the debts of the entity, and a plaintiff seeking to persuade a Delaware court to disregard the corporate structure faces "a difficult task," *Harco National Insurance Co. v. Green Farms, Inc.*, No. CIV. A. 1331, 1989 WL 110537, at *4 (Del. Ch. Sept. 19, 1989) ("*Harco*").

Nonetheless, in appropriate circumstances, the distinction between the entity and its owner "may be disregarded" to require an owner to answer for the entity's debts. *Pauley Petroleum Inc. v. Continental Oil Co.*, 239 A.2d 629, 633 (Del.1968). In general, with respect to the limited liability of owners of a corporation, Delaware law permits a court to pierce the corporate veil "where there is fraud or where [the corporation] is in fact a mere instrumentality or alter ego of its owner." *Geyer v. Ingersoll Publications Co.*, 621 A.2d 784, 793 (Del.Ch.1992). . . . Given the similar liability shields that are provided by corporations and LLCs to their respective owners, "[e]merging caselaw illustrates" that "situations that result in a piercing of the limited liability veil are similar to those [that warrant] piercing the corporate veil." J. Leet, J. Clarke, P. Nollkamper & P. Whynott, *The Limited Liability Company* § 11:130, at 11–7 (rev. ed.2007). . . .

To prevail under the alter-ego theory of piercing the veil, a plaintiff need not prove that there was actual fraud but must show a mingling of the operations of the entity and its owner plus an "overall element of injustice or unfairness." *Harco,* 1989 WL 110537, at *4.

> [A]n alter ego analysis must start with an examination of factors which reveal how the corporation operates and the particular defendant's relationship to that operation. These factors include whether the corporation was adequately capitalized for the corporate undertaking; whether the corporation was solvent; whether dividends were paid, corporate records kept, officers and directors functioned properly, and other corporate formalities were observed; whether the dominant shareholder siphoned corporate funds; and whether, in general, the corporation simply functioned as a facade for the dominant shareholder.

Id. at *4 (quoting *United States v. Golden Acres, Inc.,* 702 F.Supp. 1097, 1104 (D.Del.1988) ("*Golden Acres*"), *aff'd,* 879 F.2d 857 & 879 F.2d 860 (3d Cir.1989)).

> [N]o single factor c[an] justify a decision to disregard the corporate entity, but . . . some combination of them [i]s required, and . . . *an overall element of injustice or unfairness must always be present, as well.*

Harco, [1989 WL 110537, at *5] (quoting *Golden Acres,* 702 F.Supp. at 1104). *Harper v. Delaware Valley Broadcasters, Inc.,* 743 F.Supp. 1076, 1085 (D.Del.1990) ("*Harper*") (emphasis added), *aff'd,* 932 F.2d 959 (3d Cir.1991).

As the above discussion indicates, "[n]umerous factors come into play when discussing whether separate legal entities should be regarded as alter egos," *id.,* and "[t]he legal test for determining when a corporate form should be ignored in equity cannot be reduced to a single formula that is neither over-nor under-inclusive," *Irwin & Leighton, Inc. v. W.M. Anderson Co.,* 532 A.2d 983, 989 (Del.Ch.1987). Stated generally, the inquiry initially focuses on whether "those in control of a corporation" did not "treat[ ] the corporation as a distinct entity"; and, if they did not, the court then seeks "to evaluate the specific facts with a standard of 'fraud' or 'misuse' or some other general term of reproach in mind," *id.,* such as whether the corporation was used to engage in conduct that was "inequitable," *Mobil Oil Corp. v. Linear Films, Inc.,* 718 F.Supp. 260, 269 (D.Del.1989) ("*Mobil Oil*") (internal quotation marks omitted), or "prohibited," *David v. Mast,* No. 1369-K, 1999 WL 135244, at *2 (Del.Ch. Mar.2, 1999), or an "unfair trade practice," *id.,* or "illegal," *Martin,* 10 Del.Ch. at 219, 88 A. at 615.

Simply phrased, the standard may be restated as: "whether [the two entities] operated as a single economic entity such that it would be inequitable for th[e] Court to uphold a legal distinction between them." *Mabon, Nugent & Co.* [*v. Texas American Energy Corp.,* No. CIV. A. 8578, 1990 WL 44267, at *5 (Del.Ch. Apr.12, 1990)].

Harper, 743 F.Supp. at 1085. Our Court has stated this as a two-pronged test focusing on (1) whether the entities in question operated as a single economic entity, and (2) whether there was an overall element of injustice or unfairness. *See Fletcher v. Atex, Inc.,* 68 F.3d 1451, 1457 (2d Cir.1995).

Finally, we note that the plaintiff need not prove that the corporation was created with fraud or unfairness in mind. It is sufficient to prove that it was so used. . . .

These principles are generally applicable as well where one of the entities in question is an LLC rather than a corporation. *See, e.g., Oliver v. Boston University,* No. 16570, 2000 WL 1091480, at *9, *12 (Del.Ch. Jul.18, 2000) (holding that a Massachusetts LLC, created solely to serve the interests of its owner and completely dominated by the owner, could be fairly characterized as the alter ego of its owner). In the alter-ego analysis of an LLC, somewhat less emphasis is placed on whether the LLC observed internal formalities because fewer such formalities are legally required. *See, e.g.,* Delaware Limited Liability Company Act, Del. Code Ann. tit. 6, § 18-101 *et seq.* ("DLLCA") (requiring little more than that an LLC execute and file a proper certificate of formation, *see id.* § 18-201(a), maintain a registered office in Delaware, *see id.* § 18-104(a)(1), have a registered agent for service of process in Delaware, *see id.* § 18-104(a)(2), and maintain certain records such as membership lists and tax returns, *see id.* § 18-305(a)). On the other hand, if two entities with common ownership "failed to follow legal formalities *when contracting with each other* it would be tantamount to declaring that they are indeed one in the same." *Trustees of Village of Arden v. Unity Construction Co.,* No. C.A. 15025, 2000 WL 130627, at *3 (Del.Ch. Jan.26, 2000) (emphasis added).

. . .

3. The Evidence that LHC and Zimmerman Operated as One

With respect to the question of whether LHC and Zimmerman operated as a single entity, the record contains, *inter alia,* financial records of LHC and deposition testimony from Zimmerman and LHC's CFO, Whittier. The evidence discussed below, taken in the light most favorable to NetJets, shows, *inter alia,* that LHC, of which Zimmerman is the sole member-owner, was started with a capitalization of no more than $20,100; that LHC proceeded to invest millions of dollars supplied by Zimmerman, including some $22 million in an internet technology company eventually called Bazillion, Inc. ("Bazillion"); and that Zimmerman put money into LHC as LHC needed it, and took money out of LHC as Zimmerman needed it.

Whittier, who had known Zimmerman since 1980 and worked with him full time from 1996 until April 2002, was LHC's only officer other than Zimmerman. In addition to LHC, Zimmerman directly or indirectly owned or controlled a number of companies. . . . Whittier acted as CFO for each of those companies. During most of the period 1996 to April 2002, Whittier "got paid from either Mr. Zimmerman or one of his corporations."

Zimmerman formed LHC in 1998; for most of its operating life, it shared office space with some of Zimmerman's other companies; LHC employed no more than five-to-seven people at any given time; and some of its employees worked for both LHC and Zimmerman's other companies or for LHC and Zimmerman personally. Whittier ran much of LHC's day-to-day operations based on instructions, general or specific, received from Zimmerman.

Zimmerman formed LHC "to be used as an investment vehicle for Mr. Zimmerman for him to make investments." "With regards to investments, Mr. Zimmerman reviewed investments. If he decided to go forward after his review, he would make an investment through [LHC] to an investment corporation he wanted to invest in." Although Zimmerman sought Whittier's advice as to the best way of accomplishing something he had decided he wanted to do, the ultimate decisions were always made by Zimmerman. "There were no decisions, financial decisions, made with regard to LHC without Mr. Zimmerman's approval."

Whittier testified that LHC also "was an operating company which maintained a consulting agreement with another entity called Landtel NV." But LandTel, which was wholly owned by Zimmerman's Landover Telecom — and was apparently LHC's only paying client — did not come into existence until January 2000, and LHC records do not show receipt of any consulting fees from LandTel until July 2000. Until LandTel was formed, therefore, the day-to-day LHC operations run by Whittier apparently consisted only of making Zimmerman's investments and carrying on Zimmerman's personal business. . . . Whittier's compensation was paid sometimes by LHC and sometimes by Zimmerman personally.

In connection with Zimmerman's personal business, LHC's records show numerous transfers of money by Zimmerman to LHC, as well as numerous transfers of money from LHC to Zimmerman. Some of the transfers by Zimmerman to LHC were for the purpose of having LHC make investments, principally in Bazillion. Other transfers by Zimmerman to LHC were made for the purpose of meeting LHC's operating expenses. . . .

Whittier testified that Zimmerman would transfer funds to LHC "as needed." Often those funds would come from Zimmerman's personal bank accounts. However, because Zimmerman generally waited until the eleventh hour to provide money to meet LHC's operating needs, sometimes "shortcuts" were taken by having the money come to LHC directly from one of Zimmerman's other companies . . . , none of which had any business relationship with LHC.

Whittier testified also that "[m]onies would go . . . *out of LHC* based on the need." For example, Zimmerman would take money out of LHC to "mak[e] an investment in another entity." In addition, at several brokerage firms, Zimmerman had personal accounts that were unrelated to LHC's operations; he had many margin calls in those accounts because he "utilized margin debt very aggressively," especially with respect to two stocks whose market prices dropped sharply in 2000. Zimmerman had LHC make payments to meet some of these margin calls in his personal accounts. On May 15 and 16, 2000, for example, LHC wired a total of $2 million to Salomon Smith Barney to meet margin calls or reduce the margin debt on Zimmerman's personal brokerage accounts. On August 22 and October 6, 2000, LHC sent Paine Webber, another firm at which Zimmerman personally had "big brokerage accounts," checks totaling $2 million. Some of the money that LHC used to pay Zimmerman's margin calls was "loan money" that Zimmerman had put into LHC. Other money used to meet Zimmerman's margin calls was money that LHC received from a third party . . . purchasing a share of an LHC asset. . . .

LHC also transferred money to Zimmerman, or to third persons on his behalf, in connection with his living expenses. For example, LHC made payments to Fox Lair (consistently called "Fox Liar" in LHC's general ledger), a Zimmerman corporation that owned a $15 million New York apartment on Park Avenue, which was characterized by Zimmerman as "a corporate residence" but was used by no one other than Zimmerman and his family. Fox Lair needed money "to pay phone bills and cleaning people and things of that nature";

according to LHC's ledgers, from December 5, 2000, through July 2, 2001, Fox Lair received some $70,000 from LHC. In addition, LHC made periodic payments to the Screen Actors Guild (of which Zimmerman's wife was a member) for health insurance for Zimmerman and his family; LHC purchased a Bentley automobile at a cost of approximately $350,000 for Zimmerman's personal use, placing title in his name; and LHC made a payment of $110,000, characterized in its general ledger as "Loan receivable" and in its check register as "Interest Expense," to a person who had no connection with LHC but who held a mortgage on a property owned by Zimmerman personally.

In addition, many of the air hours to which LHC was entitled under its agreements with NetJets were used by Zimmerman personally. Of the 40-odd LHC flights invoiced by NetJets, Zimmerman acknowledges that "approximately 6" were for vacations for himself and/or his wife. But in addition to those six, there were at least an equal number of flights that apparently had no relation to LHC's business. These flights included several that transported Zimmerman's family to and from Europe or to and from one of Zimmerman's five homes. Zimmerman contends that use of LHC air hours for these purposes was "part of [his compensation] package" and "[o]ne of the perks of being the chairman." That may be; but for purposes of determining whether Zimmerman and LHC were alter egos, it is pertinent that Zimmerman made all of LHC's financial decisions; Zimmerman alone decided what his perks and package would be.

. . .

In all, LHC's financial records for the period January 1, 2000, through June 18, 2002, show — in addition to some two dozen transactions between LHC and Zimmerman's other companies — approximately 60 transfers of money directly from Zimmerman to LHC and approximately 60 transfers of money out of LHC directly to Zimmerman. In sum, there is evidence that, *inter alia*, Zimmerman created LHC to be one of his personal investment vehicles; that he was the sole decisionmaker with respect to LHC's financial actions; that Zimmerman frequently put money into LHC as LHC needed it to meet operating expenses; that LHC used some of that money, as well as some moneys it received from selling shares of one of its assets, to pay more than $4.5 million to third persons for Zimmerman's personal expenses including margin calls, mortgage payments, apartment expenses, and automobiles; and that with no written agreements or documentation or procedures in place, Zimmerman directly, on the average of twice a month for 2 1/2 years, took money out of LHC at will in order to make other investments or to meet his other personal expenses. This evidence is ample to permit a reasonable factfinder to find that Zimmerman completely dominated LHC and that he essentially treated LHC's bank account as one of his pockets, into which he reached when he needed or desired funds for his personal use. Accordingly, we reject Zimmerman's contention that the district court should have granted summary judgment in his favor on the ground that he and LHC did not operate as a single economic entity.

4. The Evidence of Fraud, Illegality, or Injustice

The district court ruled that NetJets had not adduced sufficient evidence to show that there was any fraud or unfairness in Zimmerman's operation of LHC because the court believed it could not consider, with regard to that issue, any of the factors that showed that Zimmerman and LHC operated as a single entity. . . . But nothing prevents a court, in determining whether there is sufficient evidence of fraud or unfairness, from taking into account relevant evidence that is also pertinent to the question of whether the two entities in question functioned as one.

Much of the evidence described . . . above, along with other evidence discussed below, reveals that NetJets adduced sufficient evidence of fraud, illegality, or unfairness to warrant a trial on its contract and account-stated claims against Zimmerman as LHC's alter ego. For example, in an effort to parry NetJets's contention that LHC was undercapitalized, Zimmerman submitted an affidavit from LHC's accountant stating that "it was not intended by Zimmerman to treat the monies paid into LHC as loans" and that all of Zimmerman's payments into LHC were in fact capital contributions. Yet . . . Whittier testified that Zimmerman instructed him that those payments were to be characterized as loans, in order to allow Zimmerman to take money out of LHC at will and to do so without tax consequences.

Further, although the Balaban affidavit stops short of giving an opinion as to how to characterize Zimmerman's withdrawals of money from LHC, it would appear that, if his payments to LHC were capital contributions as the Balaban affidavit opines, LHC's payments to Zimmerman would be properly characterized as distributions. Yet the DLLCA provides generally, with some qualifications, that an LLC "shall not make a distribution to a member to the extent that at the time of the distribution, after giving effect to the distribution, all liabilities of the limited liability company . . . exceed the fair value of the assets of the limited liability company." Del.Code tit. 6, § 18-607(a). Given that LHC ceased operating and was unable to pay its debt to NetJets, if Zimmerman's withdrawals left LHC in that condition those withdrawals may well have been prohibited by § 18-607(a). A factfinder could infer that Zimmerman's payments to LHC were deliberately mischaracterized as loans in order to mask the fact that Zimmerman was making withdrawals from LHC that were forbidden by law, and could thereby properly find fraud or an unfair siphoning of LHC's assets.

The record also includes other evidence from which a reasonable factfinder could find that Zimmerman operated LHC in his own self-interest in a manner that unfairly disregarded the rights of LHC's creditors. For example, it could find

— that although LHC was apparently unable in 2000 to pay its $340,840.39 (net of LHC's deposit) debt to NetJets, in that year LHC bought, and gave Zimmerman title to, a Bentley automobile for $350,210.95;

— that LHC's only paying client for its consulting services began paying LHC for those services in July 2000 (the month in which LHC terminated its agreements with NetJets), sending LHC a first payment of approximately $675,000 on July 9, and that on that day Zimmerman withdrew that amount and more from LHC;

— that from the point at which LHC terminated its relationship with NetJets in July 2000 until the end of 2001, the year in which NetJets ceased operations, LHC's records of its transactions directly with Zimmerman indicate that Zimmerman withdrew from LHC approximately $750,000 more than he put in;

— and that, excluding moneys put into LHC solely for its investments in Bazillion, the total amount of money taken out of LHC by Zimmerman and his other companies appears to exceed the amount that he and those companies put into LHC by some $3 million.

From this record, a reasonable factfinder could properly find that there was an overall element of injustice in Zimmerman's operation of LHC. Summary judgment should not have been entered dismissing NetJets's . . . claims against Zimmerman.

. . .

PROBLEM 3-4

In getting the business off the ground (see Problem 3-3), Carder has from time to time withdrawn money from the cheese shop's checking account. Over the course of six months, she has used approximately $15,000 of the cheese shop's funds without asking Drew for permission or documenting the withdrawals as loans or member distributions. She intends to repay the "borrowed" funds as soon as the online business begins to generate substantial revenues.

Unfortunately, one of the employees of the shop sold some raw milk cheese that was contaminated with *Escherichia coli* (usually abbreviated *E. coli*). The tainted cheese caused several of the cheese shop's customers to become ill, and they have now filed a lawsuit against the cheese shop.

DLLCA § 18-303(a) provides:

> Except as otherwise provided by this chapter, the debts, obligations and liabilities of a limited liability company, whether arising in contract, tort or otherwise, shall be solely the debts, obligations and liabilities of the limited liability company, and no member or manager of a limited liability company shall be obligated personally for any such debt, obligation or liability of the limited liability company solely by reason of being a member or acting as a manager of the limited liability company.

If the victims of food poisoning were successful in proving their claim against the cheese shop, would the plaintiffs be able to pierce the veil of limited liability of Turophile LLC? Would they pierce with regard to both Drew and Carder? How much would the victims be entitled to recover from the individual member(s) of the LLC?

E. FIDUCIARY DUTIES

In Chapter 1 we encountered the duty of loyalty in agency relationships, and we continued our study of fiduciary duties with partnerships in Chapter 2. The core principles underlying fiduciary law do not change substantially when we move to the LLC context, even though the LLC form creates a few new twists. As with other aspects of the law governing LLCs, fiduciary duties in the LLC context owe much to corporate law, but we attempt in this section to explore the ways in which LLCs may be distinctive.

Courts and legislatures universally impose fiduciary duties on the managers of LLCs, including members who act as managers. This reflects the policy judgment that fiduciary duties constrain the exercise of authority. It follows from this reasoning that a member in a manager-managed LLC "does not have any fiduciary duty to the company or to any other member solely by reason of being a member." RULLCA § 409(g)(5).

Generally speaking, managers owe their duties to the LLC as an entity, and some statutes impose duties to the individual members of the LLC as well. For example, RULLCA § 409(a) provides, "A member of a member-managed limited liability company owes to the company and . . . the other members the fiduciary duties of loyalty and care. . . ." When a majority member "oppresses" a minority member, courts may sustain minority owners in their claims against an oppressive majority, even if the LLC statute does not expressly provide for duties to individual members. For example, in *In re Allentown Ambassadors, Inc.,* 361 B.R. 422 (Bkrtcy. E.D. Pa., 2007), a federal bankruptcy judge rejected an argument that a manager owed no fiduciary duty to an individual member of the LLC — despite a North Carolina statute that described a duty only to the LLC — reasoning by analogy to corporate law:

> I conclude that the courts in North Carolina would hold that a manager of an LLC owes a duty to the individual members of the LLC that may be the subject of a claim for breach of fiduciary duty. I draw this conclusion from the well established principle under North Carolina law that majority shareholders owe a fiduciary duty to minority shareholders in a corporation.

We have noted in our prior discussions that fiduciary standards were first developed by courts and later codified by legislatures. Most modern LLC statutes provide for a duty of loyalty and a duty of care, with varying degrees of specificity. Interestingly, the drafters of RULLCA eliminated the following language from ULLCA: "The *only* fiduciary duties a member owes to a member-managed company and its other members are the duty of loyalty and the duty of care imposed by subsections (b) and (c)" (emphasis added). The drafters of RULLCA expressly contemplated the possible development of "other fiduciary duties," though they were vague about the precise nature of those duties. The comments indicate that the foregoing change was designed to "allow courts to continue to use fiduciary duty concepts to police disclosure obligations in member-to-member and member-LLC transactions," though the drafters offered no further elaboration of how those disclosure obligations might differ from the disclosure obligations expressly included in RULLCA § 410, which is entitled, "Right of Members, Managers, and Dissociated Members to Information."

Fiduciary duties are often said to be subject to partial or complete waiver in the operating agreement. Some scholars maintain that fiduciary law has a "mandatory core" that cannot be avoided by contract, and some LLC statutes seem to embrace this position. For example, RULLCA § 110(c) provides: "An operating agreement may not . . . eliminate the duty of loyalty, the duty of care, or any other fiduciary duty." As in RUPA, however, the statute allows the operating agreement to restrict or eliminate fiduciary duties "if not manifestly unreasonable," RULLCA § 110(d), or to "specify the method by which a specific act or transaction that would otherwise violate the duty of loyalty may be authorized or ratified." RULLCA § 110(e). On the other hand, vigorous arguments have been made in support of the possibility of complete waiver, a position embraced by the Delaware LLC statute:

>   (b) It is the policy of this chapter to give the maximum effect to the principle of freedom of contract and to the enforceability of limited liability company agreements.
>   (c) To the extent that, at law or in equity, a member or manager or other person has duties (including fiduciary duties) to a limited liability company or to another member or manager or to another person that is a party to or is otherwise bound by a limited liability company agreement, the member's or manager's or other person's duties may be expanded or restricted or eliminated by provisions in the limited liability company agreement; provided, that the limited liability company agreement may not eliminate the implied contractual covenant of good faith and fair dealing.
>   . . .
>   (e) A limited liability company agreement may provide for the limitation or elimination of any and all liabilities for breach of contract and breach of duties (including fiduciary duties) of a member, manager or other person to a limited liability company or to another member or manager or to another person that is a party to or is otherwise bound by a limited liability company agreement; provided, that a limited liability company agreement may not limit or eliminate liability for any act or omission that constitutes a bad faith violation of the implied contractual covenant of good faith and fair dealing.

Del. Code Ann. tit. 6, § 18-1101. Interpreting this provision of the DLLCA, the Delaware Court of Chancery has consistently held that participants in an LLC can limit or eliminate fiduciary duties. *See, e.g.,* Gerber v. Enter. Prods. Holdings, LLC, 2012 WL 34442, at *13 (Del. Ch. Jan. 6, 2012) ("Alternate entity legislation reflects the Legislature's decision to allow such ventures to be governed without the traditional fiduciary duties, if that is what the . . . governing document provides for, and allows conduct that, in a different context, would be sanctioned.").

But what if the participants in an LLC are silent about fiduciary duties? Should the courts impose fiduciary duties, even though the DLLCA does not expressly provide for them? In 2009 Chief Justice Myron Steele of the Delaware Supreme Court wrote a law review article arguing "that default fiduciary duties violate the strong policy favoring freedom of contract enunciated by Delaware's legislature" and that "the costs of default fiduciary duties outweigh the minimal benefits that they provide." Myron Steele, *Freedom of Contract and Default Contractual Duties in the Delaware Limited Partnerships and Limited Liability Companies*, 46 Am. Bus. L.J. 221, 223-224 (2009). In the *Auriga* case below, Chancellor Strine confronts the issue of default fiduciary duties in LLCs and reaches a different conclusion than Chief Justice Steele's.

Finally, much debate has arisen around the procedures for enforcing fiduciary duties in the LLC context. In the corporate context, shareholders sometimes are required to enforce fiduciary duties via "derivative lawsuits," that is, an action in which shareholders of a corporation sue *on behalf of* the corporation to enforce fiduciary duties against the managers of the corporation. Derivative actions are distinguished from "direct" actions, in which shareholders act on their own behalf, and this distinction has important practical implications. We deal with these implications more thoroughly in Chapter 9, but for present purposes, suffice it to say that derivative actions are subject to several constraints that make them more difficult for shareholders to sustain than direct actions. Generally speaking, therefore, shareholders prefer to pursue direct litigation, though courts routinely dismiss shareholder lawsuits on the ground that they should have been brought as derivative actions.

The line between direct and derivative actions is elusive, but courts often make this distinction by reference to the nature of the harm caused by the breach of duty. If harm was caused to the corporation — e.g., by mismanagement or theft of corporate funds — then the harm to the shareholders derives from the harm to the corporation, and a derivative lawsuit is appropriate. On the other hand, if harm was caused to the shareholders directly — e.g., by depriving shareholders of mandatory dividends based on a shareholders agreement — then the shareholders may sue directly, without the restrictions imposed on derivative actions.

We raise the issue of derivative litigation here because it has been a special point of interest in the development of the law governing LLCs. In public debates, derivative litigation is often associated with nuisance "strike suits" against large corporations brought for the settlement value, but for smaller business entities, derivative litigation is often viewed as an impractical means for minority owners to obtain redress of their grievances. Because derivative claims are made *on behalf of* the business entity, any damages should be awarded to the entity, rather than to the minority owners directly. Given the apparent injustice of this result, many courts allow minority shareholders to bring direct claims against majority shareholders, even if the claim would ordinarily be derivative in nature. In the LLC context, some courts seem to be following this pattern.

Despite the desirability of allowing direct claims in some circumstances, many LLC statutes expressly provide for the possibility of derivative litigation. *See, e.g.*, RULLCA § 902; DLLCA § 18-1001. The widely publicized case of Tzolis v. Wolff, reprinted below, on the other hand, addresses a New York statute that does not mention derivative litigation. Do you agree with the court's decision to imply a right to derivative litigation?

AURIGA CAPITAL CORPORATION v. GATZ PROPERTIES LLC

2012 WL 361677
Delaware Court of Chancery
January 27, 2012

STRINE, Chancellor.

I. INTRODUCTION

The manager of an LLC and his family acquired majority voting control over both classes of the LLC's equity during the course of its operations and thereby held a veto over any strategic option. The LLC was an unusual one that held a long-term lease on a valuable property owned by the manager and his family. The leasehold allowed the LLC to operate a golf course on the property.

The LLC intended to act as a passive operator by subleasing the golf course for operation by a large golf management corporation. A lucrative sublease to that effect was entered in 1998. The golf management corporation, however, was purchased early in the term of the sublease by owners that sought to consolidate its operations. Rather than invest in the leased property and put its full effort into making the course a success, the management corporation took short cuts, let maintenance slip, and evidenced a disinterest in the property. By as early as 2004, it was clear to the manager that the golf management corporation would not renew its lease.

This did not make the manager upset. The LLC and its investors had invested heavily in the property, building on it a first-rate Robert Trent Jones, Jr.-designed golf course and a clubhouse. If the manager and his family could get rid of the investors in the LLC, they would have an improved property, which they had reason to believe could be more valuable as a residential community. Knowing that the golf management corporation would likely not renew its sublease, the manager failed to take any steps at all to find a new strategic option for the LLC that would protect the LLC's investors. Thus, the manager did not search for a replacement management corporation, explore whether the LLC itself could manage the golf course profitably, or undertake to search for a buyer for the LLC. Indeed, when a credible buyer for the LLC came forward on its own and expressed a serious interest, the manager failed to provide that buyer with the due diligence that a motivated seller would typically provide to a possible buyer. Even worse, the manager did all it could to discourage a good bid, frustrating and misleading the interested buyer.

The manager then sought to exploit the opportunity provided by the buyer's emergence to make low-ball bids to the other investors in the LLC on the basis of materially misleading information. Among other failures, the manager made an offer at $5.6 million for the LLC without telling the investors that the buyer had expressed a willingness to discuss a price north of $6 million. The minority investors refused the manager's offer. When the minority investors asked the manager to go back and negotiate a higher price with the potential buyer, the manager refused.

This refusal reflected the reality that the manager and his family were never willing to sell the LLC. Nor did they desire to find a strategic option for the LLC that would allow it to operate profitably for the benefit of the minority investors. The manager and his family wanted to be rid of the minority investors, whom they had come to regard as troublesome bothers.

Using the coming expiration of the golf management corporation's sublease as leverage, the manager eventually conducted a sham auction to sell the LLC. The auction had all the look and feel of a distress sale, but without any of the cheap nostalgic charm of the old unclaimed freight tv commercials. Ridiculous postage stamp-sized ads were published and unsolicited junk mail was sent out. Absent was any serious marketing to a targeted group of golf course operators by a responsible, mature, respected broker on the basis of solid due diligence materials. No effort was made to provide interested buyers with a basis to assume the existing debt position of the LLC if they met certain borrower responsibility criteria. Instead, interested buyers were told that they would have to secure the bank's consent but were given an unrealistic amount of time to do so. Worst of all, interested buyers could take no comfort in the fact that the manager—who controlled the majority of the voting power of the LLC—was committed to selling the LLC to the highest bidder, as the bidding materials made clear that the manager was also planning to bid and at the same time reserved the right to cancel the auction for any reason.

When the results of this incompetent marketing process were known and the auctioneer knew that no one other than the manager was going to bid, the auctioneer told the manager that fact. The manager then won with a bid of $50,000 in excess of the LLC's debt, on which the manager was already a guarantor. Only $22,777 of the bid went to the minority investors. For his services in running this ineffective process, the auctioneer received a fee of $80,000, which was greater than the cash component of the winning bid. Despite now claiming that the LLC could not run a golf course profitably and pay off the mortgage on the property, the manager has run the course himself since the auction and is paying the debt.

A group of minority investors have sued for damages, arguing the manager breached his contractual and fiduciary duties through this course of conduct. The manager, after originally disclaiming that he owed a fiduciary duty of loyalty to the minority, now rests his defense on two primary grounds. The first is that the manager and his family were able to veto any option for the LLC as their right as members. As a result, they could properly use a chokehold over the LLC to pursue their own interests and the minority would have to live with the consequences of their freedom of action. The second defense is that by the time of the auction, the LLC was valueless.

In this post-trial decision, I find for the plaintiffs. For reasons discussed in the opinion, I explain that the LLC agreement here does not displace the traditional duties of loyalty and care that are owed by managers of Delaware LLCs to their investors in the absence of a contractual provision waiving or modifying those duties. The Delaware Limited Liability Company Act (the "LLC Act") explicitly applies equity as a default[1] and our Supreme Court, and this court, have consistently held that default fiduciary duties apply to those managers of alternative entities who would qualify as fiduciaries under traditional equitable principles, including managers of LLCs. Here, the LLC agreement makes clear that the manager could only enter into a self-dealing transaction, such as its purchase of the LLC, if it proves that the terms were fair. In other words, the LLC agreement essentially incorporates a core element of the traditional fiduciary duty of loyalty. Not only that, the LLC agreement's exculpatory provision makes clear that the manager is not exculpated for bad faith action, willful misconduct, or even grossly negligent action, *i.e.*, a breach of the duty of care.

The manager's course of conduct here breaches both his contractual and fiduciary duties. Using his control over the LLC, the manager took steps to deliver the LLC to himself and his family on unfair terms. When the LLC had a good cushion of cash from the remaining years of the lease, it was in a good position to take the time needed to responsibly identify another strategic option to generate value for the LLC and all of its investors. Although the economy was weakening, the golf course was well-designed and located in a community that is a good one for the profitable operation of a golf course. With a minimally competent and loyal fiduciary at the helm, the LLC could have charted a course that would have delivered real value to its investors.

---

1. 6 Del. C. § 18-1104.

Had the manager acted properly, for example, the buyer he rebuffed could have entered into a new lease or purchased the LLC on terms that would have at least gotten the LLC's minority investors back what they had put in and some modest return.

The manager himself is the one who has created evidentiary doubt about the LLC's value by failing to pursue any strategic option for the LLC in a timely fashion because he wished to squeeze out the minority investors. The manager's defense that his voting power gave him a license to exploit the minority fundamentally misunderstands Delaware law. The manager was free not to vote his membership interest for a sale. But he was not free to create a situation of distress by failing to cause the LLC to explore its market alternatives and then to buy the LLC for a nominal price. The purpose of the duty of loyalty is in large measure to prevent the exploitation by a fiduciary of his self-interest to the disadvantage of the minority. The fair price requirement of that duty, which is incorporated in the LLC agreement here, makes sure that if the conflicted fiduciary engages in self-dealing, he pays a price that is as much as an arms-length purchaser would pay.

The manager is in no position to take refuge in uncertainties he himself created by his own breaches of duty. He himself is responsible for the distress sale conducted in 2009. Had he acted properly, the LLC could have secured a strategic alternative in 2007, when it was in a stronger position and the economy was too. A transaction at that time would have likely yielded proceeds for the minority of a return of their invested capital plus a 10% total return, an amount which reflects the reality that the manager's desire to retain control of the LLC would have pushed up the pricing of the transaction due to his incentive to top any third-party bidder. I therefore enter a remedy to that effect, taking into account the distribution received by the plaintiffs at the auction, and add interest, compounded monthly at the legal rate, from that time period. Because the manager has made this litigation far more cumbersome and inefficient than it should have been by advancing certain frivolous arguments, I award the plaintiffs one-half of their reasonable attorneys' fees and costs. This award is justified under the bad faith exception to the American Rule, and also ensures that the disloyal manager is not rewarded for making it unduly expensive for the minority investors to pursue their legitimate claims to redress his serious infidelity. I do not award full-fee shifting because I have not adopted all of the plaintiffs' arguments and because the manager's litigation conduct, while sanctionably disappointing, was not so egregious as to justify that result.

II. Basic Factual Background

For the sake of clarity, I will make many of the key factual determinations in the course of analyzing the claims. To provide a framework for that integrated analysis, I set forth some of the key foundational facts.

A. THE PARTIES

The LLC in this case is Peconic Bay, LLC ("Peconic Bay" or the "Company"). The "Manager" of Peconic Bay is defendant Gatz Properties, LLC, an entity which is itself managed, controlled, and partially owned by defendant William Gatz. Because William Gatz as a person was the sole actor on behalf of Gatz

Properties at all times, I typically refer to "his" actions or "him," because that is what best tracks how things happened.

The plaintiffs in this case are certain minority investors in Peconic Bay: Auriga Capital Corporation, Paul Rooney, Hakan Sokmenseur, Don Kyle, Ivan Benjamin, and Glenn Morse. William Carr is the founder and principal of Auriga, which encouraged the other plaintiffs to invest in Peconic Bay. For the sake of clarity, I typically refer to the plaintiffs as the "Minority Members."

B. THE FORMATION OF PECONIC BAY

In 1997, Gatz, through Gatz Properties, and Carr, through Auriga, formed Peconic Bay for the purpose of holding a long-term leasehold in a property owned by the Gatz family (the "Property"). The idea was to develop a golf course on the Property, which was farmland in Long Island that had been in the Gatz family since the 1950s. Gatz came to this idea from reading a report authored by the National Golf Foundation predicting a boom in demand for golf courses in Long Island and opining that the area suffered a shortage of courses to meet current and future demand. He thus set out to raise cash for the construction of a golf course on the Property, and approached a local bank to gauge its interest in financing the project. The bank then referred Gatz to Carr, who had worked with the bank on a previous occasion to secure the financing for another golf course in Long Island. On this advice, Gatz reached out to Carr, and Carr agreed to commit Auriga to help finance and develop the course. Auriga agreed to assume responsibility for securing debt financing and raising additional equity, as well as overseeing the construction of the course, which would be named Long Island National Golf Course (the "Course").

Financing was located and contracts were drafted to create the structures that would reflect the parties' business dealings, including an entity — *i.e.*, Peconic Bay — in which the equity investors could hold capital. Peconic Bay took out a note worth approximately $6 million to finance the Course's construction (the "Note"), which was collateralized by the Property. The Gatz family formed Gatz Properties to hold title to the Property, which was then leased to Peconic Bay under a "Ground Lease," dated January 1, 1998.

The Ground Lease set an initial term of 40 years, with a renewal option for two 10-year extensions, which were exercisable by Peconic Bay. The terms of the Ground Lease also restricted the Property's use to a high-end daily fee public golf course. Thus, absent an agreement between Peconic Bay and the Gatz family, the Property was to be locked up for use by Peconic Bay as a golf course until 2038.

C. PECONIC BAY'S MEMBERSHIP

Peconic Bay in turn was governed by an Amended and Restated Limited Liability Company Agreement (the "LLC Agreement"). The LLC Agreement created Class A and Class B membership interests. The Class A interests comprised 86.75% of Peconic Bay's membership, and the Class B, 13.25%.

From the inception, Gatz Properties controlled the Class A vote, as it held 85.07% of the Class A interests. The rest of the Class A interests were held by Auriga and Paul Rooney.

From the time the Class B shares were first issued in 1998 until 2001, the Class B interests were more diversely held. The Gatz family and their affiliates (together with Gatz Properties, the "Gatz Members") held 39.6% of the Class B interests. The Minority Members, including non-party Hartnett, held 60.3%. But, in 2001, the Gatz Members acquired control of the Class B interests through questionable purchases of certain minority investors' Class B shares.

Obtaining control of the Class B interests was important. Under the LLC Agreement, the Manager was forbidden from making a "major decision affecting the Company" without "Majority Approval," which was defined as the vote of 66 2/3% of the Class A interests and 51% of the Class B interests. Thus, control of the Class A and Class B interests gave the Gatz Members veto power over many of Peconic Bay's key strategic options, including, most relevantly, the decision to sell the Company; enter into a long-term sublease with a golf course operator; or "otherwise deal with the [Course] in such manner as may be determined by Majority Approval of the Members," such as choosing to run the Course itself. The Gatz Members' interests in Peconic Bay were aligned and they voted their membership units as a bloc at all relevant times in this dispute.

The LLC Agreement designated Gatz Properties as Manager. Gatz, as manager of Gatz Properties, was given the "power, on behalf of [Peconic Bay], to do all things necessary or convenient to carry out the day-to-day operation of the Company." But, the role of the Manager was intended to be a limited, albeit important, one, and Gatz received no management fee in connection with his services as a reflection of this understanding. The Gatzes were instead to be compensated in two other ways: (1) through their interests as members of Peconic Bay; and (2) through rent for the Property.

The Manager's limited operational role was attributable to Peconic Bay's initial business model. Under the LLC Agreement, Peconic Bay was initially structured as a passive "black box" entity that would be a conduit for cash flows rather than actually operate the course itself. The Course was instead to be run and managed by a third-party operator. The Manager would then collect rent from that operator, make Peconic Bay's required debt payments on the Note, and then distribute the remaining cash surplus to the investors according to a distribution scheme set forth in the LLC Agreement, which called for payment of 95% of all cash distributions to go to the Class B members until they received a full return of their investment. After that point, the distributions were to be made pro rata.

D. PECONIC BAY SUBLEASES THE PROPERTY TO AMERICAN GOLF

To accomplish this business purpose, Carr brought in American Golf Corporation ("American Golf"), which was at the time one of the largest golf course operators in the country. On March 31, 1998, Peconic Bay entered into a sublease with American Golf (the "Sublease"). The Sublease was for a term of 35 years, but it gave American Golf an early termination right after the tenth full year of operation. American Golf could terminate the Sublease at its discretion and without penalty by notifying Peconic Bay within 30 days of January 1, 2010.

Peconic Bay and American Golf had high expectations for the Course's financial success. The Course was designed by a well-known golf course architect, Robert Trent Jones, Jr., and it was located in an affluent, rural part of Long Island that was described by Gatz's defense expert as "an ideal location for an affordable upscale golf facility."

The terms of the Sublease governing rent payments reflected this initial optimism. American Golf agreed to pay "Minimum Rent" according to a fixed schedule, starting at $700,000, and rising annually by $100,000 until leveling out at $1 million per year, beginning in 2003. In addition to Minimum Rent, American Golf had to pay "Ground Lease Rent" equal to 5% of its revenue from operations. Although this rent would be payable to Peconic Bay, it would pass directly through to Gatz Properties as rent under the Ground Lease between Peconic Bay and Gatz Properties.

E. A PREVIEW OF WHAT HAPPENED NEXT

This is where events took a turn for the worse. As I will discuss in more detail later, American Golf never operated the Course at a profit, and later let the Course fall into disrepair. Gatz knew in 2004 or latest 2005 that American Golf would exercise its early termination option in 2010, yet he did nothing to plan for American Golf's exit. Rather, Gatz made a series of decisions that placed Peconic Bay in an economically vulnerable position. Once Peconic Bay was in this vulnerable state, and in the midst of a down economy, Gatz decided to put Peconic Bay on the auction block without engaging a broker to market Peconic Bay to golf course managers or owners (the "Auction"). Gatz, on behalf of Gatz Properties, was the only bidder to show up. Knowing this fact before formulating his bid, Gatz purchased Peconic Bay for a nominal value over the debt, and merged Peconic Bay into Gatz Properties (the "Merger"). Gatz now operates the Course himself through a newly created entity wholly owned by Gatz Properties and seems to be paying the debt from the cash flow of the golf course operations.

III. THE PARTIES' CONTENTIONS

The first amended verified complaint pleads five counts. Counts I, II and III are related. Counts I and II allege that Gatz Properties and Gatz, respectively, breached their fiduciary duties to Peconic Bay and the Minority Members. Count III alleges that Gatz Properties breached its contractual duties under the LLC Agreement. These three counts center on the squeeze out of the Minority Members. Specifically, the Minority Members claim that Gatz breached the fiduciary duties and contractual duties owed to Peconic Bay's Minority Members by engaging in a "protracted course of self-interested conduct conceived and implemented in bad faith" for the purpose of eliminating the Minority Members' interest. The Minority Members contend that Gatz was motivated to oust the Minority Members in order to realize the upside in value that would result from eliminating Peconic Bay's long-term leasehold interest in the Property. Such actions include Gatz's failure to take any steps to evaluate strategic options for Peconic Bay based on known business realities and his discouragement of a potential third-party buyer for the Company, which entertained a willingness to make an offer that would have delivered to the Minority Members a full return of their capital investment. What's more, the Minority Members continue, Gatz used the leverage obtained from his own bad faith breaches of loyalty to make coercive buyout offers to the Minority Members, and finally to acquire Peconic Bay through a sham auction process at an unfairly low price.

For his part, Gatz maintains that he acted reasonably and in good faith throughout the entirety of events described by the Minority Members. Primarily,

Gatz grounds his defense in the argument that Gatz Properties acquired Peconic Bay for a fair price because the assets of Peconic Bay were worth less than its debt and thus the entity was insolvent. Although by the end of the trial, Gatz admitted that he and his family were never interested in selling their membership interests, he seeks to use that fact as a defensive bulwark, contending that he and his family were entitled to vote their economic interest against selling Peconic Bay to a third-party buyer and to choke off the LLC's pursuit of any other strategic options. Throughout much of the litigation, Gatz took the view that he either owed no fiduciary duties at all; that if these duties existed, they allowed him to engage in a self-dealing transaction subject only to a hands-off business judgment rule review, and that even if a more intensive review applied, Gatz ran a thorough, professional auction upon credible independent advice, thus satisfying any fairness burden. As these arguments emerged at trial as having no genuine basis in law or fact, Gatz became more nuanced and has focused on other arguments. Finally, Gatz says, even if his actions did constitute a breach of his fiduciary duties, his actions were supposedly taken in good faith and with due care, and thus he cannot be held liable due to the terms of the exculpation clause of the LLC Agreement.

Now that we have covered the basic premise of the Minority Members' claims and Gatz's arguments in response, I will consider the provisions of the LLC Agreement that govern Gatz's actions giving rise to this dispute, and assess the effect that those provisions have on the fiduciary duties owed by Gatz to the Minority Members.

IV. ANALYSIS

A. WHAT DUTIES DID GATZ OWE TO THE MEMBERS OF PECONIC BAY?

At points in this litigation, Gatz has argued that his actions were not subject to any fiduciary duty analysis because the LLC Agreement of Peconic Bay displaced any role for the use of equitable principles in constraining the LLC's Manager. As I next explain, that is not true.

The Delaware LLC Act starts with the explicit premise that "equity" governs any case not explicitly covered by the Act. But the Act lets contracting parties modify or even eliminate any equitable fiduciary duties, a more expansive constriction than is allowed in the case of corporations. For that reason, in the LLC context, it is typically the case that the evaluation of fiduciary duty claims cannot occur without a close examination of the LLC agreement itself, which often tailors the traditional fiduciary duties to address the specific relationship of the contracting parties.

I discuss these general principles and their more specific application to this case next.

1. Default Fiduciary Duties Do Exist in the LLC Context

The Delaware LLC Act does not plainly state that the traditional fiduciary duties of loyalty and care apply by default as to managers or members of a limited liability company. In that respect, of course, the LLC Act is not different than the [Delaware General Corporation Law], which does not do that either. In fact, the absence of explicitness in the DGCL inspired the case of Schnell v. Chris-Craft[, 285 A.2d 437 (Del. 1971)]. Arguing that the then newly-revised

DGCL was a domain unto itself, and that compliance with its terms was sufficient to discharge any obligation owed by the directors to the stockholders, the defendant corporation in that case won on that theory at the Court of Chancery level. But our Supreme Court reversed and made emphatic that the new DGCL was to be read in concert with equitable fiduciary duties just as had always been the case, stating famously that "inequitable action does not become legally permissible simply because it is legally possible."

The LLC Act is more explicit than the DGCL in making the equitable overlay mandatory. Specifically, § 18-1104 of the LLC Act provides that "[i]n any case not provided for in this chapter, *the rules of law and equity . . . shall govern.*" In this way, the LLC Act provides for a construct similar to that which is used in the corporate context. But unlike in the corporate context, the rules of equity apply in the LLC context by statutory mandate, creating an even stronger justification for application of fiduciary duties grounded in equity to managers of LLCs to the extent that such duties have not been altered or eliminated under the relevant LLC agreement.[2]

It seems obvious that, under traditional principles of equity, a manager of an LLC would qualify as a fiduciary of that LLC and its members. Under Delaware law, "[a] fiduciary relationship is a situation where one person reposes special trust in and reliance on the judgment of another or where a special duty exists on the part of one person to protect the interests of another."

Corporate directors, general partners and trustees are analogous examples of those who Delaware law has determined owe a "special duty." Equity distinguishes fiduciary relationships from straightforward commercial arrangements where there is no expectation that one party will act in the interests of the other.

The manager of an LLC—which is in plain words a limited liability "company" having many of the features of a corporation—easily fits the definition of a fiduciary. The manager of an LLC has more than an arms-length, contractual relationship with the members of the LLC. Rather, the manager is vested with discretionary power to manage the business of the LLC.

Thus, because the LLC Act provides for principles of equity to apply, because LLC managers are clearly fiduciaries, and because fiduciaries owe the fiduciary duties of loyalty and care, the LLC Act starts with the default that managers of LLCs owe enforceable fiduciary duties.

---

2. Section 18-1101(c) of the LLC Act provides: "*To the extent that, at law or in equity, a member or manager or other person has duties (including fiduciary duties)* to a limited liability company or to another member or manager or to another person that is a party to or is otherwise bound by a[n] [LLC] agreement, *the member's or manager's or other person's duties may be expanded or restricted or eliminated by provisions in the [LLC] agreement*; provided, that the [LLC] agreement may not eliminate the implied covenant of good faith and fair dealing." 6 Del. C. § 18-1101(c) (emphasis added). Although § 18-1101(c) allows parties to an LLC agreement to contract out of owing fiduciary duties to one another, the fact that these duties can be contractually avoided suggests that they exist by default in the first place. When read together, the most logical reading of § 18-1104 and § 18-1101(c) that results is that if, i.e., "to the extent that," equity would traditionally make a manager or member a fiduciary owing fiduciary duties, then that manager or member is a fiduciary, subject to the express right of the parties to contract out of those duties. By contrast, if a member or manager would not be considered a fiduciary owing circumstantially-relevant duties under traditional equitable principles, then the member or manager is immune from fiduciary liability, not because of the statute, but because equity itself would not consider the member or manager to have case-relevant fiduciary duties. The "to the extent that" language makes clear that the statute does not itself impose some broader scope of fiduciary coverage than traditional principles of equity.

This reading of the LLC Act is confirmed by the Act's own history. Before 2004, § 18-1101(c) of the LLC Act provided that fiduciary duties, to the extent they existed, could only be "expanded or restricted" by the LLC agreement. Following our Supreme Court's holding in *Gotham Partners*[, 817 A.2d 160 (Del. 2002)], which questioned whether default fiduciary duties could be fully eliminated in the limited partnership context when faced with similar statutory language and also affirmed our law's commitment to protecting investors who have not explicitly agreed to waive their fiduciaries' duties and therefore expect their fiduciaries to act in accordance with their interests, the General Assembly amended not only the Delaware Revised Limited Uniform Partnership Act ("DRULPA"), but also the LLC Act to permit the "eliminat[ion]" of default fiduciary duties in an LLC agreement. At the same time, the General Assembly added a provision to the LLC Act (the current § 18-1101(e)) that permits full contractual exculpation for breaches of fiduciary and contractual duties, except for the implied contractual covenant of good faith and fair dealing.

If the equity backdrop I just discussed did not apply to LLCs, then the 2004 "Elimination Amendment" would have been logically done differently. Why is this so? Because the Amendment would have instead said something like: "The managers, members, and other persons of the LLC shall owe no duties of any kind to the LLC and its members except as set forth in this statute and the LLC agreement."[3] Instead, the Amendment only made clear that an LLC agreement could, if the parties so chose, "eliminat[e]" default duties altogether, thus according full weight to the statutory policy in favor of giving "maximum effect to the principle of freedom of contract and to the enforceability of [LLC] agreements." The General Assembly left in place the explicit equitable default in § 18-1104 of the Act. Moreover, why would the General Assembly amend the LLC Act to provide for the elimination of (and the exculpation for) "something" if there were no "something" to eliminate (or exculpate) in the first place? The fact that the legislature enacted these liability-limiting measures against the backdrop of case law holding that default fiduciary duties did apply in the LLC context, and seemed to have accepted the central thrust of those decisions to be correct, provides further weight to the position that default fiduciary duties do apply in the LLC context to the extent they are not contractually altered.

Thus, our cases have to date come to the following place based on the statute. The statute incorporates equitable principles. Those principles view the manager of an LLC as a fiduciary and subject the manager as a default principle to the core fiduciary duties of loyalty and care. But, the statute allows the parties to an LLC agreement to entirely supplant those default principles or to modify them in part. Where the parties have clearly supplanted default principles in full, we give effect to the parties' contract choice. Where the parties have clearly supplanted default principles in part, we give effect to their contract choice. But,

---

3. An agreement containing a provision with this language was analyzed in *Fisk Ventures, LLC v. Segal*, 2008 WL 1961156 (Del. Ch. May 7, 2008), and the court found it to waive all fiduciary duties except those that were contractually provided for. Id. at *9 (where the provision stated: "No Member shall have any duty to any Member of the Company except as expressly set forth herein or in other written agreements. . . .").

where the core default fiduciary duties have not been supplanted by contract, they exist as the LLC statute itself contemplates.[4]

There are two issues that would arise if the equitable background explicitly contained in the statute were to be judicially excised now. The first is that those who crafted LLC agreements in reliance on equitable defaults that supply a predictable structure for assessing whether a business fiduciary has met his obligations to the entity and its investors will have their expectations disrupted. The equitable context in which the contract's specific terms were to be read will be eradicated, rendering the resulting terms shapeless and more uncertain. The fact that the implied covenant of good faith and fair dealing would remain extant would do little to cure this loss.

The common law fiduciary duties that were developed to address those who manage business entities were, as the implied covenant, an equitable gap-filler. If, rather than well thought out fiduciary duty principles, the implied covenant is to be used as the sole default principle of equity, then the risk is that the certainty of contract law itself will be undermined. The implied covenant has rightly been narrowly interpreted by our Supreme Court to apply only "when the express terms of the contract indicate that the parties would have agreed to the obligation had they negotiated the issue."[5] The implied covenant is to be used "cautious[ly]" and does not apply to situations that could be anticipated, which is a real problem in the business context, because fiduciary duty review typically addresses actions that are anticipated and permissible under the express terms of the contract, but where there is a potential for managerial abuse. For these reasons, the implied covenant is not a tool that is designed to provide a framework to govern the discretionary actions of business managers acting under a broad enabling framework like a barebones LLC agreement. In fact, if the implied covenant were used in that manner, the room for subjective judicial oversight could be expanded in an inefficient way. The default principles that apply in the fiduciary duty context of business entities are carefully tailored to avoid judicial second-guessing. A generalized "fairness" inquiry under the guise of an "implied covenant" review is an invitation to, at best, reinvent what already exists in another less candid guise, or worse, to inject unpredictability into both entity and contract law, by untethering judicial review from the well-understood frameworks that traditionally apply in those domains.

The second problem is a related one, which is that a judicial eradication of the explicit equity overlay in the LLC Act could tend to erode our state's credibility with investors in Delaware entities. To have told the investing public that the law of equity would apply if the LLC statute did not speak to the question at issue, and to have managers of LLCs easily qualify as fiduciaries under traditional and

---

4. From my experience as a trial judge, I note that few LLC agreements contain an express, general provision that states what fiduciary duties are owed in the first instance. Rather, the agreements assume that such fiduciary duties are owed, and then they proceed to cut back on liability for breaches of those duties through exculpation provisions or through provisions that displace the traditional duties in favor of a contractual standard addressing specific types of transactions or conduct.

5. Nemec v. Shrader, 991 A.2d 1120, 1127 n.20 (Del. 2010) (citing Fitzgerald v. Cantor, 1998 WL 842316, at *1 (Del. Ch. Nov. 10, 1998)); see also Katz v. Oak Indus. Inc., 508 A.2d 873, 880 (Del. Ch. 1986) (stating that the legal test for implying contractual obligations is whether it is "clear from what was expressly agreed upon that the parties who negotiated the express terms of the contract would have agreed to proscribe the act later complained of as a breach of the implied covenant of good faith — had they thought to negotiate with respect to that matter.").

settled principles of equity law in Delaware, and then to say that LLC agreements could "expan[d] or restric[t] or eliminat[e]" these fiduciary duties, would lead any reasonable investor to conclude the following: the managers of the Delaware LLC in which I am investing owe me the fiduciary duties of loyalty and care except to the extent the agreement "expand[s]," "restrict[s]," or "eliminate[s]" these duties. . . .

Reasonable minds can debate whether it would be wise for the General Assembly to create a business entity in which the managers owe the investors no duties at all except as set forth in the statute and the governing agreement. Perhaps it would be, perhaps it would not. That is a policy judgment for the General Assembly. What seems certain is that the General Assembly, and the organs of the Bar who propose alteration of the statutes to them, know how to draft a clear statute to that effect and have yet to do so. The current LLC Act is quite different and promises investors that equity will provide the important default protections it always has, absent a contractual choice to tailor or eliminate that protection. Changing that promise is a job for the General Assembly, not this court.

With that statement of the law in mind, let us turn to the relevant terms of Peconic Bay's LLC Agreement.

2. The Relevant Provisions of the LLC Agreement

I note at the outset that the Peconic Bay LLC Agreement contains no general provision stating that the only duties owed by the manager to the LLC and its investors are set forth in the Agreement itself. Thus, before taking into account the existence of an exculpatory provision, the LLC Agreement does not displace the traditional fiduciary duties of loyalty and care owed to the Company and its members by Gatz Properties and by Gatz, in his capacity as the manager of Gatz Properties. And although LLC agreements may displace fiduciary duties altogether or tailor their application, by substituting a different form of review, here § 15 of the LLC Agreement contains a clause reaffirming that a form akin to entire fairness review will apply to "Agreements with Affiliates," a group which includes Gatz Properties, that are not approved by a majority of the unaffiliated members' vote. In relevant part, § 15 provides:

> 15. *Neither the Manager nor any other Member shall be entitled to cause the Company to enter . . . into any additional agreements with affiliates on terms and conditions which are less favorable to the Company than the terms and conditions of similar agreements which could be entered into with arms-length third parties, without the consent of a majority of the non-affiliated Members* (such majority to be deemed to be the holders of 66-2/3% of all Interests which are not held by affiliates of the person or entity that would be a party to the proposed agreement).

This court has interpreted similar contractual language supplying an "arm's length terms and conditions" standard for reviewing self-dealing transactions. . . . Because the terms of § 15 only apply to Affiliate Agreements, and because these terms address the duty owed by Gatz to the Minority Members as to Affiliate Agreements, they distill the traditional fiduciary duties as to the portion of the Minority Members' claims that relates to the fairness of the Auction and Merger into a burden to prove the substantive fairness of the economic outcome. That is, § 15 distills the duty to prove the fairness of a self-dealing transaction to its economic essence. As to the rest of Gatz's conduct giving rise to this dispute — such as the failure to take steps to address the impending American Golf Sublease termination and the failure to negotiate with an interested buyer in good faith — it is governed by traditional fiduciary duties of loyalty and care because the LLC Agreement does not alter them. . . .

[Analyzing the Minority Members' claim that Gatz breached his fiduciary and contractual duties as the Manager of Peconic Bay, Chancellor Strine concludes as follows:]

The record convinces me that Gatz pursued a bad faith course of conduct to enrich himself and his family without any regard for the interests of Peconic Bay or its Minority Members. His breaches may be summarized as follows: (1) failing to take any steps for five years to address in good faith the expected loss of American Golf as an operator; (2) turning away a responsible bidder which could have paid a price beneficial to the LLC and its investors in that capacity; (3) using the leverage obtained by his own loyalty breaches to play "hardball" with the Minority Members by making unfair offers on the basis of misleading disclosures; and (4) buying the LLC at an auction conducted on terms that were well-designed to deter any third-party buyer, and to deliver the LLC to Gatz at a distress sale price.

. . .

V. Damages

A. WHAT ARE THE DAMAGES THAT GATZ OWES?

By the time of his post-trial briefs, Gatz's defense was really one based on minimizing the damages he would owe. That defense melds with his defense based on § 15 of the LLC Agreement, which is that regardless of his misconduct, Gatz Properties in fact paid a fair price for Peconic Bay at the Auction and thus complied with its core mandate that Affiliate Agreements be entered into on "arms-length" terms and conditions. . . .

I do not reach the same conclusion that Gatz does about whether he should suffer a damages award. . . . In view of the persistent and serious nature of Gatz's breaches, and in view of his own 2008 claim that he was offering a deal that would have returned to the Minority Members their full initial capital contribution, I conclude that a remedy that awards the Minority Members their full capital contribution of $725,000 plus $72,500, is the equitable result. . . . Taking into account the $20,985 that the Minority Members received through the Auction, I arrive at a remedy of $776,515. This is a modest remedy and the record could support a higher one.

PROBLEM 3-5

Having graduated from college, Drew was ready to move on with her life, so she put the cheese shop up for sale. From the beginning, Drew had faithfully distributed earnings from Turophile LLC to Carder, but Drew did not consult with Carder about the sale of the cheese shop. Carder had moved on to other ventures, and she simply did not pay much attention to the cheese shop anymore.

In negotiating the sale of Turophile LLC, Drew entered into a five-year consulting agreement with the purchaser, who wanted access to Drew's expertise. Carder initially was thrilled to hear about the sale of the company, but when she learned about Drew's consulting agreement, she became concerned about the possibility of a conflict of interest. Carder's concerns were heightened when she was told by an employee of the cheese shop that Drew was asking substantially more for the business than the ultimate sales price and that Drew agreed to the sale only after the purchaser introduced the possibility of a consulting relationship.

Turophile's LLC Agreement contains the following provisions:

- The Managers shall manage the affairs of the Company in a prudent and businesslike manner and shall devote such time to the Company affairs as they shall, in their discretion exercised in good faith, determine is reasonably necessary for the conduct of such affairs.

- In carrying out their duties hereunder, the Managers shall not be liable for money damages for breach of fiduciary duty to the Company nor to any Member for their good faith actions or failure to act, but only for their own willful or fraudulent misconduct or willful breach of their contractual or fiduciary duties under this Agreement.

The Turophile LLC Operating Agreement contains no other provisions mentioning fiduciary duties. *Would Drew be liable to Turophile LLC or Carder for breaching her fiduciary duties?*

TZOLIS v. WOLFF

2008 WL 382345
Court of Appeals of New York
February 14, 2008

SMITH, Judge.

We hold that members of a limited liability company (LLC) may bring derivative suits on the LLC's behalf, even though there are no provisions governing such suits in the Limited Liability Company Law.

FACTS AND PROCEDURAL HISTORY

Pennington Property Co. LLC was the owner of a Manhattan apartment building. Plaintiffs, who own 25% of the membership interests in the LLC, bring this action "individually and in the right and on behalf of" the company. Plaintiffs claim that those in control of the LLC, and others acting in concert with them, arranged first to lease and then to sell the LLC's principal asset for sums below market value; that the lease was unlawfully assigned; and that company fiduciaries benefited personally from the sale. Plaintiffs assert several causes of action, of which only the first two are in issue here: The first cause of action seeks to declare the sale void, and the second seeks termination of the lease.

Supreme Court dismissed these causes of action. It held that they could not be brought by plaintiffs individually, because they were "to redress wrongs suffered by the corporation." It also held, following Hoffman v. Unterberg (9 A.D.3d 386 [2d Dept. 2004]), that "New York Law does not permit members to bring derivative actions on behalf of a limited liability company." The Appellate Division, concluding that derivative suits on behalf of LLCs are permitted, reversed (39 A.D.3d 138 [1st Dept 2007]), and granted two defendants permission to appeal on a certified question. We now affirm the Appellate Division's order.

Discussion

The issue is whether derivative suits on behalf of LLCs are allowed. The basis for appellants' argument that they are not is the Legislature's decision, when the Limited Liability Company Law was enacted in 1994, to omit all reference to such suits. We hold that this omission does not imply such suits are prohibited. We base our holding on the long-recognized importance of the derivative suit in corporate law, and on the absence of evidence that the Legislature decided to abolish this remedy when it passed the Limited Liability Company Law in 1994.

I

The derivative suit has been part of the general corporate law of this state at least since 1832. It was not created by statute, but by case law. Chancellor Walworth recognized the remedy in Robinson v. Smith (3 Paige Ch. 222 [1832]), because he thought it essential for shareholders to have recourse when those in control of a corporation betrayed their duty. Chancellor Walworth applied to a joint stock corporation — then a fairly new kind of entity — a familiar principle of the law of trusts: that a beneficiary (or "*cestui que trust*") could bring suit on behalf of a trust when a faithless trustee refused to do so. Ruling that shareholders could sue on behalf of a corporation under similar circumstances, the Chancellor explained:

> The directors are the trustees or managing partners, and the stockholders are the *cestui que trusts*, and have a joint interest in all the property and effects of the corporation. . . . And no injury the stockholders may sustain by a fraudulent breach of trust can, upon the general principles of equity, be suffered to pass without a remedy. In the language of Lord Hardwicke, in a similar case [Charitable Corp. v. Sutton, 2 Atk 400, 406 (Ch. 1742)], "I will never determine that a court of equity cannot lay hold of every such breach of trust. I will never determine that frauds of this kind are out of the reach of courts of law or equity; for an intolerable grievance would follow from such a determination."

3 Paige Ch. at 232.

Eventually, the rule that derivative suits could be brought on behalf of ordinary business corporations was codified by statute. But until relatively recently, no similar statutory provision was made for another kind of entity, the limited partnership; again, the absence of a statute did not prevent courts from recognizing the remedy. In Klebanow v. New York Produce Exch. (344 F.2d 294 [2d Cir. 1965] [Friendly, J.]), the Second Circuit Court of Appeals held that limited partners could sue on a partnership's behalf. For the Second Circuit, the absence of a statutory provision was not decisive because the Court found no "clear mandate *against* limited partners' capacity to bring an action like this" (*Id.* at 298 [emphasis added]). We agreed with the holding of Klebanow in

Riviera Congress Assoc. v. Yassky (18 N.Y.2d 540, 547 [1966] [Fuld, J.]), relying, as had Chancellor Walworth long before, on an analogy with the law of trusts:

> There can be no question that a managing or general partner of a limited partnership is bound in a fiduciary relationship with the limited partners . . . and the latter are, therefore, *cestuis que trustent.* . . . It is fundamental to the law of trusts that *cestuis* have the right, 'upon the general principles of equity' (Robinson v. Smith, 3 Paige Ch. 222, 232) and 'independently of [statutory] provisions' (Brinckerhoff v. Bostwick, 88 N.Y. 52, 59), to sue for the benefit of the trust on a cause of action which belongs to the trust if 'the trustees refuse to perform their duty in that respect'. (Western R.R. Co. v. Nolan, 48 N.Y. 513, 518. . . .)

After *Klebanow* and *Riviera* were decided, the Partnership Law was amended to provide for derivative actions by limited partners.

We now consider whether to recognize derivative actions on behalf of a third kind of entity, the LLC, as to which no statutory provision for such an action exists. In addressing the question, we continue to heed the realization that influenced Chancellor Walworth in 1832, and Lord Hardwicke ninety years earlier: When fiduciaries are faithless to their trust, the victims must not be left wholly without a remedy. As Lord Hardwicke put it, to "determine that frauds of this kind are out of the reach of courts of law or equity" would lead to "an intolerable grievance" (Charitable Corp. v. Sutton, 2 Atk at 406).

To hold that there is no remedy when corporate fiduciaries use corporate assets to enrich themselves was unacceptable in 1742 and in 1832, and it is still unacceptable today. Derivative suits are not the only possible remedy, but they are the one that has been recognized for most of two centuries, and to abolish them in the LLC context would be a radical step.

Some of the problems such an abolition would create may be seen in the development of New York law since the Limited Liability Company Law, omitting all reference to derivative suits, was passed in 1994. Several courts have held that there is no derivative remedy for LLC members. But since the Legislature obviously did not intend to give corporate fiduciaries a license to steal, a substitute remedy must be devised. Perhaps responding to this need, some courts have held that members of an LLC have their own, direct claims against fiduciaries for conduct that injured the LLC—blurring, if not erasing, the traditional line between direct and derivative claims. Similarly, Supreme Court's decision in this case upheld several of plaintiffs' claims that are not in issue here, characterizing the claims as direct, though they might well be derivative under traditional analysis.

Substituting direct remedies of LLC members for the old-fashioned derivative suit-a substitution not suggested by anything in the language of the Limited Liability Company Law—raises unanswered questions. Suppose, for example, a corporate fiduciary steals a hundred dollars from the treasury of an LLC. Unquestionably he or she is liable to the LLC for a hundred dollars, a liability which could be enforced in a suit by the LLC itself. Is the same fiduciary also liable to each injured LLC member in a direct suit for the member's share of the same money? What, if anything, is to be done to prevent double liability? No doubt, if the Legislature had indeed abolished the derivative suit as far as LLCs are concerned, we could and would answer these questions and others like them. But we will not readily conclude that the Legislature intended to set us on this uncharted path.

II

As shown above, courts have repeatedly recognized derivative suits in the absence of express statutory authorization. In light of this, it could hardly be argued that the mere absence of authorizing language in the Limited Liability Company Law bars the courts from entertaining derivative suits by LLC members. It is argued, however, by appellants and by our dissenting colleagues, that here we face not just legislative silence, but a considered legislative decision not to permit the remedy. The dissent finds, in the legislative history of the Limited Liability Corporation Law, a "legislative bargain" to the effect that derivative suits on behalf of LLCs should not exist. We find no such thing. For us, the most salient feature of the legislative history is that no one, in or out of the Legislature, ever expressed a wish to *eliminate*, rather than limit or reform, derivative suits.

The Legislature clearly did decide not to enact a statute governing derivative suits on behalf of LLCs. An Assembly-passed version of the bill that became the Limited Liability Company Law included an Article IX, entitled "Derivative Claims." In the Senate-passed version, and the version finally adopted, the article was deleted, leaving a conspicuous gap; in the law as enacted, the article following Article VIII is Article X. Nothing in the legislative history discusses the omission. Our only source of information on the reason for it is a sentence written by the author of the Practice Commentaries on the Limited Liability Company Law: "Because some legislators had raised questions about the derivative rights provisions, to avoid jeopardizing passage of the balance of the entire law, Article IX was dropped" (Rich, Practice Commentaries, McKinney's Cons Laws of NY, Book 32A, Limited Liability Company Law at 181 [2007]). Nothing tells us what the "questions" were, or why they would have jeopardized the bill's passage.

The dissent attempts to fill this gap by reviewing some other events preceding the passage of the legislation. The dissent points out that New York politicians in 1993 and 1994 wanted to improve "New York's overall business climate," and that among the proposed means of doing so were "bills to *modify the treatment of* derivative lawsuits and authorize limited liability companies." But the dissent cites no evidence, and we know of none, that anyone ever suggested doing away with derivative suits entirely — a radical step, as we have already pointed out, and one that might be expected to harm the "business climate" more than help it.

In fact, the reforms of derivative suits that were under discussion in 1993-1994 came nowhere near to abolition. They were, in substance, proposals to codify and expand on our decision in Auerbach v. Bennett (47 N.Y.2d 619 [1979]), holding that a decision by disinterested directors to terminate a derivative suit would be honored by the courts. . . .

The connection, if any, between the proposed reforms of derivative suits and the fate of proposed Article IX of the Limited Liability Company Law is obscure. It seems to be true that the Senate favored a bill from which Article IX was absent, and that the Assembly acquiesced in the Senate's preference. But this does not prove that any legislator, much less the Legislature as a whole, thought that the absence of Article IX would render derivative suits non-existent — an extreme result that no legislator is known to have favored. We simply do not know what consequences the legislators expected to follow from the omission. It is possible that some legislators did expect — though no one expressed the expectation — that there would be no derivative suits. It is possible that some legislators expected the courts to follow the established case law, and to recognize derivative suits in the absence of a "clear mandate against" doing so; one witness at a legislative public hearing did express that expectation. It is possible that the Senate expected one thing, and the Assembly the other. It is even possible that neither expected anything, except that the problem would cease to be the Legislature's and become the courts'. The legislative history is, in short, far too ambiguous to permit us to infer that the Legislature intended wholly to eliminate, in the LLC context, a basic, centuries-old protection for shareholders, leaving the courts to devise some new substitute remedy.

The dissent says that, in upholding the right of LLC members to sue derivatively, we leave that right "unfettered by the prudential safeguards against abuse that the Legislature has adopted . . . in other contexts." But, the right to sue derivatively has never been "unfettered," and the limitations on it are not all of legislative origin. The case in which derivative suits originated, Robinson v. Smith, held that such a suit could be brought only on "a sufficient excuse" — *i.e.*, a showing that those in control of the corporation "refused to prosecute" because they were themselves the wrongdoers, or were in "collusion with" them (3 Paige Ch. at 232, 233). Later cases reaffirmed the rule that a derivative action could not be brought "unless it is necessary because of the neglect and refusal of the corporate body to act" (*see e.g.*, Continental Sec. Co. v. Belmont, 206 N.Y. 7, 15 [1912]). The statutes governing ordinary business corporations and limited partnerships now reflect the existence of that rule, requiring the complaint in a derivative suit to allege "the efforts of the plaintiff to secure the initiation of such action . . . or the reasons for not making such effort" (Business Corporation Law § 626[c], Partnership Law § 115-a [3]). Other statutory provisions impose other limitations (*see* Business Corporation Law § 626[b], Partnership Law § 115-a [2] [contemporaneous ownership of plaintiff's interest]; Business Corporation Law § 627, Partnership Law § 115-b [posting security for expenses]). What limitations on the right of LLC members to sue derivatively may exist is a question not before us today. We do not, however, hold or suggest that there are none.

Finding no clear legislative mandate to the contrary, we follow *Robinson, Klebanow* and *Riviera* in concluding that derivative suits should be recognized even though no statute provides for them. We therefore hold that members of LLCs may sue derivatively.

Accordingly, the order of the Appellate Division, insofar as appealed from, should be affirmed with costs and the certified question answered in the affirmative.

READ, Judge (dissenting):

The result in this case is unique in the annals of the Court of Appeals. Never before has a majority of the Court read into a statute provisions or policy choices that the enacting Legislature unquestionably considered and rejected. I respectfully dissent.

BACKGROUND AND LEGISLATIVE HISTORY

The limited liability company (LLC) first appeared in Wyoming in 1977, followed by Florida, which adopted an LLC act similar to Wyoming's in 1982. "As in Wyoming, the Florida statute was enacted to lure capital into the state," but "[a]s a result of the lingering uncertainty as to both tax treatment and the protection of the entity's members from personal liability," other states did not immediately follow suit (Keatinge *et al.*, "The Limited Liability Company: A Study of the Emerging Entity," 47 Bus. Law. 375, 383-384 [1991-1992]). After the Internal Revenue Service's public ruling in 1988 that it would treat a Wyoming LLC as a partnership for tax purposes, however, many states and drafting commissions began to consider, or experiment with, LLC laws (*Id.* at 384).

While all of this was happening, New York's Business Corporation Law was increasingly viewed as unfriendly to fledgling businesses. Indeed, in late 1993 a corporate lawyer in a major New York City law firm suggested that "[t]here are many cases where a lawyer who uses New York as the state of incorporation without discussing it in advance with his client is probably guilty of malpractice because of the many disadvantageous aspects of New York law" (Peter Blackman, "Move over Delaware! Making New York Incorporation-Friendly," 12/16/93 NYLJ 5, col. 2 [statement of Richard R. Howe]).

By the early 1990s, New York legislators and Governor Cuomo had advanced improving New York's overall business climate to the forefront of the political agenda in Albany. Although this pro-business agenda manifested itself in various ways — for example, it was in 1994 that Governor Cuomo and Chief Judge Kaye first sought to establish the Commercial Division of the Supreme Court — two of the highest-profile pro-business initiatives were "bills pending in Albany to modify the treatment of derivative lawsuits and to authorize limited liability companies" (12/16/93 NYLJ 5, col. 2). They were often cited together in reports of the Legislative and gubernatorial agenda in 1993 and 1994.

By mid-1992, "18 states permit[ted] the formation of LLCs[,] two states [] recognize[d] LLCs formed in other states[,] LLC statutes [we]re pending or [we]re being considered in approximately 28 other states, and the National Conference of Commissioners on Uniform State Laws [wa]s drafting a uniform LLC statute" (Brian L. Schorr, "Limited Liability Companies: Features and Uses," The CPA Journal 193, 193 [Dec 1994]; reprinted in 805 PLI/Corp 191). On March 19, 1992, a Joint Drafting Committee of The Association of the Bar of the City of New York and the New York State Bar Association submitted a proposed limited liability company act for the New York Legislature's consideration; by early May 1992, LLC bills had been introduced in both houses of the New York State Legislature.

A limited liability company bill was introduced in the New York State Assembly as A11016 on March 31, 1992, less than two weeks after receipt of the Joint Drafting Committee's draft. A11016 was, for purposes of this case, substantially identical to the finally enacted Limited Liability Company Law with two related exceptions: article IX of the bill authorized members to bring derivative actions; and section 610, which set out the general rule that a member may not initiate an action by or against the company, included a derivative suit under article IX as an exception to this rule. A11016 was referred to committee after its introduction; the Assembly took no further action on this bill in 1992. . . .

As the subsequent legislative history of the Limited Liability Company Law confirms, the omission of provisions authorizing derivative actions was a material — if not *the* material — term in the legislative bargain struck by the Senate and the Assembly.

As noted earlier, LLC bills were introduced, in substantially complete form, in both chambers of the Legislature in the spring of 1992. The Assembly bill (A11016) authorized derivative actions; the Senate bill (S8180) did not. After both chambers failed to pass an LLC bill in 1992, efforts to negotiate a mutually agreeable statute resumed in 1993. On January 6, 1993, an LLC bill, S27, was introduced in the Senate; neither S27 nor any of its three reprints in 1993 contained any provision authorizing derivative actions. On March 30, 1993, an LLC bill containing article IX and the accompanying language in section 610 was again introduced in the Assembly as A7127. This bill was referred to committee, and no further action was ever taken on it. On June 25, 1993, the Assembly Rules Committee introduced A8676, another LLC bill containing these same provisions authorizing derivative actions. On July 7, 1993, the Assembly passed the "B" print of this bill — which still allowed for derivative actions — and delivered it to the Senate. The Senate, which had never introduced any LLC bill sanctioning derivative actions, did not act on A8676B, thus delaying the passage of any LLC law until at least 1994.

On January 5, 1994, S27 was reintroduced. On April 5, 1994, the Assembly Rules Committee introduced A11317, a companion to S7511, which was introduced in the Senate the same day. Unlike all prior Assembly bills, A11317 did *not* authorize derivative actions; as was the case with every prior Senate bill, S7511 likewise did not authorize derivative actions. On June 30, 1994, S7511 passed the Senate and was delivered to the Assembly. That same day, the Assembly substituted S7511 for A11317, and on July 1, 1994, the Assembly passed S7511 and returned it to the Senate. The adopted bill was delivered to the Governor on July 15, 1994, and was signed into law on July 26, 1994, as Chapter 576 of the Laws of 1994.

The deletion from the adopted LLC legislation of provisions authorizing derivative actions manifests a legislative bargain: the Senate refused to pass an LLC statute if it allowed for derivative suits. Nearly finalized LLC bills appeared in the Legislature as early as Spring of 1992, and the Assembly actually passed a bill in mid-1993. Yet the Senate was unbending: At a time when serious consideration was being given to legislation cutting back on the derivative actions authorized by existing laws, the Senate refused to endorse any legislation allowing members of this new form of business entity, the LLC, to sue derivatively. It is this compromise-excision of provisions authorizing derivative actions from the Assembly bill in exchange for the Senate's agreement to the balance of the law — to which Mr. Rich, a participant in the drafting of the proposed Limited Liability Company Law, no doubt refers when he states that "[t]he absence of an Article IX from the LLCL was a conscious omission, not a typographical error, as the decision to omit derivative rights occurred late in the legislative session" (McKinney's Cons Laws of NY, Book 32/32A, Limited Liability Company Law, 181 [2007 ed]). The rejection of language authorizing derivative actions "strongly militates against a judgment that [the Legislature] intended a result that it expressly declined to enact" (Gulf Oil Corp. v. Copp Paving Co., 419 U.S. 186, 200 [1974] [conference committee deleting House language].

The majority contends, however, that the Legislature's deletion of language authorizing derivative actions does not necessarily bespeak compromise, and is, in any event, essentially unimportant because the language was superfluous. This is so because derivative rights are so well-entrenched in existing law that the Legislature might have reasonably expected the courts to do what the majority has now done: extend the right to commence a derivative action to an LLC member based on analogy to either a cestui que trust or a shareholder, both of whom historically enjoyed standing to sue derivatively, as a matter of equity in the former case and common law in the latter. To support this proposition, the majority relies on the Second Circuit's decision in Klebanow v. New York Produce Exch. (344 F.2d 294 [2d Cir1965] [Friendly, J.]), and an oblique reference to *Klebanow* and Riviera Congress Assoc. v. Yassky (18 N.Y.2d 540 [1966]) (without referring to either case by name) made by Mr. Lefkowitz in his testimony at Assembly (not Senate) hearings in 1992.

In *Klebanow*, the United States Court of Appeals for the Second Circuit held that, even in the absence of statutory authorization, a limited partner in a dissolved firm had capacity to sue on behalf of the partnership (i.e., derivatively) for injury arising out of conduct proscribed by the antitrust law where the partnership and the liquidating partner had disabled themselves or had a conflict of interest, rendering futile any demand for the partnership to sue. The Court reasoned that this was so because a limited partner was more like a shareholder (especially a preferred holder), or perhaps a cestui que trust, than a creditor.

But this case is not *Klebanow*. First, as Judge Friendly acknowledged, there was no suggestion "that the framers of the Uniform Limited Partnership Act or the legislature of 1922 had focused on the problem . . . at issue"; i.e., whether to authorize limited partners to bring derivative suits. In this case, we know that the Legislature did indeed "focus[] on the problem . . . at issue" — whether to authorize members of LLCs to bring derivative suits — and decided not to do it. Second, section 118 of the Partnership Law, captioned "Rules for cases not covered," specifies that "[i]n any case not provided for in this article the rules of law and equity, *including the law merchant,* shall govern" (emphasis added). This provision lends support for the view implicitly taken by the courts in *Klebanow* and *Riviera* that the Legislature intended judges to interpret the Partnership Law with the freedom with which they would construe and apply principles of the common law or equity to fill in perceived legislative blanks, and — without doubt — at common law a shareholder could maintain a derivative suit, which is a remedial invention of equity. There is no provision comparable to section 118 in the Limited Liability Company Law. Although one federal judge has expressed the view that "[h]ad the legislature intended to preclude derivative claims by LLC members, it easily could have written an explicit prohibition into the law" (Bischoff v. Boar's Head, 436 F. Supp. 2d 626, 632 [SD N.Y.2006]), the Legislature does not customarily write zipper clauses into its statutes, or explicitly prohibit the courts from implying rights or liabilities that it did not choose to include. Rather, the modern Legislature reasonably expects the judiciary to respect its policy choices.

Next, Mr. Lefkowitz, who testified in favor of the right of LLC members to bring derivative suits, observed that "[s]tate and federal courts in New York have permitted derivative actions by a limited partner on behalf of limited partnerships without express statutory authority"; and opined that "*if and to the extent that* members of a limited liability company are analogous to a minority shareholder or a limited partner . . . such member would, as a matter of common law precedent, have the right to bring a derivative action on behalf of a limited liability company whether or not the statute contains such right" (6/12/92 testimony of Howard Lefkowitz, at 132-133 [emphasis added]). This testimony has been cited to support the proposition that the absence of an explicit provision in the Limited Liability Company Law authorizing derivative actions does not matter because the Legislature was aware that, under settled law, these provisions were unnecessary.

[A] vacuum no doubt exists because LLCs are a fairly recent statutory innovation, unknown to the common law; a new business form combining corporate-
type limited liability with partnership tax advantages and organizational characteristics. On the matter of derivative suits in particular, there are divergent
views throughout the country. The Uniform Limited Liability Company Act
developed by the National Conference of Commissioners on Uniform State
Laws provides for derivative suits modeled on the provisions of the Revised
Uniform Limited Partnership Act. Many states have adopted laws along similar
lines. By contrast, other states, preferring the American Bar Association's Prototype Limited Liability Company Act, require disinterested members or managers to authorize litigation. The co-author of the major treatise on limited
liability companies — who (unlike the majority) questions the utility of
derivative suits in the LLC context — advocates the ABA's approach as "a reasonable compromise" (*see* Ribstein, "The Emergence of the Limited Liability
Company," 51 Bus. Law. 1, 23 [1995-1996]).

In short, there is no settled law in New York or elsewhere on the subject of
derivative rights for LLC members. Certainly, a third-party advocate's prediction
that the courts might ignore the Legislature's policy choice (which, after years of
contrary Supreme Court and Appellate Division holdings, is today made prescient) does not express or create settled law. Essentially, the majority simply
disagrees with the Legislature, calling a decision not to authorize derivative suits
in the context of LLCs a "radical step . . . that might be expected to harm the
'business climate' more than help it." But whether or not to vest LLC members
with the right to sue derivatively is the Legislature's choice to make, not ours.
Moreover, although the majority argues that *failing* to recognize a derivative
right under the statute is an "extreme result," creating an "uncharted path"
upon which "we will not readily conclude the Legislature intended to set us,"
the "uncharted path" is the one taken by the majority: judicially legislating a
cause of action that was rejected by the Legislature, and, for more than a decade
after the Limited Liability Company Law's enactment, was not recognized by any
New York court.

Our Precedents

The majority does not cite a single case where we have read into a statute a
provision or policy choice that we know the enacting Legislature rejected.
Indeed, we have never done such a thing before. We have, in fact, consistently
deferred to the Legislature in cases where the facts are far less compelling than
they are here. . . .

Conclusion

The enacting (not a subsequent) Legislature considered and explicitly rejected
language authorizing the very result that plaintiffs have successfully sought from
the judiciary in this case. Fourteen years after the fact the majority has unwound
the legislative bargain. The proponents of derivative rights for LLC members —
who were unable to muster a majority in the Senate — have now obtained from
the courts what they were unable to achieve democratically. Thanks to judicial

fiat, LLC members now enjoy the right to bring a derivative suit. And because created by the courts, this right is unfettered by the prudential safeguards against abuse that the Legislature has adopted when opting to authorize this remedy in other contexts.

Presumably, those businesses electing to organize as LLCs relied on what the Limited Liability Company Law says, and counted on the New York judiciary to interpret the statute as written. Instead, the majority has effectively rewritten the law to add a right that the Legislature deliberately chose to omit. For a Court that prides itself on resisting any temptation to usurp legislative prerogative, the outcome of this appeal is curious. I respectfully dissent.

PROBLEM 3-6

You are licensed to practice law in the State of Utopia, and you sit on a State Bar Task Force whose job is to draft the provision of the LLC statute relating to derivative litigation. Your task force is considering the following options:

- Omit any reference to derivative litigation.
- Expressly prohibit derivative litigation.
- Expressly allow derivative litigation applying the principles of derivative lawsuits applicable to corporations.
- Allow derivative litigation only if the articles of organization or the operating agreement of the LLC permits derivative actions.

Which of the foregoing is your preferred option? Would Carder's actions in Problem 3-3 require a derivative action or would Drew be allowed to sue Carder directly?

F. DISSOLUTION

In an attempt to ensure partnership tax treatment for LLCs, early LLC statutes typically provided for dissolution upon the death, insanity, bankruptcy, retirement, resignation, or expulsion of any member, thus ensuring no continuity of life. These early statutes also usually provided LLC members with the right of withdrawal (dissociation), leading to dissolution of the company. With the advent of the check-the-box regulation, most states amended their LLC statutes to remove provisions requiring dissolution upon withdrawal of a member. While some states still allow for dissociation (*see, e.g.*, RULLCA § 601), others have substantially curbed the ability of partners to withdraw, absent a provision for the right of withdrawal in the operating agreement (*see, e.g.*, DLLCA § 18-801). These statutory developments serve to "lock in" LLC members who fail to negotiate exit rights in the operating agreement. Thus, our attention is focused on the nature of negotiated exit rights, explored in Valinote v. Ballis, and in the possibility of judicial dissolution, the grounds for which are examined in Haley v. Talcott.

VALINOTE v. BALLIS

295 F.3d 666
United States Court of Appeals, Seventh Circuit
June 26, 2002

EASTERBROOK, Circuit Judge.

Omnibus Financial Group L.L.C. fell short of its founders' hopes. Formed by four investor-members in 1996, it was down to two (John Valinote and Stephen Ballis) by mid-1997, and in 1999 Valinote stopped participating in the firm's management. Early in 2000 Valinote decided to withdraw from the foundering concern and asked Ballis for an "exit strategy." This led Ballis to initiate the buy-sell clause of Omnibus's operating agreement. This procedure, common in closely held businesses, allows one investor to set a price on the shares (for an LLC, the membership interests); next the other investor decides whether to buy the first investor's interest, or sell his own, at that price. The possibility that the person naming the price can be forced either to buy or to sell keeps the first mover honest.

Nothing in the operating agreement prescribes how investments are to be valued for this purpose. (A mechanical valuation for use in the event of a member's death or resignation does not apply to voluntary transactions among members.) Ballis named a price of −$1,581.29 for each 1% interest in Omnibus, implying a total of −$79,064.25 for the 50% stake that each of the two held. Valinote then decided to sell his interest to Ballis at that price — effectively paying Ballis $79,064.25 to take his 50% off his hands. At the time (surely this was no coincidence), Omnibus owed Valinote exactly that sum to repay a loan that Valinote had made to the firm. So the bottom line was that in March 2000 Valinote surrendered his interest to Ballis, who became the sole owner of Omnibus Financial Group. No money changed hands. Valinote could have acquired Ballis's interest on the same terms but must have thought that the real value was even lower than the negative price that Ballis had specified.

Later events confirmed the dim estimate of the venture's prospects. In December 2000 Omnibus defaulted on a $200,000 debt to a bank. The bank then collected on the guarantees of this debt that Valinote and Ballis had made. Valinote demanded that Ballis indemnify him for his $100,000 share and for any future payments that Valinote may be required to make. (Omnibus has at least one other bank loan of $400,000, though it may be secured by real estate.) Ballis refused, and the district court . . . held that Ballis is under no obligation to do so. The . . . judge concluded that the purchaser in a buy-sell transaction under Omnibus's operating agreement acquires the seller's membership interest, and that any obligations of the seller to the firm are extinguished, but that obligations (such as guarantees) to third parties are unaffected. That's the implication of language dealing with obligations to the firm while omitting other obligations. Paragraph 9.J of the operating agreement requires members to indemnify each other for obligations under guarantees, but the court held that this refers to current members, not to former members such as Valinote.

The operating agreement offers some succor to former members: ¶ 9.E.1 requires indemnification of any "person" for liability reasonably incurred while that person was a member. That covers payment on a guarantee that enabled Omnibus to raise operating capital. But the indemnitor under

¶ 9.E.1 is "[t]he Company", which is to say Omnibus, and Omnibus is broke. Likewise Valinote's right to indemnity under the law of suretyship — by paying on the guarantee, Valinote stepped into the bank's shoes and acquired its $100,000 claim — is a right against Omnibus. What Valinote wants, however, is indemnity from Ballis, who unlike Omnibus remains solvent. That claim lacks support in ¶ 9.E.1 and the law of suretyship, and it runs up against the principle that corporate shareholders or LLC members are not liable for the venture's debts. That's the point of limited liability: people put at risk the amounts they invest (or contract for explicitly, as by guarantees) but not their full personal wealth. Omnibus's operating agreement makes this explicit: ¶ 9.D says that members "shall look solely to the assets of the Company for the return of their capital . . . [and] shall have no recourse against the Members, or any Member . . . except as specifically provided in this Agreement."

Valinote does not contend that anything in the operating agreement "specifically" requires indemnity from Ballis. Instead he insists that it is so strongly implicit in the buy-sell procedure that it should be treated *as if* explicit. First, he observes, the buy-sell procedure allows a member to extricate himself from the company; that can't be done unless *all* financial entanglements are wrapped up. Otherwise a departing member remains at risk for things that have passed beyond his control; the firm might be sound at the time of withdrawal and be driven to ruin by the remaining members, triggering the guarantees. That uncompensated and uncontrollable risk should be eliminated by an indemnity requirement, Valinote insists. Second, Valinote contrasts the operation of the buy-sell procedure with the consequences of an outright resignation. Under ¶ 11.C a resigning member receives the mechanically computed value of each interest and "shall . . . forfeit all further interest in the Company, but shall not be relieved of or released from any personal guarantees or other personal covenants." No such provision appears in ¶ 10, which covers the buy-sell procedure; this implies to Valinote that sellers under ¶ 10 *are* relieved of guarantees. Why would he have sold to Ballis at a negative price under ¶ 10 when he could have resigned under ¶ 11 and demanded repayment of the $79,000 loan, unless the ¶ 10 procedure shifted the financial burden of the guarantees? Third comes the *coup de grâce*: because Omnibus was a *limited liability* company, membership interests cannot be worth less than zero. Shares of a bankrupt corporation trade for a positive price as a result of limited liability, for shares are worth at worst the scrap value of the paper, and the firm might recover. Yet Ballis valued each 1% interest in Omnibus at −$1,581.29. This must mean, Valinote insists, that Ballis was covering in advance the risk of indemnity on any guarantees. How else could the price go negative?

There is some force to these observations, but not enough to justify overriding the venerable principle of limited liability, which may be vital to a business's ability to raise capital. Especially not when the operating agreement reinforces that principle by proscribing personal liability "except as specifically provided in this Agreement." The argument that "strongly implicit" is as good as "explicit" is equivalent to a plea that the *real* explicit language of the agreement — particularly the clause limiting personal liability — be overridden. That would make all contractual language unreliable, and such a step would not in the long run further the goals of investors such as Ballis and Valinote, who draft these complex agreements in the belief that what they have written will be enforced when push comes to shove. Although enforcement of the agreement may have costs — here it makes complete extrication more complex and exposes the withdrawing investor to risk if the unwinding is incomplete — these are not insuperable. Valinote could have negotiated with the bank to cancel his guarantee; the bank might have agreed, for a price, or Ballis might have agreed to assume the liability (again for a price). With so few people involved, the negotiations would not be especially costly. Far better for Valinote and Ballis to have resolved this issue between themselves *ex ante* than to ask a court to guess *ex post* what that deal would have looked like — especially when the process of guessing would override the parties' written agreement demanding specificity.

Nor is the negative price (or the contrast between buy-out under ¶ 10.C.2 and resignation under ¶ 11.C) an enigma that can be understood only by assuming that Ballis had rolled into the price the risk of indemnifying Valinote. For the operating agreement did not strictly adhere to limited liability: there *is* a veil-piercing clause that appears "specifically" in the agreement. It is ¶ 9.J, which we now reproduce in full:

> The Company, or businesses and entities with which the Company may be associated, may from time to time be required to borrow funds and, to secure such loans, to deliver guarantees by one or more Members of repayment, performance, completion, or other obligations of the Company or such associated venture. The Members covenant and agree that if any Member executes and delivers any such guarantee and if such guaranteeing Member incurs any cost or liability in connection therewith, then such cost shall be allocated among and shared by all of the Members in accordance with their respective Membership Interests.

In other words, if Member X makes good on a guarantee of the company's indebtedness, then Member Y must pick up part of the cost. This is a departure from limited liability. It also shows how the value of interests could be negative; each carries with it some risk of liability under ¶ 9.J. What is more, when one member withdraws, prospective liability under ¶ 9.J becomes concentrated on those who remain, because a *former* member is not exposed to liability under this clause-except to the extent that ¶ 11.C provides that a resigning member retains this liability. Thus the mysteries are resolved. Ballis set a negative interest value because Valinote's departure meant that he could no longer be called on for indemnity under this clause, and Ballis's expected net outlay on his own guarantees increased accordingly. Because exposure under ¶ 9.J could be substantial, something like ¶ 11.C is essential to prevent members from shucking their potential liability by resigning and walking away; but when departure is negotiated under the buy-sell provision, a price can be attached. Here the negative price compensated Ballis for giving up any opportunity to seek relief against Valinote under ¶ 9.J. (On our reading of the operating agreement, Ballis received freedom from future indemnity claims by Valinote; whether this was worth enough to reduce the net effect to zero depends on the wealth of each investor, and hence the likelihood that a demand for indemnity would be honored. The record does not reveal this information. On Valinote's reading, Ballis gave up the right to indemnification while remaining liable on his own part; the risk that Valinote might prevail in this position would be enough by itself to generate a negative price.) And if Valinote feared that what he was giving up in return (the opportunity to recover from Ballis) was worth even more, perhaps because he anticipated that under Ballis's management the chance of a draw on the guarantees would increase, he had only to buy Ballis's stake at the price Ballis set rather than sell his own. Valinote's professed fear that as sole member Ballis could transfer all of Omnibus's assets to himself, leaving Valinote holding the bag, is groundless: Such a transfer would be a fraudulent conveyance, which Valinote, as Omnibus's creditor following a call on the guarantee, could rectify by reaching Ballis's assets. Valinote does not contend, however, that any fraudulent conveyance occurred, and he does not make a claim under the law of suretyship.

Valinote would like to turn ¶ 9.J around and use it as a source of recovery: He was a member when the guaranty was written, even though not when he made good that guarantee, and thus should be entitled to spread the cost among the other members (of which Ballis is the sole remaining example). But if we were to treat "member" in this language as including former members, how could Valinote gain? He would be entitled to call on Ballis to pick up a share—but Ballis would be entitled to call on Valinote for reimbursement too, and it would be a wash. Former members could not be "members" for purposes of collection while escaping that status for purposes of liability; the requirements are symmetric. (Recall that under ¶ 10.C.2 Ballis acquired Valinote's membership interest plus Valinote's obligations "to the Company," but not Valinote's personal obligations to other members.) Like the district court, however, we think it best to read "member" to mean current member and exclude former member. This is the most natural reading; it avoids circular reimbursements; and it also avoids questions about what each person's responsibility is. Membership interests change, and Valinote's position would leave it up in the air what share each current (and former) member must pick up.

The district court read the operating agreement to mean what it says. Given ¶ 9.D, that was the most sensible course. By paying on his guarantee, Valinote was subrogated to the bank's rights and has a claim against Omnibus; and if Omnibus has a claim against Ballis, then Valinote can participate. But neither Valinote nor Ballis has a direct claim against the other; each must bear his own obligations under the guarantees. Ballis's motion for sanctions is denied, however; the appeal was not frivolous, and the operating agreement does not call for fee shifting in a dispute such as this.

HALEY v. TALCOTT

864 A.2d 86
Court of Chancery of Delaware
December 16, 2004

STRINE, Vice Chancellor.

I.   FACTUAL BACKGROUND

[Plaintiff Matthew James Haley and defendant Gregory L. Talcott each have a 50% interest in Matt & Greg Real Estate, LLC, a Delaware limited liability company (the "LLC") they formed in 2003. The creation of the company, however, is only a recent event in the history between the parties.]

Haley and Talcott have known each other since the 1980s. In 2001 Haley was the manager of the Rehoboth location of The Third Edition, a restaurant owned by Talcott that also had a location in Washington, D.C. In 2001, Haley found the location for what would become the Redfin Grill. Talcott contributed substantial start-up money and Haley managed the Redfin Grill without drawing a salary for the first year.

The structure of the agreements between the parties forming the Redfin Grill is complex and the subject of additional litigation before this court. For reasons that are not relevant, Haley and Talcott chose to create and operate the Redfin Grill as an entity solely owned by Talcott, with Haley's rights and obligations being defined by a series of contracts. Those agreements, all dated November 30, 2001, included an Employment Agreement, a Retention Bonus Agreement, and a Side Letter Agreement (together, the "Employment Contract"), as well as an Agreement regarding an option to purchase real estate (the "Real Estate Agreement").

The Employment Contract, although structured as an agreement between an employer and an employee, makes clear that the parties were operating the business as a joint venture. The Employment Contract specified that Haley reported to Talcott and that Talcott had the right to reevaluate and revise Haley's decisions, but indicated that "such action is not anticipated." It also provided that Haley's "bonus" would be one half of the net profits of the Redfin Grill, after the initial loan from Talcott was repaid. Moreover, Talcott would materially breach the Employment Contract, and Haley could end his employment for cause, if Talcott amended Haley's duties such that his position as "Operations Director" became one of "less dignity, responsibility, importance or scope." The Employment Contract further clarified Haley's importance to the enterprise by awarding him one half of any proceeds from any sale of the Redfin Grill. Finally, the Employment Contract limited Talcott's ability to remove Haley from his active role:

> [N]otwithstanding the language in the Employment Agreement relating to termination, individually, I [Talcott] will assure you that the Employment Agreement will not be terminable under any circumstances unless an event occurs that would entitle you payment of a Retention Bonus as set forth in the Retention Bonus Agreement that is part of this transaction. Such an event would be a "Business Sale". . . .

The Employment Contract therefore establishes a relationship more similar to a partnership than a typical employer/employee relationship.

The equivalent nature of the parties' contributions is further confirmed by the Real Estate Agreement. In that agreement, Talcott granted Haley the right to participate in an option to purchase the property where the Redfin Grill was situated which is located at 1111 Highway One in Bethany Beach, Delaware (the "Property"). Talcott had obtained the option personally when the Redfin Grill first leased the Property from the then-owner in February of 2001. Talcott provided this valuable right to participate for the nominal price of $10.00. The agreement provided that if the option were exercised, Haley would shoulder 50% of the burden of the purchase, and would be either a 50% owner of the land or a 50% owner of the entity formed to hold the land.

From late 2001 into 2003, under Haley's supervision, the Redfin Grill grew into a successful business. By the second year of its existence, the start-up money had been repaid to Talcott with interest, both parties were drawing salaries (Talcott's substantially smaller since he was not participating in day-to-day management), and the parties each received approximately $150,000 in profit sharing.

In 2003, the parties formed [the] LLC to take advantage of the option to purchase the Property that was the subject of the Real Estate Agreement. The option price was $720,000 and the new LLC took out a mortgage from County Bank in Rehoboth Beach, Delaware, for that amount, exercised the option, and obtained the deed to the Property on or about May 23, 2003. Importantly, both Haley and Talcott, individually, signed personal guaranties for the entire amount of the mortgage in order to secure the loan. The Redfin Grill continued to operate at the site, paying the LLC $6,000 per month in rent, a payment sufficient to cover the LLC's monthly obligation under the mortgage. Thus by mid-2003, the parties appeared poised to reap the fruits of their labors; unfortunately, at that point their personal relationship began to deteriorate.

Haley, having managed the restaurant from the time it opened in May 2001, and having formalized his management position in the Employment Contract, apparently believed that the relationship would be reformulated to provide him a direct stock ownership interest in the Redfin Grill at some point. The reasons underlying that belief are not important here, but in late October they caused a rift to develop between the parties. On or about October 27, 2003, the conflict that had been brewing between the parties led to some kind of confrontation. As a result, Talcott sent a letter of understanding to Haley dated October 27, 2003, purporting to accept his resignation and forbidding him to enter the premises of the Redfin Grill.

Haley responded on November 3, 2003 with two separate letters from his counsel to Talcott. In the first, Haley asserts that he did not resign, and that he regarded Talcott's October 27, 2003 letter of understanding as terminating him without cause in breach of the Employment Contract. Haley goes on to express his intent to pursue legal remedies, an intent that he acted upon in the related case in this court.

In his second November 3, 2003 letter, Haley purported to take several positions expressly as a 50% member in the LLC including: 1) rejecting the new lease proposed by Talcott for the Redfin Grill; 2) voting to revoke any consent to possession by the Redfin Grill and terminating any lease by which the Redfin Grill asserts the right to possession; and 3) voting that the Property be put up for sale on the open market.

Of course, as a 50% member, Haley could not force the LLC to take action on these proposals because Talcott opposed them. As a result, the pre-existing status quo continued by virtue of the stalemate — a result that Talcott favored. The Redfin Grill's lease has expired and, as a consequence, the Redfin Grill continues to pay $6,000 per month to the LLC in a month-to-month arrangement. The $6,000 rent exceeds the LLC's required mortgage payment by $800 per month, so the situation remains stable. With only a 50% ownership interest, Haley cannot force the termination of the Redfin Grill's lease and evict the Redfin Grill as a tenant; neither can he force the sale of the Property, land that was appraised as of June 14, 2004 at $1.8 million. In short, absent intervention by this court, Haley is stuck, unless he chooses to avail himself of the exit mechanism provided in the LLC Agreement.

That exit mechanism, like judicial dissolution, would provide Haley with his share of the fair market value of the LLC, including the Property. Section 18 of the LLC Agreement provides that upon written notice of election to "quit" the company, the remaining member may elect, in writing, to purchase the departing member's interest for fair market value. If the remaining member elects to purchase the departing member's interest, the parties may agree on fair value, or have the fair value determined by three arbitrators, one chosen by each member and a third chosen by the first two arbitrators. The departing member pays the reasonable expenses of the three arbitrators. Once a fair price is determined, it may be paid in cash, or over a term if secured by: 1) a note signed by the company and personally by the remaining member; 2) a security agreement; and 3) a recorded UCC lien. Only if the remaining member fails to elect to purchase the departing member's interest is the company to be liquidated.

The LLC agreement describes additional details regarding the term and interest rate of any installment payments and defines penalty, default, and acceleration terms to be contained in the securing note. Although these details are not critical to a comparison between a contractual separation under the LLC Agreement and a judicial dissolution, they demonstrate the level of detail that the parties considered in crafting the exit mechanism. But despite this level of detail, the exit provision does not expressly provide a release from the personal guaranties that both Haley and Talcott signed to secure the mortgage on the Property. Nor does the exit provision state that any member dissatisfied with the status quo must break an impasse by exit rather than a suit for dissolution.

Rather than use the exit mechanism, Haley has simultaneously sought: 1) dissolution of the LLC; and 2) relief in an employment litigation filed against Talcott and Redfin Grill, a case also pending in this court. Haley does not view himself as being obligated by the LLC Agreement to be the one who exits; moreover, he would bear the cost of the exit mechanism and that mechanism, as will be discussed, would not release him from the guaranty.

As a tactical move, Talcott — on the same day as this suit was filed — putatively reinstated Haley as a manager of the Redfin Grill, but with no duties and only $1.00 per year in pay. Talcott claims, however, to recognize Haley's right to 50% of the Redfin Grill profits. It appears that Talcott took this step as a method to preempt relief being granted to Haley by a court in lawsuits that Talcott knew were likely to be imminently filed by Haley. Despite the so-called "reinstatement," Talcott and Haley have not had any direct business contact since October 2003.

Haley has moved on since leaving the Redfin Grill in an active capacity, and now operates another restaurant in Lewes, Delaware. Despite his shift in focus, Haley continues to be interested in the Redfin Grill, and has expressed his desire to buy Talcott out of both the LLC and the Redfin Grill itself if given the opportunity. Talcott, by urging the exit remedy provided in the LLC Agreement, has expressed his desire to buy Haley out of the LLC and has no interest in selling the Redfin Grill. Haley continues to refuse to use the exit mechanism.

Pragmatically, the current impasse arises because we have two willing buyers and no willing sellers. Haley alleges that, given this practical dilemma, and his evident inability to effect his desired direction for the LLC, judicial dissolution is his only practicable remedy.

. . .

III. Legal Analysis

A. PROCEDURAL FRAMEWORK

Haley alleges that pursuant to 6 *Del. C.* § 18-802 the court should exercise its discretion and dissolve the LLC because it is not reasonably practicable for it to continue the business of the company in conformity with the LLC Agreement. Section 18-802 provides in its entirety:

> On application by or for a member or manager the Court of Chancery may decree dissolution of a limited liability company whenever it is not reasonably practicable to carry on the business in conformity with a limited liability company agreement.

Haley argues that dissolution is required because the two 50% managers cannot agree how to best utilize the sole asset of the LLC, the Property, because no provision exists for breaking a tie in the voting interests, and because the LLC cannot take any actions, such as entering contracts, borrowing or lending money, or buying or selling property, absent a majority vote of its members. Because this circumstance resembles corporate deadlock, Haley urges that 8 *Del. C.* § 273 provides a relevant parallel for analysis.

The standard Haley must meet to succeed on a motion for summary judgment is clearly established. Haley must establish that no genuine issue of law or of fact exists and that he is entitled to judgment as a matter of law. In examining the record, I must draw every rational inference in Talcott's favor. Here, even if I find that there are no facts under which the LLC could carry on business in conformity with the LLC Agreement, the remedy of dissolution, by analogy to 8 *Del. C.* § 273, remains discretionary.

Here, the key facts about the parties' ability to work together are not rationally disputable. Therefore, my decision on the motion largely turns on two legal issues: 1) if the doctrine of corporate deadlock is an appropriate analogy for the analysis of a § 18-802 claim on these facts; and 2) if so, and if action to break the stalemate is necessary to permit the LLC to function, whether, because of the contract-law foundations of the Delaware LLC Act, Haley should be relegated to the contractual exit mechanism provided in the LLC Agreement.

B. CASE LAW UNDER § 273 OF THE DELAWARE GENERAL CORPORATE LAW ("DGCL") PROVIDES AN APPROPRIATE FRAMEWORK FOR ANALYSIS

Section 18-802 of the Delaware LLC Act is a relatively recent addition to our law, and, as a result, there have been few decisions interpreting it. Nevertheless, § 18-802 has the obvious purpose of providing an avenue of relief when an LLC cannot continue to function in accordance with its chartering agreement. Thus § 18-802 plays a role for LLCs similar to the role that § 273 of the DGCL plays for joint venture corporations with only two stockholders. When a limited liability agreement provides for the company to be governed by its members, when there are only two members, and when those members are at permanent odds, § 273 provides relevant insight into what should happen. To wit, Section 273(a) provides, in relevant part, that:

> If the stockholders of a corporation of this state, having only 2 stockholders each of whom own 50% of the stock therein, shall be engaged in a joint venture and if such stockholders shall be unable to agree upon the desirability of discontinuing such

joint venture and disposing of the assets used in such venture, either stock holder may, unless otherwise provided in the certificate of incorporation of the corporation or in a written agreement between stockholders, file with the Court of Chancery a petition stating that it desires to discontinue such joint venture and to dispose of the assets used in such venture in accordance with a plan to be agreed on by both stockholders or that, if no such plan shall be agreed upon by both stockholders, the corporation be dissolved.

Section 273 essentially sets forth three pre-requisites for a judicial order of dissolution: 1) the corporation must have two 50% stockholders, 2) those stockholders must be engaged in a joint venture, and 3) they must be unable to agree upon whether to discontinue the business or how to dispose of its assets. Here, by analogy, each of the three provisions is indisputably met.

First, there is no dispute that the parties are 50% members of the LLC. The LLC agreement provided that both Haley and Talcott would have an initial 50% interest in the LLC. Although the LLC Agreement allows for adjustment to members' capital accounts based on later cash contributions, and a corresponding revision to voting power, neither party asserts that any reconfiguration has occurred. Accordingly, Haley and Talcott each remain 50% members of the LLC.

Second, there is no rational doubt that the parties intended to be and are engaged in a joint venture. While the standard for establishing a joint venture has evolved over time, it has always included the circumstances presented here, where two parties "agree[d] for their mutual benefit to combine their skills, property and knowledge, actively managing the business." The relationship between Haley and Talcott indicates active involvement by both parties in creating a restaurant for their mutual benefit and profit, and the Employment Contract shows that Haley was to be the "Operations Director" of the Redfin Grill, a position that, according to the Side Letter Agreement, would only be terminated if the restaurant was sold. Haley was also entitled to a 50% share of the Redfin Grill's profits. In short, Haley and Talcott were in it together for as long as they owned the restaurant, equally sharing the profits as provided in the Employment Contract.

Most importantly, Haley never agreed to be a passive investor in the LLC who would be subject to Talcott's unilateral dominion. Instead, the LLC agreement provided that: "no member/managers may, *without the agreement of a majority vote of the managers' interest*, act on behalf of the company." Acts of the company expressly include: borrowing money in the company name; using company property as collateral; binding the company to any obligation such as a guarantor or surety; selling, mortgaging or encumbering any personal or real property of the company except for business purposes for proper consideration; lending company funds; contracting for any debt except for a proper company purpose; and drawing checks on the company account in excess of $5,000. Under these terms, as a 50% member/manager, no major action of the LLC could be taken without Haley's approval. Thus, Haley is entitled to a continuing say in the operation of the LLC.

Finally, the evidence clearly supports a finding of deadlock between the parties about the business strategy and future of the LLC. Haley's second letter of November 3, 2003 expresses his desire to end the lease of the Redfin Grill and sell the Property at fair market value. The very fact that dissolution has not occurred, combined with Talcott's opposition in this lawsuit, leads inevitably to the conclusion that Talcott opposes such a disposition of the assets. Neither is Talcott's opposition surprising given his economic interest in the continued success of the Redfin Grill, success that one must assume relies, in part, on a continuing favorable lease arrangement with the LLC.

Talcott suggests that Haley has merely voluntarily removed himself from the management process and that no express disagreement has arisen. This court, however, may consider the totality of the circumstances in determining whether the parties disagree, and only a rational dispute of fact will preclude the entry of summary judgment. Contrary to Talcott's assertion, it is not, at least in a § 273 suit, necessary that the parties formally attempt to reach an agreement before coming to court. In any event, it is clear that, through counsel, the parties have made efforts to resolve this impasse.

Moreover, there is no evidentiary support for Talcott's suggestion that the parties are not at an impasse. The parties have not interacted since their falling out in October, 2003. Clearly, Talcott understands that the end of Haley's managerial role from the Redfin Grill profoundly altered their relationship as co-members of the LLC. After all, it has left Haley on the outside, looking in, with no power. Of course, Talcott insists that the LLC can and does continue to function for its intended purpose and in conformity with the agreement, receiving payments from the Redfin Grill and writing checks to meet its obligations under the mortgage on Talcott's authority. But that reality does not mean that the LLC is operating in accordance with the LLC Agreement. Although the LLC is technically functioning at this point, this operation is purely a residual, inertial status quo that just happens to exclusively benefit one of the 50% members, Talcott, as illustrated by the hands-tied continuation of the expired lease with the Redfin Grill. With strident disagreement between the parties regarding the appropriate deployment of the asset of the LLC, and open hostility as evidenced by the related suit in this matter, it is not credible that the LLC could, if necessary, take any important action that required a vote of the members. Abundant, uncontradicted documents in the record demonstrate the inability of the parties to function together.

For all these reasons, if the LLC were a corporation, there would be no question that Haley's request to dissolve the entity would be granted. But this case regards an LLC, not a corporation, and more importantly, an LLC with a detailed exit provision. That distinguishing factor must and is considered next.

C. EVEN GIVEN THE CONTRACTUAL EMPHASIS OF THE DELAWARE LLC ACT, THE EXIT REMEDY
    PROVIDED IN THE LLC AGREEMENT IS AN INSUFFICIENT ALTERNATIVE TO DISSOLUTION

The Delaware LLC Act is grounded on principles of freedom of contract. For that reason, the presence of a reasonable exit mechanism bears on the propriety of ordering dissolution under 6 *Del. C.* § 18-802. When the agreement itself provides a fair opportunity for the dissenting member who disfavors the inertial status quo to exit and receive the fair market value of her interest, it is at least arguable that the limited liability company may still proceed to operate practicably under its contractual charter because the charter itself provides an equitable way to break the impasse.

Here, that reasoning might be thought apt because Haley has already "voted" as an LLC member to sell the LLC's only asset, the Property, presumably because he knew he could not secure sole control of both the LLC and the Redfin Grill.

Given that reality, so long as Haley can actually extract himself fairly, it arguably makes sense for this court to stay its hand in an LLC case and allow the contract itself to solve the problem.

Notably, reasoning of this nature has been applied in the § 273 context. Even under § 273, this court's authority to order dissolution remains discretionary and may be influenced by the particular circumstances. Talcott rightly argues that the situation here is somewhat analogous to that in *In re Delaware Bay Surgical Services*, C.A. No. 2121-S (Del.Ch. Jan. 28, 2002), where this court declined to dissolve a corporation under § 273 in part because a mechanism existed for the repurchase of the complaining member's 50% interest.

But, this matter differs from *Surgical Services* in two important respects. First, in *Surgical Services*, the respondent doctor had owned the company before admitting the petitioner to his practice as a 50% stakeholder. The court found that both parties clearly intended, upon entering the contract, that if the parties ended their contractual relationship, the respondent would be the one permitted to keep the company. By contrast, no such obvious priority of interest exists here. Haley and Talcott created the LLC together and while the detailed exit provision provided in the formative LLC Agreement allows either party to leave voluntarily, it provides no insight on who should retain the LLC if both parties would prefer to buy the other out, and neither party desires to leave. In and of itself, however, this lack of priority might not be found sufficient to require dissolution, because of a case-specific fact; namely, that Haley has proposed — as a member of the LLC — that the LLC's sole asset be sold. But I need not — and do not — determine how truly distinguishing that fact is, because forcing Haley to exercise the contractual exit mechanism would not permit the LLC to proceed in a practicable way that accords with the LLC Agreement, but would instead permit Talcott to penalize Haley without express contractual authorization.[35]

Why? Because the parties agree that exit mechanism in the LLC Agreement would not relieve Haley of his obligation under the personal guaranty that he signed to secure the mortgage from County Bank. If Haley is forced to use the exit mechanism, Talcott and he both believe that Haley would still be left holding the bag on the guaranty. It is therefore not equitable to force Haley to use the exit mechanism in this circumstance. While the exit mechanism may be workable in a friendly departure when both parties cooperate to reach an adequate alternative agreement with the bank, the bank cannot be compelled to accept the removal of Haley as a personal guarantor. Thus, the exit mechanism fails as an adequate remedy for Haley because it does not equitably effect the

---

35. Stated plainly and putting aside Haley's proposal to sell the Property, it is an interesting question whether the 50% member of an LLC that operates an on-going business, and who does not favor inertial policy, must exit rather than force dissolution, particularly when the cost of the exit procedure would, as here, be borne solely by him. Arguably, it is economically more efficient — absent an explicit requirement that the party disfavoring inertia exit if he is dissatisfied — to order dissolution, and allow both parties to bid as purchasers, with the assets going to the highest bidder (inside or outside) who presumably will deploy the asset to its most valuable use. It is also concomitantly arguable that if parties wish to force the co-equal member disfavoring inertia to exit rather than seek dissolution, then they should explicitly contract upfront in the LLC agreement that exit (or the triggering of a buy-sell procedure, giving incentives for the business to be retained by the member willing to pay the highest value) is the required method of breaking any later-arising stalemate.

separation of the parties. Rather, it would leave Haley with no upside potential, and no protection over the considerable downside risk that he would have to make good on any future default by the LLC (over whose operations he would have no control) to its mortgage lender. Thus here, unlike in *Surgical Services*, the parties do not, in fact, "have at their disposal a far less drastic means to resolve their personal disagreement."

IV. CONCLUSION

For the reasons discussed above, I find that it is not reasonably practicable for the LLC to continue to carry on business in conformity with the LLC Agreement. The parties shall confer and, within four weeks, submit a plan for the dissolution of the LLC. The plan shall include a procedure to sell the Property owned by the LLC within a commercially reasonable time frame. Either party may, of course, bid on the Property.

PROBLEM 3-7

Although Drew sold the cheese shop (see Problem 3-5), she and Carder have continued to do some internet cheese sales through Turophile LLC. Carder believes that internet sales of specialty cheeses could be a very profitable business, but Drew is determined to move on with her life.

Drew remains the Manager of Turophile LLC, and she refuses to promote or expand the internet business, despite Carder's urgings. Turophile's LLC Agreement provides for the possibility of a buyout in the event of a business dispute among the members: "If a dispute relating to the affairs of the Company cannot be resolved within 15 days of such dispute arising, either party may serve a written notice that it intends to purchase the interest of the other party for a price established by the formula set out in this clause." That formula would have resulted in a purchase price well in excess of the fair market value of Drew's interest, so Carder declined to exercise her rights under the contract.

Would Drew be able to obtain a judicial dissolution of Turophile LLC in Delaware? In answering this question, consider DLLCA § 18-802, which provides as follows: "On application by or for a member or manager the Court of Chancery may decree dissolution of a limited liability company whenever it is not reasonably practicable to carry on the business in conformity with a limited liability company agreement."

NEOCLONE BIOTECHNOLOGY INTERNATIONAL LLC: A CASE STUDY

Deven McGlenn first heard about NeoClone Biotechnology International in the fall of 1999. At the time, McGlenn was sitting in his Chicago office at Arthur Andersen — then one of the "Big Five" accounting firms — where McGlenn had begun his career as a consultant two years earlier. On the other end of the telephone call was Allen Clark, a Professor of Anatomy of the University of Wisconsin Medical School. Dr. Clark's first contact with McGlenn had nothing to do with business — Clark was a neighbor and friend of the parents of McGlenn's wife — but now Clark was seeking some business advice. He had

become interested in a new technology developed at the University of
Wisconsin, and he wanted McGlenn to assist in building a business around
the technology.

The technology was a patented method of producing monoclonal antibodies.
Antibodies are proteins produced naturally by the body to fight antigens, such as
disease-causing bacteria and viruses. Each antibody is tailored to attack a specific
antigen, and some antibodies — once activated — provide ongoing protection
against future invasions by the same type of antigen (for example, antibodies
created by having the measles produce an immunity against future infections).
This immunizing attribute of antibodies makes them useful in developing vaccines. Antibodies are also used to diagnose various diseases.

Developing vaccines and diagnostic tools requires a large number of antibodies for use in research. Traditionally, scientists would produce antibodies
by injecting laboratory animals with an antigen and harvesting the antibodies
from the animal's blood. This method is slow and the resulting product is often
contaminated by other substances in the animal's blood.

Monoclonal antibody technology represented a great advance over the traditional method. Simply stated, this technology required scientists to combine
cells that produce antibodies naturally with cells that grow continually in a
cell culture. The resulting cell (called a "hybridoma") produces antibodies
continually. Because the antibodies are produced from a single cell (the hybridoma), they are called "monoclonal." These antibodies are purer and more
accurately targeted to specific antigens than the antibodies produced using
the traditional process.

The technology Clark described to McGlenn was a method of producing
monoclonal antibodies even more quickly than had previously been done, in
some instances at double the speed. Of course, the value of such a process lies
primarily in the cost savings associated with quicker production cycles. While
McGlenn knew next to nothing about the science of monoclonal antibody production, he knew a profitable business opportunity when he saw it, and this
looked like it had some potential. NeoClone, as the company came to be called,
would manufacture and sell antibodies — some "off the shelf" from NeoClone's
catalogue and others custom made.

At the time, the business consisted of three founders. Donal Kaehler and
David Largaespada were part of the research team that developed and patented
the new production process in the laboratory of a University of Wisconsin professor, Dr. Rex Risser. The third founder, Mark Jackson, was an expert in laboratory personnel and materials management, and he had worked in Risser's
laboratory after the process had been developed.

Patents relating to the new process were held by the Wisconsin Alumni
Research Foundation (WARF) — a legendary leader in technology transfer.
Founded in 1925,[1] WARF is a nonprofit organization that patents technologies

---

1. The impetus for WARF's founding was Professor Harry Steenbock's discovery that vitamin D
could be artificially manufactured and stored in foods. Steenbock recognized that his research
could lead to the elimination of rickets, and he sought the creation of WARF to ensure that his
discovery — and others like it — would reach the public. After receiving a series of patents based on
Steenbock's research, WARF granted its first license in 1927. Quaker Oats used the license to
supplement its breakfast cereals.

developed at the University of Wisconsin-Madison.[2] Mark Jackson negotiated the license of two patents from WARF on behalf of NeoClone.

Since all three founders of NeoClone were working at the University of Wisconsin, they decided to set up shop in Madison, which has an up-and-coming biotechnology industry, anchored by Promega Corporation and Third Wave Technologies and encouraged by various University initiatives.[3] McGlenn worked with the founders of NeoClone occasionally over the next two and a half years, but he kept his day job at Andersen. NeoClone hired Amy Davison Clark (Allen Clark's daughter) as its first full-time employee in April 2000, but didn't add a second employee for another year. By the spring of 2002, NeoClone was beginning to develop, and the need for a full-time manager was becoming more apparent. At the same time, life at Andersen had taken a dramatic turn for the worse for McGlenn, as the firm was enveloped by the collapse of Enron Corporation. In June 2002, McGlenn left Andersen and joined NeoClone as the Chief Executive Officer.

McGlenn immediately set to work preparing for expansion of the company. He had brought on Jeff Moore as Chief Operating Officer for this very purpose. Moore — who describes himself as a "recovering lawyer"[4] — had seven years of start-up experience with MicroCoating Technologies in Atlanta, Georgia.

Although NeoClone was generating revenues from the sale of antibodies, it needed some additional capital quickly. By the middle of October, Moore and McGlenn had successfully negotiated a $90,000 investment by a group of angel investors[5] in Madison. Although the group had begun their discussions around the idea of an equity investment, they were unable to agree on an appropriate valuation for the company.[6] Ultimately, they were able to come to terms on an investment involving convertible debt, which provides investors with the priority associated with debt in the event the company liquidates but also comes with the

---

2. Here's how it works. A researcher discloses an invention to WARF, and the WARF staff evaluates its patentability and commercial potential. If the invention is accepted, WARF provides an attorney to assist the researcher in preparing and prosecuting the patent application. In exchange, the professor assigns ownership of the future patent to WARF.

Once a patent is awarded, WARF licenses the technologies. The inventor receives 20 percent of any license revenues, and the remainder is used to support further research at the university. The University of Wisconsin, through WARF, remains consistently among the top universities in the United States in patent awards. According to WARF's Web site, nearly 100 companies based on technology developed by the University of Wisconsin are currently in operation.

3. In addition to WARF, these initiatives include a Biotechnology Center, founded in 1984 by Richard Burgess, NeoClone's current Chairman. Also, the Office of Corporate Relations has extensive programs devoted to technology transfer.

4. Although internal operations are, for the most part, beyond the scope of this case study, McGlenn credits Moore with turning NeoClone into a professional operation. Moore's background in law enabled him to take the lead on the company's contract negotiations and to deal with many other issues that otherwise would have fallen to McGlenn.

5. "Angel investor" is a term used to identify wealthy individuals who invest privately in developing firms. McGlenn cited several reasons for pursuing an angel investment as opposed to institutional venture capital: (1) angels tend to perform less "due diligence"; (2) angels are willing to take bigger risks at early stages in a company's development; and (3) angels do not require changes in the business structure. While these characterizations may not be universal, McGlenn claims that he has observed these differences across a number of investors.

6. Angel investors tend to have fewer resources at their disposal than institutional venture capitalists. As a result, negotiations over valuation can often be conducted with relatively little information. In this instance, the Madison angel investors had financial statements from NeoClone, and they called two of NeoClone's current customers. Otherwise, their approach to valuation was rather informal. In some instances, angel investors will hire an independent company to perform due diligence and provide investment advice.

prospect of obtaining common stock at some time in the future. Like most early-stage investors, these angels were willing to invest only if they had the potential to participate in the upside of the company through equity. Straight debt holds out the prospect of steady returns, but early-stage investors recognize that many of their investments will fail completely. They hope to compensate for those large failures with large successes, and the interest available from straight debt investments simply cannot reach the levels necessary to obtain such results.

In this instance, the angel investors created a company called NEOCL Investment LLC (NILLC) for the sole purpose of investing in NeoClone. In exchange for its $90,000 investment, NILLC received a Convertible Note due October 14, 2006 (exactly four years from the date of the investment). The Note would bear simple interest at a fixed rate of 12 percent, but NeoClone would not be required to make periodic cash payments. Instead, the interest would accrue and become due upon maturity of the Note.

Prior to maturity, one of four things might result in the extinguishment of the loan:

> (1) An action by NILLC to collect, prompted by an event of default by Neo-Clone. Usual events of default include the failure to make principal or interest payments — and those are included among the events of default in the Note Purchase Agreement here — but in this case, no payments of principal or interest prior to maturity were contemplated. The other events of default listed in the Note Purchase Agreement might prove more meaningful: the failure of NeoClone to observe any covenant,[7] the making of any materially untrue representation or warranty;[8] the acceleration of senior secured loans; and any voluntary or involuntary bankruptcy of NeoClone.
>
> (2) A "Qualified Financing" of NeoClone's shares. The term "Qualified Financing" is defined as follows:
>
>> (A) transaction closing on or prior to October 14, 2006 with each of the following characteristics:
>>
>>> (i) the Company (or its successor) issues equity securities in a single financing or a series of related financings;
>>>
>>> (ii) for at least $1,500,000 in cash proceeds;
>>>
>>> (iii) to one or more accredited investors (as defined in Regulation D under the Securities Act).

In all likelihood, the first financing that would meet this definition would be an investment by venture capitalists.[9] NeoClone will probably raise additional funds from angel investors prior to seeking venture capital, but angel

---

7. Most of the covenants should be relatively easy to maintain. Under the Note Purchase Agreement, NeoClone is required to furnish the angel investors with periodic financial statements, file appropriate tax returns, maintain its existence, provide notice of any actions by members, and reserve sufficient equity securities to cover the conversion of the Note. The covenant with the most important control implications is one requiring NeoClone to ensure the election of a representative of NILLC to the "Board of Advisors" (*i.e.*, the Management Committee) of NeoClone.

8. The representations and warranties included in the Note Purchase Agreement appear entirely typical for this sort of transaction. Generally speaking, NeoClone makes such representations and warranties to assure the investors that everything is as it appears with the company. For example, NeoClone represents that it is a Wisconsin LLC, that the Note Purchase Agreement has been duly authorized, that the company owns its intellectual property, and that NeoClone has no undisclosed liabilities.

9. According to McGlenn, the first venture financing will likely occur in 2004 at the earliest.

investments tend to be at amounts less than $1,500,000. In addition, NeoClone has obtained bank financing, but the definition of "Qualified Financing" is expressly limited to equity securities, thus excluding bank loans.

Upon the occurrence of a "Qualified Financing," the balance due on the Note is converted into stock of NeoClone that is "identical to the equity securities issued in the Qualified Financing except that if such securities are a senior series of a class of securities that is preferred with respect to liquidation or dividends, the Conversion Stock may be a junior series of the same class of preferred securities."

The conversion under this provision is accomplished by giving NILLC a number of shares equal to the principal balance of the Note, plus any accrued interest, divided by the "Conversion Price" (which is set in the note at 60 percent of the price per share paid in the Qualified Financing). Here's how it would work: assume that one year from the date of the angel investment, venture capitalists purchased 150,000 shares at $10 per share. The angel investors would receive $90,000 (principal) + $10,800 (one year's interest) = $100,800 ÷ $6 (that is, 60% of the $10 price paid by venture capitalists) = 16,800 shares.

(3) The sale of NeoClone. Upon the occurrence of a "Sale Event" — defined in the Note as "a sale of all or substantially all of the assets of the Company or a merger, consolidation or sale of equity interests (or stock) by the Company's members (or shareholders) immediately after which more than 50% of the equity securities of the Company are held by persons who were not members of the Company prior to such transaction" — NeoClone has the option of prepaying the Note without premium or penalty. Alternatively, the angel investors have the option of converting their debt claim into equity on the same terms as those available in a "Qualified Financing," except that the "Conversion Price" is established at "60% of the pre-conversion valuation of 100% of the Company's common equity implied by the Sale Event transaction price."

(4) An "Interim Equity Issuance" by NeoClone. The term "Interim Equity Issuance" is defined as follows:

[T]he issuance and sale by the Company of its equity securities at any time after the Company has issued, on a cumulative basis, equity securities with an aggregate purchase price of $510,000 after the date of this Note, excluding the issuance or sale of equity securities to employees or consultants of the Company.[10]

Unlike the conversion that occurs upon the completion of a "Qualified Financing," conversion under this provision is optional on the part of the angel investors. The transaction contemplated by this provision was an additional angel

10. The aggregate purchase price in this provision is not completely arbitrary. Another section of the Operating Agreement allows the company to issue additional interests, anticipating more angel investments on terms similar to the first investment:

The Members, by Majority Vote, must approve the issuance by the Company of any additional Interests except for . . . interests issuable upon conversion of up to $600,000 (original principal balance) of convertible notes in the form attached as Schedule 3.1(a)(i), of which convertible notes $90,000 principal amount is outstanding and $510,000 principal balance may be issued from and after the date of this Agreement with the approval of the Management Committee under section 5.8.

investment,[11] and the terms of the conversion would be the same as the conversion under the "Qualified Financing" provision, except that the "Conversion Price" is established at "60% of the price per share paid to the Company by the purchaser in the Interim Equity Issuance."

In addition to the foregoing provisions, the Note allows for optional conversion upon maturity. The basic idea of conversion remains the same — turning debt into equity — but the valuation in this instance cannot be tied to a "Qualified Financing," "Sale Event," or "Interim Equity Issuance." To overcome this problem, the parties simply assert that the conversion will be based on a specified valuation:

> The conversion price per share applicable to a conversion of the Note pursuant to this section 5(d) (the "Optional Conversion Stock Conversion Price") shall be an amount determined based on a $5 million pre-money valuation[12] of 100% of the Company's common equity on the date of conversion under this section 5(d) (the "Optional Conversion Date"). (For example, if there are 100,000 units of Company common equity issued and outstanding, the Optional Conversion Stock Conversion Price shall be $50.)

Given the current number of outstanding membership units (865,000, including outstanding options), the price for each additional unit would be $5.78. At this price, the angel investors would obtain just over 23,000 units,[13] which is less than 3 percent of the total equity ownership of the company.

The founders of NeoClone formed a Wisconsin LLC on July 9, 1999, and they still own a substantial majority of the membership units in NeoClone. Control of the company is specified primarily under a detailed Operating Agreement, which has been signed by all eight individual members — the three founders, Deven McGlenn, Allen Clark, Richard Burgess,[14] Nancy Thompson,[15] and Amy Davison Clark. In addition, the Operating Agreement has been signed by NeoClone's two institutional members — WARF and Breakthrough Development Co. LLC, a Madison company that provided strategic development services to NeoClone in exchange for a small equity share.

It is worth noting that the angel investors are not parties to the Operating Agreement. According to McGlenn, the angel investors were not interested in having an active involvement in the operation of NeoClone. While most of the angel investors have had long and successful business careers, they are not usually eager to spend their days running a start-up company.

---

11. According to McGlenn, NeoClone will raise additional angel financing after the initial angel investment and prior to the first venture financing.

12. "Pre-money valuation" refers to the value of the company prior to the investment contemplated. If the angel investors elect to convert their debt claim into equity, they would be effectively investing an additional $133,200 (the principal amount plus four years' interest on the note), and this amount would be added to the pre-money valuation when determining the valuation of the company after the investment ("post-money").

13. The principal amount plus four years' interest on the note would be $133,200. The amount, divided by $5.78 per share, equals approximately 23,045 units.

14. Burgess is a prominent researcher at the University of Wisconsin. He obtained a PhD in Biochemistry and Molecular Biology with Dr. James Watson at Harvard University, and he has since received numerous awards — including a Guggenheim Fellowship. He also serves as Chairman of the Board of NeoClone.

15. Thompson is an employee of Richard Burgess's laboratory who provides expertise on certain NeoClone products.

The capital structure of NeoClone consists of two major categories of claimants: members, who have equity claims, and creditors, who have debt claims. The three founders of NeoClone own 72 percent of the outstanding membership units, ignoring options and units issuable upon the conversion of a note. The creditors include banks and the angel investors discussed above. The bank extended a $75,000 equipment line of credit and a $100,000 general operating line of credit in the fall of 2000. In each instance, these loans were personally guaranteed by Mark Jackson, Donal Kaehler, Allen Clark, Richard Burgess, and Deven McGlenn.

Like most LLCs, NeoClone has some attributes that resemble a corporation and others that resemble a partnership. When analyzing the attributes of a business entity, it is common to think about "control rights" and "financial rights." While there may be some overlap — control can dictate access to the money, and financial rights can provide leverage — these are useful categories to the extent that they help to organize the many attributes of the relationship.

Control Rights

Control rights include (1) the composition and powers of the management committee; (2) the right to bind the company as an agent; (3) the right to determine membership; and (4) voting rights.

Management Committee. The Operating Agreement creates a Management Committee, which is composed of up to seven members. The Management Committee functions somewhat like a board of directors in a corporation, except that it does not possess general management authority over the LLC. Instead, all of the functions of NeoClone's Management Committee are defined in the Operating Agreement. Most important, the Management Committee must approve any fundamental transaction (for example, merger, dissolution, or sale of all or substantially all of the assets of the LLC), any amendment to the Operating Agreement, any purchase or sale of membership interests, any agreement between the LLC and a member, and any incurrence of indebtedness in excess of $100,000. In addition, the Management Committee has authority over certain ordinary business matters, such as a change in the company's principal place of business, a decision to expand the business beyond Wisconsin, allocations of profits and losses to member capital accounts, distributions to members of cash from operations, and approval of any transfers of membership interests. Finally, the Management Committee has the power to remove or replace "Managers."[16]

The Operating Agreement does not specify annual elections of the Management Committee, though such a result might be the negative implication of the Operating Agreement's statement that Managers of the LLC "shall not stand for annual election." The Operating Agreement designated Richard Burgess, Mark Jackson, Donal Kaehler, Deven McGlenn, and a representative selected by NILLC as the initial members of the Management Committee. Interestingly, as of six months after the investment, NILLC still had not found a suitable representative, and its place on the Management Committee remained vacant.

---

16. Note that "Managers" are different from members of the Management Committee — which the Operating Agreement refers to as "Representatives" — and are discussed more thoroughly below.

Power to Bind. Under the default rules of partnership law, each partner is an agent of the partnership and can bind the partnership when acting within the ordinary course of business. Shareholders, on the other hand, are not agents of the corporation simply by virtue of holding shares. Like most LLC statutes, the Wisconsin LLC statute embraces the partnership rule for member-managed firms and the corporate rule for manager-managed firms. Wis. Stat. § 183.0301.

NeoClone is a manager-managed LLC,[17] and the Operating Agreement understandably invokes the corporate rule, providing that the Managers and agents authorized by the Managers are the only people who may bind the LLC.[18] In acting on behalf of the LLC, both Managers and members — and presumably the Representatives on the Management Committee — owe fiduciary duties to the LLC. Wis. Stat. § 183.0402.

As noted above, these Managers are distinct from the Management Committee. The Operating Agreement provides for one to four Managers, who appear to be similar to officers in a corporation. Managers are not elected annually,[19] but serve at the pleasure of the Management Committee and the members. The Operating Agreement designated Mark Jackson, Donal Kaehler, and Deven McGlenn as the initial managers of the LLC, and Jeff Moore has since been added.

Membership. Membership in the LLC is regulated through a web of interlocking provisions in the Operating Agreement. The default rule under partnership law would require a vote of all partners to admit a new partner, while corporate law would allow free transfer of shares. NeoClone's Operating Agreement requires a majority vote prior to the issuance of any additional membership units, thus restricting the admission of new members to some degree, but permitting the addition of a new member with less than unanimous approval. Membership is also controlled by the classic transfer restriction, a right of first refusal. While these are not common in partnerships — where the only transferable interest in the partnership is financial and a right of first refusal is seen as unnecessary — they are *de rigueur* in closely held corporations. The right of first refusal provides that if a member receives from a third party a bona fide offer to purchase a membership interest, NeoClone retains a right to purchase the membership interest on the same terms offered by the third party. The Operating Agreement adds a partnership-like twist to this otherwise ordinary provision, in that it specifies that a nonmember purchaser of the membership interest may not exercise control rights — even after a valid purchase — unless the Management Committee of the LLC approves.[20]

17. Under the Wisconsin LLC statute, the default rule requires member management. LLCs that want to be manager-managed must make that election in the articles of organization, Wis. Stat. § 183.0401, which NeoClone has done.

18. In deciding "any matter connected with the business of" NeoClone, the Managers are required to act by majority consent. Wis. Stat. § 183.0404(1)(b).

19. Wis. Stat. § 183.0401 (providing that each manager "[s]hall hold office until a successor is elected and qualified, or until prior death, resignation or removal").

20. The Wisconsin LLC statute requires unanimous consent of the members, unless the operating agreement provides otherwise. Wis. Stat. § 183.0706.

The Operating Agreement also strictly regulates the withdrawal of members, providing that any voluntary withdrawal is considered a breach of the Operating Agreement. This portion of the agreement has a distinctly partnership feel, as it refers to "dissociation" from and "dissolution" of the LLC.[21] In most instances, the withdrawal of a member does not result in dissolution of the LLC;[22] moreover, the withdrawing member is not entitled to a buyout from the LLC.[23] Instead, the successor of the dissociated member is entitled to "receive the distributions and to share in the allocations of profits and losses to which the dissociated Member would have been entitled," but the successor cannot exercise any control rights.

Voting Rights. Under statutory default rules, partners are entitled to one vote per partner, while shareholders are entitled to as many votes as shares they own. NeoClone has embraced the corporate rule. As noted above, members of the LLC elect the Management Committee, remove or replace Managers, and exercise joint control rights with the Management Committee over such matters as the issuance of additional membership interests and the approval of fundamental transactions (just as corporate shareholders exercise joint control with boards of directors over similar matters).[24]

Financial Rights

Financial rights include (1) the right to share in profits (and the corresponding obligation to share in losses); (2) the right to a return of capital; (3) the right to distributions; and (4) limited liability.

Sharing Profits and Losses. NeoClone's allocation of profits and losses takes cues from both partnerships and corporations. Under the statutory default rules, general partnerships allocate profits and losses equally among the partners. Even if the equal-sharing rule is altered by contract, pass-through taxation requires the use of capital accounts to allocate profits and losses to the individual partners. By contrast, the default rules of corporate law do not provide for any allocation of profits and losses to common shareholders. Any profits or losses belong to the corporation itself, and common shareholders possess a claim against the residual assets of the corporation (that is, those assets that remain once all of the other obligations of the corporation have been paid). A shareholder's claim against such residual assets is based on the level of the shareholder's investment, as opposed to the equal-sharing rule of general

---

21. This follows the Wisconsin LLC statute, which uses the same sort of partnership language. Wis. Stat. § 183.0802.

22. Indeed, the Operating Agreement lists only four events that result in dissolution: (a) the sale of all or substantially all of the company's assets; (b) the majority vote of the members to dissolve; (c) the happening of any event that would make it unlawful to conduct the company's business; or (d) the entry of a decree of dissolution under the relevant section of the Wisconsin LLC statute. The Operating Agreement expressly provides that a dissociation does not lead to dissolution of the LLC unless the members vote to dissolve. Under the default rules in the Wisconsin LLC statute, NeoClone would dissolve after any dissociation unless all of the remaining members voted to continue. Wis. Stat. § 183.0901(4).

23. This changes the default rule under the Wisconsin LLC statute, which provides: "if not otherwise provided in the operating agreement, within a reasonable time after dissociation, the dissociating member is entitled to receive a distribution in complete redemption of the fair value of the member's interest in the limited liability company as of the date of dissociation. . . ." Wis. Stat. § 183.0604.

24. The right of members to vote on fundamental transactions is granted in the Wisconsin LLC statute. Wis. Stat. § 183.0404(2).

partnerships. Of course, any losses incurred by the corporation would reduce the capital of the shareholders, but losses in excess of capital contributions are capped through the rule of limited liability.

The default rule of Wisconsin's LLC statute states that "profits and losses . . . shall be allocated among the members in the manner provided in an operating agreement."[25] Under the Operating Agreement, NeoClone's members have agreed to a complex sharing of profits and losses that follows generally the investment level of the members (corporate rule), but uses capital accounts like those found in general partnerships.[26] The basic allocation provisions read as follows:

4.1 PROFITS AND LOSSES

(a) Profits. Profits shall be allocated as follows:

(i) First, to the Interest Holders, pro rata based on the Losses allocated to them pursuant to section 4.1(b)(iii) hereof until each Interest Holder has been allocated an amount of Profits pursuant to this section 4.1(a)(i) in the current and previous fiscal years that equals the Losses allocated to that Interest Holder pursuant to section 4.1(b)(iii) hereof in the previous fiscal years; (ii) Second, to the Interest Holders, pro rata based on the Losses allocated to them pursuant to section 4.1(b)(ii) hereof until each Interest Holder has been allocated an amount of Profits pursuant to this section 4.1(a)(ii) in the current and previous fiscal years that equals the Losses allocated to that Interest Holder pursuant to section 4.1(b)(ii) hereof in the previous fiscal years; and (iii) Thereafter, to all the Interest Holders, pro rata in accordance with the number of Interests held by each Interest Holder.

(b) Losses. Losses shall be allocated as follows:

(i) First, to the Interest Holders, pro rata based on the Profits allocated to them pursuant to sections 4.1(a)(iii) hereof until each Interest Holder has been allocated an amount of Losses pursuant to this section 4.1(b)(i) in the current and previous fiscal years equal to the Profits allocated to that Interest Holder pursuant to section 4.1(a)(iii) hereof in the previous fiscal years.

(ii) Second, to the Interest Holders based on their respective positive Capital Accounts, until each Interest Holder has been allocated an amount of Losses pursuant to this section 4.1(b)(ii) in the current and previous fiscal years to reduce that Interest Holder's Capital Account to zero.

(iii) Thereafter, to all the Interest Holders, pro rata based in accordance with the number of Interests held by such Interest Holder.

---

25. Wis. Stat. § 183.0503. In the absence of an operating agreement, profits and losses are allocated "on the basis of value, as stated in the [LLC's] records." *Id.*
26. The capital accounts are described in the Operating Agreement as follows:

A separate Capital Account shall be maintained for each Interest Holder. Each such Capital Account shall be increased by (a) the amount of money and the fair market value of property contributed by the Interest Holder to the Company (net of liabilities secured by such property which the Company is considered to assume or take subject to pursuant to Section 752 of the Code) and (b) allocations to the Interest Holder of Profits, and shall be decreased by (c) the amount of money and fair market value of property distributed to the Interest Holder by the Company (net of liabilities secured by such property which the Interest Holder is considered to assume or take subject to . . . Section 752 of the Code), and (d) allocations to the Interest Holder of Losses, and shall be increased or decreased by (e) special allocations of income, gain, loss or deduction as provided in sections 4.4, 4.5, 4.6, 4.7, and 4.8 of this Agreement, and (f) any other allocation or adjustment as provided under Treasury Regulations Section 1.704-1(b).

Return of Capital. Partners are entitled to a return of any capital contributions, but shareholders are not. Although NeoClone employs capital accounts to keep track of each member's contributions, the Operating Agreement expressly forswears any obligation to return capital contributions. Nevertheless, capital contributions increase a member's capital account, and the capital account is the basis for distribution upon liquidation of the LLC. As a result, capital contributions count.

Distributions. The differences between partnerships and corporations with respect to the rules governing distributions during the life of the firm are minimal. In most instances, the decision to distribute assets to equity claimants is left to the discretion of the firm's managers, whether those managers are partners or directors. The same holds true under most LLC statutes.[27] NeoClone does not break any new ground here, as it grants the Management Committee power to determine whether a distribution is in order.[28] Once the decision to make a distribution is made, it is done in accordance with each member's ownership interest.[29]

Separate distribution questions arise upon liquidation of the firm. As noted above, the use of capital accounts ensures that partners are given credit for capital contributions, while such contributions are not considered for shareholders, who receive an amount commensurate with their ownership percentage regardless of the amounts contributed to obtain that percentage. NeoClone's Operating Agreement includes a partnership-like distribution provision:

> Following the winding up of the Company, . . . the cash and other assets of the Company shall be applied first to the payment of all debts and liabilities of the Company including any loans from a Member (which for such purpose shall be treated the same as all other Company liabilities) and all expenses of liquidation, and the remainder shall be distributed to the Interest Holders in accordance with the positive balances in their Capital Accounts. . . .

Limited Liability. Obviously, one of the primary motivations for choosing an LLC over a general partnership is limited liability. NeoClone's Operating Agreement states flatly: "No Member shall be liable for the debts, obligations and liabilities of the Company except as expressly provided by the [Wisconsin LLC] Act."[30] In addition, the provision describing distributions upon liquidation of the LLC are intended to ensure that members will enjoy limited liability:

> If following the dissolution and liquidation of the Company, the Company's assets remaining after payment and discharge of the liabilities, obligations and expenses

---

27. *See, e.g.,* Wis. Stat. § 183.0601 (allowing interim distributions in accordance with the operating agreement, or, in the absence of an operating agreement, as determined by the managers).

28. The one exception here is that NeoClone follows the common practice of general partnerships in providing for an annual distribution sufficient for the payment of any tax liabilities arising from an allocation of profits.

29. *Cf.* Wis. Stat. § 183.0602 (deferring to the operating agreement, but in the absence of an operating agreement, distributions to be allocated in the same manner as profits).

30. The section of the Wisconsin LLC statute providing for limited liability (Wis. Stat. § 183.0304) expressly identifies two instances in which a member might incur personal liability. Members are responsible to follow through on promised contributions (Wis. Stat. § 183.0502), and both members and managers are responsible for wrongful distributions (Wis. Stat. § 183.0608).

of the Company, including any liabilities to any one or more of the Members, are insufficient to return any amount to a Member, such Member shall have no recourse or further right or claim against any other Member by reason of such insufficiency. No Member shall be obligated to eliminate any deficit balance in such Member's Capital Account.

Despite these provisions, members of NeoClone could be personally liable under the doctrine of "piercing the veil." Like many of its counterparts in other states, the Wisconsin LLC statute provides that "nothing in this chapter shall preclude a court from ignoring the limited liability company entity under principles of common law that are similar to those applicable to business corporations and shareholders in this state." Wis. Stat. § 183.0304(2).

QUESTIONS

1. According to McGlenn, venture capitalists have told him that the company would need to become a corporation before receiving venture capital. Can you imagine why venture capitalists would make such a demand? Why did Neo-Clone's founders decide to form an LLC?

2. Business planners have long sought to combine limited liability with pass-through taxation and have used limited partnerships and S Corporations to accomplish that purpose. LLCs provide a simple mechanism for achieving the same result. Can you see any reasons to embrace the LLC aside from this favorable combination of attributes? In other words, do the default rules in the Wisconsin LLC statute, discussed above, provide a combination of attributes that is difficult to replicate with other business forms?

3. Why did NeoClone adopt a three-tiered management structure consisting of Managers, a Management Committee, and Members?

CHAPTER
4

Organization and Structure of a Corporation

MOTIVATING HYPOTHETICAL

Josh is an Olympic swimmer who is a hometown hero in his native Chapel Hill, North Carolina. He wants to open a community swimming facility in Chapel Hill that will offer aquatic recreation to community residents and prepare up-and-coming athletes for competitive swimming. Although Josh is unfamiliar with business practices or how to operate a swimming facility, he thinks it will be successful if he takes advantage of his status in the community by using his personal brand in advertising, making personal appearances, and training at the pool in the off-season. Josh shared his idea with his swim coach, Sherrie, a former Olympic swimmer herself, who loves the idea as a way to help promote the sport. Together, they decide to move forward with the business.

We now turn to the subject that will occupy our attention throughout the remainder of the book — corporate governance. In its driest form, corporate governance can be conceived as the study of forces — both legal and nonlegal — that regulate the powers and duties of directors, officers, and shareholders. Yet, that definition misses as much as it includes, leaving out the sense of drama and conflict that imbues the study of corporate governance today. In the materials that follow, we will encounter troubling human character flaws — greed, pride, dishonesty, selfishness, and laziness — as well as some inspiring virtues. Our principal task is to explore the capacity of legal rules to encourage cooperation and constrain destructive behavior among the various participants in a corporate enterprise. Although we tend to focus on legal rules, the limits of law will become clear fairly early in our study. Markets, reputational constraints, trust, altruism, and norms pick up much of the slack. In the end, the study of corporate governance is the study of human relations. The trick is to construct a system under which the participants cooperate for mutual benefit. As you may know from your own experiences, that is easier said than done.

In thinking about corporate governance, we begin by identifying the *dramatis personae.* The American conception of corporate governance traditionally focuses on three roles: officer, director, and shareholder. Many countries outside the United States have a broader conception of corporate governance, placing creditors, employees, communities, and society at large among the relevant constituencies of corporate law. While this broader "stakeholder" conception of the corporation has occasionally prevailed in the United States, especially in the context of debates about hostile takeovers, the traditional "shareholder" conception still dominates.

Officers (with titles such as Chief Executive Officer, President, and Chief Financial Officer) are in charge of the day-to-day operations of the corporation. These are the most senior employees of the corporation, and they make many of the decisions that define a corporation's activities. Perhaps surprisingly, corporate law has little to say about officers. Instead, the law of corporations concentrates on directors and shareholders. (The top officers in the corporation typically are also members of the board of directors, which may partially explain that gap.)

Directors are elected by shareholders to supervise the officers. In short, directors are the shareholders' representatives within the corporation. For this reason, some people understand corporate governance as a species of political theory that analyzes the distribution of power within the corporation.

Directors typically have no authority to act as individuals. Instead, they act as a collective body known as a board of directors. Many of the issues that arise under corporate law relate to conflicts between the board of directors and the shareholders.

Shareholders are sometimes referred to as the "owners" of the corporation, though exactly what that means has been heavily debated. We will pursue a more textured understanding of the shareholder role by examining the rights and obligations of shareholders in some detail. For the moment, it will suffice to say that shareholders possess important control rights — including the right to elect directors and to vote on fundamental transactions, such as mergers — as well as the right to all of the assets of the corporation once the corporation's creditors have been paid in a liquidation. Unlike partners in a general partnership, shareholders are not personally liable for the obligations of the corporation; they have limited liability.

This brief description of officers, directors, and shareholders risks portraying the corporate governance system in deceptively simple terms. Indeed, the basic principles underlying the corporate governance system are fairly easy to state, but these general principles do not capture the myriad ways in which these players interact. It is in these interactions that we find most of the complexity and intrigue associated with corporate governance.

Perhaps the most important factor in determining the nature of the interaction among officers, directors, and shareholders is ownership structure. While much of corporate law applies to all corporations regardless of ownership structure, courts, legislatures, and commentators often distinguish between "public corporations" — whose shares are owned by a large number of investors and are traded in the public securities markets — and "closely held corporations" — whose shares are owned by a small number of shareholders without access to the public securities markets.

The distinction between public and closely held corporations is fundamental for a number of reasons. First, the ownership structure often determines the identities of officers, directors, and shareholders. In a public corporation, officers, directors, and shareholders typically are three distinct groups of people. While some overlap is common — for example, the chief executive officer of a public corporation is usually a director (often the chairman of the board of directors), and large shareholders sometimes have representatives on the board of directors — the distinctions among these groups are the source of many conflicts. By contrast, in a closely held corporation, overlapping roles are the norm, not the exception. It is not uncommon for one person to be simultaneously a shareholder, a director, and an officer of a close corporation.

The difference in the composition of shareholders, directors, and officers of public and close corporations elicits different mechanisms of control in the two types of corporation. In a public corporation, for example, the formal mechanisms of control are exercised primarily by the board of directors, which has the statutory power to manage the affairs of the corporation. Shareholders control the directors, if at all, through annual elections of directors and through voting on specific proposals, when allowed. Shareholder oversight in public corporations traditionally has been weak, although the increased power of institutional investors (such as state pension funds, private pension funds, or mutual funds more generally) recently has begun to change the dynamics of public corporations. Thus, it has been observed that there is a separation of ownership (the shareholders) and control (the management) in public corporations, even given activist shareholder institutional investors. In close corporations, on the other hand, the formal mechanisms of control are exercised primarily by the shareholders, who often govern by prior agreement embodied in contracts among themselves rather than by rules embodied in the corporation statutes. So dominant are shareholders in the close corporation that many states permit them to eliminate the board of directors.

A second reason that the distinction between public and closely held corporations is fundamental is that public corporations are subject to a demanding set of disclosure requirements under federal securities law. With the exception of prohibitions against fraud, which apply to all sales of securities, federal securities law is largely silent in the context of closely held corporations. The invocation of federal securities law in the public corporation context raises interesting issues of federalism (the intersection of federal and state law), which we examine in subsequent chapters.

Federal securities law requires public reporting companies to provide to the markets quarterly and annual disclosure of large quantities of specified information, including financial results, significant business risks and contingencies, financial relationships with managers and directors, significant litigation, aspects of executive compensation, information on managers' and directors' experience, and the like. Not only does this mandatory securities disclosure provide one mechanism of accountability within the corporation, but it may shape the kinds of decisions managers make (perhaps to emphasize short-term financial results over longer-term investments), and it certainly informs the investment and voting decisions shareholders make. Given the important overlay of federal securities regulation onto state corporation statutes, we emphasize federal securities regulation from the beginning in this study of corporate governance.

A third important distinction between public and closely held corporations relates to the so-called "market for corporate control." Public corporations are subject to the threat of being taken over by another company gaining control of a majority of the corporation's outstanding stock. The mechanisms for such takeovers will be studied below, but for the present, it is enough to understand that the threat of a hostile takeover is a major factor that shapes corporate law.

Indeed, today many of the most important cases examining the fiduciary duties of managers and directors involve battles for control, as do many cases about shareholder voting powers, the structure of articles of incorporation and corporate bylaws (the documents that set out the rules of the corporation and the distribution of powers between directors or officers and shareholders), and even such seemingly prosaic issues as whether a special directors' meeting was properly called. Given the importance of the market for corporate control, we will emphasize that aspect of many of the cases below.

Now that we have become acquainted with the principal players in our drama and have acquired a basic understanding of the importance of ownership structure, it is time to say a word about the sources of corporate law. Corporation statutes govern the relations among shareholders, directors, and officers of a corporation. Like general partnership statutes, corporation statutes have been adopted by all of the 50 states. Because of the so-called "internal affairs doctrine," the rules governing the relations between officers, directors, and shareholders are taken from the state of incorporation.

Delaware has long been the most popular state of incorporation for public corporations, which are said to select a state of incorporation based primarily on the sophistication of the state's corporation law, including not only the corporation statute, but also common law decisions in the state. As a result, the Delaware General Corporation Law (DGCL) is an important source of corporation law.

Closely held corporations tend to be less concerned with the sophistication of a state's corporation law because the issues resolved by a highly sophisticated system of corporation law—for example, the fiduciary standards applicable to directors in a hostile takeover—usually do not arise in a close corporation context. Founders of closely held corporations, therefore, tend to be motivated more by the initial costs of incorporation and the annual costs of maintaining the corporate form. These costs are often lowest when the incorporation occurs in the state where the business is located. Many states outside Delaware have adopted versions of the Model Business Corporation Act (Model Act), which was prepared by the Committee on Corporation Laws of the Business Law Section of the American Bar Association. As a result, in our study of corporate law we will often look both at Delaware provisions and at the provisions of the Model Act.

A. INCORPORATION

Unlike general partnerships under the Uniform Partnership Act (UPA), corporations are without question legal entities with identities separate from the owners (shareholders) of the corporation. The process by which the separate legal entity is created is called incorporation. This Section briefly discusses the mechanics of incorporation and covers certain aspects of organizing a corporation that follow incorporation.

Incorporation today is a simple process, although it was not always so. Prior to the widespread adoption of general incorporation statutes in the mid-1800s, corporations in the United States were formed only by legislative action, usually by a state legislature. This process allowed the state legislatures to exert significant control over the businesses within their respective states. Although legislatures rarely granted monopoly powers to corporations expressly, it was not uncommon for corporations to have implicit monopolies for public works projects, such as building bridges, canals, or roads. In such cases, the legislature would simply grant a charter to only one corporation, thus ensuring a monopoly. This process sometimes led to corruption, as people bribed legislatures to obtain grants of monopoly power.

During the Jacksonian period of American politics, populism swept the United States and corporate law was a prime target. The old system was displaced through the passage of general incorporation statutes — "general" because any eligible person could form a corporation without a special act of the legislature. Over time the requirements for incorporation have become exceedingly simple. Most statutes require only one person to form a corporation. Traditionally at least three incorporators and three directors were required. Although many states retain the requirement of three directors, most states allow only one incorporator. The corporation comes into existence when articles of incorporation are filed with the state, unless a later effective date is specified.

The organizing document that is used to incorporate a company is called either the "articles of incorporation" or, in Delaware, the "certificate of incorporation." We sometimes use the term "charter," which is a generic term that refers either to the articles of incorporation or to the certificate of incorporation, whichever is the name of the organizing document in a particular state. Charters are required to include certain provisions, including the name of the corporation, the number of authorized shares of stock, and the name and address of a registered agent in the state of incorporation. *See generally* DGCL § 102(a); Model Act § 2.02(a). Under Delaware law, the charter must also include the purpose of the corporation, which can be as general as "to engage in any lawful purpose for which a corporation may be organized." DGCL § 102(a)(3).

In addition to the required provisions, most well-advised corporations include some of the following additional provisions:

> *Initial Directors.* Many charters provide the names and addresses of the corporation's initial directors. If initial directors are not named in the articles of incorporation, the incorporators must hold an organizational meeting after incorporation and elect the directors. The initial directors of the corporation typically complete the organization of the corporation, which includes the appointment of officers of the corporation, the sale of shares of capital stock of the corporation, and various other administrative tasks.

> *Corporate Purposes.* A charter under the Model Act may contain a statement of the purposes of the corporation, Model Act § 2.02(b)(2)(i), and as stated above, under Delaware law the charter must contain a statement of the corporate purpose. DGCL § 102(a)(3). During the 1800s and early 1900s, a statement of purposes was important to defining the limits of a corporation's activity. When corporations were created by state legislatures, their charters typically had narrow purpose clauses, and if a corporation exceeded the purposes stated in its charter, it was said to be acting "*ultra vires,*" which means literally "beyond powers." Over time corporations were allowed to list multiple purposes in the corporate charter. By the turn of the century, most newly formed corporations listed hundreds of purposes in the charter to prevent the possibility of acting *ultra vires.* Modern incorporation statutes eliminate most cases in which *ultra vires* could be used as a claim by the corporation or any party doing business with the corporation to avoid contractual commitments.

Corporation statutes eventually permitted corporations to include a provision in the charter stating that the corporation may engage in any lawful business. Although common today, such provisions did not obtain immediate acceptance. Even today, some corporate charters limit the extent of the corporation's actions. This occurs most often because the corporation is limited by some other regulation (for example, banks and insurance companies are subject to other state and federal regulation of their activities) or because one of the founders of the corporation desires to restrict the activities of the corporation. When a limitation is expressed in the corporation's charter, there are three means of enforcing it: (1) a shareholder suit against the corporation; (2) a suit by the corporation against directors or officers for actions beyond the purpose; or (3) an involuntary judicial dissolution proceeding by the attorney general.

Management Provisions. A charter may include provisions for managing the business and regulating the affairs of the corporation. Well-written charters usually contain some such provisions. Although many management provisions are statutory or are contained in the corporation's bylaws (see below), some provisions are placed in charters to insulate them from change by the shareholders. Since under the controlling statutes only the directors may propose changes to the charter (which must be approved by the shareholders to be effective), *see* DGCL § 242(b)(1); Model Act § 10.03(a), putting management provisions in the charter protects them from shareholder-initiated changes. So, for instance, the charter may require "cause" for a director to be removed from the board at any time other than the annual shareholders' meeting. Such a "for cause" limitation on removal makes it more difficult for an outsider to take control of the firm by buying a controlling block of shares and calling a special meeting to replace the board. Other provisions are placed in the charter because the statute requires it. For example, a provision placing exclusive power to amend the bylaws with the shareholders must appear in the charter.

Bylaw Provisions. The articles of incorporation may include any provision required or permitted to be in the bylaws. The purpose of placing such a provision in the charter rather than in the bylaws is to prevent the amendment of the provision without approval by both the board of directors and the shareholders.

Director Liability. Most modern charters limit the liability of directors for money damages, subject to certain enumerated exceptions. This type of provision, called an "exculpatory provision," first appeared in corporation statutes in the mid-1980s after the Delaware Supreme Court decided in Smith v. Van Gorkom, 488 A.2d 858 (1985), that the directors of a publicly held corporation were personally liable for breach of the duty of care in a merger context. The *Van Gorkom* decision sent shock waves through boardrooms, as directors feared personal liability on a scale never before contemplated. In most states, an exculpatory provision eliminating director liability is optional, not self-executing. (Self-executing statutes appear in a few states, such as Florida, Indiana, Ohio, Maine, and Wisconsin.) A "self-executing" exculpatory statute limits director liability even absent a provision in the articles of incorporation. Even in states with optional statutes, most charters now routinely include an exculpatory provision limiting director liability.

Indemnification. Indemnification is another method of protecting directors from personal liability in their capacity as directors. Modern incorporation statutes allow a corporation to offer mandatory indemnification, subject to certain exceptions.

In addition to required and optional provisions in the corporate charter, modern incorporation statutes are notable for the things that they *do not* require. The following two types of provisions at one time were required in corporate charters:

Duration. Corporation statutes sometimes require the charter to set forth the duration of the corporation's existence and allow the duration to be perpetual. Reflecting the modern trend, Model Act § 3.02 presumes that the corporation is perpetual unless the articles of incorporation provide otherwise.

Initial Capital. Corporation statutes sometimes require the charter to set forth a certain minimum amount of capital, usually $1,000. The Model Act reflects the modern trend toward the elimination of all minimum capital requirements.

The act of incorporating seems simple enough. Indeed, it is a ministerial action that does not require specialized training. Nevertheless, corporate law is high on formality. The detailed work that accompanies an incorporation may have profound effects on the future of the company, as demonstrated in the following case. In addition to the importance of formal rules, notice the actions of the law firm. Who was the firm's client before the conflict manifested itself? Did the firm act properly in the face of conflict?

GRANT v. MITCHELL

2001 WL 221509 (unpublished)
Delaware Court of Chancery
February 23, 2001

STRINE, Vice Chancellor.

Plaintiff Ralph Grant brings this action under 8 Del. C. § 225 to determine the proper directors and officers of nominal defendant, Epasys, Inc. Grant contends that he is the sole director of Epasys, under authority of an incorporator's consent he executed on August 24, 2000.

Defendant Julee Mitchell denies Grant's contention and argues that Grant had earlier exercised his authority as sole incorporator to create a two-person board comprised of Mitchell and himself. In support of that argument, Mitchell points out that Grant signed a sworn "Foreign Corporation Certificate" on January 7, 2000 that identified Epasys's directors and officers. The Foreign Corporation Certificate identified Grant and Mitchell as the directors.

In this post-trial opinion, I conclude that it is more likely than not that Grant named an initial board of directors comprised of Mitchell and himself at or around the time Epasys was incorporated. The most reliable evidence in the record — the Foreign Corporation Certificate and documents created by the lawyers Grant chose to represent Epasys — supports this conclusion.

As a result, Grant's attempt to name himself as sole director in August 2000 was invalid and Mitchell is entitled to judgment in her favor.

I. FACTUAL BACKGROUND

A. THE GENESIS OF EPASYS

This case requires this court to address a small sliver of a much larger dispute among the founders of Epasys. The founders of Epasys were plaintiff Grant, defendant Mitchell, and non-party Jack Meltzer.

The founders began their relationship in 1998. At that time, Mitchell and Meltzer were seeking to bring a computer software program, "Monitor," to market. Monitor was designed to help businesses keep track of the federal and state environmental requirements (*e.g.*, discharge limits) that apply to their facilities and operations. Grant was then working for a systems integration business,* and had cash resources he could invest.

The founders agreed to try to develop Monitor into a commercially viable program under the rubric of a business named Phoenix Environmental, LLC ("Phoenix"), an Arizona limited liability company. Grant agreed to invest $500,000 as an initial matter, in exchange for one-third of Phoenix's stock. Mitchell and Meltzer, who are romantic as well as business partners, held the remaining two-thirds interest.

In 1999, Grant invested another $500,000 into Phoenix. In exchange, he was given 9% more stock and the right to use all of the tax losses generated by Phoenix. Thus, as of that time, Grant owned 42% of Phoenix's equity, and Mitchell and Meltzer held 29% apiece.

Later in 1999, the founders began the process of converting Phoenix from an LLC into a corporation. It was the intention of the founders to seek venture capital financing for the new corporation and to add representatives of the investors to the new corporation's board of directors. The founders were apparently optimistic that they could obtain such outside financing in a relatively short time. The founders also decided to relocate the business from Phoenix, Arizona to Boston, Massachusetts.

B. THE FOUNDERS SEEK THE ADVICE OF MCDERMOTT, WILL & EMERY

To assist them in the task of forming a new corporation, the founders consulted with John Egan, a corporate partner at the Boston office of McDermott, Will & Emery. According to Egan, he informed the founders that it was typical for a party like Grant, who was putting in cash equity, to get a preferred or priority equity position, and for sweat equity investors like Mitchell and Meltzer to get equity positions that were earned over time. The rationale for this distinction was that venture capitalists who would want to invest in the business would want assurance that the sweat equity was actually delivered before Mitchell and Meltzer became vested in their ownership positions.

Egan claims that the founders discussed the fact that Grant would have control of the corporation until the new investors came on board. Egan also says that the founders discussed the fact that Grant would be the incorporator of the new corporation, which the founders agreed to call Epasys.

Egan also testified that the founders discussed the composition of Epasys's board of directors. He says that the founders agreed that there would eventually

---

*A systems integrator combines computer hardware and software from different vendors into a coordinated whole.

be a five-person board comprised of Grant, Mitchell, and three representatives of the new outside investors.

Grant's recollection of the meeting is substantially similar to Egan's. Grant claims that it was agreed that he would have control, and that he would have the sole right to select the board as the incorporator.

Mitchell, however, denies that she was advised by Egan that Grant was to have sole power to select the board by virtue of his status as incorporator. And while she admits that Egan did discuss the priority often given to cash investors, she contends that she and Meltzer never assented to giving such priority to Grant and never would have.

C. EPASYS IS INCORPORATED

After the meeting with Egan, the founders proceeded with the creation of Epasys. On December 23, 1999, Epasys's certificate of incorporation was filed with the Secretary of State's office. The certificate named Ralph Grant as incorporator.

McDermott, Will also prepared two other documents dated December 23, 1999. One of the documents was a "Unanimous Written Consent of the Directors in Lieu of an Organizational Meeting." The directors' consent purported to adopt the second of the documents, a set of bylaws. The directors' consent also elected Ralph Grant as President, and Julee Mitchell as Treasurer and Secretary of Epasys. Finally, the directors' consent purported to ratify actions taken by Grant as incorporator in a consent dated December 22, 1999.

The directors' consent had signature lines for Grant and Mitchell, thus signifying that the creator of the document believed that they were the two initial directors of Epasys selected by Grant as incorporator. The directors' consent, however, was never executed. Nor has the incorporator's consent of December 22, 1999 emerged.

In his deposition testimony, however, Grant recalled receiving the bylaws at the time Epasys was incorporated. Grant assumed that he signed the bylaws and that the bylaws were valid.

D. THE FOUNDERS' DIVERGENT TESTIMONY ABOUT THE COMPOSITION OF EPASYS'S BOARD

Grant contends that before Epasys began doing business, he and the other founders discussed two critical subjects: (1) what equity stakes each would hold in the company; and (2) the composition of the Epasys board. As to the first subject, Grant says that the founders agreed that the initial equity stakes would be the same as their final equity positions in Phoenix. As to the composition of Epasys's board, Grant testified as follows:

> *Q:* Now, prior to the formation of Epasys, did you have any discussions with Ms.Mitchell, Mr. Meltzer, or both of them, about who would be on the board of directors of Epasys?
> *A:* Yes.
> *Q:* Please relate those discussions.
> *A:* We — I said that following John Egan's advice, it probably should be a board consisting of five people — three at the minimum, but more likely five — and that we wanted to attract people of some substance — that is, people who would give us credibility in either the marketplace or credibility with venture capitalists — and that we didn't have that credibility at that time. I wanted to wait until such time as we had something that would attract people of some stature on to the board.

Q: At any time did you ever discuss with Ms. Mitchell or Mr. Meltzer, or both of them, about putting either or both of them on the board of directors of Epasys?

A: Yes.

Q: Please relate those discussions.

A: I indicated that I thought it would be appropriate for one, not both, to be on the board, and at such time as we had three or more people that were going to be on the board.

Q: Why did you think it appropriate for only one, but not both of them, to be put on the board?

A: Because I thought that our interests at that time were close to equal, our equity interests, and that it would be inappropriate to have two of them with voting rights on the board, compared to my one vote.

Q: This discussion with Ms. Mitchell and Mr. Meltzer about putting one but not both on the board when the board of directors was five, when did that occur, if you recall?

A: I can't recall whether it was prior to Epasys — it was either immediately prior to or shortly after Epasys began operations.

Mitchell has a far different recollection. She claims that the founders had discussed the board composition issue many times and that it was agreed that all three of the founders would be on the board. Mitchell also said that the founders discussed adding outside members at some later time, but denies Grant's contention that no board was to be formed until outside investors were identified. She also claims never to have agreed to permitting Grant to be sole incorporator, and to have questioned Grant's status as sole incorporator with him when it came to her attention. Grant allegedly told her that McDermott, Will had said that it was only possible to have one incorporator.

E.   GRANT SIGNS A FOREIGN CORPORATION CERTIFICATE IDENTIFYING MITCHELL AND HIMSELF
AS THE DIRECTORS OF EPASYS

On January 7, 2000, the McDermott, Will firm delivered a Massachusetts Foreign Corporation Certificate to the offices of Epasys for signature by Grant and Mitchell. Grant was to sign in his purported capacity as President. Mitchell was to sign as Treasurer and Secretary.

The Foreign Corporation Certificate was required as a condition for Epasys to do business in Massachusetts. By law, the Foreign Corporation Certificate must identify the directors and officers of the corporation and must be signed under penalties of perjury.

The Certificate identifies the officers and directors of Epasys as follows:

11. The name and business address of the officers and the directors of the corporation are as follows:

	Name	*Business Address*
President:	Ralph Grant	163 West Newton St., Boston MA 02118
Treasurer:	Julee Mitchell	163 West Newton St., Boston MA 02118
Secretary:	Julee Mitchell	163 West Newton St., Boston MA 02118
Directors:	Ralph Grant	163 West Newton St., Boston MA 02118
	Julee Mitchell	163 West Newton St., Boston MA 02118

Grant signed the document. So did Mitchell.

Both have strikingly different recollections about doing so. Grant says he was rushed to sign it, did not read it carefully, and failed to pick up the fact that the document listed himself and Mitchell as directors. Had he seen that part of the document, Grant claims he would not have signed it because it was not correct. Grant says he knew that there was no board at that point because he was the incorporator and had not named a board. Grant further contends that he did not give McDermott, Will any information about the officers and directors of Epasys from which to prepare the Certificate and has no idea who did.

Mitchell testified that the Certificate upset her because it did not list Meltzer as a director. Mitchell claims that she raised this issue with Grant either later that same day or the next day. When confronted with this fact, Grant allegedly said that he did not know why Meltzer was not listed as a director. After discussing the issue with Meltzer privately, Mitchell says they elected not to rock the boat and to live with only herself being a director along with Grant.

F. EPASYS BEGINS OPERATING

Epasys then began to do business. The founders each held themselves out to be officers of the company when dealing with third-parties.

Consistent, however, with the lack of documentation that characterized their dealings, the founders did not issue stock to themselves in amounts reflecting their agreement as to their respective equity stakes. And while the founders met to discuss business on a regular basis, there is no evidence that Grant and Mitchell ever met formally as a board of directors.

Initially, Epasys operated out of a Boston townhouse in which Mitchell and Meltzer were living (the "Townhouse"). Grant procured a Boston apartment, which Epasys paid for.

Consistent with their prior arrangement at Phoenix, Grant provided continuing cash infusions into the company while the company sought outside investors. Because he would have simply been paying himself, Grant took no salary as President. Mitchell and Meltzer did receive salaries of $160,000 each, far more than either had ever made in a previous job.

Epasys began hiring other staff and offering them stock options. This was problematic, of course, because the founders had not even issued stock to themselves. McDermott, Will was asked to draft the stock option plan. It also worked on drafts of the documents necessary to grant equity to the founders.

Grant says that he was comfortable proceeding to fund the business while the company's equity ownership was still undocumented because it was understood that he would eventually receive additional equity in exchange for the cash he was contributing to fund Epasys's operations. In fact, Grant claims that the other founders eventually agreed that he would receive an additional 5% equity for every million dollars he put into the business.

Mitchell denies that this was the arrangement. Instead, she says that Grant agreed to provide interim funding as a low-interest rate loan until such time as Epasys could secure venture capital financing.

Neither Grant's nor Mitchell's version of what Grant was to receive for his cash support of the business is corroborated by documentary evidence or the testimony of other witnesses.

G. THE RELATIONSHIP AMONG THE FOUNDERS FALLS APART AND GRANT ACTS TO REMOVE
MITCHELL AND MELTZER FROM THEIR OFFICES

During the late spring and summer of 2000, the working relationship among the founders deteriorated. The company had not secured outside financing and its product development efforts were not as advanced as the founders wished.

According to Mitchell, Grant began to make decisions in isolation from her and Meltzer. Moreover, Grant appeared to be preoccupied with minor issues such as the need for a corporate dress code. For his part, Grant believed that Mitchell and Meltzer were not working hard and were causing morale problems among the company's other employees. After the company moved its offices out of the Townhouse, Grant says that Mitchell and Meltzer would often remain at the Townhouse during the workday and not come to Epasys's offices. Grant alleges that Mitchell and Meltzer were far behind in writing the necessary text to help Epasys's software development team update the Monitor software.

By August, Grant was set on removing Mitchell and Meltzer from their offices. As part of his justification, Grant claimed that Mitchell and Meltzer had improperly awarded themselves bonuses earlier in the year, which they had used to buy a new car. Grant also alleges that Mitchell "forged" Grant's name on a renewal of the Townhouse lease.

Grant enlisted the help of the McDermott, Will firm in August 2000 to aid him in removing Mitchell and Meltzer. McDermott, Will considered a number of issues in that regard. Most notably, the firm fixated on the question of whether Grant could remove Mitchell from the board. The documentary evidence supports the conclusion that McDermott, Will believed that Mitchell was a board member.[12]

12. The billing records and notes of McDermott, Will attorneys support the inference that the firm's lawyers came upon the argument that Mitchell was never a director as an afterthought. The primary emphasis of the firm in working with Grant at that time seemed to be on whether it was possible for Grant to remove Mitchell as a director for cause. For example, the billing records of McDermott, Will attorney Sam Webb state that he was assigned to: "Review organizational issues in light of potential Director conflict; review Restricted Stock Agreements and related documents and consider MWE's duties in the event of a conflict between Directors on a board of 2 with no stocks [*sic*] issued." JX 36 (8/15/00 time entry for MWE attorney Webb); *see also id.* (8/17/00 time entry for MWE attorney Webb referring to research on board "deadlock"). Even more revealing are the notes taken by a McDermott, Will attorney of a strategy meeting firm lawyers held about how to assist Grant in removing Mitchell and Meltzer from their positions at Epasys. The meeting notes suggest that McDermott, Will attorneys started from the premise that Mitchell was a director and brainstormed their way into the idea that she had never been put on the board in the first place. These excerpts from the notes show the backdoor way in which the idea that Mitchell had never been appointed crept into their discussion:

> Issues to be resolved: 1) Corp. Issues — Remove Julee as member of BoD . . . Legal Issues re BD (board of directors) stalemate . . . — No clear way to break logjam under DE law . . . SW [WME Attorney Webb] — Comfortable that it is in the best interests of the Company to remove directors . . . Corp. Options 1) Seek receivership in Delaware Chancery Court 2) Dissolve Entity 3) Remove Julee from BoD, Ralph Takes Control of BoD and Company (or Julee never on the BoD) (will result in litigation) . . . ? Delaware law — Can Company remove Board of Directors member for cause? Breach of Fiduciary Responsibility — Who can remove Board of Directors member? JX 46 (notes of MWE attorney Mahoney of strategy meeting in 8/21/00).

Although McDermott, Will attorneys ascribe their research into removing Mitchell as an examination of options that Grant had in the event that Mitchell claimed to be a director, the record is, on balance, more supportive of the view that the relevant McDermott, Will attorneys believed that a two-person board had been formed earlier, but then seized on the lack of documentation of that formation to come up with a creative argument for their client to use to achieve his ends.

If McDermott, Will had not earlier believed that a two-person board had been formed, it seems likely that one of the many attorneys working on the matter would have raised the issue with the founders or have instructed McDermott, Will paralegal Renee Carson to correct the documents she had prepared listing Grant and Mitchell as directors. In this regard, it is notable that the corporate notebook that McDermott, Will prepared for itself and Epasys included the unsigned directors' consent that listed Mitchell and Grant as board members. This notebook was the compilation of the company's official documents, including its charter, the December 23, 1999 bylaws, and the Foreign Corporation Certificate.

The founders engaged in some efforts to resolve their differences, which did not bear fruit. In the end, McDermott, Will and Grant decided to take an approach premised on the theory that no board of Epasys had been named as of August, 2000. Using this premise, McDermott, Will prepared a written consent of the sole incorporator in which Grant named himself as the sole director. Grant then executed a later consent as sole director naming himself to all the statutory offices at Epasys. He thereafter removed Mitchell and Meltzer from their jobs.

A flurry of litigation then ensued. Mitchell and Meltzer sued Grant in Massachusetts seeking, among other relief, a determination that they collectively owned a majority of Epasys's stock and a compulsory annual meeting. Acting as members of Phoenix, Mitchell and Meltzer removed Grant as managing director of that LLC, and demanded that Epasys cease using the Monitor software, which Mitchell and Meltzer contended was still owned by Phoenix.

Grant sought to have Epasys put into bankruptcy, under terms which would have effectively assured his control of the company. When that strategy stalled, Grant initiated this action seeking a declaration that he is the sole director of Epasys. He also filed suit in Arizona for a declaration that Phoenix was dissolved and that its assets were transferred to Epasys as of the time of Epasys's creation.

II. The Limited Purpose of This Proceeding

It is important to keep in mind the limited utility of this action in the larger scheme of the fight among Epasys's founders. Epasys is overdue for an annual meeting. As a result, any declaration I make is necessarily ephemeral.

Notably, I am not being asked to decide who owns what equity interest in Epasys. I am only being asked to decide who were the members of Epasys's initial board of directors.

Because of my limited mandate, I will endeavor to write my opinion as narrowly as possible. I am sensitive to the fact that a judicial colleague in Massachusetts will soon be asked to determine the more important issue of who owns what equity in Epasys, and I therefore do not intend to make findings of fact regarding that issue.

With that in mind, I turn to my resolution of this dispute.

III. Legal Analysis

This case does not turn on complicated questions of law, but on a single question of fact: when did Grant first exercise his authority as incorporator to name Epasys's board?

As sole incorporator, Grant had the limited but important authority spelled out in § 108(a) and (c) of Title 8:

§ 108. Organization Meeting of Incorporators or Directors Named in Certificate of Incorporation

(a) After the filing of the certificate of incorporation an organization meeting of the incorporator or incorporators, or of the board of directors if the initial directors were named in the certificate of incorporation, shall be held, either within or without this State, at the call of a majority of the incorporators or directors, as the case may be, for the purposes of adopting bylaws, electing directors (if the meeting is of the incorporators) to serve or hold office until the first annual meeting of stockholders or until their successors are elected and qualify, electing officers if the meeting is of the directors, doing any other or further acts to perfect the organizations of the corporation, and transacting such other business as may come before the meeting. . . .

(c) Any action permitted to be taken at the organization meeting of the incorporators or directors, as the case may be, may be taken without a meeting if each incorporator or director, where there is more than 1, or the sole incorporator or director where there is only 1, signs an instrument which states the action so taken.

This case turns on when Grant first exercised his authority as an incorporator. He says he did not do so until August 2000. Mitchell claims Grant did so at the latest on January 7, 2000 when he executed the Foreign Corporation Certificate.

After considering the record evidence carefully, I am persuaded that it is more probable than not that Grant acted as incorporator on or around the date of Epasys's creation to name himself and Mitchell as the initial directors of Epasys. Although it is odd to think of a single incorporator holding a meeting with himself, § 108 does not preclude a single incorporator from meeting with himself to make such a decision. Indeed, the first sentence of § 108(a) explicitly contemplates a meeting of "the incorporator." It is not inconceivable to think that a single incorporator could decide on the initial board of directors but fail to document that decision immediately. That is what most likely occurred here. In my view, Grant's sworn signature on the Foreign Corporation Certificate is the most reliable evidence of his actions. While this factual conclusion is not free from doubt, several reasons convince me it is the correct one.

First, Grant's contention that Mitchell and Meltzer would have consented to allowing him free rein to name a board without either of them on it is not convincing. Grant was making progress over the status quo at Phoenix by forming an initial Epasys board on which he would have equal say and would not be outnumbered by Mitchell and Meltzer. By even his own testimony, Grant admits that he told Mitchell and Meltzer that one of them would be on the board at the time Epasys was formed.

Second, I do not find Egan's testimony about the supposed initial deal among the founders to be particularly helpful. Grant's own testimony suggests that the founders did not follow Egan's supposed advice, because Grant himself admits that the equity interests of the founders were to be identical to those they held in Phoenix. Furthermore, Egan's testimony that Mitchell and Meltzer were mere sweat investors ignores the fact they were the ones that had developed the

Monitor software that was the heart of Epasys's business plan. This software was a tangible capital contribution that was not dependent on future sweat. Most fundamentally, however, Egan simply does not shed light on what transpired between his initial meeting with the founders and the December 23, 1999 formation of Epasys.

Third, it is clear that something transpired at or around Epasys's formation that made employees of McDermott, Will believe that a two-person board comprised of Grant and Mitchell was formed. What is striking about this belief is that the record shows that it was Grant, rather than Mitchell or Meltzer, who was in contact on a regular basis with McDermott, Will.

What is also striking is that Grant says that McDermott, Will got the officer designations correct on the Foreign Corporation Certificate. That is, Grant says that it is correct that he was to be the President and Mitchell was to be the Treasurer and Secretary. But Grant claims it was not correct that he and Mitchell were to be the directors.

It is improbable that McDermott, Will would have gotten the officers correct and the directors incorrect by sheer luck. It is also improbable that McDermott, Will would have prepared an initial consent of the directors identifying Grant and Mitchell as the directors without client input. It is much more likely that the firm received the necessary information to prepare these documents from Grant himself.

Moreover, it is clear that employees at McDermott, Will who were working on Epasys matters harbored the belief that Grant and Mitchell were directors well into the year 2000. Employees of the firm prepared various draft corporate documents identifying the two of them as the directors.

If McDermott, Will believed that Epasys had not formed a board of directors, it is somewhat difficult to imagine that the firm would not have written a memorandum to the founders suggesting the need for the company to do so promptly. After all, McDermott, Will was in the process of drafting stock option plans and the documents necessary for Epasys to issue stock to the founders. That is, the firm was drafting documents involving corporate actions typically performed by boards of directors, not incorporators. Instead of urging the formation of a board, the McDermott, Will employees involved in that process seem to have believed that Grant and Mitchell were the two directors.[17]

Furthermore, I give very little weight to McDermott, Will's after-the-fact discovery in August, 2000 that Grant did not name directors upon the formation of Epasys. For whatever reason, McDermott, Will decided to treat Grant as their sole client contact and to rely exclusively upon his word in determining what advice to give. Contrary to Grant's assertion, the record is clear that McDermott, Will undertook to represent Grant personally and aggressively against the other founders and only withdrew from that representation when the founders complained that McDermott, Will had a conflict of interest.[18]

---

17. The extent to which an incorporator can refuse to name a board of directors until the first annual meeting and manage the corporation pursuant to the powers granted by 8 Del. C. § 107 has never been decided. Most of the learned commentators wisely counsel the rapid formation of a board whenever the new corporation intends to commence genuine business activity.

18. Numerous documents illustrate the extent to which McDermott, Will aligned itself with Grant personally. The firm's lawyers counseled with Grant on how to negotiate with the other founders and considered the extent to which the threat of criminal liability could be implicitly used to induce the other founders to settle with Grant on terms favorable to him. ("Negotiating

McDermott, Will's opinion that Grant never acted as incorporator before August 2000 is the one that would be expected from lawyers who then saw themselves as zealous advocates of Grant's personal position. That creative lawyers would take such a position in the absence of a signed incorporator's minute is also to be expected. But that opinion is undercut by the pre-August 2000 evidence from McDermott, Will's own files that reflects the firm's belief that Grant had formed a board of Grant and Mitchell.

Fourth, I do not rest my decision in any way on whether Grant or Mitchell was the more credible witness. Quite candidly, parts of the testimony of each struck me as unlikely to be true. Without denigrating the basic integrity of either Grant or Mitchell, it is clear that this dispute has engendered deep feelings of ill-will on both sides, feelings that do little to instill confidence in either's recitation of the facts. If there were no documentary evidence, it would be almost impossible to decide this case.

But it is in precisely these circumstances that it is appropriate for a court to look to some more reliable indicator of what actually happened as the basis for its decision. In this case, that indicator is the Foreign Corporation Certificate. Grant signed that official document under penalty of perjury. The Foreign Corporation Certificate is a simple, easy-to-read form. It is much harder to miss the part of the document identifying the directors than it is to see it.

Fifth, I note that there is no contradiction between the formation of an initial two-person board and the founders' desire to add additional outsiders later. As the sole owners of equity in Epasys, the founders could obviously expand the board, and the bylaws drafted by McDermott, Will permitted the board to be expanded to five members without additional stockholder approval. Put simply, it was a rational business strategy to form an initial board that could be expanded, especially because the company intended to undertake initiatives, such as the creation of an employee stock option plan, that required a board's approval.

Finally, I reject Grant's inconsistent reliance on formalism as a defense. Grant insists that he could not have acted as an incorporator in December or January because he did not sign a formal written consent. He also insists he did not take a meeting with himself and make the decision to name himself and Mitchell as directors. But when confronted with his own signature under penalty of perjury on an official document identifying himself and Mitchell as directors, Grant claims that the document is not a valid recordation of his actions as incorporator because he signed it as an officer of Epasys and not as incorporator.

In this regard, it is worth noting that McDermott, Will provided Epasys with a corporate notebook comprised of the company's key documents. This notebook included not only Epasys's charter, but also the Foreign Corporation Certificate, the unsigned directors' consent, and the December 23, 1999 bylaws. Thus, the company's own compilation of its key corporate records suggested that a two-person board had been created.

Strategy — Threaten individual claim by Ralph based on forgery. Imply criminal case also but don't raise it explicitly. Part of consideration for settlement."). For example, McDermott, Will attorney Webb's notes reflect the importance Grant placed on "scaring the pants off" Mitchell and Meltzer in order to get them to compromise. Indeed, Grant ultimately asked McDermott, Will to negotiate with the other founders on his behalf, which the firm began to do. . . . McDermott, Will only withdrew from its role once Mitchell's attorney raised a conflict concern.

Grant's current litigation posture therefore emerges as a lawyer-generated strategy based on Grant's own failure to formally execute an incorporator's minute, and Grant's and Mitchell's joint failure to sign the initial directors' consent prepared by McDermott, Will. These lapses in documentation were seized upon as support for an argument that Grant never named an initial board as incorporator in December 1999 or January 2000.

The Foreign Corporation Certificate, however, as well as all the other documentary evidence suggests otherwise. All of that evidence suggests that: (1) Grant formed a two-person board of Mitchell and Grant, and (2) that the board by informal means appointed Grant as President and Mitchell as Treasurer and Secretary.

Because I conclude that Grant named an initial board of directors comprised of himself and Mitchell, his later August, 2000 attempt to name himself as sole director of Epasys was invalid. As a natural consequence, any actions he took as sole director of Epasys are equally invalid as against Mitchell and Meltzer.

This ruling leaves neither party a winner. Since August 2000, Grant has continued to provide substantial funding to Epasys. Upon this determination, Grant may well decide to stop doing so, which could force the company into bankruptcy. One hopes that the parties will consider their predicament at this point, rationally and not emotionally. It is in all of the founders' interests to work out their disputes amicably or, at the very least, promptly obtain a definitive ruling regarding their respective ownership interests in Epasys.

IV. CONCLUSION

For the foregoing reasons, Mitchell is entitled to a judgment in her favor. Counsel shall present an implementing order, agreed upon as to form, within seven days of this opinion.

PROBLEM 4-1

Because of his busy Olympic training schedule, Josh has asked Sherrie to "just get the thing rolling." Sherrie contacts Mike, a long-time friend of hers and a prominent businessman in the local community, to seek advice on how to get started. Among other things, he suggests she ought to form the business entity and consider doing so by incorporating. Sherrie searches the internet for information on how to create a North Carolina corporation. North Carolina has adopted the Model Business Corporation Act. Finding that the process doesn't seem too difficult, she decides to just do it herself. She selects a form and fills it in.

Josh and Sherrie had decided together to call the business "Fins." She lists herself as incorporator and as the registered agent, and she records her home address in Chapel Hill as Fins' address. She specifies "1,000 shares" as the number of authorized shares of stock, and lists the corporation's purpose as "to promote the sport of competitive swimming by training young athletes in developing their swimming abilities." Sherrie files the form with the North Carolina Secretary of State's Corporations Division, and she pays the appropriate incorporation fees.

If an official at the Corporations Division believes that Sherrie's statement of corporate purpose is irrelevant or ill-advised, can the official refuse to file the articles of incorporation?

If the registered address of the corporation listed by Sherrie in the articles of incorporation is incorrect, could a creditor of Fins argue successfully that the corporation was never formed (thus implying that Sherrie and Josh do not receive the benefit of limited liability)?

B. CAPITAL STRUCTURE

The capital structure of a corporation is the combination of claims sold by the corporation. Those claims generally can be divided into two types — equity claims and debt claims. Shareholders own stock, and stock is an equity claim against a corporation. "Equity" connotes a power to control, usually by voting, and the right to receive profits from the operation of the business. "Debt" connotes some fixed obligation of repayment independent of the success or failure of the business.

Equity. The articles of incorporation *authorize* the issuance of equity interests in the corporation by defining the type and number of equity interests that the corporation is allowed to sell. In some corporations, all equity holders have the same rights. Such corporations have one *class* of equity holders. If it is desirable to have equity holders with different rights — for example, if some equity holders are to receive dividends before other equity holders — the corporation will have multiple classes of equity. Sometimes people want to make distinctions within a class of equity holders, and these distinctions are accomplished by creating separate *series* within the class.

All of the equity interests of a corporation together are called the corporation's "capital stock." The individual units of capital stock are called "shares," and ownership in a corporation is quantified by saying that someone owns a certain number of shares of a certain class of capital stock of that corporation. Of course, the raw number of shares does not say anything about our shareholder's ownership relative to other shareholders. To know that would require additional knowledge about (1) what percentage of shares of the entire class our stockholder owns; and (2) what the rights are of that class of shares.

Shares are *issued* when they are sold. Shares are *outstanding* as long as shareholders hold them. If the corporation repurchases the shares, the corporation may continue to hold them as "treasury shares" (which are *issued but not outstanding*). Treasury shares are not voted by the corporation, and they may be resold for any price determined by the board, even if the price is below par value.[1] The Model Act eliminates the concept of treasury shares, providing that shares acquired by the corporation are authorized but unissued.

---

1. Many states (including Delaware) require the articles to specify a "par value" for the shares. Originally, the concept of par value evolved from the practice of financing the start-up of a corporation through pre-incorporation subscription agreements, but the meaning of "par value" gradually dissipated in the late 1800s, and it remains an anachronism today. Indeed, the Model Act has eliminated the concept entirely. For more discussion of par value and related concepts, see Chapter 5.A.

The articles of incorporation must set forth the total number of shares the corporation is authorized to issue, and if the articles authorize more than one class of shares, they must prescribe the classes and the number of shares in each class. The articles of incorporation also must prescribe a distinguishing designation for each class, and prior to the issuance of the shares, the preferences, limitations, and relative rights of that class must be described in the articles. Typical rights described in the charter are rights to dividends, liquidation rights, voting rights, conversion rights, redemption rights, and preemptive rights.

Articles of incorporation usually designate shares as "common shares" or "preferred shares." Common shares have two fundamental characteristics: (1) unlimited voting rights (including especially the right to vote for directors); (2) the right to the residual assets of the corporation (after payment of all corporate liabilities). The corporation must at all times have at least one share having each of the rights of common stock.

Preferred shares are shares that have some preference or priority in payment over common shares. The terms of the preferred shares are set out in the articles or in a separate document called a "certificate of designations." Examples of these attributes are listed in Model Act § 6.01(c) and DGCL § 151. If the articles so provide, the board of directors may designate the attributes of a class or series of shares in an amendment to the articles not requiring shareholder approval. Such shares are usually preferred shares, and are referred to as "blank check preferred."

Debt. Unlike equity, debt is not described in the articles of incorporation. The terms applying to debt securities are laid out in contracts. Many corporations borrow money and incur indebtedness by issuing "bonds" — a promise to repay a specific sum of money at a definite time, with periodic payments of interest. The bond usually refers the holder to a contract called an "indenture" for more complete information.

The indenture is entered into by the corporation and a trustee, who acts on behalf of the bondholders. It describes the procedures for issuance, payment, redemption, and discharge. It also contains extensive covenants, which are promises by the corporation to perform certain actions (for example, to make payments on time, to preserve the corporation's existence, to pay its taxes, to maintain its properties) or to refrain from certain actions (for example, making certain distributions of the corporation's money, allowing the corporation to drop below a certain net worth). An indenture also specifies the "events of default," which are certain events (for example, nonpayment of principal and interest) that will allow the bondholders to accelerate payment. Finally, the indenture defines any special terms of the debt (for example, redemption, conversion). The following are some important terms of corporate bonds:

Registered versus Bearer. The corporation makes periodic interest payments to the holders of its debt securities. "Registered securities" have the holder's name and address in a registry, and payments are made to whoever is listed in the registry (transfers of ownership must be recorded). "Bearer securities" have coupons attached, and payments are made to whoever presents the coupons.

Redemption. Debt securities are usually, but not always, subject to redemption at the option of the issuing corporation. This means that the corporation may repurchase the debt securities from the owners at a price specified in the indenture. This right is referred to as the right to "call" the bonds. Companies prefer to issue bonds that are callable, since if interest rates decline the company can borrow money at a lower interest rate and use that money to call its outstanding higher-interest bond. If the corporation wants to get rid of debt securities that are not redeemable, it must make a tender offer, usually at a substantial premium, to the owners of the securities.

Priority. Indentures define the payment priority of the debt securities in relation to existing and future debt securities. They may be "senior," "subordinated," or "senior subordinated."

Conversion. Debt securities may be convertible into capital stock of the corporation at a price and at times specified in the indenture. This is a method of allowing investors to have the protection of debt (that is, regular repayments and priority upon dissolution) while having the option of participating in the growth of the corporation.

Ratings. Debt securities issued to the public are rated by various private ratings organizations, such as Moody's and Standard & Poor's. If the securities are rated Baa or higher by Moody's or BBB or higher by Standard & Poor's (that is, if they are "medium grade obligations . . . [being] neither highly protected nor poorly secured. Such bonds have outstanding investment characteristics and in fact have speculative characteristics as well."), they are referred to as investment-grade debt. Any securities below investment grade are referred to as "junk bonds."

Given that issuing debt reduces a company's financial flexibility, since the interest payments on debt must be paid regularly as stated in the loan agreement or bond indenture agreement, or the company will be in default, it is logical to ask why a company ever issues debt instead of equity. One part of the answer is that debt has tax advantages over equity, both to the company and its investors, including that: (1) interest payments on debt are tax-deductible to the company, reducing its ultimate tax liabilities, but dividends the company pays to stockholders are not; (2) repayment of principal is a nontaxable return of capital to an investor, but dividends are ordinary income to the investor; (3) if the company fails, bad debt may be an ordinary loss but loss of stock is a capital loss to the investor. The primary risk of debt is that it requires repayment of fixed amounts at fixed intervals regardless of the success or failure of the business. By comparison, equity requires payment of dividends only when the business is successful.

Shareholders often have contrary views about debt. On the one hand, the use of debt enables the company to *leverage* the shareholders' investment. Leverage refers to the notion that borrowers may use borrowed money to generate returns greater than the cost of borrowing. In this event, the excess earnings increase the return on equity. On the other hand, borrowed money must be repaid, and the repayment obligation increases the risks associated with owning equity. Whether an additional amount of indebtedness will create benefits in excess of costs requires detailed analysis, and shareholders sometimes contract for special control rights with respect to any decisions about debt.

The following case highlights the centrality of capital structure to corporate governance. *Grimes* emphasizes the importance of capital structure by affirming the importance of the board of directors in defining the terms of stock issuances.

GRIMES v. ALTEON INC.

804 A.2d 256
Supreme Court of Delaware
July 19, 2002

VEASEY, Chief Justice.

The issue in this case is whether an alleged oral promise made to a stockholder by the CEO of a corporation to sell 10% of the corporation's future private stock offering to the stockholder, when coupled with a corresponding oral promise by the stockholder to buy that 10%, is enforceable where there has been no approval of the agreement by the board of directors and the agreement is not memorialized in a written instrument. The Court of Chancery held that the oral agreement between the stockholder and the CEO is unenforceable. We agree.

We so conclude on several grounds that are consistent with the holding of the Court of Chancery that the bilateral oral agreement creates a "right" to require the corporation to issue stock to the plaintiff within the meaning of Section 157 of the Delaware General Corporation Law, and is invalid under that section for lack of board approval and a writing. The relevant statutory scheme, including Section 157 and other provisions of the Corporation Law, establishes a policy that commitments regarding the issuance of stock must be approved in writing by the board of directors. This policy seeks to preserve the board's broad authority over the corporation and to protect the certainty of investors' expectations regarding stock.

Thus, based on the statutory structure of the Corporation Law as a whole, we affirm the judgment of the Court of Chancery.

FACTS

Alteon Inc., defendant below and appellee, is a pharmaceutical company specializing in drugs for cardiovascular and renal diseases. Charles L. Grimes, plaintiff below and appellant, is a lawyer and an investor who, along with his wife, Jane Gillespie Grimes, often purchases large blocks of stock (but below 10% to avoid insider obligations) in small technology-based companies. Grimes and his wife had held approximately 9.9% of Alteon's stock at the time of the events that have given rise to this litigation. Those events, as set forth in the complaint, may be summarized as follows.

Kenneth I. Moch, the President and Chief Executive Officer of Alteon, told Grimes that Alteon needed additional funds, and that Alteon was considering a private placement stock offering. Grimes told Moch that he was concerned about his holdings being diluted, and that he would buy 10% of any such offering. According to Grimes, Moch promised orally that he would offer Grimes 10% of the offering. In return, Grimes promised orally to buy 10% of the offering. Grimes admits that there is no writing memorializing these promises. He also admits that Alteon's board did not approve this transaction.

Subsequently, Alteon publicly announced a private placement offering. It did not allow Grimes to participate in this private placement, which presumably was fully taken by other purchasers. The stock market reacted positively to the placement, and Alteon's stock price increased from $3 to as high as $5 5/16 per share.

DECISION OF THE COURT OF CHANCERY

Grimes sued Alteon in the Delaware Court of Chancery for damages and specific performance of the oral agreement between Grimes and Moch. Alteon moved to dismiss the complaint under Court of Chancery Rule 12(b)(6) for failure to state a claim on which relief may be granted. The motion made three arguments. First, Alteon argued that any agreement between Grimes and Moch constituted a "right" under 8 Del. C. § 157, and is thus invalid because it is not written and was not approved by the board of directors. Second, Alteon argued that the agreement was a "preemptive right" under 8 Del. C. § 102(b)(3) and is thus invalid because it was not expressly provided in Alteon's certificate of incorporation. Third, Alteon argued that the agreement is too indefinite as to time, quantity, and price to constitute an enforceable contract. The Court of Chancery accepted the first ground and granted the motion to dismiss on that basis. The Court rejected the second ground, but stated that it is "highly questionable whether or not this would constitute a valid common law contract." Because of our disposition of this case, we need not reach the second and third issues.

The Vice Chancellor's rationale is expressed in a brief bench ruling holding that the agreement constituted a "right" within the meaning of 8 Del. C. § 157, and thus fails for lack of board approval and a written document evidencing it. The essence of the Vice Chancellor's bench ruling is as follows:

> I do agree with the defendants, however, that the right that is sought to be enforced here is a "right" within the meaning of Section 157. I am also satisfied that the intent of Section 157 — that is, that the overall statutory scheme that's contemplated by Section 157 and also by Section 161 — is that whenever investors are contracting to invest capital in a company or to purchase stock either directly or rights or options in stock, that the statutory scheme requires board approval and that there be a written instrument that evidences those arrangements. The reason is that where the overall capital structure of the corporation is concerned, it is a vitally important command of the law that the corporation know precisely what its capital stock is and what the potential calls on that capital will be. And it is for that reason the statute elevates that type of transaction to the level of requiring board approval and of requiring a writing. Only then will everyone know what claims on the capital will be, who has rights to invest capital, and what rights the corporation has with respect to actual or potential investors — that is, investors who have entered into contracts with the company.

Grimes has appealed to this Court the judgment of the Court of Chancery dismissing his complaint. We agree with the essential holding of the Court of Chancery that the agreement is invalid because it was not approved by the board of directors and was not memorialized in a written instrument. We do so based on the statutory scheme of the Corporation Law pertaining to stock issuance, with particular emphasis on Sections 152 and 157.

STOCK ISSUANCE AND THE DELAWARE GENERAL CORPORATION LAW STATUTORY SCHEME

Grimes argues that his arrangement with Moch does not constitute a "right" within the meaning of 8 Del. C. § 157 and, therefore, need not be approved by the board or evidenced by a written instrument as required by that statute.

Alteon argues that it does. Grimes argues that Section 157 applies only to options and "option like" rights. The fatal defect in Grimes' claim is that the agreement purports to grant a right that was not expressly approved by the board of directors as required by the statutory scheme of the Delaware General Corporation Law exemplified by Section 152 and Section 157.

The agreement purports to bind the corporation to issue to Grimes 10% of a future issuance of stock. Grimes' right to require the issuance of stock to him arises only if and when there is a public or private offering of newly issued stock. Because Grimes claims a right to require the issuance to him of 10% of any such offering, the Corporation Law applies and requires that the agreement and the issuance of the stock must be approved by the board of directors and evidenced by a written instrument.

One must read *in pari materia* the relevant statutory provisions of the Corporation Law. First there is the fundamental corporate governance principle set forth in 8 Del. C. § 141(a) that the "business and affairs of every corporation . . . shall be managed by and under the direction of" the board of directors. One then turns to the board's role in stock issuance set forth in the relevant sections of Subchapter V of Title 8. The provisions in this Subchapter relate to the issuance of capital stock, subscriptions for additional shares, options and rights agreements. Taken together, they are calculated to advance two fundamental policies of the Corporation Law: (1) to consolidate in its board of directors the exclusive authority to govern and regulate a corporation's capital structure; and (2) to ensure certainty in the instruments upon which the corporation's capital structure is based.

As this Court has stated in requiring strict adherence to statutory formality in matters relating to the issuance of capital stock, the "issuance of corporate stock is an act of fundamental legal significance having a direct bearing upon questions of corporate governance, control and the capital structure of the enterprise. The law properly requires certainty in such matters."[7] Delaware's statutory structure implements these policies through a "clear and easily followed legal roadmap" of statutory provisions.[8] This statutory scheme consistently requires board approval and a writing.

Various provisions in Subchapter V set forth the formal requirements for the issuance of capital stock, the establishment of classes of stock, the consideration for the issuance of stock, and formalities regarding rights, options and subscriptions relating to capital stock. The statutes relating to the issuance of stock that provide the policy context that is relevant here are 8 Del. C. §§ 151, 152, 153, 157, 161 and 166. Taken together, these provisions confirm the board's exclusive authority to issue stock and regulate a corporation's capital structure. To ensure certainty, these provisions contemplate board approval and a written instrument evidencing the relevant transactions affecting issuance of stock and the corporation's capital structure.

Section 151(a), relating to classes and series of stock, states that "the resolution or resolutions providing for the issue of such stock [must be] adopted by the board of directors pursuant to authority expressly vested in it by the provisions of its certificate of incorporation." Section 152, relating to the issuance of

---

7. STAAR Surgical Co. v. Waggoner, 588 A.2d 1130, 1136 (Del. 1991); *accord Kalageorgi*[v. Victor Kamkin, Inc., 750 A.2d 531, 538 (Del. Ch. 1999)].

8. *Kalageorgi*, 750 A.2d at 538.

stock, states, "The consideration . . . for subscriptions to, or the purchase of, the capital stock to be issued by a corporation shall be paid in such form and in such manner as the board of directors shall determine." Section 153, relating to the consideration for the issuance of stock, requires that such consideration shall be determined from time to time by the board of directors. Section 157, relating to rights and options respecting stock, requires board approval and a written instrument to create such rights or options. Section 161, relating to the issuance of additional stock, allows the directors to "issue or take subscriptions for additional shares of its capital stock up to the amount authorized in its certificate of incorporation." Section 166, relating to the formalities required of stock subscriptions, provides that subscription agreements are not enforceable against the subscriber unless in writing and signed by the subscriber.

The requirement of board approval for the issuance of stock is not limited to the act of transferring the shares of stock to the would-be stockholder, but includes an antecedent transaction that purports to bind the corporation to do so. As noted, Section 152 requires the directors to determine the "consideration . . . for subscriptions to, or the purchase of, the capital stock" of a corporation. Thus, director approval of the transaction fixing such consideration is required. Moreover, it is well established in the case law that directors must approve a sale of stock. This duty is considered so important that the directors cannot delegate it to the corporation's officers.

Grimes argues that the contract provides "only that *if* Alteon's board should exercise its authority to issue additional Alteon stock in a future private placement (as it did here in the private placement of 2,834,088 shares of common stock), *then* Mr. and Mrs. Grimes were obligated to purchase a certain percentage of that stock at whatever price Alteon's board set. That contract does not give Mr. and Mrs. Grimes the ability to force Alteon to issue additional stock (at any price), and thus does not implicate the board's right to regulate the company's capital structure."

This argument begs the fundamental policy question behind the statutory scheme requiring director approval for steps taken in connection with stock issuance. If the corporation is required by the Grimes agreement to issue to Grimes 10% of an offering to sell stock, the board's business judgment is or may be significantly encumbered. For example, the board would not be able to sell 91%-100% of the stock it chooses to issue to another willing purchaser or purchaser in a private placement or otherwise. It may offer those purchasers only 90% of the offering. That constraint may limit the universe of prospective investors to those who would be content to have only 90% of the stock to be issued.

An agreement that binds a company to allow a 10% stockholder to remain at a 10% holding level may be a considerable sacrifice for a corporation, or it may be a good business decision for the board to consider. Focusing, however, on the problematic aspect of such a business decision, it would seem that a 10% holding in a corporation is large enough that the investor may have considerable leverage over the corporation. Such an agreement is tantamount to an agreement to permit Grimes to have a continuing influence over the future direction of the corporation. Moreover, potential investors might be deterred from investing in a corporation that had made such a commitment. Therefore, the agreement might actually decrease the capital potentially available to a company in a future stock offering. A business decision weighing the advantages and disadvantages of the Grimes transaction would be within the discretion of the board of directors. But that choice lies only in the board's province, not that of the CEO without express board approval.

There is an important policy basis for this requirement. Shares of stock are "a species of property right" that is of "foundational importance . . . to our economic system."[12] Thus, it is "critical that the validity of those securities, especially those that are widely traded, not be easily or capriciously called into question."[13] Explicit board approval of a stock issuance or a commitment to issue stock makes it more likely that the board will have considered thoroughly the reasons for and against the issuance. Thus, director approval of stock issuance or agreements affecting the respective rights of the corporation and a putative purchaser of stock reduces later disputes about their propriety and enhances corporate stability and certainty. . . .

[Sections on 152 and 157 deleted.]

CONCLUSION

We agree with the conclusion of the Court of Chancery that the Grimes agreement is unenforceable for lack of both board approval and a written agreement. One must read together the various statutes in Subchapter V, particularly Sections 152 and 157, because the statutory scheme of the Delaware General Corporation Law requires board approval and a written instrument evidencing an agreement obligating the corporation to issue stock either unconditionally or conditionally.

PROBLEM 4-2

In building the swimming facility in Chapel Hill, Fins incurred substantial indebtedness in the form of a mortgage on the facility. *Why would Josh and Sherrie choose to finance the building of the swimming facility through a bank loan rather than by selling additional shares of stock in the company? If you were the loan officer in the bank, what sorts of restrictions, if any, would you place on Fins going forward?*

C. DIRECTORS & SHAREHOLDERS

As noted above, the management of a corporation is divided among three groups: shareholders, directors, and officers. In a public corporation, the formal mechanisms of control are exercised primarily by the board of directors, which has the statutory power to manage the affairs of the corporation, while the actual, day-to-day control resides in the top executive officers. Shareholders control the directors, if at all, through annual director elections and through voting on specific proposals, when allowed.

---

12. *Kalageorgi*, 750 A.2d at 538.
13. *Id.*

The discussion in this Section is divided between directors and shareholders. Although officers exercise the most practical control over a corporation on a daily basis, there are few corporation statutes that regulate the exercise of such control. The law focuses, instead, on directors and shareholders, both of which monitor the performance of officers, at least in theory.

Role of the board. The statutory power to manage the corporation rests with the board of directors. Each public corporation must have a board of directors, while closely held corporations can do away with the board of directors by agreement among the shareholders. Model Act §§ 8.01(a) and 7.32; Delaware General Corporation Law (DGCL) §§ 141(a) and 351. Although the charter or bylaws of a corporation may prescribe qualifications of directors (for example, they may require that the directors hold stock in the corporation or be residents of the state of incorporation), modern corporation statutes do not prescribe such qualifications. Model Act § 8.02; DGCL § 141(b). Traditionally, corporations were required to have at least three directors. Modern corporation statutes usually allow boards to have only one director, with the exact number or a range to be specified in the charter or bylaws. Model Act § 8.03(a); DGCL § 141(b).

Generally speaking, the role of the board of directors is to manage or supervise the management of the corporation. Model Act § 8.01(b); DGCL § 141(a). In a public corporation, this role includes hiring, advising, supervising, and (when necessary) firing the chief executive officer of the corporation. Boards of public corporations typically meet anywhere from four to ten times a year and tend to be nominated by and supportive of management. As a result, most boards of public corporations play a limited role in the management of the corporation except in times of crisis.

Inside versus outside directors. In talking about directors, we generally distinguish "inside" directors from "outside" directors. Inside directors are people who are employed full time by the corporation as corporate officers, in addition to their roles on the board of directors. Inside directors on the board always include the chief executive officer (CEO), and may include various other top corporate officers, such as the chief financial officer (CFO); the chief operating officer (COO); and the general counsel. Outside directors are people who don't work for the corporation, other than as members of the board. If outside directors do not have any other financial relationship with the company, they are termed "independent." So an architect who has designed theme parks for the Disney Corporation would not be considered an independent director at Disney (although an outsider), while the headmaster of a private school where the Disney CEO's children used to go to school would be considered independent. One-third of the directors of companies listed on major exchanges are the CEOs of other companies. Other board members will typically include lawyers, university presidents, former senators, ambassadors or generals, accounting professors, and even the occasional law professor. In start-up companies and high-technology companies it is typical that venture capitalists have seats on the board, but in established companies the percentage of bankers on the board has dropped sharply over the last decade, perhaps because of concerns about conflicts of interest.

During various periods of concern about corporate governance and the integrity of companies' financial and other disclosure, such as during 2001-2002's "post-Enron" period, regulators such as the New York Stock Exchange, the Securities and Exchange Commission (SEC), and Congress have emphasized the importance of having a majority of outside, independent directors on the board. It is thought that by having a majority of outside directors, the quality of boards' decision making will be enhanced, and there will be greater monitoring of officers' performance, greater independence in decision making, and fewer conflict-of-interest situations. Whether this will turn out to be true is debatable. Surveys of board members themselves show that they are aware of the difficulty of defining "independence" clearly enough: a majority of board members surveyed in 2002 thought 25 percent of their "independent" colleagues were not truly independent. Moreover, 45 percent of board members thought that they themselves didn't spend enough time on the job to be able to truly understand a company's value drivers and the risks the company faces—in other words, its business. Given the limitations of time and information inherent in a part-time job, it is inevitable that outside directors, even if theoretically "independent," will necessarily be dependent upon inside directors and other consultants for knowledge about the companies on which they sit. Also, one-third of directors are typically CEOs of other companies. There is a shared understanding that might be termed "cultural" among CEOs; and thus again there are questions about how much independence we can expect from even independent outside directors.

Terms of office. All directors are elected by the shareholders at an annual shareholders' meeting, unless their terms are staggered, Model Act § 8.03(c); DGCL § 211(b), or a vacancy in a directorship occurs mid-term. The terms "staggered" and "classified" refer to a board that allows for classes of directors to be elected for multiple-year terms. The structure of staggered boards is such that there is always a majority of directors who are continuing without need for re-election. If, for instance, a nine-person board is divided into three classes, with three-year terms, then every year, three of the directors would be elected (or re-elected) for a three-year term, and six of the directors would remain on the board without needing to be re-elected.

Having a staggered board acts as a powerful anti-takeover device. One way to take control of a public corporation where the target corporation's board is unwilling to approve the "business combination" (merger or acquisition) is to change the composition of the board through a proxy contest—that is, for an "insurgent" to nominate its own slate of nominees for the board. For reasons that will become clear in our discussion of hostile takeovers (see Chapter 13), the insurgent in such a proxy contest would typically purchase 10 to 15 percent of the firm's outstanding shares prior to the shareholder vote, and would attempt to recruit other shareholders to support its position. It would make clear in its proxy solicitation that its nominees are committed to the business combination being proposed. If a board is staggered, an insurgent would be required to win two annual elections to gain a majority of seats on the board. Given the amount of time during which the insurgent would not have control of the company but would have a large financial stake, companies with staggered boards are not often successful targets of attempted hostile takeovers.

Model Act § 8.05 specifies that each director holds office until the annual meeting following his or her election unless terms are staggered. DGCL § 141(b) states the term of directors differently: under that section, each director holds office until his or her successor is elected and qualified or until his or her earlier resignation or removal.

Removal of directors. Generally speaking, directors may be removed from the board by shareholders, with or without cause, unless the charter provides that directors may be removed only for cause. Model Act § 8.08(a); DGCL § 141(k). One important consequence of having a staggered board in Delaware is that directors may only be removed for cause, unless the charter provides otherwise. DGCL § 141(k). In other words, having a staggered board in Delaware shifts the default rule from one in which a "for cause" limitation on removal must be specified in the charter to a default rule in which there is a "for cause" limitation on removal unless the charter provides otherwise. In addition to removal by shareholders, Model Act § 8.09 provides that directors may be removed by a judicial proceeding for fraudulent or dishonest conduct or gross abuse of authority.

Vacancies. Vacancies on the board of directors may occur because of the resignation, death, or removal of a director or by the creation of a new directorship. Directors may resign at any time, usually by delivering a written notice of resignation. Model Act § 8.07(a); DGCL § 141(b). Vacancies may be filled by the remaining directors or by the shareholders. Model Act § 8.10(a); DGCL § 223(a)(1). The power of the directors to create new directorships and then fill them can be used for strategic reasons by the board or a majority faction of the board where different factions of the board disagree about an important decision.

Board meetings and directors' action on consent. Traditionally, all actions by directors had to be taken at duly called meetings of the board. Although corporation statutes at one time required boards to meet within the state of incorporation, modern statutes have eliminated that requirement. Model Act § 8.20(a); DGCL § 141(g). In a further accommodation of modern practices, corporation statutes now permit directors to be considered "present" at a meeting — even if not physically present — if the director participates in the meeting by telephone or other similar communications device that allows the directors to hear each other. Model Act § 8.20(b); DGCL § 141(i).

Modern corporation statutes also permit directors to act without holding a meeting. Model Act § 8.21 and DGCL § 141(f) allow such action by written consent if all of the directors consent to the action, as long as the charter or bylaws of the corporation do not provide otherwise. Actions by written consent are particularly common in close corporations, where informal contacts among directors are common.

Directors may act at meetings that may be held regularly, as specified in the bylaws, or at a special meeting, which requires a notice of the date, time, and place of the meeting, but not the purpose (unless the charter or bylaws so require). Model Act § 8.22. Directors may waive notice of a meeting, either in writing or simply by participating in the meeting. Model Act § 8.23. A majority of directors being present satisfies statutory quorum requirements, but the charter or bylaws of the corporation may alter the quorum requirement to specify more or less than a majority. Model Act § 8.24(a) and (b); DGCL § 141(b). Once the directors are properly assembled, a majority vote of the directors present is required to act, unless the charter or bylaws prescribe a greater number. Model Act § 8.24(c); DGCL § 141(b).

Committees of the board. The board may act through committees composed of one or more directors. Model Act § 8.25(a); DGCL § 141(c) (which authorizes committees of one or more members). In public corporations, the trend is toward companies having a number of powerful committees composed primarily or exclusively of outside directors. These committees include the audit committee, which is responsible for financial controls and risk assessment in the company; the nominating committee, which is responsible for nominating people to the board and to the committees; and the compensation committee, which is responsible for determining the compensation and other benefits of the top executive officers. In 2002 the New York Stock Exchange (NYSE) adopted corporate governance requirements for companies listed on the NYSE. These requirements substantially increased the responsibilities of these committees, including requirements that the audit and nominating committees be composed entirely of independent outside directors.

The rules governing meetings of the whole board of directors also govern meetings of the committees of the board. Model Act § 8.25(c). Actions taken by committees of the board may carry the same weight as actions by the whole board of directors, Model Act § 8.25(d); DGCL § 141(c), but the corporation statutes place some limits on the matters that may be delegated to a committee. Model Act § 8.25(e); DGCL § 141(c). Generally, actions that will need to be put to a shareholder vote may not be delegated to a board committee, nor may a committee adopt, amend, or repeal bylaws of the corporation. Model Act § 8.25(e); DGCL § 141(c)(2). Nor, in a Model Act jurisdiction, may a committee fill vacancies on the board or authorize dividends, except pursuant to formulas the whole board has adopted. Model Act § 8.25(e).

Shareholder Voting. State rules governing shareholder voting in corporations are quite simple:

(a)   Each share of common stock carries one vote. DGCL § 212(a); Model Act § 7.21(a).

(b)   Shareholders vote on the election of directors (DGCL § 211(b); Model Act §§ 8.03, 8.08), and on certain fundamental transactions: (A) Amending the corporation's charter: DGCL § 242(b); Model Act § 10.03; (B) Amending the by-laws: DGCL § 109(a); Model Act § 10.20(a); (C) Approving a merger: DGCL § 251(c); Model Act § 11.04(b); (D) Approving the sale of assets not in the ordinary course of business, i.e., selling all or substantially all of the assets of the company: DGCL § 271; Model Act § 12.02; and (E) Approving the dissolution of the company: DGCL § 275(b); Model Act § 14.02. Finally, shareholders may vote to ratify conflict-of-interest transactions: DGCL § 144(a)(2); Model Act § 8.61(b)(2).

(c)   Shareholders may vote at a shareholders' meeting either in person or by proxy. DGCL § 212(b); Model Act § 7.22(a) and 7.25(c).

(d)   Majority vote wins except in director elections, when only a plurality is required. DGCL §§ 216 (2) and (3); Model Act § 7.28 (a).

Most of these rules may be altered within prescribed limits by provisions in the corporation's charter or bylaws. In addition, the law provides that shareholders may aggregate their votes in a shareholders' agreement or a voting trust, which are different forms of contracts used to allocate control in closely held corporations but typically not public corporations.

Proxy Voting. At common law, all shareholder votes were required to be cast in person. Modern statutes allow shareholders to vote their shares either in person or by proxy. DGCL § 212(b); Model Act § 7.22(a). A "proxy" is the authorization given by a shareholder to another person to vote the shareholder's shares. The holder of a proxy is an agent subject to the control of the shareholder and having fiduciary duties to the shareholder. Although proxies may be used occasionally for voting in close corporations, especially as a control allocation device, voting by proxy is clearly the norm in public corporations. And because voting is the primary mechanism by which shareholders exert influence over the corporation, proxy voting has been a battleground in the struggle for control of public corporations.

Voting Rules. Generally, voting for directors is done by "straight voting," under which a majority voting coalition will win every seat on the board. Voting in a corporation is different from voting in a polity, because under straight voting, each shareholder votes all of his or her shares with respect to each open seat on the board. So if a person owns 100 shares of Company A and there are nine open seats on a nine-person board of directors, that person can vote 100 shares for each of the nine people nominated. Thus, if one shareholder or a voting coalition owns 51 percent of the shares of a company, under straight voting that majority block will elect each director, since they will be able to outvote the other shareholders 51 percent to 49 percent with respect to each nominee for each open seat. (Recall, however, that the overwhelming majority of board elections are uncontested and simply engender a "vote of confidence" for the nominees that the board's nominating committee has proposed.)

Another system, called "cumulative voting," allows shareholders to concentrate their voting power by "cumulating" all of the votes associated with their shares and voting them in a block for a limited number of nominees. The effect of cumulative voting is to assure minority shareholders' representation on the board in proportion to their voting strength. Thus, in the above example our hypothetical shareholder could vote her 100 shares times nine (the number of open seats), or 900 votes, and cast all 900 votes for one nominee, or she could distribute them among multiple nominees. Based on a simple mathematical formula, one can determine the maximum voting power a shareholder would have for a given number of shares and the number of open seats, and thus how many seats on the board she could be assured of winning.[1] In both the Delaware statute and the Model Act, the default rule is straight voting, while companies have the power to opt in to cumulative voting in the charter or bylaws. DGCL § 214; Model Act § 7.28(b). Cumulative voting is more common in close corporations as a control device than it is in public corporations. A study in 2001 of 350 companies going public for the first time in the 1990s showed that 13 percent of them had bylaw provisions providing for cumulative voting, so it is clearly a minority of public companies that use this voting device. *See* John C. Coates, IV, *Explaining Variation in Takeover Defenses: Blame the Lawyers*, 89 C.L.R. 1301 (2001).

Shareholder Meetings. The traditional method by which shareholders act is through voting at the annual meeting or by proxy in conjunction with the annual meeting. Corporation statutes provide for annual meetings for the election of directors, and unless directors are elected by written consent instead of at

---

1. To elect *N* number of directors, a shareholder would need $SN/(D + 1) + 1$ shares, where *S* is the number of shares voting, and *D* is the number of directors to be elected. As the number of directors to be elected goes down, as in a small board or a staggered board, the number of shares that a minority shareholder would need to hold to be assured of board representation goes up.

an annual meeting, which would be unusual in a public corporation outside of a contest for control, corporation statutes require that companies hold an annual meeting. DGCL § 211(b); Model Act § 7.01. The shareholders are given the power to seek a judicial order setting a date for the annual meeting if there has been a failure to hold the annual meeting as required. DGCL § 211(c); Model Act § 7.03(a)(1).

Corporations statutes also permit the calling of special meetings to vote on particular issues that may arise between annual meetings. DGCL § 211(d); Model Act § 7.02. Special meetings are often called to replace the directors as part of a hostile takeover attempt or to seek the shareholders' approval of a friendly takeover or merger proposal. ("Hostile" takeovers are those that do not have the support of the board of the "target" company to be taken over. "Friendly" takeovers are the merger of two companies or the acquisition of one company by another in which the boards of both companies support the business combination. The lines can blur, since in some cases a "friendly" deal is chilly, but the target board goes along with it because of the power of the acquirer to replace the board and do a hostile takeover.) In Delaware, the board has the power to call a special meeting; the shareholders may have this power if it is granted to them in the charter or bylaws. DGCL § 211(d). In a Model Act jurisdiction, the board or a 10 percent shareholder has the power to call a special meeting. Model Act § 7.02(2). Clearly, the power of the share-holders to call a special meeting, as provided for in the Model Act and in some corporations' charters or bylaws, has important implications for how power is allocated in a company between the shareholders and the directors.

Acting on Consent. Traditionally shareholders were not allowed to act except at a shareholders' meeting that had been duly noticed and at which a quorum of shareholders were present, either in person or by proxy. Modern statutes allow shareholders to act without a meeting, by written consent, unless the charter takes away that power. DGCL §§ 228, 275(c) (allowing shareholders to act by the consent of the number of shareholders that would be necessary to approve an action at a meeting, unless the articles of incorporation take away the power to act on consent); Model Act § 7.04(a) (requiring unanimous consent). These consent provisions were designed to make action by shareholders in closely held corporations easier, and yet today about half of all public corporations permit actions by shareholder consent as well. Under Delaware law, this power can be extremely useful to shareholders or to an entity seeking to take control of another company, since it means a majority coalition of shareholders can act, such as to replace the board, without having to ask the board to call a special meeting, set a meeting date, and notify shareholders of the special meet-ing. Thus, it means a majority coalition of shareholders can act without being subject to the board's tactical decisions to delay calling a special meeting. In a Model Act jurisdiction the power to act on consent is not very important because it requires unanimous shareholder consent, and it would be an extremely rare action that could garner unanimous consent.

Notice of Meetings. The process for calling a special meeting and for deciding the time and place of either a special meeting or the annual meeting appears in the charter or bylaws of a corporation. All shareholder meetings must be pre-ceded by notice to the shareholders that specifies the business to be transacted at the meeting. DGCL § 222(a); Model Act § 7.05. If notice is insufficient, actions taken at the meeting are voidable by shareholders who did not attend.

Attendance at a meeting, unless it is for the purpose of objecting to the notice, constitutes a waiver of improper notice.

Setting the Record Date. In a public corporation, where shares of stock are constantly being bought and sold, even the day before the annual meeting, special procedures have been developed to determine who has a right to vote. Notice of a meeting is provided to all shareholders who own shares as of a "record date," which is fixed by the board of directors. DGCL § 213(a); Model Act § 7.07(a). In Delaware, the record date cannot be more than 60 days before the meeting date, nor less than 10 days before the meeting date. DGCL § 213(a). In a Model Act jurisdiction, the record date cannot be more than 70 days before the meeting date. Model Act § 7.07(b). Thus, the statutes provide limits within which the board must act in determining the timing of meetings and the relationship between the record date and the meeting date. The Delaware statute also contains provisions for setting the record date for determining the shareholders eligible to be counted when they purport to act on consent. DGCL § 213(b).

Quorum Requirements. Unless the charter or bylaws provide otherwise, shareholders holding a majority of shares must be present (in person or by proxy) to constitute a quorum. DGCL § 216; Model Act § 7.25(a).

While the statutory provisions set out above are straightforward, they become problematic in cases where there is a crisis facing the corporation or there are conflicts among various groups on the board. The following case and problem not only offer a startling introduction to the rough and tumble world of battles for corporate control but highlight the striking contrast between the informality that pervades partnership law and the formality that permeates corporate law.

ADLERSTEIN v. WERTHEIMER

2002 WL 205684 (slip opinion)
Court of Chancery of Delaware
January 25, 2002

LAMB, Vice Chancellor.

I

This is an action pursuant to Section 225 of the Delaware General Corporation Law ("DGCL") brought by Joseph Adlerstein, the former Chairman and CEO of SpectruMedix Corporation ("SpectruMedix" or "the Company"), a Delaware corporation. SpectruMedix is in the business of manufacturing and selling instruments to the genetics and pharmaceutical industries and is headquartered in State College, Pennsylvania. Adlerstein's complaint is against the Company and three individuals who claim to be the current directors of the Company: Steven N. Wertheimer, Judy K. Mencher, and Ilan Reich.

At issue in the Complaint are a series of actions taken on July 9, 2001, at or in conjunction with a purported meeting of the SpectruMedix board of directors held at the New York City offices of McDermott, Will & Emery ("MW & E").[1] First, a board majority (consisting of Wertheimer and Mencher) voted to issue to the I. Reich Family Limited Partnership ("Reich Partnership"), an entity affiliated with Reich, a sufficient number of shares of a new class of supervoting preferred stock to convey to the Reich Partnership a majority of the voting power of the Company's stock. Second, the same majority voted to remove Adlerstein for cause as Chief Executive Officer of the Company, to strip him of his title as Chairman of the Board, and to appoint Reich to serve as Chief Executive Officer and as Chairman of the Board. Third, immediately after the board meeting, the Reich Partnership executed and delivered to SpectruMedix a written consent in lieu of stockholders meeting purporting to remove Adlerstein as a director. When the dust settled, the board consisted of Wertheimer, Mencher, and Reich; the Reich Partnership had replaced Adlerstein as holder of majority voting control; and Reich had replaced Adlerstein as Chairman and CEO.

Adlerstein seeks a determination that the July 9 meeting was not properly convened and, therefore, all actions taken at or in conjunction with that meeting are null and void. Adlerstein also contends that, even if the meeting was duly noticed and convened, the actions taken at the meeting by Wertheimer and Mencher were the product of a breach of the fiduciary duties they owed to him in his capacity as a director and the controlling stockholder.

II

Adlerstein is a scientist and entrepreneur. He has a Ph.D. in physics and was involved with the funding and management of a number of start-up technology companies before founding SpectruMedix (originally named Premier American Technologies Company) in 1992.

Wertheimer, an investment banker, was introduced to Adlerstein by Selbst and was elected to the board by Adlerstein on January 1, 2000. Mencher is a money manager with an expertise in high yield and distressed investments. On Wertheimer's recommendation, Adlerstein elected Mencher to the board on March 22, 2000.

In 1997, SpectruMedix completed an initial public offering of its common stock, raising net proceeds of $4.67 million, more than half of which was used to repay existing indebtedness. SpectruMedix experienced substantial net losses over the next several years, "burning" through all of the cash raised in the IPO.

In July 1999, SpectruMedix entered into a series of agreements with Applied Biosystems, Inc. and certain of its affiliates. As a result of these agreements SpectruMedix received $5 million in cash in exchange for a sublicense to certain technology licensed by SpectruMedix, shares of SpectruMedix Series A Preferred Stock, and a consulting agreement. Following this transaction, apart from a small amount of revenue from the sale of instruments and related disposable products, SpectruMedix received no other funds between July 31, 1999 and July 9, 2001.

---

1. Over the years Alderstein was represented in various personal capacities by Stephen Selbst, a partner in MW&E's New York City office. Eventually Selbst also began to serve as counsel to SpectruMedix. Selbst was present at the July 9 meeting and, as counsel to SpectruMedix, schemed with Wetheimer, Mencher, and Reich to engineer Alderstein's ouster.

In 1999, to avoid a liquidity crisis, Adlerstein loaned SpectruMedix $500,000. In exchange, SpectruMedix gave Adlerstein a note that was convertible (at Adlerstein's option) into shares of a new Series B Preferred Stock of SpectruMedix that voted with the common and carried 80,000 votes per share. In January 2000, Adlerstein converted approximately $103,000 outstanding under this loan agreement into shares of Series B Preferred Stock. As a result, although Adlerstein owned only 21.41% of the equity of SpectruMedix, he controlled 73.27% of the voting power of the Company.

Late in 1999, before joining the board, Wertheimer convinced Adlerstein to hire Manus O'Donnell, an independent management consultant, to study and report on the status of the Company's management and finances. O'Donnell conducted his study and delivered a report dated January 2, 2000, in which he concluded that, unless the Company began making sales of instruments, it had sufficient cash and cash equivalents to continue operations only until September 2001.

During September 2000, as a result of increasing concern over SpectruMedix's deteriorating financial condition, Wertheimer and Mencher convinced Adlerstein to re-hire O'Donnell. On September 15, 2000, O'Donnell updated his report, shortening the period during which sufficient cash reserves were forecasted. He stated:

> [S]ince my last forecast in December, the company burn rate has increased substantially . . . mainly due to increased headcount expense. As a result cash would last until May 2001 if grant money is received as predicted (at 115K per month from October onward). If grants are not received, then cash would be exhausted in January 2001.

As O'Donnell noted, the change in forecast was due in large part to Adlerstein's decision to increase staffing levels from 23 to 51. This headcount increase resulted in an escalation of the annual payroll by just over 100%. O'Donnell concluded by telling the board of directors that, at the then-current level of fixed expenses, SpectruMedix needed to sell and get paid for one machine per month in order to maintain an adequate cash position.

On March 28, 2001, a sexual harassment complaint was made against Adlerstein asserting that he threatened an employee's job because she objected to his inappropriate behavior toward her. An independent consultant was hired who, after an investigation, concluded that Adlerstein had been guilty of sexual harassment as defined in the Company's policy and had been less than candid in connection with the investigation. The consultant made an oral report of this conclusion to Wertheimer and Mencher on May 14, 2001. Because Adlerstein failed to pay the consultant's bill, a written report detailing the investigation was not delivered to the Company until September 2001.

On April 11, 2001, a meeting of the SpectruMedix board was held. At that meeting Adlerstein represented to the board, and the minutes of the meeting state, that three instruments had been purchased and shipped during the quarter ending March 31, 2001 and the Company was projecting sales of six to nine instruments for the quarter ending June 30, 2001. In fact, according to uncontroverted testimony, the Company sold only one instrument during the quarter ending March 31, 2001 and that sale was made on the condition that SpectruMedix would further develop the instrument to a commercially viable level of functionality.

During April 2001, Wertheimer and Mencher convinced Adlerstein to again hire O'Donnell to generate an updated report on the financial condition of the Company. The resulting report, which projected a cash balance of $66,000 for the Company as of May 31, 2001, was discussed at an April 30, 2001 meeting of the board. As reflected in the board's minutes for that meeting Adlerstein on the one hand and Wertheimer and Mencher on the other had very different reactions to the Company's financial state:

[Adlerstein] did not regard the situation as quite as desperate as the other directors. He said that the Company had previously faced similar cash crises and had weathered them. He said that he had found money to keep the Company alive in the past, and if required to do so again, he would find the resources. Mr. Wertheimer and Ms. Mencher lauded him for his past efforts to save the Company, but said that the[y] were seeking to bring the Company to a cash neutral or profitable position as promptly as possible. The point, Ms. Mencher said, was to put the Company in a position where Dr. Adlerstein wouldn't be required to keep the Company afloat personally in the future.

This divergence in perspective continued through the July 9 meeting.

The board met again on May 25, 2001. Adlerstein reported that the Company was "low on cash" but delivered an upbeat report on the status of discussions he was having with several potential strategic partners. Wertheimer and Mencher remained concerned about the Company's deteriorating financial condition and began to question seriously the information Adlerstein was providing to them. As Mencher testified:

[I]t became clear that we were not getting the entire picture of what was going on with the company and that the company was quickly heading . . . toward a major liquidity crisis — if it wasn't already in one — and that the company needed a crisis manager, just for somebody to get in and tell the board what was really going on and how long the company had to survive.

Thus, Wertheimer and Mencher suggested that the Company should again hire O'Donnell's firm to help the Company in reducing expenses and improving the instrument manufacturing process. Adlerstein agreed, and the entire board unanimously resolved to do so. O'Donnell and his colleague, Gordon Mason, agreed to take on such an assignment provided SpectruMedix execute a written consulting agreement.

During the month of June 2001, O'Donnell and members of his firm began to play a hands-on role at the Company's headquarters, reducing the number of employees while improving the instrument manufacturing process. Among other things, they drew up an organizational chart that defined lines of authority and responsibility in the Company, something Adlerstein had refused to do. These changes were met enthusiastically by the Company's senior employees.

Adlerstein conducted a rearguard action against O'Donnell's restructuring efforts. Most notably, he refused to sign a written contract with O'Donnell, notwithstanding the direction of the board that he do so. He also was frequently away from headquarters in State College during June but, when he did appear, acted to undo changes that had been implemented. Eventually, O'Donnell and

Mason stopped working. Wertheimer and Mencher concluded that Adlerstein was intentionally impeding the progress of the consultants and resolved to investigate the situation at SpectruMedix for themselves.

Wertheimer contacted three of the four department heads at the Company and learned that these individuals were planning to quit their jobs with SpectruMedix if organizational and other changes implemented by the consultants were not kept in place. On July 2, 2001, O'Donnell forwarded a report to Wertheimer and Mencher which concluded that Adlerstein was "the central problem" at the Company, because "he is totally lacking in managerial and business competence and has demonstrated an unwillingness to accept these shortcomings." O'Donnell further opined: "For SpectruMedix to have any chance, [Adlerstein] must be removed from any operating influence within the company."

In June 2001, Wertheimer contacted Reich to discuss involving him as both an investor and manager of SpectruMedix. Wertheimer knew that Reich had the personal wealth and managerial experience to take on a restructuring of SpectruMedix.[7] As he testified at trial: "Ilan was the only guy I knew that had money and had the skills to go in and . . . pull this out of the fire. . . . No institutional investor would go anywhere near a company like this. It had to be somebody that liked to get his hands dirty, who liked to go into a company and basically try and make something out of something that was in a lot of trouble." On June 27, 2001, Reich met with Selbst and O'Donnell to discuss the business of SpectruMedix. Adlerstein was unaware of this meeting. The next day, Reich and Adlerstein met in New York. Reich testified that he then determined that he would only be willing to invest in SpectruMedix if he, and not Adlerstein, were in charge of the Company. Reich thereafter executed a confidentiality agreement and received non-public information in due diligence.

On June 30, Reich sent an e-mail to Selbst that referred to an upcoming meeting between Selbst and Wertheimer for the purpose of discussing Adlerstein's Series B Preferred shares. Adlerstein was not copied on this e-mail and was not aware of this meeting. Also on June 30, Wertheimer had a discussion with Reich about firing Adlerstein.

On July 2, 2001, Reich participated in a conference call with Wertheimer and Mencher and later that day met with Wertheimer to discuss his potential investment. At that meeting, the option of firing Adlerstein for cause from his position as CEO due to his sexual harassment of a Company employee was discussed, as was Adlerstein's voting control over the Company. Adlerstein had no idea this meeting was taking place. But by this time Reich knew he would have an opportunity to take over SpectruMedix.

On July 3, 2001, Reich met with various department heads of the Company during a due diligence visit to the SpectruMedix headquarters. Aware of this visit, Adlerstein acted to discourage senior officials at State College from

7. Wertheimer was aware that in the mid-1980s Reich had pleaded guilty to federal charges of trading on inside information while he was a partner in a prominent New York City law firm and served a one-year prison sentence. Nevertheless, he also knew that, from 1998 to 2000, Reich was employed as the President and CEO of Inamed Corporation, a publicly traded company, and had accomplished a significant turnaround of that company. Wertheimer knew that Reich had left Inamed in 2001 and might be interested in a new challenge.

cooperating fully with Reich. As he e-mailed one of the Company's principal scientists:

> I am not willing to have you spend an inordinate amount of time satisfying [Reich's] . . . requests at the risk of exposing our innards (*i.e.* technologies, analysis) to someone . . . who, in the final analysis, is by no means a sure thing to invest in [SpectruMedix].

A. SPECTRUMEDIX'S INSOLVENCY

By the beginning of July 2001, if not earlier, SpectruMedix was either insolvent or operating on the brink of insolvency.[10] The Company had very little cash (or cash equivalents) and no material accounts receivable due. At the same time, the Company had substantial and increasing accounts payable, Adlerstein was not communicating with creditors, and key parts vendors were refusing to make deliveries unless paid in cash. Indisputably, SpectruMedix did not have sufficient cash on hand to meet its next employee payroll on July 13, 2001, and had no realistic expectation of receiving sufficient funds to do so from its operations. Moreover, the Company's auditors were unwilling to issue the opinion letter necessary for it to file an annual report with the SEC, which was due to be filed on July 10th.

B. THE JULY 9, 2001, BOARD MEETING

1. *Notice*

Wertheimer testified that, on or about July 5, 2001, he and Adlerstein spoke on the telephone about the deteriorating financial condition of the Company and matters relating to a significant arbitration involving SpectruMedix.[11] In that proceeding, MW & E had moved to withdraw as counsel to SpectruMedix, as a result, among other things, of disputes over non-payment of fees and expenses. Wertheimer and Adlerstein may have discussed the fact that the arbitrator planned to hold a conference on the motion to withdraw on Monday, July 9, and wished to be able to speak to Adlerstein by telephone. Wertheimer testified that, during this conversation, Adlerstein agreed to convene a meeting of the board of directors at 11 A.M. on July 9, 2001, at MW & E's New York City offices. Wertheimer further testified that Adlerstein was aware that the topics to be discussed at the meeting would be (i) SpectruMedix's dire financial condition and immediate need for cash, (ii) the arbitration, including the need to retain new counsel, (iii) the formal execution of an agreement to retain O'Donnell, and (iv) the Company's certified public accountants' refusal to issue an audit opinion. Adlerstein maintains that, while he agreed to meet with Wertheimer on July 9 in MW & E's offices, the only purpose of that meeting was to be available to speak to the arbitrator about the motion to withdraw. He denies that he ever agreed to call a board meeting for that time or knew that one was to be held.

The trial record contains plainly divergent testimony on the subject of whether Adlerstein called the July 9 meeting or was given notice of it. Mencher, Reich, and Selbst all support Wertheimer's testimony, although they all learned

---

10. According to [the defendants' exhibits], and unaudited balance sheet as of June 30, 2001, SpectruMedix had $89, 293 in cash and certificates of deposit and $2,404,135 in accounts payable.

11. The other party to the arbitration was Iowa State University Research Foundation, the licensor of core technologies used in SpectruMedix's instrumentation. The arbitration posed a substantial risk to the future viability of SpectruMedix.

about the meeting from Wertheimer. Thus, while their testimony is corroborative of his, it provides no independent evidence of Adlerstein's state of knowledge. Adlerstein's trial testimony was undermined by Karl Fazler, the Company's business manager, who spoke with Adlerstein on the morning of July 9, and remembered Adlerstein telling him that he was on his way to MW & E's offices in order to meet with the board of directors. At the same time, Adlerstein's testimony is buttressed, to some degree, by the fact that none of the directors received written notice of a meeting although, the evidence suggests, SpectruMedix usually circulated notice and a proposed agenda by e-mail.

2. Adlerstein Was Kept in the Dark About the Reich Proposal

Mencher's notes show that Reich first proposed terms for an acquisition of SpectruMedix no later than July 5. On that date, she had a teleconference with Wertheimer and Reich in which they discussed the outline of the transaction and the need to terminate Adlerstein. Her notes contain the entry "fire Joe + negotiate a settlement," followed by a summary of terms for his separation.

The documents necessary for a transaction with Reich were in draft form by July 6, 2001. Selbst sent these documents by e-mail to Wertheimer, Mencher, and Reich. He did not send them to Adlerstein, who was deliberately kept unaware that Reich had made a proposal until the July 9 meeting. At trial, Wertheimer was asked whether "[b]etween the time you got the proposal from Mr. Reich — until the time you walked in to the board meeting on July 9th, did you tell Doctor Adlerstein that you were negotiating a proposal with Ilan Reich . . . [?]" He responded that he had not:

> Because I wanted to save the company at that point. . . . So, no, I didn't tell him that this was going on, because I had no faith that he would — that he would, first of all, you know, go along with the deal; but secondly, I was also worried that he would do something to scare off the investor.

Although Adlerstein argues that the Reich proposal was finalized on Friday, July 6, the record supports the conclusion that Reich and Wertheimer were still negotiating some terms of the deal on the morning of July 9 and that final documents were not ready until that time. The deal finally negotiated provided, subject to board approval, that the Reich Partnership would invest $1 million in SpectruMedix, Reich would assume the active management of SpectruMedix, and SpectruMedix would issue shares of its Series C Preferred Stock to the Reich Partnership carrying with them voting control of the Company.

3. The Meeting Occurs

Adlerstein arrived late at MW & E's New York City offices to find Selbst and Wertheimer waiting for him. He inquired about the conference with the arbitrator and was told that the matter had been postponed. Mencher was hooked in by phone and, according to Wertheimer, Adlerstein called the meeting to order and "wanted to talk about lawyers and the arbitration." Wertheimer then interrupted and said that they needed to talk about finances. He then told Adlerstein that there was a proposal from Reich and handed him a term sheet showing the material elements of the deal.

After reviewing it, Adlerstein told Wertheimer and Mencher that he was not interested in the Reich proposal because it would dilute his shares in the

Company and result in him losing voting control. He has since testified that his lack of interest was also because he believed the price of $1 million to be insufficient for control of SpectruMedix. He did not, however, voice this concern at the time.

In response to the objection that he did voice, Wertheimer and Mencher explained that in their judgment the Company was in immediate need of funds and the investment by Reich was needed to avoid liquidation. Wertheimer asked Adlerstein directly if he was personally in a position to provide the needed funds. Adlerstein responded that he was not.

Wertheimer and Mencher tried to engage Adlerstein in further discussion about the Reich proposal, but Adlerstein sat silent. He testified that the reason for his silence was advice given to him by Selbst in the past: "when in doubt about what to do in a situation like this, keep your mouth shut." Because he and Mencher could not get Adlerstein to engage in any dialogue regarding the proposed transaction, Wertheimer moved the transaction for a vote. Wertheimer testified:

> There was no use in talking about it, because [Adlerstein] wouldn't talk. . . . So the fact that the discussion didn't go any longer, the finger should not be pointed at us, it should be pointed at the person that cut off the discussion. That is Doctor Adlerstein.

Adlerstein has testified that when the vote on the transaction was called he did not participate. The minutes of the meeting reflect that he voted "no." Each of the others present at the meeting—Wertheimer, Mencher, and Selbst—confirms the statement in the minutes.

The board then took up the question of removing Adlerstein "for cause" from his office as CEO and Chairman of SpectruMedix. The elements of "cause" assigned were mismanagement of the Company, misrepresentations to his fellow board members as to its financial situation, and sexual harassment in contravention of his employment contract. After the meeting, the Reich Partnership executed and delivered a stockholder's written consent removing Adlerstein as a director of SpectruMedix. Reich was chosen to replace him.

Some months after July 9, Adlerstein executed a written consent purporting to vote his Series B Preferred shares to remove Wertheimer and Mencher from the board. Adlerstein initiated this Section 225 action on September 11, 2001.

III

The general purpose of Section 225 is to provide "a quick method of review of the corporate election process in order to prevent a corporation from being immobilized by controversies as to who are its proper officers and directors."[20] Because it is summary in nature, a Section 225 proceeding is limited to those issues that must necessarily be considered in order to resolve a disputed corporate election process. A Section 225 action focuses narrowly on the corporate election at issue and is not an appropriate occasion to resolve matters ancillary or secondary to that election.

Here, the question is whether the meeting held on July 9 was a meeting of the board of directors or not. If it was not, Adlerstein continues to exercise a

---

20. Bossier v. Connell, 1986 Del. Ch. LEXIS 471, at *5 (Del. Ch. Oct. 7, 1986).

majority of the voting power and is now the sole lawful director. If it was, I must then address a welter of arguments advanced by Adlerstein to prove that the actions taken at the July 9 meeting ought to be invalidated because Wertheimer and Mencher (and Selbst) all operated in secret to negotiate terms with Reich while keeping Adlerstein deliberately uninformed about their plan to present the Reich proposal at the July 9 meeting. The more persuasive of these arguments are predicated largely on the decisions of the Court of Chancery in VGS, Inc. v. Castiel[23] and Koch v. Stearn.[24]

Finally, if all else fails, Adlerstein argues that Wertheimer and Mencher violated their fiduciary duties of care and loyalty to SpectruMedix in approving the Reich transaction with inadequate information and on terms that were unfair to the Company and its stockholders. He asks for an order canceling the shares and disregarding any effort by Reich to vote them.

For the reasons next discussed, I conclude that, although the meeting of July 9 was called as a board meeting, the actions taken at it must be invalidated. Thus, it is unnecessary to reach the last issue presented by Adlerstein.

A. THE CALL OF THE MEETING

On balance, the evidence at trial indicates that Adlerstein called the July 9 meeting. The procedure for giving notice of a board meeting is typically set forth in a Company's certificate or bylaws. The bylaws of SpectruMedix provide that special meetings of the board "may be called by the president on two (2) days' notice to each director by mail or forty-eight (48) hours notice to each director either personally or by telegram. . . ." I credit Wertheimer's account of his July 5 telephone call with Adlerstein. There is no reason to believe that Adlerstein would not have agreed to convene a board meeting on July 9, in view of the many urgent problems confronting SpectruMedix at that time. Fazler's testimony that Adlerstein called him on the morning of the meeting and said that he was on his way to a board meeting provides additional support for Wertheimer on this point. . . .

B. THE VALIDITY OF THE ACTIONS TAKEN AT THE JULY 9 MEETING

A more difficult issue is whether the decision of Wertheimer, Mencher, and Selbst (no doubt with the knowledge of Reich) to keep Adlerstein uninformed about their plan to present the Reich proposal for consideration at the July 9 meeting invalidates the board's approval of that proposal at the meeting.

There are several factors that weigh against a finding of invalidity. The first is the absence from SpectruMedix's bylaws of any requirement of prior notice of agenda items for meetings of the board of directors, coupled with the absence of any hard and fast legal rule that directors be given advance notice of all matters to be considered at a meeting. Second, is the good faith belief of Wertheimer and Mencher that Adlerstein should be removed from management and that, if they had told him about the Reich proposal ahead of time, he would have done something to kill the deal. Third, is the fact of SpectruMedix's insolvency and the argument that the exigencies created by that insolvency gave Wertheimer and Mencher legal warrant to "spring" the Reich proposal on Adlerstein without warning.

23. 2000 Del. Ch. LEXIS 122 (Del. Ch. Aug. 31, 2000).
24. 1992 Del. Ch. LEXIS 163 (Del. Ch. July 28, 1992).

Ultimately, I am unable to agree that these factors, either singly or in the aggregate, provide legal justification for the conduct of the July 9 meeting. Instead, I conclude that in the context of the set of legal rights that existed within SpectruMedix at the time of the July 9 meeting, Adlerstein was entitled to know ahead of time of the plan to issue new Series C Preferred Stock with the purposeful effect of destroying his voting control over the Company. This right to advance notice derives from a basic requirement of our corporation law that boards of directors conduct their affairs in a manner that satisfies minimum standards of fairness.

Here, the decision to keep Adlerstein in the dark about the plan to introduce the Reich proposal was significant because Adlerstein possessed the contractual power to prevent the issuance of the Series C Preferred Stock by executing a written consent removing one or both of Wertheimer and Mencher from the board. He may or may not have exercised this power had he been told about the plan in advance. But he was fully entitled to the opportunity to do so and the machinations of those individuals who deprived him of this opportunity were unfair and cannot be countenanced by this court.[28] . . .

Wertheimer and Mencher argue that SpectruMedix's dire financial circumstances and actual or impending insolvency justify their actions because, they believe, it was necessary to keep Adlerstein uninformed in order for them to "save the Company." From the record at trial, it is fair to conclude that SpectruMedix was insolvent as of July 9, 2001, in the sense that it was unable to meet its obligations as they came due. This was already true of ordinary supply contracts and fees for its attorneys and consultants. It was also about to be true for a payroll due a few days after the July 9 meeting. Nevertheless, I conclude that these facts do not alter the outcome of the case. Quite the opposite, it is in such times of dire consequence that the well established rules of good board conduct are most important.

While it is true that a board of directors of an insolvent corporation or one operating in the vicinity of insolvency has fiduciary duties to creditors and others as well as to its stockholders, it is not true that our law countenances, permits, or requires directors to conduct the affairs of an insolvent corporation in a manner that is inconsistent with principles of fairness or in breach of duties owed to the stockholders. . . .

There is authority in this court suggesting the possibility that a board of directors could, "consistent with its fiduciary duties, issue a dilutive option in order to protect the corporation or its minority shareholders from exploitation by a controlling shareholder who was in the process of threatening to violate his

---

28. The outcome in this case flows from the fact that Alderstein was both a director and a controlling stockholder, not from either status individually. In the absence of some special contractual right, there is no authority to support the argument that Alderstein's stockholder status entitled him to advance notice of actions proposed to be taken at a meeting of the board of directors. The actions may be voidable if improperly motivated. Condec v. Lunkenheimer, 230 A.2d 769, 775 (Del. Ch. 1967). But the absence (or presence) of notice is not a critical factor. Similarly, in the absence of a bylaw or other custom or regulation requiring that directors be given advance notice of items proposed for action at board meetings, there is no reason to believe that the failure to give such notice alone would ordinarily give rise to a claim of invalidity. Dillon v. Berg, 326 F. Supp. 1214, 1221 (D. Del.), aff'd, 453 F.2d 876 (3d Cir. 1971). Nevertheless, when a director either is the controlling stockholder or represents the controlling stockholder, our law takes a different view of the matter where the decision to withhold advance notice is done for the purpose of preventing the controlling stockholder/director from exercising his or her contractual right to put a halt to the other directors' schemes.

fiduciary duties to the corporation."[34] Nevertheless, neither this nor any other authority suggests that directors could accomplish such action through trickery or deceit, and I am not prepared to hold otherwise.[35] . . .

PROBLEM 4-3

Business has thrived at Fins. Josh, fresh off a gold medal finish at the Olympic Games, wants to take advantage of his new national fame to expand the business. He believes that his national prominence will help the expansion to be successful. He would like to expand regionally to Charlotte and Atlanta as the first steps toward a national footprint.

Sherrie is more cautious and expresses concern about overextending themselves, both personally and professionally. When a group of outside investors approaches Josh about investing in the expansion, Josh informs the investor group that his "business partner" is not keen on the idea, but Josh arranges a meeting with the investors and Sherrie. Sherrie refuses to meet with the investor group, but Josh meets with them again and likes what he hears.

Josh owns a majority of the shares of Fins, but he and Sherrie are the only two directors of the company. After Fins started to flourish, they amended the articles of incorporation to specify the composition of the board of directors. This provision prevents Josh from removing Sherrie as a director in the absence of "good cause."

Josh asks your advice about how he might proceed to pursue the expansion. Can he approve the investment in his role as majority shareholder?

D.   DIVIDENDS AND DISTRIBUTIONS

This Section addresses the most common methods corporations use to distribute money to their shareholders and the legal rules governing such distributions. The most familiar method of distributing money to shareholders is through issuing dividends. A dividend is simply a payment, usually in cash, from a corporation to its shareholders calculated on a per share basis. The timing and amount of dividends are determined by the board of directors in their discretion.

An alternative method of distributing money to shareholders is through share repurchases. When a corporation repurchases its own stock, it pays money to its shareholders and retires the shares. Unlike the redemption of debt, which reduces the outstanding claims against the corporation, the redemption of shares simply reduces the number of outstanding shares but does not change

---

34. Mendel v. Carroll, 651 A.2d 297, 306 (Del. Ch. 1994).

35. Of course, as Chancellor Allen noted in *Mendel,* "if the principal motivation for such dilution is simply to maintain corporate control . . . it would violate the norm of loyalty." 651 A.2d at 304. This principle was firmly established in *Condec,* 230 A.2d 769. The corollary proposition would appear to be equally true: *i.e.,* an action taken primarily to divest a stockholder of control and transfer that control to another would also seem afoul of "the norm of loyalty."

the fact that the shares that remain outstanding own 100 percent of the value of the corporation after all obligations of the corporation are paid.

Regardless of the form of distribution, corporation statutes limit the amount of distributions. The limits on distributions typically take two forms: a solvency test and a balance sheet test. Both are described below.

Solvency test. Most statutes (Delaware being the notable exception) impose a solvency restriction on distributions that would prohibit distributions that would result in insolvency (that is, a condition in which the corporation is unable to pay its debts as they become due in the ordinary course of business). The payment of dividends in such a circumstance also runs afoul of fraudulent conveyance laws, and creditors of the corporation will be able to avoid the payment.

Balance sheet tests. While solvency tests depend on the operations of the corporation, balance sheet tests are measured by concepts from the corporation's financial statements. The following are two different balance sheet tests:

> *"Impairment of capital" test.* Some statutes (*e.g.*, DGCL § 170) permit distributions out of "surplus," which is defined in DGCL § 154 to mean all capital in excess of the aggregate par values (for discussion of "par value," see below) of the issued shares plus any amounts the board has elected to add to its capital account.
>
> *Technical insolvency test.* Model Act § 6.40(c)(2) prohibits distributions that would result in total assets being insufficient to pay the sum of the corporation's liabilities and any liquidation preferences that would be owing if the corporation dissolved at the time of distribution.

It is useful to recognize why there are limits on the board's ability to issue dividends to shareholders. Debtholders have priority if a business fails and there is a bankruptcy proceeding. That priority means that debtholders will be fully paid before shareholders receive any money back. If a corporation approaching bankruptcy distributes all of its remaining cash or other liquid assets to its shareholders as it approaches bankruptcy, then the relative priorities of debtholders and shareholders are effectively reversed. So limits on dividends are part of a system designed to protect creditors, including debtholders, from such reversals.

Unfortunately, this relatively simple concept led to some fairly complicated rules using the concept of "legal capital." The story of legal capital begins with "par value" — a term that initially was equivalent to the sales price of shares. Legal capital is simply the par value per share times the number of shares outstanding. Distributions can only be made out of "surplus," which is all capital in excess of the legal capital. Distributions that exceed surplus result in an "impairment of capital." Today the par value of shares has no relationship to the sales price. Indeed, it is not uncommon to set the par value of shares at a penny a share, so that all of the money raised in selling shares is available as "surplus," except for the one cent per share. While the legal capital account would therefore seem to be not much of a limitation on the issuance of dividends, it is possible under DGCL § 154 to sell "no par" stock. If that is done, the board of directors must specify the amount of legal capital (called "stated capital") or all of the money raised in a no-par stock issuance would be treated as the legal capital.

The following case illustrates the legal capital system at work. Although the Model Act has eliminated legal capital, it is still an important part of the Delaware statute. *Klang* shows, however, that the board of directors has an immense amount of discretion in determining the accounting treatment for assets on their books, and thus can work within the legal capital system to accomplish their goals. One must ask, therefore, whether the goal of protecting creditors and debtholders from unwarranted preferences to the shareholders could be accomplished in a more straightforward way, perhaps as in the Model Act.

KLANG v. SMITH'S FOOD & DRUG CENTERS, INC.

702 A.2d 150
Supreme Court of Delaware
November 7, 1997

Veasey, Chief Justice.

This appeal calls into question the actions of a corporate board in carrying out a merger and self-tender offer. Plaintiff in this purported class action alleges that a corporation's repurchase of shares violated the statutory prohibition against the impairment of capital. . . .

No corporation may repurchase or redeem its own shares except out of "surplus," as statutorily defined, or except as expressly authorized by provisions of the statute not relevant here. Balance sheets are not, however, conclusive indicators of surplus or a lack thereof. Corporations may revalue assets to show surplus, but perfection in that process is not required. Directors have reasonable latitude to depart from the balance sheet to calculate surplus, so long as they evaluate assets and liabilities in good faith, on the basis of acceptable data, by methods that they reasonably believe reflect present values, and arrive at a determination of the surplus that is not so far off the mark as to constitute actual or constructive fraud.

We hold that, on this record, the Court of Chancery was correct in finding that there was no impairment of capital and there were no disclosure violations. Accordingly, we affirm.

Facts

Smith's Food & Drug Centers, Inc. ("SFD") is a Delaware corporation that owns and operates a chain of supermarkets in the Southwestern United States. Slightly more than three years ago, Jeffrey P. Smith, SFD's Chief Executive Officer, began to entertain suitors with an interest in acquiring SFD. At the time, and until the transactions at issue, Mr. Smith and his family held common and preferred stock constituting 62.1% voting control of SFD. Plaintiff and the class he purports to represent are holders of common stock in SFD.

On January 29, 1996, SFD entered into an agreement with The Yucaipa Companies ("Yucaipa"), a California partnership also active in the supermarket industry. Under the agreement, the following would take place:

> (1) Smitty's Supermarkets, Inc. ("Smitty's"), a wholly-owned subsidiary of Yucaipa that operated a supermarket chain in Arizona, was to merge into Cactus Acquisition, Inc. ("Cactus"), a subsidiary of SFD, in exchange for which SFD would deliver to Yucaipa slightly over 3 million newly-issued shares of SFD common stock;

(2) SFD was to undertake a recapitalization, in the course of which SFD would assume a sizable amount of new debt, retire old debt, and offer to repurchase up to fifty percent of its outstanding shares (other than those issued to Yucaipa) for $36 per share; and

(3) SFD was to repurchase 3 million shares of preferred stock from Jeffrey Smith and his family.

SFD hired the investment firm of Houlihan Lokey Howard & Zukin ("Houlihan") to examine the transactions and render a solvency opinion. Houlihan eventually issued a report to the SFD Board replete with assurances that the transactions would not endanger SFD's solvency, and would not impair SFD's capital in violation of 8 Del. C. § 160. On May 17, 1996, in reliance on the Houlihan opinion, SFD's Board determined that there existed sufficient surplus to consummate the transactions, and enacted a resolution proclaiming as much. On May 23, 1996, SFD's stockholders voted to approve the transactions, which closed on that day. The self-tender offer was oversubscribed, so SFD repurchased fully fifty percent of its shares at the offering price of $36 per share. . . .

PLAINTIFF'S CAPITAL-IMPAIRMENT CLAIM

A corporation may not repurchase its shares if, in so doing, it would cause an impairment of capital, unless expressly authorized by Section 160. A repurchase impairs capital if the funds used in the repurchase exceed the amount of the corporation's "surplus," defined by 8 Del. C. § 154 to mean the excess of net assets over the par value of the corporation's issued stock.

Plaintiff asked the Court of Chancery to rescind the transactions in question as violative of Section 160. As we understand it, plaintiff's position breaks down into two analytically distinct arguments. First, he contends that SFD's balance sheets constitute conclusive evidence of capital impairment. He argues that the negative net worth that appeared on SFD's books following the repurchase compels us to find a violation of Section 160. Second, he suggests that even allowing the Board to "go behind the balance sheet" to calculate surplus does not save the transactions from violating Section 160. In connection with this claim, he attacks the SFD Board's off-balance-sheet method of calculating surplus on the theory that it does not adequately take into account all of SFD's assets and liabilities. Moreover, he argues that the May 17, 1996 resolution of the SFD Board conclusively refutes the Board's claim that revaluing the corporation's assets gives rise to the required surplus. We hold that each of these claims is without merit.

SFD's Balance Sheets Do Not Establish a Violation of 8 Del. C. § 160.

In an April 25, 1996 proxy statement, the SFD Board released a pro forma balance sheet showing that the merger and self-tender offer would result in a deficit to surplus on SFD's books of more than $100 million. A balance sheet the SFD Board issued shortly after the transactions confirmed this result. Plaintiff asks us to adopt an interpretation of 8 Del. C. § 160 whereby balance-sheet net worth is controlling for purposes of determining compliance with the statute. Defendants do not dispute that SFD's books showed a negative net worth in the wake of its transactions with Yucaipa, but argue that corporations should have the presumptive right to revalue assets and liabilities to comply with Section 160.

Plaintiff advances an erroneous interpretation of Section 160. We understand that the books of a corporation do not necessarily reflect the current values of its assets and liabilities. Among other factors, unrealized appreciation or depreciation can render book numbers inaccurate. It is unrealistic to hold that a corporation is bound by its balance sheets for purposes of determining compliance with Section 160. . . .

It is helpful to recall the purpose behind Section 160. The General Assembly enacted the statute to prevent boards from draining corporations of assets to the detriment of creditors and the long-term health of the corporation. That a corporation has not yet realized or reflected on its balance sheet the appreciation of assets is irrelevant to this concern. Regardless of what a balance sheet that has not been updated may show, an actual, though unrealized, appreciation reflects real economic value that the corporation may borrow against or that creditors may claim or levy upon. Allowing corporations to revalue assets and liabilities to reflect current realities complies with the statute and serves well the policies behind this statute.

The SFD Board Appropriately Revalued Corporate Assets to Comply with 8 Del. C. § 160.

Plaintiff contends that SFD's repurchase of shares violated Section 160 even without regard to the corporation's balance sheets. Plaintiff claims that the SFD Board was not entitled to rely on the solvency opinion of Houlihan, which showed that the transactions would not impair SFD's capital given a revaluation of corporate assets. The argument is that the methods that underlay the solvency opinion were inappropriate as a matter of law because they failed to take into account all of SFD's assets and liabilities. In addition, plaintiff suggests that the SFD Board's resolution of May 17, 1996 itself shows that the transactions impaired SFD's capital, and that therefore we must find a violation of 8 Del. C. § 160. We disagree, and hold that the SFD Board revalued the corporate assets under appropriate methods. Therefore the self-tender offer complied with Section 160, notwithstanding errors that took place in the drafting of the resolution.

On May 17, 1996, Houlihan released its solvency opinion to the SFD Board, expressing its judgment that the merger and self-tender offer would not impair SFD's capital. Houlihan reached this conclusion by comparing SFD's "Total Invested Capital" of $1.8 billion—a figure Houlihan arrived at by valuing SFD's assets under the "market multiple" approach—with SFD's long-term debt of $1.46 billion. This comparison yielded an approximation of SFD's "concluded equity value" equal to $346 million, a figure clearly in excess of the outstanding par value of SFD's stock. Thus, Houlihan concluded, the transactions would not violate 8 Del. C. § 160.

Plaintiff contends that Houlihan's analysis relied on inappropriate methods to mask a violation of Section 160. Noting that 8 Del. C. § 154 defines "net assets" as "the amount by which total assets exceeds total liabilities," plaintiff argues that Houlihan's analysis is erroneous as a matter of law because of its failure to calculate "total assets" and "total liabilities" as separate variables. In a related argument, plaintiff claims that the analysis failed to take into account all of SFD's liabilities, *i.e.*, that Houlihan neglected to consider current liabilities in its comparison of SFD's "Total Invested Capital" and long-term debt. Plaintiff contends that the SFD Board's resolution proves that adding current liabilities into the mix shows a violation of Section 160. The resolution declared the value of SFD's assets to be $1.8 billion, and stated that its "total liabilities" would not exceed $1.46 billion after the transactions with Yucaipa. As noted, the $1.46 billion figure described only the value of SFD's long-term debt. Adding in SFD's $372 million in current liabilities, plaintiff argues, shows that the transactions impaired SFD's capital.

We believe that plaintiff reads too much into Section 154. The statute simply defines "net assets" in the course of defining "surplus." It does not mandate a "facts and figures balancing of assets and liabilities" to determine by what amount, if any, total assets exceeds total liabilities. The statute is merely definitional. It does not require any particular method of calculating surplus, but simply prescribes factors that any such calculation must include. Although courts may not determine compliance with Section 160 except by methods that fully take into account the assets and liabilities of the corporation, Houlihan's methods were not erroneous as a matter of law simply because they used Total Invested Capital and long-term debt as analytical categories rather than "total assets" and "total liabilities."

We are satisfied that the Houlihan opinion adequately took into account all of SFD's assets and liabilities. Plaintiff points out that the $1.46 billion figure that approximated SFD's long-term debt failed to include $372 million in current liabilities, and argues that including the latter in the calculations dissipates the surplus. In fact, plaintiff has misunderstood Houlihan's methods. The record shows that Houlihan's calculation of SFD's Total Invested Capital is already net of current liabilities. Thus, subtracting long-term debt from Total Invested Capital does, in fact, yield an accurate measure of a corporation's net assets.

The record contains, in the form of the Houlihan opinion, substantial evidence that the transactions complied with Section 160. Plaintiff has provided no reason to distrust Houlihan's analysis. In cases alleging impairment of capital under Section 160, the trial court may defer to the board's measurement of surplus unless a plaintiff can show that the directors "failed to fulfill their duty to evaluate the assets on the basis of acceptable data and by standards which they are entitled to believe reasonably reflect present values." In the absence of bad faith or fraud on the part of the board, courts will not "substitute [our] concepts of wisdom for that of the directors." Here, plaintiff does not argue that the SFD Board acted in bad faith. Nor has he met his burden of showing that the methods and data that underlay the board's analysis are unreliable or that its determination of surplus is so far off the mark as to constitute actual or constructive fraud.[12] Therefore, we defer to the board's determination of surplus, and hold that SFD's self-tender offer did not violate 8 Del. C. § 160.

On a final note, we hold that the SFD Board's resolution of May 17, 1996 has no bearing on whether the transactions conformed to Section 160. The record shows that the SFD Board committed a serious error in drafting the resolution: the resolution states that, following the transactions, SFD's "total liabilities" would be no more than $1.46 billion. In fact, that figure reflects only the

---

12. We interpret 8 Del. C. § 172 to entitle boards to rely on experts such as Houlihan to determine compliance with 8 Del. C. § 160. Plaintiff has not alleged that the SFD Board failed to exercise reasonable care in selecting Houlihan, nor that rendering a solvency opinion is outside Houlihan's realm of competence. *Compare* 8 Del. C. § 141(e) (providing that directors may rely in good faith on records, reports, experts, etc.).

value of SFD's long-term debt. Although the SFD Board was guilty of sloppy work, and did not follow good corporate practices, it does not follow that Section 160 was violated. The statute requires only that there exist a surplus after a repurchase, not that the board memorialize the surplus in a resolution. The statute carves out a class of transactions that directors have no authority to execute, but does not, in fact, require any affirmative act on the part of the board. The SFD repurchase would be valid in the absence of any board resolution. A mistake in documenting the surplus will not negate the substance of the action, which complies with the statutory scheme. . . .

The judgment of the Court of Chancery is affirmed.

PROBLEM 4-4

Despite Sherrie's initial reluctance, Josh ultimately prevailed on her to expand Fins regionally to Charlotte and Atlanta, but they agreed not to accept any outside equity investment. Instead, they have financed their expansion through a combination of personal investments, revenues from the Chapel Hill facility, and bank loans. Thus, Josh and Sherrie remain the only shareholders in Fins.

At the beginning of the third year of operation, Fins owns three facilities that appear on their balance sheet with a total valuation of $2.6 million. The properties are subject to mortgages of approximately $2.4 million. The Company has $100,000 in cash in a bank account, $40,000 in accounts receivable, and $60,000 in equipment, as well as $250,000 in accounts payable and $100,000 of loans from a line of credit from SunTrust Bank.

Josh and Sherrie are discussing the possibility of issuing dividends. Each of them has taken a modest salary from Fins, but they would both like to reap some larger rewards from their hard work, and they are considering a dividend of $100,000 ($60,000 for Josh, reflecting his 60% ownership interest, and $40,000 for Sherrie, reflecting her 40% ownership interest). Josh and Sherrie fully expect Fins to continue to pay its debts as they come due after the distribution of this dividend.

Would Josh and Sherrie be limited in the amount of dividends they can pay, even if they are the only shareholders? Should they be limited? Are there ways around these limits?

E. LIMITED LIABILITY, PIERCING THE CORPORATE VEIL, AND RELATED DOCTRINES

Limited liability and piercing the corporate veil have long been among the most controversial topics in corporate law. Scholars still do not agree about the origins of limited liability in the United States. Although some corporations received limited liability in their special charters, many special charters provided for unlimited shareholder liability. Even when special charters did not provide for direct shareholder liability, they often allowed for unlimited assessments against shareholders, thus creating indirect shareholder liability. Otherwise, the status of limited liability in late 18th-century America is unclear because no reported cases address the issue. It is clear, however, that the policy of limited liability for shareholders was not widely established by courts in the United States until some time into the 19th century. Beginning in the early 1810s, states began to adopt limited liability statutes, but attempts to revive unlimited liability persisted, and state legislatures did not consistently adopt a policy of limited liability until the 1840s. Nevertheless, by the time Joseph Angell and Samuel Ames published their famous corporate law treatise in 1832, they confidently asserted: "No rule of law we believe is better settled, than that, in general, the individual members of a private corporate body are not liable for the debts, either in their persons or in their property, beyond the amount of property which they have in stock." Joseph K. Angell and Samuel Ames, *A Treatise on the Law of Private Corporations Aggregate* 349 (1832).

Although the historical record is unclear, it appears that the availability of limited liability was a major factor in the decision to seek incorporation for many businesses in 18th-century America. During the early 1800s, there was a public outcry at what was perceived as a state-sanctioned method of avoiding responsibility for one's actions. Later, during the Jacksonian period, making limited liability accessible to the masses became a driving inspiration behind the promulgation of general incorporation statutes. Despite initial reservations, therefore, limited liability has endured; indeed, it has thrived, especially in the past decade as state legislatures continue to create new entities offering limited liability protection to investors. (See Chapter 3.) Nevertheless, the existence and recent expansion of limited liability remain one of the most talked about issues in corporate law. The following paragraphs briefly describe the justifications for limited liability and examine the situations in which the protection of limited liability is removed. Like limited liability itself, the common law doctrine of piercing the corporate veil has generated much controversy, mainly for its apparent indeterminacy.

The primary advantages of limited liability are most pronounced in public corporations, not close corporations. For example, many commentators have argued that limited liability enables shareholders to diversify more efficiently because investors made fully liable for the debts of a corporation would expose themselves to too much risk. Under this reasoning, diversification under unlimited liability actually increases risk. Investors in close corporations usually do not invest to diversify, but rather because the corporation is also their source of employment.

The previous justification for limited liability is closely related to another—namely, that limited liability permits the free transfer of shares in the public markets. If shareholders risked incurring personal liability every time they purchased shares, trading in the public markets would be severely impaired. Even if this justifies limited liability for public corporations, it says nothing about close corporations, which by definition are not publicly traded.

Another oft-cited justification for limited liability is that it reduces monitoring costs in two ways: (1) It decreases the need to monitor managers (the more risk investors bear, the more closely they monitor their "agents"); and (2) it reduces costs of monitoring other shareholders (the greater the wealth of other shareholders, the lower the probability of any one shareholder's assets being taken to satisfy a judgment). These advantages of limited liability are much less pronounced in close corporations, where shareholders and managers often are the same people.

Regardless of whether limited liability is justified, its effects are apparent. First, limited liability increases the cost of debt and decreases the cost of equity to the corporation. In other words, shareholders must pay creditors to assume some of the risk of business failure. Limited liability increases the cost of debt by reducing the creditors' sources of payment and increasing business risk (because limited liability owners have less incentive than personally liable owners to act consistently with creditor interests). Voluntary creditors will charge the firm in advance for bearing this risk.

The major potential social cost of limited liability is that people who have limited liability have an incentive to engage in riskier than optimal activities because they are not forced to bear the total costs of such behavior. This increased risk is known as "moral hazard." Moral hazard does not impose social costs in every type of transaction involving a corporation. In transactions involving the corporation and voluntary creditors (particularly lenders, but possibly including employees, consumers, and trade creditors), for example, the firm will be forced to pay for the freedom to engage in risky activities; therefore, society theoretically will bear no extra costs from limited liability. If the firm cannot make credible promises to refrain from taking excessive risks, it must pay higher interest rates. If the price that must be paid to third parties for engaging in a particular activity exceeds the benefits to the firm, the activity will not be undertaken, regardless of the liability rule.

With respect to involuntary creditors (that is, tort victims), on the other hand, there probably is some social cost to limited liability (that is, there are some costs that the corporation does not internalize but instead imposes on tort victims). Insurance may internalize some of these costs, but not all. It is for this reason that Professors Hansmann of Yale University and Kraakman of Harvard University have argued for pro rata, unlimited shareholder liability in the tort law context. *See* Henry Hansmann & Renier Kraakman, *Toward Unlimited Shareholder Liability for Corporate Torts*, 100 Yale L.J. 1879 (1991).

Special problems arise in trying to justify limited liability within corporate groups, such as a parent company and its wholly owned subsidiaries. A wholly owned subsidiary is a legal entity separately incorporated from the parent corporation, but where the parent owns 100 percent of the stock of the subsidiary. In this context it is not so clear that the various business entities should be treated as separate, rather than looking at the enterprise as one related entity. The separate legal status of parent and subsidiary corporations is respected in the majority of cases, and the "whole enterprise" theory of liability for corporate groups in the parent/subsidiary context has been soundly rejected.

Notwithstanding the usual rule of limited liability, in some instances courts will require shareholders to pay the entire amount of a contract or a judgment on a tort law claim, beyond the amount of the shareholders' investments. This is referred to as "piercing the corporate veil," for reasons shrouded in the mists of history. The following framework is used by many courts to analyze piercing cases:

Direct liability. When analyzing a claim seeking to pierce the corporate veil, a threshold question is whether liability may attach to the shareholder directly by reason of the shareholder's own actions instead of recognizing the liability as a *corporate* liability that must be paid by the shareholder personally because of the piercing analysis.

Corporate formalities. If there is no personal liability, the first question under the piercing analysis is whether corporate formalities have been carefully observed (for example, if the corporation has a separate bank account, there is no commingling of personal and corporate funds, regular meetings of directors and shareholders, or corporate records). If the formalities have been followed, few courts will pierce.

If the corporate formalities have not been observed, the analysis becomes murky. Some courts will pierce based on lack of corporate formalities alone on the theory that if the shareholder ignored the separate existence of the corporation, it would be unjust to force a creditor to respect it. But there is no logical reason to pierce the corporate veil simply because shareholders have failed to follow corporate formalities because the harm at issue in the lawsuit usually bears no relation to corporate formalities.

Fairness. Beyond a showing that the corporate formalities were not maintained, most courts require a showing of injustice or unfairness to link the wrongdoing to the harm. Two types of injustice are most common: (1) where the disregard of the corporate entity has been visible to a third party and that third party has reason to be confused about whether he or she was dealing with a corporation or an individual; (2) where the shareholder has disregarded the separateness of the corporation's funds and treated them as her own (such as through unauthorized withdrawals). Thus, if the shareholder herself seems to think it fair to treat the corporation's funds as interchangeable with her personal funds, it seems fair for the courts to do the same.

The common law doctrine of piercing the corporate veil has fascinated corporate law scholars over the years, as they have attempted to break the code used by courts to decide when to "pierce" and when to retain limited liability. One well-reasoned attempt to make sense of the piercing cases was put forward by Judge Frank Easterbrook and Professor Daniel Fischel, who contend that piercing the corporate veil cases may be understood simply as rough attempts to balance the benefits of limited liability against its costs. Frank H. Easterbrook & Daniel R. Fischel, *Limited Liability and the Corporation,* 52 U. Chi. L. Rev. 89 (1985). Based on this notion of piercing, they make the following predictions about how the cases should come out:

> *Close corporations versus public corporations.* In close corporations, those who supply the capital are usually the same people who manage the firm; therefore, there is no need to incur monitoring costs, and one of the major benefits of limited liability is gone. In addition, the costs of limited liability (that is, increased risk taking) will be more pronounced in close corporations, where the managers will capture more of any potential gains. Easterbrook and Fischel predict, therefore, that courts will often pierce in a close corporation context but not in a public corporation context.
>
> *Parent corporation versus individual shareholder.* Easterbrook and Fischel predict that courts are more likely to pierce when the shareholder is a corporation than when the shareholder is an individual because allowing creditors to reach the assets of parent corporations does not create unlimited liability for any individual; therefore, the benefits of limited liability remain largely intact. In addition, the moral hazard (that is, increased risk taking) will be more pronounced where a corporation is allowed to form a subsidiary to perform especially risky activities.
>
> *Contract cases versus tort cases.* Easterbrook and Fischel assert that courts are more likely to pierce in tort cases than in contract cases. This prediction is based on the assumption that corporations pay for risk *ex ante* under contracts but not under

torts and that courts, therefore, should be more likely to force payment *ex post* in tort cases.

Undercapitalization. Easterbrook and Fischel assert that undercapitalization is a common source of piercing, especially in tort cases because the high transaction costs preclude *ex ante* negotiation. The rationale is obvious: the lower the amount of the firm's capital, the greater the incentive to engage in risky activities.

Shortly after Easterbrook and Fischel published their analysis, Professor Robert Thompson published the results of an empirical study of 1,583 piercing cases. *See* Robert Thompson, *Piercing the Corporate Veil: An Empirical Study,* 76 Cornell L. Rev. 1036 (1991). Among Thompson's conclusions were the following:

> *Close corporations versus public corporations.* Consistent with Easterbrook and Fischel's analysis, *no case* concerned piercing the veil in a public corporation context. Stated another way, piercing the corporate veil is a doctrine reserved exclusively for close corporations.
>
> *Parent corporation versus individual shareholder.* Contrary to Easterbrook and Fischel's expectations, cases involving an individual shareholder resulted in piercing 50 percent of the time, while cases involving a parent corporation resulted in piercing 28 percent of the time.
>
> *Contract cases versus tort cases.* Again contrary to Easterbrook and Fischel's expectations, courts pierced more often in contract cases (42%) than in tort cases (31%). However, a later study found "no substantial difference between the success rate for piercing in contract cases versus tort cases." Lee C. Hodge & Andrew B. Sachs, *Piercing the Mist: Bringing the Thompson Study into the 1990s,* 43 Wake Forest L. Rev. 341 (2008).
>
> *Undercapitalization.* Again contrary to Easterbrook and Fischel, undercapitalization did not seem to play a role in a large number of piercing cases. It appeared as a factor in only 19 percent of the contract cases and 13 percent of the tort cases studied.

Of course, Thompson's study is subject to many limitations, which he acknowledges, by virtue of the fact that his data are reported cases and may not represent the total cases decided (because many decisions are not reported) or filed (since most cases are settled) and do not take account of potential cases that are not filed because the litigants are deterred by their assessment of probable outcomes. A more recent study of a large sample of complaints and counterclaims filed in federal district courts found that plaintiffs often have success with claims of veil piercing, where "success" is defined broadly to include not only success on the merits, but also success on motions that keep a case alive. Christina L. Boyd and David A. Hoffman, Disputing Limited Liability, 104 Nw. U. L. Rev. 853 (2010). With respect to the factors that drive veil piercing success, Boyd and Hoffman found, among other things, "no evidence that individual shareholders were more likely to be subject to piercing liability than corporate ones," "voluntary creditors are strong veil piercing plaintiffs," and "undercapitalization allegations are associated with a strongly increased chance of winning both veil piercing motions and cases."

The following case examines the doctrine of piercing the corporate veil and related liability claims. *Soerries* is a straightforward piercing claim based on a cause of action arising under tort law. The court cites precedent for the notion that "the concept of piercing the corporate veil is applied in Georgia to remedy injustices which arise where a party has overextended his privilege in the use of a corporate entity in order to defeat justice." Consider the evidence used to support the piercing claim and ask yourself whether piercing in this instance really accomplishes that purpose.

SOERRIES v. DANCAUSE

546 S.E.2d 356
Court of Appeals of Georgia
March 2, 2001

ELLINGTON, Judge.

In this dram shop liability case, William A. Soerries appeals from a jury verdict that pierced the corporate veil and held him personally liable for damages. Because we find that the evidence presented supported the jury's verdict, we affirm.

The facts, viewed in a light most favorable to the jury's verdict, show that Soerries was the sole shareholder of Chickasaw Club, Inc., which operated a popular nightclub in Columbus for 23 years until it closed in 1999. At approximately 11:45 P.M. on July 31, 1996, 18-year-old Aubrey Lynn Pursley was intoxicated when she entered the Chickasaw Club. Although a Columbus ordinance prohibits individuals under 21 years old from entering nightclubs, it is undisputed that club employees did not check Pursley's identification to establish her age. A friend testified that Pursley already was intoxicated when she arrived at the club. Even so, friends testified that Pursley drank additional alcohol at the club and was visibly intoxicated when she left at approximately 3:00 A.M. on August 1, 1996. Security videotapes showed that she left the club with a beer in her hand. Shortly thereafter, Pursley was killed when she lost control of her car and struck a tree.

Joseph Dancause, Pursley's stepfather, sued Chickasaw Club, Inc. and Soerries individually for the cost of the car and for punitive damages. Following a trifurcated jury trial, the trial court entered judgment on the jury's verdict, which pierced the corporate veil and found Soerries jointly liable with the corporation for $6,500 in compensatory damages and solely liable for $187,500 in punitive damages. Soerries appeals from this judgment.

Soerries argues that Dancause presented insufficient evidence to justify piercing the corporate veil. We disagree. As we have held:

> The concept of piercing the corporate veil is applied in Georgia to remedy injustices which arise where a party has overextended his privilege in the use of a corporate entity in order to defeat justice, perpetrate fraud or to evade contractual or tort responsibility. Because the cardinal rule of corporate law is that a corporation possesses a legal existence separate and apart from that of its officers and shareholders, the mere operation of corporate business does not render one personally liable for corporate acts. Sole ownership of a corporation by one person or another corporation is not a factor, and neither is the fact that the sole owner uses and controls it to promote his ends. There must be evidence of abuse of the corporate form. Plaintiff must show that the defendant disregarded the separateness of legal entities by commingling on an interchangeable or joint basis or confusing the otherwise separate properties, records or control. In deciding this enumeration of error, we are confronted with two maxims that sometimes conflict.

On the one hand, we are mindful that great caution should be exercised by the court in disregarding the corporate entity. On the other, it is axiomatic that when litigated, the issue of piercing the corporate veil is for the jury, unless there is no evidence sufficient to justify disregarding the corporate form.

J-Mart Jewelry Outlets v. Standard Design, 462 S.E.2d 406 (1995).

In this case, the jury heard testimony from Larry Jones, who managed the Chickasaw Club for 20 years. Jones testified that the club was open four nights a week and regularly admitted an average of 250 people who paid cover charges of $3 to $4 each. Additional patrons were also admitted, so that the club sometimes exceeded its capacity of 477 people. According to Jones, he and the other employees were paid each night in cash by Soerries out of the proceeds of the club. Although Jones testified that 1996 was a "bad year" for the corporation and that he was paid between $10,000 and $12,000, corporate payroll records reported his earnings as only $5,690. Jones admitted that Soerries sometimes paid him extra cash that was not reported to the club's bookkeeper.

It is undisputed that Soerries paid his employees, suppliers, and entertainers in cash and not from existing corporate checking accounts. One employee admitted he was paid "under the table." The employee never appeared on corporate payroll records, although Soerries admitted giving him money to help out around the club.

Corporate tax returns showed that, even though the Chickasaw Club was a busy nightclub, it regularly declared business losses. On cross-examination, Soerries failed to explain the substantial difference between reported income on corporate and individual tax returns and evidence regarding cash proceeds from cover charges and alcohol sales. When asked how the club paid its employees and other operating expenses while operating at a loss, Soerries explained that he often paid the corporate expenses out of his personal funds.

Soerries owned the property on which the Chickasaw Club was located and testified that he paid his $4,830 monthly mortgage note from the club's cash proceeds. Although Soerries claimed that the club's payments were rent that he then used to pay the note, personal tax returns showed that he received only $34,173 in rent in 1996, even though the corporation reported paying $43,000 in rent in its 1996 corporate tax return. Further, both figures are significantly less than the $57,960 in rent that would have been due from the corporation, based upon 12 months of $4,830 rental payments. Additional evidence showed that Soerries also owned other rental property in 1996 that would have paid $3,150 per month, making the disparity between his alleged rental earnings and his reported income even greater.

A jury could construe this evidence to demonstrate that Soerries commingled individual and corporate assets by personally assuming the corporation's financial liabilities, waiving corporate rental payments, or using corporate funds to directly pay his personal mortgage notes and other expenses. As such, the totality of the evidence presented raised a jury issue on whether Soerries

disregarded the separateness of legal entities by commingling and confusion of properties, records, control, etc. It is obvious that if the individual who is the principal shareholder or owner of the corporation conducts his private and corporate business on an interchangeable or joint basis as if they were one, then he is without standing to complain when an injured party does the same. Under such circumstances, the court may disregard the corporate entity.

Abbott Foods of Ga. v. Elberton Poultry Co., 327 S.E.2d 751.
On appeal, we construe all the evidence most strongly in support of the verdict, and if there is evidence to sustain the verdict, we cannot disturb it. We find that the evidence presented was sufficient to support the jury's decision to pierce the corporate veil.

PROBLEM 4-5

Midway through the third year of operation, revenues at all three Fins facilities dropped dramatically after it was revealed that Josh took performance-enhancing drugs prior to winning his Olympic gold medals. SunTrust Bank immediately became concerned about its ability to recover on $1.3 million in mortgage indebtedness and on approximately $250,000 owing under the line of credit.

The situation turned from bad to worse for Fins when a lifeguard at the Atlanta facility was killed in a tragic accident while cleaning the pool alone late at night. Aside from the personal tragedy, the accident was also a business setback because Fins did not carry liability insurance protecting its employees in the event of such an event. The lifeguard's young daughter was awarded a judgment of $300,000 against Fins for negligence when it turns out that key safety equipment that would have prevented the accident had not been installed.

After Fins defaults on its mortgages, SunTrust would like to pursue Josh and Sherrie personally for repayment of the Fins obligations. SunTrust argues that Josh's deceit in taking performance-enhancing drugs is a justification for piercing the corporate veil of Fins. Moreover, SunTrust argues that Fins was undercapitalized because it failed to purchase and maintain proper liability insurance.

How would a court analyze the claims by SunTrust? What facts not stated above would a court find most persuasive in determining whether to pierce the corporate veil of Fins?

CHAPTER
5

Control of the Closely Held Firm

MOTIVATING HYPOTHETICAL

James Duncan was a graduate student in Computer Science at the University of Illinois at Urbana-Champaign when the Apple iPhone was introduced in January 2007. With the support of his mother, Louise Stewart, and his long-time friend and first cousin, Thomas Luke, Duncan took a leave of absence from his studies to develop classic video game apps for the iPhone, including Donkey Kong, Frogger, Pac-Man, and Pong. He started a company called Classic Games Inc., a closely held corporation formed under the Model Business Corporation Act.

Shareholders in closely held corporations often decide to vary the default rules contained in corporation statutes. Because the number of shareholders is, by definition, small, highly tailored arrangements allocating control are often feasible. The following Sections describe myriad ways in which shareholders can structure control rights in a closely held corporation. The last Section in this chapter explores the fiduciary limits of control through the doctrine of minority oppression.

A. SHAREHOLDER AGREEMENTS

One of the most common methods of allocating control in a closely held corporation is to set up a simple contract among the shareholders. The usual thrust of such a contract is to provide protection to minority shareholders. After all, majority shareholders exercise control through the default rules of corporate law, so a contract is unnecessary to protect their interests.

Shareholders often seek to fix the composition of a board of directors through a so-called "vote pooling" agreement. Simply stated, this agreement obligates shareholders to vote together as a single block, usually for director candidates nominated by specified shareholders. Courts have long enforced vote pooling agreements, and modern corporation statutes expressly provide for such agreements. *See, e.g.,* Model Business Corporation Act (Model Act) § 7.31; Delaware General Corporation Law (DGCL) § 218(c). While vote pooling agreements sometimes purport to grant shareholders the right to "designate" or "appoint" directors, corporation statutes require director elections. Model Act § 8.03(c); DGCL § 211(b). Thus, shareholders may "nominate" candidates at a shareholders meeting or pursuant to procedures specified in the bylaws, and those candidates may stand for election to the board of directors.

The more controversial shareholder agreements are those that attempt to control the actions of the directors. Unless a minority shareholder has enough clout to obtain a majority of the director seats, representation alone offers little protection. As a result, minority shareholders frequently bargain for rights with respect to specified corporate transactions. In some instances, these are affirmative rights, such as the right to name certain corporate officers, the right to employment, or the right to certain salaries or dividends. In other instances, the protective provisions come in the form of negative covenants — rights to veto certain corporate transactions.

At one time, courts were very skeptical of shareholder agreements in which the parties attempted to make decisions otherwise vested in the board of directors. Perhaps the best known case of this kind is McQuade v. Stoneham, 189 N.E. 234 (N.Y. App. 1934), which involved the owners of the New York Giants, a professional baseball club. Charles Stoneham was the majority owner of the National Exhibition Company, which owned the Giants. Upon the sale of a minority interest in the company to Francis McQuade, Stoneham, McQuade, and John McGraw — the Hall of Fame manager of the Giants, who was also a minority shareholder of the company — entered into a shareholder agreement pursuant to which they agreed to "use their best endeavors for the purpose of continuing as directors of said Company and as officers thereof." In addition, the agreement specified each of their salaries. When the board of directors — all of whom, other than McQuade, were allegedly under Stoneham's control — terminated McQuade as treasurer of the company, and when Stoneham and McGraw subsequently failed to vote for McQuade as a director (thus resulting in his ouster from the board), McQuade sued to enforce the shareholder agreement. The court declined to enforce the agreement, however, reasoning:

> [T]he stockholders may not, by agreement among themselves, control the directors in the exercise of the judgment vested in them by virtue of their office to elect officers and fix salaries. Their motives may not be questioned so long as their acts are legal. The bad faith or the improper motives of the parties does not change the rule. Directors may not by agreements entered into as stockholders abrogate their independent judgment.

Over time, this sort of reasoning has fallen out of favor. Courts in many states have approved shareholder agreements on their own, while others have done so after being prompted by a state legislature. In either circumstance, the effect has been to allow for greater contracting freedom among shareholders. Model Act § 7.32 is an example of the legislation that validates shareholders' agreements even when they limit board powers in certain enumerated ways.

The following case construes a shareholders' agreement. How compelling is the court's rationale? And does the court address the plaintiffs' construction of the agreement in a persuasive fashion? Given the problems this badly drafted agreement created, how might the parties have better expressed what they were trying to accomplish in this agreement?

RONNEN v. AJAX ELECTRIC MOTOR CORP.

648 N.Y.S.2d 422
Court of Appeals of New York
July 9, 1996

LEVINE, Judge.

The opposing parties to this litigation are brother and sister who, with their children, collectively hold a bare majority of the issued and outstanding shares of the capital stock of Ajax Electric Motor Corp., a closely held corporation based in Rochester. Respondent Neil Norry has been the chief executive officer of Ajax. The immediate matter in dispute is the validity of the election of the board of directors of the corporation at its annual shareholders' meeting held March 13, 1995.

Central to that dispute is a March 5, 1982 shareholders' agreement between Norry (and his two sons) and his sister, appellant Deborah Ronnen, on behalf of herself and as custodian for her children. The shareholders' agreement granted Norry certain rights to vote Ronnen's stock and that of her children.

The March 13, 1995 shareholders' meeting began in acrimony between Ronnen and Norry, who initially chaired the meeting. Immediately prior to the meeting, Ronnen served Norry with a temporary restraining order prohibiting him from voting the Ronnen shares regarding proposed amendments to the Ajax bylaws and certificate of incorporation, which were on the agenda for the meeting. When the meeting convened, Ronnen's attorney had the proceedings videotaped, without prior notice to Norry. In response to these actions, Norry announced that the meeting was being adjourned. Over Ronnen's protest, [Norry] voted the Ronnen shares with the Norry shares for a combined majority vote to adjourn and left the meeting. In his absence, Ronnen and the remaining shareholders of Ajax, including appellants Bruce Lipsky and Joseph Livingston, elected a slate of directors.

Norry then brought a proceeding . . . to invalidate the election of directors in his absence and for an order directing a new election. Ronnen, Lipsky and Livingston petitioned . . . to confirm the election. Supreme Court interpreted the shareholders' agreement as giving Norry the right to vote the Ronnen shares in any election of a board of directors. This factor, together with the hostile atmosphere permeating the March 13, 1995, meeting, led Supreme Court to conclude that a new election should be held. The Appellate Division affirmed the order for a new election of directors, with two Justices dissenting on the ground that the shareholders' agreement did not transfer Ronnen's voting rights to Norry for board of directors elections and that the election was in other respects properly conducted. Ronnen, Lipsky and Livingston appeal as of right on the basis of the double dissent.

We now affirm. The parties are not in dispute over the circumstances leading up to the March 5, 1982 agreement between the Norry shareholders and Ronnen. Ajax had been a highly prosperous distributor of electric motors nationwide, founded by Irving Norry (the father of Neil Norry and Deborah Ronnen), Sydney Gilbert and David Lipsky. Irving Norry and his wife had, by 1980, transferred by gift or sale all of their shareholdings in Ajax to their two children and their families. Friction developed between Norry and Ronnen regarding, among other things: Norry's acquisition for his children of his mother's Ajax shares, upsetting the equality of the Norry siblings' interests in the corporation; Ronnen's displeasure over an irrevocable option her brother had been granted in 1967 to acquire her Ajax shares under what she considered an inadequate price formula; the level Norry had fixed for his compensation and other alleged financial self-dealing in Ajax and in Norry Electric Co., a separate family business; and Ronnen's objection to not being kept informed of financial decisions Norry made in connection with the management of both corporations. Ronnen wished to ensure that her interest in Ajax could be passed on to her children free of interference by Norry. Norry expressed willingness to accommodate Ronnen, provided he was guaranteed continued managerial control of Ajax and was given the opportunity to acquire the Ronnen shares in Ajax before they could be sold to an outsider. He also wished to buy out his sister's interest in Norry Electric Co. These various objectives of the parties were implemented in the shareholders' agreement and other contemporaneous transactions.

The shareholders' agreement recited as one of its purposes "to provide for the vote of [the Norry and Ronnen families'] Shares in order to provide for continuity in the control and management of Ajax." The primary voting control provision was set forth in paragraph 8 of the agreement. Subparagraph 8(a) provided that the Ronnen shareholders "agree that Neil Norry shall exercise voting rights over the Shares owned by them . . . with respect to any and all matters *relating to Ajax's day-to-day operations and corporate management*" (emphasis supplied). Norry was also given the right to vote the Ronnen shares regarding any sale of substantially all of Ajax's assets or stock to an outside party, provided that the transaction treated the Norry and Ronnen interests equivalently. The agreement, however, reserved to Ronnen the right to vote the Ronnen shares "[i]n connection with other major corporate policy decisions," and listed as examples of such major decisions, "other types of corporate reorganizations" and other similar actions. Subparagraph 8(b) gave Norry an irrevocable proxy to vote the Ronnen shares as provided in the preceding subparagraph.

The unambiguous words of paragraph 8 and the recital purpose clause of the agreement present an issue of pure contract interpretation for the court, and admit of no construction other than the conferral to Norry of the right to vote the Ronnen shares in any election of a board of directors of Ajax. The undisputed background facts support this interpretation as well. The parties have not cited to any provision of the Ajax certificate of incorporation transferring corporate management decisions from the board of directors to the shareholders. Therefore, management of the business of Ajax was, by statute, exclusively "under the direction of its board of directors" (Business Corporation Law § 701).

We have held that "the law in force at the time [an] agreement is entered into becomes as much a part of the agreement as though it were expressed or referred to therein, for it is presumed that the parties had such law in contemplation when the contract was made and the contract will be construed in the light of such law" (Dolman v. United States Trust Co., 2 N.Y.2d 110, 116, 157 N.Y.S.2d 537, 138 N.E.2d 784). Thus, without the right to vote the Ronnen shares to elect the directors of the corporation, the transfer of voting rights regarding "corporate management" under subparagraph 8(a) of the agreement would be essentially meaningless since management control was vested in the directors and not the shareholders. We have long and consistently ruled against any construction which would render a contractual provision meaningless or without force or effect.

The reservation to Ronnen of the right to vote the Ronnen shares "[i]n connection with . . . major corporate policy decisions" is consistent with the parties' intent to confer on Norry the right to vote the Ronnen shares in the election of board of directors, since major corporate decisions, such as corporate mergers, connote extraordinary change while director elections are the ordinary subject matter of a shareholder meeting. It, therefore, follows that by agreeing to transfer to Norry the right to vote the Ronnen shares "with respect to any and all matters relating to Ajax's . . . corporate management," the parties must have intended, on the facts of this case, to give Norry the right to vote the shares to elect a board of directors.

By the same token, in the absence of having an irrevocable proxy to vote their cumulative majority interests for the election of directors, the shareholders' agreement's recited purpose to ensure "continuity in the control and management of Ajax" could not be achieved. We should not adopt a construction of subparagraph 8(a) which would frustrate one of the explicit central purposes of the agreement.

Ronnen, however, points to the language of paragraphs 10, 12 and 14 of the shareholders' agreement as negating any inference that Norry was given the right to vote the Ronnen shares in elections of the board of directors. Paragraph 10 of the agreement recites that "[t]he parties agree that . . . they shall vote the Shares" to ensure a seat on the board of directors for Deborah Ronnen. Paragraph 12 provides that "[t]he parties agree that . . . they shall vote the Shares in the election of Directors" to ensure Ronnen's access to all reports concerning the management of Ajax, and paragraph 14 similarly requires the "parties" to "vote the Shares in the election of Directors" so as to generally cap Norry's total executive compensation at $125,000 a year.

Ronnen, thus, argues that the literal language of paragraphs 10, 12 and 14 militates against an interpretation of the agreement ceding the right of Ronnen, "a party" to the agreement, to vote the Ronnen shares for the election of directors, and that such an interpretation would deprive those provisions of any force or effect. Ronnen further argues that the use of the plural, "parties," in those paragraphs was ignored by the courts below, who rewrote the clauses in question as an agreement that, singularly, "Neil Norry shall vote the Shares" in accordance with the substantive requirements of paragraphs 10, 12 and 14. We disagree.

As we have already discussed, subparagraph 8(a) of the shareholders' agreement unequivocally guarantees the right of Norry to vote a majority block of shares on all matters "relating to . . . corporate management" of Ajax, which in this case necessarily entails majority voting rights to elect a board of directors favorable to the continuation of his corporate policies. Construing paragraphs 10, 12 and 14 literally, to permit Ronnen to vote the Ronnen shares in board of directors elections to form a majority with shareholders possibly unfavorable to Norry's management role would, thus, take away from Norry the bargained for management rights and privileges promised in paragraph 8. We have previously applied the principle that a contract which confers certain rights or benefits in one clause will not be construed in other provisions completely to undermine those rights or benefits.

Contrary to Ronnen's contention, a transfer of Ronnen's voting rights to Norry on election of a board of directors will not render paragraphs 10, 12 and 14 meaningless. These three provisions were manifestly intended to suit the purposes of Ronnen, guaranteeing her a seat on the board of directors and requiring the three Norry shareholders (Neil Norry and his sons) to vote the majority block of shares for directors who will be favorable to her position on access to corporate information and on imposing a ceiling on Norry's compensation. Thus, the pluralized language in paragraphs 10, 12 and 14 that "[t]he parties agree that . . . they shall vote the Shares" in board of directors elections can readily be construed to refer to the three Ronnens who were parties to the agreement, all of whose shares would be necessary to form a majority voting block with the Ronnen shares. That interpretation should be favored, as it would reconcile paragraphs 10, 12 and 14 with paragraph 8 of the agreement and effectuate all of the parties' objectives in entering into the agreement.

For all the foregoing reasons, we hold that the courts below properly construed the shareholder's agreement as giving Neil Norry the right to vote the Ronnen shares in board of directors elections. The position on appeal of appellants Lipsky and Livingston that, as thus construed, the shareholders' agreement is void as against public policy is unpreserved and, hence, has not been considered.

Finally, in view of the irrevocable proxy Ronnen gave Norry to vote the Ronnen shares in any election of directors, together with the other circumstances surrounding the March 13, 1995 shareholders' meeting alluded to by Supreme Court, the ordering of a new board of directors election in this case was within that court's discretionary equity powers under Business Corporation Law § 619 to "confirm the election, order a new election, or take such other action *as justice may require*" (emphasis supplied).

Accordingly, the order of the Appellate Division should be affirmed, with costs.

PROBLEM 5-1

Duncan, Stewart, and Luke own 40, 35, and 25 percent, respectively, of Classic Games Inc. The three shareholders enter into a Shareholders Agreement, which contains the following provision:

> Except as provided below, any director may be removed from office with or without cause by the affirmative vote of the holders of 60 percent of the combined voting power of the then outstanding shares of stock entitled to vote generally in the election of Directors; provided, however, that James Duncan may be removed as a director only with cause upon the unanimous affirmative vote of the other shareholders of the Company entitled to vote generally in the election of Directors.

Is this provision enforceable? If Duncan and Stewart called a shareholder meeting and voted to remove Luke as a director, would Duncan be entitled to fill the resulting vacancy on the board of directors of Classic Games Inc. over Stewart's objection?

B. TRANSFER RESTRICTIONS

Transfer restrictions are widely used to control selection of business associates, to provide certainty in estate planning, and to ensure that the corporation complies with close corporation statutes, S corporation regulations, or Securities

Act exemptions. They are imposed in the charter or bylaws of the corporation or in a separate agreement among shareholders or between shareholders and the corporation. DGCL § 202(b); Model Act § 6.27(a).

Transfer restrictions are valid if they pass a two-part test. First, the restrictions must comply with the formal requirements relating to adoption of the restriction and must be conspicuously noted on the share certificates. DGCL § 202(a) and (b); Model Act § 6.27(a) and (b). Second, the restrictions must be for a proper purpose. The general test for a proper purpose is "reasonableness." General types of transfer restrictions are laid out in DGCL § 202(c) and Model Act § 6.27(d): (1) the shareholder must offer the corporation or other shareholders the option to purchase the shares, either at a price specified by prior agreement or at the price offered by the prospective third-party purchaser (an "option"); (2) the corporation or other shareholders are obligated to purchase the shares (a "buy-sell" agreement); (3) the corporation or other shareholders must approve the transfer of the shares (a "prior approval" or "consent" requirement); (4) the shareholder is simply prohibited from transferring to certain persons or classes of persons. Options and buy-sell agreements are common forms of transfer restrictions and are usually enforced by courts. Prior approvals normally are enforceable as long as approval may not be unreasonably withheld. Flat prohibitions on transfer are viewed very skeptically by courts and usually would be struck down as unreasonable. It is important to note that all transfer restrictions may not affect shares issued before the restriction is adopted unless the holders vote in favor of the restriction. DGCL § 202(b); Model Act § 6.27(a).

The most common transfer restrictions are buy-sell agreements. Buy-sell agreements solve many problems in close corporations: (1) they provide liquidity for shareholders who wish to withdraw; (2) they determine the price of the shares at a time when none of the parties to the agreement knows which of them will be the sellers and which will be the purchasers (thus providing an incentive to all to provide for a "fair" price); and (3) they allow the principals of the corporation to plan with some certainty.

Prices in a buy-sell agreement take one of four forms: (1) fixed price, which must be updated constantly to reflect the current value of the shares; (2) book value, the most popular measure because of ease of determination, but it is based on historical costs and may not reflect true underlying values; (3) appraisal, which has the potential to be very good, but the parties should decide beforehand on what basis the business should be appraised; and (4) formula, which suffers from being very complicated.

The *Armour* case and the following Problem illustrate the use of transfer restrictions, with particular emphasis on the "reasonableness" requirement.

CAPITAL GROUP COMPANIES, INC. v. ARMOUR

2005 WL 678564
Court of Chancery of Delaware
March 15, 2005

LAMB, Vice Chancellor.

A Delaware corporation brought this suit against the two trustees of a trust, who are husband and wife, seeking a declaration that certain contractual stock transfer restrictions alleged to apply to shares of its Class A common stock owned by the trust are valid and enforceable. The two defendants are parties to a divorce proceeding pending in the Superior Court of California and, in connection with that proceeding, the wife has claimed an interest in the stock now owned by the trust. The issue is whether the stock transfer restrictions may reasonably operate to prevent the transfer to, or disposition in favor of, the wife of any legal or beneficial interest in the stock.

I.

The Capital Group Companies, Inc. ("CGC") is a privately-held Delaware corporation with its principal place of business in Los Angeles, California. The defendants are Timothy Armour and Nina Ritter, husband and wife, who are the trustees of the Ritter-Armour Revocable Trust dated August 6, 1991, as amended (the "Trust"). Armour is an Executive Vice President of Capital Research and Management Company, a subsidiary of CGC, and a director of CGC.

CGC requires all persons purchasing shares of its common stock to become parties to a Stock Restriction Agreement ("SRA") that contains several provisions relevant to this case, including a general restriction on transfer, and a right to redeem that allows the stock to be repurchased at a formula price upon its transfer to a non-authorized transferee. In general, the SRA precludes the transfer of stock to any non-employee of CGC (such as Ritter) and allows CGC the right to repurchase shares if they are transferred to a non-employee.

In 1984, Armour and Ritter were married and, in 1989, began buying CGC common stock. All stock purchased between 1989 through mid-1998 was purchased in Armour's name. In October 1998, for tax planning purposes, and with CGC's consent, the defendants placed the stock owned by Armour into the Trust. In order to comply with the SRA, and to gain CGC's consent to the transfer, the defendants amended the Trust (the "Trust Amendment"), several provisions of which are relevant to the resolution of this case. The Trust Amendment provides that the Trust may not distribute any stock held in the trust without the consent of CGC. The Trust Amendment also makes reference to the SRA and provides that, upon revocation of the Trust, if the stock is not immediately transferred to Armour, CGC has the right to repurchase it.

In connection with transferring the stock to the Trust, in their capacities as trustees, Armour and Ritter signed a so-called Joinder Agreement, agreeing to be bound by the SRA. Thereafter, through 2002, again with the consent of CGC, the parties continued to purchase stock in the name of the Trust. In connection with those purchases, defendants signed so-called Purchaser Representation Letters, again agreeing to be bound by the SRA. The Trust, as amended, provides that either Ritter or Armour may act on behalf of the Trust, but that only Armour can vote the stock held by the Trust.

In June 2003, Armour filed for divorce in California. The stock held in the Trust represents the bulk of the value of the community property from the marriage. Despite the transfer restrictions in the SRA, Ritter plans to ask for an award of a direct or indirect interest in the stock held in the Trust. Specifically, Ritter has stated that, pursuant to the divorce proceeding and the distribution of community property therewith, she will ask the California court to award the stock to Armour, and order Armour to make continuing payments to her in order to accomplish an equitable distribution of the community estate. The amount that she will request that Armour be ordered to pay will be one-half of all dividends that Armour receives from the stock and one-half of any net sale proceeds that he receives from the sale of the stock, if and when he sells the stock (the "Requested Distribution").

Anticipating that Armour or CGC, or both, would contend that the Requested Distribution is prohibited by the SRA, Ritter sought to join CGC as a party to the divorce proceeding. When that gambit failed, CGC filed this action against Ritter and Armour, in their capacity as trustees, seeking the following judgment:

> b. declaring that the SRA is valid and enforceable;
>
> . . .
>
> d. declaring that the award of a record, beneficial or other interest to Ritter in connection with the California Divorce Action would constitute an unauthorized transfer, such that CGC would be entitled to repurchase or redeem any CGC stock transferred to Ms. Ritter (directly, beneficially or otherwise) in accordance with the SRA and CGC's Certificate of Incorporation.

. . .

On November 16, 2004, CGC filed a motion for summary judgment on all claims. While not formally filing a cross-motion for summary judgment, Ritter requested in her answering brief that the court exercise its inherent power to grant summary judgment in her favor. Therefore, the court treats CGC's motion and Ritter's response as cross-motions for summary judgment.

. . .

III.

In the complaint, CGC seeks a declaration from this court that: (1) any disposition of an interest in the stock contained in the Trust, made without CGC's consent, violates the SRA; and (2) the SRA is valid and binding on Ritter. Ritter argues that the requested declaration is too vague and uncertain to be granted. She also argues that she is not bound by the SRA because, she claims, the SRA, by its terms, does not apply to the distribution of marital assets that she has requested from the California court. Finally, Ritter argues that, even if the SRA does preclude the requested distribution of marital assets, this restriction on the transfer of shares is unreasonable and, therefore, void as against public policy.

CGC counters with three arguments. First, CGC argues that the terms of the SRA specifically preclude the disposition of marital assets that Ritter has requested from the California court. Second, CGC contends that Delaware law does not require that restrictions on transfers of stock be reasonable. Finally, CGC claims that, even if Delaware law does require that restrictions on transfers of stock be reasonable, the restrictions contained in the SRA meet this test. The court will address each of these arguments in turn.

. . .

B. DOES THE SRA SPECIFICALLY PRECLUDE THE DISPOSITION OF MARITAL ASSETS THAT RITTER HAS REQUESTED FROM THE CALIFORNIA COURT?

Ritter states that, pursuant to the divorce proceeding and the distribution of community property therewith, she will ask the California court to award the stock to Armour and order Armour to continue making payments to her in order to accomplish an equitable distribution of the community estate. Ritter's Requested Distribution will be one-half of all dividends that Armour receives from the stock and one-half of any net sale proceeds that he receives from the sale of the stock, if and when he sells the stock. CGC argues that this would constitute a violation of the SRA.

Section 2.1 of the SRA states, in pertinent part:

> No Stockholder shall sell, assign, transfer (whether by merger, operation of law or otherwise), dispose of or encumber any of the Stockholder's Shares or any interest therein except as specifically provided in this Agreement. Any purported or attempted sale, assignment, transfer, disposition or encumbrance of Shares or any interest therein not in strict compliance with this Agreement shall be void and shall have no force or effect.

It is indisputable that a transfer of direct, record ownership of the stock from the Trust to Ritter would violate the SRA. However, Ritter argues that the Requested Distribution does not violate this section of the SRA because: (1) the Requested Distribution will not give Ritter an "ownership interest," (2) the Requested Distribution is not a "transfer," as that term is defined in the SRA, and (3) even if the Requested Distribution is a transfer and does give Ritter an ownership interest in the stock, the SRA does not preclude Ritter from having such an ownership interest.

First, Ritter claims that the Requested Distribution would not violate the SRA because it would not give her an ownership interest. She would not be an owner of record, and she would not have a right to vote the shares. Instead, she would have an interest in half of the dividends and half of any proceeds from the sale of the stock.

It is difficult to see how the right to receive dividends and the right to receive proceeds upon the sale of the stock does not constitute an "interest" in the stock. The rights to receive dividends and proceeds from a stock are two of the sticks in the bundle of rights that have traditionally been the hallmarks of stock ownership. In the Requested Distribution, Ritter seeks to have the California court award her these rights in the stock. Ritter tries to avoid the conclusion that this is an ownership interest by stating that she would *only* have an interest in Armour's assets directly commensurate with, and dependent upon, the proceeds he receives from the stock. This is a distinction without a difference. Under the Requested Distribution, payments to Ritter, like those to Armour (who undeniably would have an ownership interest in the stock) would be completely dependent on the distribution of dividends or the sale of stock. The Requested Distribution would give Ritter an equitable entitlement to half the proceeds from dividends paid on the stock, and half the proceeds from any sale. This is clearly an "interest," and an ownership interest, that is prohibited by the SRA.

Second, Ritter's contention that the Requested Distribution would not be a "transfer" that violates the SRA is true, but not dispositive. Section 9.39 of the SRA defines a "Transfer" as "[a] transfer of record of Shares as reflected in the stock book of CGC maintained by CGC or its stock transfer agent, as the case may be." Ritter correctly points out that, since the Requested Distribution would not make her a record holder, it would not constitute a prohibited "transfer of record." This is so because the only transfer of record ownership would be to Armour, which is permitted under the SRA. Section 2.1 of the SRA, however, precludes more than "transfers" of an interest in the stock. It also precludes dispositions and assignments, two terms not defined in the SRA. Therefore, the court must interpret these terms using their common and ordinary meaning. "Assign" generally means "to transfer to another in writing . . . ; *specif.* to transfer (property) to another in trust or for the benefit of creditors." WEBSTER'S THIRD NEW INTERNATIONAL DICTIONARY 132 (3rd ed.1976). "Dispose" generally means "to transfer into new hands or to the control of someone else (as by selling or bargaining away)." *Id.* at 654. Awarding Ritter the right to share in both the dividends paid on the stock and proceeds from its sale would qualify as both a disposition and an assignment. Therefore, it would violate the SRA.

C. DOES DELAWARE LAW REQUIRE THAT STOCK RESTRICTIONS BE REASONABLE?

Ritter also argues that the transfer restrictions found in the SRA are unreasonable and, thus, unenforceable. CGC counters that, under Delaware law, a stock restriction need not be reasonable.

The transfer restrictions contained in the SRA are governed by 8 *Del. C.*§ 202, which sets forth the requirements for a valid restriction on the transfer of securities. The first two of those requirements, that the restriction must be conspicuously noted on the stock certificate and that the restriction may be imposed either in the corporation's certificate of incorporation or in its bylaws, are not at issue. What is at issue is whether the other, substantive features of the stock transfer restrictions satisfy the remaining statutory criteria of section 202 for a legally permissible restriction on the transfer of a corporation's stock.

Before section 202's 1967 enactment, Delaware courts held that restrictions imposed by a corporation on the transfer of its stock would be upheld only if those restrictions were reasonable. Generally, a restriction was valid if it was reasonably necessary to advance the corporation's welfare or attain the objectives set forth in the corporation's charter. A determination of the validity of those restrictions required balancing the policies served by the restrictions against the traditional judicial policy favoring the free transfer of securities.

In *Lawson v. Household Fin. Corp.*, 152 A. 723 (Del. 1930), the Delaware Supreme Court held that a corporation's right of first refusal contained in its stock was reasonable, and therefore valid. The Supreme Court held that because the restriction was "necessary and convenient to the attainment of the objects for which the company was incorporated," retaining the stock ownership of the company among its employees was reasonable.

In *Greene v. E.H. Rollins & Sons*, 2 A.2d 249 (Del. Ch. 1938), this court indicated that a corporate charter provision authorizing the corporation to buy a shareholder's stock at any time at its net asset value, even from an unwilling seller, might be an invalid restriction on transfer. This court found that the only reason stated for the restriction was to perpetuate a company consisting of shareholders who were "agreeable" to the board. This court concluded that the power to redeem stock is "highly questionable if its avowed purpose was to get rid of certain stockholders of a given class solely because their presence in the stockholding group was undesirable to the rest."

After the adoption of section 202, there was some uncertainty as to whether the common law requirement of a reasonable purpose for stock transfer restrictions continued. When faced with that issue in *Grynberg v. Burke*, 378 A.2d 139

(Del. Ch. 1977), *rev'd on other grounds, Oceanic Exploration Co. v. Grynberg,* 428 A.2d 1, 8 (Del. 1981), this court held that the statute is "no more than a modern codification of the [common law] principle" and continued to apply the common law requirement that transfer restrictions serve a reasonable purpose.

In *Grynberg,* the defendants argued that the four categories of restriction contained in section 202(c) were *per se* valid. The court rejected this argument, stating that subsection (c):

> is no more than a modern codification of the principle adopted in *Lawson v. Household Finance Corp.,* namely, that a restraint on the free transferability of corporate stock . . . is permissible under our law provided it bears some reasonably necessary relation to the best interests of the corporation. § 202(e) merely backs up the provisions of § 202(c) by stating that any form of restriction other than those enumerated in subsection (c) is also permissible provided it meets the same test. If anything, it may be that § 202(c) places the burden of demonstrating the unreasonableness of such enumerated restrictions on the party attacking them.

The decision in *Grynberg* has been cited approvingly and applied in several cases in this court.

CGC asks this court to overturn *Grynberg,* solely on the basis of two non-Delaware cases decided more than 25 years ago. The first, *St. Louis Union Trust,* 562 F.2d 1040 (8th Cir.1977), decided a few months before *Grynberg,* held that section 202 had dispensed with the common law reasonableness test. In that case, the United States Court of Appeals for the Eighth Circuit based its decision on what that court viewed as the purpose of enacting the statute, *i.e.,* to broaden the circumstances in which restrictions would be enforced in order to clear up the preexisting uncertainties in the common law. In support of this proposition, the Eighth Circuit cited FOLK, THE DELAWARE GENERAL CORPORATION LAW, 198 (1972). The Eighth Circuit also relied on a Pennsylvania case construing a similar Pennsylvania statute. In the second case, *Kerrigan v. Merrill Lynch, Pierce, Fenner & Smith, Inc.,* 450 F.Supp. 639 (S.D.N.Y.1978), the United States District Court for the Southern District of New York relied almost exclusively on *St. Louis Union Trust.* Even though *Kerrigan* was decided a few months *after Grynberg, Grynberg* was not cited by the *Kerrigan* court. Therefore this court must assume that the *Kerrigan* court mistakenly concluded that no Delaware cases construing section 202 existed. Although generally well-reasoned, *St. Louis Union Trust* and *Kerrigan* can no longer be thought to reflect Delaware law. Rather, *Grynberg* has been the clearest statement of Delaware law on this subject for over 25 years, and has been cited approvingly numerous times by this court. The principle of *stare decisis* requires this court to follow *Grynberg.*

Moreover, section 202 has been amended twice since *Grynberg* was decided and on neither occasion did the General Assembly act to eliminate the reasonableness requirement found in that case. . . . For the above reasons, the court reaffirms the holding in *Grynberg* that a reasonableness inquiry is required when restrictions on the transfer of stock are contested.

D. ARE THE STOCK RESTRICTIONS CONTAINED IN THE SRA REASONABLE?

Ritter argues that, as applied to her, the restrictions in the SRA are unreasonable.

The burden of proving that a stock restriction is unreasonable lies with the party contesting the validity of the restriction. CGC has put forward numerous corporate policies that are advanced by the restrictions. However, these polices can be summarized as having two main purposes. First, CGC argues that the ownership restrictions limit the number of shareholders in the company, so that CGC need not comply with the filing and disclosure requirements that federal securities law imposes on public companies. Second, CGC argues that restricting ownership interest in the company to employees and their immediate family members aligns the interests of the employees with those of the company, thereby enabling greater returns.

CGC also relies on certain express provisions of section 202 in arguing that the restrictions are reasonable. . . .

In response, Ritter argues that, while perhaps reasonable in the abstract, the restrictions on ownership are not reasonable as they apply to her. First, the Requested Distribution will not increase the number of record shareholders, as that term is defined by SEC regulations. Therefore, the Requested Distribution will not affect CGC's filing and disclosure requirements with the SEC. Furthermore, CGC already allowed Armour to purchase more stock, which he holds in his own name. By distributing the stock held in the Trust to him, Ritter argues, the number of record shareholders would actually be reduced by one.

Second, Ritter argues that the SRA does not restrict a transfer of the stock (or an interest in the stock) to her. It only restricts such a transfer to her without CGC's consent which, she claims, has been unreasonably withheld. She notes that not all of CGC's stock is owned by CGC employees. At times, CGC has allowed charities and charitable remainder trusts to own stock. In addition, the SRA allows certain "grandfathered" stock, *i.e.* stock owned since before 1967, to be owned by the heirs and spouse of the former owner. It allows any disabled employee shareholder, who is no longer able to work for CGC, to transfer her stock to a fiduciary to act on her behalf. It also allows any employee who retires to continue to own the stock for up to six years. For the past 20 years, approximately 20% of CGC's stock has been owned by these non-employees.

1. What Is the Proper Scope of the Reasonableness Inquiry?

Ritter's argument requires this court to decide the scope of the reasonableness inquiry. The parties argue for two different standards by which the court should apply the reasonableness inquiry. First, is the actual restriction reasonable to achieve a legitimate corporate purpose (as CGC argues)? Second, is the stock transfer restriction reasonable as it applies to a particular individual (as Ritter claims)?

The Delaware courts have been reluctant to invalidate stock restrictions because they are unreasonable. In the seminal case, *Greene,* discussed *supra,* this court questioned the validity of a transfer restriction that allowed a corporation to buy back its stock at any time, even from an unwilling seller. Yet, the court did not invalidate the stock transfer restriction at issue. It decided only that a full hearing was needed to determine whether "the ends and purposes of the restraint complained against so related to the corporation's successful operation [] as to warrant the conclusion that the restraint is reasonable." Moreover, the court examined whether the restrictions were reasonable or not on their face, not in how the restrictions were applied to the particular plaintiffs.

In *Tracy v. Franklin,* 67 A.2d 56, 59-60 (Del. 1949), the Delaware Supreme Court upheld this court's invalidation of a voting trust agreement that prohibited the signatories from transferring their stock during the life of the trust.

The court found no "legally sufficient purposes to justify the restraints." The Supreme Court further noted that even if it is a stockholder agreement that restricts the transfer of shares, "some purpose must appear, other than an unexplained desire to make [the shares] inalienable." Again, the Supreme Court questioned the validity of the stock restriction on its face, and *not* how it was applied.

Since the adoption of section 202, the Delaware courts have been broadly deferential to the decisions of market participants when they decide to place restrictions on stocks. The court in *Mitchell Assocs. v. Mitchell,* 1980 WL 268106 (Del. Ch. Dec. 5, 1980), upheld the validity of a stockholder agreement that required the sale of the company's stock back to the company, at a formula price, upon the shareholder's death. The court found the restriction reasonable in relation to the company's purpose, *i.e.* "maintain[ing] some measure of choice in taking in new shareholders." Both *Grynberg* and *Agranoff v. Miller,* 1999 WL 219650 (Del. Ch. Apr. 9, 1999), place the burden of proving that a stock restriction is invalid on the party attacking the restriction. Moreover, the intention behind section 202 was to be broadly deferential to market participants. "Given the deference that should be granted toward a stock restriction that is expressly authorized by the Code, a reviewing court should not excessively scrutinize the reasonableness of the restriction." *Joslin v. S'holder Serv. Group,* 948 F.Supp. 627, 631-32 (D.Tex. 1996).

In light of the reluctance of our courts to invalidate stock restrictions and the broad deference that should be given to the decisions of market participants to enter into such restrictions, the court holds that a deferential reasonableness inquiry is required when courts are asked to invalidate a stock transfer restriction. This approach is also consistent with the general principle that Delaware corporate law is enabling and does not impose choices on market participants. Therefore, the proper inquiry is whether the actual restrictions are reasonable to achieve a legitimate corporate purpose.

2. Are the Restrictions Reasonable to Achieve a Legitimate Corporate Purpose?

The policy of restricting the number of record shareholders to avoid public company reporting and filing requirements is clearly a valid purpose under section 202(d). Not having to comply with the burdensome and costly filing and disclosure requirements is an obvious "statutory or regulatory advantage." Likewise, the Delaware Supreme Court expressly found that the alignment of the employees' interests with those of the company is a legitimate policy. In the words of the Supreme Court, a company has a legitimate interest in "the employment of trained, competent and honest persons who can always be depended upon to protect the company's interests. Such persons can best be secured by providing them with an interest in the business. . . ."

It is reasonable to conclude that CGC's purposes would not be achieved if the stock was transferable. First, transfer of the stock to a sufficiently large number of owners would destroy CGC's exemption from SEC regulations. A restriction on transfer is obviously reasonably related to this purpose. Second, restricting ownership interest in the stock to employees (or their immediate families) clearly aligns the interests of the employees with CGC. Having an ownership interest in the company gives the employees more of the benefits of the company's success, and more of the risks in the company's failure. Therefore, these restrictions are reasonably related to legitimate corporate purposes.

Ritter argues that the Requested Distribution would not violate the SRA's purpose of maintaining CGC as a private company. This is beside the point.

The Requested Distribution would violate the restrictions contained in the SRA. These restrictions were adopted to serve the proper purpose of maintaining the company as a private company and are reasonably related to this goal. The restrictions need not be the least restrictive alternative that the board could adopt. They need only be reasonable.

Furthermore, Ritter was well aware of, and specifically agreed to, the restrictions on her interest in the stock, and she agreed that she could be divested of whatever rights she had in the stock at any time. The Trust is fully revocable by either Ritter or Armour, upon written notice. Upon revocation of the Trust, the stock automatically transfers to Armour, and it cannot transfer to Ritter. Ritter also signed numerous other documents restricting any rights or interests she has in the stock. Ritter cannot now disclaim the reasonableness of these restrictions, after agreeing to them time and time again.

In addition, Ritter argues that the SRA does not *really* restrict ownership to employees because it gives CGC the discretion to waive those restrictions and because the SRA contains several exceptions. However, even Ritter admits that the vast majority of stock (approximately 80%) is employee owned. And the vast majority of stock that is not employee owned is "grandfathered" stock, stock owned before the SRA was entered into and expressly provided for in the SRA. Furthermore, while Ritter makes a great deal about the fact that CGC has allowed charities to own stock, this too is provided for in the SRA. It is also relevant that, in every instance, CGC *bought back* this stock from the charity at the formula price, usually within a month of the time the charity acquired the stock, but never more than three months after.

In contrast, a transfer to Ritter is not expressly provided for in the SRA. CGC would have to exercise its discretion and make an exception for her. While CGC most likely has the discretion to do so, it has never allowed a transfer of stock pursuant to a divorce, and asserts that it never will. In fact, should CGC make an exception for Ritter in this case, it would be more difficult for it to claim that its policy of prohibiting such transfers is reasonable in a subsequent case.

Ritter also cannot credibly argue that CGC's retention of discretion to approve an otherwise prohibited transfer is itself evidence of unreasonableness. On the contrary, it is eminently reasonable to retain the ability to adjust policy to changing circumstances. Indeed, it would perhaps have been unreasonable if CGC had not retained discretion, but had it bound itself to *never* allow a transfer not in strict compliance with the SRA.

For the foregoing reasons, the court concludes that the restrictions on the transfer of stock contained in the SRA are reasonable. . . .

V.

For the above reasons, the court concludes that CGC is entitled to declaratory relief. The court therefore declares that the restrictions on stock transfer contained in the SRA bar the disposition of record ownership of the stock to Ritter, they bar the Requested Distribution, and they bar any disposition of any ownership right in the stock to Ritter, without CGC's express prior consent. The court further declares that the restrictions contained in the SRA are valid and binding. . . . It Is So Ordered.

PROBLEM 5-2

One of the terms of the Shareholder Agreement between Duncan, Stewart, and Luke is labeled "Transfer Restrictions," and it contains the following paragraphs:

1. No stock of the Corporation shall be transferred, assigned, and/or exchanged or divided, unless or until approved by the Directors thereof;
2. If any stock be offered for sale, assigned, and/or transferred, the Corporation shall have the first opportunity of purchasing the same at no more than the book value thereof;
3. Should the Corporation be not interested in purchasing the stock, and could not economically offer to purchase said stock, any stockholder of record should be given the next opportunity to purchase said stock, at a price not to exceed the book value thereof;
4. If the Corporation was not interested in the stock, and any stockholders were not interested therein, then the same could be sold to any blood member of the family.

The book value of shares of Classic Games Inc. is approximately $3 per share, but value of these shares in an arm's length sale would be substantially higher, perhaps as high as $20 per share. Luke would like to sell his interest in the company, and he would like to use the proceeds of the sale to start his own plumbing business. Luke's uncle, Chester Petersen, has offered to purchase Luke's stock at $15 per share. Chester is the brother of Luke's mother, who is not related by blood to Duncan or Stewart.

Could Duncan and Stewart simply refuse to allow the sale by Luke? Could Duncan and Stewart force Luke to sell his shares back to the Corporation for $3 per share?

C.   VOTING TRUSTS

DGCL § 218 and Model Act § 7.30 are examples of modern statutes that authorize the use of voting trusts. Voting trusts long were frowned upon by courts as instruments of deceit. Historically, they are associated with the robber barons, who gained control over large corporations by assembling votes in voting trusts. As a result of this historical skepticism of voting trusts, even modern statutes routinely limit their duration to no longer than ten years and impose various formal requirements to prevent abuse. For example, voting trusts must be in writing and must be filed with the corporation. Litigants have often attempted to characterize agreements among shareholders as de facto voting trusts in an attempt to invalidate them; if an agreement is determined to be a de facto voting trust, the agreement inevitably will have failed to comply with the formal requirements of voting trusts and will, therefore, be invalid.

Voting trusts were created to overcome rules against irrevocable proxies.[1] Unlike proxies, in which the shareholder retains ownership of the shares but

_____

1. As noted in Chapter 6.B.1, a proxy is the authorization given by a shareholder to another person to vote the shareholder's shares. Proxies are revocable unless they are "coupled with an

simply directs the proxy holder to vote the shares, in a voting trust, legal title to shares is transferred from the shareholders to the voting trustees. Although shareholders retain the financial rights belonging to the shares, the trustees possess exclusive voting power over the shares. The voting trustees typically issue voting trust certificates to the beneficial owners of the shares. These certificates usually can be traded.

The purposes of voting trusts are varied. Generally speaking, voting trusts work to ensure continuity of management. By placing control in the hands of a trustee, shareholders are assured of consistent voting. Voting trusts are often implemented as part of a reorganization plan or to prevent dissension among various factions of stockholders.

Courts have evolved in their treatment of voting trusts. Early courts validated voting trusts only if they accomplished a legitimate purpose. The modern judicial view of voting trusts is that they are enforceable unless contrary to public policy.

The following case is the most renowned modern case involving voting trusts. The longstanding dispute among members of the Warehime family in relation to the family's business, Hanover Foods Corporation, illustrates the use of voting trusts as a control-allocation mechanism. As you can infer from the multiple opinions in the case, the Supreme Court of Pennsylvania had a difficult time with the case. Do you believe that the "good faith" standard applied by the court provides adequate protection to the dissenting members of the Warehime family?

WAREHIME v. WAREHIME

761 A.2d 1138
Supreme Court of Pennsylvania
November 27, 2000

FLAHERTY, Chief Justice.

This is an appeal by allowance from an order of Superior Court which reversed an order of the Court of Common Pleas of York County denying injunctive relief in a dispute over control of Hanover Foods Corporation (HFC), a consumer food products company. The background of the case is as follows.

Alan Warehime, the father of John A. Warehime, Michael Warehime, and Sally Warehime Yelland, was chairman and chief executive officer of HFC from 1956 to 1989. In 1988, two voting trusts were established by the Warehimes. A majority of the voting stock of HFC was placed into the trusts. One trust, containing 199,496 shares of Class B voting stock, was established by Alan

---

interest." The law traditionally had a strong presumption against irrevocability and usually would enforce an irrevocable proxy only if the interest were a charge, lien, or some property right in the shares themselves or if the shareholder had given a security interest in the shares to protect the proxy holder under a loan. More recent cases suggest that courts will enforce irrevocable proxies any time the proxy is given for the protection of the proxy holder or to ensure that the shareholder will perform some duty to the proxy holder. Despite liberalization of the common law rules governing irrevocable proxies, courts still struggle to draw the line. Model Act § 7.22 defines "coupled with an interest" in great detail in an attempt to eliminate some of the confusion over the scope of irrevocable proxies. *Cf.* DGCL § 212(e).

Warehime and his three children. The other trust, containing 15,025 Class B shares, was established by Alan Warehime and five of his grandchildren. Alan Warehime served as the sole voting trustee for both trusts.

In 1989, by appointment of Alan Warehime, John Warehime became chairman and chief executive officer of HFC. Alan Warehime continued to serve as voting trustee for the trusts, however, until his death in 1990. Thereafter, John Warehime, who had been designated by Alan Warehime as successor trustee, filled that role.

Both of the trusts were designed to expire in 1998, ten years after their creation. Anticipating this, during the 1990s Michael Warehime and Sally Warehime Yelland made it known that they were not satisfied to have John Warehime running HFC. Michael Warehime, who controls another consumer food products company, Snyder's of Hanover, expressed an interest in becoming chairman of HFC. He and the other plaintiffs in this action did not, however, develop any plans for the future of HFC; nor did they identify the management that they intended to install. Uncertainty over the course that HFC would take after expiration of the trusts caused instability within the company and cast uncertainty over its operations, with the result that relations with the company's customers and suppliers were adversely affected and it became impossible for HFC to raise needed equity capital.

In 1994, John Warehime voted all of the voting trust shares in favor of a proposal to eliminate cumulative voting in the election of HFC's directors.[1] The proposal was adopted and, as a result, John Warehime was able to exercise the voting trust shares to elect all of the board members.

In 1996, a body known as the "Independent Directors Committee" was formed by several members of the board. It was formed for the purpose of considering strategic alternatives for HFC in light of the impending expiration of the voting trusts and the dissention among members of the Warehime family. The family had not been able to set aside their differences to plan for the future of HFC. John Warehime, Michael Warehime, and Sally Warehime Yelland had engaged in very little communication with each other in recent years. The decision to form the committee was made solely by board members without advice or input from counsel or John Warehime. The committee's independence was reflected in the trial court's findings that the board rejected proposals made by John Warehime on numerous occasions and that the board would only continue to support John Warehime as chairman of HFC if he continued to perform well.

The committee commissioned various consulting firms to conduct a review of HFC. The review determined that HFC was equal or superior to its competition but that it would need approximately $30 million in new capital to sustain its competitive position. Uncertainty over HFC's future, arising from the impending 1998 expiration of the voting trusts, would make it difficult to raise this capital. The review cautioned that if uncertainty over the company's future persisted there would be a deterioration in HFC's business prospects and that the long-term interests of the company would be harmed.

In light of this situation, the committee considered various strategic alternatives. These included doing nothing and allow the voting trust to expire, with the

---

1. No challenge to the elimination of cumulative voting has been preserved by Michael Warehime and the other plaintiffs; hence, the matter is not at issue in this appeal.

result that HFC's prospects would meanwhile deteriorate. Also considered was the possibility of selling the company. The option that the committee decided upon, however, was to recommend adoption of amendments to HFC's articles of incorporation to provide a stable governance structure.

The proposed amendments permitted the issuance of 10,000 shares of Series C Convertible Preferred Stock to the HFC 401(k) plan, provided that the majority of the trustees of that plan are "disinterested directors" as defined in the Business Corporation Law. The amendments also provided a method for resolution of disputes among members of the Warehime family as to the management of HFC. Specifically, the amendments provided that in the event of a dispute among family members regarding the election of directors or other related matters during the five years after the issuance of the stock, the Series C would be entitled to 35 votes per share, and, if there is no such dispute, the Series C shares would remain non-voting. Thus, the amendments place directors serving as fiduciaries of the 401(k) plan in a position to resolve disputes over the management of HFC through exercise of their voting rights in Class C shares. John Warehime has no voting rights with regard to those shares. Because John Warehime as voting trustee of the Class B shares has control over election of the board of directors, however, the amendments have the effect of prolonging the period in which directors elected by him will have a measure of control over the company.

The shareholders of HFC were given formal notice of the proposed amendments. Soon thereafter, Michael Warehime and several other shareholders filed an action seeking a preliminary injunction to prohibit John Warehime from voting shares in the trusts in favor of the amendments. They alleged that the amendments would, in effect, allow John Warehime to extend his control of HFC beyond the termination of the voting trusts.

After a hearing, the trial court determined that the proposed amendments did not present a conflict of interest between the private interests of John Warehime and his duties as trustee of the voting trusts, that the purpose of the amendments was not to advance the personal interests of John Warehime, and that the amendments reflected a good faith effort to serve the best interests of HFC and its shareholders, including the beneficiaries of the voting trusts, since the amendments assured stability in the governance structure of HFC for a five-year period that would permit needed capital to be raised and allow the company to grow and prosper. Accordingly, on June 24, 1997, the request for a preliminary injunction was denied. The following day, John Warehime convened a meeting and voted all of the trust shares in favor of the proposed amendments; the amendments were, therefore, adopted.

Michael Warehime took an appeal to Superior Court. Superior Court held that the trial court erred in refusing to grant an injunction against John Warehime voting the trust shares in favor of the amendments and that by voting in favor of those amendments John Warehime breached his duty of loyalty to the trust beneficiaries. *Warehime v. Warehime*, 722 A.2d 1060, 1071 (Pa. Super.1998). The court stated that it was irrelevant that his actions were undertaken in good faith to benefit HFC, and that:

> [W]e cannot sanction the action of John Warehime voting the shares of the voting trusts in favor of the proposed amendments. The adoption of these amendments, while taken for the stated reasons of preserving the integrity of HFC's value and ability to function profitably, will, nonetheless, serve to perpetuate the control of

the company by John Warehime for at least another five years and preclude the other shareholders, including the beneficiaries of the trust, from the ability and opportunity to make any meaningful decision concerning the management of HFC.

In short, Superior Court held that a voting trustee's actions must be measured against a standard of conduct requiring more than good faith, i.e., a standard of absolute loyalty that bars the trustee from taking any actions that extend his influence over the corporation beyond the expiration of the trusts, irrespective of whether the actions are undertaken in good faith for the benefit the company and its shareholder beneficiaries. We do not agree that the standard of good faith was inapplicable. Accordingly, we reverse.

The Business Corporation Law expressly permits shareholders to enter into voting trust agreements and assures that the provisions of such agreements will be given effect:

> (a) Voting trusts. One or more shareholders of any business corporation may, by agreement in writing, transfer all or part of their shares to any person for the purpose of vesting in the transferee voting or other rights pertaining to the shares *upon the terms and conditions and for the period stated in the agreement.*

15 Pa.C.S. § 1768(a) (emphasis added). Nothing in this provision or elsewhere in the Business Corporation Law prevents shareholders from including in the terms and conditions of the agreement a definition of the fiduciary obligation of the trustee. The Warehime trusts include such a provision. It defines and limits the trustee's duty to the beneficiaries, as it provides:

> The Trustee will use his *best judgment* in voting upon the stock held by him, but assumes no responsibility for the consequence of any vote cast, or consent given by him, in *good faith,* and in the absence of gross negligence.

The language of the agreements is clear and unambiguous. The trustee must exercise his best judgment in voting the stock and act in good faith. Such is the extent of the fiduciary duties that the parties placed on the trustee. Other than those duties, there are no limitations set forth as to the manner in which the trustee's voting powers can be exercised.

Indeed, the trustee's powers are broadly stated in the agreements, to wit:

> [T]he *Trustee shall have the exclusive right to vote upon such stock* or to give written consents in lieu of voting thereon, subject to any limitation on the right to vote contained in the Certificate of Incorporation . . . *at any and all meetings of the stock-holders of the Corporation, for whatsoever purpose called or held,* and in any and all proceedings, whether at meetings of the stockholders or otherwise, wherein the vote or written consent of stockholders may be required. . . .

If the parties had intended to limit the trustee's authority to vote the shares in any manner, they would have included a provision setting forth the subjects on which the trustee had unrestricted voting rights and those on which the trustee did not have such rights. For example, they could have included a provision that the trustee not vote trust shares in favor of any proposal that would dilute the voting strength of shares held in trust, as occurred here through creation of the

Class C shares. Instead, they granted the trustee broad power to vote "at any and all meetings of the stockholders of the Corporation, for whatsoever purpose called or held," subject only to requirements that the trustee "use his best judgment in voting upon the stock held by him" and carry out his duties in "good faith." Such is the agreement that the parties made for themselves.

The agreement, therefore, placed the trustee in the foreseeable position of having to take actions that would benefit HFC and its shareholders while being dilutive of the voting strength of the existing trust shares. The inherent conflict between preserving the business prospects of HFC for the benefit of its share-holders and the need to take actions that might temporarily dilute the voting power of existing shares beyond expiration of the trusts did not limit the trustee from taking action.

It is undisputed that a trustee is under a duty to the beneficiaries to administer the trust solely in the interest of the beneficiaries. Here, the trial court found that John Warehime acted in good faith for the benefit of the corporation and its shareholder beneficiaries and that his actions as trustee were not taken for his own benefit. By disregarding this finding and by straying from the plain terms of the agreements which require only that the trustee exercise his best judgment and act in good faith, Superior Court erred. Accordingly, we reverse.

Order reversed, and case remanded.

SAYLOR, Justice, concurring.

Like Mr. Justice Nigro and the Superior Court majority, I see no basis upon which to distinguish voting trustees from other fiduciaries in terms of defining the general scope of their obligations owing to beneficiaries of the fiduciary relationship. Therefore, I also would hold that a duty of loyalty should ordinarily attach to the voting trustee's undertakings in relation to the trust.

Whether, and to what extent, parties may contractually alter or eliminate such duties implicates an extensive, ongoing debate in the legal community among segments sometimes denominated in the commentary as contractarians and anti-contractarians. In the present case, the majority position could perhaps be described as having a contractarian orientation, whereas the position of the Superior Court majority could be said to possess anti-contractarian over-tones. Even under contractarian theory, however, in order for general principles regarding fiduciary duty to be overridden, there must be a sufficient meeting of the minds concerning the action of the fiduciary, which I find lacking in the trust instruments at issue. While these instruments effectively conveyed a broad array of powers, I find an inherent ambiguity between the provisions limiting the effectiveness of the trusts to a fixed, ten-year term, and the utilization by the trustee of the trusts' authority to unilaterally establish an ongoing structure of corporate governance that undermines control of a corporation by majority vote of its shareholders beyond the agreed-upon time for expiration, particularly when such action is taken in contemplation of the impending termination. Therefore, I disagree with the majority that, in such circumstances, the voting trustee's obligations should be deemed limited by the written agreements. Rather, consistent with the general legal proposition advanced by Mr. Justice Nigro and the Superior Court majority, I would hold that, at least in the absence of express, unambiguous, contrary provisions within the voting trust instru-ments (or statutory prescription), the prevailing common-law standard of fiduciary conduct should control in such circumstances.

. . .

I believe that the nature of the underlying enterprise affects the character and quality of fiduciary obligations owing; therefore, I would not, as some commentators have suggested, require the wholesale prohibition of transactions in which some degree of conflict of interest is present, such as in family and close corporations. Indeed, if this were to be made the rule, the operations of a corporation having a structure and composition such as Hanover Foods Corporation ("HFC") would be substantially impeded, since the controlling interests could rarely satisfy a standard of pure, selfless disinterestedness. Rather, I believe that controlling interests bearing fiduciary duties should be permitted to exercise the implements of control, so long as they are truly operating in furtherance of the interests of the beneficiaries of the fiduciary relationship.

Pursuant to this standard, I also agree with Mr. Justice Nigro and with the Superior Court majority that alteration of the structure of corporate governance by a voting trustee is generally impermissible where the intent and effect of the action is to perpetuate the trustee's own control over the corporation beyond the life of the voting trust. In such circumstances, the conflict of interest confronting the trustee is simply too great and cannot be reconciled with his duty of loyalty. On the other hand, however, I would not foreclose the effectuation of necessary structural changes by a voting trustee under the broad form of authority conveyed by the present trust instruments where the intent underlying the changes, and their effect, are otherwise, and, after careful scrutiny of the facts, the duty of loyalty can be said to be fulfilled. Indeed, this latter form of action would seem to fall well within the scope of the parties' initial intention in entrusting their interests to a single decision maker whose own interests were, in significant part, in alignment with theirs. Thus, in my assessment, the critical questions in determining John Warehime's compliance with his fiduciary obligations in connection with the proposed amendments to HFC's articles of incorporation are: whether, and to what extent, the amendments were intended to, and/or would have the effect of, perpetuating John Warehime's control over HFC; and whether, and to what extent, the amendments would inure to the benefit (or, conversely, operate to the detriment) of the minority shareholders.

. . .

Although I believe that John Warehime was presented with an inherent conflict of interest in considering the amendments, given the realities of family-controlled corporations, I would hold that a fiduciary who is by selection self-interested may be permitted to proceed in the face of such conflicts so long as his actions inure to the benefit of minority interests. Where the minority interests themselves have conflicting interests, as the trial court found in the present case, the trustee initially, and the trial court ultimately, must necessarily make a decision that will be in derogation of some minority interests, but in furtherance of others, with the objective being to maximize the ultimate, net benefit to minority shareholders.

Here, I would find that the trial court's conclusions concerning the nature and effect of the proposed amendments vis-à-vis minority interests are mixed ones of law and fact, with the factual aspects predominating, and thus should be subject to a deferential standard of review. While acknowledging that the amendments would dilute Class B shareholders' voting interests, the trial court found this detriment substantially outweighed by the advancement of the shareholders' conflicting interest in maximizing share value, which could best be served through implementation of an effective dispute-resolution procedure. The trial court also clearly viewed such procedure as far more neutral in relation to the ongoing family dispute than did the Superior Court majority. Since I believe that the trial court's findings and conclusions in these regards are supported in the evidence and were made within the boundaries of its decision making authority, particularly as it relates to the assessment of likelihood of success on the merits on consideration of a motion for a preliminary injunction, I am able to join the majority's disposition reversing the Superior Court's order.

Nigro, Justice, dissenting.

I respectfully dissent as I believe that John Warehime's actions constituted a breach of his fiduciary duties to the trust beneficiaries, that the whole effort to retain control of the voting trusts beyond their expiration dates was a glaring example of self-dealing involving an impermissible clash between John Warehime's private interests and the interests of the beneficiaries, and that the possible outcome (e.g. alleged stability of the company) does not justify the means (breach of undivided loyalty to the beneficiaries) of achieving that result.

. . .

[A]s the treatises recognize, a voting trustee clearly has a duty of loyalty to the beneficiaries no less than the duty placed on *all* trustees of *any* trust. Nonetheless, the majority opinion seeks to sanction the actions of John Warehime by selecting a single provision of the trust documents executed by Alan Warehime as evidence that the Warehime Trust permitted the lesser standard of "best judgment" and "good faith" to govern the trustee's actions. While the two Warehime Voting Trust agreements (collectively Warehime Trust) do direct the trustee to use his "best judgment" and to act "in good faith," these terms do not pertain to the duty of loyalty imposed on a trustee. Rather, they define the required *standard of care* a trustee must use in exercising his powers. Thus, I believe that while the majority opinion properly characterizes the broadness of the scope of a trustee's *powers,* it does not adequately acknowledge the more constraining *duty* of absolute loyalty to the beneficiaries which must pervade any and all actions a trustee undertakes.

In finding that no breach of the trustee's fiduciary duty occurred here, the majority opinion places primary emphasis on the notion that the terms and conditions of the Warehime Trust agreements "could have" included a definition of the fiduciary obligation more restrictive than the standards of "best judgment" and "good faith," but did not. I do not find the omission or inclusion of such language dispositive of the intent of the trust, as the accepted tenets of the law of trusts and trustees regarding any specific trust provide that the duty of loyalty is inherent in the trust relationship itself. In other words, merely by being named trustee, the trustee's duty of complete loyalty to the beneficiaries attaches. Thus, the trustee's actions are governed *first* and foremost by the threshold "usual fiduciary principles of a trust," regardless of what standard of care is set forth in the trust documents. I would therefore read the best judgment/good faith provision of the Warehime Trust documents as presuming that the voting trustee is already acting under complete loyalty to the beneficiaries before exercising his best judgment or acting in good faith.

Furthermore, while the majority opinion focuses on the idea that specific language of the Warehime Trust agreements "could have" delineated the subjects on which the trustee had unrestricted voting rights and those on which he did not, I believe the proper focus is on the plain language of the Warehime Trust agreements that the voting trust was to expire ten years after its execution, and that no language in the agreements provides any leeway whatsoever to override that restriction. . . . I believe that focusing on what *could have* been included in the trust agreement but was not, instead of what explicitly *was* included in the agreement, is a circuitous way of giving special dispensation to John Warehime's actions. By using the trust's shares to adopt amendments that would extend the ten-year term of the voting trust another five years, John Warehime voted contrary to the trust's terms and for personal advantage, plain and simple. Had he acted with undivided loyalty to the beneficiaries, the only proper procedure would have been to allow the trusts to expire and return the right to vote their shares to the individual beneficiaries. The beneficiaries could then vote, if they so chose, to form another voting trust of designated duration and reinstate John Warehime as trustee. Instead, in using the voting trusts to perpetuate his own power to vote those shares, John Warehime not only "destroy[ed] the beneficial ownership interests" by depriving the beneficiaries of their right to vote the shares themselves, but clearly put himself in a position where his own interests—keeping control of the company—impermissibly conflicted with the interests of the trust's beneficiaries.

. . .

Finally, I note that at its core, this case is about the meaning of the word "trust"—not merely in its legal sense but pursuant to the everyday, ordinary understanding of the word, i.e., "a charge or duty imposed in faith or confidence or as a condition of some relationship . . . the obligation to promote to the largest extent possible the welfare of [those depending on the relationship]," and connotes the same qualities as the legal concept, i.e., "reliance . . . honesty . . . worthiness. . . ." *See* WEBSTER'S THIRD NEW INTERNATIONAL DICTIONARY OF THE ENGLISH LANGUAGE 2456 (1993). It is axiomatic, therefore, that regardless of whatever authority John Warehime had to exercise his "best judgment" and act in "good faith," common decency dictates that no person placed in a position of trust can meet even the everyday expectations of that status without first, last, and always being loyal to the people who placed the trust in him. Instead, John Warehime went to extraordinary legalistic lengths to attempt to defeat even the ordinary meaning of trust. I would not permit a dilution of *either* the familiar or the legal meaning of the word trust any more than I would permit a diminution of these beneficiaries' voting rights.

. . . I would find that the votes cast by John Warehime in favor of the proposed amendments should have been voided and an injunction barring him from voting in favor of the amendments to create a new class of dispute-resolution stock should have been granted.

I would therefore affirm the Superior Court based on its well-reasoned opinion.

***

Upon remand, the Court of Common Pleas denied the plaintiffs' motion for a preliminary injunction and a motion to set aside the vote of stockholders. The Superior Court of Pennsylvania then reversed, holding as follows:

John Warehime and the other directors impermissibly exercised their power to retain their own positions by purposely depriving the majority shareholders of any real opportunity to affect the outcome of any vote. Such abuse of position, even if exercised in the belief that the company was thereby well served, violates the principles of corporate democracy that enable shareholders to control their own company. Therefore, we set aside the vote taken in favor of the stock plan.

Warehime v. Warehime, 777 A.2d 469, 481 (Pa. Super. 2001). In the latest decision in the case, the Pennsylvania Supreme Court reversed the Superior Court, holding that "Michael had not adduced *any* evidence of irreparable harm" and "far greater harm would result from the granting of the preliminary injunction which would likely result in the deterioration and sale of the company." *Warehime v. Warehime*, 860 A.2d 41, 47 (Pa. 2004).

D. CLASSIFIED SHARES

Corporations statutes allow corporations to create more than one class of shares, with each class having unique rights. DGCL § 151; Model Act § 6.01. The primary purpose of classifying shares is to allocate control among the various classes of shareholders. The ways in which control may be allocated by assigning different rights to different classes of shares are infinite; they include giving a class a veto power over all decisions, giving a class no voting power (only financial rights), allowing a class to vote only on certain matters, or providing the right to board representation to certain classes.

The following case has been called a "landmark" in the venture capital industry. It explores a conflict between a venture capital firm and a bank, who had invested substantial sums in different classes of preferred stock of Juniper Financial. The investors created an elaborate system of checks and balances in the corporate charter. Delaware courts claim to interpret corporate charters as ordinary contracts, but when reading the terms of preferred stock, the Delaware courts employ a special rule of interpretation, described in the *Benchmark* opinion as follows: "any rights, preferences and limitations of preferred stock that distinguish that stock from common stock must be expressly and clearly stated [and] will not be presumed or implied." In this case, the failure of the charter to protect the venture capital firm resulted in a decision for the bank. As you read the opinion, consider whether the result is fair to the venture capital firm.

BENCHMARK CAPITAL PARTNERS IV, L.P. v. VAGUE*

2002 WL 1732423 (unpublished)
Court of Chancery of Delaware
July 15, 2002

NOBLE, Vice Chancellor.

. . .

---

*The Delaware Supreme Court affirmed this Chancery Court opinion, stating: "[T]he Court having considered this matter after oral argument and on the briefs filed by the parties has determined that the final judgment of the Court of Chancery should be affirmed on the basis of and for the reasons assigned by the Court of Chancery in its opinion dated July 15, 2002." Benchmark Capital Partners IV, L.P. v. Juniper Financial Corp., 2003 WL 1904669 (Apr. 16, 2003).

III. Factual Background

A. BENCHMARK AND CIBC INVEST IN JUNIPER

[Benchmark Capital Partners IV, L.P. ("Benchmark")] became the initial investor in [Juniper Financial Corp. ("Juniper")] when in June 2000, it invested $20 million and, in exchange, was issued Series A Preferred Shares. Juniper raised an additional $95.5 million in August 2000 by issuing its Series B Preferred Shares. Benchmark contributed $5 million in this effort. It soon became necessary for Juniper to obtain even more capital. Efforts to raise additional funds from existing investors and efforts to find new potential investors were unavailing until June 2001 when [Canadian Imperial Bank of Commerce ("CIBC")] and Juniper agreed that CIBC would invest $27 million in Juniper through a mandatory convertible note while CIBC evaluated Juniper to assess whether it was interested in acquiring the company. CIBC also agreed to provide additional capital through a Series C financing in the event that it chose not to acquire Juniper and if Juniper's efforts to find other sources for the needed funding were unsuccessful.

In July 2001, CIBC advised Juniper that it would not seek to acquire Juniper. After reviewing its options for other financing, Juniper called upon CIBC to invest the additional capital. The terms of the Series C financing were negotiated during the latter half of the summer of 2001. A representative of Benchmark, J. William Gurley, and its attorney were active participants in these negotiations. Through the Series C Transaction, which closed on September 18, 2001, CIBC invested $145 million (including the $27 million already delivered to Juniper). With its resulting Series C Preferred holdings, CIBC obtained a majority of the voting power in Juniper on an as-converted basis and a majority of the voting power of Juniper's preferred stock. CIBC also acquired the right to select six of the eleven members of Juniper's board. As required by Juniper's then existing certificate of incorporation, the approval of the holders of Series A Preferred and Series B Preferred Stock, including Benchmark, was obtained in order to close the Series C Transaction.[8]

B. THE CERTIFICATE'S PROTECTIVE PROVISIONS

In the course of obtaining that consent, CIBC had extensive negotiations regarding the provisions of Juniper's charter designed to protect the rights and interests of the holders of Series A Preferred and Series B Preferred Stock. For example, CIBC had sought the power to waive, modify or amend certain protective provisions held by the Series A Preferred and Series B Preferred stockholders. As the result of those discussions, the [Fifth Amendment and Restated Certificate of Incorporation (the "Certificate")] was adopted. CIBC obtained the right to waive certain protective voting provisions, but the right was not unlimited. A review of the Certificate's protective provisions directly involved in the pending dispute follows.

---

8. The facts giving rise to this dispute are generally uncontested. One exception is the assertion of Mr. Gurley, who, as noted, was actively involved on Benchmark's behalf in negotiating the Series C Transaction, that Juniper and CIBC promised that the Series C financing would provide Juniper with sufficient funding to implement its business plan and that no additional capital would be needed in order to achieve profitability. . . . Others, however, dispute that recollection.

Juniper's Certificate protects the holders of Series A Preferred and Series B Preferred from risks associated with the issuance of any additional equity security that would be senior to those shares by requiring their prior approval through a separate class vote as prescribed in Section C.6.a(i):

> So long as any shares of Series A Preferred Stock or Series B Preferred Stock remain outstanding, the Corporation shall not, without the vote or written consent by the holders of at least a majority of the then outstanding shares of the Series A Preferred Stock and Series B Preferred Stock, voting together as a single class; *provided, however,* that the foregoing may be amended, waived or modified pursuant to Section C.4.c: (i) Authorize or issue, or obligate itself to issue, any other equity security (including any security convertible into or exercisable for any equity security) senior to or on a parity with the Series A Preferred Stock or Series B Preferred Stock as to dividend rights or redemption rights, voting rights or liquidation preferences (other than the Series C Preferred Stock and Series C Prime Preferred Stock sold pursuant to, or issued upon the conversion of the shares sold pursuant to, the Series C Preferred Stock Purchase Agreement) . . .

Under Section C.6.a(ii), Juniper also must provide the holders of the junior preferred stock with a class vote before it may proceed to dispose of all or substantially all of its assets or to "consolidate or merge into any other Corporation (other than a wholly-owned subsidiary Corporation)." Furthermore, this right to a class vote also applies to efforts to increase the number of Juniper's directors.

Because CIBC was investing a substantial sum in Juniper, it insisted upon greater control than it would have obtained if these voting provisions (and other comparable provisions) could be exercised without limitation by the holders of Series A Preferred and Series B Preferred shares as a class. Thus, it sought and obtained a concession from the Series A Preferred and Series B Preferred holders that it could amend, waive, or modify, *inter alia,* the protective provisions of Section C.6.a. The right of CIBC to waive the voting rights of the Series A Preferred and Series B Preferred holders was limited by excluding from the scope of the waiver authority any action that "would (a) diminish or alter the liquidation preference or other financial or economic rights, modify the registration rights, or increase the obligations, indemnities or liabilities, of the holders of Series A Preferred Stock, Series A Prime Preferred Stock or Series B Preferred Stock or (b) authorize, approve or waive any action so as to violate any fiduciary duties owed by such holders under Delaware law."

Another protection afforded the holders of both the Series A Preferred and Series B Preferred Stock was set forth in Sections C.6.c(ii) & C.6.d(ii) of the Certificate. Those provisions require a vote of the holders of each series, provided that the requirement for a series vote was not amended or waived by CIBC in accordance with Section C.4.c, if that corporate action would "[m]aterially adversely change the rights, preferences and privileges of the Series A Preferred [and Series B] Preferred Stock."

C. ADDITIONAL FINANCING BECOMES NECESSARY

By early 2002, Juniper was advising its investors that even more capital would be necessary to sustain the venture. Because Juniper is in the banking business, the consequences of a capital shortage are not merely those of the typical business. Capital shortfall for a banking entity may carry the potential for significant and adverse regulatory action. Regulated not only by the Federal Reserve Board and the Federal Deposit Insurance Corporation but also by the Delaware Banking Commissioner, Juniper is required to maintain a "well-capitalized" status. Failure to maintain that standard (or to effect a prompt cure) may result in, among other things, regulatory action, conversion of the preferred stock into a "senior common stock" which could then be subjected to the imposition of additional security through the regulatory authorities, and the loss of the right to issue Visa cards and to have its customers serviced through the Visa card processing system.

Juniper, with the assistance of an investment banking firm, sought additional investors. The holders of the Series A Preferred and Series B Preferred Stock, including Benchmark, were also solicited. Those efforts failed, thus leaving CIBC as the only identified and viable participant available for the next round of financing, now known as the Series D Transaction.

D. THE SERIES D PREFERRED TRANSACTION

Thus, Juniper turned to consideration of CIBC's proposal, first submitted through a term sheet on March 15, 2002, to finance $50 million through the issuance of Series D Preferred Stock that would grant CIBC an additional 23% of Juniper on a fully-diluted basis and reduce the equity interests of the Series A Preferred and Series B Preferred holders from approximately 29% to 7%.

The board, in early April 2002, appointed a special committee to consider the CIBC proposal. As the result of the negotiations among Juniper, the special committee, and CIBC, the special committee was able to recommend the Series D Transaction with CIBC. The terms of the Series D Transaction are set forth in the "Juniper Financial Corp. Series D Preferred Stock Purchase Agreement" and the "Agreement and Plan of Merger and Reorganization by and Between Juniper Financial Corp. and Juniper Merger Corp." In general terms, the Series D Transaction consists of the following three steps:

1. Juniper will carry out a 100-1 reverse stock split of its common stock.
2. Juniper Merger Corp., a subsidiary of Juniper established for these purposes, will be merged with and into Juniper which will be the surviving corporation. The certificate of incorporation will be revised as part of the merger.
3. Series D Preferred Stock will be issued to CIBC (and, at least in theory, those other holders of Series A, B and C Preferred who may exercise preemptive rights) for $50 million.

Each share of existing Series A Preferred and each share of existing Series B Preferred will be converted into one share of new Series A Preferred or Series B Preferred, respectively, and the holders of the existing junior preferred will also receive, for each share, a warrant to purchase a small fraction of a share of common stock in Juniper and a smaller fraction of a share of common stock in Juniper.[19] A small amount of cash will also be paid. Juniper will receive no capital infusion as a direct result of the merger. Although the existing Series A Preferred and Series B Preferred shares will cease to exist and the differences

---

19. Benchmark asserts that both the warrants and the common stock are essentially worthless at this time, a contention which Juniper does not dispute. Juniper seeks to justify the warrants and the common stock as providing the Series A Preferred and Series B Preferred holders with an opportunity to participate in the future success of Juniper.

between the new and distinct Series A Preferred and Series B Preferred shares will be significant,[20] the resulting modification of Juniper's certificate of incorporation will not alter the class and series votes required by Section C.6. The changes to Juniper's charter as the result of the merger include, *inter alia,* authorization of the issuance of Series D Preferred Shares, which will be senior to the newly created Series A Preferred and Series B Preferred Stock with respect to, for example, liquidation preferences, dividends, and as applicable, redemption rights. Also the Series D Stock will be convertible into common stock at a higher ratio than the existing or newly created Series A Preferred and Series B Preferred Stock, thereby providing for a currently greater voting power. In general terms, the equity of the existing Series A Preferred and Series B Preferred holders will be reduced from approximately 29% before the merger to approximately 7% after the Series D financing, and CIBC will hold more than 90% of Juniper's voting power.

Juniper intends to proceed with the merger on July 16, 2002 and to promptly thereafter consummate the Series D financing. It projects that, without the $50 million infusion from CIBC, it will not be able to satisfy the "well-capitalized" standard as of July 31, 2002. That will trigger, or so Juniper posits, the regulatory problems previously identified and business problems, such as the risk of losing key personnel and important business relationships. Indeed, Juniper predicts that liquidation would ensue and, in that event (and Benchmark does not seriously contest this), that the holders of Series A Preferred and Series B Preferred Stock would receive nothing (or essentially nothing) from such liquidation.

IV. CONTENTIONS OF THE PARTIES

Benchmark begins its effort to earn a preliminary injunction by arguing that the junior preferred stockholders are entitled to a vote on the merger on a series basis under Sections C.6.c(ii) & C.6.d(ii) because the merger adversely affects, *inter alia,* their liquidation preference and dividend rights and on a class basis under Section C.6.a(i) because the merger, through changes to Juniper's capital structure as set forth in its revised certificate of incorporation, will authorize the issuance of a senior preferred security. Benchmark also invokes its right to a class vote to challenge the Series D Purchase Agreement under Section C.6.a(i) because that agreement obligates Juniper to issue a senior preferred security. Similarly, Benchmark challenges the issuance of the new Series D Preferred Stock after the merger because it will be issued without a class vote by the holders of either the old or the new Series A Preferred Stock and the new Series B Preferred Stock.

---

20. For example, the holders of the newly created Series A Preferred and Series B Preferred Stock will have an aggregate liquidation preference of $15 million as compared to the liquidation preference of the existing Series A Preferred and Series B Preferred holders of approximately $115 million. Moreover, "[t]he dividend payable . . . to the holders of the New Series A Stock will be reduced from $0.1068 per share to $0.020766 per share and the dividend payable . . . to the holders of the New Series B Preferred Stock will be reduced from $0.23 per share to $0.030268 per share." The redemption rights and other preferences of the existing Series A Preferred and Series B Preferred holders will similarly be comprised by the conversion to the New Series A Preferred and New Series B Preferred Stock as a result of the merger. Finally, the New Series A Preferred and the new Series B Preferred Stock will be subordinate to another series of preferred stock, the Series D Preferred Stock.

In response, Juniper and CIBC argue that the junior preferred stockholders are not entitled to a class or series vote on any aspect of the Series D financing, particularly the merger. The adverse effects of the transaction arise from the merger and not from any separate amendment of the certificate of incorporation, which would have required the exercise of the junior preferred stockholders' voting rights.[24] Juniper and CIBC emphasize that none of the junior preferred stock protective provisions expressly applies to mergers. Finally, Juniper and CIBC assert that the Series C Trump allows for the waiver of all of the voting rights at issue (except for the diminishment of the liquidation preference accomplished by the merger). Benchmark, as one might expect, maintains that the exercise of the Series C Trump is precluded because the "economic or financial rights" of the holders of the junior preferred will be adversely affected and, therefore, the limitation on CIBC's right to exercise the Series C Trump is controlling. . . .

V. ANALYSIS . . .

1. GENERAL PRINCIPLES OF CONSTRUCTION

Certificates of incorporation define contractual relationships not only among the corporation and its stockholders but also among the stockholders. Thus, the Certificate defines, as a matter of contract, both the relationship between Benchmark and Juniper and the relative relationship between Benchmark, as a holder of junior preferred stock, and CIBC, as the holder of senior preferred stock. For these reasons, courts look to general principles of contract construction in construing certificates of incorporation. . . .

These principles also apply in construing the relative rights of holders of different series of preferred stock.

2. CHALLENGES TO THE MERGER . . .

A. *Merger as Changing the Rights, Preferences and Privileges*

Benchmark looks at the Series D Preferred financing and the merger that is integral to that transaction and concludes that the authorization of the Series D Preferred Stock and the other revisions to the Juniper certificate of incorporation accomplished as part of the merger will materially adversely affect the rights, preferences, and privileges of the junior preferred shares. Among the adverse affects to be suffered by Benchmark are a significant reduction in its right to a liquidation preference, the authorization of a new series of senior

---

24. Juniper focuses on the separate statutory regimes for amendments of certificates of incorporation and for mergers. A corporation may amend its certificate of incorporation to reclassify its authorized stock, 8 Del. C. § 242(a)(3), or to create a new class of stock with rights and preferences superior to other classes of stock, 8 Del. C. § 242(a)(5). By 8 Del. C. § 242(b)(2), "[t]he holders of the outstanding shares of a class shall be entitled to vote as a class upon a proposed amendment, whether or not entitled to vote thereon by the certificate of incorporation, if the amendment would increase or decrease the aggregate number of authorized shares of such class, increase or decrease the par value of the shares of such class, or alter or change the powers, preferences, or special rights of the shares of such class so as to affect them adversely." Mergers, by contrast, are accomplished in accordance with 8 Del. C. § 251. A merger agreement, in accordance with 8 Del. C. § 251(b)(3), and a certificate of merger, in accordance with 8 Del. C. § 253(c)(4), shall state: "[I]n the case of a merger, such amendments or changes in the certificate of incorporation of the surviving corporation as are desired to be effected by the merger. . . ."

preferred stock that will further subordinate its interests in Juniper, and a reduction in other rights such as dividend priority. These adverse consequences will all be the product of the merger. Benchmark's existing Series A Preferred and Series B Preferred shares will cease to exist as of the merger and will be replaced with new Series A Preferred Stock, new Series B Preferred Stock, warrants, common stock, and a small amount of cash. One of the terms governing the new junior preferred stock will specify that those new junior preferred shares are not merely subordinate to Series C Preferred Stock, but they also will be subordinate to the new Series D Preferred Stock. Thus, the harm to Benchmark is directly attributable to the differences between the new junior preferred stock, authorized through the merger, and the old junior preferred stock as evidenced by the planned post-merger capital structure of Juniper.

Benchmark's challenge is confronted by a long line of Delaware cases which, in general terms, hold that protective provisions drafted to provide a class of preferred stock with a class vote before those shares' rights, preferences and privileges may be altered or modified do not fulfill their apparent purpose of assuring a class vote if adverse consequences flow from a merger and the protective provisions do not expressly afford protection against a merger. This result traces back to the language of 8 Del. C. § 242(b)(2), which deals with the rights of various classes of stock to vote on amendments to the certificate of incorporation that would "alter or change the powers, preferences, or special rights of the shares of such class so as to affect them adversely." That language is substantially the same as the language ("rights, preferences and privileges") of Sections C.6.c(ii) & C.6.d(ii). Where the drafters have tracked the statutory language relating to charter amendments in 8 Del. C. § 242(b), courts have been reluctant to expand those restrictions to encompass the separate process of merger as set forth in 8 Del. C. § 251, unless the drafters have made clear the intention to grant a class vote in the context of a merger. . . .

The range of Sections C.6.c(ii) and C.6.d(ii) is not expressly limited to changes in the Certificate. However, given the well established case law construing the provisions of certificates of incorporations and the voting rights of classes of preferred stockholders, I am satisfied that the language chosen by the drafters (*i.e.*, the "rights, preferences, and privileges") must be understood as those rights, preferences and privileges which are subject to change through a certificate of incorporation amendment under the standards of 8 Del. C. § 242(b) and not the standards of 8 Del. C. § 251. . . .

B. Authorization of Series D Preferred Shares Through the Merger Process

Benchmark's straightforward argument that it is entitled to a class vote on the authorization of the Series D Preferred Stock through the merger can easily be set forth. By Section C.6.a(i) of the Certificate, the holders of the Series A Preferred and Series B Preferred Stock have the right, unless that right is properly waived by CIBC, to a class vote on the authorization of a senior preferred security. The Series D Preferred Stock will be on parity with the Series C Preferred Stock and, thus, will be senior to be the existing junior preferred and the newly created junior preferred that will be created as part of the merger.[39] The

---

39. I avoid, for the moment, consideration of Juniper's argument that the Series D Preferred shares will never be senior to the existing Series A Preferred and Series B Preferred Stock because the junior preferred shares will have been extinguished by the merger when the Series D Preferred Stock are authorized.

protective provisions of the Certificate do not distinguish between authorization through amendment of the Certificate under 8 Del. C. § 242(b) and those changes in the Certificate resulting from a recapitalization accompanying a merger pursuant to 8 Del. C. § 251. Thus, according to Benchmark, it matters not how the result is achieved. Moreover, Section C.6.a(i) does not track or even resemble the "privileges, preferences and special rights" language of 8 Del. C. § 242(b)(2) that was important to the [last issue]. Benchmark thus argues that the clear and unambiguous words of Section C.6.a(i) guarantee (at least in the absence of an effective waiver by CIBC) it and the other holders of Series A Preferred and Series B Preferred shares a class vote before the Series D Preferred Stock may be authorized. While Benchmark has advanced an appealing and rational analysis, I conclude, for the reasons set forth below, that it has failed to demonstrate a reasonable probability of success on the merits of this argument.

In ascertaining whether a class of junior preferred stockholders has the opportunity to vote as a class on a proposed corporate action, the words chosen by the drafters must be read "against the background of Delaware precedent."[40] For example, Sullivan Money Management, Inc. v. FLS Holdings, Inc. involved the question of whether a class vote was required in order to change critical rights of preferred shareholders "'by amendment to the Certificate of Incorporation of [FLS Holdings, Inc.] or otherwise.'" In interpreting the charter of FLS Holdings, Inc., the Court was urged to treat the phrase "or otherwise" as including mergers. The Court, in rejecting this contention, set forth the following:

> The word "merger" is nowhere found in the provision governing the Series A Preferred Stock. The drafters' failure to express with clarity an intent to confer class voting rights in the event of a merger suggests that they had no intention of doing so, and weighs against adopting the plaintiffs' broad construction of the words "or otherwise."

Here, the authorization of the Series D Preferred Stock results from the merger and the restatement of Juniper's certificate of incorporation as part of that process. [Warner Communications, Inc. v. Chris-Craft Indus., Inc., 583 A.2d 962 (Del. Ch. 1989), aff'd, 567 A.2d 419 (Del. 1989),] and the cases following it ... demonstrate that certain rights of the holders of preferred stock that are secured by the corporate charter are at risk when a merger leads to changes in the corporation's capital structure. To protect against the potential negative effects of a merger, those who draft protective provisions have been instructed to make clear that those protective provisions specifically and directly limit the mischief that can otherwise be accomplished through a merger under 8 Del. C. § 251.

In sum, Benchmark complains of the harm which will occur because of alterations to Juniper's capital structure resulting from modifications of the certificate of incorporation emerging from the merger. General language alone granting preferred stockholders a class vote on certain changes to the corporate charter (such as authorization of a senior series of stock) will not be read to require a class vote on a merger and its integral and accompanying modifications to the corporate charter and the corporation's capital structure.

---

40. Elliot Assocs., L.P. v. Avatex Corp., 715 A2d 843, 852 (Del. 1998).

To reach the result sought by Benchmark, the protective rights "'must . . . be clearly expressed and will not be presumed.'" Unfortunately for Benchmark, the requirements of a class vote for authorization of a new senior preferred stock through a merger was not "clearly expressed" in the Certificate. . . .

3. OBLIGATION TO ISSUE AND ISSUANCE OF SERIES D PREFERRED SHARES

Under Section C.6.a(i), Juniper is also required to obtain class approval, unless effectively waived by CIBC, from its junior preferred holders before it can issue or obligate itself to issue a senior preferred stock. Juniper plans to issue its Series D Preferred Stock after the merger and at a time when the new Series A Preferred shares and the new Series B Preferred shares will be outstanding. The shares will not be issued as the result of the merger, but instead will be issued pursuant to the Purchase Agreement between CIBC and Juniper. Because the merger is not implicated by the issuance of the shares, there is no "background" precedent against which this act must be evaluated in the same sense as the case law addressing the consequences of mergers. These facts bring Juniper's proposed issuance of its Series D Preferred Stock squarely within the scope of the restrictions imposed by Section C.6.a(i) of the post-merger certificate. Specifically, to paraphrase that provision, so long as any shares of the new Series A Preferred or Series B Preferred are outstanding, Juniper may not, without the class vote or class consent of the new Series A Preferred and Series B Preferred stockholders, issue any senior equity security. While the restrictions of Section C.6.a(i) may be subject to the Series C Trump and, thus, may yet not prevent the issuance of the Series D Preferred Stock without the approval of the holders of the junior preferred stock, I am satisfied that Section C.6.a(i) applies, from the plain and unambiguous language of its text, to the issuance of Series D Preferred Stock when and as planned by Juniper. . . .

All of the class voting rights conferred upon the junior preferred holders by Section C.6.a(i) are subject to waiver by CIBC through the proper exercise of its Series C Trump. The Series C Trump is broad and (for present purposes) is restricted in application only if the corporate action for which the class vote is waived would "diminish or alter the liquidation preference or other financial or economic rights" of the holders of the junior preferred stock. Issuance of the Series D Preferred Stock will not "diminish or alter" Benchmark's liquidation preference — that was accomplished through the merger. The question thus becomes one of whether the issuance of a previously authorized senior preferred security "diminish[es] or alter[s]" the junior preferred shares' "financial or economic rights."

In some very general sense, when shares of a security with a higher priority are issued, the financial and economic rights of the holders of junior securities are adversely affected. On the other hand, that broad of a reading of "financial or economic rights" would make it difficult to find a valid waiver under the Certificate because all of the rights at issue — liquidation preferences, dividend rights, redemption rights, and even voting rights — in some sense implicate financial or economic rights and interests. In this analysis, the Court, of course, must seek to give meaning to all of the relevant provisions of the Certificate and to interpret the Certificate "as a whole."

One approach to interpreting the critical language can be drawn from the line of cases addressing the vexing issues associated with authorization of a new senior security without a class vote under 8 Del. C. § 242 such as whether that creation of a new security with priority can be construed to alter or change the preferences, special rights or powers given to any particular class of stock through the certificate of incorporation and whether that creation of a new senior security also can be deemed to affect such class adversely. Under the analytical approach suggested by these cases, the issuance of shares of a security that has priority will not adversely affect the preferences or special rights of a junior security. The argument, in general, is that the terms and powers of that particular class of junior security have not themselves been changed. That another security with priority has been issued is said to "burden" it, but its particular rights have not been modified, and thus those rights are not perceived as having been "diminished or altered." I tend toward this reading because it does interpret the preferred stock protective provisions against the "background of Delaware precedent" and because "financial and economic rights" appear in a list with other items such as liquidation preferences and registration rights which are more fairly viewed as technical and specific (as opposed to broad and general) rights.

On the other hand, "financial and economic rights" can easily be given the broad interpretation suggested by Benchmark. Moreover, if one places too much emphasis on the [aforementioned] cases for interpretive assistance, the carefully negotiated hierarchy here (right to class vote, but first subject to waiver which in turn is subject to exception) might not be fully acknowledged. Thus, the potential shortcoming of interpreting this language . . . is that the rights of the holders of the junior security in those cases are so limited that it is fair to question whether rights that narrow were intended by the parties here.

Therefore, the meaning to be given to the exception to Series C Trump or waiver is not free of ambiguity. There is no ambiguity in the actual grant of the Series C Trump to CIBC. Both sides agree that the Series C Trump, absent the exception, would provide CIBC with the authority it claims. Accordingly, the effectiveness of any exercise of the Series C Trump in this context depends upon the scope to be given to the exception. Benchmark suffers, in this context, because it must rely on the exception; terms of preferred shareholders' protective provisions "must . . . be clearly expressed and will not be presumed"; and it bears the burden as the moving party on its motion for a preliminary injunction.

A preliminary injunction necessarily involves an initial determination on [a] less than complete record and that limitation precludes a detailed consideration of extrinsic evidence. In light of the foregoing, I conclude that Benchmark has not demonstrated a reasonable probability of success on the merits of its claim that the waiver should not be available to CIBC. . . .

PROBLEM 5-3

After the introduction of the Apple iPad in April 2010, sales of Classic Games' apps doubled within two months. The company has attracted the attention of venture capitalists, who have offered to invest millions of dollars into Classic Games in exchange for convertible preferred stock.

Why would venture capitalists demand preferred stock rather than purchasing the common stock owned by the other stockholders of the company? In negotiating the terms of the preferred stock, what issues are most important to the venture capitalists?

E.   CUMULATIVE VOTING

Cumulative voting is a method of counting shareholder votes in director elections in which each shareholder is entitled to cast a number of votes equal to the product of the number of such shareholder's shares times the number of directors to be elected. Unlike "straight" voting, under cumulative voting a shareholder may cast all of his or her votes in favor of a single director rather than allocating them among the candidates. For example, if a corporation has three directors and one of the shareholders owns 500 shares of common stock, under a system of cumulative voting the shareholder is entitled to a total of 1,500 votes, which he or she may allocate among as many or as few director candidates as he or she chooses. Under straight voting, the shareholder could vote a maximum of 500 shares on any one director candidate, although the shareholder would be permitted to vote those same 500 shares for each director candidate!

The purpose of cumulative voting is to increase minority participation on the board of directors. Under straight voting, the holders of a majority of the shares would be able to elect all of the directors, but under cumulative voting, minority shareholders may be able to elect one or more directors despite the best efforts of the majority. Other methods of ensuring minority representation on the board of directors are shareholders' agreements or special classes of stock entitled to elect a certain number of directors. Model Act § 7.28(b) and DGCL § 214 provide that shareholders do not have the right to cumulate their votes for directors unless the articles of incorporation provide otherwise. These are "opt in" provisions. Many states have "opt out" provisions, and six states still have mandatory cumulative voting.

To calculate the number of shares required to elect one director under cumulative voting, the following formula is useful:

$$[\text{Shares Voting}/(\text{Directors to Be Elected} + 1)] + 1 = \text{Shares Required}$$

To illustrate the use of this formula, we assume a corporation with 1,800 shares of stock outstanding, all of which will be voted at the annual meeting in which three directors will be elected. The number of shares required to elect one of the three directors is as follows:

$$1,800/4 + 1 = 451$$

In other words, a shareholder would need *at least* 451 shares to ensure that he or she could elect one director. If a shareholder desires to elect more than one director, the following calculations are relevant:

Number of Directors to Be Elected	Number of Shares Needed
2 directors:	$3,600/4 + 1 = 901$
3 directors:	$5,400/4 + 1 = 1,351$

The shareholder described above has sufficient shares (500) to elect one director, but he does not have enough shares to elect two directors. The holders of the remaining shares (1,300) have enough to elect only two directors. As illustrated by the foregoing example, cumulative voting can be confusing to the uninitiated.

Staggering the board may defeat the effect of cumulative voting.[2] For example, in the corporation in the example, the three directors might have staggered terms of three years each; in other words, one director is elected each year. Even with cumulative voting, the shareholder who owns 500 shares would not be able to elect any directors without obtaining a majority of the outstanding shares. The formula for cumulative voting confirms that when only one director position is being filled, a majority of the shares voting is required to assure victory: $1,800/2 + 1 = 901$.

F. SUPERMAJORITY REQUIREMENTS

An easy way to ensure a minority voice in corporate affairs is to provide for supermajority quorum requirements and voting. This changes the normal corporate model of majority rule. In effect, supermajority requirements give a minority shareholder veto power over corporate decisions without offending corporate norms because corporation statutes allow high quorum and voting requirements. DGCL § 216 (if specified in the charter or bylaws); Model Act § 7.27 (if specified in the charter).

Under Delaware law, supermajority requirements can be adopted through a simple majority vote. *See, e.g.,* DGCL § 242(b)(4) (requiring a supermajority vote only when an existing supermajority voting provision is to be "altered, amended, or repealed"). By contrast, the Model Act provides that "any amendment to the articles of incorporation that adds . . . a greater quorum or voting requirement must meet the same quorum requirement and be adopted by the same vote" as required by the proposed provision. Model Act § 7.27(b).

The rules for amending or repealing supermajority requirements can be equally complex. In Delaware, the rules depend on whether the supermajority requirements appear in the charter or bylaws. When supermajority *voting* requirements appear in the charter, they can be amended or repealed only by the greater vote specified in the charter provision. DGCL § 242(b)(4). Surprisingly, there is no such statutory restriction on the amendment or repeal of supermajority voting requirements in the bylaws.[3] As a result, supermajority voting requirements that appear in the bylaws may be amended or repealed by a mere majority unless the bylaws themselves dictate that such an amendment requires a greater vote. Also, Delaware has no provision governing the amendment or repeal of supermajority quorum requirements.

2. Model Act § 8.06 refers to the process of dividing the board into different classes to be elected in alternating years as "staggering" the board. DGCL § 141(d) allows "classes" of directors. What most people called a "staggered board," therefore, becomes a "classified board" in Delaware.

3. The statutory provision governing the amendment of charter provisions was inspired by Sellers v. Joseph Bancroft & Sons Company, 2 A.2d 108 (Del. Ch. 1938), which said that an attempt to reduce supermajority voting requirements by the vote of a mere majority was "quite contrary to the evident purpose of the percentage provisions. If it be permissible, the protection to the preferred stockholders who invested their money on the faith of those percentage safeguards, was utterly illusory." *Id.* at 112. Although the Delaware legislature embraced this holding by adopting DGCL § 242(b)(4), it never adopted a similar provision for bylaw amendments.

Under the Model Act, the amendment or repeal of supermajority provisions requires a supermajority vote, Model Act § 7.27(b).

Supermajority provisions also may be applied to actions of the board of directors. DGCL § 141(b) (if specified in the charter or bylaws); Model Act § 8.24 (if specified in charter or bylaws). In close corporations, supermajority provisions often appear in shareholders' agreements. Model Act § 7.32.

Supermajority provisions may apply to certain transactions — for example, mergers or sales of all or substantially all of the assets of the corporation — or to all transactions. Of course, if supermajority provisions apply to all transactions, the possibility of deadlock increases. A common use of supermajority requirements is to protect against change in other negotiated allocations of control. For example, if the shareholders of a corporation agree to board representation of a minority shareholder and that agreement is embodied in the corporation's charter, that provision in the charter should also provide for change only upon the vote of a supermajority; in effect, changes to the provision should be subject to a minority shareholder's veto.

PROBLEM 5-4

After accepting venture capital, Duncan and Stewart owned just over 50 percent of Classic Games Inc., but both resigned from the board of directors under a cloud caused by alleged financial improprieties. Following the departure of Duncan and Stewart, the board of directors of Classic Games Inc. amended the Company's bylaws by adding the following provision to Article IX:

> The provisions contained in Sections 1 through 12 of Article III of these Bylaws shall not be amended, altered or repealed except (a) by the affirmative vote of the holders of at least eighty percent (80%) of each class of stock outstanding and entitled to vote at any meeting of the stockholders, provided notice of the proposed amendment, alteration or repeal shall have been given in the notice of such meeting or (b) by the board of directors. . . .

The sections of Article III mentioned in the foregoing provision govern matters relating to Classic Games Inc.'s board of directors, including board size. In an attempt to regain control over the board of directors, Duncan and Stewart signed a written consent deleting the sentence above that required an 80 percent supermajority vote to amend Article III. They then amended Article III to expand the board of directors from five to eleven members and elected six new directors who were aligned with Duncan and Stewart.

The directors who opposed Duncan and Stewart claimed that their actions were invalid because they should not have been allowed to remove a supermajority voting provision with less than a supermajority vote. Duncan and Stewart countered by pointing to Article II, § 8 of Classic Games Inc.'s bylaws, which provides that a simple majority vote is effective to resolve any issue unless a different vote is required by "express provision of the statutes or of the Certificate of Incorporation or . . . these Bylaws."

Should the bylaw amendment adopted by Duncan and Stewart be upheld?

G. PREEMPTIVE RIGHTS

Preemptive rights are the rights of a shareholder to subscribe to the portion of any increase in a corporation's capital stock necessary to maintain the shareholder's relative voting power as against other shareholders. If a shareholder owns 10 percent of a corporation's shares, therefore, a preemptive right would entitle the shareholder to purchase 10 percent of a subsequent issuance of shares. Up through the first part of the 20th century, preemptive rights were treated as an inherent attribute of capital stock. Preemptive rights no longer are considered inherent in capital stock, but they may be granted or denied by the articles of incorporation.

Both the DGCL and the Model Act provide for an "opt in" to preemptive rights, meaning that the default rule is against preemptive rights but that a corporation may provide for preemptive rights by including a provision to that effect in the articles of incorporation. Most state corporation statutes include an "opt out" provision for preemptive rights. The "opt in" provision reflects skepticism about the value of preemptive rights and a recognition that from the corporation's standpoint, preemptive rights simply complicate the issuance of new shares.

Because preemptive rights complicate the issuance of shares, public companies rarely have such provisions. By contrast, preemptive rights are very common in closely held corporations. The following case involves the use of preemptive rights (rights of first refusal) in the venture capital context. As you read this case, consider the incentives produced by the rights and the reasons for allowing a forced waiver of such rights.

KIMBERLIN v. CIENA CORPORATION

1998 WL 603234
United States District Court, Southern District of New York
September 11, 1998

SOTOMAYOR, District Judge.

Plaintiff Kevin Kimberlin complains to this Court that he is a victim of newer and larger investor defendants who have improperly denied the initial investor plaintiffs full participation in the growth potential of defendant Ciena Corporation. Plaintiff paints a portrait of the defendants as "the big boys repeatedly trampling the rights of the little guy who was there first." . . .

BACKGROUND

The following facts are those reasonably supported by the evidence presented, read in the light most favorable to the non-moving parties. Plaintiff Kevin Kimberlin is a New York investment banker who owns controlling or sole interests in three of the other four plaintiffs — Spencer Trask Holdings, Inc., a New York-based venture capital firm; INNO Co., a New York-based investment company; and Kevin Kimberlin L.P., a limited partnership set up by Kimberlin to hold Ciena stock. Laura McNamara, the fifth plaintiff, is a managing director of Spencer Trask.

Ciena is a manufacturer of fiber optic technology incorporated in Delaware and based in Maryland. Formerly known as Hydralite, the company's product line centers upon technology developed by its founder and Chief Technical Officer, Dr. David Huber to enable current users of fiber optic technology (*e.g.*, long-distance telephone service providers) to expand their bandwidth — that is, in effect, to create a greater data-handling capacity — without the expense of installing new fiber optic cable.

The relationship between Kimberlin and Ciena began in 1993, when Kimberlin provided Ciena with $190,000 in seed capital pursuant to a stock purchase agreement, plus a $300,000 letter of credit. At the same time, Ciena and Spencer Trask entered into a Private Placement Agreement (the "Placement Agreement") for a future capitalization effort. As Ciena grew, it attracted more investor interest, and in April 1994 Ciena issued its first series of preferred stock (the "Series A" stock issue). Spencer Trask did not, however, underwrite the Series A issue as specified in the Placement Agreement, but rather Sevin Rosen Funds, a larger venture capital firm, handled the Series A offering. Sevin Rosen had been introduced to Ciena in late 1993 and was apparently instrumental in installing defendant Patrick Nettles as director and CEO of Ciena in February 1994.

In compensation for failing to use Spencer Trask for the Series A placement, Ciena agreed to modify the Placement Agreement so that Ciena would offer its Series B preferred stock through Spencer Trask. The modified Placement Agreement contained a liquidated damages clause which stated that if Ciena did not use Spencer Trask to underwrite the Series B offering, Spencer Trask would receive a warrant for 150,000 shares of Series A stock. In addition, Kimberlin purchased (partially for himself, partially for INNO) 421,520 shares of Series A preferred stock.

In December [1994], Ciena issued its second round of private financing, the Series B preferred stock offering. The offering was made, again not through Spencer Trask, but through Charles River Ventures, another venture capital firm. When Kimberlin, through his attorneys, objected that this violated the modified Placement Agreement, Ciena forwarded the stock warrant provided for in the liquidated damages clause. Kimberlin continued to object, and ultimately a settlement was reached on February 10, 1995, which terminated the Placement Agreement and gave Kimberlin a warrant for 300,000 shares of Series B Stock. This warrant was ultimately distributed by Kimberlin as follows: Kevin Kimberlin, L.P. — 250,000 shares; Spencer Trask — 45,000 shares; and Laura McNamara — 5,000 shares. In addition, the Series B offering, which closed on December 22, 1994 without Kimberlin and INNO (both holders of Series A shares), was reopened that same day to allow Kimberlin to purchase 131,733 shares of Series B preferred stock.

During 1995, Ciena was involved in negotiations for a rather large supply contract with Sprint Corporation, a contract of significant value to Ciena. As a result of capital needs created by the contract, Ciena determined that a new round of financing, the Series C preferred stock offering, would be required. It is this Series C offering that forms the crux of the dispute in this case.

The negotiations with Sprint were included in monthly reports from Ciena at least as early as the August 1995 report (which was dated September 8). Further progress reports were included in the monthly reports for subsequent months, with the October report (dated November 9, 1995) indicating that "it appears that a contract [with Sprint] should be signed next month," and the

November report (dated December 8, 1995) indicating "Sprint Contract Negotiations near completion." The Company also published a 1996-1998 Business Plan, dated October 16, 1995, which, while not mentioning Sprint by name, indicated repeatedly that revenues for 1996 were projected from Ciena's first and sole customer and also indicated net sales in 1996 of $50 M. Although the monthly reports and the business plan were apparently distributed to the major investors, Kimberlin did not receive this information until he had a phone conversation sometime in early November with Dr. Nettles in which Kimberlin complained of the lack of information. Kimberlin subsequently received the August and October monthly reports as well as the October 16 Business Plan described above.

On October 13, 1995, the Ciena board agreed to pursue a third round of capital financing, the Series C preferred stock issue. By this point, the board of directors included the individual named defendants in this case: Jon W. Bayless, a senior executive of Sevin Rosen Funds; Michael J. Zak, a general partner of Charles River Ventures; and H. Berry Cash, a senior executive of InterWest Partners, another venture capital firm. In early November, Bayless proceeded to call the Series A and B holders to determine their interest in participating in the Series C. Kimberlin received one of these calls, informing him that Ciena was targeting a raise of $8 M from the existing investors, and that Kimberlin's pro-rata share (based on his percentage of Series A & B stock) would be 68,437 shares. Kimberlin informed Bayless that he would take his full prorata portion of Series C. On November 2, 1995, Bayless had put together a tentative list of prior investors' participation which indicated an expected purchase by the prior investors of $7.25 M-$11.5 M, but which had next to Kimberlin's name nothing but question marks. Kimberlin, in his affidavit, does not state whether his conversation with Bayless took place prior to November 2.

By November 16, 1995, agreement had apparently been reached with Weiss, Peck and Greer, a venture capital firm, to be the lead investors in the Series C round, and a term sheet was circulated to the potential investors. The term sheet showed a total financing of $15-25 M. Although Nettles asserts otherwise, Kimberlin claims he never received this term sheet. In addition, on December 8, 1995, a term sheet and a draft Series C agreement were sent to potential investors; however, the distribution list showed that Kimberlin was not included in the mailing.

Apparently, for planning purposes, Ciena used a target amount of $10 M to be raised from the existing investors, which translated into a prorata share for Kimberlin of 72,533 shares.[2] On December 15, 1995, Kimberlin faxed a letter to Joseph Chinnici, the Chief Financial Officer of Ciena, informing Chinnici that he had heard that the total Series C financing was now going to be $25 M, and that Kimberlin wished to purchase his prorata share (which, including his warrants, he calculated at 6.035%) of the entire Series C offering (not just the portion reserved for the existing investors), which he calculated as 251,526 shares, not the 72,533 already discussed. During a phone conversation with Nettles that same day, Kimberlin claims that Nettles told him that changing

---

2. $10 M at the target price of $7/share results in 1,428,571 shares. Kimberlin's beneficial ownership (*i.e.*, including INNO, of which Kimberlin owned 100%) of Series A and B shares totaled 553,253 shares out of 10,896,612 shares outstanding, resulting in a percentage ownership of 5.077%. Multiplying this percentage by 1,428,571 shares results in a prorata share of 72,533 shares of Series C.

the stock allocations at that point would destroy the financing scheme and that if he insisted on taking his full prorata share of the entire Series C, he would in fact get nothing at all. Ultimately, says Kimberlin, he was assured by Nettles that if he agreed to waive his prorata rights of first refusal, Kimberlin would be treated "like all the other existing investors," that the 72,533 shares of Series C reflected this, and that in the event of an initial public offering (IPO) of Ciena, Kimberlin would be listed as a major stockholder of the company even if his ownership at the time were less than 5% (the threshold for required reporting under SEC rules).

On that same day the Ciena board of directors met and the directors were informed that the contract with Sprint, upon which the Series C financing depended, had been executed the day prior, on December 14, 1995. The information and a copy of the contract had also been given out to some of the Series C investors, but not to Kimberlin. At the December 15 meeting, the Ciena board gave its final approval to the Series C financing. Also at this meeting, it was determined that Bessemer Ventures, one of the existing investors, would receive an additional $1 M of Series C stock, thus raising the entire Series C to its final amount of $26 M.

On December 18, 1995, the Series C Purchase Agreement was sent to all investors, including Kimberlin. The Series C agreement shows all of the existing stockholders in Ciena and also all of the Series C purchasers, including the number of shares which they would purchase at closing. Kimberlin says he "does not recall" receiving this information with the Series C agreement on December 18. Kimberlin signed and returned the signature page for the Series C agreement, which closed on December 21, 1995.

Kimberlin and his co-plaintiffs filed this suit on November 19, 1996. . . .

DISCUSSION . . .

II. THE VALIDITY OF THE TERMINATION OF THE SERIES B PREEMPTIVE RIGHTS

At the heart of all of the plaintiffs' various claims is the assertion that plaintiffs had a right under the prior stock purchase agreements to purchase a larger share of Ciena stock in the Series C offering than was actually made available by Ciena, and that this lost opportunity was caused by the defendants' wrongful conduct. Defendants counter that any such rights to a given share of Ciena stock were terminated by the vote of the other stockholders. It is clear that this question must be resolved at the outset, for if the defendants are correct, the plaintiffs could not have been damaged by the loss of their preemptive rights because there were no longer any such rights to lose. The Court agrees with defendants that the termination of the Series B preemptive rights was valid.

The Series B stock purchase agreement states as follows:

> 7.10. Right of First Refusal. The Company hereby grants to each Investor the right of first refusal to purchase, pro-rata, all (or any part) of (x) New Securities . . . that the Company may, from time to time, propose to sell and issue. . . . The Investor's pro rata share shall be the ratio of the number of Preferred Shares then held by the Investor as of the date of the Rights Notice . . . to the sum of the total number of Preferred Shares then held by all Investors . . . as of such date.

Included within the definition of "New Securities" are preferred stock issues such as the Series C stock issue in dispute here (but not the later IPO).

The Series B agreement also, however, provides for the termination of these rights of first refusal:

> 14. Modifications: Waiver. (a) . . . [A]ny provision of this Agreement may be amended and the observance of such provision may be waived (either generally or in a particular instance and either retroactively or prospectively) with (but only with) the written consent of (i) the Company, . . . (iii) in the case of any modification of [Section 7] the holders of at least 67% of the Investor Shares . . . acting together as a single class.

"Investor Shares" includes both Series A and Series B preferred stock. The new Section 7 of the Series B purchase agreement also superseded nearly identical provisions in the Series A agreement.

The effect of the above provisions gave each of the Series B investors (including all of the plaintiffs) the right to purchase a prorata share of any future rounds of stock issuance, including of course the Series C. However, it also gave the power to the holders of 67% of the combined Series A/Series B preferred shares to nullify those rights of first refusal at any time.

The key portion of the Series C purchase agreement is as follows:

> 19. Prior Agreements. . . . By execution of this Agreement, (a) the Prior Investors . . . hereby consent to the amendment of the Prior Agreements as contemplated herein, and (b) the Prior Investors waive the rights of first refusal under Section 7.10 of the Prior Agreements in respect of the issuances of Series C Preferred hereunder, such waiver to be effective on behalf of all the Investors referred to in the Prior Agreements pursuant to Section 14 thereof.

There is no dispute that both Ciena and all of the Prior Investors executed the Series C agreement which included this waiver provision, well above the 67% required to make the provision effective. The plaintiffs, of course, claim that their waivers were procured fraudulently and should not count, a proposition with which this Court agrees for purposes of this motion. However, the Kimberlin plaintiffs only held 5% of the necessary shares—close to 8% if they exercised their warrants to purchase more Series B stock—and so excluding their votes still left at least 92% voting to waive the rights of first refusal. Thus, unless this waiver vote was ineffective for some reason, plaintiffs' Series B rights of first refusal terminated as of the signing of the Series C agreement by the other investors.

The plaintiffs make two arguments in response. First, they argue that the 67% requirement has not been met because certain of the prior investors' votes should not be counted. Second, they argue that even if the 67% threshold has been crossed, the Series B purchase agreement should be interpreted as prohibiting any allocation of new stock issue which does not at least preserve each prior investor's right to purchase a pro rata share of that amount of stock which is not allocated to new investors. Neither of these contentions, however, is correct.

A. Was the 67% Threshold Met?

The plaintiffs assert that certain investors' waivers should not count because their votes were tainted, and that without these votes, the necessary 67% of Prior Investors' shares did not vote to waive the prorata allocation. The plaintiffs' arguments boil down to the assertion that certain "favored investors" were "bribed" into voting to waive the rights of first refusal because they knew that they would receive more than their prorata share of the existing investors' portion of the Series C offering. Plaintiffs contend that therefore these investors' shares "cannot legally, logically or fairly be counted" towards the 67% threshold, but precisely why this is so is unfortunately left for the Court to divine.

To the extent that, as asserted in the Complaint, the plaintiffs complain about those directors of Ciena who voted themselves a greater allocation of Series C shares, the Court assumes that plaintiffs mean to suggest that their shares should not count because this constitutes impermissible self-dealing in breach of their fiduciary duties as directors. Whether these directors had a fiduciary duty to the plaintiffs (as opposed to Ciena), whether voting their shares in such a manner breached that duty, and whether the remedy for such a breach would be the disqualification of their votes are issues which are all far from self-evident but which the Court need not reach, because of the three directors named as defendants in this case, only one wound up with a larger percentage of the existing investors' portion than his percentage ownership of Series A and B stock. . . .

InterWest and Charles River would actually, by insisting upon maintaining at least their prorata share of the Series C shares allocated to the existing investors, have wound up with more Series C stock, and thus any assertion of self-dealing on their part is simply unsupportable. . . . Thus, under the "self-dealing" theory, only Sevin Rosen's shares (along with the Kimberlin plaintiffs') should not be counted, which amounts to at most about 25% of the voting shares (Sevin Rosen's 17% plus the Kimberlin plaintiffs' 8% if they exercised their warrants). This still leaves some 75% of the existing investors waiving their rights of first refusal, and thus the waiver is still valid. . . .

[T]here are, in addition to Sevin Rosen, two other groups of prior investors, not represented on Ciena's board, who received a percentage of the Series C offering allocated to the existing investors which was higher than their percentage of Series A/B ownership: Bessemer and SVE. If these votes were not counted, along with those of Sevin Rosen and Kimberlin, then the total percentage vote for waiver would be approximately 60%, just shy of the necessary threshold for waiving the rights of first refusal.

However, the plaintiffs can point to no legal reason why the votes of SVE and Bessemer should not be counted. These shareholders had no representation on the board such that the self-dealing question raised earlier is presented. Moreover, as shareholders—and not majority or controlling shareholders—they had no fiduciary duty towards their fellow shareholders, and certainly no duty to vote their shares contrary to their own interests. Nor have the plaintiffs alleged wrongdoing of any sort on the part of these two entities. It appears from the evidence that they did no more than express an interest to the Ciena officers in receiving a larger share of Series C. Even if the Ciena board had, as the plaintiffs allege, a plan to drive out Kimberlin and his associates—and further assuming that such a plan would be impermissible in some unspecified way—the Court fails to see why such a plan should be held to deprive SVE and Bessemer—"favored investors" though they may be—of their right to vote their shares as they saw fit.

The plaintiffs' position, were it to be upheld, would require this Court to find that no prior investor could, as a matter of law, receive a larger share of the Series C offering vis-à-vis other prior investors than their holding of Series A & B. Such a position would, however, be untenable and illogical, given the plaintiffs' own admission that it was perfectly proper — even desirable — to waive the rights of first refusal to allow in new investors to Series C. After all, these new investors received a substantially — in fact, infinitely — greater share of Series C because they of course had no Series A & B shares to begin with. Plaintiffs' position would thus mean that while new investors could come in and purchase essentially any amount the Ciena board chose to sell them, the old investors — simply by virtue of their having invested in Ciena at an earlier, even less certain time — would be forever limited by their previous percentage ownership. It is difficult if not impossible to imagine a justification for such a holding. The Court thus finds that there is no fact issue as to whether the 67% level needed to waive the rights of first refusal under the Series B purchase agreement was reached.

B. Did the Series B Agreement Restrict the Power to Waive First Refusal Rights?

Having determined that the 67% threshold was reached, the Court turns to plaintiffs' next argument — namely, that even if the threshold was reached, the power of 67% of the prior investor shares to waive the right of first refusal was limited. Plaintiffs argue that, although the prorata rights of first refusal could be waived to allow in new investors, each prior investor had a right to purchase his or her prorata percentage of those shares reserved for the prior investors — a right which could not be waived by a vote of the prior investors. Plaintiffs make two arguments in this regard: (1) the Series B agreement should be interpreted this way in light of trade usage and course of dealing; and (2) such a nonwaivable right is implicit in the duty of good faith and fair dealing that is part of the Series B agreement. The Court will address each contention in turn.

1. Trade Usage and Course of Dealing

Plaintiffs' first argument urges this Court to interpret the waiver provisions in the Series B agreement to allow only a limited power of waiver — that is, while the prorata right of first refusal may be waived to allow new investors in, every prior investor maintains a right to purchase his prorata portion of those shares sold to the existing investors — a right not subject to a vote of 67% of the prior investors. Plaintiffs assert, through their expert John Mahar, that it is standard industry practice to include waivers and that such waivers "are intended to permit new investors into the financing while the remaining 'existing investors are allowed to participate in that part of the total investment that has been earmarked for them according to the pro rata calculation.'" This, the plaintiffs assert, constitutes evidence of trade usage which should be used to interpret the waiver provisions. Moreover, say plaintiffs, when the Series B offering was made, the prior investors' shares were calculated precisely in this manner, thus establishing a course of dealing which also must be used to interpret the Series B agreement.

Contrary to the plaintiffs' contentions, under Delaware law, course of dealing and trade usage are applicable to interpreting the waiver and prorata provisions of the Series B agreement only upon a threshold finding that these provisions are ambiguous. . . .

There is no ambiguity in the waiver and prorata provisions of the Series B agreement. Section 14(a) of the agreement clearly states that "any provision of this Agreement may be amended and the observance of any such provision may be waived (either generally or in a particular instance and either retroactively or prospectively" by the vote of 67% of the prior investors' shares. There is no limitation on this waiver power to be found either in Section 14 or in Section 7.10, the section granting the prorata rights, and no reasonable person could read such a limitation into this language. This is particularly true in light of the extensive and detailed nature of the stock purchase agreement, which is some 53 single-spaced pages long, and of section 7.10 in particular, which runs for several paragraphs and sets out the operation of the first refusal rights in detail. Surely such an important and easily draftable provision, if intended, would have been expressly provided for. Moreover, there is at least one provision of the Series B agreement (Section 14) which, like the plaintiffs' asserted right, is made expressly nonwaivable except by unanimous consent, so it is clear that the drafters of the purchase agreement contemplated nonwaivable provisions but did not consider the prorata rights to be one. In light of the unambiguous language of the Series B agreement, the Court cannot, and does not, consider the plaintiffs' evidence of trade usage and course of dealing.

2. Duty of Good Faith and Fair Dealing

The Series B agreement, as does every contract, carries with it an implied covenant of good faith and fair dealing. The thrust of this duty is to "require[] a party in a contractual relationship to refrain from arbitrary or unreasonable conduct which has the effect of preventing the other party to the contract from receiving the fruits of the contract." Wilgus v. Salt Pond Inves. Co., 498 A.2d 151, 159 (Del. Ch. 1985). However, "the duty arises only where it is clear from what the parties expressly agreed, that they would have proscribed the challenged conduct as a breach of the implied covenant of good faith had they thought to negotiate with respect to the matter." [Dave Greytak Enters. v. Mazda Motors of Am., 622 A.2d 14, 22-23 (Del. Ch.), *aff'd*, 609 A.2d 668 (Del. 1992).] "It follows that where the subject at issue is expressly covered by the contract, or where the contract is intentionally silent as to that subject, the implied duty to perform in good faith does not come into play." *Greytak*, 622 A.2d at 23.

In other words, the duty of good faith cannot be relied upon to alter the terms of the contract itself. As stated earlier, the Court finds the waiver provisions of the Series B agreement to be unambiguous. It is implausible, given the detailed and extensive nature of the agreement, to say that the parties simply did not consider the issue of whether waiver of the first refusal rights was limited in the way plaintiffs suggest. That the prior investors might choose to waive the prorata first refusal rights in the future was hardly unforeseen — in fact, as noted by plaintiffs' expert, such waivers are routine. Rather, it is clear that the parties chose not to place any restrictions on the right of two-thirds of the shareholders to waive these first refusal rights. To allow the plaintiffs to add this provision would be to rewrite the purchase agreement under the guise of the duty of good faith, which is plainly not consonant with principles of Delaware contract law.

In sum, then, the plaintiffs have failed to show any factual or legal basis for finding that the waiver of prorata first refusal rights from the Series B agreement was ineffective as of the execution of the Series C agreement. . . .

CONCLUSION

For the foregoing reasons, [t]he plaintiffs' contract claims . . . are dismissed without prejudice.

PROBLEM 5-5

The venture capitalists who invested in Classic Games Inc. included a Right of First Refusal (Right) in the Stock Purchase Agreement. The Right entitles the venture capitalists to purchase a "Basic Amount" of any securities offered by the company. The "Basic Amount" is defined as a "pro rata portion of the Offered Securities determined by multiplying the number of Offered Securities by a fraction, the numerator of which is the aggregate number of shares of Common Stock issued or issuable upon conversion of all Shares then held by such Qualified Purchaser and the denominator of which is the total number of shares of Common Stock then outstanding (giving effect to the conversion into Common Stock of all outstanding shares of Convertible Preferred Stock and the exercise of all outstanding options and warrants)."

How does the calculation of the Basic Amount differ from the calculation in **Kimberlin***? Why might this difference matter to investors?*

The Right does not apply to the following issuances of securities:

(i)   The issuance of any shares of Common Stock as a stock dividend to holders of Common Stock or upon any subdivision or combination of shares of Common Stock;

(ii) The issuance of any shares of Common Stock upon conversion of shares of Convertible Preferred Stock;

(iii) The issuance of shares of Common Stock, or options with respect thereto, issued or issuable to employees, directors, or officers of, or consultants to, the Company pursuant to any plan, agreement, or arrangement approved by the Board of Directors of the Company and a majority of the Board of Directors who are not employees of the Company;

(iv) The issuance of securities solely in consideration for a bona fide acquisition (whether by merger or otherwise) by the Company of all or substantially all of the stock or assets of any other entity approved by the Board of Directors of the Company;

(v)   The issuance of shares of Common Stock by the Company in a firm commitment underwritten public offering pursuant to an effective registration statement under the Securities Act.

What is the justification for each of these exclusions from the right of first refusal?

H.   DEADLOCK

Deadlocks occur when the shareholder vote is evenly divided. While deadlocks usually arise from a failure to allocate control in advance, occasionally business planners intentionally provide opportunities for deadlocks. The rationale for such planning is that some business relationships should not proceed unless there is unanimous assent to the action.

A deadlock usually leads to dissolution of a corporation. As with all fundamental decisions involving a corporation, the decision to dissolve typically requires approval by the directors and the shareholders. After dissolution is authorized, the corporation may dissolve by filing articles of dissolution with the secretary of state.

In some instances, however, shareholders cannot even agree to dissolve. When this happens, the corporation may be judicially dissolved upon a showing of deadlock. The following case involves such a dissolution. Notice that the court assigns a date of dissolution that is prior to the commencement of the lawsuit. Is this a reasonable approach in light of the statutory provisions governing judicial dissolution?

CONKLIN v. PERDUE

2002 WL 31421763 (slip opinion)
Superior Court of Massachusetts
September 17, 2002

VAN GESTEL, Justice.

This matter is before the Court for findings of fact, rulings of law and an order for judgment following a jury-waived trial.

FINDINGS OF FACT

The plaintiff, Jeffrey M. Conklin ("Conklin"), at the time of the start of the trial on June 18, 2002, was unemployed. He is a graduate of Boston College and holds a J.D. degree from Villanova University and an M.B.A. degree from Duke University.

Conklin worked for a number of years, from 1979 to 1993, at Digital Equipment Corporation ("DEC"). He started at DEC as a contract negotiator and advanced through a position as legal counsel for international purchasing to legal counsel for international matters in the financial area.

The defendant, Beth A. Perdue ("Perdue"), is a graduate of Case Western Reserve University and has a law degree from the University of Michigan. She also worked for a number of years at DEC, in the purchasing and contracts department.

While at DEC, Conklin met Perdue. They developed a personal, as well as business, relationship that included some international overlap.

Perdue left DEC in 1992, and Conklin resigned from DEC on June 4, 1993. In 1993, the two then determined to join together and establish a consulting firm to advise businesses on strategic alliances. "Strategic alliances" was a catch phrase that covered a range of activities designed to establish more positive relationships between businesses or between businesses and markets. Conklin and Perdue hoped to capitalize on their experience at DEC in understanding the intricacies of negotiating international agreements and on their knowledge of international markets, particularly in south Asia.

The entity that they formed eventually became CPInternational, Inc. ("CPI"). The "CP" stood for Conklin and Perdue.

CPI was a Massachusetts corporation which, for taxing purposes, made an election to be treated as a Subchapter S corporation. Conklin and Perdue were each directors, officers and 50% shareholders of CPI. Perdue was the president, and Conklin was the treasurer. CPI, with its two shareholders, an absence of any market for its stock, and its essentially total shareholder participation in management was a classic closely held corporation of the kind described in Donahue v. Rodd Electrotype Company of New England, Inc., 367 Mass. 578 (1975).

CPI had no capital in the beginning and, although it earned small amounts of money on a few contracts, was basically financed by Conklin, either personally or with money he borrowed from his parents. Perdue made essentially no capital contributions to CPI.

Each of Conklin and Perdue reimbursed themselves for expenses, the largest amount of which seemed to be related to international travel to countries in south Asia. Conklin and Perdue also each took from CPI what they called a "draw." One of the issues in dispute in this case is whether that draw should actually be considered a loan. The Court finds, however, that CPI's final Federal tax return, for the year 1997, includes a Schedule K-1 in the name of Perdue, listing "Property distributions (including cash) . . . reported to [her] on Form 1099" of $112,434. This $112,434 amount is the "draw" in contest. Perdue produced her own individual tax return establishing that she paid taxes on this amount.

In October of 1994, Conklin was invited to make a speech in India before the U.S./India Business Council. The U.S. Secretary of Commerce, the late Ron Brown, led the United States delegation to India in connection with the program. It being customary to give symbolic gifts in connection with such trade mission affairs, Conklin and Perdue suggested that the gift be an Internet web-page to the people of India; the web-page would demonstrate ways in which American and Indian businesses could locate, communicate and collaborate with each other. The idea was accepted, and CPI set about creating a demonstration web-page.

Because CPI had no funds to create such a web-page, it put together a consortium of four American Companies — IBM, BBN, Sun Microsystems and Bay Networks — to fund the creation of the demonstration web-page. The total funding was about $60,000. What was created was an example of how the sponsoring companies' products could be used in India. The demonstration piece had no interactive functions. The program ultimately became known at CPI as "TradeInfo."

The trade mission to India was not a success. It came at the time of a fund-raising scandal implicating the Secretary of Commerce. CPI got no follow-on consulting business from this program.

CPI did, however, make contact with the Confederation of Indian Industries ("CII"). The two entities entered into a promotional agreement whereby the CII membership list was to be put on the CPI TradeInfo program. The idea was that American companies would use the TradeInfo program with the CII database to make business-to-business contacts in India. CPI hoped that once those contacts were made, it would then be engaged by the American companies for consulting work in their negotiations of agreements with the Indian companies. In a direct sense, this program between CPI and CII was non-revenue generating and actually cost CPI some money.

In the summer of 1995, CPI started on the TradeInfo project with the CII database by beginning to create another canned demonstration similar to that used in the Indian trade mission program. CPI, which was running out of money at the time, engaged a small company in New York named Cyber House Publishing ("Cyber House") to create a web site. The web site was intended to permit U.S. companies to search the CII database for Indian companies and then call CPI for assistance in getting together.

This clearly was not a large project. Cyber House's billings only totaled $4,800. But, as an example of CPI's strained financial circumstances, even that amount was not fully paid.

What Cyber House created, however, could be accessed only by contacting Cyber House. It was, basically, a low-level prototype with no Internet address. It had no software systems, nor was it interactive or able to perform business-to-business communications.

By the end of 1995, CPI was essentially out of money, and it had only one customer, a company called HCL, which was overdue on its payments. Tensions arose between Conklin and Perdue. Conklin continued to be the sole source of money to finance CPI, and he was concerned that Perdue was not focusing adequately on the financial end of the business, nor was she contributing to it. In fact, Conklin was concerned that Perdue was an economic drain on the company.

Also by the end of 1995, CPI was located in leased space at 36 Newbury Street in Boston's Back Bay. The rent was $1,650 per month, and Conklin alone was on the lease as a guarantor.

Conklin claims — and Perdue denies the claim — that in the summer of 1995 he had her sign a promissory note reflecting the indebtedness she owed the company for the draw money she was taking. Conklin says that the note was provided to him by the company's accountants and that Perdue executed two copies thereof. He testified that he then put the two signed copies of the note in a manila envelope which he thereafter kept in a drawer of his desk. No such promissory note, nor any copy thereof, was produced at trial.

By late December 1995, Conklin concluded that CPI was not economically sustainable and had no good future prospects. He also decided that working with Perdue was difficult; and he was tired of all of the traveling.

Thus, on December 29, 1995, Conklin called Perdue and told her things were not working out; that he was in debt, and there was no security for it; and that CPI had no revenue prospects. He further told her that the 50/50 arrangement was not working out and said that he would sit down and discuss the matter with her on the day after New Year's Day.

Perdue's response was that she was "shocked." To which Conklin responded: "How can you be shocked?"

Conklin then went away for the New Year's weekend. When he returned home from the weekend, there was a voice-mail message from Perdue. It said: "I'm not going to meet. I took some records. I'll copy them and return them."

Conklin then called Perdue, and they had a brief, five-minute conversation. In the conversation, Perdue insisted that she had a legal right to do what she did. This time it was Conklin who said he was "stunned."

Conklin went to the CPI office the next day and met with the office manager, Astrid Mueller. He described the office as appearing as if it had been ransacked and looking like it had been broken into. Folders were all over the place, a computer printer was missing, and computer tapes had been taken. He also says he discovered that the promissory notes and his tax returns were no longer there.

Conklin then called Perdue and demanded that she bring everything back. She refused. He then proceeded to have the locks changed on the office doors.

However, Perdue describes the visit to the office on the New Year's weekend, and the removal of materials, somewhat differently. She says that she went to the office on Saturday, December 30, 1995, the morning after the telephone conversation with Conklin. She says that she first started to do a back-up of the computer system. She then started going through files, wondering what to take to protect the company. She says she left notes of what she had done. She specifically denies, however, taking any promissory notes — insisting that she never signed any in the first place.

Perdue concedes that on December 30, 1995, she had help from a man named Lawrence Hartford ("Hartford") in removing the files and other materials from the CPI office.

Hartford also testified about the New Year's weekend incidents — he says there were two — when he assisted Perdue in removing things from the CPI office. His story strained credulity. He described himself as a "decorative painter" who met Perdue in 1992. He evidently worked from time to time at Perdue's home, doing what sounded like interior decorating work. Hartford says he became friends with Perdue socially.

Hartford claims he received a call from Perdue on the Friday starting New Year's weekend,[3] asking for help in removing her "stuff" from the CPI office because she was going to be locked out. Hartford then says that he picked Perdue up at her home in the South End and drove to Newbury Street, arriving there at about 10:00 P.M. He then alleges that they entered the building and went up the elevator to the CPI office. There, he claims, Perdue unlocked the door, and the two of them went in. He also testified that, at Perdue's insistence, they did not put on any lights in the office because she did not want Conklin to know she was there. Then, according to Hartford, in the dark of a winter night in Boston, he and Perdue examined materials on her desk and on a secretary's desk, but Perdue took nothing therefrom, including such highly personal things as photographs of Perdue's nieces and a radio headset. Then, still in pitch dark, Hartford claims to have gone over to Conklin's desk and found a manila envelope containing two identical pages headed "promissory note." He says that he then said to Perdue: "Isn't this it?" To which he says she responded: "We should go"; and, presumably, taking nothing but the manila envelope and its contents, they left.

Hartford then says that he received a second call from Perdue on Saturday morning, as a result of which they again went to the CPI offices and removed the materials that Perdue also described in her testimony as having been removed on December 30, 1995. The materials removed on Saturday were taken by Hartford and Perdue to "Office Max" at the South Bay Center for copying. They were signed in under the name "J. Hartford" rather than Perdue in order to further conceal their whereabouts from Conklin. Eventually, Hartford says that he and [Perdue] picked up the copied materials from Office Max and took them to her home in the South End. They used two cars this time because of the documents' bulk after copying.

The Court does not credit Hartford's testimony about the dark-of-night visit to the CPI office on Friday, December 29, 1995.

---

3. The Court takes judicial notice of the fact that in 1995, the last Friday of the month was December 29, 1995, and New Year's Day was Monday January 1, 1996.

From the time of the New Year's weekend on, there initially was some effort by Conklin and Perdue to reach agreement on resolving the break-up of their relationship and resolving the affairs of CPI. Except for a few conversations and exchanges of correspondence regarding dissolution in early January 1996, however, there were no apparent efforts by either Conklin or Perdue — both law school graduates — to comply with the legal particulars regarding the winding-up of CPI's corporate affairs.

Conklin, at the same time, began a new venture on his own. On January 4, 1996, he incorporated Emerging Markets, Inc., known sometimes as Emerging Markets Business Information Services, Inc., later as TradeAccess, Inc., and now as Ozro, Inc. (herein "TradeAccess"). Conklin says the initial incorporation was simply to keep track of what he was going to do.

In an exchange of correspondence on January 15, January 17 and January 19, 1996, Conklin and Perdue reached the point where each was doing little but making accusations about the other regarding the business of CPI, and each was refusing to consent to any action by the other regarding the ongoing business of CPI or its winding-up. Also, on January 15, 1996, the small paid staff of CPI was laid off. This was the beginning of a process when each of Conklin and Perdue made allegations against the other, both in the nature of causing harm to CPI and in the nature of breaching fiduciary duties to each other. The business divorce had begun in earnest and eventually found its way, as most divorces do, into the hands of a judge for resolution of issues colored much more by emotion than economic or business reality.

The principal disagreements between Conklin and Perdue related to his allegations that Perdue's draw money was in fact a loan from the corporation and her's that Conklin, in his new venture, effectively stole corporate opportunities that belonged to CPI. Both of these issues are really derivative claims of CPI, the corporation, not of Conklin or Perdue as individuals.

For about two years thereafter, Conklin worked to make his new entity, TradeAccess, succeed. He failed, however. In the process, there was no credible evidence that he took or used materials or opportunities that belonged to CPI. He was, of course, technically still a shareholder and officer of CPI and had whatever duties that status conveyed upon him, assuming CPI remained active for such purposes.

Perdue, despite the aggressive tone in her January 1996 letters, remained remarkably passive, to the state of being essentially inactive, in any attempt to move forward with the business of CPI. Conklin, having moved on with Trade-Access, for all intents and purposes abandoned CPI to Perdue.

To be sure, of course, there were the frictions that came from communications between Conklin and entities with which he, while at CPI, had been involved. These problems mostly produced suspicions and accusations on Perdue's part that Conklin's attempts to explain his noninvolvement with CPI after January of 1996 were really attempts to destroy CPI and steal its business. This Court does not see them in such a dark light. Obviously, the parties could have accomplished the split-up much better and much more smoothly. But it was their emotional reactions to each other, not their exercise of business thievery or breaches of fiduciary duties, that were in play.

Similar suspicions were what drove the accusations that Conklin, through TradeAccess, was interfering with CPI's contractual and other advantageous relationships. As a matter of fact, there was nothing that amounted to such interference, and CPI had essentially no contracts to interfere with. TradeAccess, for one thing, was not in the same business as CPI; and, more importantly, there was no evidence that TradeAccess ever succeeded in the marketplace, except possibly for the time when it sought and received patents for its new product.

In the middle of 1998, long after CPI was in a state of total inactivity and final exhaustion, Conklin, with TradeAccess, came up with a new idea: the ability to negotiate complex business arrangements over the Internet. He then conceived of and had devised a mock-up of how this could be done. He described it as "iterative, multivariate negotiations." Through the use of this product, businesses would be able to contact each other and effectively negotiate complex transactions over the Internet. Eventually, after reducing his ideas to practice, he — and two others who worked with him — sought and received, starting in October of 2000, four patents on the process. This enabled him to attract some outside financing and seemingly to infuse life into his new business. However, this business too seems to have turned out to be an economic failure.

Significantly for this case, this Court does not find that anything in the patented process developed by Conklin and his associates, starting in 1998 and thereafter, was acquired from or was a continuation of anything that CPI was doing when it was an active corporation prior to the end of 1995. CPI never had a real product, and it certainly never had anything that allowed business-to-business iterative, multivariate negotiations over the Internet. The Patent Office's examination of prior art, and its conclusion that Conklin and his associates were entitled to four patents, enables a presumption that the patents were valid, and belies any idea that the inventors copied anything from CPI.

RULINGS OF LAW

Much turns on the status of CPI at various times, particularly in early 1996, and the consequent relationships thereto, and to each other, of CPI's two 50% shareholders, two directors and sole officers, each of the latter of which are Conklin and Perdue. Consequently, the Court first addresses the legal status of CPI as a Massachusetts corporation in January of 1996. In so doing, the Court has been made aware of a decision in the Delaware Chancery Court dealing with somewhat similar issues involving a Delaware corporation with shareholder, director and officerships quite similar to that of CPI. See Dionisi et al. v. DeCampli et al., 1995 Del. Ch. LEXIS 88 (June 28, 1995).

In *Dionisi*, Vice-Chancellor Steele was faced with the break-up of a closely held corporation basically involving two graphic designers who, after previous employment at E.I. du Pont de Nemours & Co., got together to form a small, start-up graphic design business. The entity was incorporated under Delaware law, but the parties treated it much like a joint venture. After a short few years, with very marginal economic success, the two founders had a falling out. Just as in this case, the parties in *Dionisi* sued each other for a wide array of breaches of fiduciary duties, unfair business practices, interference with contractual relations, and the like. Also, just as in this case, the parties in *Dionisi* did not avail themselves of the provisions of Delaware corporate law to effect the formal dissolution of the entity.

Vice-Chancellor Steele, in *Dionisi*, took it upon himself to dissolve the entity in the way that either of the parties could have, but failed to do. . . .

This Court finds itself in much the same position as the Delaware Chancery Court in *Dionisi*. CPI has two 50% shareholders, Conklin and Perdue. Conklin and Perdue, unlike the two shareholders in *Dionisi,* were lawyers, not graphic artists. The two shareholders here are also the only two directors and the only two executive officers of CPI. Since at least mid-January 1996, Conklin and Perdue have been deadlocked in the management of the corporate affairs of CPI and, as shareholders, have been unable to break the deadlock.

Mass. G.L. c. 156B, Sec. 99, provides in material part as follows:

> A petition for dissolution of a corporation may be filed in the supreme judicial court in the following cases: . . .
>
> (b) Such a petition may be filed by the holder or holders of not less than forty per cent of all the shares of its stock outstanding and entitled to vote thereon, treating all classes of stock entitled to vote as a single class for the purpose of determining whether the petition is brought by the holders of not less than forty per cent of the outstanding shares as aforesaid, if: . . .
>
> (1) the directors are deadlocked in the management of corporate affairs, and the shareholders are unable to break the deadlock; . . .
>
> After such notice as the court may order and after hearing, the court may decree a dissolution of the corporation, notwithstanding the fact that the business of the corporation is being conducted at a profit, if it shall find that the best interests of the stockholders will be served by such dissolution. Upon such dissolution, the existence of the corporation shall cease, subject to the provisions of sections one hundred and two, one hundred and four and one hundred and eight.

Section 102 of c. 156B is the provision that provides that dissolution under Sec. 99 shall not prevent the corporation from continuing as a body corporate for a period of three years "for the purpose of prosecuting and defending suits by and against it and/or enabling it gradually to settle and close its affairs, to dispose of and convey its property to any person and to make distributions to its stockholders of any assets remaining after payment of its debts and obligations, *but not for the purpose of continuing the business for which it was established.*" (Emphasis added.)

Can this Court, like the Delaware Chancery Court in *Dionisi*, seize upon G.L. c. 156B, Sec. 99, as a vehicle provided by the Legislature that enables the Court to do what the parties themselves did not: dissolve CPI because of the deadlock by the directors in the management of the corporation and the inability of the shareholders to break that deadlock? . . .

By the Acts of 1964, Chapter 723, the Commonwealth adopted a new Business Corporation Law, which represented the first general overhaul of the Massachusetts corporate laws since 1903. See Hosmer, *New Business Corporation Law,* 11 Ann. Survey of Massachusetts Law 1. Mr. Hosmer, Chairman of the Boston Bar Association Committee that drafted the new business corporation laws, noted that "Chapter 156B [in sec. 99] clarifies the deadlock situation for voluntary dissolution by adopting the definitions of the A.B.A. Model Act and deals with the determination of the vote required in case more than one class of stock is outstanding."

The significance of the new c. 156B to the situation before this Court was presaged, perhaps unknowingly, in Rizzuto v. Onset Cafe, Inc., [330 Mass. 595, 597-98 (1953)]. There the court said:

> The dissolution of corporations, like their creation, is primarily and fundamentally a matter of legislative and not judicial cognizance. . . . *The allegations of the bill or the*

findings of the judge do not bring this case within the scope of any statute authorizing judicial dissolution of corporations. (Emphasis added.)

Here, of course, the findings and rulings of this Court do reveal that, given the deadlock between Conklin and Perdue, the situation does fall within the scope of a statute authorizing judicial dissolution — a statute that was enacted after *Rizzuto* and was a new provision in the General Laws.

The dissolution of a corporation under c. 156B, Sec. 99 calls for the Court to apply its equitable powers. Prior to the adoption of the Massachusetts Rules of Civil Procedure in 1974, corporate dissolution proceedings generally were brought by a bill in equity. Indeed, Sec. 99 states that the result of a proceeding thereunder is for the Court to "*decree* a dissolution of the corporation." (Emphasis added.) At the time that c. 156B was enacted, "decrees" were the vehicle for resolution of matters on the equity side of the court, just as "judgments" were the vehicle on the law side. Further, the Massachusetts Rules of Civil Procedure do not apply "to proceedings pertaining to the dissolution of corporations and distribution of their assets." Mass. R. Civ. P. Rule 81(a)(1) 6.

Given all of the foregoing, this Court, believing it to be within its equitable powers, will proceed here, like the Chancery Court in *Dionisi,* to address the dissolution of CPI, as Conklin or Perdue should have done, under G.L. c. 156B, Sec. 99. In doing so, the Court must first determine when the requisite deadlock between the directors and shareholders first occurred.

As noted in the findings, there was a period from December 29, 1995 through mid-January 1996, when Conklin and Perdue — although in great discord and disarray emotionally, physically, legally and otherwise — seemed to be coming to grips with the termination of their relationship and the dissolution of CPI. Those efforts, however, erupted and imploded with the exchange of correspondence on January 15, January 17 and January 19, 1996. In that exchange, the efforts at resolution metamorphosed into recriminations and accusations, with each of Conklin and Perdue telling the other that he or she would not consent to any action the other took with regard to CPI, its business or its dissolution. The requisite deadlock had arrived, and Conklin and Perdue — CPI's sole 50% shareholders — were unable to break the deadlock. Thus, this Court, acting pursuant to its inherent equitable powers and the authority vested in G.L. c. 156B, Sec. 99, hereby determines that January 19, 1996 is the day that Conklin and Perdue were first in total deadlock regarding the management of CPI and, therefore, the date upon which the corporation is to be deemed dissolved. . . .

The Court now turns to each of the specific claims and their resolution.

Conklin makes four claims against Perdue: he charges her with money lent (Count I); money had and received (Count II); breach of contract (Count III); and breach of fiduciary duty (Count IV).

The first three claims are not Conklin's personally, but rather derivative claims of the corporation, CPI. All three relate to the issue of whether Perdue's draw was in reality a loan. On the evidence presented, this Court rules that the draw was compensation and not a loan. While a different conclusion may have been compelled if some written evidence of a loan was presented, or its absence convincingly accounted for, but it was not. Further, the fact that for S corporation tax purposes certain items needed particular handling and characterization does not change the fact. Indeed, the treatment of the K-1 for Perdue on the CPI final 1997 tax return, the issuance to her of a tax Form 1099, and her ultimate payment of income tax on the draw demonstrates quite the contrary. Counts I, II and III must be dismissed.

Count IV charges Perdue with breach of her fiduciary duties in the December 30, 1995 removal of corporate files and materials from the office. Given her position as a 50% shareholder, and Conklin's December 29, 1995 telephone call threat to the effect that CPI was over as a going operation, the charge of a breach is a close one. It need not be resolved, however, because there was no satisfactory evidence of any damage to Conklin or CPI, all of the records ultimately having been returned and always having been in the custody and control of a 50% shareholder, director and corporate officer. Indeed, it is Conklin's claim—and a major part of his defense to Perdue's claims—that CPI was effectively without any business or any prospects of business on December 29, 1995. As such, neither he nor the corporation had much, if anything, to lose.

Perdue asserts [various] claims against Conklin[, including] breach of fiduciary duty. . . .

Any fiduciary duty on Conklin's part ended on January 19, 1996, the date that this Court has ruled was the date of dissolution of the closely held corporation from which those duties flow. . . . Here, there is no showing that Conklin, prior to January 19, 1996, took any opportunity of CPI's that was not first known to and not pursued by it. Nor is there any showing that after January 19, 1996, CPI did, or purported to do, any business, or that Conklin took anything belonging to it thereafter. . . .

What is left after all of the foregoing is that neither Conklin, Perdue nor CPI are entitled to anything from the other, except that Conklin and Perdue have a theoretical right each to share one-half of the net book value of CPI as of January 19, 1996. There was, however, no evidence presented as to what that net book value might have been. Indeed, the only credible evidence presented led to the inference that it was essentially zero. . . .

I. OPPRESSION OF MINORITY SHAREHOLDERS

We have examined various methods of allocating control among shareholders in a closely held corporation, but even the best corporate planners cannot prevent conflict. The potential for conflict is especially acute when a shareholder or group of shareholders owns a controlling interest in the corporation. This situation raises the possibility of "minority oppression."

From the earliest reported cases involving shareholder disputes, courts have consistently held that the will of the majority of the shareholders governs business corporations in all actions within the bounds of the corporate charter. Nevertheless, courts are cognizant of the possibility that majority rule will lead to unfair results for minority shareholders. In the early 1800s, courts used a trust metaphor—in which directors were analogous to trustees and shareholders were analogous to beneficiaries of a trust—to impose on directors a fiduciary duty to serve *all* the stockholders, not just a select group. The clash of majority rule and universal fidelity resulted in an accommodation in which courts allowed directors to implement the will of the majority subject to limitations imposed through the doctrine of *ultra vires* and prohibitions against fraud and illegality.

Courts used this framework to adjudicate cases that today would often be resolved using the doctrine of minority oppression. Over the course of the 19th century, courts slowly changed their approach toward cases brought by minority shareholders. Having concluded that minority shareholders were beneficiaries in a trust relationship, courts were willing to override the usual binding effect of majority rule in certain circumstances. While the most important of those circumstances was labeled "fraud," this approach became an elastic concept in the hands of equity judges. Even when later judges became less willing to attach the label of "fraud" to actions of majority shareholders, however, they continued to redress the concerns of minority shareholders, increasingly under the rubric of "minority oppression."

Our study of minority oppression is split into three parts. In the first Section we explore the plight of the minority shareholder, which is the impetus for providing an oppression remedy. Observing the minority shareholder's precarious position, we ask, "What — if anything — should the law do to protect the minority shareholder against harm imposed by the majority shareholder?" As we will see, different states have different responses to this question, but most states have concluded that some action is necessary. This leads to the second Section, where we examine various possible remedies for minority oppression, including the traditional remedy of dissolution and the most common modern remedy — the buyout. As we will see, however, courts and legislatures have developed a wide range of other options. Third, we contemplate the possible meanings of "oppression" and consider whether the various definitions produce disparate results in litigated cases.

Traditional corporation laws contemplate centralized control in the board of directors and majority rule, but close corporations are characterized by shareholder participation in management and by the lack of a public market for the corporation's shares. When traditional corporation laws are applied to close corporations, minority shareholders are vulnerable to harm at the hands of the majority. In the classic oppression scenario, a majority shareholder terminates the minority shareholder's employment and refuses to declare dividends. Thus cut off from any financial benefit from his or her equity investment, the minority shareholder might attempt to exit, but the absence of a public market for the corporation's shares combined with the presence of a majority shareholder who has already manifested some hostility to minority shareholders may foreclose this option — unless, of course, the minority shareholder is willing to sell to the majority. Given the circumstances, however, one would not expect the price of such a sale to reflect the true value of the minority's shares (in the absence of oppression). In short, the minority shareholder in a closely held corporation is easily stuck.

What is the proper response to the minority shareholder's plight? The courts of Massachusetts and Delaware have developed two very different responses. In the absence of legislative guidance, the Massachusetts courts have taken it upon themselves to craft a common law of minority oppression. In the well-known case of Donahue v. Rodd Electrotype Company of New England, 328 N.E.2d 505 (Mass. 1975), the Supreme Judicial Court of Massachusetts held that majority shareholders in a closely held corporation owe each another a heightened fiduciary duty comparable to the duty that partners owe to one another. Quoting Meinhard v. Salmon, the court described this as a duty of "utmost good faith and loyalty."

The underlying facts of *Donahue* involved a repurchase of shares owned by the founder of Rodd Electrotype Company. The repurchase was authorized by the founder's sons, who remained majority shareholders. The purpose of the repurchase was to distribute assets of the company so that the 77-year-old founder could retire. The only problem with the plan was that Joseph Donahue—a longtime minority shareholder in the company—also wanted to sell his shares, but there was no ready market, and the majority shareholders were unwilling to accommodate him. The Massachusetts court held that the failure to repurchase Donahue's shares constituted a breach of duty by the controlling shareholders. In the process, the court fashioned an "equal opportunity" rule: "If the stockholder whose shares were purchased was a member of the controlling group, the controlling stockholders must cause the corporation to offer each stockholder an equal opportunity to sell a ratable number of his shares to the corporation at an identical price."

The Delaware Supreme Court responded to *Donahue* (18 years after the Massachusetts court spoke!) in Nixon v. Blackwell, 626 A.2d 1366 (Del. 1993). The Delaware court went out of its way to address the issue of "[w]hether there should be any special, judicially-created rules to 'protect' minority stockholders of closely-held Delaware corporations." The answer was resoundingly negative:

> The case at bar points up the basic dilemma of minority stockholders in receiving fair value for their stock as to which there is no market and no market valuation. It is not difficult to be sympathetic, in the abstract, to a stockholder who finds himself or herself in that position. A stockholder who bargains for stock in a closely-held corporation and who pays for those shares (unlike the plaintiffs in this case who acquired their stock through gift) can make a business judgment whether to buy into such a minority position, and if so on what terms. One could bargain for definitive provisions of self-ordering permitted to a Delaware corporation through the certificate of incorporation or by-laws. . . . Moreover, in addition to such mechanisms, a stockholder intending to buy into a minority position in a Delaware corporation may enter into definitive stockholder agreements, and such agreements may provide for elaborate earnings tests, buy-out provisions, voting trusts, or other voting agreements.
>
>   The tools of good corporate practice are designed to give a purchasing minority stockholder the opportunity to bargain for protection before parting with consideration. It would do violence to normal corporate practice and our corporation law to fashion an ad hoc ruling which would result in a court-imposed stockholder buy-out for which the parties had not contracted.

The Delaware Supreme Court was not the only court with reservations about *Donahue*. Indeed, only one year after deciding *Donahue*, the Massachusetts Supreme Judicial Court reconsidered its position in Wilkes v. Springside Nursing Home, Inc., 370 Mass. 842 (Mass. 1976), stating:

> [W]e are concerned that untempered application of the strict good faith standard enunciated in *Donahue* . . . will result in the imposition of limitations on legitimate action by the controlling group in a close corporation which will unduly hamper its effectiveness in managing the corporation in the best interests of all concerned.

Wilkes involved a corporation with four shareholders, each of whom owned an equal number of shares. According to the court, the four men had an understanding that

> each would be a director . . . and each would participate actively in the management and decision making involved in operating the corporation. It was, further, the understanding and intention of all the parties that, corporate resources permitting, each would receive money from the corporation in equal amounts as long as each assumed an active and ongoing responsibility for carrying a portion of the burdens necessary to operate the business.

The corporation operated in apparent harmony for 14 years, when two of the shareholders came to cross purposes over a property transaction. This dispute ultimately led to the isolation of one of the shareholders (Wilkes), who decided to exit. Before Wilkes could work out an amicable separation, the other three shareholders discontinued his salary and refused to reelect him as a director or officer of the company. Examining Wilkes's claim in light of *Donahue*, the court reasoned:

> [W]hen minority stockholders in a close corporation bring suit against the majority alleging a breach of the strict good faith duty owed to them by the majority, we must carefully analyze the action taken by the controlling stockholders in the individual case. It must be asked whether the controlling group can demonstrate a legitimate business purpose for its action. In asking this question, we acknowledge the fact that the controlling group in a close corporation must have some room to maneuver in establishing the business policy of the corporation. It must have a large measure of discretion, for example, in declaring or withholding dividends, deciding whether to merge or consolidate, establishing the salaries of corporate officers, dismissing directors with or without cause, and hiring and firing corporate employees.
>
> When an asserted business purpose for their action is advanced by the majority, however, we think it is open to minority stockholders to demonstrate that the same legitimate objective could have been achieved through an alternative course of action less harmful to the minority's interest. If called on to settle a dispute, our courts must weigh the legitimate business purpose, if any, against the practicability of a less harmful alternative.

Even under this less stringent application of fiduciary duty, the court held that the majority shareholders in *Wilkes* had breached their fiduciary duty: "It is an inescapable conclusion from all the evidence that the action of the majority stockholders here was a designed 'freeze out' for which no legitimate business purpose has been suggested."

The Delaware Supreme Court also had an opportunity to respond to *Wilkes*. In Riblet Products Corporation v. Nagy, 683 A.2d 37 (Del. 1996), the court considered a claim by a minority shareholder (Nagy), who was also the chief executive officer of his corporation. The lawsuit arose after Nagy was fired, in breach of his employment contract. Although the Delaware court could have ignored *Wilkes* — as the court noted, "Nagy does not allege that his termination amounted to a wrongful freeze out of his stock interest in Riblet, nor does he contend that he was harmed as a stockholder by being terminated" — it stated emphatically, "*Wilkes* has not been adopted as Delaware law." As illustrated by

Nixon and *Riblet*, minority shareholders are more vulnerable in Delaware than in any other state.

The following *Leslie* case is an excellent example of the application of that heightened duty in Massachusetts. As you read *Leslie*, consider whether the judge has remained true to the policies that animated the *Donahue* and *Wilkes* decisions. Contrast the Massachusetts and Delaware approaches and strive to understand why these two states take such different approaches.

LESLIE v. BOSTON SOFTWARE COLLABORATIVE, INC.

14 Mass. L. Rptr. 379
Superior Court of Massachusetts
February 12, 2002

VAN GESTEL, Justice.

This matter is before the Court, after a jury-waived trial, for findings of fact, rulings of law and an order for judgment.

FINDINGS OF FACT

In 1993, Mark Khayter ("Khayter"), Robert F. Goulart ("Goulart") and Dennis J. Leslie ("Leslie") entered into a simple partnership known as Boston Software Collaborative. Shortly thereafter, in September of 1994, the partnership business was incorporated in Massachusetts as Boston Software Collaborative, Inc. ("BSC"). BSC remains a corporation today.

When the partnership was established, Khayter, Goulart and Leslie each contributed $200 as start-up money.

From its inception to at least April 26, 2000, Leslie was an employee of BSC. Until June 12, 2000, he held the positions of treasurer and a director, and he at all times has been an approximately one-third shareholder.

Khayter at all times has been the president and chief executive officer of BSC, and at all times has been a director and an approximately one-third shareholder.

Goulart at all times has been the clerk of BSC, and he assumed the role of treasurer in June of 2000. He also at all times has been a director and an approximately one-third shareholder.

For tax purposes, BSC has elected to be treated as an S Corporation.

The corporate records for BSC are casual and somewhat incomplete. It is unclear, for example, whether any by-laws were ever formally adopted, although an unsigned version of a common form of by-laws — with the place for the name of the corporation to which they apply left blank — was proffered by the defendants over objection. Also, a reading of the minutes of shareholders' and directors' meetings exhibits a somewhat simplistic approach. The minutes seem more like notes of a club meeting than the formalized recording of corporate action.

Even the exact number of shares outstanding and the identity of all the shareholders is not without its uncertainty. In addition to Khayter, Goulart and Leslie, it appears that at least one other person, named Michael Bronshvayg ("Bronshvayg"), owns an inconsequentially small number of shares, and there is the possibility that a man named J. Houghton ("Houghton") may also own a still smaller number of shares. Both Bronshvayg and Houghton are employees of BSC, but not directors or officers.

BSC, in any event, is and always has been a closely-held corporation. It has a small number of shareholders, with Khayter, Goulart and Leslie each holding nearly one-third of the shares, and collectively holding in excess of 97% of all outstanding shares; there is no ready market for the BSC stock; and there is substantial majority shareholder participation in the management, direction and operations of the corporation. All of the shareholders, at least until Leslie's termination in June of 2000, were employees; and Khayter, Goulart and Leslie were, until that same time, the only directors.

Each of Khayter, Goulart and Leslie brought different skills and talents to BSC. All three were software engineers, of apparently somewhat different technical skills. Khayter seems to be the most technically proficient; Goulart's abilities are best expressed in the marketing area; and Leslie had an appetite, and some skills, for administrative and office management functions. Thus, at the start at least, they complemented each other for the general benefit of the business.

The method of compensation of the three principals created friction as the company grew. The nature of the product BSC provides is technical services in software engineering by its employees, including the principals, and by independent consultants to outside customers in need of such services for special projects. Clients, for the most part, are billed on hourly rates, and much of the work is performed physically at client sites. The analogy to a small- or medium-sized law firm is apt in many respects.

Up until early 1999, the great bulk of the compensation for the principals was allocated based upon the billings for their services. Since Leslie was doing more of the administrative and management work in the office, this scheme tended to put Leslie at the low end of the compensation ladder because office work did not result in billable hours. For example, the salaries and other compensation, not counting "distributions" which were equal for each principal, for the period from fiscal 1995 through fiscal 1998, were as follows:

	Fiscal 1995	*Fiscal 1996*	*Fiscal 1997*	*Fiscal 1998*
Khayter	$160,052	$148,195	$264,618	$151,180
Goulart	$171,990	$190,904	$265,785	$224,000
Leslie	$ 50,091	$144,382	$163,793	$103,338

Each of the principals received equal "distributions" in each of the fiscal years from 1995 through 1999 in the following amounts: 1995 — $60,000; 1996 — $80,000; 1997 — $89,280; 1998 — $47,500; and 1999 — $62,000.[4]

For the fiscal years from 1995 through 1998, the principals averaged per year the following numbers of billable hours charged to clients: Khayter — 2,065; Goulart — 2,036; and Leslie — 876.

Again, over the four fiscal years from 1995 through 1998, the total revenues brought to BSC on time and materials billing for each of the three principals were: Khayter — $788,497; Goulart — $889,565; and Leslie — $296,749.

---

4. It is not wholly clear what the "distributions" were intended to be. They were called different things by each principal. They seem somewhat like distributions of year-end profits in a partnership, although they were not always paid just at year-end; or they may be like dividends in a corporation.

In late 1998, there was a possibility of selling BSC. At about that time, the principals agreed to change to a compensation scheme that essentially equalized their total compensation without reference to billable hours, as well as their distribution. Under this plan each of the principals was to be paid at a rate of about $157,000 per year, before any distributions. Khayter and Goulart insist that this plan was only to stay in effect for about six months until the company was sold. Leslie disagrees. In any event, the plan was still in operation until the spring of 2000, and Leslie never did agree to change it.

Friction began to emerge between Leslie, on the one hand, and Khayter and Goulart, on the other. There were issues over compensation, technical proficiency, economic contributions, employee dissatisfaction and customer complaints. Essentially, Leslie felt under-compensated because he contributed more to the non-billable, office administration end of the business. Khayter and Goulart felt that they worked harder, billed more and were technically much more proficient that Leslie and, therefore, were properly compensated at a higher level.

Credible examples of complaints about Leslie from employees and customers were presented. For the most part, at least on an incident-by-incident basis, these were not matters of the magnitude that would ordinarily be seen as a justification for terminating a partner in a partnership or a shareholder in a closely held corporation.

For example, a number of employees complained that Leslie spent too much time working on personal matters while at the office, particularly emphasizing the work he did when he was in the process of building a new home in New Hampshire. Also, Leslie has an obviously brusque approach that employees found unpleasant. Some said he swore too much or at inappropriate times, and others reported on crude ethnic slurs that he tended to use.

One young employee was critical of Leslie's direction to her that she should not wear farmer-type overalls to work because "she looked like a New Hampshire hick." She was from New Hampshire. This same employee was upset that Leslie moved her desk because, he said, she was talking too much to fellow workers and was a distraction. Again from this employee, there was recited an occasion when Leslie, while driving her to a train station, first pleasantly reported to her about a raise in pay and then burst into a profanity-laced discourse about the company and another employee in particular. She felt intimidated and when she arrived home telephoned Goulart, asking for assistance.

In the late fall of 1999, three key employees threatened to quit BSC because of their concerns about working with Leslie or in a company run by him. They did not quit after discussing the matter with Goulart and receiving additional compensation.

There was a complaint in April 2000, revealed in a series of e-mails with one employee, about the timing of deposits into employees' 401(k) plans. Leslie's response to a fairly innocuous question was:

> Who the hell do you think your [sic] talking too [sic]! First of all don't take that tone of an e-mail with me . . . I have been administering the 401k for years and no one, not even you gets to talk to me in this manner. Your [sic] god damn money was sent out with everyone else's and if they haven't credited into your account we will look into it and find out what the issue is. If your [sic] having a bad day, get over it . . . Don't ever send me another e-mail like this again.

The customer complaints were generally in the nature of observations that Leslie was being billed as a senior software engineer but did not demonstrate commensurate skills, that his work took too much time to complete or was such that the customers did not want him to be assigned to their projects.

As noted above, by the end of 1999, the company not having been sold, Khayter and Goulart were anxious to return to the former time-and-materials, hourly billing method of compensation, and Leslie resisted. Finally, Khayter instructed Leslie to direct the office manager to make the change. Leslie, however, did not follow those instructions.

Leslie, in the spring of 2000, had been confiding many of his concerns about the company, its financial affairs and its future to Donald Follansbee ("Follansbee"), the new head of marketing for BSC. Near the end of April 2000, Leslie had told Follansbee of the possibility that he might leave the company. Apparently, on the evening of April 25, 2000, Leslie and his wife talked extensively about his future with BSC, and Leslie remained up the entire night considering the situation. Then, at 7:07 A.M. on April 26, 2000, Leslie sent an e-mail to Follansbee that read as follows:

> Your [*sic*] Stuck With Me . . .
>   After all that aggravation I have to go through, my wife insists that I stay. She reserves the right to shoot Bob and (or) Mark at a moments [*sic*] notice or at a minimum to severely injure them for what they are putting her through. But they are not going to take my vacation without a fight.

Later that day, Follansbee sent an e-mail to Khayter and Goulart that included Leslie's e-mail to him. Follansbee's e-mail read:

> I received this message this morning and wanted to forward it on to you. As we discussed last night I will plan to be at BSC all day on Friday. I have not sent this message through the BSC server. Millennium and Mediaone were used. I have also switched off my BSC phone because I have several messages already from Dennis and I really do not want to get into a discussion over this.

Khayter and Goulart made a joint telephone call to Leslie late in the day on April 26, 2000. They advised Leslie that he was being put on unpaid leave, that he should not come to the BSC offices, that he should not communicate with BSC personnel, and that he should appear at the offices of Palmer & Dodge, the company's counsel, on Friday, April 28, 2000, for a meeting to discuss the situation. They also told Leslie not to bring his gun to the meeting.

Leslie had a permit to carry a firearm and apparently did so from time to time. On one occasion, for example, when BSC was located at 294 Washington Street in Boston, Leslie had to go over to the post office in Post Office Square. Because he could not bring his gun with him, he put it in the drawer of the woman then acting as office manager. She protested that it made her nervous to have the gun there, but he declined to remove it.

Khayter and Goulart were concerned about the shooting threat in Leslie's April 26, 2000, e-mail to Follansbee. Leslie claims it was a "joke" and, in any event, he did not expect Follansbee to forward the e-mail on to anyone. Khayter and Goulart considered the shooting threat to be the final step in an expanding deterioration of their relationship with Leslie and, thus, put him on unpaid leave.

At the meeting at Palmer & Dodge on April 28, 2000, only the three principals were present. No lawyers were included in the conversation. Khayter and Goulart presented Leslie with a document, prepared by a Palmer & Dodge lawyer, entitled "Separation Agreement and Release." In essence, the document, in return for Leslie's termination of employment with BSC and a release of all claims against it, offered Leslie: severance of 10 weeks pay, or less if he got another job before that; a relationship with BSC in a consulting capacity if BSC chose to do so; the possibility that BSC "may attempt" to locate and provide contract opportunities for Leslie; payment of his accumulated vacation time at his current hourly rate; and continuance of his medical insurance at least until December 31, 2000. Leslie did not accept the proposal.

A modified proposal, not significantly more generous in terms, was later tendered by Khayter and Goulart and also not accepted by Leslie.

On June 6, 2000, Leslie received notice of a June 12, 2000, shareholders meeting to take place at Palmer & Dodge. The purpose for the meeting was said to be: (1) the removal of Leslie as the company's 401(k) trustee; (2) the appointment of Goulart as the company's 401(k) trustee; and (3) the removal of Leslie as a director of BSC. A proxy accompanied the notice.

Leslie did not attend the shareholders' meeting, but he did send in his proxy, which he signed and dated June 8, 2000. In his proxy, Leslie voted in favor of his own removal as the company's 401(k) trustee and the appointment of Goulart to take over that position. He voted against his removal from the board of directors. The minutes of the meeting reflect that the first two questions—Leslie's removal and Goulart's appointment as 401(k) trustee—carried with 276,000 in favor and 24,000 abstaining. The vote to remove Leslie as a director carried with 184,000 in favor, 92,000 against and 24,000 abstaining.

The shareholders' meeting minutes recite that the meeting lasted five minutes, beginning at 4:15 P.M. and adjourning at 4:20 P.M.

Also on June 12, 2000, there was a BSC directors meeting. Leslie, however, never received notice of that meeting. Its minutes recite that the meeting lasted for 10 minutes, beginning at 4:00 P.M. and adjourning at 4:10 P.M. Leslie, thus, was still a director as of the time of, and throughout, this meeting.

There were two items voted on at the directors meeting: (1) to remove Leslie as treasurer of BSC; and (2) to appoint Goulart as treasurer. Khayter and Goulart each are recorded as voting in favor, and Leslie, who was not there, is designated as "Abstained (not present)."

Leslie, aside from a distribution of $62,000 for fiscal year 1999, and being paid for his accumulated vacation, has received no further compensation payments from BSC since his termination, and no dividends or other distributions have been paid to him since that time.

Although he is said to be unemployed currently, Leslie earned between $190,000 and $230,000 in software consulting income since June of 2000.

Shortly after Leslie was terminated at BSC, Khayter and Goulart increased their personal compensation by almost the amount previously being paid in compensation to Leslie. As a result, they each started earning at a rate of approximately $240,000 per year. Also in September 2000, Khayter and Goulart, for the first time, included themselves in the employee bonus plan. As a result, they each received an additional $45,000. They also, like Leslie, cashed out their accumulated vacation pay.

There have been no further "distributions" since those made in fiscal year 1999, and the company now appears to be experiencing a time of reduced income and profits because of the current economic slowdown.

Leslie complains that, in addition to the foregoing and despite the tempered economic conditions, Khayter and Goulart are mismanaging the BSC business. He cites four things in particular: (1) raises given to certain employees; (2) expenditures to establish a presence in the Atlanta, Georgia market; (3) increasing employee benefits to give them short- and long-term disability, life insurance and dental care; and (4) moving the BSC offices from 31 Milk Street to 50 Congress Street in Boston.

Leslie also claims that the compensation currently being paid to Khayter and Goulart is excessive. On this latter point, BSC presented an expert witness skilled in assessing and advising on competitiveness and fairness in executive compensation. The Court found that while the expert was fully qualified, his testimony was of only moderate assistance because, mostly, what he did was examine information from outside website data bases, particularly that of an entity called the Economic Research Institute or "ERI." The data base of ERI seems thorough and extensive. It suggests — and the expert's additional research seems to corroborate — that Khatyer's and Goulart's current compensation falls within the mid-point to slightly higher than the mid-point of executives performing their kind of work for companies of BSC's size and earnings.

Additionally, the Court observes Leslie's August 4, 2000, e-mail in which he recommended that Follansbee be made CEO and compensated at a rate that ultimately would be higher than that now being paid to Khayter and Goulart.

Standing alone, Khayter's and Goulart's compensation is reasonable, and the Court so finds.

The Complaint is structured somewhat differently from the norm. It has two sections: one is designated Direct Action; the other is called Derivative Action. Nothing is called a "count."

In the Direct Action section, Leslie, on his own behalf, charges the defendants with: A — failure to pay dividends; B — wrongful termination; and C — freeze-out.

In the Derivative Action section, Leslie complains and seeks judgment derivatively in favor of BSC against Khayter and Goulart for waste of corporate assets and breach of fiduciary duty.

[Only the Direct Action section will be discussed in this excerpted version of the opinion.]

RULINGS OF LAW

BSC is a close corporation established under the laws of the Commonwealth. Donahue v. Rodd Electrotype Co. of New England, Inc., 367 Mass. 578, 586 (1975). It is "typified by: (1) a small number of stockholders; (2) no ready market for the corporate stock; and (3) substantial majority stockholder participation in the management, direction and operations of the corporation." Id.

Thus, BSC "bears a striking resemblance to a partnership." Id. . . .

Leslie, here, finds himself in the position of a frozen-out minority shareholder. He is "cut off from all corporation-related revenues [and] must either suffer [his] losses or seek a buyer for [his] shares. . . . [He] . . . anticipated that his salary from his position with the corporation would be his livelihood. Thus, he cannot afford to wait passively."*Id.* at 591.

Despite the [language of *Donahue*], the duties placed on shareholders in a close corporation are not meant to impose a straitjacket on legitimate corporate activity. The fiduciary duty imposed does not limit "legitimate action by the controlling group in a close corporation" that is taken to manage the corporation "in the best interests of all concerned." Wilkes v. Springside Nursing Home, Inc., 370 Mass. 842, 851 (1976).

"The controlling group in a close corporation must have some room to maneuver in establishing the business policy of the corporation."*Wilkes*, 370 Mass. at 851. This Court must, therefore, carefully analyze the action taken by Khayter and Goulart in this case. The overriding question to be determined is "whether the[y] . . . can demonstrate a legitimate business purpose for [their] action."*Id.* In this regard, Khayter and Goulart "must have a large measure of discretion, for example, in declaring or withholding dividends, . . . establishing the salaries of corporate officers, dismissing directors with or without cause, and hiring and firing corporate employees."*Id.*

"When an asserted business purpose for their action is advanced by the majority, . . . it is open to the minority . . . to demonstrate that the same legitimate objective could have been achieved through an alternative course of action less harmful to the minority's interest."*Wilkes*, 370 Mass. at 851-52. This Court must, therefore, "weigh the legitimate business purpose, if any, against the practicability of a less harmful alternative."*Wilkes*, 370 Mass. at 852.

DIRECT ACTION

Here, the majority—Khayter and Goulart—terminated Leslie's employment, removed him as company treasurer, voted him off the board of directors and since have paid him no dividends or distributions. Leslie was hardly a model employee. At the same time, as a founder and a nearly one-third minority shareholder, he was entitled to the utmost good faith and fair dealing. That he did not receive.

With an ordinary employee, not entitled to partner-like treatment, the termination of Leslie was justified. Given Leslie's enhanced status as an owner, however, Khayter and Goulart did not act in a manner demonstrating the utmost good faith.

In any event, to this Court, after weighing the situation, there appear to have been less harmful alternatives open to Khayter and Goulart than the blunt course they followed. For example, Leslie's administrative functions could have been modified such that he could have been insulated from direct contact with the BSC employees by using Follansbee as the intermediary. Leslie could have been encouraged—and assisted—in becoming more extensively involved in off-site, time-and-materials billing projects. He could have been directed to take courses and training to upgrade his technical skills. Other incentives through the use of creative compensation techniques could have been explored. Clearly, there was no demonstrated need to force him off the board of directors and thereby cut off his access and knowledge about the day-to-day affairs of the company. In short, Khayter and Goulart did not have to so completely, fully and abruptly bring Leslie's participation to a complete halt without first making a serious attempt to solve the problem in other ways.

The resolution proposed at the Palmer & Dodge meeting on April 28, 2000, can hardly be seen as a serious effort to resolve a complex corporate issue among people who were duty bound to treat each other as partners. Ten weeks' severance pay, some accrued vacation, and a non-binding suggestion of the possibility of getting some work as a consultant in return for total termination of employment and a general release do not fit any reasonable definition of acting with the "utmost good faith and loyalty" by Khayter and Goulart to their "partner," Leslie.

"Equitable remedies are flexible tools to be applied with a focus on fairness and justice." Demoulas v. Demoulas, 428 Mass. 555, 580 (1998).

What then is appropriate by way of an equitable solution for Leslie? Even he, in his opposition to a motion in limine to exclude expert valuation testimony, concedes that returning him to his former position at BSC is not a desirable remedy. He said in that opposition: "This forced continuance of the corporate marriage would most likely result in future litigation such that it is not a remedy that will resolve the damage done nor prevent further similar damage in the future."

At the same time, the case law does not support, nor does this Court think it a proper equitable resolution on the facts presented, a compelled buy-out of Leslie's shares by BSC or Khayter and Goulart at some artificially determined value. Here, unlike in *Demoulas*, 428 Mass. 555, or Crowley v. Communications for Hospitals, Inc., 30 Mass. App. Ct. 751 (1991), none of the stockholders has received any monetary benefit from the purchase or sale of their shares.

Leslie's participation as an employee is, like the fallen egg, broken beyond repair. His return to BSC, as such, would not be in the best interest of the corporation or any of its shareholders, including Leslie himself.

In exercising its "broad powers to determine the appropriate relief 'to remedy the wrong complained of and make the [judgment] effective,'" *Demoulas*, 428 Mass. at 591, three things need attention by the Court: (1) fair compensation to Leslie for his loss of employment; (2) fair compensation to Leslie for any amounts received by Khayter and Goulart in the nature of a dividend; and (3) provision for Leslie, for so long as he remains a shareholder, to be able to monitor the management of BSC and participate in the returns to shareholders, without interfering unduly therein.

Because Leslie's reinstatement as an employee is unworkable, he is entitled to a fair severance award. In assaying what is fair, the Court has considered what he was making by way of compensation as an employee when terminated, as well as the $190,000 to $230,000 he made in the period following June 2000. Under all of the circumstances, this Court considers and awards severance for the period from May 1, 2000 through December 31, 2000, at Leslie's annual rate of $157,000 per year, which here amounts to $104,667.

Additionally, this Court concludes that the $45,000 "employee bonus" payments that Khayter and Goulart awarded themselves at the end of fiscal 1999, are nothing more than distributions or dividends of the kind previously made to shareholders. Consequently, Leslie is entitled to an equal payment of $45,000.

Also, hereafter any payments made to Khayter or Goulart that are not the functional equivalent of salary for work actually performed, as opposed to net profits of BSC, and exclusive of reasonable payments in lieu of vacation and reasonable benefits, should be made in an equal amount, and at the same time, to Leslie.

Finally, Leslie should be reinstated as a full voting member of the BSC board of directors so that he may be as fully aware as that position reasonably permits about the management and operation of BSC, and so that he may constructively participate in that management insofar as a director may properly do so.

It is to be observed that none of the foregoing is meant to compel the payment of any dividends by BSC. The directors of the corporation retain their wide discretion with regard to the decision whether to declare any dividends at all, as well as the amount of any such dividends. What must not be done is to make payments only to the majority shareholders, payments having different names or styles but being in reality dividends. . . .

ORDER FOR JUDGMENT

Based upon the foregoing findings of fact and rulings of law, the Court *ORDERS* the entry of judgment in favor of the plaintiff Dennis J. Leslie, individually, against Boston Software Collaborative, Inc. only, in the amount of $149,667, together with costs and interest at the statutory rate from May 1, 2000.

The Court further *ORDERS* judgment against all defendants: that hereafter, for so long as Dennis F. Leslie remains a shareholder, any payments made to Mark Khayter or Robert F. Goulart that are not the functional equivalent of compensation for work actually performed, as opposed to net profits of Boston Software Collaborative, Inc., and exclusive of reasonable payments in lieu of vacations and reasonable benefits, shall be made in an equal amount, and at the same time, to Dennis J. Leslie; and that Dennis J. Leslie shall be reinstated forthwith as a member of the Board of Directors of Boston Software Collaborative, Inc.

Judgment shall be entered for the defendants dismissing all of the derivative claims brought by Dennis J. Leslie on behalf of Boston Software Collaborative, Inc. . . .

PROBLEM 5-6

Despite the machinations of Duncan and Stewart in Problem 5-4, the venture capital investors in Classic Games Inc. managed to regain control of the Company. Like many startup companies, however, Classic Games Inc. was losing money from its operations and desperately needed additional financing to stay alive. The venture capitalists responded to this need by initiating a series of stock issuances to themselves, thereby increasing their ownership interest in the Company to over 90 percent. Duncan and Stewart claimed that the venture capitalists used the company's difficult financial circumstances as a pretext for diluting the founders' ownership interests.

If you were representing Duncan and Stewart, what facts would be most relevant to your claim of minority oppression (breach of fiduciary duty)?

FACEBOOK, INC.: A CASE STUDY

Mark Zuckerberg was only 20 years old when he and a couple of his college roommates launched "thefacebook.com" in February 2004. Facebook, as it is now called, allows users to create a personal profile, free of charge, and use it to communicate with friends, family, and colleagues. Revenue is generated primarily through advertising. Originally open only to students from Harvard and other Ivy League schools, Facebook soon began expanding its user base to other universities. Within months, Facebook had caught the attention of outside investors, receiving its first investment in June 2004 from an "angel" investor, Peter Thiel. That same month, Facebook moved its head-quarters to Palo Alto, California. Other investments soon followed as Facebook continued to expand and attract users from universities, high schools, and workplaces worldwide. By 2006, Facebook was open to anyone age 13 and older and was already well on its way to being the number one social network-ing site in the English-speaking world. In 2012, Facebook sold shares of Class A Common Stock in an initial public offering (IPO).

Facebook's Equity

The Facebook charter divides the common stock of the company into Class A common stock and Class B common stock. Over the years, Facebook has issued Class A common stock to individuals and entities as consideration in various acquisitions and in exchange for investments from certain accredited investors. As of March 31, 2012, just prior to the IPO, Facebook had 117,549,393 shares of Class A common stock outstanding.

Class B common stock was issued to Mark Zuckerberg and to other directors, officers, employees, consultants, and service providers of Facebook, often under a stock option plan. Facebook also issued Class B common stock to individuals and entities as consideration in acquisitions. As of March 31, 2012, Facebook had 1,780,535,644 shares of Class B common stock outstanding.

In addition to these two classes of common stock, Facebook had issued a substantial number of shares of preferred stock to angel investors and venture capital firms. The largest venture investors in Facebook were Accel Partners, a well-known Silicon Valley firm, and DST Global Limited, a Russian company. Facebook sold shares of preferred stock in a number of separate transactions: Series A preferred stock (May 2005 and February 2011); Series B preferred stock (April 2006, February 2011, and December 2011); Series C preferred stock (October 2007 through March 2008); Series D preferred stock (May 2009); and Series E preferred stock (May 2009). All of the shares of Face-book's preferred stock converted into Class B common stock upon completion of the IPO.

The process of financing a company over time through multiple offerings of preferred stock is known as "staged financing," and it is an important aspect of venture capital financing. Each series of preferred stock had a package of financial and control rights. Although public information on the point is not available, the price of each round of financing typically is negotiated by a "lead investor," who has no prior investment in the company. For example, Greylock Partners led the April 2006 round in which Facebook sold Series B preferred stock. Two other venture capital firms—Accel Part-ners and Meritech Capital Partners—also participated in that round, as did angel investor Peter Thiel, who increased his personal holdings in the company.

Terms of Preferred Stock

The terms of Facebook's preferred stock — which appeared in the company's Eleventh Amended and Restated Certificate of Incorporation — included the following:

Dividends. Dividends can be a powerful constraint on managerial opportunism, at least in companies that generate free cash flow (that is, an amount of money in excess of the amount that the company can profitably invest). In such companies, dividends deplete the funds available to managers, thus eliminating the cushion between success and failure. The incentive to perform at a high level follows naturally. In the context of a high-growth company, however, free cash flow is almost never an issue because the company can profitably use large amounts of money for growth-related expenses. For example, in a January 2011 press release, Facebook announced that it had recently raised $1.5 billion. Although the press release stated that the company had "no immediate plans for these funds," they would be used to "continue investing to build and expand its operations."[1]

Even in the absence of free cash flow, the rules governing dividends may constrain opportunism by determining the allocation of funds in the event a dividend is declared. For example, many venture capital financings provide cumulative dividend rights for investors. These rights provide venture capitalists with a certain fixed return on investment, which may become important when the preferred stock is converted into common stock or upon the occurrence of certain fundamental transactions, such as a merger or public offering.

Subject to any constraints in the corporate charter and the expansive limits established by fiduciary law, the board of directors has unilateral power to declare or refrain from declaring dividends. Another important issue relating to dividends, therefore, is whether the board of directors can favor one group of investors over another. One means of restricting the power of the board in this area is to specify dividend rights among the preferences granted to preferred stock. Facebook's charter lays out a scheme according each series of preferred stock a set price per share to use in calculating the preferred stockholder's dividend. Based on that calculation, Facebook's Series A preferred stock enjoys the following dividend preference, which has the same structure as the preference awarded to every other series of preferred stock of Facebook:

> The holders of shares of Preferred Stock shall be entitled to receive dividends, out of any assets legally available therefor, prior and in preference to any declaration or payment of any dividend . . . on the Class A Common Stock or Class B Common Stock of the Corporation, at the rate of $0.00036875 per share (as adjusted for stock splits, stock dividends, reclassification and the like) per annum on each outstanding share of Series A Preferred Stock, . . . payable quarterly when, as and if declared by the Board of Directors of the Corporation. . . .

The effect of this provision is to ensure that the holders of the various series of preferred stock — the angel investors, the venture capitalists, and the other investors — understand their rights in the event the board of directors declares a dividend. Essentially, Facebook's charter makes clear that the common

---

1. Press Release, Facebook, Facebook Raises $1.5 Billion (Jan. 21, 2011), available at *http://www.facebook.com/press/releases.php?p=205070.*

stockholders cannot distribute the assets of the company without first assuring that the preferred stockholders will receive their allotted share. At the time of the IPO, Facebook had never declared or paid cash dividends.

Liquidation. The term "liquidation" is normally associated with the sale of a company's assets and the subsequent distribution of proceeds to investors. Used in this sense, liquidation is typically viewed as the necessary culmination of a business failure, and the only issue for investors is who receives the largest portion of the proceeds from the sale. To protect as much of the "principal amount" of their investment as possible, holders of preferred stock usually demand a liquidation preference — that is, the right to be repaid the original amount of the investment prior to any payment made to holders of common stock in the event of a liquidation. For example, Facebook reported in its prospectus that 44,037,540 shares of Series E preferred stock were sold on May 26, 2009, for a purchase price of $4.54 per share, and the Facebook charter grants the Series E preferred stock a liquidation preference of $4.54158 per share. By requiring the return of the original investment to preferred stockholders, liquidation rights remove any incentive that might otherwise tempt the common stockholders to liquidate opportunistically.

The venture capitalists and other preferred stockholders in Facebook received a liquidation preference, but with a twist. As in most venture capital contracts, the term "liquidation" has a broader meaning than the one suggested above. The term also includes mergers, acquisitions, and sales of all or substantially all of the assets of the company in a merger-like transaction. In short, "liquidation" may be an extremely positive event for both entrepreneurs and venture capitalists. Accordingly, many venture capitalists demand "participating preferred stock," which receives not only a liquidation preference but also a share of the assets remaining after payment of the liquidation preference. While participating preferred stock is frequently used in venture capital financings, nonparticipating preferred stock is especially attractive to the entrepreneurs, who are usually the largest common stockholders.

The holders of Facebook preferred stock negotiated liquidation rights that fall somewhere between fully participating and nonparticipating preferred stock. They negotiated the right to receive *the greater of* the amount of the liquidation preference or the amount that they would receive if they had converted their preferred shares into Class B common stock at the then-effective Conversion Price (which is described below). If any assets remain after this distribution to the preferred stockholders, "all of the remaining assets of the Corporation shall be distributed among the holders of the Class A Common Stock and Class B Common Stock pro rata based on the number of shares of Class A Common Stock and Class B Common Stock then held by them."

Voting. Voting rights are the most obvious means of controlling opportunism in the corporate setting. Venture capitalists usually receive general voting rights and targeted voting rights. The term "general voting rights" designates rights shared among all equity holders, and the term "targeted voting rights" designates rights over specified transactions that are reserved to the venture capitalists. Taken together, the general and targeted voting rights provide venture capitalists with substantial influence over the portfolio company.

Facebook's voting rights contain an additional twist, in that holders of the Class A common stock are entitled to one vote per share, while the holders of Class B common stock are entitled to ten votes per share. Both classes vote together on all matters, including the election of directors. Because the two classes have different voting rights, control of Facebook is best measured by voting power. For example, at the time of the IPO, Zuckerberg owned 533,801,850 shares of Class B common stock, representing 28.1 percent of Facebook's voting power. In addition, Zuckerberg had entered into voting agreements with various other stockholders, enabling him to control another 29.2 percent of the voting power of the company.[2] Thus, Zuckerberg had majority voting control of Facebook prior to the IPO.

The holders of Facebook preferred stock were entitled to vote as a single class with holders of common stock, in most instances. Each share of preferred stock had ten votes for each share of Class B common stock into which it could have been converted at the time of the vote. In addition, as long as they retained a specified minimum number of shares in Facebook, the holders of Series A preferred stock and Series B preferred stock were each entitled to appoint one director to Facebook's board of directors, referred to, respectively, as the "Series A Director" and the "Series B Director." An additional three directors would then be selected by the holders of Class A common stock and Class B common stock, voting together as a single class. Finally, any additional directors would be selected by the common and preferred stockholders voting as a single class. At the time of the IPO, Facebook had seven people on the board of directors.

Even though the preferred stockholders did not control the board of directors, they exerted substantial additional influence over company decision making by virtue of the following "Protective Provisions" contained in the Facebook charter:

> So long as at least 92,500,000 shares of Preferred Stock are outstanding (as adjusted for stock splits, stock dividends, reclassification and the like), the Corporation shall not (by amendment, merger, consolidation or otherwise) without first obtaining the approval (by vote or written consent, as provided by law) of the holders of at least a majority of the then outstanding shares of Preferred Stock, voting together as a class on an as-converted basis:
>
> (a) effect a Liquidation Transaction;
>
> (b) alter or change the rights, preferences or privileges of the shares of a series of Preferred Stock so as to materially and adversely affect the shares of such series in a manner that does not similarly affect all series of Preferred Stock;
>
> (c) increase or decrease (other than by conversion) the total number of authorized shares of the Preferred Stock;
>
> (d) authorize or issue, any other equity security, including any security (other than Series A, Series B, Series C, Series D or Series E Preferred Stock) convertible into or exercisable for any equity security, having a preference over, or being on a parity with, any series of Preferred Stock with respect to voting (other than the *pari passu* voting rights of Class A Common Stock or Class B Common Stock), dividends, redemption, conversion or upon liquidation;

---

2. According to the Facebook prospectus, Zuckerberg had entered into two types of voting agreements: (1) some shareholders "agreed to vote all of their shares as directed by, and granted an irrevocable proxy to, Mr. Zuckerberg at his discretion on all matters to be voted upon by stockholders"; and (2) other shareholders granted Zuckerberg "authority (and irrevocable proxy) to vote [their] shares at his discretion on all matters to be voted upon by stockholders, except for issuances of capital stock . . . in excess of 20% of . . . then outstanding stock and matters which would disproportionately, materially and adversely affect such stockholder."

(e) amend, waive, or repeal any provision of, or add any provision to, the Corporation's Certificate of Incorporation, as amended, or Bylaws; or

(f) redeem, purchase or otherwise acquire (or pay into or set aside for a sinking fund for such purpose) any share or shares of Preferred Stock, Class A Common Stock or Class B Common Stock; *provided, however,* that this restriction shall not apply to the repurchase of shares of Class A Common Stock or Class B Common Stock from employees, officers, directors, consultants or other persons performing services for the Corporation or any subsidiary pursuant to agreements under which the Corporation has the option to repurchase such shares at no greater than cost upon the occurrence of certain events, such as the termination of employment, or through the exercise of any right of first refusal.

Most venture capital investments in the United States contain a similarly long list of protective provisions, often called "negative covenants." Depending on the scope of these covenants, they may provide a fairly close substitute for majority control of the board of directors. In the case of Facebook, the covenants focus on major transactions with the potential to transfer wealth away from the preferred stockholders.

Conversion. The preferred stock issued in venture capital financings is almost always convertible into common stock of the portfolio company. Optional conversion provisions allow the venture capitalists to convert at their discretion, usually when the company is a party to a merger or acquisition and the proceeds to common stockholders are more attractive than the liquidation preference. Automatic conversion provisions require the venture capitalists to convert in specified circumstances, the most important of which is an IPO. Bernard Black and Ronald Gilson have argued that automatic conversion is part of an implicit contract over control between the entrepreneur and the venture capitalists.[3] That contract requires venture capitalists to forfeit control rights when the company meets a predefined measure of success (for example, an IPO at a specified stock price or aggregate dollar amount).

Working together, optional and automatic conversions provide the entrepreneur with incentives to create a successful company and preclude actions that would disadvantage the venture capitalist. It is not surprising, therefore, that Facebook's contracts contain both types of provisions. Although the conversion rate in most venture capital financings is simply 1:1, the contracts typically describe the conversion rate as a formula, and sometimes that formula provides investors with a premium at conversion.

The formula begins by assigning a value to each series of preferred stock, and that value is usually equivalent to the liquidation preference of the series. In the case of Facebook, for example, the value assigned to Series D preferred stock is $7.412454 per share, the same as the liquidation preference of the series. This number is divided by the "Conversion Price," which is usually set at the same value, thus producing a conversion rate of 1:1. In the case of Facebook, however, the Conversion Price of several of the series is slightly lower than the assigned value of that series, thus producing a conversion rate slightly higher than 1:1. For example, the Conversion Price of Series D preferred stock is $7.320504, thus producing a conversion rate of 1.01256:1. Stated another way, if the holders of

---

3. Bernard S. Black & Ronald J. Gilson, *Venture Capital and the Structure of Capital Markets: Banks Versus Stock Markets,* 47 J. Fin. Econ. 243 (1998).

Series D preferred stock converted their shares, they would receive 1.01256 shares of Class B common stock for each share of preferred stock.

The motivation for using a formula rather than a stated ratio is the desire to adjust the conversation rate in the event of a "down round" of financing, that is, a round of financing in which the company raises money at a lower valuation than that used by previous investors. Down rounds have the potential to *dilute* the previous investors, but adjusting the conversion rate can take some of the sting out of a down round.

To see the potential problems caused by dilution, imagine a company with a simple capital structure, including 1,000 shares of common stock and 1,000 shares of Series A preferred stock. Assume that each share of Series A preferred stock had been sold at a price of $1.00 per share, and that each of these shares was convertible on a 1:1 basis into common stock. The company would have an implied valuation of $2,000, and the preferred stockholders would own 50 percent of the company. Their shares would be worth exactly the amount of their investment, $1,000.

Now imagine that the company proposed to raise additional funds by selling 1,000 shares of common stock at a price of $.50 per share. Absent an adjustment to the conversion rate of the Series A preferred stock, the implied valuation of the company would be $1,500 (3,000 shares times $.50 per share), and the holders of the Series A preferred stock would own only 33.3 percent of the company. Their shares would be worth only $500, resulting in a dilution of their investment by half.

To protect holders of the Series A preferred stock, the contracts defining the terms of the investment might provide for adjustment of the conversion rate any time the company issues "Additional Stock" either "without consideration or for a consideration per share less than the Conversion Price of a series of Preferred Stock in effect immediately prior to the issuance of the Additional Stock." As a technical matter, the conversion rate is adjusted upward by lowering the Conversion Price. One method employed by venture capitalists is to lower the Conversion Price to the sales price of the newly issued shares. Using the numbers provided above, this so-called "ratchet method" would lower the Conversion Price of the Series A preferred stock from $1.00 per share to $.50 per share. As a result, the holders of Series A preferred stock would be entitled to convert their shares into 2,000 shares of common stock. Thus, after the sale of the new shares, the company would still have an implied valuation of $2,000 (4,000 shares times $.50 per share), the preferred stockholders would still own 50 percent of the company, and their shares would still be worth exactly the amount of their investment, $1,000.

While the ratchet method is effective at preserving value to previous venture investors, it may discourage the common stockholders from seeking new investors because the entire burden of the loss in company valuation is transferred to the common stock. As a result, most venture capitalists employ a somewhat softer adjustment to the Conversion Price, which spreads the burden across all previous investors. This "weighted average method" is illustrated by the following provision from the Facebook charter:

> The new Conversion Price . . . shall be determined by multiplying the Conversion Price then in effect by a fraction, (x) the numerator of which shall be the number of shares of [common stock] outstanding immediately prior to [the] issuance

[of Additional Shares] (the "Outstanding Common") plus a number of shares equal to the aggregate consideration received by the Corporation for such issuance divided by the Conversion Price of such series of Preferred Stock then in effect; and (y) the denominator of which shall be the number of shares of Outstanding Common plus the number of shares of such Additional Stock.

Using the numbers provided above, the Conversion Price of the Series A preferred stock ($1.00) would be adjusted downward as follows:

$$\$1.00 \times [(1,000 + 500)/2,000] = \$.75$$

Using this new Conversion Price, the holders of Series A preferred stock would be entitled to convert their shares into 1,333 shares of common stock. Thus, after the sale of the new shares, the company would have an implied valuation of $1,666.50 (3,333 shares times $.50 per share), the preferred stockholders would own approximately 40 percent of the company, and their shares would be worth approximately $666.50. As noted above, the weighted average method produces a result between no adjustment and an adjustment using the ratchet method.

The conversion rate is one of the most important features of these securities because venture capital investments are structured to result in conversion if the company executes an IPO. Unlike the optional conversion provision discussed above, the holders of preferred stock have no choice in this instance. Thus, these provisions are usually called "mandatory conversion" provisions. Facebook's charter contains a mandatory conversion provision that would be triggered in the event that Facebook undergoes an IPO. In such a case, all of the holders of preferred stock would become holders of common stock when the IPO was complete, losing all of the other rights associated with the preferred stock.

Redemption. "Redemption" is a general term that covers several different provisions. These provisions are united by the fact that each involves the repurchase of shares by the company for an amount specified in the contract. Venture capital contracts often contain provisions giving the venture capitalists an option to force the repurchase of their shares. Such an option — commonly known as a "put" — usually takes effect only after the passage of several years from the date of the investment, and the redemption price is often the same as the original issue price, though it may contain a small premium. Venture capital agreements sometimes — though rarely — give the company the right to redeem the shares owned by the venture capitalists. Such a provision — known as a "call" — allows the entrepreneur to exit, presuming that it is able to muster the necessary funds. Because call provisions would allow entrepreneurs to redeem the venture capitalists' shares when the company is very successful, venture capitalists typically will not enter into investments that contain a call provision.

Facebook is somewhat atypical in providing neither a call nor any sort of put provision. Instead, the Facebook charter declares, tersely, "[t]he Preferred Stock is not redeemable." In some ways, then, holders of Facebook preferred stock are potentially exposed to greater abuse by the entrepreneur, who typically holds common stock, than in other venture-financed corporations. However, in all cases it is rare for these provisions to be invoked. Where present, they often serve simply as leverage in negotiations with the entrepreneur because they are accompanied by an implicit threat that the venture capitalists will withdraw if the entrepreneur does not behave properly.

Registration Rights. Among the various potential means of exit, venture capitalists typically earn the highest financial and reputational returns from investments in firms that go public. Most venture investors, however, do not sell their shares in IPOs. Instead, they typically exit investments within a few years after the IPO, either by selling the shares or distributing them to their fund investors. Any offering or sale of securities in the United States—including sales by venture capitalists—must be registered with the Securities and Exchange Commission (SEC) unless the offering or sale is exempt from the registration requirements. Ostensibly to ensure their ability to sell shares into the public capital markets, venture capitalists typically contract for so-called "registration rights," which require portfolio companies to register the offering of shares by venture capitalists under specified conditions.

The investors in Facebook preferred stock received the full panoply of registration rights through the Sixth Amended and Restated Investors' Rights Agreement. (Unlike the charter, the Investors' Rights Agreement is not filed with the state of incorporation, but becomes a public document only because of the SEC's disclosure requirements when firms file for an IPO.) "Demand registration rights" would allow the investors to request registration of their securities any time after the earlier of April 17, 2013, or six months after the effective date of the IPO. "Piggyback registration rights" would allow the investors to have their shares registered, if Facebook were registering its own shares, as in the IPO. Finally, "Form S-3 registration rights" require Facebook to use "all commercially reasonable efforts" to register shares owned by the investors, if the company is eligible to register on the SEC's Form S-3, which is a simpler form of registration available to companies that have been subject to SEC disclosure requirements for 12 months and are current in all of their SEC filings.

Rights of First Refusal. The rights of first refusal—sometimes called "rights of first offer"—granted to venture capitalists are another potential control mechanism when used in conjunction with staged financing. A typical right of first refusal would require the company to give notice to holders of preferred stock of any proposed issuance, sale, or exchange of the company's securities. The preferred stock holder would then have the option to acquire a pro rata portion of the securities according to a predetermined formula. The result of such a provision would be to allow venture capitalists and other holders of preferred stock to keep pace with the growing company and maintain their position in the company relative to the other stockholders.

Certain large investors in Facebook received a right of first offer. Under the terms of this provision of the Sixth Amended and Restated Investors' Rights Agreement, if Facebook intends to offer "any shares of, or securities convertible into or exercisable for any shares of, any class of its capital stock," the investors with the right of first refusal have a right to purchase

> . . . up to that portion of such Shares which equals the proportion that the number of shares of Class A Common Stock issued and held, or issuable upon conversion and exercise of all convertible or exercisable securities then held, by such First Offeree bears to the total number of shares of Class A Common Stock outstanding immediately prior to the issuance of the Shares (assuming full conversion of the Shares and exercise of all outstanding convertible securities, rights, options and warrants).

This limitation on the number of shares subject to the right of first offer ensures that some shares would be left over. If Facebook wants to sell the excess shares, it may do so, but only "at a price not less than, and upon terms no more favorable to the offeree than" those specified for the prior investors.

Corporate Governance

Shareholders. Under Delaware law, shareholders act at an annual or special meeting or by written consent. The Facebook bylaws provide: "A special meeting of the stockholders may be called at any time by the board of directors, the chairman of the board, the president or by one or more stockholders holding shares in the aggregate entitled to cast not less than ten percent of the votes at that meeting."

While shares of stock are generally assumed to be freely transferable, the Facebook bylaws restrict the sale of shares: "No holder . . . of shares of capital stock of the corporation . . . may transfer, assign, pledge, or otherwise dispose of or encumber Shares without the prior written consent of the corporation."

Directors. Facebook's bylaws regulate the size of Facebook's board of directors: "The number of directors constituting the entire Board of Directors shall be not fewer than five (5) and not more than eight (8), with the exact number of directors to be fixed from time to time within such limit by a duly adopted resolution of the Board of Directors or the stockholders." At the time of the IPO, Facebook's board of directors consisted of seven directors, an eclectic group of investors and entrepreneurial talent. Mark Zuckerberg has been a Facebook director from the founding of the company in 2004, and he was joined on the board of directors the following year by Peter Thiel, the first angel investor in Facebook, and Jim Breyer of Accel Partners, the first venture capital investor in Facebook. Marc Andreesen, the legendary founder of Netscape and now successful venture capitalist, joined the board in 2008, and Zuckerberg's long-time friend and mentor, Donald Graham, the CEO of the Washington Post, joined the board in 2009. As is typical for a company preparing for an IPO, Facebook added new directors in preparation for filing with the SEC. Reed Hastings, CEO of Netflix, and Erskine Bowles, perhaps best known as President Bill Clinton's chief of staff, both joined the Facebook board in 2011. Thus, the board of directors of Facebook has only one employee (Zuckerberg) and six outside directors.

Officers. The officers of Facebook are very young. Zuckerberg was only 28 years old at the time of Facebook's IPO. As part of that filing, Zuckerberg included a "letter" that began "Facebook was not originally created to be a company. It was built to accomplish a social mission — to make the world more open and connected." The letter proceeds:

> Simply put: we don't build services to make money; we make money to build better services.
>
> And we think this is a good way to build something. These days I think more and more people want to use services from companies that believe in something beyond simply maximizing profits.
>
> By focusing on our mission and building great services, we believe we will create the most value for our shareholders and partners over the long term — and this in turn will enable us to keep attracting the best people and building more great services. We don't wake up in the morning with the primary goal of making money,

but we understand that the best way to achieve our mission is to build a strong and valuable company.

This is how we think about our IPO as well. We're going public for our employees and our investors. We made a commitment to them when we gave them equity that we'd work hard to make it worth a lot and make it liquid, and this IPO is fulfilling our commitment. As we become a public company, we're making a similar commitment to our new investors and we will work just as hard to fulfill it.

The oldest of the senior executive officers listed in the Facebook prospectus is Ted Ullyot, a graduate of the University of Chicago Law School and Facebook's top lawyer, who was 44 years old at the time of Facebook's IPO. Many observers credit Sheryl Sandberg, the 42-year-old chief operating officer, with making Facebook a profitable company. In a New Yorker profile of Sandberg, Ken Auletta observed, "The engineers, as at Google a decade earlier or Twitter now, were primarily interested in building a really cool site; profits, they assumed, would follow."[4] Sandberg joined Facebook in March 2008, and the company was profitable within two years.

QUESTIONS

Prior to the IPO, would the entrepreneurs or the investors (or both) make the following decisions:

- Expanding Facebook's product offerings
- Merging with Microsoft
- Selling shares by the venture capitalists
- Converting preferred stock into common stock
- Paying dividends
- Expanding the size of the board of directors
- Replacing Mark Zuckerberg as a director
- Replacing Mark Zuckerberg as an officer
- Increasing Mark Zuckerberg's salary

If the entrepreneurs want to get rid of the venture capitalists, how can they accomplish that? Under what circumstances would the venture capitalists want to redeem their shares? Under what circumstances would venture capitalists exercise their right of first refusal when a company issues additional shares? When wouldn't they?

---

4. Ken Auletta, *A Woman's Place*, The New Yorker (July 11, 2011).

Shareholder Voting in the Publicly Held Firm

MOTIVATING HYPOTHETICAL

Waste Disposal, Inc. is a publicly traded nuclear waste company based primarily in Utah but incorporated in Delaware. It has more than 3,000 employees in Utah, Washington, South Carolina, Louisiana, and Tennessee — all states that have relaxed laws on handling and processing nuclear waste. The company manages much of the country's waste through these regional disposal ports. But while the other four states help process the waste, ultimately it is shipped to Utah for disposal and management.

Lately Waste Disposal's CEO, Jim Bingham, who just came off a five-year management position at a rapidly expanding oil and gas company in Texas, has been looking for ways to expand Waste Disposal's market. His familiarity with international markets and importation of foreign energy sources has him thinking of expanding by importing foreign waste that can be processed and managed domestically. While the importation of nuclear waste could be profitable for the company, Bingham expects to face opposition to this plan from some of Waste Disposal's shareholders.

A. INTRODUCTION

In 1932 Professors Adolf Berle and Gardiner Means published *The Modern Corporation and Private Property*, an extremely influential book that described one of the defining features of a public corporation: the separation of share ownership from effective control. That is, while shareholders are understood by many to be the owners of the corporation, their powers of control over the corporation are limited compared to other types of ownership. Shareholders are generally understood to have three ways to exercise power in a public corporation: by selling their shares (the "Wall Street Rule"), which can depress the price of a company's shares if enough shareholders sell, and make the company a target for a takeover; by voting; and by suing the company's directors for breaches of their fiduciary duties. Even where shareholders have direct power, though — for example, the power to elect the board of directors — that power is reactive: shareholders react to the nominees presented by managers rather than bringing forth their own nominees in most cases. Indeed, recent efforts by shareholder activists and the SEC to give shareholders more power to nominate directors, and communicate about those nominees at the company's expense, have been unsuccessful, for reasons discussed below.

Since Berle and Means highlighted the issue of the separation of ownership from control, it has been a defining issue in debates about state corporate law and federal securities law. Distilled to its essence, the issue is this: managers and directors of large public corporations have the power to make almost all of the decisions in the corporation, from what pencils to buy to what companies to buy. Centralized power is necessary if anything is to be accomplished on a daily basis because it would be impossible to put every decision that needs to be made to a shareholder referendum. Moreover, centralized power ensures that those people with management expertise and knowledge in the relevant field are making decisions. And yet, what ensures that managers are making decisions that are in the corporation's best interest or in the shareholders' best interest, rather than in the manager's best interest? When a company buys private jets for its executives or hangs an original Van Gogh in the company's headquarters, is that decision ultimately going to be reflected in increased productivity or profitability, or an increased sense of executive self-worth, or some mixture of both? Given the broad discretion allocated to managers, what assurance is there that they will be responsible to the corporation and its shareholders, and even, perhaps, to society at large? That is the question that Berle and Means posed in 1932, and it is a question that is still at the core of the study of corporate law.

In *The Limits of Organization*, Nobel Laureate Kenneth J. Arrow provided a useful framework for thinking about the effects of shareholder participation in corporate governance. Arrow began with the observation that in virtually all organizations, centralized decision making — which Arrow called "authority" — is the rule. Arrow argued that authority has value to an organization because it coordinates the activities of members of the organization, thus economizing information costs.

On the other hand, authority also generates agency costs — the costs associated with having one person make decisions on behalf of another. In the corporate context, we conceive of the shareholders as the principals and the managers (officers and directors) as the agents. Agency costs are generated by the rules and practices that allow shareholders to monitor managerial performance (*e.g.*, the production of audited financial statements), as well as rules and practices that bond managers to shareholders (*e.g.*, the use of stock options as incentive compensation). Agency costs also include any residual costs of undeterred managerial disloyalty.

Recognizing that such costs are inherent in authority, Arrow suggested that a necessary counterweight to authority is "responsibility." Decision makers may be held responsible in various ways, for example, by subjecting their decisions to an active higher authority or to a special authority with limited jurisdiction or by allowing a higher authority to select the central decision maker at specified intervals. One key to organizational success is striking the proper balance between authority and responsibility. Arrow observes:

> To serve its functions, responsibility must be capable of correcting errors but should not be such as to destroy the genuine values of authority. Clearly, a sufficiently strict and continuous organ of responsibility can easily amount to a denial of authority. If every decision of A is to be reviewed by B, then all we have really is a shift in the locus of authority from A to B and hence no solution to the original problem. To maintain the value of authority, it would appear that responsibility must be intermittent.

One mechanism used to promote responsibility in managers of public corporations is found in the federal securities laws, including the Securities Act of 1933 and the Securities Exchange Act of 1934, both of which were passed in the shadow of Berle and Means' book. In these statutes, Congress explicitly sought to require companies to provide more information to the market on a regular basis so that investors could make informed investment and voting decisions and exercise what power they had with full and accurate information. Thus, voting rights within public corporations exist at the intersection of state corporate law (which determines, among other things, the subjects on which shareholders have voting rights) and federal securities law (which dictates many of the procedures that companies must follow and the information that must be provided when shareholders exercise their voting rights). Conflicts over the scope of federal and state power respecting corporate governance can be examined through a close study of shareholder voting rights. As this chapter reveals, dramatic increases in shareholder activism over the last two decades have brought into sharp relief the conflicts between federal and state power, and between shareholders' and managers' power.

In this chapter, we explore control of the public corporation. We begin by looking at the intersection of state and federal law, highlighted with a case study of the Enron Corporation and the Sarbanes-Oxley Act of 2002 (SOX), followed by material on the global financial crisis of 2008-2012 and the Dodd-Frank Wall Street Reform and Consumer Protection Act of 2010. We then turn to shareholder voting, examining both state and federal regulation of this most important control right in light of the increasing shareholder activism and engagement that have occurred in the last two decades.

B. CORPORATE FEDERALISM

As a general matter, state corporate law identifies the types of issues on which shareholders may or must vote, and for public corporations, federal law sets out the procedures by which voting occurs and explains what information must be provided to shareholders prior to their votes. In this Section we introduce corporate federalism, that is, the interaction of state and federal law with respect to voting and corporate governance. This background is important to understand the emerging battles between shareholders and managers that activist shareholders have initiated over the last two decades.

ENRON CORPORATION AND THE SARBANES-OXLEY ACT: A CASE STUDY

Prior to 2002, the conventional wisdom among many corporate law professors was that the regulation of the relationship among directors, managers, and shareholders was primarily a matter of state law and that federal securities law had only a minor role to play. As will be illustrated by the materials below, this conventional wisdom is not quite accurate, since one purpose of federal securities disclosure is to inform shareholders of directors' actions, including conflict-of-interest transactions between directors and the companies that they direct. Another purpose was to enhance the power of shareholders in the corporation through federal proxy regulation. Thus, the federal securities laws have always had a role to play in regulating the corporate governance relationship. Yet, prior to 2002, the federal role was largely indirect; most direct regulation of corporate governance was left to state law.

The summer of 2002 brought the beginnings of a potential shift in the balance of federal versus state power, in the form of the Sarbanes-Oxley Act of 2002 (SOX), which was itself a reaction to the collapse of the Enron Corporation. Once admired as one of the most innovative companies in America, Enron Corporation now has a legacy as one of the most spectacular frauds in business history. The rapid collapse of Enron in late 2001 resulted not only in the displacement of thousands of Enron employees and the loss of some $68 billion in stock market value, but also in significant collateral damage. Most visibly, the Enron debacle led to the implosion of Arthur Andersen, Enron's auditor and at that time one of the so-called "Big Five" accounting firms. When other firms followed in Enron's wake — the most notorious being Global Crossing and WorldCom — policymakers seized the opportunity to enact major regulatory reforms. While it is far too early to assess Enron's legacy, its collapse has already changed the legal landscape significantly. For our purposes, the most important of the post-Enron reforms was SOX. This case study will recount briefly the story of Enron Corporation[1] and will summarize the major reforms embodied in SOX.[2]

Seeds of Disaster. Enron began its corporate life as an energy company, a producer of natural gas. The company was the product of a merger of two natural gas companies in 1985,[3] and Kenneth Lay was selected to run the combined company. He immediately began the process of transforming the company into an energy trading firm. In that role, Enron was not merely an industry leader, but an industry creator.

Lay's vision for Enron did not focus on natural gas production but rather on financial intermediation. In other words, he wanted Enron to facilitate trades

---

1. The accounts of Enron's rise and fall are legion, but for background facts, we rely heavily on the first account to appear in the law reviews, the excellent article by Professor William Bratton. *See* William W. Bratton, *Enron and the Dark Side of Shareholder Value*, 76 Tul. L. Rev. 1275 (2002). For interesting insider accounts of Enron, see Brian Curver, *Anatomy of Greed: The Unshredded Truth from an Enron Insider* (2002), and Mimi Swartz & Sherron Watkins, *Power Failure: The Inside Story of the Collapse of Enron* (2003).

2. One purpose of this case study is to illustrate the legal reaction to a real-world crisis. As a result, the focus will be on SOX, rather than on subsequent developments that have arisen in the implementation of SOX. To the extent that such developments are relevant to our study of business organizations, they will be described in subsequent Sections of this book.

3. Initially, the firm was to be called "Enteron," but when someone pointed out that this word means "intestine," the name was changed to Enron. Frank Partnoy, *Infectious Greed: How Deceit and Risk Corrupted the Financial Markets* 298 (2003).

between energy producers and consumers. This was a radical notion in the mid-1980s, when electricity and natural gas production were monopolized by regulated utilities. Under Lay's leadership, Enron promoted deregulation of these industries.

Of course, an essential part of its business plan involved the lobbying of state and federal politicians. Naturally, in this context, Lay became as well known for his political ties as for his business savvy. When Enron later entered the quicksand that ultimately lead to its demise, Lay attempted to call on his political allies for assistance, but his former friends did not respond.

Two people who became crucial pieces of the Enron puzzle were added to the company in 1990. The first was Jeffrey Skilling, then a partner with the consulting firm of McKinsey & Company, who agreed to join the executive ranks at Enron. The second was Andrew Fastow, recently graduated from Northwestern University's MBA program, who joined the company's finance group. Both contributed substantially to Enron's growth — as we will see below, not always in a legitimate fashion — and both were promoted in 1997: Skilling to president and chief operating officer (COO) and Fastow to vice president of finance.

Once installed as president and COO, Skilling created a culture based on high-powered incentives. His most notorious innovation was the "rank and yank" system, described colorfully by William Bratton:

> Enron's whiz kid recruits entered a perpetual tournament. . . . Each got to pick ten other employees to rank his or her performance. But the system also allowed coworkers to make unsolicited evaluations into an online database. At year's end, Skilling threw everybody's results onto a bell curve, and those on the wrong end of the curve [the bottom 15 percent] were terminated. Those who remained scratched and clawed to get or stay in the winner's circle. Winners got million dollar bonuses and were privileged to accompany Skilling for glacier hiking in Patagonia or Land Cruiser racing in Australia.[4]

Under the influence of Lay and Skilling — with more than a small assist from the less visible Fastow, as it turns out — Enron became one of the largest corporations in the world, at least by accounting measures.[5] But the quickly constructed empire began to unravel even more quickly on October 16, 2001, when Enron announced "after-tax non-recurring charges" of $1.01 *billion* for the third quarter of the fiscal year. A week later, Fastow was placed on a leave of absence.

On October 31, William Powers, Dean of the University of Texas Law School, joined the Enron board. Powers was assigned to chair the Special Investigative Committee, whose task was to plow through Enron's records and produce a report for the directors, who wanted to know how this mess could have happened.[6] In particular, the directors wanted an explanation of various transactions between Enron and related parties, some of which are described below.

Just over a week later, Enron restated its financial statements for 1997 through the first two quarters of 2001, reducing net income from the prior statements by $586

---

4. Bratton, *supra* note 1, at 1293.
5. *See* "The 500 Largest U.S. Corporations," Fortune, April 16, 2001, at F.1 (listing Enron as the seventh largest corporation according to total revenues).
6. With the assistance of Wilmer, Cutler & Pickering, a Washington, D.C., law firm, the report — called the Report of Investigation by the Special Investigative Committee of the Board of Directors of Enron Corp. (the Powers Report) — was published on February 1, 2002.

million. On November 19, Enron filed its third-quarter Form 10-Q with the Securities and Exchange Commission (SEC). This was the document that contained financial statements showing the effects of a $1.01 billion charge. Enron's creditors were nervous. On the same day, Enron officers met with its major creditors at the Waldorf Astoria in New York City. Although Enron was then in the midst of a proposed merger with Dynegy,[7] what the creditors heard shook them.

> During this meeting, Enron informed its bankers that while the debt reflected on its third quarter 2001 balance sheet under GAAP [generally accepted accounting principles] was $12.978 billion, Enron's "debt" (as set forth in the presentation) was $38.094 billion. Thus, as Enron noted, $25.116 billion of debt was "off balance sheet," or in some cases, on the balance sheet as a liability, but classified as something other than a debt.

In re Enron Corp., First Interim Report of Neal Batson, Court-appointed Examiner (S.D.N.Y. Sept. 21, 2002).

During this time, information about the "off balance sheet" related-party transactions began to emerge, and the markets lost confidence in Enron. Enron filed for bankruptcy protection on December 2, 2001.

Accounting Problems. Enron will be remembered most as a failure of the U.S. accounting system.[8] In the wake of Enron, there seemed to be plenty of blame to go around: Enron's board of directors, its top officers (Lay, Skilling, and Fastow), its accountants, its lawyers, Wall Street analysts, the financial press, and government regulators have all been questioned. While the number of illegal transactions at Enron precludes a thorough treatment here, the following items illustrate the type of accounting tricks devised by Fastow and his minions to improve the appearance of Enron's financial statements.

1. Special purpose entities (SPEs). The Enron scandal introduced laypeople to SPEs for the first time, as news reports told of the creation of entities by Fastow with names based on *Star Wars*: Joint Energy Development Investments, L.P. (also known as JEDI) and Chewco (named after Chewbacca, the famously incoherent Wookie). Widely used by corporations for many purposes, many of which are legal, SPEs were employed illegally by Enron for the purpose of improving their financial statements.

JEDI was a limited partnership formed by Enron as general partner, with the California Public Employee Retirement System (CalPERS), as limited partner. Each invested $250 million in JEDI. Enron's investment was in the form of Enron stock while CalPERS invested cash. Each had a 50 percent interest in the partnership. JEDI was established for the purpose of making energy investments. Under U.S. accounting rules, Enron did not have to include JEDI on the Enron consolidated financial statements because it did not own a controlling interest in the firm.

When Enron asked CalPERS to invest in a larger partnership in 1997, CalPERS agreed, but only if its interest in JEDI were liquidated. Enron tried to locate a

---

7. Dynegy eventually backed away from Enron because of undisclosed liabilities. Enron sued Dynegy for wrongful termination of the merger agreement, and the parties settled in August 2002.

8. For an excellent description of the accounting problems at Enron, see George J. Benston & Al L. Hartgraves, *Enron: What Happened and What Can We Learn from It*, 21 J. Acct. & Pub. Poly. 105 (2002).

substitute investor for JEDI but was unsuccessful. As a result, Enron replaced CalPERS with SPE Chewco. According to the Powers Report, the formation of Chewco was the "first time Enron's Finance group (under Fastow) used an SPE run by an Enron employee to keep a significant investment partnership outside of Enron's financial statements."[9]

Chewco had three sources of financing: (1) a $240 million loan from Barclay's Bank, which was guaranteed by Enron; (2) a $132 million advance from JEDI, which was itself owned by Enron and Chewco; and (3) an $11.5 million equity investment from Michael J. Kopper—an Enron employee who reported to Fastow.[10] Kopper did not have $11.5 million of his own money, so he borrowed all but $125,000 from Barclay's Bank. As with the loan to Chewco, that loan was guaranteed by Enron. The executive committee of Enron's board of directors approved the Chewco investment after presentations by Skilling and Fastow. According the Powers Report, Fastow did not explain that Kopper's "equity investment" was really a loan from Barclay's Bank. *Id.* at 46.

Why did Enron go to all of this trouble? The goal was to keep JEDI's indebtedness—which was substantial, at over $1.6 billion—off Enron's financial statements. As long as Enron owned less than a majority of JEDI, GAAP did not require consolidation—that is, including JEDI's liabilities and assets on Enron's balance sheet and combining the two firms' income. The problem with Enron's decision not to consolidate JEDI was Chewco. If Enron controlled Chewco, then Enron controlled JEDI, and both Chewco and JEDI would need to be consolidated with Enron.

Whether Enron was deemed to be in control of Chewco would depend on various accounting rules, including an accounting policy adopted by the SEC known as the "3 percent rule." Under this rule, at least 3 percent of an SPE's total capital must come from an outside equity investor. In addition, the person who owns that equity must have the ability to dispose of the SPE's assets. In other words, the outside equity holder, although representing only 3 percent of the SPE's total capital, must hold a majority of the SPE's total equity, showing just how "leveraged" the capital structure of the SPE can be. In the case of Chewco, Kopper was purported to be the outside investor. But, of course, the money for Kopper's investment came from Barclay's Bank in transactions that were characterized as "equity loans." Enron attempted to structure the transactions in a manner that allowed Barclay's to treat them as loans while allowing Chewco to treat them as equity. While such a structure was apparently a common practice for SPEs, it did not satisfy the conditions of the SEC accounting policy. *Id.* at 50.

In the end, the structure of the JEDI-Chewco transaction came to light, and Enron was forced to restate its financials to reflect the consolidation of those two companies. This restatement had the effect of reducing Enron's earnings by

9. Power Report, *supra* note 5, at 41.

10. Fastow originally proposed himself as manager of Chewco, but Enron's law firm, Vinson & Elkins, said that such an arrangement would require disclosure in the company's proxy statement. In addition, Enron's Code of Conduct of Business required approval of Fastow's appointment by the chairman and CEO of Enron. Because Kopper was not a senior officer of Enron, his participation did not require disclosure in the proxy statement, though approval of the chairman and CEO was still required. According to the Powers Report, Ken Lay was both chairman and CEO at the time of the Chewco transaction, and he denied knowing Kopper. Although Skilling acknowledged approving Kopper's participation in Chewco, Skilling served as the COO at the time, and his approval was ineffective under the Code of Conduct.

$405 million, and its indebtedness was increased by $628 million for the period from 1997 through the middle of 2001.[11]

2. Fraudulent Asset Sales. GAAP typically requires assets to be recorded at their historical cost. In some instances, however, firms can "mark assets to market" — that is, change the value of assets to more fully reflect current market values. One circumstance in which mark-to-market accounting would be justified is a third-party sale. When assets are sold to a third party in an arm's length transaction, their market price is thereby established. If the seller retains similar assets, it can revalue those assets in accordance with the price established by the third-party sale. Apparently, Enron engaged in numerous transactions designed to enable this sort of revaluation, but the transactions did not involve true third-party sales.

One example involved another well-publicized Enron SPE known as LJM Cayman L.P. (LJM1).[12] Acting through a limited liability company of which he was the sole member, Fastow was the general partner of LJM1. He raised $15 million from two outside investors. In September 1999, LJM1 used a large chunk of that money to purchase a 13 percent interest in a Brazilian power plant. The sale was valued at $11.3 million.

The power plant was actually owned by a Brazilian company, of which Enron owned 65 percent. Because the plant was "experiencing significant construction problems,"[13] Enron wanted to sell some of its interest but could not find a buyer. Enter Fastow: he negotiated the sale of part of Enron's interest in the Brazilian company to LJM1. Enron claimed that this sale eliminated its control position over the Brazilian company,[14] thus allowing Enron to move the badly performing company off Enron's financial statements. In addition, one of Enron's subsidiaries had a gas supply contract with the Brazilian company, and Enron used the phony sales price to revalue the contract, booking $65 million in marked-to-market income in the second half of 1999.

Meanwhile, the power plant continued to experience construction problems. Nevertheless, nearly two years after the original transaction, Enron repurchased the interest from LJM1 for $14.4 million. According to the Powers Report, "[t]he price was calculated to provide LJM1 its maximum possible rate of return." *Id.* at 137. Apparently, this sort of transaction was not unique.

3. Derivative Transactions. Many of Enron's problems stemmed from derivative transactions. Indeed, Frank Partnoy has asserted, "Enron was, in reality, a derivatives-trading firm, not an energy firm."[15] A "derivative" is simply a financial

---

11. Frank Partnoy has observed: "Enron's dealings in JEDI and Chewco later horrified many individual investors, but the truth was that they were arguably legal, not especially unusual, mostly disclosed, and largely irrelevant to Enron's collapse." Partnoy, *supra* note 3, at 312.

12. The initials LJM represented Fastow's wife and two daughters.

13. Powers Report *supra*, at 136.

14. How Enron could plausibly take this position is not clear. *See* Benston & Hartgraves, *supra* note 7, at 113 ("Considering that 65% less 13% equals 52%, it is not clear why Andersen did not make Enron consolidate [the Brazilian company] and allowed it to record an additional gain of $65 million by marking to market a portion of a gas supply contract. . . .").

15. Partnoy, *supra* note 3, at 297. More surprisingly, Partnoy claims:

Enron's core business of derivatives trading was actually highly profitable, so profitable, in fact, that Enron almost certainly would have survived if the key parties had understood the details of its business. Instead, in late 2001, Enron was hoist with its own petard, collapsing — not because it wasn't making money — because institutional investors and credit-rating agencies abandoned the company when they learned that Enron's executives had been using derivatives to hide the risky nature of their business.

instrument whose value is derived from some other asset. For example, the value of an option to purchase stock is derived from the value of the underlying stock. As the value of the stock increases, the option to purchase that stock becomes more valuable. And vice versa.

A simple illustration of Enron's use of derivatives is provided by Enron's dealings with Chase Manhattan Bank (which later merged with J.P. Morgan and continued the types of transactions described herein). Enron wanted a loan from Chase but did not want to recognize the liability on its financial statements. To avoid this undesirable result, the two companies devised a complicated set of transactions that had the effect of a loan but the appearance of a sale. In the first set of transactions, Enron sold forward gas commodity contracts to Mahonia, Ltd., a company formed under the laws of Jersey, one of the Channel Islands. These contracts obligated Enron to sell gas to Mahonia at future dates for specified prices. In the second set of transactions, Enron purchased offsetting contracts from another Jersey company known as Stoneville Aegean Ltd. These contracts obligated Enron to buy gas from Stoneville at future dates for specified prices. Both Mahonia and Stoneville were connected to Chase.

Now comes the tricky part. Enron did not account for these mirror transactions symmetrically. It recorded the sales to Mahonia as revenues but did not count the purchases from Stoneville as expenses. Moreover, Enron collected the discounted present value of the Mahonia contracts but did not pay immediately on the Stoneville contracts. Mahonia raised the money to pay Enron by selling the forward contracts to Chase. The difference between the discounted value Enron received from Mahonia and the undiscounted value Enron would be required to pay to Stoneville was approximately equal to the interest on a 7 percent loan.

These transactions are called "prepaid swaps," and their beneficial effect on Enron's financial statements is obvious. When they were later brought to the attention of the U.S. Senate, Senator Carl Levin was astonished that these simple loans could be treated in any way other than as indebtedness. He called the transactions "phony." But, as noted by Frank Partnoy:

> These deals might have been phony, but they were both common and, arguably, legal. Numerous companies used prepaid swaps to borrow money off balance sheet, and prepaid swaps . . . were part of mainstream corporate life, even though few investors had heard of them. Yes, these deals did not fit economic reality, but in a world governed by accounting standards, economic reality was barely relevant.[16]

The Fall. As noted above, the public markets widely acknowledged Enron's troubles when the company took a massive "non-recurring" charge on its third-quarter 2001 financial statements, and shortly thereafter restated earlier financial statements. But the first hint of trouble came earlier, on August 14, when Skilling unexpectedly resigned for "personal" reasons only six months after taking the position of CEO.

Shortly after Skilling's resignation, Sherron Watkins — a former Arthur Andersen accountant and then vice president of corporate development at Enron — wrote a now-famous memo to Ken Lay expressing her concern

---

16. Partnoy, *supra* note 3, at 338.

about unusual accounting transactions like those described above.[17] Lay met personally with Watkins, then had the board of directors instruct Enron's attorneys at the Houston firm of Vinson & Elkins to investigate Watkins' charges. (This despite Watkins' specific warning that Vinson & Elkins would not be able to objectively review the transactions on which they had earlier issued favorable opinions.[18]) In an October 15 report, Vinson & Elkins concluded, "facts disclosed through our preliminary investigation do not, in our judgment, warrant a further widespread investigation by independent counsel and auditors."

Despite this report, pressure on Arthur Andersen increased. On October 23, David Duncan, the Andersen partner in charge of the Enron account, called a staff meeting, where he stressed the importance of the firm's "document retention" policy. While Duncan later testified that he did not realize his remark would lead to widespread destruction of Enron-related documents, that is exactly what happened. Over the next three days, more than a ton of documents were shredded (more than is usually shredded in an entire year), and over 30,000 e-mails were deleted. Flynn McRoberts, *Ties to Enron Blinded Andersen*, Chi. Trib. 1 (Sept. 3, 2002). Andersen was later charged and found guilty of obstruction of justice, though the jurors in post-trial interviews said that the document destruction was not the basis for their verdict. Instead, they pointed the finger at Andersen's attorney, Nancy Temple, who wrote a memo to David Duncan suggesting that she knew of the SEC's interest in Enron and was trying to keep information away from investigators. In any event, Andersen was completely destroyed as a firm.

Regulatory Response. The corporate governance system relies on a collection of intermediaries to act as watchdogs over corporate officers. Most directly, every company has a board of directors that is charged with supervising the management of the corporation. In addition, professionals outside the corporation — including accounting firms, law firms, investment bankers, institutional investors, stock analysts, and government regulators — combine to monitor corporate activity from various viewpoints. Somehow, all of these controls managed to break down in the case of Enron. This lead to a widespread belief that the system of corporate governance was broken.

Initially, it appeared that Enron would pass, like so many business failures before it, without much more than a prolonged glance from investors and regulators. When in June 2002 Global Crossing, WorldCom, and other firms revealed similar accounting problems, however, the public demanded a response, and Congress delivered in the form of SOX. The following paragraphs briefly summarize the major provisions of SOX.

1. Public Company Accounting Oversight Board: The Public Company Accounting Oversight Board was established to regulate the accounting profession. Its mission is to "oversee the audit of public companies . . . to protect the interests

---

17. As a result of this memo, Watkins became known as the "Enron whistleblower." She was subsequently chosen as one of three "Persons of the Year" by Time Magazine. *See Persons of the Year 2002: Cynthia Cooper, Coleen Rowley, and Sherron Watkins*, Time (Dec. 22, 2002).

18. Two days after Watkins' meeting with Lay, Vinson & Elkins delivered an e-mail entitled "Confidential Employee Matter" to Lay. The message read in part: "Per your request, the following are some bullet thoughts on how to manage the case with the employee who made the sensitive report. . . . Texas law does not currently protect corporate whistleblowers. The Supreme Court has twice declined to create a cause of action for whistleblowers who are discharged. . . ." *See Persons of the Year 2002: Party Crasher*, Time (Dec. 22, 2002).

of investors and further the public interest in the preparation of informative, accurate, and independent audit reports." The board is not a government agency; rather, it is a nonprofit corporation subject to oversight by the SEC. The board has authority with respect to establishing rules for audits, but it specifically has the power to adopt standards suggested by professional organizations. *See* SOX § 103(a), codified at 15 U.S.C. § 7213. The board has five members appointed by the SEC, each for a five-year term. Each of the members must serve the board full-time, and two of the members must be certified public accountants. SOX § 101(e), 15 U.S.C. § 7211.

The board was seen as potentially one of the most important reforms in SOX because it seemed to indicate more searching oversight of how the accounting industry exercised its self-regulation. It got off to a rough start, however, when the SEC nominated William Webster — former head of the FBI and CIA — as the first board chairman. The nomination was the result of a split vote (3-2) by the SEC. The dissenting Commissioners wanted someone who would be tougher on industry than Webster was expected to be. Already reeling from a series of scandals, SEC Chairman Harvey Pitt was soon forced to resign when it was revealed that Webster had been on the audit committee of U.S. Technologies when it had been charged with accounting fraud, that Chairman Pitt had known of Webster's "accounting issue," and had failed to disclose this information to the White House prior to Webster's nomination.

2. Auditor Independence: The statutory provisions attempting to encourage greater auditor independence are another important aspect of SOX. Outside auditors are understood to be important gatekeepers in the capital markets. The theory is that an independent evaluation has been done of the systems being used to generate a company's financial statements, and that based on that evaluation the auditor can say that the financial statements the company produces presents the company's financial status fairly, according to GAAP. By 2000, only about 25 percent of the "Big Five" accounting firms' income came from audit fees, however, and the balance was from non-audit services such as designing and implementing financial information systems, management consulting, bookkeeping, human resources outsourcing, and tax consulting. An important part of an audit is for the auditor to "test" the reliability of the company's information systems to see how much confidence one can have in the accuracy of the numbers being produced. If the auditor's accounting firm has set up those systems, it is impossible for the testing to be "independent," which is one of the core purposes of an audit. Moreover, if the auditor's accounting firm has given tax advice, it is impossible for that same firm independently to evaluate the amount of money being "reserved" to pay for potential taxes, or potential tax penalties and interest if questionable deductions are disallowed, for instance.

For some years prior to 2000, the SEC had been concerned about the proliferation of non-audit services by accounting firms and had been encouraging them and the AICPA (American Institute of Certified Public Accountants, one of the industry's self-regulatory agencies) to address the potential conflicts of interest and effects on auditor independence of non-audit services. Yet, the AICPA failed to act (as did Congress). Given the spectacular audit failures at Enron, WorldCom, Xerox, Global Crossing, and other companies, though, action on this issue became inevitable. SOX contained a number of provisions to try to encourage greater auditor independence, in general by prohibiting auditors from providing most non-audit services. *See* SOX § 201, 15 U.S.C. § 78j. Yet, audit companies may still provide tax-consulting services, and that is arguably the largest part of the problem of auditor non-independence: one-third of an audit firm's fees are estimated to come from tax consulting. Moreover, the board of directors may make specific exemptions to non-audit bans so long as the exemption is consistent with the protection of investors. *See id.* SOX also requires auditors to change the lead audit partner with primary responsibility for a client engagement every five years, again to try to encourage independence, although there is no requirement to change accounting firms. *See* SOX § 203, 15 U.S.C. § 78(j).

While the above provisions do not represent a shift of authority from the states to the federal government, because the SEC has had authority to regulate accountants since the 1930s (authority it has primarily delegated to accounting firms' self-regulatory organizations), many of the other provisions of SOX represent a shift in regulatory authority, leading to much greater federal involvement in corporate governance. Among the corporate governance provisions in SOX are the following:

3. Composition of Audit Committee: Every public company must have an audit committee composed exclusively of "independent directors" responsible for hiring the auditors and supervising their work. *See* SOX § 301, 15 U.S.C. § 78(j). "Independent" is defined as not having any affiliation with the audited company other than as a board member (that is, the director may not be an inside director or a major shareholder), and also not receiving any business income or consulting fees from the audited company other than income related to being a board and committee member. *See id.* SOX also directed the SEC to promulgate rules to require disclosure of whether the audit committee has at least one financial expert, and if not, why not. SOX § 407, 15 U.S.C. § 7265. (The New York Stock Exchange [NYSE] went even further and made changes to its listing standards to require that a majority of a company's board of directors be independent for a company to be listed on the NYSE.)

4. CEO and CFO Certification: SOX requires CEOs and chief financial officers (CFOs) of reporting companies to certify to the accuracy of their company's financial statements and that they have evaluated the effectiveness of their internal financial controls and have confidence in them. SOX § 302, 15 U.S.C. § 7241.

5. Internal Controls: SOX requires the SEC to develop regulations for companies to disclose, on an annual basis, how the effectiveness of internal financial controls has been evaluated. SOX § 404, 15 U.S.C. § 7262. This provision became one of the most controversial aspects of SOX, adding substantially to the costs of audits in the first years of implementation. Ultimately the SEC exempted small firms—those with a market capitalization of less than $75 million—from this requirement, and this exemption was incorporated into statute by the Dodd-Frank Act (the law passed in reaction to the financial crisis of 2008-2009, discussed below). Later evidence suggests that audits of internal financial controls actually advance investor protection. One study in 2011 found that the public companies subject to the § 404 audit experienced a 5.1 percent decline in financial statement restatements from 2009 to 2010, while smaller public companies not subject to the audit requirement experiences a 13.8 percent increase in restatements over that same period. Notwithstanding such data, in 2012 Congress passed, and the President signed, the Jumpstart Our Business Startups Act (JOBS Act), which exempts companies that go public as of 2012 from the § 404 internal controls audits for five years or until the company has $1 billion in annual income, whichever comes first.

6. Restatement of Financial Results: In the event that a company is required to restate its financial results because of "misconduct," SOX requires the CEO and CFO to reimburse the company for any bonus or other incentive-based compensation (including stock options) earned during a 12-month period following the issuance of the financial statements to be restated. SOX § 304(a), 15 U.S.C. § 7243. It also requires the CEO and CFO to reimburse the company for any profits he or she realized on the sale of company stock received during that same 12-month time. *See id.* This provision was a response to the increasing number of companies that were restating their financial statements downward during this period of time: while there were, on average, 49 restatements per year in the years 1990 to 1997, by 2000 there were 156. (Still, one must keep in mind that there were approximately 14,600 public companies in 2000, so it is not the number of restatements that suggested a need to act, but the prominence of the companies involved: Xerox, Lucent, Qualcomm, Coca-Cola, IBM, and GE, for instance.)

7. Code of Ethics: SOX directs the SEC to issue rules requiring each public reporting company to state whether it has a code of ethics for senior financial officers, and if not, why not. This section of SOX also directs the SEC to promulgate rules to require disclosure within two business days of any change in the code of ethics or waiver for senior financial officers. *See* SOX § 406, 15 U.S.C. § 7264. This latter provision was a direct response to the involvement of Michael Kopper (CFO Fastow's underling) in "investing" in the Chewco transaction. As set out in the facts above, Kopper was chosen as the person to "invest" in Chewco because his involvement would not need to be disclosed under then-existing securities regulations because he was not a senior officer of Enron.

8. Conflict-of-Interest Transactions: SOX prohibits public reporting companies from extending credit or arranging for the extending of credit, directly or indirectly, for personal loans to its executive officers or directors. SOX § 402, 15 U.S.C. § 78(m). This provision was presumably a direct response to some of the gross excesses described in the press at the Tyco Company, where the company had "loaned" CEO Dennis Kozlowski the money for not one but two multimillion dollar estates in Boca Raton, Florida. Tyco also "loaned" Kozlowski the money to purchase an apartment on Fifth Avenue in New York and to decorate the apartment with fine French antiques and (in facts that became notorious) a $6,500 shower curtain and had paid half of the $2 million tab for a birthday party for his wife on the Italian island of Sardinia, just to begin to describe the company largesse to which Mr. Kozlowski helped himself. Mr. Kozlowski, the CFO, and Tyco's general counsel were soon charged with looting the company of over $600 million, so this may not have been an example of improper company loans after all, but the facts were just beginning to be reported during the summer of 2002, and seemingly had a great impact on this provision of SOX.

9. Officers and Directors' Removal: SOX expands the SEC's ability to seek the removal of officers and directors and to seek to ban them from similar positions, due to their "unfitness." SOX § 305(a)(1), 15 U.S.C. § 78(u)(d)(2). Previously the SEC had to show "substantial unfitness" in order to remove officers or directors or to ban them from similar positions.

In addition to these provisions directed to accountants and directors or top officers, SOX also addressed the responsibility of lawyers as gatekeepers:

10. Lawyers' Responsibilities: Specifically, SOX directed the SEC to adopt rules requiring attorneys who appear before it to report "evidence" of securities laws violations, fiduciary breaches, or similar misconduct to a reporting company's chief legal counsel or CEO and, if those officers fail to act "appropriately," to the company's audit committee, its independent directors, or the board of directors as a whole. SOX § 307, 15 U.S.C. § 7245. While this provision might seem uncontroversial — after all, it is the company that hires a lawyer, so it is the company that is a lawyer's client, not the executive officers — it has spawned a storm of criticism and concern. Part of the storm arose because the SEC's first proposed rules envisioned "noisy withdrawal" — that is, a lawyer being required to notify the SEC of his or her withdrawal from representing a company if the board failed to act in response to a lawyer's report of securities law violations, fiduciary breaches, or similar violations. But even after the SEC withdrew its "noisy withdrawal" proposal and returned to "board reporting," § 307 remains controversial. Lawyers understand that "client development" often means being particularly compatible with the CEO and other top executives with whom they've developed working relationships, and such compatibility is certainly undermined by reporting differences of opinion between the CEO and lawyer to the board. Moreover, this is much more direct federal regulation of the legal profession than previously obtained, which is another source of controversy.

A number of the other provisions of SOX relate directly to required securities disclosure and regulation of the markets:

11. Real Time Disclosure: SOX amends § 13 of the Securities Exchange Act of 1934, the section establishing periodic disclosure, to require reporting companies to make "real time" disclosure of material changes in their financial condition or operations. SOX § 409, 15 U.S.C. § 78(m)(1). Previously, companies could usually wait until their next quarterly report to discuss material changes or trends affecting their financial results or operations, unless those changes were events specifically identified in Form 8-K for more immediate disclosure (such as signing a merger agreement or selling a major subsidiary). Thus, post-SOX, companies must disclose material changes "on a rapid and current basis."

12. Off-Balance Sheet Transactions Disclosure: SOX directs the SEC to promulgate rules that require disclosure of all material off-balance sheet transactions, an obvious response to the Enron off-balance sheet transactions. SOX § 401, 15 U.S.C. § 7261(c)(1). (Recall that the debt reflected on Enron's third-quarter 2001 balance sheet was $12.978 billion, while its actual debt was $39.095 billion, meaning that there was $25.116 billion of off-balance sheet debt.) Section 401(c) also directs the SEC to study the use of SPEs and their relationship to off-balance sheet transactions, and report back to Congress on whether further regulation is necessary to ensure that there is adequate financial transparency of the material risks facing companies from the use of SPEs. *See id.*

13. Whistleblower Protection: One of the ways that information was forced into the public domain at Enron was through the action of "whistleblower" Sherron Watkins. Yet, as you saw in the facts above, "whistleblowers" are often not protected under state law causes of action for wrongful discharge if they are discharged for their efforts. SOX § 806 establishes protection for whistleblowers and establishes a private right of action on behalf of whistle-blowers for compensatory damages for violations. SOX § 806(a), 18 U.S.C. § 1514A.

14. Securities Analysts' Independence: SOX requires the SEC to adopt rules governing the independence and objectivity of securities analysts. SOX § 501, 15 U.S.C. § 78o-6(a). While the Enron and WorldCom corporate governance debacles were unfolding, another series of unfortunate events began to attract public and regulatory attention, which involved conflicts of interest within securities firms. Large securities firms employ research analysts to evaluate companies and provide ideas to their clients about good stocks to buy. Large securities firms also compete to "underwrite" new stock offerings, which means to sell the offerings to the public. While the firms are supposed to ensure that the recommendations of the stock analysts are not affected by the securities offerings in which the company is involved, events in the summer of 2002 showed that any purported separation between the interests of underwriting departments and the recommendations of stock analysts was paper thin. Thus, stocks that analysts termed "dogs" and "losers" were being touted to clients when the firm was underwriter for the companies issuing such dogs and losers. Indeed, the conflicts of interest went deeper than that. Attorney General of New York Eliot Spitzer took the lead to investigate and found numerous instances in many firms where securities analysts were told to rewrite their research reports or be fired. In one particularly colorful instance, a star telecommunications analyst was alleged to have agreed to issue favorable reports on a company his securities firm was underwriting in exchange for his firm making a $1 million contribution to a private nursery school in New York so that his twin children might receive favorable consideration in their kindergarten application. (A subsequent article in the New York Times haughtily implied that such bribery would never be effective and went on to describe many, many instances of contributions to private nursery schools well in excess of $1 million — leaving the impression that it might not have been the attempted "bribery" that was the problem, but that it had been attempted on the cheap.)

15. Enhanced Criminal Penalties: In addition to all of the above (and other provisions) of SOX, the statute also enhances criminal penalties for destruction of documents and for securities fraud, leading to potential penalties of 25 years' imprisonment for securities fraud. SOX § 805, 28 U.S.C. § 994 (U.S. Sentencing Guidelines). Whether any prosecutor will ever seek such a penalty is uncertain, but clearly it will operate as a strong deterrent to intentional securities fraud of the Enron and WorldCom varieties.

1. Dodd-Frank Wall Street Reform and Consumer Protection Act of 2010

The financial crisis of 2008 derived from a number of factors that we've seen in operation in the Enron case study, albeit in the context of financial institutions rather than an operating company like Enron. Thus, special purpose entities (SPEs) creating off-balance sheet liabilities, derivatives transactions, institutional investors, and credit rating agencies all had a role.

To greatly simplify, the financial crisis was caused by large investment banks creating SPEs to hold and securitize thousands of mortgages, especially during a housing bubble in the United States from 2003 through 2007. To get a sense of the scale of this bubble, consider that between 2003 and 2005, outstanding mortgage debt in American grew by $3.7 trillion: doubling the mortgage debt that had been created between 1790 and 1990 in the United States. ("Securitization" is the process by which income-generating assets, here mortgages, are pooled together in an SPE, and the SPE issues bonds (a type of security), the payments on which will be generated by the mortgage payments on the underlying mortgages.)

These mortgage-backed securities (MBSs) were widely sold to institutional investors throughout the world, including commercial banks, pension funds, insurance companies, and hedge funds, and were valuable assets on each of these investors' balance sheets. As the market developed, credit rating agencies were hired to rate the possibility of default of different batches of MBSs, a task that became increasingly difficult as the complexity of the underlying transactions increased. In order to get better credit ratings on each batch of mortgage-backed bonds that they were selling, the investment banks would enter into derivatives transactions with third parties, called "credit default swaps" (CDSs), that acted as a type of insurance against the MBS defaulting. In essence, the "protection seller" took on the risk of default of the MBS in exchange for payments from the protection buyer. In most of these transactions, the "protection seller" was the London office of the American Insurance Group (AIG), the largest insurance group in the world.

This market functioned fine while interest rates were low, and all along this "originate-to-distribute" supply chain companies were making money. Mortgage brokers were finding new borrowers, for a fee; commercial banks were originating and funding these mortgages and then selling them on to investment banks, for a fee; the investment banks were securitizing the mortgages, for a fee; the credit rating agencies were evaluating the different batches of MBSs, for a fee; AIG was collecting what were effectively insurance premiums for its sale of CDSs without an expectation of having to pay out (and without having to set aside funds for the obligation to pay out, which would have been required with real insurance); and the investors who were in a "search for yield," given low underlying interest rates, were getting slightly higher returns from MBS investments. But, starting in 2007 the supply chain unraveled.

To continue to have product to sell, and to meet congressional demands that home-ownership expand, including ownership by lower-income borrowers, the quality of underlying mortgages had declined starting around 2003 as more and more "sub-prime" borrowers, those of lower income or with lower credit scores, were being given mortgages. In essence, all prime borrowers had already bought houses or refinanced by 2003, but the originate-to-distribute supply chain needed product to securitize and sell. Many of the mortgages sold to sub-prime borrowers were adjustable-rate mortgages (ARMs), which meant the interest rate on the mortgage went up if the underlying interest rates in the economy went up. From September 11, 2001, through June 2004, the Federal Reserve Bank's federal funds "prime rate" had been about 1 percent, but this rate rose to 4.5 percent by January 2006. This dramatic rise in the underlying interest rate caused ARM costs to rise dramatically for individual borrowers, causing defaults on mortgages to rise by late 2007, particularly among sub-prime borrowers; causing home foreclosures to increase; and causing the value of MBSs to decrease (because the security of monthly payments coming into the underlying mortgages was not as clear). Since MBSs had been widely sold to institutional investors throughout the world, including to banks, and since they were assets on all these investors' balance sheets, by 2008 there was a credit freeze: banks didn't trust each others' balance sheets and stopped lending because no one knew the real value of MBSs, and therefore the actual financial strength of potential bank counterparties (borrowers); and investors didn't trust each others' balance sheets to make short-term loans among themselves. Thus, before the end of 2008 the world was in a full-scale financial crisis, leading to the worst global economic recession since the 1930s, and leading governments around the world to step in to provide funds to unfreeze credit.

On July 21, 2010, President Barack Obama signed the Dodd-Frank Wall Street Reform and Consumer Protection Act into law in response to the financial crisis. The bill is gargantuan, encompassing 858 pages in the Daily Statute Book. One widely used summary of the bill, prepared by the corporate law firm Davis, Polk & Wardwell, is itself over 120 pages long.[19] While much of the Dodd-Frank Act deals with systemic issues, banks that are too big and too interconnected to fail, and addresses prior regulatory failures such as those with respect to derivatives, some pieces of it continue to federalize corporate governance.

For present purposes, the most important part of the new statute is Title IX, the Investor Protection and Securities Reform Act of 2010, which is an omnibus title addressing a range of issues at the SEC, and, like SOX, federalizes a number of aspects of corporate governance that had previously been the province of state corporate law. Among other provisions, it provides explicit authority to the SEC to permit shareholder proxy access to nominate directors—a provision discussed in more detail in Section C below. It also requires the disclosure of the ratio of CEO compensation to the median employee; requires disclosure of executives' hedging of their options and shares; requires "appropriate" federal regulators to work together to prohibit compensation systems that encourage excessive risk taking; adopts a comply or explain provision encouraging the separation of the CEO from the Chair position in the firm; and asks for a study of the SEC revolving door, among a long list of studies required.

There is a wealth of excellent sources of further information about the financial crisis and the Dodd-Frank Act. For a clear, and thus accessible, account, we recommend Brett McDonnell, *Don't Panic! Defending Cowardly Interventions During and After a Financial Crisis*, 116 Pa. State L. Rev. 1 (2011).

2. *Federal Proxy Regulation*

As we've seen, Sarbanes-Oxley and Dodd-Frank are each statutes that have "federalized" aspects of corporate governance that were previously the province of state corporate law. They are not the first such federal statutes, however. That trend began with the federal securities laws. Prior to 1933, there was no federal regulation of the sale of securities. Rather, 47 states regulated such sales within

---

19. Dodd-Frank Wall Street Reform and Consumer Protection Act of 2010, P.L. 111-203,124 Stat. 1376 through 124 Stat. 2228 (2010), *codified at* 12 U.S.C. §§ 5301 *et seq. See* Davis, Polk & Wardwell, *Summary of the Dodd-Frank Wall Street Reform and Consumer Protection Act, Enacted into Law on July 21, 2010,* available at *http://www.davispolk.com/files/Publication/7084f9fe-6580-413b-b870-b7c025ed2ecf /Presentation/PublicationAttachment/1d4495c7-0be0-4e9a-ba77-f786fb90464a/070910_Financial_Reform _Summary.pdf.*

their own borders under state "blue sky laws," named after the oft-repeated comment of a Kansas legislator that "some securities swindlers were so barefaced they 'would sell building lots in the blue sky.'" Joel Seligman, *The Transformation of Wall Street: A History of the Securities and Exchange Commission and Modern Corporation Finance* (2d ed. 1995). The New York Stock Exchange, where the majority of securities were bought and sold, was privately owned by its member stock brokers (as it is today) and subject to self-regulation (as it is today, though the SEC now exercises oversight over the Exchange's self-regulation).

In the early 1930s the United States and the world suffered through the first serious, global economic depression. While it is typical to talk of the "stock market crash" as part of the Great Depression, it is more historically accurate to talk of the stock market's "slow but steady decline." Thus, from September 1929 through July 1932, the aggregate value of all of the stocks traded on the New York Stock Exchange declined by more than 80 percent. In the context of great economic insecurity and loss, Wall Street, fairly or unfairly, became synonymous with the economic problems facing the nation and a favored target for Franklin Roosevelt to attack on the campaign trail. Once elected in November 1932, President Roosevelt identified the enactment of new federal laws to regulate the securities markets as one of his top priorities.

Congress agreed with President Roosevelt and enacted seven major securities statutes between 1933 and 1940 to address concerns about the management of U.S. companies and the workings of the capital markets. The two most important of these statutes for our purposes are the Securities Act of 1933 (the 1933 Act) and the Securities Exchange Act of 1934 (the 1934 Act). The 1933 Act is a transaction-specific statute that regulates sales of stocks or bonds in primary market transactions—that is, transactions in which a company like Facebook or Google sells stocks or bonds to the public and receives the money for those sales. The 1934 Act is a much more comprehensive statute that generally regulates secondary market transactions—that is, purchases and sales of securities among investors in the trading markets and exchanges—including by identifying the kinds of information public reporting companies are required to disclose to the market on a regular basis—quarterly, annually, and whenever there are significant corporate developments. "Public reporting companies" are defined as companies with securities listed on a national securities exchange (§§ 12(a) and 12(g) of the 1934 Act), or with common stock held by more than 2,000 persons or 500 "non-accredited investors" (meaning shareholders who are not wealthy, as defined by the SEC) and with assets of $10 million or more (*id.*, as further developed by Rule 12g-1), or with bonds listed on an exchange and held by more than 300 people. *Id.*, § 15(d). Given recent enactment of the JOBS Act, employee shareholders whose shares were received as part of compensation are not counted toward these shareholder limits, which will allow small start-up companies to stay private longer.

In both statutes, Congress used a number of regulatory approaches, from outright prohibitions of certain actions to standard setting for acceptable conduct with respect to other types of actions. But the regulatory approach that applies most directly to our corporate governance triumvirate—officers, directors, and shareholders—is mandatory disclosure. Congress sought to ensure that full, accurate information about public companies would be available to the markets and shareholders on a regular basis, and in proxy disclosure whenever shareholders were being asked to vote on anything, from the annual elections of directors to extraordinary transactions such as a merger.

Toward that end, there is a disclosure document, called a "proxy statement," that must be provided directly to the shareholders (or to the people who will be exercising voting power for institutional investors, such as mutual fund or pension fund managers) whenever the shareholders have the right to vote and thus whenever the shareholder's proxy is being "solicited." The requirements for the proxy statement are set out in Schedule 14A, promulgated under the authority of §14(a) of the 1934 Act. Section 14(a) is a broad delegation of authority to the SEC, which simply states:

> It shall be unlawful for any person . . . in contravention of such rules and regulations as the Commission may prescribe as necessary or appropriate in the public interest or for the protection of investors, to solicit or to permit the use of his name to solicit any proxy or consent or authorization in respect of any security [issued by a public reporting company].

The proxy solicitation process typically occurs in preparation for the annual meeting required under state law. *See* Delaware General Corporation Law (DGCL) §211(b); Model Business Corporation Act (Model Act) §7.01. Proxies can also be solicited as part of an extraordinary transaction, such as the approval of a merger in those situations where the shareholders have voting rights. Since the overwhelming majority of shareholders who vote do so in advance by giving their proxy (legal authority) to a delegee to vote their shares, the proxy solicitation process in a public corporation is the voting process, and the focus of regulatory activity is in ensuring that the proxy statement is comprehensive and accurate.

At the annual meeting, the major item of business is to elect the directors for the next year, or for the next term of years in a company with a staggered board. Other important items of business on the agenda typically include approving the accountants for the next year, and approving any executive compensation packages.[20] Moreover, there may be proposals by the board of directors to amend the certificate of incorporation for some reason, such as to authorize the issuance of new shares of stock or to adopt anti-takeover devices. Directors might also have the power to propose amendments to the bylaws under a particular company's certificate of incorporation; if so, director proposals to amend the bylaws might be on the agenda for the annual meeting.[21] Every agenda item must be fully and accurately described in the proxy statement, examples of which are easily accessible in the database of public filings at the SEC, the Electronic Data Gathering and Retrieval System (EDGAR). *See http://*

---

20. While the shareholders don't have a right to approve executive compensation packages under state law, under federal tax law there are financial advantages to the company if the shareholders have approved performance-based executive compensation packages, such as granting stock options geared to the performance of the company. Also, in 2002 the New York Stock Exchange adopted rules to expand the types of stock-based executive compensation plans that must be approved by the shareholders in firms listed on the Exchange.

21. Under Delaware law, shareholders always have the power to initiate changes to the bylaws, notwithstanding the particular company's charter, which might also give a concurrent power to the board to initiate changes to the bylaws. DGCL §109(a). The Model Act contains a similar structure of potentially concurrent power but allows the articles of incorporation to reserve the power to change the bylaws exclusively to the shareholders. Model Act §10.20 (b)(1).

www.sec.gov/edgar.html (look up your favorite companies and then look for the "Def. 14A").

Federal proxy regulations promulgated pursuant to §14(a) of the 1934 Act apply only to communications that are defined as "proxy solicitations" under Rule 14a-1. Once a communication is identified as a proxy solicitation, Rules 14a-3 to 14a-15 apply, regulating the form and content of required information that must be supplied, and providing a cause of action for material misstatements or omissions under Rule 14a-9. In the seminal case Long Island Lighting Co. v. Barbash, 779 F.2d 793 (2d Cir. 1985), the Second Circuit considered whether newspaper advertisements published in the midst of a public debate over the construction of a nuclear power plant could be considered a "proxy solicitation." The *Barbash* court held that such advertisements could be a proxy solicitation, construing the proxy rules to apply "not only to direct requests to furnish, revoke or withhold proxies, but also to communications which may indirectly accomplish such a result or constitute a step in a chain of communications designed ultimately to accomplish such a result." The major implication of a communication being held to be a proxy solicitation is that usually the party making it must send a proxy statement (as defined in Rule 14a-3 and Schedule 14A) to all of the shareholders being solicited.

In addition to items management puts on the annual meeting agenda, shareholders have an important power here: they can propose items of business for the agenda as well. Institutional investors such as public pension funds, labor funds, SRI (socially responsible investors), faith-based institutions, issue organizations such as the Center for Political Accountability or the Investor Network on Environmental Health, and governance institutions such as Governance for Owners have been using this power with increasing vigor over the last two decades. These institutional investors bring two general types of shareholder proposals:

Governance proposals: These proposals focus on board structure, such as declassifying staggered boards, compensation issues, dismantling takeover defenses, supporting majority voting rules, promoting the separation of the CEO from the board Chair, and limiting golden parachute arrangements, for instance. About 400 of these proposals are brought per year as of 2012, and about half of them receive average support of over 50 percent, the rest receiving average support of about 40 percent.

Social proposals: These proposals raise a wide variety of social and environmental issues, generally calling for reports or policy changes on issues such as political spending, climate change risk and adaptation, sustainability reporting, international human rights, industrial safety, product safety, diversity, and labor rights issues, including child labor issues. About 400 of these proposals are brought per year as well, with an average vote for these proposals in 2011 of 20 percent (compared to an average vote of 9 percent in 2002).

If a particular group of shareholders wants to put an item on the annual meeting agenda, they would send a "shareholders' proposal" and 500-word supporting statement to the company in advance of the annual meeting and ask the company to include the proposal and supporting statement in the company's proxy statement. The company will do so, reluctantly in most cases, if the proposal meets the procedural and substantive requirements that the SEC has established. Rules 14a-7 and 14a-8 are critical to the shareholders' efforts.

Rule 14a-7 obligates companies either to provide interested shareholders with a shareholders' list so that the shareholders can communicate directly with other shareholders, or obligates the company to mail soliciting materials directly to shareholders at the soliciting shareholders' expense. Rule 14a-8 sets out the procedural and substantive requirements under which companies will be required to include shareholder proposals and supporting material in the company's definitive proxy statement. The most important part of Rule 14a-8 sets out the 13 reasons that companies can exclude shareholder proposals from the company's proxy statement. Given that shareholders would far prefer their materials to be included in the company's proxy statement under Rule 14a-8 and thus mailed at the company's expense, much of the debate and legal wrangling over shareholder proposals takes place in the context of Rule 14a-8, which you'll see in the cases below.

C. SHAREHOLDER VOTING

1. *Shareholders' Voting Power Generally*

One of the clearest statements of the importance of shareholder voting comes from an opinion by Chancellor Allen in Blasius Indus., Inc. v. Atlas Corp., 564 A.2d 651 (Del. Ch. 1988). In the midst of a defense to a hostile takeover attempt by Blasius, the board of the Atlas Corporation had used powers in the company's bylaws to add new board members to three-year terms, creating a majority that could not be removed except "for cause," and thus delaying by two years the time during which shareholders could vote for new management by giving their proxy to Blasius. In discussing this "unintended breach of fiduciary duties," Chancellor Allen discussed the importance of shareholder voting as follows:

> The shareholder franchise is the ideological underpinning upon which the legitimacy of directorial power rests. Generally, shareholders have only two protections against perceived inadequate business performance. They may sell their stock (which, if done in sufficient numbers, may so affect security prices as to create an incentive for altered managerial performance), or they may vote to replace incumbent board members.
>
> It has, for a long time, been conventional to dismiss the stockholder vote as a vestige or ritual of little practical importance. It may be that we are now witnessing the emergence of new institutional voices and arrangements that will make the stockholder vote a less predictable affair than it has been. Be that as it may, however, whether the vote is seen functionally as an unimportant formalism, or as an important tool of discipline, it is clear that it is critical to the theory that legitimates the exercise of power by some (directors and officers) over vast aggregations of property that they do not own. Thus, when viewed from a broad, institutional perspective, it can be seen that matters involving the integrity of the shareholder voting process involve consideration not present in any other context in which directors exercise delegated power.

Blasius, 564 A.2d at 659.

As in so many cases, Chancellor Allen was prescient: The "emergence of new institutional voices" that he suggested in 1988 might be making shareholder voting less predictable (and thus more important) has continued to develop, as shareholders attempt to exert influence within American public corporations. In the following case we see the actions of an institutional investor, here an Australian pension fund, and the underlying power struggle between shareholders and management that shareholder activism creates. *Unisuper* is an example of one of the issues that has been at the forefront of the corporate governance agenda in recent years, namely, whether shareholders or the board should have power over the decision to sell the company. In *Unisuper*, you see an effort by activists to give shareholders power over the decision of whether to keep a "poison pill" in place or not. ("Poison pills" are rights extended to existing shareholders to buy shares at a deep discount if a hostile acquiror tries to take over the company. The existence of a pill makes companies much more expensive and difficult to take over in a hostile acquisition.) State corporate law generally permits directors to implement a poison pill without a shareholder vote, but activist shareholders have been attempting to pass bylaw amendments requiring shareholder approval of actions with respect to poison pills. *Unisuper* arose in an unusual factual context, and as we'll see shortly, may not be a typical outcome. But it raises important questions that are at the heart of debates today: If shareholders are not permitted to decide every issue of corporate governance, what is the appropriate realm of shareholder decision making? How should courts, legislatures, or regulatory agencies define the shareholder role?

UNISUPER LTD. ET AL. v. NEWS CORPORATION

2005 WL 3529317
Delaware Court of Chancery
December 20, 2005

CHANDLER, Chancellor.

This case arises from a dispute between institutional shareholders and a company whose shares the investors owned and whose corporate governance they were monitoring. Plaintiffs filed this action on October 7, 2005, against defendant News Corporation ("News Corp." or "the Company") seeking to invalidate News Corp.'s extension of its poison pill and to prohibit any further extensions absent shareholder approval. Plaintiffs allege that News Corp. contracted . . . that any extension of its poison pill would be put to a shareholder vote. When News Corp.'s board of directors extended the pill without a shareholder vote, plaintiffs filed this lawsuit. The individuals who were directors of News Corp. at the relevant times have also been named as defendants. Defendants have filed a motion to dismiss. For the reasons set forth below, I deny defendants' motion. . . .

I. BACKGROUND

On April 6, 2004, News Corp. issued a press release announcing a plan of reorganization that would include the reincorporation of News Corp. — then an

Australian corporation — as a Delaware corporation. The reorganization would be contingent on a shareholder vote of approval by each class of News Corp.'s shareholders voting separately. Because the shares beneficially owned by the Murdoch family voted as their own class, the public shareholders were in a position to prevent the reorganization if they voted as a class to reject it.

In late July 2004, the Australian Council of Super Investors Inc. ("ACSI") and Corporate Governance International ("CGI") met with News Corp. to discuss the reincorporation proposal. ACSI is a non-profit organization that advises Australian pension funds on corporate governance and CGI is an Australian proxy advisory firm. During these meetings, ACSI and CGI informed News Corp. of their concerns about the reincorporation's impact on shareholder rights and other corporate governance issues. One of the specific concerns mentioned by ACSI and GCI was that, under Delaware law, the Company's board of directors would be able to institute a poison pill without shareholder approval, while under Australian law shareholder approval is required.

After these meetings, ACSI and CGI began to develop a set of proposed changes to News Corp.'s post-reorganization, Delaware certificate of incorporation. ACSI and CGI drafted these proposed changes in the form of a "Governance Article." The Governance Article contained several provisions, including one providing that "the Board shall not have the power to, and shall not, create or implement any device, matter, or thing the purpose, nature, or effect of which is commonly described as a 'poison pill.'" On August 20, 2004, ACSI sent a copy of the Governance Article to News Corp. and requested that the proposals be included in the charter of the new Delaware corporation.

In late September 2004, News Corp. informed ACSI that the changes to the certificate of incorporation set forth in the Governance Article would not be adopted and that there would be no further negotiations. In response, ACSI issued a press release on September 27, 2004, recounting the negotiations with News Corp. and expressing ACSI's belief that the proposed reincorporation would result in the loss of shareholder protections. ACSI's September 27, 2004, press release was widely circulated and had the effect of galvanizing institutional investor opposition to the reincorporation.

On October 1, 2004, News Corp. reversed itself and initiated further negotiations with ACSI. The General Counsel for News Corp., Ian Phillip, contacted the President of ACSI, Michael O'Sullivan, and told O'Sullivan that further negotiations were possible. At this stage of the negotiations, five key issues relating to News Corp.'s corporate governance remained in contention. Three of these issues would be dealt with through the adoption of binding provisions in the new, Delaware certificate of incorporation. Only the poison pill voting issue would be dealt with through the adoption of a so-called "board policy."

The first issue was whether News Corp. would agree to retain its full foreign listing on the Australian Stock Exchange. News Corp. ultimately agreed that its Delaware certificate of incorporation would include a provision requiring that News Corp. retain its full listing on the Australian Stock Exchange. The second issue was whether News Corp. would agree to insert a provision into its Delaware certificate of incorporation stating that News Corp. would not issue new shares having more than one vote per share. The parties ultimately agreed that such a provision would be added to the new certificate of incorporation. With respect to the third issue, the parties agreed to add a provision to the certificate of incorporation providing that holders of 20 percent or more of the outstanding voting shares of News Corp. could cause a special meeting of shareholders to be called. The fourth issue was dealt with through a series of voting agreements entered into by Rupert Murdoch. These agreements provided that Murdoch would not sell any of his voting shares to a purchaser if, following such sale, the purchaser would own more than 19.9 percent of News Corp., unless such purchaser agreed to purchase all the voting and non-voting shares of News Corp. Murdoch further agreed that these voting agreements could not be terminated or amended without the affirmative vote of News Corp.'s shareholders, excluding Murdoch and his affiliates. The fifth and final of the key issues was News Corp.'s ability under Delaware law to adopt a poison pill without a shareholder vote.

During the negotiations on the fifth issue, ACSI again sought an amendment to the Company's Delaware certificate of incorporation that would require a shareholder vote approving the adoption of a poison pill. In response to this request, Phillip told O'Sullivan that an amendment to the certificate of incorporation was impractical because there was not enough time. Time was limited because of the need to hold the shareholder vote as well as the need to have the reincorporation approved by an Australian court, as required by Australian corporate law. Phillip told O'Sullivan that, in the limited time remaining, it would be too difficult to draft and finalize an amendment to the certificate of incorporation that would encompass everything that might fall within the definition of "poison pill."

Plaintiffs allege that during these conversations between ACSI and News Corp., someone on behalf of News Corp. proposed that, rather than instituting an amendment to the certificate of incorporation, the poison pill issue be addressed by means of the adoption of a board policy (the "Board Policy"). Plaintiffs allege that someone, on behalf of News Corp., further agreed that News Corp.'s board would not circumvent the voting requirement by "rolling over" a poison pill for successive one-year terms on substantially similar terms and conditions or to the same effect without shareholder approval.

On October 6, 2004, the terms of the agreement were announced in a News Corp. press release. The press release stated:

> The [News Corp.] Board has adopted a policy that if a shareholder rights plan is adopted by the Company following reincorporation, the plan would have a one year sunset clause unless shareholder approval is obtained for an extension. The policy also provides that if shareholder approval is not obtained, the Company will not adopt a successor shareholder rights plan having substantially the same terms and conditions.

On October 7, 2004, Phillip emailed the "agreed deal points" to ACSI reiterating that it was the board's policy to hold a shareholder vote on twelve-month old poison pills. Also on October 7, 2004, News Corp. sent a letter to all of its shareholders and option-holders stating:

> [T]he board . . . has established a policy that if any stockholder rights plan (known as a 'poison pill') is adopted without stockholder approval, it will expire after one year unless it is ratified by stockholders. This policy will not permit the plan to be rolled over for successive one-year terms on substantially the same terms and conditions or to the same effect without stockholder ratification.

On October 26, 2004, the shareholders and options-holders of News Corp. voted to approve the reorganization. The plaintiffs voted in favor of the reorganization and did not appear in court to object to the reorganization.

On November 8, 2004, Liberty Media Corporation ("Liberty Media") suddenly appeared as a potential hostile acquiror for News Corp. Liberty Media announced it had entered into an arrangement with a third party allowing it to acquire an additional 8% of News Corp.'s voting stock, thereby increasing its ownership to more than 17% of the voting stock. In response to this threat, News Corp.'s board adopted a poison pill, which it announced in a November 8, 2004 press release. In this press release, the board also announced that, going forward, it might or might not implement the Board Policy depending on whether it deemed the policy "appropriate in light of the facts and circumstances existing at such time."[32] One year later, on November 8, 2005, the board extended the poison pill without a shareholder vote, in contravention of the Board Policy.

Plaintiffs, a group of Australian institutional investors, filed their complaint on October 7, 2005.[34] The complaint contains five counts. Count I is for breach of contract. Count II asserts a claim for promissory estoppel. Count III is a claim for fraud. Count IV is a claim for negligent misrepresentation and equitable fraud. Count V is a claim for breach of fiduciary duties against the individual defendants. As relief for these claims, plaintiffs seek a judgment declaring the Company's poison pill invalid and enjoining defendants from extending the pill without first obtaining approval from the Company's shareholders.

II. ANALYSIS

. . .

B. COUNT I — BREACH OF CONTRACT

Plaintiffs allege that defendants entered into a contract when plaintiffs agreed to vote in favor of News Corp.'s reorganization in consideration for News Corp.'s promise to submit any extensions of its poison pill to a shareholder vote. This contract allegedly provided that News Corp. would adopt a board policy and that the board policy would not be revocable.[39] Plaintiffs assert two legal theories for

---

32. By the time of the November 8, 2004, press release, plaintiffs had already cast their votes in favor of the reincorporation.

34. Plaintiffs allege that the board's ultimate decision to extend the poison pill was foreshadowed in early August 2005. On August 10, the Company's Form 8-K filing indicated that the poison pill would be extended for two years beyond its November 8, 2005 expiration date, without shareholder approval. The 8-K made no mention of the Board Policy or explained why it would not be followed. The plaintiffs also were aware of an article published by the CEO of News Limited on August 20, 2005, that explained the board's action as follows:

> The company said it would establish a policy which it did. The company did not claim to anyone at any time, verbally or in writing, that it would never change the policy. No agreement was breached, no promise was broken and there is no credible evidence to the contrary.

39. One aspect of plaintiffs' contract theory strikes me as problematic: Plaintiffs are sophisticated investors capable of negotiating enforceable agreements to protect their interests, as is demonstrated in this case by the certificate of incorporation amendments plaintiffs managed to extract from defendants. Of the five key issues that the parties negotiated over, three were dealt with through amendments to the certificate of incorporation, and another was specifically made binding absent a shareholder vote. Thus, it is not entirely clear why in this instance plaintiffs

how the contract was formed. The first theory is that the parties entered into a written contract evidenced by the Press Release and the Letter to Shareholders. The second is that the parties entered into an oral agreement. The complaint asserts very few facts to support either of these theories. Because I am required to draw each crucial inference in plaintiffs' favor, however, I conclude that plaintiffs' breach of contract claim survives defendants' motion to dismiss.

i. Allegations of a Written Agreement: The Press Release and Letter to Shareholders

Defendants concede there was an agreement embodied in the Press Release and Letter to Shareholders by which News Corp. promised to adopt a board policy. They argue that the parties never discussed making the policy irrevocable and that, under Delaware law, a board policy is nonbinding and revocable by the board at any time. Plaintiffs counter that the contract in this case contemplated that the board would not be able to "roll over" the pill, i.e., circumvent the shareholder vote by rescinding the Board Policy.

Defendants are correct that board policies, like board resolutions, are typically revocable by the board at will. They cite *In re General Motors (Hughes) Shareholders Litigation* in support of the proposition that board policies are always revocable, in every circumstance. The board in General Motors adopted a "Board Policy Statement" setting forth procedures to be followed in the event of a material transaction between General Motors ("GM") and one of its subsidiaries, Hughes Electronics Corporation ("Hughes"). The policy required that in the event of a transfer of material assets from Hughes to GM, the GM board would be required to declare and pay a dividend to the Hughes shareholders.

In *General Motors*, this Court stated in a footnote that if a board policy has the effect of a board resolution, it might be revocable by the board at any time. This statement was phrased as a conditional statement because, as the Court noted, the complaint in General Motors contained no information with respect to the extent to which the GM board was bound to protect the rights granted to shareholders by the policy statement, i.e., the extent to which the policy had an effect greater than a simple board resolution. In contrast, *the complaint in this case alleges that the News Corp. board was contractually bound to protect the rights granted by the Board Policy.* Plaintiffs allegation is precisely that, in contrast to the facts in General Motors, the Board Policy in this case had an effect greater than that of a resolution because the board was contractually bound to keep it in place.

This Court's statement about board policies in *General Motors* simply reiterates an elementary principle of corporate law: If the board has the power to adopt resolutions (or policies), then the power to rescind resolutions (policies) must reside with the board as well. An equally strong principle is that: If a board enters into a contract to adopt and keep in place a resolution (or a policy) that others justifiably rely upon to their detriment, that contract may be enforceable, without regard to whether resolutions (or policies) are typically revocable by the board at will.

---

accepted a promise to adopt a board policy, which is a more transitory right than a charter provision, especially when sophisticated parties such as these must have understood the significant difference between a charter provision and a board policy. Nonetheless, assuming every reasonable inference in plaintiffs' favor, I cannot say at this stage that there is no set of facts that would entitle plaintiffs to prevail on their contract theory. Although plaintiffs' claim is sufficient to withstand a motion to dismiss because of the liberal standard applied in this context, it will be plaintiffs' burden going forward to demonstrate a factual and legal basis for this claim.

On their face, the Press Release and the Letter to Shareholders state that the News Corp. board would adopt a board policy. If the Press Release and the Letter to Shareholders stated nothing more, I would be inclined to grant Defendants' motion with respect to the allegations of a written contract. But both the Press Release and the Letter to Shareholders go on to state that the board policy will not permit the pill to be rolled over. The plaintiffs are entitled to all reasonable inferences, including the inference that this part of the agreement expresses an intent that the Board Policy would not be rescinded before the shareholders had a chance to vote. On this point, the meaning of the contract is ambiguous and both sides should have the opportunity to present evidence and make legal arguments concerning the proper interpretation of the agreement.[43] Whether plaintiffs will be able to adduce evidence in support of their allegations is for another day. But for now, it is sufficient that they have alleged the existence of an agreement, the existence of valuable consideration (their vote in favor of the reorganization), and that the board intentionally breached the agreement.

ii. Allegations of an Oral Contract

The complaint avers facts barely sufficient to state a claim that defendants made an oral contract with the shareholders during these conversations. The details of the alleged oral contract are not spelled out in the complaint, but what is clear is that the key term of the alleged oral contract was that shareholders would get to vote on any extension of a poison pill.

The operative sections of the complaint are paragraphs 46 and 47. The complaint makes reference to the conversations between Phillip and O'Sullivan and sets forth general facts about those conversations. Notwithstanding the dearth of factual detail about the oral contract, Rule 12(b) sets forth a "notice pleading" standard and I conclude that the complaint gives adequate notice, if barely so, as to when the alleged oral agreement was formed and as to its contents. Many of the ambiguities and gaps in the written agreement also infect the alleged oral agreement, if not more so. Nevertheless, at this early stage of the lawsuit, I must deny defendants' motion to dismiss plaintiffs' claim of an oral contract.

iii. Unenforceability

Defendants assert that, even if plaintiffs are right about the existence, substance and interpretation of the alleged contract, the contract is unenforceable as a matter of law. Defendants offer two arguments in support of this proposition.

a. Section 141(a)

Defendants first argue the alleged agreement is inconsistent with the general grant of managerial authority to the board in Section 141(a) of the Delaware General Corporation Law. According to defendants, Section 141(a) vests power to manage the corporation in the board of directors and requires that any limitation on this power be in the certificate of incorporation. Defendants contend that an agreement to hold a shareholder vote on poison pills (or any other

---

43. There are other ambiguities inherent in the alleged agreement. For example, what is the term or duration of the Board Policy? Did the parties intend to preclude the board from ever modifying the Board Policy? If the shareholders voted not to extend the poison pill, would a future board of News Corp. also be disabled from adopting a poison pill? If plaintiffs are correct about the alleged agreement, then how could the agreement have left out these crucial details?

issue affecting the business and affairs of the corporation) is unenforceable unless memorialized in the certificate of incorporation.

By definition, any contract a board could enter into binds the board and thereby limits its power. Section 141(a) does not say the board cannot enter into contracts. It simply describes who will manage the affairs of the corporation and it precludes a board of directors from ceding that power to outside groups or individuals.

The fact that the alleged contract in this case gives power to the shareholders saves it from invalidation under Section 141(a). The alleged contract with ACSI did not cede power over poison pills to an outside group; rather, it ceded that power to shareholders. In effect, defendants' argument is that the board impermissibly ceded power to the shareholders. Defendants' argument is that the contract impermissibly restricted the board's power by granting shareholders an irrevocable veto right over a question of corporate control.

Delaware's corporation law vests managerial power in the board of directors because it is not feasible for shareholders, the owners of the corporation, to exercise day-to-day power over the company's business and affairs.[48] Nonetheless, when shareholders exercise their right to vote in order to assert control over the business and affairs of the corporation the board must give way. This is because the board's power—which is that of an agent's with regard to its principal—derives from the shareholders, who are the ultimate holders of power under Delaware law.[49] . . .

III. Conclusion

The complaint adequately states [a claim] for breach of contract. . . . The burden is now on the plaintiffs to prove that a contract . . . was actually made that the Board Policy would be irrevocable. . . .

2. Shareholders' Efforts to Amend the Bylaws: Conflicts Between DGCL §§ 109 and 141(A)

We began this chapter by describing the separation of ownership and control that characterizes publicly traded corporations, and we highlighted the tension between authority and responsibility. Gone are the days, though, when shareholders followed the "Wall Street Rule" — that is, if you don't like a company's policies or strategy, don't try to change the company, just sell the shares. Given the increased demand of shareholders to participate in corporate decision making, the most important corporate governance issue of the day is the need to

---

48. Of course, the board of directors' managerial power is not unlimited; it is constrained by the directors' fiduciary duties and by shareholders' right to vote. The Delaware General Corporation Law gives shareholders an immutable right to vote on fundamental corporate changes. *See, e.g.,* 8 Del. C. § 242 (charter amendment); § 251 (merger); § 271 (sale of assets); § 275 (dissolution). In addition, the Delaware General Corporation Law vests shareholders with the power to adopt, amend or repeal bylaws relating to the business of the corporation and the conduct of its affairs. 8 Del. C. § 109.

49. The alleged agreement in this case enables a vote by all shareholders. Private agreements between the board and a few large shareholders might be troubling where the agreements restrict the board's power in favor of a particular shareholder, rather than in favor of shareholders at large.

define the acceptable scope of shareholder action. In this Section, we explore bylaw amendments under DGCL § 109 as a mechanism through which shareholders have sought to exert some control within public corporations. In Section 3 below we discuss another type of shareholder activism, that of shareholders' attempts to cause companies to change bylaws to require inclusion of shareholders' nominees for board positions in the company's proxy statement.

Even though shareholders have the right to propose bylaw amendments, there are two problems shareholders have faced trying to exercise this right. First, getting such proposals in front of the shareholders can be expensive. As a practical matter, shareholders' bylaw proposals must be included in the company's proxy statement, pursuant to the requirements of Rule 14a-8, because then the company pays for distributing the communication to the shareholder body. Rule 14a-8 provides 13 substantive bases for excluding shareholders' proposal, such as if the proposal deals with a matter relating to the company's ordinary business (Rule 14a-8(i)(7)), or relates to an election (Rule 14a-8(i)(8)), or is irrelevant (Rule 14a-8(i)(5). Under Rule 14a-8(i)(1), a proposal may be excluded from a proxy ballot if the "proposal is not a proper subject for action by shareholders under the laws of the jurisdiction of the company's organization." This basis for exclusion has been particularly critical with respect to shareholders' efforts to use their undoubted power to initiate changes to the bylaws under DGCL § 109, and this is the second hurdle shareholders have faced.

As Professor Smith and his co-authors have observed:

> The heavily-disputed question of what power shareholders have to alter or enact corporate bylaws in light of the board's authority to manage the corporation is rooted in one of corporate law's most persistent statutory knots—a Delawarean puzzle arising from the interplay between section 109 and section 141(a) of the DGCL. Any reasonable assessment of these two sections inevitably leads to one conclusion: textual analysis of the relevant statutes is not enough to solve the puzzle and, consequently, any reconciliation of the two sections must rely on policy considerations. . . . Jeffrey Gordon has described these two sections as linked in a "recursive loop:" the shareholder power to adopt, alter, or repeal bylaws is limited by "law," which includes the power of the board of directors to manage or supervise the management of the corporation detailed in section 141(a); meanwhile, the board's power to manage or supervise the management of the corporation is limited by other provisions in the DGCL, which include the shareholder power to adopt, alter or repeal bylaws found in section 109.

D. Gordon Smith, Matthew Wright, and Marcus Kai Hintze, *Private Ordering with Shareholder Bylaws*, 80 Ford. L. Rev. 125, 140-141 (2011).

In the following case, the Supreme Court of Delaware, sitting en banc, attempted to untie this "persistent statutory knot." One part of the problem had been procedural: the Delaware courts had regularly resolved binding bylaw litigation on ripeness grounds (i.e., until shareholders actually enacted a binding bylaw there was no case or controversy to determine how to resolve the conflict between §§ 109 and 141(a)), so there was no Delaware authority on how to resolve that conflict. Companies were excluding binding bylaw proposals from their proxy statements pursuant to Rule 14a-8-i(1) (on the grounds that if enacted they would be inconsistent with state law), however, and the SEC wouldn't opine on unsettled issues of Delaware law when asked by shareholders if that exclusion was proper under Rule 14a-8(i)(1)! In 2007, the Delaware General Assembly eliminated this procedural logjam by amending the Delaware Constitution to allow the Delaware Supreme Court to "hear and determine questions of law certified to it by . . . the United States Securities and Exchange Commission," a power that the SEC promptly exercised in the following case.

CA, INC. v. AFSCME EMPLOYEES PENSION PLAN

953 A.2d 227
Supreme Court of Delaware, en banc
August 15, 2008

JACOBS, Justice.

This proceeding arises from a certification by the United States Securities and Exchange Commission (the "SEC"), to this Court, of two questions of law pursuant to Article IV, Section 11(8) of the Delaware Constitution and Supreme Court Rule 41. On June 27, 2008, the SEC asked this Court to address two questions of Delaware law regarding a proposed stockholder bylaw submitted by the AFSCME Employees Pension Plan ("AFSCME") for inclusion in the proxy materials of CA, Inc. ("CA" or the "Company") for CA's 2008 annual stockholders' meeting. This Court accepted certification on July 1, 2008, and after expedited briefing, the matter was argued on July 9, 2008. This is the decision of the Court on the certified questions.

I. FACTS

CA is a Delaware corporation whose board of directors consists of twelve persons, all of whom sit for reelection each year. CA's annual meeting of stockholders is scheduled to be held on September 9, 2008. CA intends to file its definitive proxy materials with the SEC on or about July 24, 2008 in connection with that meeting.

AFSCME, a CA stockholder, is associated with the American Federation of State, County and Municipal Employees. On March 13, 2008, AFSCME submitted a proposed stockholder bylaw (the "Bylaw" or "proposed Bylaw") for inclusion in the Company's proxy materials for its 2008 annual meeting of stockholders. The Bylaw, if adopted by CA stockholders, would amend the Company's bylaws to provide as follows:

> RESOLVED, that pursuant to section 109 of the Delaware General Corporation Law and Article IX of the bylaws of CA, Inc., stockholders of CA hereby amend the bylaws to add the following Section 14 to Article II:
> The board of directors shall cause the corporation to reimburse a stockholder or group of stockholders (together, the "Nominator") for reasonable expenses ("Expenses") incurred in connection with nominating one or more candidates in a contested election of directors to the corporation's board of directors, including, without limitation, printing, mailing, legal, solicitation, travel, advertising and public relations expenses, so long as (a) the election of fewer than 50% of the directors to be elected is contested in the election, (b) one or more candidates

nominated by the Nominator are elected to the corporation's board of directors, (c) stockholders are not permitted to cumulate their votes for directors, and (d) the election occurred, and the Expenses were incurred, after this bylaw's adoption. The amount paid to a Nominator under this bylaw in respect of a contested election shall not exceed the amount expended by the corporation in connection with such election.

CA's current bylaws and Certificate of Incorporation have no provision that specifically addresses the reimbursement of proxy expenses. Of more general relevance, however, is Article SEVENTH, Section (1) of CA's Certificate of Incorporation, which tracks the language of 8 Del. C. § 141(a) and provides that:

The management of the business and the conduct of the affairs of the corporation shall be vested in [CA's] Board of Directors.

It is undisputed that the decision whether to reimburse election expenses is presently vested in the discretion of CA's board of directors, subject to their fiduciary duties and applicable Delaware law.

On April 18, 2008, CA notified the SEC's Division of Corporation Finance (the "Division") of its intention to exclude the proposed Bylaw from its 2008 proxy materials. The Company requested from the Division a "no-action letter" stating that the Division would not recommend any enforcement action to the SEC if CA excluded the AFSCME proposal. CA's request for a no-action letter was accompanied by an opinion from its Delaware counsel, Richards Layton & Finger, P.A. ("RL & F"). The RL & F opinion concluded that the proposed Bylaw is not a proper subject for stockholder action, and that if implemented, the Bylaw would violate the Delaware General Corporation Law ("DGCL").

On May 21, 2008, AFSCME responded to CA's no-action request with a letter taking the opposite legal position. The AFSCME letter was accompanied by an opinion from AFSCME's Delaware counsel, Grant & Eisenhofer, P.A. ("G & E"). The G & E opinion concluded that the proposed Bylaw is a proper subject for shareholder action and that if adopted, would be permitted under Delaware law.

The Division was thus confronted with two conflicting legal opinions on Delaware law. Whether or not the Division would determine that CA may exclude the proposed Bylaw from its 2008 proxy materials would depend upon which of these conflicting views is legally correct. To obtain guidance, the SEC, at the Division's request, certified two questions of Delaware law to this Court. Given the short timeframe for the filing of CA's proxy materials, we concluded that "there are important and urgent reasons for an immediate determination of the questions certified," and accepted those questions for review on July 1, 2008.

II. The Certified Questions

The two questions certified to us by the SEC are as follows:

1. Is the AFSCME Proposal a proper subject for action by shareholders as a matter of Delaware law?
2. Would the AFSCME Proposal, if adopted, cause CA to violate any Delaware law to which it is subject?

III. The First Question

A. PRELIMINARY COMMENTS

The first question presented is whether the Bylaw is a proper subject for shareholder action, more precisely, whether the Bylaw may be proposed and enacted by shareholders without the concurrence of the Company's board of directors. Before proceeding further, we make some preliminary comments in an effort to delineate a framework within which to begin our analysis.

First, the DGCL empowers both the board of directors and the shareholders of a Delaware corporation to adopt, amend or repeal the corporation's bylaws. 8 Del. C. § 109(a) relevantly provides that:

> After a corporation has received any payment for any of its stock, the power to adopt, amend or repeal bylaws shall be in the stockholders entitled to vote . . . ; provided, however, any corporation may, in its certificate of incorporation, confer the power to adopt, amend or repeal bylaws upon the directors. . . . The fact that such power has been so conferred upon the directors . . . shall not divest the stockholders . . . of the power, nor limit their power to adopt, amend or repeal bylaws.

Pursuant to Section 109(a), CA's Certificate of Incorporation confers the power to adopt, amend or repeal the bylaws upon the Company's board of directors. Because the statute commands that that conferral "shall not divest the stockholders . . . of . . . nor limit" their power, both the board and the shareholders of CA, independently and concurrently, possess the power to adopt, amend and repeal the bylaws.

Second, the vesting of that concurrent power in both the board and the shareholders raises the issue of whether the stockholders' power is coextensive with that of the board, and vice versa. As a purely theoretical matter that is possible, and were that the case, then the first certified question would be easily answered. That is, under such a regime any proposal to adopt, amend or repeal a bylaw would be a proper subject for either shareholder or board action, without distinction. But the DGCL has not allocated to the board and the shareholders the identical, coextensive power to adopt, amend and repeal the bylaws. Therefore, how that power is allocated between those two decision-making bodies requires an analysis that is more complex.

Moving from the theoretical to this case, by its terms Section 109(a) vests in the shareholders a power to adopt, amend or repeal bylaws that is legally sacrosanct, i.e., the power cannot be non-consensually eliminated or limited by anyone other than the legislature itself. If viewed in isolation, Section 109(a) could be read to make the board's and the shareholders' power to adopt, amend or repeal bylaws identical and coextensive, but Section 109(a) does not exist in a vacuum. It must be read together with 8 Del. C. § 141(a), which pertinently provides that:

> The business and affairs of every corporation organized under this chapter shall be managed by or under the direction of a board of directors, except as may be otherwise provided in this chapter or in its certificate of incorporation.

No such broad management power is statutorily allocated to the shareholders. Indeed, it is well-established that stockholders of a corporation subject to the DGCL may not directly manage the business and affairs of the corporation, at least without specific authorization in either the statute or the certificate of incorporation. Therefore, the shareholders' statutory power to adopt, amend or repeal bylaws is not coextensive with the board's concurrent power and is limited by the board's management prerogatives under Section 141(a).

Third, it follows that, to decide whether the Bylaw proposed by AFSCME is a proper subject for shareholder action under Delaware law, we must first determine: (1) the scope or reach of the shareholders' power to adopt, alter or repeal the bylaws of a Delaware corporation, and then (2) whether the Bylaw at issue here falls within that permissible scope. Where, as here, the proposed bylaw is one that limits director authority, that is an elusively difficult task. As one noted scholar has put it, "the efforts to distinguish by-laws that permissibly limit director authority from by-laws that impermissibly do so have failed to provide a coherent analytical structure, and the pertinent statutes provide no guidelines for distinction at all." [Lawrence A. Hamermesh, *Corporate Democracy and Stockholder-Adopted By-Laws: Taking Back the Street?*, 73 Tul. L.Rev. 409, 444 (1998); *Id.* at 416 (noting that "neither the courts, the legislators, the SEC, nor legal scholars have clearly articulated the means of . . . determining whether a stockholder-adopted by-law provision that constrains director managerial authority is legally effective.")] The tools that are available to this Court to answer those questions are other provisions of the DGCL and Delaware judicial decisions that can be brought to bear on this question.

B. ANALYSIS

1. Two other provisions of the DGCL, 8 Del. C. §§ 109(b) and 102(b)(1), bear importantly on the first question and form the basis of contentions advanced by each side. Section 109(b), which deals generally with bylaws and what they must or may contain, provides that:

> The bylaws may contain any provision, not inconsistent with law or with the certificate of incorporation, relating to the business of the corporation, the conduct of its affairs, and its rights or powers or the rights or powers of its stockholders, directors, officers or employees.

And Section 102(b)(1), which is part of a broader provision that addresses what the certificate of incorporation must or may contain, relevantly states that:

> (b) In addition to the matters required to be set forth in the certificate of incorporation by subsection (a) of this section, the certificate of incorporation may also contain any or all of the following matters:
>
> > (1) Any provision for the management of the business and for the conduct of the affairs of the corporation, and any provision creating, defining, limiting and regulating the powers of the corporation, the directors and the stockholders, or any class of the stockholders . . . ; if such provisions are not contrary to the laws of this State. Any provision which is required or permitted by any section of this chapter to be stated in the bylaws may instead be stated in the certificate of incorporation.

AFSCME relies heavily upon the language of Section 109(b), which permits the bylaws of a corporation to contain "any provision . . . relating to the . . . rights or powers of its stockholders [and] directors. . . ." The Bylaw, AFSCME argues, "relates to" the right of the stockholders meaningfully to participate in the process of electing directors, a right that necessarily "includes the right to nominate an opposing slate."

CA argues, in response, that Section 109(b) is not dispositive, because it cannot be read in isolation from, and without regard to, Section 102(b)(1). CA's argument runs as follows: the Bylaw would limit the substantive decision-making authority of CA's board to decide whether or not to expend corporate funds for a particular purpose, here, reimbursing director election expenses. Section 102(b)(1) contemplates that any provision that limits the broad statutory power of the directors must be contained in the certificate of incorporation. Therefore, the proposed Bylaw can only be in CA's Certificate of Incorporation, as distinguished from its bylaws. Accordingly, the proposed bylaw falls outside the universe of permissible bylaws authorized by Section 109(b).

Implicit in CA's argument is the premise that any bylaw that in any respect might be viewed as limiting or restricting the power of the board of directors automatically falls outside the scope of permissible bylaws. That simply cannot be. That reasoning, taken to its logical extreme, would result in eliminating altogether the shareholders' statutory right to adopt, amend or repeal bylaws. Bylaws, by their very nature, set down rules and procedures that bind a corporation's board and its shareholders. In that sense, most, if not all, bylaws could be said to limit the otherwise unlimited discretionary power of the board. Yet Section 109(a) carves out an area of shareholder power to adopt, amend or repeal bylaws that is expressly inviolate. Therefore, to argue that the Bylaw at issue here limits the board's power to manage the business and affairs of the Company only begins, but cannot end, the analysis needed to decide whether the Bylaw is a proper subject for shareholder action. The question left unanswered is what is the scope of shareholder action that Section 109(b) permits yet does not improperly intrude upon the directors' power to manage corporation's business and affairs under Section 141(a).

It is at this juncture that the statutory language becomes only marginally helpful in determining what the Delaware legislature intended to be the lawful scope of the shareholders' power to adopt, amend and repeal bylaws. To resolve that issue, the Court must resort to different tools, namely, decisions of this Court and of the Court of Chancery that bear on this question. Those tools do not enable us to articulate with doctrinal exactitude a bright line that divides those bylaws that shareholders may unilaterally adopt under Section 109(b) from those which they may not under Section 141(a). They do, however, enable us to decide the issue presented in this specific case.

2. It is well-established Delaware law that a proper function of bylaws is not to mandate how the board should decide specific substantive business decisions, but rather, to define the process and procedures by which those decisions are made. As the Court of Chancery has noted:

> Traditionally, the bylaws have been the corporate instrument used to set forth the rules by which the corporate board conducts its business. To this end, the DGCL is replete with specific provisions authorizing the bylaws to establish the procedures through which board and committee action is taken. . . . [T]here is a general consensus that bylaws that regulate the process by which the board acts are statutorily authorized.

***

. . . I reject International's argument that that provision in the Bylaw Amendments impermissibly interferes with the board's authority under § 141(a) to manage the business and affairs of the corporation. Sections 109 and 141, taken in totality. . . . make clear that bylaws may pervasively and strictly regulate the process by which boards act, subject to the constraints of equity.

Hollinger Intern., Inc. v. Black, 844 A.2d 1022, 1078-79 and 1080 n.136 (Del. Ch. 2004), *aff'd*, 872 A.2d 559 (Del. 2005).

Examples of the procedural, process-oriented nature of bylaws are found in both the DGCL and the case law. For example, 8 Del. C. §141(b) authorizes bylaws that fix the number of directors on the board, the number of directors required for a quorum (with certain limitations), and the vote requirements for board action. 8 Del. C. §141(f) authorizes bylaws that preclude board action without a meeting. And, almost three decades ago this Court upheld a shareholder-enacted bylaw requiring unanimous board attendance and board approval for any board action, and unanimous ratification of any committee action. Such purely procedural bylaws do not improperly encroach upon the board's managerial authority under Section 141(a).

The process-creating function of bylaws provides a starting point to address the Bylaw at issue. It enables us to frame the issue in terms of whether the Bylaw is one that establishes or regulates a process for substantive director decision-making, or one that mandates the decision itself. Not surprisingly, the parties sharply divide on that question. We conclude that the Bylaw, even though infelicitously couched as a substantive-sounding mandate to expend corporate funds, has both the intent and the effect of regulating the process for electing directors of CA. Therefore, we determine that the Bylaw is a proper subject for shareholder action, and set forth our reasoning below.

Although CA concedes that "restrictive procedural bylaws (such as those requiring the presence of all directors and unanimous board consent to take action) are acceptable," it points out that even facially procedural bylaws can unduly intrude upon board authority. The Bylaw being proposed here is unduly intrusive, CA claims, because, by mandating reimbursement of a stockholder's proxy expenses, it limits the board's broad discretionary authority to decide whether to grant reimbursement at all. CA further claims that because (in defined circumstances) the Bylaw mandates the expenditure of corporate funds, its subject matter is necessarily substantive, not process-oriented, and, therefore falls outside the scope of what Section 109(b) permits.[19]

Because the Bylaw is couched as a command to reimburse ("The board of directors shall cause the corporation to reimburse a stockholder"), it lends itself to CA's criticism. But the Bylaw's wording, although relevant, is not dispositive of whether or not it is process-related. The Bylaw could easily have been worded

---

19. CA actually conflates two separate arguments that, although facially similar, are analytically distinct. The first argument is that the Bylaw impermissibly intrudes upon board authority because it mandates the expenditure of corporate funds. The second is that the Bylaw impermissibly leaves no role for board discretion and would require reimbursement of the costs of a subset of CA's stockholders, even in circumstances where the board's fiduciary duties would counsel otherwise. Analytically, the first argument is relevant to the issue of whether the Bylaw is a proper subject for unilateral stockholder action, whereas the second argument more properly goes to the separate question of whether the Bylaw, if enacted, would violate Delaware law.

differently, to emphasize its process, as distinguished from its mandatory payment, component.[20] By saying this we do not mean to suggest that this Bylaw's reimbursement component can be ignored. What we do suggest is that a bylaw that requires the expenditure of corporate funds does not, for that reason alone, become automatically deprived of its process-related character. A hypothetical example illustrates the point. Suppose that the directors of a corporation live in different states and at a considerable distance from the corporation's headquarters. Suppose also that the shareholders enact a bylaw that requires all meetings of directors to take place in person at the corporation's headquarters. Such a bylaw would be clearly process-related, yet it cannot be supposed that the shareholders would lack the power to adopt the bylaw because it would require the corporation to expend its funds to reimburse the directors' travel expenses. Whether or not a bylaw is process-related must necessarily be determined in light of its context and purpose.

The context of the Bylaw at issue here is the process for electing directors — a subject in which shareholders of Delaware corporations have a legitimate and protected interest. The purpose of the Bylaw is to promote the integrity of that electoral process by facilitating the nomination of director candidates by stockholders or groups of stockholders. Generally, and under the current framework for electing directors in contested elections, only board-sponsored nominees for election are reimbursed for their election expenses. Dissident candidates are not, unless they succeed in replacing at least a majority of the entire board. The Bylaw would encourage the nomination of non-management board candidates by promising reimbursement of the nominating stockholders' proxy expenses if one or more of its candidates are elected. In that the shareholders also have a legitimate interest, because the Bylaw would facilitate the exercise of their right to participate in selecting the contestants. . . .

The shareholders of a Delaware corporation have the right "to participate in selecting the contestants" for election to the board. The shareholders are entitled to facilitate the exercise of that right by proposing a bylaw that would encourage candidates other than board-sponsored nominees to stand for election. The Bylaw would accomplish that by committing the corporation to reimburse the election expenses of shareholders whose candidates are successfully elected. That the implementation of that proposal would require the expenditure of corporate funds will not, in and of itself, make such a bylaw an improper subject matter for shareholder action. Accordingly, we answer the first question certified to us in the affirmative.

That, however, concludes only part of the analysis. The DGCL also requires that the Bylaw be "not inconsistent with law." Accordingly, we turn to the second

---

20. For example, the Bylaw could have been phrased more benignly, to provide that "[a] stockholder or group of stockholders (together, the 'Nominator') shall be entitled to reimbursement from the corporation for reasonable expenses ('Expenses') incurred in connection with nominating one or more candidates in a contested election of directors to the corporation's board of directors in the following circumstances. . . ." Although the substance of the Bylaw would be no different, the emphasis would be upon the shareholders' entitlement to reimbursement, rather than upon the directors' obligation to reimburse. As discussed in Part IV, infra, of this Opinion, in order for the Bylaw not to be "not inconsistent with law" as Section 109(b) mandates, it would also need to contain a provision that reserves the directors' full power to discharge their fiduciary duties.

certified question, which is whether the proposed By-law, if adopted, would cause CA to violate any Delaware law to which it is subject.

IV. The Second Question

In answering the first question, we have already determined that the Bylaw does not facially violate any provision of the DGCL or of CA's Certificate of Incorporation. The question thus becomes whether the Bylaw would violate any common law rule or precept. Were this issue being presented in the course of litigation involving the application of the Bylaw to a specific set of facts, we would start with the presumption that the Bylaw is valid and, if possible, construe it in a manner consistent with the law. The factual context in which the Bylaw was challenged would inform our analysis, and we would "exercise caution [before] invalidating corporate acts based upon hypothetical injuries . . ." [*Stroud v. Grace*, 606 A.2d 75, 79 (Del. 1992)]. The certified questions, however, request a determination of the validity of the Bylaw in the abstract. Therefore, in response to the second question, we must necessarily consider any possible circumstance under which a board of directors might be required to act. Under at least one such hypothetical, the board of directors would breach their fiduciary duties if they complied with the Bylaw. Accordingly, we conclude that the Bylaw, as drafted, would violate the prohibition, which our decisions have derived from Section 141(a), against contractual arrangements that commit the board of directors to a course of action that would preclude them from fully discharging their fiduciary duties to the corporation and its shareholders.

This Court has previously invalidated contracts that would require a board to act or not act in such a fashion that would limit the exercise of their fiduciary duties. In Paramount Communications, Inc. v. QVC Network, Inc., [637 A.2d 34 (Del. 1994),] we invalidated a "no shop" provision of a merger agreement with a favored bidder (Viacom) that prevented the directors of the target company (Paramount) from communicating with a competing bidder (QVC) the terms of its competing bid in an effort to obtain the highest available value for shareholders. We held that:

> The No-Shop Provision could not validly define or limit the fiduciary duties of the Paramount directors. To the extent that a contract, or a provision thereof, purports to require a board to act or not act in such a fashion as to limit the exercise of fiduciary duties, it is invalid and unenforceable. [. . .] [T]he Paramount directors could not contract away their fiduciary obligations. Since the No-Shop Provision was invalid, Viacom never had any vested contract rights in the provision.

Similarly, in Quickturn Design Systems, Inc. v. Shapiro, [721 A.2d 1281 (Del. 1998),] the directors of the target company (Quickturn) adopted a "poison pill" rights plan that contained a so-called "delayed redemption provision" as a defense against a hostile takeover bid, as part of which the bidder (Mentor Graphics) intended to wage a proxy contest to replace the target company board. The delayed redemption provision was intended to deter that effort, by preventing any newly elected board from redeeming the poison pill for six months. This Court invalidated that provision, because it would "impermissibly deprive any newly elected board of both its statutory authority to manage the corporation under 8 Del. C. § 141 (a) and its concomitant fiduciary duty pursuant to that statutory mandate." We held that:

> One of the most basic tenets of Delaware corporate law is that the board of directors has the ultimate responsibility for managing the business and affairs of a corporation. [. . .] The Quickturn certificate of incorporation contains no provision purporting to limit the authority of the board in any way. The Delayed Redemption Provision, however, would prevent a newly elected board of directors from completely discharging its fundamental management duties to the corporation and its stockholders for six months. While the Delayed Redemption Provision limits the board of directors' authority in only one respect, the suspension of the Rights Plan, it nonetheless restricts the board's power in an area of fundamental importance to the shareholders — negotiating a possible sale of the corporation. Therefore, we hold that the Delayed Redemption Provision is invalid under Section 141 (a), which confers upon any newly elected board of directors full power to manage and direct the business and affairs of a Delaware corporation.

Both QVC and Quickturn involved binding contractual arrangements that the board of directors had voluntarily imposed upon themselves. This case involves a binding bylaw that the shareholders seek to impose involuntarily on the directors in the specific area of election expense reimbursement. Although this case is distinguishable in that respect, the distinction is one without a difference. The reason is that the internal governance contract — which here takes the form of a bylaw — is one that would also prevent the directors from exercising their full managerial power in circumstances where their fiduciary duties would otherwise require them to deny reimbursement to a dissident slate. That this limitation would be imposed by a majority vote of the shareholders rather than by the directors themselves, does not, in our view, legally matter.[32]

AFSCME contends that it is improper to use the doctrine articulated in QVC and Quickturn as the measure of the validity of the Bylaw. Because the Bylaw would remove the subject of election expense reimbursement (in circumstances as defined by the Bylaw) entirely from the CA's board's discretion (AFSCME argues), it cannot fairly be claimed that the directors would be precluded from discharging their fiduciary duty. Stated differently, AFSCME argues that it is unfair to claim that the Bylaw prevents the CA board from discharging its fiduciary duty where the effect of the Bylaw is to relieve the board entirely of those duties in this specific area.

That response, in our view, is more semantic than substantive. No matter how artfully it may be phrased, the argument concedes the very proposition that renders the Bylaw, as written, invalid: the Bylaw mandates reimbursement of election expenses in circumstances that a proper application of fiduciary principles could preclude. That such circumstances could arise is not far-fetched. Under Delaware law, a board may expend corporate funds to reimburse proxy expenses "[w]here the controversy is concerned with a question of policy as distinguished from personnel o[r] management." But in a situation where the proxy contest is motivated by personal or petty concerns, or to promote interests that do not further, or are adverse to, those of the corporation, the

---

32. Only if the Bylaw provision were enacted as an amendment to CA's Certificate of Incorporation would that distinction be dispositive. See 8 Del. C. § 102 (b) (1) and § 242.

board's fiduciary duty could compel that reimbursement be denied altogether.[34]

It is in this respect that the proposed Bylaw, as written, would violate Delaware law if enacted by CA's shareholders. As presently drafted, the Bylaw would afford CA's directors full discretion to determine what amount of reimbursement is appropriate, because the directors would be obligated to grant only the "reasonable" expenses of a successful short slate. Unfortunately, that does not go far enough, because the Bylaw contains no language or provision that would reserve to CA's directors their full power to exercise their fiduciary duty to decide whether or not it would be appropriate, in a specific case, to award reimbursement at all.

***

In arriving at this conclusion, we express no view on whether the Bylaw as currently drafted, would create a better governance scheme from a policy standpoint. We decide only what is, and is not, legally permitted under the DGCL. That statute, as currently drafted, is the expression of policy as decreed by the Delaware legislature. Those who believe that CA's shareholders should be permitted to make the proposed Bylaw as drafted part of CA's governance scheme, have two alternatives. They may seek to amend the Certificate of Incorporation to include the substance of the Bylaw; or they may seek recourse from the Delaware General Assembly.

Accordingly, we answer the second question certified to us in the affirmative.

PROBLEM 6-1

After long discussions on the issue of foreign waste importation, Waste Disposal's board of directors determined that tapping into foreign markets would be financially beneficial for the company and directed the officers to begin soliciting business. Waste Disposal received a positive response from waste producers in Italy, who contracted with the company to dispose of 20,000 tons of low-level radioactive waste.

Once this transaction was picked up by the Utah media, the residents of Utah were outraged. Some shareholders likewise were outraged, principally because the way in which the issue was handled seems to have tarnished Waste Disposal's otherwise strong reputation as a responsible player in a very sensitive industry.

Certain highly motivated shareholders contended that the board did not have the authority to expand into foreign waste markets without shareholder approval. Nevertheless, the board of directors was certain that such decisions were well within its authority, and the board instructed the company's officers to move forward with the expansion and importation of foreign nuclear waste.

The shareholders are considering various actions to reverse the company's course. *If the shareholders sued, claiming that the board of directors acted beyond its authority, what issues would be relevant to the court in resolving the case? If the shareholders managed to express their opposition, via shareholder vote, to the policy of importing foreign nuclear waste, would the board be obligated to obey the shareholders? Would it*

---

34. Such a circumstance could arise, for example, if a shareholder group affiliated with a competitor of the company were to cause the election of a minority slate of candidates committed to using their director positions to obtain, and then communicate, valuable proprietary strategic or product information to the competitor.

matter if the shareholders voted to adopt a bylaw prohibiting the company from importing foreign nuclear waste? If the shareholders persuaded the board of directors to place a charter provision to the same effect up for shareholder vote, would the board be constrained by that provision?

3.   Shareholders' Efforts to Change the Procedures for the Nomination of Directors

Another particularly fruitful area for conflict has been efforts by institutional investors to require that shareholder-nominated candidates for the board of directors be included in the company's proxy statement. Previous proposals by the SEC to allow shareholders "proxy access" for their nominees, such as *Security Holder Director Nominations,* SEC Exchange Act Release No. 34-48626, 68 Fed. Reg. 60,784, 60,787 (Oct. 14, 2003) (Proposed Rule 14a-11), have been met with stiff resistance from the business community, represented by the Business Round-table (an organization of CEOs) and the U.S. Chamber of Commerce. Proposed Rule 14a-11 would have entitled a holder of at least 5 percent of the corporation's voting stock to place a nominee on the corporate ballot but only if the proxy access rule had been "activated" by one of two triggering events, including the adoption, by majority vote, of a shareholder proposal granting proxy access submitted by a holder of more than 1 percent of the corporation's voting stock.

The SEC never issued Proposed Rule 14a-11. Rather, Rule 14a-8(i)(8) permits a company to exclude a shareholder proposal "if the proposal relates to a nomination or an election for membership on the company's board of directors or analogous governing body or a procedure for such nomination or election." This language clearly allows companies to exclude shareholder-nominated candidates from the company's proxy statement, so enterprising shareholders tried another approach: bringing forth proposals to change the procedures set out in the bylaws of individual companies to allow shareholder-nominated candidates. American Federation of State, County & Municipal Employees v. American International Group, Inc., 462 F.3d 121 (2d Cir. 2006), gave this approach powerful support, creating an equally powerful response by the SEC, which almost immediately began regulatory procedures to evaluate the AFSCME decision and the whole issue of shareholder-nominated candidates. What is the right policy with regard to shareholder participation in director elections? Should shareholders be allowed to determine the ground rules for those elections? Should shareholders have the right to nominate director candidates under Rule 14a-8?

AMERICAN FEDERATION OF STATE, COUNTY & MUNICIPAL EMPLOYEES v. AMERICAN INTERNATIONAL GROUP, INC.

462 F.3d 121
United States Court of Appeals, Second Circuit
September 5, 2006

Wesley, Circuit Judge.

This case raises the question of whether a shareholder proposal requiring a company to include certain shareholder-nominated candidates for the board of directors on the corporate ballot can be excluded from the corporate proxy materials on the basis that the proposal "relates to an election" under Securities Exchange Act Rule 14a-8(i)(8) ("election exclusion" or "Rule 14a-8(i)(8)"). Complicating this question is not only the ambiguity of Rule 14a-8(i)(8) itself but also the fact that the Securities Exchange Commission (the "SEC" or "Commission") has ascribed two different interpretations to the Rule's language. The SEC's first interpretation was published in 1976, the same year that it last revised the election exclusion. The Division of Corporation Finance (the "Division"), the group within the SEC that handles investor disclosure matters and issues no-action letters,[1] continued to apply this interpretation consistently for fifteen years until 1990, when it began applying a different interpretation, although at first in an ad hoc and inconsistent manner. The result of this gradual interpretive shift is the SEC's second interpretation, as set forth in its amicus brief to this Court. We believe that an agency's interpretation of an ambiguous regulation made at the time the regulation was implemented or revised should control unless that agency has offered sufficient reasons for its changed interpretation. Accordingly, we hold that a shareholder proposal that seeks to amend the corporate bylaws to establish a procedure by which shareholder-nominated candidates may be included on the corporate ballot does not relate to an election within the meaning of the Rule and therefore cannot be excluded from corporate proxy materials under that regulation.

Background

The American Federation of State, County & Municipal Employees ("AFSCME") is one of the country's largest public service employee unions. Through its pension plan, AFSCME holds 26,965 shares of voting common stock of American International Group ("AIG" or "Company"), a multinational corporation operating in the insurance and financial services sectors. On December 1, 2004, AFSCME submitted to AIG for inclusion in the Company's 2005 proxy statement a shareholder proposal that, if adopted by a majority of AIG shareholders at the Company's 2005 annual meeting,[2] would amend the AIG bylaws to require the Company, under certain circumstances, to publish the names of shareholder-nominated candidates for director positions together with any candidates nominated by AIG's board of directors

---

1. Elaborating upon the nature of the no-action process, the Court has stated:

The no-action process works as follows: Whenever a corporation decides to exclude a shareholder proposal from its proxy materials, it "shall file" a letter with the Division explaining the legal basis for its decision. *See* Rule 14a-8(d)(3). If the Division staff agrees that the proposal is excludable, it may issue a no-action letter, stating that, based on the facts presented by the corporation, the staff will not recommend that the SEC sue the corporation for violating Rule 14a-8. . . . The no-action letter, however, is an informal response, and does not amount to an official statement of the SEC's views. . . . No-action letters are deemed interpretive because they do not impose or fix legal relationship upon any of the parties.

N.Y. City Employees' Ret. Sys. v. SEC, 45 F.3d 7, 12 (2d Cir.1995).
2. Delaware corporate law, which governs AIG's internal affairs, provides that shareholders have the power to amend bylaws by majority vote. *See* Del. Code Ann. tit. 8, § 109(a).

("Proposal").[3] AIG sought the input of the Division regarding whether AIG could exclude the Proposal from its proxy statement under the election exclusion on the basis that it "relates to an election." The Division issued a no-action letter in which it indicated that it would not recommend an enforcement action against AIG should the Company exclude the Proposal from its proxy statement. American International Group, Inc., SEC No-Action Letter, 2005 WL 372266 (Feb 14, 2005) ("AIG No-Action Letter"). Armed with the no-action letter, AIG then proceeded to exclude the Proposal from the Company's proxy statement. In response, AFSCME brought suit in the United States District Court for the Southern District of New York (Stanton, J.) seeking a court order compelling AIG to include the Proposal in its next proxy statement. The district court denied AFSCME's motion for a preliminary injunction, concluding that AFSCME's Proposal "on its face 'relates to an election.' Indeed, it relates to nothing else." Am. Fed'n of State, County & Mun. Employees Pension Plan v. Am. Int'l Group, 361 F. Supp.2d 344, 346 (S.D.N.Y.2005). After this Court denied AFSCME's motion for expedited appeal, the parties stipulated that the district court's opinion denying AFSCME's motion for a preliminary injunction "be deemed to contain the Court's complete findings of fact and conclusions of law with respect to all claims asserted by plaintiff in this action" and that it also "be deemed a final judgment on the merits with respect to all claims asserted by plaintiff in this action." Pursuant to this joint stipulation, the district court entered final judgment denying plaintiff's claims for declaratory and injunctive relief and dismissing plaintiff's complaint.

---

3. The AFSCME Proposal states in relevant part:

RESOLVED, pursuant to Section 6.9 of the By-laws (the "Bylaws") of American International Group Inc. ("AIG") and section 109(a) of the Delaware General Corporation Law, stockholders hereby amend the Bylaws to add section 6.10:

"The Corporation shall include in its proxy materials for a meeting of stockholders the name, together with the Disclosure and Statement (both defined below), of any person nominated for election to the Board of Directors by a stockholder or group thereof that satisfies the requirements of this section 6.10 (the "Nominator"), and allow stockholders to vote with respect to such nominee on the Corporation's proxy card. Each Nominator may nominate one candidate for election at a meeting.

To be eligible to make a nomination, a Nominator must:

(a) have beneficially owned 3% or more of the Corporation's outstanding common stock (the "Required Shares") for at least one year;

(b) provide written notice received by the Corporation's Secretary within the time period specified in section 1.11 of the Bylaws containing (i) with respect to the nominee, (A) the information required by Items 7(a), (b) and (c) of SEC Schedule 14A (such information is referred to herein as the "Disclosure") and (B) such nominee's consent to being named in the proxy statement and to serving as a director if elected; and (ii) with respect to the Nominator, proof of ownership of the Required Shares; and

(c) execute an undertaking that it agrees (i) to assume all liability of any violation of law or regulation arising out of the Nominator's communications with stockholders, including the Disclosure (ii) to the extent it uses soliciting material other than the Corporation's proxy materials, comply with all laws and regulations relating thereto.

The Nominator shall have the option to furnish a statement, not to exceed 500 words, in support of the nominee's candidacy (the "Statement"), at the time the Disclosure is submitted to the Corporation's Secretary. The Board of Directors shall adopt a procedure for timely resolving disputes over whether notice of a nomination was timely given and whether the Disclosure and Statement comply with this section 6.10 and SEC Rules."

DISCUSSION

Rule 14a-8(i)(8), also known as "the town meeting rule," regulates what are referred to as "shareholders proposals," that is, "recommendation[s] or requirement[s] that the company and/or its board of directors take [some] action, which [the submitting shareholder(s)] intend to present at a meeting of the company's shareholders," 17 C.F.R. § 240.14a-8(a). If a shareholder seeking to submit a proposal meets certain eligibility and procedural requirements, the corporation is required to include the proposal in its proxy statement and identify the proposal in its form of proxy, unless the corporation can prove to the SEC that a given proposal may be excluded based on one of thirteen grounds enumerated in the regulations. *Id.* § 240.14a-8(i)(1)-(13). One of these grounds, Rule 14a-8(i)(8), provides that a corporation may exclude a shareholder proposal "[i]f the proposal relates to an election for membership on the company's board of directors or analogous governing body." *Id.* § 240.14a-8(i)(8).

We must determine whether, under Rule 14a-8(i)(8), a shareholder proposal "relates to an election" if it seeks to amend the corporate bylaws to establish a procedure by which certain shareholders are entitled to include in the corporate proxy materials their nominees for the board of directors ("proxy access bylaw proposal"). "In interpreting an administrative regulation, as in interpreting a statute, we must begin by examining the language of the provision at issue." Resnik v. Swartz, 303 F.3d 147, 151-52 (2d Cir.2002) (citing New York Currency Research Corp. v. CFTC, 180 F.3d 83, 92 (2d Cir.1999)). The relevant language here — "relates to an election" — is not particularly helpful. AFSCME reads the election exclusion as creating an obvious distinction between proposals addressing a particular seat in a particular election (which AFSCME concedes are excludable) and those, like AFSCME's proposal, that simply set the background rules governing elections generally (which AFSCME claims are not excludable). AFSCME's distinction rests on Rule 14a-8(i)(8)'s use of the article "an," which AFSCME claims "necessarily implies that the phrase 'relates to an election' is intended to relate to proposals that address *particular elections*, instead of simply 'elections' generally." It is at least plausible that the words "an election" were intended to narrow the scope of the election exclusion, confining its application to proposals relating to "a particular election *and not* elections generally." It is, however, also plausible that the phrase was intended to create a comparatively broader exclusion, one covering "a particular election *or* elections generally" since any proposal that relates to elections in general will necessarily relate to an election in particular. The language of Rule 14a8(i)(8) provides no reason to adopt one interpretation over the other.

When the language of a regulation is ambiguous, we typically look for guidance in any interpretation made by the agency that promulgated the regulation in question. We are aware of two statements published by the SEC that offer informal interpretations of Rule 14a-8(i)(8). The first is a statement appearing in the amicus brief that the SEC filed in this case at our request. The second interpretation is contained in a statement the SEC published in 1976, the last time the SEC revised the election exclusion. Neither of these interpretations has the force of law. But, while agency interpretations that lack the force of law do not warrant deference when they interpret ambiguous *statutes*, they do normally warrant deference when they interpret ambiguous *regulations*.

In its amicus brief, the SEC interprets Rule 14a-8(i)(8) as permitting the exclusion of shareholder proposals that "would result in contested elections." The SEC explains that "[f]or purposes of Rule 14a-8, a proposal would result in a contested election if it is a means either to campaign for or against a director nominee or to require a company to include shareholder-nominated candidates in the company's proxy materials." Under this interpretation, a proxy access bylaw proposal like AFSCME's would be excludable under Rule 14a-8(i)(8) because it "is a means to require AIG to include shareholder-nominated candidates in the company's proxy materials." However, that interpretation is plainly at odds with the interpretation the SEC made in 1976.

In that year, the SEC amended Rule 14a-8(i)(8) in an effort to clarify the purpose of the existing election exclusion. The SEC explained that "with respect to corporate elections, [] Rule 14a-8 is not the proper means for conducting campaigns or effecting reforms in elections of that nature [i.e., "corporate, political or other elections to office"], *since other proxy rules, including Rule 14a-11, are applicable thereto.*" Proposed Amendments to Rule 14a-8, Exchange Act Release No. 34-12598, 41 Fed.Reg. 29,982, 29,9845 (proposed July 7, 1976) (emphasis added) ("1976 Statement"). The district court opinion quoted the 1976 Statement but omitted the italicized language and concluded that shareholder proposals were not intended to be used to accomplish any type of election reform. Clearly, however, that cannot be what the 1976 Statement means. Indeed, when the SEC finally adopted the revision of Rule 14a-8(i)(8) four months after publication of the 1976 Statement, it explained that it was rejecting a previous proposed rule (which would have authorized the exclusion of proposals that "relate[] to a corporate, political or other election to office") in favor of the current version (which authorizes the exclusion of proposals that simply "relate[] to an election") so as to avoid creating "the erroneous belief that the Commission intended to expand the scope of the existing exclusion to cover proposals dealing with matters previously held not excludable by the Commission, such as cumulative voting rights, general qualifications for directors, and political contributions by the issuer." Adoption of Amendments Relating to Proposals by Security Holders, Exchange Act Release No. 34-129999, 41 Fed.Reg. 52,994, 52,998 (Nov. 22, 1976) ("1976 Adoption"). And yet, all three of these shareholder proposal topics — cumulative voting rights, general qualifications for directors, and political contributions — fit comfortably within the category "election reform."

In its amicus brief, the SEC places a slightly different gloss on the 1976 Statement than did the district court. The SEC reads the 1976 Statement as implying that the purpose of Rule 14a-8(i)(8) is to authorize the exclusion of proposals that seek to effect, not election reform in general, but only certain types of election reform, namely those to which "other proxy rules, including Rule 14a-11," are generally applicable. In 1976, Rule 14a-11 was essentially the equivalent of current Rule 14a-12, which requires certain disclosures where a solicitation is made "for the purpose of opposing" a solicitation by any other person "with respect to the election or removal of directors." 17 C.F.R. § 240.14a-12(c). The SEC reasons that, based on the 1976 Statement, "a proposal may be excluded pursuant to Rule 14a-8(i)(8) if it would result in an immediate election contest (e.g., by making a director nomination for a particular meeting) or would set up a process for shareholders to conduct an election contest in the future by requiring the company to include shareholder director nominees in the company's proxy materials for subsequent meetings."

We agree with the SEC that, based on the 1976 Statement, shareholder proposals can be excluded under the election exclusion if they would result in an immediate election contest. . . .

By contrast, a proxy solicitation seeking to add a proxy access amendment to the corporate bylaws does not involve opposing solicitations dealing with "the election or removal of directors," and therefore Rule 14a-12, or, equivalently, the former Rule 14a-11, would not apply to a proposal seeking to accomplish the same end. Thus, we cannot agree with the second half of the SEC's interpretation of the 1976 Statement: that a proposal may be excluded under Rule 14a8-(i)(8) if it would simply establish a process for shareholders to wage a future election contest.

The 1976 Statement clearly reflects the view that the election exclusion is limited to shareholder proposals used to oppose solicitations dealing with an identified board seat in an upcoming election and rejects the somewhat broader interpretation that the election exclusion applies to shareholder proposals that would institute procedures making such election contests more likely. The SEC suggested as much when, four months after its 1976 Statement, it explained that the scope of the election exclusion does not cover shareholder proposals dealing with matters such as cumulative voting and general director requirements, both of which have the potential to increase the likelihood of election contests. *See* 1976 Adoption, 41 Fed.Reg. at 52,998.

That the 1976 statement adopted this narrower view of the election exclusion finds further support in the fact that it was also the view that the Division adopted for roughly sixteen years following publication of the SEC's 1976 Statement. It was not until 1990 that the Division first signaled a change of course by deeming excludable proposals that *might* result in contested elections, even if the proposal only purports to alter general procedures for nominating and electing directors.[7]

Because the interpretation of Rule 14a-8(i)(8) that the SEC advances in its amicus brief—that the election exclusion applies to proxy access bylaw proposals—conflicts with the 1976 Statement, it does not merit the usual deference we would reserve for an agency's interpretation of its own regulations. The SEC has not provided, nor to our knowledge has it or the Division ever provided, reasons for its changed position regarding the excludability of proxy access bylaw proposals. Although the SEC has substantial discretion to adopt new interpretations of its own regulations in light of, for example, changes in the capital markets or even simply because of a shift in the Commission's regulatory approach, it nevertheless has a "duty to explain its departure from prior norms." Atchison, T. & S.F. Ry. Co v. Wichita Bd. of Trade, 412 U.S. 800, 808 (1973) (citing Sec. of Agric. v. United States, 347 U.S. 645, 652-53 (1954)).

In its amicus submission, the SEC fails to so much as acknowledge a changed position, let alone offer a reasoned analysis of the change. The amicus brief is

---

7. Even then, the Division's position was far from clear-cut. Between 1990 and 1998, the Division continued to issue intermittently no-action letters adopting its prior distinction between procedures governing elections generally and those dealing with specific election contests. Since roughly 1998, the Division has consistently adopted the position expressed in the AIG No-Action Letter, which is the same position the SEC advances in its amicus brief.

curiously silent on any Division action prior to 1990 and characterizes the intermittent post-1990 no-action letters which continued to apply the pre-1990 position as mere "mistake[s]." While we by no means wish to imply that the Commission or the Division cannot correct analytical errors following a refinement of their thinking, we have a difficult time accepting the SEC's characterization of a policy that the Division consistently applied for sixteen years as nothing more than a "mistake." Although we are willing to afford the Commission considerable latitude in explaining departures from prior interpretations, its reasoned analysis must consist of something more than *mea culpas*.

Accordingly, we deem it appropriate to defer to the 1976 Statement, which represents the SEC's interpretation of the election exclusion the last time the Rule was substantively revised. We therefore interpret the election exclusion as applying to shareholder proposals that relate to a particular election and not to proposals that, like AFSCME's, would establish the procedural rules governing elections generally.

In deeming proxy access bylaw proposals non-excludable under Rule 14a-8(i)(8), we take no side in the policy debate regarding shareholder access to the corporate ballot. There might be perfectly good reasons for permitting companies to exclude proposals like AFSCME's, just as there may well be valid policy reasons for rendering them non-excludable. However, Congress has determined that such issues are appropriately the province of the SEC, not the judiciary.

CONCLUSION

For the foregoing reasons, we reverse the judgment of the district court and remand the case for entry of judgment in favor AFSCME.

***

After AFSCME v. AIG was decided, the SEC immediately announced that it would engage in rule-making in response to the Second Circuit. Its ultimate reaction represents a resounding affirmation of the status quo *ante*, sprinkled with a good deal of umbrage:

SHAREHOLDER PROPOSALS RELATING TO THE ELECTION OF DIRECTORS

SEC Release No. 34-56914
Dec. 6, 2007

Supplementary Information: We are adopting an amendment to Rule 14a-8(i)(8) under the Securities Exchange Act of 1934.

I. BACKGROUND

A. PURPOSE OF THE RULE 14A-8(i)(8) Exclusion

On July 27, 2007, the Commission published for comment the proposed amendment to Rule 14a-8(i)(8) that we are adopting today to address the uncertainty resulting from a recent decision of the U.S. Court of Appeals for the Second Circuit that did not defer to the agency's longstanding interpretation of the Rule.

Rule 14a-8, which creates a procedure under which shareholders may present certain proposals in the company's proxy materials, does not require the inclusion of any proposal that "relates to an election for membership on the company's board of directors or analogous governing body." The proper functioning of Rule 14a-8(i)(8) is particularly critical to assuring that investors receive adequate disclosure in election contests, and that they benefit from the full protection of the antifraud provisions of the securities laws. Because the inclusion of shareholder nominees for director in a company's proxy materials normally would create a contested election of directors, the protections of the proxy solicitation rules designed to provide investors with full and accurate disclosure are of vital importance in this context. An interpretation of Rule 14a-8(i)(8) that resulted in the Rule being used as a means to include shareholder nominees in company proxy materials would, in effect, circumvent the other proxy rules designed to assure the integrity of director elections. . . . [The SEC then described the company disclosures necessary to comply with Schedule 14A with respect to director nominations, and concluded:] These numerous protections of the federal proxy rules are triggered only by the presence of a solicitation made in opposition to another solicitation. Accordingly, were the election exclusion not available for proposals that would establish a process for the election of directors that circumvents the proxy disclosure rules, it would be possible for a person to wage an election contest without providing the disclosures required by the Commission's present rules governing such contests. Additionally, false and misleading disclosure in connection with such an election contest could potentially occur without liability under Exchange Act Rule 14a-9 for material misrepresentations made in a proxy solicitation. The Commission stated this rationale for the exclusion at the time it was proposed in 1976:

[T]he principal purpose of [Rule 14a-8(i)(8)] is to make clear, with respect to corporate elections, that Rule 14a-8 is not the proper means for *conducting campaigns or effecting reforms in* elections of that nature, since other proxy rules, including Rule 14a-11, are applicable thereto. (Emphasis added.)

Accordingly, the staff has determined that shareholder proposals that may result in a contested election — including those which establish a procedure to list shareholder-nominated director candidates in the company's proxy materials — fall within the election exclusion. We agree with this position and believe it is consistent with the explanation that the Commission gave.

The AIG opinion and subsequent SEC action were not the last chapter in proxy access for shareholders' board nominees, however. In 2009, Delaware passed DGCL § 112, its proxy access reform, which allows a Delaware company's bylaws to be amended to give shareholders proxy access, subject to such procedures or conditions as minimum share ownership, disclosure about the shareholder and its nominees, and so forth that an amended bylaw enacts. Shortly thereafter, the new Chair of the SEC, Mary Schapiro, stated that in light of the financial crisis the SEC would once again propose rules to permit shareholder proxy access, which it did in May 2009. While this proposed rule was again met with strong resistance from the business community, Dodd-Frank gave the SEC explicit authority to issue proxy access rules (authority it undoubtedly already had), and so on August 25, 2010, the SEC adopted two final proxy access rules.

One of these rules, Rule 14a-11, would have required companies to include shareholder-nominated directors in their proxy materials, as long as the nominating shareholders met certain conditions (holding at least 3 percent of the company's shares for at least three years). Rule 14a-8 was also revised to require companies to include shareholders' proposals to change company bylaws to allow proxy access (in essence, to adopt the holding of AFSCME v. AIG). Rule 14a-11 was immediately challenged in litigation by the Business Roundtable and the U.S. Chamber of Commerce as "arbitrary and capricious," who additionally claimed that the SEC had neglected its statutory requirement under § 3(f) of the 1934 Act to consider the effect of any rule it adopts on "efficiency, competition, and capital formation." In a stinging rebuke, the District of Columbia Circuit Court of Appeals agreed, issuing an opinion in which it seemingly culled the comments record itself and challenged the SEC's reading of the empirical evidence. Business Roundtable v. Securities and Exchange Commission, 647 F.3d 1144 (D.C. Cir. 2011) (Ginsburg, Circuit Judge). The proxy access issue remains unresolved, therefore, and will likely continue to produce activist shareholder pressure.

PROBLEM 6-2

A shareholder at Waste Disposal has submitted the following "majority vote" proposal:

> BE IT RESOLVED that the shareholders suggest that Waste adopt majority voting standards in its bylaws, such that each director who receives more "against" rather than "for" votes in annual elections will offer to resign, and the company will accept that resignation.

Would this proposal be excludable under Rule 14a-8(i)? What would be the basis for exclusion? What is the best argument for inclusion?

4. Social and Environmental Proposals

The other area of shareholder activism that has seen dramatic changes over the last two decades is social and environmental activism. Many social activist shareholder proposals are brought by members of the "socially responsible investment" (SRI) community, which are firms that evaluate companies on both financial and social and environmental grounds. SRI investors seek to screen the companies they invest in based on products or practices to avoid (typically some combination of cigarettes, gambling, alcohol, and military weapons; and some screen out contraceptives or abortifacients) or products or practices to promote (such as renewable energy, environmental sustainability, or a commitment to diversity in employment). In addition, SRI funds actively engage in discussions with companies in their portfolios to identify emerging risks from social, environmental, and human rights issues. As the corporate responsibility trend in business has strengthened, SRI investors are often seen as valuable partners with companies to help to develop best practices across a range of ESG (environmental, social, and governance) issues. Many SRI investors are members of religious communities or are fund managers who invest the pension funds of ministers, priests, rabbis, and nuns; others are members of labor unions or environmental organizations. Each of the big "fund families" (such as Fidelity, Magellan, and Vanguard) now has SRI funds. Altogether, assets in socially screened investment portfolios under professional management are $3.07 trillion in 2010, accounting for about 12 percent of money under professional management.

The shareholder proposal rule has been in force since the early 1940s, but the modern use of shareholder proposals to achieve social ends began in 1968, when religious investors and antiwar groups introduced a proxy resolution at the Dow Chemical Company asking it to amend its articles of incorporation to ensure that any napalm the company sold would not be used in the war in Vietnam. *See* Medical Comm. for Human Rights v. SEC, 432 F.2d 659, 661-662 (D.C. Cir. 1970), *vacated as moot*, 404 U.S. 403 (1972). Social activists soon saw the potential power of this technique for working with companies to encourage greater social accountability, and so the number of such proposals introduced each year gradually increased. For decades social proposals generally got votes of between 2 and 3 percent, and corporate governance proposals did not fare much better. Yet shareholder activists justified continuing to bring the proposals as a means to engage top management in discussions about various social and corporate governance issues and as the only means to raise such issues with other shareholders. The leverage of agreeing to withdraw a potentially embarrassing proposal has been used in many cases to get companies to agree to various changes at the company or to produce information to activists, and so the SRI community tracks proposals that are withdrawn as well as the votes on proposals that go to the shareholders.

The last few years have seen a dramatic change in voting tallies, however, in part in reaction to numerous well-publicized corporate governance failures (such as at Enron, WorldCom, Tyco, and HealthSouth), in part in reaction to the financial crisis, and in part as a result of shareholder activists' increasing sophistication. Today the average vote on social and environmental proposals is 20 percent. While this may seem insignificant, consider that at Exxon-Mobil 20 percent of shares in 2002 were voted in favor of having the company issue a report on its strategic initiatives to produce sustainable energy. Given that Exxon-Mobil had 6 billion shares outstanding at that time, a 20 percent vote represents 1.2 billion shares. These proposals are also gaining new allies, such as members of the Rockefeller family who announced in April 2008 that they had sponsored shareholder resolutions at Exxon-Mobil calling on the company to split the CEO and Chairman of the board, and to make greater efforts to develop renewable sources of energy. In another development, some large mutual fund families are starting to vote for social and environmental proposals, especially those related to hydraulic fracturing (average mutual fund vote 34 percent), coal combustion waste (32 percent), and disclosure of political contributions (25 percent). The two largest fund families, Vanguard and Fidelity, abstain as a voting strategy on all social and environmental proposals.

That some mutual funds are now voting with SRI shareholders was no doubt affected by a rule change in 2003, when the SEC promulgated a rule under the

Investment Company Act of 1940, Rule 30b1-4, requiring mutual fund managers by August 31, 2004, to disclose how they voted on every shareholder proposal at every company in their portfolio. This rule for proxy transparency was proposed by labor and SRI funds, and fiercely fought by the large fund families (Fidelity, Magellan, TIAA-CREF, and Vanguard, for instance), presumably in part because many previously undisclosed conflicts of interest will now be subject to scrutiny. That is, many mutual funds earn a significant part of their revenue managing the pensions of individual companies, some of which they may hold shares of in their investment portfolios. Thus, it is unlikely that the funds will vote against management's interests on shareholder proposals, since the companies can threaten to take their pension business elsewhere. So, rather than acting as shareholders' agents in voting, many mutual fund managers vote with a company's management. As proxy voting disclosure creates transparency, these conflicts of interest have been exposed, and the trend toward higher votes on shareholder proposals has continued — certainly on corporate governance proposals. On a number of issues, the average support as a percentage of votes cast was over 50 percent: majority voting rules for the election of directors (average was 56 percent); declassifying boards (61 percent); rescinding supermajority voting rules for extraordinary transactions (71 percent); requiring shareholder approval for golden parachutes (61 percent); and getting rid of poison pills or requiring a shareholder vote (58 percent).

Shareholders' developing power within the corporate governance relationship can be seen in the results of one of the AFL-CIO's Center for Working Capital and other labor pension funds' major recent efforts: to ensure that voting matters. By 2007, there were approximately 450 corporate governance proposals brought, many targeting executive pay, options back-dating, and voting rules. A substantial percentage passed, as above, with particularly successful issues in that year being proposals to give shareholders a non-binding "say on pay," as in the United Kingdom, and proposals seeking commitments from companies to institute policies ensuring that directors who do not receive a majority vote in elections will step down. This latter issue arises from the corporate "plurality voting" rules under which the directors receiving the highest number of positive votes are elected — but shares in which voting authority is withheld are ignored, and there is no option to "vote no!" Still, in reaction to labor's shareholder activism, 58 percent of the companies in the S&P 500 have now adopted majority vote bylaw changes so that a director must receive a majority of votes cast to be elected.

Given companies' understandable preference for maintaining control of the agenda and the message at the annual meeting, the major battleground for shareholder proposals is whether the shareholders can force the company, under Rule 14a-8, to include their proposal and supporting statement in the company's proxy statement as we've seen in the proxy access arena. Rule 14a-8(i), Question 9, identifies 13 reasons that companies can lawfully use to exclude shareholder proposals. Some of the most important reasons companies use include the following:

(1) *The proposal is improper under state law:* Shareholders may not command directors to do something; they must recommend or suggest action. This limitation arises

because state law provides that a public company must be managed by or under the directors, so infringements on the scope of their managerial authority are not permitted.

(5) *The proposal is not relevant:* If a proposal relates to less than 5 percent of a company's total assets or less than 5 percent of its net earnings or gross sales, it can be excluded, unless it raises significant social policy issues related to the company's business. Thus, in Lovenheim v. Iroquois Brands, Ltd., 618 F. Supp. 554 (D. C. 1985), the District Court for the District of Columbia held that the Iroquois Brands food-importing company could not exclude a resolution asking the company to stop importing pâté de foie gras, given concerns for the way the geese were force-fed to produce the pâté, even though Iroquois Brands had pâté sales of $79,000, on which it had a net loss of $3,121, as compared to annual revenues of $141 million, with $6 million in annual profits. The court ruled as it did because the ethical treatment of animals raised important social policy concerns that were related to a product the company sold, so the proposal could not be excluded.

(7) *The proposal relates to ordinary business/management functions:* If a proposal relates to operational details of how to run the business, it can be excluded, but proposals raising important public policy issues may not be excluded on this basis. The line between these two categories is constantly shifting, depending on which issues are currently a matter of public debate. For instance, while hiring decisions are ordinary business, a company's policy of discrimination on the basis of sexual preference in hiring would not be ordinary business today (but was for a time under the Cracker Barrel no-action letter, since repudiated by the SEC). This reason for excluding proposals is one of the most frequently used, and fought over.

(8) *The proposal relates to elections:* Companies may exclude proposals nominating candidates to the board or relating to elections. Some shareholder activists have been quite critical of this reason to exclude shareholder proposals, claiming that it further entrenches unresponsive management and self-perpetuating boards of directors. As a result of an increasing number of institutional investors that have tried to get election-related proposals on the agenda, such as proposed bylaw amendments to change the nomination process for the board, the SEC began a study in 2003 of the nominating and elections process.

PROBLEM 6-3

The following shareholder proposal, titled "Shareholder Proposal on Majority Votes Co-Sponsored by the Connecticut Retirement and Trust Funds Submitted on Behalf of the New York City Pension Funds by William C. Thompson, Jr., Comptroller, City of New York," was submitted to Waste Disposal for inclusion in the company's proxy statement. ***On what bases might Waste argue that the proposal is excludable? As a tactical matter, should the company seek a no-action position, or should they negotiate with the shareholders and seek withdrawal of the proposal?***

WHEREAS, in 2002, Congress, the SEC, and the stock exchanges, recognizing the urgent need to restore public trust and confidence in the capital markets, acted to strengthen accounting regulations, to improve corporate financial disclosure, independent oversight of auditors, and the independence and effectiveness of corporate boards; and

WHEREAS, we believe these reforms, albeit significant steps in the right direction, have not adequately addressed shareholder rights and the accountability of directors of corporate boards to the shareholders who elect them; and

WHEREAS, we believe the reforms have not addressed a major concern of institutional investors — the continuing failure of numerous boards of directors to adopt shareholder proposals on important corporate governance reforms despite being supported by increasing large majorities of the totals of shareholder votes cast for and against the proposals;

NOW, THEREFORE, BE IT RESOLVED: That the shareholders request the Board of Directors to adopt a policy that establishes a process and procedures for adopting shareholder proposals that are presented in the company's proxy statement, and are supported by more than 50 percent of the combined total of shares voted FOR and AGAINST such proposals, at an annual meeting of the company.

At minimum, the policy should require the Board of Directors to take the following actions:

(1) Following the official tabulation and certification of the votes, the Board of Directors will communicate directly with the proponents of such proposals to pursue constructive dialogue and agreement on the proposals. If no agreement is reached with the proponents, 60 days prior to the deadline set by the company for receiving shareholder proposals for the next annual meeting, the board will act on the proposals as follows:

(i) With respect to proposals on corporate governance reforms that would require amendments to the certificate of incorporation or bylaws, the board will propose such amendments, in the company's proxy statement, for the consideration and vote of the shareholders at the next annual meeting.

(ii) If approval of the amendments to the certificate of incorporation or bylaws require more than a simple majority vote, the board of directors will propose, for the consideration and vote for the shareholders, amendments lowering the required vote thresholds to a simple majority of the votes case for and against.

(iii) If the amendments, as presented by the Board, are supported by more than 50 percent of the combined totals of the shares voted FOR and AGAINST, the Board, at that annual meeting, will adopt the amendments.

(iv) With respect to shareholder proposals that sought the Board's adoption of governance or social policy reforms that the Board can adopt without violating the company's certificate of incorporation or bylaws, the board will adopt such shareholder proposals before the next annual meeting of the company.

PROBLEM 6-4

A shareholder of Waste Disposal has submitted the following proposal:

BE IT RESOLVED that the Board of Directors report to shareholders (at reasonable cost and omitting proprietary information) by the end of the calendar year, the risk management structure, staffing and reporting lines of the institution and how it is integrated into their business model and across all the operations of the company's business lines.

Would this proposal be excludable under Rule 14a-8(i)? What would be the basis for exclusion? What is the best argument for inclusion?

5.   Liability for Misleading Proxy Disclosure

Congress adopted mandatory disclosure as its preferred regulatory approach to protect shareholders' voting rights. And yet, if the information that a company discloses is not complete, or is not fully accurate, then it is worse than useless in empowering shareholders in the corporate governance relationship. As a result, in Rule 14a-9 the SEC has defined a cause of action for false or misleading proxy statements, and shareholders have an implied private right of action to bring claims under that Rule. *See* J.I. Case Co. v. Borak, 377 U.S. 426 (1964).

In general, it is a violation of Rule 14a-9 for a company to make a false statement of material fact or to omit to state material facts in its proxy statements. The key concept, then, is whether misstatements or omissions were of "material" facts. "Materiality" is an intellectual workhorse in securities regulation, defining both issuers' disclosure obligations *ex ante* and causes of action for securities fraud *ex post*. The definition of a "material fact" was set out in the leading case of TSC Industries v. Northway, 426 U.S. 438 (1976), as information "a reasonable shareholder would consider important in deciding how to vote." As the Court stated, "[p]ut another way, there must be a substantial likelihood that the disclosure of the omitted fact would have been viewed by the reasonable investor as having significantly altered the 'total mix' of information made available." *TSC Indus.*, 426 U.S. at 449. Whether a misstatement or omission is of a "material fact" is an inherently fact-specific inquiry, since it is necessary to examine the total mix of information available at any given time to answer the question.

In general, financial facts concerning the value of securities or the value of a transaction are material. Moreover, while it is generally true that facts concerning companies' environmental policies or social practices (such as their use of sweatshop labor or of bribes to get business) have not routinely been held to be material, today, with a growing number of investors screening their investments for such social and environmental practices, even these social and political facts can be held to be material, as in United Paperworkers International Union v. International Paper Co., 985 F.2d 1190 (2d Cir. 1993). The following problem shows the difficulty of trying to simplify the concept of "materiality" into a bright-line rule. Discussions with securities lawyers confirm that making decisions on whether information is material or not, and thus needs to be disclosed, is the most difficult part of their job. Indeed, often the problem is difficult because the lawyer views the information as material and counsels disclosing it, which the client resists because of concerns over the business impact of disclosure: if the information is likely to be considered significant to a reasonable shareholder, it is thus considered to be material.

PROBLEM 6-5

In early 2012, Waste Disposal was not in an enviable condition. It had lost 20 percent of its business due to the general slowdown in the economy, and political resistance to its strategy to expand global waste collection had solidified. Notwithstanding this discouraging statistical picture, Waste president Gerald Keegan was approached in early 2012 by top officers at Astoria Federal Recycling (Astoria), and asked whether Waste was interested in being acquired.

Astoria indicated that it would be willing to pay $18 per share for all of Waste's outstanding stock, subject to the usual due diligence. ("Due diligence" is a process whereby a buying company examines the selling company's books and records and interviews numerous employees of the selling company to assure itself that the company is worth buying, and at what price. Due diligence is done after a confidentiality agreement is negotiated so that the potential buying company cannot misuse the information it gathers.)

The next day, Keegan received a phone call from Thomas O'Brian, vice chairman of North Fork Reclamation (North Fork). O'Brian indicated that North Fork was also interested in acquiring Waste, for approximately $19 per share, subject to the usual due diligence. Keegan told O'Brian that Waste was not planning to merge and that he was unwilling to talk to O'Brian under any circumstances. The same day Keegan informed the Waste board about the Astoria offer and the North Fork expression of interest; the board authorized him to continue discussions with Astoria. Thus, Keegan continued to negotiate with Astoria, including the terms of a confidentiality order for the due diligence process, and on the terms of future employment for himself and other members of the board if the transaction went forward.

Eventually Astoria solidified its offer at $18.94 per share, and Waste prepared proxy documents to conduct a shareholder vote on the merger proposal. During the two to three weeks that had elapsed, North Fork had written numerous letters indicating its interest in a potential acquisition at $19.00 per share, or even higher, conditioned on due diligence. One day before the Waste board voted to accept Astoria's offer, North Fork was contacted by Waste's investment bank and asked if $19.00 per share was its best offer, to which North Fork replied, "Yes, until such time as we would be allowed to go in and conduct due diligence. Then we might go to $19.50."

The proxy statement that went out to the Waste shareholders for their approval of the merger with Astoria described the $18.94 per share Astoria offer as a fair price. At that time Waste stock was trading at approximately $12.00 per share. The proxy statement also described negotiations with "another organization," and stated that the other organization's offer price was $19.00; that Waste had asked the other organization to increase its price "and it declined to do so." The proxy statement failed to state that:

1. The other organization (North Fork) was a serious, motivated institution that already owned a substantial stake in Waste and had the financial ability to compete with Astoria on a level playing field if allowed to; and
2. The board may have preferred Astoria to North Fork because North Fork was not prepared to offer employment to Waste board members, including Keegan, and Astoria was.

Do the shareholders have a cause of action for material misstatements or omissions under Rule 14a-9?

CHAPTER
7

Duty of Care

MOTIVATING HYPOTHETICAL

BurgAlliance, Inc. is one of America's largest financial institutions. It was formed through one of the largest mergers in history when Burg Banking Inc. combined with Nomad Alliance Inc. BurgAlliance has established itself as a leader in the worldwide financial market, with offices in over 100 countries and accounts for over 200 million individuals. BurgAlliance stock is often seen as a safe investment for steady long-term gains and is often included in IRA and 401(k) portfolios.

Corporate directors often are viewed as "agents" in an economic sense. That is, directors do not serve their own interests, but rather the interests of a "principal." There is some debate among courts and academics as to the identity of the principal in this relationship: Is it the corporation, the shareholders, or the corporation and its shareholders together? Indeed, different professors using this book may have different views on the correct answer to that question. We challenge students to read the materials in the following chapters with a view to developing their own considered opinions.

Like the legal agents we studied in Chapter 1, directors owe various duties to their principals. Following the lead of the courts, we organize these duties under two grand headings: the duty of care and the duty of loyalty. Despite the apparent simplicity of these headings, the underlying concepts are complex and varied. In this chapter, we focus on the many aspects of the duty of care.

A.   DIRECTORS' DUTY OF CARE AND THE BUSINESS JUDGMENT RULE

Directors' duties were first developed by courts as a matter of common law. Only within the past 30 years have those duties been defined in most incorporation statutes. The Model Business Corporation Act (Model Act) first included a statement of the duty of care in 1974. *Report of Committee on Corporate Laws: Changes in the Model Business Corporation Act*, 30 Bus. Law. 501, 504-505 (1975). The

Delaware General Corporation Law (DGCL) still does not contain any general statement of directors' duties. In Delaware such duties are strictly judge-made. This section explores the directors' duty of care.

Directors are subject to a duty of care that on the surface is similar to the duty of care imposed in tort law because it flows from the same fundamental principle — namely, that a person who undertakes an action that places others at risk of injury is under a duty to act carefully and is liable for the failure to do so. In the corporate context, the duty of care generally asks whether directors have made decisions that injure the corporation. The potential liability risk from a breach of this duty is near zero in the corporate context, however, because of a powerful effect of the "business judgment rule." The significance of the business judgment rule in limiting the liability risk of directors was described by Judge Ralph Winter as follows:

> While it is often stated that corporate directors and officers will be liable for negligence in carrying out their corporate duties, all seem agreed that such a statement is misleading. Whereas an automobile driver who makes a mistake in judgment as to speed or distance injuring a pedestrian will likely be called upon to respond in damages, a corporate officer who makes a mistake in judgment as to economic conditions, consumer tastes or production line efficiency will rarely, if ever, be found liable for damages suffered by the corporation. Whatever the terminology, the fact is that liability is rarely imposed upon corporate directors or officers simply for bad judgment and this reluctance to impose liability for unsuccessful business decisions has been doctrinally labeled the business judgment rule.

Joy v. North, 692 F.2d 880, 885 (2d Cir. 1982).

But why would courts be reluctant to impose liability in the corporate context? Common justifications for the business judgment rule are that it avoids judicial interference in areas where judges have no expertise, and it encourages directors to serve by limiting their exposure to liability. These rationales for the business judgment rule are important, but do not tell the whole story. Consider other contexts: The law does not limit the liability of doctors whose treatment decisions turn out badly, or of home builders whose buildings collapse, and yet each of these is an area where judges have no expertise. Implicit in the business judgment rule is a policy judgment that permitting shareholders to enforce liability against directors for decisions that turn out badly is not a good idea. But why not?

Chancellor Allen presents his view in the following case. Chancellor Allen wrote the *Gagliardi* opinion just before he left the bench to become a faculty member at the New York University School of Law. With the exception of the classic Dodge v. Ford Motor Co. case, discussed in the last section of this chapter, all of the cases in this chapter were decided in Delaware. Over the past two decades, many states have adopted a statutory statement of the duty of care based on the Model Act. Although the Model Act first included such a statement in 1974, it did not attempt to codify the business judgment rule until 1998, when it bifurcated the standards applicable to corporate directors between "standards of conduct" (the duty of care) and "standards of liability" (the business judgment rule). *See* Model Act §§ 8.30-8.31. Cases arising under the Model Act have traditionally been analyzed in a manner similar to the Delaware cases, and they often cite major Delaware cases as precedents. Thus, we can see the importance of Delaware cases on this topic, even in jurisdictions adopting the Model Act.

GAGLIARDI v. TRIFOODS INTERNATIONAL, INC.

683 A.2d 1049
Court of Chancery of Delaware
July 19, 1996

ALLEN, Chancellor.

Currently before the Court is a motion to dismiss a shareholders action against the directors of TriFoods International, Inc. and certain partnerships and individuals that own stock in TriFoods. In broadest terms the motion raises the question, what must a shareholder plead in order to state a derivative claim to recover corporate losses allegedly sustained by reason of "mismanagement" unaffected by directly conflicting financial interests?

Plaintiff, Eugene Gagliardi, is the founder of the TriFoods, Inc. and in 1990 he induced certain persons to invest in the company by buying its stock. In 1993 he was removed as Chairman of the board and his employment with the company terminated. He continues to own approximately 13% of the company's common stock. The business of the company has, according to the allegations of the complaint, deteriorated very badly since Mr. Gagliardi's ouster. . . .

COUNT IV: NEGLIGENT MISMANAGEMENT

This count, which is asserted against all defendants, alleges that "implementation of their grandiose scheme for TriFoods' future growth . . . in only eighteen months destroyed TriFoods." Plaintiff asserts that the facts alleged, which sketch that "scheme" and those results, constitute mismanagement and waste.

The allegations of Count IV are detailed. They assert most centrally that prior to his dismissal Gagliardi disagreed with Hart [former president of TriFoods] concerning the wisdom of TriFoods manufacturing its products itself and disagreed strongly that the company should buy a plant in Pomfret, Connecticut and move its operations to that state. Plaintiff thought it foolish (and he alleges that it was negligent judgment) to borrow funds . . . for that purpose.

Plaintiff also alleges that Hart caused the company to acquire and fit-out a research or new product facility in Chadds Ford, Pennsylvania, which "duplicated one already available and under lease to Designer Foods [the predecessor name of TriFoods], and which was, therefore, a further waste of corporate assets."

Next, it is alleged that "defendants either acquiesced in or approved a reckless or grossly negligent sales commission to build volume."

Next, it is alleged that "Hart and the other defendants caused TriFoods to purchase [the exclusive rights to produce and sell a food product known as] Steak-umms from Heinz in April 1994." The price paid compared unfavorably with a transaction in 1980 in which this product had been sold and which earlier terms are detailed. "Defendants recklessly caused TriFoods to pay $15 million for Steak-umms alone (no plant, no equipment, etc.) which was then doing annual sales of only $28 million."

Next, it is alleged that "Hart caused TriFoods . . . to pay $125,000 to a consultant for its new name, logo and packaging."

Next, it is alleged that Hart destroyed customer relationships by supplying inferior products.

Next, it is alleged that "Hart refused to pay key manufacturers and suppliers . . . thus injuring TriFoods' trade relations." . . .

Do these allegations of Count IV state a claim upon which relief may be granted? In addressing that question, I start with what I take to be an elementary precept of corporation law: in the absence of facts showing self-dealing or improper motive, a corporate officer or director is not legally responsible to the corporation for losses that may be suffered as a result of a decision that an officer made or that directors authorized in good faith. There is a theoretical exception to this general statement that holds that some decisions may be so "egregious" that liability for losses they cause may follow even in the absence of proof of conflict of interest or improper motivation. The exception, however, has resulted in no awards of money judgments against corporate officers or directors in this jurisdiction and, to my knowledge, only the dubious holding in this Court of Gimbel v. Signal Companies, Inc., (Del. Ch.), 316 A.2d 599, *aff'd* (Del. Supr.) 316 A.2d 619 (1974), seems to grant equitable relief in the absence of a claimed conflict or improper motivation. Thus, to allege that a corporation has suffered a loss as a result of a lawful transaction, within the corporation's powers, authorized by a corporate fiduciary acting in a good faith pursuit of corporate purposes, does not state a claim for relief against that fiduciary no matter how foolish the investment may appear in retrospect.

The rule could rationally be no different. Shareholders can diversify the risks of their corporate investments. Thus, it is in their economic interest for the corporation to accept in rank order all positive net present value investment projects available to the corporation, starting with the highest risk adjusted rate of return first. Shareholders don't want (or shouldn't rationally want) directors to be risk averse. Shareholders' investment interests, across the full range of their diversifiable equity investments, will be maximized if corporate directors and managers honestly assess risk and reward and accept for the corporation the highest risk adjusted returns available that are above the firm's cost of capital.

But directors will tend to deviate from this rational acceptance of corporate risk if in authorizing the corporation to undertake a risky investment, the directors must assume some degree of personal risk relating to ex post facto claims of derivative liability for any resulting corporate loss.

Corporate directors of public companies typically have a very small proportionate ownership interest in their corporations and little or no incentive compensation. Thus, they enjoy (as residual owners) only a very small proportion of any "upside" gains earned by the corporation on risky investment projects. If, however, corporate directors were to be found liable for a corporate loss from a risky project on the ground that the investment was too risky (foolishly risky! stupidly risky! egregiously risky! — you supply the adverb), their liability would be joint and several for the whole loss (with I suppose a right of contribution). Given the scale of operation of modern public corporations, this stupefying disjunction between risk and reward for corporate directors threatens undesirable effects. Given this disjunction, only a very small probability of director liability based on "negligence", "inattention", "waste", etc., could induce a board to avoid authorizing risky investment projects to any extent! Obviously, it is in the shareholders' economic interest to offer sufficient protection to directors from liability for negligence, etc., to allow directors to conclude that, as a practical matter, there is no risk that, if they act in good faith and meet minimal proceduralist standards of attention, they can face liability as a result of a business loss.

The law protects shareholder investment interests against the uneconomic consequences that the presence of such second-guessing risk would have on director action and shareholder wealth in a number of ways. It authorizes corporations to pay for director and officer liability insurance and authorizes corporate indemnification in a broad range of cases, for example. But the first protection against a threat of sub-optimal risk acceptance is the so-called business judgment rule. That "rule" in effect provides that where a director is independent and disinterested, there can be no liability for corporate loss, unless the facts are such that no person could possibly authorize such a transaction if he or she were attempting in good faith to meet their duty. Saxe v. Brady, Del. Ch., 184 A.2d 602 (1962).

Thus, for example, it does not state a claim to allege that: (1) Hart caused the corporation to pay $125,000 to a consultant for the design of a new logo and packaging. On what possible basis might a corporate officer or director be put to the expense of defending such a claim? Nothing is alleged except that an expenditure of corporate funds for a corporate purpose was made. Whether that expenditure was wise or foolish, low risk or high risk is of no concern to this Court. What is alleged certainly does not bring the allegation to within shouting distance of the Saxe v. Brady principle. (2) Nor does an allegation that defendants acquiesced in a reckless commission structure "in order to build volume" state a claim; it alleges no conflicting interest or improper motivation, nor does it state facts that might come within the Saxe v. Brady principle. It alleges only an ordinary business decision with a pejorative characterization added. (3) The allegation of "duplication" of existing product research facilities similarly simply states a matter that falls within ordinary business judgment; that plaintiff regards the decision as unwise, foolish, or even stupid in the circumstances is not legally significant; indeed that others may look back on it and agree that it was stupid is legally unimportant, in my opinion. (4) That the terms of the purchase of "Steak-umms" seem to plaintiff unwise (especially when compared to the terms of a 1980 transaction involving that product) again fail utterly to state any legal claim. No self-interest, nor facts possibly disclosing improper motive or judgment satisfying the waste standard are alleged. Similarly, (5) the allegations of corporate loss resulting from harm to customer relations by delivery of poor product and (6) harm to supplier relations by poor payment practices, again state nothing that constitutes a legal claim. Certainly these allegations state facts that, if true, constitute either mistakes, poor judgment, or reflect hard choices facing a cash-pressed company, but where is the allegation of conflicting interest or suspect motivation? In the absence of such, where are the facts that, giving the pleader all reasonable inferences in his favor, might possibly make the Saxe v. Brady principle applicable? There are none. Nothing is alleged other than poor business practices. To permit the possibility of director liability on that basis would be very destructive of shareholder welfare in the long-term. . . .

Finally, . . . there is the allegation that despite warnings from plaintiff and despite the alleged fact that the Pomfret facility "was not reasonably fit" for the purpose, the directors authorized the purchase of the facility at a "grossly excessive" price in order to implement a business plan that would have the company manufacture some or all of its food products and that defendants caused the company to borrow substantial funds to accomplish that task. Once more there is no allegation of conflict of interest with respect to this transaction, nor is there any allegation of improper motivation in authorizing the transactions. There is, in effect, only an allegation that plaintiff believes the transaction represents poor business judgment and the conclusion that "no reasonable business person would have engaged in it." Thus this claim does attempt to plead the Saxe v. Brady test of corporate waste. . . .

For the foregoing reason Count IV of the amended complaint will be dismissed. . . .

PROBLEM 7-1

During the early 2000s, BurgAlliance avoided investing heavily in mortgages and mortgage-backed securities. When the housing bubble burst in 2008, BurgAlliance was in a good financial position while other banks around them began to fail. BurgAlliance saw the opportunity to buy up banks that were failing and took it, despite some analysts saying that the worst was far from over and that these banks were not a good investment at this time. The board of Burg Alliance assumed that the analysts were just being overly cautious because they had not predicted the housing market collapse and the financial crisis that went with it, and were now overcompensating.

It turned out that buying up the banks in the Fall of 2008 was not just a bad investment, it was a disastrous one. By buying up most of the failing banks, BurgAlliance took on more toxic debt than they realized, and it almost crippled the company. In 2010, investors started selling their BurgAlliance stock at an alarming rate and the company was struggling to gain back the public's confidence. In an attempt to cut costs, the board of directors authorized the closure of 30 percent of their offices.

Some of the remaining shareholders are interested in bringing a lawsuit against the directors for a breach of the duty of care. *How does the business judgment rule work into the analysis of this claim?*

B. THE DECISION-MAKING CONTEXT

The central teaching of *Gagliardi* is that courts will not second-guess the decisions of directors unless the process that generated those decisions is unsound. This is the essence of the business judgment rule. Chancellor Allen noted a "theoretical exception" to this rule for substantively "egregious" decisions, and we examine the law surrounding such decisions below under "The Waste Standard." Otherwise, generally speaking, the circumstances under which courts become suspicious of board decisions fall into two categories: (1) when directors are subject to a conflict of interest with respect to the challenged decision, courts review the decision under the standards developed under the duty of loyalty, and (2) when directors fail to gather the requisite information to make the challenged decision, courts review the decision under the "gross negligence" standard. We examine the duty of loyalty in Chapter 10, and we explore the "gross negligence" standard in the famous case of Smith v. Van Gorkom, immediately below.

In addition to the foregoing, courts have developed special standards of review for cases in which the board of directors did not actually make a decision — the so-called "oversight" cases, discussed below — as well as for cases involving mergers and acquisitions, which we cover in Chapters 12 and 13. The operation of the business judgment rule in those contexts is somewhat abstruse, so we will forgo any attempt to describe that briefly here and rely on our more thorough examination in those later sections. For the time being, we focus on Smith v. Van Gorkom, which illustrates the application of the duty of care and the business judgment rule to decision making in the context of a fundamental transaction, here the sale of a company. This is one of the few cases anywhere that imposes liability on board members based on breach of the duty of care, and it is therefore well known in corporate boardrooms.

SMITH v. VAN GORKOM

488 A.2d 858
Supreme Court of Delaware (en banc)
January 29, 1985

HORSEY, Justice (for the majority).

This appeal from the Court of Chancery involves a class action brought by shareholders of the defendant Trans Union Corporation ("Trans Union" or "the Company"), originally seeking rescission of a cash-out merger of Trans Union into the defendant New T Company ("New T"), a wholly-owned subsidiary of the defendant, Marmon Group, Inc. ("Marmon"). . . .

We hold: (1) that the Board's decision, reached September 20, 1980, to approve the proposed cash-out merger was not the product of an informed business judgment; (2) that the Board's subsequent efforts to amend the Merger Agreement and take other curative action were ineffectual, both legally and factually; and (3) that the Board did not deal with complete candor with the stockholders by failing to disclose all material facts, which they knew or should have known, before securing the stockholders' approval of the merger.

I. . . .

Trans Union was a publicly-traded, diversified holding company, the principal earnings of which were generated by its railcar leasing business. During the period here involved, the Company had a cash flow of hundreds of millions of dollars annually. However, the Company had difficulty in generating sufficient taxable income to offset increasingly large investment tax credits (ITCs). Accelerated depreciation deductions had decreased available taxable income against which to offset accumulating ITCs. The Company took these deductions, despite their effect on usable ITCs, because the rental price in the railcar leasing market had already impounded the purported tax savings.

In the late 1970's, together with other capital-intensive firms, Trans Union lobbied in Congress to have ITCs refundable in cash to firms which could not fully utilize the credit. During the summer of 1980, defendant Jerome W. Van Gorkom, Trans Union's Chairman and Chief Executive Officer, testified and lobbied in Congress for refundability of ITCs and against further accelerated depreciation. By the end of August, Van Gorkom was convinced that Congress would neither accept the refundability concept nor curtail further accelerated depreciation. . . .

On August 27, 1980, Van Gorkom met with Senior Management of Trans Union. Van Gorkom reported on his lobbying efforts in Washington and his desire to find a solution to the tax credit problem more permanent than a continued program of acquisitions. Various alternatives were suggested and discussed preliminarily, including the sale of Trans Union to a company with a large amount of taxable income.

Donald Romans, Chief Financial Officer of Trans Union, stated that his department had done a "very brief bit of work on the possibility of a leveraged buy-out." This work had been prompted by a media article which Romans had seen regarding a leveraged buy-out by management. The work consisted of a "preliminary study" of the cash which could be generated by the Company if it participated in a leveraged buy-out. As Romans stated, this analysis "was a very first and rough cut at seeing whether a cash flow would support what might be considered a high price for this type of transaction."

On September 5, at another Senior Management meeting which Van Gorkom attended, Romans again brought up the idea of a leveraged buy-out as a "possible strategic alternative" to the Company's acquisition program. Romans and Bruce S. Chelberg, President and Chief Operating Officer of Trans Union, had been working on the matter in preparation for the meeting. According to Romans: They did not "come up" with a price for the Company. They merely "ran the numbers" at $50 a share and at $60 a share with the "rough form" of their cash figures at the time. Their "figures indicated that $50 would be very easy to do but $60 would be very difficult to do under those figures." This work did not purport to establish a fair price for either the Company or 100% of the stock. It was intended to determine the cash flow needed to service the debt that would "probably" be incurred in a leveraged buy-out, based on "rough calculations" without "any benefit of experts to identify what the limits were to that, and so forth." These computations were not considered extensive and no conclusion was reached.

At this meeting, Van Gorkom stated that he would be willing to take $55 per share for his own 75,000 shares. He vetoed the suggestion of a leveraged buy-out by Management, however, as involving a potential conflict of interest for Management. Van Gorkom, a certified public accountant and lawyer, had been an officer of Trans Union for 24 years, its Chief Executive Officer for more than 17 years, and Chairman of its Board for 2 years. It is noteworthy in this connection that he was then approaching 65 years of age and mandatory retirement. . . .

Van Gorkom decided to meet with Jay A. Pritzker, a well-known corporate takeover specialist and a social acquaintance. However, rather than approaching Pritzker simply to determine his interest in acquiring Trans Union, Van Gorkom assembled a proposed per share price for sale of the Company and a financing structure by which to accomplish the sale. Van Gorkom did so without consulting either his Board or any members of Senior Management except one: Carl Peterson, Trans Union's Controller. Telling Peterson that he wanted no other person on his staff to know what he was doing, but without telling him why, Van Gorkom directed Peterson to calculate the feasibility of a leveraged buy-out at an assumed price per share of $55. Apart from the Company's historic stock market price,[5] and Van Gorkom's long association with Trans Union, the record is devoid of any competent evidence that $55 represented the per share intrinsic value of the Company.

Having thus chosen the $55 figure, based solely on the availability of a leveraged buy-out, Van Gorkom multiplied the price per share by the number of shares outstanding to reach a total value of the Company of $690 million. Van Gorkom told Peterson to use this $690 million figure and to assume a $200 million equity contribution by the buyer. Based on these assumptions, Van Gorkom directed Peterson to determine whether the debt portion of the purchase price could be paid off in five years or less if financed by Trans Union's cash flow as projected in the Five Year Forecast, and by the sale of certain weaker divisions identified in a study done for Trans Union by the Boston Consulting Group ("BCG study"). Peterson reported that, of the purchase price, approximately $50-80 million would remain outstanding after five years. Van Gorkom was disappointed, but decided to meet with Pritzker nevertheless.

Van Gorkom arranged a meeting with Pritzker at the latter's home on Saturday, September 13, 1980. Van Gorkom prefaced his presentation by stating to Pritzker: "Now as far as you are concerned, I can, I think, show how you can pay a substantial premium over the present stock price and pay off most of the loan in the first five years. . . . If you could pay $55 for this Company, here is a way in which I think it can be financed." Van Gorkom then reviewed with Pritzker his calculations based upon his proposed price of $55 per share. Although Pritzker mentioned $50 as a more attractive figure, no other price was mentioned. However, Van Gorkom stated that to be sure that $55 was the best price obtainable, Trans Union should be free to accept any better offer. Pritzker demurred, stating that his organization would serve as a "stalking horse" for an "auction contest" only if Trans Union would permit Pritzker to buy 1,750,000 shares of Trans Union stock at market price which Pritzker could then sell to any higher bidder. After further discussion on this point, Pritzker told Van Gorkom that he would give him a more definite reaction soon.

On Monday, September 15, Pritzker advised Van Gorkom that he was interested in the $55 cash-out merger proposal and requested more information on Trans Union. Van Gorkom agreed to meet privately with Pritzker, accompanied by Peterson, Chelberg, and Michael Carpenter, Trans Union's consultant from the Boston Consulting Group. The meetings took place on September 16 and 17. Van Gorkom was "astounded that events were moving with such amazing rapidity."

On Thursday, September 18, Van Gorkom met again with Pritzker. At that time, Van Gorkom knew that Pritzker intended to make a cash-out merger offer at Van Gorkom's proposed $55 per share. Pritzker instructed his attorney, a merger and acquisition specialist, to begin drafting merger documents. There was no further discussion of the $55 price. However, the number of shares of

5. The common stock of Trans Union was traded on the New York Stock Exchange. Over the five year period from 1975 through 1979, Trans Union's stock had traded within a range of a high of $39 1/2 and a low of $24 1/4. Its high and low range for 1980 through September 19 (the last trading day before announcement of the merger) was $38 1/4-$29 1/2.

Trans Union's treasury stock to be offered to Pritzker was negotiated down to one million shares; the price was set at $38 — 75 cents above the per share price at the close of the market on September 19. At this point, Pritzker insisted that the Trans Union Board act on his merger proposal within the next three days, stating to Van Gorkom: "We have to have a decision by no later than Sunday [evening, September 21] before the opening of the English stock exchange on Monday morning." Pritzker's lawyer was then instructed to draft the merger documents, to be reviewed by Van Gorkom's lawyer, "sometimes with discussion and sometimes not, in the haste to get it finished."

On Friday, September 19, Van Gorkom, Chelberg, and Pritzker consulted with Trans Union's lead bank regarding the financing of Pritzker's purchase of Trans Union. The bank indicated that it could form a syndicate of banks that would finance the transaction. On the same day, Van Gorkom retained James Brennan, Esquire, to advise Trans Union on the legal aspects of the merger. Van Gorkom did not consult with William Browder, a Vice-President and director of Trans Union and former head of its legal department, or with William Moore, then the head of Trans Union's legal staff.

On Friday, September 19, Van Gorkom called a special meeting of the Trans Union Board for noon the following day. He also called a meeting of the Company's Senior Management to convene at 11:00 A.M., prior to the meeting of the Board. No one, except Chelberg and Peterson, was told the purpose of the meetings. Van Gorkom did not invite Trans Union's investment banker, Salomon Brothers or its Chicago-based partner, to attend.

Of those present at the Senior Management meeting on September 20, only Chelberg and Peterson had prior knowledge of Pritzker's offer. Van Gorkom disclosed the offer and described its terms, but he furnished no copies of the proposed Merger Agreement. Romans announced that his department had done a second study which showed that, for a leveraged buy-out, the price range for Trans Union stock was between $55 and $65 per share. Van Gorkom neither saw the study nor asked Romans to make it available for the Board meeting.

Senior Management's reaction to the Pritzker proposal was completely negative. No member of Management, except Chelberg and Peterson, supported the proposal. Romans objected to the price as being too low;[6] he was critical of the timing and suggested that consideration should be given to the adverse tax consequences of an all-cash deal for low-basis shareholders; and he took the position that the agreement to sell Pritzker one million newly-issued shares at market price would inhibit other offers, as would the prohibitions against soliciting bids and furnishing inside information to other bidders. Romans argued that the Pritzker proposal was a "lock up" and amounted to "an agreed merger as opposed to an offer." Nevertheless, Van Gorkom proceeded to the Board meeting as scheduled without further delay.

Ten directors served on the Trans Union Board, five inside (defendants Bonser, O'Boyle, Browder, Chelberg, and Van Gorkom) and five outside (defendants Wallis, Johnson, Lanterman, Morgan and Reneker). All directors were present at the meeting, except O'Boyle, who was ill. Of the outside directors,

---

6. Van Gorkom asked Romans to express his opinion as to the $55 price. Romans stated that he "thought the price was too low in relation to what he could derive for the company in a cash sale, particularly one which enabled us to realize the values of certain subsidiaries and independent entities."

four were corporate chief executive officers and one was the former Dean of the University of Chicago Business School. None was an investment banker or trained financial analyst. All members of the Board were well informed about the Company and its operations as a going concern. They were familiar with the current financial condition of the Company, as well as operating and earnings projections reported in the recent Five Year Forecast. The Board generally received regular and detailed reports and was kept abreast of the accumulated investment tax credit and accelerated depreciation problem.

Van Gorkom began the Special Meeting of the Board with a twenty-minute oral presentation. Copies of the proposed Merger Agreement were delivered too late for study before or during the meeting. He reviewed the Company's ITC and depreciation problems and the efforts theretofore made to solve them. He discussed his initial meeting with Pritzker and his motivation in arranging that meeting. Van Gorkom did not disclose to the Board, however, the methodology by which he alone had arrived at the $55 figure, or the fact that he first proposed the $55 price in his negotiations with Pritzker.

Van Gorkom outlined the terms of the Pritzker offer as follows: Pritzker would pay $55 in cash for all outstanding shares of Trans Union stock upon completion of which Trans Union would be merged into New T Company, a subsidiary wholly-owned by Pritzker and formed to implement the merger; for a period of 90 days, Trans Union could receive, but could not actively solicit, competing offers; the offer had to be acted on by the next evening, Sunday, September 21; Trans Union could only furnish to competing bidders published information, and not proprietary information; the offer was subject to Pritzker obtaining the necessary financing by October 10, 1980; if the financing contingency were met or waived by Pritzker, Trans Union was required to sell to Pritzker one million newly-issued shares of Trans Union at $38 per share.

Van Gorkom took the position that putting Trans Union "up for auction" through a 90-day market test would validate a decision by the Board that $55 was a fair price. He told the Board that the "free market will have an opportunity to judge whether $55 is a fair price." Van Gorkom framed the decision before the Board not as whether $55 per share was the highest price that could be obtained, but as whether the $55 price was a fair price that the stockholders should be given the opportunity to accept or reject.

Attorney Brennan advised the members of the Board that they might be sued if they failed to accept the offer and that a fairness opinion was not required as a matter of law.

Romans attended the meeting as chief financial officer of the Company. He told the Board that he had not been involved in the negotiations with Pritzker and knew nothing about the merger proposal until the morning of the meeting; that his studies did not indicate either a fair price for the stock or a valuation of the Company; that he did not see his role as directly addressing the fairness issue; and that he and his people "were trying to search for ways to justify a price in connection with such a [leveraged buy-out] transaction, rather than to say what the shares are worth." Romans testified:

> I told the Board that the study ran the numbers at 50 and 60, and then the subsequent study at 55 and 65, and that was not the same thing as saying that I have a valuation of the company at X dollars. But it was a way — a first step towards reaching that conclusion.

Romans told the Board that, in his opinion, $55 was "in the range of a fair price," but "at the beginning of the range."

Chelberg, Trans Union's President, supported Van Gorkom's presentation and representations. . . .

The Board meeting of September 20 lasted about two hours. Based solely upon Van Gorkom's oral presentation, Chelberg's supporting representations, Romans' oral statement, Brennan's legal advice, and their knowledge of the market history of the Company's stock, the directors approved the proposed Merger Agreement. However, the Board later claimed to have attached two conditions to its acceptance: (1) that Trans Union reserved the right to accept any better offer that was made during the market test period; and (2) that Trans Union could share its proprietary information with any other potential bidders. While the Board now claims to have reserved the right to accept any better offer received after the announcement of the Pritzker agreement (even though the minutes of the meeting do not reflect this), it is undisputed that the Board did not reserve the right to actively solicit alternate offers.

The Merger Agreement was executed by Van Gorkom during the evening of September 20 at a formal social event that he hosted for the opening of the Chicago Lyric Opera. Neither he nor any other director read the agreement prior to its signing and delivery to Pritzker. . . .

On Monday, September 22, the Company issued a press release announcing that Trans Union had entered into a "definitive" Merger Agreement with an affiliate of the Marmon Group, Inc., a Pritzker holding company. Within 10 days of the public announcement, dissent among Senior Management over the merger had become widespread. Faced with threatened resignations of key officers, Van Gorkom met with Pritzker, who agreed to several modifications of the Agreement. Pritzker was willing to do so provided that Van Gorkom could persuade the dissidents to remain on the Company payroll for at least six months after consummation of the merger.

Van Gorkom reconvened the Board on October 8 and secured the directors' approval of the proposed amendments — sight unseen. The Board also authorized the employment of Salomon Brothers, its investment banker, to solicit other offers for Trans Union during the proposed "market test" period.

The next day, October 9, Trans Union issued a press release announcing: (1) that Pritzker had obtained "the financing commitments necessary to consummate" the merger with Trans Union; (2) that Pritzker had acquired one million shares of Trans Union common stock at $38 per share; (3) that Trans Union was now permitted to actively seek other offers and had retained Salomon Brothers for that purpose; and (4) that if a more favorable offer were not received before February 1, 1981, Trans Union's shareholders would thereafter meet to vote on the Pritzker proposal.

It was not until the following day, October 10, that the actual amendments to the Merger Agreement were prepared by Pritzker and delivered to Van Gorkom for execution. As will be seen, the amendments were considerably at variance with Van Gorkom's representations of the amendments to the Board on October 8; and the amendments placed serious constraints on Trans Union's ability to negotiate a better deal and withdraw from the Pritzker agreement. Nevertheless, Van Gorkom proceeded to execute what became the October 10 amendments to the Merger Agreement without conferring further with the Board members and apparently without comprehending the actual implications of the amendments. . . .

Salomon Brothers' efforts over a three-month period from October 21 to January 21 produced only one serious suitor for Trans Union — General Electric Credit Corporation ("GE Credit"), a subsidiary of the General Electric Company. However, GE Credit was unwilling to make an offer for Trans Union unless Trans Union first rescinded its Merger Agreement with Pritzker. When Pritzker refused, GE Credit terminated further discussions with Trans Union in early January.

In the meantime, in early December, the investment firm of Kohlberg, Kravis, Roberts & Co. ("KKR"), the only other concern to make a firm offer for Trans Union, withdrew its offer. . . .

On February 10, the stockholders of Trans Union approved the Pritzker merger proposal. Of the outstanding shares, 69.9% were voted in favor of the merger; 7.25% were voted against the merger; and 22.85% were not voted.

II.

We turn to the issue of the application of the business judgment rule to the September 20 meeting of the Board.

The Court of Chancery concluded from the evidence that the Board of Directors' approval of the Pritzker merger proposal fell within the protection of the business judgment rule. The Court found that the Board had given sufficient time and attention to the transaction, since the directors had considered the Pritzker proposal on three different occasions, on September 20, and on October 8, 1980 and finally on January 26, 1981. On that basis, the Court reasoned that the Board had acquired, over the four-month period, sufficient information to reach an informed business judgment on the cash-out merger proposal. . . .

The Court of Chancery made but one finding; *i.e.*, that the Board's conduct over the entire period from September 20 through January 26, 1981 was not reckless or improvident, but informed. . . .

Under Delaware law, the business judgment rule is the offspring of the fundamental principle, codified in 8 *Del. C.* § 141(a), that the business and affairs of a Delaware corporation are managed by or under its board of directors. In carrying out their managerial roles, directors are charged with an unyielding fiduciary duty to the corporation and its shareholders. *Loft, Inc. v. Guth*, Del.Ch., 2 A.2d 225 (1938), *aff'd*, Del.Supr., 5 A.2d 503 (1939). The business judgment rule exists to protect and promote the full and free exercise of the managerial power granted to Delaware directors. The rule itself "is a presumption that in making a business decision, the directors of a corporation acted on an informed basis, in good faith and in the honest belief that the action taken was in the best interests of the company." Thus, the party attacking a board decision as uninformed must rebut the presumption that its business judgment was an informed one.

The determination of whether a business judgment is an informed one turns on whether the directors have informed themselves "prior to making a business decision, of all material information reasonably available to them." Under the business judgment rule there is no protection for directors who have made "an unintelligent or unadvised judgment." A director's duty to inform himself in preparation for a decision derives from the fiduciary capacity in which he serves the corporation and its stockholders. Since a director is vested with the responsibility for the management of the affairs of the corporation, he must execute that duty with the recognition that he acts on behalf of others. Such obligation does not tolerate faithlessness or self-dealing. But fulfillment of the fiduciary function requires more than the mere absence of bad faith or fraud. Representation of the financial interests of others imposes on a director an affirmative duty to protect those interests and to proceed with a critical eye in assessing information of the type and under the circumstances present here.

Thus, a director's duty to exercise an informed business judgment is in the nature of a duty of care, as distinguished from a duty of loyalty. Here, there were no allegations of fraud, bad faith, or self-dealing, or proof thereof. Hence, it is presumed that the directors reached their business judgment in good faith, and considerations of motive are irrelevant to the issue before us.

The standard of care applicable to a director's duty of care has also been recently restated by this Court. In *Aronson, supra*, we stated:

> While the Delaware cases use a variety of terms to describe the applicable standard of care, our analysis satisfies us that under the business judgment rule director liability is predicated upon concepts of gross negligence. (footnote omitted)

We think the concept of gross negligence is also the proper standard for determining whether a business judgment reached by a board of directors was an informed one.

In the specific context of a proposed merger of domestic corporations, a director has a duty under 8 Del. C. § 251(b), along with his fellow directors, to act in an informed and deliberate manner in determining whether to approve an agreement of merger before submitting the proposal to the stockholders. Certainly in the merger context, a director may not abdicate that duty by leaving to the shareholders alone the decision to approve or disapprove the agreement. . . .

III.

. . . [T]he defendants contend that what the directors did and learned subsequent to September 20 and through January 26, 1981, was properly taken into account by the Trial Court in determining whether the Board's judgment was an informed one. We disagree with this *post hoc* approach.

The issue of whether the directors reached an informed decision to "sell" the Company on September 20, 1980 must be determined only upon the basis of the information then reasonably available to the directors and relevant to their decision to accept the Pritzker merger proposal. This is not to say that the directors were precluded from altering their original plan of action, had they done so in an informed manner. What we do say is that the question of whether the directors reached an informed business judgment in agreeing to sell the Company, pursuant to the terms of the September 20 Agreement presents, in reality, two questions: (A) whether the directors reached an informed business judgment on September 20, 1980; and (B) if they did not, whether the directors' actions taken subsequent to September 20 were adequate to cure any infirmity in their action taken on September 20. . . .

A

On the record before us, we must conclude that the Board of Directors did not reach an informed business judgment on September 20, 1980 in voting to "sell" the Company for $55 per share pursuant to the Pritzker cash-out merger proposal. Our reasons, in summary, are as follows:

The directors (1) did not adequately inform themselves as to Van Gorkom's role in forcing the "sale" of the Company and in establishing the per share purchase price; (2) were uninformed as to the intrinsic value of the Company; and (3) given these circumstances, at a minimum, were grossly negligent in approving the "sale" of the Company upon two hours' consideration, without prior notice, and without the exigency of a crisis or emergency.

As has been noted, the Board based its September 20 decision to approve the cash-out merger primarily on Van Gorkom's representations. None of the directors, other than Van Gorkom and Chelberg, had any prior knowledge that the purpose of the meeting was to propose a cash-out merger of Trans Union. No members of Senior Management were present, other than Chelberg, Romans and Peterson; and the latter two had only learned of the proposed sale an hour earlier. . . .

Without any documents before them concerning the proposed transaction, the members of the Board were required to rely entirely upon Van Gorkom's 20-minute oral presentation of the proposal. No written summary of the terms of the merger was presented; the directors were given no documentation to support the adequacy of $55 price per share for sale of the Company; and the Board had before it nothing more than Van Gorkom's statement of his understanding of the substance of an agreement which he admittedly had never read, nor which any member of the Board had ever seen.

Under 8 Del. C. § 141 (e), "directors are fully protected in relying in good faith on reports made by officers." The term "report" has been liberally construed to include reports of informal personal investigations by corporate officers. However, there is no evidence that any "report," as defined under § 141 (e), concerning the Pritzker proposal, was presented to the Board on September 20. Van Gorkom's oral presentation of his understanding of the terms of the proposed Merger Agreement, which he had not seen, and Romans' brief oral statement of his preliminary study regarding the feasibility of a leveraged buy-out of Trans Union do not qualify as § 141 (e) "reports" for these reasons: The former lacked substance because Van Gorkom was basically uninformed as to the essential provisions of the very document about which he was talking. Romans' statement was irrelevant to the issues before the Board since it did not purport to be a valuation study. At a minimum for a report to enjoy the status conferred by § 141 (e), it must be pertinent to the subject matter upon which a board is called to act, and otherwise be entitled to good faith, not blind, reliance. . . .

The defendants rely on the following factors to sustain the Trial Court's finding that the Board's decision was an informed one: (1) the magnitude of the premium or spread between the $55 Pritzker offering price and Trans Union's current market price of $38 per share; (2) the amendment of the Agreement as submitted on September 20 to permit the Board to accept any better offer during the "market test" period; (3) the collective experience and expertise of the Board's "inside" and "outside" directors; and (4) their reliance on Brennan's legal advice that the directors might be sued if they rejected the Pritzker proposal. We discuss each of these grounds seriatim:

(1)

A substantial premium may provide one reason to recommend a merger, but in the absence of other sound valuation information, the fact of a premium alone does not provide an adequate basis upon which to assess the fairness of an offering price. Here, the judgment reached as to the adequacy of the premium was based on a comparison between the historically depressed Trans Union market price and the amount of the Pritzker offer. Using market price as a basis for concluding that the premium adequately reflected the true value of the Company was a clearly faulty, indeed fallacious, premise, as the defendants' own evidence demonstrates.

The record is clear that before September 20, Van Gorkom and other members of Trans Union's Board knew that the market had consistently undervalued the worth of Trans Union's stock, despite steady increases in the Company's operating income in the seven years preceding the merger. . . .

The parties do not dispute that a publicly-traded stock price is solely a measure of the value of a minority position and, thus, market price represents only the value of a single share. Nevertheless, on September 20, the Board assessed the adequacy of the premium over market, offered by Pritzker, solely by comparing it with Trans Union's current and historical stock price.

Indeed, as of September 20, the Board had no other information on which to base a determination of the intrinsic value of Trans Union as a going concern. As of September 20, the Board had made no evaluation of the Company designed to value the entire enterprise, nor had the Board ever previously considered selling the Company or consenting to a buy-out merger. Thus, the adequacy of a premium is indeterminate unless it is assessed in terms of other competent and sound valuation information that reflects the value of the particular business.

Despite the foregoing facts and circumstances, there was no call by the Board, either on September 20 or thereafter, for any valuation study or documentation of the $55 price per share as a measure of the fair value of the Company in a cash-out context. . . .

We do not imply that an outside valuation study is essential to support an informed business judgment; nor do we state that fairness opinions by independent investment bankers are required as a matter of law. Often insiders familiar with the business of a going concern are in a better position than are outsiders to gather relevant information; and under appropriate circumstances, such directors may be fully protected in relying in good faith upon the valuation reports of their management. . . .

The record also establishes that the Board accepted without scrutiny Van Gorkom's representation as to the fairness of the $55 price per share for sale of the Company — a subject that the Board had never previously considered. The Board thereby failed to discover that Van Gorkom had suggested the $55 price to Pritzker and, most crucially, that Van Gorkom had arrived at the $55 figure based on calculations designed solely to determine the feasibility of a leveraged buy-out.[19] No questions were raised either as to the tax implications of a cash-out merger or how the price for the one million share option granted Pritzker was calculated. . . .

None of the directors, Management or outside, were investment bankers or financial analysts. Yet the Board did not consider recessing the meeting until a later hour that day (or requesting an extension of Pritzker's Sunday evening deadline) to give it time to elicit more information as to the sufficiency of the offer, either from inside Management (in particular Romans) or from Trans Union's own investment banker, Salomon Brothers, whose Chicago specialist in merger and acquisitions was known to the Board and familiar with Trans Union's affairs.

(2)

This brings us to the post-September 20 "market test" upon which the defendants ultimately rely to confirm the reasonableness of their September 20 decision to accept the Pritzker proposal. In this connection, the directors present a two-part argument: (a) that by making a "market test" of Pritzker's $55 per share offer a condition of their September 20 decision to accept his offer, they cannot be found to have acted impulsively or in an uninformed manner on September 20; and (b) that the adequacy of the $17 premium for sale of the Company was conclusively established over the following 90 to 120 days by the most reliable evidence available — the marketplace. . . .

Again, the facts of record do not support the defendants' argument. There is no evidence: (a) that the Merger Agreement was effectively amended to give the Board freedom to put Trans Union up for auction sale to the highest bidder; or (b) that a public auction was in fact permitted to occur. . . .

(3)

The directors' unfounded reliance on both the premium and the market test as the basis for accepting the Pritzker proposal undermines the defendants' remaining contention that the Board's collective experience and sophistication was a sufficient basis for finding that it reached its September 20 decision with informed, reasonable deliberation. . . .

(4)

Part of the defense is based on a claim that the directors relied on legal advice rendered at the September 20 meeting by James Brennan, Esquire, who was present at Van Gorkom's request. Unfortunately, Brennan did not appear and testify at trial even though his firm participated in the defense of this action. . . .

---

19. As of September 20 the directors did not know: that Van Gorkom had arrived at the $55 figure alone, and subjectively, as the figure to be used by Controller Peterson in creating a feasible structure for a leveraged buy-out by a prospective purchaser; that Van Gorkom had not sought advice, information or assistance from either inside or outside Trans Union directors as to the value of the Company as an entity or the fair price per share for 100% of its stock; that Van Gorkom had not consulted with the Company's investment bankers or other financial analysts; that Van Gorkom had not consulted with or confided in any officer or director of the Company except Chelberg; and that Van Gorkom had deliberately chosen to ignore the advice and opinion of the members of his Senior Management group regarding the adequacy of the $55 price.

Several defendants testified that Brennan advised them that Delaware law did not require a fairness opinion or an outside valuation of the Company before the Board could act on the Pritzker proposal. If given, the advice was correct. However, that did not end the matter. Unless the directors had before them adequate information regarding the intrinsic value of the Company, upon which a proper exercise of business judgment could be made, mere advice of this type is meaningless; and, given this record of the defendants' failures, it constitutes no defense here. . . .

We conclude that Trans Union's Board was grossly negligent in that it failed to act with informed reasonable deliberation in agreeing to the Pritzker merger proposal on September 20; and we further conclude that the Trial Court erred as a matter of law in failing to address that question before determining whether the directors' later conduct was sufficient to cure its initial error. . . .

V.

The defendants ultimately rely on the stockholder vote of February 10 for exoneration. The defendants contend that the stockholders' "overwhelming" vote approving the Pritzker Merger Agreement had the legal effect of curing any failure of the Board to reach an informed business judgment in its approval of the merger.

The parties tacitly agree that a discovered failure of the Board to reach an informed business judgment in approving the merger constitutes a voidable, rather than a void, act. Hence, the merger can be sustained, notwithstanding the infirmity of the Board's action, if its approval by majority vote of the shareholders is found to have been based on an informed electorate. The disagreement between the parties arises over: (1) the Board's burden of disclosing to the shareholders all relevant and material information; and (2) the sufficiency of the evidence as to whether the Board satisfied that burden. . . .

The settled rule in Delaware is that "where a majority of fully informed stockholders ratify action of even interested directors, an attack on the ratified transaction normally must fail." . . . The question of whether shareholders have been fully informed such that their vote can be said to ratify director action "turns on the fairness and completeness of the proxy materials submitted by the management to the shareholders." In *Lynch v. Vickers Energy Corp.* this Court [has] held that corporate directors owe to their stockholders a fiduciary duty to disclose all facts germane to the transaction at issue in an atmosphere of complete candor. We defined "germane" in the tender offer context as all "information such as a reasonable stockholder would consider important in deciding whether to sell or retain stock." In reality, "germane" means material facts.

Applying this standard to the record before us, we find that Trans Union's stockholders were not fully informed of all facts material to their vote on the Pritzker Merger and that the Trial Court's ruling to the contrary is clearly erroneous. We list the material deficiencies in the proxy materials:

(1) The fact that the Board had no reasonably adequate information indicative of the intrinsic value of the Company, other than a concededly depressed market price, was without question material to the shareholders voting on the merger. . . .

(2) We find false and misleading the Board's characterization of the Romans report in the Supplemental Proxy Statement. The Supplemental Proxy stated:

> At the September 20, 1980 meeting of the Board of Directors of Trans Union, Mr. Romans indicated that while he could not say that $55.00 per share was an unfair price, he had prepared a preliminary report which reflected that the value of the Company was in the range of $55.00 to $65.00 per share.

Nowhere does the Board disclose that Romans stated to the Board that his calculations were made in a "search for ways to justify a price in connection with" a leveraged buy-out transaction, "rather than to say what the shares are worth," and that he stated to the Board that his conclusion thus arrived at "was not the same thing as saying that I have a valuation of the Company at X dollars." . . .

(3) We find misleading the Board's references to the "substantial" premium offered. . . . [T]he Board did not disclose its failure to assess the premium offered in terms of other relevant valuation techniques, thereby rendering questionable its determination as to the substantiality of the premium over an admittedly depressed stock market price. . . .

For the foregoing reasons, we conclude that the director defendants breached their fiduciary duty of candor by their failure to make true and correct disclosures of all information they had, or should have had, material to the transaction submitted for stockholder approval.

VI.

To summarize: we hold that the directors of Trans Union breached their fiduciary duty to their stockholders (1) by their failure to inform themselves of all information reasonably available to them and relevant to their decision to recommend the Pritzker merger; and (2) by their failure to disclose all material information such as a reasonable stockholder would consider important in deciding whether to approve the Pritzker offer. . . .

On remand, the Court of Chancery shall conduct an evidentiary hearing to determine the fair value of the shares represented by the plaintiffs' class, based on the intrinsic value of Trans Union on September 20, 1980. . . . Thereafter, an award of damages may be entered to the extent that the fair value of Trans Union exceeds $55 per share. . . .

Reversed and remanded for proceedings consistent herewith.

McNEILLY, Justice, dissenting.

The majority opinion reads like an advocate's closing address to a hostile jury. And I say that not lightly. Throughout the opinion great emphasis is directed only to the negative, with nothing more than lip service granted the positive aspects of this case. . . .

The majority has spoken and has effectively said that Trans Union's Directors have been the victims of a "fast shuffle" by Van Gorkom and Pritzker. That is the beginning of the majority's comedy of errors. The first and most important error made is the majority's assessment of the directors' knowledge of the affairs of

Trans Union and their combined ability to act in this situation under the protection of the business judgment rule.

Trans Union's Board of Directors consisted of ten men, five of whom were "inside" directors and five of whom were "outside" directors. . . . At the time the merger was proposed the inside five directors had collectively been employed by the Company for 116 years and had 68 years of combined experience as directors. [With one exception, the "outside" directors] were all chief executive officers of Chicago based corporations that were at least as large as Trans Union. The five "outside" directors had 78 years of combined experience as chief executive officers, and 53 years cumulative service as Trans Union directors. . . .

Directors of this caliber are not ordinarily taken in by a "fast shuffle." I submit they were not taken into this multi-million dollar corporate transaction without being fully informed and aware of the state of the art as it pertained to the entire corporate panorama of Trans Union. True, even directors such as these, with their business acumen, interest and expertise, can go astray. I do not believe that to be the case here. These men knew Trans Union like the back of their hands and were more than well qualified to make on the spot informed business judgments concerning the affairs of Trans Union, including a 100% sale of the corporation. Lest we forget, the corporate world of then and now operates on what is so aptly referred to as "the fast track." These men were at the time an integral part of that world, all professional business men, not intellectual figureheads. . . .

PROBLEM 7-2

When the board of directors of BurgAlliance made the decision to invest in the failing banks, the directors acknowledged the uniqueness of the situation. Despite their many years of business experience, none of them had ever seen a situation like this one. They knew that the strategy could be harmful to the company, perhaps even devastating, but they also recognized that the economic crisis might pose a once-in-a-lifetime opportunity.

After the investments soured and the BurgAlliance stock price plummeted, The Wall Street Journal published an article about the strategy, calling it "reckless." The article detailed how the board decided to "bet the company" with only limited data about potential harms.

If shareholders brought an action for breach of fiduciary duty, how would a court evaluate claims based on "recklessness"?

C. THE WASTE STANDARD

To this point, we have focused on procedural aspects of the duty of care — that is, what procedures the board must adopt when making decisions or monitoring events at the corporation. But are there instances in which the substance of a board decision is so awful that directors may be liable for breach of the duty of care? Even if the decisions were not motivated by self-interest? Even where there is no evidence that the managers failed to gather information? Courts often discuss this prospect by invoking the concept of "waste" of the corporation's assets. Other courts speak in terms of the rationality of the decision. An influential formulation by the Delaware Supreme Court states that "[a] board of directors enjoys a presumption of sound business judgment, and its decisions will not be disturbed if they can be attributed to any rational business purpose." Sinclair Oil Corp. v. Levien, 280 A.2d 717, 720 (Del. 1971).

Today this claim of "waste" often comes up in the context of executive compensation. Over the past few decades, the levels of executive compensation in the United States increased dramatically. Between 1960 and 1992, average CEO compensation in the United States grew from 50 times the average worker's salary to about 150 times that salary. These levels became politically controversial during the recessionary years of the early 1990s, leading the Securities and Exchange Commission (SEC) to require companies to disclose more specific information on compensation of the chief executive officer (CEO) and the four most highly compensated executives, including deferred compensation such as stock options. Ironically, this disclosure may have led to even higher CEO salaries, as compensation experts and consultants used the increased financial transparency to convince CEOs that they were underpaid compared to other executives in the same field. The Internal Revenue Service (IRS) has also tried to limit companies' incentives to pay exorbitant salaries by limiting the deductibility of compensation over $1 million, unless the compensation is tied to performance goals. 26 U.S.C. § 162m (1999). Despite these legislative efforts, a recent survey of executive compensation showed that CEOs of 350 large U.S. companies had a median salary and bonuses in excess of $1.5 million annually. When stock options are added, the figures become truly eye-popping, with some CEOs reaping hundreds of millions of dollars.

Executive compensation levels in the United States are also much higher than those in Europe or Japan, where the highest-paid executives typically earn only 20 to 30 times the earnings of the lowest-paid workers in the company. By comparison, by 2002 many top executives in the United States earned over 500 times the earnings of the lowest-paid workers in their companies. Indeed, executive compensation became an important issue in the 1998 merger between Daimler-Benz of Germany and Chrysler Corporation of the United States because the Chrysler CEO was paid a total compensation of about $11 million per year — about 200 times the salary of the average Chrysler worker — while his German counterpart, Jürgen Schrempp, was paid about one-fifth of that amount — only about 20 times the earnings of the average Daimler-Benz worker.

Increasing levels of executive compensation have been widely attributed to the desire of boards to retain proven (if not spectacular) executives in the face of a relative scarcity of top corporate managers. Given pliant boards, derivative plaintiffs have recently entered the fray, claiming that "excessive" salaries are a waste of corporate assets and thus a breach of the directors' duty of care. Such a claim was one of the many claims at issue in the litigation at the Disney Corporation, which gave rise to the important decision you'll read in the next Section. In that litigation, plaintiffs challenged the terms of an employment agreement with Michael Ovitz as president of the Disney Corporation, under which Mr. Ovitz ultimately collected remuneration valued at $140 million (including stock options) for 14 months' employment. In February 2000 the Delaware

Supreme Court upheld most of the Court of Chancery's first opinion dismissing the claims against the board for breach of the duty of care with respect to the decision-making process, waste, and breach of the duty of loyalty, but dismissed with leave to amend. The court did not find the case to be an easy one, stating that:

> This is potentially a very troubling case on the merits. On the one hand, it appears from the Complaint that: (a) the compensation and termination payout for Ovitz were exceedingly lucrative, if not luxurious, compared to Ovitz' value to the Company; and (b) the processes of the boards of directors in dealing with the approval and termination of the Ovitz Employment Agreement were casual, if not sloppy and perfunctory. On the other hand, the Complaint is so inartfully drafted that it was properly dismissed under our pleading standards for derivative suits. From what we can ferret out of this deficient pleading, the processes of the Old Board [approving the employment agreement] and the New Board [approving Ovitz's termination on favorable grounds] were hardly paradigms of good corporate governance practices. Moreover, the sheer size of the payout to Ovitz, as alleged, pushes the envelope of judicial respect for the business judgment of directors in making compensation decisions. Therefore, both as to the processes of the two Boards and the waste test, this is a close case.
>
> But our concerns about lavish executive compensation and our institutional aspirations that boards of directors of Delaware corporations live up to the highest standards of good corporate practices do not translate into a holding that these plaintiffs have set forth particularized facts [necessary] . . . under our law and our pleading requirements [for derivative litigation, which is the process by which fiduciary duty claims are brought].

Brehm v. Eisner, 746 A.2d 244, 249 (Del. 2000).

With respect to the waste claim, the Court described its analysis as follows:

> The Complaint, in sum, contends that the Board committed waste by agreeing to the very lucrative payout to Ovitz under the non-fault termination provision because it had no obligation to him [since it could have terminated him "for cause"], thus taking the Board's decision outside the protection of the business judgment rule. Construed most favorably to plaintiffs, the Complaint contends that, by reason of the New Board's available arguments of resignation and good cause, it had the leverage to negotiate Ovitz down to a more reasonable payout than that guaranteed by his Employment Agreement. But the Complaint fails on its face to meet the waste test because it does not allege with particularity facts tending to show that no reasonable business person would have made the decision that the New Board made under these circumstances.

Brehm, 746 A.2d at 262.

Still, the Court dismissed with leave to amend, while seemingly skeptical about the shareholder plaintiffs' ability to overcome the formidable protections of the business judgment rule regarding the terms of compensation. As you will see in Chapter 9, plaintiffs were able to plead facts about the processes of decision making sufficient to overcome the business judgment rule presumption and take the case to trial. Ultimately, though, Disney prevailed, in an important decision that carefully considered the place of good faith within directors' fiduciary obligations.

PROBLEM 7-3

BurgAlliance was lucky in one regard in 2008, however: Because many major banks had knowingly or unknowingly "bet their company," the U.S. government ultimately needed to step in and provide emergency money to the banks in various ways, such as loans, grants, share purchases, relaxed Federal Reserve discount lending, and so forth. In the year ended September 30, 2009, BurgAlliance received $45 billion of government support. At the same time, following the worst financial results in its history, BurgAlliance CEO Jamie Blankfiend received total compensation of $27.8 million, much of it derived from guaranteed bonuses in his employment contract. When questioned about such high compensation for such dismal performance, a company spokesperson told a reporter for the Financial Times, apparently without being ironic, that competitive compensation packages were necessary, because "otherwise the firm would be unable to retain its top talent."

Outraged, social activist shareholders filed a resolution in 2010 seeking to tie Mr. Blankfiend's compensation to the social and political aspects of BurgAlliance's activities, both in the United States and around the world. The proxy resolution included the following language:

> Whereas: We believe that financial, social and environmental criteria should be taken into account in setting compensation for corporate officers. Public scrutiny on compensation is intensifying, with serious concerns being expressed about the widening chasm between the salaries of top corporate officers and their employees as well as contract workers, and a financial system that privatizes gains but socializes losses. . . .
>
> RESOLVED: Shareholders request that the Board institute an Executive Compensation Review, and prepare a report available to shareholders by October 2010 with a summary of the results and recommended changes in practice. The review should cover pay, benefits, perks, stock options, and special arrangements in the compensation packages for all top officers.
>
> The review should address:
>
> 1. Ways to link our company's executive compensation more closely to financial performance and social and environmental criteria.
> 2. Comparison of compensation packages for company officers with both the lowest and average wages for BurgAlliance's contract workers in the United States and low-wage workers in Bangalore, India, both countries where it has established call centers.
> 3. Whether a cap should be placed on compensation packages for officers to prevent our company from paying excessive compensation.

This resolution was defeated, but 14.8 percent of BurgAlliance shares (approximately 47 million shares) voted in favor of it.

Assume that shareholders are regrouping to reconsider how they might constrain the board of directors in compensating Mr. Blankfiend. *What avenues seem productive for the shareholders? Does the fact that nearly 15 percent of shares were voted to connect Mr. Blankfiend's executive compensation to the social performance of the firm indicate any potential leverage for shareholders? Would you recommend that shareholders seek to pass a binding bylaw amendment requiring a specified increase in the value of BurgAlliance's stock or a specified social performance prior to Mr. Blankfiend being paid any bonuses?*

Would shareholders be well-advised to bring a cause of action for breach of the duty of care against the board, alleging waste?

D. THE SHAREHOLDER PRIMACY NORM

We conclude our study of the duty of care by looking at the question, "To whom do directors owe their duty of care?" The Model Act requires directors to make decisions in the interests of "the corporation," and many cases state that the duty is owed to "the corporation and its shareholders." Despite the implication that "the corporation" is something more than just "the shareholders," courts have often concluded that "the shareholders" are the primary beneficiaries of the duty of care. This aspect of the duty of care is often called the "shareholder primacy norm."

The most commonly quoted judicial statement of the shareholder primacy norm was set out by the Michigan Supreme Court in Dodge v. Ford Motor Co., 170 N.W. 668 (Mich. 1919). This case involved a dispute between Henry Ford and two of the minority shareholders in the Ford Motor Company, John and Horace Dodge. The Dodge brothers owned a Detroit machine shop that supplied parts to the Ford Motor Company and had been instrumental in the early success of Ford's Model T automobile. In exchange for their contributions to the company, the brothers had been awarded 10 percent of the stock, on which they were paid millions of dollars in dividends over a period of about four years. In 1913 the Dodge brothers decided to stop supplying Ford Motor with parts and to begin building competing automobiles.

In an effort to raise capital for their venture, they attempted to sell their shares in the Ford Motor Company, but Henry Ford owned 58 percent of the stock. As with most closely held corporations, there was no market for a minority stake, especially since the majority owner was perceived as being quite eccentric. Further complicating matters for the Dodge brothers, Henry Ford decided to discontinue any special dividends to the shareholders. Ford justified the decision on grounds that he wanted to reduce the price of the Model T (even though he was selling cars as fast as he could manufacture them) and to dedicate large amounts of money to a massive expansion of the company's manufacturing capabilities. In his own words, he wanted to "employ still more men, to spread the benefits of the industrial system to the greatest possible number." Following board approval of Ford's plans, the Dodge brothers sued to force payment of dividends and to enjoin the plans to expand production and cut the prices of Ford's cars. The resulting decision favored the Dodge brothers on the dividend issue, and the court articulated its now famous version of the shareholder primacy norm:

> The difference between an incidental humanitarian expenditure of corporate funds for the benefit of the employees, like the building of a hospital for their use and the employment of agencies for the betterment of their condition, and a general purpose and plan to benefit mankind at the expense of others, is obvious. There should be no confusion (of which there is evidence) of the duties which Mr. Ford conceives that he and the stockholders owe to the general public and the duties which in law he and his codirectors owe to protesting, minority stockholders. A business corporation is organized and carried on primarily for the profit of the stockholders. The powers of the directors are to be employed for that end. The discretion of directors is to be exercised in the choice of means to attain that end, and does not extend to a change in the end itself, to the reduction of profits, or to

the nondistribution of profits among stockholders in order to devote them to other purposes.

At the same time, the court left intact Ford's plan to cut the price of the Model T and expand the company's production facilities. *Dodge* and similar cases have been widely interpreted as suggesting that directors must favor the interests of shareholders over nonshareholders (such as employees of the corporation and the public). Yet, given the business judgment rule, directors clearly have discretion to consider nonshareholder interests in decision making, so long as there is some connection with long-term shareholder interests involved in their exercise of discretion.

Given the shareholder primacy norm, capitalism in the United States and Great Britain is sometimes referred to as "shareholder capitalism," meaning that the overriding goal of the company, beyond producing needed goods and services, is to maximize shareholder wealth. In contrast, continental European and Japanese versions of capitalism are sometimes referred to as "stakeholder capitalism," because the managers of companies are understood to have broader obligations to balance shareholders' interests with the interests and concerns of employees, the community, and society as a whole. In stakeholder capitalism, these broader obligations are implemented as a part of statutory law, such as in the German system of codetermination, which gives employees places on the supervisory boards of public corporations, or as in the French corporate code, which directs managers to operate companies in the "general social interest."

The modern operation of the shareholder primacy norm in the United States is nicely illustrated in the following case, which shows that the connection between board action and long-term shareholder interests can be quite attenuated. The case involves a large charitable contribution by the Occidental Petroleum Corporation. The facts bear close attention, for you can see in them how a large transaction gets structured, what kinds of advisers are involved, and how a board protects itself from future challenges to its decision making.

KAHN v. SULLIVAN

Delaware Supreme Court
594 A.2d 48
January 10, 1992

HOLLAND, Justice.

This is an appeal from the approval of the settlement of one of three civil actions brought in the Court of Chancery by certain shareholders of Occidental Petroleum Corporation ("Occidental"). Each civil action challenged a decision by Occidental's board of directors (the "Board"), through a special committee of Occidental's outside directors ("the Special Committee"), to make a charitable donation. The purpose of the charitable donation was to construct and fund an art museum. . . .

We have concluded that the decision of the Court of Chancery must be affirmed.

Occidental is a Delaware corporation. According to the parties, Occidental has about 290 million shares of stock outstanding which are held by approximately 495 thousand shareholders. For the year ending December 31, 1988, Occidental had assets of approximately twenty billion dollars, operating revenues of twenty billion dollars and pre-tax earnings of $574 million. Its corporate headquarters are located in Los Angeles, California.

At the time of his death on December 10, 1990, Dr. [Armand] Hammer was Occidental's chief executive officer and the chairman of its board of directors. Since the early 1920's, Dr. Hammer had been a serious art collector. When Dr. Hammer died, he personally and The Armand Hammer Foundation (the "Foundation"), owned three major collections of art (referred to in their entirety as "the Art Collection"). The Art Collection, valued at $300-$400 million included: "Five Centuries of Art," more than 100 works by artists such as Rembrandt, Rubens, Renoir and Van Gogh; the Codex Hammer, a rare manuscript by Leonardo da Vinci; and the world's most extensive private collection of paintings, lithographs and bronzes by the French satirist Honore Daumier.

For many years, the Board has determined that it is in the best interest of Occidental to support and promote the acquisition and exhibition of the Art Collection. Through Occidental's financial support and sponsorship, the Art Collection has been viewed by more than six million people in more than twenty-five American cities and at least eighteen foreign countries. The majority of those exhibitions have been in areas where Occidental has operations or was negotiating business contracts. Occidental's Annual Reports to its shareholders have described the benefits and good will which it attributes to the financial support that Occidental has provided for the Art Collection.

Dr. Hammer enjoyed an ongoing relationship with the Los Angeles County Museum of Art ("LACMA") for several decades. In 1968, Dr. Hammer agreed to donate a number of paintings to LACMA, as well as funds to purchase additional art. For approximately twenty years thereafter, Dr. Hammer both publicly and privately expressed his intention to donate the Art Collection to LACMA. However, Dr. Hammer and LACMA had never entered into a binding agreement to that effect. Nevertheless, LACMA named one of its buildings the Frances and Armand Hammer Wing in recognition of Dr. Hammer's gifts.

Occidental approved of Dr. Hammer's decision to permanently display the Art Collection at LACMA. In fact, it made substantial financial contributions to facilitate that display. In 1982, for example, Occidental paid two million dollars to expand and refurbish the Hammer Wing at LACMA.

In 1987, Dr. Hammer presented Daniel N. Belin, Esquire ("Belin"), the president of LACMA's Board of Trustees, with a thirty-nine page proposed agreement which set forth the terms upon which Dr. Hammer would permanently locate the Art Collection at LACMA. LACMA and Dr. Hammer tried, but were unable to reach a binding agreement. Consequently, Dr. Hammer concluded that he would make arrangements for the permanent display of the Art Collection at a location other than at LACMA. On January 8, 1988, Dr. Hammer wrote a letter to Belin which stated that he had "decided to create my own museum to house" the Art Collection.

On January 19, 1988, at a meeting of the executive committee of Occidental's board of directors ("the Executive Committee"), Dr. Hammer proposed that Occidental, in conjunction with the Foundation, construct a museum for the Art Collection. After discussing Occidental's history of identification with the Art Collection, the Executive Committee decided that it was in Occidental's best interest to accept Dr. Hammer's proposal. The Executive Committee approved the negotiation of arrangements for the preliminary design and construction of an art museum. It would be located adjacent to Occidental's headquarters, on the site of an existing parking garage used by Occidental for its employees. The Executive Committee also decided that once the art museum project was substantially defined, a final proposal would be presented to the Board or the Executive Committee for approval and authorization.

The art museum concept was announced publicly on January 21, 1988. On February 11, 1988, the Board approved the Executive Committee's prior actions. Occidental informed its shareholders of the preliminary plan to construct The Armand Hammer Museum and Cultural Center of Art ("the Museum") in its 1987 Annual Report. In accordance with the January 19, 1988 resolutions passed by the Executive Committee, construction of a new parking garage for Occidental began in the fall of 1988. The Board approved a construction bond on November 10, 1988.

On December 15, 1988, the Board was presented with a detailed plan for the Museum proposal. The Board approved the concept and authorized a complete study of the proposal. Following the December 15th Board meeting, the law firm of Dilworth, Paxson, Kalish & Kauffman ("Dilworth") was retained by the Board to examine the Museum proposal and to prepare a memorandum addressing the issues relevant to the Board's consideration of the proposal. [At the time of its selection, Dilworth also represented Dr. Hammer personally.] The law firm of Skadden, Arps, Slate, Meagher & Flom ("Skadden Arps") was retained to represent the new legal entity which would be necessitated by the Museum proposal. Occidental's public accountants, Arthur Andersen & Co. ("Arthur Andersen"), were also asked to examine the Museum proposal.

On or about February 6, 1989, ten days prior to the Board's prescheduled February 16 meeting, Dilworth provided each member of the Board with a ninety-six page memorandum. It contained a definition of the Museum proposal and the anticipated magnitude of the proposed charitable donation by Occidental. It reviewed the authority of the Board to approve such a donation and the reasonableness of the proposed donation. The Dilworth memorandum included an analysis of the donation's effect on Occidental's financial condition, the potential for good will and other benefits to Occidental, and a comparison of the contribution by Occidental to the charitable contributions of other corporations.

The advance distribution of the Dilworth memorandum was supplemented on February 10, 1989 by a tax opinion letter from Skadden Arps. That same day, the Board also received a consulting report from the Duncan Appraisal Corporation. The latter document addressed the option price for the Museum's purchase of Occidental's headquarters building, museum facility and parking garage in thirty years as contemplated by the Museum proposal.

During the February 16 Board meeting, a Dilworth representative personally presented the basis for that law firm's analysis of the Museum proposal, as set forth in its February 6 written memorandum. The presentation reviewed again the directors' standard of conduct in considering the Museum proposal, as well as the financial and tax consequences to Occidental as a result of the donation. Following the Dilworth presentation, the Board resolved to appoint the Special Committee, comprised of its eight independent and disinterested outside directors, to further review and to act upon the Museum proposal. . . .

On February 16, 1989, following the adjournment of the Board meeting, the Special Committee met to consider the proposal presented to the full Board for establishing the Museum. The Special Committee requested the representatives of Dilworth to attend the meeting to respond to any questions relating to its February 6, 1989 opinion letter and memorandum. The Special Committee also asked representatives from Skadden Arps and Arthur Andersen to attend its meeting to address questions concerning the proposed charitable contribution.

The minutes of the February 16, 1989 meeting of the Special Committee outline its consideration of the Museum proposal. Those minutes reflect that many questions were asked by members of the Special Committee and were answered by the representatives of Dilworth, Skadden Arps, or Arthur Andersen. As a result of its own extensive discussions, and in reliance upon the experts' opinions, the Special Committee concluded that the establishment of the Museum, adjacent to Occidental's corporate offices in Los Angeles, would provide benefits to Occidental for at least the thirty-year term of the lease. The Special Committee also concluded that the proposed museum would establish a new cultural landmark for the City of Los Angeles.

On February 16, 1989, the Special Committee unanimously approved the Museum proposal, subject to certain conditions. The proposal approved by the Special Committee included the following provisions:

> (1) Occidental would construct a new museum building, renovate portions of four floors of its adjacent headquarters for use by the Museum, and construct a parking garage beneath the museum for its own use for a total cost of approximately $50 million;
>
> (2) Occidental would lease the Museum building and the four floors of its headquarters to the Museum rent-free for a term of thirty years. Occidental would continue to pay the property taxes, and the Museum would pay the utilities and maintenance expenses;
>
> (3) Occidental would purchase a thirty-year annuity at an estimated cost of $35.6 million to provide for the funding of the Museum's operations during its initial years;
>
> (4) Occidental would grant the Museum an irrevocable option to purchase the Museum building, the parking garage, and the Occidental headquarters building in thirty years for $55 million;
>
> (5) Dr. Hammer and the Foundation would transfer the Art Collection entirely to the Museum;
>
> (6) The Museum would be named for Dr. Hammer—The Armand Hammer Museum of Art and Cultural Center;
>
> (7) Occidental would have representation on the board of directors of the Museum;
>
> (8) Occidental would receive public recognition for its role in establishing the Museum, for example, by the naming of the courtyard, library, or auditorium for Occidental and Occidental would have the right to use the Museum, and be entitled to "corporate sponsor" rights. . . .

The Special Committee decided to present requests for expenditures to carry out the foregoing resolutions to the Board in the form of Authorization for Expenditures ("AFE's"). The AFE's proposed by the Special Committee were unanimously approved by the Board when it reconvened on February 16, 1989.

On April 25, 1989, Occidental reported the Special Committee's approval of the Museum proposal to its shareholders in the proxy statement for its annual meeting to be held May 26, 1989. On May 2, 1989, the first shareholder action ("the Kahn action") was filed, challenging Occidental's decision to establish and fund the Museum proposal. The Sullivan [shareholder] action was filed on May 9, 1989. . . .

Settlement negotiations were entered into almost immediately between Occidental and the attorneys for the plaintiffs in the Sullivan action. The attorney for the plaintiffs in the Kahn action was invited to attend the settlement negotiations. After the parties to the Sullivan action were in substantial agreement, the attorney for the plaintiffs in the Kahn action said it was up to his clients whether to accept the settlement, but that he was not going to recommend it.

On June 3, 1989, the parties to the Sullivan action signed a Memorandum of Understanding ("MOU") that set forth a proposed settlement in general terms. The proposed settlement was subject to the right of the plaintiffs to engage in additional discovery to confirm the fairness and adequacy of the proposed settlement.

On June 9, 1989, the plaintiffs in the Kahn action moved for a preliminary injunction to enjoin the proposed settlement in the Sullivan action and also for expedited discovery. An order granting limited expedited discovery on the motion was entered over the defendants' objection. The motion for a preliminary injunction was denied by the Court of Chancery on July 19, 1989. In denying the motion for injunctive relief, the Court of Chancery found that Kahn would suffer no irreparable harm if a proposed settlement in Sullivan was subsequently finalized and submitted for approval since Kahn, as a stockholder of Occidental, would have the opportunity to appear and object to the settlement. The Court of Chancery also identified six issues to be addressed at any future settlement hearing:

> (1) the failure of the Special Committee appointed by the directors of Occidental to hire its own counsel and advisors or even to formally approve the challenged acts; (2) the now worthlessness of a prior donation by Occidental to the Los Angeles County Museum; (3) the huge attorney fees which the parties have apparently decided to seek or not oppose; (4) the egocentric nature of some of Armand Hammer's objections to the Los Angeles County Museum being the recipient of his donation; (5) the issue of who really owns the art; and (6) the lack of any direct substantial benefit to the stockholders.

[Over the course of the next few months, Occidental's board delegated full authority to the Special Committee to settle the litigation. The Special Committee then hired independent counsel with no prior relationship with Occidental to advise it. Pursuant to its delegated authority, the Special Committee entered into a stipulation of settlement in the Sullivan action.]

[Thus,] the parties to the Sullivan action presented the Court of Chancery with a fully executed Stipulation of Compromise, Settlement and Release agreement ("the Settlement") on January 24, 1990. This agreement was only slightly changed from the June 3, 1989 Memorandum of Understanding. The Settlement, *inter alia*, provided:

(1) The Museum building shall be named the "Occidental Petroleum Cultural Center Building" with the name displayed appropriately on the building.

(2) Occidental shall be treated as a corporate sponsor by the Museum for as long as the Museum occupies the building.

(3) Occidental's contribution of the building shall be recognized by the Museum in public references to the facility.

(4) Three of Occidental's directors shall serve on the Museum's Board (or no less than one-third of the total Museum Board) with Occidental having the option to designate a fourth director.

(5) There shall be an immediate loan of substantially all of the art collections of Dr. Hammer to the Museum and there shall be an actual transfer of ownership of the collections upon Dr. Hammer's death or the commencement of operation of the Museum — whichever later occurs.

(6) All future charitable contributions by Occidental to any Hammer-affiliated charities shall be limited by the size of the dividends paid to Occidental's common stockholders. At current dividend levels, Occidental's annual contributions to Hammer-affiliated charities pursuant to this limitation could not exceed approximately three cents per share.

(7) Any amounts Occidental pays for construction of the Museum in excess of $50 million and any amounts paid to the Foundation upon Dr. Hammer's death must be charged against the agreed ceiling on limitations to Hammer-affiliated charities.

(8) Occidental's expenditures for the Museum construction shall not exceed $50 million, except that an additional $10 million may be expended through December 31, 1990 but only if such additional expenditures do not enlarge the scope of construction and if such expenditures are approved by the Special Committee. Amounts in excess of $50 million must be charged against the limitation on donations to Hammer-affiliated charities.

(9) Occidental shall be entitled to receive 50% of any consideration received in excess of a $55 million option price for the Museum property or 50% of any consideration the Museum receives from the assignment or transfer of its option or lease to a third party.

(10) Plaintiffs' attorneys' fees in the Sullivan action shall not exceed $1.4 million. . . .

On April 4, 1990, the settlement hearing in the Sullivan action was held. A number of shareholders appeared or wrote letters objecting to the Settlement. The Objectors argued that the decision of the Special Committee on February 16 to approve the charitable donation to fund the Museum proposal was neither informed nor deliberate and was not cured by any subsequent conduct. Therefore, the Objectors argued that the actions by the Special Committee were not entitled to the protection of the business judgment rule. The Objectors also argued that the charitable donation to the Museum proposal constituted a waste of Occidental's corporate assets. Consequently, in view of the merits of the claims being compromised, the Objectors submitted that the benefits of the proposed Settlement in the Sullivan action were inadequate.

On August 7, 1990, the Court of Chancery found the Settlement to be reasonable under all of the circumstances. The Court of Chancery concluded that the claims asserted by the shareholder plaintiffs would likely be dismissed before or after trial. While noting its own displeasure with the Settlement, the Court of Chancery explained that its role in reviewing the proposed Settlement was restricted to determining in its own business judgment whether, on balance, the Settlement was reasonable. The Court opined that although the benefit to be received from the Settlement was meager, it was adequate considering all the facts and circumstances.

CLAIMS AND DEFENSES

Initially, we will review the Court of Chancery's examination of the nature of the shareholder plaintiffs' claims and the possible defenses thereto, in the context of the legal and factual circumstances presented. The proponents of the Settlement argued that the business judgment rule could undoubtedly have been invoked successfully by the defendants as a complete defense to the shareholder plaintiffs' claims. The business judgment rule "creates a presumption 'that in making a business decision the directors of a corporation acted on an informed basis, in good faith and in the honest belief that the action taken was in the best interests of the corporation.'" The Objectors presented several alternative arguments in support of their contention that the shareholder plaintiffs would have been able to rebut the defense based on the protection which the presumption of the business judgment rule provides. Each of those arguments was based, at least in part, upon this Court's decision in Smith v. Van Gorkom, Del. Supr., 488 A.2d 858 (1985). . . .

[T]he Objectors argued that the presumption of the business judgment rule would have been overcome because the Special Committee proceeded initially without retaining independent legal counsel. In fact, that was a concern identified by the Court of Chancery in its July 19, 1989 opinion. However, in approving the Settlement, the Court of Chancery noted that the Special Committee had retained independent counsel, and "subsequently, and for the first time, formally approved the challenged charitable contributions." Thus, the Court of Chancery specifically found that the Special Committee had the advice of independent legal counsel before it finally approved the Museum proposal.

In this appeal, with respect to the aforementioned finding, the Objectors submit that the Court of Chancery's eventual approval of the Settlement was based upon its mistaken belief that a major judicial concern, *i.e.*, the failure of the Special Committee to retain independent counsel prior to its formal approval of the Museum proposal, had been rectified. In particular, the Objectors contend that the Special Committee formally approved the Museum proposal at its July 20, 1989 meeting. The parties all agree that the Special Committee retained its independent legal counsel on August 4, 1989. Therefore, the Objectors argue that the Court of Chancery's conclusion that the business judgment rule would apply was based upon an erroneous premise.

In response to that argument by the Objectors, the proponents of the Settlement submit the record reflects that the Special Committee reviewed and ratified all of its prior actions on September 20, 1989, after retaining independent legal counsel. Accordingly, the proponents of the Settlement contend that, whether the September 20, 1989 action by the Special Committee is characterized as the first final approval of the Museum proposal or as a re-approval of its action taken on July 20, 1989, the Special Committee's ultimate decision to proceed with the Museum proposal was based upon the advice of independent counsel.

The Objectors' third argument in the Court of Chancery, challenging the viability of the business judgment rule as a successful defense, was based upon *Van Gorkom* and contended that the Special Committee and other directors were grossly negligent in failing to inform themselves of all material information reasonably available to them.[25] Thus, the Objectors argued that even if, arguendo, the Special Committee was itself independent and formally approved the Museum proposal after its retention of independent legal counsel, such approval would not have cured the Special Committee's prior failure to exercise due care. The Court of Chancery found the record showed that the Special Committee had given due consideration to the Museum proposal and rejected the Objectors' argument to the contrary. . . .

Following its analysis and conclusion that the business judgment rule would have been applicable to any judicial examination of the Special Committee's actions, the Court of Chancery considered the shareholder plaintiffs' claim that the Board and the Special Committee's approval of the charitable donation to the Museum proposal constituted a waste of Occidental's corporate assets. In doing so, it recognized that charitable donations by Delaware corporations are expressly authorized by 8 Del. C. § 122(9). It also recognized that although § 122(9) places no limitations on the size of a charitable corporate gift, that section has been construed "to authorize any reasonable corporate gift of a charitable or educational nature." Thus, the Court of Chancery concluded that the test to be applied in examining the merits of a claim alleging corporate waste "is that of reasonableness, a test in which the provisions of the Internal Revenue Code pertaining to charitable gifts by corporations furnish a helpful guide." We agree with that conclusion.

The Objectors argued that Occidental's charitable contribution to the Museum proposal was unreasonable and a waste of corporate assets because it was excessive.[26] The Court of Chancery recognized that not every charitable gift constitutes a valid corporate action. Nevertheless, the Court of Chancery concluded, given the net worth of Occidental, its annual net income before taxes, and the tax benefits to Occidental, that the gift to the Museum was within the range of reasonableness. . . . Therefore, the Court of Chancery found that it was "reasonably probable" that plaintiffs would fail on their claim of waste. That finding is supported by the record and is the product of an orderly and logical deductive process. . . .

25. The Objectors submit that, *inter alia*, the Special Committee was apparently uninformed as to potential tax consequences of the charitable donation, the value of the Art Collection, how much of the Art Collection had been purchased with donations from Occidental, and what the cost for the Museum's rent-free use of the property would be to Occidental.

26. The Objectors also argued that the Museum project duplicated facilities previously funded by Occidental; served no social need; was designed primarily to enhance the personal reputation of Dr. Hammer; and resulted in damage (not good will) to Occidental. The Court of Chancery concluded that these concerns were ones about which reasonable minds could differ. That conclusion is also supported by the record and is the product of an orderly deductive process. . . .

CONCLUSION

The reasonableness of a particular class action settlement is addressed to the discretion of the Court of Chancery, on a case by case basis, in light of all of the relevant circumstances. In this case, we find that all of the Court of Chancery's factual findings of fact are supported by the record. We also find that all of the legal conclusions reached by the Court of Chancery were based upon a proper application of well established principles of law. Consequently, we find that the Court of Chancery did not abuse its discretion in deciding to approve the Settlement in the Sullivan action. . . .

CHIQUITA BANANAS: A CASE STUDY*

Chiquita Brands International, Inc. is the leading distributer of bananas in the United States, and an outgrowth of the famous United Fruit Company (UFC) which grew to fame — or infamy — as one of the first powerful, modern multinational corporations. United Fruit became synonymous with the term "Banana Republic" by supporting corrupt regimes throughout Latin America to assure control over their plantations.

One of the most infamous moments of oppression instituted by the UFC became known as the "Banana Massacre." In November 1928, thousands of UFC workers went on strike against UFC. The UFC used its connections within the Colombian government to break the strike, and the government ordered an attack on the strikers. When the smoke cleared, many of the strikers were dead. While the exact number proved problematic to determine, it was very likely in the hundreds. The resulting outrage among many of the people of Colombia likely led to the rise of the Fuerzas Armadas Revolucionarias de Colombia, or the Revolutionary Armed Forces of Colombia, known as the FARC, which viewed the state as one of the primary instigators of oppression in Colombia. The Banana Massacre, and other incidents like it, led to the decades of civil war that continue to ravage the country to this day.

Over the ensuing decades, the paramilitary groups used intimidation and violence to finance their activities, including kidnapping, against which protection payments were demanded, and notorious connections with the Colombian drug trade. Between 1986 and 1995, FARC nearly doubled its forces from 3,600 to 7,000 and received hundreds of millions of dollars from their illegal activities. Thus, Colombia emerged as a very difficult and dangerous place to do business. The 1980s and 1990s were especially violent, with the government continuing to struggle to make peace with the Marxist militia groups like FARC, and right-wing paramilitary groups such as the Autodefensas Unidas de Colombia, or the United Self-Defense Forces of Colombia, known as the AUC.

Chiquita ran their Latin American operations through a foreign subsidiary named Banadex. Sometime between 1987 and 1989, FARC demanded $10,000 to be paid under the threat of kidnapping. The demand made its way to a Chiquita employee named Robert Kistinger, who headed Chiquita's Latin America operations. Kistinger had the employee who had received the demand travel

---

*This case study draws heavily from the Report of the Special Litigation Committee, Chiquita Brands International, Inc. (February 2009).

to Cincinnati to meet with a number of executives including Chiquita's general counsel, Charles Morgan. After a "brief but memorable" meeting, according to Morgan, Chiquita decided to just pay the demand.

Kistinger and others recognized that this would likely be the first of other demands and retained a UK-based security consulting firm called Control Risks to establish a coherent policy to handle future demands. Control Risks, considering the political situation in Colombia, recommended trying to negotiate with the groups to keep the amount and frequency of payments low, but ultimately conceded that Chiquita likely had no practical alternative to making the payments.

This precarious political situation continued throughout the 1990s. FARC and other groups continued to attack the government and, despite the payments made by Chiquita, kidnapped Banadex employees and attacked company facilities. In 1995, a particularly terrifying attack on a bus carrying Banadex employees killed approximately 25 people. Despite a lack of evidence proving the fact, many within Chiquita at the time believed that the guerillas had targeted the bus because it was carrying individuals that supported groups in opposition to FARC's goals. Not long after, a guerilla group shot and wounded a Banadex quality control inspector as he was inspecting company farms. The Inspector then lobbied to have a high level of bulletproofing installed on company cars. This pattern contributed to the belief that Chiquita had to make the payments to avoid more serious consequences.

Chiquita had established accounting practices to monitor payments that may fall under the scope of the Foreign Corrupt Practices Act of 1977 (FCPA). The act generally bans payments made to influence foreign government officials, but does not ban "facilitating" payments that simply encourage officials to do things that are already their duty. Because the guerilla demands seemed little more than extortion, Chiquita concluded that the payments would likely not fall under the types of payments that would cause liability under the FCPA. Chiquita wanted to make sure that it established accounting procedures to properly account for any payments made to FARC or other groups.

Due to the sensitive nature of these payments, Chiquita coded the payments to cover up details about the transactions from local employees. Chiquita feared that some Banadex employees might have loyalties with groups in opposition to the guerillas receiving payments, and might tip off their contacts that Chiquita was supporting a competing group. Thus, Chiquita used an internal accounting form called Form 1016 with an accounting code that allowed the individual making the payments to make it clear to whom the payments went, and for what purpose. After the form passed through the accounting department, an intermediary made the payments in cash. Chiquita maintained that although they coded payments for security reasons, both their internal and external auditors could still track the payments.

Audits were made to attempt to monitor the payments and comply with the FCPA, which had been enacted in part to deal with past infractions by the United Fruit Company and other multinational corporations that had supported corrupt governments throughout the world. In February 1993, an in-house attorney named David Hills drafted an internal memo regarding a new Colombian law that set penalties for "paying, concealing, or failing to disclose kidnapping ransom and extortion payments." However, the Colombian Supreme Court overturned the law in June 1994, declaring that it would be unjust to punish those who made extortion payments since they acted in a "State of Necessity." Chiquita wanted to make completely sure that they had not violated Colombian law, so they retained the services of a firm expert in international affairs, Baker & McKenzie, to get a second opinion on the validity of the payments under Colombian law in 1997. Chiquita's general counsel did not know at the time that employees continued to make payments to guerilla groups, and Baker & McKenzie analyzed only historical payments. Baker & McKenzie concluded that the payments would not violate Colombian law if only made to "defend the life and freedom of individuals." Further, because the members of the government did not receive any payments, Chiquita's general counsel determined that the FCPA did not likely apply.

Despite the fact that many employees knew Chiquita was paying guerillas, the topic did not come up in board meetings. Some evidence showed that a few Banadex employees making payments, the Audit Committee tracking the money, and a few individual directors knew of the payments. But several other directors who served during the time of the payments testified that they had no idea Chiquita had been engaging in these activities.

Meanwhile, with the political situation in Colombia remaining tenuous, the right-wing nationwide paramilitary organization AUC began to assert power throughout the nation, with an emphasis in the North, near Banadex's facilities. By the mid-1990s, AUC began to push FARC and the other guerillas out of the region, and Chiquita welcomed the change. The new security did not last, however, as AUC proved to be as brutal and violent as FARC, and developed a reputation for being a "powerful, criminal group." Parallel to the rise of the AUC, the Colombian government began to support the formation of *convivir*s, which were essentially neighborhood watch groups, to support government efforts to restore order and fight both the AUC and FARC.

Sometime around early 1997, AUC leader Carlos Castaña invited Banadex employees to a "security meeting" at his compound in Medellín. Castaña knew that Banadex had been paying extortion money to guerilla groups, and stated that he would not require the types of payments that they did, but instead demanded protection money. Those attending the meeting realized that the AUC had made a threat, and that Chiquita would likely need to make the payments.

Making payments to the AUC seemed more difficult than those to the FARC had been. In fact, before long, Chiquita began making payments to the AUC through various local *convivir*s. Only about five payments were made directly to the AUC through an intermediary named "Michael."

Chiquita's Cincinnati headquarters did not know that these payments had been made, until later that year when payments to *convivir*s began to surface in Banadex's accounting records. Chiquita called a special meeting to determine the exact nature of the payments, and to learn about these new *convivir* organizations that were unfamiliar to management. At the meeting, a Banadex lawyer assured the management that the *convivir*s were completely legal and sanctioned by the government. Following the meeting, Chiquita launched its own more detailed investigation that included receiving memos from the Colombian government that the *convivir*s were indeed sanctioned by the government and contributed to the stability of the region. In fact, the Colombian lawyer recounted an incident where he had expressed concern about reports that some *convivir*s had committed human rights abuses during a meeting with then-Governor Alvaro Uribe. Uribe sent government documentation to the lawyer assuring him of the government's support for the *convivir*s. Following these assurances, Chiquita disclosed the information to their Audit Committee and began to monitor the payments as part of their FCPA duties, despite the fact that they were not payments to government officials.

In their 1997 audit, several Chiquita employees noticed $30,000 worth of sensitive payments that had been paid in the past year. Upon further investigation, Chiquita discovered that the payments were bribes paid to renew Banadex's port license. Chiquita swiftly fired or disciplined the employees involved in the payments, and while they did not voluntarily disclose the payments to any regulatory agencies, the story still leaked to the press.

Following the press coverage, the SEC subpoenaed Chiquita, and in a meeting with the Department of Justice (DOJ), SEC, and the U.S. Attorney's Office for the Southern District of New York, Chiquita volunteered detailed information about both the bribes and the extortion money paid by Chiquita to groups designated by the U.S. Department of State as a Foreign Terrorist Organization (FTO). Although the government knew the facts regarding the payments to these groups, the government agents did not raise the issue of the legality of these payments under U.S. law, except under the FCPA. In the end, the parties reached a settlement without admitting fault, and paid a $100,000 fine to the SEC regarding the bribes to government agents.

Starting in 1999, AUC came directly to Banadex demanding payment. One employee recalled "many men brandishing AK-47s," and that he "felt very scared and intimidated," as one might in such a situation. An intermediary between Banadex and the paramilitary group suggested that they pay them through a *convivir* that had been created by the AUC to raise funds.

Like the payments to FARC and to the other *convivir*s, these payments began to surface on Chiquita's FCPA reports, and Chiquita's corporate headquarters began to investigate the new *convivir*. After consulting with Colombian attorneys, they sent a corporate representative down to Colombia to assess the legitimacy of the new *convivir*. The representative found some sobering information: the *convivir* was nothing more than a front for the AUC. However, the opinion of Chiquita, even after consulting outside Colombian counsel, was that the *convivir* payments did not violate Colombian law.

A major shift occurred on September 10, 2001, when the United States listed the AUC as a foreign terrorist organization. It thus became a felony to knowingly provide "material support or resources" to the AUC. Despite the publicity in the media following the disclosure, Chiquita claimed it had no knowledge of the new designation for 18 months. The DOJ begged to differ and launched a grand jury investigation into the issue, but did not turn up any evidence to the contrary.

Meanwhile, continuing financial problems at Chiquita forced it into Chapter 11 bankruptcy. Following four months of reorganization, Chiquita emerged with five new independent members on the board. The new board then installed a new CEO, Cyrus Freidheim. In a briefing Freidheim recalled the general counsel informing him of the payments to AUC, both directly and through the *convivir*s, but assuring him that the payments raised no legal issues in the United States or Colombia outside of the FCPA, with which Chiquita complied.

A few months later, Banadex received a new demand for payment from the AUC. Apparently dissatisfied with the amount received through the *convivir*, the AUC went directly to the source. Chiquita created a new procedure for paying the paramilitary groups by taking it out of the "Manager's Expenses" account and making up for the difference by grossing up the general manager's pay. After six months, the general manager became uncomfortable with the way the payments were going, and Chiquita began to investigate other options. While running an internet search on Colombian paramilitary organizations, a Chiquita lawyer stumbled across the fact that the AUC appeared on a list of "Foreign Terrorist Organizations" kept by the State Department. He reported this to the general counsel, who very upset, reported it to outside counsel at Kirkland and Ellis ("K&E"). Up to this point, Chiquita claims that it had no knowledge that the State Department kept such a list, or that any of the groups with which they dealt would be on it.

After preliminary research by K&E, notes from a Chiquita lawyer who talked with K&E said "Bottom Line: CANNOT MAKE THE PAYMENT." Thus, all payments to the AUC stopped, but Chiquita had forgotten the connection that the *convivir* had to paramilitary groups. Two payments later, the connection was discovered, and the payments to the *convivir*s stopped as well.

After the payments were stopped, the dilemma facing Chiquita was either to make the payments and risk serious criminal charges in the United States or to stop the payments and risk the lives of Banadex employees. Ultimately, Chiquita executives decided that the only viable option was to approach the U.S. government and obtain clearance to continue making payments through the *convivir*s.

Without disclosing their client's identity, Chiquita's K&E attorneys met with the DOJ. The DOJ attorney said the decision to prosecute fell upon more senior officials than himself, and that although the payments constituted "at minimum, a technical violation" of the statute, the decision to prosecute would be entirely separate. The DOJ attorney noted, however, that the Agency would not likely give a complete "pass" to continued payments.

With this new knowledge, Chiquita called a special meeting of the Audit Committee together with the board to discuss the implications of the new developments in the law. Following a briefing by Robert Olson, Chiquita's general counsel, the board resolved to voluntarily approach the DOJ and make a full disclosure. Meanwhile, the pressures on Banadex employees to pay continued and Olson, after heated debates with Freidheim and other senior management, authorized employees to continue to make payments to AUC in an effort to protect the lives of employees in Colombia.

In April 2003, Chiquita arranged a meeting with several DOJ officials and voluntarily disclosed the payments. At first the DOJ officials "reacted in a hostile manner" to the disclosures, but after Chiquita explained the situation, the DOJ officials admitted that it was "complicated" and promised to get back to Chiquita after weighing the policy concerns. The DOJ officials also questioned why Chiquita had not considered a divestment of Banadex. Chiquita responded that the exit of a large, multinational corporation from Colombia could have other foreign policy implications that needed to be considered. Divestment was a determination that should likely be made with the cooperation of the State Department. Weighing these issues, the DOJ again acknowledged that the future payments were a "complicated issue."

Reactions and interpretations coming out of the meeting differed between the government and Chiquita – and even between Chiquita executives. Olson took the government's refusal to authorize future payments as a desire to refrain from condoning unlawful acts, but as tacit recognition that Chiquita would have to continue to make payments going forward in order to protect its employees. Also, most of the executives felt that the DOJ had essentially pledged to exercise prosecutorial discretion on behalf of Chiquita.

Meanwhile in Colombia, Banadex employees began to worry about the two months of missed payments, and sought guidance from Chiquita's headquarters in Cincinnati. A company lawyer gave the message: Keep making payments. Chiquita grappled with the decision moving forward while waiting for a decision from the DOJ. Many directors pushed for an exit from Colombia. The option appeared viable because Banacol, another Colombian banana grower, had expressed interest in a buyout almost a year before. In preparation for a potential buyout, Chiquita accepted an offer from Banacol that involved an upfront payment in exchange for a joint venture agreement for several years following at a premium price.

Discussions continued with the DOJ, and Chiquita implemented a document retention policy to make sure that they could prepare for a possible upcoming investigation. Throughout late 2003 and into early 2004, Chiquita continued to discuss the situation with the DOJ, which did not want to make any decisions on the policy matters until they had independently investigated the facts of the case. The lack of certainty worried many members of the board, who pushed toward the sale of Banadex and a greater commitment to making sure that money paid to banana suppliers was not being funneled back to the AUC and other groups.

In January 2004, Chiquita's board of directors appointed a new CEO named Fernando Aguirre, who had extensive experience in Latin America and spoke fluent Spanish. This was part of a companywide plan following their bankruptcy to change their business plan and phase out their production companies. Aguirre claimed that he did not realize the seriousness of Chiquita's problem with the DOJ regarding the Colombian situation. Within weeks, Aguirre ordered a stop to the payments. A final payment of $365,865 was made on January 24, 2004.

Two days later, Chiquita announced the planned sale of Banadex in an attempt to encourage other bids, and raise the potential sale price. No other company made bids, however, so the talks with Banacol went forward, and the board of directors eventually approved the sale. Chiquita disclosed the DOJ's ongoing investigation to Banacol, even though Chiquita worried this disclosure would give Banacol leverage to demand better terms. Banacol simply added a "break-up fee" and recognized that the DOJ might interfere with the terms moving forward. On June 28, the sale to Banacol closed. The board of directors of Chiquita, as a whole, agreed that the sale was fair and not a fire sale.

For the next year, the DOJ investigation seemed to be heading in a favorable direction for Chiquita. Then, in September 2005, a new prosecutor was appointed to the case: Assistant U.S. Attorney Jonathan Malis. He completely shifted the DOJ's approach, demanding a broader privilege waiver under the threat of considering Chiquita to be "non-cooperative." The expanded investigation led the government to subpoena directors, and outside counsel at Kirkland & Ellis. Thus, Chiquita was forced to retain Covington & Burling LLP for help in the prosecution. After about four months of deliberation, Chiquita agreed to a plea bargain that included "(i) a plea to one count of a violation of 50 U.S.C. § 1705, which prohibits knowingly engaging in transactions with a specially designated global terrorist without obtaining a license from the [U.S. Treasury's Office of Foreign Assets Control]; (ii) a maximum $25 million fine, and (iii) continued cooperation in any ongoing investigation." Chiquita thus pledged to continue to aid the DOJ in its investigation of individual officers and directors.

Following the plea deal with the DOJ, several parties brought actions against Chiquita, incensed that they had supported terrorist groups with millions of dollars over a period of nearly 15 years. Among the lawsuits, a shareholder derivative action in the United States District Court for the Southern District of Florida alleges breaches of fiduciary duty, corporate waste, and gross negligence.

Assume that you represent a large pension fund that has invested in Chiquita. Your client is one of the shareholders who initiated the derivative litigation discussed above, and your client is particularly interested in promoting corporate responsibility. Thus, your client is most concerned about Chiquita's actions after September 10, 2001, the date on which the United States designated the AUC as a foreign terrorist organization. Assuming the accuracy of the foregoing facts, answer the following questions:

1. *What is your strongest claim for breach of fiduciary duty against Chiquita's directors during the period(s) after September 10, 2001?* Note that Chiquita is a New Jersey corporation and that New Jersey law closely follows Delaware law in matters relating to fiduciary duty.

2. Looking to the future, your client would like your advice on strategies for encouraging corporate responsibility at its portfolio companies. One initiative you are aware of is that of the U.N. Special Representative on Business and Human Rights Professor John Ruggie, of Harvard University, whose Protect, Respect and Remedy Framework was approved by the U.N. Human Rights Council in 2008. That Framework rests on three pillars:

   a. The State duty to protect against human rights abuses by third parties, including business;

   b. The Corporate responsibility to respect human rights [to be operationalized by a serious due diligence process within each company]; and

   c. Greater access by victims to effective remedy, both judicial and nonjudicial.

   For further information see *http://www.reports-and-materials.org/Ruggie-protect-respect-remedy-framework.pdf* or generally *http://www.business-humanrights.org.*

   What are the pros and cons of bringing shareholder proposals asking portfolio companies to adopt the due diligence procedures suggested by the Ruggie Report as a strategy to encourage greater social responsibility?

3. One mechanism that has been used to try to promote corporate accountability in the United States for human rights violations abroad is the Alien Torts Claims Act (ATCA). The ATCA provides subject matter jurisdiction in the United States to non-U.S. citizens ("aliens") to challenge alleged violations of well-recognized international human rights, even where those challenges are brought against non-U.S. defendants (assuming there is a basis for personal jurisdiction in the United States). The ATCA has been used to bring claims against a wide range of companies for a wide range of alleged offenses, from claims of extreme environmental degradation of traditional hunting and fishing grounds brought against Texaco for its actions in Ecuador to claims of forced resettlements and "extra-judicial killings" by the state in partnership with Royal Dutch Shell, and so forth. In a recent Second

Circuit opinion, however, the court held that the corporate entity is not a "juridical person" that is directly subject to international human rights obligations. Kiobel v. Royal Dutch Shell, 621 F.3d 111 (2d Cir. 2010). While the individual corporate employees whose actions caused the alleged violations could be held liable (again, assuming personal jurisdiction in the United States), and the corporation therefore chargeable under a *respondeat superior* theory, the corporation as an entity cannot be held directly liable, according to *Kiobel*. *How, if at all, does this change your advice to the pension fund investors in Chiquita? If you were the general counsel of a multi-national enterprise such as Chiquita, how, if at all, does the Kiobel opinion change the advice you give the company with respect to its human rights obligations?*

(N.B.: The U.S. Supreme Court has granted *certiorari* in *Kiobel*, and after argument in February 2012, asked for further briefing and re-argument on the following question: "Whether and under what circumstances the Alien Tort Statute, 28 U.S.C. § 1350, allows courts to recognize a cause of action for violations of the law of nations occurring within the territory of a sovereign other than the United States." The expanded case will be re-argued during the 2012-2013 term.)

CHAPTER

8

Duty of Loyalty

MOTIVATING HYPOTHETICAL

Conrad White is the 51 percent share owner of Hollander International, a multimedia news organization that owns magazines, newspapers, commercial blogs, and Twitter accounts originating in over 80 countries. Hollander is incorporated in Delaware, with wholly owned operating subsidiaries in the major common law countries: Australia, Canada, India, Ireland, New Zealand, the United States, and the United Kingdom.

Any time a director or manager participates in a transaction involving a conflict of interest — that is, a transaction in which the director or manager may be motivated not only by the interests of the corporation but also by self-interest — the duty of loyalty is implicated. For example, when a board of directors approves a stock option plan under which the directors receive options, the directors have divided loyalties. As fiduciaries for the corporation, they should be interested in issuing the smallest number of options possible while ensuring that their compensation packages remain competitive with those of other companies. As recipients of the options, the directors will want to award the most generous options package possible. As a general rule, the duty of loyalty requires that directors serve the interests of the corporation over their self-interest, but this general rule does not resolve many of the real cases, which can be very complicated.

The complexity of the subject has encouraged courts to focus closely on context. In addition to general self-dealing, courts have developed special rules for cases involving majority or controlling shareholders. Given that many cases involving majority or controlling shareholders arise in the context of parent-subsidiary merger transactions, we postpone much of our discussion of this branch of the duty of loyalty until Chapter 10, Friendly Mergers and Acquisitions. In the meantime, we explore the statutory procedures that directors follow to remove the taint of self-interest from a transaction.

Over the past two decades, the Delaware courts have also struggled to determine whether directors have an additional and separate duty called the "duty of good faith." In this chapter, we introduce the concept of good faith because of

401

the importance of two recent Delaware Supreme Court opinions that discuss the subject in detail: In re The Walt Disney Derivative Litigation and Stone v. Ritter. In those cases, the Delaware Supreme Court ultimately held that good faith is not a freestanding duty, but rather an element of the duty of loyalty. We start with these cases, as they provide a good transition from the duty of care.

As you study these materials, keep in mind the following general points. First, because of concerns that directors have acted in their own self-interest in these transactions, courts scrutinize cases raising duty of loyalty issues much more carefully than those raising duty of care issues. While duty of loyalty cases may be treated in distinctive categories, this penchant for greater scrutiny transcends the categories. As a result, directors do not initially get the benefit of business judgment rule protection in these cases, although they can act to try to reinsert that protection through the use of various procedural mechanisms, discussed below. Second, pay close attention to the procedures companies use to approve conflict-of-interest transactions and the effects of these procedures on the judicial process. This knowledge is particularly useful for transactional lawyers, who provide advice to clients on how to structure transactions to mitigate the risk of judicial review. And third, even if companies use procedural mechanisms to remove the taint of self-interest from a transaction, courts will maintain a skeptical attitude in cases involving controlling shareholders because there is the ever-present specter of a controlling shareholder removing directors who too stubbornly refuse to approve a conflict-of-interest transaction that a controlling shareholder proposes.

A.   THE OVERSIGHT CONTEXT AND GOOD FAITH

1.   *Oversight Generally*

As noted in Chapter 7, the duty of care is primarily a procedural duty — that is, a duty to make lawful decisions in a well-informed, careful manner. A separate duty is the duty to be informed about what is happening within the corporation — that is, to provide oversight. Although providing oversight in the context of a large, decentralized, possibly global corporation includes decision making about how to monitor the affairs of the corporation, modern courts still distinguish between "decision-making" and "oversight" cases. Moreover, the Delaware courts have held that "the business judgment rule has no role in the case of inaction by the board of directors." Rattner v. Bidzos, 2003 WL 22284323 (Del. Ch. Oct. 7, 2003). As you'll see as this Section proceeds, the duty of oversight is now understood as an aspect of the duty of loyalty.

The new amendments to the Model Act codify the distinction. Although the standard of conduct under Model Act § 8.30 is the same for both classes of cases (that is, to "discharge their duties with the care that a person in a like position would reasonably believe appropriate under similar circumstances"), the oversight function merits a unique standard of liability under new Model Act § 8.31:

> A director shall not be liable to the corporation or its shareholders for any decision to take or not to take action, or any failure to take any action, as a director, unless

the party asserting liability in a proceeding establishes that . . . the challenged conduct consisted or was the result of . . . a sustained failure of the director to devote attention to ongoing oversight of the business and affairs of the corporation. . . .

Oversight cases often arise where employees of the corporation have engaged in illegal activities, and the corporation ultimately is forced to pay large penalties to the government or judgments or settlements to third parties arising from those illegal activities. Shareholders of the company then bring cases alleging that the directors breached their duty of care to the corporation by failing to ensure that the corporation had an effective law compliance system and that the directors' failure caused the economic losses to the corporation. *Caremark*, which appears below, is an example of such a case.

In the modern context, and after Sarbanes-Oxley, directors' oversight duties have been progressively expanded. Today, directors are responsible for ensuring that there are systems in place to get financial information to the board on a timely basis so that directors can determine if the company is "on target" financially; ensuring that there is reason to believe the company's financial reporting is accurate (that is, that the procedures in place make sense and that there are adequate financial controls); and ensuring that the company has a functioning law compliance structure. Moreover, well-run large companies increasingly expect directors to exercise oversight over systems put in place to evaluate and manage a wide range of risks to which companies are subject, such as operational risk, interest rate risk, currency risk, litigation risk, liability risk, social risk, environmental risk, regulatory risk and so on.

The following case became an instant classic when Chancellor Allen decided to revisit the law relating to oversight cases just before he left the bench. The decision was quite controversial in corporate boardrooms, because it seemed to portend a new source of liability. Nevertheless, Chancellor Allen notes that the plaintiffs in this case probably would not have prevailed after a trial. You should consider whether the standards enunciated by Chancellor Allen impose substantial new burdens on directors. Also, an important aspect of the case is Chancellor Allen's interpretation of Graham v. Allis-Chalmers Mfg. Co., 188 A.2d 125 (Del. 1963), a classic Delaware Supreme Court opinion.

IN RE CAREMARK INTERNATIONAL INC. DERIVATIVE LITIGATION

698 A.2d 959
Court of Chancery of Delaware
September 25, 1996

ALLEN, Chancellor.

Pending is a motion pursuant to Chancery Rule 23.1 to approve as fair and reasonable a proposed settlement of a consolidated derivative action on behalf of Caremark International, Inc. ("Caremark"). The suit involves claims that the members of Caremark's board of directors (the "Board") breached their fiduciary duty of care to Caremark in connection with alleged violations by Caremark employees of federal and state laws and regulations applicable to health care providers. . . .

Legally, evaluation of the central claim made entails consideration of the legal standard governing a board of directors' obligation to supervise or monitor corporate performance. For the reasons set forth below I conclude, in light of the discovery record, that there is a very low probability that it would be determined that the directors of Caremark breached any duty to appropriately monitor and supervise the enterprise. . . .

I. Background

[Caremark, a Delaware corporation with its headquarters in Northbrook, Illinois, was a publicly held company listed on the New York Stock Exchange. It had two main health care business segments, providing patient care and managed care services. As part of its patient care business, which accounted for the majority of Caremark's revenues, Caremark provided alternative site health care services, including infusion therapy, growth hormone therapy, HIV/AIDS-related treatments and hemophilia therapy. After extensive investigations, the federal government and a number of states indicted Caremark for paying kickbacks to doctors to induce the doctors to prescribe treatments using Caremark's infusion therapies in violation of federal Anti-Referral Payments laws applicable to Medicare and Medicaid. In return for a guilty plea to a single count of mail fraud by the corporation, the payment of a criminal fine, the payment of substantial civil damages [$250 million], and cooperation with further federal investigations, the government entities agreed to negotiate a settlement that would permit Caremark to continue participating in Medicare and Medicaid programs. On June 15, 1995, the Board approved a settlement ("Government Settlement Agreement") with the federal Department of Justice ("DOJ"), Office of the Inspector General ("OIG"), U.S. Veterans Administration, U.S. Federal Employee Health Benefits Program, federal Civilian Health and Medical Program of the Uniformed Services, and related state agencies in all fifty states and the District of Columbia. No senior officers or directors were charged with wrongdoing in the Government Settlement Agreement or in any of the prior indictments. In fact, as part of the sentencing in the Ohio action on June 19, 1995, the United States stipulated that no senior executive of Caremark participated in, condoned, or was willfully ignorant of wrongdoing in connection with the home infusion business practices. . . .]

F. THE PROPOSED SETTLEMENT

In relevant part the terms upon which the [breach of fiduciary duty] claims asserted are proposed to be settled are as follows:

1. That Caremark undertakes that it and its employees and agents not pay any form of compensation to a third party in exchange for the referral of a patient to a Caremark facility or service or the prescription of drugs marketed or distributed by Caremark for which reimbursement may be sought from Medicare, Medicaid, or a similar state reimbursement program;

2. That Caremark undertakes for itself and its employees and agents not to pay to or split fees with physicians, joint ventures, any business combination in which Caremark maintains a direct financial interest, or other health care providers with whom Caremark has a financial relationship or interest, in exchange for the referral of a patient to a Caremark facility or service or the prescription of

drugs marketed or distributed by Caremark for which reimbursement may be sought from Medicare, Medicaid, or a similar state reimbursement program;

3. That the full Board shall discuss all relevant material changes in government health care regulations and their effect on relationships with health care providers on a semi-annual basis;

4. That Caremark's officers will remove all personnel from health care facilities or hospitals who have been placed in such facility for the purpose of providing remuneration in exchange for a patient referral for which reimbursement may be sought from Medicare, Medicaid, or a similar state reimbursement program;

5. That every patient will receive written disclosure of any financial relationship between Caremark and the health care professional or provider who made the referral;

6. That the Board will establish a Compliance and Ethics Committee of four directors, two of which will be non-management directors, to meet at least four times a year to effectuate these policies and monitor business segment compliance with the ARPL, and to report to the Board semi-annually concerning compliance by each business segment; and

7. That corporate officers responsible for business segments shall serve as compliance officers who must report semi-annually to the Compliance and Ethics Committee and, with the assistance of outside counsel, review existing contracts and get advanced approval of any new contract forms.

II. Legal Principles

A. Principles Governing Settlements of Derivative Claims

[T]his Court is now required to exercise an informed judgment whether the proposed settlement is fair and reasonable in the light of all relevant factors. On an application of this kind, this Court attempts to protect the best interests of the corporation and its absent shareholders, all of whom will be barred from future litigation on these claims if the settlement is approved. The parties proposing the settlement bear the burden of persuading the court that it is in fact fair and reasonable.

B. Directors' Duties to Monitor Corporate Operations

The complaint charges the director defendants with breach of their duty of attention or care in connection with the on-going operation of the corporation's business. The claim is that the directors allowed a situation to develop and continue which exposed the corporation to enormous legal liability and that in so doing they violated a duty to be active monitors of corporate performance. The complaint thus does not charge either director self-dealing or the more difficult loyalty-type problems arising from cases of suspect director motivation, such as entrenchment or sale of control contexts. The theory here advanced is possibly the most difficult theory in corporation law upon which a plaintiff might hope to win a judgment. . . .

[This case belongs to a] class of cases in which director liability for inattention is theoretically possible [when] a loss eventuates not from a decision but, from unconsidered inaction. Most of the decisions that a corporation, acting through its human agents, makes are, of course, not the subject of director attention.

Legally, the board itself will be required only to authorize the most significant corporate acts or transactions: mergers, changes in capital structure, fundamental changes in business, appointment and compensation of the CEO, etc. As the facts of this case graphically demonstrate, ordinary business decisions that are made by officers and employees deeper in the interior of the organization can, however, vitally affect the welfare of the corporation and its ability to achieve its various strategic and financial goals. . . . Financial and organizational disasters such as these raise the question, what is the board's responsibility with respect to the organization and monitoring of the enterprise to assure that the corporation functions within the law to achieve its purposes?

Modernly this question has been given special importance by an increasing tendency, especially under federal law, to employ the criminal law to assure corporate compliance with external legal requirements, including environmental, financial, employee and product safety as well as assorted other health and safety regulations. In 1991, pursuant to the Sentencing Reform Act of 1984, the United States Sentencing Commission adopted Organizational Sentencing Guidelines which impact importantly on the prospective effect these criminal sanctions might have on business corporations. The Guidelines set forth a uniform sentencing structure for organizations to be sentenced for violation of federal criminal statutes and provide for penalties that equal or often massively exceed those previously imposed on corporations. The Guidelines offer powerful incentives for corporations today to have in place compliance programs to detect violations of law, promptly to report violations to appropriate public officials when discovered, and to take prompt, voluntary remedial efforts.

In 1963, the Delaware Supreme Court in Graham v. Allis-Chalmers Mfg. Co., addressed the question of potential liability of board members for losses experienced by the corporation as a result of the corporation having violated the antitrust laws of the United States. There was no claim in that case that the directors knew about the behavior of subordinate employees of the corporation that had resulted in the liability. Rather, as in this case, the claim asserted was that the directors ought to have known of it and if they had known they would have been under a duty to bring the corporation into compliance with the law and thus save the corporation from the loss. The Delaware Supreme Court concluded that, under the facts as they appeared, there was no basis to find that the directors had breached a duty to be informed of the ongoing operations of the firm. In notably colorful terms, the court stated that "absent cause for suspicion there is no duty upon the directors to install and operate a corporate system of espionage to ferret out wrongdoing which they have no reason to suspect exists." The Court found that there were no grounds for suspicion in that case and, thus, concluded that the directors were blamelessly unaware of the conduct leading to the corporate liability.

How does one generalize this holding today? Can it be said today that, absent some ground giving rise to suspicion of violation of law, that corporate directors have no duty to assure that a corporate information gathering and reporting system [] exists which represents a good faith attempt to provide senior management and the Board with information respecting material acts, events or conditions within the corporation, including compliance with applicable statutes and regulations? I certainly do not believe so. I doubt that such a broad generalization of the *Graham* holding would have been accepted by the Supreme Court in 1963. The case can be more narrowly interpreted as standing for the proposition that, absent grounds to suspect deception, neither corporate boards nor senior officers can be charged with wrongdoing simply for assuming the integrity of employees and the honesty of their dealings on the company's behalf.

A broader interpretation of Graham v. Allis-Chalmers — that it means that a corporate board has no responsibility to assure that appropriate information and reporting systems are established by management — would not, in any event, be accepted by the Delaware Supreme Court in 1996, in my opinion. In stating the basis for this view, I start with the recognition that in recent years the Delaware Supreme Court has made it clear — especially in its jurisprudence concerning takeovers, from Smith v. Van Gorkom through Paramount Communications v. QVC — the seriousness with which the corporation law views the role of the corporate board. Secondly, I note the elementary fact that relevant and timely information is an essential predicate for satisfaction of the board's supervisory and monitoring role under Section 141 of the Delaware General Corporation Law. Thirdly, I note the potential impact of the federal organizational sentencing guidelines on any business organization. Any rational person attempting in good faith to meet an organizational governance responsibility would be bound to take into account this development and the enhanced penalties and the opportunities for reduced sanctions that it offers.

In light of these developments, it would, in my opinion, be a mistake to conclude that our Supreme Court's statement in *Graham* concerning "espionage" means that corporate boards may satisfy their obligation to be reasonably informed concerning the corporation, without assuring themselves that information and reporting systems exist in the organization that are reasonably designed to provide to senior management and to the board itself timely, accurate information sufficient to allow management and the board, each within its scope, to reach informed judgments concerning both the corporation's compliance with law and its business performance.

Obviously the level of detail that is appropriate for such an information system is a question of business judgment. And obviously too, no rationally designed information and reporting system will remove the possibility that the corporation will violate laws or regulations, or that senior officers or directors may nevertheless sometimes be misled or otherwise fail reasonably to detect acts material to the corporation's compliance with the law. But it is important that the board exercise a good faith judgment that the corporation's information and reporting system is in concept and design adequate to assure the board that appropriate information will come to its attention in a timely manner as a matter of ordinary operations, so that it may satisfy its responsibility.

Thus, I am of the view that a director's obligation includes a duty to attempt in good faith to assure that a corporate information and reporting system, which the board concludes is adequate, exists, and that failure to do so under some circumstances may, in theory at least, render a director liable for losses caused by non-compliance with applicable legal standards. . . .

III. ANALYSIS OF THIRD AMENDED COMPLAINT AND SETTLEMENT

A. THE CLAIMS

On balance, after reviewing an extensive record in this case, including numerous documents and three depositions, I conclude that this settlement is fair and reasonable. In light of the fact that the Caremark Board already has a functioning committee charged with overseeing corporate compliance, the changes in corporate practice that are presented as consideration for the settlement do not impress one as very significant. Nonetheless, that consideration appears fully adequate to support dismissal of the derivative claims of director fault asserted, because those claims find no substantial evidentiary support in the record and quite likely were susceptible to a motion to dismiss in all events.

In order to show that the Caremark directors breached their duty of care by failing adequately to control Caremark's employees, plaintiffs would have to show either (1) that the directors knew or (2) should have known that violations of law were occurring and, in either event, (3) that the directors took no steps in a good faith effort to prevent or remedy that situation, and (4) that such failure proximately resulted in the losses complained of. . . .

1. Knowing violation of statute: Concerning the possibility that the Caremark directors knew of violations of law, none of the documents submitted for review, nor any of the deposition transcripts appear to provide evidence of it. . . . [T]he Board appears to have been informed by experts that the company's practices, while contestable, were lawful. There is no evidence that reliance on such reports was not reasonable. . . .

2. Failure to monitor: Since it does appear that the Board was to some extent unaware of the activities that led to liability, I turn to a consideration of the other potential avenue to director liability that the pleadings take: director inattention or "negligence." Generally where a claim of directorial liability for corporate loss is predicated upon ignorance of liability-creating activities within the corporation, as in *Graham* or in this case, in my opinion only a sustained or systematic failure of the board to exercise oversight — such as an utter failure to attempt to assure a reasonable information and reporting system exits — will establish the lack of good faith that is a necessary condition to liability. Such a test of liability — lack of good faith as evidenced by sustained or systematic failure of a director to exercise reasonable oversight — is quite high. But, a demanding test of liability in the oversight context is probably beneficial to corporate shareholders as a class, as it is in the board decision context, since it makes board service by qualified persons more likely, while continuing to act as a stimulus to good faith performance of duty by such directors.

Here the record supplies essentially no evidence that the director defendants were guilty of a sustained failure to exercise their oversight function. . . .

PROBLEM 8-1

Conrad White, CEO of Hollander, was in many ways an old-school newspaper guy: creative, intense, imperious, mercurial. Used to three-martini lunches and doing not very much work in the afternoons, he was also a defendant in numerous sexual harassment lawsuits by Hollander employees. (Perhaps these two facts are related.) According to an article in U.S. News & World Report, a female employee of Hollander reported White's unwelcome advances to a senior Hollander officer as early as 2000. Over the next several years, Hollander paid millions to settle multiple harassment suits against White. (The company reportedly paid $3.5 million in one case alone.)

White denied allegations of sexual harassment, and company officials claimed that the lawsuits were attempts at extortion. The women who worked for White, however, told a different story. At least five women had filed complaints with the California Department of Fair Housing and Employment, and four of those filed lawsuits against Hollander. Each of the complaints alleged that White has propositioned women employees for sex and retaliated against those who refused him.

When the board of directors first learned of the allegations is a matter of some dispute, but one director who was interviewed for the U.S. News story claimed that the board was unaware until January 2002, when the first lawsuit was filed. The board, composed exclusively of men, formed a special committee to investigate the harassment claims, and that committee hired its own lawyers. The directors on the special committee did not personally speak with any employees, but in 2005 the committee concluded that the board of directors should take a more active role in enforcing the company's sexual harassment policy.

White is said to have developed a "cult of personality" at Hollander. Indeed, according to the U.S. News story, one of the directors felt that the best way to fulfill his fiduciary duty to shareholders was to ensure that White did not get into trouble. (How exactly he was going to do that remained unspecified.) Barbara Howar, a former correspondent for CBS news, described Hollander's other managers as "obsequious and subservient to White." In short, White was the star CEO around which the company was built.

What additional facts relating to the foregoing situation would a shareholder plaintiff find most useful in mounting a case against the directors of Hollander based on a breach of the duty of oversight?

2.   The Duty of Good Faith

In *Caremark*, Chancellor Allen held that a "sustained or systematic failure of the board to exercise oversight — such as an utter failure to attempt to assure that a reasonable information and reporting system exists — will establish the lack of good faith that is a necessary condition to liability." This language suggested that plaintiffs could sustain a *duty of care* claim under *Caremark* by alleging "bad faith." Bad faith is also one way to overcome the business judgment rule, as you'll recall. Moreover, allegations of a lack of good faith have another benefit in litigation. As explored in more detail in Chapter 9, Delaware and the drafters of the Model Business Corporation Act (MBCA) reacted to Smith v. Van Gorkom by enacting legislation in 1986 that permits companies to include "exculpation clauses" in their certificate of incorporation. *See* Delaware General Corporation Law (DGCL) § 102(b)(7); MBCA § 2.02 (b)(4). An exculpation clause allows the corporation to eliminate director liability to the corporation for certain kinds of breach, including breach of the duty of care. Among other limitations, companies may not eliminate liability for acts or omissions in bad faith (Delaware) or for intentionally harming the corporation (MBCA). So allegations of a lack of good faith also serve to overcome exculpation clauses.

In the wake of *Caremark*, in light of these other doctrines, claims of lack of good faith proliferated, and the Delaware courts began to struggle with doctrinal issues such as whether a duty to act in good faith is a separate fiduciary duty, whether it is part of the duty of care as suggested in *Caremark*, whether it is part of the duty of loyalty as suggested in other cases, or whether it is part of all of the directors' fiduciary duties but not a stand-alone duty. The following two cases, decided by the Delaware Supreme Court, have answered those questions, but notice how Stone v. Ritter, decided just three months after *Disney*, both revises *Disney*'s discussion of good faith and reconceptualizes directors' *Caremark* duties to be a component of the duty of loyalty. That reconceptualization is important, because directors do not initially have the benefit of the business judgment rule for duty of loyalty claims, they cannot be exculpated for duty of loyalty violations, and they cannot be insured or indemnified for duty of loyalty violations.

IN RE THE WALT DISNEY COMPANY DERIVATIVE LITIGATION

2006 WL 1562466
Supreme Court of Delaware
June 8, 2006

JACOBS, Justice.

In August 1995, Michael Ovitz ("Ovitz") and The Walt Disney Company ("Disney" or the "Company") entered into an employment agreement under which Ovitz would serve as President of Disney for five years. In December 1996, only fourteen months after he commenced employment, Ovitz was terminated without cause, resulting in a severance payout to Ovitz valued at approximately $130 million.

In January 1997, several Disney shareholders brought derivative actions in the Court of Chancery, on behalf of Disney, against Ovitz and the directors of Disney who served at the time of the events complained of (the "Disney defendants"). The plaintiffs claimed that the $130 million severance payout was the product of fiduciary duty and contractual breaches by Ovitz, and breaches of fiduciary duty by the Disney defendants, and a waste of assets. After the disposition of several pretrial motions and an appeal to this Court, the case was tried before the Chancellor over 37 days between October 20, 2004 and January 19, 2005. In August 2005, the Chancellor handed down a well-crafted 174 page Opinion and Order, determining that "the director defendants did not breach their fiduciary duties or commit waste." The Court entered judgment in favor of all defendants on all claims alleged in the amended complaint.

The plaintiffs have appealed from that judgment, claiming that the Court of Chancery committed multitudinous errors. We conclude, for the reasons that follow, that the Chancellor's factual findings and legal rulings were correct and not erroneous in any respect. Accordingly, the judgment entered by the Court of Chancery will be affirmed.

I. THE FACTS

[The facts are recounted in fascinating detail in the Court's opinion. The basic facts for our perspective are as follows: Michael Ovitz was recruited to leave his position as one of the founders and leading partners of Creative Artists Agency

("CAA"), a powerful talent agency in Hollywood from which he was earning an annual income of over $20 million, to become his friend Michael Eisner's second in command at Disney. In order to approximate the financial aspects of his income from CAA, Ovitz negotiated hard for a generous five-year contract with Disney. The Ovitz Employment Agreement ("OEA") sought to protect both parties in the event that Ovitz's employment ended prematurely, and provided that absent defined causes, neither party could terminate the agreement before the end of its five-year term. If Ovitz walked away for any reasons other than those permitted under the OEA, he would forfeit his remaining benefits and could be enjoined from working for a competitor. If Disney fired Ovitz for any reason other than gross negligence or malfeasance, he would be entitled to generous payments under a non-fault termination ("NFT"). These included his remaining salary through the end of his five-year term; $7.5 million a year for unaccrued bonuses (which were otherwise defined in the OEA as between zero and $7.5 million per year, depending on performance); the immediate vesting of his first tranche of three million stock options; and a $10 million cash-out payment for his second tranche of options.

Ovtiz's transition from talent agent ("sell side") to creative use of talent ("buy side") went very badly. As the Court stated:

> The Court of Chancery identified three competing theories as to why Ovitz did not succeed:
> First, plaintiffs argue that Ovitz failed to follow Eisner's directives, especially in regard to acquisitions, and that generally, Ovitz did very little. Second, Ovitz contends Eisner's micromanaging prevented Ovitz from having the authority necessary to make the changes that Ovitz thought were appropriate. In addition, Ovitz believes he was not given enough time for his efforts to bear fruit. Third, the remaining defendants simply posit that Ovitz failed to transition from a private to a public company, from the "sell side to the buy side," and otherwise did not adapt to the Company culture or fit in with other executives. In the end, however, it makes no difference why Ovitz was not as successful as his reputation would have led many to expect, so long as he was not grossly negligent or malfeasant.

Although the plaintiffs attempted to show that Ovitz acted improperly (*i.e.*, with gross negligence or malfeasance) while in office, the Chancellor found that the trial record did not support those allegations.

Thus, a little over a year after he joined Disney, the Disney board granted Ovitz a non-fault termination. This decision was made after Disney's general counsel, Stanley Litvack, concluded that Disney could not fire Ovitz for cause and avoid the expensive payments associated with a non-fault termination. The effect of the non-fault termination was to provide compensation to Ovitz of $140 million for 14 months' work. Disney's shareholders sued.]

II. Summary of Appellants' Claims of Error

As noted earlier, the Court of Chancery rejected all of the plaintiff-appellants' claims on the merits and entered judgment in favor of the defendant-appellees on all counts. On appeal, the appellants claim that the adverse judgment rests upon multiple erroneous rulings and should be reversed, because the 1995 decision to approve the OEA and the 1996 decision to terminate Ovitz on a non-fault basis, resulted from various breaches of fiduciary duty by Ovitz and the Disney directors.

The appellants' claims of error are most easily analyzed in two separate groupings: (1) the claims against the Disney defendants and (2) the claims against Ovitz. The first category encompasses the claims that the Disney defendants breached their fiduciary duties to act with due care and in good faith by (1) approving the OEA, and specifically, its NFT provisions; and (2) approving the NFT severance payment to Ovitz upon his termination — a payment that is also claimed to constitute corporate waste. It is notable that the appellants do *not* contend that the Disney defendants are directly liable as a consequence of those fiduciary duty breaches. Rather, appellants' core argument is indirect, *i.e.*, that those breaches of fiduciary duty deprive the Disney defendants of the protection of business judgment review, and require them to shoulder the burden of establishing that their acts were entirely fair to Disney. That burden, the appellants contend, the Disney defendants failed to carry. [37] The appellants claim that by ruling that the Disney defendants did not breach their fiduciary duty to act with due care or in good faith, the Court of Chancery committed reversible error in numerous respects. Alternatively, the appellants claim that even if the business judgment presumptions apply, the Disney defendants are nonetheless liable, because the NFT payout constituted corporate waste and the Court of Chancery erred in concluding otherwise. . . .

[The claims against Ovitz were that he owed fiduciary duties while negotiating his employment agreement, since he started work before the contract was finalized; and in negotiating a NFT. The Court summarily rejected those claims. It found the critical terms of the OEA were negotiated before Ovitz started work, and that he had no part in the deliberations about the NFT.] . . .

IV. THE CLAIMS AGAINST THE DISNEY DEFENDANTS

We next turn to the claims of error that relate to the Disney defendants. Those claims are subdivisible into two groups: (A) claims arising out of the approval of the OEA and of Ovitz's election as President; and (B) claims arising out of the NFT severance payment to Ovitz upon his termination. We address separately those two categories and the issues that they generate.

A. CLAIMS ARISING FROM THE APPROVAL OF THE OEA AND OVITZ'S ELECTION AS PRESIDENT

As earlier noted, the appellants' core argument in the trial court was that the Disney defendants' approval of the OEA and election of Ovitz as President were not entitled to business judgment rule protection, because those actions were either grossly negligent or not performed in good faith. The Court of Chancery

---

37. The plaintiff-appellants appear to have structured their liability claim in this indirect way because Article Eleventh of the Disney Certificate of Incorporation contains an exculpatory provision modeled upon 8 *Del. C.* § 102(b)(7). That provision precludes a money damages remedy against the Disney directors for adjudicated breaches of their duty of care. For that reason the plaintiffs are asserting their due care claim as the basis for shifting the standard of review from business judgment to entire fairness, rather than as a basis for direct liability. Presumably for the sake of consistency the appellants are utilizing their good faith fiduciary claim in a like manner.

rejected these arguments, and held that the appellants had failed to prove that the Disney defendants had breached any fiduciary duty.

For clarity of presentation we address the claimed errors relating to the fiduciary duty of care rulings separately from those that relate to the directors' fiduciary duty to act in good faith.

1. The Due Care Determinations

The plaintiff-appellants advance five contentions to support their claim that the Chancellor reversibly erred by concluding that the plaintiffs had failed to establish a violation of the Disney defendants' duty of care. The appellants claim that the Chancellor erred by: (1) treating as distinct questions whether the plaintiffs had established by a preponderance of the evidence either gross negligence or a lack of good faith; (2) ruling that the old board was not required to approve the OEA; (3) determining whether the old board had breached its duty of care on a director-by-director basis rather than collectively; (4) concluding that the compensation committee members did not breach their duty of care in approving the NFT provisions of the OEA; and (5) holding that the remaining members of the old board (*i.e.*, the directors who were not members of the compensation committee) had not breached their duty of care in electing Ovitz as Disney's President.

To the extent that these claims attack legal rulings of the Court of Chancery we review them *de novo*. To the extent they attack the Court's factual findings, those findings will be upheld where they are based on the Chancellor's assessment of live testimony. The issue these claims present is whether the Court of Chancery legally (and reversibly) erred in one or more of the foregoing respects. We conclude that the Chancellor committed no error.

(a) Treating Due Care and Bad Faith as Separate Grounds for Denying Business Judgment Rule Review

This argument is best understood against the backdrop of the presumptions that cloak director action being reviewed under the business judgment standard. Our law presumes that "in making a business decision the directors of a corporation acted on an informed basis, in good faith, and in the honest belief that the action taken was in the best interests of the company." Those presumptions can be rebutted if the plaintiff shows that the directors breached their fiduciary duty of care or of loyalty or acted in bad faith. If that is shown, the burden then shifts to the director defendants to demonstrate that the challenged act or transaction was entirely fair to the corporation and its shareholders.

Because no duty of loyalty claim was asserted against the Disney defendants, the only way to rebut the business judgment rule presumptions would be to show that the Disney defendants had either breached their duty of care or had not acted in good faith. At trial, the plaintiff-appellants attempted to establish both grounds, but the Chancellor determined that the plaintiffs had failed to prove either.

The appellants' first claim is that the Chancellor erroneously (i) failed to make a "threshold determination" of gross negligence, and (ii) "conflated" the appellants' burden to rebut the business judgment presumptions, with an analysis of whether the directors' conduct fell within the 8 *Del. C.* § 102(b)(7) provision that precludes exculpation of directors from monetary liability "for acts or omissions not in good faith." The argument runs as follows: Emerald

Partners v. Berlin required the Chancellor first to determine whether the business judgment rule presumptions were rebutted based upon a showing that the board violated its duty of care, *i.e.*, acted with gross negligence. If gross negligence were established, the burden would shift to the directors to establish that the OEA was entirely fair. Only if the directors failed to meet that burden could the trial court then address the directors' Section 102(b)(7) exculpation defense, including the statutory exception for acts not in good faith.

This argument lacks merit. To make the argument the appellants must ignore the distinction between (i) a determination of bad faith for the threshold purpose of rebutting the business judgment rule presumptions, and (ii) a bad faith determination for purposes of evaluating the availability of charter-authorized exculpation from monetary damage liability after liability has been established. Our law clearly permits a judicial assessment of director good faith for that former purpose. Nothing in *Emerald Partners* requires the Court of Chancery to consider only evidence of lack of due care (*i.e.* gross negligence) in determining whether the business judgment rule presumptions have been rebutted.

Even if the trial court's analytical approach were improper, the appellants have failed to demonstrate any prejudice. The Chancellor's determinations of due care and good faith were analytically distinct and were separately conducted, even though both were done for the purpose of deciding whether to apply the business judgment standard of review. Nowhere have the appellants shown that the result would have been any different had the Chancellor proceeded in the manner that they now advocate. . . .

(d) Holding that the Compensation Committee Members Did Not Fail to Exercise Due Care in Approving the OEA

The appellants next challenge the Chancellor's determination that although the compensation committee's decision-making process fell far short of corporate governance "best practices," the committee members breached no duty of care in considering and approving the NFT terms of the OEA. That conclusion is reversible error, the appellants claim, because the record establishes that the compensation committee members did not properly inform themselves of the material facts and, hence, were grossly negligent in approving the NFT provisions of the OEA.

The appellants advance five reasons why a reversal is compelled: (i) not all committee members reviewed a draft of the OEA; (ii) the minutes of the September 26, 1995 compensation committee meeting do not recite any discussion of the grounds for which Ovitz could receive a non-fault termination; (iii) the committee members did not consider any comparable employment agreements or the economic impact of extending the exercisability of the options being granted to Ovitz; (iv) Crystal did not attend the September 26, 1995, committee meeting, nor was his letter distributed to or discussed with Poitier and Lozano; and (v) Poitier and Lozano did not review the spreadsheets generated by Watson. These contentions amount essentially to an attack upon underlying factual findings that will be upheld where they result from the Chancellor's assessment of live testimony.

Although the appellants have balkanized their due care claim into several fragmented parts, the overall thrust of that claim is that the compensation committee approved the OEA with NFT provisions that could potentially result in an enormous payout, without informing themselves of what the full magnitude of that payout could be. Rejecting that claim, the Court of Chancery found that the compensation committee members were adequately informed. The issue thus becomes whether that finding is supported by the evidence of record. We conclude that it is.

In our view, a helpful approach is to compare what actually happened here to what would have occurred had the committee followed a "best practices" (or "best case") scenario, from a process standpoint. In a "best case" scenario, all committee members would have received, before or at the committee's first meeting on September 26, 1995, a spreadsheet or similar document prepared by (or with the assistance of) a compensation expert (in this case, Graef Crystal). Making different, alternative assumptions, the spreadsheet would disclose the amounts that Ovitz could receive under the OEA in each circumstance that might foreseeably arise. One variable in that matrix of possibilities would be the cost to Disney of a non-fault termination for each of the five years of the initial term of the OEA. The contents of the spreadsheet would be explained to the committee members, either by the expert who prepared it or by a fellow committee member similarly knowledgeable about the subject. That spreadsheet, which ultimately would become an exhibit to the minutes of the compensation committee meeting, would form the basis of the committee's deliberations and decision.

Had that scenario been followed, there would be no dispute (and no basis for litigation) over what information was furnished to the committee members or when it was furnished. Regrettably, the committee's informational and decision-making process used here was not so tidy. That is one reason why the Chancellor found that although the committee's process did not fall below the level required for a proper exercise of due care, it did fall short of what best practices would have counseled.

The Disney compensation committee met twice: on September 26 and October 16, 1995. The minutes of the September 26 meeting reflect that the committee approved the terms of the OEA (at that time embodied in the form of a letter agreement), except for the option grants, which were not approved until October 16 — after the Disney stock incentive plan had been amended to provide for those options. At the September 26 meeting, the compensation committee considered a "term sheet" which, in summarizing the material terms of the OEA, relevantly disclosed that in the event of a non-fault termination, Ovitz would receive: (i) the present value of his salary ($1 million per year) for the balance of the contract term, (ii) the present value of his annual bonus payments (computed at $7.5 million) for the balance of the contract term, (iii) a $10 million termination fee, and (iv) the acceleration of his options for 3 million shares, which would become immediately exercisable at market price.

Thus, the compensation committee knew that in the event of an NFT, Ovitz's severance payment alone could be in the range of $40 million cash,[77] plus the

---

77. The cash portion of the NFT payout after one year would be the sum of: (i) the present value of Ovitz's remaining salary over the life of the contract (4 years × $1 million/yr = $4 million, reduced to present value), plus (ii) the present value of his unpaid annual bonus payments ($7.5 million/yr × 4 years = $30 million, discounted to present value), plus (iii) $10 million cash for the second tranche of options. These amounts total $44 million before discounting the $34 million of annual salaries and bonuses to present value. The actual cash payment to Ovitz was $38.5 million, which, it would appear, reflects the then-present value of the $34 million of salaries and bonuses.

value of the accelerated options. Because the actual payout to Ovitz was approximately $130 million, of which roughly $38.5 million was cash, the value of the options at the time of the NFT payout would have been about $91.5 million. Thus, the issue may be framed as whether the compensation committee members knew, at the time they approved the OEA, that the value of the option component of the severance package could reach the $92 million order of magnitude if they terminated Ovitz without cause after one year. The evidentiary record shows that the committee members were so informed.

On this question the documentation is far less than what best practices would have dictated. There is no exhibit to the minutes that discloses, in a single document, the estimated value of the accelerated options in the event of an NFT termination after one year. The information imparted to the committee members on that subject is, however, supported by other evidence, most notably the trial testimony of various witnesses about spreadsheets that were prepared for the compensation committee meetings.

The compensation committee members derived their information about the potential magnitude of an NFT payout from two sources. The first was the value of the "benchmark" options previously granted to Eisner and Wells and the valuations by Watson of the proposed Ovitz options. Ovitz's options were set at 75% of parity with the options previously granted to Eisner and to Frank Wells. Because the compensation committee had established those earlier benchmark option grants to Eisner and Wells and were aware of their value, a simple mathematical calculation would have informed them of the potential value range of Ovitz's options. Also, in August and September 1995, Watson and Russell met with Graef Crystal to determine (among other things) the value of the potential Ovitz options, assuming different scenarios. Crystal valued the options under the Black-Scholes method, while Watson used a different valuation metric. Watson recorded his calculations and the resulting values on a set of spreadsheets that reflected what option profits Ovitz might receive, based upon a range of different assumptions about stock market price increases. Those spreadsheets were shared with, and explained to, the committee members at the September meeting.

The committee's second source of information was the amount of "downside protection" that Ovitz was demanding. Ovitz required financial protection from the risk of leaving a very lucrative and secure position at CAA, of which he was a controlling partner, to join a publicly held corporation to which Ovitz was a stranger, and that had a very different culture and an environment which prevented him from completely controlling his destiny. The committee members knew that by leaving CAA and coming to Disney, Ovitz would be sacrificing "booked" CAA commissions of $150 to $200 million — an amount that Ovitz demanded as protection against the risk that his employment relationship with Disney might not work out. Ovitz wanted at least $50 million of that compensation to take the form of an "up-front" signing bonus. Had the $50 million bonus been paid, the size of the option grant would have been lower. Because it was contrary to Disney policy, the compensation committee rejected the up-front signing bonus demand, and elected instead to compensate Ovitz at the "back end," by awarding him options that would be phased in over the five-year term of the OEA.

It is on this record that the Chancellor found that the compensation committee was informed of the material facts relating to an NFT payout. If measured in terms of the documentation that would have been generated if "best practices" had been followed, that record leaves much to be desired. The Chancellor acknowledged that, and so do we. But, the Chancellor also found that despite its imperfections, the evidentiary record was sufficient to support the conclusion that the compensation committee had adequately informed itself of the potential magnitude of the entire severance package, including the options, that Ovitz would receive in the event of an early NFT.

The OEA was specifically structured to compensate Ovitz for walking away from $150 million to $200 million of anticipated commissions from CAA over the five-year OEA contract term. This meant that if Ovitz was terminated without cause, the earlier in the contract term the termination occurred the larger the severance amount would be to replace the lost commissions. Indeed, because Ovitz was terminated after only one year, the total amount of his severance payment (about $130 million) closely approximated the lower end of the range of Ovitz's forfeited commissions ($150 million), less the compensation Ovitz received during his first and only year as Disney's President. Accordingly, the Court of Chancery had a sufficient evidentiary basis in the record from which to find that, at the time they approved the OEA, the compensation committee members were adequately informed of the potential magnitude of an early NFT severance payout. . . .

2. The Good Faith Determinations

The Court of Chancery held that the business judgment rule presumptions protected the decisions of the compensation committee and the remaining Disney directors, not only because they had acted with due care but also because they had not acted in bad faith. That latter ruling, the appellants claim, was reversible error because the Chancellor formulated and then applied an incorrect definition of bad faith.

In its Opinion the Court of Chancery defined bad faith as follows:

> Upon long and careful consideration, I am of the opinion that the concept of *intentional dereliction of duty*, a *conscious disregard for one's responsibilities*, is an appropriate (although not the only) standard for determining whether fiduciaries have acted in good faith. Deliberate indifference and inaction *in the face of a duty to act* is, in my mind, conduct that is clearly disloyal to the corporation. It is the epitome of faithless conduct.

The appellants contend that definition is erroneous for two reasons. First they claim that the trial court had adopted a different definition in its 2003 decision denying the motion to dismiss the complaint, and the Court's post-trial (2005) definition materially altered the 2003 definition to appellants' prejudice. Their argument runs as follows: under the Chancellor's 2003 definition of bad faith, the directors must have "*consciously and intentionally disregarded their responsibilities*, adopting a 'we don't care about the risks' attitude concerning a material corporate decision." Under the 2003 formulation, appellants say, "directors violate their duty of good faith if they are making material decisions without adequate information and without adequate deliberation[,]" but under the 2005 post-trial definition, bad faith requires proof of a subjective bad motive or intent. This definitional change, it is claimed, was procedurally prejudicial because appellants relied on the 2003 definition in presenting their evidence of bad faith at the trial. Without any intervening change in the law, the Court of Chancery could not unilaterally alter its definition and then hold the appellants to a higher, more stringent standard.

Second, the appellants claim that the Chancellor's post-trial definition of bad faith is erroneous substantively. They argue that the 2003 formulation was (and is) the correct definition, because it is "logically tied to board decision-making under the duty of care." The post-trial formulation, on the other hand, "wrongly incorporated substantive elements regarding the rationality of the decisions under review rather than being constrained, as in a due care analysis, to strictly procedural criteria." We conclude that both arguments must fail.

The appellants' first argument — that there is a real, significant difference between the Chancellor's pre-trial and post-trial definitions of bad faith — is plainly wrong. We perceive no substantive difference between the Court of Chancery's 2003 definition of bad faith — a "conscious[] and intentional[] disregard[][of] responsibilities, adopting a 'we don't care about the risks' attitude . . ." — and its 2005 post-trial definition — an "intentional dereliction of duty, a conscious disregard for one's responsibilities." Both formulations express the same concept, although in slightly different language.

The most telling evidence that there is no substantive difference between the two formulations is that the appellants are forced to contrive a difference. Appellants assert that under the 2003 formulation, "directors violate their duty of good faith if they are making material decisions without adequate information and without adequate deliberation." For that *ipse dixit* they cite no legal authority. That comes as no surprise because their verbal effort to collapse the duty to act in good faith into the duty to act with due care, is not unlike putting a rabbit into the proverbial hat and then blaming the trial judge for making the insertion.

The appellants essentially concede that their proof of bad faith is insufficient to satisfy the standard articulated by the Court of Chancery. That is why they ask this Court to treat a failure to exercise due care as a failure to act in good faith. Unfortunately for appellants, that "rule," even if it were accepted, would not help their case. If we were to conflate these two duties and declare that a breach of the duty to be properly informed violates the duty to act in good faith, the outcome would be no different, because, as the Chancellor and we now have held, the appellants failed to establish any breach of the duty of care. To say it differently, even if the Chancellor's definition of bad faith were erroneous, the error would not be reversible because the appellants cannot satisfy the very test they urge us to adopt.

For that reason, our analysis of the appellants' bad faith claim could end at this point. In other circumstances it would. This case, however, is one in which the duty to act in good faith has played a prominent role, yet to date is not a well-developed area of our corporate fiduciary law. Although the good faith concept has recently been the subject of considerable scholarly writing,[99] which includes

---

99. *See, e.g.,* Hillary A. Sale, *Delaware's Good Faith,* 89 Cornell L.Rev. 456 (2004); Matthew R. Berry, *Does Delaware's Section 102(b)(7) Protect Reckless Directors From Personal Liability? Only If Delaware Courts Act in Good Faith,* 79 Wash. L.Rev. 1125 (2004); John L. Reed and Matt Neiderman, *Good Faith and the Ability of Directors to Assert § 102(b)(7) of the Delaware Corporation Law as a Defense to Claims Alleging Abdication, Lack of Oversight, and Similar Breaches of Fiduciary Duty,* 29 Del. J. Corp. L. 111 (2004); David Rosenberg, *Making Sense of Good Faith in Delaware Corporate Fiduciary Law: A Contractarian Approach,* 29 Del. J. Corp. L. 491 (2004); Sean J. Griffith, *Good Faith Business Judgment: A Theory of*

articles focused on this specific case,[100] the duty to act in good faith is, up to this point relatively uncharted. Because of the increased recognition of the importance of good faith, some conceptual guidance to the corporate community may be helpful. For that reason we proceed to address the merits of the appellants' second argument.

The precise question is whether the Chancellor's articulated standard for bad faith corporate fiduciary conduct — intentional dereliction of duty, a conscious disregard for one's responsibilities — is legally correct. In approaching that question, we note that the Chancellor characterized that definition as "*an appropriate (although not the only)* standard for determining whether fiduciaries have acted in good faith." That observation is accurate and helpful, because as a matter of simple logic, at least three different categories of fiduciary behavior are candidates for the "bad faith" pejorative label.

The first category involves so-called "subjective bad faith," that is, fiduciary conduct motivated by an actual intent to do harm. That such conduct constitutes classic, quintessential bad faith is a proposition so well accepted in the liturgy of fiduciary law that it borders on axiomatic. We need not dwell further on this category, because no such conduct is claimed to have occurred, or did occur, in this case.

The second category of conduct, which is at the opposite end of the spectrum, involves lack of due care — that is, fiduciary action taken solely by reason of gross negligence and without any malevolent intent. In this case, appellants assert claims of gross negligence to establish breaches not only of director due care but also of the directors' duty to act in good faith. Although the Chancellor found, and we agree, that the appellants failed to establish gross negligence, to afford guidance we address the issue of whether gross negligence (including a failure to inform one's self of available material facts), without more, can also constitute bad faith. The answer is clearly no.

From a broad philosophical standpoint, that question is more complex than would appear, if only because (as the Chancellor and others have observed) "issues of good faith are (to a certain degree) inseparably and necessarily intertwined with the duties of care and loyalty. . . ." But, in the pragmatic, conduct-regulating legal realm which calls for more precise conceptual line drawing, the answer is that grossly negligent conduct, without more, does not and cannot constitute a breach of the fiduciary duty to act in good faith. The conduct that is the subject of due care may overlap with the conduct that comes within the rubric of good faith in a psychological sense,[104] but from a legal standpoint those duties are and must remain quite distinct. Both our legislative history

---

Rhetoric in Corporate Law Jurisprudence, 55 Duke L.J. 1 (2005) ("Griffith"); Melvin A. Eisenberg, *The Duty of Good Faith in Corporate Law,* 31 Del. J. Corp. L. 1 (2005); Filippo Rossi, *Making Sense of the Delaware Supreme Court's Triad of Fiduciary Duties* (June 22, 2005), *available at http://ssrn.com /abstract= 755784;* Christopher M. Bruner, *"Good Faith," State of Mind, and the Outer Boundaries of Director Liability in Corporate Law* (Boston Univ. Sch. of Law Working Paper No. 05-19), *available at http://ssrn.com/abstract= 832944;* Sean J. Griffith & Myron T. Steele, *On Corporate Law Federalism Threatening the Thaumatrope,* 61 Bus. Law. 1 (2005).

100. *See, e.g.,* Robert Baker, *In Re Walt Disney: What It Means To The Definition Of Good Faith, Exculpatory Clauses, and the Nature of Executive Compensation,* 4 Fla. St. U. Bus. Rev. 261 (2004-2005); Tara L. Dunn, *The Developing Theory of Good Faith In Director Conduct: Are Delaware Courts Ready To Force Corporate Directors To Go Out-Of-Pocket After Disney IV?,* 83 Denv. U.L.Rev. 531 (2005).

104. An example of such overlap might be the hypothetical case where a director, because of subjective hostility to the corporation on whose board he serves, fails to inform himself of, or to devote sufficient attention to, the matters on which he is making decisions as a fiduciary. In such a

and our common law jurisprudence distinguish sharply between the duties to exercise due care and to act in good faith, and highly significant consequences flow from that distinction.

The Delaware General Assembly has addressed the distinction between bad faith and a failure to exercise due care (*i.e.*, gross negligence) in two separate contexts. The first is Section 102(b)(7) of the DGCL, which authorizes Delaware corporations, by a provision in the certificate of incorporation, to exculpate their directors from monetary damage liability for a breach of the duty of care. That exculpatory provision affords significant protection to directors of Delaware corporations. The statute carves out several exceptions, however, including most relevantly, "for acts or omissions not in good faith. . . ." Thus, a corporation can exculpate its directors from monetary liability for a breach of the duty of care, but not for conduct that is not in good faith. To adopt a definition of bad faith that would cause a violation of the duty of care automatically to become an act or omission "not in good faith," would eviscerate the protections accorded to directors by the General Assembly's adoption of Section 102(b)(7).

A second legislative recognition of the distinction between fiduciary conduct that is grossly negligent and conduct that is not in good faith, is Delaware's indemnification statute, found at 8 *Del. C.* § 145. To oversimplify, subsections (a) and (b) of that statute permit a corporation to indemnify *(inter alia)* any person who is or was a director, officer, employee or agent of the corporation against expenses (including attorneys' fees), judgments, fines and amounts paid in settlement of specified actions, suits or proceedings, where (among other things): (i) that person is, was, or is threatened to be made a party to that action, suit or proceeding, and (ii) that person "acted in good faith and in a manner the person reasonably believed to be in or not opposed to the best interests of the corporation. . . ." Thus, under Delaware statutory law a director or officer of a corporation can be indemnified for liability (and litigation expenses) incurred by reason of a violation of the duty of care, but not for a violation of the duty to act in good faith.

Section 145, like Section 102(b)(7), evidences the intent of the Delaware General Assembly to afford significant protections to directors (and, in the case of Section 145, other fiduciaries) of Delaware corporations. To adopt a definition that conflates the duty of care with the duty to act in good faith by making a violation of the former an automatic violation of the latter, would nullify those legislative protections and defeat the General Assembly's intent. There is no basis in policy, precedent or common sense that would justify dismantling the distinction between gross negligence and bad faith.

That leaves the third category of fiduciary conduct, which falls in between the first two categories of (1) conduct motivated by subjective bad intent and (2) conduct resulting from gross negligence. This third category is what the Chancellor's definition of bad faith—intentional dereliction of duty, a conscious disregard for one's responsibilities—is intended to capture. The

---

case, two states of mind coexist in the same person: subjective bad intent (which would lead to a finding of bad faith) and gross negligence (which would lead to a finding of a breach of the duty of care). Although the coexistence of both states of mind may make them indistinguishable from a psychological standpoint, the fiduciary duties that they cause the director to violate—care and good faith—are legally separate and distinct.

question is whether such misconduct is properly treated as a non-exculpable, nonindemnifiable violation of the fiduciary duty to act in good faith. In our view it must be, for at least two reasons.

First, the universe of fiduciary misconduct is not limited to either disloyalty in the classic sense (*i.e.*, preferring the adverse self-interest of the fiduciary or of a related person to the interest of the corporation) or gross negligence. Cases have arisen where corporate directors have no conflicting self-interest in a decision, yet engage in misconduct that is more culpable than simple inattention or failure to be informed of all facts material to the decision. To protect the interests of the corporation and its shareholders, fiduciary conduct of this kind, which does not involve disloyalty (as traditionally defined) but is qualitatively more culpable than gross negligence, should be proscribed. A vehicle is needed to address such violations doctrinally, and that doctrinal vehicle is the duty to act in good faith. . . .

Second, the legislature has also recognized this intermediate category of fiduciary misconduct, which ranks between conduct involving subjective bad faith and gross negligence. Section 102(b)(7)(ii) of the DGCL expressly denies money damage exculpation for "acts or omissions not in good faith or which involve intentional misconduct or a knowing violation of law." By its very terms that provision distinguishes between "intentional misconduct" and a "knowing violation of law" (both examples of subjective bad faith) on the one hand, and "acts . . . not in good faith," on the other. Because the statute exculpates directors only for conduct amounting to gross negligence, the statutory denial of exculpation for "acts . . . not in good faith" must encompass the intermediate category of misconduct captured by the Chancellor's definition of bad faith.

For these reasons, we uphold the Court of Chancery's definition as a legally appropriate, although not the exclusive, definition of fiduciary bad faith. We need go no further. To engage in an effort to craft (in the Court's words) "a definitive and categorical definition of the universe of acts that would constitute bad faith"[112] would be unwise and is unnecessary to dispose of the issues presented on this appeal.

Having sustained the Chancellor's finding that the Disney directors acted in good faith when approving the OEA and electing Ovitz as President, we next address the claims arising out of the decision to pay Ovitz the amount called for by the NFT provisions of the OEA.

B. CLAIMS ARISING FROM THE PAYMENT OF THE NFT SEVERANCE PAYOUT TO OVITZ

The appellants advance three alternative claims (each accompanied by assorted subsidiary arguments) whose overall thrust is that even if the OEA approval was legally valid, the NFT severance payout to Ovitz pursuant to the OEA was not. Specifically, the appellants contend that: (1) only the full Disney board with the concurrence of the compensation committee—but not Eisner alone—was authorized to terminate Ovitz; (2) because Ovitz could have been terminated for cause, Litvack and Eisner acted without due care and in bad faith in reaching the contrary conclusion; and (3) the business judgment rule presumptions did

---

112. For the same reason, we do not reach or otherwise address the issue of whether the fiduciary duty to act in good faith is a duty that, like the duties of care and loyalty, can serve as an independent basis for imposing liability upon corporate officers and directors. That issue is not before us on this appeal.

not protect the new Disney board's acquiescence in the NFT payout, because the new board was not entitled to rely upon Eisner's and Litvack's contrary advice. Appellants urge that in rejecting these claims the Court of Chancery committed reversible error. We disagree. . . .

At the trial level, the appellants attempted to show, as a factual matter, that Ovitz's conduct as President met the standard for a termination for cause, because (i) Ovitz intentionally failed to follow Eisner's directives and was insubordinate, (ii) Ovitz was a habitual liar, and (iii) Ovitz violated Company policies relating to expenses and to reporting gifts he gave while President of Disney. The Court found the facts contrary to appellants' position. As to the first accusation, the Court found that many of Ovitz's efforts failed to produce results "often because his efforts reflected an opposite philosophy than that held by Eisner, Iger, and Roth. This does not mean that Ovitz intentionally failed to follow Eisner's directives or that he was insubordinate." As to the second, the Court found that:

> In the absence of any concrete evidence that Ovitz told a material falsehood during his tenure at Disney, plaintiffs fall back on alleging that Ovitz's disclosures regarding his earn-out with, and past income from, CAA, were false or materially misleading. As a neutral fact-finder, I find that the evidence simply does not support either of those assertions.

And, as to the third accusation, the Court found "that Ovitz was not in violation of The Walt Disney Company's policies relating to expenses or giving and receiving gifts." Accordingly, the appellants' claim that the Chancellor incorrectly determined that Ovitz could not legally be terminated for cause lacks any factual foundation. . . .

****

To summarize, the Court of Chancery correctly determined that the decisions of the Disney defendants to approve the OEA, to hire Ovitz as President, and then to terminate him on an NFT basis, were protected business judgments, made without any violations of fiduciary duty. Having so concluded, it is unnecessary for the Court to reach the appellants' contention that the Disney defendants were required to prove that the payment of the NFT severance to Ovitz was entirely fair. . . .

STONE v. RITTER

2006 WL 3169168
Supreme Court of Delaware
November 6, 2006

HOLLAND, Justice:

This is an appeal from a final judgment of the Court of Chancery dismissing a derivative complaint against fifteen present and former directors of AmSouth Bancorporation ("AmSouth"), a Delaware corporation. The plaintiffs-appellants, William and Sandra Stone, are AmSouth shareholders and filed their derivative complaint without making a pre-suit demand on AmSouth's board of directors (the "Board"). The Court of Chancery held that the plaintiffs had failed to adequately plead that such a demand would have been futile.

The Court, therefore, dismissed the derivative complaint under Court of Chancery Rule 23.1.

The Court of Chancery characterized the allegations in the derivative complaint as a "classic *Caremark* claim," a claim that derives its name from *In re Caremark Int'l Deriv. Litig.*[698 A.2d 959 (Del.Ch.1996).]. In *Caremark*, the Court of Chancery recognized that: "[G]enerally where a claim of directorial liability for corporate loss is predicated upon ignorance of liability creating activities within the corporation . . . only a sustained or systematic failure of the board to exercise oversight — such as an utter failure to attempt to assure a reasonable information and reporting system exists-will establish the lack of good faith that is a necessary condition to liability."

In this appeal, the plaintiffs acknowledge that the directors neither "knew [n]or should have known that violations of law were occurring," *i.e.*, that there were no "red flags" before the directors. Nevertheless, the plaintiffs argue that the Court of Chancery erred by dismissing the derivative complaint which alleged that "the defendants had utterly failed to implement any sort of statutorily required monitoring, reporting or information controls that would have enabled them to learn of problems requiring their attention." The defendants argue that the plaintiffs' assertions are contradicted by the derivative complaint itself and by the documents incorporated therein by reference.

Consistent with our opinion in In re Walt Disney Co. Deriv Litig, [906 A.2d 27 (Del.2006),] we hold that *Caremark* articulates the necessary conditions for assessing director oversight liability. We also conclude that the *Caremark* standard was properly applied to evaluate the derivative complaint in this case. Accordingly, the judgment of the Court of Chancery must be affirmed.

FACTS

This derivative action is brought on AmSouth's behalf by William and Sandra Stone, who allege that they owned AmSouth common stock "at all relevant times." The nominal defendant, AmSouth, is a Delaware corporation with its principal executive offices in Birmingham, Alabama. During the relevant period, AmSouth's wholly-owned subsidiary, AmSouth Bank, operated about 600 commercial banking branches in six states throughout the southeastern United States and employed more than 11,600 people.

In 2004, AmSouth and AmSouth Bank paid $40 million in fines and $10 million in civil penalties to resolve government and regulatory investigations pertaining principally to the failure by bank employees to file "Suspicious Activity Reports" ("SARs"), as required by the federal Bank Secrecy Act ("BSA") and various anti-money-laundering ("AML") regulations. Those investigations were conducted by the United States Attorney's Office for the Southern District of Mississippi ("USAO"), the Federal Reserve, FinCEN and the Alabama Banking Department. No fines or penalties were imposed on AmSouth's directors, and no other regulatory action was taken against them.

The government investigations arose originally from an unlawful "Ponzi" scheme operated by Louis D. Hamric, II and Victor G. Nance. In August 2000, Hamric, then a licensed attorney, and Nance, then a registered investment advisor with Mutual of New York, contacted an AmSouth branch bank in Tennessee to arrange for custodial trust accounts to be created for "investors" in a "business venture." That venture (Hamric and Nance represented) involved the construction of medical clinics overseas. In reality, Nance had convinced more than forty of his clients to invest in promissory notes bearing high rates of return, by misrepresenting the nature and the risk of that investment. Relying on similar misrepresentations by Hamric and Nance, the AmSouth branch employees in Tennessee agreed to provide custodial accounts for the investors and to distribute monthly interest payments to each account upon receipt of a check from Hamric and instructions from Nance.

The Hamric-Nance scheme was discovered in March 2002, when the investors did not receive their monthly interest payments. Thereafter, Hamric and Nance became the subject of several civil actions brought by the defrauded investors in Tennessee and Mississippi (and in which AmSouth also was named as a defendant), and also the subject of a federal grand jury investigation in the Southern District of Mississippi. Hamric and Nance were indicted on federal money-laundering charges, and both pled guilty.

The authorities examined AmSouth's compliance with its reporting and other obligations under the BSA. On November 17, 2003, the USAO advised AmSouth that it was the subject of a criminal investigation. On October 12, 2004, AmSouth and the USAO entered into a Deferred Prosecution Agreement ("DPA") in which AmSouth agreed: first, to the filing by USAO of a one-count Information in the United States District Court for the Southern District of Mississippi, charging AmSouth with failing to file SARs; and second, to pay a $40 million fine. In conjunction with the DPA, the USAO issued a "Statement of Facts," which noted that although in 2000 "at least one" AmSouth employee suspected that Hamric was involved in a possibly illegal scheme, AmSouth failed to file SARs in a timely manner. In neither the Statement of Facts nor anywhere else did the USAO ascribe any blame to the Board or to any individual director.

On October 12, 2004, the Federal Reserve and the Alabama Banking Department concurrently issued a Cease and Desist Order against AmSouth, requiring it, for the first time, to improve its BSA/AML program. That Cease and Desist Order required AmSouth to (among other things) engage an independent consultant "to conduct a comprehensive review of the Bank's AML Compliance program and make recommendations, as appropriate, for new policies and procedures to be implemented by the Bank." KPMG Forensic Services ("KPMG") performed the role of independent consultant and issued its report on December 10, 2004 (the "KPMG Report").

Also on October 12, 2004, FinCEN and the Federal Reserve jointly assessed a $10 million civil penalty against AmSouth for operating an inadequate anti-money-laundering program and for failing to file SARs. In connection with that assessment, FinCEN issued a written Assessment of Civil Money Penalty (the "Assessment"), which included detailed "determinations" regarding AmSouth's BSA compliance procedures. FinCEN found that "AmSouth violated the suspicious activity reporting requirements of the Bank Secrecy Act," and that "[s]ince April 24, 2002, AmSouth has been in violation of the anti-money-laundering program requirements of the Bank Secrecy Act." Among FinCEN's specific determinations were its conclusions that "AmSouth's [AML compliance] program lacked adequate board and management oversight," and that "reporting to management for the purposes of monitoring and oversight of compliance activities was materially deficient." AmSouth neither admitted nor denied FinCEN's determinations in this or any other forum. . . .

[The Court first discussed certain procedural aspects of "derivative litigation," which is the procedure that we will study in the next chapter by which shareholders are entitled to cause the corporation to bring claims of breach of fiduciary duty.] Critical to the [plaintiffs' argument that they were entitled to start the derivative litigation because defendants faced personal liability and so could not be trusted to decide to start the litigation] is the fact that the directors' potential personal liability depends upon whether or not their conduct can be exculpated by the section 102(b)(7) provision contained in the AmSouth certificate of incorporation. Such a provision can exculpate directors from monetary liability for a breach of the duty of care, but not for conduct that is not in good faith or a breach of the duty of loyalty. The standard for assessing a director's potential personal liability for failing to act in good faith in discharging his or her oversight responsibilities has evolved beginning with our decision in Graham v. Allis-Chalmers Manufacturing Company, through the Court of Chancery's *Caremark* decision to our most recent decision in *Disney*. A brief discussion of that evolution will help illuminate the standard that we adopt in this case.

GRAHAM AND CAREMARK

Graham was a derivative action brought against the directors of Allis-Chalmers for failure to prevent violations of federal anti-trust laws by Allis-Chalmers employees. There was no claim that the Allis-Chalmers directors knew of the employees' conduct that resulted in the corporation's liability. Rather, the plaintiffs claimed that the Allis-Chalmers directors *should have known* of the illegal conduct by the corporation's employees. In *Graham*, this Court held that "*absent cause for suspicion* there is no duty upon the directors to install and operate a corporate system of espionage to ferret out wrongdoing which they have no reason to suspect exists."

In *Caremark*, the Court of Chancery reassessed the applicability of our holding in *Graham* when called upon to approve a settlement of a derivative lawsuit brought against the directors of Caremark International, Inc. The plaintiffs claimed that the Caremark directors should have known that certain officers and employees of Caremark were involved in violations of the federal Anti-Referral Payments Law. That law prohibits health care providers from paying any form of remuneration to induce the referral of Medicare or Medicaid patients. The plaintiffs claimed that the Caremark directors breached their fiduciary duty for having "allowed a situation to develop and continue which exposed the corporation to enormous legal liability and that in so doing they violated a duty to be active monitors of corporate performance."

In evaluating whether to approve the proposed settlement agreement in *Caremark*, the Court of Chancery narrowly construed our holding in *Graham* "as standing for the proposition that, absent grounds to suspect deception, neither corporate boards nor senior officers can be charged with wrongdoing simply for assuming the integrity of employees and the honesty of their dealings on the company's behalf." The *Caremark* Court opined it would be a "mistake" to interpret this Court's decision in *Graham* to mean that:

corporate boards may satisfy their obligation to be reasonably informed concerning the corporation, without assuring themselves that information and reporting systems exist in the organization that are reasonably designed to provide to senior management and to the board itself timely, accurate information sufficient to allow management and the board, each within its scope, to reach informed judgments concerning both the corporation's compliance with law and its business performance.

To the contrary, the *Caremark* Court stated, "it is important that the board exercise a good faith judgment that the corporation's information and reporting system is in concept and design adequate to assure the board that appropriate information will come to its attention in a timely manner as a matter of ordinary operations, so that it may satisfy its responsibility." The *Caremark* Court recognized, however, that "the duty to act in good faith to be informed cannot be thought to require directors to possess detailed information about all aspects of the operation of the enterprise." The Court of Chancery then formulated the following standard for assessing the liability of directors where the directors are unaware of employee misconduct that results in the corporation being held liable:

> Generally where a claim of directorial liability for corporate loss is predicated upon ignorance of liability creating activities within the corporation, as in *Graham* or in this case, . . . only a sustained or systematic failure of the board to exercise oversight — such as an utter failure to attempt to assure a reasonable information and reporting system exists — will establish the lack of good faith that is a necessary condition to liability.

Caremark Standard Approved

As evidenced by the language quoted above, the *Caremark* standard for so-called "oversight" liability draws heavily upon the concept of director failure to act in good faith. That is consistent with the definition(s) of bad faith recently approved by this Court in its recent *Disney* decision, where we held that a failure to act in good faith requires conduct that is qualitatively different from, and more culpable than, the conduct giving rise to a violation of the fiduciary duty of care (i.e., gross negligence). In *Disney*, we identified the following examples of conduct that would establish a failure to act in good faith:

> A failure to act in good faith may be shown, for instance, where the fiduciary intentionally acts with a purpose other than that of advancing the best interests of the corporation, where the fiduciary acts with the intent to violate applicable positive law, or where the fiduciary intentionally fails to act in the face of a known duty to act, demonstrating a conscious disregard for his duties. There may be other examples of bad faith yet to be proven or alleged, but these three are the most salient.

The third of these examples describes, and is fully consistent with, the lack of good faith conduct that the *Caremark* court held was a "necessary condition" for director oversight liability, i.e., "a sustained or systematic failure of the board to exercise oversight — such as an utter failure to attempt to assure a reasonable information and reporting system exists. . . ." Indeed, our opinion in *Disney* cited *Caremark* with approval for that proposition. Accordingly, the Court of Chancery applied the correct standard in assessing whether demand was excused in this case where failure to exercise oversight was the basis or theory of the plaintiffs' claim for relief.

It is important, in this context, to clarify a doctrinal issue that is critical to understanding fiduciary liability under *Caremark* as we construe that case. The phraseology used in *Caremark* and that we employ here — describing the lack of good faith as a "necessary condition to liability" — is deliberate. The purpose of that formulation is to communicate that a failure to act in good faith is not conduct that results, *ipso facto,* in the direct imposition of fiduciary liability. The failure to act in good faith may result in liability because the requirement to act in good faith "is a subsidiary element[,]" i.e., a condition, "of the fundamental duty of loyalty." It follows that because a showing of bad faith conduct, in the sense described in *Disney* and *Caremark,* is essential to establish director oversight liability, the fiduciary duty violated by that conduct is the duty of loyalty.

This view of a failure to act in good faith results in two additional doctrinal consequences. First, although good faith may be described colloquially as part of a "triad" of fiduciary duties that includes the duties of care and loyalty,[29] the obligation to act in good faith does not establish an independent fiduciary duty that stands on the same footing as the duties of care and loyalty. Only the latter two duties, where violated, may directly result in liability, whereas a failure to act in good faith may do so, but indirectly. The second doctrinal consequence is that the fiduciary duty of loyalty is not limited to cases involving a financial or other cognizable fiduciary conflict of interest. It also encompasses cases where the fiduciary fails to act in good faith. As the Court of Chancery aptly put it in Guttman v. Huang [823 A.2d 492, 506 n. 34 (Del. Ch. 2003), "[a] director cannot act loyally towards the corporation unless she acts in the good faith belief that her actions are in the corporation's best interest."

We hold that *Caremark* articulates the necessary conditions predicate for director oversight liability: (a) the directors utterly failed to implement any reporting or information system or controls; *or* (b) having implemented such a system or controls, consciously failed to monitor or oversee its operations thus disabling themselves from being informed of risks or problems requiring their attention. In either case, imposition of liability requires a showing that the directors knew that they were not discharging their fiduciary obligations. Where directors fail to act in the face of a known duty to act, thereby demonstrating a conscious disregard for their responsibilities, they breach their duty of loyalty by failing to discharge that fiduciary obligation in good faith.

CHANCERY COURT DECISION

The plaintiffs contend that demand is excused under Rule 23.1 because AmSouth's directors breached their oversight duty and, as a result, face a "substantial likelihood of liability" as a result of their "utter failure" to act in good faith to put into place policies and procedures to ensure compliance with BSA and AML obligations. The Court of Chancery found that the plaintiffs did not plead the existence of "red flags" — "facts showing that the board ever was

---

29. *See* Cede & Co. v. Technicolor, Inc., 634 A.2d 345, 361 (Del.1993).

aware that AmSouth's internal controls were inadequate, that these inadequacies would result in illegal activity, and that the board chose to do nothing about problems it allegedly knew existed." In dismissing the derivative complaint in this action, the Court of Chancery concluded:

> This case is not about a board's failure to carefully consider a material corporate decision that was presented to the board. This is a case where information was not reaching the board because of ineffective internal controls. . . . With the benefit of hindsight, it is beyond question that AmSouth's internal controls with respect to the Bank Secrecy Act and anti-money laundering regulations compliance were inadequate. Neither party disputes that the lack of internal controls resulted in a huge fine — $50 million, alleged to be the largest ever of its kind. The fact of those losses, however, is not alone enough for a court to conclude that a majority of the corporation's board of directors is disqualified from considering demand that AmSouth bring suit against those responsible.

This Court reviews *de novo* a Court of Chancery's decision to dismiss a derivative suit under Rule 23.1.

REASONABLE REPORTING SYSTEM EXISTED

The KPMG Report evaluated the various components of AmSouth's longstanding BSA/AML compliance program. The KPMG Report reflects that AmSouth's Board dedicated considerable resources to the BSA/AML compliance program and put into place numerous procedures and systems to attempt to ensure compliance. According to KPMG, the program's various components exhibited between a low and high degree of compliance with applicable laws and regulations.

The KPMG Report describes the numerous AmSouth employees, departments and committees established by the Board to oversee AmSouth's compliance with the BSA and to report violations to management and the Board:

> **BSA Officer.** Since 1998, AmSouth has had a "BSA Officer" "responsible for all BSA/AML-related matters including employee training, general communications, CTR reporting and SAR reporting," and "presenting AML policy and program changes to the Board of Directors, the managers at the various lines of business, and participants in the annual training of security and audit personnel[;]"
> **BSA/AML Compliance Department.** AmSouth has had for years a BSA/AML Compliance Department, headed by the BSA Officer and comprised of nineteen professionals, including a BSA/AML Compliance Manager and a Compliance Reporting Manager;
> **Corporate Security Department.** AmSouth's Corporate Security Department has been at all relevant times responsible for the detection and reporting of suspicious activity as it relates to fraudulent activity, and William Burch, the head of Corporate Security, has been with AmSouth since 1998 and served in the U.S. Secret Service from 1969 to 1998; and
> **Suspicious Activity Oversight Committee.** Since 2001, the "Suspicious Activity Oversight Committee" and its predecessor, the "AML Committee," have actively overseen AmSouth's BSA/AML compliance program. The Suspicious Activity Oversight Committee's mission has for years been to "oversee the policy, procedure, and process issues affecting the Corporate Security and BSA/AML

> Compliance Programs, to ensure that an effective program exists at AmSouth to
> deter, detect, and report money laundering, suspicious activity and other fraudu-
> lent activity."

The KPMG Report reflects that the directors not only discharged their oversight responsibility to establish an information and reporting system, but also
proved that the system was designed to permit the directors to periodically
monitor AmSouth's compliance with BSA and AML regulations. For example,
as KPMG noted in 2004, AmSouth's designated BSA Officer "has made annual
high-level presentations to the Board of Directors in each of the last five years."
Further, the Board's Audit and Community Responsibility Committee (the
"Audit Committee") oversaw AmSouth's BSA/AML compliance program on
a quarterly basis. The KPMG Report states that "the BSA Officer presents
BSA/AML training to the Board of Directors annually," and the "Corporate
Security training is also presented to the Board of Directors."

The KPMG Report shows that AmSouth's Board at various times enacted
written policies and procedures designed to ensure compliance with the BSA
and AML regulations. For example, the Board adopted an amended bank-wide
"BSA/AML Policy" on July 17, 2003—four months before AmSouth became
aware that it was the target of a government investigation. That policy was
produced to plaintiffs in response to their demand to inspect AmSouth's
books and records pursuant to section 220 and is included in plaintiffs' appen-
dix. Among other things, the July 17, 2003, BSA/AML Policy directs all AmSouth
employees to immediately report suspicious transactions or activity to the BSA/
AML Compliance Department or Corporate Security.

COMPLAINT PROPERLY DISMISSED

In this case, the adequacy of the plaintiffs' assertion that demand is excused
depends on whether the complaint alleges facts sufficient to show that the
defendant *directors* are potentially personally liable for the failure of non-
director bank *employees* to file SARs. Delaware courts have recognized that
"[m]ost of the decisions that a corporation, acting through its human agents,
makes are, of course, not the subject of director attention." [*Caremark*] Consequently, a claim that directors are subject to personal liability for employee
failures is "possibly the most difficult theory in corporation law upon which a
plaintiff might hope to win a judgment."

For the plaintiffs' derivative complaint to withstand a motion to dismiss, "only
a sustained or systematic failure of the board to exercise oversight—such as an
utter failure to attempt to assure a reasonable information and reporting system
exists—will establish the lack of good faith that is a necessary condition to
liability." As the *Caremark* decision noted:

> Such a test of liability—lack of good faith as evidenced by sustained or systematic
> failure of a director to exercise reasonable oversight—is quite high. But, a
> demanding test of liability in the oversight context is probably beneficial to cor-
> porate shareholders as a class, as it is in the board decision context, since it makes
> board service by qualified persons more likely, while continuing to act as a stimulus
> to *good faith performance of duty* by such directors.

The KPMG Report—which the plaintiffs explicitly incorporated by reference into their derivative complaint—refutes the assertion that the directors "never took the necessary steps . . . to ensure that a reasonable BSA compliance and reporting system existed." KPMG's findings reflect that the Board received and approved relevant policies and procedures, delegated to certain employees and departments the responsibility for filing SARs and monitoring compliance, and exercised oversight by relying on periodic reports from them. Although there ultimately may have been failures by employees to report deficiencies to the Board, there is no basis for an oversight claim seeking to hold the directors personally liable for such failures by the employees.

With the benefit of hindsight, the plaintiffs' complaint seeks to equate a bad outcome with bad faith. The lacuna in the plaintiffs' argument is a failure to recognize that the directors' good faith exercise of oversight responsibility may not invariably prevent employees from violating criminal laws, or from causing the corporation to incur significant financial liability, or both, as occurred in *Graham, Caremark* and this very case. In the absence of red flags, good faith in the context of oversight must be measured by the directors' actions "to assure a reasonable information and reporting system exists" and not by second-guessing after the occurrence of employee conduct that results in an unintended adverse outcome.[43] Accordingly, we hold that the Court of Chancery properly applied *Caremark* and dismissed the plaintiffs' derivative complaint for failure to excuse demand by alleging particularized facts that created reason to doubt whether the directors had acted in good faith in exercising their oversight responsibilities.

CONCLUSION

The judgment of the Court of Chancery is affirmed.

PROBLEM 8-2

Reconsider the facts of Problem 8-1 in light of *Disney* and Stone v. Ritter. *How, if at all, do these cases change your analysis? How, if at all, do these cases change the incentives of directors or the company to settle cases early? Are the directors exposed to a higher risk of personal liability after* Disney *and Stone v. Ritter? What are some of the implications of these decisions for the kinds of protections directors might negotiate for when being asked to join a board of directors?*

B.   CONFLICT-OF-INTEREST TRANSACTIONS GENERALLY

Notwithstanding the greater scrutiny of conflict-of-interest transactions, the law tolerates these transactions because their benefits often are so high. A director

---

43. *Id.* at 967-68, 971.

of a closely held corporation may be the only individual willing to enter into a transaction with the corporation, for example. In such a circumstance, a court could rightly be accused of overzealousness if it prohibited a transaction that would benefit all associated with the corporation. In public corporations, most directors are successful business people with financial interests in multiple companies. To the extent that directors are involved in multiple companies that do business with each other or have corporate relationships such as parent/subsidiary relationships, conflicts are endemic. To prohibit all conflict-of-interest transactions in this context might sharply limit the pool of people who would be willing to serve as directors of America's public companies. Instead, corporate law attempts to identify "bad" transactions—those that are unfair to the company and its shareholders—while allowing "good" transactions—those that are fair—to go forward. This winnowing of fair from unfair is done using a collection of substantive and procedural rules under corporate law that we'll study in this chapter. Securities law often plays a role as well, if the underlying transaction needs shareholder approval, but securities law focuses primarily on the accurate disclosure of conflict-of-interest transactions, not their substantive fairness.

1. Majority or Controlling Shareholders

Like directors and officers, majority or controlling shareholders are fiduciaries of the corporation, and thus have duties to the corporation and its minority shareholders. These duties require that the majority or controlling shareholders not cause the corporation to effect transactions that would uniquely benefit the fiduciary or that would benefit the fiduciary at the expense of the minority shareholders.

A majority or controlling shareholder standing on both sides of a transaction — such as a parent corporation and its controlled subsidiary signing a contract with each other — bears the burden of proving the entire fairness of its actions, that is, the fairness of the procedure developed to approve a transaction, and the fairness of the price of the transaction. Weinberger v. UOP, Inc., 457 A.2d 701, 710 (Del. 1983). Because most of those cases arise in the context of parent-subsidiary merger transactions, we have included the major cases on this issue in Chapter 10, Friendly Mergers and Acquisitions.

In the case below, we consider the meaning of "controlling shareholder." The definition of a majority shareholder is clear: a shareholder who owns more than 50 percent of a corporation's outstanding voting rights. The definition of "controlling shareholder" is less clear, but the following case offers a thorough investigation of that issue. As you read the case, ask yourself: Why are non-controlling shareholders allowed to pursue their own self-interest, while controlling shareholders are constrained by fiduciary duties? Does your answer to this question help you to draw the line between controlling and non-controlling shareholders? In Problem 8-3, following the next case, you will have the opportunity to consider the scope of fiduciary constraints on controlling shareholders in the challenging context of a dilutive financing.

WILLIAMSON v. COX COMMUNICATIONS, INC.

2006 WL 1586375
Court of Chancery of Delaware
June 5, 2006

CHANDLER, Chancellor:

Two cable companies shared joint control over an Internet service provider ("ISP") in which they held minority equity stakes. The ISP was in the business of providing Internet services to customers of the cable companies. The cable companies sold their joint control to a third cable company through a transaction that is alleged to have been unfair to the ISP. At issue in this litigation is whether the cable companies were actually "controlling shareholders" for the purposes of this transaction and whether the transaction was unfair to the minority shareholders?

Plaintiff—the court appointed representative of the bondholders of At Home Corporation ("At Home" or the "Company")—challenges the fairness of agreements At Home entered into in March 2000 with its three cable partners: defendant Comcast Corporation ("Comcast"), defendant Cox Communications ("Cox"), and non-party AT&T Corp. ("AT&T"). These three cable partners were At Home's largest and, plaintiff alleges, controlling shareholders. Plaintiff alleges that Cox and Comcast, together with their two designees to the At Home Board of directors—individual defendants David Woodrow and Brian Roberts—breached fiduciary duties to At Home by causing the Company to enter into the March 2000 Transactions.

I. FACTS

A. THE FORMATION OF AT HOME

Telecommunications Inc. ("TCI"), a cable company, founded At Home in March 1995. At Home, a Delaware corporation, was founded to provide high-speed Internet access to customers through cable television lines. In August 1996, Cox and Comcast, also cable companies, acquired minority stockholdings in the Company. Following the investment by Cox and Comcast, At Home sold stocks and bonds to public investors.

B. TCI'S INITIAL CONTROL OVER AT HOME

At the outset, TCI controlled At Home through its ownership of the At Home series B super-voting common stock. Ownership of these shares provided TCI with in excess of 70% of the voting power of At Home stock.

TCI's representatives on the At Home board had the power to control board decisions. At Home's board of directors was divided into six series A directors and five series B directors. At Home's certificate of incorporation required that board decisions be approved by a majority of the five series B directors. Appointment of the series B directors was governed by a stockholders' agreement between TCI, Cox and Comcast (the "Stockholders' Agreement"). The Stockholders' Agreement provided Cox and Comcast with the right to each designate one series B director, with the remaining three being appointed by TCI.

C. THE ORIGINAL MASTER DISTRIBUTION AGREEMENTS

At Home was in the business of providing high-speed Internet access to cable subscribers of TCI, Cox and Comcast (collectively, the "Cable Companies"). The partnership between At Home, on the one hand, and the Cable Companies, on the other, was governed by agreements called Master Distribution Agreements ("MDAs"). The first set of MDAs (the "Original MDAs") provided that At Home would provide Internet services to cable customers. In return, At Home would be entitled to a 35% share of the subscription revenues paid by the cable company subscribers to the Cable Companies for high-speed Internet access provided by At Home. The MDAs also provided that the Cable Companies would use At Home as their exclusive provider of high-speed Internet access (the "Exclusivity Obligation").

D. AT&T'S ACQUISITION OF TCI AND AT&T'S BREACH OF THE MDAS

AT&T acquired TCI in June 1998. AT&T stepped into TCI's shoes with regard to the MDAs and the ownership and control of At Home. Soon after its acquisition of TCI, AT&T breached the MDAs. The MDAs provided that if AT&T (formerly TCI) was unable to sign-up a certain number of At Home high-speed Internet customers by a specified date, Cox and Comcast could terminate the Exclusivity Obligation. AT&T failed to sign up the required number of subscribers by the specified date.

To induce Cox and Comcast not to terminate the Exclusivity Obligation, AT&T agreed to amend At Home's Certificate of Incorporation to provide that At Home board action required approval by four of the five Series B directors. Because Cox and Comcast had the right to appoint one series B director each, this amendment to the Certificate of Incorporation effectively gave Cox and Comcast the power to veto board decisions if their board designees voted together.

E. THE MARCH 2000 AGREEMENTS

The complaint alleges that AT&T quickly realized that splitting up control over board decisions among the three Cable Companies had been a mistake. On March 28, 2000, AT&T, Cox, and Comcast entered into a series of agreements (the "March 2000 Agreements") that transferred complete control back to AT&T and that, the complaint alleges, greatly benefited each of the Cable Companies at the expense of At Home. The complaint further alleges that the Cable Companies *actually* exerted their control over At Home in order to cause At Home to take steps that were necessary to implement the March 2000 Agreements. In order to facilitate the transfer of control back to AT&T, defendants Woodrow and Roberts voted to amend At Home's Certificate of Incorporation to provide that AT&T would thereafter have the right to appoint all five of the At Home series B directors. Woodrow and Roberts then resigned from the At Home board of directors.

Defendants also allegedly caused At Home to enter into new Master Distribution Agreements (the "March 2000 MDAs"). In their final form, the March 2000 MDAs gave Cox and Comcast the right to break the Exclusivity Obligation and to demand "exit services" from At Home when they exited the business. These "exit services" included technical assistance to be provided by At Home, as well as the transfer of certain At Home assets to Cox and Comcast. Defendants also allegedly used their control over At Home to cause the Company to enter into one-sided service level agreements. These agreements obligated At Home to pay Cox and Comcast penalties in the event that At Home failed to maintain minimum service level requirements.

At Home created a special committee to consider the March 2000 Transactions. The special committee, however, was not created until *twenty-four hours* before the full At Home board was scheduled to meet to vote on the March 2000 Transactions. Moreover, the special committee's review occurred *after* all of the terms of the March 2000 Transactions had already been negotiated and reduced to writing and the review occurred without the benefit of independent legal or financial advisors. Additionally, the special committee lacked the power or authority to negotiate better terms because it was merely asked to recommend the March 2000 Transactions to the full board of directors. Finally, the full board of directors did not have the power to approve or disapprove the transaction because that power was entirely in the hands of the series B directors. When the At Home board met to vote on the March 2000 Agreements, each of the five series B directors (including defendants Woodrow and Roberts) voted in favor of the March 2000 Transactions.

The March 2000 Transactions were conditioned on approval by At Home's stockholders of the proposed amendments to At Home's Certificate of Incorporation. At Home shareholders voted in favor of the proposed amendments to the Certificate of Incorporation. The vote was not conditioned on approval by a majority of the minority shareholders. Cox, Comcast and AT&T controlled more than 63% of the vote.

F. AT HOME'S BANKRUPTCY FILING

At Home filed for bankruptcy in September 2001 and ceased commercial operations in early 2002. As of the filing of the complaint, At Home's assets were in the process of being sold, liquidated or transferred pursuant to a plan of reorganization. Plaintiff brings this action pursuant to an order issued by the United States Bankruptcy Court for the Northern District of California transferring to the Bondholders Liquidating Trust the Company's causes of action against Cox and Comcast and the individual defendants. Plaintiff asserts a single cause of action for breach of fiduciary duty against Cox, Comcast, Woodrow and Roberts. Defendants Cox and Comcast, together with their board designees, have each filed motions to dismiss.

At Home first filed a breach of fiduciary duty claim against defendants in connection with the March 2000 Transactions on September 24, 2002, in the United States District Court for the District of Delaware. This breach of fiduciary duty claim was asserted as a pendent claim (the third cause of action) to At Home's federal claims (the first and second causes of action) for illegal "short swing profits" arising out of the March 2000 Transactions. After transfer of the case to the Southern District of New York, defendants filed motions to dismiss plaintiff's federal claims on the basis of statute of limitations and failure to state a claim. The Federal Court granted defendants' motions to dismiss the short swing profits claims and, with the parties' agreement, dismissed the breach of fiduciary duty claim without prejudice pursuant to 28 § U.S.C. 1367(c)(3). The parties signed a tolling agreement ("Tolling Agreement") that tolled the statute of limitations for the breach of fiduciary duty claim, the third cause of action in the previously filed federal action.

. . .

III. ANALYSIS

A. PLAINTIFF'S FIDUCIARY DUTY CLAIM AGAINST COX AND COMCAST

A shareholder does not owe a fiduciary duty to the company's other shareholders unless she is a "controlling shareholder." The test for control has two prongs: A shareholder is a "controlling" one if she owns more than 50% of the voting power in a corporation *or* if she "exercises control over the business and affairs of the corporation."[42] Where a shareholder stands on both sides of a transaction and is found to be a controlling shareholder, the transaction will be viewed under the entire fairness standard as opposed to the more deferential business judgment standard.

To survive defendants' motions to dismiss, plaintiff must allege domination and control by Cox and Comcast through *actual* control of corporate conduct. Simply alleging that they had the *potential* ability to exercise control is not sufficient. It is not necessary, however, for plaintiff to plead actual control by Cox and Comcast over the day-to-day operations of At Home. Plaintiff can survive the motion to dismiss by alleging actual control with regard to the particular transaction that is being challenged.

Based on the particular facts of this case as alleged in the complaint, together with all the reasonable inferences granted at this stage of the litigation, I conclude that the complaint contains facts that do support, at a minimum, the *inference* that Cox and Comcast were controlling shareholders. I summarize the well-plead facts that support this inference below.

1. Cox and Comcast's Designees to the At Home Board of Directors

The fact that an allegedly controlling shareholder appointed its affiliates to the board of directors is one of many factors Delaware courts have considered in analyzing whether a shareholder is controlling. Cox and Comcast each appointed a designee to be one of the five At Home series B directors. AT&T appointed the remaining three series B directors. The net effect of this arrangement was that control of the At Home board was split between the representatives of the three Cable Companies. Cox appointed Woodrow, a senior Cox executive, and Comcast appointed Roberts, who was at all relevant times the President of Comcast Corporation and one of its directors. Woodrow and Roberts could not be considered, in any sense of the word, independent of Cox and Comcast, and at this stage of the litigation I must infer that they acted as the representatives of their employer's interests.[49]

The fact that Cox and Comcast nominated directors to the At Home board does not, without more, establish actual domination or control. To hold otherwise would have a chilling effect on transactions that depend on a particular shareholder being able to appoint representatives to an investee's

---

42. *Kahn v. Lynch Commc'n Sys., Inc.*, 638 A.2d 1110, 1113-14 (Del.1994).

49. As directors of At Home, the individual defendants owed fiduciary duties to the Company. Plaintiff alleges that the individual defendants breached their duties by voting in favor of the March 2000 Transactions. The individual defendants allegedly voted in favor of the March 2000 Agreements in order to further Cox and Comcast's interests, not At Home's. Plaintiff also alleges the individual defendants voted to approve the March 2000 Agreements even though they knew that AT&T planned to use its control position to plunder the assets of the Company. These allegations (which are accepted as true at this stage) are sufficient to support a claim for breach of the duty of loyalty against the individual defendants.

board of directors. But this is not a case where plaintiff alleges control based solely, or even primarily, on the fact that defendants appointed two directors. As discussed below, plaintiff also points to Cox and Comcast's business relationship with At Home and their control over At Home board decisions.

2. *The Business Relationship Between At Home and Cox and Comcast*

The Cable Companies were At Home's only significant customers and At Home depended on their cooperation as customers if it was going to operate its business profitably. Plaintiff alleges that, under the revenue sharing agreement between At Home and the Cable Companies, the Cable Companies were able to (and did) exert control over At Home by influencing the flow of revenue to At Home. These allegations support the inference that the Cable Companies had significant leverage over At Home and were able to dictate to At Home the terms of the March 2000 Agreements.

3. *Cox and Comcast's "Veto" Power*

There is no case law in Delaware, nor in any other jurisdiction that this Court is aware of, holding that board veto power *in and of itself* gives rise to a shareholder's controlling status. Delaware law requires actual control, not merely the potential to control, and in this case plaintiff makes no allegation that Cox and Comcast ever affirmatively vetoed any At Home board decisions.

Cox and Comcast's potential veto power is significant for analysis of the control issue, however, because it supports plaintiff's allegation that Cox and Comcast had coercive leverage over At Home. Cox and Comcast had the ability to shut down the effective operation of the At Home board of directors by vetoing board actions. Plaintiff may be able to prove facts showing that this leverage (together with the special business relationships and other circumstances mentioned above) was enough for Cox and Comcast to obtain a far better deal then they would have in an arm's-length transaction.[52]

. . .

IV. Conclusion

The question whether a shareholder is a controlling one is highly contextualized and is difficult to resolve based solely on the complaint. No single allegation in plaintiff's complaint is sufficient on its own to defeat defendants' motions to dismiss. Designating directors to the board of directors or entering into business agreements with an investee is not sufficient to trigger a finding of "controlling" status. Nor is the allegation that Cox, Comcast and AT&T had parallel interests sufficient to allege that the Cable Companies were part of a "controlling group."

---

52. Given that plaintiff alleges the March 2000 Agreements were a way for AT&T to acquire sole control of At Home, it is tempting to conclude that AT&T effectively represented At Home's interests in the negotiations with Cox and Comcast. From this, one might conclude that At Home enjoyed the benefit of AT&T's negotiating leverage, which even the complaint alleges to have been substantial. The reason this is not persuasive at this stage of the case is that the complaint also alleges that AT&T's interests were *not* aligned with At Home's. According to plaintiff, the March 2000 Agreements were the culmination of a process by which AT&T, Cox and Comcast agreed to carve-up the assets of At Home amongst themselves, with no regard for the interests of At Home's other shareholders.

The complaint succeeds because it pleads a nexus of facts all suggesting that the Cable Companies were in a controlling position and that they exploited that control for their own benefit. The well-pled facts taken together give rise to the inference that the March 2000 Agreements were the culmination of a process by which AT&T, Cox and Comcast agreed to carve-up the assets of At Home among themselves, with no regard for the interests of At Home's other shareholders. The complaint's allegations, therefore, are sufficient to withstand a motion to dismiss. The motion to dismiss is denied.

PROBLEM 8-3

At a certain point in 2011, the social networking and media industries began to experience a frothy run of valuations. LinkedIn, a professional networking site, engaged in an Initial Public Offering (sold shares of stock to the public for the first time) that at the end of the first day of trading valued the company at $9 billion. Goldman Sachs, the investment bank, purchased a major interest in Facebook that implied a valuation of $50 billion for that social networking company. In that context, Hollander, a mostly old media company, found itself in need of cash. Rather than sell shares to raise that cash, Hollander entered into a transaction that raised $230.8 million as follows:

> Three separate lines of credit which are guaranteed by three different entities for a total of $230.8 million in bank financing for the Company. Conrad White, the Company's majority stockholder and CEO, is the lead guarantor, providing a guarantee of $110.8 million. Two other Hollander-associated guarantors have guaranteed a total of $120 million. Upon the closing of the lines of credit, the Company issued warrants to the guarantors to purchase 2,776,664 shares of its common stock at an exercise price of $4.75 per share. The warrants are exercisable immediately and expire in ten years. The Company has estimated the fair market value of the warrants to be $1.50 per warrant or $4,164,996 for the 2,776,664 issued and outstanding warrants.

Hollander turned to loan guarantees by White and two Hollander-associated investors for two reasons. First, it could not borrow funds conventionally; the banks would not lend the needed funds on Hollander's credit alone, given how badly over-extended it was in debt financing, and given how little it had ventured into new media. Second, White was concerned that the issuance of more stock would dilute his equity interest in Hollander.

Based on the information provided, do you believe that Hollander's controlling share-holder has acted in accordance with his fiduciary duties to the minority in the Loan Guarantee Transaction?

2.   Judicial Review

At one time courts dealt with the possible harms inherent in self-interested transactions by making such transactions void or voidable by the corporation or a complaining shareholder. But this posture introduced a high degree of uncertainty into the binding effect of conflict-of-interest transactions, and eventually it was abandoned in favor of a narrower rule. Modern statutes like the former Modern Business Corporations Act (Model Act) §8.31 (which has been replaced by Subchapter F of the Model Act but still is in force in many states) and Delaware General Corporation Law (DGCL) §144 provide that conflict-of-interest transactions are not void or voidable if: (1) the material facts are disclosed to the board of directors or shareholders, *and* (2) either the disinterested directors or the disinterested shareholders authorize, approve, or ratify the transaction. Alternatively, conflict-of-interest transactions are not void or voidable if they are fair to the corporation. Although the statutes are disjunctive — implying that conflict-of-interest transactions are not void or voidable if they are *either* procedurally *or* substantively fair — most courts require some evidence of substantive fairness even when the procedural requirements have been met, particularly where the transaction is between the corporation and a controlling shareholder, as will be seen below. The substantive fairness of a conflict-of-interest transaction is demonstrated by showing both fair price and fair dealing.

In the mid-1990s, the Model Act was amended to clarify the implications of approval by disinterested directors or shareholders. The amended Model Act applies only to "director's conflicting interest transactions," a term that is defined to include any transaction in which the beneficial financial interest of a director is of such financial significance to the director that the interest "would reasonably be expected to exert an influence on the director's judgment if [he or she] were called upon to vote on the transaction." Under Model Act §8.61, interested transactions may not be enjoined if (a) the board approves the transaction in accordance with Model Act §8.62; (b) the shareholders approve the transaction in accordance with Model Act §8.63; or (c) the transaction is fair to the corporation at the time it is authorized. The first two are *procedural* protections designed to remove the taint of self-interest. The third is a *substantive* protection designed to allow fair transactions even if they have never been approved by disinterested parties. Note that if approval were obtained in accordance with the statute, this would not necessarily validate the transaction; it would simply eliminate the interested-director cloud. The decision would still be subject to a challenge based on the duty of care, albeit with the powerful protection of the business judgment rule.

The following case illustrates the treatment of conflict-of-interest transactions under the two procedural prongs of DGCL §144. *Wheelabrator* involves approval by disinterested shareholders under DGCL §144(a)(2). Set in the context of a merger, *Wheelabrator* foreshadows some of the loyalty issues that we will examine in Chapter 10, Friendly Mergers and Acquisitions. For the present, notice the important difference in the substantive standard of review courts apply to controlling shareholder transactions versus conflict-of-interest transactions without a controlling shareholder, as discussed in *Wheelabrator*.

IN RE WHEELABRATOR TECHNOLOGIES INC. SHAREHOLDERS LITIGATION

663 A.2d 1194
Court of Chancery of Delaware
May 18, 1995

JACOBS, Vice Chancellor.

This shareholder class action challenges the September 7, 1990 merger (the "merger") of Wheelabrator Technologies, Inc. ("WTI") into a wholly-owned subsidiary of Waste Management, Inc. ("Waste"). The plaintiffs are share-holders of WTI. The named defendants are WTI and the eleven members of WTI's board of directors at the time the merger was negotiated and approved.[1]

The plaintiffs claim that WTI and the director defendants breached their fiduciary obligation to disclose to the class material information concerning the merger. The plaintiffs also claim that in negotiating and approving the merger, the director defendants breached their fiduciary duties of loyalty and care. The defendants deny that they breached any duty of disclosure. They further contend that because the merger was approved by a fully informed shareholder vote, that vote operates as a complete defense to, and extinguishes, the plaintiffs' fiduciary claims.

This is the Opinion of the Court on the defendants' motion for summary judgment. For the reasons elaborated below, the Court concludes that: (1) the plaintiffs have failed to adduce evidence sufficient to defeat summary judgment on their duty of disclosure claim, and that (2) the fully informed shareholder vote approving the merger operated to extinguish the plaintiffs' duty of care claims, but not their duty of loyalty claim. Accordingly, the defendants' summary judgment motion is granted in part and denied in part.

I. Procedural Background

On April 5, 1990, the plaintiffs commenced these class actions (which were later consolidated) challenging the then-proposed merger with Waste. After expedited discovery, the plaintiffs moved for a preliminary injunction. That motion was denied, In re Wheelabrator Technologies, Inc. Shareholders Litig., Del. Ch., Cons. C.A. No. 11495, Jacobs, V.C., 1990 WL 131351 (Sept. 6, 1990) ("*Wheelabrator I*"), and the merger was approved by WTI's shareholders, specifically, by a majority of WTI's shareholders other than Waste. On July 22, 1991, the plaintiffs filed a Second Amended Consolidated Class Action Complaint, which the defendants moved to dismiss pursuant to Chancery Court Rule 12(b)(6). That motion was denied in part and granted in part. In re Wheelabrator Technologies, Inc. Shareholders Litig., Del. Ch., Cons. C.A. No. 11495, Jacobs, V.C., 1992 WL 212595 (Sept. 1, 1992). As a result of that ruling, all but three claims alleged in the complaint were dismissed.

The first remaining claim is Count I of the complaint, which alleges that the defendants violated their duty to disclose all material facts related to the merger in the proxy statement issued in connection with the transaction. More specifically, plaintiffs allege that (i) the proxy statement falsely represented that the merger negotiations lasted one week, whereas in fact agreement on all essential merger terms had been reached on the first day; (ii) the proxy statement disclosed that WTI's negotiators had successfully extracted concessions from Waste, whereas in fact Waste had dictated the merger terms to WTI; and (iii) the proxy statement disclosed that WTI's board had carefully considered

---

1. Three of the eleven individual director defendants, Paul M. Montrone, Rodney C. Gilbert, and Paul M. Meister, were all members of WTI's management. Four directors, Dean L. Buntrock, William P. Hulligan, Phillip B. Rooney, and Donald F. Flynn were officers of Waste Management. The remaining four directors, Michael D. Dengman, Gerald J. Lewis, Thomas P. Stafford, and Edward Montgomery, were outside directors.

the merger agreement before approving and recommending it to shareholders, whereas in fact the board did not consider the matter carefully before it acted.

Count III alleges that the defendants breached their duty of care by failing adequately to investigate alternative transactions, neglecting to consider certain nonpublic information regarding certain of Waste's potential legal liabilities, failing to appoint a committee of independent directors to negotiate the merger, and failing adequately to consider the merger terms.

Count IV alleges that the defendants breached their duty of loyalty, in that a majority of WTI's eleven directors had a conflict of interest that caused them not to seek or obtain the best possible value for the company's shareholders in the merger.

On December 30, 1992, the defendants filed the pending summary judgment motion seeking dismissal of these claims. Following discovery and briefing, that motion was argued on March 3, 1995.

II. RELEVANT FACTS

WTI, a publicly held Delaware corporation headquartered in New Hampshire, is engaged in the business of developing and providing refuse-to-energy services. Waste, a Delaware corporation with principal offices in Illinois, provides waste management services to national and international commercial, industrial, and municipal customers.

In August 1988, Waste and WTI entered into a transaction (the "1988 transaction") to take advantage of their complementary business operations. In the 1988 transaction, Waste acquired a 22% equity interest in WTI in exchange for certain assets that Waste sold to WTI. The two companies also entered into other agreements that concerned WTI's rights to ash disposal, the purchase of real estate for future refuse-to-energy facilities, and other business development opportunities. As a result of the 1988 transaction, Waste became WTI's largest (22%) stockholder and was entitled to nominate four of WTI's eleven directors.

Over the next two years, Waste and WTI periodically discussed other ways to reduce perceived inefficiencies by coordinating their operations. Those discussions intensified in December 1989, when Waste acquired a refuse-to-energy facility in West Germany. That acquisition raised concerns that the four Waste designees to WTI's board of directors might have future conflicts of interest if WTI later decided to enter the West German market.

Prompted by these and other concerns, Waste began, in December 1989, to consider either acquiring a majority equity interest in WTI or, alternatively, divesting all of its WTI stock. After several discussions, both companies agreed that Waste would increase its equity position in WTI. On March 22, 1990, Waste proposed a stock-for-stock, market-to-market (*i.e.* no premium) exchange in which Waste would become WTI's majority stockholder. WTI declined that proposal, and insisted on a transaction in which its shareholders would receive a premium above the current market price of their shares.

The following day, March 23, 1990, representatives of WTI and Waste met in New York City. Accompanying WTI's representatives were members of WTI's investment banking firm, Lazard Freres. At that meeting, Waste's representatives expressed Waste's interest in acquiring an additional 33% of WTI, thereby making Waste the owner of 55% of WTI's outstanding shares. The parties ultimately agreed on that concept. They also agreed to structure the transaction as a stock-for-stock merger that would be conditioned upon the approval of a majority of WTI's disinterested stockholders, *i.e.*, a majority of WTI's stockholders other than Waste. Waste agreed to pay a 10% premium for the additional shares required to reach the 55% equity ownership level. Finally, it was agreed that the merger would involve no "lockup," breakup fees, or other arrangements that would impede WTI from considering alternative transactions.

During the following week, additional face-to-face meetings and telephone conversations took place between the two companies' representatives. Those negotiations resulted in five "ancillary agreements" that gave WTI certain funding and business opportunity options, as well as licenses to use certain Waste-owned intellectual property.

On March 30, 1990, agreement on the final merger exchange ratio was reached. The parties agreed that WTI shareholders would receive 0.574 shares of WTI stock plus 0.469 shares of Waste stock for each of their pre-merger WTI shares. That same day, March 30, 1990, WTI's board of directors held a special meeting to consider the merger agreement. All board members attended except the four Waste designees, who had recused themselves. Also present were WTI's "in-house" and outside counsel, and representatives of Lazard Freres and Salomon Brothers. The WTI board members reviewed copies of the draft merger agreement and materials furnished by the investment bankers concerning the financial aspects of the transaction. The directors also heard presentations from the investment bankers and from legal counsel, who opined that the transaction was fair. A question and answer session followed.

The seven board members present then voted unanimously to approve the merger and to recommend its approval by WTI's shareholders. After that vote, the four Waste-designated board members joined the meeting, and the full board then voted unanimously to approve and recommend the merger.

On July 30, 1990, WTI and Waste disseminated a joint proxy statement to WTI shareholders, disclosing the recommendation of both boards of directors that their shareholders approve the transaction. At a special shareholders meeting held on September 7, 1990, the merger was approved by a majority of WTI shareholders other than Waste.

III. The Parties' Contentions

The defendants seek the dismissal of plaintiffs' remaining disclosure claim on the ground that it has no evidentiary support. The defendants further contend that the effect of the fully informed shareholder vote approving the merger was to ratify the directors' actions in negotiating and approving the merger, and thereby extinguish the plaintiffs' claims that those actions constituted breaches of fiduciary duty.

The plaintiffs respond that they have raised genuine issues of material fact that preclude the grant of summary judgment on their disclosure claim. They further argue that even if the disclosure claim were dismissed, that would not result in the extinguishment of their breach of loyalty claim. Plaintiffs maintain that the only effect of shareholder ratification would be to impose upon them the burden of proving that the merger was unfair to the corporation, with entire fairness being the applicable standard of judicial review. . . .

IV. The Disclosure Claim

[The Court first analyzed the plaintiffs' disclosure claims and ruled against the plaintiffs, finding there was insufficient evidentiary support for the plaintiffs' contentions.]

For the foregoing reasons, summary judgment will be granted dismissing the remaining duty of disclosure claim.

V. The Fiduciary Duty Claims

In rejecting the disclosure claim, the Court necessarily has determined that the merger was approved by a fully informed vote of a majority of WTI's disinterested stockholders. That determination requires the Court to confront the defendants' argument that that vote constituted shareholder ratification which operated as a complete defense to, and consequently extinguished, the claims that the defendants breached their fiduciary duties of care and loyalty.

The plaintiffs do not dispute that if the WTI shareholder vote was fully informed, it operated to extinguish their due care claim in this case. They avidly insist, however, that that vote could not, as a legal matter, extinguish their duty of loyalty claim. Plaintiffs argue that because the merger was an "interested" transaction subject to the entire fairness standard of review, the sole effect of shareholder ratification was to shift to plaintiffs the burden of proving that the merger was unfair.

I conclude, for the reasons next discussed, that (1) the effect of the informed shareholder vote was to extinguish the plaintiffs' due care claim; (2) that vote did not operate either to extinguish the duty of loyalty claim (as defendants contend), or to shift to the plaintiffs the burden of proving that the merger was unfair (as plaintiffs contend); and (3) the effect of the shareholder vote in this case is to invoke the business judgment standard, which limits review to issues of gift or waste with the burden of proof resting upon the plaintiffs. Because the parties have not yet been heard on the question of how the business judgment standard would apply to these facts, summary judgment with respect to the duty of loyalty claim must be denied.

A. THE DUTY OF CARE CLAIM

As noted, the plaintiffs concede that if the WTI shareholder vote was fully informed, the effect of that informed vote would be to extinguish the claim that the WTI board failed to exercise due care in negotiating and approving the merger. Given the ratification holding of Smith v. Van Gorkom, Del. Supr., 488 A.2d 858, 889-90 (1985), that concession is not surprising. In *Van Gorkom*, the defendant directors argued that the shareholder vote approving a challenged merger agreement "had the legal effect of curing any failure of the board to reach an informed business judgment in its approval of the merger." *Id.* at 889. Accepting that legal principle (but not its application to the facts before it), the Supreme Court stated:

> The parties tacitly agree that a discovered failure of the Board to reach an informed business judgment constitutes a voidable, rather than a void, act. Hence, the merger can be sustained, notwithstanding the infirmity of the Board's actions, if

its approval by majority vote of the shareholders is found to have been based on an informed electorate.

Id. at 889.

Accordingly, summary judgment dismissing the plaintiffs' due care claim will be granted. That leaves for decision the legal effect of the informed shareholder vote on the duty of loyalty claims alleged in Count IV of the complaint.

B. THE DUTY OF LOYALTY CLAIM

The defendants contend that the informed shareholder approval of the WTI-Waste merger also operated to extinguish the claim that the directors' approval of the merger violated their duty of loyalty to WTI and its stockholders. The plaintiffs counter that a fully informed shareholder vote cannot, as a matter of law, operate to extinguish a duty of loyalty claim. At most, plaintiffs argue, the informed shareholder vote in this case would only shift to the plaintiff the burden of showing that the merger was unfair. Having considered the relevant authorities, and the law on this subject generally, I conclude that neither side's position is correct.

1.

I begin with the candid observation that the defendants' "claim extinguishment" argument is squarely supported by two decisions of this Court, one handed down in this very case. *Wheelabrator I, supra,* Mem. Op. at 19-20; Weiss v. Rockwell, Int'l. Corp., Del. Ch., C.A. No. 8811, Jacobs, V.C. (July 19, 1989), *aff'd per curiam,* Del. Supr., 574 A.2d 264 (1990).

In *Weiss,* this Court dismissed a fiduciary duty of loyalty claim that the directors of Rockwell International had approved a charter amendment creating a new class of super-voting stock for the sole purpose of entrenching themselves in office. Citing *Van Gorkom,* this Court held, without extended analysis, that the fully informed shareholder approval of the amendment extinguished the duty of loyalty claim. *Weiss, supra,* Letter Op. at 10. The Supreme Court affirmed that dismissal without comment in a *per curiam* opinion. 574 A.2d 264 (1990). In *Wheelabrator I,* this Court, citing *Van Gorkom* and *Weiss,* denied the plaintiffs' motion for a preliminary injunction against the merger at issue here, on the ground (*inter alia*) that if WTI's shareholders approved the merger, that ratifying vote would extinguish the plaintiffs' so-called "*Revlon*" claim.

In *Weiss* and *Wheelabrator I,* this Court reached that result by extending to a duty of loyalty claim the "extinguishment" doctrine applied to a duty of care claim in *Van Gorkom.* Although this Court did not articulate the propriety of that extension in doctrinal or policy terms, the result it reached was informed by the Supreme Court's statement in *Van Gorkom* that:

> where a majority of fully informed stockholders ratify action *of even interested directors,* an attack on the ratified transaction normally must fail.

488 A.2d at 890 (emphasis added). That language suggested that the Supreme Court would endorse the application of its "claim extinguishment" doctrine to duty of loyalty claims.

Not surprisingly, the defendants here argue that *Weiss* and *Wheelabrator I* impel the Court to reach the same result, that is to conclude that the plaintiffs' duty of loyalty claims were automatically extinguished by virtue of shareholder ratification. My difficulty with the defendants' position is that since 1990 the law has changed, and there is now significant reason to conclude that *Wheelabrator I* and *Weiss* would not be regarded as good law today. Not only has the Delaware Supreme Court never endorsed the view adopted in those cases, the decisions that postdate *Weiss* and *Wheelabrator I* persuasively indicate that the Supreme Court would not hold that shareholder approval of board action claimed to violate the fiduciary duty of loyalty would operate automatically to extinguish a duty of loyalty claim.

2.

The question of whether or not shareholder ratification should operate to extinguish a duty of loyalty claim cannot be decided in a vacuum, divorced from the broader issue of what generally are the legal consequences of a fully-informed shareholder approval of a challenged transaction. The Delaware case law addressing that broader topic is not reducible to a single clear rule or unifying principle. Indeed, the law in that area might be thought to lack coherence because the decisions addressing the effect of shareholder "ratification" have fragmented that subject into three distinct compartments, only one of which involves "claim extinguishment."

The basic structure of stockholder ratification law is, at first glance, deceptively simple. Delaware law distinguishes between acts of directors (or management) that are "void" and acts that are "voidable." As the Supreme Court stated in Michelson v. Duncan, 407 A.2d 211, 218-19 (1979):

> The essential distinction between voidable and void acts is that the former are those which may be found to have been performed in the interest of the corporation but beyond the authority of management, as distinguished from acts which are *ultra vires*, fraudulent, or waste of corporate assets. The practical distinction, for our purposes, is that voidable acts are susceptible to cure by shareholder approval while void acts are not.

One possible reading of *Michelson* is that all "voidable" acts are "susceptible to cure by shareholder approval." Under that reading, shareholder ratification might be thought to constitute a "full defense" (407 A.2d at 219) that would automatically extinguish all claims challenging such acts as a breach of fiduciary duty. Any such reading, however, would be overbroad, because the case law governing the consequences of ratification does not support that view and, in fact, is far more complex.

The Delaware Supreme Court has found shareholder ratification of "voidable" director conduct to result in claim-extinguishment in only two circumstances. The first is where the directors act in good faith, but exceed the board's de jure authority. In that circumstance, *Michelson* holds that "a validly accomplished shareholder ratification relates back to cure otherwise unauthorized acts of officers and directors." 407 A.2d at 219. The second circumstance is where the directors fail "to reach an informed business judgment" in approving a transaction. *Van Gorkom*, 488 A.2d at 889.

Except for these two situations, no party has identified any type of board action that the Delaware Supreme Court has deemed "voidable" for claim extinguishment purposes. More specifically, no Supreme Court case has held that shareholder ratification operates automatically to extinguish a duty of loyalty claim. To the contrary, the ratification cases involving duty of loyalty claims have uniformly held that the effect of shareholder ratification is to alter the standard of review, *or* to shift the burden of proof, *or* both. Those cases further frustrate any effort to describe the "ratification" landscape in terms of a simple rule.

The ratification decisions that involve duty of loyalty claims are of two kinds: (a) "interested" transaction cases between a corporation and its directors (or between the corporation and an entity in which the corporation's directors are also directors or have a financial interest), and (b) cases involving a transaction between the corporation and its controlling shareholder.

Regarding the first category, 8 Del. C. § 144(a)(2) pertinently provides that an "interested" transaction of this kind will not be voidable if it is approved in good faith by a majority of disinterested stockholders. Approval by fully informed, disinterested shareholders pursuant to § 144(a)(2) invokes "the business judgment rule and limits judicial review to issues of gift or waste with the burden of proof upon the party attacking the transaction." Marciano v. Nakash, Del. Supr., 535 A.2d 400, 405 n. 3 (1987). The result is the same in "interested" transaction cases not decided under § 144:

> Where there has been independent shareholder ratification of interested director actions, the objecting stockholder has the burden of showing that no person of ordinary sound business judgment would say that the consideration received for the options was a fair exchange for the options granted.

Michelson, 407 A.2d at 224 (quoting Kaufman v. Shoenberg, Del. Ch., 91 A.2d 786, 791 (1952), at 791); *see also* Gottlieb v. Heyden Chem. Corp., Del. Supr., 91 A.2d 57, 59 (1952); and Citron v. E.I. Du Pont de Nemours & Co., 584 A.2d 490, 501 (citing authorities reaching the same result in mergers involving fiduciaries that were not controlling stockholders).

The second category concerns duty of loyalty cases arising out of transactions between the corporation and its controlling stockholder. Those cases involve primarily parent-subsidiary mergers that were conditioned upon receiving "majority of the minority" stockholder approval. In a parent-subsidiary merger, the standard of review is ordinarily entire fairness, with the directors having the burden of proving that the merger was entirely fair. Weinberger v. UOP, Inc., 457 A.2d 701, 703. But where the merger is conditioned upon approval by a "majority of the minority" stockholder vote, and such approval is granted, the standard of review remains entire fairness, but the burden of demonstrating that the merger was unfair shifts to the plaintiff. Kahn v. Lynch Communication Sys. Del. Supr., 638 A.2d 1110 (1994); Rosenblatt v. Getty Oil Co., 493 A.2d 929, 937-38 (1985); *Weinberger*, at 710; *Citron*, at 502. That burden-shifting effect of ratification has also been held applicable in cases involving mergers with a de facto controlling stockholder, and in a case involving a transaction other than a merger [where there was a controlling shareholder]. . . .

To repeat: in only two circumstances has the Delaware Supreme Court held that a fully-informed shareholder vote operates to extinguish a claim: (1) where the board of directors takes action that, although not alleged to constitute *ultra vires*, fraud, or waste, is claimed to exceed the board's authority; and (2) where it is claimed that the directors failed to exercise due care to adequately inform themselves before committing the corporation to a transaction. In no case has the Supreme Court held that stockholder ratification automatically extinguishes a claim for breach of the directors' duty of loyalty. Rather, the operative effect of shareholder ratification in duty of loyalty cases has been either to change the standard of review to the business judgment rule, with the burden of proof resting upon the plaintiff, *or* to leave "entire fairness" as the review standard, but shift the burden of proof to the plaintiff. Thus, the Supreme Court ratification decisions do not support the defendants' position.

That being the present state of the law, the question then becomes whether there exists a policy or doctrinal basis that would justify extending the claim-extinguishing effect of shareholder ratification to cases involving duty of loyalty claims. *Van Gorkom* does not articulate a basis, and the parties have suggested none. The defendants rely solely upon the argument that *Weiss* and *Wheelabrator I* continue to be good law. That position requires this Court to revisit these decisions.

3.

As earlier noted, *Weiss* and *Wheelabrator I* are the sole authorities upon which the defendants' "claim extinguishment" argument rests. In those cases this Court extended *Van Gorkom* (which validated the extinguishment of a duty of care claim) to extinguish a duty of loyalty claim. Plausible as that extension might have been in 1989 and 1990 when *Weiss* and *Wheelabrator I* were decided, later Supreme Court decisions persuasively indicate that that view is no longer tenable.

In Kahn v. Lynch Communication Sys., *supra*, an "interested" cash out merger between a corporation and its de facto controlling stockholder was challenged as a breach of the directors' duty of loyalty. Had *Weiss* or *Wheelabrator I* been viewed as the correct ratification rule, the Supreme Court could have stated that the effect of shareholder ratification would be to extinguish the duty of loyalty claim. Instead, however, the Supreme Court held that in an interested merger with a controlling stockholder, the applicable judicial review standard is entire fairness, and shareholder ratification merely shifts the burden of proof on the fairness issue from the controlling stockholder to the challenging plaintiff. 638 A.2d at 1117. The *Kahn* Court disclaimed any suggestion that shareholder ratification obviates further judicial review, by noting that "the unchanging nature of the underlying 'interested' transaction requires careful scrutiny." *Id.* at 1116.

Stroud v. Grace, [606 A.2d 75, 85 (Del. 1992)], is similarly instructive. There, as in *Weiss*, the claim was that certain charter amendments proposed by the board whose members were also the corporation's controlling stockholders, were unfair and a breach of the directors' duty of loyalty to the minority stockholders. The charter amendments were found to have been approved by the fully-informed vote of a majority of the minority stockholders. Had *Weiss* (which was also a charter amendment case) been viewed as the correct approach, the Supreme Court could simply have held, without further analysis, that the duty of loyalty claims were extinguished by the informed shareholder vote. But, the Court did not do that. It ruled that the ratifying vote "[shifted] the burden of proof to the [plaintiffs] to prove that the transaction was unfair," 606 A.2d at 90, and then proceeded to consider the plaintiffs' claim that the charter amendments were unfair because (*inter alia*) they were intended to interfere with the shareholder franchise.

From these decisions I conclude that in duty of loyalty cases arising out of transactions with a controlling shareholder, our Supreme Court would reject the proposition that the Delaware courts will have no reviewing function in cases where the challenged transaction is approved by an informed shareholder vote. *Kahn* makes explicit the Supreme Court's concern that even an informed shareholder vote may not afford the minority sufficient protection to obviate the judicial oversight role. Even if the ratified transaction does not involve a controlling stockholder, the result would not be to extinguish a duty of loyalty claim. In such cases the Supreme Court has held that the effect of shareholder ratification is to make business judgment the applicable review standard and shift the burden of proof to the plaintiff stockholder. None of these authorities holds that shareholder ratification operates automatically to extinguish a duty of loyalty claim.

For these reasons, and in the absence of any policy or doctrinal basis to conclude otherwise, I find that insofar as *Weiss* and *Wheelabrator I* hold that shareholder ratification extinguishes a duty of loyalty claim, those cases would not be regarded today as good law. If the contrary view is to prevail, its source must be the Delaware Supreme Court, which is the only Court that can authoritatively rationalize and bring needed coherence to this important area of our corporate law. Accordingly, the defendants' "claim extinguishment" argument, in the duty of loyalty context, must be rejected.

C. THE APPROPRIATE REVIEW STANDARD AND BURDEN OF PROOF

Having determined what effect shareholder ratification does *not* have, the Court must now determine what effect it does have. The plaintiffs argue that their duty of loyalty claim is governed by the entire fairness standard, with ratification operating only to shift the burden on the fairness issue to the plaintiffs. That is incorrect, because this merger did not involve an interested and controlling stockholder.

In both *Kahn* and *Stroud*, the Supreme Court determined that the effect of a fully informed shareholder vote was to shift the burden of proof within the entire fairness standard of review. *Kahn*, 638 A.2d at 1117; *Stroud*, 606 A.2d at 90. Critical to the result in those cases was that the transaction involved a de facto (*Kahn, supra*) or de jure (*Stroud, supra*) controlling stockholder. That circumstance brought those cases within the purview of the ratification doctrine articulated in *Rosenblatt, supra*, Bershad v. Curtiss-Wright-Corp., Del. Supr., 535 A.2d 840 (1987), and Citron v. E.I. Du Pont de Nemours & Co., *supra*, all involving mergers between a corporation and its majority stockholder-parent. The participation of the controlling interested stockholder is critical to the application of the entire fairness standard because, as *Kahn* and *Stroud* recognize, the potential for process manipulation by the controlling stockholder, and the concern that the controlling stockholder's continued presence might influence even a fully informed shareholder vote, justify the need for the exacting judicial scrutiny and procedural protection afforded by the entire fairness form of review.

In this case, there is no contention or evidence that Waste, a 22% stockholder of WTI, exercised de jure or de facto control over WTI. Therefore, neither the holdings of or policy concerns underlying *Kahn* and *Stroud* are implicated here. Accordingly, the review standard applicable to this merger is business judgment, with the plaintiffs having the burden of proof.[8]

---

8. The result is reached not only by process of elimination but also by application of 8 Del. C. §144(a)(1). That statute provides that when a majority of fully informed, disinterested directors (even if less than a quorum) approve a transaction in which other directors are interested, the

The final question concerns the proper application of that review standard to the facts at bar. Because no party has yet been heard on that subject, that issue cannot be determined on this motion. Its resolution must await further proceedings, which counsel may present (if they so choose) on a supplemental motion for summary judgment. . . .

For the foregoing reasons, the defendants' motion for summary judgment (1) is granted as to the disclosure claim, (2) is granted as to the duty of care claim, and (3) is denied as to the duty of loyalty claims. Counsel shall submit an appropriate implementing form of order.

PROBLEM 8-4

The capital structure of Hollander was not helpful to its efforts to raise money. It was capitalized with three separate classes of stock — Class A preferred stock, Class B preferred stock, and common stock. Mr. White, and entities controlled by him, own 61.1 percent of the Class A preferred shares; 11.3 percent of the Class B preferred shares, and 43.1 percent of the company's common shares. The Class A shares had a liquidation preference four times that of Class B shares.

As of 2012, the price of Hollander common stock was languishing in the range of $6 to $7 per share. At the same time, the company had an unpaid dividend arrearage owed to Class A holders of $234.6 million and a $172.9 million dividend arrearage owed to the Class B holders. Thus, the common stock would not be paying dividends in the near future, one could surmise. Contemplating this situation, the board of Hollander determined that market analysts were having a hard time determining Hollander's true value because of its complicated capital structure. Thus, a recapitalization was in order. Under the recapitalization plan that the board approved, the Class A and Class B shares' accrued and unpaid dividends would be wiped out. Each Class A share would be reclassified and changed into 20 common shares and one warrant to purchase an additional share for $12.50 (above the market price, clearly). (A "warrant" is a long-term option to buy the common stock of a corporation granted by the corporation.) Each Class B share would be reclassified and changed into one-third of a common share and warrants to purchase five additional shares at $12.50 per share. Each common share would be converted to one-tenth of a common share and three-tenths of a warrant to purchase a share for $12.50.

The plan was approved and recommended by a committee of the board made up of outside directors. In order to be adopted, the plan was put to a vote that required approval of a simple majority of all three classes. After the plan was publicly announced, in connection with the filing of the proxy statement with the Securities and Exchange Commission (SEC) in preparation for the vote, Class A shares rose in value dramatically while Class B shares lost half of their value. At a special shareholders' meeting held in May 2012, each voting class approved the plan. The votes in favor of the plan were 82.7 percent of the

transaction will not be void or voidable by reason of the conflict of interest. Under § 144(a)(1), a ratifying disinterested director vote has the same procedural effect as a ratifying disinterested shareholder vote under § 144(a)(2). *See Marciano*, 535 A.2d at 405, n. 3. Here, it is disputed that the merger was approved by the fully informed vote of WTI's disinterested directors. Those directors were fully aware of both the obvious conflict of the Waste designees and of the conflict of three other directors, created by the prospect of accelerated stock options and of future employment.

outstanding Class A shares, 68.8 percent of the outstanding Class B shares, and 53.2 percent of the old common shares. After the recapitalization was effected, the common shares still traded well below the warrant price of $12.50, and the warrants themselves traded at $.50 per warrant.

Former holders of Class B shares are interested in evaluating whether they have a cause of action against the board for breach of the duty of loyalty or for various disclosure violations. They point to the market reaction as evidence that the plan unfairly favored Class A shareholders at the expense of Class B shareholders. They also contend that the proxy statement contained the following material misrepresentations or omissions:

1. It failed to disclose the projected value of the new common stock despite the fact that the board had that projection;
2. It failed to estimate the value of the warrants, despite the fact that the board had that estimate; and
3. It failed to disclose that the investment banker who gave the fairness opinion anticipates getting further work from Hollander-related entities.

How do you advise the Class B shareholders? What additional information do you need prior to giving advice? Who would have the burden of proof in the litigation, and what would that party have to prove? How does the shareholder vote affect your analysis?

C. OFFICERS' FIDUCIARY DUTIES

For many years, the Delaware courts have assumed that the fiduciary duties of officers are identical to those of directors, without having an opportunity to directly so hold. In *Gantler v. Stephens,* the Delaware Supreme Court took that opportunity, since one of the defendants whose actions were alleged to violate fiduciary duties was an officer but not a director. As you read this case, notice also the court's useful discussion of the content of directors' and officers' fiduciary duty of disclosure.

GANTLER v. STEPHENS

965 A.2d 695
Supreme Court of Delaware
January 27, 2009

Jacobs, Justice.

First Niles, a Delaware corporation headquartered in Niles, Ohio, is a holding company whose sole business is to own and operate the Home Federal Savings and Loan Association of Niles ("Home Federal" or the "Bank"). The Bank is a federally chartered stock savings association that operates a single branch in Niles, Ohio.

. . .

In late 2003, First Niles was operating in a depressed local economy, with little to no growth in the Bank's assets and anticipated low growth for the future. At that time [William L.] Stephens, who was Chairman, President, CEO and founder of First Niles and the Bank, was beyond retirement age and there was no heir apparent among the Company's officers. The acquisition market for banks like Home Federal was brisk, however, and First Niles was thought to be an excellent acquisition for another financial institution. Accordingly, the First Niles Board sought advice on strategic opportunities available to the Company, and in August 2004, decided that First Niles should put itself up for sale (the "Sales Process").

After authorizing the sale of the Company, the First Niles Board specially retained an investment bank, Keefe, Bruyette & Woods (the "Financial Advisor"), and a law firm, Silver, Freedman & Taft ("Legal Counsel"). At the next Board meeting in September 2004, Management advocated abandoning the Sales Process in favor of a proposal to "privatize" the Company. Under Management's proposal, First Niles would delist its shares from the NASDAQ SmallCap Market, convert the Bank from a federally chartered to a state chartered bank, and reincorporate in Maryland. The Board did not act on that proposal, and the Sales Process continued.

In December 2004, three potential purchasers — Farmers National Banc Corp. ("Farmers"), Cortland Bancorp ("Cortland"), and First Place Financial Corp. ("First Place") — sent bid letters to Stephens. Farmers stated in its bid letter that it had no plans to retain the First Niles Board, and the Board did not further pursue the Farmers offer. In its bid letter, Cortland offered $18 per First Niles share, 49% in cash and 51% in stock, representing a 3.4% premium over the current First Niles share price. Cortland also indicated that it would terminate all the incumbent Board members, but would consider them for future service on Cortland's board. First Place's bid letter, which made no representation regarding the continued retention of the First Niles Board, proposed a stock-for-stock transaction valued at $18 to $18.50 per First Niles Share, representing a 3.4% to 6.3% premium.

The Board considered these bids at its next regularly scheduled meeting in December 2004. At that meeting the Financial Advisor opined that all three bids were within the range suggested by its financial models, and that accepting the stock-based offers would be superior to retaining First Niles shares. The Board took no action at that time. Thereafter, at that same meeting, Stephens also discussed in further detail Management's proposed privatization.

On January 18, 2005, the Board directed the Financial Advisor and Management to conduct due diligence in connection with a possible transaction with First Place or Cortland. The Financial Advisor met with Stephens and [Lawrence Safarek, the treasurer and vice president of both First Niles and the Bank,] and all three reviewed Cortland's due diligence request. Stephens and Safarek agreed to provide the materials Cortland requested and scheduled a due diligence session for February 6. Cortland failed to receive the materials it requested, canceled the February 6 meeting, and demanded the submission of those materials by February 8. The due diligence materials were never furnished, and Cortland withdrew its bid for First Niles on February 10. Management did not inform the Board of these due diligence events until after Cortland had withdrawn its bid.

First Place made its due diligence request on February 7, 2005, and asked for a due diligence review session the following week. Initially, Stephens did not provide the requested materials to First Place and resisted setting a date for a due diligence session. After Cortland withdrew its bid, however, Stephens agreed to schedule a due diligence session.

First Place began its due diligence review on February 13, 2005, and submitted a revised offer to First Niles on March 4. As compared to its original offer, First Place's revised offer had an improved exchange ratio. Because of a decline in First Place's stock value, the revised offer represented a lower implied price per share ($17.25 per First Niles share), but since First Niles' stock price had also declined, the revised offer still represented an 11% premium over market price. The Financial Advisor opined that First Place's revised offer was within an acceptable range, and that it exceeded the mean and median comparable multiples for previous acquisitions involving similar banks.

On March 7, 2005, at the next regularly scheduled Board meeting, Stephens informed the directors of First Place's revised offer. Although the Financial Advisor suggested that First Place might again increase the exchange ratio, the Board did not discuss the offer. Stephens proposed that the Board delay considering the offer until the next regularly scheduled Board meeting. After the Financial Advisor told him that First Place would likely not wait two weeks for a response, Stephens scheduled a special Board meeting for March 9 to discuss the First Place offer.

On March 8, First Place increased the exchange ratio of its offer to provide an implied value of $17.37 per First Niles share. At the March 9 special Board meeting, Stephens distributed a memorandum from the Financial Advisor describing First Place's revised offer in positive terms. Without any discussion or deliberation, however, the Board voted 4 to 1 to reject that offer, with only Gantler voting to accept it. After the vote, Stephens discussed Management's privatization plan and instructed Legal Counsel to further investigate that plan.

C. The Reclassification Proposal

Five weeks later, on April 18, 2005, Stephens circulated to the Board members a document describing a proposed privatization of First Niles ("Privatization Proposal"). That Proposal recommended reclassifying the shares of holders of 300 or fewer shares of First Niles common stock into a new issue of Series A Preferred Stock on a one-to-one basis (the "Reclassification"). The Series A Preferred Stock would pay higher dividends and have the same liquidation rights as the common stock, but the Preferred holders would lose all voting rights except in the event of a proposed sale of the Company. The Privatization Proposal claimed that the Reclassification was the best method to privatize the Company because it allowed maximum flexibility for future capital management activities, such as open market purchases and negotiated buy-backs. Moreover, First Niles could achieve the Reclassification without having to buy back shares in a fair market appraisal.

On April 20, 2005, the Board appointed [Ralph A. Zuzolo, a director and corporate board secretary of First Niles and the Bank,] to chair a special committee to investigate issues relating to the Reclassification, specifically: (1) reincorporating in a state other than Delaware, (2) changing the Bank's charter from a federal to a state charter, (3) deregistering from NASDAQ, and

(4) delisting. However, Zuzolo passed away before any other directors were appointed to the special committee.

On December 5, 2005, Powell Goldstein, First Niles' outside counsel specially retained for the Privatization ("Outside Counsel"), orally presented the Reclassification proposal to the Board. The Board was not furnished any written materials. After the presentation, the Board voted 3 to 1 to direct Outside Counsel to proceed with the Reclassification program. [Leonard T. Gantler, a First Niles shareholder and director,] cast the only dissenting vote.

Thereafter, the makeup of the Board changed. [Zuzolo and Gantler were replaced] in April of 2006. . . . On June 5, 2006, the Board determined, based on the advice of Management and First Niles' general counsel, that the Reclassification was fair both to the First Niles shareholders who would receive newly issued Series A Preferred Stock, and to those shareholders who would continue to hold First Niles common stock. On June 19, the Board voted unanimously to amend the Company's certificate of incorporation to reclassify the shares held by owners of 300 or fewer shares of common stock into shares of Series A Preferred Stock that would have the features and terms described in the Privatization Proposal.

D. The Reclassification Proxy and the Shareholder Vote

On June 29, 2006, the Board submitted a preliminary proxy to the United States Securities and Exchange Commission ("SEC"). An amended version of the preliminary proxy was filed on August 10. Plaintiffs initiated this lawsuit after the amended filing, claiming that the preliminary proxy was materially false and misleading in various respects. On November 16, 2006, the Board, after correcting some of the alleged deficiencies, disseminated a definitive proxy statement ("Reclassification Proxy" or "Proxy") to the First Niles shareholders. On November 20, the plaintiffs filed an amended complaint, alleging (inter alia) that the Reclassification Proxy contained material misstatements and omissions.

In the Reclassification Proxy, the Board represented that the proposed Reclassification would allow First Niles to "save significant legal, accounting and administrative expenses" relating to public disclosure and reporting requirements under the Exchange Act. The Proxy also disclosed the benefits of deregistration as including annual savings of $142,500 by reducing the number of common shareholders, $81,000 by avoiding Sarbanes-Oxley related compliance costs, and $174,000 by avoiding a one-time consulting fee to design a system to improve the Company's internal control structure. The negative features and estimated costs of the transaction included $75,000 in Reclassification-related expenses, reduced liquidity for both the to-be-reclassified preferred and common shares, and the loss of certain investor protections under the federal securities laws.

The Reclassification Proxy also disclosed alternative transactions that the Board had considered, including a cash-out merger, a reverse stock-split, an issue tender offer, expense reduction and a business combination. The Proxy stated that each of the directors and officers of First Niles had "a conflict of interest with respect to [the Reclassification] because he or she is in a position to structure it in such a way that benefits his or her interests differently from the interests of unaffiliated shareholders." The Proxy further disclosed that the Company had received one firm merger offer, and that "[a]fter careful deliberations, the board determined in its business judgment the proposal was not in the best interests of the Company or our shareholders and rejected the proposal."

The Company's shareholders approved the Reclassification on December 14, 2006. Taking judicial notice of the Company's Rule 13e-3 [Going Private] Transaction Statement, the trial court concluded that of the 1,384,533 shares outstanding and eligible to vote, 793,092 shares (or 57.3%) were voted in favor and 11,060 shares abstained. Of the unaffiliated shares, however, the proposal passed by a bare 50.28% majority vote.

. . .

B. The Court of Chancery Misapplied the Business Judgment Standard

[Count I alleges that the defendants breached their fiduciary duties to the First Niles shareholders by rejecting the First Place merger offer and abandoning the Sales Process.]

The plaintiffs . . . claim that the legal sufficiency of Count I should have been reviewed under the entire fairness standard. That claim is assessed within the framework of the business judgment standard, which is "a presumption that in making a business decision the directors of a corporation acted on an informed basis, in good faith and in the honest belief that the action taken was in the best interests of the company." *Aronson v. Lewis*, 473 A.2d 805, 812 (Del. 1984).

Procedurally, the plaintiffs have the burden to plead facts sufficient to rebut that presumption. On a motion to dismiss, the pled facts must support a reasonable inference that in making the challenged decision, the board of directors breached either its duty of loyalty or its duty of care. If the plaintiff fails to satisfy that burden, "a court will not substitute its judgment for that of the board if the . . . decision can be 'attributed to any rational business purpose.' "

We first consider the sufficiency of Count I as against the Director Defendants. That Count alleges that those defendants (together with non-party director Zuzolo) improperly rejected a value-maximizing bid from First Place and terminated the Sales Process. Plaintiffs allege that the defendants rejected the First Place bid to preserve personal benefits, including retaining their positions and pay as directors, as well as valuable outside business opportunities. The complaint further alleges that the Board failed to deliberate before deciding to reject the First Place bid and to terminate the Sales Process. Indeed, plaintiffs emphasize, the Board retained the Financial Advisor to advise it on the Sales Process, yet repeatedly disregarded the Financial Advisor's advice.

A board's decision not to pursue a merger opportunity is normally reviewed within the traditional business judgment framework. In that context the board is entitled to a strong presumption in its favor, because implicit in the board's statutory authority to propose a merger, is also the power to decline to do so.

Our analysis of whether the Board's termination of the Sales Process merits the business judgment presumption is two pronged. First, did the Board reach its decision in the good faith pursuit of a legitimate corporate interest? Second, did the Board do so advisedly? For the Board's decision here to be entitled to the business judgment presumption, both questions must be answered affirmatively.

We consider first whether Count I alleges a cognizable claim that the Board breached its duty of loyalty. In *TW Services v. SWT Acquisition Corporation*, the Court of Chancery recognized that a board's decision to decline a merger is often rooted in distinctively corporate concerns, such as enhancing the corporation's long term share value, or "a plausible concern that the level of debt likely to be borne by [the target company] following any merger would be detrimental to the long term function of th[at] [c]ompany." A good faith pursuit of legitimate concerns of this kind will satisfy the first prong of the analysis.

Here, the plaintiffs allege that the Director Defendants had a disqualifying self-interest because they were financially motivated to maintain the status quo. A claim of this kind must be viewed with caution, because to argue that directors have an entrenchment motive solely because they could lose their positions following an acquisition is, to an extent, tautological. By its very nature, a board decision to reject a merger proposal could always enable a plaintiff to assert that a majority of the directors had an entrenchment motive. For that reason, the plaintiffs must plead, in addition to a motive to retain corporate control, other facts sufficient to state a cognizable claim that the Director Defendants acted disloyally.

The plaintiffs have done that here. . . .

In dismissing Count I as to the Officer Defendants, the Court of Chancery . . . erred. The Court of Chancery has held, and the parties do not dispute, that corporate officers owe fiduciary duties that are identical to those owed by corporate directors. That issue — whether or not officers owe fiduciary duties identical to those of directors — has been characterized as a matter of first impression for this Court. In the past, we have implied that officers of Delaware corporations, like directors, owe fiduciary duties of care and loyalty, and that the fiduciary duties of officers are the same as those of directors. We now explicitly so hold.[1] The only question presented here is whether the complaint alleges sufficiently detailed acts of wrongdoing by Stephens and Safarek to state a claim that they breached their fiduciary duties as officers. We conclude that it does.

Stephens and Safarek were responsible for preparing the due diligence materials for the three firms that expressed an interest in acquiring First Niles. The alleged facts that make it reasonable to infer that Stephens violated his duty of loyalty as a director, also establish his violation of that same duty as an officer. It also is reasonably inferable that Safarek aided and abetted Stephens' separate loyalty breach. Safarek, as First Niles' Vice President and Treasurer, depended upon Stephen's continued good will to retain his job and the benefits that it generated. Because Safarek was in no position to act independently of Stephens, it may be inferred that by assisting Stephens to "sabotage" the due diligence process, Safarek also breached his duty of loyalty.

The Court of Chancery found otherwise. Having characterized Safarek's actions as causing "a delay of a matter of days, or at most a couple of weeks," the Vice Chancellor observed that he could not see how that "conceivably could be a breach of Safarek's fiduciary duties." This analysis is inappropriate on a motion to dismiss. The complaint alleges that Safarek never responded to Cortland's due diligence requests and that as a result, Cortland withdrew a competitive bid for First Niles. Those facts support a reasonable inference that Safarek and Stephens attempted to sabotage the Cortland and First Place due diligence process. On a motion to dismiss, the Court of Chancery was not free to disregard

---

1. That does not mean, however, that the consequences of a fiduciary breach by directors or officers, respectively, would necessarily be the same. Under 8 Del. C. 102 (b)(7), a corporation may adopt a provision in its certificate of incorporation exculpating its directors from monetary liability for an adjudicated breach of their duty of care. Although legislatively possible, there currently is no statutory provision authorizing comparable exculpation of corporate officers.

that reasonable inference, or to discount it by weighing it against other, perhaps contrary, inferences that might also be drawn. By dismissing Count I as applied to Stephens and Safarek as officers of First Niles, the trial court erred.

. . .

SALOMON BROTHERS: A CASE STUDY

The U.S. Treasury Department generally sells its bills (less than one year's maturity); notes (one to five years' maturity); and bonds (over five years' maturity) using a closed-bid, multiple-price auction system and holding more than 150 auctions a year. Under that system, the U.S. government does not set a price for the securities it is selling. Rather, the government announces the quantity and maturity of securities it intends to sell (for instance, $9 billion of five-year U.S. Treasury notes), and potential purchasers submit bids indicating the quantity of securities they want to purchase and the price that they would be willing to pay for those securities. Prior to 1990, if auctions were oversubscribed, the Treasury Department had a policy of limiting sales to any one purchaser to 35 percent of the securities being auctioned. In such cases, the Department would recognize bids above 35 percent but fill the bids it had received by prorating each bidder's total bid. Under the pre-July 1990 rules, bidders might thus decide to submit a bid for more than 35 percent of the total being auctioned to increase their chances of getting the full number of securities they wanted, after proration.

In 1990, Salomon Brothers' managing director, Paul M. Mozer, who was the head of Salomon's Government [Bond] Trading Desk, became particularly aggressive in bidding for more than 35 percent of securities being auctioned. Indeed, in one July 1990 auction Mozer bid for more than 100 percent of the securities being auctioned, prompting a call from a senior Treasury official, Michael Basham, who asked Mozer not to be so aggressive in his bidding.

Mozer was noncommital in his response to Basham, which is odd enough in a relationship between the regulated and a top regulator, but then bid for more than 100 percent of the securities being auctioned in the very next auction. When Basham tried to call Mozer to criticize the aggressive bidding in this auction, Mozer refused to return Basham's phone call. The next day, the Treasury Department changed its rules, stating that in future auctions no bidder could bid (either for its own account or for a customer) at any one price for more than 35 percent of the securities being auctioned. Mozer was publicly critical of both the rule change and of Michael Basham, including being quoted in the New York Times as saying that the rule change was unnecessary and that the Treasury Department did not understand the market. On Wall Street, the rule became known as the "Mozer/Basham" rule.

Privately, Mozer took other actions in response to the rule change. Beginning in December 1990, Mozer began occasionally submitting unauthorized customer bids for more than 35 percent of securities being auctioned. In a number of auctions, Mozer submitted bids allegedly for Salomon's customers, without the customers' knowledge or authorization, and then "sold" the securities purchased through the unauthorized bids to Salomon Brothers for the Government Trading Desk's own account (securities Salomon owned for investment or resale). According to standard Salomon procedures, the submission of the bid, the purchase from the Treasury Department, and the subsequent "sale" to Salomon all should have generated customer confirmations — that is, a written notice to the customer of the activity in its account. Mozer, who was a highly placed Salomon employee, was able to ensure that no confirmation was sent at any of these three points in the transaction by issuing "Do Not Confirm" instructions for the unauthorized trades. Between July 1990 and July 1991, Mozer submitted partially or wholly unauthorized customer bids, and engaged in other trading irregularities, in seven auctions. Each unauthorized customer bid submitted by Mozer to the Treasury Department was a crime by virtue of 18 U.S.C. §1001, which prohibits knowingly making false statements to the government.

One of the auctions in which Mozer submitted unauthorized bids and suppressed customer confirmations was an auction on February 21, 1991, of $9 billion of five-year U.S. Treasury notes. In that auction, Mozer submitted a bid for $3.15 billion of the notes (35 percent) for Salomon's account, at a yield of 7.51 percent to maturity. Thus, according to the Treasury Department rules, Salomon was prohibited from submitting any other bids at 7.51 percent. Mozer, however, submitted two additional unauthorized $3.15 billion bids at 7.51 percent in the name of two of its established customers: the Quantum Fund, and Mercury Asset Management (Mercury). The Federal Reserve Bank of New York (the Fed), which administered the auction, prorated each of the $3.15 billion bids at 54 percent, awarding $1.701 billion of the securities on each bid. Since each of the bids was actually Mozer's bid for Salomon's account, Salomon ended up with a total of $5.103 billion of the notes, or 56.7 percent of the securities being auctioned.

In the February 21, 1991, auction just described, a primary dealer named S.G. Warburg also submitted a bid at 7.51 percent for $100 million of securities. S.G. Warburg and Mercury Asset Management were both subsidiaries of the same holding company, S.G. Warburg, PLC, so if their bids were aggregated they had bid over the 35 percent limit, in violation of the new Treasury Department rules. On February 21, 1991, the Fed notified the Treasury Department of this fact, but employees of the Treasury Department decided not to reduce the amount of either bid for purposes of determining the results of the auction, in particular since proration in the auction was so significant. At the same time, the Treasury Department decided to investigate Warburg and Mercury's corporate relationship to determine if their bids should be aggregated for purposes of the 35 percent rule in the future. Ultimately concluding that aggregation was appropriate, the Treasury Department wrote a letter on April 17, 1991, to Warburg, PLC, discussing the February 21, 1991, bids by S.G. Warburg and Mercury, and informing Warburg, PLC that in the future S.G. Warburg and Mercury's bids would be aggregated for determining compliance with the 35 percent rule. Copies of the letter were sent to Mercury and to Mozer.

The Treasury Department letter clearly presented a problem for Mozer, since Mercury had not actually submitted a bid in the February 21 auction. Mozer first called a managing director at Mercury, said that a clerk at Salomon Brothers had made a mistake and had incorrectly placed Mercury's name on a bidding sheet, that the problem had been corrected internally, and that Mozer would be grateful if the Mercury director would keep the matter confidential. Mozer then went to the office of his boss, John Meriwether, and showed Meriwether the Treasury Department letter. John Meriwether was a vice-chairman of Salomon Brothers in charge of the firm's fixed income (bond) and proprietary trading (trading for Salomon's own account). When Meriwether finished reading the letter, Mozer told him that Mercury had not bid in the auction nor authorized the bid, and that the bid had been for Salomon Brothers. Meriwether was shocked at Mozer's confession, and told Mozer that the incident was "career-threatening" and that Meriwether would have to immediately discuss the matter with Thomas Strauss, the president of Salomon Brothers. Meriwether asked Mozer if Mozer had ever submitted other unauthorized customer bids, and Mozer incorrectly said no.

Over the course of the following days, a number of conversations took place between John Meriwether, Thomas Strauss, John Gutfreund (chairman and CEO of Salomon), and Salomon's chief legal officer, Donald Feuerstein. (Gutfreund and Strauss were both directors of Salomon, as well as being top executive officers.) Feuerstein's legal advice, in summary, was that the unauthorized bid was a crime and that while there was probably no legal duty to report the unauthorized bid (based on existing securities law doctrine), Salomon Brothers should report it to the government as a matter of good judgment. Meriwether, Strauss, Gutfreund, and Feuerstein came away from the discussions with the sense that a decision had been made to report the unauthorized bid to the government but no clear sense of who was going to make the report, and to whom the report would be made. As the SEC put it in their eventual consent settlement of the matter:

> Meriwether stated that he believed that Strauss would make an appointment to report the matter to Gerald Corrigan, the President of the Federal Reserve Bank of New York. Feuerstein stated that he believed that Gutfreund wanted to think further about how the bid should be reported . . . [but] that [Feuerstein] believed the report should be made to the Federal Reserve Bank of New York, which could then, if it wanted, pass the information on to the Treasury department. Strauss stated that he believed that he and Gutfreund would report the matter in a personal visit with Corrigan. . . . Gutfreund stated that he believed that a decision had been made that he and Strauss, either separately or together, would speak to Corrigan about the matter.

In re John H. Gutfreund, Thomas W. Strauss and John. W. Meriwether, 51 S.E.C. 93 (1992).

Over the next few months, Feuerstein and Gutfreund had occasional conversations about the matter, but no report was made to the government.

During the course of the April discussions, there was no discussion of undertaking further investigations of Mozer's actions, nor of putting limits on his authority to submit bids in future U.S. Treasury auctions. After Mozer's disclosure to his superiors of one unauthorized customer bid in the February 21 auction, he submitted two additional unauthorized bids. These additional bidding irregularities, as well as the other previous unauthorized customer bids, only came to light after other conduct by Mozer (alleged antitrust violations with respect to the securities sold in the May 22, 1991, Treasury auction) prompted an internal investigation of Mozer's actions.

In early July, Salomon Brothers engaged an outside law firm to conduct an investigation into Mozer's activities with respect to the May 22, 1991, auction, since by then it was clear that the government was investigating alleged antitrust problems. By mid-July, the law firm suggested broadening the scope of the investigation, because they had begun to get information about unauthorized customer bids. That investigation concluded in early August, by which point the

law firm had uncovered evidence of bidding irregularities by Mozer in five Treasury auctions. The results of the investigation were reported to Feuerstein on
August 6, 1991, and to Gutfreund, Strauss, and Meriwether on August 7. After
consultation with counsel and public relations advisors, Salomon issued a press
release on Friday, August 9, stating that it had "uncovered irregularities and rule
violations in connection with its submission of bids in certain auctions of Treasury
securities." The press release described the bidding violations and stated that
Salomon had "suspended two managing directors on the Government Trading
Desk and two other employees," with pay, until further facts were known. The
August 9 press release made no mention of Gutfreund, Strauss, Meriwether, and
Feuerstein's knowledge for four months of one unauthorized customer bid.

Late in the evening of Thursday, August 8, as the press release was being
drafted, Strauss and Feuerstein arranged to have a telephone conversation
with a Salomon board member and major stockholder, who ultimately became
quite important to keeping Salomon Brothers alive: Warren Buffett. Buffett,
who is sometimes referred to as the "Oracle of Omaha" (because he lives in
Omaha, Nebraska, and because of his ability to pick winning investments), is one
of the country's wealthiest individuals, with a reputation for tough-minded honesty. His company, Berkshire Hathaway, is a holding company that owns various
other companies (including textile, insurance, and financial services companies). Berkshire Hathaway often seeks to buy companies outright, but occasionally it will take a major stake in a company, as it did in 1987 when it invested $700
million in Salomon in return for 9 percent preferred stock that was convertible
into a 12 percent stake in the company. Buffett also got a seat on Salomon's
board of directors. When Buffett spoke with Strauss and Feuerstein on the night
of August 8, he was told in general terms about Mozer's actions, and was read the
press release. Based on that phone conversation, Buffett thought the problem
was being handled appropriately and that the press release was adequate.

Buffett's business partner, Charlie Munger, who is a lawyer, heard things
differently that Thursday night, as the press release was being drafted. Munger
had been told in a telephone conversation with Feuerstein that "one part of the
problem had been known since April," and Munger immediately wanted to
know what had been known, and by whom. When he was told that Gutfreund,
Strauss, Meriwether, and Feuerstein had known of one unauthorized bid since
April and had failed to notify the Fed, Munger argued that the press release must
make that fact clear. Feuerstein disagreed, stating that Salomon's management
was concerned that disclosure of those facts, not clearly required by securities
law precedent, could have a negative impact on Salomon's ability to fund its
ongoing operations. However, Munger was on vacation on an island in Minnesota and was unable to talk to Buffett until after the press release was issued.
Thus, the strategy that was developed and implemented was for Salomon to call
its directors and regulators on August 9, as it issued the press release, and tell
them that management had known of one unauthorized customer bid since
April but not to include that fact in the press release.

Hindsight shows that Salomon's August 9 press strategy was a disaster. Various
Treasury Department and Federal Reserve Bank officials were furious that top
managers had known since April of one of Mozer's unauthorized bids and had
not told the government immediately about the problem. (This fury was exacerbated by the fact that Gutfreund had met with top Treasury officials in June to
discuss the antitrust allegations about the May 22, 1991, auction, and had not

brought up the subject of the unauthorized customer bid.) Thus, when reporters called administration officials on August 9 to get reactions to the press release, all they heard about was that "management had known about this," which set off a wild round of press accounts speculating about whether top management had been involved in the illegality or whether the facts that were known were just the tip of the iceberg of what would be discovered to be widespread illegality (neither of which proved to be the case).

By early the next week, it was clear that Salomon would need to disclose further facts, given all the press speculation. Moreover, once Buffett and Munger had had an opportunity to talk, Buffett began to press for further disclosure. Thus, Salomon scheduled a board of directors meeting for Wednesday, August 14, and at that meeting a more descriptive press release was approved. The August 14 press release included specific details about each of the bidding violations that had been uncovered and stated that certain top managers had known of one unauthorized bid since April 1991 and had failed to disclose it to the government. At the same time, the board was not told that on the previous day, the Fed had delivered a letter to Gutfreund calling into question whether Salomon could continue to submit bids for its customers in Treasury auctions and asking for a complete report within ten days of all of the "irregularities, violations, and oversights" of which Salomon was aware. Carol J. Loomis, *Warren Buffett's Wild Ride at Salomon*, Fortune, Oct. 27, 1997, at 114. As Buffett interpreted these events, Fed president Corrigan expected the letter to be given to the board and also expected that the board would recognize that top management needed to be ousted based on the seriousness with which the regulators viewed their lack of disclosure. When the board failed to act to force Gutfreund's resignation, according to Buffett, "[u]nderstandably, the Fed felt at this point that the directors had joined with management in spitting in its face."

Two days later, Gutfreund and Strauss resigned under pressure, and Buffett agreed to take on the role of interim chairman of Salomon, Inc., for the princely sum of $1 per year. (At the time of Gutfreund's and Strauss's resignations, Meriwether's continued employment at Salomon was uncertain. Meriwether determined a few days after Buffett took over that it would be best for the firm for Meriwether to resign, which he did. Soon after, Feuerstein was forced to resign.) Buffett's actions are generally credited with having been critical in Salomon's survival. He has tremendous credibility with regulators, with Congress (which immediately began investigations of the matter, given the importance to the national interest of the integrity of the market for U.S. Treasury securities), with market participants, and with the press. Moreover, Buffett acted immediately and decisively to distance himself and the new management team from the problems of the past management team, calling their delay in notifying regulators of Mozer's illegal conduct "inexcusable and inexplicable"; implementing new procedures to prohibit overriding the customer confirmation system; and promising — and delivering — full cooperation with the government in fully investigating the extent of Mozer's wrongdoing. To emphasize the extent of his commitment to ethical business, Buffett sent a memo to each of Salomon's 8,000 employees soon after he took over indicating that there would be no tolerance for unethical misconduct:

> If you lose money for the firm by bad decisions, I will be very understanding. If you lose reputation for the firm, I will be ruthless. There is plenty of money to be

made — and I want to make it — playing straight down the center of the court. I don't want anyone playing close to the line.

The memo concluded by saying that Buffett wanted to know of any ethical or legal violations, with the exception of minor traffic violations, and underlining the seriousness of his commitment by including his home telephone number.

These events, lavishly reported in the press (particularly since August is typically a slow news month), had a predictable effect on Salomon's stock price: it dropped. From a high of $36 dollars per share prior to the first press release, the stock fell 25 percent to $27 per share after the second release. There were other effects as well: The Fed suspended Salomon's ability to bid in auctions for customers; large institutional investors, such as state pension funds, suspended their dealings with Salomon Brothers; Salomon's underwriting business dried up; and Salomon's bond ratings were downgraded by Moody's and other bond rating companies. The stock price drop, combined with these corollary effects, had another predictable effect: it led to litigation. First, Salomon's stockholders brought federal securities litigation challenging the accuracy of Salomon's press disclosures. Next, Salomon's stockholders brought derivative litigation challenging Gutfreund's, Strauss's, Meriwether's, and Mozer's exercise of their duty of care. The derivative plaintiffs made the following assertions in their Amended Consolidated Derivative Complaint:

¶ 4. As set forth in greater detail below, the head of Salomon's Government Trading Desk, Paul Mozer, aided and abetted by his closest associates and assistants, implemented a campaign to wrongfully manipulate the trading of United States Treasury securities in at least eight different treasury auctions in and prior to 1991. The violations included placing bids in the names of customers that were actually intended for Salomon's own account and maintaining false books and records intended to avoid detection by proper governmental authorities. These manipulations enabled Salomon to receive more than 35% of the securities offered at some Treasury auctions in violation of applicable laws and regulations, and in one case, enabled Salomon to receive 94% of the securities available at an auction. Mozer and others under his control sought to take advantage of Salomon's resulting market power by negotiating unfairly favorable terms on transactions involving the Treasury securities that Salomon acquired so as to increase the profits generated through their trading activities and thereby increase their compensation and their status both within the firm and outside.

¶ 5. Salomon's then most senior executives, including defendants John Gutfreund (Chairman of the Board and CEO), Thomas Strauss (then Vice-Chairman) and John Meriwether (chief of Salomon's fixed-income securities trading), were advised of Mozer's misconduct by Mozer no later than late April 1991 and determined that disclosure to appropriate government authorities should be promptly made. In breach of their fiduciary obligations, and contrary to the best interests of Salomon and its shareholders, these senior executives wrongfully delayed advising relevant government officials, misinformed government officials of the true facts and took no steps to prevent or investigate the underlying wrongdoing or discipline the known perpetrators. The Individual Defendants failed to reveal these facts to government regulators, the investing public and the full Salomon board until disclosure was forced by the inquiries of government officials and the results of a confidential investigation by outside counsel which they had no role in initiating.

¶ 6. Largely as a result of the wrongful failures by Gutfreund, Strauss and Meriwether to promptly investigate, discipline, report and prevent the wrongful bidding practices, and their affirmative concealment of the underlying misconduct from senior government officials, Salomon, upon public revelation of the facts, was threatened by total expulsion from the Treasury bidding market which, if such penalty had been exacted, would have had devastating consequences for the totality of its business and potentially forced the Company into bankruptcy. As it was, the Company suffered a major and costly suspension of [its ability to enter bids for customers for close to a year], and, in addition, the image and reputation of Salomon was severely damaged and Salomon has incurred over $290 million in civil fines, penalties and payments and has suffered other serious loss of business and commercial or financial repercussions, among other resulting injuries.

¶ 19. By reason of their positions and because of their ability to control the business and corporate affairs of Salomon Brothers at all relevant times, the Individual Defendants owed . . . fiduciary obligations of fidelity, trust, loyalty, and due care and were and are required to use their utmost ability to control, supervise and manage Salomon and its subsidiaries in a fair, just and equitable manner and to act in furtherance of the best interests of Salomon and its stockholders and to exercise due care and loyalty in the management and administration of the affairs of Salomon Brothers and in the use and preservation of their properties and assets.

¶ 21. The Individual Defendants, because of their positions of control and authority as officers and senior executives of Salomon Brothers, were able to and did, directly or indirectly, control the operations of Salomon's Government Trading Desk and the reporting of misdeeds by Mozer and others to the Federal Reserve, Treasury and other relevant government agencies. The Individual Defendants participated in the alleged wrongdoing, in part, in order to (i) conceal and cover up their own prior misconduct and mismanagement of Salomon and avoid being held responsible therefor; (ii) protect their executive positions and the substantial compensation they obtained thereby; (iii) obtain enhanced and/or bonus compensation pursuant to management incentive plans; and/or (iv) inflate and maintain the price of Salomon's securities which the Individual Defendants owned or had options to purchase at favorable prices.

As members of the board or senior officers, Gutfreund, Strauss and Meriwether were covered by Salomon's D&O insurance policy, and indemnified "to the full extent of Delaware law." Thus, Salomon's Certificate of Incorporation stated that:

To the extent permitted by law, as the same exists or may hereafter be amended (but, in the case of such amendment, only to the extent that such amendment permits the Corporation to provide broader indemnification rights than said law permitted to the Corporation prior to such amendment) the Corporation shall indemnify any person against any and all judgments, fines, amounts paid in settling or otherwise disposing of threatened, pending or completed actions, suits or proceedings, whether by reason of the fact that he, his testator or intestate representative, is or was a director or officer of (or a plan fiduciary or plan administrator of any employee benefit plan sponsored by) the Corporation or of (or by) any other corporation of any type or kind, domestic or foreign, which he served in any capacity at the request of the corporation. The foregoing right of indemnification shall in no way be exclusive of any other rights or indemnification to which any such person may be entitled, under any By-law, agreement, vote of shareholders or disinterested directors or otherwise, and shall inure to the benefit of the heirs, executors and administrators of such person.

QUESTIONS

1. Analyze the plaintiffs' fiduciary duty claims against Gutfreund, Strauss, and Meriwether. How, if at all, do *Caremark* and Stone v. Ritter affect your strategy? If you represented Salomon Brothers, what arguments would you make? How would you advise the Company to proceed in this litigation?

2. Soon after the litigation ensued, Gutfreund, Strauss, and Meriwether, each represented by separate counsel, sought a commitment from Salomon Brothers that it would advance the costs of defending them in the litigation, pursuant to the above provision in its Certificate of Incorporation that promised such defense to "the full extent of the law." As part of its "new broom sweeps clean" strategy, the board of directors wanted to deny those requests in order to emphasize the differences between the philosophies of the new management team versus the old one and to signal that it was no longer "business as usual" at Salomon. How would you advise the board on this issue?

3. If you represented the plaintiffs and wanted to bring a claim against the board as a whole, instead of against individual officers, how would you structure the complaint? What additional facts would you need to investigate? What are the advantages of bringing such a claim, in contrast to the claim analyzed in Question (1), above? What are the disadvantages?

4. What advice would you give the board on changes they could make with respect to structure and functioning to give greater emphasis to law compliance at the board level? What additional facts do you need to investigate prior to making recommendations? What are the risks to the board from implementing a changed law compliance structure while litigation is pending?

CHAPTER
9

Litigation to Enforce Fiduciary Duties

MOTIVATING HYPOTHETICAL

On January 14, 2012, two large banks — Grenfell & Company and Bank Won — published a joint press release announcing that they had agreed upon a merger, which had been unanimously approved by their respective boards of directors. Pursuant to the agreement, Grenfell would acquire Bank Won by issuing shares of its common stock to Bank Won stockholders at a premium of 14 percent over the closing price of Bank Won common stock on the date of the announcement of the merger. The combined company would be called Grenfell Bank.

The merger agreement also laid out the succession plan for Grenfell Bank. After the merger, the CEO of Grenfell & Company, Henry Harrison, would serve as CEO of Grenfell Bank for two years, after which time the CEO of Bank Won, James Diamond, would succeed. During the interim two years, Diamond would serve as president and chief operating officer. Harrison, who was chairman of the board of Grenfell & Company before the merger, would continue in that role indefinitely beyond the two years.

Not disclosed in the joint press release, or joint proxy statement, was the fact that Bank Won's CEO, James Diamond, had proposed a no-premium merger if he were immediately promoted to CEO of the resulting entity. The CEO of the acquirer, Harrison, in consultation with the Grenfell & Company board of directors, refused that offer, choosing instead to pay the premium for the target's stack and retain his title.

A. THE DEMAND REQUIREMENT

When directors breach their fiduciary duties, often it is the company itself that is directly harmed and should have the right to enforce a claim. But a company acts through its directors and officers — the very people who have breached their fiduciary duties. Of course, we cannot expect the directors and officers to sue themselves. Recognizing this problem, courts of equity gave shareholders the right to sue in such cases. A shareholder suit of this type is known as "derivative litigation," a designation acknowledging that the shareholders' claim is not a claim of direct harm, but a claim that is derived from harm to the corporation. We have seen derivative litigation in prior chapters. For example, the *Disney* litigation for excessive executive compensation, and Kahn v. Sullivan challenging Occidental Petroleum's charitable contributions, were both derivative actions.

The courts have described derivative claims as being two actions combined in one. The first action is a suit by the shareholders against the corporation to compel the corporation to sue. In derivative litigation, therefore, the corporation is a nominal defendant, even though the real defendants are the directors. The second action is by the corporation against the directors, and the shareholders are, in a sense, only the nominal plaintiffs. They are suing on behalf of the corporation.

Because the claim belongs to the corporation — not the shareholders — any recovery goes to the corporation. This feature of derivative litigation introduces a potential problem: Why would any shareholder bear all of the costs of litigation with the prospect of receiving only a portion of the benefits (equal to the shareholder's ownership interest in the corporation)? In most cases, the answer is simple: The shareholders themselves would not sue under those circumstances.

This was a real problem for the courts of equity, which recognized the potential benefits from derivative litigation. Not only could such litigation provide compensation to an injured corporation, but the fear of litigation could deter future breaches of fiduciary duty. In short, the courts of equity wanted to encourage derivative claims . . . at least, *meritorious* derivative claims.

To address the incentive problem, courts of equity decided that they would award attorneys' fees for successful lawsuits. This mechanism for encouraging derivative litigation has profound effects on the frequency and efficacy of claims. The obvious implication is that the shareholders are not the real party in interest: The attorneys have assumed that role.

Providing incentives to attorneys, however, can be a dangerous thing. Attorneys may be less concerned about the merits of the claim than they are about its settlement value. And, of course, no case would settle under this regime without an agreement on behalf of the defendants to pay fees for the plaintiffs' attorneys. Unmeritorious claims — commonly known as "strike suits" — became the next challenge.

The courts decided to meet that challenge by erecting various procedural obstacles: (1) Plaintiffs must have been shareholders at the time of the alleged breach of duty ("contemporaneous ownership" rule); (2) plaintiffs must remain shareholders throughout the litigation ("standing requirement"); (3) shareholders must "demand" that the board of directors take action before the shareholder assumes control of the litigation ("demand requirement"); and (4) once a derivative claim is filed, the court must approve any settlement. The standing requirement has been embraced by the Delaware courts as a matter of common law. *See* Lewis v. Anderson, 477 A.2d 1040, 1046 (Del. 1984). The other three requirements are embodied in Delaware Chancery Rule 23.1.

The idea behind these procedures was that good derivative suits would work their way through the obstacles, while bad derivative suits would falter. Of course, whether this aspiration would be realized would depend in large part on the manner in which the courts enforced the procedures. By far the most important decisions in this regard relate to the demand requirement.

The Delaware courts have not interpreted the demand requirement as mandatory. In some instances, the courts have been willing to "excuse" demand. These are cases in which directors—as a result of some conflict of interest or where the challenged action presents a real risk of fiduciary liability—would not be willing to act upon a demand. The courts describe those as cases in which a demand would be futile.

While this exception to the demand requirement might seem sensible enough at first blush, the effect of "demand futility" on derivative litigation has become the subject of persistent debate. The source of the controversy is the fact that Delaware courts review claims differently depending on whether demand is excused or has already been refused by the board of directors. If a plaintiff makes a demand and the board of directors refuses to act, the Delaware courts review the board's decision to refuse the demand. In other words, the case becomes a "wrongful refusal" case. Moreover, in deciding wrongful refusal cases, the Delaware courts have held that by making a demand, a shareholder tacitly acknowledges the board's independence and concedes the board's capacity to evaluate that demand. As a result, the court reviews the board's decision to refuse the demand under the deferential business judgment rule.

By contrast, if a plaintiff bypasses the board of directors and argues that a demand would be futile, the Delaware courts may scrutinize the case more carefully, as described in Aronson v. Lewis, 473 A.2d 805 (Del. 1984). The facts of that case are rather mundane: A stockholder of Meyers Parking System challenged certain transactions (namely, an employment agreement and interest-free loans) between the company and a 47 percent stockholder, who was also a director and officer of the company. The Court of Chancery refused to grant the defendant directors' motion to dismiss for failure to make a demand, holding that the plaintiff's allegations raised a "reasonable inference that the business judgment rule is not applicable for purposes of considering a pre-suit demand pursuant to Rule 23.1." In deciding whether a "reasonable inference" exists, the court examined the challenged transactions (that is, the employment agreement and the interest-free loans). If these transactions did not receive the protection of the business judgment rule, the court reasoned, then the directors who approved the transactions would become potentially liable for a breach of their fiduciary duty. As a result, they would not be capable of impartially considering a stockholder's demand.

In an interlocutory appeal, the defendants argued that the Court of Chancery had been too lax in its interpretation of the demand requirement. Observing that the board of directors is central to the management structure of a Delaware corporation, the defendants argued that the demand requirement could not be waived merely because the directors had approved the challenged transactions. If this were the standard, then demand would be waived in almost every case. Of course, the plaintiff countered by arguing that the board of directors was incapable of entertaining a demand with requisite impartiality because all of the directors had been selected for the board by the stockholder whose transactions were being challenged. These are all entirely predictable arguments, but the Delaware Supreme Court decided to seize the opportunity to revisit the standard for determining demand futility.

The Supreme Court began with the cardinal precept of Delaware corporate law that "directors, rather than shareholders, manage the business and affairs of the corporation." The demand requirement acknowledges the board's central role, but "where officers and directors are under an influence which sterilizes their discretion, they cannot be considered proper persons to conduct litigation on behalf of the corporation." *Aronson*, 473 A.2d at 814. The question thus became, under what circumstances would a board's discretion become sterilized? It would require something more than approval of the challenged transaction (for this would disqualify almost every board, and the demand requirement would become meaningless). Instead, the court offered the following standard:

> Our view is that in determining demand futility the Court of Chancery in the proper exercise of its discretion must decide whether, under the particularized facts alleged, a reasonable doubt is created that: (1) the directors *are* disinterested and independent [*or*] (2) the challenged transaction *was* otherwise the product of a valid exercise of business judgment. (Emphasis added.)

The easiest way for a plaintiff to meet this standard is to show that a majority of the current directors were interested in the challenged transaction. Unfortunately for many plaintiffs, such a showing does not fit the facts. The following statements from *Aronson* highlight the difficulty of making such a showing:

- [E]ven proof of majority ownership of a company [by a controlling shareholder who proposed a conflict-of-interest transaction] does not strip the directors of the presumptions of independence, and that their acts have been taken in good faith and in the best interests of the corporation. There must be coupled with the allegation of control such facts as would demonstrate that through personal or other relationships the directors are beholden to the controlling person.
- [I]t is not enough to charge that a director was nominated by or elected at the behest of those controlling the outcome of a corporate election. That is the usual way a person becomes a corporate director. It is the care, attention and sense of individual responsibility to the performance of one's duties, not the method of election, that generally touches on independence.
- Plaintiff's final argument is the incantation that demand is excused because the directors otherwise would have to sue themselves, thereby placing the conduct of the litigation in hostile hands and preventing its effective prosecution. . . . Its acceptance would effectively abrogate Rule 23.1 and weaken the managerial power of directors. Unless facts are alleged with particularity to overcome the presumptions of independence and a proper exercise of business judgment, in which case the directors could not be expected to sue themselves, a bare claim of this sort raises no legally cognizable issue under Delaware corporate law.

Initially, *Aronson* offered plaintiffs a Hobson's choice: make a demand and bring a wrongful refusal case under the business judgment rule, or avoid the demand and hope to show that the board of directors was interested. In the ensuing years, the Delaware courts have loosened the standards for demand futility somewhat. The case below, Beam ex rel. Martha Stewart Living Omnimedia, Inc. v. Martha Stewart, is an excellent example of the modern application of the *Aronson* standards.

All of this should be read in contrast to the Model Business Corporation Act ("Model Act"), which has short-circuited the drama over demand futility by adopting a universal demand requirement, under which plaintiffs must always first bring demand to the board that it initiate derivative litigation for breach of fiduciary duty. *See* Model Act § 7.42. If, after 90 days, the board has not acted, then the plaintiffs (who are, in every case, shareholders) can initiate litigation. *See* Model Act § 7.42(2). The drafters of the Model Act adopted a universal demand approach for two reasons. First, they envision it as a sort of alternative dispute resolution mechanism. Thus, by bringing demand to the board, the board would have the opportunity to recognize problems with the actions they have taken and to take steps to address the plaintiffs' concerns without litigation. Second, given how much time in litigation is spent on the question of whether demand is required or excused, the drafters felt that eliminating that potential issue would save time and money and streamline the process of litigation.

BEAM EX REL. MARTHA STEWART LIVING OMNIMEDIA, INC. v. STEWART

845 A.2d 1040
Supreme Court of Delaware
March 31, 2004

VEASEY, Chief Justice.

In this appeal we review and affirm the judgment of the Court of Chancery in dismissing under Rule 23.1 a claim in a derivative suit because the plaintiff failed to make presuit demand on the corporation's board of directors and failed to demonstrate demand futility. In his opinion, the Chancellor dealt with several issues and provided a detailed account of the facts of the case. We summarize only those facts most pertinent to this appeal. The single issue before us is that of demand futility, no appeal having been taken on the other issues. . . .

FACTS

The plaintiff, Monica A. Beam, owns shares of Martha Stewart Living Omnimedia, Inc. (MSO). Beam filed a derivative action in the Court of Chancery against Martha Stewart [and] the five other members of MSO's board of directors. . . . In four counts, Beam's amended complaint challenged three types of activity by Stewart and the MSO board. The Court of Chancery dismissed three of the four claims under Court of Chancery Rule 12(b)(6). Those dismissals were not appealed and are not before us.

In the single claim at issue on appeal (Count 1), Beam alleged that Stewart breached her fiduciary duties of loyalty and care by illegally selling ImClone stock in December of 2001 and by mishandling the media attention that followed, thereby jeopardizing the financial future of MSO. The Court of Chancery dismissed Count 1 under Court of Chancery Rule 23.1 because Beam failed to plead particularized facts demonstrating presuit demand futility.

When Beam filed the complaint in the Court of Chancery, the MSO board of directors consisted of six members: Stewart, Sharon L. Patrick, Arthur C. Martinez, Darla D. Moore, Naomi O. Seligman, and Jeffrey W. Ubben. The Chancellor concluded that the complaint alleged sufficient facts to support the conclusion that two of the directors, Stewart and Patrick, were not disinterested or independent for purposes of considering a presuit demand.

The Court of Chancery found that Stewart's potential civil and criminal liability for the acts underlying Beam's claim rendered Stewart an interested party and therefore unable to consider demand.[1] The Court also found that Patrick's position as an officer and inside director,[2] together with the substantial compensation she receives from the company, raised a reasonable doubt as to her ability objectively to consider demand. The defendants do not challenge the Court's conclusions with respect to Patrick and Stewart.

We now address the plaintiff's allegations concerning the independence of the other board members. We must determine if the following allegations of the complaint, and the reasonable inferences that may flow from them, create a reasonable doubt of the independence of . . . Martinez, Moore or Seligman:

4. Defendant Arthur C. Martinez ("Martinez") is a director of the Company, a position that he has held since January 2001. Until December 2000, Martinez served as Chairman of the board of directors of Sears Roebuck and Co., and was its Chief Executive Officer from August 1995 until October 2000. Martinez joined Sears, Roebuck and Co. in September 1992 as the Chairman and Chief Executive Officer of Sears Merchandise Group, Sears's former retail arm. From 1990 to 1992, he was Vice Chairman of Saks Fifth Avenue and was a member of Saks Fifth Avenue's board of directors. Martinez is currently a member of the board of directors of PepsiCo, Inc., Liz Claiborne, Inc. and International Flavors & Fragrances, Inc., and is the Chairman of the Federal Reserve Bank of Chicago. *Martinez is a longstanding personal friend of defendants Stewart and Patrick. While at Sears, Martinez established a relationship with the Company, which marketed a substantial volume of products through Sears. Martinez was recruited for the board by Stewart's longtime personal friend, Charlotte Beers. Defendant Patrick was quoted in an article dated March 22, 2001 appearing in Directors & Board as follows: "Arthur is an old friend to both me and Martha."*

5. Defendant Darla D. Moore ("Moore") is a director of the Company, a position she has held since September 2001. Moore has been a partner of Rainwater, Inc., a private investment firm, since 1994. Before that, Moore was a Managing Director of Chase Bank. Moore is also a trustee of Magellan Health Services, Inc. *Moore is a longstanding friend of defendant Stewart. In November 1995, she attended a wedding reception hosted by Stewart's personal lawyer, Allen Grubman, for his daughter. Also in attendance were Stewart and Stewart's friend, Samuel Waksal. In August 1996, Fortune carried an article highlighting Moore's close personal relationship with Charlotte Beers and defendant Stewart. When Beers, a longtime friend and confidante to Stewart, resigned from the Company's board in September 2001, Moore was nominated to replace her.*

6. Defendant Naomi O. Seligman ("Seligman") is a director of the Company, a position that she has held since September 1999. Seligman was a co-founder of Cassius Advisers, an e-commerce consultancy, where she has served as a senior partner since 1999, and is a co-founder of the Research Board, Inc., an information technology research group, where she served as a senior partner from 1975 until

---

1. Stewart was, at all relevant times, MSO's chairman and chief executive. She controls over 94% of the shareholder vote. She also personifies MSO's brands and was its primary creative force.
2. Patrick is the president and chief operating officer of MSO.

1999. Seligman currently serves as a director of Akamai Technologies, Inc., The Dun & Bradstreet Corporation, John Wiley & Sons and Sun Microsystems, Inc. *According to a story appearing on July 2, 2002 in The Wall Street Journal, Seligman contacted the Chief Executive Officer of John Wiley & Sons (a publishing house) at defendant Stewart's behest last year to express concern over its planned publication of a biography that was critical of Stewart.*

***

8. Martinez, Moore, Seligson [*sic*], and Ubben are hereinafter referred to collectively as the Director Defendants. By reason of Stewart's overwhelming voting control over the Company, each of the Director Defendants serves at her sufferance. Each of the Director Defendants receive [*sic*] valuable perquisites and benefits by reason of their service on the Company's Board. . . .

***

DEMAND ALLEGATIONS

73. . . . No demand on the Board of Directors was made prior to institution of this action, as a majority of the Board of Directors is not independent or disinterested with respect to the claims asserted herein.

***

77. *Defendant Martinez is not disinterested in view of his longstanding personal friendship with both Patrick and Stewart.*

78. *Defendant Moore is not disinterested in view of her longstanding personal relationship with defendant Stewart.*

79. *Defendant Seligman is not disinterested; she has already shown that she will use her position as a director at another corporation to act at the behest of defendant Stewart when she contacted the Chief Executive Officer of John Wiley & Sons in an effort to dissuade the publishing house from publishing a biography that was critical of Stewart.*

80. The Director Defendants are not disinterested as they are jointly and severally liable with Stewart in view of their failure to monitor Stewart's actions. Moreover, pursuit of these claims would imperil the substantial benefits that accrue to them by reason of their service on the Board, given Stewart's voting control.

DEMAND FUTILITY AND DIRECTOR INDEPENDENCE

. . .

Under the first prong of *Aronson*,[14] a stockholder may not pursue a derivative suit to assert a claim of the corporation unless: (a) she has first demanded that the directors pursue the corporate claim and they have wrongfully refused to do so; or (b) such demand is excused because the directors are deemed incapable of making an impartial decision regarding the pursuit of the litigation. The issue in this case is the quantum of doubt about a director's independence that is "reasonable" in order to excuse a presuit demand. The parties argue opposite sides of that issue.

The key principle upon which this area of our jurisprudence is based is that the directors are entitled to a *presumption* that they were faithful to their fiduciary

---

14. See Aronson v. Lewis, 473 A.2d 805, 814 (Del.1984) (setting forth two steps of a demand futility analysis: whether (1) "the directors are disinterested and independent and (2) the challenged transaction was otherwise the product of a valid exercise of business judgment").

duties. In the context of presuit demand, the burden is upon the plaintiff in a derivative action to overcome that presumption. The Court must determine whether a plaintiff has alleged particularized facts creating a reasonable doubt of a director's independence to rebut the presumption at the pleading stage. If the Court determines that the pleaded facts create a reasonable doubt that a majority of the board could have acted independently in responding to the demand, the presumption is rebutted for pleading purposes and demand will be excused as futile.

A director will be considered unable to act objectively with respect to a presuit demand if he or she is interested in the outcome of the litigation or is otherwise not independent. A director's interest may be shown by demonstrating a potential personal benefit or detriment to the director as a result of the decision. "In such circumstances, a director cannot be expected to exercise his or her independent business judgment without being influenced by the . . . personal consequences resulting from the decision."[22] The primary basis upon which a director's independence must be measured is whether the director's decision is based on the corporate merits of the subject before the board, rather than extraneous considerations or influences. This broad statement of the law requires an analysis of whether the director is disinterested in the underlying transaction and, even if disinterested, whether the director is otherwise independent. More precisely in the context of the present case, the independence inquiry requires us to determine whether there is a reasonable doubt that any one of these three directors is capable of objectively making a business decision to assert or not assert a corporate claim against Stewart.

INDEPENDENCE IS A CONTEXTUAL INQUIRY

Independence is a fact-specific determination made in the context of a particular case. The court must make that determination by answering the inquiries: independent from whom and independent for what purpose? To excuse presuit demand in this case, the plaintiff has the burden to plead particularized facts that create a reasonable doubt sufficient to rebut the presumption that . . . Moore, Seligman or Martinez was independent of defendant Stewart.

In order to show lack of independence, the complaint of a stockholder-plaintiff must create a reasonable doubt that a director is not so "beholden" to an interested director (in this case Stewart) that his or her "discretion would be sterilized."[24] Our jurisprudence explicating the demand requirement is designed to create a balanced environment which will: (1) on the one hand, deter costly, baseless suits by creating a screening mechanism to eliminate claims where there is only a suspicion expressed solely in conclusory terms; and (2) on the other hand, permit suit by a stockholder who is able to articulate particularized facts showing that there is a reasonable doubt either that (a) a majority of the board is independent for purposes of responding to the demand, or (b) the underlying transaction is protected by the business judgment rule.

The "reasonable doubt" standard "is sufficiently flexible and workable to provide the stockholder with 'the keys to the courthouse' in an appropriate

---

22. Rales v. Blasband, 634 A.2d 927, 936 (Del.1993).
24. *Id.*

case where the claim is not based on mere suspicions or stated solely in conclusory terms."[26]

PERSONAL FRIENDSHIP

A variety of motivations, including friendship, may influence the demand futility inquiry. But, to render a director unable to consider demand, a relationship must be of a bias-producing nature. Allegations of mere personal friendship or a mere outside business relationship, standing alone, are insufficient to raise a reasonable doubt about a director's independence. In this connection, we adopt as our own the Chancellor's analysis in this case:

> [S]ome professional or personal friendships, which may border on or even exceed familial loyalty and closeness, may raise a reasonable doubt whether a director can appropriately consider demand. This is particularly true when the allegations raise serious questions of either civil or criminal liability of such a close friend. Not all friendships, or even most of them, rise to this level and the Court cannot make a *reasonable* inference that a particular friendship does so without specific factual allegations to support such a conclusion.

The facts alleged by Beam regarding the relationships between Stewart and these other members of MSO's board of directors largely boil down to a "structural bias" argument, which presupposes that the professional and social relationships that naturally develop among members of a board impede independent decisionmaking. This Court addressed the structural bias argument in Aronson v. Lewis:

> Critics will charge that [by requiring the independence of only a majority of the board] we are ignoring the structural bias common to corporate boards throughout America, as well as the other unseen socialization processes cutting against independent discussion and decisionmaking in the boardroom. The difficulty with structural bias in a demand futile case is simply one of establishing it in the complaint for purposes of Rule 23.1. We are satisfied that discretionary review by the Court of Chancery of complaints alleging specific facts pointing to bias on a particular board will be sufficient for determining demand futility.[30]

In the present case, the plaintiff attempted to plead affinity beyond mere friendship between Stewart and the other directors, but her attempt is not sufficient to demonstrate demand futility. Even if the alleged friendships may have preceded the directors' membership on MSO's board and did not necessarily arise out of that membership, these relationships are of the same nature as those giving rise to the structural bias argument.

Allegations that Stewart and the other directors moved in the same social circles, attended the same weddings, developed business relationships before

---

26. Grimes v. Donald, 673 A.2d 1207, 1217 (Del.1996).
30. 473 A.2d 805, 815 n. 8 (Del.1984). Although the *Aronson* Court spoke of "discretionary" review by the Court of Chancery, a concept that was changed by this Court in Brehm v. Eisner, 746 A.2d 244, 253 (Del.2000), when we stated that our review of the Court of Chancery decision on presuit demand is de novo, the same principles apply as stated in *Aronson*.

joining the board, and described each other as "friends," even when coupled with Stewart's 94% voting power, are insufficient, without more, to rebut the presumption of independence. They do not provide a sufficient basis from which reasonably to infer that Martinez, Moore and Seligman may have been beholden to Stewart. Whether they arise before board membership or later as a result of collegial relationships among the board of directors, such affinities — standing alone — will not render presuit demand futile.

The Court of Chancery in the first instance, and this Court on appeal, must review the complaint on a case-by-case basis to determine whether it states with articularity facts indicating that a relationship — whether it preceded or followed board membership — is so close that the director's independence may *reasonably* be doubted. This doubt might arise either because of financial ties, familial affinity, a particularly close or intimate personal or business affinity or because of evidence that in the past the relationship caused the director to act non-independently vis à vis an interested director. No such allegations are made here. Mere allegations that they move in the same business and social circles, or a characterization that they are close friends, is not enough to negate independence for demand excusal purposes.

That is not to say that personal friendship is always irrelevant to the independence calculus. But, for presuit demand purposes, friendship must be accompanied by substantially more in the nature of serious allegations that would lead to a reasonable doubt as to a director's independence. That a much stronger relationship is necessary to overcome the presumption of independence at the demand futility stage becomes especially compelling when one considers the risks that directors would take by protecting their social acquaintances in the face of allegations that those friends engaged in misconduct. To create a reasonable doubt about an outside director's independence, a plaintiff must plead facts that would support the inference that because of the nature of a relationship or additional circumstances other than the interested director's stock ownership or voting power, the non-interested director would be more willing to risk his or her reputation than risk the relationship with the interested director.

SPECIFIC ALLEGATIONS CONCERNING SELIGMAN AND MOORE[33]

1. SELIGMAN

Beam's allegations concerning Seligman's lack of independence raise an additional issue not present in the Moore and Martinez relationships. Those allegations are not necessarily based on a purported friendship between Seligman and

---

33. In her reply brief in this Court the plaintiff appears to have abandoned any serious contention that she has properly alleged a reasonable doubt that Martinez is independent, focusing instead on her contention that the Chancellor erred in dismissing her complaint as to Moore and Seligman. In her reply brief the plaintiff states:

What Plaintiff has asked is that the Court apply the law of Delaware to the allegations in the Amended Complaint. Had the Court of Chancery done so and heeded its expressed doubts, it would not have dismissed the Amended Complaint, because Moore and Seligman (as well as Stewart and Patrick) are not capable of impartially considering demand.

Accordingly, we do not analyze separately the allegations concerning Martinez. Moreover, since it is clear that the plaintiff has not pleaded facts raising a reasonable doubt as to Seligman and Moore, *a fortiori*, the plaintiff's weaker allegations concerning Martinez must fail.

Stewart. Rather, they are based on a specific past act by Seligman that, Beam claims, indicates Seligman's lack of independence from Stewart. Beam alleges that Seligman called John Wiley & Sons (Wiley) at Stewart's request in order to prevent an unfavorable publication reference to Stewart. The Chancellor concluded, properly in our view, that this allegation does not provide particularized facts from which one may reasonably infer improper influence.

The bare fact that Seligman contacted Wiley, on whose board Seligman also served, to dissuade Wiley from publishing unfavorable references to Stewart, even if done at Stewart's request, is insufficient to create a reasonable doubt that Seligman is capable of considering presuit demand free of Stewart's influence. Although the court should draw all *reasonable* inferences in Beam's favor, neither improper influence by Stewart over Seligman nor that Seligman was beholden to Stewart is a reasonable inference from these allegations.

Indeed, the reasonable inference is that Seligman's purported intervention on Stewart's behalf was of benefit to MSO and *its* reputation, which is allegedly tied to *Stewart's* reputation, as the Chancellor noted. A motivation by Seligman to benefit the company every bit as much as Stewart herself is the only reasonable inference supported by the complaint, when all of its allegations are read in context.[35]

2. MOORE

The Court of Chancery concluded that the plaintiff's allegations with respect to Moore's social relationship with Stewart presented "quite a close call" and suggested ways that the "balance could have been tipped." Although we agree that there are ways that the balance could be tipped so that mere allegations of social relationships would become allegations casting reasonable doubt on independence, we do not agree that the facts as alleged present a "close call" with respect to Moore's independence. These allegations center on: (a) Moore's attendance at a wedding reception for the daughter of Stewart's lawyer where Stewart and Waksal were also present; (b) a *Fortune* magazine article focusing on the close personal relationships among Moore, Stewart and Beers; and (c) the fact that Moore replaced Beers on the MSO board. In our view, these bare social relationships clearly do not create a reasonable doubt of independence.

---

35. The complaint alleges:

16. The Company is highly dependent upon Stewart; as the Company's prospectus for the public offering indicated:
**
We are highly dependent upon our founder, Chairman and Chief Executive Officer, Martha Stewart. . . . The diminution or loss of the services of Martha Stewart, and any negative market or industry perception arising from that diminution or loss, would have a material adverse effect on our business. . . . Martha Stewart remains the personification of our brands as well as our senior executive and primary creative force.

17. The prospectus for the public offering also warned that the Company's business would be affected adversely if "Martha Stewart's public image or reputation were to be tarnished. Martha Stewart, as well as her name, her image and the trademarks and other intellectual property rights relating to these, are integral to our marketing efforts and form the core of our brand name. Our continued success and the value of our brand name therefore depends, to a large degree, on the reputation of Martha Stewart."

3. STEWART'S 94% STOCK OWNERSHIP

Beam attempts to bolster her allegations regarding the relationships between Stewart and Seligman and Moore by emphasizing Stewart's overwhelming voting control of MSO. That attempt also fails to create a reasonable doubt of independence. A stockholder's control of a corporation does not excuse presuit demand on the board without particularized allegations of relationships between the directors and the controlling stockholder demonstrating that the directors are beholden to the stockholder. As noted earlier, the relationships alleged by Beam do not lead to the inference that the directors were beholden to Stewart and, thus, unable independently to consider demand. Coupling those relationships with Stewart's overwhelming voting control of MSO does not close that gap.[38]

A Word About the Oracle Case

In his opinion, the Chancellor referred several times to the Delaware Court of Chancery decision in In re Oracle Corp. Derivative Litigation, 824 A.2d 917 (Del.Ch. 2003). Indeed, the plaintiff relies on the *Oracle* case in this appeal. *Oracle* involved the issue of the independence of the Special Litigation Committee (SLC) appointed by the Oracle board to determine whether or not the corporation should cause the dismissal of a corporate claim by stockholder-plaintiffs against directors. The Court of Chancery undertook a searching inquiry of the relationships between the members of the SLC and Stanford University in the context of the financial support of Stanford by the corporation and its management. The Vice Chancellor concluded, after considering the SLC Report and the discovery record, that those relationships were too close for purposes of the SLC analysis of independence.

An SLC is a unique creature that was introduced into Delaware law by Zapata v. Maldonado, [430 A.2d 779 (Del. Supr. 1981)]. The SLC procedure is a method sometimes employed where presuit demand has already been excused and the SLC is vested with the full power of the board to conduct an extensive investigation into the merits of the corporate claim with a view toward determining whether — in the SLC's business judgment — the corporate claim should be pursued. Unlike the demand-excusal context, where the board is presumed to be independent, the SLC has the burden of establishing its own independence by a yardstick that must be "like Caesar's wife" — "above reproach."[43] Moreover, unlike the presuit demand context, the SLC analysis contemplates not only a shift in the burden of persuasion but also the availability of discovery into various issues, including independence.

We need not decide whether the substantive standard of independence in an SLC case differs from that in a presuit demand case. As a practical matter, the procedural distinction relating to the diametrically-opposed burdens and the availability of discovery into independence may be outcome-determinative on

---

38. The plaintiff's counsel was asked at oral argument in this Court if she had any authority for the proposition that social friendship plus such strong voting power of the interested director was sufficient to create a reasonable doubt of independence alone. Counsel admitted that she could point to no such authority.

43. Lewis v. Fuqua, 502 A.2d 962, 967 (Del.Ch.1985).

the issue of independence. Moreover, because the members of an SLC are vested with enormous power to seek dismissal of a derivative suit brought against their director-colleagues in a setting where presuit demand is already excused, the Court of Chancery must exercise careful oversight of the bona fides of the SLC and its process. Aside from the procedural distinctions, the Stanford connections in *Oracle* are factually distinct from the relationships present here.

CONCLUSION

Because Beam did not plead facts sufficient to support a reasonable inference that at least one MSO director in addition to Stewart and Patrick was incapable of considering demand, Beam was required to make demand on the board before pursuing a derivative suit. Hence, presuit demand was not excused. The Court of Chancery did not err by dismissing Count 1 under Rule 23.1. The judgment of the Court of Chancery is affirmed. . . .

PROBLEM 9-1

Plaintiff shareholders of the acquiring firm Grenfell & Company sued its directors, alleging breaches of fiduciary duty with regard to the acquisition. Plaintiffs claim that the acquirer paid too much for the acquired bank simply to mollify Grenfell's CEO, Harrison, who was unwilling to give up his position as CEO in order to let James Diamond take over. The Grenfell board has 12 directors, including Harrison and the company's chief financial officer. In addition to challenging Harrison for his conflict of interest and challenging the CFO's independence, plaintiffs assert that four other directors lack independence. Thus, plaintiffs claim that demand is excused. Evaluate the independence of the following Grenfell directors, based on the specific allegations found in the complaint, and determine if plaintiffs' assertion of demand being excused is correct:

1. *Riley Hunter*

Hunter is the chairman, CEO, and a director of Hunter Corporation, one of the largest privately held companies in the United States. The plaintiffs allege that Hunter is not independent because Hunter Corporation does business with the Trade Bank of Iraq, which is managed by Grenfell & Company. The plaintiffs claim that Hunter Corporation has received $2 billion from the Trade Bank in connection with the reconstruction of Iraq following the Iraq War. The plaintiffs further allege that Hunter is not independent because Grenfell & Company and Hunter Corporation share other financial interests. As an example, the plaintiffs cite an investment partnership that is jointly owned by partners of Hunter Corporation and a private equity firm affiliated with Grenfell & Company.

2. *Lawrence Honeywell*

The plaintiffs question the independence of Honeywell because his son is employed as a Grenfell & Company vice president. The plaintiffs contend that Honeywell would be unable to vote against Harrison because his vote would potentially endanger his son's career.

3. Elaine Flutter

Flutter is the president, as well as a trustee, of The American Museum of Natural History. The plaintiffs claim that Flutter cannot act independently because Grenfell & Company is a significant benefactor to the museum, having donated over $18 million to the museum since 1990. The plaintiffs also claim that Flutter cannot act independently because Grenfell & Company employed her brother-in-law as a managing director.

4. Anthony Burnside

Burnside is the chairman emeritus and former CEO of Traylor Systems, Inc., a large transportation company. Grenfell & Company serves as indenture trustee for Traylor when it raises funds publicly through the sale of bonds, including in its recent registration of $800 million of securities. Plaintiffs claim that the financial relations between Grenfell & Company and Traylor impedes Burnside's ability to act as an independent director.

B. DIRECT VERSUS DERIVATIVE CLAIMS

We have examined the procedural rules governing derivative litigation, but when is a claim a derivative claim and when is it a direct claim? The answer to this question is not always as simple as it might sound, as the following case shows.

TOOLEY v. DONALDSON, LUFKIN, & JENRETTE, INC.

845 A.2d 1031
Supreme Court of Delaware
April 2, 2004

VEASEY, Chief Justice:

Plaintiff-stockholders brought a purported class action in the Court of Chancery, alleging that the members of the board of directors of their corporation breached their fiduciary duties by agreeing to a 22-day delay in closing a proposed merger. Plaintiffs contend that the delay harmed them due to the lost time-value of the cash paid for their shares. The Court of Chancery granted the defendants' motion to dismiss on the sole ground that the claims were, "at most," claims of the corporation being asserted derivatively. They were, thus, held not to be direct claims of the stockholders, individually. Thereupon, the Court held that the plaintiffs lost their standing to bring this action when they tendered their shares in connection with the merger.

Although the trial court's legal analysis of whether the complaint alleges a direct or derivative claim reflects some concepts in our prior jurisprudence, we believe those concepts are not helpful and should be regarded as erroneous. We set forth in this Opinion the law to be applied henceforth in determining whether a stockholder's claim is derivative or direct. That issue must turn *solely* on the following questions: (1) who suffered the alleged harm (the corporation or the suing stockholders, individually); and (2) who would receive the benefit of any recovery or other remedy (the corporation or the stockholders, individually)?

To the extent we have concluded that the trial court's analysis of the direct vs. derivative dichotomy should be regarded as erroneous, we view the error as harmless in this case because the complaint does not set forth *any* claim upon which relief can be granted. In its opinion, the Court of Chancery properly found on the facts pleaded that the plaintiffs have no separate contractual right to the alleged lost time-value of money arising out of extensions in the closing of a tender offer. These extensions were made in connection with a merger where the plaintiffs' right to any payment of the merger consideration had not ripened at the time the extensions were granted. No other individual right of these stockholders having been asserted in the complaint, it was correctly dismissed.

In affirming the judgment of the trial court as having correctly dismissed the complaint, we reverse only its dismissal with prejudice. We remand this action to the Court of Chancery with directions to amend its order of dismissal to provide that: (a) the action is dismissed for failure to state a claim upon which relief can be granted; and (b) that the dismissal is without prejudice. Thus, plaintiffs will have an opportunity to replead, if warranted under Court of Chancery Rule 11.

FACTS

Patrick Tooley and Kevin Lewis are former minority stockholders of Donaldson, Lufkin & Jenrette, Inc. (DLJ), a Delaware corporation engaged in investment banking. DLJ was acquired by Credit Suisse Group (Credit Suisse) in the Fall of 2000. Before that acquisition, AXA Financial, Inc. (AXA), which owned 71% of DLJ stock, controlled DLJ. Pursuant to a stockholder agreement between AXA and Credit Suisse, AXA agreed to exchange with Credit Suisse its DLJ stock-holdings for a mix of stock and cash. The consideration received by AXA consisted primarily of stock. Cash made up one-third of the purchase price. Credit Suisse intended to acquire the remaining minority interests of publicly-held DLJ stock through a cash tender offer, followed by a merger of DLJ into a Credit Suisse subsidiary.

The tender offer price was set at $90 per share in cash. The tender offer was to expire 20 days after its commencement. The merger agreement, however, authorized two types of extensions. First, Credit Suisse could unilaterally extend the tender offer if certain conditions were not met, such as SEC regulatory approvals or certain payment obligations. Alternatively, DLJ and Credit Suisse could agree to postpone acceptance by Credit Suisse of DLJ stock tendered by the minority stockholders.

Credit Suisse availed itself of both types of extensions to postpone the closing of the tender offer. The tender offer was initially set to expire on October 5, 2000, but Credit Suisse invoked the five-day unilateral extension provided in the agreement. Later, by agreement between DLJ and Credit Suisse, it postponed the merger a second time so that it was then set to close on November 2, 2000.

Plaintiffs challenge the second extension that resulted in a 22-day delay. They contend that this delay was not properly authorized and harmed minority stock-holders while improperly benefitting AXA. They claim damages representing the time-value of money lost through the delay.

THE DECISION OF THE COURT OF CHANCERY

The order of the Court of Chancery dismissing the complaint, and the Memorandum Opinion upon which it is based, state that the dismissal is based on the plaintiffs' lack of standing to bring the claims asserted therein. Thus, when plaintiffs tendered their shares, they lost standing under Court of Chancery Rule 23.1, the contemporaneous holding rule. The ruling before us on appeal is that the plaintiffs' claim is derivative, purportedly brought on behalf of DLJ. The Court of Chancery, relying upon our confusing jurisprudence on the direct/derivative dichotomy, based its dismissal on the following ground: "Because this delay affected all DLJ shareholders equally, plaintiffs' injury was not a special injury, and this action is, thus, a derivative action, at most."

Plaintiffs argue that they have suffered a "special injury" because they had an alleged contractual right to receive the merger consideration of $90 per share without suffering the 22-day delay arising out of the extensions under the merger agreement. But the trial court's opinion convincingly demonstrates that plaintiffs had no such contractual right that had ripened at the time the extensions were entered into. . . . Moreover, no other individual right of these stockholder-plaintiffs was alleged to have been violated by the extensions.

That conclusion could have ended the case because it portended a definitive ruling that plaintiffs have no claim whatsoever on the facts alleged. But the defendants chose to argue, and the trial court chose to decide, the standing issue, which is predicated on an assertion that this claim is a derivative one asserted on behalf of the corporation, DLJ.

The Court of Chancery correctly noted that "[t]he Court will independently examine the nature of the wrong alleged and any potential relief to make its own determination of the suit's classification. . . . Plaintiffs' classification of the suit is not binding." The trial court's analysis was hindered, however, because it focused on the confusing concept of "special injury" as the test for determining whether a claim is derivative or direct. The trial court's premise was as follows:

> In order to bring a *direct* claim, a plaintiff must have experienced some "special injury."[citing Lipton v. News Int'l, 514 A.2d 1075, 1079 (Del.1986)]. A special injury is a wrong that "is separate and distinct from that suffered by other shareholders, . . . or a wrong involving a contractual right of a shareholder, such as the right to vote, or to assert majority control, which exists independently of any right of the corporation."[citing Moran v. Household Int'l. Inc., 490 A.2d 1059, 1070 (Del.Ch.1985), *aff'd* 500 A.2d 1346 (Del.1986 [1985])].

In our view, the concept of "special injury" that appears in some Supreme Court and Court of Chancery cases is not helpful to a proper analytical distinction between direct and derivative actions. We now disapprove the use of the concept of "special injury" as a tool in that analysis.

THE PROPER ANALYSIS TO DISTINGUISH BETWEEN DIRECT AND DERIVATIVE ACTIONS

The analysis must be based solely on the following questions: Who suffered the alleged harm — the corporation or the suing stockholder individually — and who would receive the benefit of the recovery or other remedy? This simple analysis is well imbedded in our jurisprudence, but some cases have complicated it by injection of the amorphous and confusing concept of "special injury."

The Chancellor, in the very recent *Agostino* case,[3] correctly points this out and strongly suggests that we should disavow the concept of "special injury." In a scholarly analysis of this area of the law, he also suggests that the inquiry should be whether the stockholder has demonstrated that he or she has suffered an injury that is not dependent on an injury to the corporation. In the context of a claim for breach of fiduciary duty, the Chancellor articulated the inquiry as follows: "Looking at the body of the complaint and considering the nature of the wrong alleged and the relief requested, has the plaintiff demonstrated that he or she can prevail without showing an injury to the corporation?" We believe that this approach is helpful in analyzing the first prong of the analysis: what person or entity has suffered the alleged harm? The second prong of the analysis should logically follow.

A Brief History of Our Jurisprudence

The derivative suit has been generally described as "one of the most interesting and ingenious of accountability mechanisms for large formal organizations."[10] It enables a stockholder to bring suit on behalf of the corporation for harm done to the corporation. Because a derivative suit is being brought on behalf of the corporation, the recovery, if any, must go to the corporation. A stockholder who is directly injured, however, does retain the right to bring an individual action for injuries affecting his or her legal rights as a stockholder. Such a claim is distinct from an injury caused to the corporation alone. In such individual suits, the recovery or other relief flows directly to the stockholders, not to the corporation.

Determining whether an action is derivative or direct is sometimes difficult and has many legal consequences, some of which may have an expensive impact on the parties to the action . . . . The decision whether a suit is direct or derivative may be outcome-determinative. Therefore, it is necessary that a standard to distinguish such actions be clear, simple and consistently articulated and applied by our courts.

In Elster v. American Airlines, Inc., [100 A.2d 219, 222 (Del.Ch.1953),] the stockholder sought to enjoin the grant and exercise of stock options because they would result in a dilution of her stock personally. In *Elster*, the alleged injury was found to be derivative, not direct, because it was essentially a claim of mismanagement of corporate assets. Then came the complication in the analysis: The Court held that where the alleged injury is to both the corporation *and* to the stockholder, the stockholder must allege a "special injury" to maintain a direct action. The Court did not define "special injury," however. By implication, decisions in later cases have interpreted *Elster* to mean that a "special injury" is alleged where the wrong is inflicted upon the stockholder alone or where the stockholder complains of a wrong affecting a particular right. Examples would be a preemptive right as a stockholder, rights involving control of the

---

3. Agostino v. Hicks, 2004 WL 443987 (Del.Ch. March 11, 2004).

10. Kramer v. Western Pacific Industries, Inc., 546 A.2d at 351 (quoting R. Clark, *Corporate Law* 639-40 (1986)).

corporation or a wrong affecting the stockholder, qua individual holder, and not the corporation.

In Bokat v. Getty Oil Co., [262 A.2d 246 (Del.1970),] a stockholder of a subsidiary brought suit against the director of the parent corporation for causing the subsidiary to invest its resources wastefully, resulting in a loss to the subsidiary. The claim in *Bokat* was essentially for mismanagement of corporate assets. Therefore, the Court held that any recovery must be sought on behalf of the corporation, and the claim was, thus, found to be derivative.

In describing how a court may distinguish direct and derivative actions, the *Bokat* Court stated that a suit must be maintained derivatively if the injury falls equally upon all stockholders. Experience has shown this concept to be confusing and inaccurate. It is confusing because it appears to have been intended to address the fact that an injury to the corporation tends to diminish each share of stock equally because corporate assets or their value are diminished. In that sense, the *indirect* injury to the stockholders arising out of the harm to the corporation comes about solely by virtue of their stockholdings. It does not arise out of any independent or direct harm to the stockholders, individually. That concept is also inaccurate because a direct, individual claim of stockholders that does not depend on harm to the corporation can also fall on all stockholders equally, without the claim thereby becoming a derivative claim.

In Lipton v. News International, Plc., [514 A.2d 1075, 1 1078,] this Court applied the "special injury" test. There, a stockholder began acquiring shares in the defendant corporation presumably to gain control of the corporation. In response, the defendant corporation agreed to an exchange of its shares with a friendly buyer. Due to the exchange and a supermajority voting requirement on certain stockholder actions, the management of the defendant corporation acquired a veto power over any change in management.

The *Lipton* Court concluded that the critical analytical issue in distinguishing direct and derivative actions is whether a "special injury" has been alleged. There, the Court found a "special injury" because the board's manipulation worked an injury upon the plaintiff-stockholder unlike the injury suffered by other stockholders. That was because the plaintiff-stockholder was actively seeking to gain control of the defendant corporation. Therefore, the Court found that the claim was direct. Ironically, the Court could have reached the same correct result by simply concluding that the manipulation directly and individually harmed the stockholders, without injuring the corporation.

In Kramer v. Western Pacific Industries, Inc., [546 A.2d 348, 352 (Del.1988),] this Court found to be derivative a stockholder's challenge to corporate transactions that occurred six months immediately preceding a buy-out merger. The stockholders challenged the decision by the board of directors to grant stock options and golden parachutes to management. The stockholders argued that the claim was direct because their share of the proceeds from the buy-out sale was reduced by the resources used to pay for the options and golden parachutes. Once again, our analysis was that to bring a direct action, the stockholder must allege something other than an injury resulting from a wrong to the corporation. We interpreted *Elster* to require the court to determine the nature of the action based on the "nature of the wrong alleged" and the relief that could result. That was, and is, the correct test. The claim in *Kramer* was essentially for mismanagement of corporate assets. Therefore, we found the claims to be derivative. That was the correct outcome.

In Grimes v. Donald, [673 A.2d 1207, 1213 (Del.1996),] we sought to distinguish between direct and derivative actions in the context of employment agreements granted to certain officers that allegedly caused the board to abdicate its authority. Relying on the *Elster* and *Kramer* precedents that the court must look to the nature of the wrong and to whom the relief will go, we concluded that the plaintiff was not seeking to recover any damages for injury to the corporation. Rather, the plaintiff was seeking a declaration of the invalidity of the agreements on the ground that the board had abdicated its responsibility to the stockholders. Thus, based on the relief requested, we affirmed the judgment of the Court of Chancery that the plaintiff was entitled to pursue a direct action.

Grimes was followed by Parnes v. Bally Entertainment Corp., [722 A.2d 1243, 1245 (Del.1999),] which held, among other things, that the injury to the stockholders must be "independent of any injury to the corporation." As the Chancellor correctly noted in *Agostino*, neither *Grimes* nor *Parnes* applies the purported "special injury" test.

Thus, two confusing propositions have encumbered our caselaw governing the direct/derivative distinction. The "special injury" concept, applied in cases such as *Lipton*, can be confusing in identifying the nature of the action. The same is true of the proposition that stems from *Bokat*—that an action cannot be direct if all stockholders are equally affected or unless the stockholder's injury is separate and distinct—from that suffered by other stockholders. The proper analysis has been and should remain that stated in *Grimes, Kramer* and *Parnes*. That is, a court should look to the nature of the wrong and to whom the relief should go. The stockholder's claimed direct injury must be independent of any alleged injury to the corporation. The stockholder must demonstrate that the duty breached was owed to the stockholder and that he or she can prevail without showing an injury to the corporation.

Standard to Be Applied in This Case

In this case it cannot be concluded that the complaint alleges a derivative claim. There is no derivative claim asserting injury to the corporate entity. There is no relief that would go the corporation. Accordingly, there is no basis to hold that the complaint states a derivative claim.

But, it does not necessarily follow that the complaint states a direct, individual claim. While the complaint purports to set forth a direct claim, in reality, it states no claim at all. The trial court analyzed the complaint and correctly concluded that it does not claim that the plaintiffs have any rights that have been injured. Their rights have not yet ripened. The contractual claim is nonexistent until it is ripe, and that claim will not be ripe until the terms of the merger are fulfilled, including the extensions of the closing at issue here. Therefore, there is no direct claim stated in the complaint before us.

Accordingly, the complaint was properly dismissed. But, due to the reliance on the concept of "special injury" by the Court of Chancery, the ground set forth for the dismissal is erroneous, there being no derivative claim. That error is harmless, however, because, in our view, there is no direct claim either.

Conclusion

For purposes of distinguishing between derivative and direct claims, we expressly disapprove both the concept of "special injury" and the concept that a claim is necessarily derivative if it affects all stockholders equally. In our view, the tests going forward should rest on those set forth in this opinion.

We affirm the judgment of the Court of Chancery dismissing the complaint, although on a different ground from that decided by the Court of Chancery. We reverse the dismissal with prejudice and remand this matter to the Court of Chancery to amend the order of dismissal: (a) to state that the complaint is dismissed on the ground that it does not state a claim upon which relief can be granted; and (b) that the dismissal is without prejudice.

Because our determination that there is no valid claim whatsoever in the complaint before us was not argued by the defendants and was not the basis of the ruling of the Court of Chancery, the interests of justice will be best served if the dismissal is without prejudice, and plaintiffs have an opportunity to replead if they have a basis for doing so under Court of Chancery Rule 11. This result — permitting plaintiffs to replead — is unusual, but not unprecedented. . . .

PROBLEM 9-2

In challenging the acquisition of Bank Won, Grenfell & Company shareholder plaintiffs challenge the 14 percent premium paid in the exchange of Grenfell & Company's shares for Bank Won shares. They claim the premium was higher than necessary only because Grenfell & Company CEO Harrison wanted to keep his position as CEO. This premium, the plaintiffs argue, prevented them from receiving their fair share of the resulting business combination, causing them to be harmed directly through dilution of their collective ownership percentage.

Applying Tooley, analyze whether the plaintiffs are correct that this is a direct, and not a derivative, claim.

C. SPECIAL LITIGATION COMMITTEES

In most cases where demand is properly excused, the company would still like to take control of the litigation. This is done by appointing a special litigation committee (SLC) (which sometimes might require expanding the size of the board and appointing new, disinterested directors), and then delegating power to the SLC to determine if it is in the company's best interest to proceed with the litigation. It would not be surprising to learn that it is the rare case in which the SLC recommends proceeding with the litigation.

In Zapata Corp. v. Maldonado, 430 A.2d 779 (Del. 1980), the Delaware Supreme Court articulated the principles that Delaware courts use to evaluate a SLC's decision to terminate litigation. *Zapata* first came to the Delaware courts as a demand futility case. Several years after commencement of the case, a number of the defendant directors had been replaced by outside directors. The board of Zapata created an independent investigation committee (Committee), composed of two outside directors, to determine whether continued litigation was in the best interests of the corporation. The Committee examined not only the Delaware litigation but related litigation arising out of the same matter in New York and Texas.

Following an investigation, the Committee concluded that all of the pending derivative lawsuits should be dismissed, and the company subsequently moved for summary judgment. The District Court for the Southern District of New York granted Zapata's motion, applying its interpretation of Delaware law, under which the Committee's action would be evaluated under the business judgment rule. Prior to the Delaware litigation in *Zapata* itself, most courts reviewed actions by SLCs under the business judgment rule, virtually ensuring the dismissal of every derivative claim subject to SLC review.

Contrary to the federal court in New York, the Delaware Court of Chancery denied Zapata's motion and held that the business judgment rule did not confer power "to a corporate board of directors to terminate a derivative suit." This conclusion is undoubtedly correct. As noted by the Delaware Supreme Court in reviewing this decision, the business judgment rule does not create authority. The authority, if any exists, emanates from Delaware General Corporation Law (DGCL) § 141(a). The business judgment rule, by contrast, "evolved to give recognition and deference to directors' business expertise when exercising their managerial power under § 141(a)." The issue with respect to SLCs, therefore, was whether the business judgment rule dictated deference.

To speak of deference to an SLC in this context may seem to be putting the cart in front of the horse. After all, the shareholder had properly initiated a derivative lawsuit. Why should the board have any continuing role? The Delaware Supreme Court addresses this question as follows:

> At the risk of stating the obvious, the problem is relatively simple. If, on the one hand, corporations can consistently wrest bona fide derivative actions away from well-meaning derivative plaintiffs through the use of the committee mechanism, the derivative suit will lose much, if not all, of its generally-recognized effectiveness as an intra-corporate means of policing boards of directors. If, on the other hand, corporations are unable to rid themselves of meritless or harmful litigation and strike suits, the derivative action, created to benefit the corporation, will produce the opposite, unintended result. It thus appears desirable to us to find a balancing point where bona fide stockholder power to bring corporate causes of action cannot be unfairly trampled on by the board of directors, but the corporation can rid itself of detrimental litigation.

430 A.2d at 786.

Assuming the board retains a continuing oversight role, the question becomes: When, if at all, should an authorized board committee be permitted to cause litigation, properly initiated by a derivative stockholder in his own right, to be dismissed? The federal court in New York had held that an authorized board committee could dismiss litigation as long as that decision passed muster under the business judgment rule, but the Delaware Supreme Court found this standard too lax. In a foreshadowing of standards later employed in the hostile takeover context, the court reasoned:

We are not satisfied, however, that acceptance of the "business judgment" rationale at this stage of derivative litigation is a proper balancing point. While we admit an analogy with a normal case respecting board judgment, it seems to us that there is sufficient risk in the realities of a situation like the one presented in this case to justify caution beyond adherence to the theory of business judgment.

The context here is a suit against directors where demand on the board is excused. We think some tribute must be paid to the fact that the lawsuit was properly initiated. It is not a board refusal case. . . .

Moreover, notwithstanding our conviction that Delaware law entrusts the corporate power to a properly authorized committee, we must be mindful that directors are passing judgment on fellow directors in the same corporation and fellow directors, in this instance, who designated them to serve both as directors and committee members. The question naturally arises whether a "there but for the grace of God go I" empathy might not play a role. And the further question arises whether inquiry as to independence, good faith and reasonable investigation is sufficient safeguard against abuse, perhaps subconscious abuse.

We thus steer a middle course between those cases which yield to the independent business judgment of a board committee and this case as determined below which would yield to unbridled plaintiff stockholder control. . . . The Court should apply a two-step test to the motion.

First, the Court should inquire into the independence and good faith of the committee and the bases supporting its conclusions. Limited discovery may be ordered to facilitate such inquiries. The corporation should have the burden of proving independence, good faith and a reasonable investigation, rather than presuming independence, good faith and reasonableness. If the Court determines either that the committee is not independent or has not shown reasonable bases for its conclusions, or, if the Court is not satisfied for other reasons relating to the process, including but not limited to the good faith of the committee, the Court shall deny the corporation's motion. If, however, the Court is satisfied under Rule 56 standards that the committee was independent and showed reasonable bases for good faith findings and recommendations, the Court may proceed, in its discretion, to the next step.

The second step provides, we believe, the essential key in striking the balance between legitimate corporate claims as expressed in a derivative stockholder suit and a corporation's best interests as expressed by an independent investigating committee. The Court should determine, applying its own independent business judgment, whether the motion should be granted. This means, of course, that instances could arise where a committee can establish its independence and sound bases for its good faith decisions and still have the corporation's motion denied. The second step is intended to thwart instances where corporate actions meet the criteria of step one, but the result does not appear to satisfy its spirit, or where corporate actions would simply prematurely terminate a stockholder grievance deserving of further consideration in the corporation's interest. The Court of Chancery of course must carefully consider and weigh how compelling the corporate interest in dismissal is when faced with a non-frivolous lawsuit. The Court of Chancery should, when appropriate, give special consideration to matters of law and public policy in addition to the corporation's best interests.

If the Court's independent business judgment is satisfied, the Court may proceed to grant the motion, subject, of course, to any equitable terms or conditions the Court finds necessary or desirable.

430 A.2d at 787-788.

The notion that courts should apply their "own independent business judgment" was viewed as quite innovative. In the wake of *Zapata*, courts outside Delaware reconsidered the standards used to evaluate actions by special litigation committees. Some courts remain deferential to SLC actions, *see* Houle v. Low, 556 N.E.2d 51 (Mass. 1990) (upholding such actions as long as they are "reasoned and principled"), while other courts view such decisions with great suspicion and employ standards of review similar to those of *Zapata*. *See* Alford v. Shaw, 358 S.E.2d 323 (N.C. 1987) (holding that *Zapata*-like standards should be employed in both demand-excused and demand-refused cases). The following is a Delaware case applying the *Zapata* standards in an unusual context. The case summarizes important developments in Delaware law governing SLCs. Moreover, it raises important questions about the role of SLCs in derivative litigation. As you read the case, consider whether the Delaware courts have properly extended the teachings of *Zapata*.

IN RE ORACLE CORP. DERIVATIVE LITIGATION

824 A.2d 917
Court of Chancery of Delaware
June 17, 2003

STRINE, Vice Chancellor.

In this opinion, I address the motion of the special litigation committee ("SLC") of Oracle Corporation to terminate this action, "the Delaware Derivative Action," and other such actions pending in the name of Oracle against certain Oracle directors and officers. These actions allege that these Oracle directors engaged in insider trading while in possession of material, non-public information showing that Oracle would not meet the earnings guidance it gave to the market for the third quarter of Oracle's fiscal year 2001. The SLC bears the burden of persuasion on this motion and must convince me that there is no material issue of fact calling into doubt its independence. This requirement is set forth in Zapata Corp. v. Maldonado and its progeny.

The question of independence "turns on whether a director is, *for any substantial reason*, incapable of making a decision with only the best interests of the corporation in mind." That is, the independence test ultimately "focus[es] on impartiality and objectivity." In this case, the SLC has failed to demonstrate that no material factual question exists regarding its independence.

During discovery, it emerged that the two SLC members — both of whom are professors at Stanford University — are being asked to investigate fellow Oracle directors who have important ties to Stanford, too. Among the directors who are accused by the derivative plaintiffs of insider trading are: (1) another Stanford professor, who taught one of the SLC members when the SLC member was a Ph.D. candidate and who serves as a senior fellow and a steering committee member alongside that SLC member at the Stanford Institute for Economic Policy Research or "SIEPR"; (2) a Stanford alumnus who has directed millions of dollars of contributions to Stanford during recent years, serves as Chair of SIEPR's Advisory Board and has a conference center named for him at SIEPR's facility, and has contributed nearly $600,000 to SIEPR and the Stanford Law School, both parts of Stanford with which one of the SLC members is closely affiliated; and (3) Oracle's CEO, who has made millions of dollars in donations to Stanford through a personal foundation and large donations indirectly through Oracle, and who was considering making donations of his $100 million house and $170 million for a scholarship program as late as August 2001, at around the same time period the SLC members were added to the Oracle board. Taken together, these and other facts cause me to harbor a reasonable doubt about the impartiality of the SLC.

It is no easy task to decide whether to accuse a fellow director of insider trading. For Oracle to compound that difficulty by requiring SLC members to consider accusing a fellow professor and two large benefactors of their university of conduct that is rightly considered a violation of criminal law was unnecessary and inconsistent with the concept of independence recognized by our law. The possibility that these extraneous considerations biased the inquiry of the SLC is too substantial for this court to ignore. I therefore deny the SLC's motion to terminate.

I. FACTUAL BACKGROUND

A. SUMMARY OF THE PLAINTIFFS' ALLEGATIONS

The Delaware Derivative Complaint centers on alleged insider trading by four members of Oracle's board of directors—Lawrence Ellison, Jeffrey Henley, Donald Lucas, and Michael Boskin (collectively, the "Trading Defendants"). Each of the Trading Defendants had a very different role at Oracle.

Ellison is Oracle's Chairman, Chief Executive Officer, and its largest stockholder, owning nearly twenty-five percent of Oracle's voting shares. By virtue of his ownership position, Ellison is one of the wealthiest men in America. By virtue of his managerial position, Ellison has regular access to a great deal of information about how Oracle is performing on a week-to-week basis. Henley is Oracle's Chief Financial Officer, Executive Vice President, and a director of the corporation. Like Ellison, Henley has his finger on the pulse of Oracle's performance constantly. Lucas is a director who chairs Oracle's Executive Committee and its Finance and Audit Committee. Although the plaintiffs allege that Lucas's positions gave him access to material, non-public information about the company, they do so cursorily. On the present record, it appears that Lucas did not receive copies of week-to-week projections or reports of actual results for the quarter to date. Rather, his committees primarily received historical financial data. Boskin is a director, Chairman of the Compensation Committee, and a member of the Finance and Audit Committee. As with Lucas, Boskin's access to information was limited mostly to historical financials and did not include the week-to-week internal projections and revenue results that Ellison and Henley received.

According to the plaintiffs, each of these Trading Defendants possessed material, non-public information demonstrating that Oracle would fail to meet the earnings and revenue guidance it had provided to the market in December 2000. In that guidance, Henley projected—subject to many disclaimers, including the possibility that a softening economy would hamper Oracle's ability to achieve these results—that Oracle would earn 12 cents per share and generate revenues of over $2.9 billion in the third quarter of its fiscal year 2001 ("3Q FY 2001"). Oracle's 3Q FY 2001 ran from December 1, 2000 to February 28, 2001.

The plaintiffs allege that this guidance was materially misleading and became even more so as early results for the quarter came in. To start with, the plaintiffs assert that the guidance rested on an untenably rosy estimate of the performance of an important new Oracle product, its "Suite 11i" systems integration product that was designed to enable a business to run all of its information systems using a complete, integrated package of software with financial, manufacturing, sales, logistics, and other applications features that were "inter-operable." The reality, the plaintiffs contend, was that Suite 11i was riddled with bugs and not ready for prime time. As a result, Suite 11i was not in a position to make a material contribution to earnings growth.

In addition, the plaintiffs contend more generally that the Trading Defendants received material, non-public information that the sales growth for Oracle's other products was slowing in a significant way, which made the attainment of the earnings and revenue guidance extremely difficult. This information grew in depth as the quarter proceeded, as various sources of information that Oracle's top managers relied upon allegedly began to signal weakness in the company's revenues. These signals supposedly included a slowdown in the "pipeline" of large deals that Oracle hoped to close during the quarter and weak revenue growth in the first month of the quarter.

During the time when these disturbing signals were allegedly being sent, the Trading Defendants engaged in the following trades:

- On January 3, 2001, Lucas sold 150,000 shares of Oracle common stock at $30 per share, reaping proceeds of over $4.6 million. These sales constituted 17% of Lucas's Oracle holdings.
- On January 4, 2001, Henley sold one million shares of Oracle stock at approximately $32 per share, yielding over $32.3 million. These sales represented 7% of Henley's Oracle holdings.
- On January 17, 2001, Boskin sold 150,000 shares of Oracle stock at over $33 per share, generating in excess of $5 million. These sales were 16% of Boskin's Oracle holdings.
- From January 22 to January 31, 2001, Ellison sold over 29 million shares at prices above $30 per share, producing over $894 million. Despite the huge proceeds generated by these sales, they constituted the sale of only 2% of Ellison's Oracle holdings.

Into early to mid-February, Oracle allegedly continued to assure the market that it would meet its December guidance. Then, on March 1, 2001, the company announced that rather than posting 12 cents per share in quarterly earnings and 25% license revenue growth as projected, the company's earnings for the quarter would be 10 cents per share and license revenue growth only 6%. The stock market reacted swiftly and negatively to this news, with Oracle's share price dropping as low as $15.75 before closing at $16.88—a 21% decline in one day. These prices were well below the above $30 per share prices at which the Trading Defendants sold in January 2001.

Oracle, through Ellison and Henley, attributed the adverse results to a general weakening in the economy, which led Oracle's customers to cut back sharply on purchases. Because (the company claimed) most of its sales close in the late days of quarters, the company did not become aware that it would miss its projections until shortly before the quarter closed. The reasons given by Ellison and Henley subjected them to sarcastic rejoinders from analysts, who noted that they had only recently suggested that Oracle was better-positioned than other companies to continue to deliver growth in a weakening economy.

B. THE PLAINTIFFS' CLAIMS IN THE DELAWARE DERIVATIVE ACTION

The plaintiffs make two central claims in their amended complaint in the Delaware Derivative Action. First, the plaintiffs allege that the Trading Defendants breached their duty of loyalty by misappropriating inside information and using it as the basis for trading decisions. This claim rests its legal basis on the venerable case of Brophy v. Cities Service Co., 70 A.2d 5 (Del. Ch. 1949). Its factual foundation is that the Trading Defendants were aware (or at least possessed information that should have made them aware) that the company would miss its December guidance by a wide margin and used that information to their advantage in selling at artificially inflated prices.

Second, as to the other defendants — who are the members of the Oracle board who did not trade — the plaintiffs allege a *Caremark* violation, in the sense that the board's indifference to the deviation between the company's December guidance and reality was so extreme as to constitute subjective bad faith.

. . .

D. THE FORMATION OF THE SPECIAL LITIGATION COMMITTEE

On February 1, 2002, Oracle formed the SLC in order to investigate the Delaware Derivative Action and to determine whether Oracle should press the claims raised by the plaintiffs, settle the case, or terminate it. Soon after its formation, the SLC's charge was broadened to give it the same mandate as to all the pending derivative actions, wherever they were filed. The SLC was granted full authority to decide these matters without the need for approval by the other members of the Oracle board.

E. THE MEMBERS OF THE SPECIAL LITIGATION COMMITTEE

Two Oracle board members were named to the SLC. Both of them joined the Oracle board on October 15, 2001, more than a half a year after Oracle's 3Q FY 2001 closed. The SLC members also share something else: both are tenured professors at Stanford University.

Professor Hector Garcia-Molina is Chairman of the Computer Science Department at Stanford and holds the Leonard Bosack and Sandra Lerner Professorship in the Computer Science and Electrical Engineering Departments at Stanford. A renowned expert in his field, Garcia-Molina was a professor at Princeton before coming to Stanford in 1992. Garcia-Molina's appointment at Stanford represented a homecoming of some sort, because he obtained both his undergraduate and graduate degrees from Stanford.

The other SLC member, Professor Joseph Grundfest, is the W.A. Franke Professor of Law and Business at Stanford University. He directs the University's well-known Directors' College and the Roberts Program in Law, Business, and Corporate Governance at the Stanford Law School. Grundfest is also the principal investigator for the Law School's Securities Litigation Clearinghouse. Immediately before coming to Stanford, Grundfest served for five years as a Commissioner of the Securities and Exchange Commission. Like Garcia-Molina, Grundfest's appointment at Stanford was a homecoming, because he obtained his law degree and performed significant post-graduate work in economics at

Stanford. As will be discussed more specifically later, Grundfest also serves as a steering committee member and a senior fellow of the Stanford Institute for Economic Policy Research, and releases working papers under the "SIEPR" banner.

For their services, the SLC members were paid $250 an hour, a rate below that which they could command for other activities, such as consulting or expert witness testimony. Nonetheless, during the course of their work, the SLC members became concerned that (arguably scandal-driven) developments in the evolving area of corporate governance as well as the decision in Telxon v. Meyerson, 802 A.2d 257 (Del. 2002), might render the amount of their compensation so high as to be an argument against their independence. Therefore, Garcia-Molina and Grundfest agreed to give up any SLC-related compensation if their compensation was deemed by this court to impair their impartiality.

F. THE SLC MEMBERS ARE RECRUITED TO THE BOARD

The SLC members were recruited to the board primarily by defendant Lucas, with help from defendant Boskin. The wooing of them began in the summer of 2001. Before deciding to join the Oracle board, Grundfest, in particular, did a good deal of due diligence. His review included reading publicly available information, among other things, the then-current complaint in the Federal Class Action.

Grundfest then met with defendants Ellison and Henley, among others, and asked them some questions about the Federal Class Action. The claims in the Federal Class Action are predicated on facts that are substantively identical to those on which the claims in the Delaware Derivative Action are based. Grundfest received answers that were consistent enough with what he called the "exogenous" information about the case to form sufficient confidence to at least join the Oracle board. Grundfest testified that this did not mean that he had concluded that the claims in the Federal Class Action had no merit, only that Ellison's and Henley's explanations of their conduct were plausible. Grundfest did, however, conclude that these were reputable businessmen with whom he felt comfortable serving as a fellow director, and that Henley had given very impressive answers to difficult questions regarding the way Oracle conducted its financial reporting operations.

G. THE SLC'S ADVISORS

The most important advisors retained by the SLC were its counsel from Simpson Thacher & Bartlett LLP. Simpson Thacher had not performed material amounts of legal work for Oracle or any of the individual defendants before its engagement, and the plaintiffs have not challenged its independence. National Economic Research Advisors ("NERA") was retained by the SLC to perform some analytical work. The plaintiffs have not challenged NERA's independence.

H. THE SLC'S INVESTIGATION AND REPORT

The SLC's investigation was, by any objective measure, extensive. The SLC reviewed an enormous amount of paper and electronic records. SLC counsel interviewed seventy witnesses, some of them twice. SLC members participated in several key interviews, including the interviews of the Trading Defendants.

Importantly, the interviewees included all the senior members of Oracle's management most involved in its projection and monitoring of the company's financial performance, including its sales and revenue growth. These interviews combined with a special focus on the documents at the company bearing on these subjects, including e-mail communications.

The SLC also asked the plaintiffs in the various actions to identify witnesses the Committee should interview. The Federal Class Action plaintiffs identified ten such persons and the Committee interviewed all but one, who refused to cooperate. The Delaware Derivative Action plaintiffs and the other derivative plaintiffs declined to provide the SLC with any witness list or to meet with the SLC.

During the course of the investigation, the SLC met with its counsel thirty-five times for a total of eighty hours. In addition to that, the SLC members, particularly Professor Grundfest, devoted many more hours to the investigation.

In the end, the SLC produced an extremely lengthy Report totaling 1,110 pages (excluding appendices and exhibits) that concluded that Oracle should not pursue the plaintiffs' claims against the Trading Defendants or any of the other Oracle directors serving during the 3Q FY 2001. The bulk of the Report defies easy summarization. I endeavor a rough attempt to capture the essence of the Report in understandable terms, surfacing some implicit premises that I understand to have undergirded the SLC's conclusions. Here goes.

Having absorbed a huge amount of material regarding Oracle's financial condition during the relevant period, the flow of information to top Oracle executives, Oracle's business and its products, and the general condition of the market at that time, the SLC concluded that even a hypothetical Oracle executive who possessed all information regarding the company's performance in December and January of 3Q FY 2001 would not have possessed material, non-public information that the company would fail to meet the earnings and revenue guidance it provided the market in December. Although there were hints of potential weakness in Oracle's revenue growth, especially starting in mid-January 2001, there was no reliable information indicating that the company would fall short of the mark, and certainly not to the extent that it eventually did. . . . [The SLC also extensively evaluated various other elements of the insider trading claims under federal securities law and found them to be without merit — for instance, that the defendants did not act with scienter.]

Of course, the amount of the proceeds each of the Trading Defendants generated was extremely large. By selling only two percent of his holdings, Ellison generated nearly a billion dollars, enough to flee to a small island nation with no extradition laws and to live like a Saudi prince. But given Oracle's fundamental health as a company and his retention of ninety-eight percent of his shares, Ellison (the SLC found) had no need to take desperate — or, for that matter, even slightly risky — measures. The same goes for the other Trading Defendants; there was simply nothing special or urgent about their financial circumstances in January 2001 that would have motivated (or did motivate, in the SLC's view) the Trading Defendants to cash out because they believed that Oracle would miss its earnings guidance. And, of course, the SLC found that none of them possessed information that indicated that Oracle would, in fact, miss its mark for 3Q FY 2001.

For these and other reasons, the SLC concluded that the plaintiffs' allegations that the Trading Defendants had breached their fiduciary duty of loyalty by using inside information about Oracle to reap illicit trading gains were without merit. The SLC also determined that, consistent with this determination, there was no reason to sue the other members of the Oracle board who were in office as of 3Q FY 2001. Therefore, the SLC determined to seek dismissal of the Delaware Derivative Action and the other derivative actions.

II.   THE SLC MOVES TO TERMINATE

Consistent with its Report, the SLC moved to terminate this litigation. The plaintiffs were granted discovery focusing on three primary topics: the independence of the SLC, the good faith of its investigative efforts, and the reasonableness of the bases for its conclusion that the lawsuit should be terminated. Additionally, the plaintiffs received a large volume of documents comprising the materials that the SLC relied upon in preparing its Report.

III.   THE APPLICABLE PROCEDURAL STANDARD

In order to prevail on its motion to terminate the Delaware Derivative Action, the SLC must persuade me that: (1) its members were independent; (2) that they acted in good faith; and (3) that they had reasonable bases for their recommendations. If the SLC meets that burden, I am free to grant its motion or may, in my discretion, undertake my own examination of whether Oracle should terminate and permit the suit to proceed if I, in my oxymoronic judicial "business judgment," conclude that procession is in the best interests of the company. This two-step analysis comes, of course, from *Zapata*.

In this case, the plaintiffs principally challenge the SLC's independence and the reasonableness of its recommendation. For reasons I next explain, I need examine only the more difficult question, which relates to the SLC's independence.

IV.   IS THE SLC INDEPENDENT?

A.   THE FACTS DISCLOSED IN THE REPORT

In its Report, the SLC took the position that its members were independent. In support of that position, the Report noted several factors including:

- the fact that neither Grundfest nor Garcia-Molina received compensation from Oracle other than as directors;
- the fact that neither Grundfest nor Garcia-Molina were on the Oracle board at the time of the alleged wrongdoing;
- the fact that both Grundfest and Garcia-Molina were willing to return their compensation as SLC members if necessary to preserve their status as independent;
- the absence of any other material ties between Oracle, the Trading Defendants, and any of the other defendants, on the one hand, and Grundfest and Garcia-Molina, on the other; and

- the absence of any material ties between Oracle, the Trading Defendants, and any of the other defendants, on the one hand, and the SLC's advisors, on the other.

Noticeably absent from the SLC Report was any disclosure of several significant ties between Oracle or the Trading Defendants and Stanford University, the university that employs both members of the SLC. In the Report, it was only disclosed that:

- defendant Boskin was a Stanford professor;
- the SLC members were aware that Lucas had made certain donations to Stanford; and
- among the contributions was a donation of $50,000 worth of stock that Lucas donated to Stanford Law School after Grundfest delivered a speech to a venture capital fund meeting in response to Lucas's request. It happens that Lucas's son is a partner in the fund and that approximately half the donation was allocated for use by Grundfest in his personal research.

B. THE "STANFORD" FACTS THAT EMERGED DURING DISCOVERY

In view of the modesty of these disclosed ties, it was with some shock that a series of other ties among Stanford, Oracle, and the Trading Defendants emerged during discovery. Although the plaintiffs have embellished these ties considerably beyond what is reasonable, the plain facts are a striking departure from the picture presented in the Report.

Before discussing these facts, I begin with certain features of the record — as I read it — that are favorable to the SLC. Initially, I am satisfied that neither of the SLC members is compromised by a fear that support for the procession of this suit would endanger his ability to make a nice living. Both of the SLC members are distinguished in their fields and highly respected. Both have tenure, which could not have been stripped from them for making a determination that this lawsuit should proceed.

Nor have the plaintiffs developed evidence that either Grundfest or Garcia-Molina have fundraising responsibilities at Stanford. Although Garcia-Molina is a department chairman, the record is devoid of any indication that he is required to generate contributions. And even though Grundfest heads up Stanford's Directors' College, the plaintiffs have not argued that he has a fundraising role in that regard. For this reason, it is important to acknowledge up front that the SLC members occupy positions within the Stanford community different from that of the University's President, deans, and development professionals, all of whom, it can be reasonably assumed, are required to engage heavily in the pursuit of contributions to the University. . . .

With this question in mind, I begin to discuss the specific ties that allegedly compromise the SLC's independence, beginning with those involving Professor Boskin.

1. Boskin

Defendant Michael J. Boskin is the T.M. Friedman Professor of Economics at Stanford University. During the Administration of President George H.W. Bush, Boskin occupied the coveted and important position of Chairman of the

President's Council of Economic Advisors. He returned to Stanford after this government service, continuing a teaching career there that had begun many years earlier.

During the 1970s, Boskin taught Grundfest when Grundfest was a Ph.D. candidate. Although Boskin was not Grundfest's advisor and although they do not socialize, the two have remained in contact over the years, speaking occasionally about matters of public policy.

Furthermore, both Boskin and Grundfest are senior fellows and steering committee members at the Stanford Institute for Economic Policy Research, which was previously defined as "SIEPR." According to the SLC, the title of senior fellow is largely an honorary one. According to SIEPR's own web site, however, "[s]enior fellows actively participate in SIEPR research and participate in its governance."

Likewise, the SLC contends that Grundfest went MIA as a steering committee member, having failed to attend a meeting since 1997. The SIEPR web site, however, identifies its steering committee as having the role of "advising the director [of SIEPR] and guiding [SIEPR] on matters pertaining to research and academics." Because Grundfest allegedly did not attend to these duties, his service alongside Boskin in that capacity is, the SLC contends, not relevant to his independence.

That said, the SLC does not deny that both Boskin and Grundfest publish working papers under the SIEPR rubric and that SIEPR helps to publicize their respective works. Indeed, as I will note later in this opinion, Grundfest, in the same month the SLC was formed, addressed a meeting of some of SIEPR's largest benefactors — the so-called "SIEPR Associates." The SLC just claims that the SIEPR affiliation is one in which SIEPR basks in the glow of Boskin and Grundfest, not the other way around, and that the mutual service of the two as senior fellows and steering committee members is not a collegial tie of any significance.

With these facts in mind, I now set forth the ties that defendant Lucas has to Stanford.

2. Lucas

As noted in the SLC Report, the SLC members admitted knowing that Lucas was a contributor to Stanford. They also acknowledged that he had donated $50,000 to Stanford Law School in appreciation for Grundfest having given a speech at his request. About half of the proceeds were allocated for use by Grundfest in his research.

But Lucas's ties with Stanford are far, far richer than the SLC Report lets on. To begin, Lucas is a Stanford alumnus, having obtained both his undergraduate and graduate degrees there. By any measure, he has been a very loyal alumnus, [donating $4.1 million to Stanford, including $424,000 to SIEPR and $149,000 to Stanford Law School]. . . .

With these facts in mind, it remains to enrich the factual stew further, by considering defendant Ellison's ties to Stanford.

3. Ellison

There can be little doubt that Ellison is a major figure in the community in which Stanford is located. The so-called Silicon Valley has generated many success stories, among the greatest of which is that of Oracle and its leader, Ellison.

One of the wealthiest men in America, Ellison is a major figure in the nation's increasingly important information technology industry. Given his wealth, Ellison is also in a position to make — and, in fact, he has made — major charitable contributions.

Some of the largest of these contributions have been made through the Ellison Medical Foundation, which makes grants to universities and laboratories to support biomedical research relating to aging and infectious diseases. Ellison is the sole director of the Foundation . . . and Stanford has nonetheless been the beneficiary of grants from the Ellison Medical Foundation — to the tune of nearly $10 million in paid or pledged funds. . . .

During the time Ellison has been CEO of Oracle, the company itself has also made over $300,000 in donations to Stanford. Not only that, when Oracle established a generously endowed educational foundation — the Oracle Help Us Help Foundation — to help further the deployment of educational technology in schools serving disadvantaged populations, it named Stanford as the "appointing authority," which gave Stanford the right to name four of the Foundation's seven directors. Stanford's acceptance reflects the obvious synergistic benefits that might flow to, for example, its School of Education from the University's involvement in such a foundation, as well as the possibility that its help with the Foundation might redound to the University's benefit when it came time for Oracle to consider making further donations to institutions of higher learning.

Taken together, these facts suggest that Ellison (when considered as an individual and as the key executive and major stockholder of Oracle) had, at the very least, been involved in several endeavors of value to Stanford.

Beginning in the year 2000 and continuing well into 2001 — the same year that Ellison made the trades the plaintiffs contend were suspicious and the same year the SLC members were asked to join the Oracle board — Ellison and Stanford discussed a much more lucrative donation [to establish the Ellison Scholars Program, to bring students from around the world for two-year interdisciplinary research in economics, political science, and computer technology].

. . . According to the Wall Street Journal, Ellison was considering the possibility of donating $150 million to either Harvard or Stanford for the purpose of creating an interdisciplinary (political science, economics, and technology) academic program. And, according to Fortune, Ellison said in an interview with *Fortune* correspondent Brent Schlender: "[O]ne of the other philanthropic things I'm doing is talking to Harvard and Stanford and MIT about creating a research program that looks at how technology impacts [*sic*] economics, and in turn how economics impacts the way we govern ourselves." It is significant that the latter article was published in mid-August 2001 — around the same time that the SLC members were considering whether to join the Oracle board and within a calendar year of the formation of the SLC itself. Importantly, these public statements supplement other private communications by Stanford officials treating the Ellison Scholars Program as an idea under serious consideration by Ellison. . . .

C. THE SLC'S ARGUMENT

The SLC contends that even together, these facts regarding the ties among Oracle, the Trading Defendants, Stanford, and the SLC members do not impair the SLC's independence. In so arguing, the SLC places great weight on the fact that none of the Trading Defendants have the practical ability to deprive either Grundfest or Garcia-Molina of their current positions at Stanford. Nor, given their tenure, does Stanford itself have any practical ability to punish them for taking action adverse to Boskin, Lucas, or Ellison — each of whom, as we have seen, has contributed (in one way or another) great value to Stanford as an institution. As important, neither Garcia-Molina nor Grundfest are part of the official fundraising apparatus at Stanford; thus, it is not their on-the-job duty to be solicitous of contributors, and fundraising success does not factor into their treatment as professors.

In so arguing, the SLC focuses on the language of previous opinions of this court and the Delaware Supreme Court that indicates that a director is not independent only if he is dominated and controlled by an interested party, such as a Trading Defendant. The SLC also emphasizes that much of our jurisprudence on independence focuses on economically consequential relationships between the allegedly interested party and the directors who allegedly cannot act independently of that director. Put another way, much of our law focuses the bias inquiry on whether there are economically material ties between the interested party and the director whose impartiality is questioned, treating the possible effect on one's personal wealth as the key to the independence inquiry. Putting a point on this, the SLC cites certain decisions of Delaware courts concluding that directors who are personal friends of an interested party were not, by virtue of those personal ties, to be labeled non-independent.

More subtly, the SLC argues that university professors simply are not inhibited types, unwilling to make tough decisions even as to fellow professors and large contributors. What is tenure about if not to provide professors with intellectual freedom, even in non-traditional roles such as special litigation committee members? No less ardently — but with no record evidence that reliably supports its ultimate point — the SLC contends that Garcia-Molina and Grundfest are extremely distinguished in their fields and were not, in fact, influenced by the facts identified heretofore. Indeed, the SLC argues, how could they have been influenced by many of these facts when they did not learn them until the post-Report discovery process? If it boils down to the simple fact that both share with Boskin the status of a Stanford professor, how material can this be when there are 1,700 others who also occupy the same position?

D. THE PLAINTIFFS' ARGUMENTS

The plaintiffs confronted these arguments with less nuance than was helpful. Rather than rest their case on the multiple facts I have described, the plaintiffs chose to emphasize barely plausible constructions of the evidence, such as that Grundfest was lying when he could not recall being asked to participate in the Ellison Scholars Program. From these more extreme arguments, however, one can distill a reasoned core that emphasizes what academics might call the "thickness" of the social and institutional connections among Oracle, the Trading Defendants, Stanford, and the SLC members. These connections, the plaintiffs argue, were very hard to miss — being obvious to anyone who entered the SIEPR facility, to anyone who read the *Wall Street Journal, Fortune,* or the *Washington Post,* and especially to Stanford faculty members interested in their own university community and with a special interest in Oracle. Taken in their totality, the plaintiffs contend, these connections simply constitute too great a bias-producing factor for the SLC to meet its burden to prove its independence.

Even more, the plaintiffs argue that the SLC's failure to identify many of these connections in its Report is not an asset proving its independence, but instead a fundamental flaw in the Report itself, which is the document in which the SLC is supposed to demonstrate its own independence and the reasonableness of its investigation. By failing to focus on these connections when they were obviously discoverable and when it is, at best, difficult for the court to believe that at least some of them were not known by the SLC — *e.g.*, Boskin's role at SIEPR and the fact that the SIEPR Conference Center was named after Lucas — the SLC calls into doubt not only its independence, but its competence. If it could not ferret out these things, by what right should the court trust its investigative acumen?

In support of its argument, the plaintiffs note that the Delaware courts have adopted a flexible, fact-based approach to the determination of directorial independence. This test focuses on whether the directors, for any substantial reason, cannot act with only the best interests of the corporation in mind, and not just on whether the directors face pecuniary damage for acting in a particular way.

E. THE COURT'S ANALYSIS OF THE SLC'S INDEPENDENCE

Having framed the competing views of the parties, it is now time to decide.

I begin with an important reminder: the SLC bears the burden of proving its independence. It must convince me.

But of what? According to the SLC, its members are independent unless they are essentially subservient to the Trading Defendants — *i.e.*, they are under the "domination and control" of the interested parties. If the SLC is correct and this is the central inquiry in the independence determination, they would win. Nothing in the record suggests to me that either Garcia-Molina or Grundfest are dominated and controlled by any of the Trading Defendants, by Oracle, or even by Stanford.

But, in my view, an emphasis on "domination and control" would serve only to fetishize much-parroted language, at the cost of denuding the independence inquiry of its intellectual integrity. Take an easy example. Imagine if two brothers were on a corporate board, each successful in different businesses and not dependent in any way on the other's beneficence in order to be wealthy. The brothers are brothers, they stay in touch and consider each other family, but each is opinionated and strong-willed. A derivative action is filed targeting a transaction involving one of the brothers. The other brother is put on a special litigation committee to investigate the case. If the test is domination and control, then one brother could investigate the other. Does any sensible person think that is our law? I do not think it is.

And it should not be our law. Delaware law should not be based on a reductionist view of human nature that simplifies human motivations on the lines of the least sophisticated notions of the law and economics movement. *Homo sapiens* is not merely *homo economicus*. We may be thankful that an array of other motivations exist that influence human behavior; not all are any better than greed or avarice, think of envy, to name just one. But also think of motives like love, friendship, and collegiality, think of those among us who direct their behavior as best they can on a guiding creed or set of moral values.[47]

---

47. In an interesting work, Professor Lynn Stout has argued that there exists an empirical basis to infer that corporate directors are likely to be motivated by altruistic impulses and not simply by a concern for their own pocketbooks. *See* Lynn A. Stout, *In Praise of Procedure: An Economic and Behavioral Defense of* Smith v. Van Gorkom *and the Business Judgment Rule*, 96 Nw. U.L. Rev. 675, 677-78 (2002).

Nor should our law ignore the social nature of humans. To be direct, corporate directors are generally the sort of people deeply enmeshed in social institutions. Such institutions have norms, expectations that, explicitly and implicitly, influence and channel the behavior of those who participate in their operation. Some things are "just not done," or only at a cost, which might not be so severe as a loss of position, but may involve a loss of standing in the institution. In being appropriately sensitive to this factor, our law also cannot assume — absent some proof of the point — that corporate directors are, as a general matter, persons of unusual social bravery, who operate heedless to the inhibitions that social norms generate for ordinary folk.

For all these reasons, this court has previously held that the Delaware Supreme Court's teachings on independence can be summarized thusly:

> At bottom, the question of independence turns on whether a director is, *for any substantial reason*, incapable of making a decision with only the best interests of the corporation in mind. That is, the Supreme Court cases ultimately focus on impartiality and objectivity.

This formulation is wholly consistent with the teaching of *Aronson*, which defines independence as meaning that "a director's decision is based on the corporate merits of the subject before the board rather than extraneous considerations or influences." As noted by Chancellor Chandler recently, a director may be compromised if he is beholden to an interested person. Beholden in this sense does not mean just owing in the financial sense, it can also flow out of "personal or other relationships" to the interested party. . . .

1. The Contextual Nature of the Independence Inquiry Under Delaware Law

In examining whether the SLC has met its burden to demonstrate that there is no material dispute of fact regarding its independence, the court must bear in mind the function of special litigation committees under our jurisprudence. Under Delaware law, the primary means by which corporate defendants may obtain a dismissal of a derivative suit is by showing that the plaintiffs have not met their pleading burden under the test of Aronson v. Lewis, [473 A.2d 805 (Del. 1985),] or the related standard set forth in Rales v. Blasband[, 634 A.2d 927 (Del. 1993)]. In simple terms, these tests permit a corporation to terminate a derivative suit if its board is comprised of directors who can impartially consider a demand.

Special litigation committees are permitted as a last chance for a corporation to control a derivative claim in circumstances when a majority of its directors cannot impartially consider a demand. By vesting the power of the board to determine what to do with the suit in a committee of independent directors, a corporation may retain control over whether the suit will proceed, so long as the committee meets the standard set forth in *Zapata*. . . .

Thus, in assessing the independence of the Oracle SLC, I necessarily examine the question of whether the SLC can independently make the difficult decision entrusted to it: to determine whether the Trading Defendants should face suit for insider trading-based allegations of breach of fiduciary duty. An affirmative answer by the SLC to that question would have potentially huge negative consequences for the Trading Defendants, not only by exposing them to the possibility of a large damage award but also by subjecting them to great reputational harm. To have Professors Grundfest and Garcia-Molina declare that Oracle should press insider trading claims against the Trading Defendants would have been, to put it mildly, "news." Relatedly, it is reasonable to think that an SLC determination that the Trading Defendants had likely engaged in insider trading would have been accompanied by a recommendation that they step down as fiduciaries until their ultimate culpability was decided.

The importance and special sensitivity of the SLC's task is also relevant for another obvious reason: investigations do not follow a scientific process like an old-fashioned assembly line. The investigators' mindset and talent influence, for good or ill, the course of an investigation. Just as there are obvious dangers from investigators suffering from too much zeal, so too are dangers posed by investigators who harbor reasons not to pursue the investigation's targets with full vigor.

The nature of the investigation is important, too. Here, for example, the SLC was required to undertake an investigation that could not avoid a consideration of the subjective state of mind of the Trading Defendants. Their credibility was important, and the SLC could not escape making judgments about that, no matter how objective the criteria the SLC attempted to use.

Therefore, I necessarily measure the SLC's independence contextually, and my ruling confronts the SLC's ability to decide impartially whether the Trading Defendants should be pursued for insider trading. This contextual approach is a strength of our law, as even the best minds have yet to devise across-the-board definitions that capture all the circumstances in which the independence of directors might reasonably be questioned. By taking into account all circumstances, the Delaware approach undoubtedly results in some level of indeterminacy, but with the compensating benefit that independence determinations are tailored to the precise situation at issue.

Likewise, Delaware law requires courts to consider the independence of directors based on the facts known to the court about them specifically, the so-called "subjective 'actual person' standard."

That said, it is inescapable that a court must often apply to the known facts about a specific director a consideration of how a reasonable person similarly situated to that director would behave, given the limited ability of a judge to look into a particular director's heart and mind. This is especially so when a special litigation committee chooses, as was the case here, to eschew any live witness testimony, a decision that is, of course, sensible lest special litigation committee termination motions turn into trials nearly as burdensome as the derivative suit the committee seeks to end. But with that sensible choice came an acceptance of the court's need to infer that the special litigation committee members are persons of typical professional sensibilities.

2. The SLC Has Not Met Its Burden to Demonstrate the Absence
of a Material Dispute of Fact About Its Independence

Using the contextual approach I have described, I conclude that the SLC has not met its burden to show the absence of a material factual question about its independence. I find this to be the case because the ties among the SLC, the Trading Defendants, and Stanford are so substantial that they cause reasonable doubt about the SLC's ability to impartially consider whether the Trading Defendants should face suit. . . .

The pertinent question is whether, given *all* the facts, the SLC has met its independence burden.

When viewed in that manner, the facts [as set out above] about Ellison buttress the conclusion that the SLC has not met its burden. Whether the SLC members had precise knowledge of all the facts that have emerged is not essential, what is important is that by any measure this was a social atmosphere painted in too much vivid Stanford Cardinal red for the SLC members to have reasonably ignored it. Summarized fairly, two Stanford professors were recruited to the Oracle board in summer 2001 and soon asked to investigate a fellow professor and two benefactors of the University. On Grundfest's part, the facts are more substantial, because his connections — through his personal experiences, SIEPR, and the Law School — to Boskin and to Lucas run deeper.

It seems to me that the connections outlined in this opinion would weigh on the mind of a reasonable special litigation committee member deciding whether to level the serious charge of insider trading against the Trading Defendants. As indicated before, this does not mean that the SLC would be less inclined to find such charges meritorious, only that the connections identified would be on the mind of the SLC members in a way that generates an unacceptable risk of bias. That is, these connections generate a reasonable doubt about the SLC's impartiality because they suggest that material considerations other than the best interests of Oracle could have influenced the SLC's inquiry and judgments. . . .

The SLC has made the argument that a ruling against it will chill the ability of corporations to locate qualified independent directors in the academy. This is overwrought. If there are 1,700 professors at Stanford alone, as the SLC says, how many must there be on the west coast of the United States, at institutions without ties to Oracle and the Trading Defendants as substantial as Stanford's? Undoubtedly, a corporation of Oracle's market capitalization could have found prominent academics willing to serve as SLC members, about whom no reasonable question of independence could have been asserted.

Rather than form an SLC whose membership was free from bias-creating relationships, Oracle formed a committee fraught with them. As a result, the SLC has failed to meet its *Zapata* burden, and its motion to terminate must be denied. Because of this reality, I do not burden the reader with an examination of the other *Zapata* factors. In the absence of a finding that the SLC was independent, its subjective good faith and the reasonableness of its conclusions would not be sufficient to justify termination. Without confidence that the SLC was impartial, its findings do not provide the assurance our law requires for the dismissal of a derivative suit without a merits inquiry.

V. CONCLUSION

The SLC's motion to terminate is DENIED. IT IS SO ORDERED.

PROBLEM 9-3

Assume that the four outside directors mentioned in Problem 9-1 were members of a Special Litigation Committee (SLC) rather than merely members of the board of directors. *Is there any difference in the analysis of their independence in these two different procedural contexts? (Recall that the SLC bears the burden of establishing its independence.) What factors ought a court to consider in the second step of Zapata when the court exercises its business judgment in determining if the case against Grenfell directors should be dismissed? What additional facts would you need to know?*

D. STATUTORY EXCULPATION FROM LIABILITY

In Chapter 6 we saw how weak standards of care and the protection of the business judgment rule make breach of duty claims difficult for plaintiffs to sustain. Directors also are protected from personal liability for some breaches by exculpation clauses often found in the articles of incorporation. DGCL § 102(b)(7) and Model Act § 2.02(b)(4) allow corporations to limit or eliminate director liability for money damages for certain types of wrongdoing, most clearly eliminating liability for breaches of the duty of care. Under the Model Act, the articles of incorporation may "eliminate or limit the liability of a director to the corporation or its shareholders for money damages for any action taken, or any failure to take any action" in breach of the duty of care, including breaches that constitute an intentional violation of civil law. Model Act § 2.02(b)(4)(D). The articles may not exculpate directors for receiving financial benefits to which they are not entitled, for approving improper dividends, for intentionally harming the corporation, or for intentional violations of criminal law. Model Act § 2.02(b)(4). DGCL § 102(b)(7) permits narrower exculpation. Under Delaware law the corporation may not exculpate its directors for breaches of the duty of loyalty, or for "acts or omission not in good faith or which involve intentional misconduct or a knowing violation of law," either civil or criminal. Exculpation clauses do not prevent a stockholder from pursuing other remedies, for example, an injunction, if the directors have breached their duty of care. Exculpation statutes were passed in the wake of *Smith v. Van Gorkom* (Chapter 6) and have been criticized by those who believe that directors should be more accountable to shareholders. Moreover, the Model Act standards have been criticized as demonstrating an insufficient concern with law compliance, since directors may be exculpated even for intentional violations of law, albeit not criminal law.

The procedural impact of exculpation provisions under Delaware law has been enormous and, at times, confusing. Defendants are understandably eager to have claims against them dismissed, and this eagerness has led to many battles over the proper scope and application of exculpatory provisions in shareholder litigation. Exculpatory clauses explicitly protect directors from personal liability for breaches of the duty of care, and so such claims will be dismissed on the basis of a provision in a company's charter tracking § 102(b)(7), *Malpiede v. Townson,* 780 A.2d 1075 (Del. 2001), whereas duty of loyalty claims cannot be exculpated. The sticking point has been claims of a lack of good faith, which also cannot be exculpated. Ever since *Caremark* held that failures of oversight could constitute a lack of good faith in some circumstances, plaintiffs have been structuring their derivative allegations to fit within *Caremark*'s rubric of a "sustained or systematic failure of the board to exercise oversight — such as an utter failure to attempt to assure a reasonable information and reporting system exists" in order to allege the lack of good faith that could overcome an exculpatory clause. *In re Caremark Int'l Deriv. Litig.*, 698 A.2d 959, 971 (Del. Ch. 1996) (Allen, Ch.). The theoretic risk of this type of good-faith liability was arguably heightened in Stone v. Ritter when the Delaware Supreme Court adopted the *Caremark* framework for evaluating failures of oversight, but held that oversight is an aspect of the duty of loyalty, not care, given its source in directors' obligations to act in good faith. Stone v. Ritter, 911 A.2d 362 (Del. 2006). The *Stone* Court also clarified that "the imposition of liability requires a showing that the directors knew that they were not discharging their fiduciary obligations." *Stone*, 911 A.2d at 370.

Recent cases suggest, however, that it will be the rare case indeed where directors' lack of oversight will be sufficient to constitute a lack of good faith, and thus not be conduct protected by an exculpation clause. As the Delaware Supreme Court stated in *Lyondell Chemical v. Ryan*, 970 A.2d 235, 245 (Del. 2009), "there is a vast difference between an inadequate or flawed effort to carry out fiduciary duties and a conscious disregard for those duties," as required under Stone v. Ritter. The following case challenging Goldman Sachs compensation policies and actions during the sub-prime housing bubble suggests that plaintiffs will still attempt to bring oversight claims within the contours of *Caremark* and *Stone*, but that these efforts will continue to be unsuccessful given the powerful effects of § 102(b)(7) exculpation provisions.

IN RE THE GOLDMAN SACHS GROUP, INC. SHAREHOLDER LITIGATION

2011 WL 4826104
Delaware Court of Chancery
October 12, 2011

GLASSCOCK, Vice Chancellor.

The Delaware General Corporation Law is, for the most part, enabling in nature. It provides corporate directors and officers with broad discretion to act as they find appropriate in the conduct of corporate affairs. It is therefore left to Delaware case law to set a boundary on that otherwise unconstrained realm of action. The restrictions imposed by Delaware case law set this boundary by requiring corporate officers and directors to act as faithful fiduciaries to the corporation and its stockholders. Should these corporate actors perform in such a way that they are violating their fiduciary obligations — their core duties of care or loyalty — their faithless acts properly become the subject of judicial action in vindication of the rights of the stockholders. Within the boundary of fiduciary duty, however, these corporate actors are free to pursue corporate opportunities in any way that, in the exercise of their business judgment on behalf of the corporation, they see fit. It is this broad freedom to pursue opportunity on behalf of the corporation, in the myriad ways that may be revealed to creative human minds, that has made the corporate structure a supremely effective engine for the production of wealth. Exercising that freedom is precisely what directors and officers are elected by their shareholders to do. So long as such individuals act within the boundaries of their fiduciary duties, judges are ill-suited by training (and should be disinclined by temperament) to second-guess the business decisions of those chosen by the stockholders to fulfill precisely that function. This case, as in so many corporate matters considered by this Court, involves whether actions taken by certain director defendants fall outside of the fiduciary boundaries existing under Delaware case law—and are therefore subject to judicial oversight—or whether the acts complained of are within those broad boundaries, where a law-trained judge should refrain from acting.

This matter is before me on a motion to dismiss, pursuant to Court of Chancery Rule 23.1 for failure to make a pre-suit demand upon the board, and Court of Chancery rule 12(b)(6). for failure to state a claim. The Plaintiffs contend that Goldman's compensation structure created a divergence of interest between Goldman's management and its stockholders. The Plaintiffs allege that because Goldman's directors have consistently based compensation for the firm's management on a percentage of net revenue, Goldman's employees had a motivation to grow net revenue at any cost and without regard to risk.

The Plaintiffs allege that under this compensation structure, Goldman's employees would attempt to maximize short-term profits, thus increasing their bonuses at the expense of stockholders' interests. The Plaintiffs contend that Goldman's employees would do this by engaging in highly risky trading practices and over-leveraging the company's assets. If these practices turned a profit, Goldman's employees would receive a windfall; however, losses would fall on the stockholders.

The Plaintiffs allege that the Director Defendants breached their fiduciary duties by approving the compensation structure discussed above. Additionally, the Plaintiffs claim that the payments under this compensation structure constituted corporate waste. Finally, the Plaintiffs assert that this compensation structure led to overly-risky business decisions and unethical and illegal practices, and that the Director Defendants failed to satisfy their oversight responsibilities with regard to those practices.

The Defendants seek dismissal of this action on the grounds that the Plaintiffs have failed to make a pre-suit demand on the board and have failed to state a claim. For the reasons stated below, I find that the Plaintiffs' complaint must be dismissed.

I. Facts

The facts below are taken from the second amended complaint. All reasonable inferences are drawn in the Plaintiffs' favor.

A. PARTIES

Co-lead plaintiffs Southeastern Pennsylvania Transportation Authority and International Brotherhood of Electrical Workers Local 98 Pension Fund ("the Plaintiffs") are stockholders of Goldman Sachs Group, Inc. ("Goldman"), and have continuously held Goldman stock during all relevant times.

Defendant Goldman is a global financial services firm which provides investment banking, securities, and investment management services to consumers, businesses, and governments. Goldman is a Delaware corporation with its principal executive offices in New York, NY. The complaint also names fourteen individual current and former directors and officers of Goldman as defendants . . . collectively referred to as the "Director Defendants." . . .

Goldman engages in three principal business segments: investment banking, asset management and securities services, and trading and principal investments. The majority of Goldman's revenue comes from the trading and principal investment segment. In that segment Goldman engages in market making, structuring and entering into a variety of derivative transactions, and the proprietary trading of financial instruments. ["Proprietary Trading" refers to a firm's trades for its own benefit with its own money.]

Since going public in 1999, Goldman's total assets under management and common stockholder equity have substantially increased. In 1999, Goldman had $258 billion of assets under management and $10 billion of common shareholder equity. By 2010, those numbers had grown to $881 billion of assets under management and $72.94 billion of common shareholder equity. Corresponding with this increase in assets under management and common shareholder equity was a hike in the percentage of Goldman's revenue that was generated by the trading and principal investment segment. In 1999, the trading and principal investment segment generated 43% of Goldman's revenue; by 2007 the segment generated over 76% of Goldman's revenue.

As the revenue generated by the trading and principal investment segment grew, so did the trading department's stature within Goldman. The traders "became wealthier and more powerful in the bank." The Plaintiffs allege that the compensation for these traders was not based on performance and was unjustifiable because Goldman was doing "nothing more than compensat[ing] employees for results produced by the vast amounts of shareholder equity that Goldman ha[d] available to be deployed."

Goldman employed a "pay for performance" philosophy linking the total compensation of its employees to the company's performance. Goldman has used a Compensation Committee since at least 2006 to oversee the development and implementation of its compensation scheme. The Compensation Committee was responsible for reviewing and approving the Goldman executives' annual compensation. To fulfill their charge, the Compensation Committee consulted with senior management about management's projections of net revenues and the proper ratio of compensation and benefits expenses to net revenues (the "compensation ratio"). Additionally, the Compensation Committee compared Goldman's compensation ratio to that of Goldman's competitors such as Bear Stearns, Lehman Brothers, Merrill Lynch, and Morgan Stanley. The Compensation Committee would then approve a ratio and structure that Goldman would use to govern Goldman's compensation to its employees.

The Plaintiffs allege that from 2007 through 2009, the Director Defendants approved a management-proposed compensation structure that caused management's interests to diverge from those of the stockholders. According to the Plaintiffs, in each year since 2006 the Compensation Committee approved the management-determined compensation ratio, which governed "the total amount of funds available to compensate all employees including senior executives," without any analysis.[17] Although the total compensation paid by Goldman varied significantly each year, total compensation as a percentage of net revenue remained relatively constant. Because management was awarded a relatively constant percentage of total revenue, management could maximize their compensation by increasing Goldman's total net revenue and total stockholder equity. The Plaintiffs contend that this compensation structure led management to pursue a highly risky business strategy that emphasized short term profits in order to increase their yearly bonuses.

D. BUSINESS RISK

The Plaintiffs allege that management achieved Goldman's growth "through extreme leverage and significant uncontrolled exposure to risky loans and credit risks." The trading and principal investment segment is the largest contributor to Goldman's total revenues; it is also the segment to which Goldman commits the largest amount of capital. [The segment generated 76% of Goldman's revenues in 2009, and as of December 2009, the segment also utilized 78% of the firm's assets.] Plaintiffs argue that this was a risky use of Goldman's assets, pointing out that Goldman's Value at Risk (VAR) increased between 2007 and 2009, and that in 2007 Goldman had a leverage ratio of 25 to 1, exceeding that of its peers.

The Plaintiffs charge that this business strategy was not in the best interest of the stockholders, in part, because the stockholders did not benefit to the same degree that management did. Stockholders received roughly 2% of the revenue generated in the form of dividends — but if the investment went south, it was the stockholders' equity at risk, not that of the traders.

The Plaintiffs point to Goldman's performance in 2008 as evidence of these alleged diverging interests. In that year, "the Trading and Principal Investment segment produced $9.06 billion in net revenue, but as a result of discretionary bonuses paid to employees *lost* more than $2.7 billion." This contributed to Goldman's 2008 net income falling by $9.3 billion. The Plaintiffs contend that, but for a cash infusion from Warren Buffett, federal government intervention and Goldman's conversion into a bank holding company, Goldman would have gone into bankruptcy.

The Plaintiffs acknowledge that during this time Goldman had an Audit Committee in charge of overseeing risk. . . . In addition to having an Audit Committee in place, Goldman managed risk associated with the trading and principal investment section by hedging its positions — sometimes taking positions opposite to the clients that it was investing with, advising, and financing. Since 2002, Goldman has acknowledged that possible conflicts could occur and that it seeks to "manage" these conflicts. The Plaintiffs allege that if the Audit Committee had been properly functioning, the board should have been forewarned about conflicts of interest between Goldman and its clients.

The Plaintiffs contend that these conflicts of interest came to a head during the mortgage and housing crisis. In December 2006, Goldman's CFO, in a meeting with Goldman's mortgage traders and risk managers, concluded that

---

17. Goldman's total net revenue was $46 billion in 2007, $22.2 billion in 2008, and $45.2 billion in 2009. Goldman paid its employees total compensation of $20.2 billion in 2007, $10.9 billion in 2008, and $16.2 billion in 2009. As a percentage of total net revenue, the total compensation paid by Goldman was 44% in 2007, 48% in 2008, and 36% in 2009. The total compensation initially approved in 2007, by the Compensation Committee, was $16.7 billion or 47% of total revenue; however, this amount was changed after public outcry.

the firm was over-exposed to the subprime mortgage market and decided to reduce Goldman's overall exposure. In 2007, as the housing market began to decline, a committee of senior executives, including Viniar, Cohn, and Blankfein, took an active role in monitoring and overseeing the mortgage unit. The committee's job was to examine mortgage products and transactions while protecting Goldman against risky deals. The committee eventually decided to take positions that would allow Goldman to profit if housing prices declined. When the subprime mortgage markets collapsed, not only were Goldman's long positions hedged, Goldman actually profited more from its short positions than it lost from its long positions. The Plaintiffs allege that Goldman's profits resulted from positions that conflicted with its clients' interests to the detriment of the company's reputation.

As an example of these conflicts of interest, the Plaintiffs point to the infamous Abacus transaction. In the Abacus transaction, hedge fund manager John Paulson, a Goldman client, had a role in selecting the mortgages that would ultimately be used to back a collateralized debt obligation (CDO).[39] Paulson took a short position that would profit if the CDO fell in value. Goldman sold the long positions to other clients without disclosing Paulson's involvement. On April 16, 2010, the SEC charged Goldman and a Goldman employee with fraud for their actions related to the Abacus transaction. On July 14, 2010, Goldman settled the case with the SEC and agreed to pay a civil penalty of $535 million and to disgorge the $15 million in profits it made on the transaction. Goldman also agreed to review its internal processes related to mortgage securities transactions.

To demonstrate further examples of conflicts of interest, the Plaintiffs rely on a April 26, 2010 memorandum, from Senators Carl Levin and Tom Coburn to the Members of the Permanent Subcommittee on Investigations, entitled "Wall Street and the Financial Crisis: The Role of Investment Banks" ("Permanent Subcommittee Report"), that highlighted three mortgage-related products that Goldman sold to its clients. These transactions involved synthetic CDOs,[46] where Goldman sold long positions to clients while Goldman took the short positions. Unlike the Abacus transaction, these three transactions did not end with SEC involvement, but the Plaintiffs allege that investors who lost money are "reviewing their options, including possibly bringing lawsuits."

E. THE PLAINTIFFS' CLAIMS

The Plaintiffs allege that the Director Defendants breached their fiduciary duties by (1) failing to properly analyze and rationally set compensation levels for Goldman's employees and (2) committing waste by "approving a

39. A CDO is a type of asset-backed security backed by a pool of bonds, loans, or other assets. The underlying assets' cash flow is used to make interest and principal payments to the holders of the CDO securities. CDO securities are issued in different classes, or tranches, that vary by their level of risk and maturity date. The senior tranches are paid first, while the junior tranches have higher interest rates or lower prices to compensate for the higher risk of default.

46. Synthetic CDOs are CDOs structured out of credit default swaps. A credit default swap (CDS) can essentially be thought of as an insurance policy on an asset such as a CDO or CDO tranche. The purchaser of the CDS pays a fixed amount at certain intervals to the seller of the CDS. If the CDO maintains its value, the seller of the CDS retains the money paid by the purchaser of the CDS; however, if the CDO falls in value, the seller of the CDS must pay the purchaser of the CDS for losses. Synthetic CDOs package CDSs together and use the cash flows from the CDSs to pay the purchasers of the CDO.

compensation ratio to Goldman employees in an amount so disproportionately large to the contribution of management, as opposed to capital as to be unconscionable." The Plaintiffs also allege that the Director Defendants violated their fiduciary duties by failing to adequately monitor Goldman's operations and by "allowing the Firm to manage and conduct the Firm's trading in a grossly unethical manner."

II. Legal Standards

The Plaintiffs have brought this action derivatively on behalf of Goldman "to redress the breaches of fiduciary duty and other violations of law by [the] Defendants." The Defendants have moved to dismiss, pursuant to Court of Chancery Rule 23.1, for failure to make a pre-suit demand upon the board, and Court of Chancery Rule 12(b)(6) for failure to state a claim.

A. RULE 12(B)(6)

As our Supreme Court has recently made clear, "the governing pleading standard in Delaware to survive a motion to dismiss is reasonable 'conceivability.' *Cent. Mortgage Capital Holdings v. Morgan Stanley*, 2011 WL 3612992, at *5 (Del. Aug. 18, 2011).* Under this minimal standard, when considering a motion to dismiss, the trial court must accept "even vague allegations in the Complaint as 'well-pleaded' if they provide the defendant notice of the claim." The trial court must "draw all reasonable inferences in favor of the plaintiff, and deny the motion unless the plaintiff could not recover under any reasonably conceivable set of circumstances susceptible of proof." This is true even if, "as a factual matter," it may "ultimately prove impossible for the plaintiff to prove his claims at a later stage of a proceeding."

B. RULE 23.1

"[T]he pleading burden imposed by Rule 23.1 . . . is more onerous than that demanded by Rule 12(b)(6)." Though a complaint may plead a "conceivable" allegation that would survive a motion to dismiss under Rule 12(b)(6), "vague allegations are . . . insufficient to withstand a motion to dismiss pursuant to Rule 23.1." This difference reflects the divergent reasons for the two rules: Rule 12(b)(6) is designed to ensure a decision on the merits of any potentially valid claim, excluding only clearly meritless claims; Rule 23.1 is designed to vindicate the authority of the corporate board, except in those cases where the board will not or (because of conflicts) cannot exercise its judgment in the interest of the corporation. Rule 23.1 requires that "a plaintiff shareholder . . . make a demand upon the corporation's current board to pursue derivative claims owned by the corporation before a shareholder is permitted to pursue legal action on the corporation's behalf." Demand is required because "[t]he decision whether to initiate or pursue a lawsuit on behalf of the corporation is generally within the power and responsibility of the board of directors." Accordingly, the complaint must allege "with particularity the efforts, if any, made by the plaintiff to obtain the action the plaintiff desires from the directors or comparable authority and the reasons for the plaintiff's failure to obtain the action or for not making the effort."

If, as here, a stockholder does not first demand that the directors pursue the alleged cause of action, he must establish that demand is excused by satisfying "stringent [pleading] requirements of factual particularity" by "set [ting] forth particularized factual statements that are essential to the claim" in order to demonstrate that making demand would be futile. Pre-suit demand is futile if a corporation's board is "deemed incapable of making an impartial decision regarding the pursuit of the litigation." Under the two-pronged test, first explicated in *Aronson*, when a plaintiff challenges a conscious decision of the board, a plaintiff can show demand futility by alleging particularized facts that create a reasonable doubt that either (1) the directors are disinterested and independent or (2) "the challenged transaction was otherwise the product of a valid exercise of business judgment." *Aronson v. Lewis*, 473 A.2d 805, 814 (Del. 1984).

On the other hand, when a plaintiff complains of board *inaction*, "there is no 'challenged transaction,' and the ordinary *Aronson* analysis does not apply." Instead, the board's inaction is analyzed under *Rales v. Blasband*, 634 A.2d 927 (Del. 1993). Under the *Rales* test, a plaintiff must plead particularized facts that "create a reasonable doubt that, as of the time the complaint [was] filed, the board of directors could have properly exercised its independent and disinterested business judgment in responding to a demand."

Here, the Plaintiffs concede that they have not made demand upon Goldman's board of directors, but they assert that such demand would be futile for numerous reasons. First, they argue that Goldman's board of directors is interested or lacks independence because of financial ties between the Director Defendants and Goldman. Next, they allege that there is a reasonable doubt as to whether the board's compensation structure was the product of a valid exercise of business judgment. The Plaintiffs further assert that there is a substantial likelihood that the Director Defendants will face personal liability for the dereliction of their duty to oversee Goldman's operations.

I evaluate the Plaintiffs' claims involving active decisions by the board under *Aronson*. I evaluate the Plaintiffs' oversight claims against the Director Defendants for the failure to monitor Goldman's operations under *Rales*.

III. ANALYSIS

A. APPROVAL OF THE COMPENSATION SCHEME

The Plaintiffs challenge the Goldman board's approval of the company's compensation scheme on three grounds. They allege (1) that the majority of the board was interested or lacked independence when it approved the compensation scheme, (2) the board did not otherwise validly exercise its business judgment, and (3) the board's approval of the compensation scheme constituted waste. Because the approval of the compensation scheme was a conscious decision by the board, the Plaintiffs must satisfy the *Aronson* test to successfully plead demand futility. I find that under all three of their challenges to the board's approval of the compensation scheme, the Plaintiffs have failed to adequately plead demand futility. . . .

1. Independence and Disinterestedness of the Board

[The Court first held that plaintiffs had failed to provide particularized facts establishing that a majority of the board was interested or lacked independence, applying the standards of *Beam ex. rel. Martha Stewart Living* to evaluate the alleged lack of independence of the outside directors based on charitable contributions that Goldman had made to individual director's institutions or business relationships between Goldman and firms with which other directors were associated.]

B. OTHERWISE THE PRODUCT OF A VALID EXERCISE OF BUSINESS JUDGMENT

Having determined that the Plaintiffs have not pled particularized factual allegations that raise a reasonable doubt as to a majority of the Director Defendants' disinterestedness and independence, I must now apply the second prong of *Aronson* and determine whether the Plaintiffs have pled particularized facts that raise a reasonable doubt that Goldman's compensation scheme was otherwise the product of a valid exercise of business judgment. To successfully plead demand futility under the second prong of *Aronson*, the Plaintiffs must allege "particularized facts sufficient to raise (1) a reason to doubt that the action was taken honestly and in good faith or (2) a reason to doubt that the board was adequately informed in making the decision." Goldman's charter has an 8 Del. C. § 102 (b)(7) provision, providing that the directors are exculpated from liability except for claims based on 'bad faith' conduct; therefore, the Plaintiffs must also plead particularized facts that demonstrate that . . . there was an "intentional dereliction of duty" or "a conscious disregard" for their responsibilities, amounting to bad faith. *In re Walt Disney Co. Derivative Litig.*, 907 A.2d 693, 755 (Del. Ch. 2005) (Disney III).

The Plaintiffs assert that the Director Defendants owed "a fiduciary duty to assess continually Goldman's compensation scheme to ensure that it reasonably compensated employees and reasonably allocated the profit of Goldman's activities according to the contributions of shareholder capital and the employees of the Company." The Plaintiffs contend that the entire compensation structure put in place by the Director Defendants was done in bad faith and that the Director Defendants were not properly informed when making compensation awards. I find that the Plaintiffs have not provided particularized factual allegations that raise a reasonable doubt whether the process by which Goldman's compensation scheme allocated profits between the employees and shareholders was implemented in good faith and on an informed basis.

1. Good Faith

"[A] failure to act in good faith requires conduct that is qualitatively different from, and more culpable than, the conduct giving rise to a violation of the fiduciary duty of care (i.e., gross negligence)." *Stone v. Ritter*, 911 A.2d 362, 369 (Del. 2006). Examples of this include situations where the fiduciary intentionally breaks the law, "where the fiduciary intentionally acts with a purpose other than that of advancing the best interests of the corporation," or "where the fiduciary intentionally fails to act in the face of a known duty to act, demonstrating a conscious disregard for his duties." *In re Walt Disney Co. Derivative Litig.* 906 A.2d 27, 67 (Del. 2006) (Disney IV). While this is not an exclusive list, "these three are the most salient." . . .

The Plaintiffs' main contention is that Goldman's compensation scheme itself was approved in bad faith. The Plaintiffs allege that "[n]o person acting in good faith on behalf of Goldman consistently could approve the payment of between 44% and 48% of net revenues to Goldman's employees year in and year out" and that accordingly the Director Defendants abdicated their duties by engaging in these "practices that overcompensate management." The complaint is entirely silent with respect to any individual salary or bonus; the Plaintiffs' allegation is that the scheme so misaligns incentives that it cannot have been the product of a good faith board decision. . . .

The decision as to how much compensation is appropriate to retain and incentivize employees, both individually and in the aggregate, is a core function of a board of directors exercising its business judgment. The Plaintiffs' pleadings fall short of creating a reasonable doubt that the Director Defendants have failed to exercise that judgment here. The Plaintiffs acknowledge that the compensation plan authorized by Goldman's board, which links compensation to revenue produced, was intended to align employee interests with those of the stockholders and incentivize the production of wealth. To an extent, it does so: extra effort by employees to raise corporate revenue, if successful, is rewarded. The Plaintiffs' allegations mainly propose that the compensation scheme implemented by the board does not perfectly align these interests; and that, in fact, it may encourage employee behavior incongruent with the stockholders' interest. This may be correct, but it is irrelevant. The fact that the Plaintiffs may desire a different compensation scheme does not indicate that equitable relief is warranted. Such changes may be accomplished through directorial elections, but not, absent a showing unmet here, through this Court. . . .

2. Adequately Informed

The Plaintiffs also contend that the board was uninformed in making its compensation decision. "Pre-suit demand will be excused in a derivative suit only if the . . . particularized facts in the complaint create a reasonable doubt that the informational component of the directors' decisionmaking process, *measured by concepts of gross negligence,* included consideration of all material information reasonably available." Here, Goldman's charter has a 8 Del. C. § 102(b)(7) provision, so gross negligence, by itself, is insufficient basis upon which to impose liability. The Plaintiffs must allege particularized facts creating a reasonable doubt that the directors acted in good faith. . . .

[T]the Plaintiffs acknowledge that Goldman has a compensation committee that reviews and approves the annual compensation of Goldman's executives. The Plaintiffs also acknowledge that Goldman has adopted a "pay for performance" philosophy, that Goldman represents as a way to align employee and shareholder interests. . . . Finally, the Plaintiffs note that the compensation committee reviewed information relating to the compensation ratio of Goldman's "core competitors that are investment banks (Bear Stearns, Lehman Brothers, Merrill Lynch, and Morgan Stanley)."

Rather than suggesting that the Director Defendants acted on an uninformed basis, the Plaintiffs' pleadings indicate that the board adequately informed itself before making a decision on compensation. The Director Defendants considered other investment bank comparables, varied the total percent and the total dollar amount awarded as compensation, and changed the total amount of compensation in response to changing public opinion. None of the Plaintiffs' allegations suggests gross negligence on the part of the Director Defendants, and the conduct described in the Plaintiffs' allegations certainly does not rise to the level of bad faith such that the Director Defendants would lose the protection of an 102(b)(7) exculpatory provision. . . .

D. THE PLAINTIFFS' *CAREMARK* CLAIM

In addition to the claims addressed above, the Plaintiffs assert that the board breached its duty to monitor the company as required under *Caremark*. Because this claim attacks a failure to act, rather than a specific transaction, the *Rales* standard applies. The *Rales* standard addresses whether the "board that would be addressing the demand can impartially consider its merits without being influenced by improper considerations." To properly plead demand futility under *Rales*, a plaintiff must allege particularized facts which create a reasonable doubt that "the board of directors could have properly exercised its independent and disinterested business judgment in responding to a demand."

"Under *Rales*, defendant directors who face a *substantial* likelihood of personal liability are deemed interested in the transaction and thus cannot make an impartial decision." A simple allegation of potential directorial liability is insufficient to excuse demand, else the demand requirement itself would be rendered toothless, and directorial control over corporate litigation would be lost. The likelihood of directors' liability is significantly lessened where, as here, the corporate charter exculpates the directors from liability to the extent authorized by 8 Del. C. § 102(b)(7). Because Goldman's charter contains such a provision, shielding directors from liability for breaches of the duty of care (absent bad faith) "a serious threat of liability may only be found to exist if the plaintiff pleads a *non-exculpated* claim against the directors based on particularized facts." This means that "plaintiffs must plead particularized facts showing bad faith in order to establish a substantial likelihood of personal directorial liability."

The Plaintiffs' contentions that the Director Defendants face a substantial likelihood of personal liability are based on oversight liability, as articulated by then-Chancellor Allen in *Caremark*. In *Caremark*, Chancellor Allen held that a company's board of directors could not "satisfy [its] obligation to be reasonably informed . . . without assuring [itself] that information and reporting systems exist[ed] in the organization." These systems are needed to provide the board with accurate information so that the board may reach "informed judgments concerning both the corporation's compliance with law and its business performance." A breach of oversight responsibilities is a breach of the duty of loyalty, and thus not exculpated under section 102(b)(7).

To face a substantial likelihood of oversight liability for a *Caremark* claim, the Director Defendants must have "(a) . . . utterly failed to implement any reporting or information system or controls" (which the Plaintiffs concede is not the case here); "*or* (b) having implemented such a system or controls, consciously failed to monitor or oversee its operations thus disabling themselves from being informed of risks or problems requiring their attention." Furthermore, "where a claim of directorial liability for corporate loss is predicated upon ignorance of liability creating activities within the corporation . . . only a sustained or systematic failure of the board to exercise oversight—such as an utter failure to attempt to assure a reasonable information and reporting system [exists]—will establish the lack of good faith that is a necessary condition to liability."

The Plaintiffs specifically contend that the Director Defendants created a compensation structure that caused management's interests to diverge from the stockholders' interests. As a result, management took risks which eventually led to unethical behavior and illegal conduct that exposed Goldman to financial liability. According to the Plaintiffs, after the Director Defendants created Goldman's compensation structure, they had a duty to ensure protection from abuses by management, which were allegedly made more likely due to the form of that structure. Instead of overseeing management, however, the Director Defendants abdicated their oversight responsibilities.

Unlike the original and most subsequent *Caremark* claims, where plaintiffs alleged that liability was predicated on a failure to oversee corporate conduct leading to violations of law, the Plaintiffs here argue that the Director Defendants are also liable for oversight failure relating to Goldman's business performance. Because the oversight of legal compliance and the oversight of business risk raise distinct concerns, I shall examine those issues separately.

1. Unlawful Conduct

As described above, the Plaintiffs must plead particularized facts suggesting that the board failed to implement a monitoring and reporting system or consciously disregarded the information provided by that system. Here, the Plaintiffs assert that the Goldman employees engaged in unethical trading practices in search of short term revenues. Although the Plaintiffs' allegations fall short of the florid contentions about the corporation made elsewhere,[187] the Plaintiffs provide examples, based on the Permanent Subcommittee report, of conduct they believe was unethical and harmful to the company. The Plaintiffs argue that the Director Defendants should have been aware of purportedly unethical conduct such as securitizing high risk mortgages, shorting the mortgage market, using naked credit default swaps, and "magnifying risk" through the creation of synthetic CDOs. The Plaintiffs also allege that Goldman's trading business often put Goldman in potential conflicts of interest with its own clients and that the Director Defendants were aware of this and have embraced this goal.

Illegal corporate conduct is not loyal corporate conduct. "[A] fiduciary of a Delaware corporation cannot be loyal to a Delaware corporation by knowingly causing it to seek profit by violating the law." The "unethical" conduct the Plaintiffs allege here, however, is not the type of wrongdoing envisioned by *Caremark*. The conduct at issue here involves, for the most part, *legal* business decisions that were firmly within management's judgment to pursue. There is nothing intrinsic in using naked credit default swaps or shorting the mortgage market that makes these actions illegal or wrongful. These are actions that Goldman managers, presumably using their informed business judgment, made to hedge the Corporation's assets against risk or to earn a higher return. Legal, if risky, actions that are within management's discretion to pursue are not "red flags" that would put a board on notice of unlawful conduct.

. . .

---

187. *See* Matt Taibbi, *The Great American Bubble Machine*, Rolling Stone Magazine, July 9–23, 2009, at 52 ("[Goldman] is a great vampire squid wrapped around the face of humanity, relentlessly jamming its blood funnel into anything that smells like money.").

2. Business Risk

Part of the Plaintiffs' *Caremark* claim stems from the Director Defendants' oversight of Goldman's business practices. As a preliminary matter, this Court has not definitively stated whether a board's *Caremark* duties include a duty to monitor business risk. In *Citigroup*, then-Chancellor Chandler posited that "it may be possible for a plaintiff to meet the burden under some set of facts." *Citigroup*, 964 A.2d at 126. . . .

As was the case in *Citigroup*, however, the facts pled here do not give rise to a claim under *Caremark*, and thus I do not need to reach the issue of whether the duty of oversight includes the duty to monitor business risk.

As the Court observed in *Citigroup*, "imposing *Caremark*-type duties on directors to monitor business risk is fundamentally different" from imposing on directors a duty to monitor fraud and illegal activity. Risk is "the chance that a return on an investment will be different than expected." Consistent with this, "a company or investor that is willing to take on more risk can earn a higher return." The manner in which a company "evaluate[s] the trade-off between risk and return" is "[t]he essence of . . . business judgment." The Plaintiffs here allege that Goldman was over-leveraged, engaged in risky business practices, and did not set enough money aside for future losses. As a result, the Plaintiffs assert, Goldman was undercapitalized, forcing it to become a bank holding company and to take on an onerous loan from Warren Buffett.

Although the Plaintiffs have molded their claims with an eye to the language of *Caremark*, the essence of their complaint is that I should hold the Director Defendants "personally liable for making (or allowing to be made) business decisions that, in hindsight, turned out poorly for the Company." If an actionable duty to monitor business risk exists,[217] it cannot encompass any substantive evaluation by a court of a board's determination of the appropriate amount of risk. Such decisions plainly involve business judgment.

The Plaintiffs' remaining allegations in essence seek to hold the Director Defendants "personally liable to the Company because they failed to fully recognize the risk posed by subprime securities." The Plaintiffs charge that the entire board was aware of, or should have been aware of, "the details of the trading business of Goldman and failed to take appropriate action." The Plaintiffs note that "[a]s the housing market began to fracture in early 2007, a committee of senior Goldman executives . . . including Defendants Viniar, Cohn, and Blankfein and those helping to manage Goldman's mortgage, credit and legal operations, took an active role in overseeing the mortgage unit." "[This] committee's job was to vet potential new products and transactions, being wary

---

217. While a valid claim against a board of directors in a hierarchical corporation for failure to monitor risk undertaken by corporate employees is a theoretical possibility, it would be, appropriately, a difficult cause of action on which to prevail. Assuming excessive risk-taking at some level becomes the misconduct contemplated by *Caremark*, the plaintiff would essentially have to show that the board *consciously* failed to implement any sort of risk monitoring system or, having implemented such a system, *consciously* disregarded red flags signaling that the company's employees were taking facially improper, and not just ex-post ill-advised or even bone-headed, business risks. Such bad-faith indifference would be formidably difficult to prove.

This heavy burden serves an important function in preserving the effectiveness of 8 Del. C. §102(b)(7) exculpatory provisions. If plaintiffs could avoid the requirement of showing bad faith by twisting their duty of care claims into *Caremark* loyalty claims, such a scenario would eviscerate the purpose of 8 Del. C. §102(b)(7) and could potentially chill the service of qualified directors.

of deals that exposed Goldman to too much risk." This committee eventually decided that housing prices would decline and decided to take a short position in the mortgage market. The Plaintiffs contend that the Director Defendants were "fully aware of the extent of Goldman's RMBS and CDO securities market activities." The Plaintiffs point out that the Director Defendants were informed about the business decisions Goldman made during the year including an "intensive effort to not only reduce its mortgage risk exposure, but profit from high risk RMBS and CDO Securities incurring losses." The Plaintiffs further allege that because of this the Director Defendants "understood that these efforts involved very large amounts of Goldman's capital that exceeded the Company's Value-at-Risk measures." Finally, the Plaintiffs allege that the practices allowed by the board, including transactions in which Goldman's risk was hedged, imposed reputational risk upon the corporation.

Thus, the Plaintiffs do not plead with particularity anything that suggests that the Director Defendants acted in bad faith or otherwise consciously disregarded their *oversight* responsibilities in regards to Goldman's business risk. Goldman had an Audit Committee in place that was "charged with assisting the Board in its oversight of the Company's management of market, credit liquidity and other financial and operational risks." The Director Defendants exercised their business judgment in choosing and implementing a risk management system that they presumably believed would keep them reasonably informed of the company's business risks. As described in detail above, the Plaintiffs admit that the Director Defendants were "fully aware of the extent of Goldman's RMBS and CDO securities market activities."

"Oversight duties under Delaware law are not designed to subject directors, even expert directors, to *personal liability* for failure to predict the future and to properly evaluate business risk." No reasonable inference can be made from the pleadings that the Director Defendants consciously disregarded their duty to be informed about business risk (assuming such a duty exists). On the contrary, the pleadings suggest that the Director Defendants kept themselves reasonably informed and fulfilled their duty of oversight in good faith. Good faith, not a good result, is what is required of the board.

Goldman's board and management made decisions to hedge exposure during the deterioration of the housing market, decisions that have been roundly criticized in Congress and elsewhere. Those decisions involved taking objectively large risks, including particularly reputational risks. The outcome of that risk-taking may prove ultimately costly to the corporation. The Plaintiffs, however, have failed to plead with particularity that the Director Defendants consciously and in bad faith disregarded these risks; to the contrary, the facts pled indicate that the board kept itself informed of the risks involved. The Plaintiffs have failed to plead facts showing a substantial likelihood of liability on the part of the Director Defendants under *Caremark*.

. . .

PROBLEM 9-4

In addition to challenging the premium Grenfell & Company paid in the Bank Won acquisition, plaintiff Grenfell & Company shareholders assert that the Grenfell & Company board of directors breached its duty to monitor the company as required under *Caremark*. In particular, plaintiffs contend that the Grenfell & Company board of directors was entirely too passive during the nego-tiation process, letting CEO Harrison do all of the negotiating and letting him control the flow of information to them. The board has a three-member executive committee composed of outside directors, but it did not meet during the period of time of the negotiations to discuss Harrison's role either during the negotia-tions or after the two companies were combined. During the board discussion of the transaction the board did ask for comparables concerning the premiums in other bank mergers, but those discussions occurred after Harrison had presented the 14 percent premium deal to the board as a "hell of a deal," while also men-tioning the at-market deal if he were willing to step down. The board approved the 14 percent deal prior to receiving the materials on comparables.

Grenfell & Company has an exculpatory clause that incorporates the lan-guage of § 102(b)(7). *What effect will the exculpatory clause have on plaintiffs' claim (a) that the premium was too high and (b) that the board had failed in its Caremark duties?*

E. INSURANCE AND INDEMNIFICATION

Another way that companies protect directors from personal liability for their actions as directors is by providing insurance, referred to as directors' and offi-cers' insurance (or usually just "D&O insurance"). Professors Tom Baker and Sean Griffith have been studying D&O insurers to determine their role in the corporate governance system. The professors write:

> D&O insurers have three ways of furthering the deterrence objectives of corporate and securities law liability and, in order to minimize their own payout obligations, ample incentive to do so. First, they can price their insurance based on their best assessment of the liability risk of each individual corporation, thereby providing an incentive for corporations to minimize that risk. Second, they can monitor and seek to improve the corporate governance practices of the corporations they insure. Third, they can manage the defense and settlement of corporate and securities lawsuits so that only meritorious claims are paid.

Tom Baker & Sean J. Griffith, *The Missing Monitor in Corporate Governance: The Directors' and Officers' Liability Insurer*, 95 Geo. L.J. 1795, 1797 (2007). Baker and Griffith find evidence that D&O insurers attempt to price on the basis of risk, but conclude that "the highly discretionary nature of the D&O insurance under-writing process and the competitive pressures of the insurance underwriting cycle limit the ability of corporate and securities law deterrence objectives to be fully reflected in the pricing of D&O insurance." *Id.* at 1798. Based on inter-views with insurers, these authors also conclude that D&O insurers do not actively monitor corporate governance, a finding that, according to the authors, "raises substantial questions about the deterrent effect of corporate and private securities law liability." *Id.* at 1799.

In this section, we focus on the third means of pursuing deterrence: manage-ment of the defense and settlement of lawsuits. As with any insurance, on public policy grounds the company cannot insure against losses arising out of intentional misconduct or dishonesty; nor will insurance companies write policies to insure against directors' breaches of loyalty. Moreover, companies maintain "reimbursement insurance" to provide reimbursement to the company for any payments to third parties or the government (penalties, judgments, settlements, and the costs of the company defending itself) arising from actions of their directors and employees. Both D&O policies and the company's reimbursement policy will typically require the insurance company to defend its insureds (the company and the directors and officers) when a lawsuit is brought that states a claim for an "insurable event." Unfortunately, insurance companies and their insureds often disagree about whether a lawsuit states a claim for an insurable event. Thus, one stage in many complex commercial litigations is a declaratory judgment action between the insurance company and its insured about the potential scope of coverage and the insurance company's "duty to defend" its insured.

In addition to providing its directors and officers with insurance, companies will enter into indemnification agreements with top executives and its board of directors, typically by specifying such parties' indemnification rights in its bylaws. In typical bylaw provisions, the company agrees to pay ("indemnify") the directors and officers for any losses arising out of their service to the corporation (including the costs of defending lawsuits), subject to specified limitations, usually the limits provided in the jurisdiction's controlling statutes. Such agreements or bylaw provisions supplement common law principles of agency law, under which a principal is generally obligated to indemnify an agent against losses that arise out of the agency relationship, assuming the agent's actions were authorized and taken in good faith. *See* Restatement (Second) of Agency §§ 438-440. From the perspective of directors and officers, whether they are indemnified by the company or insured against losses by insurance policies the company pays for is important if the company's future solvency is problematic (such as in a Silicon Valley start-up with excellent prospects but no actual products to market at the time of incorporation). Prudent directors and officers seek — and typically get — both types of protection.

As might be anticipated, both the Delaware General Corporation Law and the Model Business Corporation Act specify indemnification rights and the limits thereto. Neither makes for scintillating reading, but because these issues are a part of most complex corporate litigation, it is important to have at least a glancing familiarity with the provisions. In general, the key issue that determines indemnification rights is whether the directors, officers, employees, or agents (DOEA) acted in good faith and in a manner reasonably anticipated to be in (or not opposed to) the corporation's best interest. DGCL § 145; Model Act §§ 8.51-8.57. If the DOEA are successful on the merits, then the company must indemnify them for their attorneys' fees and expenses.

The statutes also regulate the advancement of expenses. DGCL § 145(e) and Model Act § 8.53 permit advancement of expenses prior to the final disposition of a lawsuit, and many corporations make such advancement mandatory, either by contract or bylaw.

A final type of agreement that often comes into play in litigation challenging the legality of actions of the directors or employees of a company is seen in the case below, here called a "forbearance agreement," and often called a "standstill agreement." The need for these agreements arises from a conflict between the corporation and the DOEA. Remember that the corporation can act only through its agents, including its board of directors and its employees. If these agents are alleged to have violated the law, the corporation as well as the agents will potentially be liable to third parties or to the government based on the doctrine of *respondeat superior*—*even* where the agent's actions were against explicit company policy.

Such vicarious liability creates a dilemma for the corporation in litigation: while wanting to assert to third parties or to the government that there were no violations of law, the corporation may want to maintain its ability to seek compensation (maintain its right of "contribution") against its directors or employees if there is ultimately a settlement or judgment that costs the company money, particularly where the corporation views the directors' or employees' actions with disfavor. Conversely, the directors or employees want to protect their rights to indemnification and insurance but recognize that it may not be strategically smart to have the company litigating their good faith (on which insurance and indemnification rights depend) at the beginning of the legal proceedings. In such situations, the company and its directors or employees will often sign a "standstill agreement." Such an agreement typically freezes each party's claims against the other for a specified period of time and provides other protection (such as providing that neither party will raise statute of limitations defenses in any subsequent litigation or making explicit provision for advancing defense costs subject to a right of reimbursement). Through such an agreement, the company and the directors or employees can present a more united front against third parties or the government without unduly compromising their claims against each other. You can see the interaction of various of the above types of protection in Problem 9-5.

Problem 9-5

As word leaked out that Grenfell could have done a no-premium deal with Bank Won, a spate of shareholder lawsuits (and an SEC investigation into the accuracy of the joint proxy statement describing the terms of the deal) followed. Harrison, members of the board, and Grenfell itself were named as defendants.

As pressure on Harrison mounted, he entered into a forbearance agreement with Grenfell in August 2011. Under that agreement, both Dunlap and Sunbeam agreed to freeze any litigation against each other for 180 days. Nevertheless, other litigation proceeded, and Harrison's legal bills began to mount quickly. In December 2011, Grenfell paid a law firm $123,548 for services rendered to Harrison and Russell A. Kersh, Grenfell's executive vice president for disclosure policy and administration. A few months later, however, Grenfell's board of directors voted to refuse further requests for advances. In considering the propriety of the board's actions, read section 8.1 of Grenfell's bylaws:

> To the extent permitted by law, as the same exists or may hereafter be amended (but, in the case of such amendment, only to the extent that such amendment permits the Corporation to provide broader indemnification rights than said law permitted to the Corporation prior to such amendment) the Corporation shall indemnify any person against any and all judgments, fines, amounts paid in settling or otherwise disposing of threatened, pending or completed actions, suits or

proceedings, whether by reason of the fact that he, his testator or intestate representative, is or was a director or officer of (or a plan fiduciary or plan administrator of any employee benefit plan sponsored by) the Corporation or of (or by) any other corporation of any type or kind, domestic or foreign, which he served in any capacity at the request of the corporation. Expenses so incurred by any such person in defending or investigating a threatened or pending civil or criminal action or proceedings shall at his request be paid by the Corporation in advance of the final disposition of such action or proceeding upon receipt of an undertaking by or on behalf of such director or officer to repay such amount if it shall be ultimately determined that such person is not entitled to be indemnified by the Corporation as authorized by this Article VIII. The foregoing right of indemnification shall in no way be exclusive of any other rights of indemnification to which any such person may be entitled, under any bylaw, agreement, vote of shareholders or disinterested directors, or otherwise, and shall inure to the benefit of the heirs, executors, and administrators of such person.

In addition to the foregoing, consider the following Paragraph 3 of the forbearance agreement:

Grenfell agrees to advance to the Individuals [Harrison and Kersh] their out-of-pocket expenses, costs, and legal fees incurred by them in connection with: (i) certain litigations in which they are named as defendants by reason of the fact that they were officers and/or directors of Sunbeam, which litigations are identified in Schedule A to this agreement, and any future litigations in which they are named as defendants by reason of the fact that they were officers and/or directors of Grenfell, Inc. and (ii) the investigation of Grenfell currently being carried out by the Division of Enforcement of the Securities and Exchange Commission (SEC) and any future investigation relating in any way to the Individuals' performance of their duties at Grenfell which may be carried out by the SEC or any other governmental agency in accordance with and subject to limitations of reasonableness contained in any employment agreements entered into between the Individuals and Grenfell, Grenfell's bylaws, and Delaware law. Such advancement shall be subject to the receipt by Grenfell of an appropriate undertaking by each of the Individuals to repay any amounts so advanced if it shall be ultimately determined that the Individual is not entitled to be indemnified by Grenfell for such expenses, costs, or fees (the "Undertaking"). Nothing in this Agreement shall constitute a waiver by Grenfell of any claim for recoupment or repayment of any amounts so advanced, nor shall anything in this Agreement constitute a waiver by the Individuals or a limitation on the individuals with respect to any right to be indemnified by Grenfell in accordance with applicable law, the bylaws of Grenfell, or the Individuals' respective Employment Agreements or to have continued coverage under Grenfell's Directors' and Officers' Liability Insurance Policy. Grenfell hereby acknowledges that it has received the Undertaking from the Individuals.

In light of these provisions and the underlying statutes, must Grenfell advance expenses to Harrison and Kersh? What difficulties, if any, does this advancement pose as a practical matter in the litigation?

DOW CHEMICAL COMPANY: A CASE STUDY

On February 9, 2009, plaintiff shareholder Michael Blum filed the following derivative complaint against the Dow Chemical Company. Dow has fully exculpated its directors pursuant to §102(b)(7), and fully indemnified them according to § 145. Analyze this complaint to determine (a) whether plaintiff is correct that demand is excused, and therefore whether defendant's motion to dismiss for failure to make demand should be denied; and (b) what the likely effect of the Dow Chemical Company's § 145 promise will be on the litigation. In addressing that latter question, remember that a key consideration for § 145 indemnification is whether the officers and directors acted in good faith.

Verified Shareholder Derivative Complaint:

Plaintiff Michael D. Blum, by his undersigned attorneys, submits this Verified Shareholder Derivative Complaint (Complaint) in the name and on behalf of nominal defendant The Dow Chemical Company (Dow or the Company) against certain officers and directors of Dow (Defendants). Plaintiff bases his allegations on actual knowledge as to his own acts and on information and belief as to all other allegations after due investigation.

Summary of the Allegations

1.   Dow—based in Midland, Michigan—has been one of the giants of the American chemical industry practically since it was founded in 1897. In recent years, however, growing competition at home and abroad has chipped away at the Company's profit margins on commodity chemicals, its traditional mainstay. Accordingly, successive managers have sought ways to leverage the Company's holdings in specialty chemicals, such as plastics and polymers, and to increase its commitment to these higher-margin businesses.

2.   Thus, in 2008, Dow—led by Defendants—embarked upon a new strategy. Under this strategy, the Company would monetize its basic chemicals business—for example, by selling off assets or entering into joint ventures whereby 50-percent interests would be sold for cash to third parties, with the Company often continuing to operate the businesses. Proceeds would be invested in specialty chemicals.

3.   While the new strategy may have been sound at its inception, as executed by Defendants, it took a bizarre and catastrophic turn. Under the leadership of Andrew N. Liveris, whom the other Defendants had allowed to assume unquestioned operational and financial control of the Company, Dow entered into two, multi-billion dollar transactions almost simultaneously—and did so in so grossly reckless a manner that today, only months after the second of those deals was announced, the Company, by its own admission, sits on the precipice of an unmitigated financial disaster.

4.   In the first deal, Dow signed a memorandum of understanding (the MOU) with the Petrochemical Industries Company of the State of Kuwait (Kuwait). In this venture, known as K-Dow, the Company was to sell a 50-percent interest in certain of its commodities chemicals businesses to Kuwait in exchange for $10 billion in cash proceeds.

5.   In the second deal, Dow agreed to acquire the Rohm & Haas Company (R&H), a long-time producer of specialty chemicals, for $19 billion in cash. This deal is referred to throughout this Complaint as the Merger or the R&H Merger.

6.   Defendants intended to use the proceeds from the K-Dow venture to fund Dow's purchase obligation under the R&H Merger. In fact, undisclosed to Company shareholders, Dow would be unable to finance that Merger without closing K-Dow.

7. Whatever promise this All at Once plan may once have held for Dow, it is almost impossible to conceive of how it could have been carried out more recklessly, or with more utter disregard for the grave and foreseeable risks to Dow, than it was by Defendants.

8. The K-Dow MOU was signed first, in December 2007. It was a tentative agreement, subject to the completion of definitive agreements, customary conditions, regulatory approvals, and various other conditions. The venture was not even expected to close and get underway until a full year later, December 2008. Moreover, in pursuing this venture, Dow was partnering with a Third World government entity known for its unpredictability.

9. Seven months later, as K-Dow meandered to fruition, Dow — again spearheaded by Chairman Liveris and his compliant Board — entered into the deal (the Merger Agreement) with R&H. The Merger Agreement, as negotiated by Liveris's managers and approved by all Defendants, was the polar opposite of K-Dow: It was a definitive agreement. It was with a sophisticated, U.S.-based counterparty. It called for a quick closing — just two business days after all regulatory approvals were obtained. It did not contain any of the customary out clauses — such as intervening economic or industry downturns that the vast majority of would-be acquirors were insisting upon at the time given the severe tightening of credit that was already well underway in the U.S. and world economies. It was not contingent upon Dow obtaining adequate financing. To the contrary, the Haas family, which controlled R&H, pointedly refused to sell their company unless Dow would covenant the attainment of the financing necessary to close. Most alarming of all, the Haas family demanded, and Defendants consented to, a clause providing for specific performance (i.e., compelled implementation) of the Merger if Defendants did not close it for any reason.[1]

10. Thus, Defendants had matters 180 degrees backwards from where they should have been had they exercised their business judgment in good faith. To protect the Company, the basic chemicals joint venture that was to net cash for Dow should have been a definitive agreement, with no contingencies, with a reliable counterparty, and set to close quickly — or some combination of those features. By contrast, the specialty chemicals investment, which drained cash, should have contained an out for an intervening economic deterioration, set to close after the joint venture, been substantially contingent upon Dow obtaining the necessary financing, and/or limited in consequences, should Dow renege, to reasonable liquidated damages.

11. Beginning in the fall of 2008, the foreseeable consequences of Defendants' dereliction began to play out. The world economy did not improve from its July levels, and credit shrank even more. Dow's earnings and share price declined precipitously. Kuwait demanded a $500 million price reduction, to which Defendants consented. Dow's cash reserves plummeted, and, although Defendants claimed they had arranged bridge financing for the R&H Merger on very favorable terms, the Company's ability to tap alternative lines of credit evaporated. Defendants came to realize two things: first, Dow would not have sufficient cash or financing to sustain the R&H Merger following the closing, unless K-Dow also immediately closed; and second, given the Company's

---

1. In addition, Dow obligated itself to pay a ticking fee to R&H of $100 million for each month that the Merger did not close. The ticking fee is ticking now, and Dow owes R&H over $50 million as of today's date.

debilitated financial condition, if it had to close the R&H Merger without the proceeds from K-Dow in hand, that would trigger a cascading series of credit instrument defaults that would quickly drive Dow into deep insolvency. None of these facts were shared with stockholders, however. To the contrary, Defendants continued to reassure the market that the R&H Merger categorically did not depend on K-Dow, and that Dow had access to all the credit it needed to close the Merger.

12. When December arrived, Defendants watched as one regulatory approval after another fell into place, signaling the impending close of the R&H Merger. They took desperate measures to delay the close, lest proceeds from K-Dow be not yet in hand — at one point in December even visiting Washington to lobby the FTC for a delay in issuing an antitrust approval. But by the last week in December, all indications were that the final approval would be received on January 8, and the Merger would have to close by January 12, 2009. In the nick of time, Dow received final clearance from Kuwait on the K-Dow venture, and a closing date for that deal was set for January 2, 2009.

13. It was at this point that the ticking bomb lying at the heart of Defendants' dereliction went off. On December 28, 2008, Kuwait cabled that the K-Dow venture was off — per the Kuwait Supreme Petroleum Council, which had rescinded its prior approval without explanation. Defendants scrambled to renegotiate the closing with R&H, but R&H — unsurprisingly, given that it had pointedly bargained for an ironclad closing — declined. Finally, on January 25, 2009, Liveris sent a letter to R&H's CEO, Raj Gupta, delivering the news: Dow could not, and would not, close by January 27, 2009 (the current operative deadline). One day later, R&H sued Dow in this Court, demanding specific performance of the $19 billion cash Merger. Trial is set for March 9, 2009.

14. Dow is fully cognizant that, as a result of Defendants' actions, it has no defenses to R&H's suit. The Company filed an Answer (a copy of which is attached hereto as Exhibit A) in which it essentially admitted its legal breach of the Merger Agreement and appealed to equity to forgo specific performance and instead allow Dow to cram down a delayed closing on R&H. Remarkably, Defendants admit in the Answer that the completion of the R&H Merger was, all along, dependent on receiving cash from the closing of K-Dow — belying Defendants' protestations to the contrary for the last half year and causing Dow to take a position radically inconsistent with the position it took in the negotiations with R&H. Defendants also caused Dow to file a lawsuit against Kuwait which Defendants cannot reasonably expect to progress to a favorable conclusion for Dow.

15. Even worse, the Majlis Al-Umma — the National Assembly of Kuwait — has launched an investigation into bribery by Dow of Kuwaiti state oil officials to obtain their cooperation in agreeing to the K-Dow venture. The Assembly's investigation is ongoing.

16. Dow, in the hands of Defendants, now perches on the horns of an appalling dilemma. If it goes through with the R&H Merger, voluntarily or otherwise, it will — by Defendants' own admission — career into almost immediate insolvency. If it does not go through with the Merger, it will be liable for astronomical damages, which if measured by the intervening fall in R&H's share price from the agreed upon consideration of $78 per share, could reach approximately $10 billion. With its word no longer its bond, its ability to conduct acquisitions and other major transactions curtailed, and is access to credit markets frozen, Dow now faces a bleak and uncertain future. The harm is already

quantifiable: the Company's debt rating has been cut to just above junk, and it is incurring a $100 million obligation to R&H with every month the closing is delayed — on top of increased costs of capital and other measurable consequences.

17. Accordingly, Michael D. Blum, who is now and has at all relevant times been a shareholder of Dow, brings this action on behalf of the Company against Defendants for their abdication of their most basic duty to act in good faith and to bring rational business judgment to bear on the affairs of the enterprise. Defendants have breached their fiduciary duties of care, oversight, good faith, candor, and loyalty by, inter alia: (a) deciding to enter into an ironclad agreement in July 10, 2008 to purchase R&H for $18.8 billion, without any contingencies for failure of financing (including a contingency if the K-Dow deal were to fall through) or other material adverse events, at a time when they lacked a reasonable certainty of obtaining sufficient funds to complete the deal in the time allotted; (b) deciding to withhold from shareholders the fact that the R&H purchase depended on the Company successfully closing the K-Dow deal and instead encouraging shareholders to believe otherwise; (c) deciding to enter into a draconian Merger with R&H without first reaching a definitive agreement on, closing, and obtaining the proceeds from, the K-Dow venture with Kuwait, relying instead on a tentative agreement subject to many, highly uncertain contingencies, and on bribery of officials of the Kuwait state-run oil syndicate and/or the strength of the Company's relationships with such officials, and bypassing others in the Kuwaiti government who had veto power and whose continued support was vital; and (d) deciding to enter into temporary and longer-term financing arrangements with various banks and third parties that contained multiple cross-default provisions and that were all premised, at root, on Dow receiving $9 billion from Kuwait in the K-Dow deal, at a time when the K-Dow deal was far from certain and the failure of that deal would cause multiple, cascading defaults on Dow's finances and push the Company into insolvency. These acts were not, and could not have been, the product of Defendants' informed business judgment.

18. In addition, Defendants' acts constituted bad faith and gross recklessness, in that each of the Defendants willfully or recklessly ignored information that would have led to the discovery and prevention of the misconduct at issue. In particular, before approving the R&H Merger, the Board had available to it the following facts: (a) the deal involved a 75 percent premium to R&H's current stock price; (b) the deal contained no out clauses protecting Dow; (c) the deal required a quick closing and was not made conditional on achieving funding; (d) the deal was dependent for its funding on a prior, highly tentative transaction with a Third World government entity with a closing date that was still months away; (e) the K-Dow transaction consisted simply of an MOU, and no definitive agreement was in sight for many months; (f) Dow had recently paid a $325,000 fine to the United States Securities and Exchange Commission and admitted to having paid over $200,000 in bribes to officials of the Central Insecticide Board, Ministry of Agriculture, Government of India, and agriculture extension officials in Maharashtra, India, in connection with achieving expedited registration of three pesticides for the Indian market; and (g) the entire Board of Dow was flown to Kuwait for the final week of negotiations and signing of the K-Dow MOU and had direct exposure to the key government officials of Kuwait involved in the K-Dow venture.

19.   Moreover, the terms in the R&H deal were so extreme and one-sided to Dow's disadvantage, and the terms of the K-Dow deal were so nebulous and unprotective of Dow, as to have placed the Board on notice that Dow was relying on the K-Dow deal without a reasonable basis — including possibly by the strength of extra-contractual relationships such as bribes or other questionable relationships. Indeed, Dow had a Code of Conduct that applied Company-wide and was part of its organic corporate governance documentation. That Code provided, among other things, that:

> It is against Dow policy to make unlawful, improper or other kinds of questionable payments to customers, government employees or officials, or other parties. . . . We will not offer expensive gifts, bribes or any other kind of payment or benefit to representatives of customers, suppliers, competitors, government or governmental agencies. This applies to any individual or organization at any level, within or outside the U.S.

20.   This action seeks relief in the form of the implementation of specific corporate reforms at Dow — including procedures for greater shareholder input into the actions of the Board, safeguards for the conduct of mergers and acquisitions, the termination of Liveris, the replacement of Liveris and several other directors on the Board, and the separation of key executive positions from other positions and from Board chairmanship — as well as monetary damages and attorneys' fees.

The Parties

21.   Plaintiff Michael D. Blum has been a continuous owner of Dow common stock since 2000, and remains so today.

22.   Nominal defendant The Dow Chemical Company is a corporation organized and existing under the laws of the State of Delaware, with its principal place of business in Midland, Michigan. Dow is a diversified chemical company engaged in the manufacture and sale of chemicals, plastic materials, and agricultural and other specialized products and services.

23.   Defendant Andrew N. Liveris (Liveris) has complete hegemony over the Company and is, and at all relevant times has been, President, Chief Executive Officer, Chief Operating Officer, and Chairman of the Board of Directors of Dow, as well as serving as Chairman of the Executive Committee of the Company. . . . [Further allegations about each Director are reprinted below.]

24.   Defendant Geoffrey E. Merszei (Merszei) is, and at all relevant times has been, the Chief Financial Officer and a member of Dow's Board of Directors, in both capacities since 2005, and a member of the Executive Committee of the Board of the Company. Received stock awards, restricted stock units, and other compensation from the Company in 2007.

25.   Defendant James A. Bell (Bell) is, and at all relevant times has been, a member of Dow's Board of Directors since 2005 and a member of the Audit Committee and the Governance Committee of the Board of the Company.

26.   Defendant Barbara Hackman Franklin (Franklin) is, and at all relevant times has been, a member of Dow's Board of Directors, since 1980, except for a brief interruption in 1992-93. Franklin also currently serves on three of the Board's Committees: as Chair of the Audit Committee, a member of the Governance Committee, and a member of the Executive Committee.

27.   Defendant John B. Hess (Hess) is, and at all relevant times has been, a member of Dow's Board of Directors, since 2006, and a member of the Compensation Committee.

28.   Defendant Dennis H. Reilley (Reilley) is, and at all relevant times has been, a member of Dow's Board of Directors, since August 2007, and a member of the Audit Committee of the Board of the Company.

29.   Defendant Ruth G. Shaw (Shaw) is, and at all relevant times has been, a member of Dow's Board of Directors, since 2005, and a member of the Compensation Committee.

30.   Defendant Paul G. Stern (Stern) is, and at all relevant times has been, a member of Dow's Board of Directors, since May 2006, and a member of three committees of the Board: Chair of the Governance Committee; a member of the Audit Committee; and a member of the Executive Committee.

31.   Defendant James M. Ringler (Ringler) is, and at all relevant times has been, a member of Dow's Board of Directors, since 2001, and Chair of the Compensation Committee of the Board of the Company.

32.   Defendant Jacqueline K. Barton (Barton) is, and at all relevant times has been, a member of Dow's Board of Directors, since 1993, and a member of the Compensation Committee of the Board of the Company.

33.   Defendant Jeff M. Fettig (Fettig) is, and at all relevant times since 2003 has been, a member of Dow's Board of Directors, and a member of the Audit Committee and the Governance Committee.

34.   Defendant Arnold A. Allemang (Allemang) is, and at all relevant times has been, a member of Dow's Board of Directors, since 1996. Allemang was an officer or employee of Dow for 43 years, and served as a Vice President at the same time that Liveris also served as a Vice President of Dow.

35.   Defendant Michael Gambrell (Gambrell) is, and at all relevant times has been, the Executive Vice President for Basic Plastics and Chemicals of Dow. . . . Gambrell was one of several key officers of Dow involved in implementing and attempting to close the K-Dow venture with Kuwait.

Derivative Allegations

36.   Plaintiff brings this action derivatively in the right and for the benefit of Dow to redress injuries suffered, and to be suffered, by Dow as a direct result of Defendants' breaches of fiduciary duties by virtue of the wrongs alleged herein, including, among other things, insider selling, unjust enrichment, and waste of corporate assets. Dow is named as a nominal defendant solely in a derivative capacity.

37.   Plaintiff will adequately and fairly represent the interests of Dow in enforcing and prosecuting its rights.

38.   Plaintiff was an owner of Dow common stock at all relevant times and continues to own Dow stock at this time.

39.   Prosecution of this action, independent of the Dow Board, is in the best interests of the Company.

Demand Is Futile and Therefore Excused

40.   Demand upon the Dow Board that they institute this action in the Company's name would be entirely futile, and is therefore excused.

41.   First, the acts and decisions of the Board — as catalogued herein — constituted a breach of Defendants' fiduciary duties of care, oversight, good faith,

candor, and loyalty. These decisions were not, and could not have been, the product of the Board's good faith, informed business judgment. As such, and for this separate and independent ground alone, demand on the Board to bring these claims on the Company's behalf would be utterly futile, and is excused.

42.   Second, the Board of Dow is subject to numerous conflicts of interest, interlocking relationships, governance defects, and other features that prevent it from objectively considering a demand to bring these claims. The Board consists of twelve (12) individuals: Defendants Liveris, Merszei, Allemang, Barton, Bell, Fettig, Franklin, Hess, Reilley, Ringler, Shaw, and Stern. As discussed herein at least six of these individuals are not disinterested and independent with respect to the acts and omissions alleged herein:

(a) Liveris dominates and controls all other directors. Liveris, who is the President, Chief Executive Officer, Chairman of the Board of Directors of Dow, and de facto Chief Operating Officer of the Company, has spent years in high-level executive positions at Dow and controls the compensation and other benefits paid to the other directors, what committees they sit on, what role they play in governance, and other processes. With respect to the control and management of the Company, there is no meaningful distinction between Dow and Liveris himself. Unlike other large companies, Dow has no single shareholder, or group of shareholders with aligned interests, who own a major portion of the Company's stock and who can exert a mediating influence on either Liveris or the Board he controls.

(b) Liveris's domination of Dow and its Board is illustrated by an episode that occurred in early 2007. By that time, the drag on Dow's results from its low-margin basic chemicals business was well known. In response, two officers of Dow, Romeo Kreinberg and then-CFO and Director J. Pedro Reinhard urged action upon Liveris to sell off the Company's basic chemicals business and focus exclusively on specialty chemicals. When this appeal fell on deaf ears, the two executives searched for possible transactions with third parties that could help Dow and its shareholders unlock more value. A potential leveraged buyout deal was arranged with a foreign sovereign wealth fund. When news reached Liveris, he moved swiftly to block Kreinberg and Reinhard and oust them from the Company — prevailing upon the Board, the following morning, to terminate their employment, invoke punitive damages clauses in their contracts, and cut off roughly $45 million in vested equity and other compensation. The Board followed Liveris's directive, without conducting an independent investigation of the events, without forming a Special Committee, and without addressing the advisability of the financial and structural changes being proposed by Kreinberg and Reinhard. The two men sued for defamation, and Dow promptly settled, restoring most of the withheld compensation. Dow publicly acknowledged the two executives' substantial contributions to Dow over their lengthy and illustrious careers at Dow. Although Kreinberg and Reinhard acknowledged that their actions had been unduly secretive, the net result of the episode was that Liveris had gotten rid of Kreinberg and Reinhard, the Board had fallen into line without protest or significant inquiry, and the two men's idea of selling the basic chemicals businesses outright was never taken up by the Board again.

(c) Defendants Liveris, Merszei, and Allemang are high-level, highly-compensated executive officers of Dow, and the Company acknowledged in the 2008 Proxy that they are not independent under either the listing standards of the New York Stock Exchange or the Company's own Director Independence Standards.

(d) Defendants Bell, Hess, Reilley, Shaw and Stern joined the Board in 2005 or later, after Liveris had become Chairman and CEO, were hand picked or approved by Liveris, and are beholden to him for their positions.

(e) The Company lacks the normal checks and balances that arise from a healthy competition of interests among directors, managers, and shareholders, allowing Liveris to step into the breach and assume complete command of the Company, controlling groups of managers and fellow directors who will not question or challenge his decisions. Governance at Dow violates basic standards of good corporate governance, reflected, among other things in: Liveris's domination of the Board and the entire Company; the overlapping Committee assignments set forth herein; the participation of Merszei as both Chief Financial Officer and a Board member; the participation of Liveris both as CEO, COO, and President, and as Chairman of the Board and Chairman of the Executive Committee; the multiple ties and entanglements among Liveris and other Board members outside of Dow; Franklin's chairmanship of the Audit Committee, which should be occupied by a person of unquestioned independence, despite the fact that she is a close confidant of Liveris and serves on the Executive Committee with him; the near-100% overlap between the Audit Committee and the Governance Committee; and the presence of Executive Committee member Stern on the Audit Committee.

(f) Defendant Liveris is a member of the Board of Directors of Citigroup, Inc., which is a lead agent on the $13 billion bridge facility that is providing short-term financing to Dow and which Dow argues would be breached if it is compelled to go through with the merger with R&H, thereby rendering Dow insolvent. As such, Liveris has a conflict of interest that precludes him from exercising independent and disinterested judgment with respect to these claims on behalf of Dow.

(g) Defendants Franklin (Chair), Bell, Fettig, Reilley, and Stern sit on the Audit Committee, which allowed Dow to engage in transactions with Kuwait and R&H that were grossly reckless and patently unreasonable and which were not the product of prudent and reasonable business judgment, and which have needlessly exposed Dow to the risk of catastrophic failure. Having participated in the wrongs and material breaches of fiduciary duly alleged herein, these directors cannot be expected to be disinterested and independent in connection with rectifying the same.

(h) Defendants Franklin, Bell, Fettig, and Stern played a disproportionately significant role in the oversight of the Company as it engaged in the K-Dow and R&H transactions because each of these Defendants sits on both the Audit Committee and the Governance Committee of Dow's Board. These two Committees have the exact same membership, except that the Audit Committee has one additional member, and in fact, pursuant to the Audit Committee's Charter, the Governance Committee appointed the various members of the Audit Committee.[3] This means that Franklin, Bell, Fettig, and Stern, as Liveris's direction, appointed themselves as the Company's auditors.

(i) Defendant Franklin is not independent of Liveris for the further reason that she shares close personal and social relationships with him outside of Dow. Franklin joined the Board of the US-China Business Council, the leading organization of U.S. companies engaged in business with the People's Republic of China, in June 2008, at the same time that Liveris became Chairman thereof. In addition, Franklin will not sue other members of the Board of Directors, or the other Defendants, because her very livelihood depends on being identified as a counselor and advocate for the Boards of Directors of American companies doing business in international markets, especially China, and instituting these claims would destroy her reputation among her customer base.

(j) Defendants concede that several Board members have significant existing commercial relationships and entanglements. Those relationships have prevented them and continue to prevent them from taking the actions requested by Plaintiff herein. For example, defendants Liveris, Franklin, Fettig, Hess, Stern and Reilley face debilitating conflicts of interest and will take no action against one another or the other Defendants related to the harm complained of herein, for the following reasons, among others:

   (i)   Hess and Liveris serve as members of The Business Council and The National Petroleum Council, two prominent business councils;

   (ii) Franklin and Liveris serve as directors of the U.S.-China Business Council, a prominent international business council. A third director, W. James McNerney, Jr., is the Chairman and CEO of Boeing Company, where Dow director Bell is employed as CFO; thus, Bell cannot be independent of Franklin or Liveris in determining whether to pursue claims against them, in that Franklin or Liveris might then disparage him to McNerney, his boss and their colleague on the USCBC.

   (iii) Hess and Franklin both hold prominent positions at J.P. Morgan Chase & Co. — one of the nation's pre-eminent investment banking firms — with Hess serving as Director of the National Advisory Board of J.P. Morgan, and Franklin serving as Director of JP Morgan Value Opportunities Fund, Inc;

   (iv) Stern and Fettig are both members of the Board of Directors of Whirlpool, where Fettig serves as Chairman of the Board of Directors and Chief Executive Officer; Fettig recruited Stern to Whirlpool, and Stern has sat on the nominating and corporate governance committee of Whirlpool since 1990, recently acquiescing in a $10.3 million pay package to Fettig in 2006, and a $15.5 million payout in 2007, despite the fact that Whirlpool's stock price had made no progress in that two-year period and paid only a 2.5 percent dividend yield;

   (v)   Stern and Hess are both members of the Council of Foreign Relations, a prominent council that offers advice to domestic companies and politicians on foreign business and business practices; and

3. From the Governance Committee Charter: The members of the Audit Committee shall be appointed by the Board on the recommendation of the Governance Committee.

    (vi) Liveris and Reilley are both members of the prestigious American Chemistry Council, where Liveris is currently Chairman Emeritus and where Reilley served as former Chairman.

(k) Based on their knowledge of material, non-public information, defendants Allemang and Gambrell, while in possession of material, non-public information regarding the shakiness of the K-Dow and R&H deals and their potential to cause catastrophic failure at the Company, sold over $7.4 million in Dow stock since mid-April 2008, inconsistent with their past sales patterns and practices, as follows:

    (i) On or about April 16, 2008, defendant Allemang sold the vast majority of his Dow shares at prices as high as $46.75 per share, to realize gross proceeds of over $5.8 million; and

    (ii) On or about April 16 and April 17, 2008, Gambrell sold material amounts of his Dow shares at prices as high as $39.45 per share, to realize gross proceeds of over $1.6 million.

Substantial Threat of Liability for Breach of Duties

43.   Third, as set forth herein, Defendants face a substantial threat of liability for their breaches of fiduciary duty set forth herein. Indeed, the various Committees of the Board were specifically tasked with control and oversight over the very conduct that went so fatally awry at Dow. Each of Defendants sat on at least one — and in most cases, several — of the Board's Committees during the relevant period and thus had direct responsibility for ensuring various aspects of the Company's operations. Each of the Committees was charged with making regular reports to the Board of Directors. [Plaintiffs allege that the Audit, Compensation, and Governance committees failed to exercise proper oversight over the conduct that led to Dow's problems.]

CHAPTER
10

Friendly Mergers and Acquisitions

MOTIVATING HYPOTHETICAL

One of the many industries thrown into turmoil by computers is the publishing industry. E-books are simply the most visible dagger in the heart of beautifully produced and illustrated books, but changes in publishing go much further, affecting suppliers of paper and ink, typesetters, copyediting services, proofreading services, and so forth, even as new computer-assisted design and illustration specialities emerge. Still, publishing houses can be valuable businesses, as Emily and Caroline Kamm, family owners of Portland-based publishing company Dutch Masters, can attest. Dutch Masters specializes in publishing books on art, dance, theater, and architecture, with high-quality reproductions of major works of art as their trademark. Dutch Masters went public in 1997, using a dual class capitalization, with 13.6 million shares of publicly traded Class A common stock outstanding, and 13.4 million shares of Class B common stock outstanding. Class A shares have one vote per share, and Class B shares have ten votes per share. Notwithstanding the voting disparity, the company's certificate of incorporation provides for equal consideration in the event of a sale or merger. The Kamm sisters own 162 shares of Class A stock and 9.9 million shares of Class B stock. This constitutes 67 percent of the voting power in the corporation.

Lawyers divide business combinations into two categories: "friendly" and "hostile." Friendly deals are negotiated by the respective managers of two companies, while hostile acquisitions take place notwithstanding the resistance of the target company's management. Despite this nomenclature, not all friendly deals are in fact marked by real friendliness. In some instances a board of directors of a target company will agree to a takeover plan because it knows that the acquiror will be able take control anyway, particularly if the target company does not have effective anti-takeover devices in place. For example, the Lotus Company agreed to be acquired by IBM, notwithstanding initial resistance, when IBM's lawyers pointed out that under the Lotus Company's charter, the shareholders could act by written consent pursuant to Delaware General Corporation Law (DGCL) §228, and thus IBM could simply buy a majority of

Lotus's stock, act by written consent to replace the incumbent directors, and have the new directors agree to the acquisition.

Friendly deals predominate in the market for corporate control. Fewer than 2 percent of completed transactions in an average year arise as hostile acquisitions. Yet some of the most contested legal issues involve hostile acquisitions, in part because they often sharply raise the issue of whether the board of directors or the shareholders should have the power to make fundamental decisions about a company's future. Both friendly and hostile deals involve the same duties we have seen in previous chapters (loyalty, care, good faith, disclosure), but because the factual circumstances in which they come into play are different in friendly rather than hostile deals, and the legal analysis of whether there has been a breach differs in the two situations, we will look at each separately.

A. STRUCTURING AN ACQUISITION

There are three ways to structure an acquisition under state statutory law: as a merger or consolidation; as a purchase of the assets and liabilities of the selling company; or as a purchase of 100 percent of the stock of the selling company. While the ultimate effect of using any one of these three mechanisms may be essentially equivalent in any given case — Corporation A acquires Corporation B — there are different implications for a number of important issues depending on which form is used. Thus, there will be important differences in tax treatment; in which shareholders get voting rights to approve or disapprove of the combination; in whether all of the liabilities of the acquired firm get transferred to the acquiring firm; and what remedies there are for dissenting shareholders. This is an area of corporate law where form predominates over substance, and which form is used matters a great deal.

Merger or Consolidation. A merger is a procedure under which one company is entirely subsumed by another through the operation of law. *See* DGCL § 251; Model Business Corporation Act (Model Act) § 11.02. A "merger" occurs when the surviving company is one of the two companies that entered into the process. By contrast, a "consolidation" occurs when two companies use the statutory merger procedure to combine to form a new company. In a merger or consolidation, all of the assets and all of the liabilities of the company or companies being merged out of existence transfer automatically when (a) the boards of directors of both companies approve a plan of merger; (b) the shareholders with voting rights approve the plan of merger; and (c) the surviving company files the plan of merger in its state of incorporation. The consideration used by the acquiring company to pay the selling company may be stock of the acquiring company, bonds, cash, securities of another company (such as a parent corporation), or some combination of these. *See* DGCL § 251(b); Model Act § 11.02(c)(3). If stocks or bonds constitute at least 50 percent of the merger consideration, then this is a nontaxable transaction for the acquiring corporation, for the selling corporation, and for the seller's shareholders. If cash is more than 50 percent of the consideration, the transaction is taxable.

Because a merger or consolidation involves fundamental changes in the target company, shareholders of that company are given the right to vote on the transaction, except in the case of a "short form merger," described below. *See* DGCL § 251(c); Model Act § 11.04(b). In some instances, shareholders of the surviving (acquiring) company are given voting rights, but only if the charter of the surviving company will be amended by the merger, the rights or privileges attached to shares of the surviving company will be changed by the merger, or the surviving company is going to issue new shares of stock equal to 20 percent or more of the common stock outstanding prior to the merger in order to pay for the merger. *See* DGCL § 251(f); Model Act § 11.04(g). The theory behind these limitations is that shareholder votes should be required only "if the transaction fundamentally alters the character of the enterprise or substantially reduces the shareholders' participation in voting or profit distribution." Official Comment, Model Act, § 11.04. It is only when there are amendments to the charter, changes to the features of the shares, or vote dilution greater than 20 percent that the transaction is treated as fundamentally altering the character of the company in which the acquiring company's shareholders are invested.

Even these voting rights for the surviving company's shareholders can be eliminated in some cases, however, by using a "triangular" merger structure. In a triangular merger, the surviving company establishes a wholly owned subsidiary (the parent company owns 100 percent of the stock) and capitalizes the subsidiary with the merger consideration, which can include the parent's stock, cash, bonds, or some combination of stock, cash, and bonds. *See* DGCL § 251(b); Model Act § 11.02(c)(3). The subsidiary and the selling company then enter into a merger agreement, which both boards of directors approve, and the selling company's shareholders vote on the plan. Now the only shareholder of the acquiror that has voting rights is the parent company itself, which has already approved the transaction by virtue of its board's approval, thus eliminating the time, expense, and uncertainty of a shareholder vote.

The voting rights of the target company's shareholders may be eliminated through a "short-form" merger. In this transaction, a parent company owns 90 percent or more of the stock of the target corporation. The parent is allowed to merge the subsidiary into itself using simplified procedures, including the avoidance of a shareholder vote. *See* DGCL § 253; Model Act § 11.05. The simplified procedures include notifying minority shareholders of the target corporation that the merger has occurred, offering them the merger consideration for their shares that the parent has determined is fair, and notifying any dissenting shareholders of their right to an "appraisal" — a judicial proceeding to determine the fair value of the shares. We discuss appraisal proceedings in more detail below.

Generally, it is clear in a merger which shareholders have voting rights and which do not. Thus, the planning issue that arises is to structure the transaction in such a way that a shareholder vote can be avoided where the outcome of the vote seems doubtful or just needlessly expensive or time-consuming. The time factor is of particular importance, because according to SEC rules a shareholder vote must be preceded by the issuance of a proxy statement, and then 20 days must elapse before the vote. Effectively, then, a month is required for a shareholder vote, during which time another company may come forward to try to buy one of the partners, including using a hostile takeover. Thus, transactions are often structured as a triangular merger (or reverse triangular merger) in order to avoid a shareholder vote in order to protect the deal.

Purchase of Assets. A purchase of assets under state law is exactly what it sounds like — that is, a negotiated transaction to purchase specified assets and liabilities of another company. *See* DGCL § 271; Model Act § 12.02. Unlike a merger, the selling company's assets and liabilities do not transfer automatically by operation of law. Rather, the liabilities that are assumed by the purchasing company and those that remain with the selling company are subject to negotiation. One of the advantages of a sale of assets, therefore, is the increased discretion of the parties with regard to the transfer of assets and liabilities. (Note that the doctrine of "successor liability" permits tort claims to be asserted against the successor company notwithstanding the contractual arrangements made by the two companies. In fact, the Model Act permits such claims to be asserted against shareholders of the selling company, pro rata, for five years after the sale of assets. *See* Model Act § 14.07.)

The procedure for accomplishing a sale of assets is as follows: as with a merger, both boards of directors adopt resolutions authorizing the transaction. If the selling company is selling "substantially all" of its assets, then its shareholders have the right to vote to approve the sale. *See* DGCL § 271(a); Model Act § 12.02(a). The Model Act has adopted a fairly clear rule regarding the sale of "substantially all" of the assets of the company. The rule states that neither voting rights nor appraisal rights are available if the company will be left with at least 25 percent of its presale assets and either 25 percent of after-tax operating income or 25 percent of revenues. Model Act § 12.02(a). The Delaware analysis is less precise, since the courts have defined "substantially all" assets through common law adjudication. The Delaware courts emphasize a disjunctive qualitative/quantitative test that looks at both the quantitative importance of the assets being sold to the company and their qualitative importance. In the leading case, the Delaware Chancery Court stated that "all or substantially all" of the assets are involved if the sale is of assets "quantitatively vital to the operation of the corporation and is out of the ordinary and substantially affects the existence and purpose of the corporation." Gimbel v. Signal Cos., 316 A.2d 599, 606 (Del. Ch. 1974).

If the selling company is selling part but not substantially all of its assets, then its shareholders do not have voting rights. The purchasing company's shareholders don't have voting rights in an asset purchase transaction (except, under the Model Act, if the company will issue shares greater than 20 percent of outstanding shares before the purchase in exchange for the assets to be a purchased). *See* Model Act § 6.21(f). In Model Act jurisdictions, dissenting shareholders in the selling company have appraisal rights (discussed below) except if their shares are publicly traded and they are receiving either cash or publicly traded shares. *See* Model Act § 13.02(b). In Delaware dissenting shareholders don't have appraisal rights. A sale of assets for cash is a taxable transaction for the selling shareholders (the cash will be treated as a dividend), while a sale of assets for stock is nontaxable.

Once the shareholders have approved the sale, the assets and liabilities agreed to in negotiations between the two companies are transferred in exchange for the merger consideration. At the same time, the selling board adopts a resolution dissolving the corporation, paying any creditors that have not agreed to the substitution of a new debtor, canceling the outstanding stock, and distributing any remaining proceeds from the merger consideration to the selling company's shareholders.

Purchase of Stock. A purchase of the stock of a company can occur in a friendly transaction, with the support of the target board, but also can occur in a hostile transaction. In both cases, an acquirer gains control of a majority or even all the shares of a company by making an offer directly to shareholders to purchase their shares for a premium — that is, at an above-market price. This procedure is called a "tender offer," and it is regulated in large part by the Williams Act, which is part of federal securities law. We examine the Williams Act briefly in the context of hostile tender offers in Chapter 11.

In a tender offer, shareholders decide individually whether to participate, so this is not a case like a merger or sale of assets where a majority of shareholders acting as a group must approve the transaction for it to go forward. If enough individual shareholders tender their shares, however, an acquirer can gain control of a majority of shares and thus control the company. This is how a tender offer works in a hostile acquisition to go over the target company's board of directors and directly to the target company's shareholders. Although modern acquisitions practice has developed strategies called "rights plans" or "poison pills" that are useful in resisting hostile tender offers, determined acquirors are usually successful.

Tender offers are used in a variety of contexts, including "self-tenders" by a corporation of its own stock, or a tender offer by a controlling shareholder, such as a parent corporation, as the first step in "squeezing out" or "cashing out" minority shareholders. In this latter case, the controlling shareholder will first launch a tender offer in the hope of obtaining more than 90 percent of the shares. After the controlling shareholder acquires more than 90 percent ownership, it can consummate a short-form merger to cash out the remaining minority shareholders. If the controlling shareholder doesn't acquire more than 90 percent ownership because too few shareholders tender, the controlling shareholder will still be in a controlling position and can then effect a regular cash-out merger of the minority shareholders by "persuading" the controlled board of the subsidiary company to adopt a resolution approving an agreement to merge with the parent company. This agreement to merge would then be put to a shareholders' vote in the subsidiary, and if a majority of the minority shareholders vote for the merger, the merger will go forward. You will see this technique in a number of the cases below.

Appraisal. As indicated above, shareholders whose investment is fundamentally changed by a business combination usually are given the right to approve or disapprove the transaction. Shareholders who are given voting rights under state law usually receive the right to challenge the merger price in an appraisal proceeding. *See* DGCL § 262; Model Act § 13.02. Moreover, shareholders in a short-form merger are given appraisal rights even though they don't have voting rights.

An important exception to the availability of appraisal rights occurs when selling shareholders have the right to vote on a merger but start out with stock of a publicly held company and end up with stock of another publicly held company. In this circumstance, the shareholders do not have appraisal rights. The theory behind this exception is that if shareholders do not like the transaction, they can sell their shares in the market. When shareholders have the option of asserting their right to an appraisal, they must vote against the transaction, notify the company within a specified period of time that they might assert their appraisal rights, and then actually assert those rights within the time specified in the controlling statute. *See* DGCL § 262(d); Model Act § 13.22(b)(2)(ii).

In the following case study, you can see some of the tactical issues that are involved in utilizing various statutory approaches to structure an acquisition. Moreover, in the contract provisions included in the case study, you will also see some ways that deals get "protected" from interlopers during the considerable amount of time that can elapse between two boards deciding on a business combination and the transaction closing. We'll see additional examples of those "deal protection devices" in later cases.

DAIMLER-CHRYSLER: A CASE STUDY

One of the most celebrated mergers of all time occurred in 1998, when "Big Three" automaker Chrysler Corporation combined with German powerhouse Daimler Benz AG.[1] Although negotiated and publicized as a "merger of equals," it became apparent fairly quickly after the merger was consummated that Daimler was in control of the combined company.[2] That combined company was never successful, and the merger was undone in 2007, when Chrysler was sold to Cerberus Capital Management, a private equity firm specializing in restructuring troubled companies. The two parties to the original merger are now known as Daimler AG and Chrysler Group LLC. Despite the ultimate failure of the combination, the issues that drove the negotiations and the contracts that ultimately led to one of the biggest corporate combinations in history remain interesting and instructive.

Prelude to Merger: The Kerkorian Threat

On December 14, 1990, Chrysler Corp. announced that Beverly Hills billionaire Kirk Kerkorian had accumulated 22 million shares of its common stock. The stake represented 9.8 percent of Chrysler's 224 million shares outstanding and was purchased at a total cost of $272 million. Kerkorian was then Chrysler's largest shareholder.

Kerkorian stated in an SEC filing that the shares, purchased through Kerkorian's investment firm, Tracinda Corp., were acquired for investment purposes only and resulted from the high regard he held for Chrysler's then CEO and chairman, Lee Iacocca. Upon learning of Kerkorian's purchases on December 14, 1990, Iacocca called a special meeting of Chrysler's board. The board reacted quickly by strengthening Chrysler's poison pill, reducing the trigger from 20 percent to 10 percent. Chrysler officials maintained that the move was simply precautionary, while Kerkorian's spokesman called it an overreaction.

In the period following Kerkorian's initial investment until November 1994, Kerkorian's participation in Chrysler's affairs was muted. It appeared that he would stick to his declared intention to remain a passive investor, as he remained quiet and simply maintained his holdings by purchasing enough shares from new offerings to remain at 9.8 percent.

Chrysler's performance during this time was poor, as the company weathered the economic downturn of the early 1990s. In March 1991, Chrysler cut the 30-cent quarterly dividend in half and engaged in other cost-cutting measures to help

---

1. "AG" is short for Aktiengesellschaft, the German equivalent of a publicly traded corporation in the United States.

2. For an entire book dedicated to this thesis, see Bill Vlasic & Bradley A. Stertz, *Taken for a Ride* (2001).

minimize losses. However, the automaker's fortunes turned around in 1992 as the economy strengthened. Chrysler was poised with a new lineup of vehicles, including the Dodge Viper, the Jeep Grand Cherokee, and a trio of midsize sedans.

In 1992 Iacocca's relationship with Kerkorian blossomed as Iacocca stepped down from his post. Chrysler appointed Robert J. Eaton, a former GM executive, as his successor. Before retiring, Iacocca complained privately that he was being treated shabbily by the board by being forced to move on too quickly. Kerkorian responded by issuing a letter to Chrysler's board threatening to seek board representation to rectify concerns over "Mr. Iacocca's continued leadership role in the company." However, after a meeting with Iacocca, Eaton, and another board member, Kerkorian became convinced that "the interests of Chrysler's shareholders [were] being well represented" and dropped his threat to take a more active role in Chrysler's management. In exchange the board acknowledged that Iacocca would represent Kerkorian's interest on the board.

In November 1994, Kerkorian again began to feel dissatisfied with Chrysler's stock performance. This time he pointed the finger at Chrysler's cash stockpile. In a filing with the SEC and a letter to Chrysler's board, Kerkorian detailed his proposals for increasing the value of his investment, which included instituting a stock repurchase program, effecting a 2-for-1 stock split, and raising the quarterly dividend. He also declared his intention to increase his stake in Chrysler to 15 percent. Accordingly, he asked Chrysler's board to redeem its poison pill takeover defense, which had a 10 percent threshold. This move focused attention on the cash stockpile Chrysler was amassing, which, at the time of Kerkorian's announcement, was approximately $6.6 billion. Chrysler was intent on saving at least $7.5 billion to continue its aggressive product development through the next economic downturn. Many of Chrysler's large investors supported Kerkorian's push for a stock repurchase and an increased dividend.

The Chrysler board met on December 1, 1994, to respond to Kerkorian's proposals. The board appeased Kerkorian by raising Chrysler's quarterly dividend 60 percent — from 25 cents to 40 cents — by announcing a $1 billion stock buyback program, and by raising its poison pill threshold from 10 percent to 15 percent. Chrysler was able to approve these measures and still remain on track to reach its $7.5 billion cash goal by the end of 1995. The move was pleasing overall to Kerkorian, although he continued to hold out hope for a stock split. He subsequently purchased an additional 4 million shares, raising his total share in the company to 10.16 percent. Despite the actions taken by the board, the stock price languished, dropping to a low of $38.25 in late March 1995.

On April 12, 1995, Kerkorian and Iacocca tendered an unsolicited bid for Chrysler at $55 a share. Kerkorian's plan amounted to a leveraged buyout with $12 to $13 billion in loans, $2 billion from Kerkorian's continued equity holdings, another $3 billion from additional equity partners, and $5.5 billion from Chrysler's cash. The $55-a-share offering price represented a 40 percent premium over market price.

Reaction to the offer was mostly negative. Auto workers and management spoke out against Kerkorian's proposal to use up the majority of Chrysler's cash cushion; however, a few institutional investors appeared to embrace the offer. Whatever support Kerkorian may have had initially was withdrawn when it was discovered that he did not have financing arranged prior to launching the bid. He was unable to gain financial backing from banks who do business with Chrysler, because they were concerned, under pressure from Chrysler, about the proposed use of Chrysler's cash.

Kerkorian then shifted his focus to mounting a possible proxy fight. He sent a letter to Robert Eaton proposing that the board let the shareholders vote on his offer, or, alternatively, let them vote on the idea of raising the annual dividend to $5 per share. Kerkorian purchased an additional 1.9 million shares in the open market at $50 to $52, pushing his share of the company to 14.1 percent.

After these transactions, both sides attempted to curry favor with investors in preparation for an increasingly likely proxy fight. On September 5, 1995, Kerkorian hired former Chrysler CFO and board member Jerome B. York to serve as Tracinda Corporation's vice chairman. The move gave Kerkorian a legitimate candidate through which he could pursue board representation. Along with Kerkorian's increased stake in the company, the hiring of York also reestablished Kerkorian's credibility. Chrysler countered by doubling the stock repurchase program to $2 billion and by sending Eaton to meet with Chrysler's big investors. Chrysler even took out newspaper and magazine ads defending the company's record. York countered Chrysler's posturing by focusing attention on Chrysler's vehicle quality problems.

On October 25, 1995, in a letter to Eaton, York demanded a seat on Chrysler's board. York's demand also included a proposal to add two board seats to be filled by persons mutually agreed upon. The letter also asked Chrysler to appoint a committee of outside directors to examine Chrysler's cash management policy, adopt an anti-greenmail bylaw, require shareholder approval of any issuance of blank check preferred stock, and to raise the poison pill threshold from 15 percent to 20 percent. Chrysler's board met the following week and responded by commissioning a 90-day review of its corporate governance policies and board membership.

On February 8, 1996, Kerkorian signed a five-year standstill agreement that prohibited him from purchasing Chrysler shares in exchange for a board seat, filled by Kerkorian aide James D. Aljian; an increase in the stock repurchase program to $3 billion; an increased dividend; and an end to the feud between Iacocca and Chrysler involving his stock options. The agreement appears to have been motivated by findings made during the 90-day review. York said that after visiting other shareholders, it became clear that a settlement was something investors wanted. As agreed, Chrysler boosted the quarterly dividend again on May 16, 1996, to 70 cents. In addition, Chrysler declared a 2-for-1 stock split.

Consolidating Power at Daimler-Benz

At the same time Chrysler was settling with Kerkorian, Daimler's CEO, Jürgen Schrempp, was battling to establish control of his company. Unlike Robert Eaton, however, Schrempp's opponent was inside the company. Helmut Werner was the CEO of Mercedes-Benz, the powerful automobile subsidiary of Daimler. While Schrempp was forced to answer to Daimler's shareholders — including, most significantly, Deutsche Bank — Werner answered to Schrempp, at least nominally. In reality, he had insulated himself from Schrempp and had become the most powerful executive in the company. Schrempp felt the need for change.

At the beginning of 1996, Daimler was in trouble. The company's woes were caused primarily by some unwise acquisitions during the 1980s. When Schrempp assumed office in 1995, his first task was to slash jobs. This did not endear Schrempp to German labor, which held half of the seats on Daimler's supervisory board. (By law, the supervisory board of a German corporation must be equally divided between management representatives and labor representatives, with management having the tie-breaking vote.) Schrempp concluded that retrenchment was the only path to safety.

Schrempp also decided to streamline Daimler's cumbersome governance system. As a corporation, Daimler was managed by a supervisory board and a management board. Schrempp controlled the management board, but the supervisory board was led by Hilmar Kopper, the head of Deutsche Bank, which was Daimler's largest shareholder. (Many German corporations have large banks as substantial shareholders. Some commentators have argued that this concentration of ownership is useful in mitigating the agency costs that inevitably arise in the corporate context.)

But Daimler was not just a corporation, it was a conglomerate, a holding company with numerous subsidiary businesses each reporting to Schrempp. The problem—from Schrempp's standpoint—was that he was required to answer to Kopper and other members of the supervisory board, but the operational decisions were made by Werner and his counterparts at Daimler's other subsidiaries. Within months of taking office, therefore, Schrempp resolved to merge Mercedes into Daimler, thus consolidating control of the most important assets of the company and removing Werner as a rival.

As one would expect, Werner did not go along with this plan quietly. The first battle occurred in the management board, which consisted of eight members, including Schrempp and Werner. After multiple meetings and some backroom negotiations, Schrempp convinced the members of the management board of the merits of his proposal, which prevailed by a 7-to-1 vote (with Werner dissenting). The battle then moved to the supervisory board, but with the management board's approval and Kopper's support, Schrempp made fast work of the supervisory board. Werner resigned, and leadership of the company belonged to Schrempp.

The Search for a Deal

In the wake of this extended battle with Kerkorian, Chrysler's management felt the need to do some forward thinking. Perceiving the trend toward consolidation in the automobile industry, Eaton decided that Chrysler must seek a strategic partner. At the same time, Schrempp was searching for ways to double Daimler's revenues. Further conglomeration was not the answer; after all, he had spent the first part of his tenure overseeing the retrenchment from failed conglomeration efforts. Instead, Schrempp concluded that Daimler must expand its automobile operations by manufacturing not only premium cars but also cars for the masses.

It didn't take long for the companies to find each other. Under Schrempp's predecessor, the two companies had entertained briefly the idea of forming a strategic partnership, but both sides had concluded that the timing was wrong. When Schrempp approached Chrysler in 1997, however, he found a receptive audience. Over the next several months, the parties spoke informally and then more seriously about a merger. Finally, on May 7, 1998, they publicly announced the merger.

Constructing the Deal

Moving from the idea of a merger to the details of a merger is a protracted and sometimes painful process. The business combination agreement that the parties signed on May 7 described the obligations of each party in some detail, thus providing the framework for the transaction. Of course, other contracts and regulatory filings were required to execute the plan, but the combination agreement provided the basic form. The following paragraphs summarize a few of the issues that occupied the parties during their negotiations.

Headquarters. When the parties initiated merger discussions, they left open the question of where the company would be headquartered. This might be viewed as one of the most important decisions to be made, at least for the ongoing health of the combined company. When the time came to actually make the decision, Schrempp insisted that the company reside in Germany. According to *Taken for a Ride,*

> Schrempp knew there was no way he could merge Daimler and Chrysler as an American corporation. His supervisory board would not accept it, his employees would not accept it, and Germany would not accept it. Schrempp's global perspective and ambitions had their limits. He could bring Chrysler into the fold but could never move Daimler out of Germany. In Germany, companies are governed by "codetermination," in which half the members of the supervisory board are elected representatives of the labor force. Codetermination was an absolute tenet of German democracy, one that even Schrempp could not overcome.

Id. at 201.

General Structure. The transaction contemplated three parties: Daimler, Chrysler, and Oppenheim AG, which was referred to as "Newco" in the combination agreement. Newco was formed as a wholly owned subsidiary of Daimler specifically to facilitate this transaction. Newco was to play three critical roles: (1) it would acquire shares of Daimler common stock (as well as American depository shares[3] representing Daimler stock) through an exchange offer; (2) it would acquire shares of Chrysler through an exchange offer; and (3) it would merge with Daimler to create the new Daimler-Chrysler.

Once the shareholders of Daimler and Chrysler approved the merger (on the topic of shareholder approval, see below), Newco was committed to offer an exchange of one share of its own common stock for one "ordinary share" of Daimler stock. In addition, Newco offered to exchange one Newco ADS for one Daimler-Benz ADS. These exchanges together would consolidate all of the ordinary shares of Daimler in Newco and turn the former shareholders of Daimler into shareholders of Newco. In addition, Newco would change its name to "Daimler Chrysler Aktiengesellschaft."

"As promptly as possible following the date" of the combination agreement, Newco was to appoint an exchange agent in the United States who would form and hold all of the stock of a Delaware corporation known as "Chrysler Merger Sub." Immediately after consummation of the exchange offer discussed above, Chrysler Merger Sub would be merged into Chrysler, with Chrysler remaining as

---

3. "American depository shares" (ADSs) are securities that are created by non-U.S. companies to facilitate ownership and trading of the company's shares by U.S. investors. The shares are issued by a U.S. commercial bank, which acts as the depository, and the shares represent a bundle of control and financial rights that are associated with underlying shares of a company's stock. The underlying shares are held by a correspondent bank in the home country of the company. ADSs are evidenced by physical certificates called American depository receipts, or ADRs.

the surviving company. The terms of that merger would require the conversion of shares of Chrysler common stock into the right to receive Newco ADSs.

Meanwhile, the exchange agent would become the sole shareholder of the surviving company (Chrysler). This was to be only temporary, of course, as the parties wanted Chrysler and Daimler to be consolidated into the same firm. As soon as possible after the merger became effective, therefore, Newco would issue its own ordinary shares to the exchange agent — these are the shares that would underlie the Newco ADSs — and the exchange agent would in turn transfer all shares of Chrysler common stock to Newco.

The most difficult aspect of the merger agreement is the provision that dictates the value of Chrysler shares under the exchange just described. Prior to the Chrysler merger, the former shareholders of Daimler would be 100 percent owners of Newco. After the Chrysler merger, the former shareholders of Daimler and the former shareholders of Chrysler would share ownership of Newco. Their relative ownership interests would be dictated by the relative values of the two companies, which were negotiated in the merger talks.

The thing that makes the valuation provision so complicated is the lag time between the date of the negotiations and the date of the exchange. Between those two dates, the market values of the two companies could be affected by myriad factors. The valuation provision attempts to anticipate and account for changes. Of course, the currency here is Newco shares. Under the exchange offer, every ordinary share of Daimler was worth one share of Newco. The relative values of Daimler and Chrysler, therefore, were dictated by the exchange rate of Chrysler shares for Newco shares. The combined effect of the merger and the exchange offer was that (1) Newco owned all of the shares of Chrysler *and* all of the shares of Daimler; and (2) the former shareholders of Chrysler and Daimler together owned all of the shares of Newco.

Only one step remained to complete the transaction: the merger of Daimler into Newco, with Newco (which, as noted above, had been renamed "Daimler Chrysler Aktiengesellschaft") as the surviving corporation. Under the German stock corporation law — as under corporation law in the United States — Newco succeeded to all rights, assets, liabilities, and obligations of Daimler by operation of law. As part of the merger, all shareholders who still held shares of Daimler (that is, those who did not exchange their shares pursuant to the exchange offer) would automatically become shareholders of Newco at the same one-to-one conversion rate that prevailed in the exchange offer.

Shareholder Approval. Two shareholders needed to be convinced. On the Chrysler side, Tracinda Corporation still controlled a substantial percentage of Chrysler's shares. On the Daimler side, Deutsche Bank AG was a substantial shareholder and creditor. In addition to these major shareholders, the parties needed to obtain the approval of at least 90 percent of the outstanding shares of each company to qualify for the favorable pooling-of-interests accounting treatment.[4]

---

4. As its description implies, the effect of "pooling of interests" accounting is to treat two merged entities as if they had never been separate. This approach allows the company that survives a merger to carry forward all assets at their historical cost. Contrast this to "purchase" accounting, which treats a merger as a purchase of one entity by another and thus revalues the assets of the acquired entity. Although many companies found "pooling of interests" accounting more favorable, the Financial Accounting Standards Board eliminated it as an option in 2001.

The combination agreement required Chrysler to hold a special shareholder meeting "as promptly as practicable after the F-4 Registration Statement is declared effective under the Securities Act." Daimler, in turn, was required to schedule a shareholder meeting "so that the vote necessary to obtain the Chrysler Stockholder Approval occurs simultaneously with the Daimler-Benz Stockholder Approval."

Post-Merger Governance Structure. With the decision to form the new company in Germany, a host of other corporate governance issues fell into place automatically. In accordance with German company law, the new company would have a two-tiered governance structure comprising a supervisory board (*Aufsichtsrat*) and a management board (*Vorstand*). Under the German Co-Determination Law of 1976, half of the supervisory board must be composed of representatives elected by the company's employees. In addition, the combination agreement specifies that the remaining representatives would be divided equally between Daimler and Chrysler. The parties also agreed that the chairman of Newco's supervisory board would be the then-current chairman of Daimler's supervisory board.

Control over the management board was also dictated by the combination agreement:

> The Management Board (*Vorstand*) of Newco AG shall consist of 18 members. In general, 50% of such members shall be those designated by Chrysler, and 50% of such members shall be those designated by Daimler-Benz, and there will be two additional members with responsibility for Daimler-Benz's non-automotive businesses.

Deal Protection Devices. As in any well-constructed merger, the combination agreement provided various mechanisms to increase the likelihood that the transaction would actually be consummated. The most conspicuous provision of the combination agreement in this regard was the "no-shop" clause, which prohibited both parties from soliciting, initiating, or encouraging the making of a takeover proposal or participating in discussions regarding a takeover proposal. This included a prohibition on furnishing information to prospective acquirors. An exception arises "if the party's Board of Directors (or the Management Board (*Vorstand*) in the case of Daimler-Benz) determines in good faith, after receiving the advice of outside counsel, that its failure to do so may result in a breach of its fiduciary duties to its stockholders under applicable law." This is the provision commonly known as a "fiduciary out."

Conclusion and Denouement

The creation of Daimler-Benz was completed on November 17, 1998, when the company's shares began trading on the New York Stock Exchange. The shareholders of both corporations had overwhelmingly approved the combination (98 percent for Chrysler and 99 percent for Daimler). A short time after the shareholder meetings, Standard & Poors announced that Chrysler would be removed from the S&P 500 stock index and the new Daimler-Benz would not be selected to replace it — only American companies are allowed in this club. The stock prices of both Chrysler and Daimler fell on this news in anticipation of index funds selling their shares. Within a short time after the combination, it became apparent that this was not the "merger of equals" that Robert Eaton had demanded, but a takeover by Schrempp. This revelation led to a class action lawsuit by institutions who had been investors in Chrysler and a separate lawsuit by Kerkorian. Both lawsuits claimed that Daimler had misrepresented the deal as a "merger of equals," and that if it had been clear that Daimler was acquiring Chrysler, the Chrysler shareholders would have insisted on a control premium. Daimler-Chrysler settled the class action claims for $300 million in August 2003, but Kerkorian's claim for losses of $8 billion proceeded to trial, leading to a victory for Daimler-Chrysler on all counts that was upheld on appeal. Tracinda Corp. v. Daimler Chrysler AG, 502 F.3d 212 (3d Cir. 2007).

Litigation was not the only bump in the road for Daimler Chrysler. Difficulties integrating the two companies led to disappointing results, particularly on the Chrysler side. When Chrysler's losses in 2006 hit $1.5 billion, Daimler decided to call it mostly quits, selling an 80.1 percent share of the company for $7.4 billion to Cerebus Capital Management, L.P., a private equity firm. Most of that money went into paying Chrysler's debts, and Daimler was required to pay into the Chrysler pension fund and pay closing costs to get the deal done. So Daimler ended up paying $650 million to transfer this ownership interest to Cerebus.

The private equity firm model uses investors' capital to purchase undervalued and underperforming companies and, as Cerebus puts it, "to transform them into industry leaders," at which point the companies are brought back to the public capital markets with a public stock flotation. But the timing was bad for Cerebus: Its purchase of Chrysler from Daimler was concluded in 2007, just as problems in the financial markets were becoming evident and car sales in the United States were collapsing. Chrysler's losses of $8 billion in 2008 compressed Cerebus's time frame for reselling, which would typically occur three to five years after a private equity investment. Thus, Cerebus looked for an investor for a strategic alliance that would provide Chrysler with a more global presence and greater expertise in smaller, more fuel-efficient vehicles. This search led to serious discussions with Fiat, and as Chrysler's financial position became more dire in 2009, those discussions intensified. *See* In re: Chrysler LLC, 405 B.R. 94, 90 (Bankr. S.D.N.Y. 2009).

Meanwhile, Chrysler's deteriorating financial condition required U.S. government assistance, in the form of a $4 billion loan from the U.S. Treasury in December 2008, and then an additional $8.5 billion injection of U.S. cash early in the administration of President Barack Obama. The first loan was conditioned on Chrysler developing strategies for its long-term viability, and of the strategies proposed to the government's Auto Task Force, a strategic partnership with Fiat was concluded to be the most promising alternative. Negotiations with Fiat and Chrysler stakeholders ultimately produced a sale of 35 percent of Chrysler to Fiat, with an option to bring Fiat's ownership to 55 percent if certain performance benchmarks were met. The contract of sale was dated April 30, 2009—the same day Chrysler filed for bankruptcy, using what's called a § 363 plan of reorganization as its mechanism for entering and emerging from bankruptcy in 41 days. (For discussion of the bankruptcy implications of Chrysler's (and GM's) use of the § 363 mechanism on Chapter 11 bankruptcies, see Ralph Brubaker & Charles Jordan Tabb, *Bankruptcy Reorganizations and the Troubling Legacy of Chrysler and GM*, 2010 U. Il. L. Rev. 1375-1410.) At that point 55 percent of Chrysler was transferred to a voluntary employee benefit association (VEBA) to settle a class action brought by the United Auto Workers against Cerebus for failing to make good on health care promises to

Chrysler's retirees. Remaining ownership was held by the U.S. and Canadian governments. Daimler, meanwhile, in a somewhat later transaction, was able to "redeem" its 19.9 percent stake in Chrysler by agreeing to pay $600 million into Chrysler's pension fund over three years.

Three years later, the strategic alliance with Fiat seemed to be a real success. Integration of the two companies' design and engineering functions goes forward, with excellent product innovation on both sides of the Atlantic, and sales are booming. In April 2012, Chrysler's sales were up 20 percent as compared to April 2011, and the company enjoyed its twenty-fifth consecutive month of year-over-year sales increases (comparing each month to the same month of the prior year). Sales of Fiat cars in the United States, which was part of Fiat's interest in this transaction, were up 336 percent as compared to the year prior. Still, as Daimler's wild ride shows, results in the automotive industry are highly cyclical, so we can be cautiously optimistic, at most, about the continuing success of this international strategic partnership.

QUESTIONS

1. In a transaction of this size and complexity, how do the parties assure themselves that there are no "skeletons on the closet"? For example, how does each party know that the other is not hiding a potentially large liability? What specific kinds of future liabilities must be considered in structuring the agreement?

2. In the wake of highly publicized accounting scandals, wouldn't the parties be concerned about the possibility that the other side is fabricating or materially misstating its financial statements? What kinds of provisions may be included in the merger agreement to protect against this concern?

3. What issues arise with respect to compliance with the various laws governing both companies? Does Chrysler simply trust Daimler to ensure that all of the requirements of German law are met? And vice versa?

4. The parties included in the combination agreement an obligation on all sides to use "reasonable best efforts" to consummate the transaction. Why would the parties think such a provision necessary or useful?

B.   FIDUCIARY DUTIES IN FRIENDLY TRANSACTIONS

As in any transaction in which the directors make decisions that affect the shareholders of the company, directors authorizing a merger, sale of assets, or sale of stock must fulfill their duties of care and loyalty in evaluating and approving the transaction, and they must generally act in good faith. They also must fulfill their fiduciary and federal securities law duties to disclose all material facts to the shareholders in the proxy statement soliciting shareholders' votes, or in the notice the company sends out describing the transaction, as in a short-form merger.

Courts calibrate their review of director actions to fit the context. In an arm's length transaction between two unrelated companies, as in Smith v. Van Gorkom (Chapter 7), courts normally apply the (usually) deferential business judgment rule. This decision seems to reflect some faith in the ability of shareholders to protect themselves through the required vote. When shareholders are unable to protect themselves — most importantly, in a transaction involving a controlling shareholder — courts apply a more searching standard of review to the merger. As you might imagine, the Delaware courts have struggled mightily to develop appropriate standards for the myriad cases involving controlling shareholders, and much of our study of fiduciary duties in friendly mergers focuses on this challenging factual context.

1. The Entire Fairness Standard

The following is the foundational Delaware case for evaluation of fiduciary duties in controlling shareholder transactions. As we saw in Chapter 8, the "entire fairness" standard created in *Weinberger* is central to all conflict of interest cases, but it has special resonance in the takeover context. While *Weinberger* is a relatively old decision (1983), clearly its analysis is still vital, and thus it bears careful attention. *Weinberger* is important not only for its analysis of the duty of loyalty issues, here inherent in a negotiated merger between a parent/controlling shareholder and its minority-owned subsidiary, but also for its discussion of the remedy of appraisal for shareholders who don't agree with a transaction, and therefore vote against it. Note in particular the court's discussion of the "exclusivity" of the appraisal remedy. We'll return to that issue in Section C of this chapter.

WEINBERGER v. UOP, INC.

457 A.2d 701
Supreme Court of Delaware (en banc)
February 1, 1983

MOORE, Justice.

This post-trial appeal was reheard en banc from a decision of the Court of Chancery. It was brought by the class action plaintiff below, a former shareholder of UOP, Inc., who challenged the elimination of UOP's minority shareholders by a cash-out merger between UOP and its majority owner, The Signal Companies, Inc. Originally, the defendants in this action were Signal, UOP, certain officers and directors of those companies, and UOP's investment banker, Lehman Brothers Kuhn Loeb, Inc. The present Chancellor held that the terms of the merger were fair to the plaintiff and the other minority shareholders of UOP. Accordingly, he entered judgment in favor of the defendants. [This appeal followed.] . . .

I.

The facts found by the trial court, pertinent to the issues before us, are supported by the record, and we draw from them as set out in the Chancellor's opinion.

Signal is a diversified, technically based company operating through various subsidiaries. Its stock is publicly traded on the New York, Philadelphia and Pacific Stock Exchanges. UOP, formerly known as Universal Oil Products Company, was a diversified industrial company engaged in various lines of business, including petroleum and petro-chemical services and related products, construction, fabricated metal products, transportation equipment products, chemicals and plastics, and other products and services including land development, lumber products and waste disposal. Its stock was publicly held and listed on the New York Stock Exchange.

In 1974 Signal sold one of its wholly-owned subsidiaries for $420,000,000 in cash. *See* Gimbel v. Signal Companies, Inc., Del. Ch., 316 A.2d 599, *aff'd*, Del. Supr., 316 A.2d 619 (1974). While looking to invest this cash surplus, Signal became interested in UOP as a possible acquisition. Friendly negotiations ensued, and Signal proposed to acquire a controlling interest in UOP at a price of $19 per share. UOP's representatives sought $25 per share. In the arm's length bargaining that followed, an understanding was reached whereby Signal agreed to purchase from UOP 1,500,000 shares of UOP's authorized but unissued stock at $21 per share.

This purchase was contingent upon Signal making a successful cash tender offer for 4,300,000 publicly held shares of UOP, also at a price of $21 per share. This combined method of acquisition permitted Signal to acquire 5,800,000 shares of stock, representing 50.5% of UOP's outstanding shares. The UOP board of directors advised the company's shareholders that it had no objection to Signal's tender offer at that price. Immediately before the announcement of the tender offer, UOP's common stock had been trading on the New York Stock Exchange at a fraction under $14 per share.

The negotiations between Signal and UOP occurred during April 1975, and the resulting tender offer was greatly oversubscribed. However, Signal limited its total purchase of the tendered shares so that, when coupled with the stock bought from UOP, it had achieved its goal of becoming a 50.5% shareholder of UOP.

Although UOP's board consisted of thirteen directors, Signal nominated and elected only six. Of these, five were either directors or employees of Signal. The sixth, a partner in the banking firm of Lazard Freres & Co., had been one of Signal's representatives in the negotiations and bargaining with UOP concerning the tender offer and purchase price of the UOP shares.

However, the president and chief executive officer of UOP retired during 1975, and Signal caused him to be replaced by James V. Crawford, a long-time employee and senior executive vice president of one of Signal's wholly-owned subsidiaries. Crawford succeeded his predecessor on UOP's board of directors and also was made a director of Signal.

By the end of 1977 Signal basically was unsuccessful in finding other suitable investment candidates for its excess cash, and by February 1978 considered that it had no other realistic acquisitions available to it on a friendly basis. Once again its attention turned to UOP.

The trial court found that at the instigation of certain Signal management personnel, including William W. Walkup, its board chairman, and Forrest N. Shumway, its president, a feasibility study was made concerning the possible acquisition of the balance of UOP's outstanding shares. This study was performed by two Signal officers, Charles S. Arledge, vice president (director of planning), and Andrew J. Chitiea, senior vice president (chief financial officer). Messrs. Walkup, Shumway, Arledge and Chitiea were all directors of UOP in addition to their membership on the Signal board.

Arledge and Chitiea concluded that it would be a good investment for Signal to acquire the remaining 49.5% of UOP shares at any price up to $24 each. Their report was discussed between Walkup and Shumway who, along with Arledge, Chitiea and Brewster L. Arms, internal counsel for Signal, constituted Signal's senior management. In particular, they talked about the proper price to be paid if the acquisition was pursued, purportedly keeping in mind that as UOP's majority shareholder, Signal owed a fiduciary responsibility to both its own stockholders as well as to UOP's minority. It was ultimately agreed that a meeting of Signal's executive committee would be called to propose that Signal acquire the remaining outstanding stock of UOP through a cash-out merger in the range of $20 to $21 per share.

The executive committee meeting was set for February 28, 1978. As a courtesy, UOP's president, Crawford, was invited to attend, although he was not a member of Signal's executive committee. On his arrival, and prior to the meeting, Crawford was asked to meet privately with Walkup and Shumway. He was then told of Signal's plan to acquire full ownership of UOP and was asked for his reaction to the proposed price range of $20 to $21 per share. Crawford said he thought such a price would be "generous," and that it was certainly one which should be submitted to UOP's minority shareholders for their ultimate consideration. He stated, however, that Signal's 100% ownership could cause internal problems at UOP. He believed that employees would have to be given some assurance of their future place in a fully-owned Signal subsidiary. Otherwise, he feared the departure of essential personnel. Also, many of UOP's key employees had stock option incentive programs which would be wiped out by a merger. Crawford therefore urged that some adjustment would have to be made, such as providing a comparable incentive in Signal's shares, if after the merger he was to maintain his quality of personnel and efficiency at UOP.

Thus, Crawford voiced no objection to the $20 to $21 price range, nor did he suggest that Signal should consider paying more than $21 per share for the minority interests. Later, at the executive committee meeting the same factors were discussed, with Crawford repeating the position he earlier took with Walkup and Shumway. Also considered was the 1975 tender offer and the fact that it had been greatly oversubscribed at $21 per share. For many reasons, Signal's management concluded that the acquisition of UOP's minority shares provided the solution to a number of its business problems.

Thus, it was the consensus that a price of $20 to $21 per share would be fair to both Signal and the minority shareholders of UOP. Signal's executive committee authorized its management "to negotiate" with UOP "for a cash acquisition of the minority ownership in UOP, Inc., with the intention of presenting a proposal to [Signal's] board of directors . . . on March 6, 1978." Immediately after this February 28, 1978, meeting, Signal issued a press release stating:

> The Signal Companies, Inc. and UOP, Inc. are conducting negotiations for the acquisition for cash by Signal of the 49.5 per cent of UOP which it does not presently own, announced Forrest N. Shumway, president and chief executive officer of Signal, and James V. Crawford, UOP president.

> Price and other terms of the proposed transaction have not yet been finalized and would be subject to approval of the boards of directors of Signal and UOP, scheduled to meet early next week, the stockholders of UOP and certain federal agencies.

The announcement also referred to the fact that the closing price of UOP's common stock on that day was $14.50 per share.

Two days later, on March 2, 1978, Signal issued a second press release stating that its management would recommend a price in the range of $20 to $21 per share for UOP's 49.5% minority interest. This announcement referred to Signal's earlier statement that "negotiations" were being conducted for the acquisition of the minority shares.

Between Tuesday, February 28, 1978 and Monday, March 6, 1978, a total of four business days, Crawford spoke by telephone with all of UOP's non-Signal, *i.e.*, outside, directors. Also during that period, Crawford retained Lehman Brothers to render a fairness opinion as to the price offered the minority for its stock. He gave two reasons for this choice. First, the time schedule between the announcement and the board meetings was short (by then only three business days) and since Lehman Brothers had been acting as UOP's investment banker for many years, Crawford felt that it would be in the best position to respond on such brief notice. Second, James W. Glanville, a long-time director of UOP and a partner in Lehman Brothers, had acted as a financial advisor to UOP for many years. Crawford believed that Glanville's familiarity with UOP, as a member of its board, would also be of assistance in enabling Lehman Brothers to render a fairness opinion within the existing time constraints.

Crawford telephoned Glanville, who gave his assurance that Lehman Brothers had no conflicts that would prevent it from accepting the task. Glanville's immediate personal reaction was that a price of $20 to $21 would certainly be fair, since it represented almost a 50% premium over UOP's market price. Glanville sought a $250,000 fee for Lehman Brothers' services, but Crawford thought this too much. After further discussions Glanville finally agreed that Lehman Brothers would render its fairness opinion for $150,000.

During this period Crawford also had several telephone contacts with Signal officials. In only one of them, however, was the price of the shares discussed. In a conversation with Walkup, Crawford advised that as a result of his communications with UOP's non-Signal directors, it was his feeling that the price would have to be the top of the proposed range, or $21 per share, if the approval of UOP's outside directors was to be obtained. But again, he did not seek any price higher than $21.

Glanville assembled a three-man Lehman Brothers team to do the work on the fairness opinion. These persons examined relevant documents and information concerning UOP, including its annual reports and its Securities and Exchange Commission filings from 1973 through 1976, as well as its audited financial statements for 1977, its interim reports to shareholders, and its recent and historical market prices and trading volumes. In addition, on Friday, March 3, 1978, two members of the Lehman Brothers team flew to UOP's headquarters in Des Plaines, Illinois, to perform a "due diligence" visit, during the course of which they interviewed Crawford as well as UOP's general counsel, its chief financial officer, and other key executives and personnel.

As a result, the Lehman Brothers team concluded that "the price of either $20 or $21 would be a fair price for the remaining shares of UOP." They telephoned this impression to Glanville, who was spending the weekend in Vermont.

On Monday morning, March 6, 1978, Glanville and the senior member of the Lehman Brothers team flew to Des Plaines to attend the scheduled UOP directors meeting. Glanville looked over the assembled information during the flight. The two had with them the draft of a "fairness opinion letter" in which the price had been left blank. Either during or immediately prior to the directors' meeting, the two-page "fairness opinion letter" was typed in final form and the price of $21 per share was inserted.

On March 6, 1978, both the Signal and UOP boards were convened to consider the proposed merger. Telephone communications were maintained between the two meetings. Walkup, Signal's board chairman, and also a UOP director, attended UOP's meeting with Crawford in order to present Signal's position and answer any questions that UOP's non-Signal directors might have. Arledge and Chitiea, along with Signal's other designees on UOP's board, participated by conference telephone. All of UOP's outside directors attended the meeting either in person or by conference telephone.

First, Signal's board unanimously adopted a resolution authorizing Signal to propose to UOP a cash merger of $21 per share as outlined in a certain merger agreement and other supporting documents. This proposal required that the merger be approved by a majority of UOP's outstanding minority shares voting at the stockholders meeting at which the merger would be considered, and that the minority shares voting in favor of the merger, when coupled with Signal's 50.5% interest would have to comprise at least two-thirds of all UOP shares. Otherwise the proposed merger would be deemed disapproved.

UOP's board then considered the proposal. Copies of the agreement were delivered to the directors in attendance, and other copies had been forwarded earlier to the directors participating by telephone. They also had before them UOP financial data for 1974-1977, UOP's most recent financial statements, market price information, and budget projections for 1978. In addition they had Lehman Brothers' hurriedly prepared fairness opinion letter finding the price of $21 to be fair. Glanville, the Lehman Brothers partner, and UOP director, commented on the information that had gone into preparation of the letter.

Signal also suggests that the Arledge-Chitiea feasibility study, indicating that a price of up to $24 per share would be a "good investment" for Signal, was discussed at the UOP directors' meeting. The Chancellor made no such finding, and our independent review of the record, detailed *infra*, satisfies us by a preponderance of the evidence that there was no discussion of this document at UOP's board meeting. Furthermore, it is clear beyond peradventure that nothing in that report was ever disclosed to UOP's minority shareholders prior to their approval of the merger.

After consideration of Signal's proposal, Walkup and Crawford left the meeting to permit a free and uninhibited exchange between UOP's non-Signal directors. Upon their return a resolution to accept Signal's offer was then proposed and adopted. While Signal's men on UOP's board participated in various aspects of the meeting, they abstained from voting. However, the minutes show that each of them "if voting would have voted yes."

On March 7, 1978, UOP sent a letter to its shareholders advising them of the action taken by UOP's board with respect to Signal's offer. This document pointed out, among other things, that on February 28, 1978 "both companies had announced negotiations were being conducted."

Despite the swift board action of the two companies, the merger was not submitted to UOP's shareholders until their annual meeting on May 26, 1978. In the notice of that meeting and proxy statement sent to shareholders in May, UOP's management and board urged that the merger be approved. The proxy statement also advised:

> The price was determined after *discussions* between James V. Crawford, a director of Signal and Chief Executive Officer of UOP, and officers of Signal which took place during meetings on February 28, 1978, and in the course of several subsequent telephone conversations. (Emphasis added.)

In the original draft of the proxy statement the word "negotiations" had been used rather than "discussions." However, when the Securities and Exchange Commission sought details of the "negotiations" as part of its review of these materials, the term was deleted and the word "discussions" was substituted. The proxy statement indicated that the vote of UOP's board in approving the merger had been unanimous. It also advised the shareholders that Lehman Brothers had given its opinion that the merger price of $21 per share was fair to UOP's minority. However, it did not disclose the hurried method by which this conclusion was reached.

As of the record date of UOP's annual meeting, there were 11,488,302 shares of UOP common stock outstanding, 5,688,302 of which were owned by the minority. At the meeting only 56%, or 3,208,652, of the minority shares were voted. Of these, 2,953,812, or 51.9% of the total minority, voted for the merger, and 254,840 voted against it. When Signal's stock was added to the minority shares voting in favor, a total of 76.2% of UOP's outstanding shares approved the merger while only 2.2% opposed it.

By its terms the merger became effective on May 26, 1978, and each share of UOP's stock held by the minority was automatically converted into a right to receive $21 cash.

II.

A.

A primary issue mandating reversal is the preparation by two UOP directors, Arledge and Chitiea, of their feasibility study for the exclusive use and benefit of Signal. This document was of obvious significance to both Signal and UOP. Using UOP data, it described the advantages to Signal of ousting the minority at a price range of $21-$24 per share. Mr. Arledge, one of the authors, outlined the benefits to Signal: [Handwritten comments of Mr. Arledge are indicated in parentheses.]

PURPOSE OF THE MERGER

1) Provides an outstanding investment opportunity for Signal — (Better than any recent acquisition we have seen.)
2) Increases Signal's earnings.

3) Facilitates the flow of resources between Signal and its subsidiaries — (Big factor — works both ways.)

4) Provides cost savings potential for Signal and UOP.

5) Improves the percentage of Signal's "operating earnings" as opposed to "holding company earnings."

6) Simplifies the understanding of Signal.

7) Facilitates technological exchange among Signal's subsidiaries.

8) Eliminates potential conflicts of interest.

Having written those words, solely for the use of Signal, it is clear from the record that neither Arledge nor Chitiea shared this report with their fellow directors of UOP. We are satisfied that no one else did either. This conduct hardly meets the fiduciary standards applicable to such a transaction. While Mr. Walkup, Signal's chairman of the board and a UOP director, attended the March 6, 1978 UOP board meeting and testified at trial that he had discussed the Arledge-Chitiea report with the UOP directors at this meeting, the record does not support this assertion. Perhaps it is the result of some confusion on Mr. Walkup's part. In any event Mr. Shumway, Signal's president, testified that he made sure the Signal outside directors had this report prior to the March 6, 1978 Signal board meeting, but he did not testify that the Arledge-Chitiea report was also sent to UOP's outside directors.

Mr. Crawford, UOP's president, could not recall that any documents, other than a draft of the merger agreement, were sent to UOP's directors before the March 6, 1978 UOP meeting. Mr. Chitiea, an author of the report, testified that it was made available to Signal's directors, but to his knowledge it was not circulated to the outside directors of UOP. He specifically testified that he "didn't share" that information with the outside directors of UOP with whom he served. . . .

Actually, it appears that a three-page summary of figures was given to all UOP directors. Its first page is identical to one page of the Arledge-Chitiea report, but this dealt with nothing more than a justification of the $21 price. Significantly, the contents of this three-page summary are what the minutes reflect Mr. Walkup told the UOP board. However, nothing contained in either the minutes or this three-page summary reflects Signal's study regarding the $24 price.

The Arledge-Chitiea report speaks for itself in supporting the Chancellor's finding that a price of up to $24 was a "good investment" for Signal. It shows that a return on the investment at $21 would be 15.7% versus 15.5% at $24 per share. This was a difference of only two-tenths of one percent, while it meant over $17,000,000 to the minority. Under such circumstances, paying UOP's minority shareholders $24 would have had relatively little long-term effect on Signal, and the Chancellor's findings concerning the benefit to Signal, even at a price of $24, were obviously correct. Levitt v. Bouvier, Del. Supr., 287 A.2d 671, 673 (1972).

Certainly, this was a matter of material significance to UOP and its shareholders. Since the study was prepared by two UOP directors, using UOP information for the exclusive benefit of Signal, and nothing whatever was done to disclose it to the outside UOP directors or the minority shareholders, a question of breach of fiduciary duty arises. This problem occurs because there were common Signal-UOP directors participating, at least to some extent, in the UOP board's decision-making processes without full disclosure of the conflicts they faced.[7]

B.

In assessing this situation, the Court of Chancery was required to:

> examine what information defendants had and to measure it against what they gave to the minority stockholders, in a context in which "complete candor" is required. In other words, the limited function of the Court was to determine whether defendants had disclosed all information in their possession germane to the transaction in issue. And by "germane" we mean, for present purposes, information such as a reasonable shareholder would consider important in deciding whether to sell or retain stock.
>
> . . . Completeness, not adequacy, is both the norm and the mandate under present circumstances.

Lynch v. Vickers Energy Corp., Del. Supr., 383 A.2d 278, 281 (1977) (*Lynch I*).

This is merely stating in another way the long-existing principle of Delaware law that these Signal designated directors on UOP's board still owed UOP and its shareholders an uncompromising duty of loyalty. The classic language of Guth v. Loft, Inc., Del. Supr., 5 A.2d 503, 510 (1939), requires no embellishment:

> A public policy, existing through the years, and derived from a profound knowledge of human characteristics and motives, has established a rule that demands of a corporate officer or director, peremptorily and inexorably, the most scrupulous observance of his duty, not only affirmatively to protect the interests of the corporation committed to his charge, but also to refrain from doing anything that would work injury to the corporation, or to deprive it of profit or advantage which his skill and ability might properly bring to it, or to enable it to make in the reasonable and lawful exercise of its powers. The rule that requires an undivided and unselfish loyalty to the corporation demands that there shall be no conflict between duty and self-interest.

Given the absence of any attempt to structure this transaction on an arm's length basis, Signal cannot escape the effects of the conflicts it faced, particularly when its designees on UOP's board did not totally abstain from participation in the matter. There is no "safe harbor" for such divided loyalties in Delaware. When directors of a Delaware corporation are on both sides of a transaction, they are required to demonstrate their utmost good faith and the most scrupulous inherent fairness of the bargain. Gottlieb v. Heyden Chemical Corp., Del. Supr., 91 A.2d 57, 57-58 (1952). The requirement of fairness is unflinching in its demand that where one stands on both sides of a transaction, he has the burden

---

7. Although perfection is not possible, or expected, the result here could have been entirely different if UOP had appointed an independent negotiating committee of its outside directors to deal with Signal at arm's length. *See, e.g.*, Harriman v. E.I. duPont de Nemours & Co., 411 F. Supp. 133 (D. Del.1975). Since fairness in this context can be equated to conduct by a theoretical, wholly independent, board of directors acting upon the matter before them, it is unfortunate that this course apparently was neither considered nor pursued. Johnston v. Greene, Del. Supr., 121 A.2d 919, 925 (1956). Particularly in a parent-subsidiary context, a showing that the action taken was as though each of the contending parties had in fact exerted its bargaining power against the other at arm's length is strong evidence that the transaction meets the test of fairness. Getty Oil Co. v. Skelly Oil Co., Del. Supr., 267 A.2d 883, 886 (1970); Puma v. Marriott, Del. Ch., 283 A.2d 693, 696 (1971).

of establishing its entire fairness, sufficient to pass the test of careful scrutiny by the courts. . . .

There is no dilution of this obligation where one holds dual or multiple directorships, as in a parent-subsidiary context. Levien v. Sinclair Oil Corp., Del. Ch., 261 A.2d 911, 915 (1969). Thus, individuals who act in a dual capacity as directors of two corporations, one of whom is parent and the other subsidiary, owe the same duty of good management to both corporations, and in the absence of an independent negotiating structure (see note 7, *supra*), or the directors' total abstention from any participation in the matter, this duty is to be exercised in light of what is best for both companies. Warshaw v. Calhoun, Del. Supr., 221 A.2d 487, 492 (1966). The record demonstrates that Signal has not met this obligation.

C.

The concept of fairness has two basic aspects: fair dealing and fair price. The former embraces questions of when the transaction was timed, how it was initiated, structured, negotiated, disclosed to the directors, and how the approvals of the directors and the stockholders were obtained. The latter aspect of fairness relates to the economic and financial considerations of the proposed merger, including all relevant factors: assets, market value, earnings, future prospects, and any other elements that affect the intrinsic or inherent value of a company's stock. . . . However, the test for fairness is not a bifurcated one as between fair dealing and price. All aspects of the issue must be examined as a whole since the question is one of entire fairness. However, in a non-fraudulent transaction we recognize that price may be the preponderant consideration outweighing other features of the merger. Here, we address the two basic aspects of fairness separately because we find reversible error as to both.

D.

Part of fair dealing is the obvious duty of candor required by *Lynch I, supra.* . . . With the well-established Delaware law on the subject, and the Court of Chancery's findings of fact here, it is inevitable that the obvious conflicts posed by Arledge and Chitiea's preparation of their "feasibility study," derived from UOP information, for the sole use and benefit of Signal, cannot pass muster.

The Arledge-Chitiea report is but one aspect of the element of fair dealing. How did this merger evolve? It is clear that it was entirely initiated by Signal. The serious time constraints under which the principals acted were all set by Signal. It had not found a suitable outlet for its excess cash and considered UOP a desirable investment, particularly since it was now in a position to acquire the whole company for itself. For whatever reasons, and they were only Signal's, the entire transaction was presented to and approved by UOP's board within four business days. Standing alone, this is not necessarily indicative of any lack of fairness by a majority shareholder. It was what occurred, or more properly, what did not occur, during this brief period that makes the time constraints imposed by Signal relevant to the issue of fairness.

The structure of the transaction, again, was Signal's doing. So far as negotiations were concerned, it is clear that they were modest at best. Crawford, Signal's man at UOP, never really talked price with Signal, except to accede to its management's statements on the subject, and to convey to Signal the UOP outside directors' view that as between the $20-$21 range under consideration, it would have to be $21. The latter is not a surprising outcome, but hardly arm's length negotiations. Only the protection of benefits for UOP's key employees and the issue of Lehman Brothers' fee approached any concept of bargaining.

As we have noted, the matter of disclosure to the UOP directors was wholly flawed by the conflicts of interest raised by the Arledge-Chitiea report. All of those conflicts were resolved by Signal in its own favor without divulging any aspect of them to UOP. . . .

Finally, the minority stockholders were denied the critical information that Signal considered a price of $24 to be a good investment. Since this would have meant over $17,000,000 more to the minority, we cannot conclude that the shareholder vote was an informed one. Under the circumstances, an approval by a majority of the minority was meaningless. *Lynch I*, 383 A.2d at 279, 281; Cahall v. Lofland, Del. Ch., 114 A. 224 (1921).

Given these particulars and the Delaware law on the subject, the record does not establish that this transaction satisfies any reasonable concept of fair dealing, and the Chancellor's findings in that regard must be reversed.

E.

Turning to the matter of price, plaintiff also challenges its fairness. His evidence was that on the date the merger was approved the stock was worth at least $26 per share. In support, he offered the testimony of a chartered investment analyst who used two basic approaches to valuation: a comparative analysis of the premium paid over market in ten other tender offer-merger combinations, and a discounted cash flow analysis.

. . . [The Court then rejected prior Delaware case law that had used only one method of valuing stock, holding that] a more liberal approach must include proof of value by any techniques or methods which are generally considered acceptable in the financial community and otherwise admissible in court. . . .

The plaintiff has not sought an appraisal, but rescissory damages of the type contemplated by Lynch v. Vickers Energy Corp., Del. Supr., 429 A.2d 497, 505-06 (1981) (*Lynch II*). In view of the approach to valuation that we announce today, we see no basis in our law for *Lynch II*'s exclusive monetary formula for relief. On remand the plaintiff will be permitted to test the fairness of the $21 price by the standards we herein establish, in conformity with the principle applicable to an appraisal — that fair value be determined by taking "into account all relevant factors" [*see* 8 Del. C. § 262(h), *supra*]. In our view this includes the elements of rescissory damages if the Chancellor considers them susceptible of proof and a remedy appropriate to all the issues of fairness before him. To the extent that *Lynch II*, 429 A.2d at 505-06, purports to limit the Chancellor's discretion to a single remedial formula for monetary damages in a cash-out merger, it is overruled.

While a plaintiff's monetary remedy ordinarily should be confined to the more liberalized appraisal proceeding herein established [taking into account "all relevant factors" in determining the value of shares, as required under DGCL § 262(h)], we do not intend any limitation on the historic powers of the Chancellor to grant such other relief as the facts of a particular case may dictate. The appraisal remedy we approve may not be adequate in certain cases, particularly where fraud, misrepresentation, self-dealing, deliberate waste of corporate assets, or gross and palpable overreaching are involved. Cole v. National Cash Credit Association, Del. Ch., 156 A. 183, 187 (1931). Under such circumstances, the Chancellor's powers are complete to fashion any form of equitable and monetary relief as may be appropriate, including rescissory damages. Since it is apparent that this long completed transaction is too involved to undo, and in view of the Chancellor's discretion, the award, if any, should be in the form of monetary damages based upon entire fairness standards, *i.e.*, fair dealing and fair price.

Obviously, there are other litigants, like the plaintiff, who abjured an appraisal and whose rights to challenge the element of fair value must be preserved. Accordingly, the quasi-appraisal remedy we grant the plaintiff here will apply only to: (1) this case; (2) any case now pending on appeal to this Court; (3) any case now pending in the Court of Chancery which has not yet been appealed but which may be eligible for direct appeal to this Court; (4) any case challenging a cash-out merger, the effective date of which is on or before February 1, 1983; and (5) any proposed merger to be presented at a shareholders' meeting, the notification of which is mailed to the stockholders on or before February 23, 1983. Thereafter, the provisions of 8 Del. C. § 262, as herein construed, respecting the scope of an appraisal and the means for perfecting the same, shall govern the financial remedy available to minority shareholders in a cash-out merger. Thus, we return to the well established principles of Stauffer v. Standard Brands, Inc., Del. Supr., 187 A.2d 78 (1962) and David J. Greene & Co. v. Schenley Industries, Inc., Del. Ch., 281 A.2d 30 (1971), mandating a stockholder's recourse to the basic remedy of an appraisal.

The judgment of the Court of Chancery, finding both the circumstances of the merger and the price paid the minority shareholders to be fair, is reversed. The matter is remanded for further proceedings consistent herewith. Upon remand the plaintiff's post-trial motion to enlarge the class should be granted.

Reversed and Remanded.

PROBLEM 10-1

In the early fall of 2011, a European publishing company, Swedish Match, approached the Kamms and expressed an interest in buying out all of the Class A public shareholders and all of the Class B shares not owned by the Kamms. With the assistance of another board member, Peter Solomon, and his financial advising firm, Peter J. Solomon & Co., the Kamms arrived at an understanding with Swedish Match that they would sell Swedish Match one-third of their Class B shares for $15.00 per share; immediately after that sale, Dutch Masters would cash out the public, unaffiliated shareholders for $15.00 per share in a cash-out merger; Emily and Caroline would retain their positions as chair and CEO of the surviving company for three years and have the power to appoint a majority of the board. Part of the agreement was that if this agreement did not go forward, the Kamms could not vote their shares for any other transaction for one year. This provision was designed to keep the Kamms from trying to "shop" the company. Even after the proposed sale the Kamm sisters would continue to have voting control over the company because of the disproportionate 10:1 voting strength of the Class B shares the Kamms would retain.

How would you advise the Kamm sisters to proceed with respect to the above transaction? What procedural mechanisms should they institute to ensure that the transaction is above reproach? In the unhappy event of litigation, how would the entire fairness standard of review be applied?

2. *The Independent Board Committees*

Weinberger's entire fairness standard emphasized both procedure ("fair dealing") and substance ("fair price"), but most of the subsequent developments in this area of the law have concentrated on procedures that might serve to cleanse controlling shareholder transactions of the taint of self-interest. One of the most important of these procedures is the use of an independent board committee. In the case below, the Delaware Supreme Court evaluates the use of an independent board committee and explores the potential effects of such a device on the burdens of proof in fiduciary litigation.

KAHN v. LYNCH COMMUNICATION SYSTEMS, INC.

638 A.2d 1110
Supreme Court of Delaware
April 5, 1994

HOLLAND, Justice.

This is an appeal by the plaintiff-appellant, Alan R. Kahn ("Kahn"), from a final judgment of the Court of Chancery which was entered after a trial. The action, instituted by Kahn in 1986, originally sought to enjoin the acquisition of the defendant-appellee, Lynch Communication Systems, Inc. ("Lynch"), by the defendant-appellee, Alcatel U.S.A. Corporation ("Alcatel"), pursuant to a tender offer and cash-out merger. Kahn amended his complaint to seek monetary damages after the Court of Chancery denied his request for a preliminary injunction. The Court of Chancery subsequently certified Kahn's action as a class action on behalf of all Lynch shareholders, other than the named defendants, who tendered their stock in the merger, or whose stock was acquired through the merger.

A three-day trial was held April 13-15, 1993. Kahn alleged that Alcatel was a controlling shareholder of Lynch and breached its fiduciary duties to Lynch and its shareholders. According to Kahn, Alcatel dictated the terms of the merger; made false, misleading, and inadequate disclosures; and paid an unfair price.

The Court of Chancery concluded that Alcatel was, in fact, a controlling shareholder that owed fiduciary duties to Lynch and its shareholders. It also concluded that Alcatel had not breached those fiduciary duties. Accordingly, the Court of Chancery entered judgment in favor of the defendants.

Kahn has raised three contentions in this appeal. Kahn's first contention is that the Court of Chancery erred by finding that "the tender offer and merger were negotiated by an independent committee," and then placing the burden of persuasion on the plaintiff, Kahn. Kahn asserts the uncontradicted testimony in the record demonstrated that the committee could not and did not bargain at arm's length with Alcatel. Kahn's second contention is that Alcatel's Offer to Purchase was false and misleading because it failed to disclose threats made by Alcatel to the effect that if Lynch did not accept its proposed price, Alcatel would institute a hostile tender offer at a lower price. Third, Kahn contends that the merger price was unfair. Alcatel contends that the Court of Chancery was correct in its findings, with the exception of concluding that Alcatel was a controlling shareholder.

This Court has concluded that the record supports the Court of Chancery's finding that Alcatel was a controlling shareholder. However, the record does not support the conclusion that the burden of persuasion shifted to Kahn. Therefore, the burden of proving the *entire* fairness of the merger transaction remained on Alcatel, the controlling shareholder. Accordingly, the judgment of the Court of Chancery is reversed. The matter is remanded for further proceedings in accordance with this opinion.

FACTS

Lynch, a Delaware corporation, designed and manufactured electronic telecommunications equipment, primarily for sale to telephone operating companies. Alcatel, a holding company, is a subsidiary of Alcatel (S.A.), a French company involved in public telecommunications, business communications, electronics, and optronics. Alcatel (S.A.), in turn, is a subsidiary of Compagnie Generale d'Electricite ("CGE"), a French corporation with operations in energy, transportation, telecommunications and business systems.

In 1981, Alcatel acquired 30.6 percent of Lynch's common stock pursuant to a stock purchase agreement. As part of that agreement, Lynch amended its certificate of incorporation to require an 80 percent affirmative vote of its shareholders for approval of any business combination. In addition, Alcatel obtained proportional representation on the Lynch board of directors and the right to purchase 40 percent of any equity securities offered by Lynch to third parties. The agreement also precluded Alcatel from holding more than 45 percent of Lynch's stock prior to October 1, 1986. By the time of the merger which is contested in this action, Alcatel owned 43.3 percent of Lynch's outstanding stock; designated five of the eleven members of Lynch's board of directors; two of three members of the executive committee; and two of four members of the compensation committee.

In the spring of 1986, Lynch determined that in order to remain competitive in the rapidly changing telecommunications field, it would need to obtain fiber optics technology to complement its existing digital electronic capabilities. Lynch's management identified a target company, Telco Systems, Inc. ("Telco"), which possessed both fiber optics and other valuable technological assets. The record reflects that Telco expressed interest in being acquired by Lynch. Because of the supermajority voting provision, which Alcatel had negotiated when it first purchased its shares, in order to proceed with the Telco combination Lynch needed Alcatel's consent. In June 1986, Ellsworth F. Dertinger ("Dertinger"), Lynch's CEO and chairman of its board of directors, contacted Pierre Suard ("Suard"), the chairman of Alcatel's parent company, CGE, regarding the acquisition of Telco by Lynch. Suard expressed Alcatel's opposition to Lynch's acquisition of Telco. Instead, Alcatel proposed a combination of Lynch and Celwave Systems, Inc. ("Celwave"), an indirect subsidiary of CGE engaged in the manufacture and sale of telephone wire, cable and other related products.

Alcatel's proposed combination with Celwave was presented to the Lynch board at a regular meeting held on August 1, 1986. Although several directors expressed interest in the original combination which had been proposed with Telco, the

Alcatel representatives on Lynch's board made it clear that such a combination would not be considered before a Lynch/Celwave combination. According to the minutes of the August 1 meeting, Dertinger expressed his opinion that Celwave would not be of interest to Lynch if Celwave was not owned by Alcatel.

At the conclusion of the meeting, the Lynch board unanimously adopted a resolution establishing an Independent Committee, consisting of Hubert L. Kertz ("Kertz"), Paul B. Wineman ("Wineman"), and Stuart M. Beringer ("Beringer"), to negotiate with Celwave and to make recommendations concerning the appropriate terms and conditions of a combination with Celwave. On October 24, 1986, Alcatel's investment banking firm, Dillon, Read & Co., Inc. ("Dillon Read") made a presentation to the Independent Committee. Dillon Read expressed its views concerning the benefits of a Celwave/Lynch combination and submitted a written proposal of an exchange ratio of 0.95 shares of Celwave per Lynch share in a stock-for-stock merger. [In a stock-for-stock merger, the consideration that the Celwave shareholders would receive for selling their company would be Lynch stock. The exchange ratio reflects the relative values of the companies and of their stock.]

However, the Independent Committee's investment advisors, Thomson McKinnon Securities Inc. ("Thomson McKinnon") and Kidder, Peabody & Co. Inc. ("Kidder Peabody"), reviewed the Dillon Read proposal and concluded that the 0.95 ratio was predicated on Dillon Read's overvaluation of Celwave. Based upon this advice, the Independent Committee determined that the exchange ratio proposed by Dillon Read was unattractive to Lynch. The Independent Committee expressed its unanimous opposition to the Celwave/Lynch merger on October 31, 1986.

Alcatel responded to the Independent Committee's action on November 4, 1986, by withdrawing the Celwave proposal. Alcatel made a simultaneous offer to acquire the entire equity interest in Lynch, constituting the approximately 57 percent of Lynch shares not owned by Alcatel. The offering price was $14 cash per share.

On November 7, 1986, the Lynch board of directors revised the mandate of the Independent Committee. It authorized Kertz, Wineman, and Beringer to negotiate the cash merger offer with Alcatel. At a meeting held that same day, the Independent Committee determined that the $14 per share offer was inadequate. The Independent Committee's own legal counsel, Skadden, Arps, Slate, Meagher & Flom ("Skadden Arps"), suggested that the Independent Committee should review alternatives to a cash-out merger with Alcatel, including a "white knight" third party acquiror, a repurchase of Alcatel's shares, or the adoption of a shareholder rights plan.

On November 12, 1986, Beringer, as chairman of the Independent Committee, contacted Michiel C. McCarty ("McCarty") of Dillon Read, Alcatel's representative in the negotiations, with a counteroffer at a price of $17 per share. McCarty responded on behalf of Alcatel with an offer of $15 per share. When Beringer informed McCarty of the Independent Committee's view that $15 was also insufficient, Alcatel raised its offer to $15.25 per share. The Independent Committee also rejected this offer. Alcatel then made its final offer of $15.50 per share.

At the November 24, 1986 meeting of the Independent Committee, Beringer advised its other two members that Alcatel was "ready to proceed with an unfriendly tender at a lower price" if the $15.50 per share price was not recommended by the

Independent Committee and approved by the Lynch board of directors. Beringer also told the other members of the Independent Committee that the alternatives to a cash-out merger had been investigated but were impracticable.[3] After meeting with its financial and legal advisors, the Independent Committee voted unanimously to recommend that the Lynch board of directors approve Alcatel's $15.50 cash per share price for a merger with Alcatel. The Lynch board met later that day. With Alcatel's nominees abstaining, it approved the merger.

ALCATEL DOMINATED LYNCH CONTROLLING SHAREHOLDER STATUS

This Court has held that "a shareholder owes a fiduciary duty only if it owns a majority interest in or *exercises control* over the business affairs of the corporation." Ivanhoe Partners v. Newmont Mining Corp., Del. Supr., 535 A.2d 1334, 1344 (1987) (emphasis added). With regard to the exercise of control, this Court has stated:

> [A] shareholder who owns less than 50% of a corporation's outstanding stocks does not, without more, become a controlling shareholder of that corporation, with a concomitant fiduciary status. For a dominating relationship to exist in the absence of controlling stock ownership, a plaintiff must allege domination by a minority shareholder through actual control of corporation conduct.

Citron v. Fairchild Camera & Instrument Corp., Del. Supr., 569 A.2d 53, 70 (1989) (quotations and citation omitted).

Alcatel held a 43.3 percent minority share of stock in Lynch. Therefore, the threshold question to be answered by the Court of Chancery was whether, despite its minority ownership, Alcatel exercised control over Lynch's business affairs. Based upon the testimony and the minutes of the August 1, 1986 Lynch board meeting, the Court of Chancery concluded that Alcatel did exercise control over Lynch's business decisions. . . . The record supports the Court of Chancery's factual finding that Alcatel dominated Lynch.

At the August 1 meeting, Alcatel opposed the renewal of compensation contracts for Lynch's top five managers. According to Dertinger, Christian Fayard ("Fayard"), an Alcatel director, told the board members, "[y]ou must listen to us. We are 43 percent owner. You have to do what we tell you." The minutes confirm Dertinger's testimony. They recite that Fayard declared, "you are pushing us very much to take control of the company. Our opinion is not taken into consideration."

Although Beringer and Kertz, two of the independent directors, favored renewal of the contracts, according to the minutes, the third independent director, Wineman, admonished the board as follows:

> Mr. Wineman pointed out that the vote on the contracts is a "watershed vote" and the motion, due to Alcatel's "strong feelings," might not carry if taken now.

---

3. The minutes reflect that Beringer told the Committee the "white knight" alternative "appeared impractical with the 80% approval requirement"; the repurchase of Alcatel's shares would produce a "highly leveraged company with a lower book value" and was an alternative "not in the least encouraged by Alcatel"; and a shareholder rights plan was not viable because of the increased debt it would entail.

Mr. Wineman clarified that "you [management] might win the battle and lose the war." With Alcatel's opinion so clear, Mr. Wineman questioned "if management wants the contracts renewed under these circumstances." He recommended that management "think twice." Mr. Wineman declared: "I want to keep the management. I can't think of a better management." Mr. Kertz agreed, again advising consideration of the "critical" period the company is entering.

The minutes reflect that the management directors left the room after this statement. The remaining board members then voted not to renew the contracts.

At the same meeting, Alcatel vetoed Lynch's acquisition of the target company, which, according to the minutes, Beringer considered "an immediate fit" for Lynch. Dertinger agreed with Beringer, stating that the "target company is extremely important as they have the products that Lynch needs now." Nonetheless, Alcatel prevailed. The minutes reflect that Fayard advised the board: "Alcatel, with its 44% equity position, would not approve such an acquisition as . . . it does not wish to be diluted from being the main shareholder in Lynch." From the foregoing evidence, the Vice Chancellor concluded:

> . . . Alcatel did control the Lynch board, at least with respect to the matters under consideration at its August 1, 1986 board meeting. The interplay between the directors was more than vigorous discussion, as suggested by defendants. The management and independent directors disagreed with Alcatel on several important issues. However, when Alcatel made its position clear, and reminded the other directors of its significant stockholdings, Alcatel prevailed. Dertinger testified that Fayard "scared [the non-Alcatel directors] to death." While this statement undoubtedly is an exaggeration, it does represent a first-hand view of how the board operated. I conclude that the non-Alcatel directors deferred to Alcatel because of its position as a significant stockholder and not because they decided in the exercise of their own business judgment that Alcatel's position was correct [citation omitted].

The record supports the Court of Chancery's underlying factual finding that "the non-Alcatel [independent] directors deferred to Alcatel because of its position as a significant stockholder and not because they decided in the exercise of their own business judgment that Alcatel's position was correct." The record also supports the subsequent factual finding that, notwithstanding its 43.3 percent minority shareholder interest, Alcatel did exercise actual control over Lynch by dominating its corporate affairs. The Court of Chancery's legal conclusion that Alcatel owed the fiduciary duties of a controlling shareholder to the other Lynch shareholders followed syllogistically as the logical result of its cogent analysis of the record.

ENTIRE FAIRNESS REQUIREMENT DOMINATING INTERESTED SHAREHOLDER

A controlling or dominating shareholder standing on both sides of a transaction, as in a parent-subsidiary context, bears the burden of proving its entire fairness. Weinberger v. UOP, Inc., Del. Supr., 457 A.2d 701, 710 (1983).

See Rosenblatt v. Getty Oil Co., Del. Supr., 493 A.2d 929, 937 (1985). The demonstration of fairness that is required was set forth by this Court in *Weinberger:*

> The concept of fairness has two basic aspects: fair dealing and fair price. The former embraces questions of when the transaction was timed, how it was initiated, structured, negotiated, disclosed to the directors, and how the approvals of the directors and the stockholders were obtained. The latter aspect of fairness relates to the economic and financial considerations of the proposed merger, including all relevant factors: assets, market value, earnings, future prospects, and any other elements that affect the intrinsic or inherent value of a company's stock. However, the test for fairness is not a bifurcated one as between fair dealing and price. All aspects of the issue must be examined as a whole since the question is one of entire fairness.

Weinberger v. UOP, Inc., 457 A.2d at 711 (citations omitted).

The logical question raised by this Court's holding in *Weinberger* was what type of evidence would be reliable to demonstrate entire fairness. That question was not only anticipated but also initially addressed in the *Weinberger* opinion. *Id.* at 709-10 n.7. This Court suggested that the result "could have been entirely different if UOP had appointed an independent negotiating committee of its outside directors to deal with Signal at arm's length," because "fairness in this context can be equated to conduct by a theoretical, wholly independent, board of directors." *Id.* Accordingly, this Court stated, "a showing that the action taken was as though each of the contending parties had in fact exerted its bargaining power against the other at arm's length is strong *evidence* that the transaction meets the test of fairness." *Id.* (emphasis added). . . .

Once again, this Court holds that the exclusive standard of judicial review in examining the propriety of an interested cash-out merger transaction by a controlling or dominating shareholder is entire fairness. Weinberger v. UOP, Inc., 457 A.2d at 710-11. The initial burden of establishing entire fairness rests upon the party who stands on both sides of the transaction. *Id.* However, an approval of the transaction by an independent committee of directors or an informed majority of minority shareholders shifts the burden of proof on the issue of fairness from the controlling or dominating shareholder to the challenging shareholder-plaintiff. *See* Rosenblatt v. Getty Oil Co., 493 A.2d at 937-38. Nevertheless, even when an interested cash-out merger transaction receives the informed approval of a majority of minority stockholders or an independent committee of disinterested directors, an entire fairness analysis is the only proper standard of judicial review. *See id.*

INDEPENDENT COMMITTEES INTERESTED MERGER TRANSACTIONS

. . . In *Weinberger*, this Court noted that "[p]articularly in a parent-subsidiary context, a showing that the action taken was as though each of the contending parties had *in fact* exerted its bargaining power against the other at arm's length is strong evidence that the transaction meets the test of fairness." 457 A.2d at 709-10 n.7 (emphasis added). *Accord* Rosenblatt v. Getty Oil Co., 493 A.2d at 937-38 & n.7. In *Rosenblatt*, this Court pointed out that "[an] independent bargaining structure, while not conclusive, is strong evidence of the fairness" of a merger transaction. Rosenblatt v. Getty Oil Co., 493 A.2d at 938 n.7.

The same policy rationale which requires judicial review of interested cash-out mergers exclusively for entire fairness also mandates careful judicial scrutiny of a special committee's real bargaining power before shifting the burden of proof on the issue of entire fairness. A recent decision from the Court of Chancery articulated a two-part test for determining whether burden shifting is appropriate in an interested merger transaction. Rabkin v. Olin Corp., Del. Ch., C.A. No. 7547 (Consolidated), Chandler, V.C., 1990 WL 47648, slip op. at 14-15 (Apr. 17, 1990), *reprinted in* 16 Del. J. Corp. L. 851, 861-62 (1991), *aff'd*, Del. Supr., 586 A.2d 1202 (1990). In *Olin*, the Court of Chancery stated:

> The mere existence of an independent special committee . . . does not itself shift the burden. At least two factors are required. First, the majority shareholder must not dictate the terms of the merger. Rosenblatt v. Getty Oil Co., Del. Ch., 493 A.2d 929, 937 (1985). Second, the special committee must have real bargaining power that it can exercise with the majority shareholder on an arms length basis.

Id., slip op. at 14-15, 16 Del. J. Corp. L. at 861-62. This Court expressed its agreement with that statement by affirming the Court of Chancery decision in *Olin* on appeal.

LYNCH'S INDEPENDENT COMMITTEE

In the case *sub judice*, the Court of Chancery observed that although "Alcatel did exercise control over Lynch with respect to the decisions made at the August 1, 1986 board meeting, it does not necessarily follow that Alcatel also controlled the terms of the merger and its approval." This observation is theoretically accurate, as this opinion has already stated. Weinberger v. UOP, Inc., 457 A.2d at 709-10 n.7. However, the performance of the Independent Committee merits careful judicial scrutiny to determine whether Alcatel's demonstrated pattern of domination was effectively neutralized so that "each of the contending parties had in fact exerted its bargaining power against the other at arm's length." *Id.* The fact that the same independent directors had submitted to Alcatel's demands on August 1, 1986 was part of the basis for the Court of Chancery's finding of Alcatel's domination of Lynch. Therefore, the Independent Committee's ability to bargain at arm's length with Alcatel was suspect from the outset.

The Independent Committee's original assignment was to examine the merger with Celwave which had been proposed by Alcatel. The record reflects that the Independent Committee effectively discharged that assignment and, in fact, recommended that the Lynch board reject the merger on Alcatel's terms. Alcatel's response to the Independent Committee's adverse recommendation was not the pursuit of further negotiations regarding its Celwave proposal, but rather its response was an offer to buy Lynch. That offer was consistent with Alcatel's August 1, 1986 expressions of an intention to dominate Lynch, since an acquisition would effectively eliminate once and for all Lynch's remaining vestiges of independence.

The Independent Committee's second assignment was to consider Alcatel's proposal to purchase Lynch. The Independent Committee proceeded on that task with full knowledge of Alcatel's demonstrated pattern of domination. The Independent Committee was also obviously aware of Alcatel's refusal to negotiate with it on the Celwave matter.

BURDEN OF PROOF SHIFTED COURT OF CHANCERY'S FINDING

The Court of Chancery began its factual analysis by noting that Kahn had "attempted to shatter" the image of the Independent Committee's actions as having "appropriately simulated" an arm's length, third-party transaction. The Court of Chancery found that "to some extent, [Kahn's attempt] was successful." The Court of Chancery gave credence to the testimony of Kertz, one of the members of the Independent Committee, to the effect that he did not believe that $15.50 was a fair price but that he voted in favor of the merger because he felt there was no alternative.

The Court of Chancery also found that Kertz understood Alcatel's position to be that it was ready to proceed with an unfriendly tender offer at a lower price if Lynch did not accept the $15.50 offer, and that Kertz perceived this to be a threat by Alcatel. The Court of Chancery concluded that Kertz ultimately decided that, "although $15.50 was not fair, a tender offer and merger at that price would be better for Lynch's stockholders than an unfriendly tender offer at a significantly lower price." The Court of Chancery determined that "Kertz failed either to satisfy himself that the offered price was fair or oppose the merger."

In addition to Kertz, the other members of the Independent Committee were Beringer, its chairman, and Wineman. Wineman did not testify at trial. Beringer was called by Alcatel to testify at trial. Beringer testified that at the time of the Committee's vote to recommend the $15.50 offer to the Lynch board, he thought "that *under the circumstances*, a price of $15.50 was fair and should be accepted" (emphasis added).

Kahn contends that these "circumstances" included those referenced in the minutes for the November 24, 1986 Independent Committee meeting: "Mr. Beringer added that Alcatel is 'ready to proceed with an unfriendly tender at a lower price' if the $15.50 per share price is not recommended to, and approved by, the Company's Board of Directors." In his testimony at trial, Beringer verified, albeit reluctantly, the accuracy of the foregoing statement in the minutes: "[Alcatel] *let us know* that they were giving serious consideration to making an unfriendly tender" (emphasis added). . . .

According to the Court of Chancery, the Independent Committee rejected three lower offers for Lynch from Alcatel and then accepted the $15.50 offer "after being advised that [it] was fair and after considering the absence of alternatives." The Vice Chancellor expressly acknowledged the impracticability of Lynch's Independent Committee's alternatives to a merger with Alcatel:

> Lynch was not in a position to shop for other acquirors, since Alcatel could block any alternative transaction. Alcatel also made it clear that it was not interested in having its shares repurchased by Lynch. The Independent Committee decided that a stockholder rights plan was not viable because of the increased debt it would entail.

Nevertheless, based upon the record before it, the Court of Chancery found that the Independent Committee had "appropriately simulated a third-party transaction, where negotiations are conducted at arms-length and there is no compulsion to reach an agreement." The Court of Chancery concluded that the Independent Committee's actions "as a whole" were "sufficiently well informed . . . and aggressive to simulate an arms-length transaction," so that the burden of proof as to entire fairness shifted from Alcatel to the contending Lynch shareholder, Kahn. The Court of Chancery's reservations about that finding are apparent in its written decision.

The Power to Say No, the Parties' Contentions, Arm's Length Bargaining

The Court of Chancery properly noted that limitations on the alternatives to Alcatel's offer did not mean that the Independent Committee should have agreed to a price that was unfair:

> The power to say no is a significant power. It is the duty of directors serving on [an independent] committee to approve only a transaction that is in the best interests of the public shareholders, to say no to any transaction that is not fair to those shareholders and is not the best transaction available. It is not sufficient for such directors to achieve the best price that a fiduciary will pay if that price is not a fair price.

(Quoting In re First Boston, Inc. Shareholders Litig., Del. Ch., C.A. 10338 (Consolidated), Allen, C., 1990 WL 78836, slip op. at 15-16 (June 7, 1990)). . . .

Kahn contends the record reflects that the conduct of Alcatel deprived the Independent Committee of an effective "power to say no." Kahn argues that Alcatel not only threatened the Committee with a hostile tender offer in the event its $15.50 offer was not recommended and approved, but also directed the affairs of Lynch for Alcatel's benefit in such a way as to make it impossible for Lynch to continue as a public company under Alcatel's control without injury to itself and its minority shareholders. In support of this argument, Kahn relies upon another proceeding wherein the Court of Chancery has been previously presented with factual circumstances comparable to those of the case *sub judice*, albeit in a different procedural posture. *See* American Gen. Corp. v. Texas Air Corp., Del. Ch., C.A. Nos. 8390, 8406, 8650 & 8805, Hartnett, V.C., 1987 WL 6337 (Feb. 5, 1987), *reprinted in* 13 Del. J. Corp. L. 173 (1988).

In *American General*, in the context of an application for injunctive relief, the Court of Chancery found that the members of the Special Committee were "truly independent and . . . performed their tasks in a proper manner," but it also found that "at the end of their negotiations with [the majority shareholder] the Committee members were issued an ultimatum and told that they must accept the $16.50 per share price or [the majority shareholder] would proceed with the transaction without their input." *Id.*, slip op. at 11-12, 13 Del. J. Corp. L. at 181. The Court of Chancery concluded based upon this evidence that the Special Committee had thereby lost "its ability to negotiate in an arms-length manner" and that there was a reasonable probability that the burden of proving entire fairness would remain on the defendants if the litigation proceeded to trial. *Id.*, slip op. at 12, 13 Del. J. Corp. L. at 181.

Alcatel's efforts to distinguish *American General* are unpersuasive. Alcatel's reliance on *Braunschweiger* is also misplaced. In *Braunschweiger*, the Court of Chancery pointed out that "[p]laintiffs do not allege that [the management-affiliated merger partner] ever used the threat of a hostile takeover to influence the special committee." Braunschweiger v. American Home Shield Corp., slip op. at 13, 17 Del. J. Corp. L. at 219. Unlike *Braunschweiger*, in this case the coercion was extant and directed to a specific price offer which was, in effect, presented in the form of a "take it or leave it" ultimatum by a controlling sharcholder with the capability of following through on its threat of a hostile takeover.

Alcatel's Entire Fairness Burden Did Not Shift to Kahn

A condition precedent to finding that the burden of proving entire fairness has shifted in an interested merger transaction is a careful judicial analysis of the factual circumstances of each case. Particular consideration must be given to evidence of whether the special committee was truly independent, fully informed, and had the freedom to negotiate at arm's length. Weinberger v. UOP, Inc., Del. Supr., 457 A.2d 701, 709-10 n.7 (1983). *See also* American Gen. Corp. [*supra*], Hartnett, V.C., 1987 WL 6337, slip op. at 11 (Feb. 5, 1987), *reprinted in* 13 Del. J. Corp. L. 173, 181 (1988). "Although perfection is not possible," unless the controlling or dominating shareholder can demonstrate that it has not only formed an independent committee but also replicated a process "as though each of the contending parties had in fact exerted its bargaining power at arm's length," the burden of proving entire fairness will not shift. *Weinberger*, 457 A.2d at 709-10 n.7. *See also* Rosenblatt v. Getty Oil Co., Del. Supr., 493 A.2d 929, 937-38 (1985). . . .

The Court of Chancery's determination that the Independent Committee "appropriately simulated a third-party transaction, where negotiations are conducted at arm's-length and there is no compulsion to reach an agreement," is not supported by the record. Under the circumstances present in the case *sub judice*, the Court of Chancery erred in shifting the burden of proof with regard to entire fairness to the contesting Lynch shareholder-plaintiff, Kahn. The record reflects that the ability of the Committee effectively to negotiate at arm's length was compromised by Alcatel's threats to proceed with a hostile tender offer if the $15.50 price was not approved by the Committee and the Lynch board. The fact that the Independent Committee rejected three initial offers, which were well below the Independent Committee's estimated valuation for Lynch and were not combined with an explicit threat that Alcatel was "ready to proceed" with a hostile bid, cannot alter the conclusion that any semblance of arm's length bargaining ended when the Independent Committee surrendered to the ultimatum that accompanied Alcatel's final offer. *See* Rabkin v. Philip A. Hunt Chem. Corp., Del. Supr., 498 A.2d 1099, 1106 (1985).

Conclusion

Accordingly, the judgment of the Court of Chancery is reversed. This matter is remanded for further proceedings consistent herewith, including a redetermination of the entire fairness of the cash-out merger to Kahn and the other Lynch minority shareholders with the burden of proof remaining on Alcatel, the dominant and interested shareholder.

PROBLEM 10-2

Once the negotiations between Dutch Masters and Swedish Match reached agreement on the general parameters of the sale ($15.00 per share for both Class A common and Class B super-voting shares), Dutch Masters appointed a special committee consisting of three outside directors, Dan W. Lufkin, Thomas C. Israel, and Frances T. Vincent, Jr., to decide if the transaction was advisable. The committee had independent legal advice from Wachtell, Lipton, Rosen & Katz, and had independent financial advice from Deutsche Bank Securities. In early January 2012 the special committee received copies of the proposed agreements and then, based on advice from their legal and financial advisors, negotiated directly with Swedish Match. As a result of their negotiation, the purchase price for the publicly owned Class A and B shares was increased from $15.00 to $15.25 per share, and the restriction on the Kamms voting for an alternative transaction was extended from 12 months to 18 months. On January 19, 2012, the special committee unanimously recommended approval of the transaction. That same day, the Dutch Masters board also unanimously recommended approval.

Assume that a number of Class A stockholders who want to enjoin the transaction come to you for advice on challenging the merger. They suggest the following facts about directors Lufkin, Israel, and Vincent. Directors Israel and Vincent had longstanding (15-year) business relationships with the Kamms, including as board members of Dutch Masters or its predecessors since 1996. Director Lufkin was a founder of Donaldson, Lufkin & Jenrette (DLJ), a securities firm, and lead underwriter in Dutch Masters' 1997 IPO, earning a substantial fee as a result. The stockholders contend that Director Lufkin couldn't possibly hope to attract any future Dutch Masters business if he voted against the merger. In addition, Class A shareholders challenge the independence of other directors. Director Barnet, they claim, has a financial interest in the merger because he will be a director in the surviving company. Director Bernbach has a consulting agreement with Dutch Masters for $75,000 per year, and the Class A shareholders assert that this agreement would not be extended if Director Bernbach voted against the merger. Director Solomon has an interest in the transaction because his company stands to gain $3.3 million if the merger is consummated. (Dutch Masters has a nine-person board.)

How do you analyze whether or not to proceed with this case? Who will have the burden of proof, and what will the burden be? What additional facts do you need to advise Class A stockholders on whether to challenge this transaction?

3. "Majority of the Minority" Provisions

Another important procedural device for enhancing the procedural fairness of merger transactions is the affirmative vote of a "majority of the minority" shareholders of the target company. Parties to a merger often include a "majority of the minority" provision in the merger agreement, precisely to improve the quality of the merger procedures that will be reviewed in anticipated future litigation. Even in the absence of an express agreement, a majority of the minority vote may enhance perceived fairness of the transaction. In the following opinion, Vice Chancellor Strine examines the reach of the entire fairness standard, then proceeds to evaluate the effect of a "majority of the minority" provision.

IN RE PNB HOLDING CO. SHAREHOLDERS LITIGATION

2006 WL 2403999
Court of Chancery of Delaware
August 18, 2006

STRINE, Vice Chancellor.

This post-trial opinion addresses the claims of stockholders of a rural Illinois bank holding company, PNB Holding Company, who were cashed out in a merger that had the purpose and effect of allowing PNB to reclassify itself as a subchapter S corporation (the "Merger"). To have that effect, the Merger had to reduce the number of PNB stockholders remaining after the Merger to no more than seventy-five. The stockholders of PNB were offered $41.00 per share in the Merger. Several stockholders dissented from the Merger and perfected their appraisal rights. The remaining stockholders accepted the Merger consideration but through class counsel now complain that the directors of PNB breached their fiduciary duties and that the Merger was unfair. That is, this opinion resolves both an appraisal claim and an equitable challenge to the Merger.

A major issue decided in this opinion is whether the Merger is subject to entire fairness review. The plaintiffs claim that it is subject to heightened review because the PNB directors, and many members of their families, remained in the "golden circle" of PNB ownership after its conversion into an S corporation while the numerical majority of PNB stockholders were cashed-out. Because the directors and their family members who would remain collectively held 59.5% of the stock, the plaintiffs claim the Merger was destined to receive the required vote. As a result, the plaintiffs argue that this case should be analyzed as a controlling stockholder merger, governed by Kahn v. Lynch Communications Systems, Inc. I reject that argument, however, because the largest bloc held by any PNB director was 10.6%, and the directors were not bound together by voting agreements or other material, economic bonds to justify treating them as a unified group.

Although I do not believe *Lynch* governs review of the Merger, I do find that the Merger is presumptively subject to entire fairness review. By deciding to embark on the Merger, the PNB directors created a zero-sum game. Each of

them (and their family members) stood to gain by paying as little as possible to
the departing PNB stockholders. The Merger contemplated only sixty-eight of
PNB's more than 300 stockholders remaining in the new S corporation. The
reality, then, was that the PNB directors were assured of remaining in this golden
circle and far more than half of the remaining PNB stockholders would be on
the outside. In this conflicted situation, the PNB directors are bound to show
that the Merger was fair to the departing stockholders or to point to the presence of a cleansing device, such as approval by a special committee of
independent directors or an informed majority-of-the-minority vote, in order
to justify review under the business judgment rule. The first device was not
employed here, and a majority of the minority was not obtained. Therefore,
the entire fairness standard applies.

The question then becomes whether certain members of the equitable class
are precluded from recovery. I conclude that those stockholders who voted for
the Merger are barred from recovery. The PNB directors, I find, despite the
plaintiffs' arguments to the contrary, disclosed all material facts in connection
with the Merger. Thus, these plaintiffs are barred by the doctrine of acquiescence from challenging the fairness of the Merger. By contrast, I conclude that
those stockholders who did not vote for the Merger, but who simply forewent
appraisal and accepted the Merger consideration, are not barred from recovery.
The consequence of that ruling is that those members of the plaintiff class will
receive the difference between the fair value of PNB's shares on the Merger date
and the consideration paid to them in the Merger. That is, the recovery of the
stockholders who did not seek appraisal will track the recovery of the plaintiffs
who perfected their appraisal rights. After performing an independent valuation, I conclude that the fair value of a share of PNB on the date of the Merger
was $52.34, which is $11 .34 per share higher than the consideration offered in
the Merger. Therefore, the appraisal plaintiffs are entitled to $52.34 per share,
while the remaining plaintiffs (all of whom accepted the Merger consideration)
will receive $11.34-the damages resulting from the unfair Merger. Those awards
will be subject to pre-judgment interest at the legal rate, compounded quarterly.

I. FACTUAL BACKGROUND

These are the facts as I find them after trial. [Chancellor Strine then elaborates
upon the above facts in colorful detail, but the general point is clear: the Board
has agreed to a transaction in which they are assured of remaining shareholders
and getting the tax benefits of investing in an S corporation, such that entire
fairness is the standard of review unless it could point to a cleansing mechanism
that would reinstate business judgment review. We turn directly to the cleansing
mechanism of a "majority of the minority" vote.]

. . .

In view of all the facts, the PNB board majority was not positioned to make a
judgment about the Merger consideration that is entitled, as a presumptive
matter, to business judgment rule protection. Rather, the conflict they faced
requires that they prove the fairness of the price paid, unless they can point to
some other circumstance relieving them of that burden. Those circumstances
traditionally include approval of the transaction by disinterested directors, pref-
erably constituting a board majority or as a special committee. But the PNB

board all suffered the same conflict and made no attempt to add directors representing the stockholders to be cashed-out. At best, the board employed an investment bank to give them an opinion about the price to be paid. But that move, in itself, does nothing to invoke the business judgment rule.

Therefore, the only basis for the defendants to escape entire fairness review is by showing that an informed majority of the departing PNB stockholders approved the Merger. I turn to that issue next.

III. Did a Majority of Disinterested Shareholders Approve, and Ratify, the Merger?

Having determined that the directors were interested in the Merger, subjecting the Merger to entire fairness review, I must now address the consequences for that entire fairness review, if any, of the shareholder vote on the Merger. As discussed, the Merger was conditioned upon stockholder approval "by a majority vote," not a vote of a majority-of-the-minority. Under Delaware law, however, the mere fact that an interested transaction was not made expressly subject to a non-waivable majority-of-the-minority vote condition has not made the attainment of so-called "ratification effect" impossible. Rather, outside the *Lynch* context,[71] proof that an informed, non-coerced majority of the disinterested stockholders approved an interested transaction has the effect of invoking business judgment rule protection for the transaction and, as a practical matter, insulating the transaction from revocation and its proponents from liability.

Essentially, the most important preliminary issue raised by the plaintiffs in response to the defendants' ratification argument is mathematical. The plaintiffs question whether or not a majority of the disinterested shareholders in fact voted in favor of the Merger. That this issue even requires discussion now results largely from the plaintiffs' failure to raise the issue of numerical adequacy until trial. I therefore permitted the defendants to submit additional evidence after trial. With that evidence, and with helpful commentary from the parties on that evidence and the stipulated facts in the pre-trial order, I was able to make a responsible count. That count, as noted previously, indicates that only 48.8% of the 94,742 departing shares voted for the Merger.

Recognizing that result, the defendants advance an argument that I reject. The defendants argue that the only relevant question is whether a majority of the departing shareholders who returned a proxy cast a vote in favor of the Merger. Thus, in the defendants' view, departing stockholders who did not return a proxy do not count in the denominator. I disagree.

The cleansing effect of ratification depends on the intuition that when most of the affected minority affirmatively approves the transaction, their self-interested decision to approve is sufficient proof of fairness to obviate a judicial examination of that question. I do not believe that the same confidence flows

---

71. In the context of a going private transaction with a controlling stockholder, there are reasons why the simple fact that a majority of the disinterested electorate votes yes on a merger might be deemed insufficient to be given ratification effect. As noted in other decisions, in that special context, an alteration of *Lynch* to give more effect to disinterested stockholder choice might more soundly rest on a requirement, at the very least, that the transaction be expressly conditioned, on a non-waivable basis, on approval by a majority of the minority, and that such approval be preceded by negotiation and approval of the transaction by disinterested directors.

when the transaction simply garners more votes in favor than votes against, or abstentions from, the merger from the minority who actually vote. That position requires an untenable assumption that those who did not return a proxy were members of a "silent affirmative majority of the minority." That is especially so in the merger context when a refusal to return a proxy (if informedly made) is more likely a passive dissent. Why? Because under 8 Del. C. § 251, a vote of a "majority of the outstanding stock of the corporation entitled to vote" is required for merger approval, and a failure to cast a ballot is a *de facto* no vote. Therefore, giving ratification effect only if a majority of the disinterested shares outstanding were cast in favor of the transaction also coheres with § 251.[74]

Because a majority of the minority did not vote for the Merger, the directors cannot look to our law's cleansing mechanism of ratification to avoid entire fairness review. The most they can expect to do is to bar those stockholders who voted in favor of the Merger from recovery based on the doctrine of acquiescence. To invoke that doctrine, though, the defendants must show that the yes voters were informed of the material facts. I turn to that issue now.

[The Court proceeded to hold that "there were no disclosure violations and that the proxy statement fairly disclosed the material facts bearing on the advisability of the Merger." The Court then held that "stockholders who do not vote for a transaction and who simply accept the transactional consideration rather than seek appraisal are not barred from making or participating in an equitable challenge to the transaction." These holdings led the Court to the issue of "fair price." Vice-Chancellor Strine reasoned:

> Having concluded that the Merger is subject to entire fairness review and determined which stockholders are eligible to benefit from any finding of unfairness, I reach the confluence of two jurisprudential rivers. The first is that of equity. Here, although I do not find any evidence that the defendants consciously intended to pay an unfair price, the only procedural safeguard used was the employment of an investment bank to give a fairness opinion, and the record does not give one confidence that the work of Prairie Capital was a sufficient guarantee that a fair price was paid. As in most fairness cases, the ultimate issue of fairness turns on my perception of the economics. That is, did the defendants cause the corporation to pay a fair price? Here, where there is no useful market information about PNB's value, the court must necessarily look to valuation metrics. In other words, to measure whether the Merger price was unfair, the court must conduct the same essential inquiry as in an appraisal, albeit with more leeway to consider fairness as a range and to consider the remedial objectives of equity.

After working through the evidence and testimony on the fair price of PNB, the Court concluded that the Merger price was unfair. The fair value of a PNB share on the date of the Merger was $52.34, and the Merger consideration was $41.00.]

---

74. I need not, and do not, hold that a qualifying ratification vote always needs to track the percentage approval required for the underlying transaction. One can posit a situation when a particular type of transaction requires, by charter, a 66.67% supermajority vote, and a conflicted stockholder holds 40% of the total vote, with the rest of the votes held by disinterested stockholders. To promote fair treatment, the board makes approval subject to a majority of the minority vote condition. Nothing in this opinion suggests that ratification effect would not be given if an informed majority of the minority of the remaining 60% of the electorate voted in favor of the transaction.

PROBLEM 10-3

Approval of the merger of Dutch Masters and Swedish Match required that a majority of the unaffiliated shareholders of Class A stock, voting separately as a class, vote in favor of the transaction in which they'd receive $15.25 a share. In April a majority of the unaffiliated Class A shareholders overwhelmingly voted for the transaction: 10,009,994 shares in favor; 24,686 against; and 9,353 abstentions. This was perhaps not a surprising outcome because the merger consideration of $15.25 per share represented a 30 percent premium to the Class A shareholders.

How does this vote affect the burden of proof for Class A challengers of the transaction? How does it affect the standard of proof? (Recall In re: Wheelabrator, Chapter 8, in forming your analysis.) How, if at all, does it affect a lawyer's analysis of the strengths and weaknesses of her potential case?

4. Tender Offers

As we have seen in the Daimler-Chrysler Case Study and in Weinberger v. UOP and Kahn v. Lynch, the acquisition of one company by another often is accomplished through a tender offer. The following case discusses in elegant detail a perplexing feature of Delaware corporate law: the content of fiduciary duties, even in a parent/controlling shareholder and subsidiary/minority shareholder context, is fundamentally affected by whether the transaction uses a negotiated merger structure or a tender offer structure.

IN RE PURE RESOURCES, INC. SHAREHOLDERS LITIGATION
808 A.2d 421
Delaware Court of Chancery
October 7, 2002

STRINE, Vice Chancellor.

This is the court's decision on a motion for preliminary injunction. The lead plaintiff in the case holds a large block of stock in Pure Resources, Inc., 65% of the shares of which are owned by Unocal Corporation. The lead plaintiff and its fellow plaintiffs seek to enjoin a now-pending exchange offer (the "Offer") by which Unocal hopes to acquire the rest of the shares of Pure in exchange for shares of its own stock.

The plaintiffs believe that the Offer is inadequate and is subject to entire fairness review, consistent with the rationale of Kahn v. Lynch Communication Systems, Inc. and its progeny. Moreover, they claim that the defendants, who include Unocal and Pure's board of directors, have not made adequate and non-misleading disclosure of the material facts necessary for Pure stockholders to make an informed decision whether to tender into the Offer.

By contrast, the defendants argue that the Offer is a non-coercive one that is accompanied by complete disclosure of all material facts. As such, they argue that the Offer is not subject to the entire fairness standard, but to the standards set forth in cases like Solomon v. Pathe Communications Corp., standards which they argue have been fully met.

In this opinion, I conclude that the Offer is subject, as a general matter, to the *Solomon* standards, rather than the *Lynch* entire fairness standard. I conclude, however, that many of the concerns that justify the *Lynch* standard are implicated by tender offers initiated by controlling stockholders, which have as their goal the acquisition of the rest of the subsidiary's shares [either in the tender offer itself, or in combination with a later short-form merger]. These concerns should be accommodated within the *Solomon* form of review, by requiring that tender offers by controlling shareholders be structured in a manner that reduces the distorting effect of the tendering process on free stockholder choice and by ensuring minority stockholders a candid and unfettered tendering recommendation from the independent directors of the target board. In this case, the Offer for the most part meets this standard, with one exception that Unocal may cure.

. . .

I.

These are the key facts as I find them for purposes of deciding this preliminary injunction motion.

A.

Unocal Corporation is a large independent natural gas and crude oil exploration and production company with far-flung operations. In the United States, its most important operations are currently in the Gulf of Mexico. Before May 2000, Unocal also had operations in the Permian Basin of western Texas and southeastern New Mexico. During that month, Unocal spun off its Permian Basin unit and combined it with Titan Exploration, Inc. Titan was an oil and gas company operating in the Permian Basin, south central Texas, and the central Gulf Coast region of Texas. It also owned mineral interests in the southern Gulf Coast.

The entity that resulted from that combination was Pure Resources, Inc. Following the creation of Pure, Unocal owned 65.4% of Pure's issued and outstanding common stock. The remaining 34.6% of Pure was held by Titan's former stockholders, including its managers who stayed on to run Pure. The largest of these stockholders was Jack D. Hightower, Pure's Chairman and Chief Executive Officer, who now owns 6.1% of Pure's outstanding stock before the exercise of options. As a group, Pure's management controls between a quarter and a third of the Pure stock not owned by Unocal, when options are considered.

B.

Several important agreements were entered into when Pure was formed. The first is a Stockholders Voting Agreement. That Agreement requires Unocal and Hightower to vote their shares to elect to the Pure board five persons designated by Unocal (so long as Unocal owns greater than 50% of Pure's common stock), two persons designated by Hightower, and one person to be jointly agreed upon by Unocal and Hightower. Currently, the board resulting from the implementation of the Voting Agreement is comprised as follows:

UNOCAL DESIGNEES:

- Darry D. Chessum — Chessum is Unocal's Treasurer and is the owner of one share of Pure stock.
- Timothy H. Ling — Ling is President, Chief Operating Officer, and director of Unocal. He owns one share of Pure stock.
- Graydon H. Laughbaum, Jr. — Laughbaum was an executive for 34 years at Unocal before retiring at the beginning of 1999. For most of the next three years, he provided consulting services to Unocal. Laughbaum owns 1,301 shares of Pure stock.
- HD Maxwell — Maxwell was an executive for many years at Unocal before 1992. Maxwell owns one share of Pure stock.
- Herbert C. Williamson, III — Williamson has no material ties to Unocal. He owns 3,364 shares of Pure stock.

HIGHTOWER DESIGNEES:

- Jack D. Hightower — As mentioned, he is Pure's CEO and its largest stockholder, aside from Unocal.
- George G. Staley — Staley is Pure's Chief Operating Officer and also a large stockholder, controlling 625,261 shares.

JOINT DESIGNEE OF UNOCAL AND HIGHTOWER:

- Keith A. Covington — Covington's only tie to Unocal is that he is a close personal friend of Ling, having gone to business school with him. He owns 2,401 Pure shares.

As part of the consideration it received in the Titan combination, Unocal extracted a "Business Opportunities Agreement" ("BOA") from Titan. So long as Unocal owns at least 35% of Pure, the BOA limits Pure to the oil and gas exploration and production business in certain designated areas, which were essentially co-extensive with the territories covered by Titan and the Permian Basin operations of Unocal as of the time of the combination. The BOA includes an acknowledgment by Pure that it has no business expectancy in opportunities outside the limits set by the contract. This limitation is not reciprocal, however.

By contrast, the BOA expressly states that Unocal may compete with Pure in its areas of operation. Indeed, it implies that Pure board members affiliated with Unocal may bring a corporate opportunity in Pure's area of operation to Unocal for exploitation, but may not pursue the opportunity personally.

Another protection Unocal secured in the combination was a Non-Dilution Agreement. That Agreement provides Unocal with a preemptive right to maintain its proportionate ownership in the event that Pure issues new shares or undertakes certain other transactions.

Finally, members of Pure's management team entered into "Put Agreements" with Unocal at the time of the combination. The Put Agreements give the managers — including Hightower and Staley — the right to put their Pure stock to Unocal upon the occurrence of certain triggering events — among which would be consummation of Unocal's Offer.

The Put Agreements require Unocal to pay the managers the "per share net asset value" or "NAV" of Pure, in the event the managers exercise their Put rights within a certain period after a triggering event. One triggering event is a transaction in which Unocal obtains 85% of Pure's shares, which could include the Offer if it results in Unocal obtaining that level of ownership. The NAV of Pure is determined under a complex formula dependent largely on Pure's energy reserves and debt. Notably, Pure's NAV for purposes of the Put Agreement could fall below or exceed the price of a triggering transaction, but in the latter event the triggering transaction would provide the Put holders with the right to receive the higher NAV. Although it is not clear whether the Put holders can tender themselves into the Offer in order to create a triggering transaction and receive the higher of the Offer price or the NAV, it is clear that the Put Agreements can create materially different incentives for the holders than if they were simply holders of Pure common stock.

In addition to the Put Agreements, senior members of Pure's management team have severance agreements that will (if they choose) be triggered in the event the Offer succeeds. In his case, Hightower will be eligible for a severance payment of three times his annual salary and bonus, or nearly four million dollars, an amount that while quite large, is not substantial in comparison to the economic consequences of the treatment of his equity interest in Pure. Staley has a smaller, but similar package, and the economic consequences of the treatment of his equity also appear to be more consequential than any incentive to receive severance.

II.

A.

With these agreements in mind, I now turn to the course of events leading up to Unocal's offer.

From its formation, Pure's future as an independent entity was a subject of discussion within its board. Although Pure's operations were successful, its status as a controlled subsidiary of another player in the oil and gas business suggested that the day would come when Pure either had to become wholly-owned by Unocal or independent of it.

This reality was made manifest as Pure's management undertook to expand its business. On several occasions, this resulted in requests by Pure for limited waivers of the BOA to enable Pure to take advantage of opportunities beyond the areas designated in that contract. Unocal granted these waivers in each case. Another aspect of this subject also arose, as Unocal considered re-entering areas of geographical operation core to Pure's operations. Concerns arose in the minds of Unocal's lawyers about the extent to which the BOA could truly protect those Unocal officers (*i.e.*, Chessum and Ling) who sat on the Pure board from claims of breach of fiduciary duty in the event that Unocal were to pursue, for example, an opportunity in the Permian Basin. Because Unocal owed an indemnification obligation to Chessum and Ling and because it would be difficult to get officers to serve on subsidiary boards if Unocal did not back them, Unocal obviously was attentive to this uncertainty. Stated summarily, some, if not all, the complications that the BOA was designed to address remained a concern — a concern that would be eradicated if Unocal purchased the rest of Pure.

The aggressive nature of Pure's top management also fed this furnace. Hightower is an assertive deal-maker with plans to make Pure grow. To his mind, Unocal should decide on a course of action: either let Pure expand as much it could profitably do or buy the rest of Pure. In one of the negotiations over a limited waiver of the BOA, Hightower put this choice to Unocal in more or less these terms.

During the summer of 2001, Unocal explored the feasibility of acquiring the rest of Pure. On behalf of Unocal, Pure directors Maxwell and Laughbaum collected non-public information about Pure's reserves, production capabilities, and geographic assets and reported back to Unocal. This was done with the permission of Pure's management. By September 2001, it appeared that Unocal might well propose a merger, but the tragic events of that month and other more mundane factors resulted in the postponement of any proposal. Unocal's Chief Financial Officer informed Hightower of Unocal's decision not to proceed and that "all evaluation work on such a transaction ha[d] ceased."

That last statement was only fleetingly true. The record contains substantial evidence that Unocal's management and board soon renewed their consideration of taking Pure private. Pure director Ling knew that this renewed evaluation was going on, but it appears that he never shared that information with his fellow Pure directors. Nor did Unocal ever communicate to Pure that its September 2001 representation that all evaluation work had ceased was no longer correct. Nonetheless, during this period, Unocal continued to have access to non-public information from Pure.

Supplementing the pressure for a transaction that was generated by Hightower's expansion plans was a specific financing vehicle that Hightower sought to have the Pure board pursue. In the spring of 2002, Pure's management began seriously considering the creation of a "Royalty Trust." The Royalty Trust would monetize the value of certain mineral rights owned by Pure by selling portions of those interests to third parties. This would generate a cash infusion that would reduce Pure's debt and potentially give it capital to expand. By August of 2002, Hightower was prepared to push hard for this transaction, subject to ensuring that it could be accounted for on a favorable basis with integrity and would not have adverse tax effects.

For its part, Unocal appears to have harbored genuine concerns about the transaction, in addition to its shared concern about the accounting and tax implications of the Royalty Trust. Among its worries was that the Royalty Trust would simply inflate the value of the Put rights of management by delivering Pure (and increasing its NAV) without necessarily increasing its stock price. The Royalty Trust also complicated any future acquisition of Pure because the formation of the Trust would leave Unocal entangled with the third-parties who invested in it, who might be classified as holding a form of equity in Pure.

Although the record is not without doubt on the point, it appears that the Pure board decided to pursue consideration of the Royalty Trust during mid-August 2002. During these meetings, however, Chessum raised a host of issues that needed to be resolved favorably before the board could ultimately agree to consummate a Royalty Trust transaction. The plaintiffs argue that Chessum was buying time and trying to throw sand in the gears. Although I believe Unocal was worried about the transaction's effect, I am not prepared to say that Chessum's concerns were illegitimate. Indeed, many of them were shared by Hightower. Nonetheless, what is more evident is that the Royalty Trust discussions put pressure on Unocal to decide whether to proceed with an acquisition offer and that the Royalty Trust was likely not the method of financing that Unocal would use if it wholly owned Pure.

I infer that Hightower knew this. Simultaneous with pushing the Royalty Trust, Hightower encouraged Unocal to make an offer for the rest of Pure. Hightower suggested that Unocal proceed by way of a tender offer, because he believed that his Put rights complicated the Pure board's ability to act on a merger proposal.

B.

Despite his entreaties, Hightower was surprisingly surprised by what came next, as were the members of the Pure board not affiliated with Unocal. On August 20, 2002, Unocal sent the Pure board a letter that stated in pertinent part that:

> It has become clear to us that the best interests of our respective stockholders will be served by Unocal's acquisition of the shares of Pure Resources that we do not already own. . . . Unocal recognizes that a strong and stable on-shore, North America production base will facilitate the execution of its North American gas strategy. The skills and technology required to maximize the benefits to be realized from that strategy are now divided between Union Oil and Pure. Sound business strategy calls for bringing those assets together, under one management, so that they may be deployed to their highest and best use. For those reasons, we are not interested in selling our shares in Pure. Moreover, if the two companies are combined, important cost savings should be realized and potential conflicts of interest will be avoided.
>
> Consequently, our Board of Directors has authorized us to make an exchange offer pursuant to which the stockholders of Pure (other than Union Oil) will be offered 0.6527 shares of common stock of Unocal for each outstanding share of Pure common stock they own in a transaction designed to be tax-free. Based on the $34.09 closing price of Unocal's shares on August 20, 2002, our offer provides a value of approximately $22.25 per share of Pure common stock and a 27% premium to the closing price of Pure common stock on that date.
>
> Unocal's offer is being made directly to Pure's stockholders. . . .
>
> Our offer will be conditioned on the tender of a sufficient number of shares of Pure common stock such that, after the offer is completed, we will own at least 90% of the outstanding shares of Pure common stock and other customary conditions. . . . Assuming that the conditions to the offer are satisfied and that the offer is completed, we will then effect a "short form" merger of Pure with a subsidiary of Unocal as soon as practicable thereafter. In this merger, the remaining Pure public stockholders will receive the same consideration as in the exchange offer, except for those stockholders who choose to exercise their appraisal rights.
>
> We intend to file our offering materials with the Securities and Exchange Commission and commence our exchange offer on or about September 5, 2002. Unocal is not seeking, and as the offer is being made directly to Pure's stockholders, Delaware law does not require approval of the offer from Pure's Board of Directors. We, however, encourage you to consult with your outside counsel as to the obligations of Pure's Board of Directors under the U.S. tender offer rules to advise the stockholders of your recommendation with respect to our offer [as required under Rule 14D-9]. . . .

Unocal management asked Ling and Chessum to make calls to the Pure board about the Offer. In their talking points, Ling and Chessum were instructed to suggest that any Special Committee formed by Pure should have powers "limited to hiring independent advisors (bank and lawyers) and to coming up with a recommendation to the Pure shareholders as to whether or not to accept UCL's offer; any greater delegation is not warranted."

The next day the Pure board met to consider this event. Hightower suggested that Chessum and Ling recuse themselves from the Pure board's consideration of the Offer. They agreed to do so. After that, the Pure board voted to establish a Special Committee comprised of Williamson and Covington to respond to the Unocal bid. Maxwell and Laughbaum were omitted from the Committee because of their substantial employment histories with Unocal. Despite their work with Unocal in assessing the advisability of a bid for Pure in 2001, however, Maxwell and Laughbaum did not recuse themselves generally from the Pure board's process of reacting to the Offer. Hightower and Staley were excluded from the Committee because there were circumstances in which the Put Agreements could provide them with incentive to support the procession of the Offer, not because the Offer was at the most favorable price, but because it would trigger their right to receive a higher price under the NAV formula in the Put Agreements.

The precise authority of the Special Committee to act on behalf of Pure was left hazy at first, but seemed to consist solely of the power to retain independent advisors, to take a position on the offer's advisability on behalf of Pure, and to negotiate with Unocal to see if it would increase its bid. Aside from this last point, this constrained degree of authority comported with the limited power that Unocal had desired.

During the early days of its operation, the Special Committee was aided by company counsel, Thompson & Knight, and management in retaining its own advisors and getting started. Soon, though, the Special Committee had retained two financial advisors and legal advisors to help it.

For financial advisors, the Special Committee hired Credit Suisse First Boston ("First Boston"), the investment bank assisting Pure with its consideration of the Royalty Trust, and Petrie Parkman & Co., Inc., a smaller firm very experienced in the energy field. The Committee felt that the knowledge that First Boston had gleaned from its Royalty Trust work would be of great help to the Committee, especially in the short time frame required to respond to the Offer, which was scheduled to expire at midnight on October 2, 2002.

For legal advisors, the Committee retained Baker Botts and Potter Anderson & Corroon. Baker Botts had handled certain toxic tort litigation for Unocal and was active as lead counsel in representing an energy consortium of which Unocal is a major participant in a major piece of litigation. Nonetheless, the Committee apparently concluded that these matters did not materially compromise Baker Botts' ability to act aggressively towards Unocal.

After the formation of the Special Committee, Unocal formally commenced its Offer, which had these key features:

- An exchange ratio of 0.6527 of a Unocal share for each Pure share.
- A non-waivable majority of the minority tender provision, which required a majority of shares not owned by Unocal to tender. Management of Pure, including Hightower and Staley, are considered part of the minority for

purposes of this condition, not to mention Maxwell, Laughbaum, Chessum, and Ling.

- A waivable condition that a sufficient number of tenders be received to enable Unocal to own 90% of Pure and to effect a short-form merger under 8 Del. C. § 253.
- A statement by Unocal that it intends, if it obtains 90%, to consummate a short-form merger as soon as practicable at the same exchange ratio.

As of this time, this litigation had been filed and a preliminary injunction hearing was soon scheduled. Among the issues raised was the adequacy of the Special Committee's scope of authority.

Thereafter, the Special Committee sought to, in its words, "clarify" its authority. The clarity it sought was clear: the Special Committee wanted to be delegated the full authority of the board under Delaware law to respond to the Offer. With such authority, the Special Committee could have searched for alternative transactions, speeded up consummation of the Royalty Trust, evaluated the feasibility of a self-tender, and put in place a shareholder rights plan (*a.k.a.*, poison pill) to block the Offer.

What exactly happened at this point is shrouded by invocations of privilege. But this much is clear. Having recused themselves from the Pure board process before, Chessum and Ling reentered it in full glory when the Special Committee asked for more authority. Chessum took the lead in raising concerns and engaged Unocal's in-house and outside counsel to pare down the resolution proposed by the Special Committee. After discussions between Counsel for Unocal and the Special Committee, the bold resolution drafted by Special Committee counsel was whittled down to take out any ability on the part of the Special Committee to do anything other than study the Offer, negotiate it, and make a recommendation on behalf of Pure in the required 14D-9.

The record does not illuminate exactly why the Special Committee did not make this their Alamo. It is certain that the Special Committee never pressed the issue to a board vote and it appears that the Pure directors never seriously debated the issue at the board table itself. The Special Committee never demanded that Chessum and Ling recuse themselves from consideration of this issue, much less Maxwell and Laughbum.

At best, the record supports the inference that the Special Committee believed some of the broader options technically open to them under their preferred resolution (*e.g.*, finding another buyer) were not practicable. As to their failure to insist on the power to deploy a poison pill — the by-now *de rigeur* tool of a board responding to a third-party tender offer — the record is obscure. The Special Committee's brief suggests that the Committee believed that the pill could not be deployed consistently with the Non-Dilution Agreement protecting Unocal, but nowhere indicates how Unocal's contractual right to preserve its 65% position precluded a rights plan designed solely to keep it at that level. The Special Committee also argues that the pill was unnecessary because the Committee's ability to make a negative recommendation — coupled with High-tower's and Staley's by-then apparent opposition to the Offer — were leverage and protection enough.

My ability to have confidence in these justifications has been compromised by the Special Committee's odd decision to invoke the attorney-client privilege as to its discussion of these issues. Because the Committee delegated to its legal advisors the duty of negotiating the scope of the Committee's authority and seems to have acquiesced in their acceptance of defeat at the hands of Unocal's lawyers, invocation of the privilege renders it impossible for me know what really went on.

The most reasonable inference that can be drawn from the record is that the Special Committee was unwilling to confront Unocal as aggressively as it would have confronted a third-party bidder. No doubt Unocal's talented counsel made much of its client's majority status and argued that Pure would be on uncertain legal ground in interposing itself — by way of a rights plan — between Unocal and Pure's stockholders. Realizing that Unocal would not stand for this broader authority and sensitive to the expected etiquette of subsidiary-parent relations, the Pure board therefore decided not to vote on the issue, and the Special Committee's fleeting act of boldness was obscured in the rhetoric of discussions about "clarifying its authority."

Contemporaneous with these events, the Special Committee met on a more or less continuous basis. On a few occasions, the Special Committee met with Unocal and tried to persuade it to increase its offer. On September 10, for example, the Special Committee asked Unocal to increase the exchange ratio from 0.6527 to 0.787. Substantive presentations were made by the Special Committee's financial advisors in support of this overture.

After these meetings, Unocal remained unmoved and made no counteroffer. Therefore, on September 17, 2002, the Special Committee voted not to recommend the Offer, based on its analysis and the advice of its financial advisors. The Special Committee prepared the 14D-9 on behalf of Pure, which contained the board's recommendation not to tender into the Offer. Hightower and Staley also announced their personal present intentions not to tender, intentions that if adhered to would make it nearly impossible for Unocal to obtain 90% of Pure's shares in the Offer.

During the discovery process, a representative of the lead plaintiff, which is an investment fund, testified that he did not feel coerced by the Offer. The discovery record also reveals that a great deal of the Pure stock held by the public is in the hands of institutional investors.

III.   THE PLAINTIFFS' DEMAND FOR A PRELIMINARY INJUNCTION

A.   THE MERITS

The plaintiffs advance an array of arguments, not all of which can be dealt with in the time allotted to me for decision. . . .

Distilled to the bare minimum, the plaintiffs argue that the Offer should be enjoined because: (i) the Offer is subject to the entire fairness standard and the record supports the inference that the transaction cannot survive a fairness review; (ii) in any event, the Offer is actionably coercive and should be enjoined on that ground; and (iii) the disclosures provided to the Pure stockholders in connection with the Offer are materially incomplete and misleading. . . .

B.   THE PLAINTIFFS' SUBSTANTIVE ATTACK ON THE OFFER

1.

The primary argument of the plaintiffs is that the Offer should be governed by the entire fairness standard of review. In their view, the structural power of

Unocal over Pure and its board, as well as Unocal's involvement in determining the scope of the Special Committee's authority, make the Offer other than a voluntary, non-coercive transaction. In the plaintiffs' mind, the Offer poses the same threat of (what I will call) "inherent coercion" that motivated the Supreme Court in Kahn v. Lynch Communication Systems, Inc., 638 A.2d 1110 (Del. 1994) to impose the entire fairness standard of review on any interested merger involving a controlling stockholder, even when the merger was approved by an independent board majority, negotiated by an independent special committee, and subject to a majority of the minority vote condition.

In support of their argument, the plaintiffs contend that the tender offer method of acquisition poses, if anything, a greater threat of unfairness to minority stockholders and should be subject to the same equitable constraints. More case-specifically, they claim that Unocal has used inside information from Pure to foist an inadequate bid on Pure stockholders at a time advantageous to Unocal. Then, Unocal acted self-interestedly to keep the Pure Special Committee from obtaining all the authority necessary to respond to the Offer. As a result, the plaintiffs argue, Unocal has breached its fiduciary duties as majority stockholder, and the Pure board has breached its duties by either acting on behalf of Unocal (in the case of Chessum and Ling) or by acting supinely in response to Unocal's inadequate offer (the Special Committee and the rest of the board). Instead of wielding the power to stop Unocal in its tracks and make it really negotiate, the Pure board has taken only the insufficient course of telling the Pure minority to say no.

In response to these arguments, Unocal asserts that the plaintiffs misunderstand the relevant legal principles. Because Unocal has proceeded by way of an exchange offer and not a negotiated merger, the rule of *Lynch* is inapplicable. Instead, Unocal is free to make a tender offer at whatever price it chooses so long as it does not: i) "structurally coerce" the Pure minority by suggesting explicitly or implicitly that injurious events will occur to those stockholders who fail to tender; or ii) mislead the Pure minority into tendering by concealing or misstating the material facts. This is the rule of law articulated by, among other cases, Solomon v. Pathe Communications Corp., 672 A.2d 35 (Del. 1996). Because Unocal has conditioned its Offer on a majority of the minority provision and intends to consummate a short-form merger at the same price, it argues that the Offer poses no threat of structural coercion and that the Pure minority can make a voluntary decision. Because the Pure minority has a negative recommendation from the Pure Special Committee and because there has been full disclosure (including of any material information Unocal received from Pure in formulating its bid), Unocal submits that the Pure minority will be able to make an informed decision whether to tender. For these reasons, Unocal asserts that no meritorious claim of breach of fiduciary duty exists against it or the Pure directors.

2.

This case therefore involves an aspect of Delaware law fraught with doctrinal tension: what equitable standard of fiduciary conduct applies when a controlling shareholder seeks to acquire the rest of the company's shares? . . .

At present, the Delaware case law has two strands of authority that answer these questions differently. In one strand, which deals with situations in which controlling stockholders negotiate a merger agreement with the target board to buy out the minority, our decisional law emphasizes the protection of minority stockholders against unfairness. In the other strand, which deals with situations when a controlling stockholder seeks to acquire the rest of the company's shares through a tender offer followed by a short-form merger under 8 Del. C. § 253, Delaware case precedent facilitates the free flow of capital between willing buyers and willing sellers of shares, so long as the consent of the sellers is not procured by inadequate or misleading information or by wrongful compulsion.

These strands appear to treat economically similar transactions as categorically different simply because the method by which the controlling stockholder proceeds varies. This disparity in treatment persists even though the two basic methods (negotiated merger versus tender offer/short-form merger) pose similar threats to minority stockholders. Indeed, it can be argued that the distinction in approach subjects the transaction that is more protective of minority stockholders when implemented with appropriate protective devices—a merger negotiated by an independent committee with the power to say no and conditioned on a majority of the minority vote — to more stringent review than the more dangerous form of a going private deal — an unnegotiated tender offer made by a majority stockholder. The latter transaction is arguably less protective than a merger of the kind described, because the majority stockholder-offeror has access to inside information, and the offer requires disaggregated stockholders to decide whether to tender quickly, pressured by the risk of being squeezed out in a short-form merger at a different price later or being left as part of a much smaller public minority. This disparity creates a possible incoherence in our law.

3.

To illustrate this possible incoherence in our law, it is useful to sketch out these two strands. I begin with negotiated mergers. In Kahn v. Lynch Communication Systems, Inc., the Delaware Supreme Court addressed the standard of review that applies when a controlling stockholder attempts to acquire the rest of the corporation's shares in a negotiated merger pursuant to 8 Del. C. § 251. The Court held that the stringent entire fairness form of review governed regardless of whether: i) the target board was comprised of a majority of independent directors; ii) a special committee of the target's independent directors was empowered to negotiate and veto the merger; and iii) the merger was made subject to approval by a majority of the disinterested target stockholders. . . . [The Court then described the rationale of *Lynch.*]

The policy balance struck in *Lynch* continues to govern negotiated mergers between controlling stockholders and subsidiaries. If anything, later cases have extended the rule in *Lynch* to a broader array of transactions involving controlling shareholders. [*See, e.g.*, Emerald Partners v. Berlin, 787 A.2d 85, 93 n.52 (Del. 2001); Kahn v. Tremont Corp., 694 A.2d 422, 428 (Del. 1997).]

4.

The second strand of cases involves tender offers made by controlling stockholders — *i.e.*, the kind of transaction Unocal has proposed. The prototypical transaction addressed by this strand involves a tender offer by the controlling stockholder addressed to the minority stockholders. In that offer, the controlling stockholder promises to buy as many shares as the minority will sell but may subject its offer to certain conditions. For example, the controlling stockholder might condition the offer on receiving enough tenders for it to obtain 90% of the subsidiary's shares, thereby enabling the controlling stockholder to consummate a short-form merger under 8 Del. C. § 253 at either the same or a different price.

As a matter of statutory law, this way of proceeding is different from the negotiated merger approach in an important way: neither the tender offer nor the short-form merger requires any action by the subsidiary's board of directors. The tender offer takes place between the controlling shareholder and the minority shareholders so long as the offering conditions are met. And, by the explicit terms of § 253, the short-form merger can be effected by the controlling stockholder itself, an option that was of uncertain utility for many years because it was unclear whether § 253 mergers were subject to an equitable requirement of fair process at the subsidiary board level. That uncertainty was recently resolved in Glassman v. Unocal Exploration Corp., 777 A.2d 242 (Del. 2001), an important recent decision, which held that a short-form merger was not reviewable in an action claiming unfair dealing, and that, absent fraud or misleading or inadequate disclosures, could be contested only in an appraisal proceeding that focused solely on the adequacy of the price paid.

Before *Glassman*, transactional planners had wondered whether the back-end of the tender offer/short-form merger transaction would subject the controlling stockholder to entire fairness review. *Glassman* seemed to answer that question favorably from the standpoint of controlling stockholders, and to therefore encourage the tender offer/short-form merger form of acquisition as presenting a materially less troublesome method of proceeding than a negotiated merger.

Why? Because the legal rules that governed the front end of the tender offer/ short-form merger method of acquisition had already provided a more flexible, less litigious path to acquisition for controlling stockholders than the negotiated merger route. Tender offers are not addressed by the Delaware General Corporation Law ("DGCL"), a factor that has been of great importance in shaping the line of decisional law addressing tender offers by controlling stockholders — but not, as I will discuss, tender offers made by third parties.

Because no consent or involvement of the target board is statutorily mandated for tender offers, our courts have recognized that "[i]n the case of totally voluntary tender offers . . . courts do not impose any right of the shareholders to receive a particular price. Delaware law recognizes that, as to allegedly voluntary tender offers (in contrast to cash-out mergers), the determinative factors as to voluntariness are whether coercion is present, or whether there are materially false or misleading disclosures made to stockholders in connection with the offer." Solomon v. Pathe Communications Corp., 672 A.2d 35, 39 (Del. 1996) (citations and quotations omitted). In two recent cases, this court has followed *Solomon*'s articulation of the standards applicable to a tender offer, and held that the "Delaware law does not impose a duty of entire fairness on controlling stockholders making a non-coercive tender or exchange offer to acquire shares directly from the minority holders."

The differences between this approach, which I will identify with the *Solomon* line of cases, and that of *Lynch* are stark. To begin with, the controlling stockholder is said to have no duty to pay a fair price, irrespective of its power over the subsidiary. Even more striking is the different manner in which the coercion concept is deployed. In the tender offer context addressed by *Solomon* and its progeny, coercion is defined in the more traditional sense as a wrongful threat that has the effect of forcing stockholders to tender at the wrong price to avoid an even worse fate later on, a type of coercion I will call structural coercion. The inherent coercion that *Lynch* found to exist when controlling stockholders seek to acquire the minority's stake is not even a cognizable concern for the common law of corporations if the tender offer method is employed.

This latter point is illustrated by those cases that squarely hold that a tender [offer] is not actionably coercive if the majority stockholder decides to: (i) condition the closing of the tender offer on support of a majority of the minority and (ii) promise that it would consummate a short-form merger on the same terms as the tender offer. In those circumstances, at least, these cases can be read to bar a claim against the majority stockholder even if the price offered is below what would be considered fair in an entire fairness hearing ("fair price") or an appraisal action ("fair value"). That is, in the tender offer context, our courts consider it sufficient protection against coercion to give effective veto power over the offer to a majority of the minority. Yet that very same protection is considered insufficient to displace fairness review in the negotiated merger context. . . .

6.

Because tender offers are not treated exceptionally in the third-party context, it is important to ask why the tender offer method should be consequential in formulating the equitable standards of fiduciary conduct by which courts review acquisition proposals made by controlling stockholders. Is there reason to believe that the tender offer method of acquisition is more protective of the minority, with the result that less scrutiny is required than of negotiated mergers with controlling stockholders?

Unocal's answer to that question is yes and primarily rests on an inarguable proposition: in a negotiated merger involving a controlling stockholder, the controlling stockholder is on both sides of the transaction. That is, the negotiated merger is a self-dealing transaction, whereas in a tender offer, the controlling stockholder is only on the offering side and the minority remain free not to sell.

As a formal matter, this distinction is difficult to contest. When examined more deeply, however, it is not a wall that can bear the full weight of the *Lynch/Solomon* distinction. In this regard, it is important to remember that the overriding concern of *Lynch* is the controlling shareholders have the ability to take retributive action in the wake of rejection by an independent board, a special committee, or the minority shareholders. That ability is so influential that the usual cleansing devices that obviate fairness review of interested transactions cannot be trusted.

The problem is that nothing about the tender offer method of corporate acquisition makes the 800-pound gorilla's [the controlling shareholder's] retributive capabilities less daunting to minority stockholders. Indeed, many commentators would argue that the tender offer form is more coercive than a merger vote. In a merger vote, stockholders can vote no and still receive the transactional consideration if the merger prevails. In a tender offer, however, a non-tendering shareholder individually faces an uncertain fate. That stockholder could be one of the few who holds out, leaving herself in an even more thinly traded stock with little hope of liquidity and subject to a § 253 merger at a lower price or at the same price but at a later (and, given the time value of money, a less valuable) time. The 14D-9 warned Pure's minority stockholders of just this possibility. For these reasons, some view tender offers as creating a prisoner's dilemma — distorting choice and creating incentives for stockholders to tender into offers that they believe are inadequate in order to avoid a worse fate. But whether or not one views tender offers as more coercive of shareholder choice than negotiated mergers with controlling stockholders, it is difficult to argue that tender offers are materially freer and more reliable measures of stockholder sentiment. . . .

7.

The absence of convincing reasons for this disparity in treatment inspires the plaintiffs to urge me to apply the entire fairness standard of review to Unocal's offer. Otherwise, they say, the important protections set forth in the *Lynch* line of cases will be rendered useless, as all controlling stockholders will simply choose to proceed to make subsidiary acquisitions by way of a tender offer and later short-form merger. [Although "troubled by the imbalance in Delaware law exposed by the *Solomon/Lynch* line of cases," the Court determined that *Solomon* applied.]

8.

To be more specific about the application of *Solomon* in these circumstances, it is important to note that the *Solomon* line of cases does not eliminate the fiduciary duties of controlling stockholders or target boards in connection with tender offers made by controlling stockholders. Rather, the question is the contextual extent and nature of those duties, a question I will now tentatively, and incompletely, answer.

The potential for coercion and unfairness posed by controlling stockholders who seek to acquire the balance of the company's shares by acquisition requires some equitable reinforcement, in order to give proper effect to the concerns undergirding *Lynch*. In order to address the prisoner's dilemma problem, our law should consider an acquisition tender offer by a controlling stockholder non-coercive only when: 1) it is subject to a non-waivable majority of the minority tender condition; 2) the controlling stockholder promises to consummate a prompt § 253 merger at the same price if it obtains more than 90% of the shares; and 3) the controlling stockholder has made no retributive threats. . . .

The informational and timing advantages possessed by controlling stockholders also require some countervailing protection if the minority is to truly be afforded the opportunity to make an informed, voluntary tender decision. In this regard, the majority stockholder owes a duty to permit the independent directors on the target board both free rein and adequate time to react to the tender offer, by (at the very least) hiring their own advisors, providing the minority with a recommendation as to the advisability of the offer, and disclosing adequate information for the minority to make an informed judgment. For their part, the independent directors have a duty to undertake these tasks in good faith and diligently, and to pursue the best interests of the minority.

When a tender offer is non-coercive in the sense I have identified and the independent directors of the target are permitted to make an informed recommendation and provide fair disclosure, the law should be chary about superimposing the full fiduciary requirement of entire fairness upon the statutory tender offer process. Here, the plaintiffs argue that the Pure board breached its fiduciary duties by not giving the Special Committee the power to block the

Offer by, among other means, deploying a poison pill. Indeed, the plaintiffs argue that the full board's decision not to grant that authority is subject to the entire fairness standard of review because a majority of the full board was not independent of Unocal.

That argument has some analytical and normative appeal, embodying as it does the rough fairness of the goose and gander rule.[49] I am reluctant, however, to burden the common law of corporations with a new rule that would tend to compel the use of a device [the poison pill] that our statutory law only obliquely sanctions and that in other contexts is subject to misuse, especially when used to block a high value bid that is not structurally coercive. When a controlling stockholder makes a tender offer that is not coercive in the sense I have articulated, therefore, the better rule is that there is no duty on its part to permit the target board to block the bid through use of the pill. Nor is there any duty on the part of the independent directors to seek blocking power. But it is important to be mindful of one of the reasons that make a contrary rule problematic — the awkwardness of a legal rule requiring a board to take aggressive action against a structurally non-coercive offer by the controlling stockholder that elects it. This recognition of the sociology of controlled subsidiaries puts a point on the increased vulnerability that stockholders face from controlling stockholder tenders, because the minority stockholders are denied the full range of protection offered by boards in response to third party offers. This factor illustrates the utility of the protective conditions that I have identified as necessary to prevent abuse of the minority.

9.

Turning specifically to Unocal's Offer, I conclude that the application of these principles yields the following result. The Offer, in its present form, is coercive because it includes within the definition of the "minority" those stockholders who are affiliated with Unocal as directors and officers. It also includes the management of Pure, whose incentives are skewed by their employment, their severance agreements, and their Put Agreements. This is, of course, a problem that can be cured if Unocal amends the Offer to condition it on approval of a majority of Pure's unaffiliated stockholders. Requiring the minority to be defined exclusive of stockholders whose independence from the controlling stockholder is compromised is the better legal rule (and result). Too often, it will be the case that officers and directors of controlled subsidiaries have voting incentives that are not perfectly aligned with their economic interest in their stock and who are more than acceptably susceptible to influence from controlling stockholders. Aside, however, from this glitch in the majority of the minority condition, I conclude that Unocal's Offer satisfies the other requirements of "non-coerciveness." Its promise to consummate a prompt

---

49. Management-side lawyers must view this case, and the recent *Digex* case, *see* In re Digex Inc. S'holders Litig., 789 A.2d 1176 (Del. Ch. 2000), as boomerangs. Decades after their invention, tools designed to help management stay in place are now being wielded by minority stockholders. I note that the current situation can be distinguished from *Digex*, insofar as in that case the controlling stockholder forced the subsidiary board to take action only beneficial to it, whereas here the Pure board simply did not interpose itself between Unocal's Offer and the Pure minority.

§253 merger is sufficiently specific,[51] and Unocal has made no retributive threats.

Although Unocal's Offer does not altogether comport with the above-described definition of non-coercive, it does not follow that I believe that the plaintiffs have established a probability of success on the merits as to their claim that the Pure board should have blocked that Offer with a pill or other measures. Putting aside the shroud of silence that cloaked the board's (mostly, it seems, behind the scenes) deliberations, there appears to have been at least a rational basis to believe that a pill was not necessary to protect the Pure minority against coercion, largely, because Pure's management had expressed adamant opposition to the Offer. Moreover, the board allowed the Special Committee a free hand: to recommend against the Offer — as it did; to negotiate for a higher price — as it attempted to do; and to prepare the company's 14D-9 — as it did.

For all these reasons, therefore, I find that the plaintiffs do not have a probability of success on the merits of their attack on the Offer, with the exception that the majority of the minority condition is flawed.

PROBLEM 10-4

Analyzing the Dutch Masters/Swedish Match transaction in light of In re: Pure Resources, what are the advantages and disadvantages of proceeding by a negotiated merger versus a tender offer mechanism? Why wouldn't every transaction use a tender offer mechanism, given the more limited judicial review possible if the transaction were challenged?

C. THE APPRAISAL REMEDY

As we've seen above, a majority shareholder (usually a parent company) has the power to "cash out" the minority shareholders (usually a subsidiary), using either a merger or a short-form merger. (This could also be structured as a sale of assets, although that would not be as common.) The question then arises: what protects the minority shareholder in this situation from being cashed out at a price that is unfair? As always, the law relies on the constraints of fiduciary duty — the board that approves either the merger or the short-form merger must act in good faith, consistent with its duties of loyalty, due care, and full disclosure. Moreover, even if the board acts consistent with those duties, the shareholders may have a remedy if they believe that the price at which they were cashed out does not represent "fair value" for their shares. This remedy is a specific type of proceeding called an "appraisal." *See* DGCL § 262; Model Act § 13.02.

---

51. A note is in order here. I believe Unocal's statement of intent to be sufficiently clear as to expose it to potential liability in the event that it were to obtain 90% and not consummate the short-form merger at the same price (*e.g.*, if it made the exchange ratio in the short-form merger less favorable). The promise of equal treatment in short-form merger is what renders the tender decision less distorting.

While you've seen language in Weinberger v. UOP stating that appraisal is the "exclusive" remedy for dispossessed shareholders in a cash-out merger, in fact appraisal is only the exclusive remedy when price is the only issue. So where plaintiffs claim that the price at which they were cashed out is unfair *and* that there were other breaches (of fiduciary duty in the process of deciding on a merger, or of disclosure duties in proxy solicitations to approve the merger, for instance), then plaintiffs may bring an equitable action to try to stop the merger or an action for equitable damages such as rescission after the fact, or they may initiate fiduciary duty litigation. There is one sense in which an appraisal proceeding really is exclusive, however, and that is that only the fairness of the price can be litigated in an appraisal action. So if plaintiffs in an appraisal proceeding uncover breaches of fiduciary duty through discovery, they will be forced into parallel litigation.

The perils of this "parallel litigation" procedure are well illustrated in a convoluted litigation in Delaware, Cinerama, Inc. v. Technicolor (also referred to as Cede & Co. v. Technicolor after the name of the depository company, Cede & Co., in whose name many shares of stock owned by institutions and brokerage firms are held). This litigation, which lasted almost 23 years, generated six opinions by the Delaware Supreme Court; double that number of opinions by the Delaware Court of Chancery; a spontaneous recusal by a Delaware Chancellor, who was apparently fed up with the latest Supreme Court remand; and numerous unpublished interim and discovery orders. As the chancery court recognized in denying an interlocutory appeal of its order setting out trial procedures in 2001 for the second trial in the appraisal action,

> [t]he long history of the dispute between these parties is well known not only to the parties, but also to all those who are familiar with Delaware corporate law. As Cinerama continues to battle its seemingly eternal adversary, Technicolor, the present appraisal proceeding is all that remains after almost two decades of fierce litigation. As these parties launch their final campaign, the conflict between them not only appears to sustain both combatants, but has in part come to define them.

Cede v. Technicolor, 2001 WL 515106 (Del. Ch. 2001).

The *Technicolor* litigation began in 1983 as an appraisal proceeding, but the plaintiffs, Cinerama, who were minority shareholders in the target company, Technicolor, Inc., soon uncovered information leading them to believe that at least some members of the board had breached their fiduciary duties. Their claim was that two of Technicolor's board members, including its chief executive officer, had secretly been negotiating with executives of the potential acquirer, MacAndrews & Forbes Group, Inc., and giving them information on how to structure a winning bid, and that the "tainted" board members had pushed the transaction on the Technicolor board without disclosing these facts. Further, plaintiffs claimed, the process the board had used to determine the price at which to sell Technicolor was not adequate. In the litigation, because the alleged breaches were uncovered after the plaintiffs had already begun an appraisal proceeding and because price is the only permissible issue in an appraisal proceeding, the Delaware Supreme Court allowed both a personal liability action and an appraisal action to go forward in the Court of Chancery, in parallel, and consolidated through trial. Timing problems in the parallel actions have perhaps caused the Delaware Supreme Court to regret that ruling, which resulted in the case bouncing back and forth between the Court of Chancery and the Delaware Supreme Court for years. In 1995, on the third appeal, the Delaware Supreme Court upheld a finding of entire fairness by the board (finding that the conflict of interest on the part of two members of the board did not "taint" the entire board's procedures).

The appraisal proceeding was not resolved until 2005. The Court of Chancery held another trial on the appraisal action in May 2003, producing a judgment for the plaintiffs in the amount of $4,422,376 plus interest from August 2, 1991. On the sixth appeal in the case, the Delaware Supreme Court affirmed the valuation model used by the lower court, but reversed again with respect to the actual calculations under that model. Fortunately, the Supreme Court was able to specify the correct calculations, and concluded its opinion with the following sentence: "We remand this case with instructions to enter judgment consistent with this opinion so that this litigation, at long last, is brought to an end." Cede & Co. v. Technicolor, Inc., 884 A.2d 26, 43 (2005).

Appraisal as a remedy is not very satisfactory to many potential plaintiffs for reasons in addition to the limited nature of the proceeding, particularly in Delaware, which is perhaps why fewer than 10 percent of eligible shareholders ever seek appraisal. (The following analysis draws upon the excellent work of Professors Klein and Coffee in William A. Klein & John C. Coffee, Jr., *Business Organization and Finance: Legal and Economic Principles* (8th ed. 2002)). First, appraisal actions are individual actions, not class actions, so shareholders must exercise the initiative to perfect their appraisal rights on their own. While the court may ultimately consolidate the individual actions, this can be a formidable obstacle, particularly to an out-of-state shareholder. In contrast, a claim of breach of fiduciary duty can be asserted by a single shareholder representing the interests of all shareholders in a class action. Second, dissenters must initially bear all of the costs of litigation, and while the court may ultimately assess costs against the company, it need not. Third, shareholders do not get paid until the end of the litigation, and while the court has the power to award reasonable interest, the amount of interest awarded may be far less than the amount of money the shareholder could have earned on the same amount of money invested elsewhere. Finally, the shareholder receives no dividends (if the consideration was stock in a privately held company) and has no voting rights during the appraisal proceeding.

The Model Act attempts to ameliorate some of these difficulties. Probably most important to shareholders, the company must pay dissenters the merger consideration at the beginning of the litigation if the dissenter deposits the shares with the company. *See* Model Act § 13.24. In addition to payment, the company is asked to provide additional information so the shareholder can decide whether to settle the action. If within 60 days the shareholder has not decided to settle the action, the corporation must institute, and pay for, an appraisal proceeding. *See* Model Act § 13.30(a). Ultimately the court may assess costs against the dissenters, but at least under this procedure it is the company that is out of pocket for the costs of litigation during the pendency of the proceeding.

The following case explores an issue that has generated substantial litigation over the past decade—namely, whether a court that is determining the value of a minority shareholder's claim should apply a discount to reflect the lack of marketability or lack of control of a minority stake in a privately held company.

At first glance, this issue may seem arcane and uninteresting, but whether a discount is applied makes a substantial difference in the price paid to minority shareholders. Moreover, this issue goes to the heart of the appraisal remedy: what is its ultimate purpose? Perhaps predictably, courts have differed in their approach to this fundamental question, as ably discussed by the Supreme Court of Colorado.

PUEBLO BANCORPORATION v. LINDOE, INC.

63 P.3d 353
Supreme Court of Colorado (en banc)
January 21, 2003

RICE, Justice.

In this dissenter's rights action, Petitioner, Pueblo Bancorporation, appeals the court of appeals' reversal of the trial court's determination of the fair value of the shares owned by Lindoe, Inc., a minority shareholder in Pueblo Bancorporation. The parties do not disagree over the value of Pueblo Bancorporation; the only issue is whether the trial court, in assigning a specific "fair value" to Lindoe's shares, should apply a discount to reflect the shares' lack of marketability. The trial court applied such a discount, but the court of appeals reversed and held, as a matter of law, no marketability discount may be applied. We granted certiorari to resolve a conflict in the court of appeals regarding the meaning of "fair value." We hold that "fair value" under the Colorado dissenters' rights statute means the shareholder's proportionate ownership interest in the value of the corporation. Therefore, no marketability discount may be applied. The court of appeals decision is affirmed.

I. FACTS AND PROCEDURAL HISTORY

Petitioner, Pueblo Bancorporation ("Holding Company"), a Colorado corporation, is a bank holding company whose principal asset is The Pueblo Bank and Trust, a commercial bank with several branches throughout southeastern Colorado. In November of 1997, Holding Company had 114,217 outstanding shares, owned by thirty-eight shareholders — including twenty-nine individuals, two corporations, and seven retirement trusts.

One of Holding Company's corporate shareholders was Respondent, Lindoe, Inc. Lindoe, which is also a bank holding company, first purchased shares in 1988 and has since acquired additional shares as they became available. By November of 1997, Lindoe owned 6,525 (5.71%) of Holding Company's outstanding shares and was its sixth-largest shareholder.

This dispute was set in motion by a change in federal tax law. Prior to 1997, Holding Company was taxed as a corporation under subchapter C of the Internal Revenue Code. I.R.C. § 1361(a)(2). The earnings of a C corporation are subject to double taxation; earnings are taxed once at the corporate level and then taxed a second time at the individual level when distributed to shareholders. In contrast, corporations which qualify under subchapter S of the Internal Revenue Code are not generally subject to double taxation; corporate earnings are not taxed at the corporate level but pass through to the share-holders, who pay tax on the corporate income according to their proportionate ownership interest in the entity. I.R.C. § 1363. There are narrow restrictions on the types of corporations that may qualify as S corporations, and prior to 1997, Holding Company could not qualify. However, in 1997, because of certain changes to the rules governing S corporations, Holding Company became eligible to elect S corporation status.

Because of the opportunity to eliminate the double tax, Holding Company's board of directors sought to convert the company into an S corporation. However, they faced two potential obstacles. First, under the Code, an S corporation cannot have a corporation as a shareholder. I.R.C. § 1361(b)(1)(B). Several of Holding Company's shareholders, including Lindoe, would not qualify to hold stock in Holding Company if it were an S corporation. Second, an election to become an S corporation requires the unanimous approval of its shareholders; a single dissenting vote can block the conversion. I.R.C. § 1362(a)(2).

To avoid both of these potential pitfalls, Holding Company devised a plan to accomplish the conversion through merger. Holding Company created a second corporation, Pueblo Bancorp Merger Corporation (Merger Corp.), which was organized as an S corporation. Three of Holding Company's directors served as directors of Merger Corp. and the officers of the two entities were the same. The two companies entered into a merger agreement, subsequently approved by the shareholders of both companies. The resulting entity was an S corporation which continued operating under the name Pueblo Bancorporation; however, only those shareholders who could legally own shares in an S corporation were eligible to remain shareholders of the surviving corporation. Shareholders, such as Lindoe, that were ineligible to receive shares of the surviving entity received a cash payout in exchange for their Holding Company stock.

After an appraisal of the value of its shares, Holding Company offered $341 per share to the cashed out shareholders. Several shareholders accepted the amount and tendered their stock. Lindoe, however, chose to dissent and seek a higher amount. Pursuant to the procedure set out in Colorado's dissenters' rights statute, Lindoe sent a notice to Holding Company rejecting Holding Company's fair value determination and providing its own estimate of fair value: $775 per share. Disputing Lindoe's estimate, Holding Company initiated this action in order to obtain the court's determination of the fair value of Lindoe's shares.

The trial to determine fair value was a classic battle of experts. Holding Company's expert concluded that Holding Company, as an entity, was worth $72.9 million, or $638 per share. Lindoe provided two valuation experts whose estimates regarding the value of Holding Company ranged from $82.8 million to $88.5 million, a per share value of $725 to $775. The primary source of disagreement throughout the proceeding was whether the court should apply a minority or marketability discount to determine the fair value of Lindoe's shares.[2] Holding Company's expert, arguing that the court must apply both a minority

---

2. The distinction between a minority discount and a marketability discount is important. A minority discount adjusts the value of specific minority shares to reflect the fact that the shares lack sufficient voting power to control corporate decisions and policies. A marketability discount adjusts the value of specific shares to reflect the fact that there is no ready trading market for the shares. Because there are a small number of potential buyers of closely-held corporate stock, a shareholder may be unable to secure a willing buyer if he decides to cash out of his investment. *See* Edwin T. Hood *et al.*, *Valuation of Closely Held Business Interests*, 65 UMKC L. Rev. 399, 438 (1997).

and marketability discount in order to accurately reflect the value of Lindoe's shares, applied both discounts to arrive at his final opinion that the shares had a fair value of $344 per share. Lindoe's experts argued that application of discounts was inappropriate; the fair value of the shares in their opinion was between $725 and $775 per share.

The trial court first determined the value of Holding Company as an entity by combining the opinions of two of the experts. It concluded that the enterprise value of Holding Company was $76,087,723, or $666.16 per share. On the issue of discounts, the court was persuaded by Holding Company and applied both a minority discount and a marketability discount to arrive at its fair value determination of $362.03. Because Lindoe had already received $341 for its shares, the court entered judgment in favor of Lindoe in the amount of $137,220.75 ($21.03 times 6,525, the number of shares held by Lindoe).

On appeal, the primary issue, as it was in the trial court, was whether it was appropriate to apply a minority or marketability discount. The court of appeals sided with Lindoe and reversed the trial court, holding that the court erred in applying the discounts. Pueblo Bancorporation v. Lindoe, Inc., 37 P.3d 492 (Colo. App. 2001).

We granted certiorari to resolve a conflict in the court of appeals regarding the question of whether a marketability discount may be applied in determining "fair value" under the Colorado dissenters' rights statute.[3]

II. ANALYSIS

Under Colorado's dissenters' rights statute, a dissenting shareholder must follow certain procedures in order to receive the fair value of his shares. First, upon majority shareholder approval of certain corporate actions, the dissenting shareholder must notify the company of his intention to demand dissenters' rights. Upon receiving notice, the company must pay the dissenting shareholder the amount which the company estimates to be the fair value of the dissenter's shares. If the dissenting shareholder is dissatisfied with the company's estimate of fair value, he must provide his own estimate and demand payment in that amount from the company. Upon receiving such a demand from the dissenting shareholder, the company must either pay the amount of the dissenter's estimate or commence a proceeding for a judicial determination of fair value.

Throughout the entire process, the statutory standard of value to which a dissenting shareholder is entitled is "fair value":

> "Fair Value," with respect to a dissenter's shares, means the value of the shares immediately before the effective date of the corporate action to which the dissenter objects, excluding any appreciation or depreciation in anticipation of the corporate action except to the extent that exclusion would be inequitable.

§ 7-113-101(4), 2 C.R.S. (2002).

---

3. We granted certiorari review only on the issue of whether a marketability discount may be applied. We do not review the court of appeals' conclusion that a minority discount should not be applied in determining fair value.

This case requires us to determine what the General Assembly meant by "fair value." . . .

Because we are unable to resolve the meaning of "fair value" by reference to the plain language of the statute, and because of the conflicting interpretations of the term found in prior case law, it is the role of this court to determine the meaning of this statutory phrase. Of course, if the legislature disapproves of our interpretation, it has the power to amend the statute to make its intention clear.

In our view, the term "fair value" could reasonably be subject to one of three interpretations. One possible interpretation, urged by Lindoe, is that fair value requires the court to value the dissenting shares by looking at what they represent: the ownership of a certain percentage of the corporation. In this case, the trial court found that Holding Company, as an entity, was worth $76.1 million. Lindoe owned 5.71 percent of Holding Company and therefore, under this view, Lindoe is entitled to 5.71 percent of Holding Company's value, or just over $4.3 million. Because the proper measure of value is the shareholder's proportionate interest in the value of the entity, discounts at the shareholder level are inapplicable.

Another interpretation of fair value is to value the dissenters' specific allotment of shares, just as one would value the ownership of a commodity. Under this view, although Lindoe's shares represent ownership of 5.71 percent of Holding Company, the "fair value" of its ownership interest is only the amount a willing buyer would pay to acquire the shares. In effect, this interpretation reads fair value as synonymous with fair market value. An investor who wants to buy a minority allotment of shares in a closely-held corporation would discount the price he was otherwise willing to pay for the shares because the shares are a minority interest in the company and are a relatively illiquid investment. Likewise, under this interpretation, the trial court should usually apply minority and marketability discounts.

The third possible interpretation of fair value is a case-by-case approach which allows the trial court to adapt the meaning of fair value to the specific facts of the case. In some circumstances, fair value of a dissenter's shares will mean his proportionate interest in the corporation; in other cases it will mean the fair market value of specific shares valued as a commodity.

For the reasons set forth below, we first hold that the meaning of "fair value" is a question of law, not an issue of fact to be opined on by appraisers and decided by the trial court on a case-by-case basis.

Next, we conclude that fair value must have a definitive meaning; either it is the shareholder's proportionate ownership interest in the corporation or it is the value of the shareholder's specific allotment of shares. We conclude that the legislature chose the term "fair value" for a reason and therefore it must mean something different than "fair market value." To determine the precise meaning of "fair value," we consider the purpose underlying the dissenters' rights statute and the interpretation of "fair value" provided by courts and commentators from around the country.

Finally, we hold that the proper interpretation of fair value is the shareholder's proportionate interest in the value of the corporation. Therefore, a marketability discount should not be applied at the shareholder level to determine the "fair value" of the dissenter's shares.

A.   THE ERROR OF A CASE-BY-CASE APPROACH

Holding Company urges this court to adopt a case-by-case approach to the meaning of "fair value." This approach would leave the decision of whether to apply a marketability discount in the discretion of the trial court. . . .

A case-by-case interpretation of "fair value" results in a definition that is too imprecise to be useful to the business community. . . .

We conclude that a case-by-case approach to the definition of "fair value" is untenable. "Fair value" must have a definitive meaning; either it is the value of the shareholder's proportionate interest in the value of the corporation as an entity, or it is the value of the specific shares in the hands of that particular shareholder. To the extent [that prior cases] embraced a case-by-case determination of the meaning of "fair value," they are overruled.

We now turn to the language and purpose of the statute to determine which of these two interpretations the legislature intended.

B.   FAIR VALUE DOES NOT MEAN FAIR MARKET VALUE

The interpretation of "fair value" advocated by Holding Company reads the term as synonymous with "fair market value." Under a fair market value standard a marketability discount should be applied because the court is, by definition, determining the price at which a specific allotment of shares would change hands between a willing buyer and a willing seller. However, in a dissenters' rights action, the dissenting shareholder is not in the same position as a willing seller on the open market — he is an unwilling seller with little or no bargaining power. We are convinced that "fair value" does not mean "fair market value."

In the sixty year history of Colorado's dissenters' rights statute, the measure of compensation has changed from "value" to "fair value," but the legislature has never required that dissenters be paid "fair market value" for their shares.

Fair market value is typically defined as the price at which property would change hands between a willing buyer and a willing seller when neither party is under an obligation to act. If the General Assembly intended to create a fair market value measure for the price of a dissenter's shares, it knew how to provide it; the phrase has been used many times in a wide variety of other statutes.

We conclude that if the General Assembly intended a dissenter to receive the fair market value for his shares, it would have said so. . . .

Although the plain language of the statute is ambiguous, we conclude that "fair value" is not synonymous with "fair market value." To determine the precise meaning of the term, we next consider the purpose of the statute and the interpretation of "fair value" provided by courts and commentators around the country.

C.   "FAIR VALUE" MEANS THE SHAREHOLDER'S PROPORTIONATE OWNERSHIP INTEREST IN THE CORPORATION

We hold that the proper interpretation of fair value is the shareholder's proportionate ownership interest in the value of the corporation, without discounting for lack of marketability. This view is consistent with the underlying purpose of the dissenters' rights statute and the strong national trend against applying discounts.

1. Purpose of the Dissenters' Rights Statute

Historically, the dissenters' rights statutes were intended to compensate minority shareholders for the loss of their veto power and to provide liquidity for dissenting shareholders who found themselves trapped in an involuntarily altered investment. *See* Barry M. Wertheimer, *The Purpose of the Shareholders' Appraisal Remedy*, 65 Tenn. L. Rev. 661 (1998); Mary Siegel, *Back to the Future: Appraisal Rights in the Twenty-First Century*, 32 Harv. J. on Legis. 79, 93-97 (1995).

In recent years, the purpose of modern dissenters' rights statutes has been vigorously debated by commentators. The consensus that has developed among courts and commentators is that the modern dissenters' rights statute exists to protect minority shareholders from oppressive conduct by the majority.

The necessity of a dissenters' rights statute for protection of minority shareholders is illustrated by examining the situations in which the remedy is typically used today. The original concern of the appraisal remedy was for shareholders who were trapped in a post-merger investment that did not resemble their original investment. Today, financial practice and legal environments have changed such that mergers are often used solely to cash out minority shareholders.

In a typical cash-out merger, a corporation creates a shell company which is owned by the corporation's majority shareholders. The original corporation and the shell company merge and only the majority shareholders continue as shareholders of the surviving company; the minority shareholders are involuntarily cashed out of their investment.

The dissenters' rights statute serves as the primary assurance that minority shareholders will be properly compensated for the involuntary loss of their investment. The remedy protects the minority shareholders *ex ante*, by deterring majority shareholders from engaging in wrongful transactions, and *ex post*, by providing adequate compensation to minority shareholders.

In this case, the sole purpose of the merger between Holding Company and Merger Corp. was to cash out minority shareholders, such as Lindoe, who did not qualify to hold stock in an S corporation. The time and price at which Lindoe was cashed out was determined entirely by Holding Company.

The purpose of the dissenters' rights statute would best be fulfilled through an interpretation of "fair value" which ensures minority shareholders are compensated for what they have lost, that is, their proportionate ownership interest in a going concern. A marketability discount is inconsistent with this interpretation; it injects unnecessary speculation into the appraisal process and substantially increases the possibility that a dissenting shareholder will be undercompensated for his ownership interest. An interpretation of "fair value" that gives minority shareholders "less than their proportionate share of the whole firm's fair value would produce a transfer of wealth from the minority shareholders to the shareholders in control. Such a rule would inevitably encourage corporate squeeze-outs." In re Valuation of Common Stock of McLoon Oil Co., 565 A.2d 997 (Me. 1989).

2. The National Trend

The interpretation of fair value which we adopt today is the clear majority view. It has been adopted by most courts that have considered the issue, the authors of the Model Business Corporation Act, and the American Law Institute.

a.   Other Jurisdictions

Our interpretation of "fair value" is consistent with the interpretation adopted by most courts that have considered the issue. The interpretation of other states is especially persuasive for two reasons. First, the language of the Colorado statute, because it was based on the Model Act, is nearly identical to the language of dissenters' rights statutes around the country. . . .

Second, we believe that one of the purposes of the MBCA was to facilitate a degree of national uniformity among state corporate law. Because the General Assembly enacted Colorado's corporate code based largely on the Model Act, we presume that it intended, to some degree, to place Colorado's corporate law in step with the law of other states. Holding Company's interpretation of "fair value" conflicts with the interpretation adopted by most courts that have already considered the issue.

In the leading case regarding discounts, Cavalier Oil Corp. v. Harnett, 564 A.2d 1137 (Del. 1989), the Delaware Supreme Court held that discounts should not be used in determining the "fair value" of a dissenters' shares. In that case, the majority shareholders of a closely-held Delaware corporation, in order to consolidate ownership of the company, approved a short-form merger. The dissenting shareholder, who owned just 1.5 percent of the company's outstanding shares, exercised his dissenters' rights. In determining the fair value of his shares, the Delaware Court of Chancery refused to apply a discount at the shareholder level. The supreme court affirmed:

> [T]he appraisal process is not intended to reconstruct a pro forma sale but to assume that the shareholder was willing to maintain his investment position, however slight, had the merger not occurred. Discounting individual share holdings injects into the appraisal process speculation on the various factors which may dictate the marketability of minority shareholdings. More important, to fail to accord to a minority shareholder the full proportionate value of his shares imposes a penalty for lack of control, and unfairly enriches the majority shareholders who may reap a windfall from the appraisal process by cashing out a dissenting shareholder, a clearly undesirable result.

Cavalier, 564 A.2d at 1145.

Since Cavalier, courts across the country have considered the issue of marketability discounts and have generally followed Delaware's lead. Of the jurisdictions with "fair value" statutes, courts in fifteen states have held that a marketability discount should not be applied in determining fair value.

In addition, five state legislatures have already adopted the 1999 amendments to the MBCA's fair value definition which explicitly prohibit minority and marketability discounts.

Finally, several other states, while not specifically addressing the issue of marketability discounts, have expressed the view that the proper interpretation of "fair value" is the shareholder's proportionate interest of the corporation as a going concern, not the specific stock valued as a commodity.

In contrast, only six states with "fair value" statutes have clearly concluded that fair value may include marketability discounts.

The clear majority trend is to interpret fair value as the shareholder's proportionate ownership of a going concern and not to apply discounts at the shareholder level. The interpretation urged by Holding Company would position Colorado among a shrinking minority of jurisdictions in the country. We decline to do so. Although corporate law varies widely among the states, we believe there is some benefit to a consistent interpretation of the same statutory language from one jurisdiction to the next.

b.   The 1999 Amendments to the Model Business Corporation Act

We also find the recent amendments to the Model Business Corporation Act to be persuasive. In 1999, the MBCA amended its definition of fair value to reflect the national trend against discounts in fair value appraisals. "Fair value," according to the amended definition:

> means the value of the corporation's shares determined: . . .
>   (iii) without discounting for lack of marketability or minority status except, if appropriate, for amendments to the articles pursuant to section 13.02(a)(5).

Model Bus. Corp. Act 3d § 13.01(4)(iii) (1984) (amended 1999). The commentary to the 1999 amendments makes clear that the change was an adoption of the "more modern view that appraisal should generally award a shareholder his or her proportional interest in the corporation after valuing the corporation as a whole, rather than the value of the shareholder's shares when valued alone." MBCA § 13.01 official cmt. 2.

The MBCA has long been the source of Colorado's corporate law, including the dissenters' rights statute. Colorado's first dissenters' rights statute was enacted in 1941 and has undergone numerous revisions since that time. Since 1958, when Colorado adopted the first Model Business Corporation Act, the corporate code of this state has been largely modeled after the amendments and revisions to the Model Act.

In 1984, the Revised Model Business Corporation Act was published. The General Assembly followed suit in 1993 by repealing the entire Corporate Code and enacting, in large part, the 1984 Act. The current version of Colorado's dissenters' rights statute, although amended in 1996, remains substantially the same as the 1984 Model Act. The most important part of the statute for the purpose of this case, the definition of "fair value," is nearly identical to the definition found in the 1984 Model Act.

Holding Company argues that because the General Assembly has not adopted the 1999 MBCA amendments we should infer that it has rejected them. We are not persuaded. It has been less than four years since the MBCA was amended, too short a period of time to infer intent from legislative inaction. Because the legislature has consistently relied on the MBCA when fashioning the corporate laws of this state we find the views of the MBCA on this issue to be persuasive.

c.   The American Law Institute

Finally, we are persuaded by the recommendations of the American Law Institute regarding the interpretation of "fair value." The ALI has endorsed the national trend of interpreting fair value as the proportionate share of a going concern "without any discount for minority status or, absent extraordinary circumstances, lack of marketability." A.L.I., *Principles of Corporate Governance: Analysis and Recommendations* § 7.22(a) (1994). To determine fair value, the trial court must determine the aggregate value for the firm as an entity, and then simply allocate that value pro rata in accordance with the shareholders' percentage ownership. A.L.I. § 7.22 cmt. *d*. . . .

III. CONCLUSION

We hold that the term "fair value," for the purpose of Colorado's dissenters' rights statute, means the dissenting shareholder's proportionate interest in the corporation valued as a going concern. The trial court must determine the value of the corporate entity and allocate the dissenting shareholder his proportionate ownership interest of that value, without applying a marketability discount at the shareholder level. The court of appeals decision is affirmed.

Justice KOURLIS dissenting.

In my view, defining "fair value" so to extinguish the possibility of marketability discounts in dissenters' rights actions represents a policy decision that the General Assembly must make. Our statute is, as the majority notes, ambiguous. Colorado courts, with the exception of the court of appeals' decision in this case, have never interpreted the language of the statute as precluding trial courts from considering a marketability discount in valuing dissenters' shares. We must presume that the General Assembly is aware of those cases.

Despite the national trend to eliminate the marketability discount and the 1999 amendments to the Model Business Corporations Act ("MBCA"), also eliminating marketability discounts, the Colorado General Assembly has made no movement to change the Colorado statute. In my view, we cannot infer from any legislative history surrounding the dissenters' rights statute that the General Assembly has or would mandatorily exclude the use of marketability discounts in arriving at valuation.

Hence, absent a clear legislative declaration, an interpretation of the term "fair value" that essentially gives a shareholder more money for its shares because of a merger than the shareholder would have received immediately prior to the corporate action does not, in my view, comport with the language of the statute or with this state's prior case law. . . .

CHAPTER
11

Defending Against Hostile Takeovers

MOTIVATING HYPOTHETICAL

Multiply Marketplace Inc. (Multiply) was incorporated in Delaware in 2007 to facilitate peer-to-peer lending, a form of "crowdfunding" in which one person loans money to another without using a traditional bank as an intermediary. Multiply was launched at the commencement of the global financial crisis, when many traditional banks had ceased making new loans. Although it focused originally on personal loans — mostly for mortgages, education, and debt consolidation — Multiply quickly evolved into business lending. With the passage of the Jumpstart Our Business Startups (JOBS) Act in 2012, Multiply has expanded further into equity financing, and in the summer of 2012 Multiply completed a wildly successful initial public offering of its common stock. Emboldened by its success in the public capital markets, Multiply has begun to explore the possibility of expanding through acquisitions.

As discussed in previous chapters, mergers and acquisitions either can be negotiated transactions between the managements of two corporations, called "friendly" transactions, or can be "hostile" transactions, in which one company is taken over by another company or by a determined bidder, in spite of resistance from the target company's board of directors. Business lawyers create governance structures that give companies the tools they need to resist being taken over in hostile transactions. This often is done by adopting defense mechanisms, such as "poison pills," which limit the ability of a potential acquirer to purchase shares, and by enacting charter provisions that create staggered boards or supermajority voting requirements — both of which effectively limit the voting power of shareholders.

In the face of a threatened takeover, the adoption of any of these techniques raises stark fiduciary duty issues, and one central question: By acting to remain independent, were the directors acting in the interests of the corporation and its shareholders or were they acting to entrench themselves — that is, to perpetuate themselves in office? This question arises when a board adopts defensive measures because target shareholders often benefit from a free-flowing market for corporate control. Target shareholders typically receive takeover premiums (increases) of between 40 percent (in friendly deals) and 50 percent (in hostile bids) for their shares. If a shareholder holds stock in Intel, for example, at $100.00 per share, she will typically be paid between $140 and $150 per share if Intel is acquired. So when a board of directors takes defensive actions to rebuff a takeover, those actions may prevent shareholders from getting a takeover premium for their shares.

Ironically, one effect of takeover defenses in many cases is to enhance the ultimate financial return for the target shareholders. In many cases, the effect of a board taking defensive action is that another bidder enters the fray, or management is given more leverage in negotiating with the first bidder, forcing that bidder to offer more money. The ultimate impact of defensive measures in those cases is that the company is sold for a higher price, and the shareholders get a higher premium. On the other hand, where the target company has a staggered board and a poison pill, the hopeful acquirer may give up. In this situation, the target firm would remain independent, and the target share-holders are denied a premium.

In current mergers and acquisitions practice, boards of directors know that whatever defensive measures they take will be tested in litigation because litigation is an inevitable part of hostile acquisitions and attempted hostile acqui-sitions. Thus, fiduciary duty litigation has an important role to play in providing a forum in which the courts evaluate whether the directors are acting in the interests of the corporation and its shareholders by adopting defensive measures or whether the directors are acting to entrench themselves and maintain their positions. You will see that this issue is the subtext in just about every hostile takeover case.

A.   A BRIEF HISTORY OF HOSTILE TAKEOVERS

One underlying issue in many hostile takeover cases is where to locate power in the corporation — in the shareholders or in the managers. Resolving this issue requires courts to grapple with a more fundamental issue, namely, whether corporations are simply vehicles to maximize shareholder wealth, in which case hostile tender offers would presumably flourish, or whether corporations are social entities with relationships to employees, creditors, communities, and shareholders that can be undermined by hostile takeovers and some of the resulting dislocations. This consideration comes into focus only upon learning the history of hostile takeovers in the 1980s, when the foundational cases in Delaware arose.

Hostile takeovers are concluded either through a tender offer or a proxy contest. In a tender offer, a bidder offers to buy shares directly from existing shareholders in the target company. If the bidder succeeds in buying a control-ling stake in the target company, the bidder uses that control to elect a new board of directors. Thus, the tender offer is simply an offer to buy shares at a premium, and it is made to all shareholders in their individual capacity. The offer bypasses the board completely, and if the potential acquirer holds a substantial number of shares before making the offer, it is possible that the tender offer can result in the transfer of control, even though less than a majority of shareholders accept the offer.

Federal securities law regulates the tender offer process pursuant to amendments to the Securities Exchange Act of 1934, principally found in §§ 13(d) and 14(d) of the Williams Act. These statutory provisions seek to reduce some coercive aspects of tender offers by regulating the timing of tender offers (they must stay open for 20 days), by regulating the disclosure a tender offeror and target must provide to shareholders, and by providing certain rules to ensure fairness. These rules include requirements that bidders must buy shares *pro rata* from shareholders rather than buying shares on a first-come, first-served basis, and that bidders must pay every shareholder who tenders the highest price in the tender offer. This protects shareholders who tender early from missing out on later, higher tender offer prices. The focus of these regulations is to slow down the process, providing shareholders with enough information to make intelligent decisions about whether to tender their shares, and to some extent reducing the incentives shareholders might otherwise feel to tender early so as not to miss out on a tender offer premium.

In a proxy contest, as you have seen in previous chapters, a suitor seeks proxy voting authority from enough shareholders to put its slate of directors in power on the board. In this procedure, the potential acquirer bypasses the board, but needs to persuade a majority of shareholders to vote for the acquirer's slate to be successful. Of the two, hostile tender offers are the more secure: If the acquirer can arrange the financing necessary to purchase 51 percent of the shares at a premium, it can be certain to be successful in taking over another company, assuming majority voting rules and a board that is not staggered. Moreover, since the tender offeror sets the conditions for actually purchasing shares in the tender offer, the offeror will be under no obligation to purchase shares if the requisite number of shareholders refuse to tender. As you will see, legislatures have acted to make hostile acquisitions by tender offer much more difficult, as has the poison pill, so proxy contests have assumed more importance.

Tender offers permitting hostile takeovers have existed for decades but were not used with any regularity until a period beginning in the late 1970s, with their use dramatically increasing in a period beginning in about 1985. This market shift seems to have been fueled primarily by a shift in norms among investment bankers as to whether it was proper to provide funding for a hostile tender offer to effect a takeover. As Professors Gilson and Black have stated,

> Until 1975, no major investment banking firm would participate in a hostile takeover attempt. But once Morgan Stanley, the most conservative of the leading firms, legitimized hostile takeovers by participating in a hostile tender offer for International Nickel in 1975, the conduct of parties to acquisitions moved farther and farther from the image of "gentlemen" conducting business in a restrained and courteous fashion. Increasingly, the dominant metaphor was war.

Ronald J. Gilson & Bernard S. Black, *The Law and Finance of Corporate Acquisitions* (2d ed. 1995).

Many of the hostile takeovers of the 1980s were quite different from earlier waves of takeovers, in that the suitor did not seek to acquire a company to run it better than existing management or to create a conglomerate of unrelated products. Rather, hostile takeovers in the 1980s were often "bust-up" takeovers, in which a company was purchased at a premium and then the different subsidiaries or operating divisions were sold to pay off the debt incurred in buying the company. (That debt would be incurred in buying target shares at a premium in the tender offer to shareholders.)

The takeovers of the 1980s were also different in the way they were financed. The new financing mechanism, called "high-yield bonds" or "junk bonds," allowed many of these hostile takeovers to go forward with very little money of the purchaser in the deal—often 10 percent or even less—and lots of debt. The market for junk bonds was the creation of Michael Milken, of Drexel Burnham Lambert, a now-defunct securities firm. These bonds were high-yield because they were high-risk, having repayments dependent on companies with an uncertain future. However, they provided a way to raise much larger amounts of money than banks would typically provide in their lending. As a result of the existence of junk bond financing, the size of transactions increased, and the ratio of debt to equity increased.

When RJR Nabisco was taken over by Kohlberg Kravis Roberts (KKR) in 1989, after a bruising fight with then-CEO Ross Johnson, who sought control, the ultimate price paid for the company was $24.8 billion, well beyond the financing capacity of most acquirers in prior decades. Because these transactions exhibited highly leveraged financial structures, they were called leveraged buyouts, or "LBOs." If management were buying out the company in a leveraged transaction, it was called a management buyout, or "MBO," and this class of transactions creates special fiduciary duty issues because of the inherent conflict of interest. Takeover specialists such as T. Boone Pickens, KKR, or Forstmann, Little ended up making a lot of money by engaging in bust-up takeovers, and were either vilified or venerated, depending on one's perspective, in movies such as *Wall Street* (roughly based on Michael Milken and Ivan Boesky); *Barbarians at the Gate* (the story of the RJR Nabisco takeover); and *Other People's Money* (depicting takeover specialists generally).

In about 1990, this type of takeover activity cooled. Junk bonds dried up as a financing mechanism when Michael Milken was indicted in 1990 and then went to jail in 1991 for numerous violations of federal securities laws. His firm declared bankruptcy. State anti-takeover legislation, which had been passed in many states in the mid-1980s, was upheld against constitutional attacks in the late 1980s. Moreover, there was an economic downturn in 1990-1992, which depressed mergers and acquisitions as bankruptcies replaced deals at the center of high-stakes business practices.

Law professors and legal commentators continue to debate whether the transactions of the 1980s were good for society or not. Many economists would say that these bust-up takeovers in the 1980s were simply necessary divestitures of unrelated businesses and subsidiaries that allowed companies to unwind the conglomerates that had been put together in the 1960s and 1970s. Those conglomerates, it is argued, had too many disparate units in too many different businesses and thus were underperforming the market. If existing management saw the value of "deconglomerization," assets could be sold without a bust-up takeover, but if existing management did not see this strategic necessity, a hostile takeover would be necessary to wrest control from management and put these assets to their highest-value use. Many politicians, managers, labor advocates, and reporters saw the social dislocations these takeovers caused, the jobs lost, and the communities affected by corporate downsizing or by relocations outside the United States and felt that the social costs were too high to justify whatever economic benefits these types of takeovers produced.

In response, most states enacted protective legislation in the late 1980s to make hostile takeovers more difficult. The first type of state legislation imposed disclosure obligations in addition to those in the Williams Act, and created state regulatory agencies that had to approve takeover bids. But in 1982, the U.S. Supreme Court held that this type of statute was an unconstitutional interference with interstate commerce. Edgar v. MITE Corp., 457 U.S. 624 (1982). In response, state legislatures passed "second-generation" protective legislation that has, so far, withstood constitutional challenge. *See* CTS Corp. v. Dynamics Corp., 481 U.S. 69 (1987) (Indiana's control share statute is not preempted by the Williams Act, nor does it violate the Commerce Clause); Amanda Acquisition Corp. v. Universal Foods, 877 F.2d 496 (7th Cir. 1989) (Easterbrook, J.) (same result regarding Wisconsin's moratorium statute). These statutes take a number of forms, but for purposes of this discussion, it is only necessary to highlight their impact, which was twofold: They essentially shut down some of the most coercive tender offers, and they rendered hostile takeovers using tender offers rather than proxy contests virtually impossible in many states. And if the statutes hadn't done that, poison pills would have. Thus, in combination with opinions in Delaware upholding the legality of poison pills, by the end of the 1980s the power of the board to fend off hostile takeovers was well established, although not unlimited.

And yet takeovers, both hostile and friendly, flourished from 1993 until the stock market began to decline in 2000. Each year from 1995 through 1999 records were broken regarding the value of negotiated deals. These deals were valued at $1.75 trillion in 1999, up from $1.65 trillion in 1998. Hostile takeovers occurred as well during this period, notwithstanding state legislative impediments and companies' adoption of shark repellents and poison pills. Thus, in 1995 there were nearly 70 hostile takeover bids, compared to 88 hostile takeover bids in 1988, the peak year for hostile takeovers in the 1980s. As Professor John Coates puts it, "At a minimum, the roaring mergers and acquisitions market [of the late 1990s] shows that defenses are not major impediments to the movement of assets to 'higher valuing users' via the market for corporate control." John C. Coates IV, *Takeover Defenses in the Shadow of the Pill: A Critique of the Scientific Evidence*, 79 Tex. L. Rev. 271 (2000). And a robust mergers and acquisitions market is not just a U.S. phenomenon: worldwide, the value of mergers and acquisitions in 1999 was $3.4 trillion, a 40 percent increase from the previous record of $2.5 trillion in 1998. Cross-border mergers were also on the rise during this period: The dollar value of cross-border mergers in 1999, $1.1 trillion, was almost double the value of cross-border mergers in 1998 and accounted for nearly 33 percent of the value of all worldwide deals.

Takeovers in the 1990s and 2000s were different from those of the 1980s, however. First, a majority were not cash acquisitions, which the acquirer financed with junk bonds. Rather, given soaring stock prices, 55 percent of acquirers used shares of their company's stock as the consideration in share-for-share exchanges. A second difference from the 1980 takeovers is that many of these transactions were strategic acquisitions in which an acquirer sought to increase its size or expand its business operations by acquiring other companies in the same or a related field. Acquiring lots of small phone companies (and one large one, MCI) is how WorldCom grew from a small, start-up phone company based in Clinton, Mississippi, to an industry behemoth, servicing 20 percent of consumers' telephone needs and 50 percent of internet traffic in the United States at the time of its bankruptcy in 2002. So, unlike the acquisitions of the 1960s and 1970s, these acquisitions for the most part did not create conglomerates of unrelated businesses within the same corporate structure; they were acquisitions of related businesses. And unlike in the 1980s, these acquisitions did not lead to "busting up" the companies being purchased. While many of the mergers and acquisitions of the 1990s and 2000s led to layoffs from "synergies" — that is, companies could eliminate overlapping or redundant operations — takeovers didn't lead to the same hostility and political response as did takeovers in the 1980s. Perhaps this is because states had already passed protective legislation giving the board the power to ward off unsolicited tender offers. Perhaps it was because 50 percent of Americans were stockholders by the 1990s, either directly or through their pension funds, and were happy with what their stock portfolios were doing. In any case, political debate about takeovers in the 1990s and 2000s in the United States was just about nonexistent.

Yet within the corporate governance community, questions about the distribution of powers between shareholders and directors to respond to hostile takeover attempts and about directors' fiduciary duties remain central. You will see these questions developed in the cases set out below. The first series of cases, Unocal Corp. v. Mesa Petroleum Co. and its progeny, evaluates defensive measures that boards take to determine if those measures are consistent with the board's duties of care and loyalty to the corporation and its shareholders. Given the importance of poison pills as a particular defensive technique, we will look at the legitimacy of pills and the latest variations on them (so-called "dead-hand" and "no-hand" pills), and then turn to other recent applications of *Unocal.* The second series of cases, the *Revlon* line, seeks to determine if there has been a change-of-control transaction and evaluates the board's duties once it is no longer defending the company against an unwanted suitor, but is actively selling the company. As you will see below, a quite different legal analysis obtains if the company is being sold versus being defended.

B. DELAWARE'S "INTERMEDIATE SCRUTINY" OF DEFENSIVE MEASURES

Unocal Corp. v. Mesa Petroleum Co. describes the standards employed by the Delaware courts to evaluate the use of defensive measures by the board of directors of a Delaware corporation. *Unocal* is widely considered one of the most important and innovative cases in the history of Delaware corporate law. Piecing together prior cases, it constructs a new method of analyzing defensive measures.

After *Unocal* was decided, the Securities and Exchange Commission (SEC) promulgated Rule 14(d)-10, based on the authority of § 14 of the 1934 Act. Rule 14(d)-10 prohibits selective tender offers and requires all tendering securities holders to be paid the highest price paid to anyone in the tender offer. Thus, Rule 14(d)-10 now prohibits the selective self-tender upheld by the *Unocal* court. *Unocal* is still an extremely important case, however, since the standard used by the court to evaluate the Unocal board's defensive actions remains the standard used in Delaware to analyze all cases involving defensive actions.

UNOCAL CORP. v. MESA PETROLEUM CO.

493 A.2d 946
Supreme Court of Delaware
June 10, 1985

MOORE, Justice.

We confront an issue of first impression in Delaware — the validity of a corporation's self-tender for its own shares which excludes from participation a stockholder making a hostile tender offer for the company's stock.

The Court of Chancery granted a preliminary injunction to the plaintiffs, Mesa Petroleum Co., Mesa Asset Co., Mesa Partners II, and Mesa Eastern, Inc. (collectively "Mesa"),[1] enjoining an exchange offer of the defendant, Unocal Corporation (Unocal) for its own stock. The trial court concluded that a selective exchange offer, excluding Mesa, was legally impermissible. We cannot agree with such a blanket rule. The factual findings of the Vice Chancellor, fully supported by the record, establish that Unocal's board, consisting of a majority of independent directors, acted in good faith, and after reasonable investigation found that Mesa's tender offer was both inadequate and coercive. Under the circumstances the board had both the power and duty to oppose a bid it perceived to be harmful to the corporate enterprise. On this record we are satisfied that the device Unocal adopted is reasonable in relation to the threat posed, and that the board acted in the proper exercise of sound business judgment. We will not substitute our views for those of the board if the latter's decision can be "attributed to any rational business purpose." Sinclair Oil Corp. v. Levien, Del. Supr., 280 A.2d 717, 720 (1971). Accordingly, we reverse the decision of the Court of Chancery and order the preliminary injunction vacated.

I.

On April 8, 1985, Mesa, the owner of approximately 13% of Unocal's stock, commenced a two-tier "front loaded" cash tender offer for 64 million shares, or approximately 37%, of Unocal's outstanding stock at a price of $54 per share. The "back-end" was designed to eliminate the remaining publicly held shares by an exchange of securities purportedly worth $54 per share. However, pursuant to an order entered by the United States District Court for the Central District of California on April 26, 1985, Mesa issued a supplemental proxy statement to Unocal's stockholders disclosing that the securities offered in the second-step merger would be highly subordinated, and that Unocal's capitalization would differ significantly from its present structure. Unocal has rather aptly termed such securities "junk bonds."

---

1. T. Boone Pickens, Jr., is President and Chairman of the Board of Mesa Petroleum and President of Mesa Asset and controls the related Mesa entities.

Unocal's board consists of eight independent outside directors and six insiders. It met on April 13, 1985, to consider the Mesa tender offer. Thirteen directors were present, and the meeting lasted nine and one-half hours. The directors were given no agenda or written materials prior to the session. However, detailed presentations were made by legal counsel regarding the board's obligations under both Delaware corporate law and the federal securities laws. The board then received a presentation from Peter Sachs on behalf of Goldman Sachs & Co. (Goldman Sachs) and Dillon, Read & Co. (Dillon Read) discussing the bases for their opinions that the Mesa proposal was wholly inadequate. Mr. Sachs opined that the minimum cash value that could be expected from a sale or orderly liquidation for 100% of Unocal's stock was in excess of $60 per share. In making his presentation, Mr. Sachs showed slides outlining the valuation techniques used by the financial advisors, and others, depicting recent business combinations in the oil and gas industry. The Court of Chancery found that the Sachs presentation was designed to apprise the directors of the scope of the analyses performed rather than the facts and numbers used in reaching the conclusion that Mesa's tender offer price was inadequate.

Mr. Sachs also presented various defensive strategies available to the board if it concluded that Mesa's two-step tender offer was inadequate and should be opposed. One of the devices outlined was a self-tender by Unocal for its own stock with a reasonable price range of $70 to $75 per share. The cost of such a proposal would cause the company to incur $6.1-6.5 billion of additional debt, and a presentation was made informing the board of Unocal's ability to handle it. The directors were told that the primary effect of this obligation would be to reduce exploratory drilling, but that the company would nonetheless remain a viable entity.

The eight outside directors, comprising a clear majority of the thirteen members present, then met separately with Unocal's financial advisors and attorneys. Thereafter, they unanimously agreed to advise the board that it should reject Mesa's tender offer as inadequate, and that Unocal should pursue a self-tender to provide the stockholders with a fairly priced alternative to the Mesa proposal. The board then reconvened and unanimously adopted a resolution rejecting as grossly inadequate Mesa's tender offer. Despite the nine and one-half hour length of the meeting, no formal decision was made on the proposed defensive self-tender.

On April 15, the board met again with four of the directors present by telephone and one member still absent. This session lasted two hours. Unocal's Vice President of Finance and its Assistant General Counsel made a detailed presentation of the proposed terms of the exchange offer. A price range between $70 and $80 per share was considered, and ultimately the directors agreed upon $72. The board was also advised about the debt securities that would be issued, and the necessity of placing restrictive covenants upon certain corporate activities until the obligations were paid. The board's decisions were made in reliance on the advice of its investment bankers, including the terms and conditions upon which the securities were to be issued. Based upon this advice, and the board's own deliberations, the directors unanimously approved the exchange offer. Their resolution provided that if Mesa acquired 64 million shares of Unocal stock through its own offer (the Mesa Purchase Condition), Unocal would buy the remaining 49 percent outstanding for an exchange of debt securities having an aggregate par value of $72 per share. The board resolution also stated that the offer would be subject to other conditions that had been described to the board at the meeting, or which were deemed necessary by Unocal's officers, including the exclusion of Mesa from the proposal (the Mesa exclusion). Any such conditions were required to be in accordance with the "purport and intent" of the offer.

Unocal's exchange offer was commenced on April 17, 1985, and Mesa promptly challenged it by filing this suit in the Court of Chancery. On April 22, the Unocal board met again and was advised by Goldman Sachs and Dillon Read to waive the Mesa Purchase Condition as to 50 million shares. This recommendation was in response to a perceived concern of the shareholders that, if shares were tendered to Unocal, no shares would be purchased by either offeror. The directors were also advised that they should tender their own Unocal stock into the exchange offer as a mark of their confidence in it.

Another focus of the board was the Mesa exclusion. Legal counsel advised that under Delaware law Mesa could only be excluded for what the directors reasonably believed to be a valid corporate purpose. The directors' discussion centered on the objective of adequately compensating shareholders at the "back-end" of Mesa's proposal, which the latter would finance with "junk bonds." To include Mesa would defeat that goal, because under the proration aspect of the exchange offer (49%) every Mesa share accepted by Unocal would displace one held by another stockholder. Further, if Mesa were permitted to tender to Unocal, the latter would in effect be financing Mesa's own inadequate proposal. . . .

[After hearings on Mesa's motion for a temporary restraining order (TRO) and preliminary injunction (PI), and subsequent to the Delaware Supreme court posing questions of fact for the chancery court to consider in its hearing for a PI,] the Vice Chancellor issued an unreported opinion on May 13, 1985 granting Mesa a preliminary injunction. Specifically, the trial court noted that "[t]he parties basically agree that the directors' duty of care extends to protecting the corporation from perceived harm whether it be from third parties or shareholders." The trial court also concluded in response to the second inquiry in the Supreme Court's May 2 order, that "[a]lthough the facts, . . . do not appear to be sufficient to prove that Mesa's principle objective is to be bought off at a substantial premium, they do justify a reasonable inference to the same effect."

As to the third and fourth questions posed by this Court, the Vice Chancellor stated that they "appear to raise the more fundamental issue of whether directors owe fiduciary duties to shareholders who they perceive to be acting contrary to the best interests of the corporation as a whole." While determining that the directors' decision to oppose Mesa's tender offer was made in a good faith belief that the Mesa proposal was inadequate, the court stated that the business judgment rule does not apply to a selective exchange offer such as this.

On May 13, 1985 the Court of Chancery certified this interlocutory appeal to us as a question of first impression, and we accepted it on May 14. The entire matter was scheduled on an expedited basis.

II.

The issues we address involve these fundamental questions: Did the Unocal board have the power and duty to oppose a takeover threat it reasonably perceived to be harmful to the corporate enterprise, and if so, is its action here entitled to the protection of the business judgment rule?

Mesa contends that the discriminatory exchange offer violates the fiduciary duties Unocal owes it. Mesa argues that because of the Mesa exclusion the business judgment rule is inapplicable, because the directors by tendering their own shares will derive a financial benefit that is not available to *all* Unocal stockholders. Thus, it is Mesa's ultimate contention that Unocal cannot establish that the exchange offer is fair to *all* shareholders, and argues that the Court of Chancery was correct in concluding that Unocal was unable to meet this burden.

Unocal answers that it does not owe a duty of "fairness" to Mesa, given the facts here. Specifically, Unocal contends that its board of directors reasonably and in good faith concluded that Mesa's $54 two-tier tender offer was coercive and inadequate, and that Mesa sought selective treatment for itself. Furthermore, Unocal argues that the board's approval of the exchange offer was made in good faith, on an informed basis, and in the exercise of due care. Under these circumstances, Unocal contends that its directors properly employed this device to protect the company and its stockholders from Mesa's harmful tactics.

III.

We begin with the basic issue of the power of a board of directors of a Delaware corporation to adopt a defensive measure of this type. Absent such authority, all other questions are moot. Neither issues of fairness nor business judgment are pertinent without the basic underpinning of a board's legal power to act.

The board has a large reservoir of authority upon which to draw. Its duties and responsibilities proceed from the inherent powers conferred by 8 Del. C. § 141(a), respecting management of the corporation's "business and affairs." Additionally, the powers here being exercised derive from 8 Del. C. § 160(a), conferring broad authority upon a corporation to deal in its own stock. From this it is now well established that in the acquisition of its shares a Delaware corporation may deal selectively with its stockholders, provided the directors have not acted out of a sole or primary purpose to entrench themselves in office. Cheff v. Mathes, Del. Supr., 199 A.2d 548, 554 (1964); [other citations].

Finally, the board's power to act derives from its fundamental duty and obligation to protect the corporate enterprise, which includes stockholders, from harm reasonably perceived, irrespective of its source. Thus, we are satisfied that in the broad context of corporate governance, including issues of fundamental corporate change, a board of directors is not a passive instrumentality.

Given the foregoing principles, we turn to the standards by which director action is to be measured. In Pogostin v. Rice, Del. Supr., 480 A.2d 619 (1984), we held that the business judgment rule, including the standards by which director conduct is judged, is applicable in the context of a takeover. *Id.* at 627. The business judgment rule is a "presumption that in making a business decision the directors of a corporation acted on an informed basis, in good faith and in the honest belief that the action taken was in the best interests of the company." Aronson v. Lewis, Del. Supr., 473 A.2d 805, 812 (1984) (citations omitted). A hallmark of the business judgment rule is that a court will not substitute its judgment for that of the board if the latter's decision can be "attributed to any rational business purpose." Sinclair Oil Corp. v. Levien, Del. Supr., 280 A.2d 717, 720 (1971).

When a board addresses a pending takeover bid it has an obligation to determine whether the offer is in the best interests of the corporation and its shareholders. In that respect a board's duty is no different from any other responsibility it shoulders, and its decisions should be no less entitled to the respect they otherwise would be accorded in the realm of business judgment. There are, however, certain caveats to a proper exercise of this function. Because of the omnipresent specter that a board may be acting primarily in its own interests, rather than those of the corporation and its shareholders, there is an enhanced duty which calls for judicial examination at the threshold before the protections of the business judgment rule may be conferred.

This Court has long recognized that:

> We must bear in mind the inherent danger in the purchase of shares with corporate funds to remove a threat to corporate policy when a threat to control is involved. The directors are of necessity confronted with a conflict of interest, and an objective decision is difficult.

Bennett v. Propp, Del. Supr., 187 A.2d 405, 409 (1962). In the face of this inherent conflict directors must show that they had reasonable grounds for believing that a danger to corporate policy and effectiveness existed because of another person's stock ownership. Cheff v. Mathes, 199 A.2d at 554-55. However, they satisfy that burden "by showing good faith and reasonable investigation. . . ." *Id.* at 555. Furthermore, such proof is materially enhanced, as here, by the approval of a board comprised of a majority of outside independent directors who have acted in accordance with the foregoing standards. *See* Aronson v. Lewis, 473 A.2d at 812, 815. . . .

IV.

A.

In the board's exercise of corporate power to forestall a takeover bid our analysis begins with the basic principle that corporate directors have a fiduciary duty to act in the best interests of the corporation's stockholders. As we have noted, their duty of care extends to protecting the corporation and its owners from perceived harm whether a threat originates from third parties or other shareholders. But such powers are not absolute. A corporation does not have unbridled discretion to defeat any perceived threat by any Draconian means available.

The restriction placed upon a selective stock repurchase is that the directors may not have acted solely or primarily out of a desire to perpetuate themselves in office. *See* Cheff v. Mathes, 199 A.2d at 556; Kors v. Carey, 158 A.2d at 140. Of course, to this is added the further caveat that inequitable action may not be taken under the guise of law. Schnell v. Chris-Craft Industries, Inc., Del. Supr., 285 A.2d 437, 439 (1971). The standard of proof established in Cheff v. Mathes . . . is designed to ensure that a defensive measure to thwart or impede a takeover is indeed motivated by a good faith concern for the welfare of the corporation and its stockholders, which in all circumstances must be free of any fraud or other misconduct. Cheff v. Mathes, 199 A.2d at 554-55. However, this does not end the inquiry.

B.

A further aspect is the element of balance. If a defensive measure is to come within the ambit of the business judgment rule, it must be reasonable in relation to the threat posed. This entails an analysis by the directors of the nature of the takeover bid and its effect on the corporate enterprise. Examples of such concerns may include: inadequacy of the price offered, nature and timing of the offer, questions of illegality, the impact on "constituencies" other than shareholders (*i.e.*, creditors, customers, employees, and perhaps even the community generally), the risk of nonconsummation, and the quality of securities being offered in the exchange. While not a controlling factor, it also seems to us that a board may reasonably consider the basic stockholder interests at stake, including those of short term speculators, whose actions may have fueled the coercive aspect of the offer at the expense of the long term investor.[11] Here, the threat posed was viewed by the Unocal board as a grossly inadequate two-tier coercive tender offer coupled with the threat of greenmail.

Specifically, the Unocal directors had concluded that the value of Unocal was substantially above the $54 per share offered in cash at the front end. Furthermore, they determined that the subordinated securities to be exchanged in Mesa's announced squeeze out of the remaining shareholders in the "back-end" merger were "junk bonds" worth far less than $54. It is now well recognized that such offers are a classic coercive measure designed to stampede shareholders into tendering at the first tier, even if the price is inadequate, out of fear of what they will receive at the back end of the transaction. Wholly beyond the coercive aspect of an inadequate two-tier tender offer, the threat was posed by a corporate raider with a national reputation as a "greenmailer."[13]

In adopting the selective exchange offer, the board stated that its objective was either to defeat the inadequate Mesa offer or, should the offer still succeed, provide the 49% of its stockholders, who would otherwise be forced to accept

11. There has been much debate respecting such stockholder interests. One rather impressive study indicates that the stock of over 50 percent of target companies, who resisted hostile takeovers, later traded at higher market prices than the rejected offer price, or were acquired after the tender offer was defeated by another company at a price higher than the offer price. *See* Lipton, [*Takeover Bids in the Target's Boardroom*, 35 Bus. Law. 101,] 106-109, 132-133. Moreover, an update by Kidder Peabody & Company of this study, involving the stock prices of target companies that have defeated hostile tender offers during the period from 1973 to 1982 demonstrates that in a majority of cases the target's shareholders benefitted from the defeat. The stock of 81% of the targets studied has, since the tender offer, sold at prices higher than the tender offer price. When adjusted for the time value of money, the figure is 64%. *See* Lipton & Brownstein, *supra* ABA Institute at 10. The thesis being that this strongly supports application of the business judgment rule in response to takeover threats. There is, however, a rather vehement contrary view. *See* Easterbrook & Fischel, [The Proper Rule of a Target's Management in Responding to a Tender Offer, 94 Harv. L. Rev. 1161, 1739-1745 (1981)].

13. The term "greenmail" refers to the practice of buying out a takeover bidder's stock at a premium that is not available to other shareholders in order to prevent the takeover. The Chancery Court noted that "Mesa has made tremendous profits from its takeover activities although in the past few years it has not been successful in acquiring any of the target companies on an unfriendly basis." Moreover, the trial court specifically found that the actions of the Unocal board were taken in good faith to eliminate both the inadequacies of the tender offer and to forestall the payment of "greenmail."

"junk bonds," with $72 worth of senior debt. We find that both purposes are valid.

However, such efforts would have been thwarted by Mesa's participation in the exchange offer. First, if Mesa could tender its shares, Unocal would effectively be subsidizing the former's continuing effort to buy Unocal stock at $54 per share. Second, Mesa could not, by definition, fit within the class of shareholders being protected from its own coercive and inadequate tender offer.

Thus, we are satisfied that the selective exchange offer is reasonably related to the threats posed. It is consistent with the principle that "the minority stock-holder shall receive the substantial equivalent in value of what he had before." Sterling v. Mayflower Hotel Corp., Del. Supr., 93 A.2d 107, 114 (1952). *See also* Rosenblatt v. Getty Oil Co., Del. Supr., 493 A.2d 929, 940 (1985). This concept of fairness, while stated in the merger context, is also relevant in the area of tender offer law. Thus, the board's decision to offer what it determined to be the fair value of the corporation to the 49% of its shareholders, who would otherwise be forced to accept highly subordinated "junk bonds," is reasonable and consistent with the directors' duty to ensure that the minority stockholders receive equal value for their shares.

V.

Mesa contends that it is unlawful, and the trial court agreed, for a corporation to discriminate in this fashion against one shareholder. It argues correctly that no case has ever sanctioned a device that precludes a raider from sharing in a benefit available to all other stockholders. However, as we have noted earlier, the principle of selective stock repurchases by a Delaware corporation is neither unknown nor unauthorized. Cheff v. Mathes, 199 A.2d at 554; 8 Del. G.C.L. § 160. The only difference is that heretofore the approved transaction was the payment of "greenmail" to a raider or dissident posing a threat to the corporate enterprise. All other stockholders were denied such favored treatment, and given Mesa's past history of greenmail, its claims here are rather ironic.

However, our corporate law is not static. It must grow and develop in response to, indeed in anticipation of, evolving concepts and needs. Merely because the General Corporation Law is silent as to a specific matter does not mean that it is prohibited. In the days when *Cheff, Bennett, Martin* and *Kors* were decided, the tender offer, while not an unknown device, was virtually unused, and little was known of such methods as two-tier "front-end" loaded offers with their coercive effects. Then, the favored attack of a raider was stock acquisition followed by a proxy contest. Various defensive tactics, which provided no benefit whatever to the raider, evolved. Thus, the use of corporate funds by management to counter a proxy battle was approved. Litigation, supported by corporate funds, aimed at the raider has long been a popular device.

More recently, as the sophistication of both raiders and targets has developed, a host of other defensive measures to counter such ever mounting threats has evolved and received judicial sanction. These include defensive charter amend-ments and other devices bearing some rather exotic, but apt, names: Crown Jewel, White Knight, Pac Man, and Golden Parachute. Each has highly selective features, the object of which is to deter or defeat the raider.

Thus, while the exchange offer is a form of selective treatment, given the nature of the threat posed here the response is neither unlawful nor unreasonable. If the board of directors is disinterested, has acted in good faith and with due care, its decision in the absence of an abuse of discretion will be upheld as a proper exercise of business judgment.

To this Mesa responds that the board is not disinterested, because the directors are receiving a benefit from the tender of their own shares, which because of the Mesa exclusion, does not devolve upon *all* stockholders equally. *See* Aronson v. Lewis, Del. Supr., 473 A.2d 805, 812 (1984). However, Mesa concedes that if the exclusion is valid, then the directors and all other stockholders share the same benefit. The answer of course is that the exclusion is valid, and the directors' participation in the exchange offer does not rise to the level of a disqualifying interest.

Nor does this become an "interested" director transaction merely because certain board members are large stockholders. As this Court has previously noted, that fact alone does not create a disqualifying "personal pecuniary interest" to defeat the operation of the business judgment rule. Cheff v. Mathes, 199 A.2d at 554.

Mesa also argues that the exclusion permits the directors to abdicate the fiduciary duties they owe it. However, that is not so. The board continues to owe Mesa the duties of due care and loyalty. But in the face of the destructive threat Mesa's tender offer was perceived to pose, the board had a supervening duty to protect the corporate enterprise, which includes the other shareholders, from threatened harm.

Mesa contends that the basis of this action is punitive, and solely in response to the exercise of its rights of corporate democracy. Nothing precludes Mesa, as a stockholder, from acting in its own self-interest. However, Mesa, while pursuing its own interests, has acted in a manner which a board consisting of a majority of independent directors has reasonably determined to be contrary to the best interests of Unocal and its other shareholders. In this situation, there is no support in Delaware law for the proposition that, when responding to a perceived harm, a corporation must guarantee a benefit to a stockholder who is deliberately provoking the danger being addressed. There is no obligation of self-sacrifice by a corporation and its shareholders in the face of such a challenge.

Here, the Court of Chancery specifically found that the "directors' decision [to oppose the Mesa tender offer] was made in the good faith belief that the Mesa tender offer is inadequate." Given our standard of review under Levitt v. Bouvier, Del. Supr., 287 A.2d 671, 673 (1972), and Application of Delaware Racing Association, Del. Supr., 213 A.2d 203, 207 (1965), we are satisfied that Unocal's board has met its burden of proof. Cheff v. Mathes, 199 A.2d at 555.

VI.

In conclusion, there was directorial power to oppose the Mesa tender offer, and to undertake a selective stock exchange made in good faith and upon a reasonable investigation pursuant to a clear duty to protect the corporate enterprise. Further, the selective stock repurchase plan chosen by Unocal is reasonable in relation to the threat that the board rationally and reasonably believed was posed by Mesa's inadequate and coercive two-tier tender offer. Under those circumstances the board's action is entitled to be measured by the standards of the business judgment rule. Thus, unless it is shown by a preponderance of the evidence that the directors' decisions were primarily based on perpetuating themselves in office, or some other breach of fiduciary duty such as fraud, overreaching, lack of good faith, or being uninformed, a Court will not substitute its judgment for that of the board.

In this case that protection is not lost merely because Unocal's directors have tendered their shares in the exchange offer. Given the validity of the Mesa exclusion, they are receiving a benefit shared generally by all other stockholders except Mesa. In this circumstance the test of Aronson v. Lewis, 473 A.2d at 812, is satisfied. If the stockholders are displeased with the action of their elected representatives, the powers of corporate democracy are at their disposal to turn the board out. Aronson v. Lewis, Del. Supr., 473 A.2d 805, 811 (1984). *See also* 8 Del. C. §§ 141(k) and 211(b).

With the Court of Chancery's findings that the exchange offer was based on the board's good faith belief that the Mesa offer was inadequate, that the board's action was informed and taken with due care, that Mesa's prior activities justify a reasonable inference that its principle objective was greenmail, and implicitly, that the substance of the offer itself was reasonable and fair to the corporation and its stockholders if Mesa were included, we cannot say that the Unocal directors have acted in such a manner as to have passed an "unintelligent and unadvised judgment." The decision of the Court of Chancery is therefore REVERSED, and the preliminary injunction is VACATED.

PROBLEM 11-1

After considering various strategic options, Multiply decided to expand through the acquisition of regional banks. By offering traditional banking services alongside innovative crowdfunding solutions, Multiply hopes to attract more customers that have been reluctant to participate in crowdfunding.

Path Bank Inc. (Path) is a regional bank serving six states in the Intermountain West. Path is publicly traded on the New York Stock Exchange. Path weathered the global financial crisis, but after several years of austerity, the bank was looking for new opportunities. When Multiply proposed a merger, the top executives were immediately intrigued, and the two companies quickly negotiated a merger agreement under which Multiply agreed to pay approximately $400 million in a stock-for-stock transaction. In this transaction, Path would merge into Multiply, and the shareholders of Path would receive shares of Multiply in exchange for their Path shares.

The merger agreement contained several provisions requested by Multiply designed to ensure that Path would consummate the transaction. First, the parties negotiated a termination fee, under which Path would pay Multiply $20 million (5 percent of the merger consideration) if Path failed to consummate the transaction because Path's board of directors accepted a competing offer or changed its recommendation in favor of the transaction, causing Multiply to terminate the merger agreement rather than proceed with the shareholder vote. Second, the parties agreed to a "no-shop" provision, which prohibited Path from "tak[ing] any action to solicit, initiate, encourage or assist the submission of any proposal, negotiation or offer from any person or entity other than Multiply relating to the sale or issuance, of any of the capital stock of the Company or the acquisition, sale, lease, license or other disposition of the Company or any material part of the stock or assets of the Company."

Termination fee provisions, no-shop provisions, and other so-called "deal protection devices" are common in merger agreements. Until a deal is closed, acquirers are concerned that a third party may enter the negotiations with a superior bid. Deal protection devices are intended to discourage third party bids or, where the bids are not discouraged, to provide compensation to the acquirer for initiating the acquisition.

Should deal protection devices be subject to analysis under the **Unocal** *standard?*

C. POISON PILLS

The *Unocal* standard is often referred to as an "enhanced scrutiny" or "intermediate scrutiny" standard because the board is neither given the benefit of the business judgment rule nor placed under the burden of proving the entire fairness of the transaction. Rather, the court employs a two-step analysis: (1) the board must show that it had reasonable grounds to believe there was a threat to an important corporate policy from an offer (the "threat analysis"); and (2) the board must show that the means used to defend against that threat were proportionate to the threat (the "proportionality review").

The threat analysis involves an inquiry into the same issues that arise under the business judgment rule—did the board act in good faith and pursuant to a reasonable investigation in determining that there was a threat posed to the shareholders or to an important corporate policy by the takeover bid? The only difference lies in the burden of proof, which is shifted to the defendant in *Unocal* cases. Subsequent decisions suggest that burden-shifting here does not affect the outcome of the cases, as directors almost always prevail on this part of the analysis. Particularly if they have financial advisors who opine that the price of a takeover bid is too low, the directors will be able to show that the takeover bid is a threat to shareholders: A price that is too low is always a threat to the shareholders.

The more innovative and controversial aspect of *Unocal* was the proportionality review. This part of the analysis seems to contemplate a substantive review of board decisions by the court. Perhaps driven by the same deference that animates the business judgment rule, the Delaware Supreme Court has, until recently, been reluctant to second-guess directors' actions, notwithstanding the "enhanced" scrutiny under *Unocal*. That has not stopped the court from tinkering with the proportionality review. In Unitrin, Inc. v. American General Corp., 651 A.2d 1361 (Del. 1995), the court held that the proportionality review required two levels of inquiry. At the first level, the court would determine whether the challenged defensive action was "coercive" or "preclusive." A defensive measure is "coercive" if it is "aimed at 'cramming down' on its shareholders a management-sponsored alternative" to an outside bid, and a defensive measure is "preclusive" if it prevents any bidder from being able to successfully take over the company, including by using a proxy contest.

If the board's action is neither coercive nor preclusive, the court must still evaluate the action to determine whether it falls within the "range of reasonableness."

In other words, a defensive action constitutes a breach of fiduciary duty if it is unreasonable in light of the threat posed by a bid, even if it is not so extreme as to be coercive or preclusive. At this stage of the inquiry, however, the court is again deferential to the board. In the words of the *Unitrin* court:

> The *ratio decidendi* for the "range of reasonableness" standard is a need of the board of directors for latitude in discharging its fiduciary duties to the corporation and its shareholders when defending against perceived threats. The concomitant requirement is for judicial restraint. Consequently, if the board of directors' defensive response is not draconian (preclusive or coercive) and is within a "range of reasonableness," a court must not substitute its judgment for the board's.

According to the *Unocal* court, the two steps in the analysis are a "threshold" to be crossed on the way to the business judgment rule. If the defendants carry their burden, therefore, the plaintiffs theoretically have the opportunity to show that there is some other reason to rebut the business judgment rule. As noted by Vice-Chancellor Strine in In re Gaylord Container Corp. S'holders Litig., 753 A.2d 462, 475-476 (Del. Ch. 2000), this structure simply does not make sense:

> It is not at all apparent how a plaintiff could meet this burden in a circumstance where the board met its burden under *Unocal*. To the extent that the plaintiff has persuasive evidence of disloyalty (for example, that the board acted in a self-interested or bad-faith fashion), this would fatally undercut the board's *Unocal* showing. Similarly, it is hard to see how a plaintiff could rebut the presumption of the business judgment rule by demonstrating that the board acted in a grossly careless manner in a circumstance where the board had demonstrated that it had acted reasonably and proportionately. Least of all could a plaintiff show that the board's actions lacked a rational business purpose in a context where the board had already demonstrated that those actions were reasonable, *i.e.*, rational.

Poison pills give the board substantial leverage in negotiations with potential acquirers. Poison pills usually involve the distribution of "rights" to existing shareholders pursuant to Delaware General Corporation Law (DGCL) § 157. These rights allow the shareholders to buy shares of the acquiring company ("flip-over pills") or the target company ("flip-in pills") at a deep discount — typically half price — if any bidder acquires a certain percentage of the target's shares (called the "trigger"), usually 10 or 15 percent, without the board's approval. If the rights are triggered, the bidder's stake will immediately be diluted as existing shareholders exercise their rights to buy shares at bargain basement prices, which would then require the bidder to buy substantially more shares to take control.

Poison pills are intended to substantially increase the cost of a hostile acquisition. As a result, bidders rarely purchase more shares than the "trigger." Poison pills are the most important arrow in a company's quiver of defenses, because they can be adopted unilaterally by the board in response to an identified threat, and they can be "redeemed" (eliminated) by the board by paying a nominal amount to the shareholders to allow a merger with a favored acquisition partner. Poison pills force would-be acquirers to either negotiate with the board of directors or engage in a proxy fight to elect a board that is committed to replacing the board of directors and then redeeming the pill. In Delaware, however, if the board is staggered, two annual elections are needed to take majority control of the target's board, because staggering the board implies a "for cause" limitation on removal of board members; thus even a proxy fight requires two years. The combination of a pill and a staggered board is a powerful anti-takeover device, and it is probably for this reason that as of 1998, 59 percent of public companies in the United States had staggered boards, as did 82 percent of companies going public for the first time in 2001. *See* Lucian Bebchuk, John Coates & Guhan Subramanian, *The Powerful Antitakeover Force of Staggered Boards: Theory, Evidence and Policy*, 54 Stan. L. Rev. 887, 888 (2002).

The "ballot box" alternative to negotiating with the target board would seem to offer a real alternative to potential acquirers and thus to pose a threat to boards determined to stay independent. As a result, stronger variations of the pill were developed. Carmody v. Toll Brothers, 723 A.2d 1180 (Del. Ch. 1998), for example, involved a poison pill with a "continuing director" provision, which proscribed the removal of the poison pill by anyone other than the directors who adopted the pill or their approved successors. These provisions have been called "dead-hand poison pills." Vice Chancellor Jacobs of the Delaware Court of Chancery struck down the provision, concluding that the dead-hand pill was preclusive under *Unitrin* because it made the "bidder's ability to wage a successful proxy contest and gain control either 'mathematically impossible' or 'realistically unattainable.'" Carmody, 723 A.2d at 1195.

In response to the *Carmody* decision, the board of directors of Quickturn Design Systems, Inc. amended its poison pill by eliminating its "dead-hand" feature and replacing it with a deferred redemption provision, under which no newly elected board could redeem the rights plan for six months after taking office, if the purpose or effect of the redemption would be to facilitate a transaction with an "interested person," defined as anyone who proposed, nominated, or financially supported the election of the new directors to the board. This new version of the poison pill, dubbed the "no-hand" poison pill, was invalidated by the Delaware Supreme Court, not on the ground that a deferred redemption provision is coercive or preclusive, but on the ground that it "violates fundamental Delaware law." In Quickturn Design Sys., Inc. v. Shapiro, 721 A.2d 1281 (Del. 1998), the court reasoned:

> The Delayed Redemption Provision . . . would prevent a newly elected board of directors from completely discharging its fundamental management duties to the corporation and its stockholders for six months. While the Delayed Redemption Provision limits the board of directors' authority in only one respect, the suspension of the Rights Plan, it nonetheless restricts the board's power in an area of fundamental importance to the shareholders — negotiating a possible sale of the corporation. Therefore, we hold that the Delayed Redemption Provision is invalid under Section 141(a), which confers upon any newly elected board of directors full power to manage and direct the business and affairs of a Delaware corporation.

Id. at 1291-1292.

Even though these innovative poison pills have been invalidated in Delaware, a company that has a staggered board in its charter and is either incorporated in Delaware or has a for-cause limitation on removing directors can impose significant delay on a hostile bidder, requiring two annual elections before an acquirer is able to take control. We will see the effects of that delay in Air

Products and Chemicals, Inc. v. Airgas, Inc. later in this chapter. In the meantime, the next case examines another innovative poison pill, the so-called "NOL pill," which is designed to help certain companies preserve a valuable tax attribute called "net operating loss carryforwards." Unlike the dead-hand poison pill and the no-hand poison pill, the NOL pill does not restrict the ability of the board of directors to redeem the shareholder rights. Instead, it lowers the trigger below 5 percent, thus making a successful ballot box challenge more difficult.

VERSATA ENTERPRISES, INC. v. SELECTICA, INC.

5 A.3d 586
Supreme Court of Delaware
October 4, 2010

HOLLAND, Justice:

. . .

Since it became a public company in March 2000, Selectica, Inc. ("Selectica" or the "Company") has lost a substantial amount of money and failed to turn an annual profit, despite routinely projecting near-term profitability. Its IPO price of $30 per share has steadily fallen and now languishes below $1 per share, placing Selectica's market capitalization at roughly $23 million as of the end of March 2009. By Selectica's own admission, its value today "consists primarily in its cash reserves, its intellectual property portfolio, its customer and revenue base, and its accumulated [net operating loss carryforwards ("NOLs")]." By consistently failing to achieve positive net income, Selectica has generated an estimated $160 million in NOLs for federal tax purposes over the past several years.

. . .

NOLs are tax losses, realized and accumulated by a corporation, that can be used to shelter future (or immediate past) income from taxation. If taxable profit has been realized, the NOLs operate either to provide a refund of prior taxes paid or to reduce the amount of future income tax owed. Thus, NOLs can be a valuable asset, as a means of lowering tax payments and producing positive cash flow. NOLs are considered a contingent asset, their value being contingent upon the firm's reporting a future profit or having an immediate past profit.

Should the firm fail to realize a profit during the lifetime of the NOL (twenty years), the NOL expires. The precise value of a given NOL is usually impossible to determine since its ultimate use is subject to the timing and amount of recognized profit at the firm. If the firm never realizes taxable income, at dissolution its NOLs, regardless of their amount, would have zero value.

In order to prevent corporate taxpayers from benefiting from NOLs generated by other entities, Internal Revenue Code Section 382 establishes limitations on the use of NOLs in periods following an "ownership change." If Section 382 is triggered, the law restricts the amount of prior NOLs that can be used in subsequent years to reduce the firm's tax obligations. Once NOLs are so impaired, a substantial portion of their value is lost.

The precise definition of an "ownership change" under Section 382 is rather complex. At its most basic, an ownership change occurs when more than 50% of a firm's stock ownership changes over a three-year period. Specific provisions in Section 382 define the precise manner by which this determination is made. Most importantly for purposes of this case, the only shareholders considered when calculating an ownership change under Section 382 are those who hold, or have obtained during the testing period, a 5% or greater block of the corporation's shares outstanding.

. . .

Trilogy Buys Selectica Stock

On the evening of November 10, 2008, [Trilogy chief financial officer Sean Fallon] contacted [Brenda Zawatski, co-chair of the Selectica Board of Directors (the "Board"),] and informed her that Trilogy had purchased more than 5% of Selectica's outstanding stock and would be filing a Schedule 13D shortly, which it did on November 13. On a subsequent call with Zawatski and [investment banker Jim Reilly of Needham & Company], Fallon explained that Trilogy had begun buying because it believed that "the company should work quickly to preserve whatever shareholder value remained and that we were interested in seeing this process that they announced with Needham, that we were interested in seeing that accelerate. . . ." Within four days of its 13D filing, Trilogy had acquired more than 320,000 additional shares, representing an additional 1% of the Company's outstanding shares.

NOL Poison Pill Adopted

In the wake of Trilogy's decision to begin acquiring Selectica shares, the Board took actions to gauge the impact of these acquisitions, if any, on the Company's NOLs, and to determine whether anything needed to be done to mitigate their effects. . . .

The Board met on November 16 to discuss the situation and to consider amending Selectica's Shareholder Rights Plan, which had been in place since February 2003. As with many Rights Plans employed as protection devices against hostile takeovers, Selectica's Rights Plan had a 15% trigger. The Board considered an amendment that would reduce that threshold trigger to 4.99% in order to prevent additional 5% owners from emerging and potentially causing a change-in-control event, thereby devaluing Selectica's NOLs. . . .

[After hearing from financial and legal advisors,] the Board . . . unanimously passed a resolution amending Selectica's Shareholder Rights Plan, by decreasing the beneficial ownership trigger from 15% to 4.99%, while grandfathering in existing 5% shareholders and permitting them to acquire up to an additional 0.5% (subject to the original 15% cap) without triggering the NOL Poison Pill. . . .

Trilogy Triggers NOL Poison Pill

The Board publicly announced the amendment of Selectica's Rights Plan on Monday, November 17. Early the following morning, Fallon e-mailed Trilogy's broker, saying "[W]e need to stop buying SLTC. They announced a new pill and we need to understand it." Fallon also sent [Trilogy founder and 85% stockholder, Joseph Liemandt,] a copy of Selectica's 8-K containing the amended language of the NOL Poison Pill. Trilogy immediately sought legal advice about the NOL Poison Pill. The following morning, Liemandt e-mailed Price, with a copy to Fallon, asking, "What percentage of [Selectica] would we need to buy to ruin the tax attributes . . . ?" They concluded that they would need to acquire 23% to trigger a change-in-control event.

Later that week, Trilogy sent Selectica a letter [requesting a meeting with] Selectica. . . . Fallon, Liemandt, and Jacops from Trilogy, along with Zawatski, Thanos, and Heaps from Selectica met on December 17. The parties' discussions at this meeting are protected by a confidentiality agreement that had been circulated in advance. However, Selectica contends that "based solely on statements and conduct outside that meeting, it is evident that Trilogy threatened to trigger the NOL Poison Pill deliberately unless Selectica agreed to Trilogy's renewed efforts to extract money from the Company."

On December 18, Trilogy purchased an additional 30,000 Selectica shares, and Trilogy management verified with Liemandt his intention to proceed with "buying through" the NOL Poison Pill. The following morning, Trilogy purchased an additional 124,061 shares of Selectica, bringing its ownership share to 6.7% and thereby becoming an "Acquiring Person" under the NOL Poison Pill. Liemandt testified that the rationale behind triggering the pill was to "bring accountability" to the Board and "expose" what Liemandt characterized as "illegal behavior" by the Board in adopting a pill with such a low trigger. Fallon asserted that the reason for triggering the NOL Poison Pill was to "bring some clarity and urgency" to their discussions with Selectica . . . by "setting a time frame that might help accelerate discussions" on the direction of the business. . . .

Board Considers Options and Requests a Standstill

The Selectica Board had a telephonic meeting on Saturday, December 20. . . . The Board discussed "the desirability of taking steps to ensure the validity of the Shareholder Rights Plan," and ultimately passed a resolution authorizing the filing of this lawsuit, which occurred the following day. On December 22, Trilogy filed an amended Schedule 13D disclosing its ownership percentage and again the Selectica Board met telephonically to discuss the litigation. It eventually agreed to have a representative contact Trilogy to seek a standstill on any additional open market purchases while the Board used the ten-day clock under the NOL Poison Pill to determine whether to consider Trilogy's purchases "exempt" under the Rights Plan, and if not, how Selectica would go about implementing the pill.

The amended Rights Plan allowed the Board to declare Trilogy an "Exempt Person" during the ten-day period following the trigger, if the Board determined that Trilogy would not "jeopardize or endanger the availability to the Company of the NOLs. . . ." The Board could also decide during this window to exchange the rights (other than those held by Trilogy) for shares of common stock. If the Board did nothing, then after ten days the rights would "flip in" automatically, becoming exercisable for $36 worth of newly-issued common stock at a price of $18 per right.

The Board met [several more times between December 23 and December 31 to discuss options under the NOL Poison Pill. During this period, Selectica inquired whether Trilogy would be willing "to negotiate a standstill agreement that might make triggering the remedies available under the Shareholder Rights Plan, as amended, unnecessary at this time." Fallon responded that Trilogy did not want to agree to a standstill, that relief from the NOL Poison Pill was not

Trilogy's goal, and that Trilogy expected that the NOL Poison Pill would apply to it.]

The Board discussed Trilogy's actions at some length, ultimately concluding that they "were very harmful to the Company in a number of respects," and that "implementing the exchange was reasonable in relation to the threat imposed by Trilogy." In particular, that was because (1) the NOLs were seen as "an important corporate asset that could significantly enhance stockholder value," and (2) Trilogy had intentionally triggered the NOL Poison Pill, publicly suggested it might purchase additional stock, and had refused to negotiate a standstill agreement, even though an additional 10% acquisition by a 5% share-holder would likely trigger an ownership change under Section 382.

. . .

Board Adopts Reloaded Pill and Dilutes Trilogy Holdings

On January 2, the Board . . . passed a resolution [delegating] authority to [a] Committee . . . to effect an exchange of the rights under the NOL Poison Pill and to declare a new dividend of rights under an amended Rights Plan (the "Reloaded NOL Poison Pill"). The Board then adjourned and the Committee — comprised of Sems and Arnold — met with legal and financial advisors.

. . .

The Committee concluded that Trilogy should not be deemed an "Exempt Person," that its purchase of additional shares should not be deemed an "Exempt Transaction," that an exchange of rights for common stock (the "Exchange") should occur, and that a new rights dividend on substantially similar terms should be adopted. The Committee passed resolutions implementing those conclusions, thereby adopting the Reloaded NOL Poison Pill and instituting the Exchange.

The Exchange doubled the number of shares of Selectica common stock owned by each shareholder of record, other than Trilogy or Versata, thereby reducing their beneficial holdings from 6.7% to 3.3%. The implementation of the Exchange led to a freeze in the trading of Selectica stock from January 5, 2009 until February 4, 2009, with the stock price frozen at $0.69. The Reloaded NOL Poison Pill will expire on January 2, 2012, unless the expiration date is advanced or extended, or unless these rights are exchanged or redeemed by the Board some time before.

ANALYSIS

Unocal Standard Applies

In *Unocal*, this Court recognized that "our corporate law is not static. It must grow and develop in response to, indeed in anticipation of, evolving concepts and needs." The Court of Chancery concluded that the protection of company NOLs may be an appropriate corporate policy that merits a defensive response when they are threatened. We agree.

The *Unocal* two part test is useful as a judicial analytical tool because of the flexibility of its application in a variety of fact scenarios. Delaware courts have approved the adoption of a Shareholder Rights Plan as an antitakeover device, and have applied the *Unocal* test to analyze a board's response to an actual or potential hostile takeover threat. Any NOL poison pill's principal intent, however, is to prevent the inadvertent forfeiture of potentially valuable assets, not to protect against hostile takeover attempts. Even so, any Shareholder Rights Plan, by its nature, operates as an antitakeover device. Consequently, notwithstanding its primary purpose, a NOL poison pill must also be analyzed under *Unocal* because of its effect and its direct implications for hostile takeovers.

Threat Reasonably Identified

The first part of *Unocal* review requires a board to show that it had reasonable grounds for concluding that a threat to the corporate enterprise existed. The Selectica Board concluded that the NOLs were an asset worth preserving and that their protection was an important corporate objective. Trilogy contends that the Board failed to demonstrate that it conducted a reasonable investigation before determining that the NOLs were an asset worth protecting. We disagree.

The record reflects that the Selectica Board met for more than two and a half hours on November 16. . . . The record shows that the Board first analyzed the NOLs in September 2006, and sought updated Section 382 analyses . . . in March 2007, June 2007, and July 2008. At the November 16 meeting, the Board [was advised] that the NOLs were a "significant asset" based on his recently updated calculations of the NOLs' magnitude. [A]n investment banker similarly advised the Board that the NOLs were worth protecting given the possibility of a sale of Selectica or its assets. Accordingly, the record supports the Court of Chancery's factual finding that the Board acted in good faith reliance on the advice of experts in concluding that "the NOLs were an asset worth protecting and thus, that their preservation was an important corporate objective."

The record also supports the reasonableness of the Board's decision to act promptly by reducing the trigger on Selectica's Rights Plan from 15% to 4.99%. . . .

Selectica Defenses Not Preclusive

The second part of the *Unocal* test requires an initial evaluation of whether a board's defensive response to the threat was preclusive or coercive and, if neither, whether the response was "reasonable in relation to the threat" identified. Under *Unitrin*, a defensive measure is disproportionate and unreasonable *per se* if it is draconian by being either coercive or preclusive. A coercive response is one that is "aimed at 'cramming down' on its shareholders a management-sponsored alternative."

A defensive measure is preclusive where it "makes a bidder's ability to wage a successful proxy contest and gain control either 'mathematically impossible' or 'realistically unattainable.'" A successful proxy contest that is mathematically impossible is, *ipso facto*, realistically unattainable. Because the "mathematically impossible" formulation in *Unitrin* is subsumed within the category of preclusivity described as "realistically unattainable," there is, analytically speaking, only one test of preclusivity: "realistically unattainable."

Trilogy claims that a Rights Plan with a 4.99% trigger renders the possibility of an effective proxy contest realistically unattainable. In support of that position, Trilogy argues that, because a proxy contest can only be successful where the challenger has sufficient credibility, the 4.99% pill trigger prevents a potential dissident from signaling its financial commitment to the company so as to establish such credibility. . . .

This Court first examined the validity of a Shareholder Rights Plan in *Moran v. Household International, Inc.*[25] In *Moran* the Rights Plan at issue had a 20% trigger. We recognized that, while a Rights Plan "does deter the formation of proxy efforts of a certain magnitude, it does not limit the voting power of individual shares." In *Moran*, we concluded that the assertion that a Rights Plan would frustrate proxy fights was "highly conjectural" and pointed to "recent corporate takeover battles in which insurgents holding less than 10% stock ownership were able to secure corporate control through a proxy contest or the threat of one."

The 5% trigger that is necessary for a NOL poison pill to serve its primary objective imposes a lower threshold than the Rights Plan thresholds that have traditionally been adopted and upheld as acceptable anti-takeover defenses by Delaware courts. Selectica submits that the distinguishing feature of the NOL Poison Pill and Reloaded NOL Poison Pill — the 5% trigger — is not enough to differentiate them from other Rights Plans previously upheld by Delaware courts, and that there is no evidence that a challenger starting below 5% could not realistically hope to prevail in a proxy contest at Selectica. In support of those arguments Selectica presented expert testimony from Professor John C. Coates IV and Peter C. Harkins.

Professor Coates identified more than fifty publicly held companies that have implemented NOL poison pills with triggers at roughly 5%, including several large, well-known corporations, some among the Fortune 1000. Professor Coates noted that 5% Rights Plans are customarily adopted where issuers have "ownership controlled" assets, such as the NOLs at issue in this case. Professor Coates also testified that Selectica's 5% Rights Plan trigger was narrowly tailored to protect the NOLs because the relevant tax law, Section 382, measures ownership changes based on shareholders who own 5% or more of the outstanding stock.

Moreover, and as the Court of Chancery noted, shareholder advisory firm RiskMetrics Group now supports Rights Plans with a trigger below 5% on a case-by-case basis if adopted for the stated purpose of preserving a company's net operating losses. The factors RiskMetrics will consider in determining whether to support a management proposal to adopt a NOL poison pill are the pill's trigger, the value of the NOLs, the term of the pill, and any corresponding shareholder protection mechanisms in place, such as a sunset provision causing the pill to expire upon exhaustion or expiration of the NOLs.

Selectica expert witness Harkins of the D.F. King & Co. proxy solicitation firm analyzed proxy contests over the three-year period ending December 31, 2008. He found that of the fifteen proxy contests that occurred in micro-cap companies where the challenger controlled less than 5.49% of the outstanding shares, the challenger successfully obtained board seats in ten contests, five of which involved companies with classified boards. Harkins opined that Selectica's unique shareholder profile would considerably reduce the costs associated with a proxy fight, since seven shareholders controlled 55% of Selectica's shares, and twenty-two shareholders controlled 62%. Harkins testified that "if you have a compelling platform, which is critical, it would be easy from a logistical perspective; and from a cost perspective, it would be *de minimis* expense to communicate with those investors, among others." Harkins noted that to win

---

25. *Moran v. Household Int'l, Inc.*, 500 A.2d 1346, 1356 (Del.1985).

a proxy contest at Selectica, one would need to gain only the support of owners of 43.2% plus one share.

The Court of Chancery concluded that the NOL Poison Pill and Reloaded NOL Poison Pill were not preclusive. For a measure to be preclusive, it must render a successful proxy contest realistically unattainable given the specific factual context. The record supports the Court of Chancery's factual determination and legal conclusion that Selectica's NOL Poison Pill and Reloaded NOL Poison Pill do not meet that preclusivity standard.

Our observation in *Unitrin* is also applicable here: "[I]t is hard to imagine a company more readily susceptible to a proxy contest concerning a pure issue of dollars." The key variable in a proxy contest would be the merit of the bidder's proposal and not the magnitude of its stockholdings. The record reflects that Selectica's adoption of a 4.99% trigger for its Rights Plan would not preclude a hostile bidder's ability to marshal enough shareholder votes to win a proxy contest.

Trilogy argues that, even if a 4.99% shareholder could realistically win a proxy contest "the preclusiveness question focuses on whether a challenger could realistically attain sufficient board control to remove the pill." Here, Trilogy contends, Selectica's charter-based classified board effectively forecloses a bid conditioned upon a redemption of the NOL Poison Pill, because it requires a proxy challenger to launch and complete two successful proxy contests in order to change control. Therefore, Trilogy argues that even if a less than 5% shareholder could win a proxy contest, Selectica's Rights Plan with a 4.99% trigger in combination with Selectica's charter-based classified board, makes a successful proxy contest for control of the board "realistically unattainable."

Trilogy's preclusivity argument conflates two distinct questions: first, is a successful proxy contest realistically attainable; and second, will a successful proxy contest result in gaining control of the board at the next election? Trilogy argues that unless both questions can be answered affirmatively, a Rights Plan and a classified board, viewed collectively, are preclusive. If that preclusivity argument is correct, then it would apply whenever a corporation has both a classified board and a Rights Plan, irrespective whether the trigger is 4.99%, 20%, or anywhere in between those thresholds.

Classified boards are authorized by statute and are adopted for a variety of business purposes. Any classified board also operates as an antitakeover defense by preventing an insurgent from obtaining control of the board in one election. . . . The fact that a combination of defensive measures makes it more difficult for an acquirer to obtain control of a board does not make such measures realistically unattainable, i.e., preclusive.

In *Moran*, we rejected the contention "that the Rights Plan strips stockholders of their rights to receive tender offers, and that the Rights Plan fundamentally restricts proxy contests." We explained that "the Rights Plan will not have a severe impact upon proxy contests and it will not *preclude* all hostile acquisitions of Household." In this case, we hold that the combination of a classified board and a Rights Plan do not constitute a preclusive defense.

Range of Reasonableness

If a defensive measure is neither coercive nor preclusive, the *Unocal* proportionality test "requires the focus of enhanced judicial scrutiny to shift to 'the range of reasonableness.'" . . . Trilogy asserts that the NOL Poison Pill, the

Exchange, and the Reloaded NOL Poison Pill were not a reasonable collective response to the threat of the impairment of Selectica's NOLs.

The critical facts do not support that assertion. On November 20, within days of learning of the NOL Poison Pill, Trilogy sent Selectica a letter, demanding a conference. . . . The parties met on December 17, and the following day, Trilogy resumed its purchases of Selectica stock.

. . .

Trilogy's deliberate trigger started a ten business day clock under the terms of the NOL Poison Pill. If the Board took no action during that time, then the rights (other than those belonging to Trilogy) would "flip-in" and become exercisable for deeply discounted common stock. Alternatively, the Board had the power to exchange the rights (other than those belonging to Trilogy) for newly-issued common stock, or to grant Trilogy an exemption. Three times in the two weeks following the triggering, Selectica offered Trilogy an exemption in exchange for an agreement to stand still and to withdraw its threat to impair the value and usability of Selectica's NOLs. Three times Trilogy refused and insisted instead that Selectica repurchase its stock, terminate a license agreement with an important client, sign over intellectual property, and pay Trilogy millions of dollars. After three failed attempts to negotiate with Trilogy, it was reasonable for the Board to determine that they had no other option than to implement the NOL Poison Pill.

The Exchange employed by the Board was a more proportionate response than the "flip-in" mechanism traditionally envisioned for a Rights Plan. Because the Board opted to use the Exchange instead of the traditional "flip-in" mechanism, Trilogy experienced less dilution of its position than a Rights Plan is traditionally designed to achieve.

The implementation of the Reloaded NOL Poison Pill was also a reasonable response. The Reloaded NOL Poison Pill was considered a necessary defensive measure because, although the NOL Poison Pill and the Exchange effectively thwarted Trilogy's immediate threat to Selectica's NOLs, they did not eliminate the general threat of a Section 382 change-in-control. Following implementation of the Exchange, Selectica still had a roughly 40% ownership change for Section 382 purposes and there was no longer a Rights Plan in place to discourage additional acquisitions by 5% holders. Selectica argues that the decision to adopt the Reloaded NOL Poison Pill was reasonable under those circumstances. We agree.

The record indicates that the Board was presented with expert advice that supported its ultimate findings that the NOLs were a corporate asset worth protecting, that the NOLs were at risk as a result of Trilogy's actions, and that the steps that the Board ultimately took were reasonable in relation to that threat.[44] Outside experts were present and advised the Board on these matters at both the November 16 meeting at which the NOL Poison Pill was adopted and at the Board's December 29 meeting. The Committee also heard from expert advisers a third time at the January 2 meeting prior to instituting the Exchange and adopting the Reloaded NOL Poison Pill.

Under part two of the *Unocal* test, the Court of Chancery found that the combination of the NOL Poison Pill, the Exchange, and the Reloaded NOL

---

44. Del.Code Ann. tit. 8, § 141(e) (2010).

Poison Pill was a proportionate response to the threatened loss of Selectica's NOLs. Those findings are not clearly erroneous. They are supported by the record and the result of a logical deductive reasoning process. Accordingly, we hold that the Selectica directors satisfied the second part of the *Unocal* test by showing that their defensive response was proportionate by being "reasonable in relation to the threat" identified.

Context Determines Reasonableness

Under a *Unocal* analysis, the reasonableness of a board's response is determined in relation to the "specific threat," at the time it was identified. Thus, it is the specific nature of the threat that "sets the parameters for the range of permissible defensive tactics" at any given time. The record demonstrates that a longtime competitor sought to increase the percentage of its stock ownership, not for the purpose of conducting a hostile takeover but, to intentionally impair corporate assets, or else coerce Selectica into meeting certain business demands under the threat of such impairment. Only in relation to that specific threat have the Court of Chancery and this Court considered the reasonableness of Selectica's response.

The Selectica Board carried its burden of proof under both parts of the *Unocal* test. Therefore, at this time, the Selectica Board has withstood the enhanced judicial scrutiny required by the two part *Unocal* test. That does not, however, end the matter.

As we held in *Moran*, the adoption of a Rights Plan is not absolute. In other cases, we have upheld the adoption of Rights Plans in specific defensive circumstances while simultaneously holding that it may be inappropriate for a Rights Plan to remain in place when those specific circumstances change dramatically. The fact that the NOL Poison Pill was reasonable under the specific facts and circumstances of this case, should not be construed as generally approving the reasonableness of a 4.99% trigger in the Rights Plan of a corporation with or without NOLs.

To reiterate *Moran*, "the ultimate response to an actual takeover bid must be judged by the Directors' actions at that time." If and when the Selectica Board "is faced with a tender offer and a request to redeem the [Reloaded NOL Poison Pill], they will not be able to arbitrarily reject the offer. They will be held to the same fiduciary standards any other board of directors would be held to in deciding to adopt a defensive mechanism." The Selectica Board has no more discretion in refusing to redeem the Rights Plan "than it does in enacting any defensive mechanism." Therefore, the Selectica Board's future use of the Reloaded NOL Poison Pill must be evaluated if and when that issue arises.

. . .

Conclusion

The judgments of the Court of Chancery are affirmed.

PROBLEM 11-2

Even after its acquisition of Path (see Problem 11-1), Multiply's founder and CEO, Jason Conrad, held approximately 30 percent of the outstanding shares of Multiply, and he was eager to maintain control of the company.

Thus, when Multiply began to hear rumors that it was a potential takeover target, Conrad encouraged the board of directors of Multiply to adopt a poison pill with a 5 percent trigger.

Before the board could act, WFC Bank (WFC), a large multinational financial services company, filed a Schedule 13D with the SEC, disclosing that WFC owned approximately 7 percent of Multiply's common stock. As required by the SEC rules, WFC disclosed that the purpose of its investment was to explore the possibility of acquiring Multiply. On the day WFC filed its Schedule 13D, the CEO of WFC called Conrad and requested a meeting. Conrad declined to meet.

In response to this filing, the board of directors of Multiply adopted a Shareholder Rights Plan that would be triggered when a shareholder or group of shareholders acquired over 10 percent of Multiply's outstanding shares of common stock. The pill's 10 percent trigger would not apply to Conrad, however, as his ownership stake was grandfathered under the terms of the pill. Nevertheless, the pill specified that Conrad could not increase his ownership of the company.

After the adoption of the poison pill, WFC filed a lawsuit in the Delaware Court of Chancery alleging that the board of directors of Multiply breached its fiduciary duties by adopting the poison pill. While conceding that the pill is not preclusive, WFC argued that it is beyond the range of reasonable responses to any threat posed by WFC. More specifically, WFC argued that Conrad's large stake in Multiply makes the use of a 10 percent trigger unreasonable because the low trigger unfairly and unreasonably tilts the electoral playing field against WFC. In connection with this argument, WFC notes that it has never proposed a hostile takeover of Multiply; therefore, WFC claims it is unreasonable overkill for the board of directors of Multiply to prevent WFC from buying additional shares up to the level of Conrad's ownership in the company.

Was the decision by the Multiply board of directors to adopt a poison pill with a 10 percent threshold beyond the range of reasonableness?

D. CHANGE-OF-CONTROL TRANSACTIONS

Shortly after creating the *Unocal* standard for evaluating defensive actions, the Delaware Supreme Court introduced another new judicial standard for evaluating the actions of directors when there is a "change-of-control" transaction. The *Revlon* case involves some defensive actions—which generated *Unocal* claims by the plaintiffs—but the Delaware Supreme Court saw a separate set of issues when the board of directors of Revlon decided to stop resisting a takeover and instead pursued a sale of the company. As you read the case, see if you can discern the answer to the two questions that challenged courts in the wake of *Revlon*: (1) When are *Revlon*'s special duties triggered? and (2) What do those duties specifically require?

REVLON, INC. v. MacANDREWS & FORBES HOLDINGS., INC.

506 A.2d 173
Supreme Court of Delaware
March 13, 1986

Moore, Justice.

In this battle for corporate control of Revlon, Inc. (Revlon), the Court of Chancery enjoined certain transactions designed to thwart the efforts of Pantry Pride, Inc. (Pantry Pride) to acquire Revlon. The defendants are Revlon, its board of directors, and Forstmann Little & Co. and the latter's affiliated limited partnership (collectively, Forstmann). The injunction barred consummation of an option granted Forstmann to purchase certain Revlon assets (the lock-up option), a promise by Revlon to deal exclusively with Forstmann in the face of a takeover (the no-shop provision), and the payment of a $25 million cancellation fee to Forstmann if the transaction was aborted. The Court of Chancery found that the Revlon directors had breached their duty of care by entering into the foregoing transactions and effectively ending an active auction for the company. The trial court ruled that such arrangements are not illegal per se under Delaware law, but that their use under the circumstances here was impermissible. We agree. *See* MacAndrews & Forbes Holdings, Inc. v. Revlon, Inc., Del. Ch., 501 A.2d 1239 (1985). Thus, we granted this expedited interlocutory appeal to consider for the first time the validity of such defensive measures in the face of an active bidding contest for corporate control. Additionally, we address for the first time the extent to which a corporation may consider the impact of a takeover threat on constituencies other than shareholders. *See* Unocal Corp. v. Mesa Petroleum Co., Del. Supr., 493 A.2d 946, 955 (1985).

In our view, lock-ups and related agreements are permitted under Delaware law where their adoption is untainted by director interest or other breaches of fiduciary duty. The actions taken by the Revlon directors, however, did not meet this standard. Moreover, while concern for various corporate constituencies is proper when addressing a takeover threat, that principle is limited by the requirement that there be some rationally related benefit accruing to the stockholders. We find no such benefit here. Thus, under all the circumstances we must agree with the Court of Chancery that the enjoined Revlon defensive measures were inconsistent with the directors' duties to the stockholders. Accordingly, we affirm.

I.

[The facts of the case, distilled to their essence, are as follows. This case arose from Pantry Pride's efforts, at the behest of Ronald O. Perelman, chairman and chief executive officer, to buy the Revlon company, whose chairman and CEO Michel C. Bergerac, wanted nothing to do with being sold. Pantry Pride's initial approach, on August 14, was to suggest a negotiated deal at $42-$43 per share, or a hostile tender offer at $45 per share. Revlon's 14-member board met, and on the advice of its investment bankers, concluded that $45 per share was an inadequate price. (Of the 14 members, only two were independent: six were members of senior management; two were major stockholders; and four had significant business relationships with Revlon.) Upon determining that the price was inadequate, the directors adopted a poison pill, and authorized a self-tender for 5 million of its 30 million outstanding shares. Pantry Pride responded on August 23 with a cash tender offer for 100 percent of outstanding shares at $47.50 per common share and $26.67 per preferred share, conditioned upon Pantry Pride getting financing and Revlon getting rid of its poison pill. Revlon responded on August 29 by starting its own tender offer, now for up to 10 million shares, offering to exchange each common share tendered for one senior subordinated note (the Note) of $47.50 principal at 11.75 percent interest, due 1995, and one-tenth of a share of $9.00 cumulative convertible preferred stock valued at $100 per share. The new Notes contained a promise (called a "covenant" in financial circles) that Revlon would not take on any additional debt, sell assets, or pay dividends unless approved by the independent members of the board. Pantry Pride remained determined to acquire Revlon, offering $50 per share in September, then $53 per share, and $56.25 per share in early October, each offer conditioned on the board removing the poison pill.

Facing this determined acquiror, the Revlon board authorized management to try to shop the company to other potential acquirers, eventually bringing forth two competitors to Pantry Pride: Forstmann, Little and Adler & Shaykin — both "investment groups" engaged in buying and selling companies. At a time when Pantry Pride was offering $53 per share, Revlon's board unanimously agreed to be acquired by Forstmann at $56 per share. Forstmann agreed to take on the $475 million of debt Revlon had taken on to fund the self-tender, and in exchange Revlon would remove the poison pill and, significantly, would waive the Note covenants to allow the company to take on more debt or sell assets. When this news became public, the price of the Notes started to fall, and directors reported being "deluged" with angry Noteholders threatening litigation. Pantry Pride, Revlon, and Forstmann met to try to negotiate a solution. Negotiations then broke down, but not before Pantry Pride announced that it would engage in "fractional bidding" to outbid any Forstmann offer.

By this point in the fracas, Revlon had provided its confidential financial data to Forstmann, not Pantry Pride, so Forstmann was in a position to make a higher offer: $57.25 per share, with several conditions. These included Revlon's agreement to a lock-up option (a right to buy valuable Revlon divisions at a $100-$175 million discount if another acquirer got 40 percent of Revlon's shares), a no-shop provision, its agreement to waive the Note covenants and remove the pill, and its agreement to a $25 million cancellation fee. Forstmann also agreed to support the falling Note values by an exchange of new Notes. In response Pantry Pride announced a new tender offer, at $58 per share in cash, and brought an action to enjoin Revlon from performing any of its obligations under its contract with Forstmann.]

II.

To obtain a preliminary injunction, a plaintiff must demonstrate both a reasonable probability of success on the merits and some irreparable harm which will occur absent the injunction. Gimbel v. Signal Companies, Del. Ch., 316 A.2d 599, 602 (1974), *aff'd*, Del. Supr., 316 A.2d 619 (1974). Additionally, the Court shall balance the conveniences of and possible injuries to the parties. *Id.*

A.

We turn first to Pantry Pride's probability of success on the merits. The ultimate responsibility for managing the business and affairs of a corporation falls on its board of directors. In discharging this function the directors owe fiduciary duties of care and loyalty to the corporation and its shareholders. These principles apply with equal force when a board approves a corporate merger pursuant to 8 Del. C. § 251(b), and of course they are the bedrock of our law regarding corporate takeover issues. While the business judgment rule may be applicable to the actions of corporate directors responding to takeover threats, the principles upon which it is founded — care, loyalty and independence — must first be satisfied.

If the business judgment rule applies, there is a "presumption that in making a business decision the directors of a corporation acted on an informed basis, in good faith and in the honest belief that the action taken was in the best interests of the company." Aronson v. Lewis, 473 A.2d [805, 812 (1984)]. However, when a board implements anti-takeover measures there arises "the omnipresent specter that a board may be acting primarily in its own interests, rather than those of the corporation and its shareholders. . . ." Unocal Corp. v. Mesa Petroleum Co., 493 A.2d at 954. This potential for conflict places upon the directors the burden of proving that they had reasonable grounds for believing there was a danger to corporate policy and effectiveness, a burden satisfied by a showing of good faith and reasonable investigation. *Id.* at 955. In addition, the directors must analyze the nature of the takeover and its effect on the corporation in order to ensure balance — that the responsive action taken is reasonable in relation to the threat posed. *Id.*

B.

The first relevant defensive measure adopted by the Revlon board was the Rights Plan, which would be considered a "poison pill" in the current language of corporate takeovers — a plan by which shareholders receive the right to be bought out by the corporation at a substantial premium on the occurrence of a stated triggering event. By 8 Del. C. §§ 141 and 122(13), the board clearly had the power to adopt the measure. *See* Moran v. Household International, Inc., 500 A.2d at 1351. Thus, the focus becomes one of reasonableness and purpose.

The Revlon board approved the Rights Plan in the face of an impending hostile takeover bid by Pantry Pride at $45 per share, a price which Revlon reasonably concluded was grossly inadequate. Lazard Freres had so advised the directors, and had also informed them that Pantry Pride was a small, highly leveraged company bent on a "bust-up" takeover by using "junk bond" financing to buy Revlon cheaply, sell the acquired assets to pay the debts incurred, and retain the profit for itself. In adopting the Plan, the board protected the shareholders from a hostile takeover at a price below the company's intrinsic value, while retaining sufficient flexibility to address any proposal deemed to be in the stockholders' best interests.

To that extent the board acted in good faith and upon reasonable investigation. Under the circumstances it cannot be said that the Rights Plan as employed was unreasonable, considering the threat posed. Indeed, the Plan was a factor in causing Pantry Pride to raise its bids from a low of $42 to an eventual high of $58. At the time of its adoption the Rights Plan afforded a measure of protection consistent with the directors' fiduciary duty in facing a takeover threat perceived as detrimental to corporate interests. Far from being a "show-stopper," as the plaintiffs had contended in *Moran*, the measure spurred the bidding to new heights, a proper result of its implementation. *See Moran*, 500 A.2d at 1354, 1356-67.

Although we consider adoption of the Plan to have been valid under the circumstances, its continued usefulness was rendered moot by the directors' actions on October 3 and October 12. At the October 3 meeting the board redeemed the Rights conditioned upon consummation of a merger with Forstmann, but further acknowledged that they would also be redeemed to facilitate any more favorable offer. On October 12, the board unanimously passed a resolution redeeming the Rights in connection with any cash proposal of $57.25 or more per share. Because all the pertinent offers eventually equalled or surpassed that amount, the Rights clearly were no longer any impediment in the contest for Revlon. This mooted any question of their propriety under *Moran* or *Unocal*.

C.

The second defensive measure adopted by Revlon to thwart a Pantry Pride takeover was the company's own exchange offer for 10 million of its shares. The directors' general broad powers to manage the business and affairs of the corporation are augmented by the specific authority conferred under 8 Del. C. § 160(a), permitting the company to deal in its own stock. However, when exercising that power in an effort to forestall a hostile takeover, the board's actions are strictly held to the fiduciary standards outlined in *Unocal*. These standards require the directors to determine the best interests of the corporation and its stockholders, and impose an enhanced duty to abjure any action that is motivated by considerations other than a good faith concern for such interests.

The Revlon directors concluded that Pantry Pride's $47.50 offer was grossly inadequate. In that regard the board acted in good faith, and on an informed basis, with reasonable grounds to believe that there existed a harmful threat to the corporate enterprise. The adoption of a defensive measure, reasonable in relation to the threat posed, was proper and fully accorded with the powers, duties, and responsibilities conferred upon directors under our law.

D.

However, when Pantry Pride increased its offer to $50 per share, and then to $53, it became apparent to all that the break-up of the company was inevitable. The Revlon board's authorization permitting management to negotiate a merger or buyout with a third party was a recognition that the company was for sale. The duty of the board had thus changed from the preservation of Revlon as a corporate entity to the maximization of the company's value at a sale for the stockholders' benefit. This significantly altered the board's responsibilities under the *Unocal* standards. It no longer faced threats to corporate policy and effectiveness, or to the stockholders' interests, from a grossly inadequate bid. The whole question of defensive measures became moot. The directors' role changed from defenders of the corporate bastion to auctioneers charged with getting the best price for the stockholders at a sale of the company.

III.

This brings us to the lock-up with Forstmann and its emphasis on shoring up the sagging market value of the Notes in the face of threatened litigation by their holders. Such a focus was inconsistent with the changed concept of the directors' responsibilities at this stage of the developments. The impending waiver of the Notes covenants had caused the value of the Notes to fall, and the board was aware of the noteholders' ire as well as their subsequent threats of suit. The directors thus made support of the Notes an integral part of the company's dealings with Forstmann, even though their primary responsibility at this stage was to the equity owners.

The original threat posed by Pantry Pride — the break-up of the company — had become a reality which even the directors embraced. Selective dealing to fend off a hostile but determined bidder was no longer a proper objective. Instead, obtaining the highest price for the benefit of the stockholders should have been the central theme guiding director action. Thus, the Revlon board could not make the requisite showing of good faith by preferring the noteholders and ignoring its duty of loyalty to the shareholders. The rights of the former already were fixed by contract. Wolfensohn v. Madison Fund, Inc., Del. Supr., 253 A.2d 72, 75 (1969); Harff v. Kerkorian, Del. Ch., 324 A.2d 215 (1974). The noteholders required no further protection, and when the Revlon board entered into an auction-ending lock-up agreement with Forstmann on the basis of impermissible considerations at the expense of the shareholders, the directors breached their primary duty of loyalty.

The Revlon board argued that it acted in good faith in protecting the noteholders because *Unocal* permits consideration of other corporate constituencies. Although such considerations may be permissible, there are fundamental limitations upon that prerogative. A board may have regard for various constituencies in discharging its responsibilities, provided there are rationally related benefits accruing to the stockholders. *Unocal*, 493 A.2d at 955. However, such concern for non-stockholder interests is inappropriate when an auction among active bidders is in progress, and the object no longer is to protect or maintain the corporate enterprise but to sell it to the highest bidder.

Revlon also contended that by Gilbert v. El Paso Co., Del. Ch., 490 A.2d 1050, 1054-55 (1984), it had contractual and good faith obligations to consider the noteholders. However, any such duties are limited to the principle that one may not interfere with contractual relationships by improper actions. Here, the rights of the noteholders were fixed by agreement, and there is nothing of substance to suggest that any of those terms were violated. The Notes covenants specifically contemplated a waiver to permit sale of the company at a fair price. The Notes were accepted by the holders on that basis, including the risk of an adverse market effect stemming from a waiver. Thus, nothing remained for Revlon to legitimately protect, and no rationally related benefit thereby accrued to the stockholders. Under such circumstances we must conclude that the merger agreement with Forstmann was unreasonable in relation to the threat posed.

A lock-up is not per se illegal under Delaware law. Its use has been approved in an earlier case. Thompson v. Enstar Corp., Del. Ch., [1984 WL 8240] (1984). Such options can entice other bidders to enter a contest for control of the corporation, creating an auction for the company and maximizing shareholder profit. Current economic conditions in the takeover market are such that a "white knight" like Forstmann might only enter the bidding for the target company if it receives some form of compensation to cover the risks and costs involved. However, while those lock-ups which draw bidders into the battle benefit shareholders, similar measures which end an active auction and foreclose further bidding operate to the shareholders' detriment. . . .

The Forstmann option had a . . . destructive effect on the auction process. Forstmann had already been drawn into the contest on a preferred basis, so the result of the lock-up was not to foster bidding, but to destroy it. The board's stated reasons for approving the transactions were: (1) better financing, (2) note-holder protection, and (3) higher price. As the Court of Chancery found, and we agree, any distinctions between the rival bidders' methods of financing the proposal were nominal at best, and such a consideration has little or no significance in a cash offer for any and all shares. The principal object, contrary to the board's duty of care, appears to have been protection of the noteholders over the shareholders' interests.

While Forstmann's $57.25 offer was objectively higher than Pantry Pride's $56.25 bid, the margin of superiority is less when the Forstmann price is adjusted for the time value of money. In reality, the Revlon board ended the auction in return for very little actual improvement in the final bid. The principal benefit went to the directors, who avoided personal liability to a class of creditors to whom the board owed no further duty under the circumstances. Thus, when a board ends an intense bidding contest on an insubstantial basis, and where a significant by-product of that action is to protect the directors against a perceived threat of personal liability for consequences stemming from the adoption of previous defensive measures, the action cannot withstand the enhanced scrutiny which *Unocal* requires of director conduct.

In addition to the lock-up option, the Court of Chancery enjoined the no-shop provision as part of the attempt to foreclose further bidding by Pantry Pride. The no-shop provision, like the lock-up option, while not per se illegal, is impermissible under the *Unocal* standards when a board's primary duty becomes that of an auctioneer responsible for selling the company to the highest bidder. The agreement to negotiate only with Forstmann ended rather than intensified the board's involvement in the bidding contest.

It is ironic that the parties even considered a no-shop agreement when Revlon had dealt preferentially, and almost exclusively, with Forstmann throughout the contest. After the directors authorized management to negotiate with other parties, Forstmann was given every negotiating advantage that Pantry Pride had been denied: cooperation from management, access to financial data, and the exclusive opportunity to present merger proposals directly to the board of directors. Favoritism for a white knight to the total exclusion of a hostile bidder might be justifiable when the latter's offer adversely affects shareholder interests, but when bidders make relatively similar offers, or dissolution of the company becomes inevitable, the directors cannot fulfill their enhanced *Unocal* duties by playing favorites with the contending factions. Market forces must be allowed to operate freely to bring the target's shareholders the best price available for their equity. Thus, as the trial court ruled, the shareholders' interests necessitated that the board remain free to negotiate in the fulfillment of that duty. . . .

V.

In conclusion, the Revlon board was confronted with a situation not uncommon in the current wave of corporate takeovers. A hostile and determined bidder sought the company at a price the board was convinced was inadequate. The initial defensive tactics worked to the benefit of the shareholders, and thus the board was able to sustain its *Unocal* burdens in justifying those measures. However, in granting an asset option lock-up to Forstmann, we must conclude that under all the circumstances the directors allowed considerations other than the maximization of shareholder profit to affect their judgment, and followed a course that ended the auction for Revlon, absent court intervention, to the ultimate detriment of its shareholders. No such defensive measure can be sustained when it represents a breach of the directors' fundamental duty of care. In that context the board's action is not entitled to the deference accorded it by the business judgment rule. The measures were properly enjoined. The decision of the Court of Chancery, therefore, is Affirmed.

PROBLEM 11-3

Assume for the sake of discussing this problem that WFC Bank was unsuccessful in persuading the Court of Chancery to invalidate Multiply's poison pill (see Problem 11-2). Following the disposition of that action, WFC announced its intention to commence an all-cash tender offer for all outstanding shares of Multiply's common stock, conditioned on (a) the valid tender of enough of the outstanding shares of Multiply common stock to give WFC majority ownership of Multiply; and (b) the Multiply board of directors redeeming Multiply's poison pill. WFC made redemption of the pill a condition of the tender offer because Multiply has a classified board of directors; therefore, even if WFC obtained majority ownership of Multiply, WFC could not obtain control of the board of directors without going through two election cycles.

The announced tender offer price represented a 30 percent premium above the market price of the shares. Upon WFC's announcement, Multiply engaged Goldman Sachs to advise it on the tender offer price. Goldman Sachs reviewed both publicly and privately available financial data and interviewed top executives and operations executives at Multiply. Based on that analysis, it concluded that the tender offer price was inadequate. In part, this conclusion was based on the fact that Multiply had achieved record financial results in the prior fiscal year and quarter, which it believed was just the beginning of the benefits it would receive from its acquisition of Path Bank.

Meanwhile, nearly 80 percent of Multiply's shareholders other than Conrad had tendered into the offer, representing enough shares to give WFC majority ownership of Multiply. Nonetheless, the board of directors of Multiply determined the offer was inadequate and refused to redeem the pill.

May the board of directors of Multiply "just say no" to the WFC offer under these circumstances?

E. THE EVOLVING STANDARDS

In the immediate wake of *Unocal* and *Revlon*, it was far from clear to the Delaware Court of Chancery what the Delaware Supreme Court had done. In his earliest opinion after *Revlon*, Chancellor Allen concluded that *Revlon* "should not . . . be interpreted as representing a sharp turn in our law." City Capital Associates Ltd. Partnership v. Interco Inc., 551 A.2d 787, 802 (Del. Ch. Nov. 1, 1988). By this, Chancellor Allen meant that, absent conflicts, the directors' actions should be subjected to business judgment review.

Justice Moore, the author of *Revlon*, struck back against this view in Mills Acquisition Co. v. Macmillan, Inc., 559 A.2d 1261 (Del. 1989), emphasizing the importance of "enhanced scrutiny" in the *Revlon* context:

> As we held in *Revlon*, when management of a target company determines that the company is for sale, the board's responsibilities under the enhanced *Unocal* standards are significantly altered. Although the board's responsibilities under *Unocal* are far different, the enhanced duties of the directors in responding to a potential shift in control, recognized in *Unocal*, remain unchanged. The principle pervades *Revlon*, and when directors conclude that an auction is appropriate, the standard by which their ensuing actions will be judged continues to be the enhanced standard imposed by this Court in *Unocal*.

Exactly what "enhanced scrutiny" means under *Revlon* and how that relates to the *Unocal* standard has been explored in many other cases. In Paramount Communications, Inc. v. Time Inc., 571 A.2d 1140 (Del. 1989), for example, the Delaware Supreme Court examined the action of the board of directors of Time Inc., who elected to merge with Warner Communication, Inc. instead of accepting what many Time shareholders thought was a superior bid by Paramount Communications, Inc. Like many hostile takeover cases, this one involved both *Unocal* and *Revlon* claims, and the Court treated them separately.

The *Unocal* claim was straightforward: Time's directors breached their fiduciary duty by rejecting a superior, non-threatening offer by Paramount. The crux of Paramount's argument was that an all-cash tender offer does not constitute a threat for purposes of the *Unocal* standard. The Delaware Supreme Court rejected this argument, that "narrow and rigid construction of *Unocal*," because "it would involve the court in substituting its judgment as to what is a 'better' deal for that of a corporation's board of directors." This part of the opinion gave rise to the question, raised in Problem 11-3 and addressed by Chancellor Chandler below in Air Products and Chemicals, Inc. v. Airgas, Inc., whether a target board of directors could "just say no" to a non-threatening bid for the company.

The *Revlon* claim allowed the Court to address the question raised above: When are *Revlon*'s special duties triggered? According to the Court:

> Under Delaware law, there are, generally speaking and *without excluding other possibilities*, two circumstances which may implicate *Revlon* duties. The first, and clearer one, is when a corporation initiates an active bidding process seeking to sell itself or to effect a business reorganization involving a clear break up of the company. However, *Revlon* duties may also be triggered where, in response to a

bidder's offer, a target abandons its long-term strategy and seeks an alternative transaction involving the breakup of the company.

The Court later came to regret this overly formalistic statement of the *Revlon* standard. In Paramount Communications Inc. v. QVC Network Inc., 637 A.2d 34 (Del. 1994), the plaintiffs argued that *Time* required a "break up of the company" before *Revlon* would be triggered, but the Delaware Supreme Court rejected this argument:

> [W]hen a corporation undertakes a transaction which will cause: (a) a change in corporate control; *or* (b) a break-up of the corporate entity, the directors' obliga-tion is to seek the best value reasonably available to the stockholders. . . . Neither *Time-Warner* nor any other decision of this Court holds that a "break-up" of the company is essential to give rise to this obligation where there is a sale of control.

Id. at 48.

QVC represented an important conceptual turn for Delaware's *Unocal* and *Revlon* jurisprudence. As evident in both of the original opinions, the enhanced scrutiny of *Unocal* and *Revlon* was justified when a board of directors was subject to a conflict of interest. In *QVC*, however, the Court held that change-of-control transactions are so important that courts should review the reasonableness of director action, even if the directors are disinterested.

The *QVC* case is also known for the Court's attempt to unify the *Unocal* standard and the *Revlon* standard into a single "enhanced scrutiny" test:

> The key features of an enhanced scrutiny test are: (a) a judicial determination regarding the adequacy of the decisionmaking process employed by the directors, including the information on which the directors based their decision; and (b) a judicial examination of the reasonableness of the directors' action in light of the circumstances then existing. The directors have the burden of proving that they were adequately informed and acted reasonably.

Id. at 45.

This awkward formulation has never taken hold, but the Delaware courts have successfully distinguished the *Revlon* standard from the business judgment rule. *In re Netsmart Technologies, Inc. Shareholders Litigation* states:

> What is important and different about the Revlon standard is the intensity of judicial review that is applied to the directors' conduct. Unlike the bare rationality standard applicable to garden variety decisions subject to the business judgment rule, the Revlon standard contemplates a judicial examination of the reasonable-ness of the board's decision making process. Although linguistically not obvious, this reasonableness review is more searching than rationality review, and there is less tolerance for slack by the directors. Although the directors have a choice of means, they do not comply with their Revlon duties unless they undertake reason-able steps to get the best deal.

In the meantime, the *Unocal* standard also continues to develop. After *Unitrin* modified the *Unocal* standard in 1995, it is hard to imagine any defensive measure that would be invalidated, other than the dead-hand and no-hand poison pills, which the Delaware courts referred to as "show stoppers." The

Delaware Supreme Court seemed so deferential to target boards that Professors Robert Thompson and Gordon Smith declared *Unocal* a "dead letter." Robert B. Thompson & D. Gordon Smith, *Toward a New Theory of the Shareholder Role: "Sacred Space" in Corporate Takeovers*, 80 Tex. L. Rev. 261, 286 (2001). Although *Unocal* has invalidated some corporate actions, it remains a very deferential standard, as illustrated by the following case.

AIR PRODUCTS AND CHEMICALS, INC. v. AIRGAS, INC.

2011 WL 806417
Delaware Court of Chancery
February 15, 2011

CHANDLER, Chancellor.

This case poses the following fundamental question: Can a board of directors, acting in good faith and with a reasonable factual basis for its decision, when faced with a structurally non-coercive, all-cash, fully financed tender offer directed to the stockholders of the corporation, keep a poison pill in place so as to prevent the stockholders from making their own decision about whether they want to tender their shares — even after the incumbent board has lost one election contest, a full year has gone by since the offer was first made public, and the stockholders are fully informed as to the target board's views on the inadequacy of the offer? If so, does that effectively mean that a board can "just say never" to a hostile tender offer?

The answer to the latter question is "no." A board cannot "*just* say no" to a tender offer. Under Delaware law, it must first pass through two prongs of exacting judicial scrutiny by a judge who will evaluate the actions taken by, and the motives of, the board. Only a board of directors found to be acting in good faith, after reasonable investigation and reliance on the advice of outside advisors, which articulates and convinces the Court that a hostile tender offer poses a legitimate threat to the corporate enterprise, may address that perceived threat by blocking the tender offer and forcing the bidder to elect a board majority that supports its bid.

In essence, this case brings to the fore one of the most basic questions animating all of corporate law, which relates to the allocation of power between directors and stockholders. That is, "when, if ever, will a board's duty to 'the corporation and its shareholders' require [the board] to abandon concerns for 'long term' values (and other constituencies) and enter a current share value maximizing mode?"[1] More to the point, in the context of a hostile tender offer, who gets to decide when and if the corporation is for sale?

Since the Shareholder Rights Plan (more commonly known as the "poison pill") was first conceived and throughout the development of Delaware corporate takeover jurisprudence during the twenty-five-plus years that followed, the debate over who ultimately decides whether a tender offer is adequate and should be accepted — the shareholders of the corporation or its board of directors — has raged on. Starting with *Moran v. Household International, Inc.*[2] in 1985, when the Delaware Supreme Court first upheld the adoption of the poison pill

---

1. *TW Servs., Inc. v. SWT Acquisition Corp.*, 1989 WL 20290, at *8 (Del.Ch. Mar.2, 1989).
2. 490 A.2d 1059 (Del.1985).

as a valid takeover defense, through the hostile takeover years of the 1980s, and in several recent decisions of the Court of Chancery and the Delaware Supreme Court,[3] this fundamental question has engaged practitioners, academics, and members of the judiciary, but it has yet to be confronted head on.

For the reasons much more fully described in the remainder of this Opinion, I conclude that, as Delaware law currently stands, the answer must be that the power to defeat an inadequate hostile tender offer ultimately lies with the board of directors. As such, I find that the Airgas board has met its burden under *Unocal* to articulate a legally cognizable threat (the allegedly inadequate price of Air Products' offer, coupled with the fact that a majority of Airgas's stockholders would likely tender into that inadequate offer) and has taken defensive measures that fall within a range of reasonable responses proportionate to that threat. I thus rule in favor of defendants. Air Products' and the Shareholder Plaintiffs' requests for relief are denied, and all claims asserted against defendants are dismissed with prejudice.

INTRODUCTION

This is the Court's decision after trial, extensive post-trial briefing, and a supplemental evidentiary hearing in this long-running takeover battle between Air Products & Chemicals, Inc. ("Air Products") and Airgas, Inc. ("Airgas"). The now very public saga began quietly in mid-October 2009 when John McGlade, President and CEO of Air Products, privately approached Peter McCausland, founder and CEO of Airgas, about a potential acquisition or combination. After McGlade's private advances were rebuffed, Air Products went hostile in February 2010, launching a public tender offer for all outstanding Airgas shares.

Now, over a year since Air Products first announced its all-shares, all-cash tender offer, the terms of that offer (other than price) remain essentially unchanged. After several price bumps and extensions, the offer currently stands at $70 per share and is set to expire today, February 15, 2011—Air Products' stated "best and final" offer. The Airgas board unanimously rejected that offer as being "clearly inadequate." The Airgas board has repeatedly expressed the view that Airgas is worth at least $78 per share in a sale transaction—and at any rate, far more than the $70 per share Air Products is offering.

So, we are at a crossroads. Air Products has made its "best and final" offer—apparently its offer to acquire Airgas has reached an end stage. Meanwhile, the Airgas board believes the offer is clearly inadequate and its value in a sale transaction is at least $78 per share. At this stage, it appears, neither side will budge. Airgas continues to maintain its defenses, blocking the bid and effectively denying shareholders the choice whether to tender their shares. Air Products and Shareholder Plaintiffs now ask this Court to order Airgas to redeem its poison pill and other defenses that are stopping Air Products from moving forward with its hostile offer, and to allow Airgas's stockholders to decide for themselves

---

3. *See, e.g., Yucaipa Am. Alliance Fund II, L.P. v. Riggio*, 1 A.3d 310, 351 n.229 (Del. Ch.2010); *eBay Domestic Holdings, Inc. v. Newmark*, 2010 WL 3516473 (Del.Ch. Sept.9, 2010); *Versata Enters., Inc. v. Selectica, Inc.*, 5 A.3d 586 (Del.2010).

whether they want to tender into Air Products' (inadequate or not) $70 "best and final" offer.

A week-long trial in this case was held from October 4, 2010 through October 8, 2010. . . .

Now, having thoroughly read, reviewed, and reflected upon all of the evidence presented to me, and having carefully considered the arguments made by counsel, I conclude that the Airgas board, in proceeding as it has since October 2009, has not breached its fiduciary duties owed to the Airgas stockholders. I find that the board has acted in good faith and in the honest belief that the Air Products offer, at $70 per share, is inadequate.

Although I have a hard time believing that inadequate price alone (according to the target's board) in the context of a non-discriminatory, all-cash, all-shares, fully financed offer poses any "threat" — particularly given the wealth of information available to Airgas's stockholders at this point in time — under existing Delaware law, it apparently does. Inadequate price has become a form of "substantive coercion" as that concept has been developed by the Delaware Supreme Court in its takeover jurisprudence. That is, the idea that Airgas's stockholders will disbelieve the board's views on value (or in the case of merger arbitrageurs who may have short-term profit goals in mind, they may simply ignore the board's recommendations), and so they may mistakenly tender into an inadequately priced offer. Substantive coercion has been clearly recognized by our Supreme Court as a valid threat.

Trial judges are not free to ignore or rewrite appellate court decisions. Thus, for reasons explained in detail below, I am constrained by Delaware Supreme Court precedent to conclude that defendants have met their burden under *Unocal* to articulate a sufficient threat that justifies the continued maintenance of Airgas's poison pill. That is, assuming defendants have met their burden to articulate a legally cognizable threat (prong 1), Airgas's defenses have been recognized by Delaware law as reasonable responses to the threat posed by an inadequate offer — even an all-shares, all-cash offer (prong 2).

In my personal view, Airgas's poison pill has served its legitimate purpose. Although the "best and final" $70 offer has been on the table for just over two months (since December 9, 2010), Air Products' advances have been ongoing for over sixteen months, and Airgas's use of its poison pill — particularly in combination with its staggered board — has given the Airgas board over a full year to inform its stockholders about its view of Airgas's intrinsic value and Airgas's value in a sale transaction. It has also given the Airgas board a full year to express its views to its stockholders on the purported opportunistic timing of Air Products' repeated advances and to educate its stockholders on the inadequacy of Air Products' offer. It has given Airgas *more time than any litigated poison pill in Delaware history* — enough time to show stockholders four quarters of improving financial results, demonstrating that Airgas is on track to meet its projected goals. And it has helped the Airgas board push Air Products to raise its bid by $10 per share from when it was first publicly announced to what Air Products has now represented is its highest offer. The record . . . confirm[s] that Airgas's stockholder base is sophisticated and well-informed, and that essentially all the information they would need to make an informed decision is available to them. In short, there seems to be no threat here — the stockholders know what they need to know (about both the offer and the Airgas board's opinion of the offer) to make an informed decision.

That being said, however, as I understand binding Delaware precedent, I may not substitute my business judgment for that of the Airgas board.[4] The Delaware Supreme Court has recognized inadequate price as a valid threat to corporate policy and effectiveness.[5] The Delaware Supreme Court has also made clear that the "selection of a time frame for achievement of corporate goals . . . may not be delegated to the stockholders."[6] Furthermore, in powerful dictum, the Supreme Court has stated that "[d]irectors are not obliged to abandon a deliberately conceived corporate plan for a short-term shareholder profit unless there is clearly no basis to sustain the corporate strategy."[7] Although I do not read that dictum as eliminating the applicability of heightened *Unocal* scrutiny to a board's decision to block a non-coercive bid as underpriced, I do read it, along with the actual holding in *Unitrin*, as indicating that a board that has a good faith, reasonable basis to believe a bid is inadequate may block that bid using a poison pill, irrespective of stockholders' desire to accept it.

Here, even using heightened scrutiny, the Airgas board has demonstrated that it has a reasonable basis for sustaining its long term corporate strategy—the Airgas board is independent, and has relied on the advice of three different outside independent financial advisors in concluding that Air Products' offer is inadequate. Air Products' *own three nominees* who were elected to the Airgas board in September 2010 have joined wholeheartedly in the Airgas board's determination, and when the Airgas board met to consider the $70 "best and final" offer in December 2010, it was one of those Air Products Nominees who said, "We have to protect the pill." Indeed, one of Air Products' *own directors* conceded at trial that the Airgas board members had acted within their fiduciary duties in their desire to "hold out for the proper price," and that "if an offer was made for Air Products that [he] considered to be unfair to the stockholders of Air Products . . . [he would likewise] use every legal mechanism available" to hold out for the proper price as well. Under Delaware law, the Airgas directors have complied with their fiduciary duties. Thus, as noted above, and for the reasons more fully described in the remainder of this Opinion, I am constrained to deny Air Products' and the Shareholder Plaintiffs' requests for relief.

. . .

III. ANALYSIS

A.   HAS THE AIRGAS BOARD ESTABLISHED THAT IT REASONABLY PERCEIVED THE EXISTENCE OF A LEGALLY COGNIZABLE THREAT?

1. Process

Under the first prong of *Unocal*, defendants bear the burden of showing that the Airgas board, "after a reasonable investigation . . . determined in good faith, that the [Air Products offer] presented a threat . . . that warranted a defensive

---

4. *Paramount Commc'ns, Inc. v. Time, Inc.*, 571 A.2d 1140, 1154 (Del.1990); *see City Capital Assocs. Ltd. P'ship v. Interco, Inc.*, 551 A.2d 787 (Del.Ch.1988); *Grand Metro. Pub. Ltd. Co. v. Pillsbury Co.*, 558 A.2d 1049 (Del.Ch.1988).

5. *See Unitrin, Inc. v. Am. Gen. Corp.*, 651 A.2d 1361, 1384 (Del.1995) ("This Court has held that the 'inadequate value' of an all cash for all shares offer is a 'legally cognizable threat.'") (quoting *Paramount Commc'ns, Inc. v. Time, Inc.*, 571 A.2d 1140, 1153 (Del.1990)).

6. *Paramount*, 571 A.2d at 1154.

7. *Id.*

response." I focus my analysis on the defendants' actions in response to Air Products' current $70 offer, but I note here that defendants would have cleared the *Unocal* hurdles with greater ease when the relevant inquiry was with respect to the board's response to the $65.50 offer.[8]

In examining defendants' actions under this first prong of *Unocal*, "the presence of a majority of outside independent directors coupled with a showing of reliance on advice by legal and financial advisors, 'constitute[s] a prima facie showing of good faith and reasonable investigation."[9] Here, it is undeniable that the Airgas board meets this test.

First, it is currently comprised of a majority of outside independent directors — including the three recently-elected insurgent directors who were nominated to the board by Air Products. Air Products does not dispute the independence of the Air Products Nominees, and the evidence at trial showed that the rest of the Airgas board, other than McCausland, are outside, independent directors who are not dominated by McCausland.

Second, the Airgas board relied on not one, not two, but three outside independent financial advisors in reaching its conclusion that Air Products' offer is "clearly inadequate." Credit Suisse, the third outside financial advisor . . . was selected by the entire Airgas board, was approved by the three Air Products Nominees, and its independence and qualifications are not in dispute. In addition, the Airgas board has relied on the advice of legal counsel, and the three Air Products Nominees have retained their own additional independent legal counsel (Skadden, Arps). In short, the Airgas board's process easily passes the smell test.

2. What Is the "Threat"?

Although the Airgas board meets the threshold of showing good faith and reasonable investigation, the first part of *Unocal* review requires more than that; it requires the board to show that its good faith and reasonable investigation ultimately gave the board "grounds for concluding that a threat to the corporate enterprise existed."[10] In the supplemental evidentiary hearing, Airgas (and its lawyers) attempted to identify numerous threats posed by Air Products' $70 offer: It is coercive. It is opportunistically timed. It presents the stockholders with a "prisoner's dilemma." It undervalues Airgas — it is a "clearly inadequate" price. The merger arbitrageurs who have bought into Airgas need to be "protected from themselves." The arbs are a "threat" to the minority. The list goes on.

The reality is that the Airgas board discussed essentially none of these alleged "threats" in its board meetings, or in its deliberations on whether to accept or reject Air Products' $70 offer, or in its consideration of whether to keep the pill in place. The board did not discuss "coercion" or the idea that Airgas's stockholders would be "coerced" into tendering. The board did not discuss the concept of a "prisoner's dilemma." The board did not discuss Air Products'

8. There are a number of reasons for this. For example, the inadequacy of the price was even greater at $65.50. More importantly, Air Products had openly admitted that it was willing to pay more for Airgas. The pill was serving an obvious purpose in providing leverage to the Airgas board. The collective action problem is lessened when the bidder has made its "best and final" offer, provided it is in fact its best and final offer.

9. *Selectica Inc. v. Versata Enters., Inc.*, 2010 WL 703062, at *12 (Del.Ch. Feb.26, 2010).

10. *Versata Enters., Inc. v. Selectica, Inc.*, 5 A.3d 586, 599 (Del.2010).

offer in terms of any "danger" that it posed to the corporate enterprise. In the October trial, Airgas had likewise failed to identify threats other than that Air Products' offer undervalues Airgas. In fact, there has been no specific board discussion since the October trial over whether to keep the poison pill in place (other than Clancey's "protect the pill" line).

Airgas's board members testified that the concepts of coercion, threat, and the decision whether or not to redeem the pill were nonetheless "implicit" in the board's discussions due to their knowledge that a large percentage of Airgas's stock is held by merger arbitrageurs who have short-term interests and would be willing to tender into an inadequate offer. But the only threat that the board discussed — the threat that has been the central issue since the beginning of this case — is the inadequate price of Air Products' offer. Thus, inadequate price, coupled with the fact that a majority of Airgas's stock is held by merger arbitrageurs who might be willing to tender into such an inadequate offer, is the only real "threat" alleged. . . .

In the end, it really is "All About Value." Airgas's directors and Airgas's financial advisors concede that the Airgas stockholder base is sophisticated and well-informed, and that they have all the information necessary to decide whether to tender into Air Products' offer.

. . .

c.   Substantive Coercion

Inadequate price and the concept of substantive coercion are inextricably related. The Delaware Supreme Court has defined substantive coercion . . . as "the risk that [Airgas's] stockholders might accept [Air Products'] inadequate Offer because of 'ignorance or mistaken belief' regarding the Board's assessment of the long-term value of [Airgas's] stock." In other words, if management advises stockholders, in good faith, that it believes Air Products' hostile offer is inadequate because in its view the future earnings potential of the company is greater than the price offered, Airgas's stockholders might nevertheless reject the board's advice and tender.

In the article that gave rise to the concept of "substantive coercion," Professors Gilson and Kraakman argued that, in order for substantive coercion to exist, two elements are necessary: (1) management must actually expect the value of the company to be greater than the offer — and be correct that the offer is in fact inadequate, and (2) the stockholders must reject management's advice or "*believe* that management will not deliver on its promise."[11] Both elements must be present because "[w]ithout the first element, shareholders who accept a structurally non-coercive offer have not made a mistake. Without the second element, shareholders will believe management and reject underpriced offers."

Defendants' argument involves a slightly different take on this threat, based on the particular composition of Airgas's stockholders (namely, its large "short-term" base). In essence, Airgas's argument is that "the substantial ownership of Airgas stock by these short-term, deal-driven investors poses a threat to the company and its shareholders" — the threat that, because it is likely that the arbs would support the $70 offer, "shareholders will be coerced into tendering into an inadequate offer." The threat of "arbs" is a new facet of substantive

---

11. Ronald Gilson & Reinier Kraakman, *Delaware's Intermediate Standard for Defensive Tactics: Is There Substance to Proportionality Review?*, 44 Bus. Law. 247, 260 (1989).

coercion. . . . [D]efendants' claim is not about "confusion" or "mistakenly tendering" (or even "disbelieving" management) — Air Products' offer has been on the table for over a year, Airgas's stockholders have been barraged with information, and there is no alternative offer to choose that might cause stockholders to be confused about the terms of Air Products' offer. Rather, Airgas's claim is that it needs to maintain its defensive measures to prevent control from being surrendered for an unfair or inadequate price. The argument is premised on the fact that a large percentage (almost half) of Airgas's stockholders are merger arbitrageurs — many of whom bought into the stock when Air Products first announced its interest in acquiring Airgas, at a time when the stock was trading much lower than it is today — who would be willing to tender into an inadequate offer because they stand to make a significant return on their investment even if the offer grossly undervalues Airgas in a sale. "They don't care a thing about the fundamental value of Airgas." In short, the risk is that a majority of Airgas's stockholders will tender into Air Products' offer despite its inadequate price tag, leaving the minority "coerced" into taking $70 as well. The defendants do not appear to have come to grips with the fact that the arbs bought their shares from long-term stockholders who viewed the increased market price generated by Air Products' offer as a good time to sell.

The threat that merger arbs will tender into an inadequately priced offer is only a legitimate threat if the offer is indeed inadequate. "The only way to protect stockholders [from a threat of substantive coercion] is for courts to ensure that the threat is real and that the board asserting the threat is not imagining or exaggerating it." Air Products and Shareholder Plaintiffs attack two main aspects of Airgas's five year plan — (1) the macroeconomic assumptions relied upon by management, and (2) the fact that Airgas did not consider what would happen if the economy had a "double-dip" recession.

Plaintiffs argue that reasonable stockholders may disagree with the board's optimistic macroeconomic assumptions. McCausland did not hesitate to admit during the supplemental hearing that he is "very bullish" on Airgas. "It's an amazing company," he said. He testified that the company has a shot at making its 2007 five year plan "despite the fact that the worst recession since the Great Depression landed right in the middle of that period. [W]e're in a good business, and we have a unique competitive advantage in the U.S. market." And it's not just Airgas that McCausland is bullish about — he's "bullish on the United States [ ] economy" as well.

So management presented a single scenario in its revised five-year plan — no double dip recession; reasonably optimistic macroeconomic growth assumptions. Everyone at trial agreed that "reasonable minds can differ as to the view of future value." But nothing in the record supported a claim that Airgas fudged any of its numbers, nor was there evidence that the board did not act at all times in good faith and in reasonable reliance on its outside advisors. The Air Products Nominees found the assumptions to be "reasonable." They do not see "any indication of a double-dip recession."

The next question is, if a majority of stockholders *want* to tender into an inadequately priced offer, is that substantive coercion? Is that a threat that justifies continued maintenance of the poison pill? Put differently, is there evidence in the record that Airgas stockholders are so "focused on the short-term" that they would "take a smaller harvest in the swelter of August over a larger one in Indian Summer"? Air Products argues that there is none whatsoever. They argue that there is "no evidence in the record that [Airgas's short-term] holders [i.e., arbitrageurs and hedge funds] would not [ ] reject the $70 offer if it was viewed by them to be inadequate. . . . Defendants have not demonstrated a single fact supporting their argument that a threat to Airgas stockholders exists because the Airgas stock is held by investors with varying time horizons."

But there is at least some evidence in the record suggesting that this risk may be real. Moreover, both Airgas's expert as well as *Air Products' own expert* testified that a large number — if not all — of the arbitrageurs who bought into Airgas's stock at prices significantly below the $70 offer price would be happy to tender their shares at that price regardless of the potential long-term value of the company. Based on the testimony of both expert witnesses, I find sufficient evidence that a majority of stockholders might be willing to tender their shares regardless of whether the price is adequate or not — thereby ceding control of Airgas to Air Products. . . .

Ultimately, it all seems to come down to the Supreme Court's holdings in *Paramount* and *Unitrin*. In *Unitrin*, the Court held: "[T]he directors of a Delaware corporation have the prerogative to determine that the market undervalues its stock and to protect its stockholders from offers that do not reflect the long-term value of the corporation under its present management plan."[12] . . . The Supreme Court has unequivocally "endorse[d the] conclusion that it is not a breach of faith for directors to determine that the present stock market price of shares is not representative of true value or that there may indeed be several market values for any corporation's stock." [B]ased on all of the facts presented to me, I find that the Airgas board acted in good faith and relied on the advice of its financial and legal advisors in coming to the conclusion that Air Products' offer is inadequate. And as the Supreme Court has held, a board that in good faith believes that a hostile offer is inadequate may "properly employ[ ] a poison pill as a proportionate defensive response to protect its stockholders from a 'low ball' bid."

B. IS THE CONTINUED MAINTENANCE OF AIRGAS'S DEFENSIVE MEASURES PROPORTIONATE TO THE "THREAT" POSED BY AIR PRODUCTS' OFFER?

Turning now to the second part of the *Unocal* test, I must determine whether the Airgas board's defensive measures are a proportionate response to the threat posed by Air Products' offer. Where the defensive measures "are inextricably related, the principles of *Unocal* require that [they] be scrutinized collectively as

---

12. *Unitrin*, 651 A.2d 1361, 1376 (citing *Paramount*, 571 A.2d at 1153). Vice Chancellor Strine has pointed out that "[r]easonable minds can and do differ on whether it is appropriate for a board to consider an all cash, all shares tender offer as a threat that permits any response greater than that necessary for the target board to be able to negotiate for or otherwise locate a higher bid and to provide stockholders with the opportunity to rationally consider the views of both management and the prospective acquiror before making the decision to sell their personal property." *In re Gaylord Container Corp. S'holders Litig.*, 753 A.2d 462, 478 n. 56 (Del.Ch.2000). But the Supreme Court cited disapprovingly to the approach taken in *City Capital Associates v. Interco, Inc.*, 551 A.2d 787 (Del.Ch.1988), which had suggested that an all-cash, all-shares bid posed a limited threat to stockholders that justified leaving a poison pill in place only for some period of time while the board protects stockholder interests, but "[o]nce that period has closed . . . and [the board] has taken such time as it required in good faith to arrange an alternative value-maximizing transaction, then, in most instances, the legitimate role of the poison pill in the context of a noncoercive offer will have been fully satisfied." The Supreme Court rejected that understanding as "not in keeping with a proper *Unocal* analysis."

a unitary response to the perceived threat." Defendants bear the burden of showing that their defenses are not preclusive or coercive, and if neither, that they fall within a "range of reasonableness."

1. Preclusive or Coercive

A defensive measure is coercive if it is "aimed at 'cramming down' on its shareholders a management-sponsored alternative."[13] Airgas's defensive measures are certainly not coercive in this respect, as Airgas is specifically *not* trying to cram down a management sponsored alternative, but rather, simply wants to maintain the status quo and manage the company for the long term.

A response is preclusive if it "makes a bidder's ability to wage a successful proxy contest and gain control [of the target's board] . . . 'realistically unattainable.'"[14] Air Products and Shareholder Plaintiffs argue that Airgas's defensive measures are preclusive because they render the possibility of an effective proxy contest realistically unattainable. What the argument boils down to, though, is that Airgas's defensive measures make the possibility of Air Products obtaining control of the Airgas board and removing the pill realistically unattainable *in the very near future*, because Airgas has a staggered board in place. Thus, the real issue posed is whether defensive measures are "preclusive" if they make gaining control of the board realistically unattainable in the short term (but still realistically attainable sometime in the future), or if "preclusive" actually means "preclusive" — i.e. forever unattainable. In reality, or perhaps I should say in practice, these two formulations ("preclusive for now" or "preclusive forever") may be one and the same when examining the combination of a staggered board plus a poison pill, because no bidder to my knowledge has ever successfully stuck around for two years and waged two successful proxy contests to gain control of a classified board in order to remove a pill. So does that make the combination of a staggered board and a poison pill preclusive?

This precise question was asked and answered four months ago in *Versata Enterprises, Inc. v. Selectica, Inc.* There, Trilogy (the hostile acquiror) argued that in order for the target's defensive measures not to be preclusive: (1) a successful proxy contest must be realistically attainable, and (2) the successful proxy contest must result in gaining control of the board at the next election. The Delaware Supreme Court rejected this argument, stating that "[i]f that preclusivity argument is correct, then it would apply whenever a corporation has both a classified board and a Rights Plan. . . . *[W]e hold that the combination of a classified board and a Rights Plan do not constitute a preclusive defense.*"[15]

The Supreme Court explained its reasoning as follows:

> Classified boards are authorized by statute and are adopted for a variety of business purposes. Any classified board also operates as an antitakeover defense by preventing an insurgent from obtaining control of the board in one election. More than a decade ago, in *Carmody [v. Toll Brothers, Inc.]*, the Court of Chancery noted

---

13. *Selectica*, 5 A.3d at 601 (quoting *Unitrin*, 651 A.2d at 1387).

14. *Id.* (citing *Carmody v. Toll Bros., Inc.*, 723 A.2d 1180, 1195 (Del.Ch.1998)). Until *Selectica*, the preclusive test asked whether defensive measures rendered an effective proxy contest "'mathematically impossible' or 'realistically unattainable,'" but since "realistically unattainable" subsumes "mathematically impossible," the Supreme Court in *Selectica* explained that there is really "only one test of preclusivity: 'realistically unattainable.'" *Id.*

15. *Selectica*, 5 A.3d 586, 604 (Del.2010) (emphasis added).

"because only one third of a classified board would stand for election each year, a classified board would *delay — but not prevent — a hostile acquiror from obtaining control of the board*, since a determined acquiror could wage a proxy contest and obtain control of two thirds of the target board over a two year period, as opposed to seizing control in a single election."

The Court concluded: "The fact that a combination of defensive measures makes it more difficult for an acquirer to obtain control of a board does not make such measures realistically unattainable, i.e., preclusive." Moreover, citing *Moran*, the Supreme Court noted that pills do not fundamentally restrict proxy contests. . . . Arguably the combination of a staggered board plus a pill is at least *more* preclusive than the use of a rights plan by a company with a pill alone. . . . In any event, though, the Supreme Court in *Selectica* suggests that this is a distinction without a significant difference, and very clearly held that the combination of a classified board and a Rights Plan is not preclusive, and that the combination may only "delay—but not prevent—a hostile acquiror from obtaining control of the board."

. . .

I am thus bound by this clear precedent to proceed on the assumption that Airgas's defensive measures are not preclusive if they delay Air Products from obtaining control of the Airgas board (even if that delay is significant) so long as obtaining control at some point in the future is realistically attainable. I now examine whether the ability to obtain control of Airgas's board in the future is realistically attainable.

Air Products has already run one successful slate of insurgents. Their three independent nominees were elected to the Airgas board in September. Airgas's next annual meeting will be held sometime around September 2011. Accordingly, if Airgas's defensive measures remain in place, Air Products has two options if it wants to continue to pursue Airgas at this time: (1) It can call a special meeting and remove the entire board with a supermajority vote of the outstanding shares, or (2) [i]t can wait until Airgas's 2011 annual meeting to nominate a slate of directors. [Chancellor Chandler concluded that both of these options were viable.]

2. *Range of Reasonableness*

. . .

Here, the record demonstrates that Airgas's board, composed of a majority of outside, independent directors, acting in good faith and with numerous outside advisors concluded that Air Products' offer clearly undervalues Airgas in a sale transaction. The board believes in good faith that the offer price is inadequate by no small margin. Thus, the board is responding to a legitimately articulated threat.

This conclusion is bolstered by the fact that the three Air Products Nominees on the Airgas board have now wholeheartedly joined in the board's determination — what is more, they believe it is their fiduciary duty to keep Airgas's defenses in place. And Air Products' *own directors* have testified that (1) they have no reason to believe that the Airgas directors have breached their fiduciary duties, (2) even though plenty of information has been made available to the stockholders, they "agree that Airgas management is in the best position to understand the intrinsic value of the company," and (3) if the shoe were on the other foot, they would act in the same way as Airgas's directors have.

In addition, Air Products made a tactical decision to proceed with its offer for Airgas in the manner in which it did. First, Air Products made a choice to launch a proxy contest in connection with its tender offer. It could have — at that point, in February 2010 — attempted to call a special meeting to remove the entire board. The 67% vote requirement was a high hurdle that presented uncertainty, so it chose to proceed by launching a proxy contest in connection with its tender offer.

Second, Air Products chose to replace a minority of the Airgas board with three *independent directors* who promised to take a "fresh look." Air Products ran its nominees expressly premised on that independent slate. It could have put up three nominees premised on the slogan of "shareholder choice." It could have run a slate of nominees who would promise to remove the pill if elected. It could have gotten three directors elected who were resolved to fight back against the rest of the Airgas board.

Certainly what occurred here is not what Air Products expected to happen. Air Products ran its slate on the promise that its nominees would "consider without any bias [the Air Products] Offer," and that they would "be willing to be out-spoken in the boardroom about their views on these issues." Air Products *got what it wanted.* Its three nominees got elected to the Airgas board and then questioned the directors about their assumptions. (They got answers.) They looked at the numbers themselves. (They were impressed.) They requested outside legal counsel. (They got it.) They requested a third outside financial advisor. (They got it.) And in the end, they *joined in the board's view* that Air Products' offer was inadequate. John Clancey, one of the Air Products Nomi-nees, grabbed the flag and championed Airgas's defensive measures, telling the rest of the board, "*We have to protect the pill.*" David DeNunzio, Airgas's new independent financial advisor from Credit Suisse who was brought in to take a "fresh look" at the numbers, concluded in his professional opinion that the fair value of Airgas is in the "mid to high seventies, and well into the mid eighties." In Robert Lumpkins' opinion (one of the Air Products Nominees), "the company on its own, its own business will be worth $78 or more in the not very distant future because of its own earnings and cash flow prospects . . . as a standalone company."

The Supreme Court has clearly held that "the 'inadequate value' of an all cash for all shares offer is a 'legally cognizable threat.'" Moreover, "[t]he fiduciary duty to manage a corporate enterprise includes the selection of a time frame for achievement of corporate goals. *That duty may not be delegated to the stockholders.*" The Court continued, "Directors are not obligated to abandon a deliberately conceived corporate plan for a short-term shareholder profit unless there is clearly no basis to sustain the corporate strategy." Based on all of the foregoing factual findings, I cannot conclude that there is "clearly no basis" for the Airgas board's belief in the sustainability of its long-term plan.

On the contrary, the maintenance of the board's defensive measures must fall within a range of reasonableness here. The board is not "cramming down" a management-sponsored alternative — or *any* company-changing alternative. Instead, the board is simply maintaining the status quo, running the company for the long-term, and consistently showing improved financial results each passing quarter. The board's actions do not *forever* preclude Air Products, or any bidder, from acquiring Airgas or from getting around Airgas's defensive measures if the price is right. In the meantime, the board is preventing a change of control from occurring at an inadequate price. This course of action has been clearly recognized under Delaware law: "[D]irectors, when acting deliberately, in an informed way, and in the good faith pursuit of corporate interests, may follow a course designed to achieve long-term value even at the cost of immediate value maximization."

Conclusion

. . .

There is no question that poison pills act as potent anti-takeover drugs with the potential to be abused. Counsel for plaintiffs (both Air Products and Shareholder Plaintiffs) make compelling policy arguments in favor of redeeming the pill in this case — to do otherwise, they say, would essentially make all companies with staggered boards and poison pills "takeover proof." The argument is an excellent sound bite, but it is ultimately not the holding of this fact-specific case, although it does bring us one step closer to that result.

As this case demonstrates, in order to have any effectiveness, pills do not — and cannot — have a set expiration date. To be clear, though, this case does not endorse "just say never." What it does endorse is Delaware's long-understood respect for reasonably exercised managerial discretion, so long as boards are found to be acting in good faith and in accordance with their fiduciary duties (after rigorous judicial fact-finding and enhanced scrutiny of their defensive actions). The Airgas board serves as a quintessential example.

Directors of a corporation still owe fiduciary duties to *all stockholders* — this undoubtedly includes short-term as well as long-term holders. At the same time, a board cannot be forced into *Revlon* mode any time a hostile bidder makes a tender offer that is at a premium to market value. The mechanisms in place to get around the poison pill — even a poison pill in combination with a staggered board, which no doubt makes the process prohibitively more difficult — have been in place since 1985, when the Delaware Supreme Court first decided to uphold the pill as a legal defense to an unwanted bid. That is the current state of Delaware law until the Supreme Court changes it.

For the foregoing reasons, Air Products' and the Shareholder Plaintiffs' requests for relief are denied, and all claims asserted against defendants are dismissed with prejudice. The parties shall bear their own costs.

PROBLEM 11-4

After losing the foregoing case, Air Products dropped its bid to acquire Airgas. In a press release issued that day, John E. McGlade, Air Products' chairman, president, and chief executive officer, said, "While acquiring Airgas at an appropriate price would have been a value-creating opportunity, Air Products has many other compelling growth opportunities around the world that we are continuing to pursue. Our business is performing extremely well as evidenced by our most recent results, and we remain focused on executing against our strategic plan and delivering strong results for our shareholders."

The *Airgas* decision has been a frequent topic of conversation among scholars and practicing attorneys. The following is a March 31, 2011, report from the Deal Professor, Steven M. Davidoff, who teaches at the Moritz College of Law, The Ohio State University:

> A mergers and acquisitions panel at the Tulane Corporate Law Institute focused on the future of the poison pill takeover defense on Thursday after Airgas won its battle against its hostile bidder, Air Products and Chemicals. That future is hazy.
>
> The debate centered on whether the *Airgas* decision was rightly decided in Delaware Chancery Court and also on how the case would be applied in the future. Given that the panel included four expert New York takeover [defense] lawyers, it was not surprising that they largely thought the decision was a good one. . . .
>
> The one possible dissenter on the panel appeared to be the most important one, Vice Chancellor Leo E. Strine, Jr. of the Delaware court. While he avoided the question of whether the case was rightly decided by his colleague, Chancellor William B. Chandler III, he did say it was still an open question in Delaware. This is because the *Airgas* case was decided in the lower court, not the higher Delaware Supreme Court and 1980s precedent might still allow a court to rule the other way.

For purposes of discussing this problem, assume that Air Products did not drop its bid to acquire Airgas after Chancellor Chandler issued his opinion. Instead, Air Products appealed to the Delaware Supreme Court.

Could Chancellor Chandler's decision be reversed under the existing Delaware precedent? If not and you were a member of the Delaware Supreme Court, would you change that precedent?

CHAPTER
12

Regulation of Disclosure, Fraud, and Insider Trading

MOTIVATING HYPOTHETICAL

Over the past several decades, advances in the theory of corporate finance have resulted in many financial innovations. One set of innovations that attracted a great deal of attention during the global financial crisis of 2007-2009 is the practice of "securitization." "Securitizing" is the general process of bundling thousands of assets that are producing an income stream, such as home loans, credit cards, auto loans, or student loans, transferring that bundle to a separately incorporated legal entity called an SPV ("special purpose vehicle") or SIV ("special investment vehicle"), and then issuing new securities, most often bonds, whose interest payments will come from the consumers making payments on the underlying mortgages, auto loans, or what have you. In some instances, the bonds issued by SPVs would be bundled and transferred to a new SPV, which would issue a new batch of bonds. These second-order securitized instruments are most often called CDOs, or "collateralized debt obligations." As problems unfolded in the financial crisis, CDOs composed of securitized mortgages became a particular source of financial instability, and a fertile field for the growth of securities fraud claims.

In Chapter 6, we examined the federal securities law that applies to proxy communications with shareholders and saw that there is a private cause of action under Section 14(a) of the Securities Exchange Act of 1934 (the Exchange Act or 1934 Act) and Rule 14a-9 for any material misstatement or omission in a proxy communication. The purpose of that cause of action is to encourage companies to provide full and accurate disclosure to shareholders in conjunction with every shareholder vote. Yet many statements companies make are not made in the context of proxy solicitations, but rather are general statements to the press, to securities analysts, and to the public. Other sections of the federal securities laws have as their goal ensuring that companies' statements to the capital markets generally embody full and fair disclosure.

By far the most important of these other sections is Section 10(b) of the Exchange Act, and Rule 10b-5 promulgated thereunder. Together these create a cause of action for fraud for any material misstatement or omission in connection with the purchase or sale of securities that has caused damages. Liability under Section 10(b) and Rule 10b-5 reaches not only statements contained in required disclosure documents such as quarterly and annual reports, but also every public statement a company's authorized agent makes, such as in a press release, news conference, or response to reporters' questions. Pick up any newspaper in the United States and you can read about either the Securities and Exchange Commission (SEC) or private investors as a class suing a company for securities fraud — for instance, because the financial statements overstate revenues by a few billion dollars — and the odds are overwhelming that a violation of Section 10(b) and Rule 10b-5 has been alleged. This chapter begins with an examination of the more important elements of a cause of action for fraud generally under Section 10(b) and Rule 10b-5. We then move on to look at a specific species of fraud under Section 10(b) and Rule 10b-5 that is of particular interest because it raises both corporate governance and securities law issues: insider trading. Bear in mind that a detailed examination of these topics is beyond the scope of this casebook, but you can look forward to such an examination by taking an upper-level securities class.

A.   SECTION 10(b) AND RULE 10b-5

Section 10 of the Securities Exchange Act of 1934, 15 U.S.C. § 78j, provides in relevant part:

> It shall be unlawful for any person, directly or indirectly, by the use of any means or instrumentality of interstate commerce or of the mails, or of any facility of any national securities exchange . . .
> (b) To use or employ, in connection with the purchase or sale of any security . . . any manipulative or deceptive device or contrivance in contravention of such rules and regulations as the Commission may prescribe as necessary or appropriate in the public interest or for the protection of investors.

Rule 10b-5, 17 C.F.R. § 240.10b-5 (2000), provides:

> It shall be unlawful for any person, directly or indirectly, by the use of any means or instrumentality of interstate commerce, or of the mails or of any facility of any national securities exchange,
> (a) to employ any device, scheme, or artifice to defraud,
> (b) to make any untrue statement of a material fact or to omit to state a material fact necessary in order to make the statements made, in the light of the circumstances under which they were made, not misleading, or
> (c) to engage in any act, practice, or course of business which operates or would operate as a fraud or deceit upon any person, in connection with the purchase or sale of any security.

Based on this statutory and regulatory language, the elements of a cause of action are a (1) misstatement or omission of a (2) material fact on which the plaintiff (3) relied (4) in connection with the (5) purchase or sale of securities, (6) causing (7) damages. We will discuss all but the damages element below.

Traditionally, courts have treated Section 10b and Rule 10b-5 as concerned primarily with the accuracy of disclosure, and not concerned with corporate governance or enforcing fiduciary duties. In Santa Fe v. Green, for example, the majority shareholders in a short-form merger notified plaintiffs that their shares would be purchased for $150 per share. (Recall that a short-form merger is one in which a parent company owning more than 90 percent of the shares of a subsidiary can cause a merger with the subsidiary without the requirement of a shareholder vote.) As part of the disclosure document notifying the minority shareholders of the merger and of their appraisal rights, the majority shareholders told the minority they had obtained independent appraisals of the company's physical assets (land, timber, buildings, and machinery), which showed those assets were worth $640 per share. The minority shareholders sued under Section 10(b) and Rule 10b-5, claiming that the use of the short-form merger procedure was a scheme or an artifice to defraud the minority of the fair value of their shares. The U.S. Supreme Court rejected the minority's claim, stating that "our cases have rejected the view that a breach of fiduciary duty by majority stockholders, without any deception, misrepresentation, or nondisclosure, violates the statute and the Rule." Santa Fe v. Green, 430 U.S. 462, 467 (1977).

More recently, courts seem to have started to come to view Section 10(b)/Rule 10b-5 as an important mechanism regulating corporate governance insofar as disclosure brings to light conflicts of interest and enhances shareholder power. This development, which is shown in the insider trading case presented later in this chapter (United States v. O'Hagan) and in the *Zandford* case, will also likely be seen as the courts start to interpret Sarbanes-Oxley, which explicitly federalizes some aspects of corporate governance. Thus, while in this Section we explore some of the more important technical requirements of a cause of action under Section 10(b)/Rule 10b-5, the larger issue on which to focus is how this cause of action mitigates conflicts between managers and shareholders.

1. Misstatements and Omissions

To demonstrate liability under Section 10(b) and Rule 10b-5, plaintiffs must first show that the defendant misstated a material fact or omitted to state a material fact necessary to make the statements that were made not misleading. For instance, if a company states that "to date, the FDA has not disapproved any drug that we are developing," it would be a material omission not to also state, "but we have been advised that the FDA staff is recommending that approval be denied of our most promising drug," if those were the circumstances. Thus, although the first statement is literally true, it would be held to be a half-truth if not elaborated upon in the manner indicated.

By far the most difficult issues that arise with respect to this element of a cause of action under Section 10(b) and Rule 10b-5 concern omissions, since "silence, absent a duty to speak, is not misleading under Rule 10b-5." Basic Inc. v. Levinson, 485 U.S. 224, 239 n.17 (1988). The question arises, then, when is there a duty to speak — that is, a duty to disclose a fact that was omitted? Such a duty to avoid half-truths can arise, as in the example in the paragraph above. A duty to speak may arise because a company is selling new securities to the public and thus needs to file a disclosure document (a "prospectus") under the Securities Act of 1933. The contents of the prospectus will be specified by line-item instructions in Regulation S-K (which contains integrated instructions for disclosure documents under both the 1933 Act and the 1934 Act). Prospectus disclosure is also guided by Rule 408, which requires any additional disclosure necessary to make the statements not misleading that are made in response to line-item disclosure under Regulation S-K. When a public company files quarterly reports or annual reports, again, Regulation S-K sets out the required disclosure, and again there is a requirement to avoid half-truths. If a company is buying back its own stock, there is a duty to disclose all material information that might affect the value of the stock in order to avoid liability, because a company has a fiduciary duty to its shareholders, arising from agency law, to disclose material information when it buys securities from them. Or in the context of a proxy statement, either in advance of the annual meeting or in conjunction with a special meeting, there is a duty to speak. Thus, there are very many points in time when there is a duty to speak, and failure to speak (an omission) will create liability.

Yet, as the following case indicates, we do not have a disclosure regimen requiring immediate disclosure of every material event. Rather, the SEC has promulgated Form 8-K, which requires disclosure within four business days of specified events, such as a change in control of the registrant, the acquisition or disposition of major assets not in the ordinary course of business, resignation of the company's accountant or directors, or a bankruptcy filing. Sarbanes-Oxley directed the SEC to develop rules to identify which kinds of material changes in the financial condition or operations of the issuer must be disclosed "on a rapid and current basis," § 409 of Sarbanes-Oxley, 15 U.S.C. § 78m(l), pursuant to which the SEC shortened the time for Form 8-K disclosure from 15 days to the current four business days. Section 409 moves capital market regulation in the direction of "continuous disclosure," as defined in the following case, and yet the United States still allows a few days to elapse before the disclosure of material events is required. The enclosed case is a good overview of the duty to disclose and the underlying philosophy of U.S. securities regulation.

GALLAGHER v. ABBOTT LABORATORIES

269 F.3d 806
United States Court of Appeals, Seventh Circuit
October 17, 2001

Easterbrook, Circuit Judge.

Year after year the Food and Drug Administration inspected the Diagnostic Division of Abbott Laboratories, found deficiencies in manufacturing quality control, and issued warnings. The Division made efforts to do better, never to the FDA's satisfaction, but until 1999 the FDA was willing to accept Abbott's promises and remedial steps. On March 17, 1999, the FDA sent Abbott another letter demanding compliance with all regulatory requirements and threatening severe consequences. This could have been read as more saber rattling — Bloomberg News revealed the letter to the financial world in June, and Abbott's stock price did not even quiver — but later developments show that it was more ominous. By September 1999 the FDA was insisting on substantial penalties plus changes in Abbott's methods of doing business. On September 29, 1999, after the markets had closed, Abbott issued a press release describing the FDA's position, asserting that Abbott was in "substantial" compliance with federal regulations, and revealing that the parties were engaged in settlement talks. Abbott's stock fell more than 6%, from $40 to $37.50, the next business day. On November 2, 1999, Abbott and the FDA resolved their differences, and a court entered a consent decree requiring Abbott to remove 125 diagnostic products from the market until it had improved its quality control and to pay a $100 million civil fine. Abbott took an accounting charge of $168 million to cover the fine and worthless inventory. The next business day Abbott's stock slumped $3.50, which together with the earlier drop implied that shareholders saw the episode as costing Abbott (in cash plus future compliance costs and lost sales) more than $5 billion. (Neither side has used the capital asset pricing model or any other means to factor market movements out of these price changes, so we take them at face value.)

Plaintiffs in these class actions under § 10(b) of the Securities Exchange Act of 1934, and the SEC's Rule 10b-5 contend that Abbott committed fraud by deferring public revelation. The classes comprise all buyers of Abbott's securities between March 17 and November 2. (One class consists of persons who bought securities in ALZA, a firm that Abbott proposed to acquire through an exchange of securities and whose market price thus tracked Abbott's. For simplicity we treat these plaintiffs as purchasers of Abbott stock.) The district judge dismissed the complaints under Fed. R. Civ. P. 12(b)(6) for failure to state a claim on which relief may be granted. The market's non-reaction to Bloomberg's disclosure shows, the judge thought, that the FDA's letter was not by itself material or that the market price had earlier reflected the news; only later developments contained material information, which Abbott disclosed in September and November. Moreover, the judge concluded, plaintiffs had not identified any false or fraudulent statement by Abbott, as opposed to silence in the face of bad news. We are skeptical that these shortcomings justify dismissal for failure to state a claim on which relief may be granted; the judge's reasons seem more akin to an invocation of Fed. R. Civ. P. 9(b), which requires fraud to be pleaded with particularity, or the extra pleading requirements for securities cases created by the Private Securities Litigation Reform Act of 1995. But it is not necessary to decide whether Rule 12(b)(6), Rule 12(c), Rule 9(b), or the Reform Act supplies the best basis of decision. Nor is it necessary to decide whether the news was "material" before the FDA's negotiating position stiffened, to decide whether Abbott acted with the state of mind necessary to support liability under Rule 10b-5, or to address other potential stumbling blocks. What sinks plaintiffs' position is their inability to identify any false statement — or for that matter any truthful statement made misleading by the omission of news about the FDA's demands.

Much of plaintiffs' argument reads as if firms have an absolute duty to disclose all information material to stock prices as soon as news comes into their possession. Yet that is not the way the securities laws work. We do not have a system of continuous disclosure. Instead firms are entitled to keep silent (about good news as well as bad news) unless positive law creates a duty to disclose. Until the Securities Act of 1933 there was no federal regulation of corporate disclosure. The 1933 Act requires firms to reveal information only when they issue securities, and the duty is owed only to persons who buy from the issuer or an underwriter distributing on its behalf; every other transaction is exempt under § 4. (No member of either class contends that he purchased securities from Abbott, or an underwriter on Abbott's behalf, between March 17 and November 2.) Section 13 of the Securities Exchange Act of 1934, 15 U.S.C. § 78m, adds that the SEC may require issuers to file annual and other periodic reports—with the emphasis on *periodic* rather than continuous. Section 13 and the implementing regulations contemplate that these reports will be snapshots of the corporation's status on or near the filing date, with updates due not when something "material" happens, but on the next prescribed filing date.

Regulations implementing § 13 require a comprehensive annual filing, the Form 10-K report, and less extensive quarterly supplements on Form 10-Q. The supplements need not bring up to date everything contained in the annual 10-K report; counsel for the plaintiff classes conceded at oral argument that nothing in Regulation S-K (the SEC's list of required disclosures) requires either an updating of Form 10-K reports more often than annually, or a disclosure in a quarterly Form 10-Q report of information about the firm's regulatory problems. The regulations that provide for disclosures on Form 10-Q tell us *which* items in the annual report must be updated (a subset of the full list), and how often (quarterly).

Many proposals have been made to do things differently—to junk this combination of sale-based disclosure with periodic follow-up and replace it with a system under which *issuers* rather than *securities* are registered and disclosure must be continuous. *E.g.*, American Law Institute, *Federal Securities Code* xxvii-xxviii, § 602 & commentary (1978); Securities and Exchange Commission, *Report of the Advisory Committee on the Capital Formation and Regulatory Process* 9-14, 36-38 (1996). Regulation S-K goes some distance in this direction by defining identical items of disclosure for registration of stock and issuers' subsequent reports, and by authorizing the largest issuers to use their annual 10-K reports as the kernels of registration statements for new securities. But Regulation S-K does not replace periodic with continuous disclosure, and the more ambitious proposals to do this have not been adopted.

The ALI's proposal, for example, was embraced by the SEC, *see* 1933 Act Release No. 6242 (Sept. 18, 1980); 1933 Act Release No. 6377 (Jan. 31, 1982), but never seriously pursued, and revisions of Regulation S-K satisfied many of the original supporters of the ALI's proposal. The advisory committee report, prepared by a distinguished group of scholars and practitioners under the leadership of Commissioner Steven M.H. Wallman, did not persuade the SEC's other members and was not taken up by the agency as a legislative plan or even as the basis of a demonstration project. Whatever may be said for and against these proposals, they must be understood as projects for legislation (and to a limited extent for the use of the SEC's rulemaking powers); judges have no authority to scoop the political branches and adopt continuous disclosure under the banner of Rule 10b-5. *Especially* not under that banner, for Rule 10b-5 condemns only fraud, and a corporation does not commit fraud by standing on its rights under a periodic-disclosure system. The Supreme Court has insisted that this judicially created right of action be used only to implement, and not to alter, the rules found in the text of the 1933 and 1934 Acts.

Trying to locate some statement that was either false or materially misleading because it did not mention the FDA's position, plaintiffs pointed in the district court to several reports filed or statements made by Abbott before November 2, 1999. All but two of these have fallen by the wayside on appeal. What remain are Abbott's Form 10-K annual report for 1998 filed in March 1999 and an oral statement that Miles White, Abbott's CEO, made at the annual shareholders' meeting the next month.

Plaintiffs rely principally on Item 303(a)(3)(ii) of Regulation S-K, which provides that registration statements and annual 10-K reports must reveal

> any known trends or uncertainties that have had or that the registrant reasonably expects will have a material favorable or unfavorable impact on net sales or revenues or income from continuing operations.

The FDA's letter, and its negotiating demands, are within this description, according to the plaintiff classes. We shall assume that this is so. The 10-K report did state that Abbott is "subject to comprehensive government regulation" and that "[g]overnment regulatory actions can result in . . . sanctions." Plaintiffs say that this is too general in light of the FDA's letter and Abbott's continuing inability to satisfy the FDA's demands. Again we shall assume that plaintiffs are right. But there is a fundamental problem: The 10-K report was filed on March 9, 1999, and the FDA's letter is dated March 17, eight days later. Unless Abbott had a time machine, it could not have described on March 9 a letter that had yet to be written.

Attempting to surmount this temporal problem, plaintiffs insist that Abbott had a "duty to correct" the 10-K report. Yet a statement may be "corrected" only if it was *in*correct when made, and nothing said as of March 9 was incorrect. . . .

As for White's statements at the annual meeting: he said very little that was concrete (as opposed to puffery), and everything concrete was true. White said, for example:

> The outcome [of our efforts] has been growth more than five times faster than the diagnostics market. We expect this trend to continue for the foreseeable future, due to the unprecedented state of our new product cycle. By supplementing our internal investment with opportunistic technology acquisitions, Abbott's diagnostics pipeline is fuller than ever before.

The statement about past performance was accurate, and the plaintiffs have not given us any reason to doubt that White honestly believed that similar growth would continue, or that White honestly believed "Abbott's diagnostics pipeline [to be] fuller than ever before." Even with the benefit of hindsight these statements cannot be gainsaid. Here is where Rule 9(b) pinches: Plaintiffs have done nothing to meet the requirements for pleading fraud with respect to the annual meeting, even if it were possible (which we doubt) to treat as "fraud" the predictive components in White's boosterism.

Affirmed.

2. *Materiality and Reliance*

We have already seen the definition of a "material" fact or omission in Chapter 6: a fact a reasonable investor would consider significant in the total mix of information available about a company. We have also already seen that this definition is quite fact- and context-specific, and that in recent years the parameters of what "reasonable investors" want to know about a company are expanding from financial information, which is presumably always material, to social and environmental information in some instances.

One of the more interesting problems in securities regulation and Section 10(b)/Rule 10b-5 causes of action concerns the materiality of speculative or future facts. After all, an investment today in a company is an indication of the investor's view of the company's future, and any reasonable investor would want that view to be as informed as management's concerning current trends, risks, and business developments that might affect the future of the company. The following case, Basic Inc. v. Levinson, sets out the process of analysis for determining whether speculative future events are material. This case is also of major importance in understanding the scope of Section 10(b)/Rule 10b-5's reliance requirement, so that part of the opinion is also included. To understand the significance of the discussion of reliance, some context is in order.

Under the common law of fraud, plaintiffs must show that they relied upon a material misstatement of fact to their economic detriment. Section 10(b) was enacted to expand the scope of the common law cause of action for fraud, though, because in the early 1930s common law remedies were thought to have been inadequate to protect investors during the Roaring Twenties. Two related problems with the common law reliance element are discussed in Basic Inc. v. Levinson: First, while reliance is an element of a plaintiff's case in a face-to-face transaction, what sort of reliance must be proved in a "market" transaction (on an exchange or over NASDAQ)? Second, Section 10(b) expanded the scope of the common law cause of action for fraud beyond *misstatements* of fact to *omissions* to state necessary facts. But how can one "rely" on an omission? Basic Inc. v. Levinson's "fraud on the market" theory addresses the first problem, and the Court's discussion of Affiliated Ute Citizens v. United States summarizes its prior resolution of the second problem.

BASIC INC. v. LEVINSON

485 U.S. 224
Supreme Court of the United States
March 7, 1988

Justice BLACKMUN.

This case requires us to apply the materiality requirement of § 10(b) of the Securities Exchange Act of 1934 (1934 Act), 48 Stat. 881, as amended, 15 U.S.C. § 78a *et seq.*, and the Securities and Exchange Commission's Rule 10b-5, 17 CFR § 240.10b-5 (1987), promulgated thereunder, in the context of preliminary corporate merger discussions. We must also determine whether a person who traded a corporation's shares on a securities exchange after the issuance of a materially misleading statement by the corporation may invoke a rebuttable presumption that, in trading, he relied on the integrity of the price set by the market.

I

Prior to December 20, 1978, Basic Incorporated was a publicly traded company primarily engaged in the business of manufacturing chemical refractories for the steel industry. As early as 1965 or 1966, Combustion Engineering, Inc., a company producing mostly alumina-based refractories, expressed some interest in acquiring Basic, but was deterred from pursuing this inclination seriously because of antitrust concerns it then entertained. . . . In 1976, however, regulatory action opened the way to a renewal of Combustion's interest. The "Strategic Plan," dated October 25, 1976, for Combustion's Industrial Products Group included the objective: "Acquire Basic Inc. $30 million." . . .

Beginning in September 1976, Combustion representatives had meetings and telephone conversations with Basic officers and directors, including petitioners here [members of the board of directors], concerning the possibility of a merger. During 1977 and 1978, Basic made three public statements denying that it was engaged in merger negotiations.[4] On December 18, 1978, Basic asked the New York Stock Exchange to suspend trading in its shares and issued a release stating that it had been "approached" by another company concerning a merger. *Id.*, at 413. On December 19, Basic's board endorsed Combustion's offer of $46 per share for its common stock, *id.*, at 335, 414-416, and on the following day publicly announced its approval of Combustion's tender offer for all outstanding shares.

Respondents are former Basic shareholders who sold their stock after Basic's first public statement of October 21, 1977, and before the suspension of trading in December 1978. Respondents brought a class action against Basic and its directors, asserting that the defendants issued three false or misleading public statements and thereby were in violation of § 10(b) of the 1934 Act and of Rule 10b-5. Respondents alleged that they were injured by selling Basic shares at artificially depressed prices in a market affected by petitioners' misleading statements and in reliance thereon.

---

4. On October 21, 1977, after heavy trading and a new high in Basic stock, the following news item appeared in the Cleveland Plain Dealer:

"[Basic] President Max Muller said the company knew no reason for the stock's activity and that no negotiations were under way with any company for a merger. He said Flintkote recently denied Wall Street rumors that it would make a tender offer of $25 a share for control of the Cleveland-based maker of refractories for the steel industry." App. 363.

On September 25, 1978, in reply to an inquiry from the New York Stock Exchange, Basic issued a release concerning increased activity in its stock and stated that

"management is unaware of any present or pending company development that would result in the abnormally heavy trading activity and price fluctuation in company shares that have been experienced in the past few days." *Id.*, at 401.

On November 6, 1978, Basic issued to its shareholders a "Nine Months Report 1978." This Report stated:

"With regard to the stock market activity in the Company's shares we remain unaware of any present or pending developments which would account for the high volume of trading and price fluctuations in recent months." *Id.*, at 403.

The District Court adopted a presumption of reliance by members of the plaintiff class upon petitioners' public statements that enabled the court to conclude that common questions of fact or law predominated over particular questions pertaining to individual plaintiffs. *See* Fed. Rule Civ. Proc. 23(b)(3). The District Court therefore certified respondents' class. On the merits, however, the District Court granted summary judgment for the defendants. It held that, as a matter of law, any misstatements were immaterial: there were no negotiations ongoing at the time of the first statement, and although negotiations were taking place when the second and third statements were issued, those negotiations were not "destined, with reasonable certainty, to become a merger agreement in principle." . . .

The United States Court of Appeals for the Sixth Circuit affirmed the class certification, but reversed the District Court's summary judgment, and remanded the case. 786 F.2d 741 (1986). The court reasoned that while petitioners were under no general duty to disclose their discussions with Combustion, any statement the company voluntarily released could not be "'so incomplete as to mislead.'" *Id.*, at 746, quoting SEC v. Texas Gulf Sulphur Co., 401 F.2d 833, 862 (2d Cir. 1968) (en banc). In the Court of Appeals' view, Basic's statements that no negotiations were taking place, and that it knew of no corporate developments to account for the heavy trading activity, were misleading. With respect to materiality, the court rejected the argument that preliminary merger discussions are immaterial as a matter of law, and held that "once a statement is made denying the existence of any discussions, even discussions that might not have been material in absence of the denial are material because they make the statement made untrue." 786 F.2d, at 749.

The Court of Appeals joined a number of other Circuits in accepting the "fraud-on-the-market theory" to create a rebuttable presumption that respondents relied on petitioners' material misrepresentations, noting that without the presumption it would be impractical to certify a class under Federal Rule of Civil Procedure 23(b)(3). *See* 786 F.2d, at 750-751.

We granted certiorari, 479 U.S. 1083 (1987), to resolve the split, *see* Part III, *infra*, among the Courts of Appeals as to the standard of materiality applicable to preliminary merger discussions, and to determine whether the courts below properly applied a presumption of reliance in certifying the class, rather than requiring each class member to show direct reliance on Basic's statements.

II

The 1934 Act was designed to protect investors against manipulation of stock prices. *See* S. Rep. No. 792, 73d Cong., 2d Sess., 1-5 (1934). Underlying the adoption of extensive disclosure requirements was a legislative philosophy: "There cannot be honest markets without honest publicity. Manipulation and dishonest practices of the market place thrive upon mystery and secrecy." H.R. Rep. No. 1383, 73d Cong., 2d Sess., 11 (1934). This Court "repeatedly has described the 'fundamental purpose' of the Act as implementing a 'philosophy of full disclosure.'" Santa Fe Industries, Inc. v. Green, 430 U.S. 462, 477-478 (1977), quoting SEC v. Capital Gains Research Bureau, Inc., 375 U.S. 180, 186 (1963).

Pursuant to its authority under § 10(b) of the 1934 Act, 15 U.S.C. § 78j, the Securities and Exchange Commission promulgated Rule 10b-5. Judicial interpretation and application, legislative acquiescence, and the passage of time have removed any doubt that a private cause of action exists for a violation of § 10(b) and Rule 10b-5, and constitutes an essential tool for enforcement of the 1934 Act's requirements. *See, e.g.*, Ernst & Ernst v. Hochfelder, 425 U.S. 185, 196 (1976); Blue Chip Stamps v. Manor Drug Stores, 421 U.S. 723, 730 (1975).

The Court previously has addressed various positive and common-law requirements for a violation of § 10(b) or of Rule 10b-5. *See, e.g.*, Santa Fe Industries, Inc. v. Green, *supra* ("manipulative or deceptive" requirement of the statute); Blue Chip Stamps v. Manor Drug Stores, *supra* ("in connection with the purchase or sale" requirement of the Rule); Dirks v. SEC, 463 U.S. 646 (duty to disclose); Chiarella v. United States, 445 U.S. 222 (1980) (same); Ernst & Ernst v. Hochfelder, *supra* (scienter). *See also* Carpenter v. United States, 484 U.S. 19 (1987) (confidentiality). The Court also explicitly has defined a standard of materiality under the securities laws, *see* TSC Industries, Inc. v. Northway, Inc., 426 U.S. 438 (1976), concluding in the proxy-solicitation context that "[a]n omitted fact is material if there is a substantial likelihood that a reasonable shareholder would consider it important in deciding how to vote." *Id.*, at 449. Acknowledging that certain information concerning corporate developments could well be of "dubious significance," *id.*, at 448, the Court was careful not to set too low a standard of materiality; it was concerned that a minimal standard might bring an overabundance of information within its reach, and lead management "simply to bury the shareholders in an avalanche of trivial information — a result that is hardly conducive to informed decisionmaking." *Id.*, at 448-449. It further explained that to fulfill the materiality requirement "there must be a substantial likelihood that the disclosure of the omitted fact would have been viewed by the reasonable investor as having significantly altered the 'total mix' of information made available." *Id.*, at 449. We now expressly adopt the *TSC Industries* standard of materiality for the § 10(b) and Rule 10b-5 context.

III

The application of this materiality standard to preliminary merger discussions is not self-evident. Where the impact of the corporate development on the target's fortune is certain and clear, the *TSC Industries* materiality definition admits straightforward application. Where, on the other hand, the event is contingent or speculative in nature, it is difficult to ascertain whether the "reasonable investor" would have considered the omitted information significant at the time. Merger negotiations, because of the ever-present possibility that the contemplated transaction will not be effectuated, fall into the latter category.

A

Petitioners urge upon us a Third Circuit test for resolving this difficulty. . . . Under this approach, preliminary merger discussions do not become material until "agreement-in-principle" as to the price and structure of the transaction has been reached between the would-be merger partners. *See* Greenfield v. Heublein, Inc., 742 F.2d 751, 757 (3d Cir. 1984), *cert. denied*, 469 U.S. 1215 (1985). By definition, then, information concerning any negotiations not yet at the agreement-in-principle stage could be withheld or even misrepresented without a violation of Rule 10b-5.

Three rationales have been offered in support of the "agreement-in-principle" test. The first derives from the concern expressed in *TSC Industries* that an investor not be overwhelmed by excessively detailed and trivial information, and focuses on the substantial risk that preliminary merger discussions may collapse: because such discussions are inherently tentative, disclosure of their existence itself could mislead investors and foster false optimism. *See* Greenfield v. Heublein, Inc., 742 F.2d, at 756; Reiss v. Pan American World Airways, Inc., 711 F.2d 11, 14 (2d Cir. 1983). The other two justifications for the agreement-in-principle standard are based on management concerns: because the requirement of "agreement-in-principle" limits the scope of disclosure obligations, it helps preserve the confidentiality of merger discussions where earlier disclosure might prejudice the negotiations; and the test also provides a usable, bright-line rule for determining when disclosure must be made. *See* Greenfield v. Heublein, Inc., 742 F.2d, at 757; Flamm v. Eberstadt, 814 F.2d 1169, 1176-1178 (7th Cir. 1987).

None of these policy-based rationales, however, purports to explain why drawing the line at agreement-in-principle reflects the significance of the information upon the investor's decision. The first rationale, and the only one connected to the concerns expressed in *TSC Industries*, stands soundly rejected, even by a Court of Appeals that otherwise has accepted the wisdom of the agreement-in-principle test. "It assumes that investors are nitwits, unable to appreciate — even when told — that mergers are risky propositions up until the closing." Flamm v. Eberstadt, 814 F.2d, at 1175. Disclosure, and not paternalistic withholding of accurate information, is the policy chosen and expressed by Congress. We have recognized time and again, a "fundamental purpose" of the various Securities Acts, "was to substitute a philosophy of full disclosure for the philosophy of *caveat emptor* and thus to achieve a high standard of business ethics in the securities industry." SEC v. Capital Gains Research Bureau, Inc., 375 U.S., at 186. . . . The role of the materiality requirement is not to "attribute to investors a child-like simplicity, an inability to grasp the probabilistic significance of negotiations," Flamm v. Eberstadt, 814 F.2d, at 1175, but to filter out essentially useless information that a reasonable investor would not consider significant, even as part of a larger "mix" of factors to consider in making his investment decision. TSC Industries, Inc. v. Northway, Inc., 426 U.S., at 448-449.

The second rationale, the importance of secrecy during the early stages of merger discussions, also seems irrelevant to an assessment whether their existence is significant to the trading decision of a reasonable investor. To avoid a "bidding war" over its target, an acquiring firm often will insist that negotiations remain confidential, *see, e.g.*, In re Carnation Co., Exchange Act Release No. 22214, 33 S.E.C. Docket 1025 (1985), and at least one Court of Appeals has stated that "silence pending settlement of the price and structure of a deal is beneficial to most investors, most of the time." Flamm v. Eberstadt, 814 F.2d at 1177.

We need not ascertain, however, whether secrecy necessarily maximizes shareholder wealth — although we note that the proposition is at least disputed as a matter of theory and empirical research — for this case does not concern the *timing* of a disclosure; it concerns only its accuracy and completeness. We face here the narrow question whether information concerning the existence and status of preliminary merger discussions is significant to the reasonable investor's trading decision. Arguments based on the premise that some disclosure would be "premature" in a sense are more properly considered under the rubric of an issuer's duty to disclose. The "secrecy" rationale is simply inapposite to the definition of materiality.

The final justification offered in support of the agreement-in-principle test seems to be directed solely at the comfort of corporate managers. A bright-line rule indeed is easier to follow than a standard that requires the exercise of judgment in the light of all the circumstances. But ease of application alone is not an excuse for ignoring the purposes of the Securities Acts and Congress' policy decisions. Any approach that designates a single fact or occurrence as always determinative of an inherently fact-specific finding such as materiality must necessarily be overinclusive or underinclusive. In *TSC Industries* this Court explained: "The determination [of materiality] requires delicate assessments of the inferences a 'reasonable shareholder' would draw from a given set of facts and the significance of those inferences to him. . . ." 426 U.S., at 450. . . .

We therefore find no valid justification for artificially excluding from the definition of materiality information concerning merger discussions, which would otherwise be considered significant to the trading decision of a reasonable investor, merely because agreement-in-principle as to price and structure has not yet been reached by the parties or their representatives. . . .

C

Even before this Court's decision in *TSC Industries*, the Second Circuit had explained the role of the materiality requirement of Rule 10b-5, with respect to contingent or speculative information or events, in a manner that gave that term meaning that is independent of the other provisions of the Rule. Under such circumstances, materiality "will depend at any given time upon a balancing of both the indicated probability that the event will occur and the anticipated magnitude of the event in light of the totality of the company activity." SEC v. Texas Gulf Sulphur Co., 401 F.2d, at 849. Interestingly, neither the Third Circuit decision adopting the agreement-in-principle test nor petitioners here take issue with this general standard. Rather, they suggest that with respect to preliminary merger discussions, there are good reasons to draw a line at agreement on price and structure.

In a subsequent decision, the late Judge Friendly, writing for a Second Circuit panel, applied the *Texas Gulf Sulphur* probability/magnitude approach in the specific context of preliminary merger negotiations. After acknowledging that materiality is something to be determined on the basis of the particular facts of each case, he stated:

> "Since a merger in which it is bought out is the most important event that can occur in a small corporation's life, to wit, its death, we think that inside information, as regards a merger of this sort, can become material at an earlier stage than would be the case as regards lesser transactions — and this even though the mortality rate of mergers in such formative stages is doubtless high." SEC v. Geon Industries, Inc., 531 F.2d 39, 47-48 (2d Cir. 1976).

We agree with that analysis.

Whether merger discussions in any particular case are material therefore depends on the facts. Generally, in order to assess the probability that the event will occur, a factfinder will need to look to indicia of interest in the transaction at the highest corporate levels. Without attempting to catalog all such possible factors, we note by way of example that board resolutions, instructions to investment bankers, and actual negotiations between principals or their intermediaries may serve as indicia of interest. To assess the magnitude of the transaction to the issuer of the securities allegedly manipulated, a factfinder will need to consider such facts as the size of the two corporate entities and of the potential premiums over market value. No particular event or factor short of closing the transaction need be either necessary or sufficient by itself to render merger discussions material.[17]

As we clarify today, materiality depends on the significance the reasonable investor would place on the withheld or misrepresented information. The fact-specific inquiry we endorse here is consistent with the approach a number of courts have taken in assessing the materiality of merger negotiations. Because the standard of materiality we have adopted differs from that used by both courts below, we remand the case for reconsideration of the question whether a grant of summary judgment is appropriate on this record.

IV

A

We turn to the question of reliance and the fraud-on-the-market theory. Succinctly put:

> "The fraud on the market theory is based on the hypothesis that, in an open and developed securities market, the price of a company's stock is determined by the available material information regarding the company and its business. . . . Misleading statements will therefore defraud purchasers of stock even if the purchasers do not directly rely on the misstatements. . . . The causal connection between the defendants' fraud and the plaintiffs' purchase of stock in such a case is no less significant than in a case of direct reliance on misrepresentations." Peil v. Speiser, 806 F.2d 1154, 1160-1161 (3d Cir. 1986).

Our task, of course, is not to assess the general validity of the theory, but to consider whether it was proper for the courts below to apply a rebuttable presumption of reliance, supported in part by the fraud-on-the-market theory. *Cf.* the comments of the dissent, *post*, at 994-995. . . .

We agree that reliance is an element of a Rule 10b-5 cause of action. *See* Ernst & Ernst v. Hochfelder, 425 U.S., at 206 (quoting Senate Report). Reliance provides the requisite causal connection between a defendant's misrepresentation and a plaintiff's injury. There is, however, more than one way to demonstrate the causal connection. Indeed, we previously have dispensed with a requirement of positive proof of reliance, where a duty to disclose material information had been breached [an omission case], concluding that the necessary nexus between the

---

17. To be actionable, of course, a statement must also be misleading. Silence, absent a duty to disclose, is not misleading under Rule 10b-5. "No comment" statements are generally the functional equivalent of silence. *See* In re Carnation Co., Exchange Act Release No. 22214, 33 S.E.C. Docket 1025 (1985). *See also* New York Stock Exchange Listed Company Manual § 202.01, reprinted in 3 CCH Fed. Sec. L. Rep. ¶ 23,515 (1987) (premature public announcement may properly be delayed for valid business purpose and where adequate security can be maintained); American Stock Exchange Company Guide §§ 401-405, reprinted in 3 CCH Fed. Sec. L. Rep. ¶ ¶ 23,124A-23,124E (1985) (similar provisions).

plaintiffs' injury and the defendant's wrongful conduct had been established. *See* Affiliated Ute Citizens v. United States, 406 U.S., at 153-154. Similarly, we did not require proof that material omissions or misstatements in a proxy statement decisively affected voting, because the proxy solicitation itself, rather than the defect in the solicitation materials, served as an essential link in the transaction. *See* Mills v. Electric Auto-Lite Co., 396 U.S. 375, 384-385 (1970).

The modern securities markets, literally involving millions of shares changing hands daily, differ from the face-to-face transactions contemplated by early fraud cases, and our understanding of Rule 10b-5's reliance requirement must encompass these differences.[22]

> "In face-to-face transactions, the inquiry into an investor's reliance upon information is into the subjective pricing of that information by that investor. With the presence of a market, the market is interposed between seller and buyer and, ideally, transmits information to the investor in the processed form of a market price. Thus the market is performing a substantial part of the valuation process performed by the investor in a face-to-face transaction. The market is acting as the unpaid agent of the investor, informing him that given all the information available to it, the value of the stock is worth the market price." In re LTV Securities Litigation, 88 F.R.D. 134, 143 (ND Tex. 1980).

B

Presumptions typically serve to assist courts in managing circumstances in which direct proof, for one reason or another, is rendered difficult. *See, e.g.,* 1 D. Louisell & C. Mueller, *Federal Evidence* 541-542 (1977). The courts below accepted a presumption, created by the fraud-on-the-market theory and subject to rebuttal by petitioners, that persons who had traded Basic shares had done so in reliance on the integrity of the price set by the market, but because of petitioners' material misrepresentations that price had been fraudulently depressed. Requiring a plaintiff to show a speculative state of facts, *i.e.,* how he would have acted if omitted material information had been disclosed, *see* Affiliated Ute Citizens v. United States, 406 U.S., at 153-154 or if the misrepresentation had not been made, *see* Sharp v. Coopers & Lybrand, 649 F.2d 175, 188 (3d Cir. 1981), would place an unnecessarily unrealistic evidentiary burden on the Rule 10b-5 plaintiff who has traded on an impersonal market. *Cf.* Mills v. Electric Auto-Lite Co., 396 U.S., at 385. . . .

Indeed, nearly every court that has considered the proposition has concluded that where materially misleading statements have been disseminated into an impersonal, well-developed market for securities, the reliance of individual plaintiffs on the integrity of the market price may be presumed. Commentators generally have applauded the adoption of one variation or another of the fraud-on-the-market theory. An investor who buys or sells stock at the price set by the market does so in reliance on the integrity of that price. Because most publicly available information is reflected in market price, an investor's reliance on any public material misrepresentations, therefore, may be presumed for purposes of a Rule 10b-5 action.

---

22. Actions under Rule 10b-5 are distinct from common-law deceit and misrepresentation claims, *see* Blue Chip Stamps v. Manor Drug Stores, 421 U.S. 723, 744-745 (1975), and are in part designed to add to the protections provided investors by the common law, *see* Herman & MacLean v. Huddleston, 459 U.S. 375, 388-389 (1983).

Any showing that severs the link between the alleged misrepresentation and either the price received (or paid) by the plaintiff, or his decision to trade at a fair market price, will be sufficient to rebut the presumption of reliance. For example, if petitioners could show that the "market makers" were privy to the truth about the merger discussions here with Combustion, and thus that the market price would not have been affected by their misrepresentations, the causal connection could be broken: the basis for finding that the fraud had been transmitted through market price would be gone. Similarly, if, despite petitioners' allegedly fraudulent attempt to manipulate market price, news of the merger discussions credibly entered the market and dissipated the effects of the misstatements, those who traded Basic shares after the corrective statements would have no direct or indirect connection with the fraud. . . .

V

The judgment of the Court of Appeals is vacated, and the case is remanded to that court for further proceedings consistent with this opinion.

It is so ordered.

Justice WHITE, with whom Justice O'CONNOR joins, concurring in part and dissenting in part.

I join Parts I-III of the Court's opinion, as I agree that the standard of materiality we set forth in TSC Industries, Inc. v. Northway, Inc., 426 U.S. 438, 449 (1976), should be applied to actions under §10(b) and Rule 10b-5. But I dissent from the remainder of the Court's holding because I do not agree that the "fraud-on-the-market" theory should be applied in this case.

I

Even when compared to the relatively youthful private cause-of-action under §10(b), *see* Kardon v. National Gypsum Co., 69 F. Supp. 512 (E.D. Pa. 1946), the fraud-on-the-market theory is a mere babe.[1] Yet today, the Court embraces this theory with the sweeping confidence usually reserved for more mature legal doctrines. In so doing, I fear that the Court's decision may have many adverse, unintended effects as it is applied and interpreted in the years to come. . . .

C.

At the bottom of the Court's conclusion that the fraud-on-the-market theory sustains a presumption of reliance is the assumption that individuals rely "on the integrity of the market price" when buying or selling stock in "impersonal, well-developed market[s] for securities." *Ante,* at 991-992. Even if I was prepared to accept (as a matter of common sense or general understanding) the assumption that most persons buying or selling stock do so in response to the market price,

---

1. The earliest Court of Appeals case adopting this theory cited by the Court is Blackie v. Barrack, 524 F.2d 891 (CA 9 1975), *cert. denied,* 429 U.S. 816, 97 S. Ct. 57, 50 L. Ed. 2d 75 (1976). Moreover, widespread acceptance of the fraud-on-the-market theory in the Courts of Appeals cannot be placed any earlier than five or six years ago. *See ante,* at 991, n.24; Brief for Securities and Exchange Commission as *Amicus Curiae* 21, n.24.

the fraud-on-the-market theory goes further. For in adopting a "presumption of reliance," the Court *also* assumes that buyers and sellers rely—not just on the market price—but on the "*integrity*" of that price. It is this aspect of the fraud-on-the-market hypothesis which most mystifies me.

To define the term "integrity of the market price," the majority quotes approvingly from cases which suggest that investors are entitled to "'rely on the price of a stock as a reflection of its value.'" *Ante*, at 990 (quoting Peil v. Speiser, 806 F.2d 1154, 1161 (3d Cir. 1986)). But the meaning of this phrase eludes me, for it implicitly suggests that stocks have some "true value" that is measurable by a standard other than their market price. While the scholastics of medieval times professed a means to make such a valuation of a commodity's "worth," I doubt that the federal courts of our day are similarly equipped.

Even if securities had some "value"—knowable and distinct from the market price of a stock—investors do not always share the Court's presumption that a stock's price is a "reflection of [this] value." Indeed, "many investors purchase or sell stock because they believe the price *inaccurately* reflects the corporation's worth." *See* Black, *Fraud on the Market: A Criticism of Dispensing with Reliance Requirements in Certain Open Market Transactions*, 62 N.C. L. Rev. 435, 455 (1984) (emphasis added). If investors really believed that stock prices reflected a stock's "value," many sellers would never sell, and many buyers never buy (given the time and cost associated with executing a stock transaction). As we recognized just a few years ago: "[I]nvestors act on inevitably incomplete or inaccurate information, [consequently] there are always winners and losers; but those who have 'lost' have not necessarily been defrauded." Dirks v. SEC, 463 U.S. 646, 667, n.27 (1983). Yet today, the Court allows investors to recover who can show little more than that they sold stock at a lower price than what might have been.

I do not propose that the law retreat from the many protections that § 10(b) and Rule 10b-5, as interpreted in our prior cases, provide to investors. But any extension of these laws, to approach something closer to an investor insurance scheme, should come from Congress, and not from the courts. . . .

PROBLEM 12-1

Wilson and Levy, a Wall Street investment bank, created a batch of securitized mortgages using an SPE called PERSIA. All of Wilson and Levy's marketing materials for PERSIA (the term sheet and offering memorandum) represented that the collection of mortgages underlying PERSIA was selected by a third party, PERSIA Management, with great experience in analyzing the credit risks of each individual mortgage. (The "credit risk" is the risk that the borrower will not repay his or her mortgage.) Direct statements in both the term sheet and the offering memorandum were that "this is a high-quality group of mortgages that would continue to be paid off in timely fashion, and the risk of default is low."

Not disclosed in the marketing materials was the information that a large hedge fund, Olsen & Co., with economic interests directly adverse to investors in the PERSIA entity, had played a significant role in selecting the mortgages to be put into the PERSIA entity. Olsen & Co. had been the one to suggest to Wilson and Levy that Olsen & Co. should have a role in selecting the likely-to-go-into-default package of mortgages that PERSIA actually comprised. Through a series of financial transactions called "short sales" and "credit default swaps," the details of which are not important for present purposes, Olsen & Co. stood to make money if PERSIA lost money. In other words, given its financial short interest, Olsen & Co. had an economic incentive to choose mortgages to put into PERSIA that it expected to experience negative credit events—borrowers defaulting on paying their mortgages and going into foreclosure.

When the deal closed, the entire batch of PERSIA securities were purchased in a private offering by two institutional investors, a German institutional investor and a Chicago bank. Within six months, 83 percent of the underlying mortgages in the package had been downgraded (their credit evaluation had worsened), and within one year, 99 percent of the mortgages were on a credit watch. As a result, investors in the PERSIA entity lost over $1 billion. Olsen, however, made over $1 billion.

Analyze this transaction. Has there been a material misstatement or omission? Can the investors rely on either the **Affiliated Ute** *presumption or the fraud on the market presumption in bringing their Section 10(b) claim?*

3. Scienter

One of the most important bulwarks against liability under Section 10(b)/Rule 10b-5 is the requirement that plaintiffs allege, and eventually prove, that the defendant's misstatement or omission of material fact was made with "scienter"—that is, with an intent to deceive. *See* Ernst & Ernst v. Hockfelder, 425 U.S. 185, 193 (1976). *Ernst & Ernst* involved a company, First Securities, whose president, Leston B. Nay, defrauded investors for decades by encouraging them to invest in "escrow funds" that paid a high rate of return. In fact, there were no such funds, but rather a variation on a Ponzi scheme: As long as Nay could continue to get new investors, he could pay out high rates of return to prior investors and skim generous funds off the top for himself, and everyone was happy. Events eventually caused the scheme to unravel, though, as these schemes invariably do, and Nay committed suicide, leaving a note that described the firm as bankrupt and the escrow accounts as "spurious." Plaintiffs brought a cause of action against Nay's estate and against First Securities' accountants, Ernst & Ernst, claiming the accountants aided and abetted Nay's securities fraud by their negligent failure to uncover odd rules at First Securities, including that only Nay could open the mail. Had Ernst & Ernst conducted a proper audit, the fraud would have been discovered decades earlier, plaintiffs claimed, and their funds would not have been depleted.

The Court rejected the SEC's argument that negligent behavior could suffice to set out a cause of action under Section 10(b)/Rule 10b-5:

> Section 10(b) makes unlawful the use or employment of "any manipulative or deceptive device or contrivance" in contravention of Commission rules. The words "manipulative or deceptive" used in conjunction with "device or contrivance" strongly suggest that §10(b) was intended to proscribe knowing or intentional misconduct.
>
> In its *Amicus curiae* brief, however, the Commission contends that nothing in the language "manipulative or deceptive device or contrivance" limits its operation to knowing or intentional practices. In support of its view, the Commission cites the

overall congressional purpose in the 1933 and 1934 Acts to protect investors against false and deceptive practices that might injure them. . . . The Commission then reasons that since the "effect" upon investors of given conduct is the same regardless of whether the conduct is negligent or intentional, Congress must have intended to bar all such practices and not just those done knowingly or intentionally. The logic of this effect-oriented approach would impose liability for wholly faultless conduct where such conduct results in harm to investors, a result the Commission would be unlikely to support. But apart from where its logic might lead, the Commission would add a gloss to the operative language of the statute quite different from its commonly accepted meaning. . . . The argument simply ignores the use of the words "manipulative," "device," and "contrivance" terms that make unmistakable a congressional intent to proscribe a type of conduct quite different from negligence. Use of the word "manipulative" is especially significant. It is and was virtually a term of art when used in connection with securities markets. It connotes intentional or willful conduct designed to deceive or defraud investors by controlling or artificially affecting the price of securities.

Ernst & Ernst v. Hockfelder, 425 U.S. 185, 193 (1976).

The *Ernst & Ernst* court left open whether recklessness would suffice to show scienter under Section 10(b)/Rule 10b-5, *id.* at 193 n.12, but the federal circuit courts of appeals have found recklessness to be sufficient to set out a cause of action under Section 10(b)/Rule 10b-5 as well. *See* Hollinger v. Titan Capital Corp., 914 F.2d 1564, 1568 n.6 (9th Cir. 1990) (citing opinions from every circuit holding that recklessness is sufficient).

Notwithstanding the requirement to plead that defendants acted with scienter, and the general requirement under the Federal Rules of Civil Procedure to allege fraud with particularity, *see* Rule 9(b), Fed. R. Civ. P., in December 1995 Congress amended the federal securities laws to make it even more difficult for private plaintiffs (but not the SEC) to bring claims under Section 10(b)/Rule 10b-5. These amendments were made in response to the perception that there was too much securities litigation in the United States, and that such litigation was undermining U.S. economic competitiveness. Ironically, this perception was fueled by high technology firms in California, which also fueled the technology stock price bubble that burst starting in March 2000, wiping out 70 percent of the value of the "technology-heavy" NASDAQ trading market. The 1995 amendments, called the Private Securities Litigation Reform Act of 1995 (PSLRA), did not purport to change the scienter requirement under Section 10(b)/Rule 10b-5, but amended the pleading requirements, requiring plaintiffs to state facts that provide a "strong inference" that the defendants acted with the required mental state to set out a cause of action. The Circuit Courts of Appeal have struggled with how to interpret the "strong inference" pleading requirement since PSLRA was enacted in 1995. The Supreme Court finally provided guidance on that issue in the following case. After reading the case, evaluate whether the facts set out in Problem 14-2 meet the "strong inference" of the intent to defraud necessary to state a cause of action under Section 10(b)/ Rule 10b-5.

TELLABS, INC. v. MAKOR ISSUES & RIGHTS, LTD.

127 S. Ct. 2499
United States Supreme Court
June 21, 2007

GINSBURG, Justice.

This Court has long recognized that meritorious private actions to enforce federal antifraud securities laws are an essential supplement to criminal prosecutions and civil enforcement actions brought, respectively, by the Department of Justice and the Securities and Exchange Commission (SEC). See, e.g., Dura Pharmaceuticals, Inc. v. Broudo, 544 U.S. 336, 345 (2005). Private securities fraud actions, however, if not adequately contained, can be employed abusively to impose substantial costs on companies and individuals whose conduct conforms to the law. See Merrill Lynch, Pierce, Fenner & Smith Inc. v. Dabit, 547 U.S. 71, 81 (2006). As a check against abusive litigation by private parties, Congress enacted the Private Securities Litigation Reform Act of 1995 (PSLRA), 109 Stat. 737.

Exacting pleading requirements are among the control measures Congress included in the PSLRA. The Act requires plaintiffs to state with particularity both the facts constituting the alleged violation, and the facts evidencing scienter, i.e., the defendant's intention "to deceive, manipulate, or defraud." This case concerns the latter requirement. As set out in § 21D(b)(2) of the PSLRA, plaintiffs must "state with particularity facts giving rise to a strong inference that the defendant acted with the required state of mind." 15 U.S.C. § 78u-4(b)(2).

Congress left the key term "strong inference" undefined, and Courts of Appeals have divided on its meaning. In the case before us, the Court of Appeals for the Seventh Circuit held that the "strong inference" standard would be met if the complaint "allege[d] facts from which, if true, a reasonable person could infer that the defendant acted with the required intent." 437 F.3d 588, 602 (2006). That formulation, we conclude, does not capture the stricter demand Congress sought to convey in § 21D(b)(2). It does not suffice that a reasonable factfinder plausibly could infer from the complaint's allegations the requisite state of mind. Rather, to determine whether a complaint's scienter allegations can survive threshold inspection for sufficiency, a court governed by § 21D(b)(2) must engage in a comparative evaluation; it must consider, not only inferences urged by the plaintiff, as the Seventh Circuit did, but also competing inferences rationally drawn from the facts alleged. An inference of fraudulent intent may be plausible, yet less cogent than other, nonculpable explanations for the defendant's conduct. To qualify as "strong" within the intendment of § 21D(b)(2), we hold, an inference of scienter must be more than merely plausible or reasonable — it must be cogent and at least as compelling as any opposing inference of nonfraudulent intent.

I

Petitioner Tellabs, Inc., manufactures specialized equipment used in fiber optic networks. During the time period relevant to this case, petitioner Richard Notebaert was Tellabs' chief executive officer and president. Respondents

(Shareholders) are persons who purchased Tellabs stock between December 11, 2000, and June 19, 2001. They accuse Tellabs and Notebaert (as well as several other Tellabs executives) of engaging in a scheme to deceive the investing public about the true value of Tellabs' stock. Beginning on December 11, 2000, the Shareholders allege, Notebaert (and by imputation Tellabs) "falsely reassured public investors, in a series of statements . . . that Tellabs was continuing to enjoy strong demand for its products and earning record revenues," when, in fact, Notebaert knew the opposite was true. From December 2000 until the spring of 2001, the Shareholders claim, Notebaert knowingly misled the public in four ways. First, he made statements indicating that demand for Tellabs' flagship networking device, the TITAN 5500, was continuing to grow, when in fact demand for that product was waning. Second, Notebaert made statements indicating that the TITAN 6500, Tellabs' next-generation networking device, was available for delivery, and that demand for that product was strong and growing, when in truth the product was not ready for delivery and demand was weak. Third, he falsely represented Tellabs' financial results for the fourth quarter of 2000 (and, in connection with those results, condoned the practice of "channel stuffing," under which Tellabs flooded its customers with unwanted products). Fourth, Notebaert made a series of overstated revenue projections, when demand for the TITAN 5500 was drying up and production of the TITAN 6500 was behind schedule. Based on Notebaert's sunny assessments, the Shareholders contend, market analysts recommended that investors buy Tellabs' stock.

The first public glimmer that business was not so healthy came in March 2001 when Tellabs modestly reduced its first quarter sales projections. In the next months, Tellabs made progressively more cautious statements about its projected sales. On June 19, 2001, the last day of the class period, Tellabs disclosed that demand for the TITAN 5500 had significantly dropped. Simultaneously, the company substantially lowered its revenue projections for the second quarter of 2001. The next day, the price of Tellabs stock, which had reached a high of $67 during the period, plunged to a low of $15.87.

On December 3, 2002, the Shareholders filed a class action in the District Court for the Northern District of Illinois. Their complaint stated, inter alia, that Tellabs and Notebaert had engaged in securities fraud in violation of § 10(b) of the Securities Exchange Act of 1934, and SEC Rule 10b-5, also that Notebaert was a "controlling person" under § 20(a) of the 1934 Act, and therefore derivatively liable for the company's fraudulent acts. Tellabs moved to dismiss the complaint on the ground that the Shareholders had failed to plead their case with the particularity the PSLRA requires. The District Court agreed, and therefore dismissed the complaint without prejudice. See Johnson v. Tellabs, Inc., 303 F.Supp.2d 941, 945 (N.D.Ill.2004).

The Shareholders then amended their complaint, adding references to 27 confidential sources and making further, more specific, allegations concerning Notebaert's mental state. The District Court again dismissed, this time with prejudice. The Shareholders had sufficiently pleaded that Notebaert's statements were misleading, the court determined, but they had insufficiently alleged that he acted with scienter.

The Court of Appeals for the Seventh Circuit reversed in relevant part. Like the District Court, the Court of Appeals found that the Shareholders had pleaded the misleading character of Notebaert's statements with sufficient particularity. Unlike the District Court, however, the Seventh Circuit concluded that the Shareholders had sufficiently alleged that Notebaert acted with the requisite state of mind. Id., at 603-605.

The Court of Appeals recognized that the PSLRA "unequivocally raise[d] the bar for pleading scienter" by requiring plaintiffs to "plea[d] sufficient facts to create a strong inference of scienter." Id., at 601 (internal quotation marks omitted). In evaluating whether that pleading standard is met, the Seventh Circuit said, "courts [should] examine all of the allegations in the complaint and then . . . decide whether collectively they establish such an inference." Ibid. "[W]e will allow the complaint to survive," the court next and critically stated, "if it alleges facts from which, if true, a reasonable person could infer that the defendant acted with the required intent. . . . If a reasonable person could not draw such an inference from the alleged facts, the defendants are entitled to dismissal." Id., at 602.

In adopting its standard for the survival of a complaint, the Seventh Circuit explicitly rejected a stiffer standard adopted by the Sixth Circuit, i.e., that "plaintiffs are entitled only to the most plausible of competing inferences." Id., at 601, 602 (quoting Fidel v. Farley, 392 F.3d 220, 227 (C.A.6 2004)). The Sixth Circuit's standard, the court observed, because it involved an assessment of competing inferences, "could potentially infringe upon plaintiffs' Seventh Amendment rights." 437 F.3d, at 602. We granted certiorari to resolve the disagreement among the Circuits on whether, and to what extent, a court must consider competing inferences in determining whether a securities fraud complaint gives rise to a "strong inference" of scienter.

II

Section 10(b) of the Securities Exchange Act of 1934 forbids the "use or employ, in connection with the purchase or sale of any security . . . , [of] any manipulative or deceptive device or contrivance in contravention of such rules and regulations as the [SEC] may prescribe as necessary or appropriate in the public interest or for the protection of investors." 15 U.S.C. § 78j(b). SEC Rule 10b-5 implements § 10(b) by [here the Court set out the text of Rule 10b-5.] . . .

The "strong inference" standard "unequivocally raise[d] the bar for pleading scienter," 437 F.3d, at 601, and signaled Congress' purpose to promote greater uniformity among the Circuits. But "Congress did not . . . throw much light on what facts . . . suffice to create [a strong] inference," or on what "degree of imagination courts can use in divining whether" the requisite inference exists. While adopting the Second Circuit's "strong inference" standard, Congress did not codify that Circuit's case law interpreting the standard. With no clear guide from Congress other than its "inten[tion] to strengthen existing pleading requirements," Court of Appeals have diverged again, this time in construing the term "strong inference." Among the uncertainties, should courts consider competing inferences in determining whether an inference of scienter is "strong"? See 437 F.3d, at 601-602 (collecting cases). Our task is to prescribe a workable construction of the "strong inference" standard, a reading geared to the PSLRA's twin goals: to curb frivolous, lawyer-driven litigation, while preserving investors' ability to recover on meritorious claims.

III

A

We establish the following prescriptions: First, faced with a Rule 12(b)(6) motion to dismiss a § 10(b) action, courts must, as with any motion to dismiss for failure to plead a claim on which relief can be granted, accept all factual allegations in the complaint as true. On this point, the parties agree. Second, courts must consider the complaint in its entirety, as well as other sources courts ordinarily examine when ruling on Rule 12(b)(6) motions to dismiss, in particular, documents incorporated into the complaint by reference, and matters of which a court may take judicial notice. The inquiry, as several Courts of Appeals have recognized, is whether all of the facts alleged, taken collectively, give rise to a strong inference of scienter, not whether any individual allegation, scrutinized in isolation, meets that standard.

Third, in determining whether the pleaded facts give rise to a "strong" inference of scienter, the court must take into account plausible opposing inferences. The Seventh Circuit expressly declined to engage in such a comparative inquiry. A complaint could survive, that court said, as long as it "alleges facts from which, if true, a reasonable person could infer that the defendant acted with the required intent"; in other words, only "[i]f a reasonable person could not draw such an inference from the alleged facts" would the defendant prevail on a motion to dismiss. But in § 21D(b)(2), Congress did not merely require plaintiffs to "provide a factual basis for [their] scienter allegations," i.e., to allege facts from which an inference of scienter rationally could be drawn. Instead, Congress required plaintiffs to plead with particularity facts that give rise to a "strong," i.e., a powerful or cogent-inference.

The strength of an inference cannot be decided in a vacuum. The inquiry is inherently comparative: How likely is it that one conclusion, as compared to others, follows from the underlying facts? To determine whether the plaintiff has alleged facts that give rise to the requisite "strong inference" of scienter, a court must consider plausible nonculpable explanations for the defendant's conduct, as well as inferences favoring the plaintiff. The inference that the defendant acted with scienter need not be irrefutable, i.e., of the "smoking-gun" genre, or even the "most plausible of competing inferences." Recall in this regard that § 21D(b)'s pleading requirements are but one constraint among many the PSLRA installed to screen out frivolous suits, while allowing meritorious actions to move forward. Yet the inference of scienter must be more than merely "reasonable" or "permissible" — it must be cogent and compelling, thus strong in light of other explanations. A complaint will survive, we hold, only if a reasonable person would deem the inference of scienter cogent and at least as compelling as any opposing inference one could draw from the facts alleged.

B

Tellabs contends that when competing inferences are considered, Notebaert's evident lack of pecuniary motive will be dispositive. The Shareholders, Tellabs stresses, did not allege that Notebaert sold any shares during the class period. See Brief for Petitioners 50 ("The absence of any allegations of motive color all the other allegations putatively giving rise to an inference of scienter."). While it is true that motive can be a relevant consideration, and personal financial gain may weigh heavily in favor of a scienter inference, we agree with the Seventh

Circuit that the absence of a motive allegation is not fatal. As earlier stated, allegations must be considered collectively; the significance that can be ascribed to an allegation of motive, or lack thereof, depends on the entirety of the complaint.

Tellabs also maintains that several of the Shareholders' allegations are too vague or ambiguous to contribute to a strong inference of scienter. For example, the Shareholders alleged that Tellabs flooded its customers with unwanted products, a practice known as "channel stuffing." But they failed, Tellabs argues, to specify whether the channel stuffing allegedly known to Notebaert was the illegitimate kind (e.g., writing orders for products customers had not requested) or the legitimate kind (e.g., offering customers discounts as an incentive to buy). We agree that omissions and ambiguities count against inferring scienter, for plaintiffs must "state with particularity facts giving rise to a strong inference that the defendant acted with the required state of mind." We reiterate, however, that the court's job is not to scrutinize each allegation in isolation but to assess all the allegations holistically. In sum, the reviewing court must ask: When the allegations are accepted as true and taken collectively, would a reasonable person deem the inference of scienter at least as strong as any opposing inference?

IV

Accounting for its construction of § 21D(b)(2), the Seventh Circuit explained that the court "th[ought] it wis[e] to adopt an approach that [could not] be misunderstood as a usurpation of the jury's role." 437 F.3d, at 602. In our view, the Seventh Circuit's concern was undue. A court's comparative assessment of plausible inferences, while constantly assuming the plaintiff's allegations to be true, we think it plain, does not impinge upon the Seventh Amendment right to jury trial. Congress, as creator of federal statutory claims, has power to prescribe what must be pleaded to state the claim, just as it has power to determine what must be proved to prevail on the merits. It is the federal lawmaker's prerogative, therefore, to allow, disallow, or shape the contours of—including the pleading and proof requirements for—§ 10(b) private actions. No decision of this Court questions that authority in general, or suggests, in particular, that the Seventh Amendment inhibits Congress from establishing whatever pleading requirements it finds appropriate for federal statutory claims. . . .

In the instant case, provided that the Shareholders have satisfied the congressionally "prescribe[d] . . . means of making an issue," *Fidelity & Deposit Co. of Maryland v. U.S.*, 187 U.S., at 320, 23 S. Ct. 120, the case will fall within the jury's authority to assess the credibility of witnesses, resolve any genuine issues of fact, and make the ultimate determination whether Notebaert and, by imputation, Tellabs acted with scienter. We emphasize, as well, that under our construction of the "strong inference" standard, a plaintiff is not forced to plead more than she would be required to prove at trial. A plaintiff alleging fraud in a § 10(b) action, we hold today, must plead facts rendering an inference of scienter at least as likely as any plausible opposing inference. At trial, she must then prove her case by a "preponderance of the evidence." Stated otherwise, she must demonstrate that it is more likely than not that the defendant acted with scienter.

See Herman & MacLean v. Huddleston, 459 U.S. 375, 390, 103 S. Ct. 683, 74 L.Ed.2d 548 (1983).

While we reject the Seventh Circuit's approach to § 21D(b)(2), we do not decide whether, under the standard we have described, see supra, at 2509-2511, the Shareholders' allegations warrant "a strong inference that [Notebaert and Tellabs] acted with the required state of mind," 15 U.S.C. § 78u-4(b)(2). Neither the District Court nor the Court of Appeals had the opportunity to consider the matter in light of the prescriptions we announce today. We therefore vacate the Seventh Circuit's judgment so that the case may be reexamined in accord with our construction of § 21D(b)(2). . . . The judgment of the Court of Appeals is vacated, and the case is remanded for further proceedings consistent with this opinion.

It is so ordered.

Justice SCALIA, concurring in the judgment.

I fail to see how an inference that is merely "at least as compelling as any opposing inference," ante, at 2505, can conceivably be called what the statute here at issue requires: a "strong inference," 15 U.S.C. § 78u-4(b)(2). If a jade falcon were stolen from a room to which only A and B had access, could it possibly be said there was a "strong inference" that B was the thief? I think not, and I therefore think that the Court's test must fail. In my view, the test should be whether the inference of scienter (if any) is more plausible than the inference of innocence. . . .

Even if I agreed with the Court's interpretation of "strong inference," I would not join the Court's opinion because of its frequent indulgence in the last remaining legal fiction of the West: that the report of a single committee of a single House expresses the will of Congress. The Court says, for example, that "Congress'[s] purpose" was "to promote greater uniformity among the Circuits," relying for that certitude upon the statement of managers accompanying a House Conference Committee Report whose text was never adopted by the House, much less by the Senate, and as far as we know was read by almost no one. The Court is sure that Congress "'inten[ded] to strengthen existing pleading requirements,'" because—again—the statement of managers said so. I come to the same conclusion for the much safer reason that the law which Congress adopted (and which the Members of both Houses actually voted on) so indicates. And had the legislation not done so, the statement of managers assuredly could not have remedied the deficiency.

With the above exceptions, I am generally in agreement with the Court's analysis, and so concur in its judgment.

(Justice ALITO concurrence in the judgment is omitted.)

Justice STEVENS, dissenting.

As the Court explains, when Congress enacted a heightened pleading requirement for private actions to enforce the federal securities laws, it "left the key term 'strong inference' undefined." It thus implicitly delegated significant lawmaking authority to the Judiciary in determining how that standard should operate in practice. Today the majority crafts a perfectly workable definition of the term, but I am persuaded that a different interpretation would be both easier to apply and more consistent with the statute.

The basic purpose of the heightened pleading requirement in the context of securities fraud litigation is to protect defendants from the costs of discovery and trial in unmeritorious cases. Because of its intrusive nature, discovery may also invade the privacy interests of the defendants and their executives. Like citizens suspected of having engaged in criminal activity, those defendants should not be required to produce their private effects unless there is probable cause to believe them guilty of misconduct. Admittedly, the probable-cause standard is not capable of precise measurement, but it is a concept that is familiar to judges. As a matter of normal English usage, its meaning is roughly the same as "strong inference." Moreover, it is most unlikely that Congress intended us to adopt a standard that makes it more difficult to commence a civil case than a criminal case.[1]

In addition to the benefit of its grounding in an already familiar legal concept, using a probable-cause standard would avoid the unnecessary conclusion that "in determining whether the pleaded facts give rise to a 'strong' inference of scienter, the court must take into account plausible opposing inferences." *Ante*, at 2509 (emphasis added). There are times when an inference can easily be deemed strong without any need to weigh competing inferences. For example, if a known drug dealer exits a building immediately after a confirmed drug transaction, carrying a suspicious looking package, a judge could draw a strong inference that the individual was involved in the aforementioned drug transaction without debating whether the suspect might have been leaving the building at that exact time for another unrelated reason.

If, using that same methodology, we assume (as we must, *see ante*, at 2509-2510, 2511) the truth of the detailed factual allegations attributed to 27 different confidential informants described in the complaint, and view those allegations collectively, I think it clear that they establish probable cause to believe that Tellabs' chief executive officer "acted with the required intent," as the Seventh Circuit held. The "channel stuffing" allegations in ¶¶ 62-72 of the amended complaint, App. 110-113, are particularly persuasive. Contrary to petitioners' arguments that respondents' allegations of channel stuffing "are too vague or ambiguous to contribute to a strong inference of scienter," *ante*, at 2511, this portion of the complaint clearly alleges that Notebaert himself had specific knowledge of illegitimate channel stuffing during the relevant time period. *See*, e.g., App. 111, ¶ 67 ("Defendant Notebaert worked directly with Tellabs' sales personnel to channel stuff SBC"); id., at 110-112 (alleging, in describing such channel stuffing, that Tellabs took "extraordinary" steps that amounted to "an abnormal practice in the industry"; that "distributors were upset and later

---

1. The meaning of a statute can only be determined on a case by case basis and will, in each case, turn differently on the clarity of the statutory language, its context, and the intent of its drafters. Here, in my judgment, a probable-cause standard is more faithful to the intent of Congress, as expressed in both the specific pleading requirement and the statute as a whole, than the more defendant-friendly interpretation that Justice Scalia prefers. He is clearly wrong in concluding that in divining the meaning of this term, we can merely "read the language for what it says," and that it is susceptible to only one reading. *Ante*, at 2514 (opinion concurring in judgment). He argues that we "must be content to give 'strong inference' its normal meaning," *ibid.*, and yet the "normal meaning" of a term such as "strong inference" is surely in the eye of the beholder. As the Court's opinion points out, Courts of Appeals have divided on the meaning of the standard, and today, the Members of this Court have done the same. Although Justice Scalia may disagree with the Court's reading of the term, he should at least acknowledge that, in this case, the term itself is open to interpretation.

returned the inventory" (and, in the case of Verizon's Chairman, called Tellabs to complain); that customers "did not want" products that Tellabs sent and that Tellabs employees wrote purchase orders for; that "returns were so heavy during January and February 2001 that Tellabs had to lease extra storage space to accommodate all the returns"; and that Tellabs "backdat[ed] sales" that actually took place in 2001 to appear as having occurred in 2000). If these allegations are actually taken as true and viewed in the collective, it is hard to imagine what competing inference could effectively counteract the inference that Notebaert and Tellabs "'acted with the required state of mind.'" *Ante*, at 2513 (opinion of the Court) (quoting 15 U.S.C. § 78u-4(b)(2)).]

Accordingly, I would affirm the judgment of the Court of Appeals.

PROBLEM 12-2

Hancock Brothers, another Wall Street investment bank, engaged in so-called "Repo 105 transactions," by which Hancock was able to move liabilities off its balance sheet at the end of each quarter over a period of years. A "repo," or repurchase transaction, is a two-step transaction that may be used to obtain short-term funding. In the first step, the entity needing funds transfers securities or other assets to a counter-party in exchange for cash, while at the same time agreeing to repurchase the transferred assets at a future date for an amount equal to the cash exchanged plus an agreed-upon charge. In the second stage, the transferor pays the counter-party the original cash amount plus the agreed-upon interest, and the counter-party returns the originally transferred assets.

A repo is thus like a loan, and, if accounted for properly, does not raise any particular problems. But Hancock's Repo 105 transactions were not accounted for properly. The asset used as collateral in a Repo 105 transaction was treated as though it actually had been sold and, therefore, removed from Hancock's balance sheet. Hancock used the cash received in the first step to pay down other existing liabilities. The effect of this treatment was to lower Hancock's leverage, and thus make the company look financially stronger than it was. Some investors in Hancock brought a securities class action lawsuit against Hancock, alleging that Hancock repeatedly used Repo 105 transactions near the end of its quarterly reporting periods to temporarily remove tens of billions of dollars from its balance sheet, usually for a period of seven to ten days. As Hancock's financial health deteriorated, the amounts of the Repo 105 transactions increased.

Ruling on Hancock's Motion to Dismiss these claims, a federal district court judge stated that the securities fraud claims involved enough red flags to establish an inference of scienter about the misleading character of the Repo 105 transactions, even though Hancock's outside auditor had approved the accounting for them. The court explained that "red flags may exist if the complaint alleges the existence of transactions that were large, recurrent, timed near the end of a reporting period, and obviously lacking in business purpose. This may be true even if the registrant's outside auditor has opined that the company's financial statements were presented in accordance with GAAP."

Assume that you've been retained to evaluate Hancock's arguments for a possible appeal. Assuming that this case has been brought as a class action, analyze the court's ruling in light of Tellabs.

4. "In Connection With"

While it would seem to be obvious whether a misstatement or omission was made "in connection with" a purchase or sale of securities, the *Zandford* case and United States v. O'Hagan, are expanding the definition of when a misstatement or omission is in connection with a purchase or sale of securities. In both cases, the expansion changes the focus of the Section 10(b)/Rule 10b-5 violation to enforcing fiduciary duties, as you'll see below.

SECURITIES & EXCHANGE COMMN. v. ZANDFORD

535 U.S. 813
Supreme Court of the United States
June 3, 2002

STEVENS, Justice.

The Securities and Exchange Commission (SEC) filed a civil complaint alleging that a stockbroker violated both §10(b) of the Securities Exchange Act of 1934 and the SEC's Rule 10b-5, by selling his customer's securities and using the proceeds for his own benefit without the customer's knowledge or consent. The question presented is whether the alleged fraudulent conduct was "in connection with the purchase or sale of any security" within the meaning of the statute and the rule.

I

Between 1987 and 1991, respondent was employed as a securities broker in the Maryland branch of a New York brokerage firm. In 1987, he persuaded William Wood, an elderly man in poor health, to open a joint investment account for himself and his mentally retarded daughter. According to the SEC's complaint, the "stated investment objectives for the account were 'safety of principal and income.'" The Woods granted respondent discretion to manage their account and a general power of attorney to engage in securities transactions for their benefit without prior approval. Relying on respondent's promise to "conservatively invest" their money, the Woods entrusted him with $419,255. Before Mr. Wood's death in 1991, all of that money was gone.

In 1991, the National Association of Securities Dealers (NASD) conducted a routine examination of respondent's firm and discovered that on over 25 separate occasions, money had been transferred from the Woods' account to accounts controlled by respondent. In due course, respondent was indicted in the United States District Court for the District of Maryland on 13 counts of wire fraud in violation of 18 U.S.C. §1343. The first count alleged that respondent sold securities in the Woods' account and then made personal use of the proceeds. Each of the other counts alleged that he made wire transfers between Maryland and New York that enabled him to withdraw specified sums from the Woods' accounts. Some of those transfers involved respondent writing checks to himself from a mutual fund account held by the Woods, which required liquidating securities in order to redeem the checks. Respondent was convicted on all counts, sentenced to prison for 52 months, and ordered to pay $10,800 in restitution.

After respondent was indicted, the SEC filed a civil complaint in the same District Court alleging that respondent violated § 10(b) and Rule 10b-5 by engaging in a scheme to defraud the Woods and by misappropriating approximately $343,000 of the Woods' securities without their knowledge or consent. The SEC moved for partial summary judgment after respondent's criminal conviction, arguing that the judgment in the criminal case estopped respondent from contesting facts that established a violation of § 10(b). Respondent filed a motion seeking discovery on the question whether his fraud had the requisite "connection with" the purchase or sale of a security. The District Court refused to allow discovery and entered summary judgment against respondent. It enjoined him from engaging in future violations of the securities laws and ordered him to disgorge $343,000 in ill-gotten gains.

The Court of Appeals for the Fourth Circuit reversed the summary judgment and remanded with directions for the District Court to dismiss the complaint. It first held that the wire fraud conviction, which only required two findings — (1) that respondent engaged in a scheme to defraud and (2) that he used interstate wire communications in executing the scheme — did not establish all the elements of a § 10(b) violation. Specifically, the conviction did not necessarily establish that his fraud was "in connection with" the sale of a security. The court then held that the civil complaint did not sufficiently allege the necessary connection because the sales of the Woods' securities were merely incidental to a fraud that "lay in absconding with the proceeds" of sales that were conducted in "a routine and customary fashion." Respondent's "scheme was simply to steal the Woods' assets" rather than to engage "in manipulation of a particular security." Ultimately, the court refused "to stretch the language of the securities fraud provisions to encompass every conversion or theft that happens to involve securities." Adopting what amounts to a "fraud on the market" theory of the statute's coverage, the court held that without some "relationship to market integrity or investor understanding," there is no violation of § 10(b).

We granted the SEC's petition for a writ of certiorari to review the Court of Appeals' construction of the phrase "in connection with the purchase or sale of any security." Because the Court of Appeals ordered the complaint dismissed rather than remanding for reconsideration, we assume the allegations contained therein are true and affirm that disposition only if no set of facts would entitle petitioner to relief. We do not reach the question whether the record supports the District Court's grant of summary judgment in the SEC's favor — a question that requires all potential factual disputes to be resolved in respondent's favor. We merely hold that the allegations of the complaint, if true, entitle the SEC to relief; therefore, the Court of Appeals should not have directed that the complaint be dismissed.

II

Section 10(b) of the Securities Exchange Act makes it "unlawful for any person . . . [t]o use or employ, in connection with the purchase or sale of any security . . . , any manipulative or deceptive device or contrivance in contravention of such rules and regulations as the [SEC] may prescribe." Rule 10b-5, which implements this provision, forbids the use, "in connection with the purchase or sale of any security," of "any device, scheme, or artifice to defraud" or any other "act, practice, or course of business" that "operates . . . as a fraud or deceit." Among Congress' objectives in passing the Act was "to insure honest securities markets and thereby promote investor confidence" after the market crash of 1929. United States v. O'Hagan, 521 U.S. 642, 658 (1997). More generally, Congress sought "'to substitute a philosophy of full disclosure for the philosophy of *caveat emptor* and thus to achieve a high standard of business ethics in the securities industry.'" Affiliated Ute Citizens of Utah v. United States, 406 U.S. 128, 151 (1972) (quoting SEC v. Capital Gains Research Bureau, Inc., 375 U.S. 180, 186 (1963)).

Consequently, we have explained that the statute should be "construed 'not technically and restrictively, but flexibly to effectuate its remedial purposes.'" 406 U.S., at 151 (quoting *Capital Gains Research Bureau, Inc.*, 375 U.S., at 195). In its role enforcing the Act, the SEC has consistently adopted a broad reading of the phrase "in connection with the purchase or sale of any security." It has maintained that a broker who accepts payment for securities that he never intends to deliver, or who sells customer securities with intent to misappropriate the proceeds, violates § 10(b) and Rule 10b-5. *See, e.g.*, In re Bauer, 26 S.E.C. 770, 1947 WL 24474 (1947); In re Southeastern Securities Corp., 29 S.E.C. 609, 1949 WL 36491 (1949). This interpretation of the ambiguous text of § 10(b), in the context of formal adjudication, is entitled to deference if it is reasonable. For the reasons set forth below, we think it is. While the statute must not be construed so broadly as to convert every common-law fraud that happens to involve securities into a violation of § 10(b), neither the SEC nor this Court has ever held that there must be a misrepresentation about the value of a particular security in order to run afoul of the Act.

The SEC claims respondent engaged in a fraudulent scheme in which he made sales of his customer's securities for his own benefit. Respondent submits that the sales themselves were perfectly lawful and that the subsequent misappropriation of the proceeds, though fraudulent, is not properly viewed as having the requisite connection with the sales; in his view, the alleged scheme is not materially different from a simple theft of cash or securities in an investment account. We disagree.

According to the complaint, respondent "engaged in a scheme to defraud" the Woods beginning in 1988, shortly after they opened their account, and that scheme continued throughout the 2-year period during which respondent made a series of transactions that enabled him to convert the proceeds of the sales of the Woods' securities to his own use. The securities sales and respondent's fraudulent practices were not independent events. This is not a case in which, after a lawful transaction had been consummated, a broker decided to steal the proceeds and did so. Nor is it a case in which a thief simply invested the proceeds of a routine conversion in the stock market. Rather, respondent's fraud coincided with the sales themselves.

Taking the allegations in the complaint as true, each sale was made to further respondent's fraudulent scheme; each was deceptive because it was neither authorized by, nor disclosed to, the Woods. With regard to the sales of shares in the Woods' mutual fund, respondent initiated these transactions by writing a check to himself from that account, knowing that redeeming the check would require the sale of securities. Indeed, each time respondent "exercised his power of disposition for his own benefit," that conduct, "without more," was a fraud. United States v. Dunn, 268 U.S. 121, 131 (1925). In the aggregate, the sales are properly viewed as a "course of business" that operated as a fraud or deceit on a stockbroker's customer.

Insofar as the connection between respondent's deceptive practices and his sale of the Woods' securities is concerned, the case is remarkably similar to Superintendent of Ins. of N.Y. v. Bankers Life & Casualty Co., 404 U.S. 6 (1971). In that case the directors of Manhattan Casualty Company authorized the sale of the company's portfolio of treasury bonds because they had been "duped" into believing that the company would receive the proceeds of the sale. We held that "Manhattan was injured as an investor through a deceptive device which deprived it of any compensation for the sale of its valuable block of securities." *Id.*, at 10. In reaching this conclusion, we did not ask, as the Fourth Circuit did in this case, whether the directors were misled about the value of a security or whether the fraud involved "manipulation of a particular security." In fact, we rejected the Second Circuit's position in Superintendent of Ins. of N.Y. v. Bankers Life & Casualty Co., 430 F.2d 355, 361 (C.A. 2 1970), that because the fraud against Manhattan did not take place within the context of a securities exchange it was not prohibited by § 10(b). We refused to read the statute so narrowly, noting that it "must be read flexibly, not technically and restrictively." *Id.*, at 12. Although we recognized that the interest in "'preserving the integrity of the securities markets,'" was one of the purposes animating the statute, we rejected the notion that § 10(b) is limited to serving that objective alone.

Like the company directors in *Bankers Life*, the Woods were injured as investors through respondent's deceptions, which deprived them of any compensation for the sale of their valuable securities. They were duped into believing respondent would "conservatively invest" their assets in the stock market and that any transactions made on their behalf would be for their benefit for the "'safety of principal and income.'" The fact that respondent misappropriated the proceeds of the sales provides persuasive evidence that he had violated § 10(b) when he made the sales, but misappropriation is not an essential element of the offense. Indeed, in *Bankers Life*, we flatly stated that it was "irrelevant" that "the proceeds of the sale that were due the seller were misappropriated." 404 U.S., at 10. It is enough that the scheme to defraud and the sale of securities coincide. . . .

As in *Bankers Life*, . . . and *O'Hagan* [which we will read, below], the SEC complaint describes a fraudulent scheme in which the securities transactions and breaches of fiduciary duty coincide.[4] Those breaches were therefore "in connection with" securities sales within the meaning of § 10(b). Accordingly, the judgment of the Court of Appeals is reversed, and the case is remanded for further proceedings consistent with this opinion.

It is so ordered.

---

4. Contrary to the Court of Appeals' prediction, our analysis does not transform every breach of fiduciary duty into a federal securities violation. If, for example, a broker embezzles cash from a client's account or takes advantage of the fiduciary relationship to induce his client into a fradulent real estate transaction, than the fraud would not include the requisite connection to a purchase or sale of securities. Likewise if the broker told his client he was stealing the client's assets, that breach of fiduciary duty might be in connection with a sale of securities, but it would not involve a deceptive device or fraud.

5.   *Causation*

In addition to the other elements of the Section 10(b)/Rule 10b-5 case discussed above, plaintiffs must allege and prove that the defendant's misstatement or omission caused the financial loss of which plaintiffs' complain. Traditional tort law established two aspects to the causation requirement for fraud, that of "transaction causation" and "loss causation." Transaction causation refers to the requirement that the plaintiff allege and ultimately prove that the misstatement or omission caused the plaintiff to engage in the transaction in the first place. This element of the common law cause of action for fraud has been subsumed in the reliance element of Section 10b/Rule 10b-5, met through the Basic v. Levinson presumption of reliance, at least where the market for a company's stock is an efficient one (a major exchange), or through the *Affiliated Ute* presumption. Loss causation refers to the requirement that the plaintiff allege and ultimately prove that her financial loss was caused by the misstatement or omission. In a capital markets transaction, this element is met by showing that the stock price dropped after true facts about the company emerged. In the following case, the Supreme Court clarifies the plaintiff's burden with respect to loss causation.

DURA PHARMACEUTICALS, INC. v. BROUDO

544 U.S. 336
United States Supreme Court
April 19, 2005

BREYER, Justice.

A private plaintiff who claims securities fraud must prove that the defendant's fraud caused an economic loss. 15 U.S.C. § 78u-4(b)(4). We consider a Ninth Circuit holding that a plaintiff can satisfy this requirement—a requirement that courts call "loss causation"—simply by alleging in the complaint and subsequently establishing that "the price" of the security "*on the date of purchase* was inflated because of the misrepresentation." 339 F.3d 933, 938 (9th Cir.2003) (internal quotation marks omitted). In our view, the Ninth Circuit is wrong, both in respect to what a plaintiff must prove and in respect to what the plaintiffs' complaint here must allege.

I.

Respondents are individuals who bought stock in Dura Pharmaceuticals, Inc., on the public securities market between April 15, 1997, and February 24, 1998. They have brought this securities fraud class action against Dura and some of its managers and directors (hereinafter Dura) in federal court. In respect to the question before us, their detailed amended (181 paragraph) complaint makes substantially the following allegations:

1. Before and during the purchase period, Dura (or its officials) made false statements concerning both Dura's drug profits and future Food and Drug

Administration (FDA) approval of a new asthmatic spray device. See, *e.g.*, App. 45a, 55a, 89a.

2. In respect to drug profits, Dura falsely claimed that it expected that its drug sales would prove profitable. See, *e.g., id.,* at 66a-69a.

3. In respect to the asthmatic spray device, Dura falsely claimed that it expected the FDA would soon grant its approval. See, *e.g., id.,* at 89a-90a, 103a-104a.

4. On the last day of the purchase period, February 24, 1998, Dura announced that its earnings would be lower than expected, principally due to slow drug sales. *Id.,* at 51a.

5. The next day Dura's shares lost almost half their value (falling from about $39 per share to about $21). *Ibid.*

6. About eight months later (in November 1998), Dura announced that the FDA would not approve Dura's new asthmatic spray device. *Id.,* at 110a.

7. The next day Dura's share price temporarily fell but almost fully recovered within one week. *Id.,* at 156a.

Most importantly, the complaint says the following (and nothing significantly more than the following) about economic losses attributable to the spray device misstatement: *"In reliance on the integrity of the market, [the plaintiffs] . . . paid artificially inflated prices for Dura securities"* and the plaintiffs suffered *"damage[s]"* thereby. *Id.,* at 139a (emphasis added).

The District Court dismissed the complaint. In respect to the plaintiffs' drug-profitability claim, it held that the complaint failed adequately to allege an appropriate state of mind, *i.e.,* that defendants had acted knowingly, or the like. In respect to the plaintiffs' spray device claim, it held that the complaint failed adequately to allege "loss causation."

The Court of Appeals for the Ninth Circuit reversed. In the portion of the court's decision now before us — the portion that concerns the spray device claim — the Circuit held that the complaint adequately alleged "loss causation." The Circuit wrote that "plaintiffs establish loss causation if they have shown that the price *on the date of purchase* was inflated because of the misrepresentation." 339 F.3d, at 938 (emphasis in original; internal quotation marks and citation omitted). It added that "the injury occurs at the time of the transaction." *Ibid.* Since the complaint pleaded "that the price at the time of purchase was overstated," and it sufficiently identified the cause, its allegations were legally sufficient. *Ibid.*

Because the Ninth Circuit's views about loss causation differ from those of other Circuits that have considered this issue, we granted Dura's petition for certiorari. We now reverse.

II.

Private federal securities fraud actions are based upon federal securities statutes and their implementing regulations. Section 10(b) of the Securities Exchange Act of 1934 forbids (1) the "use or employ[ment] . . . of any . . . deceptive device," (2) "in connection with the purchase or sale of any security," and (3) "in contravention of" Securities and Exchange Commission "rules and regulations." 15 U.S.C. §78j(b). Commission Rule 10b-5 forbids, among other things, the making of any "untrue statement of a material fact" or the omission of any material fact "necessary in order to make the statements made . . . not misleading." 17 CFR § 240.10b-5 (2004). The courts have implied from these statutes and Rule a private damages action, which resembles, but is not identical to, common-law tort actions for deceit and misrepresentation. And Congress has imposed statutory requirements on that private action. *E.g.*, 15 U.S.C. § 78u-4(b)(4).

In cases involving publicly traded securities and purchases or sales in public securities markets, the action's basic elements include:

> (1) *a material misrepresentation (or omission);* (2) *scienter, i.e.,* a wrongful state of mind; (3) *a connection with the purchase or sale of a security;* (4) *reliance,* often referred to in cases involving public securities markets (fraud-on-the-market cases) as "transaction causation," see *Basic, supra,* at 248-249, 108 S.Ct. 978 (nonconclusively presuming that the price of a publicly traded share reflects a material misrepresentation and that plaintiffs have relied upon that misrepresentation as long as they would not have bought the share in its absence); (5) *economic loss;* and (6) *"loss causation", i.e.,* a causal connection between the material misrepresentation and the loss.

Dura argues that the complaint's allegations are inadequate in respect to these last two elements.

A.

We begin with the Ninth Circuit's basic reason for finding the complaint adequate, namely, that at the end of the day plaintiffs need only "establish," *i.e.,* prove, that "the price *on the date of purchase* was inflated because of the misrepresentation." 339 F.3d, at 938 (internal quotation marks and citation omitted). In our view, this statement of the law is wrong. Normally, in cases such as this one (*i.e.,* fraud-on-the-market cases), an inflated purchase price will not itself constitute or proximately cause the relevant economic loss.

For one thing, as a matter of pure logic, at the moment the transaction takes place, the plaintiff has suffered no loss; the inflated purchase payment is offset by ownership of a share that *at that instant* possesses equivalent value. Moreover, the logical link between the inflated share purchase price and any later economic loss is not invariably strong. Shares are normally purchased with an eye toward a later sale. But if, say, the purchaser sells the shares quickly before the relevant truth begins to leak out, the misrepresentation will not have led to any loss. If the purchaser sells later after the truth makes its way into the marketplace, an initially inflated purchase price *might* mean a later loss. But that is far from inevitably so. When the purchaser subsequently resells such shares, even at a lower price, that lower price may reflect, not the earlier misrepresentation, but changed economic circumstances, changed investor expectations, new industry-specific or firm-specific facts, conditions, or other events, which taken separately or together account for some or all of that lower price. (The same is true in respect to a claim that a share's higher price is lower than it would otherwise have been-a claim we do not consider here.) Other things being equal, the longer the time between purchase and sale, the more likely that this is so, *i.e.,* the more likely that other factors caused the loss.

Given the tangle of factors affecting price, the most logic alone permits us to say is that the higher purchase price will *sometimes* play a role in bringing about a future loss. It may prove to be a necessary condition of any such loss, and in that sense one might say that the inflated purchase price suggests that the misrepresentation (using language the Ninth Circuit used) "touches upon" a later economic loss. *Ibid.* But, even if that is so, it is insufficient. To "touch upon" a loss is not to *cause* a loss, and it is the latter that the law requires. . . .

Given the common-law roots of the securities fraud action (and the common-law requirement that a plaintiff show actual damages), it is not surprising that other Courts of Appeals have rejected the Ninth Circuit's "inflated purchase price" approach to proving causation and loss. Indeed, the Restatement of Torts, in setting forth the judicial consensus, says that a person who "misrepresents the financial condition of a corporation in order to sell its stock" becomes liable to a relying purchaser "for the loss" the purchaser sustains "when the facts . . . become generally known" and "as a result" share value "depreciate[s]." § 548A, Comment *b*, at 107. Treatise writers, too, have emphasized the need to prove proximate causation. Prosser and Keeton § 110, at 767 (losses do "not afford any basis for recovery" if "brought about by business conditions or other factors").

We cannot reconcile the Ninth Circuit's "inflated purchase price" approach with these views of other courts. And the uniqueness of its perspective argues against the validity of its approach in a case like this one where we consider the contours of a judicially implied cause of action with roots in the common law. . . .

The statute . . . makes clear Congress' intent to permit private securities fraud actions for recovery where, but only where, plaintiffs adequately allege and prove the traditional elements of causation and loss. By way of contrast, the Ninth Circuit's approach would allow recovery where a misrepresentation leads to an inflated purchase price but nonetheless does not proximately cause any economic loss. That is to say, it would permit recovery where these two traditional elements in fact are missing.

In sum, we find the Ninth Circuit's approach inconsistent with the law's requirement that a plaintiff prove that the defendant's misrepresentation (or other fraudulent conduct) proximately caused the plaintiff's economic loss. We need not, and do not, consider other proximate cause or loss-related questions.

B.

Our holding about plaintiffs' need to *prove* proximate causation and economic loss leads us also to conclude that the plaintiffs' complaint here failed adequately to *allege* these requirements. We concede that the Federal Rules of Civil Procedure require only "a short and plain statement of the claim showing that the pleader is entitled to relief." Fed. Rule Civ. Proc. 8(a)(2). And we assume, at least for argument's sake, that neither the Rules nor the securities statutes impose any special further requirement in respect to the pleading of proximate causation or economic loss. But, even so, the "short and plain statement" must provide the defendant with "fair notice of what the plaintiff's claim is and the grounds upon which it rests." Conley v. Gibson, 355 U.S. 41, 47, 78 S. Ct. 99, 2 L.Ed.2d 80 (1957). The complaint before us fails this simple test.

As we have pointed out, the plaintiffs' lengthy complaint contains only one statement that we can fairly read as describing the loss caused by the defendants' "spray device" misrepresentations. That statement says that the plaintiffs "paid artificially inflated prices for Dura['s] securities" and suffered "damage[s]." App. 139a. The statement implies that the plaintiffs' loss consisted of the "artificially inflated" purchase "prices." The complaint's failure to claim that Dura's share price fell significantly after the truth became known suggests that the plaintiffs considered the allegation of purchase price inflation alone sufficient. The complaint contains nothing that suggests otherwise.

For reasons set forth in Part II-A, *supra*, however, the "artificially inflated purchase price" is not itself a relevant economic loss. And the complaint nowhere else provides the defendants with notice of what the relevant economic loss might be or of what the causal connection might be between that loss and the misrepresentation concerning Dura's "spray device." . . .

For these reasons, we find the plaintiffs' complaint legally insufficient. We reverse the judgment of the Ninth Circuit, and we remand the case for further proceedings consistent with this opinion.

It is so ordered.

B. INSIDER TRADING

1. *The Classical Theory*

The classical theory of insider trading is concerned with corporate insiders' unfair use of corporate information to make a profit at the expense of outsiders who couldn't possibly, by dint of hard work, discover the information. For instance, if a person studied all of the available public information about data warehousing companies and decided that she thought Company A was well positioned to get a large contract that the U.S. Post Office just announced it would be awarding, she would have no legal duty to disclose that analysis prior to buying Company A's stock. (This assumes that the investor is not an employee or director or other fiduciary of Company A.) And if Company A did get the contract and the stock price went up, she can go out and celebrate without fear of an unpleasant future meeting with the SEC or an assistant U.S. attorney. But if an employee of Company A has just heard through the corporate grapevine that the company got the U.S. Post Office contract, under the classical theory she would have a legal duty to disclose that information prior to trading, or to abstain from trading.

This proposition, that an insider with knowledge of material nonpublic information is prohibited from trading in the company's stock, was derived initially from the duties of full disclosure required of any agent under state fiduciary duty law and then imported into federal securities law. (The following discussion is based on Richard W. Painter, Kimberly D. Krawiec, & Cynthia A. Williams, *Don't Ask, Just Tell: Insider Trading After* United States v. O'Hagan, 84 Va. L. Rev. 153 (1988).) At first these federal decisions were limited to face-to-face transactions. For instance, in Speed v. Transamerica Corp., 99 F. Supp. 808, 828-829 (D. Del. 1951), the court held that "[i]t is unlawful [under Rule 10b-5] for an insider, such as a majority stockholder, to purchase the stock of minority stockholders without disclosing material facts affecting the value of the stock, known to the majority stockholder by virtue of his inside position." Beginning in 1961 the SEC began to take the position that a similar "disclose or abstain" rule applied in open market transactions, *see* Cady, Roberts & Co., 40 S.E.C. 907 (1961), as did the federal courts. One of the most important of these federal decisions, which you'll see discussed in the case below, was SEC v. Texas Gulf Sulphur, 401 F.2d 833 (2d Cir. 1968) (en banc). In that case, the Texas Gulf Sulphur company had geological reports indicating huge, easily extractable mineral deposits of extremely valuable minerals on land it owned (and on neighboring pieces it was busily buying up). The company continued to downplay the finds, or deny them altogether, even as word started to leak out and reporters started asking questions. Meanwhile a number of insiders were also busily buying the company's stock, surmising that when the true state of the facts became known the stock price would increase. Finding a violation of Section 10(b) and Rule 10b-5, the Second Circuit en banc held that "anyone in possession of material inside information must either disclose it to the investing public, or . . . must abstain from trading." SEC v. Texas Gulf Sulphur, *supra*. The source of this duty to disclose is the fiduciary duty of full disclosure the insiders, as agents, owe to the shareholders, as principals. This has come to be called the "classical" theory of insider trading liability, and it specifically targets trading activity by people inside the firm, such as officers, directors, and employees, as well as "temporary insiders" such as a company's accountants or lawyers. In contrast, the "misappropriation theory," to be examined in the next section, prohibits some people outside the firm from trading without disclosure of material, nonpublic information where that information has been misappropriated in violation of fiduciary duties to the source of the information — such as a law clerk trading on information gained in a clerkship.

The following case presents a charge of insider trading under the classical theory, but addresses one of the unresolved issues: Is it enough to show that the insider "possessed" material nonpublic information when trading, or must a plaintiff or the government show that the insider actually used the information in deciding to trade? While that question might seem murky, the court below provides a clear articulation of both the issue and the answer. The case involves the materiality of forward-looking information, so serves as a good review of that issue as well.

UNITED STATES v. SMITH

155 F.3d 1051
United States Court of Appeals, Ninth Circuit
August 25, 1998

O'SCANNLAIN, Circuit Judge.

In this appeal from an insider securities trading conviction, we must decide difficult evidentiary issues involving an illegal interception of voicemail, as well as whether internal corporate earnings projections may constitute "material" inside information and whether conviction requires proof of actual use of that inside information.

I

PDA Engineering, Inc. ("PDA") was, in 1993, a software design firm with head-quarters in Orange County, California. Shares in PDA were publicly traded on the National Association of Securities Dealers Exchange (commonly referred to as "NASDAQ"). Richard Smith served as PDA's Vice President for North American Sales and worked in PDA's Nashville, Tennessee, office. By early 1993, after nearly three years with PDA, Smith had accumulated 51,445 shares of PDA stock.

In a series of transactions between June 10 and June 18, 1993, Smith liqui-dated his entire position in PDA. In addition to selling his own shares, Smith "sold short"[1] 25,000 shares on July 8, and another 10,000 shares on July 20. Smith's parents also sold and sold short a total of 12,000 shares.

Amidst this flurry of sales activity, on June 19, Smith telephoned Angela Bravo de Rueda ("Bravo"), an employee in the Los Angeles office of PDA, and left her the following voicemail message:

Hi, Angie, Rich. . . . I talked to Tom last night after I left you some messages and he and Lou discovered that there was about a million and a half dollar mistake in the budget, so now we're back at ground zero and we've got to scramble for the next few days. Anyway, finally I sold all my stock off on Friday and I'm going to short the stock because I know its going to go down a couple of points here in the next week as soon as Lou releases the information about next year's earnings. I'm more concerned about this year's earnings actually.

Unbeknownst to either Smith or Bravo, another Los Angeles-based PDA employee, Linda Alexander-Gore ("Gore"), guessed correctly Bravo's voice-mail password and accessed Bravo's mailbox. When Gore encountered Smith's message, she forwarded it to her own mailbox. In order to retrieve it, she then called her own voicemail from her home telephone, played the message, and recorded it with a handheld audiotape recorder. [The Court observed in a footnote that "[t]he record does not reveal the precise reason for Gore's curi-osity."] After recording the message, Gore approached a co-worker, Robert Phillips ("Phillips"). She informed him of the general nature of the communi-cation and provided him with a copy of the recording.

Phillips listened to the message and telephoned the United States Attorney's Office for the Central District of California, where he spoke to Assistant United States Attorney Bart Williams ("Williams"). Phillips told Williams that he believed he had information, in the form of an audiotape, that indicated possible criminal activity. He played the tape for Williams approximately four times and attempted to answer several questions about the contents of the recording. He informed Williams that he believed that the speaker on the tape was Smith and that the references in the message to "Tom" and "Lou" were probably to Tom Curry and

---

1. "Short selling is a device whereby the speculator sells stock which he does not own, antici-pating that the price will decline and that he will thereby be enabled to 'cover,' or make delivery of the stock sold, by purchasing it at the lesser price. If the decline materializes, the short seller realizes as a profit the differential between the sales price and the lower purchase or covering price." Louis Loss & Joel Seligman, *Fundamentals of Securities Regulation* 699 (3d ed. 1988) (quoting Stock Exchange Practices, Report of Comm. on Banking & Currency, S. Rep. No. 1455, 73d Cong., 2d Sess. 50-51 (1934)) (internal quotation marks omitted).

Lou Delmonico, both corporate officers at PDA. Phillips offered to send Williams a copy of the tape itself, but Williams declined. Phillips never spoke to Williams again.

Williams referred the matter to Special Agent Maura Kelly ("Kelly") of the Federal Bureau of Investigation ("FBI"). Kelly contacted the Pacific Regional Office of the Securities and Exchange Commission ("SEC") and relayed to a staff attorney that an "anonymous informant had told [Williams] about insider trading in the stock of a company called PDA Engineering by a person named Richard Smith and that the anonymous informant had a tape of a conversation involving an individual purporting to be Smith discussing insider trading." In November 1993, the SEC issued a formal order of investigation against Smith. Over the course of the ensuing eight months, the SEC obtained documentary evidence from various sources and deposed a number of witnesses. Sometime during the seventh month of its eight-month investigation (in July 1994), the SEC obtained via administrative subpoena an audiotape copy of the recorded voicemail message.

In September 1994, the SEC referred the matter back to the United States Attorney in Los Angeles for possible criminal prosecution. Throughout the next eighteen months, the United States Attorney's Office and the FBI conducted substantial additional investigation, during which they interviewed fifteen individuals and subpoenaed sixteen additional boxes of documents.

Smith was indicted on eleven counts of insider trading in violation of § 10(b) of the Securities Exchange Act of 1934, 15 U.S.C. § 78j(b), and SEC Rule 10b-5, 17 C.F.R. § 240.10b-5, and on one count of obstruction of justice in violation of 18 U.S.C. § 1505. Smith moved to suppress the evidence supporting the eleven insider trading counts and to dismiss the indictment as a whole, including the obstruction-of-justice count. After an extensive hearing, the district court suppressed the voicemail message itself, but refused to exclude the remainder of the government's evidence, concluding that it was not "derived from" the initial illegal recording. Although the court granted Smith's motion to dismiss the obstruction count, it denied his motion to dismiss with respect to the insider trading counts.

After a week-long trial, a jury returned guilty verdicts on all eleven insider trading counts. Smith filed a motion for judgment of acquittal or, in the alternative, for a new trial. The district court denied the motion, and Smith appealed.

Smith's contentions on appeal are essentially these: (1) that the government's evidence of insider trading was "derived from" an illegal wiretap and, therefore, should have been excluded pursuant to 18 U.S.C. § 2515; (2) that the information he possessed was forward-looking, or "soft," information, and hence was not "material" within the meaning of Rule 10b-5; and (3) that the district court erroneously instructed the jury that it could convict Smith based upon his mere possession, as opposed to his use, of inside information.

II

[The court first determined that the tape of the voicemail had been properly excluded by the district court but that the evidence that had been developed independently was not required to be suppressed.]

III

[The court first set out the text of Section 10(b) and Rule 10b-5.] A violation of Rule 10b-5 comprises four elements: a (1) misleading (2) statement or omission (3) of a "material" fact (4) made with scienter. *See* SEC v. Fehn, 97 F.3d 1276, 1289 (9th Cir. 1996). Under the "classical theory" of insider trading liability, a violation of Rule 10b-5 occurs "when a corporate insider trades in the securities of his corporation on the basis of material, nonpublic information." United States v. O'Hagan, 521 U.S. 642, 651 (1997); *accord* SEC v. Clark, 915 F.2d 439, 443 (9th Cir. 1990) ("[A] person violates Rule 10b-5 by buying or selling securities on the basis of material nonpublic information if . . . he is an insider of the corporation in whose shares he trades.") (quoting Barbara Bader Aldave, *Misappropriation: A General Theory of Liability for Trading on Nonpublic Information,*13 Hofstra L. Rev. 101, 101-02 (1984)).

. . . Smith does not contend that the information he possessed falls outside the Basic Inc. v. Levenson definition of materiality — that a reasonable investor would not have considered it useful or significant.[20] Rather, he argues that "[t]his Circuit has set limits on the type of information that may be considered material as a matter of law." Specifically, Smith says, "this Court has repeatedly held that forecasts of future sales and revenue are too speculative to constitute material facts." Smith contends that both the government's indictment and its proof at trial centered on his possession of "soft" information in the form of quarterly revenue projections. For instance, Smith points out, the indictment alleged that Smith knew in April 1993 that PDA "actually *expected* to realize" roughly 16% percent less in revenues for the fiscal year's fourth quarter than it had projected (a shortfall of approximately $2.3 million), and that Smith knew in June 1993 (in light of revised sales figures) that PDA "actually *expected*" to come up about 12% short. The government's evidence at trial, Smith maintains, mirrored the allegations in the indictment. Specifically, it elicited testimony from Smith's supervisor that Smith knew, both in April and in June, that PDA *was not likely* to meet fourth quarter revenue projections. When Smith traded on the basis of his knowledge of a fourth-quarter shortfall, the government's case went, he violated § 10(b) and Rule 10b-5.

In support of his contention that "soft" information cannot, as a matter of law, be "material" within the meaning of Rule 10b-5, Smith invokes a handful of Ninth Circuit cases [citations omitted] and a recent First Circuit decision. These cases, however, cannot bear the weight of the extreme interpretation with which Smith has saddled them. The decisions Smith cites stand for a more modest proposition, namely, that, *in the circumstances presented in those individual cases*, the disputed information was not sufficiently certain or significant to be considered material. We have never held — nor even hinted — that forward-looking information or intra-quarter data cannot, *as a matter of law*, be material. Nor has any other court for that matter, at least to the best of our knowledge. Indeed, both the Supreme Court's landmark decision in *Basic* and preexisting Ninth Circuit

20. Indeed, to do so would, as the SEC argues, "defy logic and experience." After all, investors are concerned, perhaps above all else, with the future cash flows of the companies in which they invest. Surely, the average investor's interest would be piqued by a company's internal projections of economic downturn.

authority confirm that so-called "soft" information can, under the proper circumstances, be "material" within the meaning of Rule 10b-5. . . .

There is, quite simply, no case law to support Smith's blanket assertion that forward-looking statements cannot, as a matter of law, constitute "material" information within the meaning of Rule 10b-5. Indeed, both the Supreme Court and this court have held to the contrary and have observed that determining materiality requires a nuanced, case-by-case approach. Consequently, we reject Smith's contentions that the district court erred (1) in refusing to dismiss the indictment, (2) in denying his motion for a judgment of acquittal, and (3) in instructing the jury based upon the *Basic* definition of materiality.

IV

With respect to Smith's state of mind, the district court instructed the jury as follows:

> In order for you to find the defendant guilty on [the insider trading counts] of the indictment, the government must prove a causal relationship between the material nonpublic information in the defendant's possession and the defendant's trading.
>
> That is, the government must prove that the defendant sold or sold short PDA stock because of material nonpublic information that he knowingly possessed. It is not sufficient that the government proves that the defendant sold or sold short PDA stock while knowingly in possession of the material nonpublic information. However, the government need not prove that the defendant sold or sold short PDA stock solely because of the material nonpublic information. It is enough if the government proves that such inside information was a significant factor in defendant's decision to sell or sell short PDA stock.

Although he accedes in much of the instruction, Smith objects to the final two sentences, arguing that they "confused the jury" by providing that the government need only demonstrate that the inside information was a "significant factor" in his decision to trade, and not "the reason." The government and the SEC counter by arguing that, in fact, the district court's instruction "exceeded the requirements of existing law." They insist that there is no "causation" element to an insider trading prosecution. Rather, they contend, "[w]hen a corporate insider like Smith has information relating to his company that he knows (or is reckless in not knowing) to be material and nonpublic and he trades in the company's stock, he violates the antifraud provisions of the federal securities laws, *whether or not the information is a factor in his decision to trade.*" In other words, the government contends, it needed only to prove that Smith knowingly *possessed* material nonpublic information, not that he actually *used* the information in deciding to buy or sell.

A

Although the use-possession debate has attracted a good deal of attention from academic commentators, very few courts (and none in this circuit) have addressed the issue head on. In support of their proposed "possession-only" standard, the government and the SEC rely principally upon dictum from a Second Circuit case, United States v. Teicher, 987 F.2d 112, 119 (2d Cir.

1993). The court in *Teicher* suggested, without squarely deciding, that proof of "knowing possession" is sufficient to sustain an insider trading prosecution and that the government need not affirmatively prove that the investor used the information in formulating his trade. For support, the court pointed to "a number of factors." *Id.* at 120. First, it asserted that the SEC has "consistently endorsed" a knowing-possession standard, and that the agency's interpretation of Rule 10b-5 in that respect is "entitled to some consideration." *Id.* Second, the court found the less exacting knowing-possession standard to be more consistent with the language of §10(b) and Rule 10b-5, both of which require only that a deceptive trade practice be conducted "in connection with" the purchase or sale of a security. *See id.* Third, the court observed that a knowing-possession standard "comports with the oft-quoted maxim that one with a fiduciary or similar duty to hold material nonpublic information in confidence must either 'disclose or abstain' with regard to trading." *Id.* (quoting Chiarella v. United States, 445 U.S. 222, 227 (1980)). Finally, the *Teicher* court pointed to what it believed to be the probable, yet subtle (indeed perhaps unconscious), effect that inside information has on traders:

> Because the advantage [an inside trader has over other traders] is in the form of information, it exists in the mind of the trader. Unlike a loaded weapon which may stand ready but unused, material information can not lay idle in the human brain.

Id. at 120-121.

Despite the Second Circuit's thoughtful analysis, we believe that the weight of authority supports a "use" requirement. Perhaps most significantly, the Supreme Court has consistently suggested, albeit in dictum, that Rule 10b-5 requires that the government prove causation in insider trading prosecutions. Indeed, just last Term, in United States v. O'Hagan, 521 U.S. 642 (1997), the Court indicated that an insider trading suspect must actually use the information to which he is privy, observing that "[u]nder the 'traditional' or 'classical theory' of insider trading liability, §10(b) and Rule 10b-5 are violated when a corporate insider trades in the securities of his corporation *on the basis of* material, nonpublic information." *Id.* 117 S. Ct. at 2207 (emphasis added). The *O'Hagan* Court was even more explicit in a separate portion of the opinion: "[T]he fiduciary's fraud is consummated, not when the fiduciary gains the confidential information, but when, without disclosure to his principal, he *uses the information* to purchase or sell securities." *Id.* 117 S. Ct. at 2209 (emphasis added). The Court's earlier decisions sound a similar theme. *See, e.g.,* Dirks v. SEC, 463 U.S. 646, 653 n.10 (1983) (referring to "duty that insiders owe . . . not to trade on inside information"); *id.* at 654 (referring to "duty to disclose before trading on material nonpublic information"); *id.* at 658-59 (referring to "trad[ing] on" inside information); *id.* at 662 (observing that "a purpose of the securities laws was to eliminate 'use of inside information for personal advantage'"; quoting In re Cady, Roberts & Co., 40 S.E.C. 907, 912 n.15 (1961)); *Chiarella*, 445 U.S. at 226 (referring to "the unfairness of allowing a corporate insider to take advantage of [inside] information by trading without disclosure"); *id.* at 229, 100 S. Ct. 1108 (observing that "[t]he federal courts have found violations of §10(b) where corporate insiders used undisclosed information for their own benefit").

In addition to suggestions from the Supreme Court, the only court of appeals squarely to consider the causation issue concluded that Rule 10b-5 does, in fact, entail a "use" requirement. *See* SEC v. Adler, 137 F.3d 1325, 1337-39 (11th Cir. 1998). In reaching its decision, the Eleventh Circuit pointed out that the SEC's position with regard to causation has not been nearly as "consistent" as the Second Circuit implied in *Teicher*; rather, it has "fluctuat[ed] over time." *Id.* at 1336. Although the SEC's current policy appears to be that "Rule 10b-5 does not require a showing that an insider sold his securities for the purpose of taking advantage of material non-public information," In re Sterling Drug, Inc., Fed. Sec. L. Rep. (CCH) ¶ 81,570, at 80,295 (April 18, 1978), such has not always been the case. In fact, in the not-too-distant past, the SEC concluded that an essential element of an insider trading violation was that the inside information "be a factor in [the insider's] decision to effect the transaction." In re Investors Management Co., Fed. Sec. L. Rep. (CCH) ¶ 78,163, at 80,514 (July 29, 1971). Of course, the fact that the SEC's position with respect to the causation issue has flip-flopped is not fatal to its claim to deference. *See* NLRB v. Local Union No. 103, 434 U.S. 335, 351 (1978) ("An administrative agency is not disqualified from changing its mind; and when it does, the courts . . . should not approach the statutory construction issue de novo and without regard to the administrative understanding of the statutes."). Nor, however, is the agency's about-face irrelevant to our inquiry. *See* Skidmore v. Swift & Co., 323 U.S. 134, 140 (1944) (listing "consistency with earlier and later pronouncements" as a pertinent consideration in determining the persuasiveness of an agency ruling). . . .

We do not take lightly the SEC's argument that a "use" requirement poses difficulties of proof. . . . We appreciate that a "use" requirement renders criminal prosecutions marginally more difficult for the government to prove. The difficulties, however, are by no means insuperable. It is certainly not necessary that the government present a smoking gun in every insider trading prosecution. (Not that a smoking gun will always be beyond the government's reach; consider, for instance, that in this case Bravo might herself have gone to the authorities with Smith's statement that "I'm going to short the stock because I know its going to go down a couple of points here in the next week as soon as Lou releases the information about next year's earnings.") Any number of types of circumstantial evidence might be relevant to the causation issue. Suppose, for instance, that an individual who has never before invested comes into possession of material nonpublic information and the very next day invests a significant sum of money in substantially out-of-the-money call options.[26] We are confident that the government would have little trouble demonstrating "use" in such a situation, or in other situations in which unique trading patterns or unusually large trading quantities suggest that an investor had used inside information.

Consequently, we reject the government's proffered "knowing possession" standard for insider trading violations as contrary [to] the weight of existing authority. Rather, we hold that Rule 10b-5 requires that the government (or the SEC, as the case may be) demonstrate that the suspected inside trader actually used material nonpublic information in consummating his transaction.

---

26. "An 'out-of-the-money' call option allows a person purchasing the option to buy stock during a limited period in the future at a fixed price (the 'strike price'). That price is higher than the current market price. Thus, the option holder essentially is betting that the market price will rise over the strike price within the limited time period. The time period limitations make such investments extremely speculative." United States v. Grossman, 843 F.2d 78, 81 n.1 (2d Cir. 1988).

B

Smith contends that the district court's instructions in this case were insufficient as a matter of law. Specifically, he complains that "a jury instruction which allows the government to obtain a conviction *without* proof that the defendant traded in stock '*because of* the material nonpublic information' that he possessed, effectively wipes out the scienter requirement as defined by this Court and the Supreme Court." As a legal matter, he is correct. The trouble for Smith lies not in the law but in the facts, because the district court in this case *did* require proof of causation. It specifically instructed the jury that "the government must prove that the defendant sold or sold short PDA stock *because of* material nonpublic information that he knowingly possessed" and cautioned that "[i]t is *not* sufficient that the government proves that the defendant sold or sold short PDA stock while knowingly in possession of the material nonpublic information." In other words, even under the more rigorous "use" standard that we adopt today, Smith has nothing to complain about. We must therefore reject Smith's challenge to the district court's state-of-mind instruction.

V

For the foregoing reasons, the district court's decision is affirmed in all respects.

2.   The Misappropriation Theory

Since the law of insider trading has been treated as a species of Section 10(b) and Rule 10b-5, there have been serious difficulties in defining who beyond insiders is under a duty to abstain or disclose. This is because "silence, absent a duty to disclose, is not deceptive," Basic, Inc. v. Levinson, 485 U.S. 224, 239 n.17 (1988), and deception (scienter) is part of the cause of action under Section 10(b) and Rule 10b-5. For insiders, the duty to disclose arises from the fiduciary duty that every agent owes his or her principal — here, the shareholders of the company or persons about to be shareholders. But "outsiders" to a company, such as a company's outside counsel, owe fiduciary duties to the company, not to the shareholders individually. And the farther you go "outside" the company, the more attenuated any potential disclosure claims based on fiduciary duty become. What duty might a law clerk have to the shareholders of a company, when aware of an opinion being drafted that may have an impact on the company's share price? Clearly there is a fiduciary duty to the judge for whom the clerk works, but not to the shareholders of a company that may be affected by the judge's ruling. What duty might a hairdresser have, when a CEO's husband tells him that the CEO's company is just about to purchase another company? These questions present gaps in the law of insider trading where an outsider having no fiduciary duty to the trading partner, either a purchaser or seller, may be able to trade on material, nonpublic information without liability under Section 10(b)/Rule 10b-5.

Until 1980, a number of courts and the SEC interpreted Section 10(b) and Rule 10b-5 not to distinguish between insiders and outsiders, but rather to impose on anyone in possession of material, nonpublic information an obligation either to disclose that information or to refrain from trading. Although

Texas Gulf Sulphur had involved insiders, the language it used could be more broadly construed to prohibit anyone from trading on the basis of material, nonpublic information. *See* SEC v. Texas Gulf Sulphur, 401 F. 2d 833, 848 (2d Cir. 1968) (in discussing the obligations of corporate insiders, the court stated that "anyone in possession of material inside information must either disclose it to the investing public, or . . . must abstain from trading). In 1980, though, the Supreme Court rejected this "equality of access" theory of insider trading in Chiarella v. United States, 445 U.S. 222 (1980). *Chiarella* involved an employee of a financial printer who worked on tender offer documents. Mr. Chiarella was able to determine from those documents which companies were going to be the targets in hostile takeover attempts, and he bought stock in those companies before the tender offers were publicly announced. (It is typical to either leave the names blank in such sensitive documents until the final printing, or to use false names that get replaced at the last moment, but Mr. Chiarella was able to figure out the true targets from other information in the documents. Ultimately he made $30,000 from the appreciation in the stock he bought.) The Second Circuit had upheld his conviction for insider trading, but the Supreme Court reversed, rejecting the equality of access theory of insider trading:

> When an allegation of fraud is based upon nondisclosure, there can be no fraud absent a duty to speak. . . . The element required to make silence fraudulent—a duty to disclose—is absent in this case. No duty could arise from petitioner's relationship with the sellers of the target company's securities, for petitioner had no prior dealings with them. He was not their agent, he was not a fiduciary, he was not a person in whom the sellers had placed their trust and confidence. He was, in fact, a complete stranger who dealt with the sellers only through impersonal market transactions. We cannot affirm petitioner's conviction without recognizing a general duty between all participants in market transactions to forgo actions based on material, nonpublic information. Formulation of such a broad duty, which departs radically from the established doctrine that duty arises from a specific relationship between two parties, should not be undertaken absent some explicit evidence of congressional intent.

Chiarella v. United States, 445 U.S. 222, 235 (1980).

A concurrence in *Chiarella* by Justice Stevens discussed with some approval an alternative theory of liability, which has come to be known as the misappropriation theory of insider trading, although Justice Stevens recognized that the misappropriation theory could not be the basis on which to uphold the conviction against Mr. Chiarella because it had not been presented at trial. Under this theory, the deception necessary to ground liability consists of fraud on the source of the information. *Chiarella*, 445 U.S. at 238. The fraud in *Chiarella*, under this theory, consisted of Mr. Chiarella's misappropriating the information the acquiring companies had entrusted to his employer and using it for his personal financial gain. And yet, the misappropriation theory was dictum discussed in a concurrence, so it hardly provided a clear answer to the question of who beyond insiders must disclose material nonpublic information or abstain from trading.

The following case, after 25 years of lower court development and SEC endorsement of the misappropriation theory post-*Chiarella*, provides the Supreme Court's ultimate endorsement of the theory. Note that this theory grounds liability on deception based on a breach of fiduciary duty between an agent (*e.g.*, the law clerk, in the previous example) and a principal (*e.g.*, the judge), not on a breach of a fiduciary duty of disclosure between a company insider and the buyer and seller of stock. As such, notice the extent to which securities liability here reinforces core concepts of the principal/agent relationship and the fiduciary duties inherent in that relationship.

UNITED STATES v. O'HAGAN

521 U.S. 642
Supreme Court of the United States
June 25, 1997

GINSBURG, Justice.

This case concerns the interpretation and enforcement of § 10(b) . . . of the Securities Exchange Act of 1934, and [the rule] made by the Securities and Exchange Commission pursuant [thereto], Rule 10b-5. . . . [W]e address and resolve [this issue]: (1) Is a person who trades in securities for personal profit, using confidential information misappropriated in breach of a fiduciary duty to the source of the information, guilty of violating § 10(b) and Rule 10b-5? Our answer to the . . . question is yes. . . .

I

Respondent James Herman O'Hagan was a partner in the law firm of Dorsey & Whitney in Minneapolis, Minnesota. In July 1988, Grand Metropolitan PLC (Grand Met), a company based in London, England, retained Dorsey & Whitney as local counsel to represent Grand Met regarding a potential tender offer for the common stock of the Pillsbury Company, headquartered in Minneapolis. Both Grand Met and Dorsey & Whitney took precautions to protect the confidentiality of Grand Met's tender offer plans. O'Hagan did no work on the Grand Met representation. Dorsey & Whitney withdrew from representing Grand Met on September 9, 1988. Less than a month later, on October 4, 1988, Grand Met publicly announced its tender offer for Pillsbury stock.

On August 18, 1988, while Dorsey & Whitney was still representing Grand Met, O'Hagan began purchasing call options for Pillsbury stock. Each option gave him the right to purchase 100 shares of Pillsbury stock by a specified date in September 1988. Later in August and in September, O'Hagan made additional purchases of Pillsbury call options. By the end of September, he owned 2,500 unexpired Pillsbury options, apparently more than any other individual investor. O'Hagan also purchased, in September 1988, some 5,000 shares of Pillsbury common stock, at a price just under $39 per share. When Grand Met announced its tender offer in October, the price of Pillsbury stock rose to nearly $60 per share. O'Hagan then sold his Pillsbury call options and common stock, making a profit of more than $4.3 million.

The Securities and Exchange Commission (SEC or Commission) initiated an investigation into O'Hagan's transactions, culminating in a 57-count indictment.

The indictment alleged that O'Hagan defrauded his law firm and its client, Grand Met, by using for his own trading purposes material, nonpublic information regarding Grand Met's planned tender offer. According to the indictment, O'Hagan used the profits he gained through this trading to conceal his previous embezzlement and conversion of unrelated client trust funds. O'Hagan was charged with 20 counts of mail fraud, in violation of 18 U.S.C. § 1341; 17 counts of securities fraud, in violation of § 10(b) of the Securities Exchange Act of 1934 (Exchange Act), and SEC Rule 10b-5; 17 counts of fraudulent trading in connection with a tender offer, in violation of § 14(e) of the Exchange Act, and SEC Rule 14e-3(a); and 3 counts of violating federal money laundering statutes. A jury convicted O'Hagan on all 57 counts, and he was sentenced to a 41-month term of imprisonment.

A divided panel of the Court of Appeals for the Eighth Circuit reversed all of O'Hagan's convictions. Liability under § 10(b) and Rule 10b-5, the Eighth Circuit held, may not be grounded on the "misappropriation theory" of securities fraud on which the prosecution relied. . . .

Decisions of the Courts of Appeals are in conflict on the propriety of the misappropriation theory under § 10(b) and Rule 10b-5. . . . We granted certiorari and now reverse the Eighth Circuit's judgment.

II

We address . . . the Court of Appeals' reversal of O'Hagan's convictions under § 10(b) and Rule 10b-5. Following the Fourth Circuit's lead, *see* United States v. Bryan, 58 F.3d 933, 943-959 (1995), the Eighth Circuit rejected the misappropriation theory as a basis for § 10(b) liability. We hold, in accord with several other Courts of Appeals, that criminal liability under § 10(b) may be predicated on the misappropriation theory.

A

. . .

Under the "traditional" or "classical theory" of insider trading liability, § 10(b) and Rule 10b-5 are violated when a corporate insider trades in the securities of his corporation on the basis of material, nonpublic information. Trading on such information qualifies as a "deceptive device" under § 10(b), we have affirmed, because "a relationship of trust and confidence [exists] between the shareholders of a corporation and those insiders who have obtained confidential information by reason of their position with that corporation." Chiarella v. United States, 445 U.S. 222, 228 (1980). That relationship, we recognized, "gives rise to a duty to disclose [or to abstain from trading] because of the 'necessity of preventing a corporate insider from . . . tak[ing] unfair advantage of . . . uninformed . . . stockholders.'" *Id.*, at 228-229. The classical theory applies not only to officers, directors, and other permanent insiders of a corporation, but also to attorneys, accountants, consultants, and others who temporarily become fiduciaries of a corporation. *See* Dirks v. SEC, 463 U.S. 646, 655, n.14 (1983).

The "misappropriation theory" holds that a person commits fraud "in connection with" a securities transaction, and thereby violates § 10(b) and Rule 10b-5, when he misappropriates confidential information for securities trading purposes, in breach of a duty owed to the source of the information. Under this theory, a fiduciary's undisclosed, self-serving use of a principal's information to purchase or sell securities, in breach of a duty of loyalty and confidentiality, defrauds the principal of the exclusive use of that information. In lieu of premising liability on a fiduciary relationship between company insider and purchaser or seller of the company's stock, the misappropriation theory premises liability on a fiduciary-turned-trader's deception of those who entrusted him with access to confidential information.

The two theories are complementary, each addressing efforts to capitalize on nonpublic information through the purchase or sale of securities. The classical theory targets a corporate insider's breach of duty to shareholders with whom the insider transacts; the misappropriation theory outlaws trading on the basis of nonpublic information by a corporate "outsider" in breach of a duty owed not to a trading party, but to the source of the information. . . .

In this case, the indictment alleged that O'Hagan, in breach of a duty of trust and confidence he owed to his law firm, Dorsey & Whitney, and to its client, Grand Met, traded on the basis of nonpublic information regarding Grand Met's planned tender offer for Pillsbury common stock. This conduct, the Government charged, constituted a fraudulent device in connection with the purchase and sale of securities.

B

We agree with the Government that misappropriation, as just defined, satisfies § 10(b)'s requirement that chargeable conduct involve a "deceptive device or contrivance" used "in connection with" the purchase or sale of securities. We observe, first, that misappropriators, as the Government describes them, deal in deception. A fiduciary who "[pretends] loyalty to the principal while secretly converting the principal's information for personal gain," "dupes" or defrauds the principal. *See* Aldave, *Misappropriation: A General Theory of Liability for Trading on Nonpublic Information*, 13 Hofstra L. Rev. 101, 119 (1984). . . .

Deception through nondisclosure is central to the theory of liability for which the Government seeks recognition. As counsel for the Government stated in explanation of the theory at oral argument: "To satisfy the common law rule that a trustee may not use the property that [has] been entrusted [to] him, there would have to be consent. To satisfy the requirement of the Securities Act that there be no deception, there would only have to be disclosure." *[S]ee generally* Restatement (Second) of Agency §§ 390, 395 (1958) (agent's disclosure obligation regarding use of confidential information).

The misappropriation theory advanced by the Government is consistent with Santa Fe Industries, Inc. v. Green, 430 U.S. 462 (1977), a decision underscoring that § 10(b) is not an all-purpose breach of fiduciary duty ban; rather, it trains on conduct involving manipulation or deception. In contrast to the Government's allegations in this case, in *Santa Fe Industries*, all pertinent facts were disclosed by the persons charged with violating § 10(b) and Rule 10b-5; therefore, there was no deception through nondisclosure to which liability under those provisions could attach. Similarly, full disclosure forecloses liability under the misappropriation theory: Because the deception essential to the misappropriation theory involves feigning fidelity to the source of information, if the fiduciary discloses to the source that he plans to trade on the nonpublic information, there is no "deceptive device" and thus no § 10(b) violation — although the fiduciary-turned-trader may remain liable under state law for breach of a duty of loyalty.[7]

We turn next to the § 10(b) requirement that the misappropriator's deceptive use of information be "in connection with the purchase or sale of [a] security." This element is satisfied because the fiduciary's fraud is consummated, not when the fiduciary gains the confidential information, but when, without disclosure to his principal, he uses the information to purchase or sell securities. The securities transaction and the breach of duty thus coincide. This is so even though the person or entity defrauded is not the other party to the trade, but is, instead, the source of the nonpublic information. A misappropriator who trades on the basis of material, nonpublic information, in short, gains his advantageous market position through deception; he deceives the source of the information and simultaneously harms members of the investing public. . . .

The Government notes another limitation on the forms of fraud § 10(b) reaches: "The misappropriation theory would not . . . apply to a case in which a person defrauded a bank into giving him a loan or embezzled cash from another, and then used the proceeds of the misdeed to purchase securities." In such a case, the Government states, "the proceeds would have value to the malefactor apart from their use in a securities transaction, and the fraud would be complete as soon as the money was obtained." In other words, money can buy, if not anything, then at least many things; its misappropriation may thus be viewed as sufficiently detached from a subsequent securities transaction that § 10(b)'s "in connection with" requirement would not be met.

Justice Thomas' charge that the misappropriation theory is incoherent because information, like funds, can be put to multiple uses misses the point. The Exchange Act was enacted in part "to insure the maintenance of fair and honest markets," 15 U.S.C. § 78b, and there is no question that fraudulent uses of confidential information fall within § 10(b)'s prohibition if the fraud is "in connection with" a securities transaction. It is hardly remarkable that a rule suitably applied to the fraudulent uses of certain kinds of information would be stretched beyond reason were it applied to the fraudulent use of money. . . .

The misappropriation theory comports with § 10(b)'s language, which requires deception "in connection with the purchase or sale of any security," not deception of an identifiable purchaser or seller. The theory is also well tuned to an animating purpose of the Exchange Act: to insure honest securities markets and thereby promote investor confidence. *See* 45 Fed. Reg. 60412 (1980) (trading on misappropriated information "undermines the integrity of, and investor confidence in, the securities markets"). Although informational disparity is inevitable in the securities markets, investors likely would hesitate to venture their capital in a market where trading based on misappropriated nonpublic information is unchecked by law. An investor's informational disadvantage vis-à-vis a misappropriator with material, nonpublic information stems from contrivance, not luck; it is a disadvantage that cannot be overcome with research or skill.

In sum, considering the inhibiting impact on market participation of trading on misappropriated information, and the congressional purposes underlying § 10(b), it makes scant sense to hold a lawyer like O'Hagan a § 10(b) violator if

7. Where, however, a person trading on the basis of material, nonpublic information owes a duty of loyalty and confidentiality to two entities or persons — for example, a law firm and its client — but makes disclosure to only one, the trader may still be liable under the misappropriation theory.

he works for a law firm representing the target of a tender offer, but not if he works for a law firm representing the bidder. The text of the statute requires no such result. The misappropriation at issue here was properly made the subject of a § 10(b) charge because it meets the statutory requirement that there be "deceptive" conduct "in connection with" securities transactions. . . .

The judgment of the Court of Appeals for the Eighth Circuit is reversed, and the case is remanded for further proceedings consistent with this opinion.

It is so ordered.

Justice SCALIA, concurring in part and dissenting in part.

. . . I do not agree . . . with Part II of the Court's opinion, containing its analysis of respondent's convictions under § 10(b) and Rule 10b-5. . . .

While the Court's explanation of the scope of § 10(b) and Rule 10b-5 would be entirely reasonable in some other context, it does not seem to accord with the principle of lenity we apply to criminal statutes (which cannot be mitigated here by the Rule, which is no less ambiguous than the statute). In light of that principle, it seems to me that the unelaborated statutory language: "[t]o use or employ, in connection with the purchase or sale of any security . . . any manipulative or deceptive device or contrivance,"§ 10(b), must be construed to require the manipulation or deception of a party to a securities transaction.

Justice THOMAS, with whom THE CHIEF JUSTICE joins, concurring in the judgment in part and dissenting in part.

Today the majority upholds respondent's convictions for violating § 10(b) of the Securities Exchange Act of 1934, and Rule 10b-5 promulgated thereunder, based upon the Securities and Exchange Commission's "misappropriation theory." Central to the majority's holding is the need to interpret § 10(b)'s requirement that a deceptive device be "use[d] or employ [ed], in connection with the purchase or sale of any security." Because the Commission's misappropriation theory fails to provide a coherent and consistent interpretation of this essential requirement for liability under § 10(b), I dissent. . . .

I

I do not take issue with the majority's determination that the undisclosed misappropriation of confidential information by a fiduciary can constitute a "deceptive device" within the meaning of § 10(b). Nondisclosure where there is a pre-existing duty to disclose satisfies our definitions of fraud and deceit for purposes of the securities laws.

Unlike the majority, however, I cannot accept the Commission's interpretation of when a deceptive device is "use[d] . . . in connection with" a securities transaction. Although the Commission and the majority at points seem to suggest that *any* relation to a securities transaction satisfies the "in connection with" requirement of § 10(b), both ultimately reject such an overly expansive construction and require a more integral connection between the fraud and the securities transaction. The majority states, for example, that the misappropriation theory applies to undisclosed misappropriation of confidential information "for securities trading purposes," thus seeming to require a particular intent by the misappropriator in order to satisfy the "in connection with" language. The Commission goes further, and argues that the misappropriation theory satisfies the "in connection with" requirement because it "depends on an *inherent* connection between the deceptive conduct and the purchase or sale of a security."

The Commission's construction of the relevant language in § 10(b), and the incoherence of that construction, become evident as the majority attempts to describe why the fraudulent theft of information falls under the Commission's misappropriation theory, but the fraudulent theft of money does not. The majority correctly notes that confidential information "qualifies as property to which the company has a right of exclusive use." It then observes that the "undisclosed misappropriation of such information, in violation of a fiduciary duty, . . . constitutes fraud akin to embezzlement—the fraudulent appropriation to one's own use of the money or goods entrusted to one's care by another." So far the majority's analogy to embezzlement is well taken, and adequately demonstrates that undisclosed misappropriation can be a fraud on the source of the information.

What the embezzlement analogy does not do, however, is explain how the relevant fraud is "use[d] or employ[ed], in connection with" a securities transaction. And when the majority seeks to distinguish the embezzlement of funds from the embezzlement of information, it becomes clear that neither the Commission nor the majority has a coherent theory regarding § 10(b)'s "in connection with" requirement.

Turning first to why embezzlement of information supposedly meets the "in connection with" requirement, the majority asserts that the requirement "is satisfied because the fiduciary's fraud is consummated, not when the fiduciary gains the confidential information, but when, without disclosure to his principal, he uses the information to purchase or sell securities. The securities transaction and the breach of duty thus coincide."

The majority later notes, with apparent approval, the Government's contention that the embezzlement of funds used to purchase securities would *not* fall within the misappropriation theory. The misappropriation of funds used for a securities transaction is not covered by its theory, the Government explains, because "the proceeds would have value to the malefactor apart from their use in a securities transaction, and the fraud would be complete as soon as the money was obtained."

Accepting the Government's description of the scope of its own theory, it becomes plain that the majority's explanation of how the misappropriation theory supposedly satisfies the "in connection with" requirement is incomplete. The touchstone required for an embezzlement to be "use[d] or employ[ed], in connection with" a securities transaction is not merely that it "coincide" with, or be consummated by, the transaction, but that it is *necessarily* and *only* consummated by the transaction. Where the property being embezzled has value "apart from [its] use in a securities transaction"—even though it is in fact being used in a securities transaction—the Government contends that there is no violation under the misappropriation theory. . . .

Once the Government's construction of the misappropriation theory is accurately described and accepted—along with its implied construction of § 10(b)'s "in connection with" language—that theory should no longer cover cases, such as this one, involving fraud on the source of information where the source has no connection with the other participant in a securities transaction. It seems obvious that the undisclosed misappropriation of confidential information is not necessarily consummated by a securities transaction. In this case, for example, upon learning of Grand Met's confidential takeover plans, O'Hagan could have done any number of things with the information: He could have sold it to a newspaper for publication; he could have given or sold the information to Pillsbury itself; or he could even have kept the information and used it solely for his personal amusement, perhaps in a fantasy stock trading game.

Any of these activities would have deprived Grand Met of its right to "exclusive use" of the information and, if undisclosed, would constitute "embezzlement" of Grand Met's informational property. Under *any* theory of liability, however, these activities would not violate § 10(b) and, according to the Commission's monetary embezzlement analogy, these possibilities are sufficient to preclude a violation under the misappropriation theory even where the informational property *was* used for securities trading. That O'Hagan actually did use the information to purchase securities is thus no more significant here than it is in the case of embezzling money used to purchase securities. In both cases the embezzler *could have* done something else with the property, and hence the Commission's necessary "connection" under the securities laws would not be met.[2] . . .

In upholding respondent's convictions under the new and improved misappropriation theory, the majority also points to various policy considerations underlying the securities laws, such as maintaining fair and honest markets, promoting investor confidence, and protecting the integrity of the securities markets. But the repeated reliance on such broad-sweeping legislative purposes reaches too far and is misleading in the context of the misappropriation theory. It reaches too far in that, regardless of the overarching purpose of the securities laws, it is not illegal to run afoul of the "purpose" of a statute, only its letter. The majority's approach is misleading in this case because it glosses over the fact that the supposed threat to fair and honest markets, investor confidence, and market integrity comes not from the supposed fraud in this case, but from the mere fact that the information used by O'Hagan was nonpublic.

As the majority concedes, because "the deception essential to the misappropriation theory involves feigning fidelity to the source of information, if the fiduciary discloses *to the source* that he plans to trade on the nonpublic information, there is no 'deceptive device' and thus no § 10(b) violation." Indeed, were the source expressly to authorize its agents to trade on the confidential information—as a perk or bonus, perhaps—there would likewise be no § 10(b) violation. Yet in either case—disclosed misuse or authorized use—the hypothesized "inhibiting impact on market participation," would be identical to that from behavior violating the misappropriation theory: "Outsiders" would still be trading based on nonpublic information that the average investor has no hope of obtaining through his own diligence.

. . . The absence of a coherent and consistent misappropriation theory and, by necessary implication, a coherent and consistent application of the statutory "use or employ, in connection with" language, is particularly problematic in the context of this case. The Government claims a remarkable breadth to the

---

2. Indeed, even if O'Hagan or someone else thereafter used the information to trade, the misappropriation would have been complete before the trade and there should be no § 10(b) liability. The most obvious real-world example of this scenario would be if O'Hagan had simply tipped someone else to the information. The mere act of passing the information along would have violated O'Hagan's fiduciary duty and, if undisclosed, would be an "embezzlement" of the confidential information, regardless of whether the tippee later traded on the information.

delegation of authority in § 10(b), arguing that "the very aim of this section was to pick up unforeseen, cunning, deceptive devices that people might cleverly use in the securities markets." As the Court aptly queried, "[t]hat's rather unusual, for a criminal statute to be that open-ended, isn't it?" Unusual indeed. Putting aside the dubious validity of an open-ended delegation to an independent agency to go forth and create regulations criminalizing "fraud," in this case we do not even have a formal regulation embodying the agency's misappropriation theory. Certainly Rule 10b-5 cannot be said to embody the theory—although it deviates from the statutory language by the addition of the words "any person," it merely repeats, unchanged, § 10(b)'s "in connection with" language. Given that the validity of the misappropriation theory turns on the construction of that language in § 10(b), the regulatory language is singularly uninformative. . . .

PROBLEM 12-3

About two years after PERSIA lost $1 billion (see Problem 12-1), Wilson and Levy's John Tower, the main architect of the PERSIA deal, got word that the SEC was investigating him and Wilson and Levy for the events surrounding PERSIA's losses. Such an investigation is required to be announced in quarterly filing of a public company like Wilson and Levy. Before the company's quarterly filing deadline, Tower started to get nervous, had trouble sleeping, and found himself losing his appetite for the wine, women, and song that had been such a big part of his life. He made an appointment to get a thorough physical, and his doctor asked if anything was troubling Tower at work. Tower mentioned the SEC investigation.

As it turned out, Tower's doctor owned a substantial amount of Wilson and Levy stock, and understood that there might be a stock price drop if the SEC investigation ever led to charges being filed. Thus, Tower's doctor arranged to sell about 80 percent of his holdings.

Under the reasoning of O'Hagan, would Tower's doctor be guilty of insider trading for misappropriation of confidential information? Does Rule 10b5-2 make your analysis any easier?

C. REGULATION FD

Although Congress and the SEC have for the most part regulated insider trading through Section 10(b) and Rule 10b-5, it has not done so entirely. In 1984, Congress enacted the Insider Trading Sanctions Act of 1984, which makes it illegal to trade options and other derivative securities in circumstances where it would be illegal to trade in the underlying security. Insider Trading Sanctions Act of 1984, Pub. L. No. 98-376, 98 Stat. 1264, 1265 (codified in scattered subsections of 15 U.S.C. § 78). In 1988 Congress amended the Exchange Act to provide a remedy for contemporaneous traders against "any person who violates any provision of this title or the rules or regulations thereunder by purchasing or selling a security while in possession of material, nonpublic information."

Section 20A of the 1934 Act, enacted as the Insider Trading and Securities Fraud Enforcement Act of 1988. Moreover, in Rule 14e-3 the SEC prohibited most trading on the basis of material, nonpublic information about a pending tender offer (a direct response to *Chiarella*). (The potential tender offeror may continue to buy securities up to the 5 percent "trigger" of §13(d), which then requires public disclosure of the purchases and the purpose of the purchases — that is, whether they are for investment or as the first step in a takeover attempt.) And in §16 of the Exchange Act, Congress specifically addressed insider trading by requiring insiders to disgorge any profits from "short-swing" sales in their company's stock — that is, a purchase followed within six months by a sale or vice versa. Securities Exchange Act of 1934, §16, 15 U.S.C. §78p (1994).

Probably the most controversial action taken by the SEC to regulate the trading on material, nonpublic information is Regulation Fair Disclosure (Reg. FD), promulgated in 1999. Regulation FD states that if a company discloses material, nonpublic information to brokers or dealers, investment advisors, investment companies, securities analysts, or large shareholders, it must publicly disclose the same information either simultaneously, in the case of intentional disclosure, or promptly, in the case of nonintentional disclosure. The purpose of Regulation FD is to create a level playing field, and stop the selective disclosure of material, nonpublic information to securities professionals in conference calls, conversations between institutional investors and the company, and similar nonpublic formats. Conference calls between companies and securities analysts and other market professionals were a regular feature of communications between companies and the market prior to Regulation FD. Selective disclosures to market professionals were not violations of insider trading law under existing Supreme Court precedent prior to Regulation FD because of a loophole left by Dirks v. SEC, 463 U.S. 646 (1983). In that case, the Supreme Court had analyzed the potential liability of Raymond Dirks, an officer of a broker-dealer firm, who had received information (making him a "tippee") from company insiders ("tippers") suggesting massive fraud at the company. Dirks had investigated the information, discussing it with other broker-dealers and with clients along the way, and was ultimately successful in bringing the fraud to light — and was then prosecuted by the SEC for his efforts. The Court in *Dirks* exonerated Dirks, holding that "tippee" liability is a derivative form of liability, and depends on whether the insider/tipper breached a duty owed to shareholders. *Dirks*, 463 U.S. at 654. If the insider disclosed the information without breaching a fiduciary duty to the company or personally benefiting — such as when a company insider discusses the company with securities analysts and other market professionals — there is no breach by the tipper and thus no derivative breach by the tippee. This interpretation of *Dirks* had allowed selective disclosure to market professionals to flourish, leading the SEC to enact Regulation FD.

Regulation FD is controversial precisely because it keeps information from the market by keeping it from securities professionals. As you read the following case, consider whether the goal of fairness to "the market" is advanced by Regulation FD, whether that benefit is worth the cost of decreased information to market professionals and thus to the market generally, and whether there are alternative ways the SEC could have regulated selective disclosure.

SECURITIES AND EXCHANGE COMMISSION v. SIEBEL SYSTEMS, INC.

2005 WL 2100269
Southern District of New York
September 1, 2005

DANIELS, District Judge.

Plaintiff, the Securities and Exchange Commission ("SEC"), commenced this action, against Siebel Systems, Inc. ("Siebel Systems"), Siebel Systems's Chief Financial Officer, Kenneth Goldman, and one of Siebel Systems's Senior Vice Presidents, Mark Hanson. The SEC charges the defendants with, *inter alia*, violations of, or aiding and abetting in the violation of, Regulation FD ("Fair Disclosure). In general terms, Regulation FD prohibits a company and its senior officials from privately disclosing any material nonpublic information regarding the company or its securities to certain persons such as analysts and institutional investors.

Defendants moved, pursuant to Fed.R.Civ.P. 12(b)(6), to dismiss the complaint for failure to state a claim upon which relief may be granted on the grounds that the statements disclosed were neither material nor nonpublic. Defendants' motion is granted. The nature and content of the statements that the SEC alleges violate Regulation FD do not support the Commission's claim that Siebel Systems or its senior officials privately disclosed material nonpublic information.

Regulation FD requires an issuer, to make public material information disclosed to security market professionals or holders of the issuer's securities who are reasonably likely to trade on the basis of that information. Where the issuer's selective disclosure of material nonpublic information is intentional, the issuer is to simultaneously make public disclosure. In the case of non-intentional disclosure, public disclosure must be promptly made. "'Promptly' means as soon as reasonably practicable (but in no event after the later of 24 hours or the commencement of the next day's trading on the New York Stock Exchange) after a senior official of the issuer, . . . learns that there has been a non-intentional disclosure by the issuer or person acting on behalf of the issuer of information that the senior official knows, or is reckless in not knowing, is both material and nonpublic." 17 C.F.R. § 243.101(d).

The gravamen of the complaint is that defendant Goldman made positive comments about the company's business activity levels and sales transaction pipeline[3] at two private events on April 30th, 2003, attended by institutional investors and by defendant Hanson. The SEC alleges that, at these two events, Mr. Goldman privately disclosed material nonpublic information by stating that Siebel Systems's activity levels were "good" or "better," that new deals were coming back into the pipeline, that the pipeline was "building" and "growing," and that "there were some $5 million deals in Siebel's pipeline." The complaint alleges that immediately following the disclosure of this information or soon thereafter, certain attendants of the meetings and their associates made substantial purchases of shares of Siebel Systems's stock. The SEC alleges "by

---

3. The SEC alleges that "[f]or shareholders or potential investors, information concerning the status of the Company's pipeline — whether it is lagging, static or growing — and the activity levels of the sale force — whether they are active or inactive — is important to making an investment decision because such information is an indicator of the Company's ability to generate revenues."

disclosing that Siebel's business activity levels were 'good' and 'better,' and that its sales transaction pipeline was 'growing' and 'building,' Goldman communicated to his private audiences that Siebel's business was improving as the result of new business, and that the increase in the Company's guidance for the second quarter was not simply because deals that had slipped from the first quarter were closing."

The SEC claims that these statements materially contrasted with public statements made by Thomas Siebel [Siebel Systems' founder, chairman, and CEO] during conference calls on April 4th and 23rd, and at an April 28th conference. In the complaint, the SEC sets forth, in great detail, the contents of Mr. Siebel's public statements of April 4th, April 23rd, and April 28th. Those statements provided information about the company's "performance in the first quarter of 2003 and its expected performance in the second quarter of 2003." The SEC alleges that in these statements it was reported that: (1) Siebel Systems's first quarter results were poor because the economy was poor and because some deals that were expected to close in the previous quarter did not, *i.e.*, deals had "slipped" into the second quarter; (2) Siebel Systems's software license revenues were expected to be higher in the second quarter than in the first quarter, but the company conditioned its estimate on the performance of the overall economy; and (3) there were no indications that the existing poor economic conditions were [improving]. "In each statement, the Company [allegedly] characterized the economy negatively (as not improved or not improving)." . . .

The SEC contends that "[b]ased on these disclosures, the total mix of information available to investors was that Siebel's business had performed poorly in the first quarter and would improve in the second quarter only if the economy improved." Allegedly, Mr. Goldman's "statements materially contrasted with the public statements that Thomas Siebel made during the April 4 and 23 conference calls and at the . . . conference on April 28. For example, in contrast to the apocalyptic economic environment that Thomas Siebel described at the [April 28th] conference, Goldman's disclosure at the April 30 [events] were significantly more positive and upbeat. Unlike the Company's prior public disclosure about its prospective performance in the second quarter, Goldman's statements about the Company's business were not linked to or conditioned upon the performance of the economy." . . .

VIOLATION OF REGULATION FD

The complaint alleges four nonpublic material disclosures made by Mr. Goldman which are the basis for the SEC's claims for violations of Regulation FD: (1) that there were some *five million dollar deals* in the company's pipeline for the second quarter of 2003; (2) that *new deals* were coming into the sales pipeline; (3) that the company's sales pipeline was "*growing*" or "*building*"; and (4) that the company's sales or business activity levels were "*good*" or "*better*." The complaint relies on no statements regarding specific earnings or sales figures. Defendants argue that dismissal of the complaint is warranted because the four statements at issue cannot support a conclusory allegation that these statements were either material or nonpublic.

Regulation FD does not contain definitions for the terms "material" or "nonpublic." In the SEC's release discussing the proposed adoption of the regulation

("Proposing Release"), the SEC "recognize[d] that materiality judgments can be difficult." *Proposed Rule: Selective Disclosure and Insider Trading,* 64 Fed. Reg. 72590, 72594 (Dec. 28, 1999) ("Proposing Release").

. . .

Despite its previous acknowledgment, in the Proposing Release, that materiality judgments can be difficult, the SEC did not find that the "appropriate answer to this difficulty is to set forth a bright-line test, or an exclusive list of material items for purpose of Regulation FD." *Id.* at 51721. Although the SEC declined to set forth an all-inclusive list of what matters are to be deemed material, it did provide seven categories of information or events that have a higher probability of being considered material. The seven enumerated categories are:

(1) Earnings information; (2) mergers, acquisitions, tender offers, joint ventures, or changes in assets; (3) new products or discoveries, or developments regarding customers or supplies (e.g., the acquisition or loss of a contract); (4) changes in control or in management; (5) change in auditors or auditor notification that the issuer may no longer rely on an auditor's audit report; (6) events regarding the issuer's securities—e.g., defaults on strict securities, calls of securities for redemption, repurchase plans, stock splits or changes in dividends, changes to rights of security holders, public or private sales of additional securities; and (7) bankruptcies and receiverships.

The specific matters included in the list, however, are not *per se* material.

Although Regulation FD does not contain definitions for the terms "material" or "nonpublic," the Adopting Release advises that those terms are to be defined as they have been in previous case law. . . .

In applying the aforementioned [materiality] principles to the case at bar, the allegations in the complaint fail to demonstrate that Regulation FD was violated. Regulation FD was never intended to be utilized in the manner attempted by the SEC under these circumstances. The statements relied upon in the complaint cannot support a conclusion that material information privately provided by Mr. Goldman was unavailable to the public. Specifically, Mr. Goldman's private statement regarding the existence of five million dollar deals in the company's pipeline for the second quarter was equivalent in substance to the information previously disclosed by Mr. Siebel. With regard to the guidance for the second quarter, Mr. Siebel stated at the April 23rd conference call:

Our guidance and license revenue for the quarter is 120 to 140 million range. I think that we'll see lots of small deals. We'll see some medium deals. We'll see a number of deals over a million dollars. And I suspect we'll see some *greater than five.* And now that's what the mix will look like.

The SEC argues that Mr. Goldman's statement, in contrast, was in the *present* tense, and hence constitutes a factually different material statement than that made by Mr. Siebel. The SEC contends that unlike Mr. Goldman's statement, Mr. Siebel's statement was in the *future* tense, and Mr. Siebel's use of the word "suspect" indicates his statement was not a present fact, but rather was forward looking.

It would appear that in examining publicly and privately disclosed information, the SEC has scrutinized, at an extremely heightened level, every particular word used in the statement, including the tense of verbs and the general syntax of each sentence. No support for such an approach can be found in Regulation FD itself, or in the Proposing and Adopting Releases. Such an approach places an unreasonable burden on a company's management and spokespersons to become linguistic experts, or otherwise live in fear of violating Regulation FD should the words they use later be interpreted by the SEC as connoting even the slightest variance from the company's public statements.

Regulation FD does not require that corporate officials only utter verbatim statements that were previously publicly made. In Kennecott Copper Corp. v. Curtiss-Wright Corp., 584 F.2d 1195 (2d Cir.1978), which concerned the adequacy of a proxy disclosure, the Second Circuit advised that, in analyzing the disclosure of material statements, "nit-picking should not become the name of the game. . . . There is no requirement that a material fact be expressed in certain words or in a certain form of language. Fair accuracy, not perfection, is the appropriate standard." *Kennecott Copper Corp.*, 584 F.2d at 2000. To require a more demanding standard, in the context of Regulation FD, could compel companies to discontinue any spontaneous communications so that the content of any intended communication may be examined by a lexicologist to ensure that the proposed statement discloses the exact information in the same form as was publicly disclosed. If Regulation FD is applied in such a manner, the very purpose of the regulation, *i.e.*, to provide the public with a broad flow of relevant investment information, would be thwarted. . . .

Similarly unavailing are the SEC's claims that Mr. Goldman's private statements regarding new business in the pipeline and that the pipeline was "growing" or "building" was information which was not previously disclosed to the public. The SEC argues that Mr. Siebel "did not describe the status of the Company's pipeline." (Pl.'s Opp'n Mem. at 6). However, at the April 23rd conference call, a question was posed regarding the makeup of the pipeline with respect to "new versus exist[ing] customers." The verbatim transcript on which the SEC relies indicates that in response thereto, Mr. Siebel publicly stated, "every quarter will be some place between 45 and 55 percent of our business with new customers." Such a statement clearly indicated that the second quarter pipeline would include new deals. . . .

The SEC further alleges that Regulation FD was violated as a result of Mr. Goldman's private statements that Siebel Systems's sales or business activity levels were "good" or "better." Mr. Goldman's private statement that the activity levels were "good" or "better" was based on information available to the public since Siebel Systems publicly reported that it anticipated a future increase in the company's performance. The terms "better" and "good" are merely generalized descriptive labels based on the underlying quantitative information provided publicly by Siebel Systems. Given the detailed and specific information revealed in the company's public disclosures, Mr. Goldman's description of the company's performance and activity level as being "good" and "better" imparted no greater information to his private audiences than Siebel Systems had already disclosed to the public at large. Hence, the statements regarding the company's performance or activity levels being "good" or "better" did not alter the total mix of information already available to the reasonable investor.

The SEC maintains that Mr. Goldman's statements constituted nonpublic material information because his statements forecasted overall positive growth for the company, whereas the company's public statements avoided making such a positive affirmation. Although the SEC is not disputing that the public information was that the second quarter guidance was higher than the first quarter's actual results, the SEC asserts that this is not dispositive of whether business was improving. However, the information available to the public provides a sufficient factual basis for a reasonable investor to conclude that business was improving.

The SEC places great emphasis on the alleged actions taken by certain individuals who were in attendance at Mr. Goldman's private speaking engagements. The complaint alleges that certain attendees, and other individuals with whom they communicated, purchased Siebel Systems stock almost immediately after Mr. Goldman's private statements or soon thereafter, causing the market for Siebel Systems stock to significantly rise and for trading to surge. The SEC argues that taking these allegations as true, and drawing all reasonable inferences in its favor, leads to the conclusion that Mr. Goldman disclosed information that was both new and material.

A major factor in determining whether information is material is the importance attached to it by those who were exposed to the information as may be expressed by their reaction to the information. Although stock movement is a relevant factor to be considered in making the determination as to materiality, it is not, however, a sufficient factor alone to establish materiality.

An examination of the public and private statements do not support a conclusory allegation that Mr. Goldman's statements were the disclosure of non-public material information. The actions taken by those in attendance at Mr. Goldman's speaking engagements, although a relevant consideration, do not change the nature or content of Mr. Goldman's statements. Regulation FD deals exclusively with the disclosure of material information. The regulation does not prohibit persons speaking on behalf of an issuer, from providing mere positive or negative characterizations, or their optimistic or pessimistic subjective general impressions, based upon or drawn from the material information available to the public. The mere fact that analysts might have considered Mr. Goldman's private statements significant is not, standing alone, a basis to infer that Regulation FD was violated. *See*, 65 Fed.Reg. 51716, 51722 ("Regulation FD will not be implicated where an issuer discloses immaterial information whose significance is discerned by the analyst. ... The focus of Regulation FD is on whether the issuer discloses material nonpublic information, not on whether an analyst, through some combination of persistence, knowledge, and insight, regards as material information whose significance is not apparent to the reasonable investor."). . . .

Significantly, none of the statements challenged by the SEC falls squarely within the seven enumerated categories listed by the SEC, in the Adopting Release, as being more likely to be considered material. Applying Regulation FD in an overly aggressive manner cannot effectively encourage full and complete public disclosure of facts reasonably deemed relevant to investment decisionmaking. It provides no clear guidance for companies to conform their conduct in compliance with Regulation FD. Instead, the enforcement of Regulation FD by excessively scrutinizing vague general comments has a potential chilling effect which can discourage, rather than, encourage public disclosure of material information.

In accepting the factual allegations in the complaint as true and drawing all reasonable inferences in the SEC's favor, the statements relied upon in the complaint fail to support its conclusory allegation that material Information in private by Mr. Goldman, had not already been publicly disclosed by Siebel Systems. Accordingly, the complaint fails to sufficiently allege that Regulation FD was violated.

. . .

The defendants' motion to dismiss the complaint, pursuant to Fed.R.Civ.P. 12(b)(6), is granted. The case is dismissed in its entirety.

PROBLEM 12-4

One of the concerns about Regulation FD is that it reduces, rather than expands, the amount of information made available to securities analysts and the market. Thus, when analysts call a company to ask questions company officials may refuse to answer, citing Reg. FD, rather than disclose negative trends or conclusions to market professionals generally. This dynamic has been observed by analysts at the Calvert family of funds, among others. Calvert is one of the oldest "socially responsible investment" (SRI) mutual fund companies, with a range of different mutual funds that are designed to help investors "achieve financial security while helping to build a sustainable world and protect our quality of life." Currently it manages $8.5 billion in assets. Like most SRI funds, Calvert screens the companies in which it invests for both their financial performance and their social performance, evaluating a broad range of issues and information concerning companies' "triple-bottom line" (economic, environmental, and social impacts).

One source of data that is particularly useful to SRI analysts in evaluating environmental performance is the Toxic Release Inventory (TRI). TRI was established by a federal statute that since 1986 has required manufacturing companies to report annually on the levels of specified toxic chemicals that they've released. TRI reporting is done facility by facility and chemical by chemical, so SRI analysts need to perform significant work to aggregate reports in order to develop an accurate assessment of a company's environmental practices. After Reg. FD was promulgated, Calvert analysts had a number of experiences of calling specific companies to ask questions like "Why do your TRI data show a 40% increase in emissions over the last year?" or "Why are your facilities in X state showing a significant increase in emissions?" and having the companies refuse to answer the questions, citing Reg. FD. Some companies even refuse to answer more general questions now, such as what their safety policies are or what steps they take to produce their TRI data. Although Calvert's policy is to ask companies to disclose their answers publicly, not just to Calvert, that seems to be part of the problem, because under Reg. FD, if the information is material and it is disclosed to one analyst, it must be disclosed generally, and companies prefer non-disclosure of negative information when possible. Prior to Reg. FD more companies would answer these questions. The strategy of using Reg. FD as a shield against disclosure may be counterproductive with SRI firms, since analysts assume that it is primarily poor performers who refuse to answer. Still, the phenomenon raises the general question of whether Reg. FD has advanced its own policy goals, or whether it is unintentionally inhibiting them.

What does it say about the materiality of environmental information that a company refuses to answer questions about its TRI data, citing Reg. FD? What time frame should be used to determine the materiality of environmental information, given the long latency of some environmental harms and the long-term risks those harms pose to companies and their shareholders? Is there any way to revise Reg. FD to advance the goal of inhibiting selective disclosure without suffering the "chilling effect"? Should analysts who work hard to synthesize data that is generally available, such as TRI data, in order to ask probing questions be rewarded with answers without imposing a general disclosure obligation on the company? If such select disclosure is allowed, how does one avoid the conflicts of interest that led to Reg. FD in the first place — that is, favored analysts being given at mid-quarter more information on financial projections or significant corporate developments?

D.   FIDUCIARY DUTY OF DISCLOSURE UNDER STATE LAW

An important requirement protecting the shareholders' power to vote is that they must be adequately and accurately informed by the directors prior to voting. The duty of disclosure — sometimes called the "duty of candor" — occupies an important niche in the panoply of director duties. As discussed in Chapter 6 and in this chapter, the mandatory disclosure system under federal securities law determines in large part the scope and substance of corporate disclosure obligations, at least with respect to public companies. Nevertheless, the Delaware courts guard jealously the place of state fiduciary law in regulating disclosure. Indeed, beginning with Lynch v. Vickers Energy Corp., 383 A.2d 278 (Del. 1977), the Delaware courts developed an expansive notion of the fiduciary duty of disclosure that began to compete with federal disclosure rules.

Lynch was far from the first case to articulate a fiduciary duty of disclosure,[1] but its description of a duty of "complete candor" prompted widespread interest among litigants. *Lynch* involved a classic conflict of interest — a tender offer by a majority shareholder for the shares held by the minority shareholders — and thus fit comfortably under a fairly conventional and well-established theory of shareholder approval for conflict-of-interest transactions under Delaware General Corporation Law (DGCL) §144(b). To the extent that *Lynch* was describing a duty to provide full information in such a context, it was completely unremarkable. Indeed, for the next several years, application of the duty of candor was limited to cases involving conflict-of-interest transactions.

The turning point for the duty of disclosure was Smith v. Van Gorkom, 488 A.2d 858 (Del. 1985), a case typically cited for other reasons. The Delaware Supreme Court's discussion of the duty of disclosure is important because *Van Gorkom* did not involve a conflict-of-interest transaction. Nevertheless, the court held that the directors of Trans Union breached their fiduciary duty of disclosure "by their failure to disclose all material information such as a reasonable stockholder would consider important" in voting on the merger proposal. *Id.* at 893.

Van Gorkom opened whole new possibilities for the duty of disclosure, and the Delaware courts soon found themselves attempting to cage this new duty. By the

---

1. For an excellent history of the duty of disclosure in Delaware, see Lawrence A. Hamermesh, *Calling Off the Lynch Mob: A Corporate Director's Fiduciary Disclosure Duty*, 49 Vand. L. Rev. 1087 (1996).

time of Stroud v. Grace, 606 A.2d 75 (Del. 1992), decided seven years after *Van Gorkom*, the Delaware Supreme Court was comfortable asserting that the duty of candor "represents nothing more than the well-recognized proposition that directors of Delaware corporations are under a fiduciary duty to disclose fully and fairly all material information within the board's control when it seeks shareholder action." *Id.* at 84. But the *Stroud* court went one step further, holding that "in the absence of a proxy solicitation," corporate managers have a duty of disclosure contiguous with the requirements of the DGCL, and those requirements are fairly flimsy. In the context of charter amendments to be approved at an annual meeting—the issue in *Stroud*—the only state statutory disclosure requirements are a duty to provide notice of the meeting (DGCL §222(a)) and a duty to set forth and summarize the proposed amendment (DGCL §242(b)(1)).

Stroud was expressly "limited to non-public, privately-held corporations," *id.* at 86, and thus did not raise questions regarding the interface of federal and state disclosure duties. Defining the intersection of those two regulatory regimes became more urgent in 1995, when Congress adopted the PSLRA, which raised the pleading standards for disclosure actions in federal courts by adopting the strong inference pleading standard discussed above. By increasing the burdens on federal disclosure claims, PSLRA necessarily made state disclosure claims more attractive. This was particularly true of Delaware disclosure claims, which did not require proof of reliance, causation, or quantifiable monetary damages. In short, they carried a "virtual per se rule of damages for breach of the fiduciary duty of disclosure." In re Tri-Star Pictures, Inc. Litigation, 634 A.2d 319, 333 (Del. 1993).

Sensing that the PSLRA was being undermined by increasing state litigation, Congress responded by passing the Securities Litigation Uniform Standards Act of 1998 (SLUSA). The purpose of the statute was to preempt state securities fraud class actions, but it explicitly preserved some of those actions through a provision tagged as the "Delaware carve-outs":

> (A) Actions preserved.— . . . [A] covered class action described in sub-paragraph (B) of this paragraph that is based upon the statutory or common law of the State in which the issuer is incorporated . . . may be maintained in a State or Federal court by a private party.
>
> (B) Permissible actions.—A covered class action is described in this subpara-graph if it involves:
>
> (i) the purchase or sale of securities by the issuer or an affiliate of the issuer exclusively from or to holders of equity securities of the issuer; or
>
> (ii) any recommendation, position, or other communication with respect to the sale of securities of the issuer that—
>
> (I) is made by or on behalf of the issuer or an affiliate of the issuer to holders of equity securities of the issuer; and
>
> (II) concerns decisions of those equity holders with respect to voting their securities, acting in response to a tender or exchange offer, or exercising dissenters' or appraisal rights.

Securities Act of 1933, §16, 15 U.S.C. §77 (2003).

This provision played a central role in Malone v. Brincat, 722 A.2d 5 (Del. 1998), the Delaware Supreme Court's attempt to clarify the respective domains of federal and state securities law. *Malone* considered a claim by shareholders of

Mercury Finance Company (Mercury), which became infamous for massive accounting fraud. Once unearthed, the fraud led to the quick demise of the company—a loss of approximately $2 billion in shareholder value. The distinguishing feature of the *Malone* claim is that the plaintiffs had not purchased or sold securities in reliance on the misstatements, nor were they claiming to have taken a particular action that was influenced by the misstatements.

The Court of Chancery dismissed the complaint on the ground that federal securities law—not state fiduciary law—was responsible for "ensur[ing] the timely release of accurate information into the marketplace." From the plaintiffs' perspective, the problem with this holding was that they did not qualify for a federal securities law claim. One of the elements of such a claim is that the plaintiff be a purchaser or seller of securities. In *Malone* the plaintiffs were shareholders who had purchased prior to the fraudulent disclosures and held throughout the relevant time periods.

The Delaware Supreme Court was less willing to cede ground. While stopping short of imposing a duty of continuous disclosure, the court held that general fiduciary principles require honest disclosure:

> The shareholder constituents of a Delaware corporation are entitled to rely upon their elected directors to discharge their fiduciary duties at all times. Whenever directors communicate publicly or directly with shareholders about the corporation's affairs, with or without a request for shareholder action, directors have a fiduciary duty to shareholders to exercise due care, good faith and loyalty. It follows *a fortiori* that when directors communicate publicly or directly with shareholders about corporate matters the *sine qua non* of directors' fiduciary duty to shareholders is honesty.

Malone, 722 A.2d at 10. The court then proceeded to define the respective domains of federal and state disclosure obligations.

Federal Securities Law. In *Malone*, the Delaware Supreme Court articulated a rather narrow view of its unique place in disclosure regulation:

> In deference to the panoply of federal protections that are available to investors in connection with the purchase or sale of securities of Delaware corporations, this Court has decided not to recognize a state common law cause of action against the directors of Delaware corporations for "fraud on the market." Here, it is to be noted, the claim appears to be made by those who did not sell and, therefore, would not implicate federal securities laws which relate to the purchase or sale of securities.

Malone, 722 A.2d at 13.

State Fiduciary Law: Action Requested. Delaware courts had long recognized a duty of disclosure in the context of a request for shareholder action. As noted above, this became the standard description of the domain of the duty of disclosure by the time of *Stroud*. *Malone* affirmed this tradition and stated that requests for shareholder action are the *only* contexts in which plaintiffs may assert a "duty of disclosure":

> The duty of disclosure is, and always has been, a specific application of the general fiduciary duty owed by directors. The duty of disclosure obligates directors

> to provide the stockholders with accurate and complete information material to a transaction or other corporate event that is being presented to them for action.
>
> The issue in this case is not whether Mercury's directors breached their duty of disclosure. It is whether they breached their more general fiduciary duty of loyalty and good faith by knowingly disseminating to the stockholders false information about the financial condition of the company. The directors' fiduciary duties include the duty to deal with their stockholders honestly.

Malone, 722 A.2d at 10.

As these paragraphs make clear, the "duty of disclosure" in Delaware is a term of art that does not cover all cases in which disclosure is at issue. In some instances — notably in *Malone* itself — failures of disclosure are dealt with under the more general rubrics of duty of loyalty or duty of care.

State Fiduciary Law: No Action Requested. Perhaps *Malone*'s most important holding was that directors do, in fact, owe a fiduciary duty, even when no shareholder action is requested. There appears to be some overlap with federal securities law here, but the court affirmed the continuing vitality of state fiduciary duties in this context:

> When the directors disseminate information to stockholders when no stockholder action is sought, the fiduciary duties of care, loyalty and good faith apply. Dissemination of false information could violate one or more of those duties.

Malone, 722 A.2d at 12.

While the SLUSA did not apply to the transactions in *Malone*, which occurred prior to the passage of the statute, the court was mindful of its message and its apparent accommodation of overlap between federal and state claims. Still, the court commented, "The historic roles played by state and federal law in regulating corporate disclosures have been not only compatible but complementary," *Malone*, 722 A.2d at 13.

Despite the Court's efforts in *Malone* to clarify the line between federal and state disclosure actions, questions remained. In the following case, the Supreme Court broadly construes the scope of SLUSA preemption, suggesting that it might similarly construe broad federal authority over disclosure should that case ultimately come before it. Still, the Delaware courts have shown no tendency to want to cede authority over corporate governance to the federal government, while the federal government has only episodically sought to wrest such authority from Delaware.

MERRILL LYNCH, PIERCE, FENNER & SMITH, INC. v. DABIT

547 U.S. 71
United States Supreme Court
March 21, 2006

Justice STEVENS delivered the opinion of the Court, in which all other Members joined, except ALITO, J., who took no part in the consideration or decision of the case.

Title I of the Securities Litigation Uniform Standards Act of 1998 (SLUSA) provides that "[n]o covered class action" based on state law and alleging "a misrepresentation or omission of a material fact in connection with the purchase or sale of a covered security" "may be maintained in any State or Federal court by any private party." § 101(b), 112 Stat. 3227 (codified at 15 U.S.C. § 78bb(f)(1)(A)). In this case the Second Circuit held that SLUSA only pre-empts state-law class-action claims brought by plaintiffs who have a private remedy under federal law. 395 F.3d 25 (2005). A few months later, the Seventh Circuit ruled to the contrary, holding that the statute also pre-empts state-law class-action claims for which federal law provides no private remedy. Kircher v. Putnam Funds Trust, 403 F.3d 478 (C.A.7 2005). The background, the text, and the purpose of SLUSA's pre-emption provision all support the broader interpretation adopted by the Seventh Circuit.

I

Petitioner Merrill Lynch, Pierce, Fenner & Smith, Inc. (Merrill Lynch), is an investment banking firm that offers research and brokerage services to investors. Suspicious that the firm's loyalties to its investment banking clients had produced biased investment advice, the New York attorney general in 2002 instituted a formal investigation into Merrill Lynch's practices. The investigation sparked a number of private securities fraud actions, this one among them.

Respondent, Shadi Dabit, is a former Merrill Lynch broker. He filed this class action in the United States District Court for the Western District of Oklahoma on behalf of himself and all other former or current brokers who, while employed by Merrill Lynch, purchased (for themselves and for their clients) certain stocks between December 1, 1999, and December 31, 2000. Rather than rely on the federal securities laws, Dabit invoked the District Court's diversity jurisdiction and advanced his claims under Oklahoma state law. The gist of Dabit's complaint was that Merrill Lynch breached the fiduciary duty and covenant of good faith and fair dealing it owed its brokers by disseminating misleading research and thereby manipulating stock prices. Dabit's theory was that Merrill Lynch used its misinformed brokers to enhance the prices of its investment banking clients' stocks: The research analysts, under management's direction, allegedly issued overly optimistic appraisals of the stocks' value; the brokers allegedly relied on the analysts' reports in advising their investor clients and in deciding whether or not to sell their own holdings; and the clients and brokers both continued to hold their stocks long beyond the point when, had the truth been known, they would have sold. The complaint further alleged that when the truth was actually revealed (around the time the New York attorney general instituted his investigation), the stocks' prices plummeted.

Dabit asserted that Merrill Lynch's actions damaged the class members in two ways: The misrepresentations and manipulative tactics caused them to hold onto overvalued securities, and the brokers lost commission fees when their clients, now aware that they had made poor investments, took their business elsewhere.

In July 2002, Merrill Lynch moved to dismiss Dabit's complaint. It argued, first, that SLUSA pre-empted the action and, second, that the claims alleged were not cognizable under Oklahoma law. The District Court indicated that it was "not impressed by" the state-law argument, but agreed that the federal statute pre-empted at least some of Dabit's claims. The court noted that the complaint alleged both "claims and damages based on wrongfully-induced purchases" and "claims and damages based on wrongfully-induced holding." While the "holding" claims, the court suggested, might not be pre-empted, the "purchasing" claims certainly were. The court dismissed the complaint with leave to amend to give Dabit the opportunity to untangle his "hopeless melange of purchase-related and holding-related assertions."

Dabit promptly filed an amended complaint that omitted all direct references to purchases. What began as a class of brokers who "purchased" the subject securities during the class period became a class of brokers who "owned and continued to own" those securities.

Meanwhile, dozens of other suits, based on allegations similar to Dabit's, had been filed against Merrill Lynch around the country on both federal- and state-law theories of liability. The Judicial Panel on Multidistrict Litigation transferred all of those cases, along with this one, to the United States District Court for the Southern District of New York for consolidated pretrial proceedings. Merrill Lynch then filed its second motion to dismiss Dabit's complaint. Senior Judge Milton Pollack granted the motion on the ground that the claims alleged fell "squarely within SLUSA's ambit." In re Merrill Lynch & Co., Inc., 2003 WL 1872820, *1 (Apr. 10, 2003).

The Court of Appeals for the Second Circuit, however, vacated the judgment and remanded for further proceedings. 395 F.3d, at 51. It concluded that the claims asserted by holders did not allege fraud "in connection with the purchase or sale" of securities under SLUSA. Although the court agreed with Merrill Lynch that that phrase, as used in other federal securities laws, has been defined broadly by this Court, it held that Congress nonetheless intended a narrower meaning here—one that incorporates the "standing" limitation on private federal securities actions adopted in Blue Chip Stamps v. Manor Drug Stores, 421 U.S. 723 (1975). Under the Second Circuit's analysis, fraud is only "in connection with the purchase or sale" of securities, as used in SLUSA, if it is alleged by a purchaser or seller of securities. Thus, to the extent that the complaint in this action alleged that brokers were fraudulently induced, not to sell or purchase, but to retain or delay selling their securities, it fell outside SLUSA's pre-emptive scope.

After determining that the class defined in Dabit's amended complaint did not necessarily exclude purchasers, the panel remanded with instructions that the pleading be dismissed without prejudice. The court's order would permit Dabit to file another amended complaint that defines the class to exclude "claimants who purchased in connection with the fraud and who therefore could meet the standing requirement" for a federal damages action, and to include only those "who came to hold [a Merrill Lynch] stock before any relevant misrepresentation." Under the Second Circuit's analysis, a class action so limited could be sustained under state law. For the reasons that follow, we disagree.

II

The magnitude of the federal interest in protecting the integrity and efficient operation of the market for nationally traded securities cannot be overstated. In response to the sudden and disastrous collapse in prices of listed stocks in 1929, and the Great Depression that followed, Congress enacted the Securities Act of 1933 (1933 Act), and the Securities Exchange Act of 1934 (1934 Act). Since their enactment, these two statutes have anchored federal regulation of vital elements of our economy.

Securities and Exchange Commission (SEC) Rule 10b-5, promulgated in 1942 pursuant to § 10(b) of the 1934 Act, is an important part of that regulatory scheme. The Rule, like § 10(b) itself, broadly prohibits deception, misrepresentation, and fraud "in connection with the purchase or sale of any security." The SEC has express statutory authority to enforce the Rule. Although no such authority is expressly granted to private individuals injured by securities fraud, in 1946 Judge Kirkpatrick of the United States District Court for the Eastern District of Pennsylvania, relying on "the general purpose" of the Rule, recognized an implied right of action thereunder. Kardon v. National Gypsum Co., 69 F. Supp. 512, 514. His holding was adopted by an "overwhelming consensus of the District Courts and Courts of Appeals," *Blue Chip Stamps*, 421 U.S., at 730, and endorsed by this Court in Superintendent of Ins. of N.Y. v. Bankers Life & Casualty Co., 404 U.S. 6 (1971).

A few years after Kardon was decided, the Court of Appeals for the Second Circuit limited the reach of the private right of action under Rule 10b-5. In Birnbaum v. Newport Steel Corp., 193 F.2d 461 (C.A.2 1952), a panel composed of Chief Judge Swan and Judges Augustus and Learned Hand upheld the dismissal of a suit brought on behalf of a corporation and a class of its stockholders alleging that fraud "in connection with" a director's sale of his controlling block of stock to third parties violated Rule 10b-5. The court held that the Rule could only be invoked by a purchaser or seller of securities to remedy fraud associated with his or her own sale or purchase of securities, and did not protect those who neither purchased nor sold the securities in question but were instead injured by corporate insiders' sales to third parties. While the Birnbaum court did not question the plaintiffs' "standing" to enforce Rule 10b-5, later cases treated its holding as a standing requirement.

By the time this Court first confronted the question, literally hundreds of lower court decisions had accepted "Birnbaum's conclusion that the plaintiff class for purposes of § 10(b) and Rule 10b-5 private damages actions is limited to purchasers and sellers." *Blue Chip Stamps*, 421 U.S., at 731-732. Meanwhile, however, cases like *Bankers Life & Casualty Co.* had interpreted the coverage of the Rule more broadly to prohibit, for example, "deceptive practices touching [a victim's] sale of securities as an investor." 404 U.S., at 12-13. The "judicial oak which ha[d] grown from little more than a legislative acorn," as then-Justice Rehnquist described the rules governing private Rule 10b-5 actions, *Blue Chip Stamps*, 421 U.S., at 737, had thus developed differently from the law defining what constituted a substantive violation of Rule 10b-5. Ultimately, the Court had to decide whether to permit private parties to sue for any violation of Rule 10b-5 that caused them harm, or instead to limit the private remedy to plaintiffs who were themselves purchasers or sellers.

Relying principally on "policy considerations" which the Court viewed as appropriate in explicating a judicially crafted remedy, and following judicial precedent rather than "the many commentators" who had criticized the Birnbaum rule as "an arbitrary restriction which unreasonably prevents some deserving plaintiffs from recovering damages," the Court in *Blue Chip Stamps* chose to limit the private remedy. The main policy consideration tipping the scales in favor of precedent was the widespread recognition that "litigation under Rule 10b-5 presents a danger of vexatiousness different in degree and in kind from that which accompanies litigation in general." Even weak cases brought under the Rule may have substantial settlement value, the Court explained, because "[t]he very pendency of the lawsuit may frustrate or delay normal business activity." *Blue Chip Stamps*, at 740. Cabining the private cause of action by means of the purchaser-seller limitation would, in the Court's view, minimize these ill effects. The limitation of course had no application in Government enforcement actions brought pursuant to Rule 10b-5.

III

Policy considerations similar to those that supported the Court's decision in *Blue Chip Stamps* prompted Congress, in 1995, to adopt legislation targeted at perceived abuses of the class-action vehicle in litigation involving nationally traded securities. While acknowledging that private securities litigation was "an indispensable tool with which defrauded investors can recover their losses," the House Conference Report accompanying what would later be enacted as the Private Securities Litigation Reform Act of 1995 (Reform Act) identified ways in which the class action device was being used to injure "the entire U.S. economy." H.R.Rep. No. 104-369, p. 31 (1995). According to the Report, nuisance filings, targeting of deep-pocket defendants, vexatious discovery requests, and "manipulation by class action lawyers of the clients whom they purportedly represent" had become rampant in recent years. Proponents of the Reform Act argued that these abuses resulted in extortionate settlements, chilled any discussion of issuers' future prospects, and deterred qualified individuals from serving on boards of directors.

Title I of the Reform Act, captioned "Reduction of Abusive Litigation," represents Congress' effort to curb these perceived abuses. Its provisions limit recoverable damages and attorney's fees, provide a "safe harbor" for forward-looking statements, impose new restrictions on the selection of (and compensation awarded to) lead plaintiffs, mandate imposition of sanctions for frivolous litigation, and authorize a stay of discovery pending resolution of any motion to dismiss. Title I also imposes heightened pleading requirements in actions brought pursuant to §10(b) and Rule 10b-5; it "insists that securities fraud complaints 'specify' each misleading statement; that they set forth the facts 'on which [a] belief' that a statement is misleading was 'formed'; and that they 'state with particularity facts giving rise to a strong inference that the defendant acted with the required state of mind.'" Dura Pharmaceuticals, Inc. v. Broudo, 544 U.S. 336, 345 (2005).

The effort to deter or at least quickly dispose of those suits whose nuisance value outweighs their merits placed special burdens on plaintiffs seeking to bring federal securities fraud class actions. But the effort also had an unintended consequence: It prompted at least some members of the plaintiffs' bar to avoid the federal forum altogether. Rather than face the obstacles set in their path by the Reform Act, plaintiffs and their representatives began bringing class actions under state law, often in state court. The evidence presented to Congress during a 1997 hearing to evaluate the effects of the Reform Act suggested that this phenomenon was a novel one; state-court litigation of class actions involving nationally traded securities had previously been rare. To stem this "shif[t] from Federal to State courts" and "prevent certain State private securities class action lawsuits alleging fraud from being used to frustrate the objectives of" the Reform Act, SLUSA §§ 2(2), (5), Congress enacted SLUSA.

IV

[The Court then set out the core pre-emptive provision of SLUSA, inserted into both the Securities Act and the Exchange Act, as follows:]

> "Class Action Limitations. — No covered class action based upon the statutory or common law of any State or subdivision thereof may be maintained in any State or Federal court by any private party alleging —
> "(A) a misrepresentation or omission of a material fact in connection with the purchase or sale of a covered security; or
> "(B) that the defendant used or employed any manipulative or deceptive device or contrivance in connection with the purchase or sale of a covered security."

A "covered class action" is a lawsuit in which damages are sought on behalf of more than 50 people. A "covered security" is one traded nationally and listed on a regulated national exchange. Respondent does not dispute that both the class and the securities at issue in this case are "covered" within the meaning of the statute, or that the complaint alleges misrepresentations and omissions of material facts. The only disputed issue is whether the alleged wrongdoing was "in connection with the purchase or sale" of securities.

Respondent urges that the operative language must be read narrowly to encompass (and therefore pre-empt) only those actions in which the purchaser-seller requirement of *Blue Chip Stamps* is met. Such, too, was the Second Circuit's view. But insofar as the argument assumes that the rule adopted in *Blue Chip Stamps* stems from the text of Rule 10b-5-specifically, the "in connection with" language, it must be rejected. Unlike the Birnbaum court, which relied on Rule 10b-5's text in crafting its purchaser-seller limitation, this Court in *Blue Chip Stamps* relied chiefly, and candidly, on "policy considerations" in adopting that limitation. 421 U.S., at 737. The *Blue Chip Stamps* Court purported to define the scope of a private right of action under Rule 10b-5-not to define the words "in connection with the purchase or sale." *Id.*, at 749 ("No language in either [§ 10(b) or Rule 10b-5] speaks at all to the contours of a private cause of action for their violation"). Any ambiguity on that score had long been resolved by the time Congress enacted SLUSA. . . .

Congress can hardly have been unaware of the broad construction adopted by both this Court and the SEC when it imported the key phrase — "in connection with the purchase or sale" — into SLUSA's core provision. And when "judicial interpretations have settled the meaning of an existing statutory provision, repetition of the same language in a new statute indicates, as a general matter, the intent to incorporate its . . . judicial interpretations as well." Application of that presumption is particularly apt here; not only did Congress use the same words as are used in § 10(b) and Rule 10b-5, but it used them in a provision that appears in the same statute as § 10(b). Generally, "identical words used in different parts of the same statute are . . . presumed to have the same meaning."

The presumption that Congress envisioned a broad construction follows not only from ordinary principles of statutory construction but also from the particular concerns that culminated in SLUSA's enactment. A narrow reading of the statute would undercut the effectiveness of the 1995 Reform Act and thus run contrary to SLUSA's stated purpose, viz., "to prevent certain State private securities class action lawsuits alleging fraud from being used to frustrate the objectives" of the 1995 Act. As the *Blue Chip Stamps* Court observed, class actions brought by holders pose a special risk of vexatious litigation. It would be odd, to say the least, if SLUSA exempted that particularly troublesome subset of class actions from its pre-emptive sweep.

Respondent's preferred construction also would give rise to wasteful, duplicative litigation. Facts supporting an action by purchasers under Rule 10b-5 (which must proceed in federal court if at all) typically support an action by holders as well, at least in those States that recognize holder claims. The prospect is raised, then, of parallel class actions proceeding in state and federal court, with different standards governing claims asserted on identical facts. That prospect, which exists to some extent in this very case, squarely conflicts with the congressional preference for "national standards for securities class action lawsuits involving nationally traded securities."

In concluding that SLUSA pre-empts state-law holder class-action claims of the kind alleged in Dabit's complaint, we do not lose sight of the general "presum[ption] that Congress does not cavalierly pre-empt state-law causes of action." But that presumption carries less force here than in other contexts because SLUSA does not actually pre-empt any state cause of action. It simply denies plaintiffs the right to use the class action device to vindicate certain claims. The Act does not deny any individual plaintiff, or indeed any group of fewer than 50 plaintiffs, the right to enforce any state-law cause of action that may exist. Moreover, the tailored exceptions to SLUSA's pre-emptive command demonstrate that Congress did not by any means act "cavalierly" here. The statute carefully exempts from its operation certain class actions based on the law of the State in which the issuer of the covered security is incorporated, actions brought by a state agency or state pension plan, actions under contracts between issuers and indenture trustees, and derivative actions brought by shareholders on behalf of a corporation. The statute also expressly preserves state jurisdiction over state agency enforcement proceedings. The existence of these carve-outs both evinces congressional sensitivity to state prerogatives in this field and makes it inappropriate for courts to create additional, implied exceptions.

Finally, federal law, not state law, has long been the principal vehicle for asserting class-action securities fraud claims. Prior to the passage of the Reform Act, there was essentially no significant securities class action litigation brought in State court. More importantly, while state-law holder claims were theoretically available both before and after the decision in *Blue Chip Stamps*, the actual assertion of such claims by way of class action was virtually unheard of before SLUSA was enacted; respondent and his amici have identified only one pre-SLUSA case involving a state-law class action asserting holder claims. This is hardly a situation, then, in which a federal statute has eliminated a historically entrenched state-law remedy. . . .

The holder class action that respondent tried to plead, and that the Second Circuit envisioned, is distinguishable from a typical Rule 10b-5 class action in only one respect: It is brought by holders instead of purchasers or sellers. For purposes of SLUSA pre-emption, that distinction is irrelevant; the identity of the plaintiffs does not determine whether the complaint alleges fraud "in connection with the purchase or sale" of securities. The misconduct of which respondent complains here — fraudulent manipulation of stock prices — unquestionably qualifies as fraud "in connection with the purchase or sale" of securities as the phrase is defined in *Zandford*, 535 U.S., at 820, 822, and *O'Hagan*, 521 U.S., at 651.

The judgment of the Court of Appeals for the Second Circuit is vacated, and the case is remanded for further proceedings consistent with this opinion.

It is so ordered.

Table of Cases

Index